Case Studies in Finance

Managing for
Corporate Value
Creation

Case Studies in Finance

Managing for Corporate Value Creation

Fifth Edition

Robert F. Bruner

McGraw-Hill
Irwin

Boston   Burr Ridge, IL   Dubuque, IA   Madison, WI   New York   San Francisco   St. Louis
Bangkok   Bogotá   Caracas   Kuala Lumpur   Lisbon   London   Madrid   Mexico City
Milan   Montreal   New Delhi   Santiago   Seoul   Singapore   Sydney   Taipei   Toronto

**McGraw-Hill
Irwin**

CASE STUDIES IN FINANCE: MANAGING FOR CORPORATE VALUE CREATION
Published by McGraw-Hill/Irwin, a business unit of The McGraw-Hill Companies, Inc., 1221
Avenue of the Americas, New York, NY, 10020. Copyright © 2007 by The McGraw-Hill
Companies, Inc. All rights reserved. No part of this publication may be reproduced or
distributed in any form or by any means, or stored in a database or retrieval system, without
the prior written consent of The McGraw-Hill Companies, Inc., including, but not limited to,
in any network or other electronic storage or transmission, or broadcast for distance learning.

Some ancillaries, including electronic and print components, may not be available to
customers outside the United States.

This book is printed on acid-free paper.

1 2 3 4 5 6 7 8 9 0 DOC/DOC 0 9 8 7 6

ISBN-13: 978-0-07-299475-9
ISBN-10: 0-07-299475-4

Editorial director: *Brent Gordon*
Publisher: *Stephen M. Patterson*
Executive editor: *Michele Janicek*
Editorial coordinator: *Barbara Hari*
Executive marketing manager: *Rhonda Seelinger*
Lead producer, Media technology: *Kai Chiang*
Project manager: *Jim Labeots*
Production supervisor: *Gina Hangos*
Senior designer: *Adam Rooke*
Lead media project manager: *Becky Szura*
Cover design: *Jillian Lindner*
Typeface: *10/12 Times Roman*
Compositor: *Techbooks*
Printer: *R. R. Donnelley*

Library of Congress Cataloging-in-Publication Data

Bruner, Robert F., 1949-
    Case studies in finance: managing for corporate value creation / Robert F. Bruner. — 5th ed.
      p. cm. — (The McGraw-Hill/Irwin series in finance, insurance and real estate)

    ISBN-13: 978-0-07-299475-9 (alk. paper)
    ISBN-10: 0-07-299475-4 (alk. paper)

    1. Corporations—Finance—Case studies. 2. International business enterprises—Finance—
Case studies. I. Title. II. Series.
HG4015.5.B78 2007
658.15—dc22
                                                2006012345

www.mhhe.com

The McGraw-Hill/Irwin Series in Finance, Insurance and Real Estate

Stephen A. Ross
Franco Modigliani Professor of Finance and Economics
Sloan School of Management
Massachusetts Institute of Technology
Consulting Editor

FINANCIAL MANAGEMENT

Smith
The Modern Theory of Corporate Finance
Second Edition

White
Financial Analysis with an Electronic Calculator
Sixth Edition

INVESTMENTS

Bodie, Kane and Marcus
Essentials of Investments
Sixth Edition

Bodie, Kane and Marcus
Investments
Sixth Edition

Cohen, Zinbarg and Zeikel
Investment Analysis and Portfolio Management
Fifth Edition

Corrado and Jordan
Fundamentals of Investments: Valuation and Management
Third Edition

Hirt and Block
Fundamentals of Investment Management
Eighth Edition

FINANCIAL INSTITUTIONS AND MARKETS

Cornett and Saunders
Fundamentals of Financial Institutions Management

Rose and Hudgins
Bank Management and Financial Services
Sixth Edition

Rose and Marquis
Money and Capital Markets: Financial Institutions and Instruments in a Global Marketplace
Ninth Edition

Santomero and Babbel
Financial Markets, Instruments, and Institutions
Second Edition

Saunders and Cornett
Financial Institutions Management: A Risk Management Approach
Fifth Edition

Saunders and Cornett
Financial Markets and Institutions: An Introduction to the Risk Management Approach
Third Edition

INTERNATIONAL FINANCE

Beim and Calomiris
Emerging Financial Markets

Eun and Resnick
International Financial Management
Fourth Edition

Kuemmerle
Case Studies in International Entrepreneurship: Managing and

Financing Ventures in the Global Economy
First Edition

Levich
International Financial Markets: Prices and Policies
Second Edition

Dedication

In dedication to Henry Pfeiffer Bruner and Marjorie Williamson Bruner

One looks back with appreciation to the brilliant teachers, but with gratitude to those who touched our human feelings. The curriculum is so much necessary raw material, but warmth is the vital element for the growing plant and for the soul of the child.
—Carl Jung

Robert F. Bruner is Dean of the Darden Graduate School of Business Administration, Distinguished Professor of Business Administration and Charles C. Abbott Professor of Business Administration at the University of Virginia. He has taught and written in various areas, including corporate finance, mergers and acquisitions, investing in emerging markets, innovation, and technology transfer. In addition to *Case Studies in Finance,* his books include *Finance Interactive,* multimedia tutorial software in Finance (Irwin/McGraw-Hill 1997), *The Portable MBA* (Wiley 2003), *Applied Mergers and Acquisitions (*Wiley, 2004), and *Deals from Hell: M&A Lessons that Rise Above the Ashes* (Wiley, 2005). He has been recognized in the United States and Europe for his teaching and casewriting. *BusinessWeek* magazine cited him as one of the "masters of the MBA classroom." He is the author or co-author of over 400 case studies and notes. His research has been published in journals such as *Financial Management, Journal of Accounting and Economics, Journal of Applied Corporate Finance, Journal of Financial Economics, Journal of Financial and Quantitative Analysis,* and *Journal of Money, Credit, and Banking.* Industrial corporations, financial institutions, and government agencies have retained him for counsel and training. He has been on the faculty of the Darden School since 1982, and has been a visiting professor at various schools including Columbia, INSEAD, and IESE. Formerly he was a loan officer and investment analyst for First Chicago Corporation. He holds the B.A. degree from Yale University and the M.B.A. and D.B.A. degrees from Harvard University. Copies of his papers and essays may be obtained from his Web site, http://faculty.darden.edu/brunerb/. He may be reached via email at brunerr@virginia.edu.

Contents

Setting Some Themes

Financial Analysis and Forecasting

Estimating the Cost of Capital

Capital Budgeting and Resource Allocation

Management of the Firm's Equity: Dividends, Repurchases, Initial Offerings

Management of the Corporate Capital Structure

7 Analysis of Financing Tactics: Leases, Options, and Foreign Currency

8 Valuing the Enterprise: Acquisitions and Buyouts

Foreword

by R. Glenn Hubbard
Dean and Russell L. Carson Professor of Finance and Economics
Columbia Business School

In business, the future is a moving target. So is "best practice." Practices, processes, and business models that were conventional wisdom not long ago are no longer best practice. Some of them were bad ideas to begin with, others have simply been superseded by what Joseph Schumpeter called "the perennial gale of creative destruction" in business that continually challenges and uproots old ways of doing business. The field of finance has witnessed some of the most dramatic changes, including the advent of asset-pricing and option-pricing models; the rise of new markets for high-yield securities, derivatives, bonds, and stock; dramatic growth among financial institutions and the invention of completely new classes of institutions, such as hedge funds; and growing globalization of markets. In an environment such as this, the best practitioner thinks critically about the changing world, pays attention to new evidence, and adapts in sensible ways. Business schools play a critical role in the change process: Theory suggests new approaches, empirical research tests them, and classroom teaching promotes knowledge transfer. The development of new teaching materials is vital to the task of conveying best practice in compelling new ways.

The teaching case studies in finance have evolved markedly in the past 40 years. On one hand, this shift mirrors the revolutionary changes in markets and organization seen in the business world. On the other hand, it reflects the many major advances in finance theory and empirical research. Because case studies are an important avenue along which scholars, students, and practitioners communicate, it is very important that this body of cases grow along with practice and the theoretical and large-sample empirical scholarship in finance.

I am glad to introduce the reader to Robert Bruner's *Case Studies in Finance*. He exemplifies the practice-oriented scholar who has an understanding of the economic foundations of finance and the extensive varieties of practice. He translates business phenomena into material that is accessible both to the serious practitioner and novice in finance.

Bob Bruner has contributed significantly to the growth and change of finance cases. First, his cases link managerial decisions to capital markets and the expectations of investors. At the core of almost all of his cases is a valuation task that requires the student to look to financial markets for guidance in resolving the case problem. Second, he has brought into case studies a wide range of contemporary problems of interest to scholars and practitioners, including cases in real and financial options, agency conflicts, financial innovation, investing in emerging markets, and corporate control. As the body of cases continues to mature, we should look for more of this kind of presentation of financial economic research. At the same time, he has presented clear expressions of classic problems in finance, including dividend policy, the mix of debt and equity, financing, the estimation of future financial requirements, and the choice between mutually exclusive investments. Third, his cases invite the student to apply modern information technology (in the form of computers and the Internet) to the analysis of managerial decisions. Instructors in finance need to be able to serve up case problems that invite students to harness technology that they will use in the workplace and that can help them penetrate to key insights effectively.

This collection of cases will help students, scholars, and practitioners sharpen their decision-making ability. And it will advance further the body of cases in finance.

November, 2005
New York City

The inexplicable is all around us. So is the incomprehensible. So is the unintelligible. Interviewing Babe Ruth[1] in 1928, I put it to him, "People come and ask what's your system for hitting home runs—that so?" "Yes," said the Babe, "and all I can tell 'em is I pick a good one and sock it. I get back to the dugout and they ask me what it was I hit and I tell 'em I don't know except it looked good."

—Carl Sandburg[2]

Managers are not confronted with problems that are independent of each other, but with dynamic situations that consist of complex systems of changing problems that interact with each other. I call such situations messes . . . managers do not solve problems: they manage messes.

—Russell Ackoff[3]

Orientation of the Book

Practitioners tell us that much in finance is inexplicable, incomprehensible, and unintelligible. Like Babe Ruth, their explanations for their actions often amount to "I pick a good one and sock it." Fortunately for a rising generation of practitioners, tools and concepts of modern finance provide a language and approach for excellent performance. The aim of this book is to illustrate and exercise the application of these tools and concepts in a messy world.

Focus on Value

The subtitle of this book is *Managing for Corporate Value Creation*. Economics teaches us that value creation should be an enduring focus of concern because value is the foundation of survival and prosperity of the enterprise. The focus on value also helps managers understand the impact of the firm on the world around it. These cases harness and exercise this economic view of the firm. It is the special province of finance to highlight value as a legitimate concern for managers. The cases in this book exercise valuation analysis over a wide range of assets, debt, equities, and options, and a wide range of perspectives, such as investor, creditor, and manager.

Linkage to Capital Markets

An important premise of these cases is that managers should take cues from the capital markets. The cases in this volume help the student learn to look at the capital markets in four ways. First, they illustrate important players in the capital markets such as individual exemplars like Warren Buffett and Bill Miller and institutions like

---

[1]George Herman "Babe" Ruth (1895–1948) was one of the most famous players in the history of American baseball, leading the league in home runs for 10 straight seasons, setting a record of 60 home runs in one season, and hitting 714 home runs in his career. Ruth was also known as the "Sultan of the Swat."

[2]Carl Sandburg, "Notes for Preface," in *Harvest Poems* (New York: Harcourt Brace Jovanovich, 1960), p.11.

[3]Russell Ackoff, "The Future of Operational Research is Past," *Journal of Operational Research Society,* 30, 1 (Pergamon Press, Ltd., 1979): 93–104.

investment banks, commercial banks, rating agencies, hedge funds, merger arbitrageurs, private equity firms, lessors of industrial equipment, and so on. Second, they exercise the students' abilities to interpret capital market conditions across the economic cycle. Third, they explore the design of financial securities, and illuminate the use of exotic instruments in support of corporate policy. Finally, they help students understand the implications of transparency of the firm to investors, and the impact of news about the firm in an efficient market.

Respect for the Administrative Point of View

The real world is messy. Information is incomplete, arrives late, or is reported with error. The motivations of counterparties are ambiguous. Resources often fall short. These cases illustrate the immense practicality of finance theory in sorting out the issues facing managers, assessing alternatives, and illuminating the effects of any particular choice. A number of the cases in this book present practical ethical dilemmas or moral hazards facing managers—indeed, this edition debuts a new chapter, "Ethics in Finance," right at the beginning, where ethics belongs. Most of the cases (and teaching plans in the associated instructor's resource manual) call for *action plans* rather than mere analyses or descriptions of a problem.

Contemporaneity

Over three-quarters of the cases in this book are set in the year 2000 or after. Thirty-six percent of these cases and technical notes are new, or significantly updated. The mix of cases reflects the global business environment: 46 percent of the cases in this book are set outside the United States, or have strong cross-border elements. Finally the blend of cases continues to reflect the growing role of women in managerial ranks: 40 percent of the cases present women as key protagonists and decision-makers. Generally, these cases reflect the increasingly diverse world of business participants.

Plan of the Book

The cases may be taught in many different combinations. The sequence indicated by the table of contents corresponds to course designs used at Darden. Each cluster of cases in the Table of Contents suggests a concept module, with a particular orientation.

1. **Setting Some Themes.** These cases introduce basic concepts of value creation, assessment of performance against a capital-market benchmark, and capital-market efficiency that reappear throughout a case course. The numerical analysis required of the student is relatively light. The synthesis of case facts into an important framework or perspective is the main challenge. The case, "Warren E. Buffett, 2005," sets the nearly universal theme of this volume: the need to think like an investor. "Bill Miller and Value Trust," explores a basic question about performance measurement: what is the right benchmark against which to evaluate success? "Ben & Jerry's Homemade" invites a consideration of "value" and the ways to measure it. The cases about FedEx versus United Parcel Service and Coca-Cola versus PepsiCo (in the third section) use "economic profit" (or EVA®)

to explore the origins of value creation and destruction, and its competitive implications for the future.

2. **Financial Analysis and Forecasting.** In this section, students are introduced to the crucial skills of financial-statement analysis, break-even analysis, ratio analysis, and financial-statement forecasting. One case ("The Body Shop International PLC, 2001: An Introduction to Financial Modeling") takes the student step-by-step through the preparation of forecasts, both by hand and with the aid of a computer-spreadsheet program. Other cases address issues in the analysis of working-capital management, and credit analysis. A new case, "Krispy Kreme Doughnuts, Inc.," confronts issues regarding the quality of reported financial results.

3. **Estimating the Cost of Capital.** This module begins with a discussion of "best practices" among leading firms. The cases exercise skills in estimating the cost of capital for firms and their business segments. The cases aim to exercise and solidify students' mastery of the capital-asset pricing model, the dividend-growth model, and the weighted average cost of capital formula. "Nike, Inc.: Cost of Capital" presents an introductory exercise in the estimation of the weighted average cost of capital. "Teletech Corporation, 2005," explores the implications of mean-variance analysis to business segments within a firm, and gives a useful foundation for discussing value-additivity. A new case, "The Boeing 7E7," presents a dramatic exercise in the estimation of a discount rate for a major corporate project.

4. **Capital Budgeting and Resource Allocation.** The focus of these cases is the evaluation of investment opportunities and entire capital budgets. The analytical challenges range from simple time value of money problems to setting the entire capital budget for a resource-constrained firm. Key issues in this module include the estimation of free cash flows, the comparison of various investment criteria (NPV, IRR, payback, and equivalent annuities), the treatment of issues in mutually exclusive investments, and capital budgeting under rationing. "Genzyme/GelTex Pharmaceuticals Joint Venture," explores the economics of staged investing versus investing in a lump sum. A new case, "Compass Records," considers the dilemma of a small recording company regarding the best terms for engaging an artist.

5. **Management of the Firm's Equity Dividends, Repurchases, Initial Offerings.** This module seeks to develop practical principles about dividend policy and share issues by drawing on concepts about dividend irrelevance, signaling, investor clienteles, bonding, and agency costs. "Gainesboro Machine Tools Corporation" explores decisions about dividends and share repurchase through the lenses of a range of theoretical concepts, including signaling, clientele effects, and residual policies. The new case, "JetBlue Airways IPO Valuation," considers numerous issues in initial public offerings, including underpricing, choice of comparables, and underwriter risk. Another new case, "Purinex, Inc.," explores the decision of a young company to issue new equity to angel investors and venture capitalists.

6. **Management of the Corporate Capital Structure.** The problem of setting capital structure targets is introduced in this module. Prominent issues are the use and

creation of debt tax shields, the role of industry economics and technology, the influence of corporate competitive strategy, the tradeoffs between debt policy, dividend policy, and investment goals, and the avoidance of costs of distress. The new case, "The Wm. Wrigley Jr. Company: Capital Structure, Valuation, and Cost of Capital," addresses the classic dilemma entailed in optimizing the use of debt tax shields and providing financial flexibility—this theme is extended in another new case, "Deluxe Corporation," that asks how much flexibility a firm needs. A third new case in this section is "Deutsche Bank Securities: Financing the Acquisition of Consolidated Supply S.A." that takes the view of a lender in a large leveraged acquisition to explore the relation between firm value and debt capacity.

7. **Analysis of Financing Tactics: Leases, Options, and Foreign Currency.** While the preceding module is concerned with setting debt targets, this module addresses a range of tactics a firm might use to pursue those targets, hedge risk, and exploit market opportunities. Included are domestic and international debt offerings, leases, currency hedges, weather derivatives, warrants, and convertibles. With these cases, students will exercise techniques in securities valuation, including the use of option-pricing theory. This module includes two new cases. "Carrefour S.A." gives a problem in currency risk management. "Primus Automation Division, 2002" explores the challenges of a lessor attempting to set the terms of a lease.

8. **Valuing the Enterprise: Acquisitions and Buyouts.** This module exercises students' skills in valuing the firm. The focus includes valuation using DCF and multiples, techniques of valuing highly leveraged firms, reallocation of value in financial distress, and distribution of joint value in merger negotiation. This module features two merger negotiation exercises and a technical note on hostile takeovers. A new case, "General Electric's Proposed Acquisition of Honeywell," invites students to take the perspective of a merger arbitrage firm in evaluating a proposed deal. The cases in this module are excellent vehicles for end-of-course classes, student term papers, and/or presentations by teams of students.

This edition offers a number of cases that give insights about investing or financing decisions in emerging markets. These include "Deutsche Brauerei," "Kota Fibres, Ltd.," "Rosario Acero S.A.," "Star River Electronics Ltd.," and "Structuring Repsol's Acquisition of YPF S.A."

Summary of Changes from the Fourth Edition

The fifth edition represents a substantial change from the fourth edition.

This edition offers 18 new and significantly updated cases, or 36 percent of the total. All of the cases are set in 1996 or after, and the vast majority is set in 2000 or later. Time marches on. In the interest of presenting a fresh and contemporary collection, older cases have been updated and/or replaced with new case situations. Several of the most favorite "classic" cases from the first four editions are available online from Irwin/McGraw-Hill, where instructors who adopt this edition may copy them for classroom use. All cases and teaching notes have been edited to sharpen the opportunities for student analysis.

The book continues with a strong international aspect (23 of the cases, 46 percent, are set outside the United States or feature significant cross-border issues). Also, the collection continues to feature female decision-makers and protagonists prominently (20, or 40 percent, of the cases).

Supplements

The case studies in this volume are supported by various resources that help make student engagement a success:

*   Spreadsheet files support student and instructor preparation of the cases. They are located on the book's Web site at www.mhhe.com/bruner5e.

*   A guide to the novice on case preparation, "Note to the Student: How to Study and Discuss Cases," appear in this volume.

*   Five cases in the instructor's resource manual provide counterparty roles for two negotiation exercises, or present detailed discussions of case outcomes (i.e., the "B" case to cases appearing in this volume). These supplemental cases can significantly extend student learning and expand the opportunities for classroom discussion.

*   An instructor's resource manual of about 1,000 pages in length containing teaching notes for each case. Each teaching note includes suggested assignment questions, a hypothetical teaching plan, and a prototypical finished case analysis.

*   Web site addresses in many of the teaching notes. These provide a convenient avenue for updates on the performance of undisguised companies appearing in the book.

*   Notes in the instructor's manual on how to design a case method course, on using computers with cases, and on preparing to teach a case.

*   A companion book by Robert Bruner titled, *Socrates' Muse: Reflections on Excellence in Case Discussion Leadership* (Irwin/McGraw-Hill, 2002), is available to instructors who adopt the book for classroom use. This book offers useful tips on case method teaching.

*   Several "classic" cases and their associated teaching notes were among the most popular and durable cases in the first four editions of *Case Studies in Finance*. Instructors adopting this volume for classroom use may request permission to reproduce them for their courses.

Acknowledgments

This book would not be possible without the contributions of many other people. Colleagues at Darden who have taught, co-authored, contributed to, or commented on these cases are Brandt Allen, Yiorgos Allayannis, Sam Bodily, Karl-Adam Bonnier, Susan Chaplinsky, John Colley, Bob Conroy, Ken Eades, Mark Eaker, Bob Fair, Paul Farris, Jim Freeland, Sherwood Frey, Bob Harris, Mark Haskins, Michael Ho, Charles Meiburg, Jud Reis, Michael Schill, William Sihler and Robert Spekman. I am grateful for their collegiality and for the support for my casewriting efforts from the Darden School Foundation, the Batten Institute, the Citicorp Global Scholars Program, Columbia Business School, and INSEAD.

Lee Remmers of INSEAD contributed the case, "Merton Electronics," which I am delighted to present in this collection. Colleagues at other schools provided worthy insights and encouragement toward the development of the five editions of *Case Studies in Finance*. I am grateful to the following persons (listed with the schools with which they were associated at the time of my correspondence or work with them):

Michael Adler, *Columbia*

Raj Aggarwal, *John Carroll*

Turki Alshimmiri, *Kuwait Univ.*

Ed Altman, *NYU*

James Ang, *Florida State*

Paul Asquith, *M.I.T.*

Geert Bekaert, *Stanford*

Michael Berry, *James Madison*

Randy Billingsley, *VPI&SU*

Gary Blemaster, *Georgetown*

Rick Boebel, *University Otago, New Zealand*

Oyvind Bohren, *BI, Norway*

John Boquist, *Indiana*

Michael Brennan, *UCLA*

Duke Bristow, *UCLA*

Ed Burmeister, *Duke*

Kirt Butler, *Michigan State*

Don Chance, *VPI&SU*

Andrew Chen, *Southern Methodist*

Barbara J. Childs, *University of Texas at Austin*

C. Roland Christensen, *Harvard*

Thomas E. Copeland, *McKinsey*

Jean Dermine, *INSEAD*

Michael Dooley, *UVA Law*

Barry Doyle, *University of San Francisco*

Bernard Dumas, *INSEAD*

Peter Eisemann, *Georgia State*

Javier Estrada, *IESE*

Ben Esty, *Harvard*

Thomas H. Eyssell, *Missouri*

Pablo Fernandez, *IESE*

Kenneth Ferris, *Thunderbird*

John Finnerty, *Fordham*

Joseph Finnerty, *Illinois*

Steve Foerster, *Western Ontario*

Günther Franke, *Konstanz*

Bill Fulmer, *George Mason*

Louis Gagnon, *Queens*

Dan Galai, *Jerusalem*

Jim Gentry, *Illinois*

Stuart Gilson, *Harvard*

Robert Glauber, *Harvard*

Mustafa Gultekin, *North Carolina*

Benton Gup, *Alabama*

Jim Haltiner, *William & Mary*

Rob Hansen, *VPI&SU*

Philippe Haspeslagh, *INSEAD*

Pekka Hietala, *INSEAD*

Rocky Higgins, *Washington*

Pierre Hillion, *INSEAD*

Laurie Simon Hodrick, *Columbia*

John Hund, *Texas*

Arthur Houston, *San Diego State University*

Daniel Indro, *Kent State*

Thomas Jackson, *UVA Law*

Pradeep Jalan, *Regina*

Michael Jensen, *Harvard*

Randy D. Jorgensen, *Creighton University*

Sreeni Kamma, *Indiana*

Steven Kaplan, *Chicago*

Andrew Karolyi, *Western Ontario*

James Kehr, *Miami University Ohio*

Kathryn Kelm, *Emporia State*

Carl Kester, *Harvard*

Herwig Langohr, *INSEAD*

Dan Laughhunn, *Duke*

Ken Lehn, *Pittsburgh*

Saul Levmore, *UVA Law*

Wilbur Lewellen, *Purdue*

Scott Linn, *Oklahoma*

Dennis Logue, *Dartmouth*

Robert A. Lutz, *University of Utah*

Paul Mahoney, *UVA Law*

Paul Malatesta, *Washington*

Wesley Marple, *Northeastern*

Felicia Marston, *UVA (McIntire)*

John Martin, *Texas*

Ronald Masulis, *Vanderbilt*

John McConnell, *Purdue*

Wm R. McDaniel, *Florida Atlantic Univ.*

Catherine McDonough, *Babson*

Richard McEnally, *North Carolina*

Wayne Mikkelson, *Oregon*

Michael Moffett, *Thunderbird*

Nancy Mohan, *Dayton*

Ed Moses, *Rollins*

Charles Moyer, *Wake Forest*

David W. Mullins, Jr., *Harvard*

James T. Murphy, *Tulane*

Chris Muscarella, *Penn State*

Robert Nachtmann, *Pittsburgh*

Tom C. Nelson, *University of Colorado*

Ben Nunnally, *UNC-Charlotte*

Richard E. Ottoo, *Pace University*

Robert Parrino, *Texas (Austin)*

Luis Pereiro, *Universidad Torcuato di Tella*

Pamela Peterson, *Florida State*

Larry Pettit, *Virginia (McIntire)*

Tom Piper, *Harvard*

Gordon Philips, *Maryland*

John Pringle, *North Carolina*

Ahmad Rahnema, *IESE*

Al Rappaport, *Northwestern*

Allen Rappaport, *Northern Iowa*

Raghu Rau, *Purdue*

David Ravenscraft, *North Carolina*

Henry B. Reiling, *Harvard*

Lee Remmers, *INSEAD*

Jay Ritter, *Michigan*

Richard Ruback, *Harvard*

Art Selander, *Southern Methodist*

Israel Shaked, *Boston*

Dennis Sheehan, *Penn State*

J.B. Silvers, *Case Western*

Betty Simkins, *Oklahoma State*

Luke Sparvero, *Texas*

Richard Stapleton, *Lancaster*

Laura Starks, *Texas*

Jerry Stevens, *Richmond*

John Strong, *William & Mary*

Marti Subrahmanyam, *NYU*

Anant Sundaram, *Thunderbird*

Rick Swasey, *Northeastern*

Bob Taggart, *Boston College*

Udin Tanuddin, *University Surabaya, Indonesia*

Anjan Thakor, *Indiana*

Thomas Thibodeau, *Southern Methodist*

Clifford Thies, *Shenandoah University*

James G. Tompkins, *Kenesaw State*

Walter Torous, *UCLA*

Max Torres, *IESE*

Nick Travlos, *Boston College*

Lenos Trigeorgis, *Cyprus*

George Tsetsekos, *Drexel*

Peter Tufano, *Harvard*

James Van Horne, *Stanford*

Nick Varaiya, *San Diego State*

Theo Vermaelen, *INSEAD*

Michael Vetsuypens, *Southern Methodist*

Claude Viallet, *INSEAD*

Ingo Walter, *NYU*

J.F. Weston, *UCLA*

Peter Williamson, *Dartmouth*

Brent Wilson, *Brigham Young*

Kent Womack, *Dartmouth*

Karen Wruck, *Ohio State*

Fred Yeager, *St. Louis*

Betty Yobaccio, *Framingham State*

Ken Yook, *Johns Hopkins University*

Marc Zenner, *North Carolina*

I am also grateful to the following practitioners (listed here with affiliated companies at the time of my work with them):

Norm Bartczak, *Center for Financial Strategy*

Bo Brookby, *First Wachovia*

Alison Brown, *Compass Records*

W.L. Lyons Brown, *Brown-Forman*

Bliss Williams Browne, *First Chicago*

George Bruns, *BankBoston*

Ian Buckley, *Henderson Investors*

Ned Case, *General Motors*

Daniel Cohrs, *Marriott*

David Crosby, *Johnson & Johnson*

Jinx Dennett, *BankBoston*

Barbara Dering, *Bank of New York*

Ty Eggemeyer, *McKinsey*

Geoffrey Elliott, *Morgan Stanley*

Louis Elson, *Palamon Capital Partners*

Christine Eosco, *BankBoston*

Catherine Friedman, *Morgan Stanley*

Carl Frischkorn, *Threshold Sports*

Charles Griffith, *AlliedSignal*

Ian Harvey, *BankBoston*

David Herter, *Fleet Boston*

Christopher Howe, *Kleinwort Benson*

Paul Hunn, *Manufacturers Hanover*

Kristen Huntley, *Morgan Stanley*

James Gelly, *General Motors*

Ed Giera, *General Motors*

Betsy Hatfield, *Bank Boston*

Denis Hamboyan, *Bank Boston*

Thomas Jasper, *Salomon Brothers*

Andrew Kalotay, *Salomon Brothers*

Lisa Levine, *Equipment Leasing*

Mary Lou Kelley, *McKinsey*

Francesco Kestenholz, *UBS*

Eric Linnes, *Kleinwort Benson*

Peter Lynch, *Fidelity Investments*

Mary McDaniel, *SNL Securities*

Jean McTighe, *BankBoston*

Frank McTigue, *McTigue Associates*

David Meyer, *J.P. Morgan*

Michael Melloy, *Planet*

Jeanne Mockard, *Putnam Investments*

Pascal Montiero de Barros, *Planet*

Lin Morison, *BankBoston*

John Muleta, *PSINet*

Dennis Neumann, *Bank of New York*

John Newcomb, *BankBoston*

Ralph Norwood, *Polaroid*

Marni Gislason Obernauer, *J.P. Morgan*

Michael Pearson, *McKinsey*

Nancy Preis, *Kleinwort Benson*

Joe Prendergast, *First Wachovia*

Luis Quartin-Bastos, *Planet*

Jack Rader, *FMA*

Christopher Reilly, *S.G. Warburg*

Emilio Rottoli, *Glaxo*

Gerry Rooney, *NationsBank*

Craig Ruff, *AIMR*

Barry Sabloff, *First Chicago*

Linda Scheuplein, *J.P. Morgan*

Keith Shaughnessy, *Bank Boston*

Jack Sheehan, *Johnstown*

Katrina Sherrerd, *AIMR*

John Smetanka, *Security Pacific*

John Smith, *General Motors*

Raj Srinath, *AMTRAK*

Rick Spangler, *First Wachovia*

Kirsten Spector, *BankBoston*

Martin Steinmeyer, *MediMedia*

Bill Stilley, *Adenosine Therapeutics*

Stephanie Summers, *Lehman Brothers*

Sven-Ivan Sundqvist, *Dagens Nyheter*

Patrick Sweeney, *ServerVault*

Peter Thorpe, *Citicorp.*

Katherine Updike, *Excelsior*

Tom Verdoorn, *Land O'Lakes*

Frank Ward, Corp. *Performance Systems*

David Wake Walker, *Kleinwort Benson*

Garry West, *Compass Records*

Ulrich Wiechmann, *UWINC*

Scott Williams, *McKinsey*

Harry You, *Salomon Brothers*

Research assistants working under my direction have helped gather data and prepare drafts. My principal assistant for this fifth edition was Sean Carr. His distinguished contribution was multifaceted: research assistant to me, primary author of some cases under my direction, editor and reviser of material, and generally, manager of this very complex project. He has been a pleasure to work with: a skilled analyst and word-smith, a leader of others, a passionate artist of the case study, devoted to the learning challenge of the student and the opportunities for classroom discussion. Research assistants who contributed to various cases in this and previous editions include Darren Berry, Anna Buchanan, Anne Campbell, Jessica Chan, David Eichler, Dennis Hall, Jerry Halpin, Peter Hennessy, Casey Opitz, Katarina Paddack, Chad Rynbrandt, Michael Schill, John Sherwood, Jane Sommers-Kelly, Thien Pham, Carla Stiassni,

Sanjay Vakharia, Larry Weatherford, and Steve Wilus. I have supervised numerous others in the development of individual cases—those worthy contributors are recognized in the first footnote of each case.

A busy professor soon learns the wisdom in the adage, "Many hands make work light." I am very grateful to the staff of the Darden School for its support in this project. Excellent editorial assistance at Darden was provided by Stephen Smith and Catherine Wiese (Darden's nonpareil editors) and their associates in Darden Business Publishing and the Darden Case Collection, Sherry Alston, Kathie Amato, Amy Lemley, Jamie Miller, Heidi White, and Beth Woods. Betty Sprouse and Ginny Fisher gave stalwart secretarial support. Valuable library research support was given by Karen Marsh King, Nancy Newins, and Susan Norrisey. The patience, care, and dedication of these people are richly appreciated.

At McGraw-Hill/Irwin, Michele Janicek has served as Executive Editor for this book. Mike Junior, now Vice President of eProduct Development, recruited me into this project years ago; the legacy of our early vision-setting continues in this edition. James Labeots was Project Manager; and Barbara Hari served as Development Editor and Editorial Coordinator on this edition.

Of all the contributors, my wife, Barbara McTigue Bruner, and two sons, Jonathan and Alexander, have endured great sacrifices to see this book appear. As Milton said, "They also serve who only stand and wait." Development of this fifth edition would not have been possible without their fond patience.

All these acknowledgments notwithstanding, responsibility for these materials is mine. I welcome suggestions for their enhancement. Please let me know of your experience with these cases, either through McGraw-Hill/Irwin, or at the coordinates given below.

Robert F. Bruner
Dean,
Charles C. Abbott Professor of Business Administration, and
Distinguished Professor of Business Administration
Darden Graduate School of Business
University of Virginia
brunerr@virginia.edu[*]

Individual copies of all the Darden cases in this and previous editions may be obtained promptly from McGraw-Hill/Irwin's *Primis Online* (www.mhhe.com/primis/) or from Darden Business Publishing (telephone: 800-246-3367; mailto: sales@dardenpublishing.com). Proceeds from these case sales support casewriting efforts. Please respect the copyrights on these materials.

---

[*]Students should know that I am unable to offer any comments that would assist their preparation of these cases without the prior express request of their instructors with agreement by me.

Note to the Student: How to Study and Discuss Cases

Get a good idea and stay with It. Dog it and work at it until it's done, and done right.
—Walt Disney

You enroll in a "case method" course, pick up the book of case studies or the stack of loose-leaf cases, and get ready for the first class meeting. If this is your first experience with case discussions, the odds are that you are clueless and a little anxious about how to prepare for this course. That is fairly normal, but something you should try to break through quickly in order to gain the maximum benefit from your studies. Quick breakthroughs come from a combination of good attitude, good "infrastructure," and good execution—this note offers some tips.

Good Attitude

Students learn best that which they teach themselves. Passive and mindless learning is ephemeral. Active, mindful learning simply sticks. The case method makes learning sticky by placing you in situations that require the invention of tools and concepts *in your own terms*. The most successful case method students share a set of characteristics that drive self-teaching:

1. **Personal initiative, self-reliance.** Case studies rarely suggest how to proceed. Professors are more like guides on a long hike: they can't carry you, but they can show you the way. You must arrive at the destination under your own power. You must figure out the case on your own. To teach yourself means that you must sort ideas out in ways that make sense to you personally. To teach yourself is to give yourself two gifts: the idea you are trying to learn and greater self-confidence in your own ability to master the world.

2. **Curiosity, a zest for exploration as an end in itself.** Richard P. Feynman, who won the Nobel Prize in Physics in 1965, was once asked whether his key discovery was worth it. He replied, "[The Nobel Prize is] a pain in the. . . . I don't like honors. . . . The prize is the pleasure of finding the thing out, the kick in the discovery, the observation that other people use it [my work]—those are the real things; the honors are unreal to me."[1]

3. **A willingness to take risks.** Risk-taking is at the heart of all learning. Usually, one learns more from failures than from successes. Banker Walter Wriston once said, "Good judgment comes from experience. Experience comes from bad judgment."

4. **Patience and persistence.** Case studies are messy, a realistic reflection of the fact that managers don't manage problems, they manage messes. Initially, reaching a solution will seem to be the major challenge. But once you reach *a* solution, you may discover other possible solutions and then face the choice among the best alternatives.

5. **An orientation to community and discussion.** Much of the power of the case method derives from a willingness to *talk* with others about your ideas and your points of confusion. This is one of the paradoxes of the case method: you must teach yourself, but not in a vacuum. The poet T. S. Eliot said, "There is no life not lived in community." Talking seems like such an inefficient method of sorting through the case, but if exploration is an end in itself, then talking is the only way. Furthermore, talking is an excellent means of testing your own mastery of ideas, of rooting out points of confusion, and, generally, of preparing yourself for professional life.

6. **Trust in the process.** The learnings from a case-method course are impressive. They arrive cumulatively over time. In many cases, the learnings continue well after the course has finished. Occasionally, those learnings hit you with the force of a tsunami. But generally, the learnings creep in quietly, but powerfully, like the tide. After the case course, you will look back and see that your thinking, mastery, and appreciation have changed dramatically. The key point is that you should not measure the success of your progress on the basis of any single case discussion. Trust that, in the cumulative work over many cases, you will gain the mastery you seek.

Good Infrastructure

"Infrastructure" consists of all the resources that the case-method student can call upon. Some of this is simply given to you by the professor: case studies, assignment questions, supporting references to textbooks or articles, and computer data or models. But you can go much further to help yourself. Consider these steps:

1. **Find a quiet place to study. Spend at least 90 minutes there for each case study.** Each case has subtleties to it that you will miss unless you can concentrate.

---

[1]Richard P. Feynman, *The Pleasure of Finding Things Out* (Cambridge, Mass.: Perseus Publishing, 1999), 12.

After two or three visits, your quiet place will take on the attributes of a habit: you will slip into a working attitude more easily. Be sure to spend enough time in the quiet place to give yourself a chance to really engage the case.

2. **Get a business dictionary.** If you are new to business and finance, some of the terms will seem foreign; if English is not your first language, *many* of the terms will seem foreign, if not bizarre. Get into the habit of looking up terms that you don't know. The benefit of this becomes cumulative.

3. **Skim a business newspaper each day; read a business magazine; follow the markets.** Reading a newspaper or magazine helps build a *context* for the case study you are trying to solve at the moment, and helps you make connections between the case study and current events. The terminology of business and finance that you see in the publications helps to reinforce your use of the dictionary, and hastens your mastery of the terms that you will see in the cases. Your learning by reading business periodicals is cumulative. Some students choose to follow a good business news Web site on the Internet. Those Web sites have the virtue of being inexpensive and efficient, but they tend to screen too much. Having the printed publication in your hands and leafing through it help the process of *discovery,* which is the whole point of the exercise.

4. **Learn the basics of spreadsheet modeling on a computer.** Many case studies now have supporting data available for analysis in spreadsheet files, such as Microsoft Excel. Analyzing the data on a computer rather than by hand both speeds up your work and extends your reach.

5. **Form a study group.** The ideas in many cases are deep; the analysis can get complex. *You will learn more and perform better in class participation by discussing the cases together in a learning team.* Your team should devote an average of an hour to each case. High-performance teams show a number of common attributes:

   a.   The members commit to the success of the team.

   b.   The team plans ahead, leaving time for contingencies.

   c.   The team meets regularly.

   d.   Team members show up for meetings and are *prepared* to contribute.

   e.   There may or may not be a formal leader, but the assignments are clear. Team members meet their assigned obligations.

6. **Get to know your professor.** In the case method, students inevitably learn more from one another than from the instructor. But the teacher is part of the learning infrastructure, too: a resource to be used wisely. Never troll for answers in advance of a case discussion. Do your homework; use classmates and learning teams to clear up most of your questions so that you can focus on the meatiest issues with the teacher. Be very organized and focused about what you would like to discuss. Remember that teachers like to learn, too: if you reveal a new insight about a case or bring a clipping about a related issue in current events, both the professor and the student can gain from their time together. Ultimately, the best payoff to the professor is the "aha" in the student's eyes when he or she masters an idea.

Good Execution

Good attitude and infrastructure must be employed properly—one needs good execution. The extent to which a student learns depends on how the case study is approached. What can one do to gain the maximum from the study of those cases?

1. **Reading the case.** The very first time you read any case, look for the forest, not the trees. This requires that your first reading be quick. Do not begin taking notes on the first round; instead, read the case like a magazine article. The first few paragraphs of a well-constructed case usually say something about the problem—read those carefully. Then quickly read the rest of the case, mainly seeking a sense of the scope of the problems and what information the case contains to help resolve them. Leaf through the exhibits, looking for what information they hold rather than for any analytical insights. At the conclusion of the first pass, read any supporting articles or notes that your instructor may have recommended.

2. **Getting into the case situation. Develop your "awareness."** With the broader perspective in mind, the second and more detailed reading will be more productive. The reason is that, as you now encounter details, your mind will be able to organize them in some useful fashion rather than inventorying them randomly. Making links among case details is necessary for solving the case. At this point, you can take the notes that will set up your analysis.

   The most successful students project themselves into the position of the decision maker because this perspective helps them link case details as well as develop a stand on the case problem. Assignment questions may help you do this, but it is a good idea to get into the habit of doing it yourself. Here are the kinds of questions you might try to answer in preparing every case:

   - Who are the protagonists in the case? Who must take action on the problem? What do they have at stake? What pressures are they under?

   - What business is the company in? What is the nature of its product? What is the nature of demand for that product? What is the firm's distinctive competence? With whom does it compete?[2] What is the structure of the industry? Is the firm comparatively strong or weak? In what ways?

   - What are the goals of the firm? What is the firm's strategy in pursuit of those goals? (The goals and strategy may be explicitly stated, or they may be implicit in the way the firm does business.) What are the firm's apparent functional policies in marketing (e.g., push versus pull strategy), production (e.g., labor relations, use of new technology, distributed production versus centralized), and finance (e.g., the use of debt financing, payment of dividends)? Financial and business strategies

---

[2]Think broadly about competitors. In *A Connecticut Yankee in King Arthur's Court,* Mark Twain wrote, "The best swordsman in the world doesn't need to fear the second best swordsman in the world; no, the person for him to be afraid of is some ignorant antagonist who has never had a sword in his hand before; he doesn't do the thing he ought to do, and so the expert isn't prepared for him; he does the thing he ought not to do; and it often catches the expert out and ends him on the spot."

can be inferred from an analysis of the financial ratios and a sources-and-uses-of-funds statement.

- How well has the firm performed in pursuit of its goals? (The answer to this question calls for simple analysis using financial ratios, such as the DuPont system, compound growth rates, and measures of value creation.)

The larger point of this phase of your case preparation is to broaden your awareness of the issues. Warren Buffett, perhaps the most successful investor in history, said, "Any player unaware of the fool in the market probably *is* the fool in the market." Awareness is an important attribute of successful managers.

3. **Defining the problem.** A common trap for many executives is to assume that the issue at hand is the real problem most worthy of their time, rather than a symptom of some larger problem that *really* deserves their time. For instance, a lender is often asked to advance funds to help tide a firm over a cash shortfall. Careful study may reveal that the key problem is not a cash shortfall, but rather product obsolescence, unexpected competition, or careless cost management. Even in cases where the decision is fairly narrowly defined (e.g., a capital-expenditure choice), the "problem" generally turns out to be the believability of certain key assumptions. Students who are new to the case method tend to focus narrowly in defining problems and often overlook the influence that the larger setting has on the problem. In doing that, the student develops narrow specialist habits, never achieving the general-manager perspective. It is useful and important for you to define the problem yourself and, in the process, validate the problem as suggested by the protagonist in the case.

4. **Analysis: run the numbers and go to the heart of the matter.** Virtually all finance cases require numerical analysis. This is good because figure-work lends rigor and structure to your thinking. But some cases, reflecting reality, invite you to explore blind alleys. If you are new to finance, even those explorations will help you learn.[3] The best case students develop an instinct for where to devote their analysis. Economy of effort is desirable. If you have invested wisely in problem definition, economical analysis tends to follow. For instance, a student might assume that a particular case is meant to exercise financial forecasting skills and will spend two or more hours preparing a detailed forecast, instead of preparing a simpler forecast in one hour and conducting a sensitivity analysis based on key assumptions in the next hour. An executive rarely thinks of a situation as having to do with a forecasting method or discounting or any other technique, but rather thinks of it as a problem of judgment, deciding on which people or concepts or environmental conditions to bet. The best case analyses get down to the *key bets* on which the executive is wagering the prosperity of the firm and his or her career. Get to the business issues quickly, and avoid lengthy churning through relatively unimportant calculations.

---

[3]Case analysis is often iterative: an understanding of the big issues invites an analysis of details—then the details may restructure the big issues and invite the analysis of other details. In some cases, getting to the heart of the matter will mean just such iteration.

5. **Prepare to participate: take a stand.** To develop analytical insights without making recommendations is useless to executives and drains the case-study experience of some of its learning power. A stand means having a point of view about the problem, a recommendation, and an analysis to back up both of them. The lessons most worth learning all come from taking a stand. From that truth flows the educative force of the case method. In the typical case, the student is projected into the position of an executive who must do something in response to a problem. It is this choice of what to do that constitutes the executive's stand. Over the course of a career, an executive who takes stands gains wisdom. If the stand provides an effective resolution of the problem, so much the better for all concerned. If it does not, however, the wise executive analyzes the reasons for the failure and may learn even more than from a success. As Theodore Roosevelt wrote:

> The credit belongs to the man[4] who is actually in the arena—whose face is marred by dust and sweat and blood . . . who knows the great enthusiasms, the great devotions—and spends himself in a worthy cause—who, at best, if he wins, knows the thrills of high achievement—and if he fails, at least fails while daring greatly so that his place shall never be with those cold and timid souls who know neither victory nor defeat.

6. **In class: participate actively in support of your conclusions, but be open to new insights.** Of course, one can have a stand without the world being any wiser. To take a stand in case discussions means to participate actively in the discussion and to advocate your stand until new facts or analyses emerge to warrant a change.[5] Learning by the case method is not a spectator sport. A classic error many students make is to bring into the case-method classroom the habits of the lecture hall (i.e., passively absorbing what other people say). These habits fail miserably in the case-method classroom because they only guarantee that one absorbs the truths and fallacies uttered by others. The purpose of case study is to develop and exercise one's *own* skills and judgment. This takes practice and participation, just as in a sport. Here are two good general suggestions: (1) defer significant note taking until after class and (2) strive to contribute to every case discussion.

7. **Immediately after class: jot down notes, corrections, and questions.** Don't overinvest in taking notes during class—that just cannibalizes "air time" in which you could be learning through discussing the case. But immediately after class, collect your learnings and questions in notes that will capture your thinking. Of course, ask a fellow student or your teacher questions to help clarify issues that still puzzle you.

8. **Once a week, flip through notes. Make a list of your questions, and pursue answers.** Take an hour each weekend to review your notes from class discussions

---

[4]Today, a statement such as this would surely recognize women as well.

[5]There is a difference between taking a stand and pigheadedness. Nothing is served by clinging to your stand to the bitter end in the face of better analysis or common sense. Good managers recognize new facts and good arguments as they come to light and adapt.

during the past week. This will help build your grasp of the flow of the course. Studying a subject by the case method is like building a large picture with small mosaic tiles. It helps to step back to see the big picture. But the main objective should be to make an inventory of anything you are unclear about: terms, concepts, and calculations. Work your way through this inventory with classmates, learning teams, and, ultimately, the instructor. This kind of review and follow-up builds your self-confidence and prepares you to participate more effectively in future case discussions.

Conclusion: Focus on Process and Results Will Follow

View the case-method experience as a series of opportunities to test your mastery of techniques and your business judgment. If you seek a list of axioms to be etched in stone, you are bound to disappoint yourself. As in real life, there are virtually no "right" answers to these cases in the sense that a scientific or engineering problem has an exact solution. Jeff Milman has said, "The answers worth getting are never found in the back of the book." What matters is that you obtain a way of thinking about business situations that you can carry from one job (or career) to the next. In the case method, it is largely true that *how you learn is what you learn.*[6]

---

[6]In describing the work of case teachers, John H. McArthur has said, "How we teach is what we teach."

Ethics in Finance

The first thing is character, before money or anything else.

—J. P. Morgan (in testimony before the U.S. Congress)

The professional concerns himself with doing the right thing rather than making money, knowing that the profit takes care of itself if the other things are attended to.

—Edwin LeFevre, *Reminiscences of a Stock Operator*

Integrity is paramount for a successful career in finance and business, as practitioners remind us. One learns, rather than inherits, integrity. And the lessons are everywhere, even in case studies about finance. To some people, the world of finance is purely mechanical, devoid of ethical considerations. The reality is that ethical issues are pervasive in finance. **Exhibit 1** gives a list of prominent business scandals around the turn of the twenty-first century. One is struck by the wide variety of industrial settings and especially by the recurrent issues rooted in finance and accounting. Still, the disbelief that ethics matter in finance can take many forms.

"It's not my job," says one person, thinking that a concern for ethics belongs to a CEO, an ombudsperson, or a lawyer. But if you passively let someone else do your thinking, you expose yourself to complicity in the unethical decisions of others. Even worse is the possibility that if everyone assumes that someone else owns the job of ethical practice, then perhaps *no one* owns it and that therefore the enterprise has no moral compass at all.

Another person says, "When in Rome, do as the Romans do. It's a dog-eat-dog world. We have to play the game their way if we mean to do business there." Under that view, it is assumed that everybody acts ethically relative to his local environment so that it is inappropriate to challenge unethical behavior. This is moral relativism. The problem with this view is that it presupposes that you have no identity, that, like a chameleon, you are defined by the environment around you. Relativism is the enemy

---

This technical note was prepared by Robert F. Bruner and draws segments from two of his books, *Applied Mergers and Acquisitions* (John Wiley & Sons, copyright © 2004 by Robert F. Bruner) and *Deals from Hell: Lessons That Rise Above the Ashes* (John Wiley & Sons, copyright © 2005 by Robert F. Bruner). These segments are used here with his permission.

of personal identity and character. You *must* have a view, if you are rooted in any cultural system. Prepare to take a stand.

A third person says, "It's too complicated. Civilization has been arguing about ethics for 3,000 years. You expect me to master it in my lifetime?" The response must be that we use complicated systems dozens of times each day without a full mastery of their details. Perhaps the alternative would be to live in a cave, which is a simpler life but much less rewarding. Moreover, as courts have been telling the business world for centuries, ignorance of the law is no defense. If you want to succeed in the field of finance, you must grasp the norms of ethical behavior.

There is no escaping the fact that ethical reasoning is vital to the practice of business and finance. Tools and concepts of ethical reasoning belong in the financial toolkit alongside other valuable instruments of financial practice.

Ethics and economics were once tightly interwoven. The patriarch of economics, Adam Smith, was actually a scholar of moral philosophy. Although the two fields may have diverged in the last century, they remain strong complements.[1] Morality concerns norms and teachings. Ethics concerns the process of making morally *good* decisions or, as Andrew Wicks wrote, "Ethics has to do with pursuing—and achieving—laudable ends."[2] The *Oxford English Dictionary* defines moral as follows: "Of knowledge, opinions, judgments, etc.; relating to the nature and application of the distinction between right and wrong."[3] Ethics, however, is defined as the "science of morals."[4] To see how the decision-making processes in finance have ethical implications, consider the following case study.

Minicase: WorldCom Inc.[5]

The largest corporate fraud in history entailed the falsification of $11 billion in operating profits at WorldCom Inc. WorldCom was among the three largest long-distance telecommunications providers in the United States, the creation of a rollup acquisition strategy by its CEO, Bernard Ebbers. WorldCom's largest acquisition, MCI Communications in 1998, capped the momentum-growth story. This, combined with the buoyant stock market of the late 1990s, increased the firm's share price dramatically.

By early 2001, it dawned on analysts and investors that the United States was greatly oversupplied with long-distance telecommunications capacity. Much of that capacity had been put in place with unrealistic expectations of growth in Internet use. With the collapse of the Internet bubble, the future of telecom providers was suddenly in doubt.

---

[1]Sen (1987) and Werhane (1999) have argued that Smith's masterpiece, *Wealth of Nations*, is incorrectly construed as a justification for self-interest and that it speaks more broadly about virtues such as prudence, fairness, and cooperation.

[2]Wicks (2003), 5.

[3]*Oxford English Dictionary* (1989), vol. IX, 1068.

[4]*Oxford English Dictionary* (1989), vol. V, 421.

[5]This case is based on facts drawn from Pulliam (2003), Blumenstein and Pulliam (2003), Blumenstein and Solomon (2003), and Solomon (2003).

WorldCom had leased a significant portion of its capacity to both Internet service providers and telecom service providers. Many of those lessees declined and, starting in 2000, entered bankruptcy. In mid-2000, Ebbers and WorldCom's chief financial officer (CFO), Scott Sullivan, advised Wall Street that earnings would fall below expectations. WorldCom's costs were largely fixed—the firm had high operating leverage. With relatively small declines in revenue, earnings would decline sharply. In the third quarter of 2000, WorldCom was hit with $685 million in write-offs as its customers defaulted on capacity-lease commitments. In October 2000, Sullivan pressured three midlevel accounting managers at WorldCom to draw on reserve accounts set aside for other purposes to cover operating expenses, which reduced the reported operating expenses and increased profits. The transfer violated rules regarding the independence and purpose of reserve accounts. The three accounting managers acquiesced, but later regretted their action. They considered resigning, but were persuaded to remain with the firm through its earnings crisis. They hoped or believed that a turnaround in the firm's business would make their action an exception.

Conditions worsened in the first quarter of 2001. Revenue fell further, producing a profit shortfall of $771 million. Again, Sullivan prevailed on the three accounting managers to shift operating costs—this time, to capital-expenditure accounts. Again, the managers complied. This time, they backdated entries in the process. In the second, third, and fourth quarters of 2001, they transferred $560 million, $743 million, and $941 million, respectively. In the first quarter of 2002, they transferred $818 million.

The three accounting managers experienced deep emotional distress over their actions. In April 2002, when they discovered that WorldCom's financial plan for 2002 implied that the transfers would continue until the end of the year, the three managers vowed to cease making transfers and to look for new jobs. But inquiries by the U.S. Securities and Exchange Commission (SEC) into the firm's suspiciously positive financial performance triggered an investigation by the firm's head of internal auditing. Feeling the heat of the investigation, the three managers met with representatives from the SEC, the U.S. Federal Bureau of Investigation (FBI), and the U.S. attorney's office on June 24, 2002. The next day, WorldCom's internal auditor disclosed to the SEC the discovery of $3.8 billion in fraudulent accounting. On June 26, the SEC charged WorldCom with fraud.

But the scope of the fraud grew. In addition to the $3.8 billion reallocation of operating expenses to reserves and capital expenditures, WorldCom had shifted another $7.2 billion to its MCI subsidiary, which affected the tracking stock on that entity.

As news of the size of the fraud spread, WorldCom's stock price sank. From its peak in late 2000 until it filed for bankruptcy in July 2002, about $180 billion of WorldCom's equity-market value evaporated. In March 2003, WorldCom announced that it would write off $79.8 billion in assets following an impairment analysis: $45 billion of the write-off arose from the impairment of goodwill.

The three accounting managers had hoped that they would be viewed simply as witnesses. On August 1, they were named by the U.S. attorney's office as unindicted co-conspirators in the fraud. WorldCom fired them immediately. Unable to cope with the prospect of large legal bills for their defense, they pleaded guilty to securities fraud and conspiracy to commit fraud. The charges carried a maximum of 15 years in prison.

Bernard Ebbers and Scott Sullivan were charged with fraud. A study conducted by the bankruptcy examiner concluded that Ebbers had played a role in inflating the firm's revenues. One example cited in the report was the firm's announcement of the acquisition of Intermedia Communications Inc. in February 2001. Even before World-Com's board had approved the deal, the firm's lawyers made it look as if the board had approved the deal by creating false minutes.

WorldCom emerged from bankruptcy in 2004 with a new name, MCI Communications. On March 2, 2004, Sullivan pleaded guilty to fraud. Ebbers continued to protest his innocence, arguing that the fraud was masterminded by Sullivan without Ebbers's knowledge. A jury found Ebbers guilty on March 15, 2005. In the summer of 2005, MCI agreed to be acquired by Verizon, a large regional telephone company in the United States.

This case illustrates how unethical behavior escalates over time. Such behavior is costly to companies, investors, and employees. It damages investor confidence and trust—and it is invariably uncovered. Fraud and earnings management share a common soil: a culture of aggressive growth. Although growth is one of the foremost aims in business, the mentality of growth at any price can warp the thinking of otherwise honorable people.

The shields against fraud are a culture of integrity, strong governance, and strong financial monitoring. Yet in some circumstances, such shields fail to forestall unethical behavior. Michael Jensen (2005) explored an important circumstance associated with managerial actions: when the stock price of a firm is inflated beyond its intrinsic (or true) value. Jensen pointed to the scandals that surfaced during and after a period of overvaluation in share prices between 1998 and 2001. He argued that "society seems to overvalue what is new." When a firm's equity becomes overvalued, it motivates behavior that poorly serves the interests of those investors on whose behalf the firm is managed. Managers whose compensation is tied to increases in share price are motivated to "game the system" by setting targets and managing earnings in ways that yield large bonuses. This behavior is a subset of problems originating from target-based corporate-budgeting systems.

Jensen argues that the market for corporate control solves the problem of *under*valued equity (i.e., firms operating at low rates of efficiency) with the instruments of hostile takeovers, proxy fights, leveraged buyouts, and so on. But he points out that there is little remedy for the opposite case, *over*valued equity. Equity-based compensation—in the form of stock options, shares of stock, stock-appreciation rights, and so on—merely adds fuel to the fire.

Paradoxically, a high stock price would seem to be desirable. But occasionally, stock prices become detached from the fundamental basis for their valuation—that is, when the price exceeds the intrinsic value of the shares. Jensen defines overvalued stock as occurring when the performance necessary to produce that price cannot be attained except by good fortune. The problem is that managers fail to face the facts and explain to investors the overvaluation of shares. Instead, they take actions that prolong, or even worsen, the overvaluation. Those actions destroy value in the long run, even though they may appear to create or preserve value in the short run—as was the case with WorldCom. A little of this behavior begins to stimulate more; soon, a sense of proportion is lost and the organization eventually turns to fraud. The hope is to postpone the inevitable correction in price until after the executive has moved on to another firm or retired. Telling the truth to investors about overvaluation is extremely painful. The firm's stock price falls, executive bonuses dwindle, and the directors listen to outraged investors.

What the tragedies of WorldCom and the other firms cited in **Exhibit 1** share is that, like Peter Pan, those companies refused to grow up. They refused to admit frankly to their shareholders and to themselves that their very high rates of growth were unsustainable.

Why One Should Care about Ethics in Finance

Managing in ethical ways is not merely about avoiding bad outcomes. There are at least five positive arguments for bringing ethics to bear on financial decision making.

Sustainability. Unethical practices are not a foundation for an enduring, sustainable enterprise. This first consideration focuses on the *legacy* one creates through one's financial transactions. What legacy do you want to leave? To incorporate ethics into our finance mind set is to think about the kind of world that we would like to live in and that our children will inherit. One might object that, in a totally anarchic world, unethical behavior might be the only path in life. But this view only begs the point: we don't live in such a world. Instead, our world of norms and laws ensures a corrective process against unethical behavior.

Ethical behavior builds trust. Trust rewards. The branding of products seeks to create a bond between producer and consumer: a signal of purity, performance, or other attributes of quality. This bond is built by trustworthy behavior. As markets reveal, successfully branded products command a premium price. Bonds of trust tend to pay. If the field of finance were purely a world of one-off transactions, it would seem ripe for opportunistic behavior. But in the case of repeated entry into financial markets and transactions by, for example, active buyers, intermediaries, and advisers, reputation can count for a great deal in shaping the expectations of counterparties. This implicit bond, trust, or reputation can translate into more effective and economically attractive financial transactions and policies.

Surely, ethical behavior should be an end in itself. If you are behaving ethically only to get rich, then you are hardly committed to that behavior. But it is a useful encouragement that ethical behavior need not entail pure sacrifice. Some might even see ethical behavior as an imperfect means by which justice expresses itself.

Ethical behavior builds teams and leadership, which underpin process excellence. Standards of global best-practice emphasize that good business processes drive good outcomes. Stronger teams and leaders result in more agile and creative responses to problems. Ethical behavior contributes to the strength of teams and leadership by aligning employees around shared values and by building confidence and loyalty.

An objection to this argument is that, in some settings, promoting ethical behavior is no guarantee of team building. Indeed, teams might blow apart over disagreements about what is ethical or what action is appropriate to take. But typically, this is not the fault of ethics, but rather that of the teams' processes for handling disagreements.

Ethics sets a higher standard than laws and regulations. To a large extent, the law is a crude instrument. It tends to trail rather than anticipate behavior. It contains gaps that become recreational exploitation for the aggressive businessperson. Justice may be neither swift nor proportional to the crime; as Andrew Wicks said, it "puts you in an adversarial posture with respect to others, which may be counterproductive to other objectives in facing a crisis."[6] To use only the law as a basis for ethical thinking is to settle for the lowest common denominator of social norms. As Richard Breeden, the former SEC chair, said, "It is not an adequate ethical standard to want to get through the day without being indicted."[7]

Some might object to that line of thinking by claiming that, in a pluralistic society, the law is the only baseline of norms on which society can agree. Therefore, isn't the law a "good-enough" guide to ethical behavior? Lynn Paine argued that this view leads to a "compliance" mentality and that ethics takes one further. She wrote, "Attention to law, as an important source of managers' rights and responsibilities, is integral to, but not a substitute for, the ethical point of view—a point of view that is attentive to rights, responsibilities, relationships, opportunities to improve and enhance human well-being, and virtue and moral excellence."[8]

Reputation and conscience. Motivating ethical behavior only by trumpeting its financial benefits without discussing its costs is inappropriate. By some estimates, the average annual income for a lifetime of crime (even counting years spent in prison) is large—it seems that crime *does* pay. If income were all that mattered, most of us would switch to this lucrative field. The business world features enough cheats and scoundrels who illustrate that there are myriad opportunities for any professional to break promises—or worse—for money. Ethical professionals decline those opportunities for reasons having to do with the kind of people they want to be. Amar Bhide and Howard Stevenson wrote:

> The businesspeople we interviewed set great store on the regard of their family, friends, and the community at large. They valued their reputations, not for some nebulous financial gain but because they took pride in their good names. Even more important, since outsiders cannot easily judge trustworthiness, businesspeople seem guided by their inner voices, by their consciences. . . . We keep promises because it is right to do so, not because it is good business.[9]

For Whose Interests Are You Working?

Generally, the financial executive or deal designer is an agent acting on behalf of others. For whom are you the agent? Two classic schools of thought emerge.

- *Stockholders.* Some national legal frameworks require directors and managers to operate a company in the interests of its shareholders. This shareholder focus affords a clear objective: do what creates shareholder wealth. This approach

---

[6]Wicks (2003), 11.

[7]K. V. Salwen, "SEC Chief's Criticism of Ex-Managers of Salomon Suggests Civil Action is Likely," *Wall Street Journal,* 20 November 1991, A10.

[8]Paine (1999), 194–195.

[9]Bhide and Stevenson (1990), 127–128.

would seem to limit charitable giving, "living-wage" programs, voluntary reduction of pollution, and enlargement of pension benefits for retirees, all of which can be loosely gathered under the umbrella of the social responsibility movement in business. Milton Friedman (1962), perhaps the most prominent exponent of the stockholder school of thought, has argued that the objective of business is to return value to its owners, and that to divert the objective to other ends is to expropriate shareholder value and threaten the survival of the enterprise. Also, the stockholder view would argue that, if all the companies deviated, the price system would cease to function well as a carrier of information about the allocation of resources in the economy. The stockholder view is perhaps dominant in the United States, the United Kingdom, and other countries in the Anglo-Saxon sphere.

• *Stakeholders*. The alternative view admits that stockholders are an important constituency of the firm, but that other groups such as employees, customers, suppliers, and the community also have a stake in the activities and the success of the firm. Edward Freeman (1984) argued that the firm should be managed in the interest of the broader spectrum of constituents. The manager would necessarily be obligated to account for the interests and concerns of the various constituent groups in arriving at business decisions. The aim would be to satisfy them all, or at least the most concerned stakeholders, on each issue. The complexity of that kind of decision-making can be daunting and slows the process. In addition, it is not always clear which stakeholder interests are relevant in making specific decisions. Such a definition seems to depend largely on the specific context, which would seem to challenge the ability to achieve equitable treatment of different stakeholder groups across time. But the important contribution of this view is to suggest a relational view of the firm and to stimulate the manager to consider the diversity of those relationships.

Adding complexity to the question of whose interests one serves is the fact that one often has many allegiances—not only to the firm or the client, but also to one's community, family, etc. One's obligations as an employee or as a professional are only a subset of one's total obligations.

What is "Good"? Consequences, Duties, Virtues

One confronts ethical issues when one must choose among alternatives on the basis of right versus wrong. The ethical choices may be stark where one alternative is truly right and the other truly wrong. But in professional life, the alternatives typically differ more subtly, as in choosing which alternative is *more* right or *less* wrong. Ernest Hemingway said that what is moral is what makes one feel good after and what is immoral is what makes one feel bad after. Because feelings about an action could vary tremendously from one person to the next, this simplistic test would seem to admit moral relativism as the only course, an ethical "I'm OK, you're OK" approach. Fortunately 3,000 years of moral reasoning provide frameworks for a better definition of what is right and wrong.

Right and wrong as defined by consequences. An easy point of departure is to focus on outcomes. An action might be weighed in terms of its utility[10] for society. Who is hurt or helped must be taken into consideration. Utility can be assessed in terms of the pleasure or pain for people. People choose to maximize utility. Therefore, the right action is that which produces the greatest good for the greatest number of people.

Utilitarianism has proven to be a controversial ideal. Some critics have argued that this approach might endorse gross violations of the norms that society holds dear, including the right to privacy, the sanctity of contracts, and property rights, when weighed against the consequences for all. And the calculation of utility might be subject to special circumstances or open to interpretation, making the assessment rather more situation-specific than some philosophers could accept.

Utilitarianism was the foundation for modern neoclassical economics. Utility has proved to be difficult to measure rigorously, and remains a largely theoretical idea. Yet utility-based theories are at the core of welfare economics, and underpin analyses of such widely varying phenomena as government policies, consumer preferences, and investor behavior.

Right and wrong as defined by duty or intentions. Immoral actions are ultimately self-defeating. The practice of writing bad checks, for instance, if practiced universally, would result in a world without check-writing and probably very little credit, too. Therefore, you should act on rules that you would be required to apply universally.[11] You should treat a person as an end, never as a means. It is vital to ask whether an action would show respect for others and whether that action was something a rational person would do: "If everyone behaved this way, what kind of world would we have?"

Critics of that perspective argue that its universal view is too demanding, indeed, even impossible for a businessperson to observe. For instance, the profit motive focuses on the manager's duty to just one company. But Norman Bowie responds, "Perhaps focusing on issues other than profits . . . will actually enhance the bottom line. . . . Perhaps we should view profits as a consequence of good business practices rather than as the goal of business."[12]

Right and wrong as defined by virtues. Finally, a third tradition[13] in philosophy argues that the debate over values is misplaced. The focus should instead be on *virtues* and the qualities of the practitioner. The attention to consequences or duty is fundamentally a focus on *compliance.* Rather, one should consider whether an action is consistent with being a virtuous person. This view argues that personal happiness flows from being virtuous and not merely from comfort (utility) or observance (duty).

---

[10]The Utilitarian philosophers, Jeremy Bentham (1748–1832), James Mill (1773–1836), and John Stuart Mill (1806–1873), argued that the utility (or usefulness) of ideas, actions, and institutions could be measured in terms of their consequences.

[11]The philosopher Immanuel Kant (1724–1804) sought a foundation for ethics in the purity of one's motives.

[12]Bowie (1999), 13.

[13]This view originated in ancient Greek philosophy, starting with Socrates, Plato, and Aristotle.

It acknowledges that vices are corrupting. And it focuses on personal pride: "If I take this action, would I be proud of what I see in the mirror? If it were reported tomorrow in the newspaper, would I be proud of myself?" Warren Buffett, chief executive officer (CEO) of Berkshire Hathaway, and one of the most successful investors in modern history, issued a letter to each of his operating managers every year emphasizing the importance of personal integrity. He said that Berkshire could afford financial losses, but not losses in reputation. He also wrote, "Make sure everything you do can be reported on the front page of your local newspaper written by an unfriendly, but intelligent reporter."[14]

Critics of virtue-based ethics raise two objections. First, a virtue to one person may be a vice to another. Solomon (1999) points out that Confucius and Friedrich Nietzsche, two other virtue ethicists, held radically different visions of virtue. Confucius extolled such virtues as respect and piety, whereas Nietzsche extolled risk-taking, war-making, and ingenuity. Thus, virtue ethics may be context-specific. Second, virtues can change over time. What may have been regarded as gentlemanly behavior in the nineteenth century might have been seen by feminists in the late twentieth century as insincere and manipulative.

A discrete definition of right and wrong remains the subject of ongoing discourse. But the practical person can abstract from those and other perspectives useful guidelines toward ethical conduct:

- How will my action affect others? What are the consequences?
- What are my motives? What is my duty here? How does this decision affect them?
- Does this action serve the best that I can be?

What Can *You* Do to Promote Ethical Behavior in Your Firm?

An important contributor to unethical business practices is the existence of a work environment that promotes such behavior. Leaders in corporate workplaces need to be proactive in shaping a high-performance culture that sets high ethical expectations. The leader can take a number of steps to shape an ethical culture.

Adopt a code of ethics. One dimension of ethical behavior is to acknowledge some code by which one intends to live. Corporations, too, can adopt codes of conduct that shape ethical expectations. Firms recognize the "problem of the commons" inherent in unethical behavior by one or a few employees. In 1909, the U.S. Supreme Court decided that a corporation could be held liable for the actions of its employees.[15] Since then, companies have sought to set corporate expectations for employee behavior, including codes of ethics.[16] **Exhibit 2** gives an example of one such code, from General Electric Company. Those norms are one page of a 35-page document outlining the code, to whom it applies, special responsibilities for employees and

---

[14]Russ Banham, "The Warren Buffett School," *Chief Executive* (December 2002): http://www.robertpmiles.com/BuffettSchool.htm (accessed on 19 May 2003).

[15]See *New York Central v. United States*, 212 U.S. 481.

[16]Murphy (1997) compiled 80 exemplary ethics statements.

leaders, specific codes of conduct with respect to customers and suppliers, government business, competition, health, safety, employment, and the protection of GE's assets. Corporate codes are viewed by some critics as cynical efforts that seem merely to respond to executive liability that might arise from white collar and other economic crimes. Companies and their executives may be held liable for an employee's behavior, even if the employee acted contrary to the company's instructions. Mere observance of guidelines in order to reduce liability is a legalistic approach to ethical behavior. Instead, Lynn Paine (1994) has urged firms to adopt an "integrity strategy" that uses ethics as the driving force within a corporation. Deeply held values would become the foundation for decision making across the firm, and would yield a frame of reference that would integrate functions and businesses. By that view, ethics defines what a firm stands for.

In addition, an industry or a professional group can adopt a code of ethics. One example relevant to finance professionals is the Code of Ethics of the CFA Institute, the group that confers the Chartered Financial Analyst (CFA) designation on professional securities analysts and portfolio managers. Excerpts from the CFA Institute's Code of Ethics and Standards of Professional Conduct are given in **Exhibit 3.**

Talk about ethics within your team and firm. Many firms seek to reinforce a culture of integrity with a program of seminars and training in ethical reasoning. A leader can stimulate reflection through informal discussion of ethical developments (e.g., indictments, convictions, civil lawsuits) in the industry or profession, or of ethical issues that the team may be facing. This kind of discussion (without preaching) signals that it is on the leader's mind and is a legitimate focus of discussion. One executive regularly raises issues such as those informally over lunch or morning coffee. Leaders believe that ethical matters are important enough to be the focus of team discussions.

Reflect on your dilemmas. The challenge for many finance practitioners is that ethical dilemmas do not readily lend themselves to the structured analysis that one would apply to valuing a firm or balancing the books. Nevertheless, one can harness the questions raised in the field of ethics to lend some rigor to one's reflections. Laura Nash (1981) abstracted a list of 12 questions on which the thoughtful practitioner might reflect in grappling with an ethical dilemma:

1. Have I defined the problem correctly and accurately?
2. If I stood on the other side of the problem, how would I define it?
3. What are the origins of this dilemma?
4. To whom and to what am I loyal, as a person and as a member of a firm?
5. What is my intention in making this decision?
6. How do the likely results compare with my intention?
7. Can my decision injure anyone? How?
8. Can I engage the affected parties in my decision before I decide or take action?
9. Am I confident that my decision will be as valid over a long period as it may seem at this moment?

10. If my boss, the CEO, the directors, my family, or the community learned about this decision, would I have misgivings about my actions?

11. What signals (or symbols) might my decision convey, if my decision were understood correctly? If misunderstood?

12. Are there exceptions to my position, perhaps special circumstances under which I might make a different decision?

Act on your reflections. This may be the toughest step of all. The field of ethics can lend structure to one's thinking, but has less to say about the action to be taken. When confronting a problem of ethics within a team or an organization, one can consider a hierarchy of responses, from questioning and coaching to whistle-blowing (either to an internal ombudsperson or, if necessary, to an outside entity) and, possibly, leaving the organization.

Conclusion

An analysis of finance's ethical issues is vital. The cases of WorldCom and other major business scandals show that ethical issues pervade the financial environment. Ethics is one of the pillars on which stands success in finance—it builds sustainable enterprise, trust, organizational strength, and personal satisfaction. Therefore, the financial decision-maker must learn to identify, analyze, and act on the ethical issues that may arise. Consequences, duties, and virtues stand out as three important benchmarks for ethical analysis. Nevertheless, the results of such analysis are rarely clear-cut. But real business leaders will take the time to sort through the ambiguities and do "the right thing" in the words of Edwin LeFevre. These and other ethical themes will appear throughout finance case studies and one's career.

References and Recommended Readings

Achampong, F., and W. Zemedkun. "An Empirical and Ethical Analysis of Factors Motivating Managers' Merger Decisions." *Journal of Business Ethics* 14 (1995): 855–865.

Bhide, A., and H. H. Stevenson. "Why be Honest if Honesty Doesn't Pay." *Harvard Business Review* (September–October 1990): 121–129.

Bloomenthal, Harold S. *Sarbanes-Oxley Act in Perspective.* (St. Paul, MN: West Group), 2002.

Blumenstein, R., and S. Pulliam. "WorldCom Report Finds Ebbers Played Role in Inflating Revenue." *Wall Street Journal.* 6 June 2003, downloaded from http://online.wsj.com/article_print/0,,SB105485251027721500,00.html.

Blumenstein, R., and D. Solomon. "MCI is Expected to Pay Massive Fine in SEC Deal." *Wall Street Journal.* 19 May 2003, downloaded from http://online.wsj.com/article_print/0,,SB105329362774148600,00.html.

Boatright, J. R. *Ethics in Finance.* (Oxford: Blackwell Publishers), 1999.

Bowie, N. E. "A Kantian Approach to Business Ethics." in *A Companion to Business Ethics*. R. E. Frederick, ed. (Malden, MA: Blackwell), 1999, 3–16.

Carroll, A. B. "Ethics in Management." in *A Companion to Business Ethics*. R. E. Frederick, ed. (Malden, MA: Blackwell), 1999, 141–152.

Frederick, R. E. *A Companion to Business Ethics*. (Oxford: Blackwell Publishers).

Freeman, R. E. *Strategic Management: A Stakeholder Approach*. (Boston, MA: Pittman), 1984.

Friedman, M. *Capitalism and Freedom*. (Chicago, IL: University of Chicago Press), 1962.

General Electric Company. "Integrity: The Spirit and Letter of our Commitment." February 2004. http://www.ge.com/files/usa/en/commitment/social/integrity/downloads/english.pdf.

Jensen, M. "The Agency Costs of Overvalued Equity." *Financial Management* (Spring 2005): 5–19.

Kidder, R. "Ethics and the Bottom Line: Ten Reasons for Businesses to do Right." *Insights on Global Ethics* (Spring 1997): 7–9.

Murphy, P. E. "80 Exemplary Ethics Statements." in L. H. Newton, "A Passport for the Corporate Code: From Borg Warner to the Caux Principles." in R. E. Frederick, ed. *A Companion to Business Ethics*. (Malden, MA: Blackwell), 1999, 374–385.

Nash, L. L. "Ethics without the Sermon," *Harvard Business Review* (November–December 1981): 79–90.

Paine, L. S. "Managing for Organizational Integrity." *Harvard Business Review* (March–April 1994): 106–117.

———. "Law, Ethics, and Managerial Judgment," in R. E. Frederick, ed. *A Companion to Business Ethics*. (Malden, MA: Blackwell), 1999, 194–206.

Paine, L. S. *Value Shift: Why Companies Must Merger Social and Financial Imperatives to Achieve Superior Performance*. (New York: McGraw-Hill), 2003.

Pulliam, S. "A Staffer Ordered to Commit Fraud Balked, and then Caved." *Wall Street Journal*. 23 June 2003, A1.

Sen, A. *On Ethics and Economics*. (Oxford: Blackwell Publishers), 1987.

Shafer, W. "Effects of Materiality, Risk, and Ethical Perceptions on Fraudulent Reporting by Financial Executives." *Journal of Business Ethics* 38, 3 (2002): 243–263.

Solomon, R. "Business Ethics and Virtue." in R. E. Frederick, ed. *A Companion to Business Ethics*. (Malden, MA: Blackwell), 1999, 30–37.

Solomon, D. "WorldCom Moved Expenses to the Balance Sheet of MCI." *Wall Street Journal*. 31 March 2003, http://online.wsj.com/article_print/0,,SB104907054486790100,00.html.

Werhane, P. "Two Ethical Issues in Mergers and Acquisitions." *Journal of Business Ethics* 7 (1988): 41–45.

———. "Mergers, Acquisitions, and the Market for Corporate Control." *Public Affairs Quarterly* 4, 1 (1990): 81–96.

———. "A Note on Moral Imagination." Charlottesville, VA: University of Virginia Darden School of Business Case Collection (UVA-E-0114), 1997.

———. "Business Ethics and the Origins of Contemporary Capitalism: Economics and Ethics in the Work of Adam Smith and Herbert Spencer." in R. E. Frederick, ed. *A Companion to Business Ethics*. (Malden, MA: Blackwell), 1999, 325–341.

Wicks, A. "A Note on Ethical Decision Making." Charlottesville, VA: University of Virginia Darden School of Business Case Collection (UVA-E-0242), 2003.

EXHIBIT 1 | Prominent Business Scandals Revealed between 1998 and 2002

The companies and their alleged or admitted accounting issues are as follows:
- Adelphia (loans and looting)
- Bristol-Myers (improper inflation of revenues through use of sales incentives)
- CMS Energy (overstatement of revenues through round-trip energy trades)
- Computer Associates (inflation of revenues)
- Dynegy (artificial increase of cash flow)
- Elan (use of off-balance-sheet entities)
- Enron (inflation of earnings and use of off-balance-sheet entities)
- Global Crossing (artificial inflation of revenues)
- Halliburton (improper revenue recognition)
- Kmart (accounting for vendor allowances)
- Lucent Technologies (revenue accounting and vendor financing)
- Merck (revenue recognition)
- MicroStrategy (backdating of sales contracts)
- Network Associates (revenue and expense recognition)
- PNC Financial Services (accounting for the transfer of loans)
- Qwest (revenue inflation)
- Reliance Resources (revenue inflation through round-trip energy trades)
- Rite Aid (inflation of earnings)
- Tyco International (improper use of "cookie jar" reserves and acquisition accounting)
- Vivendi Universal (withholding information about liquidity troubles)
- WorldCom (revenue and expense recognition)
- Xerox (revenue and earnings inflation)

These cases and their points of controversy are summarized in Bloomenthal (2002), Appendices E-1 and E-2.

EXHIBIT 2 | General Electric's (GE) Code of Conduct

- Obey the applicable laws and regulations governing our business conduct worldwide.
- Be honest, fair, and trustworthy in all your GE activities and relationships.
- Avoid all conflicts of interest between work and personal affairs.
- Foster an atmosphere in which fair employment practices extend to every member of the diverse GE community.
- Strive to create a safe workplace and to protect the environment.
- Through leadership at all levels, sustain a culture where ethical conduct is recognized, valued, and exemplified by all employees.

Source: General Electric Company, "Integrity: The Spirit and Letter of Our Commitment," February 2004, 5. A longer version of this resource is also available on the company's Web site at http://www.ge.com/files/usa/en/commitment/social/integrity/downloads/ english.pdf.

EXHIBIT 3 | Excerpts from the CFA Institute's Code of Ethics and Standards of Professional Conduct: January 1, 2006

CFA Institute's Code of Ethics

- Act with integrity, competence, diligence, respect, and in an ethical manner with the public, clients, prospective clients, employers, employees, colleagues in the investment profession, and other participants in the global capital markets.
- Place the integrity of the investment profession and the interests of clients above their own personal interests.
- Use reasonable care and exercise independent professional judgment when conducting investment analysis, making investment recommendations, taking investment actions, and engaging in other professional activities.
- Practice and encourage others to practice in a professional and ethical manner that will reflect credit on themselves and the profession.
- Promote the integrity of, and uphold the rules governing, capital markets.
- Maintain and improve their professional competence and strive to maintain and improve the competence of other investment professionals.

CFA Institute's Standards of Professional Conduct (*excerpts that suggest the scope and detail of the complete standards*)

Members and candidates must:

- Understand and comply with all applicable laws, rules, and regulations . . .
- Use reasonable care and judgment to achieve and maintain independence and objectivity in their professional activities. Members and candidates must not offer, solicit, or accept any gift, benefit, compensation, or consideration that reasonably could be expected to compromise their own or another's independence and objectivity.
- Not knowingly make any misrepresentations relating to investment analysis, recommendations, actions, or other professional activities.
- Not engage in any professional conduct involving dishonesty, fraud, or deceit, or commit any act that reflects adversely on their professional reputation, integrity, or competence.
- Not act or cause others to act on the [material, nonpublic] information.
- Not engage in practices that distort prices or artificially inflate trading volume with the intent to mislead market participants.
- Have a duty of loyalty to their clients and must act with reasonable care and exercise prudent judgment. Members and candidates must act for the benefit of their clients and place their clients' interests before their employer's or their own interests. . . .
- Deal fairly and objectively with all clients. . . .
- Keep information about current, former, and prospective clients confidential. . . .
- Act for the benefit of their employer and not deprive their employer of the advantage of their skills and abilities, divulge confidential information, or otherwise cause harm to their employer.
- Not accept gifts, benefits, compensation, or consideration that competes with, or might reasonably be expected to create a conflict of interest with, their employer's interest. . . .
- Make reasonable efforts to detect and prevent violations of applicable laws, rules, regulations, and the Code and Standards by anyone subject to their supervision or authority.
- Disclose to clients and prospective clients the basic format and general principles of the investment processes used . . . Use reasonable judgment in identifying which factors are important to their investment analyses, recommendations, or actions and include those factors in communications with clients and prospective clients. . . . Distinguish between fact and opinion in the presentation of investment analysis and recommendations. . . .

Source: CFA Institute, *Code of Ethics and Standards of Professional Conduct* (Charlottesville, VA: CFA Institute), 2006, http://www.cfainstitute.org/cfacentre/pdf/English2006CodeandStandards.pdf.

PART 1

Setting Some Themes

Warren E. Buffett, 2005

On May 24, 2005, Warren E. Buffett, the chairperson and chief executive officer (CEO) of Berkshire Hathaway Inc., announced that MidAmerican Energy Holdings Company, a subsidiary of Berkshire Hathaway, would acquire the electric utility PacifiCorp. In Buffett's largest deal since 1998, and the second largest of his entire career, MidAmerican would purchase PacifiCorp from its parent, Scottish Power plc, for $5.1 billion in cash and $4.3 billion in liabilities and preferred stock. "The energy sector has long interested us, and this is the right fit," Buffett said. At the announcement, Berkshire Hathaway's Class A shares closed up 2.4 percent for the day, for a gain in market value of $2.17 billion.[1] Scottish Power's share price also jumped 6.28 percent on the news[2]; the S&P 500 Composite Index closed up 0.02 percent. **Exhibit 1** illustrates the recent share-price performance for Berkshire Hathaway, Scottish Power, and the S&P 500 Index.

The acquisition of PacifiCorp renewed public interest in its sponsor, Warren Buffett. In many ways, he was an anomaly. One of the richest individuals in the world (with an estimated net worth of about $44 billion), he was also respected and even beloved. Though he had accumulated perhaps the best investment record in history (a compound annual increase in wealth for Berkshire Hathaway of 24 percent from 1965 to 2004),[3] Berkshire paid him only $100,000 per year to serve as its CEO. While Buffett and other insiders controlled 41.8 percent of Berkshire Hathaway, he ran the company in the interests of all shareholders. "We will not take cash compensation, restricted stock, or option grants that would make our results superior to [those of Berkshire's investors]," Buffett said. "I will keep well over 99 percent of my net worth in Berkshire. My wife and I have never sold a share nor do we intend to."[4]

---

[1]The per-share change in Berkshire Hathaway's Class A share price at the date of the announcement was $2,010. The company had 1,267,197 Class A shares outstanding.

[2]The per-share change in Scottish Power's share price at the date of the announcement was (British pounds) GBP27.75. The company had 466,112,000 shares outstanding.

[3]In comparison, the annual average total return on all large stocks from 1965 to the end of 2004 was 10.5 percent. *Stocks, Bonds, Bills, and Inflation 2005 Yearbook* (Chicago: Ibbotson Associates, 2005), 217.

[4]Warren Buffett, Annual Letter to Shareholders, 2001.

Buffett was the subject of numerous laudatory articles and at least eight biographies, yet he remained an intensely private individual. Though acclaimed by many as an intellectual genius, he shunned the company of intellectuals and preferred to affect the manner of a down-home Nebraskan (he lived in Omaha) and a tough-minded investor. In contrast to investing's other "stars," Buffett acknowledged his investment failures both quickly and publicly. Although he held an MBA from Columbia University and credited his mentor, Professor Benjamin Graham, with developing the philosophy of value-based investing that had guided Buffett to his success, he chided business schools for the irrelevance of their finance and investing theories.

Numerous writers sought to distill the essence of Buffett's success. What were the key principles that guided Buffett? Could those principles be applied broadly in the 21st century, or were they unique to Buffett and his time? From an understanding of those principles, analysts hoped to illuminate the acquisition of PacifiCorp. What were Buffett's probable motives in the acquisition? What did Buffett's offer say about his valuation of PacifiCorp, and how would it compare with valuations for other regulated utilities? Would Berkshire's acquisition of PacifiCorp prove to be a success? How would Buffett define success?

Berkshire Hathaway Inc.

Berkshire Hathaway was incorporated in 1889 as Berkshire Cotton Manufacturing, and eventually grew to become one of New England's biggest textile producers, accounting for 25 percent of the United States' cotton textile production. In 1955, Berkshire merged with Hathaway Manufacturing and began a secular decline due to inflation, technological change, and intensifying competition from foreign competitors. In 1965, Buffett and some partners acquired control of Berkshire Hathaway, believing that its financial decline could be reversed.

Berkshire Hathaway "Class A" vs. S&P 500 Composite Index

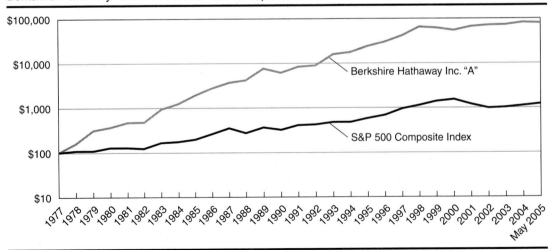

Over the next 20 years, it became apparent that large capital investments would be required to remain competitive and that even then the financial returns would be mediocre. Fortunately, the textile group generated enough cash in the initial years to permit the firm to purchase two insurance companies headquartered in Omaha: National Indemnity Company and National Fire & Marine Insurance Company. Acquisitions of other businesses followed in the 1970s and 1980s; Berkshire Hathaway exited the textile business in 1985.

The investment performance of a share in Berkshire Hathaway had astonished most observers. In 1977, the firm's year-end closing share price was $102; on May 24, 2005, the closing price on its Class A shares reached $85,500. Over the same period, the Standard & Poor's 500 Index grew from 96 to 1,194. Some observers called for Buffett to split[5] the firm's share price to make it more accessible to the individual investor. He steadfastly refused.[6]

In 2004, Berkshire Hathaway's annual report described the firm as "a holding company owning subsidiaries engaged in a number of diverse business activities."[7] Berkshire's portfolio of businesses included:

- **Insurance:** The largest component of Berkshire's portfolio focused on property and casualty insurance, on both a direct and a reinsurance basis (for example, GEICO, General Re).

- **Apparel:** Manufacturing and distribution of a variety of footwear and clothing products, including underwear, active-wear, children's clothes, and uniforms (for example, Fruit of the Loom, Garan, Fechheimer Brothers, H.H. Brown Shoe, Justin Brands).

- **Building products:** Manufacturing and distribution of a variety of building materials, and related products and services (for example, Acme Building Brands, Benjamin Moore, Johns Manville, MiTek).

- **Finance and financial products:** Proprietary investing, manufactured housing and related consumer financing, transportation equipment leasing, furniture leasing, life annuities and risk management products (for example, BH Finance, Clayton Homes, XTRA, CORT, Berkshire Hathaway Life, and General Re Securities).

- **Flight services:** Training to operators of aircraft and ships, and providing fractional ownership programs for general aviation aircraft (for example, FlightSafety, NetJets).

---

[5]A split was an increase in the number of a firm's outstanding shares that did not cause a change in the shareholders' equity. A two-for-one split would entail a 50 percent reduction in the stock's price at the time of the split. Company directors authorized stock splits to make the company's shares affordable to a broader range of investors.

[6]In 1996, Berkshire Hathaway issued Class B shares, which had an economic interest equal to 1/30 and a voting interest equal to 1/200 that of the firm's Class A shares.

[7]Berkshire Hathaway Inc., 2004 Annual Report, 1.

- **Retail:** Retail sales of home furnishings, appliances, electronics, fine jewelry and gifts (for example, Nebraska Furniture Mart, R.C. Willey Home Furnishings, Star Furniture Company, Jordan's Furniture, Borsheim's, Helzberg Diamond Shops, Ben Bridge Jeweler).

- **Grocery distribution:** Wholesale distributing of groceries and nonfood items (for example, McLane Company).

- **Carpet and floor coverings:** Manufacturing and distribution of carpet and floor coverings under a variety of brand names (for example, Shaw Industries).

Berkshire also owned an assortment of smaller businesses[8] generating about $3 billion in revenues. **Exhibit 2** gives a summary of revenues, operating profits, capital expenditures, depreciation, and assets for Berkshire's various business segments. The company's investment portfolio also included equity interests in numerous publicly traded companies, which are summarized in **Exhibit 3.** In addition, the company owned about $21.4 billion of foreign exchange contracts at year end, spread among 12 currencies. Prior to March 2002, neither Buffett nor Berkshire had ever traded in currencies, but Buffett had developed serious concerns about the United States' large current account deficits, and he hoped that his currency bets would offset the growing pressure on the dollar.

Buffett's Investment Philosophy

Warren Buffett was first exposed to formal training in investing at Columbia University where he studied under Professor Benjamin Graham. A coauthor of the classic text *Security Analysis,* Graham developed a method of identifying undervalued stocks (that is to say, stocks whose prices were less than their intrinsic value). This became the cornerstone of modern value investing. Graham's approach was to focus on the value of assets such as cash, net working capital, and physical assets. Eventually, Buffett modified that approach to focus also on valuable franchises that were unrecognized by the market.

Over the years, Buffett had expounded his philosophy of investing in his chairperson's letter to the shareholders in Berkshire Hathaway's annual report. By 2005, those lengthy letters had accumulated a broad following because of their wisdom and their humorous, self-deprecating tone. The letters emphasized the following elements:

1. *Economic reality, not accounting reality.* Financial statements prepared by accountants conformed to rules that might not adequately represent the *economic* reality of a business. Buffett wrote:

---

[8]These included Scott Fetzer, a diversified manufacturer and distributor of commercial and industrial products; Buffalo News, a newspaper publisher in western New York; International Dairy Queen, which licensed and serviced a system of 6,000 Dairy Queen stores; See's Candies, a manufacturer and distributor of boxed chocolates and other confectionery products; Larson-Juhl, which designed, manufactured, and distributed custom picture-framing products; CTB International, a manufacturer of equipment and systems for the poultry, hog, egg production, and grain industries; and the Pampered Chef, a direct seller of kitchen tools.

Because of the limitations of conventional accounting, consolidated reported earnings may reveal relatively little about our true economic performance. Charlie [Munger, Buffett's business partner] and I, both as owners and managers, virtually ignore such consolidated numbers. . . . Accounting consequences do not influence our operating or capital-allocation process.[9]

Accounting reality was conservative, backward-looking, and governed by generally accepted accounting principles (GAAP). Investment decisions, on the other hand, should be based on the economic reality of a business. In economic reality, intangible assets such as patents, trademarks, special managerial expertise, and reputation might be very valuable, yet under GAAP, they would be carried at little or no value. GAAP measured results in terms of net profit; in economic reality, the results of a business were its *flows of cash*.

A key feature to Buffett's approach defined economic reality at the level of the business itself, not the market, the economy, or the security—he was a *fundamental analyst* of the business. His analysis sought to judge the simplicity of the business, the consistency of its operating history, the attractiveness of its long-term prospects, the quality of management, and the firm's capacity to create value.

2. *The cost of the lost opportunity.* Buffett compared an investment opportunity against the next best alternative, the "lost opportunity." In his business decisions, he demonstrated a tendency to frame his choices as either/or decisions rather than yes/no decisions. Thus, an important standard of comparison in testing the attractiveness of an acquisition was the potential rate of return from investing in the common stocks of other companies. Buffett held that there was no fundamental difference between buying a business outright, and buying a few shares of that business in the equity market. Thus, for him, the comparison of an investment against other returns available in the market was an important benchmark of performance.

3. *Value creation: time is money.* Buffett assessed intrinsic value as the present value of future expected performance:

[All other methods fall short in determining whether] an investor is indeed buying something for what it is worth and is therefore truly operating on the principle of obtaining value for his investments. . . . Irrespective of whether a business grows or doesn't, displays volatility or smoothness in earnings, or carries a high price or low in relation to its current earnings and book value, the investment shown by the discounted-flows-of-cash calculation to be the cheapest is the one that the investor should purchase.[10]

Enlarging on his discussion of intrinsic value, Buffett used an educational example:

We define intrinsic value as the discounted value of the cash that can be taken out of a business during its remaining life. Anyone calculating intrinsic value necessarily comes up with a highly subjective figure that will change both as estimates of future cash flows are revised and as interest rates move. Despite its fuzziness, however, intrinsic value is all important and is the only logical way to evaluate the relative attractiveness of investments and businesses.

---

[9]Berkshire Hathaway Inc., 2004 Annual Report, 2.

[10]Berkshire Hathaway Inc., 1992 Annual Report, 14.

To see how historical input (book value) and future output (intrinsic value) can diverge, let us look at another form of investment, a college education. Think of the education's cost as its "book value." If it is to be accurate, the cost should include the earnings that were foregone by the student because he chose college rather than a job. For this exercise, we will ignore the important non-economic benefits of an education and focus strictly on its economic value. First, we must estimate the earnings that the graduate will receive over his lifetime and subtract from that figure an estimate of what he would have earned had he lacked his education. That gives us an excess earnings figure, which must then be discounted, at an appropriate interest rate, back to graduation day. The dollar result equals the intrinsic economic value of the education. Some graduates will find that the book value of their education exceeds its intrinsic value, which means that whoever paid for the education didn't get his money's worth. In other cases, the intrinsic value of an education will far exceed its book value, a result that proves capital was wisely deployed. In all cases, what is clear is that book value is meaningless as an indicator of intrinsic value.[11]

To illustrate the mechanics of this example, consider the hypothetical case presented in **Exhibit 4.** Suppose an individual has the opportunity to invest $50 million in a business—this is its cost or book value. This business will throw off cash at the rate of 20 percent of its investment base each year. Suppose that instead of receiving any dividends, the owner decides to reinvest all cash flow back into the business—at this rate, the book value of the business will grow at 20 percent per year. Suppose that the investor plans to sell the business for its book value at the end of the fifth year. Does this investment create value for the individual? One determines this by discounting the future cash flows to the present at a cost of equity of 15 percent. Suppose that this is the investor's opportunity cost, the required return that could have been earned elsewhere at comparable risk. Dividing the present value of future cash flows (i.e., Buffett's intrinsic value) by the cost of the investment (i.e., Buffett's book value) indicates that every dollar invested buys securities worth $1.23. Value is created.

Consider an opposing case, summarized in **Exhibit 5.** The example is similar in all respects except for one key difference: the annual return on the investment is 10 percent. The result is that every dollar invested buys securities worth $0.80. Value is destroyed.

Comparing the two cases in **Exhibits 4** and **5,** the difference in value creation and destruction is driven entirely by the relationship between the expected returns and the discount rate: in the first case, the spread is positive; in the second case, it is negative. Only in the instance where expected returns equal the discount rate will book value equal intrinsic value. In short, book value or the investment outlay may not reflect the economic reality. One needs to focus on the prospective rates of return, and how they compare to the required rate of return.

4. *Measure performance by gain in intrinsic value, not accounting profit.* Buffett wrote:

---

[11]Berkshire Hathaway Inc., 1994 Annual Report, 7.

Our long-term economic goal . . . is to maximize Berkshire's average annual rate of gain in intrinsic business value on a per-share basis. We do not measure the economic significance or performance of Berkshire by its size; we measure by per-share progress. We are certain that the rate of per-share progress will diminish in the future—a greatly enlarged capital base will see to that. But we will be disappointed if our rate does not exceed that of the average large American corporation.[12]

The gain in intrinsic value could be modeled as the value added by a business above and beyond the charge for the use of capital in that business. The gain in intrinsic value was analogous to the economic-profit and market-value-added measures used by analysts in leading corporations to assess financial performance. Those measures focus on the ability to earn returns in excess of the cost of capital.

5. *Risk and discount rates.* Conventional academic and practitioner thinking held that the more risk one took, the more one should get paid. Thus, discount rates used in determining intrinsic values should be determined by the risk of the cash flows being valued. The conventional model for estimating discount rates was the capital asset pricing model (CAPM), which added a risk premium to the long-term risk-free rate of return, such as the U.S. Treasury bond yield.

Buffett departed from conventional thinking by using the rate of return on the long-term (for example, 30-year) U.S. Treasury bond to discount cash flows.[13] Defending this practice, Buffett argued that he avoided risk, and therefore should use a "risk-free" discount rate. His firm used almost no debt financing. He focused on companies with predictable and stable earnings. He or his vice chair, Charlie Munger, sat on the boards of directors, where they obtained a candid, inside view of the company and could intervene in managements' decisions if necessary. Buffett once said, "I put a heavy weight on certainty. If you do that, the whole idea of a risk factor doesn't make sense to me. Risk comes from not knowing what you're doing."[14] He also wrote:

We define risk, using dictionary terms, as "the possibility of loss or injury." Academics, however, like to define "risk" differently, averring that it is the relative volatility of a stock or a portfolio of stocks—that is, the volatility as compared to that of a large universe of stocks. Employing databases and statistical skills, these academics compute with precision the "beta" of a stock—its relative volatility in the past—and then build arcane investment and capital allocation theories around this calculation. In their hunger for a single statistic to measure risk, however, they forget a fundamental principle: it is better to be approximately right than precisely wrong.[15]

---

[12]Berkshire Hathaway Inc., 2004 Annual Report, 74.

[13]The yield on the 30-year U.S. Treasury bond on May 24, 2005, was 5.76 percent. The beta of Berkshire Hathaway was 0.75.

[14]Quoted in Jim Rasmussen, "Buffett Talks Strategy with Students," *Omaha World-Herald,* 2 January 1994, 26.

[15]Berkshire Hathaway Inc., 1993 Annual Report. Republished in Andrew Kilpatrick, *Of Permanent Value: The Story of Warren Buffett* (Birmingham, AL: AKPE, 1994), 574.

6. *Diversification*. Buffett disagreed with conventional wisdom that investors should hold a broad portfolio of stocks in order to shed company-specific risk. In his view, investors typically purchased far too many stocks rather than waiting for one exceptional company. Buffett said,

> Figure businesses out that you understand and concentrate. Diversification is protection against ignorance, but if you don't feel ignorant, the need for it goes down drastically.[16]

7. *Investing behavior should be driven by information, analysis, and self-discipline, not by emotion or "hunch."* Buffett repeatedly emphasized awareness and information as the foundation for investing. He said, "Anyone not aware of the fool in the market probably is the fool in the market."[17] Buffett was fond of repeating a parable told to him by Benjamin Graham:

> There was a small private business and one of the owners was a man named Market. Every day, Mr. Market had a new opinion of what the business was worth, and at that price stood ready to buy your interest or sell you his. As excitable as he was opinionated, Mr. Market presented a constant distraction to his fellow owners. "What does he know?" they would wonder, as he bid them an extraordinarily high price or a depressingly low one. Actually, the gentleman knew little or nothing. You may be happy to sell out to him when he quotes you a ridiculously high price, and equally happy to buy from him when his price is low. But the rest of the time, you will be wiser to form your own ideas of the value of your holdings, based on full reports from the company about its operation and financial position.[18]

Buffett used this allegory to illustrate the irrationality of stock prices as compared to true intrinsic value. Graham believed that an investor's worst enemy was not the stock market, but oneself. Superior training could not compensate for the absence of the requisite temperament for investing. Over the long term, stock prices should have a strong relationship with the economic progress of the business. But daily market quotations were heavily influenced by momentary greed or fear, and were an unreliable measure of intrinsic value. Buffett said,

> As far as I am concerned, the stock market doesn't exist. It is there only as a reference to see if anybody is offering to do anything foolish. When we invest in stocks, we invest in businesses. You simply have to behave according to what is rational rather than according to what is fashionable.[19]

Accordingly, Buffett did not try to "time the market" (i.e., trade stocks based on expectations of changes in the market cycle)—his was a strategy of patient,

---

[16]Quoted in *Forbes* (19 October 1993). Republished in Andrew Kilpatrick, *Of Permanent Value,* 574.

[17]Quoted in Michael Lewis, *Liar's Poker* (New York: Norton, 1989), 35.

[18]Originally published in Berkshire Hathaway Inc., 1987 Annual Report. This quotation was paraphrased from James Grant, *Minding Mr. Market* (New York: Times Books, 1993), xxi.

[19]Peter Lynch, *One Up on Wall Street* (New York: Penguin Books, 1990), 78.

long-term investing. As if in contrast to Mr. Market, Buffett expressed more contrarian goals: "We simply attempt to be fearful when others are greedy and to be greedy only when others are fearful."[20] Buffett also said, "Lethargy bordering on sloth remains the cornerstone of our investment style,"[21] and "The market, like the Lord, helps those who help themselves. But unlike the Lord, the market does not forgive those who know not what they do."[22]

Buffett scorned the academic theory of capital-market efficiency. The efficient markets hypothesis (EMH) held that publicly known information was rapidly impounded into share prices, and that as a result, stock prices were fair in reflecting what was known about a company. Under EMH, there were no bargains to be had and trying to outperform the market would be futile. "It has been helpful to me to have tens of thousands turned out of business schools taught that it didn't do any good to think," Buffett said.[23]

I think it's fascinating how the ruling orthodoxy can cause a lot of people to think the earth is flat. Investing in a market where people believe in efficiency is like playing bridge with someone who's been told it doesn't do any good to look at the cards.[24]

8. *Alignment of agents and owners.* Explaining his significant ownership interest in Berkshire Hathaway, Buffett said, "I am a better businessman because I am an investor. And I am a better investor because I am a businessman."[25]

As if to illustrate this sentiment, he said:

A managerial "wish list" will not be filled at shareholder expense. We will not diversify by purchasing entire businesses at control prices that ignore long-term economic consequences to our shareholders. We will only do with your money what we would do with our own, weighing fully the values you can obtain by diversifying your own portfolios through direct purchases in the stock market.[26]

For four of Berkshire's six directors, over 50 percent of their family net worth was represented by shares in Berkshire Hathaway. The senior managers of Berkshire Hathaway subsidiaries held shares in the company, or were compensated under incentive plans that imitated the potential returns from an equity interest in their business unit or both.[27]

---

[20]Berkshire Hathaway Inc., 1986 Annual Report, 16.

[21]Berkshire Hathaway Inc., 1990 Annual Report, 15.

[22]Berkshire Hathaway Inc., Letters to Shareholders, 1977–83, 53.

[23]Quoted in Andrew Kilpatrick, *Of Permanent Value,* 353.

[24]Quoted in L. J. Davis, "Buffett Takes Stock," *New York Times,* 1 April 1990, 16.

[25]Quoted in *Forbes* (19 October 1993). Republished in Andrew Kilpatrick, *Of Permanent Value,* 574.

[26]"Owner-Related Business Principles," in Berkshire Hathaway's 2004 Annual Report, 75.

[27]In April 2005, the U.S. Securities and Exchange Commission interviewed Warren Buffett in connection with an investigation into the insurance giant AIG and its dealings with Berkshire Hathaway's General Re insurance unit. Buffett reported that he had questioned General Re's CEO about the transactions with AIG, but that he never learned any details.

MidAmerican Energy Holdings Company

MidAmerican Energy Holdings Company, a subsidiary of Berkshire Hathaway Inc., was a leader in the production of energy from diversified sources, including geothermal, natural gas, hydroelectric, nuclear power, and coal. Based in Des Moines, Iowa, the company was a major supplier and distributor of energy to over 5 million customers in the United States and Great Britain. Through its HomeServices of America division, MidAmerican also owned the second-largest full-service independent real-estate brokerage in the United States. **Exhibit 6** provides condensed, consolidated financial statements for MidAmerican for the years 2000 through 2004.

Berkshire Hathaway took a major stake in MidAmerican on March 14, 2000, with a $1.24 billion investment in common stock and a non-dividend-paying convertible preferred stock.[28] This investment gave Berkshire about a 9.7 percent voting interest and a 76 percent economic interest in MidAmerican. "Though there are many regulatory constraints in the utility industry, it's possible that we will make additional commitments in the field," Buffett said, at the time. "If we do, the amounts could be large."[29] Subsequently, in March 2002, Berkshire acquired another 6.7 million shares of MidAmerican's convertible stock for $402 million, giving Berkshire a 9.9 percent voting interest and an 83.7 percent economic interest in the equity of MidAmerican (80.5 percent on a diluted basis).

At the time of Berkshire's initial investment in MidAmerican, Buffett explained that acquisitions in the electric utility industry were complicated by a variety of regulations, including the Public Utility Holding Company Act of 1935 (PUHCA), which was intended to prevent conglomerates from owning utilities and to impede the formation of massive national utilities that regulators could not control. This regulation made it necessary for Berkshire to structure its investment in MidAmerican such that it would not have voting control. Buffett had said he was eager to have PUHCA scaled back, and that if it were repealed he would invest $10 billion to $15 billion in the electric utility industry.[30]

PacifiCorp

For the past several years, Berkshire Hathaway had been unsuccessful in identifying attractive acquisition opportunities. In 2001, Buffett addressed the issue head-on in his annual letter to shareholders:

> Some years back, a good $10 million idea could do wonders for us (witness our investment in the Washington Post in 1973 or GEICO in 1976). Today, the combination of *ten* such

---

[28]Berkshire acquired 900,942 shares of common stock and 34,563,395 shares of convertible preferred stock of MidAmerican. Convertible preferred stock was preferred stock that carried the right to be exchanged by the investor for common stock. The exchange, or conversion, right was like a call option on the common stock of the issuer. The terms of the convertible preferred stated the price at which common shares could be acquired in exchange for the principal value of the convertible preferred stock.

[29]Berkshire Hathaway Inc., 1999 Annual Report, 11.

[30]Rebecca Smith and Karen Richardson, *Wall Street Journal,* 25 May 2005, A1.

ideas and a triple in the value of *each* would increase the net worth of Berkshire by only ¼ of 1 percent. We need "elephants" to make significant gains now—and they are hard to find.[31]

By 2004, Berkshire's fruitless search for "elephants" had begun to take its toll. In his annual letter that year, Buffett lamented his failure to make any multibillion-dollar acquisitions, and he bemoaned Berkshire's large cash balance that had been accumulating since 2002. "We don't enjoy sitting on $43 billion of cash equivalents that are earning paltry returns," Buffett said. "What Charlie [Munger] and I would like is a little action now."[32]

The announcement that Berkshire's wholly owned subsidiary, MidAmerican Energy Holdings Company, would acquire PacifiCorp seemed to indicate that Buffett had found an "elephant." PacifiCorp was a leading, low-cost energy producer and distributor that served 1.6 million customers in six states in the western United States. Based in Portland, Oregon, PacifiCorp generated power through company-owned coal, hydrothermal, renewable wind power, gas-fired combustion, and geothermal facilities. The company had merged with Scottish Power in 1999. **Exhibit 7** presents PacifiCorp's most recent financial statements.

The PacifiCorp announcement renewed general interest in Buffett's approach to acquisitions. **Exhibit 8** gives the formal statement of acquisition criteria contained in Berkshire Hathaway's 2004 Annual Report. In general, the policy expressed a tightly disciplined strategy that refused to reward others for actions that Berkshire Hathaway might just as easily take on its own. Analysts scrutinized the PacifiCorp deal for indications of how it fit Berkshire's criteria. Several noted that the timing of Berkshire Hathaway's bid closely followed Duke Energy's bid to acquire Cinergy for $9 billion. The PacifiCorp deal was expected to close after the federal and state regulatory reviews were completed, sometime in the next 12 to 18 months.

Exhibit 9 provides company descriptions and key financial data for comparable firms in the regulated electric utility business. **Exhibit 10** presents a range of enterprise values and equity market values for PacifiCorp implied by the multiples of comparable firms.

Conclusion

Conventional thinking held that it would be difficult for Warren Buffett to maintain his record of 24 percent annual growth in shareholder wealth. Buffett acknowledged that "a fat wallet is the enemy of superior investment results."[33] He stated that it was the firm's goal to meet a 15 percent annual growth rate in intrinsic value. Would the PacifiCorp acquisition serve the long-term goals of Berkshire Hathaway? Was the bid price appropriate? Because PacifiCorp was privately held by Scottish Power, how did Berkshire's offer measure up against the company's valuation implied by the multiples for comparable firms? What might account for the share-price increase for Berkshire Hathaway at the announcement?

---

[31]Berkshire Hathaway Inc., 2001 Annual Report, 17.

[32]Berkshire Hathaway Inc., 2001 Annual Report, 17.

[33]Quoted in Garth Alexander, "Buffett Spends $2bn on Return to His Roots," *Times* (London), 17 August 1995.

EXHIBIT 1 | Relative Share Price Performance of Berkshire Hathaway "Class A" & Scottish Power plc vs. S&P 500 Index (January 3, 2005–May 24, 2005)

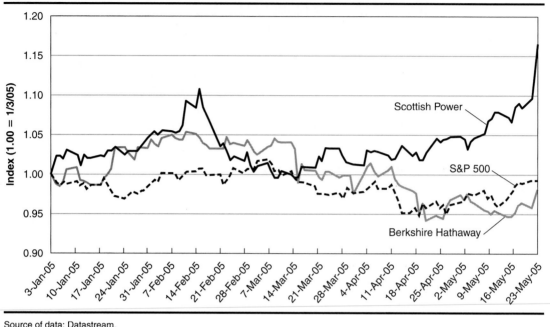

Source of data: Datastream.

EXHIBIT 2 | Business-Segment Information for Berkshire Hathaway Inc. (dollars in millions)

Segment	Revenues		Earnings (loss) before Taxes		Capital Expenditures		Depreciation[1]		Identifiable Assets	
	2004	2003	2004	2003	2004	2003	2004	2003	2004	2003
Insurance	$23,927	$24,731	$4,375	$4,941	$ 52	$ 55	$ 52	$ 63	$114,759	$109,004
Apparel	2,200	2,075	325	289	51	71	52	51	1,582	1,523
Building products	4,337	3,846	643	559	219	170	172	174	2,803	2,593
Financial products	3,774	3,045	584	619	296	232	183	161	30,086	28,338
Flight services	3,244	2,431	191	72	155	150	146	136	2,823	2,875
Grocery distribution	23,373	13,743	228	150	136	51	107	59	2,349	2,243
Retail	2,601	2,311	163	165	126	106	56	51	1,669	1,495
Carpet & floor coverings	5,174	4,660	466	436	125	120	99	91	2,153	1,999
Other businesses	3,213	3,040	465	486	41	47	44	43	1,875	1,813
Total	$71,843	$59,882	$7,440	$7,717	$1,201	$1,002	$911	$829	$160,099	$151,883

[1]Excludes capital expenditures which were part of business acquistions.

Source of data: Berkshire Hathaway Inc., 2004 Annual Report.

EXHIBIT 3 | Major Investees of Berkshire Hathaway (dollars in millions)

Company	Shares	% of Co. Owned	Cost[1]	Market Value
American Express Company[2]	151,610,700	12.1	$1,470	$ 8,546
The Coca-Cola Company[2]	200,000,000	8.3	1,299	8,328
The Gillette Company[2]	96,000,000	9.7	600	4,299
H&R Block, Inc.	14,350,600	8.1	223	703
M&T Bank Corporation	6,708,760	5.8	103	723
Moody's Corporation	24,000,000	16.2	499	2,084
PetroChina "H" shares	2,338,961,000	1.3	488	1,249
The Washington Post Company	1,727,765	18.1	11	1,698
Wells Fargo & Company[2]	56,448,380	3.3	463	3,508
White Mountain Insurance	1,724,200	16.0	369	1,114
Others			3,531	5,465
Total Common Stocks			$9,056	$37,717

[1]This was both Berkshire's actual purchase price and tax basis; GAAP "cost" differed in a few cases because of write-ups or write-downs that had been required.

[2]Buffett referred to this group of companies as Berkshire Hathaway's "Big Four." Berkshire invested $3.83 billion in the four through multiple transactions between May 1988 and October 2003; on a composite basis, Berkshire's dollar-weighted purchase date was July 1992. By year-end 2004, Berkshire had held these interests, on a weighted basis, for about 12.5 years.

Source of data: Berkshire Hathaway Inc., 2004 Annual Report, 16.

EXHIBIT 4 | Hypothetical Example of Value Creation

Assume:

- 5-year investment horizon, when you liquidate at "book" or accumulated investment value
- initial investment is $50 million
- no dividends are paid, all cash flows are reinvested
- return on equity = 20%
- cost of equity = 15%

Year	0	1	2	3	4	5
Investment or **Book** Equity Value	50	60	72	86	104	124

Market Value (or Intrinsic Value) = Present value @ 15% of 124 = $61.65

Market/Book = $61.65/50.00 = $1.23

Value created: $1.00 invested becomes $1.23 in market value.

Source: Case writer analysis.

EXHIBIT 5 | Hypothetical Example of Value Destruction

Assume:

- 5-year investment horizon, when you liquidate at "book" or accumulated investment value
- initial investment of $50 million
- no dividends are paid, all cash flows are reinvested
- return on equity = 10%
- cost of equity = 15%

Year	0	1	2	3	4	5
Investment or **Book** Equity Value	50	55	60	67	73	81

Market Value (or intrinsic value) = Present value @ 15% of $81 = $40.30

Market/Book = $40.30/50.00   = $0.80

Value destroyed: $1.00 invested becomes $0.80 in market value.

Source: Case writer analysis.

EXHIBIT 6 | MidAmerican Energy Holdings Co.: Condensed Consolidated Financial
Statements (dollars in millions)

	2000	2001	2002	2003	2004
Balance sheets					
Assets:					
Properties, plants, and equipment, net	$ 5,349	$ 6,537	$10,285	$11,181	$11,607
Goodwill	3,673	3,639	4,258	4,306	4,307
Other assets	2,659	2,450	3,892	3,658	3,990
	$11,681	$12,626	$18,435	$19,145	$19,904
Liabilities and shareholders' equity:					
Debt, except debt owed to Berkshire	$ 5,919	$ 7,163	$10,286	$10,296	$10,528
Debt owed to Berkshire	1,032	455	1,728	1,578	1,478
Other liabilities and minority interest	3,154	3,300	4,127	4,500	4,927
	10,105	10,918	16,141	16,374	16,933
Shareholders' equity	1,576	1,708	2,294	2,771	2,971
	$11,681	$12,626	$18,435	$19,145	$19,904
Income statements					
Operating revenue and other income	$ 4,013	$ 4,973	$ 4,903	$ 6,143	$ 6,727
Costs and expenses:					
Cost of sales and operating expenses	3,100	3,522	3,092	3,913	4,390
Depreciation and amortization	383	539	530	603	638
Interest expense – debt held by Berkshire	40	50	118	184	170
Other interest expense	336	443	640	716	713
	3,859	4,554	4,380	5,416	5,911
Earnings before taxes	154	419	523	727	816
Income taxes and minority interests	73	276	126	284	278
Earnings from continuing operations	81	143	397	443	538
Loss on discontinued operations	—	—	(17)	(27)	(368)
Net earnings	$ 81	$ 143	$ 380	$ 416	$ 170

Source of data: Berkshire Hathaway regulatory filings.

EXHIBIT 7 | PacifiCorp Consolidated Financial Statements (millions of dollars)

	Year Ended March 31,	
	2004	**2005**
Balance sheets		
Assets:		
Current assets	$ 756.4	$ 1,214.3
Properties, plants, and equipment, net	9,036.5	9,490.6
Other assets	1,884.2	1,816.0
	$11,677.1	$12,520.9
Liabilities and shareholders' equity:		
Current liabilities	$ 1,074.3	$ 1,597.7
Deferred credits	$ 3,706.3	$ 3,868.3
Long-term debt and capital lease obligations	3,520.2	3,629.0
Preferred stock subject to mandatory redemption	56.3	48.8
	8,357.1	9,143.8
Shareholders' equity	3,320.0	3,377.1
	$11,677.1	$12,520.9
Income statements		
Operating revenue and other income	$ 3,194.5	$ 3,048.8
Costs and expenses:		
Operating expenses	2,147.8	1,955.5
Depreciation and amortization	428.8	436.9
Income from operations	617.9	656.4
Interest expense	224.4	236.2
Income from operations before income tax expense	393.5	420.2
Cumulative effect of accounting change	(0.9)	—
Income tax expense	144.5	168.5
Net income	$ 248.1	$ 251.7

Source of data: PacifiCorp 10-K regulatory filing.

EXHIBIT 8 | Berkshire Hathaway Acquisition Criteria

We are eager to hear *from principals or their representatives* about businesses that meet all of the following criteria:

1. Large purchases (at least $75 million of pretax earnings unless the business will fit into one of our existing units).
2. Demonstrated consistent earning power (Future projections are of no interest to us, nor are "turnaround" situations.)
3. Businesses earning good returns on equity while employing little or no debt.
4. Management in place (We can't supply it.)
5. Simple businesses (If there's lots of technology, we won't understand it.)
6. An offering price (We don't want to waste our time or that of the seller by talking, even preliminarily, about a transaction when price is unknown.)

The larger the company, the greater will be our interest: We would like to make an acquisition in the $5 billion to $20 billion range. *We are not interested, however, in receiving suggestions about purchases we might make in the general stock market.*

We will not engage in unfriendly takeovers. We can promise complete confidentiality and a very fast answer—customarily within five minutes—as to whether we're interested. We prefer to buy for cash, but will consider issuing stock when we receive as much in intrinsic business value as we give. *We don't participate in auctions.*

Charlie and I frequently get approached about acquisitions that don't come close to meeting our tests: We've found that if you advertise an interest in buying collies, a lot of people will call hoping to sell you their cocker spaniels. A line from a country song expresses our feeling about new ventures, turnarounds, or auction-like sales: "When the phone don't ring, you'll know it's me."

Source: Berkshire Hathaway Inc., 2004 Annual Report, 28.

EXHIBIT 9 | Comparable Regulated Energy Firms

		Price Per Share						(Dollars in Millions)							
	Beta	Shares O/S (millions)	Low	High	Div. Per Share	S&P Rating	Total Assets	Total Liabilities	Cash and Equiv.	ST Debt	LT Debt	Net Debt	Rev	EBITDA	EBIT	Net Income
Alliant Energy Corp.	0.85	115.74	$23.50	$28.80	$1.01	na	$ 8,275	$ 5,470	$276	$ 243	$2,300	$2,267	$2,959	$ 752	$ 420	$164
Cinergy Corp.	0.85	187.53	$34.90	$42.60	$1.88	BBB+	$14,982	$10,804	$165	$1,179	$4,228	$5,242	$4,688	$1,198	$ 738	$404
NSTAR	0.70	106.55	$22.70	$27.20	$1.13	A	$ 7,117	$ 5,633	$ 23	$ 311	$2,101	$2,389	$2,954	$ 702	$ 455	$190
SCANA Corp.	0.75	113.00	$32.80	$39.70	$1.46	na	$ 8,996	$ 6,430	$120	$ 415	$3,186	$3,481	$3,885	$ 861	$ 596	$264
Wisconsin Energy Corp.	0.70	116.99	$29.50	$34.60	$0.83	BBB+	$ 9,565	$ 7,043	$ 36	$ 439	$3,240	$3,643	$3,431	$ 857	$ 530	$306
PacifiCorp	na	312.18	na	na	na	na	$12,521	$ 9,144	$199	$ 270	$3,629	$3,700	$3,049	$1,093	$ 656	$252

ALLIANT: Alliant Energy's utilities, Interstate Power and Light (IPL), and Wisconsin Power and Light (WPL) provided electricity to more than 970,000 customers and natural gas to about 412,000 customers in four states.

CINERGY: Its traditional operating units generated, transmitted, and distributed electricity to more than 1.5 million customers and natural gas to 500,000 in Ohio, Indiana, and Kentucky. Cinergy had agreed to be acquired by utility behemoth, Duke Energy, in a $9 billion stock swap.

NSTAR: Utility holding company transmitted and distributed electricity to 1.4 million homes and businesses in Massachusetts; also served some 300,000 natural-gas customers. The company marketed wholesale electricity, operated liquefied natural-gas processing and storage facilities, provided district heating and cooling services, and offered fiber-optic telecommunications services.

SCANA: The holding company served more than 585,000 electricity customers and 690,000 gas customers in South and North Carolina and the neighboring states through utilities South Carolina Electric & Gas and Public Service Company of North Carolina.

WISCONSIN ENERGY: The company's utilities provided electricity to nearly 1.1 million customers and natural gas to 1 million customers in eastern and northern Wisconsin and Michigan's Upper Peninsula.

Sources of data: Value Line Investment Survey; Standard & Poor's (case writer's analysis).

EXHIBIT 10 | Valuation Multiples for Comparable Regulated Energy Firms

	(Dollars in Millions)				Enterprise Value as Multiple of:				MV Equity as Multiple of:	
	MV Equity	Enterprise Value	Book Value	EPS	Rev	EBIT	EBITDA	Net Income	EPS	Book Value
Alliant Energy Corp.	$3,333	$ 5,600	$2,805	$ 1.42	1.89x	13.33x	7.45x	34.15x	20.33x	1.19x
Cinergy Corp.	$7,989	$13,231	$4,178	$ 2.15	2.82x	17.93x	na	32.75x	19.77x	1.91x
NSTAR	$2,898	$ 5,287	$1,484	$ 1.78	1.79x	11.62x	7.53x	27.83x	15.25x	1.95x
SCANA Corp.	$4,486	$ 7,967	$2,566	$ 2.34	2.05x	13.37x	9.25x	30.18x	16.99x	1.75x
Wisconsin Energy Corp.	$4,048	$ 7,691	$2,522	$ 2.62	2.24x	14.51x	8.97x	25.13x	13.23x	1.61x
Median	$4,048	$ 7,691	$2,566	$ 2.15	2.05x	13.37x	8.25x	30.18x	16.99x	1.75x
Mean	$4,551	$ 7,955	$2,711	$ 2.06	2.16x	14.15x	8.30x	30.01x	17.11x	1.68x
Implied Value of PacifiCorp[1]			$3,377	$ 0.81	$6,252	$8,775	$9,023	$7,596	$4,277	$5,904
					$6,584	$9,289	$9,076	$7,553	$4,308	$5,678

[1]Implied values for PacifiCorp's Enterprise Value and Market Value of Equity are derived using the Median (top) and Mean (bottom) multiples of the comparable firms.

Sources of data: Value Line Investment Survey; Standard & Poor's (case writer's analysis).

Bill Miller and Value Trust

Bill Miller's success is so far off the charts that you have to ask whether it is superhuman. Quite simply, fund mangers are not supposed to be this good. Is it mortal genius, or is it celestial luck?[1]

By the middle of 2005, Value Trust, an $11.2-billion mutual fund[2] managed by William H. (Bill) Miller III, had outperformed its benchmark index, the Standard & Poor's 500 Index (S&P 500), for an astonishing 14 years in a row. This record marked the longest streak of success for any manager in the mutual-fund industry; the next longest period of sustained performance was only half as long. For many fund managers, simply beating the S&P 500 in any *single* year would have been an accomplishment, yet Miller had achieved consistently better results during both the bull markets of the late 1990s and the bear markets of the early 2000s.

Over the previous 15 years, investors in Value Trust, one of a family of funds managed by the Baltimore, Maryland–based Legg Mason, Inc., could look back on the fund's remarkable returns: an average annual total return of 14.6 percent, which surpassed the S&P 500 by 3.67 percent per year. An investment of $10,000 in Value Trust at its inception, in April 1982, would have grown to more than $330,000 by March 2005. Unlike the fund's benchmark, which was a capitalization-weighted index composed of 500 widely held common stocks, Value Trust only had 36 holdings, 10 of which accounted for nearly 50 percent of the fund's assets. **Exhibit 1** presents a summary of Legg Mason Value Trust, Inc., as it stood in August 2005.

While Miller rarely had the best overall performance among fund managers in any given year, and while some managers had beaten his results over short-term periods, no one had ever matched his consistent index-beating record. Miller's results seemed to contradict conventional theories, which suggested that, in markets characterized by

---

[1] James K. Glassman, "More Than Pure Luck," *Washington Post,* 14 January 2004, F-01.

[2] A mutual fund was an investment vehicle that pooled the funds of individual investors to buy a portfolio of securities, stocks, bonds, and money-market instruments; investors owned a pro rata share of the overall investment portfolio.

high competition, easy entry, and informational efficiency, it would be extremely difficult to beat the market on a sustained basis. Observers wondered what might explain Miller's performance.

The U.S. Mutual-Fund Market[3]

The U.S. mutual-fund market was the largest in the world, accounting for half of the $16.2 trillion in mutual-fund assets reported worldwide. The aggregate figures somewhat masked the continual growth of mutual funds as an investment vehicle. Between 1995 and 2005, mutual-fund assets grew from $2.8 trillion to $8.1 trillion. Ninety-two million individuals, or nearly half of all households, owned mutual funds in 2004, compared with less than 6 percent in 1980. In 2004, individual investors held about 90 percent of all mutual-fund assets.

Mutual funds served several economic functions for investors. First, they afforded the individual investor the opportunity to diversify (own many different stocks) his or her portfolio efficiently without having to invest the sizable amount of capital usually necessary to achieve efficiency. Efficiency was also reflected in the ability of mutual funds to exploit scale economies in trading and transaction costs, economies unavailable to the typical individual investor. Second, in theory, mutual funds provided the individual investor with the professional expertise necessary to earn abnormal returns through successful analysis of securities. A third view was that the mutual-fund industry provided, according to one observer, "an insulating layer between the individual investor and the painful vicissitudes of the marketplace":

> This service, after all, allows individuals to go about their daily lives without spending too much time on the aggravating subject of what to buy and sell and when, and it spares them the even greater aggravation of kicking themselves for making the wrong decision. . . . Thus, the money management industry is really selling "more peace of mind" and "less worry," though it rarely bothers to say so.[4]

Between 1970 and 2005, the number of all mutual funds grew from 361 to 8,044. This total included many different kinds of funds; each one pursued a specific investment focus and was categorized into several acknowledged segments of the industry: aggressive growth (capital-appreciation-oriented), equity income, growth, growth and income, international, option, specialty, small company, balanced, and a variety of bond or fixed-income funds.[5] Funds whose principal focus of investing was common stocks comprised the largest sector of the industry.

---

[3]*Investment Company Fact Book,* 45th ed. (Investment Company Institute, 2005).

[4]Contrarious, "Good News and Bad News," *Personal Investing* (26 August 1987): 128.

[5]Aggressive growth funds sought to maximize capital gains, so current income was of little concern. Growth funds invested in better-known companies with steadier track records. Growth and income funds invested in companies with longer track records that were expected to increase in value and provide a steady income stream. International funds invested in foreign companies. Option funds sought to maximize current returns by investing in dividend-paying stocks on which call options were traded. Balanced funds attempted to conserve principal while earning both current income and capital gains.

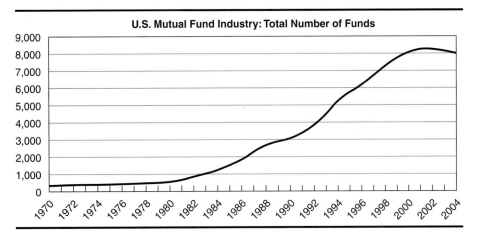

U.S. Mutual Fund Industry: Total Number of Funds

Source: Investment Company Institute Fact Book 2005.

To some extent, the growth in the number and types of mutual funds reflected the increased liquidity in the market and the demand by investors for equity. More importantly, it reflected the effort by mutual-fund organizations to segment the market (i.e., to identify the specialized and changing needs of investors, and to create products to meet those needs). One important result was a broader customer base for the mutual-fund industry as well as a deeper penetration of the total market for financial services.

Another important result of this development was that it added a degree of complexity to the marketplace that altered the investment behavior of some equity investors. In particular, the breadth of mutual-fund alternatives tended to encourage fund switching, especially from one type of fund to another within a family of funds. This reflected the greater range of mutual funds from which to choose, the increased volatility in the market, and the increased trend toward timing-oriented investment strategies. In short, as the mutual-fund industry grew, mutual-fund money became "hotter" (tended to turn over faster).

Institutional investors that managed mutual funds, pension funds, and hedge funds[6] on the behalf of individual investors dominated the market for common stocks in the United States in the mid 2000s. Indeed, at the end of 2004, mutual funds alone owned more than 20 percent of the outstanding stock of U.S. companies. The sheer dominance of those money managers appeared not only in the amount of assets held, but also in their trading muscle—their ability to move huge sums of money in and out of

---

[6]Hedge funds, like mutual funds, pooled investors' money and invested those funds in financial instruments to generate a positive return. Hedge-fund managers typically charged fees of 1 percent to 2 percent of the fund's assets plus a performance fee of 20 percent of profits. Participation in a fund was usually limited to a small number of high net-worth individuals, who were required to "lock up" their invested capital for a year or more. Worldwide growth in hedge funds had exploded in recent years, rising from approximately 600 funds with $38 billion in assets in 1990, to more than 8,000 funds with $1 trillion in assets in 2004. Many hedge funds took speculative, value-driven trading positions, believed to enhance market volatility and liquidity. Traditionally, hedge funds had been little known and unregulated, but their recent growth as an investment vehicle had brought about increasing regulatory scrutiny in the United States.

stocks on short notice. The rising dominance of institutional investors resulted in the growth of trading volume, average trade size, and, especially, block trading (individual trades of more than 10,000 shares), which had increased from about 15 percent of all trading volume 30 years ago to about one-third in 2004. Accordingly, money managers were the principal price-setters (lead steers) in the stock market.

Mutual-Fund Basics

When individuals invested in a mutual fund, their ownership was proportional to the number of shares purchased. The value of each share was called the fund's *net asset value* (NAV). The NAV was computed as the fund's total assets less liabilities, divided by the number of mutual-fund shares outstanding, or:

$$\text{Net asset value (NAV)} = \frac{\text{Market value of fund assets} - \text{Liabilities}}{\text{Fund shares outstanding}}$$

The performance of a mutual fund could thus be measured as the increase or decrease in net asset value plus the fund's income distributions (i.e., dividends and capital gains), expressed as a percentage of the fund's NAV at the beginning of the investment period, or:

$$\frac{\text{Annual}}{\text{total return}} = \frac{\text{Change in net asset value} + \text{Dividends} + \text{Capital-gain distributions}}{\text{NAV (at the beginning of the year)}}$$

Advisers, or managers, of mutual funds were compensated by investors through one-time transaction fees and annual payments. A fund's transaction fees, or loads, covered brokerage expenses and were rarely higher than 6 percent of an individual's investment in the fund. Annual payments were calculated as a percentage of the fund's total assets (called its *expense ratio*), and were charged to all shareholders proportionally. The expense ratio covered the fund's management fees, administrative costs, and advertising and promotion expenses. Expense ratios ranged from as low as 0.2 percent to as high as 2.0 percent. The average expense ratio was around 1.3 percent to 1.5 percent. Because the expense ratio was regularly deducted from the portfolio, it reduced the fund's NAV, thereby lowering the fund's gross returns. Depending on the magnitude of the fund's expense ratio, the net effect of loads and expense ratios on shareholder returns could be dramatic.[7]

Another drag on shareholders' returns was the fund's tendency to keep about 8 percent of its assets in cash to meet redemptions or to invest in unexpected bargains. One observer of the industry, economist Henry Kaufman, warned that a sudden economy-wide shock from interest rates or commodity prices could spook investors into panic-style redemptions from mutual funds, which themselves would liquidate investments and send security prices into a tailspin. Unlike the banking industry, which enjoyed the liquidity afforded by the U.S. Federal Reserve System to respond to the effects of panic by depositors, the mutual-fund industry enjoyed no such government-backed reserve.

---

[7]For instance, suppose that you invested $10,000 in a fund that would appreciate at 10 percent annually, which you then sold out after three years. Also, suppose that the advisory firm had an expense ratio of 2 percent and a front-end load of 4 percent. The fees would cut your pretax profit by 35 percent—from $3,310 to $2,162.

Performance of the Mutual-Fund Industry

The two most frequently used measures of performance were (1) the percentage of annual growth rate of NAV assuming reinvestment (the total return on investment) and (2) the absolute dollar value today of an investment made at some time in the past. Those measures were then compared with the performance of a benchmark portfolio such as the Russell 2000 Index or the S&P 500 Composite Index. **Exhibit 2** provides performance data on a range of mutual-fund categories and comparative indices. The Russell, S&P 500, Dow Jones, and Value Line indices offered benchmarks for the investment performance of hypothetical stock portfolios.[8]

Academicians criticized those performance measures because they failed to adjust for the relative risk of the mutual fund. Over long periods, as **Exhibit 3** shows, different types of securities yielded different levels of total return. **Exhibit 4** shows that each of those types of securities was associated with differing degrees of risk (measured as the standard deviation of returns). Thus, the relationship between risk and return was reliable both on average and over time. For instance, it should be expected that a conservatively managed mutual fund would yield a lower return—precisely because it took fewer risks.

After adjusting for the risk of the fund, academic studies reported that mutual funds were able to perform up to the market on a gross-returns basis; however, when expenses were factored in, they underperformed the market. For instance, Michael Jensen, in a paper published in 1968, reported that gross risk-adjusted returns were −0.4 percent and that net risk-adjusted returns (i.e., net of expenses) were −1.1 percent. In 1977, Main updated the study and found that, for a sample of 70 mutual funds, net risk-adjusted returns were essentially zero. Some analysts attributed this general result to the average 1.3 percent expense ratio of mutual funds and their desire to hold cash.

Most mutual-fund managers relied on some variation of the two classic schools of analysis:

Technical analysis: This involved the identification of profitable investment opportunities based on trends in stock prices, volume, market sentiment, Fibonacci numbers,[9] etc.

Fundamental analysis: This approach relied on insights afforded by an analysis of the economic fundamentals of a company and its industry: supply and demand costs, growth prospects, etc.

---

[8]The Dow Jones indices of industrial companies, transportation companies, and utilities reflected the stocks of a small number (e.g., 30) of large, blue-chip companies, all traded on the New York Stock Exchange (NYSE) and the NASDAQ. The S&P 500 was an index of shares of the 500 largest companies, traded on both the New York and American Stock Exchanges. The Value Line Index was an equal-weighted stock index containing 1,700 companies from the NYSE, American Stock Exchange, NASDAQ, and over-the-counter market; it was also known as the Value Line Investment Survey. The Russell 2000 measured the performance of 2,000 of the smallest companies in the Russell 3000 index of the biggest U.S. stocks. As any index sample became larger, it reflected a greater weighting of smaller, high-growth companies.

[9]The sequence, named for Leonard Fibonacci (1175–1240), consisted of the numbers 1, 1, 2, 3, 5, 8, 13 and so on. Each number after the first two equals the sum of the two numbers before it. No academic research associates this sequence with a consistent ability to earn supernormal returns from investing in the market.

While variations on those approaches often produced supernormal returns in certain years, there was no guarantee that they would produce such returns consistently over time.

Burton Malkiel, an academic researcher, concluded that a passive buy-and-hold strategy (of a large, diversified portfolio) would do as well for the investor as the average mutual fund:

> Even a dart-throwing chimpanzee can select a portfolio that performs as well as one carefully selected by the experts. This, in essence, is the practical application of the theory of efficient markets. . . . The theory holds that the market appears to adjust so quickly to information about individual stocks and the economy as a whole, that no technique of selecting a portfolio—neither technical nor fundamental analysis—can consistently outperform a strategy of simply buying and holding a diversified group of securities such as those that make up the popular market averages. . . . [o]ne has to be impressed with the substantial volume of evidence suggesting that stock prices display a remarkable degree of efficiency. . . . If some degree of mispricing exists, it does not persist for long. "True value will always out" in the stock market.[10]

Many scholars accepted that view. They argued that the stock market followed a "random walk," where the price movements of tomorrow were essentially uncorrelated with the price movements of today. In essence, this denied the possibility that there could be momentum in the movements of common stock prices. According to this view, technical analysis was the modern-day equivalent of alchemy. Fundamental analysis, too, had its academic detractors. They argued that capital markets' information was efficient, and that the insights available to any one fundamental analyst were bound to be impounded quickly into share prices.

The notion that capital markets incorporated all the relevant information into existing securities' prices was known as the *efficient market hypothesis* (EMH), and was widely, though not universally, accepted by financial economists. If EMH were correct and all current prices reflected the true value of the underlying securities, then arguably it would be impossible to beat the market with superior skill or intellect.

Economists defined three levels of market efficiency, which were distinguished by the degree of information believed to be reflected in current securities' prices. The *weak* form of efficiency maintained that all past prices for a stock were impounded into today's price; prices today simply followed a random walk with no correlation with past patterns. *Semistrong* efficiency held that today's prices reflected not only all past prices, but also all publicly available information. Finally, the *strong* form of market efficiency held that today's stock price reflected *all* the information that could be acquired through a close analysis of the company and the economy. "In such a market," as one economist said, "we would observe lucky and unlucky investors, but we wouldn't find any superior investment managers who can consistently beat the market."[11]

---

[10]Burton G. Malkiel, *A Random Walk Down Wall Street* (New York: Norton, 1990), 186, 211.

[11]Richard A. Brealey, Stewart C. Myers, and Franklin Allen, *Principles of Corporate Finance,* 8th ed. (New York: McGraw–Hill Irwin, 2006), 337.

By implication, proponents of those academic theories were highly critical of the services provided by active mutual-fund managers. Paul Samuelson, the Nobel Prize-winning economist, said:

> [E]xisting stock prices already have discounted in them an allowance for their future prospects. Hence . . . one stock [is] about as good or bad a buy as another. To [the] passive investor, chance alone would be as good a method of selection as anything else.[12]

Various popular tests of this thinking seemed to support that view. For instance, *Forbes* magazine chose 28 stocks by throwing darts in June 1967 and invested $1,000 in each. By 1984, the $28,000 investment was worth $131,697.61, for a 9.5 percent compound rate of return. This beat the broad market averages and almost all mutual funds. *Forbes* concluded, "It would seem that a combination of luck and sloth beats brains."[13]

Yet, the nagging problem remained that there were still some superstar money managers—like Bill Miller—who, over long periods, greatly outperformed the market. In reply, Malkiel suggested that beating the market was much like participating in a coin-tossing contest where those who consistently flip heads are the winners.[14] In a coin-tossing game with 1,000 contestants, half will be eliminated on the first flip. On the second flip, half of those surviving contestants are eliminated. And so on, until, on the seventh flip, only eight contestants remain. To the naïve observer, the ability to flip heads consistently looks like extraordinary skill. By analogy, Malkiel suggested that the success of a few superstar portfolio managers could be explained as luck.

As might be expected, the community of money managers received those scholarly theories with great hostility. And even in the ranks of academicians, dissension appeared in the form of the burgeoning field of "behavioral finance," which suggested that greed, fear, and panic were much more significant factors in the setting of stock prices than the mainstream theory would permit. For instance, to many observers, the Internet bubble of the late 1990s seemed to be totally inconsistent with the view of markets as fundamentally rational and efficient. Professor Robert Shiller of Yale University said:

> Evidence from behavioral finance helps us to understand . . . that the recent stock market boom, and then crash after 2000, had its origins in human foibles and arbitrary feedback relations and must have generated a real and substantial misallocation of resources. The challenge for economists is to make this reality a better part of their models.[15]

Similarly, the stock-market crash of October 1987 had also seemed to undermine the strength of the EMH. Professor Lawrence Summers of Harvard argued that the 1987

[12]Malkiel, *Random Walk,* 182.

[13]Malkiel, *Random Walk,* 164.

[14]Malkiel, *Random Walk,* 175–176.

[15]Robert J. Shiller, "From Efficient Markets Theory to Behavioral Finance," *Journal of Economic Perspectives* (winter 2003): 102.

crash was a "clear gap with the theory. If anyone did seriously believe that price movements are determined by changes in information about economic fundamentals, they've got to be disabused of that notion by [the] 500-point drop."[16] Shiller said, "The efficient market hypothesis is the most remarkable error in the history of economic theory. This is just another nail in its coffin."[17]

Academic research exposed other inconsistencies with the EMH. Those included apparently predictable stock-price patterns indicating reliable, abnormally positive returns in early January of each year (the "January effect"), and a "blue Monday" effect, where average stock returns were negative from the close of trading on Friday to the close of trading on Monday. Other evidence suggested that stocks with low price-to-earnings (P/E) multiples tended to outperform those with high P/E multiples. Finally, some evidence emerged for positive serial correlation (that is, momentum) in stock returns from week to week or from month to month. Those results were inconsistent with a random walk of prices and returns. Yet, despite the existence of those anomalies, the EMH remained the dominant paradigm in the academic community.

Bill Miller and Value Trust

Exhibit 5 presents a 10-year summary of the annual returns for Value Trust and eight other Legg Mason equity funds. Morningstar, the well-known statistical service for the investment community, gave Value Trust a five-star rating, its highest for investment performance. Some observers attributed this success to the fund manager's conscious strategy of staying fully invested at all times rather than attempting to time the extent of market investments. Another popular explanation for the fund's performance was the unusual skill of Bill Miller, the fund's portfolio manager.

Miller started investing when he was about 9 years old; he later bought his first stock, RCA, when he was 16. During the Vietnam War, Miller served in military intelligence, and afterward earned a doctorate in philosophy from Johns Hopkins University. He eventually joined Legg Mason, Inc., in 1981. Miller was an adherent of fundamental analysis, an approach to equity investing he had gleaned from a number of sources:

> I had read a bunch of stuff on investing ever since I had gotten interested: *Supermoney,* about Ben Graham and Warren Buffett; Graham's *Intelligent Investor; Security Analysis;* David Dreman's *Psychology in the Stock Market.* Combine those books and those approaches, and what you have is basically a contrarian, value-based methodology, which, psychologically, was very compatible with the way I tended to think about things. I tend to think stocks are more attractive at lower prices rather than higher prices.[18]

---

[16]B. Donnelly, "Efficient-Market Theorists Are Puzzled by Recent Gyrations in Stock Market," *Wall Street Journal,* 23 October 1987, 7.

[17]B. Donnelly, "Efficient-Market Theorists."

[18]Jack Otter, "Meet Mr. Market," www.smartmoney.com, 5 May 2005, accessed 15 September 2005.

Miller's approach was research-intensive and highly concentrated. Nearly 50 percent of Value Trust's assets were invested in just 10 large-capitalization companies. While most of Miller's investments were value stocks, he was not averse to taking large positions in the stocks of growth companies.[19] Generally speaking, Miller's style was eclectic and difficult to distill. "He almost takes pleasure in having people think he's crazy," one industry veteran said of him. "It means he's doing well."[20] By the early 2000s, however, several key elements of Miller's contrarian strategy had begun to emerge:

- *Buy low-price, high intrinsic-value stocks:* "We want to know how stock prices depart from underlying value and why. That can be on the upside as we saw with the Internet, when most companies weren't worth anything like what the market thought they were worth. What we want is the reverse—tremendous pessimism, people believing that a business is broken, scandal, something everybody is fleeing."[21]

- *Take heart in pessimistic markets:* "Bargain prices do not occur when the consensus is cheery, the news is good, and investors are optimistic. Our research efforts are usually directed at precisely the area of the market the news media tells you has the least promising outlook, and we are typically selling those stocks that you are reading have the greatest opportunity for near-term gain."[22]

- *Remember that the lowest average cost wins:* "For most investors, if a stock starts behaving in a way that is different from what they think it ought to be doing—say, it falls 15 percent—they will probably sell. In our case, when a stock drops and we believe in the fundamentals, the case for future returns goes up. Think of it like this: If the underlying business is worth $40, and the stock is $20, my rate of return is 100 percent. The lower the shares go, the higher the future rate of return and the more money you should invest in them."[23]

- *Be wary of valuation illusions:* "I'll give you two historical valuation illusions: Wal-Mart stores and Microsoft. From the day they came public, they looked expensive. Nonetheless, if you bought Wal-Mart when it went public at an expensive-looking 20+ times earnings, you would have the returns of many thousands percent on that. The same goes for Microsoft. Until a couple of years ago, Microsoft went up an average 1 percent every week it was public, despite the fact

---

[19]The stock of a corporation that exhibited faster-than-average gains in earnings during recent periods was typically considered a growth stock. Growth stocks were generally riskier than the average stock, and they often had higher price-to-earnings ratios and paid little to no dividends. A value stock tended to trade at a lower price relative to its earnings, and it usually carried a high dividend yield and low price-to-book or price-to-earnings ratio.

[20]Christopher Davis, co-manager of the Davis Funds, quoted in Matthew Heimer, "Bill Miller," www.smartmoney.com, 1 July 2005.

[21]"Miller's Tale: Legg Mason's Revered Fund Steward Talks about Value, Metrics, and His Optimism," *Barron's* (3 February 2003).

[22]Ian McDonald, "Miller Finds Value in Dreary Places," *Wall Street Journal,* 16 May 2002.

[23]"Bill Miller: How to Profit from Falling Prices," *Fortune* (3 September 2003).

that it looked expensive. Had we known the growth that was in front of it, we would have known it was actually a bargain."[24]

- *Take the long view:* "Portfolio turnover is over 100 percent for the average mutual fund, implying a 10- or 11-month holding period even though the short term is pretty well reflected in stock prices. The biggest opportunity for investors is really thinking out longer term. [P]eople need to think long term. People tend to react and not anticipate. And what they react to is what they wish they'd done a year ago, or two years ago."[25, 26]

- *Look for cyclical and secular underpricing*: "Most value people tend to own stocks that are cyclically underpriced. Most growth people own stocks that are secularly underpriced: things that can grow for long periods of time. Our portfolios historically tended to be, though I wouldn't say they are now, better diversified along both cyclical and secular lines. And our portfolio tries to look at underpricing or mispricing along both of those dimensions so that we're not caught in one or the other."[27]

- *Buy low-expectation stocks:* "I think buying low-expectation stocks, buying higher dividend-yielding stocks, staying away from things with high expense ratios, and most important, the key thing would be—as Warren Buffett says—you need to be fearful when others are greedy, and greedy when others are fearful. So when the market's been down for a while, and it looks bad, then you should be more aggressive, and when it's been up for a while, then you should be less aggressive."[28]

- *Take risks:* "As Earl Weaver[29] used to say, you win more games on three-run homers than sacrifice bunts. That's the thing people in the markets don't understand as well as they should. A lot of people look to hit singles and sacrifice bunts and make small returns.[30] But statistically you are far better off with huge gains because you are going to make mistakes. And if you are playing small ball and you make a few mistakes, you can't recover."[31]

Value Trust had earned a cumulative return of more than 830 percent over the previous 14 years, more than double that of its average peer and the index, according to Morningstar. Even so, Miller remained modest about this record: "The evidence is pretty

---

[24]"Miller's Tale."

[25]McDonald, "Bill Miller Dishes on His Streak and His Strategy," *Wall Street Journal,* 6 January 2005.

[26]Otter, "Meet Mr. Market."

[27]Otter, "Meet Mr. Market."

[28]Otter, "Meet Mr. Market."

[29]Earl Sidney Weaver was a long-time manager of the Baltimore Orioles, an American baseball team. During his tenure, the Orioles won six division titles, four league pennants, and the World Series championship. Bill Miller was widely known as an ardent Orioles fan.

[30]In American baseball, a homer (home run) was a hit that allowed a batter to circle all the bases and score a run. A bunt occurred when the batter hit the ball by positioning the bat in front of his body, rather than by swinging at it; a sacrifice bunt was a bunt that resulted in a base runner advancing and the batter being put out. A single was a batted ball that allowed a batter to reach first base only.

[31]"Bill Miller: How to Profit."

compelling that the market is pretty efficient and will beat most people most of the time."[32] He acknowledged that his much ballyhooed streak could just as easily have been an accident of the calendar. "If the year ended on different months, it wouldn't be there, and at some point those mathematics will hit us," Miller said. "We've been lucky. Well, maybe it's not 100 percent luck. Maybe 95 percent luck."[33] According to Morningstar, Miller's fund lagged behind the S&P 500 in 32 12-month periods out of a total of 152 12-month periods, from the beginning of the streak through July 2004.

Conclusion

Judged from almost any perspective, Miller's investment success was remarkable. His long-run, market-beating performance defied conventional academic theories. Investors, scholars, and market observers wondered about the sources of Miller's superior performance and about its sustainability. As of the middle of 2005, was it rational for an equity investor to buy shares in Value Trust?

At 55, Bill Miller was hardly considered old. Warren Buffett was 74, and he remained an active and visible investor through his company, Berkshire Hathaway, Inc. But investors and other observers had begun to wonder how long Miller would remain at the helm of Value Trust and whether his successor could sustain his exemplary record.

In addition to managing the $11.2-billion Value Trust, Miller also guided the $3.2-billion Legg Mason Opportunity Trust and the $3.2-billion Legg Mason Special Investment Trust. Miller also served as the chief executive officer of Legg Mason Capital Management, which had about $40 billion in assets under its management.

---

[32]McDonald, "Bill Miller Dishes."

[33]McDonald, "Bill Miller Dishes."

EXHIBIT 1 | Morningstar Report on Legg Mason Value Trust, Inc.

Legg Mason Value Prim

Governance and Management

Stewardship Grade B

Portfolio Manager(s)

Longtime manager Bill Miller has vastly outperformed his average peer and the index during his tenure. Assistant manager Nancy Dennin, who focused mostly on administrative tasks, recently stepped down. Some of her duties are being taken on by David Nelson, manager of American Leading Companies. The firm has hired a new research director. Ira Malis, and a chief strategist, Michael Mauboussin along with a handful of new analysis.

Strategy

Bill Miller looks for companies that are trading cheaply relative to his estimated of what they're worth. This often leads him to beaten-down turnaround plays. Unlike many value managers, however. Miller is willing make fairly optimistic assumptions about growth, and he doesn't shy away from owning companies in traditional growth sectors. In this portfolio, pricey Internet stocks rub elbows with bargain-priced financials and turnaround plays. Miller will also let favored names run, allowing top positions to soak up a large percentage of assets.

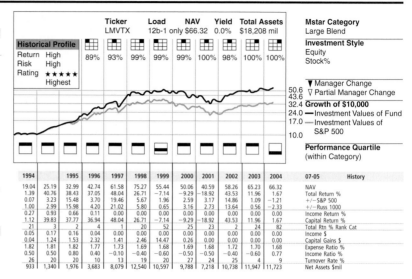

	Ticker	Load	NAV	Yield	Total Assets
	LMVTX	12b-1 only	$66.32	0.0%	$18,208 mil

Historical Profile
Return High
Risk High
Rating ★★★★★
Highest

89% | 93% | 99% | 99% | 99% | 100% | 98% | 100% | 100%

Mstar Category
Large Blend

Investment Style
Equity
Stock%

▼ Manager Change
▽ Partial Manager Change
Growth of $10,000
— Investment Values of Fund
— Investment Values of S&P 500

50.6
43.6
32.4
24.0
17.0
10.0

Performance Quartile
(within Category)

	1994	1995	1996	1997	1998	1999	2000	2001	2002	2003	2004	07-05	History
	19.04	25.19	32.99	42.74	61.58	75.27	55.44	50.06	40.59	58.26	65.23	66.32	NAV
	1.39	40.76	38.43	37.05	48.04	26.71	-7.14	-9.29	-18.92	43.53	11.96	1.67	Total Return %
	0.07	3.23	15.48	3.70	19.46	5.67	1.96	2.59	3.17	14.86	1.09	-1.21	+/-S&P 500
	1.00	2.99	15.98	4.20	21.02	5.80	0.65	3.16	2.73	13.64	0.56	-2.33	+/-Russ 1000
	0.27	0.93	0.66	0.11	0.00	0.00	0.00	0.00	0.00	0.00	0.00	0.00	Income Return %
	1.12	39.83	37.77	36.94	48.04	26.71	-7.14	-9.29	-18.92	43.53	11.96	1.67	Capital Return %
	21	3	2	4	1	20	52	25	23	2	24	82	Total Rtn % Rank Cat
	0.05	0.17	0.16	0.04	0.00	0.00	0.00	0.00	0.00	0.00	0.00	0.00	Income $
	0.04	1.24	1.53	2.32	1.41	2.46	14.47	0.26	0.00	0.00	0.00	0.00	Capital Gains $
	1.82	1.81	1.82	1.77	1.73	1.69	1.68	1.69	1.68	1.72	1.70	1.68	Expense Ratio %
	0.50	0.50	0.80	0.40	-0.10	-0.40	-0.60	-0.50	-0.50	-0.40	-0.60	0.77	Income Ratio %
	26	20	20	10	13	19	20	27	24	25	4	9	Turnover Rate %
	933	1,340	1,976	3,683	8,079	12,540	10,597	9,788	7,218	10,738	11,947	11,723	Net Assets $mil

Performance 02.31.05

	1st Qtr	2nd Qtr	3rd Qtr	4th Qtr	Total
2001	-3.08	7.33	-20.01	9.02	-9.29
2002	-3.66	-13.73	-13.96	13.38	-18.92
2003	-2.91	25.48	3.54	13.79	43.53
2004	-1.22	4.59	-5.80	15.04	11.96
2005	-5.95	3.52	—	—	—

Trailing	Total Return %	+/- S&P 500	+/- Russ 1000	% Rank Cat	Growth of $10,000
3 Mo	11.31	4.14	3.30	5	11,131
6 Mo	5.45	0.00	-1.24	45	10,545
1 Yr	19.54	5.50	3.34	10	11,954
3 Yr Avg	19.87	7.26	6.41	1	17,224
5 Yr Avg	2.93	4.28	3.73	12	11,553
10 Yr Avg	15.96	5.98	5.79	1	43,962
15 Yr Avg	14.88	3.94	3.62	2	80,106

Tax Analysis	Tax-Adj Rtn %	% Rank Cat	Tax-Cost Rat	% Rank Cat
3 Yr (estimated)	19.87	1	0.00	1
5 Yr (estimated)	2.39	11	0.52	29
10 Yr (estimated)	14.88	1	0.93	28

Potential Capital Gain Exposure: 31% of assets

Rating and Risk

Time Period	Load-Adj Return %	Morningstar Rtn vs Cat	Morningstar Risk vs Cat	Morningstar Risk-Adj Rating
1 Yr	19.54			
3 Yr	19.87	High	High	★★★★★
5 Yr	2.93	+Avg	High	★★★★
10 Yr	15.96	High	High	★★★★★
Incept	16.64			

Other Measures	Standard Index S&P 500	Best Fit Index Russ 1000
Alpha	3.6	2.4
Beta	1.31	1.33
R-Squared	88	89

Standard Deviation	18.25
Mean	19.87
Sharpe Ratio	1.00

Portfolio Analysis 03-31-05

Share change since 12-04 Total Stocks:36

	Sector	PE	Tot Ret %	% Assets
Nextel Communications	Telecom	13.3	15.96	7.57
⊖ UnitedHealth Group	Health	24.8	18.86	7.22
Tyco International	Ind Mtrls	26.0	-14.20	6.96
AES	Utilities	24.7	17.41	5.16
⊕ Amazon.com	Consumer	36.1	1.94	4.88
⊕ IAC/InterActiveCorp	Consumer	NMF	-3.33	4.58
⊕ J.P. Morgan Chase & Co.	Financial	27.9	-7.32	3.98
Eastman Kodak	Goods	—	-16.31	3.35
⊕ Aetna	Financial	18.3	24.09	3.18
McKesson	Health	—	43.48	2.97
⊖ MGIC Investment	Financial	11.0	-0.11	2.80
⊕ eBay	Consumer	68.5	-28.18	2.71
⊖ Waste Management	Business	17.5	-4.80	2.69
⊖ Washington Mutual	Financial	13.8	3.92	2.56
Electronic Arts	Software	36.2	-6.61	2.54
⊖ Qwest Communications Int	Telecom	—	-13.96	2.49
Citigroup	Financial	13.2	-7.12	2.45
⊖ The Directv Group	Media	—	-8.00	2.44
WPP Grp	Business	—	—	2.34
Home Depot	Consumer	18.6	2.31	2.31

Current Investment Style

Value Blnd Growth

	Market cap	%
	Giant	34.8
	Large	54.2
	Mid	11.0
	Small	0.0
	Micro	0.0

Avg $mil:
26,231

Value Measures		Rel Category
Price/Earnings	16.91	1.06
Price/Book	2.10	0.88
Price/Sales	1.01	0.72
Price/Cash Flow	9.92	1.27
Dividend Yield %	2.37	1.37

Growth Measures	%	Rel Category
Long-Term Erngs	13.08	1.16
Book Value	9.87	1.06
Sales	6.87	0.92
Cash Flow	27.70	2.89
Historical Erngs	0.40	0.03

Profitability	%	Rel Category
Return on Equity	12.99	0.72
Return on Assets	7.48	0.80
Net Margin	9.99	0.81

Sector Weightings	% of Stocks	Rel S&P 500	3 Year High Low	
⟳ Info	24.08	1.17		
🖥 Software	4.12	1.02	5	0
🖲 Hardware	3.70	0.37	4	2
📶 Media	6.17	1.81	7	5
☎ Telecom	10.09	3.36	12	10
☁ Service	60.41	1.32		
🏥 Health	13.38	1.03	16	12
🛒 Consumer	18.93	1.99	23	19
💲 Business	7.35	1.98	7	6
💲 Financial	20.75	1.05	24	21
⚒ Mfg	15.51	0.46		
🔧 Goods	3.07	0.37	6	3
🔩 Ind Mtrls	6.98	0.58	7	5
🔋 Energy	0.00	0.00	0	0
🔌 Utilities	5.17	1.53	5	2

Composition

● Cash 0.3
● Stocks 99.7
● Bonds 0.0
⊕ Others 0.0
Foreign 2.3
(% of stock)

Morningstar's Take by Christopher Traulsen 08-01-05

Size isn't yet a big problem for this fund, but we're keeping an eye on the matter.

If you count all the money that manager Bill Miller and his team are running in this style, it totals $38 billion. That's a sizable sum, particularly when one considers that other large names than William Danoff's $38 billion Fidelity Contrafund. Indeed, the typical actively managed domestic stock mutual fund with at least $35 billion in assets holds 265 stocks and stashed 22% of assets in its top 10 holdings. As of March 31, 2005, the fund held just 36 stocks and squeezed 50% of its assets into its top 10 holdings.

The worry is that as the fund grows, Miller will be forced to deviate from those ideas he thinks have the highest probability of success because he already owns too much of them. Miller discounts this as a real negative, noting that he can just buy highly correlated names if need be. However, doing so still runs the risk that those names wont be as strong as the best

opportunities identified by his research. It's worth noting, though, that other aspects of Miller's style make him well-suited to running such a large portfolio. First, he usually isn't competing for liquidity with the hordes of traders that a less contrarian manager might be. Miller also just doesn't trade much: The fund's turnover rate hasn't cracked 30% since 1992.

It's obvious that Miller is a brilliant portfolio manager—to glean that much, one just needs to look at his record and speak to him about how he thinks about investment opportunities. And we do not think the fund's current size is cause for concern. However, Legg Mason's recent deal with Citigroup means that a lot more brokers may suddenly be selling this fund (though it could also mean the share classes with cheaper ongoing expenses may proliferate). Add to that the fact that as CEO of the fund advisor, Miller has little incentive to close this offering and slow the growth of his group's business, and we think the issue bears close watching.

Address:	100 Light St. Baltimore MD 21203 800-577-8589	Minimum Purchase: Min Auto Inv Plan: Sales Fees:	$1000 $1000 0.70%B, 0.25%S	Add: $100 Add: $50	IRA: $1000
Web Address:	www.leggmason.com	Management Fee:	0.65%		
Inception:	04-16-82	Actual Fees:	Mgt:0.66%	Dist:0.95%	
Advisor:	Legg Mason Funds Management Inc.	Expense Projections:	3Yr:$536	5Yr:$923	10Yr:$2009
Subadvisor:	None	Income Distrib:	Annually		

NTF Plans: DATALynx NTF, TD Waterhouse Ins NT

EXHIBIT 2 | Morningstar Performance Comparison of Mutual-Fund Categories and Broad Market Indices (Performance Close-Ups)

Benchmark Performance

No. of Funds	Total Assets $Bil	Category	TR% YTD 10-14-05	Total Return % through 09-30-05				Annualized			Annual Return						
				1Mo	3Mo	6Mo	1Yr	3Yr	5Yr	10Yr	1998	1999	2000	2001	2002	2003	2004
7502	2320	**Domestic Stock**	0.05	0.98	4.68	7.14	15.85	18.19	0.03	8.80	16.19	29.22	-0.03	-9.21	-22.05	33.39	12.40
1190	0.0	Large Value	0.08	0.90	3.55	4.77	13.67	17.75	4.45	9.27	11.31	5.72	9.74	-3.08	-18.36	28.57	12.99
1683	860.9	Large Blend	-0.17	1.01	4.06	5.57	13.17	15.72	-1.17	8.23	21.33	20.43	-4.06	-11.42	-21.81	27.53	10.08
1482	654.0	Large Growth	-0.66	1.08	4.78	7.52	13.39	14.62	-7.28	6.94	33.00	38.92	-12.90	-21.12	-27.10	28.99	7.78
325	113.4	Mid-Cap Value	1.37	0.50	4.20	6.86	18.77	22.14	10.85	11.87	2.44	8.42	21.02	6.60	-12.80	36.29	18.55
423	121.8	Mid-Cap Blend	1.74	0.90	5.08	7.93	19.33	21.57	6.52	11.22	9.82	21.47	10.14	1.26	-16.30	36.77	16.23
850	191.7	Mid-Cap Growth	1.30	1.48	6.27	9.75	20.29	19.58	-4.36	8.17	17.95	59.61	-2.88	-18.62	-26.61	36.28	13.19
308	79.7	Small Value	0.19	0.27	4.46	7.49	18.61	24.23	14.59	13.04	-5.85	6.90	17.86	16.29	-10.05	43.95	20.81
505	160.9	Small Blend	0.26	0.63	5.25	8.69	19.24	23.25	10.07	11.77	-4.96	14.05	13.84	8.37	-15.68	42.81	18.72
736	137.7	Small Growth	-1.27	1.05	5.61	9.47	18.53	21.17	-1.45	8.13	6.19	62.84	-4.62	-8.45	-27.94	45.44	12.20
		S&P 500 Index	-0.77	0.81	3.60	5.02	12.25	16.71	-1.49	9.48	28.58	21.04	-9.10	-11.88	-22.09	28.67	10.87
		S&P MidCap 400	3.56	0.77	4.88	9.35	22.14	22.09	7.04	14.13	19.11	14.72	17.49	-0.60	-14.53	35.59	16.47
		Russell 2000	—	0.31	4.69	9.21	17.95	24.12	6.45	9.37	-2.55	21.26	-3.02	2.49	-20.48	47.25	18.33
1903	771	**International Stock**	8.06	4.16	11.24	11.68	27.60	24.99	3.95	7.18	6.78	50.82	-15.34	-16.69	-14.55	39.91	18.57
99	26.8	Europe Stock	7.64	1.89	9.82	9.25	27.79	26.94	6.45	10.09	15.25	33.81	-5.10	-16.46	-11.41	39.64	21.73
16	2.9	Latin Amer Stock	33.90	15.45	29.43	42.55	77.07	56.46	17.63	13.41	-37.07	60.18	-15.58	-5.91	-19.95	61.74	38.26
190	63.2	Div Emerging Mkts	16.31	8.58	17.33	21.77	44.04	36.80	14.08	6.70	-26.37	70.37	-29.86	-3.04	-5.72	55.51	23.80
21	2.2	Div Pac/Asia	11.71	7.78	14.73	14.81	29.60	23.03	3.63	4.47	-1.59	87.73	-30.50	-17.84	-10.74	41.05	17.39
87	9.3	Pac/Asia ex-Japan	9.73	4.85	9.65	12.99	28.48	26.57	9.31	4.34	-7.61	72.75	-23.59	-2.08	-9.32	52.82	13.22
42	10.9	Japan Stock	12.39	8.10	18.20	15.73	26.39	18.04	-3.45	1.15	6.29	111.88	-34.01	-30.52	-12.86	38.40	14.18
161	115.3	Foreign Large Value	6.77	3.65	10.04	8.99	24.65	25.34	7.76	9.24	10.77	25.71	-2.15	-13.52	-11.35	39.36	21.90
549	209.0	Foreign Large Blend	6.71	3.85	11.08	10.21	25.15	22.03	1.15	6.25	13.24	39.79	-15.86	-21.73	-16.86	33.38	17.31
204	83.7	Foreign Large Growth	6.21	3.86	11.27	10.86	24.73	21.46	-0.95	5.36	14.48	55.97	-19.86	-23.45	-18.91	34.86	15.90
54	33.9	Foreign Sm/Mid Val	9.61	2.92	9.86	9.45	28.59	29.43	12.74	10.86	5.07	33.86	-5.39	-8.30	-3.02	50.19	24.22
99	21.4	Foreign Sm Mid Grth	12.84	4.12	13.52	13.59	35.66	32.02	3.56	13.91	19.75	89.46	-15.83	-24.65	-14.73	54.13	23.73
381	192.6	World Stock	3.93	2.44	7.89	9.03	21.21	21.04	0.51	7.91	14.57	42.38	-8.24	-16.15	-19.12	34.98	15.24
		MSCI EAFE	—	4.45	10.38	9.26	25.79	24.61	3.13	5.83	19.93	27.03	-14.19	-21.42	-15.94	38.59	20.25
		MSCI Emerging Markets	—	9.09	17.01	20.53	42.48	35.45	11.37	3.56	-27.67	64.09	-31.90	-4.68	-7.97	51.59	22.45
1161	221	**Specialty Stock**	4.76	2.47	8.15	14.62	22.82	23.97	1.63	10.56	8.40	32.02	12.80	-13.71	-17.84	40.80	15.67
37	3.2	Communications	1.31	2.21	7.86	14.33	25.69	32.49	-11.13	7.18	42.58	58.01	-29.54	-28.73	-39.66	44.63	21.80
121	11.0	Financial	-3.13	0.61	1.48	5.21	9.40	16.65	7.40	12.85	6.35	-2.24	27.62	-2.70	-9.74	32.74	13.81
188	50.5	Health	4.42	0.50	7.02	14.35	15.93	16.43	-0.82	11.62	21.01	19.24	56.86	-11.24	-26.74	31.32	9.57
125	45.9	Natural Resources	28.86	5.72	21.88	24.59	48.39	37.78	17.33	15.07	-24.90	30.95	29.63	-10.79	-3.50	32.64	27.28
51	8.7	Precious Metals	7.96	16.62	20.65	19.54	13.78	23.41	27.49	4.01	-10.49	6.11	16.71	18.84	62.93	58.49	-8.30
254	50.8	Real Estate	3.22	0.42	3.30	16.65	26.23	25.93	18.54	15.05	-15.86	-2.80	26.87	9.80	4.21	37.06	32.12
286	34.1	Technology	-3.07	2.12	7.70	11.30	17.85	24.67	-17.51	5.08	51.58	126.37	-31.73	-35.41	-42.22	57.04	4.32
99	16.8	Utilities	10.83	3.42	8.29	16.02	33.54	25.76	1.23	10.04	20.95	18.45	10.89	-20.66	-24.09	23.32	23.82

EXHIBIT 2 | Morningstar Performance Comparison of Mutual-Fund Categories and Broad Market Indices (Performance Close-Ups)
(continued)

Benchmark Performance

No. of Funds	Total Assets $Bil	Category	TR% YTD 10-14-05	Total Return % through 09-30-05				Annualized			Annual Return						
				1Mo	3Mo	6Mo	1Yr	3Yr	5Yr	10Yr	1998	1999	2000	2001	2002	2003	2004
1752	**713**	**Hybrid**	**0.70**	**0.49**	**2.73**	**4.50**	**9.57**	**11.56**	**2.69**	**7.59**	**12.16**	**11.25**	**2.68**	**−3.65**	**−9.02**	**18.86**	**8.11**
516	103.3	Conservative Alloc	0.32	−0.04	1.37	3.13	5.95	7.90	3.44	6.56	10.59	5.63	4.37	0.02	−3.50	12.42	5.39
79	15.1	Convertible	−0.70	1.39	4.88	6.10	9.55	14.47	2.43	8.63	5.04	28.84	1.26	−6.36	−8.00	26.56	8.72
1084	499.3	Moderate Allocation	0.85	0.61	3.10	5.00	10.81	12.40	2.21	7.65	13.89	11.09	2.35	−4.58	−11.38	20.20	8.80
73	94.9	World Allocation	2.62	1.34	4.31	5.47	14.83	16.63	7.64	9.33	9.14	15.34	1.65	−3.08	−1.90	25.00	14.46
875	**240**	**Specialty Bond**	**0.38**	**−0.48**	**1.14**	**2.92**	**6.37**	**12.36**	**7.03**	**6.57**	**1.12**	**4.84**	**−1.67**	**3.22**	**3.79**	**20.78**	**9.32**
67	29.0	Bank Loan	3.44	0.39	1.65	2.23	4.81	6.73	4.70	5.10	6.28	5.91	5.33	1.63	0.75	10.32	5.09
464	125.1	High Yield Bond	0.34	−0.75	1.30	3.21	6.13	13.93	5.81	5.64	0.00	4.74	−6.96	2.40	−1.34	24.54	9.95
144	43.2	Multisector Bond	0.41	−0.43	0.74	2.92	6.06	10.60	7.49	6.72	0.80	3.26	1.06	3.67	6.89	17.05	8.28
149	31.9	World Bond	−2.99	−1.10	−0.20	−0.28	4.56	8.20	7.71	6.37	9.62	−2.52	3.37	2.06	13.83	13.57	8.91
51	10.5	Emerg Mkts Bd	6.50	2.08	4.13	11.48	16.96	22.35	15.58	14.57	−21.03	27.82	12.06	13.06	12.75	30.79	12.49
		CSFB High Yield		*−0.97*	*0.91*	*2.82*	*6.31*	*15.55*	*8.56*	*7.37*	*0.58*	*3.28*	*−5.21*	*5.78*	*3.11*	*27.93*	*11.96*
1522	**499**	**General Bond**	**0.84**	**−0.71**	**−0.34**	**1.81**	**2.26**	**3.61**	**5.48**	**5.50**	**6.88**	**−0.31**	**9.14**	**7.51**	**7.26**	**4.50**	**3.31**
80	13.0	Long-Term Bond	0.73	−1.20	−0.91	2.33	4.04	7.27	7.61	6.77	5.85	−3.38	9.48	8.42	8.57	9.89	6.44
968	372.0	Interm-Term Bond	0.74	−0.97	−0.59	1.99	2.43	4.01	5.98	5.78	7.37	−1.32	9.77	7.71	8.17	5.06	3.92
366	82.5	Short-Term Bond	0.85	−0.29	0.06	1.31	1.31	2.13	4.14	4.80	6.16	2.20	7.76	7.23	5.52	2.67	1.64
108	31.3	Ultrashort Bond	1.79	0.16	0.67	1.45	2.25	1.78	3.05	4.42	5.06	4.48	6.74	5.77	2.74	1.56	1.25
		Lehman Bros Aggregate		*−1.03*	*−0.67*	*2.31*	*2.80*	*3.96*	*6.62*	*6.55*	*8.69*	*−0.82*	*11.63*	*8.44*	*10.25*	*4.10*	*4.34*
616	**158**	**Government Bond**	**0.90**	**−0.70**	**−0.49**	**1.82**	**2.35**	**2.37**	**5.15**	**5.23**	**7.43**	**−0.93**	**10.75**	**6.79**	**9.09**	**2.09**	**3.15**
85	24.5	Long Govt	1.68	−1.31	−1.25	3.20	5.45	5.11	8.35	7.04	10.55	−7.75	20.29	3.54	16.42	4.25	7.24
358	106.5	Interm Govt	0.85	−0.77	−0.53	1.81	2.28	2.47	5.34	5.41	7.51	−1.39	10.99	6.93	9.40	2.14	3.37
173	27.6	Short Govt	0.63	−0.37	−0.13	1.21	1.09	1.45	4.10	4.68	6.49	1.22	8.33	7.20	6.82	1.39	1.33
		Lehman Bros Govt		*−1.18*	*−0.94*	*2.39*	*2.47*	*2.85*	*6.28*	*6.34*	*9.85*	*−2.23*	*13.24*	*7.23*	*11.50*	*2.36*	*3.48*
1187	**221**	**Municipal Bond**	**1.52**	**−0.62**	**−0.17**	**2.31**	**3.10**	**3.20**	**5.24**	**4.99**	**5.41**	**−3.70**	**10.23**	**4.20**	**8.01**	**4.41**	**3.32**
89	37.3	High Yield Muni	4.53	−0.65	0.57	3.77	7.60	6.10	6.31	5.36	5.36	−4.65	5.63	4.98	6.09	6.91	6.48
263	70.9	Muni National Long	1.79	−0.74	−0.21	2.55	3.56	3.49	5.52	5.17	5.30	−4.76	11.27	3.86	8.45	4.84	3.72
211	53.0	Muni National Interm	0.82	−0.56	−0.31	2.05	2.01	2.74	5.02	4.85	5.53	−2.35	9.34	4.35	8.58	4.14	2.80
249	15.8	Muni Single ST Long	1.69	−0.67	−0.20	2.35	3.38	3.36	5.44	5.11	5.35	−4.76	11.19	4.24	8.14	4.65	3.65
260	16.4	Muni Single ST Intr	0.99	−0.63	−0.34	2.05	2.27	2.83	5.07	4.92	5.46	−3.05	9.86	4.29	8.44	4.13	2.89
115	28.0	Muni Short	0.70	0.04	0.24	1.16	1.06	1.59	3.30	3.62	4.55	0.69	5.73	4.80	5.03	2.37	1.16
		Lehman Bros Muni		*−0.67*	*−0.12*	*2.80*	*4.05*	*4.18*	*6.34*	*6.06*	*6.48*	*−2.06*	*11.68*	*5.13*	*9.60*	*5.31*	*4.48*
16518	**5143**	**Total Fund Average**	**1.60**	**0.91**	**4.05**	**6.39**	**13.18**	**14.53**	**2.69**	**6.95**	**10.08**	**18.84**	**2.10**	**−5.07**	**−10.37**	**25.00**	**10.39**

Source: Morningstar, Inc.

EXHIBIT 3 | Long-Term Cumulative Returns for Major Asset Categories

Investments in the U.S. Capital Markets	Year-end 2004
Year-end 1925 = $1.00	
Small company stocks	$12,968.48
Large company stocks	$2,533.20
Long-term government bonds	$65.72
Treasury bills	$17.87
Inflation	$10.62

Source of data: *Stocks, Bonds, Bills, and Inflation 2005 Yearbook* (Chicago: Ibbotson Associates, 2005), 28.

EXHIBIT 4 | Mean Returns and Standard Deviation of Returns by Major Asset Category

Series (from 1926 to 2004)	Geometric Mean	Arithmetic Mean	Standard Deviation
Large company stocks	10.4%	12.4%	20.3%
Small company stocks	12.7	17.5	33.1
Long-term corporate bonds	5.9	6.2	8.6
Long-term government	5.4	5.8	9.3
Intermediate-term government	5.4	5.5	5.7
U.S. Treasury bills	3.7	3.8	3.1
Inflation	3.0%	3.1%	4.3%

Source of data: *Stocks, Bonds, Bills, and Inflation 2005 Yearbook* (Chicago: Ibbotson Associates, 2005), 33.

EXHIBIT 5 | Average Annual Performance of Legg Mason Equity Funds

Fund Name	Average Annual Total Returns as of September 30, 2005 (%)					
	One Year	Three Year	Five Year	Seven Year	Ten Year	Since Inception
American Leading Companies Trust	17.87	19.75	4.22	6.93	9.83	9.37
Classic Valuation Fund	18.69	18.59	3.78	—	—	5.21
Value Trust, Inc.*	**14.25**	**21.86**	**2.07**	**9.41**	**15.04**	**16.39**
Growth Trust	12.81	27.39	4.51	8.93	11.44	11.74
Special Investment Trust*	18.95	27.31	9.24	16.06	14.62	13.75
U.S. Small-Capitalization Value Trust	15.02	22.23	16.24	12.11	—	8.01
Balanced Trust	9.31	10.15	1.94	2.97	—	4.34
Financial Services Fund	12.19	17.28	10.67	—	—	8.99
Opportunity Trust*	24.36	34.02	9.31	—	—	9.81

*Managed by Bill Miller.

Source of data: Company reports.

Ben & Jerry's Homemade

JERRY: What's interesting about me and my role in the company is I'm just this guy on the street. A person who's fairly conventional, mainstream, accepting of life as it is.

BEN: Salt of the earth. A man of the people.

JERRY: But then I've got this friend, Ben, who challenges everything. It's against his nature to do anything the same way anyone's ever done it before. To which my response is always, "I don't think that'll work."

BEN: To which my response is always, "How do we know until we try?"

JERRY: So I get to go through this leading-edge, risk-taking experience with Ben— even though I'm really just like everyone else.

BEN: The perfect duo. Ice cream and chunks. Business and social change. Ben and Jerry.

Ben & Jerry's Double-Dip

As Henry Morgan's plane passed over the snow-covered hills of Vermont's dairy land, through his mind passed the events of the last few months. It was late January 2000. Morgan, the retired dean of Boston University's business school, knew well the trip to Burlington. As a member of the board of directors of Ben & Jerry's Homemade for the past 13 years, Morgan had seen the company grow both in financial and social stature. The company was now not only an industry leader in the super-premium ice cream market, but also commanded an important leadership position in a variety of social causes from the dairy farms of Vermont to the rainforests of South America.

Increased competitive pressure and Ben & Jerry's declining financial performance had triggered a number of takeover offers for the resolutely independent-minded company. Today's board meeting had been convened to consider the pending offers.

This case was prepared by Professor Michael J. Schill with research assistance from Daniel Burke, Vern Hines, Sangyeon Hwang, Wonsang Kim, Vincente Ladinez, and Tyrone Taylor. It was written as a basis for class discussion rather than to illustrate effective or ineffective handling of an administrative situation. Copyright © 2001 by the University of Virginia Darden School Foundation, Charlottesville, VA. All rights reserved. *To order copies, send an e-mail to* sales@dardenpublishing.com. *No part of this publication may be reproduced, stored in a retrieval system, used in a spreadsheet, or transmitted in any form or by any means—electronic, mechanical, photocopying, recording, or otherwise—without the permission of the Darden School Foundation.* Rev. 10/03.

Morgan expected a lively debate. Cofounders Ben Cohen and Jerry Greenfield knew the company's social orientation required corporate independence. In stark contrast, chief executive Perry Odak felt that Ben and Jerry's shareholders would be best served by selling out to the highest bidder.

Ben & Jerry's Homemade

Ben & Jerry's Homemade, a leading distributor of super-premium ice creams, frozen yogurts, and sorbets, was founded in 1978 in an old gas station in Burlington, Vermont. Cohen and Greenfield recounted their company's beginnings:

> One day in 1977, we [Cohen and Greenfield] found ourselves sitting on the front steps of Jerry's parents' house in Merrick, Long Island, talking about what kind of business to go into. Since eating was our greatest passion, it seemed logical to start with a restaurant. . . . We wanted to pick a product that was becoming popular in big cities and move it to a rural college town, because we wanted to live in that kind of environment. We wanted to have a lot of interaction with our customers and enjoy ourselves. And, of course, we wanted a product that we liked to eat. . . . We found an ad for a $5 ice-cream-making correspondence course offered through Penn State. Due to our extreme poverty, we decided to split one course between us, sent in our five bucks, read the material they sent back, and passed the open-book tests with flying colors. That settled it. We were going into the ice cream business.
>
> Once we'd decided on an ice cream parlor, the next step was to decide where to put it. We knew college students eat a lot of ice cream; we knew they eat more of it in warm weather. Determined to make an informed decision (but lacking in technological and financial resources), we developed our own low-budget "manual cross-correlation analysis." Ben sat at the kitchen table, leafing through a U.S. almanac to research towns that had the highest average temperatures. Jerry sat on the floor; reading a guide to American colleges, searching for the rural towns that had the most college kids. Then we merged our lists. When we investigated the towns that came up, we discovered that apparently someone had already done this work ahead of us. All the warm towns that had a decent number of college kids already had homemade ice-cream parlors. So we threw out the temperature criterion and ended up in Burlington, Vermont. Burlington had a young population, a significant college population, and virtually no competition. Later, we realized the reason why there was no competition. It's so cold in Burlington for so much of the year, and the summer season is so short, it was obvious (to everyone except us) that there was no way an ice cream parlor could succeed there. Or so it seemed.[1]

By January 2000, Cohen and Greenfield's ice cream operation in Burlington, Ben & Jerry's Homemade, had become a major premium ice cream producer with over 170 stores (scoop shops) across the United States and overseas, and had developed an important presence on supermarket shelves. Annual sales had grown to $237 million, and the company's equity was valued at $160 million (**Exhibits 1** and **2**). The

---

[1] Ben Cohen and Jerry Greenfield, *Ben & Jerry's Double-Dip* (New York: Simon & Schuster, 1997), 15–17.

company was known for such zany ice cream flavors as Chubby Hubby, Chunky Monkey, and Bovinity Divinity. **Exhibit 3** provides a selected list of flavors from its scoop-shop menu.

Ben & Jerry's Social Consciousness

Ben & Jerry's was also known for its emphasis on socially progressive causes and its strong commitment to the community. Although unique during the company's early years, Ben & Jerry's community orientation was no longer that uncommon. Companies such as Patagonia (clothing), Odwalla (juice), The Body Shop (body-care products), and Tom's of Maine (personal-care products) shared similar visions of what they termed "caring capitalism."

Ben & Jerry's social objective permeated every aspect of the business. One dimension was its tradition of generous donations of its corporate resources. Since 1985, Ben & Jerry's donated 7.5 percent of its pretax earnings to various social foundations and community-action groups. The company supported causes such as Greenpeace International and the Vietnam Veterans of America Foundation by signing petitions and recruiting volunteers from its staff and the public. The company expressed customer appreciation with an annual free cone day at all of its scoop shops. During the event, customers were welcome to enjoy free cones all day.

Although the level of community giving was truly exceptional, what really made Ben & Jerry's unique was its commitment to social objectives in its marketing, operations, and finance policies. Cohen and Greenfield emphasized that their approach was fundamentally different from the self-promotion-based motivation of social causes supported by most corporations.

> At its best, cause-related marketing is helpful in that it uses marketing dollars to help fund social programs and raise awareness of social ills. At its worst, it's "greenwashing"—using philanthropy to convince customers the company is aligned with good causes, so the company will be seen as good, too, whether it is or not. . . . They understand that if they dress themselves in that clothing, slap that image on, that's going to move product. But instead of just slapping the image on, wouldn't it be better if the company actually did care about its consumers and the community?[2]

An example of Ben & Jerry's social-value-led marketing included its development of an ice cream flavor to provide demand for harvestable tropical-rainforest products. The product's sidebar described the motivation:

> This flavor combines our super creamy vanilla ice cream with chunks of Rainforest Crunch, a cashew & Brazil nut buttercrunch made for us by our friends at Community Products in Montpelier, Vermont. The cashews & Brazil nuts in this ice cream are harvested in a sustainable way from tropical rainforests and represent an economically viable long-term alternative to cutting these trees down. Enjoy!
>
> *Ben & Jerry*

---

[2]Ben Cohen and Jerry Greenfield, *Ben & Jerry's Double-Dip* (New York: Simon & Schuster, 1997), 33.

Financing decisions were also subject to community focus. In May of 1984, Ben & Jerry's initiated its first public equity financing. Rather than pursue a broad traditional public offering, the company issued 75,000 shares at $10.50 a share exclusively to Vermont residents. By restricting the offering to Vermonters, Cohen hoped to offer those who had first supported the company with the opportunity to profit from its success. To provide greater liquidity and capital, a traditional broad offering was later placed and the shares were then listed and traded on the NASDAQ. Despite Ben & Jerry's becoming a public company, Cohen and Greenfield did not always follow traditional investor-relations practices. "Chico" Lager, the general manager at the time, recalled the following Ben Cohen interview transcript that he received before its publication in the *Wall Street Transcript:*

> TWST: Do you believe you can attain a 15 percent increase in earnings each year over the next five years?
>
> COHEN: I got no idea.
>
> TWST: Umm-hmm. What do you believe your capital spending will be each year over the next five years?
>
> COHEN: I don't have any ideas as to that either.
>
> TWST: I see. How do you react to the way the stock market has been treating you in general and vis-à-vis other companies in your line?
>
> COHEN: I think the stock market goes up and down, unrelated to how a company is doing. I never expected it to be otherwise. I anticipate that it will continue to go up and down, based solely on rumor and whatever sort of manipulation those people who like to manipulate the market can accomplish.
>
> TWST: What do you have for hobbies?
>
> COHEN: Hobbies. Let me think. Eating, mostly. Ping-Pong.
>
> TWST: Huh?
>
> COHEN: Ping-Pong.[3]

Solutions to corporate operating decisions were also dictated by Ben & Jerry's interest in community welfare. The disposal of factory wastewater provided an example.

> In 1985, when we moved into our new plant in Waterbury, we were limited in the amount of wastewater that we could discharge into the municipal treatment plant. As sales and production skyrocketed, so did our liquid waste, most of which was milky water. [We] made a deal with Earl, a local pig farmer, to feed our milky water to his pigs. (They loved every flavor except Mint with Oreo Cookies, but Cherry Garcia was their favorite.) Earl's pigs alone couldn't handle our volume, so eventually we loaned Earl $10,000 to buy 200 piglets. As far as we could tell, this was a win-win solution to a tricky environ-

---

[3]Fred "Chico" Lager, *Ben & Jerry's: The Inside Scoop* (New York: Crown Publishers, 1994), 124–125.

mental problem. The pigs were happy. Earl was happy. We were happy. The community was happy.[4]

Ben & Jerry's social orientation was balanced with product and economic objectives. Its mission statement included all three dimensions, and stressed seeking new and creative ways of fulfilling each without compromising the others:

Product: To make, distribute, and sell the finest quality all-natural ice cream and related products in a wide variety of innovative flavors made from Vermont dairy products.

Economic: To operate the company on a sound financial basis of profitable growth, increasing value for our shareholders, and creating career opportunities and financial rewards for our employees.

Social: To operate the company in a way that actively recognizes the central role that business plays in the structure of society by initiating innovative ways to improve the quality of life of the broad community—local, national, and international.

Management discovered early on that the company's three objectives were not always in harmony. Cohen and Greenfield told of an early example:

One day we were talking [about our inability to make a profit] to Ben's dad, who was an accountant. He said, "Since you're gonna make such a high-quality product . . . why don't you raise your prices?" At the time, we were charging fifty-two cents a cone. Coming out of the '60s, our reason for going into business was that ours was going to be "ice cream for the people." It was going to be great quality products for everybody— not some elitist treat. . . . Eventually we said, Either we're going to raise our prices or we're going to go out of business. And then where will the people's ice cream be? They'll have to get their ice cream from somebody else. So we raised the prices. And we stayed in business.[5]

At other times, management chose to sacrifice short-term profits for social gains. Greenfield tells of one incident with a supplier:

Ben went to a Social Ventures Network meeting and met Bernie Glassman, a Jewish-Buddhist former nuclear-physicist monk. Bernie had a bakery called Greyston in inner-city Yonkers, New York. It was owned by a nonprofit religious institution; its purpose was to train and employ economically disenfranchised people [and] to fund low-income housing and other community-service activities. Ben said, "We're looking for someone who can bake these thin, chewy, fudgy brownies. If you could do that, we could give you some business, and you could make us the brownies we need, and that would be great for both of us." . . . The first order we gave Greyston was for a couple of tons. For us, that was a small order. For Greyston, it was a huge order. It caused their system to break down. The brownies were coming off the line so fast that they ended up getting packed hot. Then they

---

[4]*Ben & Jerry's Double-Dip,* 154.

[5]*Ben & Jerry's Double-Dip,* 154.

needed to be frozen. Pretty soon, the bakery freezer was filled up with these steaming 50-pound boxes of hot brownies. The freezer couldn't stay very cold, so it took days to freeze the brownies. By the time they were frozen, [they] had turned into 50-pound blocks of brownie. And that's what Greyston shipped to us. So we called up Bernie and we said, "Those two tons you shipped us were all stuck together. We're shipping them back." Bernie said, "I can't afford that. I need the money to meet my payroll tomorrow. Can't you unstick them?" And we said, "Bernie, this really gums up the works over here." We kept going back and forth with Greyston, trying to get the brownies right. Eventually we created a new flavor, Chocolate Fudge Brownie, so we could use the brownie blocks.[6]

Asset Control

The pursuit of a nonprofit-oriented policy required stringent restrictions on corporate control. For Ben & Jerry's, asset control was limited through elements of the company's corporate charter, differential stock-voting rights, and a supportive Vermont legislature.

Corporate Charter Restrictions

At the 1997 annual meeting, Ben & Jerry's shareholders approved amendments to the charter that gave the board greater power to perpetuate the mission of the firm. The amendments created a staggered board of directors, whereby the board was divided into three classes with one class of directors being elected each year for a three-year term. A director could only be removed with the approval of a two-thirds vote of all shareholders. Also, any vacancy resulting from the removal of a director could be filled by two-thirds vote of the directors who were then in office. Finally, the stockholders increased the number of votes required to alter, amend, repeal, or adopt any provision inconsistent with those amendments to at least two-thirds of shareholders. See **Exhibit 4** for a summary of the current board composition.

Differential Voting Rights

Ben & Jerry's had three equity classes: class A common, class B common, and class A preferred. The holders of class A common were entitled to one vote for each share held. The holders of class B common, reserved primarily for insiders, were entitled to 10 votes for each share held. Class B common was not transferable, but could be converted into class A common stock on a share-for-share basis and was transferable thereafter. The company's principals—Ben Cohen, Jerry Greenfield, and Jeffrey Furman—effectively held 47 percent of the aggregate voting power, with only 17 percent of the aggregate common equity outstanding. Nonboard members, however, still maintained 51 percent of the voting power (see **Exhibit 5**). The class A preferred stock was held exclusively by the Ben & Jerry's Foundation, a community-action group. The class A preferred gave the foundation a special voting right to act with respect to certain business combinations and the authority to limit the voting rights of common

---

[6]*Ben & Jerry's Double-Dip,* 154.

stockholders in certain transactions such as mergers and tender offers, even if the common stockholders favored such transactions.

Vermont Legislature

In April 1998, the Vermont Legislature amended a provision of the Vermont Business Corporation Act, which gave the directors of any Vermont corporation the authority to consider the interests of the corporation's employees, suppliers, creditors, and customers when determining whether an acquisition offer or other matter was in the best interest of the corporation. The board could also consider the economy of the state in which the corporation was located and whether the best interests of the company could be served by the continued independence of the corporation.

Those and other defense mechanisms strengthened Ben & Jerry's ability to remain an independent, Vermont-based company, and to focus on carrying out the threefold corporate mission, which management believed was in the best interest of the company, its stockholders, employees, suppliers, customers, and the Vermont community at large.

The Offers

Morgan reviewed the offers on the table. Discussion with potential merger partners had been ongoing since the previous summer. In August 1999, Pillsbury (maker of the premium ice cream Haagen-Dazs) and Dreyer's announced the formation of an ice cream joint venture. Under past distribution agreements, Pillsbury-Dreyer's would become the largest distributor of Ben & Jerry's products. In response, the Ben & Jerry's board had authorized Odak to pursue joint-venture and merger discussions with Unilever and Dreyer's. By December, the joint-venture arrangements had broken down, but the discussions had resulted in takeover offers for Ben & Jerry's of between $33 and $35 a share from Unilever, and an offer of $31 a share from Dreyer's. Just yesterday, Unilever had raised its offer to $36, and two private investment houses, Meadowbrook Lane Capital and Chartwell Investments, had made two separate additional offers. The offer prices represented a substantial premium over the preoffer-announcement share price of $21.[7] See **Exhibit 6** for a comparison of investor-value measures for Ben & Jerry's and the select competitors.

Dreyer's Grand Ice Cream

Dreyer's Grand Ice Cream sold premium ice cream and other frozen desserts under the Dreyer's and Edy's brands and some under nonbranded labels. The Dreyer's and

---

[7]Recent food-company acquisitions included Kraft's $270-million acquisition of Balance Bar and Kellogg's $308-million acquisition of Worthington Foods. Balance Bar and Worthington—both health-food companies—sold at takeover premia of 76 percent and 88 percent, respectively. The mean acquisition premium offered by successful bidders in a large sample of U.S. multiple-bid contests was found to be 70 percent. See S. Betton and B. E. Eckbo, "Toeholds, Bid Jumps, and Expected Payoffs in Takeovers," *Review of Financial Studies* 13, 4 (winter 2000): 841–882.

Edy's lines were distributed through a direct store-delivery system. Total sales were over $1 billion, and company stock traded at a total capitalization of $450 million. Dreyer's was also involved in community-service activities. In 1987, the company established the Dreyer's Foundation to provide focused community support, particularly for youth and K–12 public education.

Unilever

Unilever manufactured branded consumer goods, including foods, detergents, and other home- and personal-care products. The company's ice cream division included the Good Humor, Breyers, Klondike, Dickie Dee, and Popsicle brands, and was the largest producer of ice cream in the world. Good Humor-Breyers was headquartered in Green Bay, Wisconsin, with plants and regional sales offices located throughout the United States. Unilever had a total market capitalization of $18 billion.

Meadowbrook Lane Capital

Meadowbrook Lane Capital was a private investment fund that portrayed itself as socially responsible. The firm was located in Northampton, Massachusetts. The Meadowbrook portfolio included holdings in Hain Foods, a producer of specialty health-oriented food products. Meadowbrook proposed acquiring a majority ownership interest through a tender offer to Ben & Jerry's shareholders.

Chartwell Investments

Chartwell Investments was a New York City private-equity firm that invested in growth financings and management buyouts of middle-market companies. Chartwell proposed investing between $30 million and $50 million in Ben & Jerry's in exchange for a convertible preferred-equity position that would allow Chartwell to obtain majority representation on the board of directors.

Morgan summarized the offers as follows:

Bidder	Offering Price	Main Proposal
Dreyer's Grand	$31 (stock)	• Maintain B&J management team • Operate B&J as a quasi-autonomous business unit • En courage some social endeavors
Unilever	$36 (cash)	• Maintain select members of B&J management team • Integrate B&J into Unilever's frozen desserts division • Restrict social commitments and interests
Meadowbrook Lane	$32 (cash)	• Install new management team • Allow B&J to operate as an independent company controlled under the Meadowbrook umbrella • Maintain select social projects and interests
Chartwell	Minority interest	• Install new management team • Allow B&J to continue as an independent company

Conclusion

Henry Morgan doubted that the social mission of the company would survive a takeover by a large traditional company. Despite his concern for Ben & Jerry's social interests, Morgan recognized that, as a member of the board, he had been elected to represent the interests of the shareholders. A financial reporter, Richard McCaffrey, expressed the opinion of many shareholders:

> Let's jump right into the fire and suggest, depending upon the would-be acquiring company's track record at creating value, that it makes sense for the company [Ben & Jerry's] to sell. Why? At $21 a share, Ben & Jerry's stock has puttered around the same level, more or less, for years despite regular sales and earnings increases. For a company with a great brand name, about a 45 percent share of the super-premium ice cream market, successful new-product rollouts, and decent traction in its international expansion efforts, the returns should be better. Some of the reasons for underperformance, such as the high price of cream and milk, aren't factors the company can control. That's life in the ice cream business. But Ben & Jerry's average return on shareholders' equity, a measure of how well it's employing shareholders' money, stood at 7 percent last year, up from 5 percent in 1997. That's lousy by any measure, although it's improved this year and now stands at about 9 percent. This isn't helped by the company's charitable donations, of course, but if you're an investor in Ben & Jerry's you knew that going in—it's an ironclad part of corporate culture, and has served the company well. Still, Ben & Jerry's has to find ways to create value.[8]

The plane banked over icy Lake Champlain and began its descent into Burlington as Morgan collected his thoughts for what would undoubtedly be an emotional and

---

[8]Richard McCaffrey, "In the Hunt for Ben & Jerry's," *Fool.com* (2 December 1999).

EXHIBIT 1 | Ben & Jerry's Homemade Financial Statements and Financial Ratios (in millions, except for per-share figures)

	1999	1998	1997	1996	1995	1994
1 Net sales	$237.0	$209.2	$174.2	$167.2	$155.3	$148.8
2 Cost of sales	145.3	136.2	114.3	115.2	109.1	109.8
3 Gross profit	91.8	73.0	59.9	51.9	46.2	39.0
4 Selling, general, & administrative expenses	82.9*	63.9	53.5	45.5	36.4	36.3
5 Earnings before interest and taxes	8.9*	9.1	6.4	6.4	9.8	2.8
6 Net income	8.0*	6.2	3.9	3.9	5.9	(1.9)
7 Working capital	$ 42.8	$ 48.4	$ 51.4	$ 50.1	$ 51.0	$ 37.5
8 Total assets	150.6	149.5	146.5	$136.7	131.1	120.3
9 Long-term debt and obligations	16.7	20.5	25.7	31.1	32.0	32.4
10 Stockholders' equity	89.4	90.9	86.9	82.7	78.5	72.5
Per-share figures:						
Sales	$31.34					
Earnings	$ 1.06*					
Book equity	$11.82					
Gross margin (3 ÷ 1)	38.7%	34.9%	34.4%	31.0%	29.7%	26.2%
Operating margin (5 ÷ 1)	3.8%*	4.3%	3.7%	3.8%	6.3%	1.9%
Net income margin (6 ÷ 1)	3.4%*	3.0%	2.2%	2.3%	3.8%	−1.3%
Asset turnover (1 ÷ 8)	1.6	1.4	1.2	1.2	1.2	1.2
Working capital turnover (1 ÷ 7)	5.5	4.3	3.4	3.3	3.0	4.0
ROA (5 × [1 − 40%] ÷ 8)	3.5%*	3.7%	2.6%	2.8%	4.5%	1.4%
ROE (6 ÷ 10)	8.9%*	6.8%	4.5%	4.7%	7.5%	−2.6%
Yield to maturity on 30-year U.S. Treasury bonds (DataStream)	6.5%	5.1%	5.9%	6.6%	6.0%	7.9%

*Adjusted by case writer for 50% of 1999 $8.6-million special charge for asset write-off and employee severance associated with frozen novelty manufacturing facility.

Source: SEC filings.

EXHIBIT 2 | Ben & Jerry's Homemade Stock-Price Performance

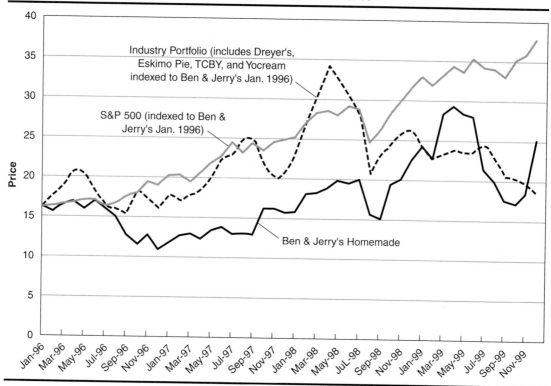

EXHIBIT 3 | Ben & Jerry's Selected List of Flavors (January 2000)

Bovinity Divinity	Milk-chocolate ice cream and white-chocolate cows swirled with white-chocolate ice cream and dark fudge cows
Cherry Garcia	Cherry ice cream with cherries and fudge flakes
Chocolate Chip Cookie Dough	Vanilla ice cream with gobs of chocolate-chip cookie dough
Chocolate Fudge Brownie	Chocolate ice cream with fudgy brownies
Chubby Hubby	Chocolate-covered, peanut-butter-filled pretzels in vanilla-malt ice cream with fudge and peanut-butter swirls
Chunky Monkey	Banana ice cream with walnuts and chocolate chunks
Coconut Almond Fudge Chip	Coconut ice cream with almonds and fudge chips
Coffee, Coffee, BuzzBuzzBuzz!	Coffee ice cream with espresso-fudge chunks
Deep Dark Chocolate	Very chocolaty ice cream
New York Super Fudge Chunk	Chocolate ice cream with white- and dark-chocolate chunks, pecans, walnuts, and chocolate-covered almonds
Peanut Butter Cup	Peanut-butter ice cream with peanut-butter cups
Phish Food	Milk-chocolate ice cream with marshmallow nougat, caramel swirls, and fudge fish
Pistachio Pistachio	Pistachio ice cream with pistachios
S'mores	Chocolate low-fat ice cream with marshmallow swirls and graham-cracker wedges
Southern Pecan Pie	Brown-sugar ice cream with roasted pecans, chunks of pecan-pie pieces, and a pecan-caramel swirl

EXHIBIT 4 | Composition of Board of Directors

Name	Age	Office	Year Elected
Jerry Greenfield	48	Chairperson, Director	1990
Ben Cohen	48	Vice Chairperson, Director	1977
Perry Odak	54	Chief Executive Officer, President, and Director	1997
Pierre Ferrari	49	Director, Self-Employed Consultant	1997
Jeffrey Furman	56	Director, Self-Employed Consultant	1982
Jennifer Henderson	46	Director, President of leadership-consulting firm—Strategic Interventions	1996
Frederick A. Miller	53	Director, President of management-consulting firm—Kaleel Jamison Consulting Group	1992
Henry Morgan	74	Director, Dean Emeritus of Boston University School of Management	1987
Bruce Bowman	47	Senior Director of Operations	1995
Charles Green	45	Senior Director of Sales and Distribution	1996
Michael Sands	35	Chief Marketing Officer	1999
Frances Rathke	39	Chief Financial Officer and Secretary	1990

*Occupations of directors who were neither employed at Ben & Jerry's nor the Ben & Jerry's Foundation, Inc., as of March 25, 1999, are as follows:

Ben Cohen: Cofounder of Ben & Jerry's, and served as a director at Blue Fish Clothing, Community Products, Inc., Social Venture Network, and Greenpeace International.

Pierre Ferrari: President of Lang International, a marketing-consulting firm.

Jeffrey Furman: Self-employed consultant.

Jennifer Henderson: Director of Training at the Center for Community Change, and President of Strategic Interventions, a leadership- and management-consulting firm.

Frederick A. Miller: President of Kaleel Jamison Consulting Group, a strategic-culture-change and management-consulting firm.

Henry Morgan: Dean Emeritus of the Boston University School of Management. Also served as a director at Cambridge Bancorporation, Southern Development Bancorporation, and Cleveland Development Bancorporation.

Source: SEC filings.

EXHIBIT 5 | Beneficial-Ownership Structure of Ben & Jerry's Homemade

	Class A Common Stock		Class B Common Stock		Preferred Stock	
	# Shares	% Outstanding Shares	# Shares	% Outstanding Shares	# Shares	% Outstanding Shares
Ben Cohen	413,173	6.1%	488,486	60.9%	—	—
Jerry Greenfield	130,000	1.9%	90,000	11.2%	—	—
Jeffrey Furman	17,000	*	30,300	3.8%	—	—
Perry Odak	368,521	5.5%	—	—	—	—
Pierre Ferrari	8,121	*	—	—	—	—
Jennifer Henderson	1,138	*	—	—	—	—
Frederick A. Miller	4,345	*	—	—	—	—
Henry Morgan	5,845	*	—	—	—	—
Bruce Bowman	46,064	*	—	—	—	—
Charles Green	17,809	*	—	—	—	—
Frances Rathke	51,459	*	—	—	—	—
Credit Suisse Asset Management	860,500	12.7%	—	—	—	—
Dimensional Fund Advisors	359,000	5.3%	—	—	—	—
All officers & directors as a group of 15 persons	1,115,554	16.5%	608,786	75.9%	—	—
Ben & Jerry's Foundation, Inc.	—	—	—	—	900	100.0%
Total shares outstanding (12/25/1999)	6,759,276		801,813		900	

*Less than 1%.

Source: SEC filings.

EXHIBIT 6 | Investor-Value Measures: Ben & Jerry's and Industry Comparables

	Price/Earnings	Price/Book
Dreyer's Grand	47.2	7.8
Eskimo Pie	30.7	1.1
TCBY Enterprises	12.5	1.2
Yocream International	9.4	1.8
Ben & Jerry's	19.8	1.8

Source: Case writer analysis.

The Battle for Value, 2004: FedEx Corp. vs. United Parcel Service, Inc.

FedEx will produce superior financial returns for shareowners by providing high value-added supply chain, transportation, business, and related information services through focused operating companies competing collectively, and managed collaboratively, under the respected FedEx brand.

    FedEx Mission Statement (Excerpt)

We serve the evolving distribution, logistics, and commerce needs of our customers worldwide, offering excellence and value in all we do. We sustain a financially strong company, with broad employee ownership, that provides a long-term competitive return to our shareowners.

    UPS Mission Statement (Excerpt)

On June 18, 2004, the United States and China reached a landmark air-transportation agreement that quintupled the number of commercial cargo flights between the two countries. The agreement also allowed for the establishment of air-cargo hubs in China and landing rights for commercial airlines at any available airport. The pact represented the most dramatic liberalization of air traffic in the history of the two nations, and FedEx Corporation and United Parcel Service, Inc. (UPS), the only U.S. all-cargo carriers then permitted to serve the vast Chinese market,[1] were certain to be the primary beneficiaries of this opportunity.

News of the transportation agreement did not come as a major surprise to most observers as U.S. and Chinese negotiators had been in talks since at least February. The stock prices of both companies had been rising steadily since those talks began,

---

[1]Northwest Airlines served China through both all-cargo and all-passenger services.

This case was prepared by Robert F. Bruner and Sean D. Carr as a basis for classroom discussion rather than to illustrate effective or ineffective management. The case complements "Battle for Value: Federal Express Corporation vs. United Parcel Service of America, Inc." (UVA-F-1115), prepared by Robert F. Bruner and Derick Bulkley. Copyright © 2005 by the University of Virginia Darden School Foundation, Charlottesville, VA. All rights reserved. *To order copies, send an e-mail to* sales@dardenpublishing.com. *No part of this publication may be reproduced, stored in a retrieval system, used in a spreadsheet, or transmitted in any form or by any means—electronic, mechanical, photocopying, recording, or otherwise—without the permission of the Darden School Foundation.*

but FedEx's share price had rocketed at a rate nearly five times faster than UPS's.[2] **Exhibit 1** presents an illustration of recent stock-price patterns for the two firms relative to the S&P 500 Index. FedEx had the largest foreign presence in China, with 11 weekly flights—almost twice as many as UPS. The company served 220 Chinese cities, and flew directly to Beijing, Shenzhen, and Shanghai. FedEx's volumes in China had grown by more than 50 percent between 2003 and 2004.

While UPS lagged behind FedEx in the Chinese market, it was still the world's largest package-delivery company and the dominant parcel carrier in the United States. UPS had been active in China since 1988 and was the first carrier in the industry to offer nonstop service from the United States. By 2003, UPS had six weekly Boeing 747 flights to China, with direct flights to Beijing and Shanghai, serving nearly 200 cities. UPS reported a 60 percent growth in traffic on its principal U.S.–Shanghai route since initiating that service in 2001, and it predicted that peak-season demand would exceed its capacity.

As the U.S. package-delivery segment matured, the international markets—and especially China—became a battleground for the two package-delivery giants. FedEx had virtually invented customer logistical management, and was widely perceived as innovative, entrepreneurial, and an operational leader. Historically, UPS had a reputation for being big, bureaucratic, and an industry follower, but "Big Brown" was aggressively shedding its plodding image, as it too became an innovator and a tenacious adversary. UPS had recently undergone a major overhaul of its image, and was repositioning itself as a leading provider of logistics and supply-chain management services.

The 2004 air-transportation agreement between China and the United States was a watershed moment for the international package-delivery business—more than 100 new weekly all-cargo flights were up for grabs with the United States' largest trading partner. There was, however, no guarantee for exactly how those new cargo routes would be allocated between UPS and FedEx, companies that had been battling each other for dominance for more than 30 years. Moreover, the eventual assignment to the region of other carriers would test each company's ability to fend off emerging competitive threats.

Against this backdrop, industry observers wondered how the titanic struggle between FedEx and UPS would develop, particularly for investors in the two firms. Was the performance of the companies in recent years predictive of the future? Success in China was widely seen as the litmus test for corporate survival in the new millennium. Which company was better positioned to attract the capital necessary to win this competitive battle?

FedEx Corporation

FedEx first took form as Fred Smith's undergraduate term paper for a Yale University economics class. Smith's strategy dictated that FedEx would purchase the planes that it required to transport packages, whereas all other competitors used the cargo

---

[2]Between February 18 and June 18, 2004, FedEx's stock price rose 13.9 percent, whereas UPS's grew 3.1 percent.

space available on passenger airlines. In addition to using his own planes, Smith's key innovation was a hub-and-spoke distribution pattern, which permitted cheaper and faster service to more locations than his competitors could offer. In 1971, Smith invested his $4-million inheritance, and raised $91 million in venture capital to launch the firm—the largest venture-capital start-up at the time.

In 1973, on the first night of continuous operation, 389 FedEx employees delivered 186 packages overnight to 25 U.S. cities. In those early years FedEx, then known as Federal Express Corporation, experienced severe losses, and Smith was nearly ousted from his chair position. By 1976, FedEx finally saw a modest profit of $3.6 million on an average daily volume of 19,000 packages. Through the rest of the 1970s, FedEx continued to grow by expanding services, acquiring more trucks and aircraft, and raising capital. The formula was successful. In 1981, FedEx generated more revenue than any other U.S. air-delivery company.

By 1981, competition in the industry had started to rise. Emery Air Freight began to imitate FedEx's hub system and to acquire airplanes, and UPS began to move into the overnight air market. The United States Postal Service (USPS) positioned its overnight letter at half the price of FedEx's, but quality problems and FedEx's "absolutely positively overnight" ad campaign quelled that potential threat. In 1983, FedEx reached $1 billion in revenues and seemed poised to own the market for express delivery.

During the 1990s, FedEx proved itself as an operational leader, even receiving the prestigious Malcolm Baldrige National Quality Award from the President of the United States. FedEx was the first company ever to win in the service category. Part of this success could be attributed to deregulation and to operational strategy, but credit could also be given to FedEx's philosophy of "People-Service-Profit," which reflected its emphasis on customer focus, total quality management, and employee participation. Extensive attitude surveying, a promote-from-within policy, effective grievance procedures that sometimes resulted in a chat with Fred Smith himself, and an emphasis on personal responsibility and initiative not only earned FedEx a reputation as a great place to work, but also helped to keep the firm largely free of unions.

FedEx's growth occurred within the context of fundamental change in the business environment. Deregulation of the domestic airline industry permitted larger planes to replace smaller ones, thereby permitting FedEx to purchase several Boeing 727s, which helped reduce its unit costs. Trucking industry deregulation also permitted FedEx to establish an integrated regional trucking system that lowered its unit costs on short-haul trips, enabling the company to compete more effectively with UPS. Rising inflation and global competitiveness compelled manufacturers to manage inventories more closely and to emulate the just-in-time (JIT) supply programs of the Japanese, creating a heightened demand for FedEx's rapid and carefully monitored movement of packages. And, finally, technological innovations enabled FedEx to achieve important advances in customer ordering, package tracking, and process monitoring.

By the end of 2003, FedEx had nearly $15.4 billion in assets and net income of $830 million on revenues of about $22.5 billion. **Exhibit 2** provides FedEx's financial and analytical ratios. The company had about 50,000 ground vehicles, 625 aircraft, 216,500 full- and part-time employees, and shipped more than 5.4 million packages daily.

United Parcel Service, Inc.

Founded in 1907, United Parcel Service, Inc., was the largest package-delivery company in the world. Consolidated parcel delivery, both on the ground and through the air, was the primary business of the company, although increasingly the company offered more specialized transportation and logistics services.

Known in the industry as Big Brown, UPS had its roots in Seattle, Washington, where 19-year-old Jim Casey started a bicycle-messenger service called American Messenger Company. After merging with a rival firm, Motorcycle Delivery Company, the company focused on department-store deliveries, and that remained true until the 1940s. Renamed United Parcel Service of America, UPS started an air-delivery service in 1929 by putting packages on commercial passenger planes. The company entered its strongest period of growth during the post–World War II economic boom and, by 1975, UPS had reached a milestone when it could promise package delivery to every address in the continental United States. That same year the company expanded outside the country with its first delivery to Ontario, Canada. The following year, UPS began service in West Germany with 120 of its trademark-brown delivery vans.

The key to the success of UPS, later headquartered in Atlanta, Georgia, was efficiency. According to *BusinessWeek*, "Every route is timed down to the traffic light. Each vehicle was engineered to exacting specifications. And the drivers . . . endure a daily routine calibrated down to the minute."[3] But this demand for machinelike precision met with resistance by UPS's heavily unionized labor force. Of those demands, UPS driver Mark Dray said:

> . . . drivers are expected to keep precise schedules (with hours broken down into hundredths) that do not allow for variables such as weather, traffic conditions, and package volume. If they're behind, they're reprimanded, and if they're ahead of schedule, their routes are lengthened.[4]

In its quest for efficiency, UPS experienced several major strikes resulting from changes in labor practices and driver requirements. In August 1997, the 190,000 teamsters employed at UPS went on strike for 15 days before agreeing to a new five-year contract. In addition to large wage increases, the new agreement called for the creation of 10,000 new full-time jobs and the shifting of 10,000 part-time workers into full-time positions. The strike cost UPS $700 million in lost revenue, resulting in less than 1 percent sales growth for the year (1996) and a decline in profits to $909 million from $1.15 billion.

---

[3]Todd Vogel and Chuck Hawkins, "Can UPS Deliver the Goods in a New World?" *BusinessWeek* (4 June 1990).

[4]Jill Hodges, "Driving Negotiations; Teamsters Survey Says UPS Drivers among Nation's Most Stressed Workers," *Star Tribune* (9 June 1993).

For most of the company's history, UPS stock was owned solely by UPS's managers, their families, former employees, or charitable foundations owned by UPS. The company acted as the market-maker in its own shares, buying or selling shares at a fair market value[5] determined by the board of directors each quarter. By the end of the millennium, however, having shrugged off the lingering effects of the strike and having emerged as a newly revitalized company with strong forward momentum, company executives determined that UPS needed the added flexibility of publicly traded stock in order to pursue a more aggressive acquisition strategy.

In November 1999, UPS initiated a two-for-one stock split, whereby the company exchanged each existing UPS share for two Class A shares. The company then sold 109.4 million newly created Class B shares on the New York Stock Exchange in an initial public offering (IPO) that raised $5.266 billion, net of issuance costs. UPS used the majority of these proceeds to repurchase 68 million shares of the Class A stock. Following a holding period after the IPO, Class A shares were convertible to Class B, and could be traded or sold accordingly. Although both shares of stock had the same economic interest in the company, Class A shares entitled holders to ten votes per share while the Class B shareowners were entitled to one vote.

Until the stock split and IPO in 1999, the financially and operationally conservative company had been perceived as slow and plodding. Although much larger than FedEx, UPS had not chosen to compete directly in the overnight delivery market until 1982, largely because of the enormous cost of building an air fleet. But after going public UPS initiated an aggressive series of acquisitions, beginning with a Miami-based freight carrier operating in Latin America and a franchise-based chain of stores providing packing, shipping, and mail services called Mail Boxes Etc. (later renamed the UPS Store) with more than 4,300 domestic and international locations.

More assertive than ever before, the UPS of the new millennium was the product of extensive reengineering efforts and a revitalized business focus. While the company had traditionally been the industry's low-cost provider, in recent years the company had been investing heavily in information technology, aircraft, and facilities to support service innovations, maintain quality, and reduce costs. In early 2003, the company revamped its logo for the first time since 1961, and emphasized its activities in the wider supply-chain industry. "The small-package market in the United States is about a $60-billion market. The worldwide supply-chain market is about a $3.2-trillion market," said Mike Eskew, UPS's chair and CEO. "It's everything from the moment something gets made until it gets delivered for final delivery, and then after market, its parts replacement."[6]

---

[5]In setting its share price, the board considered a variety of factors, including past and current earnings, earnings estimates, the ratio of UPS's common stock to its debt, the business and outlook of UPS, and the general economic climate. The opinions of outside advisers were sometimes considered. The stock price had never decreased in value. The employee stock purchases were often financed with stock hypothecation loans from commercial banks. As the shares provided the collateral for those loans, the assessment made by the outside lenders provided some external validation for the share price.

[6]Harry R. Weber, "UPS, FedEx Rivalry: A Study in Contrasts," *Associated Press Newswires,* 21 May 2004.

By 2003, UPS offered package-delivery services throughout the United States and in more than 200 countries and territories, and moved more than 13 million packages and documents through its network every day. Domestic package operations accounted for 76 percent of revenues in 2002; international (15 percent); nonpackage (9 percent). In the United States, it was estimated that the company's delivery system carried goods having a value in excess of 6 percent of the U.S. gross domestic product.[7] The company employed 360,000 people (of whom 64 percent were unionized), and owned 88,000 ground vehicles and 583 aircraft.

At year-end 2003, UPS reported assets, revenues, and profits of $28.9 billion, $33.4 billion, and $2.9 billion, respectively. **Exhibit 3** provides UPS's financial and analytical ratios. The company's financial conservatism was reflected in its AAA bond rating.

Competition in the Express-Delivery Market

The $45-billion domestic U.S. package-delivery market could be segmented along at least three dimensions: weight, mode of transit, and timeliness of service. The weight categories consisted of letters (weighing 0–2.0 pounds), packages (2.0–70 pounds), and freight (over 70 pounds). The mode of transit categories were simply air and ground. Finally, time categories were overnight, deferred delivery (second-day), three-day delivery, and, lastly, regular delivery, which occurred four or more days after pickup.

The air-express segment was a $25-billion portion of the U.S. package-delivery industry, and was concentrated in letters and packages, overnight and deferred, and air or air-and-ground. While virtually all of FedEx's business activities were in the air-express segment of the package-delivery industry, only about 22 percent of UPS's revenues were derived from its next-day air business. FedEx and UPS's competition for dominance of the $25-billion domestic air-express delivery market foreshadowed an unusually challenging future.

Exhibit 4 provides a detailed summary of the major events marking the competitive rivalry between FedEx and UPS. Significant dimensions of this rivalry included the following:

- **Customer focus.** Both companies emphasized their focus on the customer. This meant listening carefully to the customer's needs, providing customized solutions rather than standardized products, and committing to service relationships.

- **Price competition.** UPS boldly entered the market by undercutting the price of FedEx's overnight letter by half. But by the late 1990s, both firms had settled into a predictable pattern of regular price increases. **Exhibit 5** provides a summary of recent rate increases.

- **Operational reengineering.** Given the intense price competition, the reduction of unit costs became a priority. Cost reduction was achieved through the exploitation

---

[7]"United Parcel Service, Inc.– SWOT Analysis," *Datamonitor Company Profiles* (16 July 2004).

of economies of scale, investment in technology, and business-process reengineering, which sought to squeeze unnecessary steps and costs out of the service process.

- **Information technology.** Information management became central to the operations of both UPS and FedEx. Every package handled by FedEx, for instance, was logged into COSMOS (Customer, Operations, Service, Master On-line System), which transmitted data from package movements, customer pickups, invoices, and deliveries to a central database at the Memphis, Tennessee, headquarters. UPS relied on DIADs (Delivery Information Acquisition Devices), which were handheld units that drivers used to scan package barcodes and record customer signatures.

- **Service expansion.** FedEx and UPS increasingly pecked at each other's service offerings. FedEx, armed with volume discounts and superb quality, went after the big clients that had previously used UPS without thought. UPS copied FedEx's customer interfaces by installing 11,500 drop-off boxes to compete with FedEx's 12,000 boxes, 165 drive-through stations, and 371 express-delivery stores. UPS also began Saturday pickups and deliveries to match FedEx's schedule. FedEx bought $200 million in ground vehicles to match UPS.

- **Logistics services.** The largest innovations entailed offering integrated logistics services to large corporate clients. These services were aimed at providing total inventory control to customers, including purchase orders, receipt of goods, order entry and warehousing, inventory accounting, shipping, and accounts receivable. The London design-company Laura Ashley, for instance, retained FedEx to store, track, and ship products quickly to individual stores worldwide. Similarly, Dell Computer retained UPS to manage its total inbound and outbound shipping.

The impact of the fierce one-upmanship occurring between FedEx and UPS was clearly reflected in their respective investment expenditures. Between 1992 and 2003, capital expenditures for FedEx and UPS rose at an annualized rate of 34.64 percent and 36.78 percent, respectively. During this period, the two companies matched each other's investments in capital almost exactly. (**Exhibit 6** provides a graphical representation of the firms' cumulative capital-investment expenditures.)

International Package-Delivery Market

By 2004, express cargo aircraft carried nearly 50 percent of all international trade, measured by value.[8] Yet throughout the 1990s, international delivery had remained only a small part of the revenues for UPS and FedEx. After making significant investments in developing European delivery capabilities, FedEx eventually relinquished its hub in Europe in 1992 by selling its Brussels, Belgium, operation to DHL. Analysts estimated that FedEx had lost $1 billion in Europe since its entry there in 1984. FedEx would continue to deliver to Europe, but relied on local partners. In 1995, FedEx expanded

---

[8]Alexandara Harney and Dan Roberts, "Comment & Analysis," *Financial Times,* 9 August 2004.

its routes in Latin America and the Caribbean, and later introduced FedEx AsiaOne, a next-business-day service between Asian countries and the United States via a hub in Subic Bay, Philippines.

UPS did not break into the European market in earnest until 1988, with the acquisition of 10 European courier services. To enhance its international delivery systems, UPS created a system that coded and tracked packages and automatically billed customers for customs' duties and taxes. UPS hoped that its international service would account for one-third of total revenue by 2000. In May 1995, it announced that it would spend more than $1 billion to expand its European operations during the next five years. **Exhibit 7** presents international and domestic (U.S.) segment data for FedEx and UPS.

According to economic and industry experts, China would become the world's second-largest economy within 11 years and the largest by 2039. It was already the world's largest market for mobile phones and a key center for the production of textiles, computer chips, and other high-tech products. According to recent economic projections, inter-Asia trade was projected to grow at a rate of 16.8 percent annually through 2005.[9]

The overall market for air cargo in China had been growing at 30 percent a year and was expected to increase at nearly that pace for the next five years.[10] FedEx and UPS focused primarily on the import/export package market and not the intra-China domestic market, using local partners to pick up and deliver parcels within the country (although, by December 2005, each company would be permitted to own completely package operations in China). One industry source believed the domestic parcel market was approximately $800 million, while China's export-import market was nearly $1 billion. "As it becomes the workshop of the world," one observer noted, "teeming factories along the Pearl and Yangtze river deltas represent both the start of the world's supply chain and the source of some of its biggest transport bottlenecks."[11]

The newly announced U.S.–China air-service agreement would allow an additional 195 weekly flights for each country—111 by all-cargo carriers and 84 by passenger airlines—resulting in a total of 249 weekly flights by the end of a six-year phase-in period. The two countries also agreed to allow their carriers to serve any city in the other country. Until that time, Chinese carriers were limited to twelve U.S. cities, and U.S. passenger carriers could fly to only five Chinese cities. The agreement also provided that when carriers established cargo hubs in the other country, they would be granted a high degree of operating flexibility. According to U.S. Transportation Secretary Norman Mineta, "This agreement represents a giant step forward in creating an international air-transportation system that meets the needs of the new global marketplace."

UPS and FedEx both welcomed the news. "This provides an extraordinary opportunity for strengthening commercial supply chains that support growing international trade between the United States and China and throughout the world," said Mike Eskew, UPS chair and CEO, who added that the hub provision in the agreement would

---

[9]UPS press release, 4 November 2004.

[10]Morgan Stanley, 6 April 2004.

[11]Alexandara Harney and Dan Roberts, "Comment & Analysis," *Financial Times*, 9 August 2004.

facilitate that process. Fred Smith, chair and CEO of FedEx, said, "We think China is a huge opportunity for the company. We have significant expansion plans in the country, reflecting its fantastic growth and unique position as one of the world's top manufacturing centers."[12]

Performance Assessment

Virtually all interested observers—customers, suppliers, investors, and employees—watched the competitive struggle between UPS and FedEx for hints about the next stage of the drama. The conventional wisdom was that if a firm were operationally excellent, strong financial performance would follow. Indeed, FedEx had set a goal of producing "superior financial returns," while UPS targeted "a long-term competitive return." Had the two firms achieved their goals? Moreover, did the trends in financial performance suggest whether strong performance could be achieved in the future? In pursuit of the answers to those questions, the following exhibits afford several possible avenues of analysis.

EPS, Market Values, and Returns

Exhibit 8 presents the share prices, earnings per share (EPS), and price-earnings ratios for the two firms. Also included is the annual total return from holding each share (percentage gain in share price plus dividend yield). Some analysts questioned the appropriateness of using UPS's fair market-value share price before the 1999 IPO, because it had been set by the board of directors rather than in an open market.

Ratio Analysis

Exhibits 2 and **3** present a variety of analytical ratios computed from the financial statements of each firm.

Economic Profit (Economic Value Added, or EVA™) Analysis

EVA reflects the value created or destroyed each year by deducting a charge for capital from the firm's net operating profit after taxes (NOPAT).

$$\text{EVA} = \text{Operating profits} - \text{Capital charge}$$
$$= \text{NOPAT} - (K \times \text{Capital})$$

The capital charge was determined by multiplying the cost of capital, K, by the capital employed in the business or operation. This computation could be done by either of two methods, both of which would yield the same answer; they are presented in the exhibits for the sake of illustration. The *operating approach* works with the asset side of the balance sheet, and computes NOPAT directly from the income statement. The *capital approach* works with the right-hand side of the balance sheet, and computes NOPAT indirectly (i.e., by adjusting net income).

---

[12]Dan Roberts, "FedEx Plans Expanded Services in China," *Financial Times,* 23 June 2004.

Estimating Capital   Exhibits **9** and **10** calculate the actual amount of capital from both an operating and a capital approach. Included in capital are near-capital items that represent economic value employed on behalf of the firm, such as the present value of operating leases, amortized goodwill, and losses. The rationale for including losses and write-offs in continuing capital is that such losses represent unproductive assets or a failed investment. Were they excluded from the capital equation, the sum would only count successful efforts and would not accurately reflect the performance of the firm.

Estimating NOPAT   Exhibits **9** and **10** calculate NOPAT with a similar regard for losses and write-offs. Here, the aim is to arrive at the actual cash generated by the concern. To do so, the exhibits add increases in deferred taxes back into income because it is not a cash expense, and calculate the interest expense of the leased operating assets as if they were leased capital assets.

Estimating Cost of Capital   The capital charge applied against NOPAT should be based on a blend of the costs of all the types of capital the firm employs, or the weighted-average cost of capital (WACC). The cost of debt (used for both debt and leases) is the annual rate consistent with each firm's bond rating (BBB for FedEx and AAA for UPS). The cost of equity may be estimated in a variety of ways. In the analysis here, the capital asset pricing model (CAPM)[13] was employed. FedEx's beta and cost of equity are used in estimating FedEx's cost of capital. Because UPS's beta was unobservable, the analysis that follows uses the average annual betas for UPS's publicly held peer firms: FedEx, Air Express, Airborne Freight, Roadway, Yellow Transport, and J.B. Hunt Transport.

Estimating EVA and MVA   In Exhibits **9** and **10,** the stock of capital and the flow of cash are used to calculate the actual return and, with the introduction of the WACC, to calculate the EVA. These exhibits present the EVA calculated each year and cumulatively over time. The panel at the bottom of each exhibit estimates the market value created or destroyed (or the market value added [MVA]) over the observation period. MVA is calculated as the difference between the current market value of the company and its investment base. The market value created could be compared with cumulative EVA. In theory, the following relationships would hold:

$$MVA = \text{Present value of all future EVA}$$

$$MVA = \text{Market value of debt and equity} - \text{Capital}$$

Thus,

$$\text{Market value} = \text{Capital} + \text{Present value of all future EVA}$$

---

[13]The CAPM describes the cost of equity as the sum of the risk-free rate of return and a risk premium. The risk premium is the average risk premium for a large portfolio of stocks times the risk factor (beta) for the company. A beta equal to 1.0 suggests that the company is just as risky as the market portfolio; less than 1.0 suggests lower risk; greater than 1.0 implies greater risk.

In other words, maximizing the present value of EVA would amount to maximizing the market value of the firm.

Outlook for FedEx and UPS

About 70 percent[14] of FedEx's common shares were held by institutional investors that, it could be assumed, were instrumental in setting the prices for the company's shares. Typically, those investors absorbed the thinking of the several securities analysts who followed FedEx and UPS in 2004. **Exhibit 11** contains excerpts from various equity reports, which indicate the outlook held by those analysts.

Observers of the air-express package-delivery industry pondered the recent performance of the two leading firms and their prospects. What had been the impact of the intense competition between the two firms? Which firm was doing better? The companies faced a watershed moment with the dramatic liberalization of the opportunities in China. Might their past performance contain clues about the prospects for future competition?

---

[14]Officers, directors, and employees of FedEx owned 7 percent of the shares; the remainder, about 23 percent, was owned by individual investors not affiliated with the company.

EXHIBIT 1 | UPS and FedEx Price Patterns June 18, 2003 to
September 3, 2004

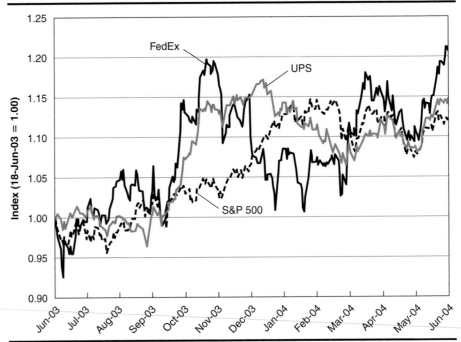

Source of data: Datastream (case writer's analysis).

EXHIBIT 2 | Financial and Analytical Ratios for FedEx

FEDEX CORP	1992	1993	1994	1995	1996	1997	1998	1999	2000	2001	2002	2003	
Activity Analysis													
Average days outstanding	44.10	42.60	41.82	41.79	42.67	44.11	39.74	44.57	46.98	46.98	44.25	41.54	365/receivables turnover
Working capital turnover	(42.21)	(817.85)	37.64	103.73	93.51	67.84	208.05	47.08	46.37	98.37	28.50	37.11	Sales/average net working capital
Fixed assets turnover	2.21	2.25	2.46	2.53	2.50	2.49	2.67	2.56	2.58	2.42	2.48	2.58	Sales/average net fixed assets
Total asset turnover	1.38	1.35	1.42	1.46	1.53	1.51	1.64	1.58	1.58	1.47	1.49	1.46	Sales/average total assets
Liquidity Analysis													
Current ratio	0.87	0.99	1.15	1.05	1.07	1.09	1.03	1.13	1.14	1.06	1.25	1.18	Current assets/current liab.
Cash ratio	0.06	0.11	0.26	0.20	0.06	0.06	0.08	0.12	0.02	0.04	0.11	0.16	(Cash + mkt. securities)/curr. liab.
Cash from operations ratio	0.38	0.50	0.50	0.58	0.58	0.51	0.61	0.64	0.56	0.63	0.76	0.56	Cash from operations/curr.liab.
Defensive interval	0.70	0.78	0.91	0.92	0.68	0.72	0.80	0.92	0.94	0.87	0.92	1.02	(Cash + AR + cash taxes)/ (rents + gross CAPEX)
Long-Term Debt and Solvency Analysis													
Debt/equity ratio	1.24	1.21	0.95	0.70	0.52	0.51	0.41	0.29	0.37	0.36	0.28	0.28	Total debt/total equity
Times interest earned	1.36	1.82	2.92	3.73	4.31	5.06	6.42	7.78	7.83	6.58	6.98	10.51	EBIT/interest expense
Fixed-charge coverage ratio	0.34	0.46	0.64	0.65	0.61	0.57	0.74	0.75	0.72	0.65	0.61	0.83	EBIT/((rental exp. and int. exp.)
Capital expenditure ratio	0.15	0.21	0.22	0.28	0.23	0.22	0.29	0.27	0.23	0.25	0.27	0.22	Cash from operations/CAPEX
Cash from operations/ debt ratio	0.27	0.36	0.42	0.65	0.71	0.66	1.04	1.29	0.91	0.96	1.23	0.93	Cash from operations/total debt
Profitability Analysis													
Margin before interest and tax	3.67%	4.67%	6.26%	6.29%	6.07%	5.94%	6.82%	6.93%	6.69%	6.09%	5.79%	6.54%	EBIT/sales
Net profit margin	(1.51%)	0.69%	2.41%	3.17%	3.00%	3.14%	3.17%	3.76%	3.77%	2.98%	3.45%	3.69%	Net income/sales
Return on assets	1.63%	4.38%	6.45%	7.09%	6.75%	6.51%	6.94%	7.33%	7.32%	5.74%	6.38%	6.30%	(NI + int. exp.)/avg. total assets
Return on total equity	(7.20%)	3.22%	10.62%	13.25%	11.95%	12.19%	12.70%	13.54%	14.38%	9.90%	10.85%	11.39%	Net income/average total equity
Financial leverage effect	(21.85%)	7.43%	26.64%	28.87%	32.51%	35.85%	29.48%	35.63%	42.35%	28.59%	31.87%	44.36%	Net income/operating income

Growth	'92–'93	'93–'94	'94–'95	'95–'96	'96–'97	'97–'98	'98–'99	'99–'00	'00–'01	'01–'02	'02–'03	CAGR	('92–'03)
Sales	3.42%	8.60%	10.76%	9.39%	12.13%	37.79%	5.67%	8.84%	7.52%	4.98%	9.12%	11.53%	('92–'03)
Book assets	6.04%	3.44%	7.36%	4.13%	13.83%	27.02%	9.93%	8.25%	15.73%	3.54%	11.39%	9.81%	('92–'03)
Net income before unusual (gain) loss	(196.51%)	86.11%	45.61%	3.42%	17.37%	37.91%	26.73%	9.03%	(15.10%)	24.07%	14.48%	25.20%	('93–'03)
Net income	(147.34%)	279.40%	45.61%	3.42%	17.37%	39.26%	25.51%	9.03%	(15.10%)	21.50%	16.90%	35.51%	('93–'03)
Operating income	31.67%	45.51%	11.40%	5.53%	9.65%	58.27%	7.43%	4.99%	(2.14%)	(0.16%)	23.30%	13.64%	('92–'03)

Source of data: DataStream (Thomson Financial).

EXHIBIT 3 | Financial and Analytical Ratios for UPS

UPS	1992	1993	1994	1995	1996	1997	1998	1999	2000	2001	2002	2003	
Activity Analysis													
Average days outstanding	23.13	23.11	25.66	30.50	34.81	38.57	37.68	39.67	44.79	53.16	54.92	51.60	365/receivables turnover
Working capital turnover	267.78	4,748.29	161.79	80.63	20.39	20.81	14.51	3.90	11.35	10.33	9.82	7.72	Sales/average net working capital
Fixed assets turnover	2.59	2.63	2.52	2.34	2.19	2.04	2.18	2.34	2.41	2.28	2.30	2.41	Sales/average net fixed assets
Total asset turnover	1.83	1.86	1.75	1.66	1.50	1.41	1.45	1.17	1.37	1.24	1.19	1.16	Sales/average total assets
Liquidity Analysis													
Current ratio	1.03	1.00	1.04	1.09	1.35	1.32	1.46	2.65	1.58	1.64	1.57	1.79	Current assets/current liab.
Cash ratio	0.06	0.12	0.09	0.07	0.12	0.14	0.44	1.50	0.43	0.35	0.54	0.72	(Cash + mkt. securities)/curr.liab.
Cash from operations ratio	0.69	0.74	0.56	0.66	0.60	0.73	0.77	0.53	0.61	0.84	1.01	0.84	Cash from operations/curr. liab.
Defensive interval	1.71	1.83	1.47	1.36	1.38	1.60	3.12	5.13	3.07	2.82	4.98	4.57	(Cash + AR + cash taxes)/(rents + gross CAPEX)
Long-Term Debt and Solvency Analysis													
Debt/equity ratio	0.23	0.22	0.24	0.34	0.44	0.43	0.36	0.19	0.37	0.50	0.37	0.26	Total debt/total equity
Times interest earned	18.68	23.59	20.85	17.19	13.71	7.38	12.17	16.08	19.58	16.83	23.15	36.41	EBIT/interest expense
Fixed-charge coverage ratio	18.68	23.59	20.85	17.19	13.71	7.38	12.17	16.08	19.58	16.83	23.15	36.41	EBIT/(rental exp. and int.exp.)
Capital expenditure ratio	0.23	0.26	0.21	0.22	0.19	0.22	0.25	0.19	0.22	0.29	0.41	0.33	Cash from operations/CAPEX
Cash from operations/debt ratio	1.67	2.04	1.43	1.13	0.74	0.94	1.10	0.92	0.76	0.75	1.22	1.22	Cash from operations/total debt
Profitability Analysis													
Margin before interest and tax	7.74%	8.20%	7.95%	10.29%	9.07%	7.56%	12.47%	14.74%	15.19%	12.69%	12.81%	13.16%	EBIT/sales
Net profit margin	3.12%	4.55%	4.82%	4.96%	5.12%	4.05%	7.02%	3.26%	9.86%	7.83%	10.18%	8.65%	Net income/sales
Return on assets	6.47%	9.10%	9.10%	9.24%	8.65%	7.16%	11.69%	4.91%	14.61%	10.68%	12.73%	10.44%	(NI + int. exp.)/avg. total assets
Return on total equity	13.87%	20.53%	20.30%	20.25%	19.42%	14.93%	24.27%	7.08%	30.14%	23.41%	25.55%	19.51%	Net income/average total equity
Financial leverage effect	35.59%	46.16%	58.39%	53.41%	60.16%	36.82%	60.70%	39.72%	107.00%	61.51%	56.55%	62.38%	Net income/operating income

Growth		'92–'93	'93–'94	'94–'95	'95–'96	'96–'97	'97–'98	'98–'99	'99–'00	'00–'01	'01–'02	'02–'03	CAGR	
Sales		7.65%	10.08%	7.51%	6.29%	0.40%	10.37%	9.13%	10.05%	2.94%	2.04%	7.08%	7.32%	('92–'03)
Book assets		5.93%	16.80%	13.08%	18.26%	6.41%	7.26%	35.01%	(5.99%)	13.73%	6.99%	9.68%	8.12%	('92–'03)
Net income before unusual (gain) loss		5.82%	16.51%	10.57%	9.88%	(20.68%)	91.53%	(49.28%)	232.28%	(17.35%)	34.19%	(10.94%)	14.25%	('92–'03)
Net income		56.86%	16.51%	10.57%	9.88%	(20.68%)	91.53%	(49.28%)	232.28%	(18.23%)	32.64%	(8.93%)	18.83%	('92–'03)
Operating income		14.08%	6.74%	39.21%	(6.33%)	(16.31%)	81.98%	29.06%	13.39%	(14.02%)	3.01%	10.01%	12.35%	('92–'03)

Source of data: DataStream (Thomson Financial).

EXHIBIT 4 | Timeline of Competitive Developments

FedEx Corp.		United Parcel Service, Inc.
• Offers 10:30 A.M. delivery	1982	• Establishes next-day air service
• Acquires Gelco Express and launches operations in Asia-Pacific	1984	
• Establishes European hub in Brussels	1985	• Begins intercontinental air service between United States and Europe
• Introduces handheld barcode scanner to capture detailed package information	1986	
• Offers warehouse services for IBM, National Semiconductor, Laura Ashley	1987	
	1988	• Establishes UPS's first air fleet • Offers automated customs service
• Acquires Tiger International to expand its international presence	1989	• Expands international air service to 180 countries
• Wins Malcolm Baldrige National Quality Award	1990	• Introduces 10:30 A.M. guarantee for next-day air
	1991	• Begins Saturday delivery • Offers electronic-signature tracking
• Offers two-day delivery	1992	• Expands delivery to over 200 countries
	1993	• Provides supply-chain solutions through UPS Logistics Group
• Launches Web site for package tracking	1994	• Launches Web site for package tracking
• Acquires air routes serving China	1995	• Offers guaranteed 8 A.M. overnight delivery
• Establishes Latin American division		
• Creates new hub at Roissy–Charles de Gaulle Airport in France	1999	• Makes UPS stock available through a public offering
• Launches business-to-consumer home-delivery service	2000	• Acquires all-cargo air service in Latin America
• Carries U.S. Postal Service packages	2001	• Acquires Mail Boxes Etc. retail franchise
• Acquires American Freightways Corp.		• Begins direct flights to China
• Expands home delivery to cover 100% of the U.S. population	2002	• Offers guaranteed next-day home delivery
• Acquires Kinko's retail franchise	2003	• Contracts with Yangtze River Express for package delivery within China
• Establishes Chinese headquarters		• Reduces domestic ground-delivery time

EXHIBIT 5 | Summary of Announced List-Rate Increases

UPS	1998	1999	2000	2001	2002	2003	2004	Average
Date implemented	2/8/02	2/9/03	2/8/04	2/6/05	1/8/06	1/7/07	1/6/08	
UPS ground	3.6%	2.5%	3.1%	3.1%	3.5%	3.9%	1.9%	3.1%
U.S. domestic air	3.3%	2.5%	3.5%	3.7%	4.0%	3.2%	2.9%	3.3%
U.S. export	0.0%	0.0%	2.9%	2.9%	3.9%	2.9%	2.9%	2.2%
Residential premium[1]	*$1.00*	*$1.00*	*$1.00*	*$1.05*	*$1.10*	*$1.15*	*$1.40*	
Commercial premium[2]	*N/A*	*N/A*	*N/A*	*N/A*	*N/A*	*N/A*	*$1.00*	
FedEx	**1998**	**1999**	**2000**	**2001**	**2002**	**2003**	**2004**	**Average**
Date implemented	2/16/02	2/9/03	2/2/04	2/2/05	1/8/06	1/7/07	1/6/08	
FedEx ground	3.6%	2.5%	3.1%	3.1%	3.5%	3.9%	1.9%	3.1%
U.S. domestic air	3.5%	2.8%	0.0%	4.9%	3.5%	3.5%	2.5%	3.0%
U.S. export	0.0%	0.0%	0.0%	2.9%	3.5%	3.5%	2.5%	1.8%
Residential premium-express[1]	*N/A*	*N/A*	*N/A*	*N/A*	*$1.35*	*$1.40*	*$1.75*	
Residential premium-ground,	*N/A*	*N/A*	*N/A*	*$1.30*	*$1.35*	*$1.40*	*$1.75*	
Residential premium-home delivery[1]	*N/A*	*N/A*	*N/A*	*$1.05*	*$1.10*	*$1.15*	*$1.40*	
Commercial premium-express[2]	*N/A*	*N/A*	*N/A*	*N/A*	*$1.50*	*$1.75*	*$1.00*	
Commercial premium-ground[2]	*N/A*	*N/A*	*N/A*	*N/A*	*N/A*	*N/A*	*$1.00*	

Sources of data: UPS, FedEx, and Morgan Stanley.

[1]The residential premium was an additional charge for deliveries of express letters and packages to residential addresses to offset the higher cost of providing service to them.

[2]The commercial premium was applied to products shipped to remote locations and/or select zip codes.

EXHIBIT 6 | Cumulative Capital Expenditures for FedEx and UPS

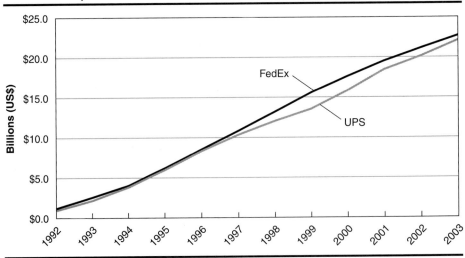

Sources of data: Company regulatory filings.

EXHIBIT 7 | Geographic Segment Information (values in millions of U.S. dollars)

FedEx Corp.	1992	1993	1994	1995	1996	1997	1998[a]	1999	2000	2001	2002	2003
U.S. domestic												
Revenue	5,195	5,668	5,195	6,839	7,466	8,322	9,665	12,910	13,805	14,858	15,968	17,277
Identifiable assets	3,941	4,433	4,884	5,322	5,449	6,123	6,873	6,506	7,224	8,637	8,627	9,908
International												
Revenue	2,355	2,140	2,280	2,553	2,807	3,198	3,589	3,863	4,452	4,771	4,639	5,210
Identifiable assets	1,522	1,360	1,109	1,112	1,250	1,503	1,503	1,001	7,224	1,254	1,520	1,536
Consolidated												
Revenue	7,550	7,808	7,474	9,392	10,274	11,520	13,255	16,773	18,257	19,629	20,607	22,487
Identifiable assets	5,463	5,793	5,992	6,433	6,699	7,625	8,376	7,507	14,448	9,891	10,147	11,444

United Parcel Service Inc.	1992	1993	1994	1995	1996	1997	1998[a]	1999	2000	2001	2002	2003
U.S. domestic												
Revenue	14,722	15,823	17,298	18,243	20,108	20,238	22,252	24,093	26,325	26,163	26,284	26,968
Identifiable assets	7,873	8,539	9,902	11,157	9,376	10,063	9,832	10,725	12,477	13,717	14,129	14,915
International												
Revenue	1,797	1,960	2,278	2,802	2,260	2,220	2,536	2,959	3,446	4,158	4,988	6,517
Identifiable assets	1,164	1,214	1,280	1,488	1,323	1,372	1,810	2,111	2,061	3,050	2,874	3,567
Consolidated												
Revenue	16,519	17,782	19,576	21,045	22,368	22,458	24,788	27,052	29,771	30,321	31,272	33,485
Identifiable assets	9,038	9,754	11,182	12,645	10,699	11,435	11,642	12,836	14,538	16,767	17,003	18,482

Sources of data: Company regulatory filings.

[a] FASB Statement No. 131 (Disclosures about Segments of an Enterprise and Related Information), established the standard to be used by enterprises to identify and report information about operating segments and for related disclosures about products and services, geographic areas, and major customers.

EXHIBIT 8 | Equity Prices and Returns for FedEx and UPS

United Parcel Service, Inc.	1992	1993	1994	1995	1996	1997	1998	1999	2000	2001	2002	2003
Stock price[1], December 31	$9.25	$10.38	$11.75	$13.13	$14.63	$15.38	$20.00	$69.00	$58.75	$54.50	$63.08	$74.55
Dividends per share[1]	$0.25	$0.25	$0.28	$0.32	$0.34	$0.35	$0.22	$0.58	$0.68	$0.76	$0.76	$0.92
EPS, basic incl. extra items[1]	$0.44	$0.70	$0.81	$0.92	$1.00	$0.82	$1.59	$0.79	$2.54	$2.13	$2.84	$2.57
P/E multiple[1]	21.26	14.82	14.42	14.34	14.55	18.64	12.58	87.34	23.13	25.59	22.21	29.01
Capital appreciation		12.16%	13.25%	11.70%	11.43%	5.13%	30.08%	245.00%	(14.86%)	(7.23%)	15.74%	18.18%
Cumul. compound annual return[2]		12.16%	27.03%	41.89%	58.11%	66.22%	116.22%	645.95%	535.14%	489.19%	581.95%	705.95%

FedEx Corp.	1992	1993	1994	1995	1996	1997	1998	1999	2000	2001	2002	2003
Stock price, December 31	$10.19	$12.25	$19.13	$14.97	$19.16	$26.19	$32.06	$54.81	$35.50	$40.00	$53.95	$63.98
Dividends per share	$0.00	$0.00	$0.00	$0.00	$0.00	$0.00	$0.00	$0.00	$0.00	$0.00	$0.00	0.20
EPS, basic incl. extra items	($0.53)	$0.25	$0.91	$1.32	$1.35	$1.56	$1.72	$2.13	$2.36	$2.02	$2.38	$2.79
P/E multiple	nmf	50.00	20.96	11.36	14.22	16.79	18.70	25.73	15.04	19.80	22.67	22.93
Capital appreciation		20.25%	56.12%	(21.73%)	27.97%	36.70%	22.43%	70.96%	(35.23%)	12.68%	34.88%	18.59%
Cumul. compound annual return[2]		20.25%	87.73%	46.93%	88.04%	157.06%	214.72%	438.04%	248.47%	292.64%	429.57%	528.02%

Standard & Poor's 500 Index	1992	1993	1994	1995	1996	1997	1998	1999	2000	2001	2002	2003
Index level	435.71	466.45	459.27	615.93	740.74	970.43	1,229.23	1,469.25	1,320.28	1,148.08	879.82	1,111.92
Annual return		7.06%	(1.54%)	34.11%	20.26%	31.01%	26.67%	19.53%	(10.14%)	(13.04%)	(23.37%)	26.38%
Cumul. compound annual return[2]		7.06%	5.41%	41.36%	70.01%	122.72%	182.12%	237.21%	203.02%	163.50%	101.93%	155.20%

Cumul. Market-Adjusted Returns	1993	1994	1995	1996	1997	1998	1999	2000	2001	2002	2003
UPS	5.11%	21.62%	0.53%	(11.90%)	(56.51%)	(65.90%)	408.74%	332.12%	325.69%	480.02%	550.75%
FedEx	13.19%	82.32%	5.57%	18.03%	34.33%	32.60%	200.83%	45.45%	129.14%	327.64%	372.83%

Source of data: Standard & Poor's *Research Insight*, annual reports.

[1] These data have been adjusted for the two-for-one stock split and initial public offering completed by UPS in November 1999. Prior to 1999, UPS shares were not publicly traded and the company acted as a market-maker for its own stock.

[2] Compound annual return calculation: (Current year price–Beginning year price)/Beginning year price.

EXHIBIT 9 | Economic Profit Analysis for FedEx

FedEx Corp.	1992	1993	1994	1995	1996	1997	1998	1999	2000	2001	2002	2003
Return on Net Assets (RONA)												
Net operating profit after tax ($mm)	$187	$176	$363	$405	$419	$499	$727	$726	$866	$750	$881	$1,418
Beginning capital ($mm)	$4,078	$4,344	$4,456	$4,655	$5,081	$5,663	$6,882	$7,863	$8,636	$10,090	$10,870	$12,050
RONA (NOPAT/beginning capital)	4.59%	4.05%	8.16%	8.70%	8.25%	8.82%	10.56%	9.23%	10.03%	7.43%	8.10%	11.77%
Weighted-Average Cost of Capital (WACC)												
Long-term debt ($mm)	$1,798	$1,882	$1,632	$1,325	$1,325	$1,398	$1,385	$1,360	$1,776	$1,900	$1,800	$1,709
Shares outstanding (mm)	216	219	224	225	228	230	295	298	284	297	298	299
Share price ($)	$10	$12	$19	$15	$19	$26	$32	$55	$36	$40	$54	$64
Market value of equity ($mm)	$2,205	$2,682	$4,274	$3,363	$4,359	$6,018	$9,453	$16,333	$10,098	$11,893	$16,087	$19,104
Tax rate (%)	23%	46%	46%	43%	43%	43%	45%	41%	39%	37%	38%	38%
Long-term U.S. gov't. bonds (%)	7.97%	6.80%	7.53%	7.01%	7.07%	6.89%	5.94%	5.79%	6.19%	5.65%	5.55%	4.76%
Senior Baa-rated debt (%)	9.20%	8.11%	8.71%	8.27%	8.46%	8.16%	7.33%	7.69%	8.87%	7.94%	7.96%	6.58%
Risk premium (%)	5.6%	5.6%	5.6%	5.6%	5.6%	5.6%	5.6%	5.6%	5.6%	5.6%	5.6%	5.6%
Beta	1.10	1.15	1.20	1.20	1.40	1.35	1.30	1.15	1.20	1.20	1.20	1.10
Cost of equity[1] (%)	14.13%	13.24%	14.25%	13.73%	14.91%	14.45%	13.22%	12.23%	12.91%	12.37%	12.27%	10.92%
WACC	10.99%	9.72%	11.61%	11.18%	12.56%	12.61%	12.05%	11.64%	11.79%	11.35%	11.53%	10.36%
Economic Value Added (EVA)												
RONA (NOPAT/beginning capital)	4.59%	4.05%	8.16%	8.70%	8.25%	8.82%	10.56%	9.23%	10.03%	7.43%	8.10%	11.77%
WACC	10.99%	9.72%	11.61%	11.18%	12.56%	12.61%	12.05%	11.64%	11.79%	11.35%	11.53%	10.36%
Spread	(6.39%)	(5.67%)	(3.46%)	(2.48%)	(4.30%)	(3.79%)	(1.48%)	(2.41%)	(1.75%)	(3.92%)	(3.43%)	1.41%
X beginning capital ($mm)	$4,078	$4,344	$4,456	$4,655	$5,081	$5,663	$6,882	$7,863	$8,636	$10,090	$10,870	$12,050
EVA (annual)	($261)	($246)	($154)	($115)	($219)	($215)	($102)	($190)	($151)	($396)	($373)	$170
EVA (cumulative)	($261)	($507)	($661)	($777)	($995)	($1,210)	($1,312)	($1,502)	($1,653)	($2,049)	($2,422)	($2,252)
Market Value Added (MVA)												
Market value of equity ($mm)	$2,205	$2,682	$4,274	$3,363	$4,359	$6,018	$9,453	$16,333	$10,098	$11,893	$16,087	$19,104
Long-term debt ($mm)	1,798	1,882	1,632	1,325	1,325	1,398	1,385	1,360	1,776	1,900	1,800	1,709
Capital (market value) ($mm)	4,002	4,565	5,907	4,687	5,684	7,416	10,838	17,693	11,874	13,793	17,887	20,813
Book value of equity ($mm)	1,580	1,671	1,925	2,246	2,576	2,963	3,961	4,664	4,785	5,900	6,545	7,288
Long-term debt ($mm)	1,798	1,882	1,632	1,325	1,325	1,398	1,385	1,360	1,776	1,900	1,800	1,709
Capital (book value) ($mm)	3,378	3,554	3,557	3,570	3,901	4,360	5,346	6,023	6,561	7,801	8,345	8,997
MVA (market value - book value)	$625	$1,011	$2,350	$1,117	$1,783	$3,056	$5,492	$11,670	$5,313	$5,993	$9,542	$11,816

Source of data: *Value Line Investment Survey,* Standard & Poor's *Research Insight,* Bloomberg LP, Datastream.

[1]The cost of equity was derived using the capital asset pricing model (CAPM).

EXHIBIT 10 | Economic Profit Analysis for UPS

United Parcel Service, Inc.	1992	1993	1994	1995	1996	1997	1998	1999	2000	2001	2002	2003
Return on Net Assets (RONA)												
Net operating profit after tax ($mm)	$914	$888	$944	$1,448	$1,545	$1,379	$1,909	$3,215	$2,955	$2,846	$2,589	$3,309
Beginning capital ($mm)	$6,932	$7,195	$8,280	$9,679	$11,796	$12,514	$13,350	$18,845	$17,161	$20,007	$20,802	$23,391
RONA (NOPAT/beginning capital)	13.19%	12.34%	11.40%	14.96%	13.10%	11.02%	14.30%	17.06%	17.22%	14.23%	12.45%	14.15%
Weighted-Average Cost of Capital (WACC)												
Long-term debt ($mm)	$862	$852	$1,127	$1,729	$2,573	$2,583	$2,191	$1,912	$2,981	$4,648	$3,495	$3,149
Shares outstanding[1] (mm)	1,190	1,160	1,160	1,140	1,140	1,124	1,095	1,211	1,135	1,121	1,123	1,129
Share price[1] ($)	$9	$10	$12	$13	$15	$15	$20	$69	$59	$55	$63	$75
Market value of equity[1] ($mm)	$11,008	$12,035	$13,630	$14,963	$16,673	$17,282	$21,896	$83,538	$66,663	$61,068	$70,839	$84,167
Tax rate (%)	40%	43%	40%	39%	40%	41%	40%	58%	39%	38%	35%	34%
Long-term U.S. govt. bonds (%)	7.97%	6.80%	7.53%	7.01%	7.07%	6.89%	5.94%	5.79%	6.19%	5.65%	5.55%	4.76%
Senior Baa-rated debt (%)	8.34%	7.36%	8.08%	7.71%	7.78%	7.53%	6.71%	6.90%	7.99%	7.16%	6.66%	5.47%
Risk premium (%)	5.6%	5.6%	5.6%	5.6%	5.6%	5.6%	5.6%	5.6%	5.6%	5.6%	5.6%	5.6%
Beta[2]	1.24	1.13	1.16	1.18	1.18	1.14	1.08	1.15	1.11	1.09	0.95	0.80
Cost of equity[3] (%)	14.92%	13.15%	14.02%	13.64%	13.68%	13.27%	11.99%	12.23%	12.41%	11.75%	10.87%	9.24%
WACC	14.20%	12.58%	13.32%	12.72%	12.47%	12.12%	11.26%	12.02%	12.09%	11.23%	10.56%	9.04%
Economic Value Added (EVA)												
RONA (NOPAT/beginning capital)	13.19%	12.34%	11.40%	14.96%	13.10%	11.02%	14.30%	17.06%	17.22%	14.23%	12.45%	14.15%
WACC	14.20%	12.58%	13.32%	12.72%	12.47%	12.12%	11.26%	12.02%	12.09%	11.23%	10.56%	9.04%
Spread	(1.01%)	(0.24%)	(1.91%)	2.24%	0.63%	(1.10%)	3.04%	5.04%	5.13%	2.99%	1.89%	5.11%
X beginning capital ($mm)	$6,932	$7,195	$8,280	$9,679	$11,796	$12,514	$13,350	$18,845	$17,161	$20,007	$20,802	$23,391
EVA (annual) ($mm)	($70)	($17)	($158)	$217	$74	($138)	$405	$949	$881	$599	$392	$1195
EVA (cumulative) ($mm)	($70)	($87)	($246)	($28)	$45	($92)	$313	$1,262	$2,143	$2,741	$3,133	$4,328
Market Value Added (MVA)												
Market value of equity[1] ($mm)	$11,008	$12,035	$13,630	$14,963	$16,673	$17,282	$21,896	$83,538	$66,663	$61,068	$70,839	$84,167
Long-term debt ($mm)	862	852	1,127	1,729	2,573	2,583	2,191	1,912	2,981	4,648	3,495	3,149
Capital (market value) ($mm)	11,870	12,887	14,757	16,692	19,246	19,865	24,087	85,450	69,644	65,716	74,334	87,316
Book value of equity ($mm)	3,720	3,945	4,647	5,151	5,901	6,087	7,173	12,474	9,735	10,248	12,455	14,852
Long-term debt ($mm)	862	852	1,127	1,729	2,573	2,583	2,191	1,912	2,981	4,648	3,495	3,149
Capital (book value) ($mm)	4,583	4,797	5,775	6,880	8,474	8,670	9,364	14,386	12,716	14,896	15,950	18,001
MVA (market value - book value)	$7,287	$8,090	$8,983	$9,812	$10,772	$11,195	$14,723	$71,064	$56,928	$50,820	$58,384	$69,315

Source of data: Value Line Investment Survey, Standard & Poor's Research Insight, Bloomberg LP, DataStream.

[1]These data have been adjusted for the two-for-one stock split and initial public offering completed by UPS in November 1999. Prior to 1999, UPS shares were not publicly traded and the company acted as a market-maker for its own stock.

[2]For the period 1992–2001, this figure reflects the average betas for peer firms.

[3]The cost of equity was derived using the capital asset pricing model (CAPM).

EXHIBIT 11 | Equity Analysts' Outlook for FedEx and UPS

FedEx Corporation	
Analyst	**Comments**
Morgan Stanley's J.J. Valentine, April 6, 2004	It was refreshing to hear FedEx's management highlight some of the risks in China as we sense these issues are too often overlooked by the bulls. Some of these issues include:
	• lack of legal framework
	• different interpretations of laws by regional and local governments
	• nonperforming loans that put pressure on China's banking sector
	• liability by government for retirement program of state-owned enterprises
	• widening gap between the urban and the rural standard of living
	• government that often dictates commercial relationships
	One issue that's not as much a risk as it is a challenge is finding skilled, educated labor. This was a recurring theme that we heard during our visit to Asia, namely that China has a large unskilled workforce to produce cheap products, but it is becoming increasingly difficult to find skilled labor for the service industry, such as parcel delivery or logistics.
Value Line Investment Survey's W.R. Perkowitz Jr., Dec. 12, 2003	The international business should drive long-term growth. Unlike the domestic express business, which has reached maturity, the international market remains in the growth stage. Indeed, growth rates in this sector mirror the rate of domestic expansion in the late 1980s. Furthermore, demand for this service should rise going forward, as a greater amount of manufacturing capacity is outsourced to Asia. Finally, since a large portion of FedEx's cost structure is fixed, and it has ample capacity to serve additional business, any increases in volume should flow directly to the bottom line.

United Parcel Service Inc.	
Analyst	**Comments**
Value Line Investment Survey's D. Y. Fung, Dec. 12, 2003	United Parcel Service's third-quarter 2003 results were better than we expected. . . . This gain was driven by record-breaking results in the international and nonpackage segments. Indeed, both units experienced advances in volume and margins, which led to bottom-line increases of 171% and 61% respectively. Importantly, growth of these two businesses has resulted in greater earnings diversity at UPS. This has helped to protect investors from the cyclical downturn in the U.S. economy in the past two years. Going forward, we believe international and nonpackage will continue along their positive growth trajectory, while generating a higher portion of the company's net earnings.

PART 2

Financial Analysis and Forecasting

The Financial Detective, 2005

Financial characteristics of companies vary for many reasons. The two most prominent drivers are industry economics and firm strategy.

Each industry has a financial norm around which companies within the industry tend to operate. An airline, for example, would naturally be expected to have a high proportion of fixed assets (airplanes), while a consulting firm would not. A steel manufacturer would be expected to have a lower gross margin than a pharmaceutical manufacturer because commodities such as steel are subject to strong price competition, while highly differentiated products like patented drugs enjoy much more pricing freedom. Because of unique economic features of each industry, average financial statements will vary from one industry to the next.

Similarly, companies *within* industries have different financial characteristics, in part, because of the diverse strategies that can be employed. Executives choose strategies that will position their company favorably in the competitive jockeying within an industry. Strategies typically entail making important choices in how a product is made (e.g., capital intensive versus labor intensive), how it is marketed (e.g., direct sales versus the use of distributors), and how the company is financed (e.g., the use of debt or equity). Strategies among companies in the same industry can differ dramatically. Different strategies can produce striking differences in financial results for firms in the same industry.

The following paragraphs describe pairs of participants in a number of different industries. Their strategies and market niches provide clues as to the financial condition and performance that one would expect of them. The companies' common-sized financial statements and operating data, as of early 2005, are presented in a standardized format in **Exhibit 1.** It is up to you to match the financial data with the company descriptions. Also, try to explain the differences in financial results *across* industries.

This case was prepared by Sean Carr, under the direction of Robert F. Bruner. It was written as a basis for class discussion rather than to illustrate effective or ineffective handling of an administrative situation. Copyright © 2005 by the University of Virginia Darden School Foundation, Charlottesville, VA. All rights reserved. *To order copies, send an e-mail to* sales@dardenpublishing.com. *No part of this publication may be reproduced, stored in a retrieval system, used in a spreadsheet, or transmitted in any form or by any means—electronic, mechanical, photocopying, recording, or otherwise—without the permission of the Darden School Foundation.*

Health Products

Companies A and B manufacture and market health-care products. One firm is the world's largest prescription-pharmaceutical company. This firm has a very broad and deep pipeline of ethical pharmaceuticals, supported by a robust research and development budget. In recent years, the company has divested several of its nonpharmaceutical businesses, and it has come to be seen as the partner of choice for licensing deals with other pharmaceutical and biotechnology firms.

The other company is a diversified health-products company that manufactures and mass markets a broad line of prescription pharmaceuticals, over-the-counter remedies (i.e., nonprescription drugs), consumer health and beauty products, and medical diagnostics and devices. For its consumer segment, brand development and management are a major element of this firm's mass-market-oriented strategy.

Beer

Of the beer companies, C and D, one is a national brewer of mass-market consumer beers sold under a variety of brand names. This company operates an extensive network of breweries and distribution systems. The firm also owns a number of beer-related businesses, such as snack and aluminum-container manufacturing, and several major theme parks.

The other company produces seasonal and year-round beers with smaller production volume and higher prices. This company outsources most of its brewing activity. The firm is financially conservative, and has recently undergone a major cost-savings initiative to counterbalance the recent surge in packaging and freight costs.

Computers

Companies E and F sell computers and related equipment. One company focuses exclusively on mail-order sales of built-to-order PCs, including desktops, laptops, notebooks, servers, workstations, printers, and handheld devices. The company is an assembler of PC components manufactured by its suppliers. The company allows its customers to design, price, and purchase through its Web site.

The other company sells a highly differentiable line of computers, consumer-oriented electronic devices, and a variety of proprietary software products. Led by its charismatic founder, the company has begun to recover from a dramatic decline in its market share. The firm has an aggressive retail strategy intended to drive traffic through its stores and to expand its installed base of customers by showcasing its products in a user-friendly retail atmosphere.

Books and Music

The book and music retailers are companies G and H. One focuses on selling primarily to customers through a vast retail-store presence. The company is the leader in traditional book retailing, which it fosters through its "community store" concept and regular discount policy. The firm also maintains an on-line presence and owns a publishing imprint.

The other company sells books, music, and videos solely through its Internet Web site. While more than three-quarters of its sales are media, it also sells electronics and other general merchandise. The firm has only recently become profitable, and it has followed an aggressive strategy of acquiring related on-line businesses in recent years.

Paper Products

Companies I and J are both paper manufacturers. One company is the world's largest maker of paper, paperboard, and packaging. This vertically integrated company owns timberland; numerous lumber, paper, paperboard, and packing-products facilities; and a paper-distribution network. The company has spent the last few years rationalizing capacity by closing inefficient mills, implementing cost-containment initiatives, and selling nonessential assets.

The other firm is a small producer of printing, writing, and technical specialty papers, as well as towel and tissue products. Most of the company's products are marketed under branded labels. The company purchases the wood fiber used in its paper-making process on the open market.

Hardware and Tools

Companies K and L manufacture and sell hardware and tools. One of the companies is a global manufacturer and marketer of power tools and power-tool accessories, hardware and home-improvement products, and fastening systems. The firm sells primarily to retailers, wholesalers, and distributors. Its products appear under a variety of well-known brand names and are geared for the end user.

The other tool company manufactures and markets high-quality precision tools and diagnostic-equipment systems for professional users. The firm offers a broad range of products, which it sells via its own technical representatives and mobile franchise dealers. The company also provides financing for franchisees and for customers' large purchases.

Retailing

Companies M and N are two large discount retailers. One firm carries a wide variety of nationally advertised general merchandise. The company is known for its low prices, breadth of merchandise, and volume-oriented strategy. Most of its stores are leased and are located near the company's expanding network of distribution centers. The company has begun to implement plans to expand both internationally and in large urban areas.

The other firm is a rapidly growing chain of upscale discount stores. The company competes by attempting to match other discounters' prices on similar merchandise and by offering deep discounts on its differentiated items. Additionally, the company has partnerships with several leading designers. Recently, the firm has divested several nondiscount department-store businesses. To support sales and earnings growth, this company offers credit to qualified customers.

Newspapers

Companies O and P own newspapers. One is a diversified media company that generates most of its revenues through newspapers sold around the country and around the world. Because the company is centered largely on one product, it has strong central controls. Competition for subscribers and advertising revenues in this firm's segment is fierce. The company has also recently built a large office building for its headquarters.

The other firm owns a number of newspapers in relatively small communities throughout the Midwest and the Southwest. Some analysts view this firm as holding a portfolio of small local monopolies in newspaper publishing. This company has a significant amount of goodwill on its balance sheet, stemming from acquisitions. Key to this firm's operating success is a strategy of decentralized decision making and administration.

EXHIBIT 1 | Common-Sized Financial Data and Ratios

	Health Prod.		Beer		Computers		Books & Music		Paper		Tools		Retail		Newspapers	
Assets	A	B	C	D	E	F	G	H	I	J	K	L	M	N	O	P
Cash & Short Term Investments	24.2	16.1	1.4	55.6	42.2	67.9	54.8	16.2	7.6	5.9	9.3	6.5	4.6	7.0	0.6	1.1
Receivables	12.8	8.1	4.3	11.9	19.0	13.0	nmf	2.3	8.8	10.9	18.9	23.7	1.4	17.0	4.6	9.9
Inventories	7.0	5.4	4.3	11.7	2.0	1.3	14.8	38.6	7.9	14.4	17.8	14.9	24.5	16.7	0.8	0.8
Current Assets-Other	7.2	2.5	1.3	2.4	9.5	5.5	8.6	2.6	3.0	1.4	7.0	6.9	1.5	2.5	0.7	3.8
Current Assets-Total	51.2	32.1	11.2	81.7	72.8	87.6	78.2	59.7	27.2	32.6	52.9	52.1	32.0	43.1	6.6	2.5
Net Fixed Assets	19.6	14.9	54.7	16.0	7.3	8.8	7.6	24.4	50.8	62.5	13.6	13.7	57.0	52.2	14.1	34.6
Assets-Other	6.9	3.8	7.2	1.0	1.3	2.4	9.3	4.9	5.4	3.1	11.8	8.9	2.0	4.0	0.1	7.2
Intangibles	22.2	46.1	7.4	1.3	0.0	1.2	4.4	11.1	14.6	1.9	21.4	22.3	9.0	0.6	76.8	37.1
Investments & Advances	0.1	3.1	2.9	0.0	18.6	0.0	0.0	0.0	0.0	0.0	0.0	3.0	0.0	0.0	0.7	0.0
Assets-Total	100.0	100.0	100.0	100.0	100.0	100.0	100.0	100.0	100.0	100.0	100.0	100.0	100.0	100.0	100.0	100.0
Liabilities & Equity																
Accounts Payable	9.8	2.2	7.4	9.1	38.3	18.0	35.1	22.6	6.7	8.5	8.4	8.5	18.0	17.9	1.4	4.8
Debt in Current Liabilities	0.5	9.1	0.0	0.0	0.0	0.0	0.1	0.0	1.5	0.0	3.5	5.6	6.5	1.6	0.8	14.9
Income Taxes Payable	2.8	1.6	0.9	1.7	0.0	0.0	0.0	0.0	0.0	1.2	0.9	1.0	1.1	0.9	0.3	nmf
Current Liabilities-Other	13.0	8.5	3.8	13.7	22.6	15.3	14.7	17.6	6.1	7.1	19.5	14.4	10.1	5.1	5.1	8.7
Current Liabilities-Total	26.1	21.4	12.2	24.4	60.9	33.3	49.9	40.2	14.2	16.7	32.4	29.4	35.7	25.5	7.5	28.3
Long-Term Debt	4.8	5.9	51.2	1.9	2.2	0.0	56.9	7.4	41.3	18.3	21.7	8.9	19.7	28.0	14.4	11.9
Deferred Taxes	0.8	10.2	10.7	0.7	0.0	0.0	nmf	5.9	5.0	12.0	3.1	3.3	3.0	3.0	15.0	3.3
Liabilities-Other	8.6	7.3	9.5	0.7	8.9	3.7	0.2	11.0	10.9	12.4	14.6	8.9	2.5	3.2	0.7	17.5
Liabilities-Total	40.3	44.8	83.5	27.1	72.1	36.9	107.0	64.7	75.9	59.5	71.8	51.5	58.9	59.7	37.5	64.5
Stockholders' Equity	59.7	55.2	16.5	72.9	27.9	63.1	(7.0)	35.3	24.1	40.5	28.2	48.5	41.1	40.3	62.5	35.5
Total Liabilities & Equity	100.0	100.0	100.0	100.0	100.0	100.0	100.0	100.0	100.0	100.0	100.0	100.0	100.0	100.0	100.0	100.0
Income/Expenses																
Sales-Net	100.0	100.0	100.0	100.0	100.0	100.0	100.0	100.0	100.0	100.0	100.0	100.0	100.0	100.0	100.0	100.0
Cost of Goods Sold	23.9	11.1	53.9	38.5	81.0	70.9	75.8	69.5	75.3	82.9	61.0	51.6	75.3	67.1	49.7	40.5
Gross Profit	76.1	88.9	46.1	61.5	19.0	29.1	24.2	30.5	24.7	17.1	39.0	48.4	24.7	32.9	50.3	59.5
SG&A Expense	44.5	46.7	17.3	50.5	9.7	23.1	16.9	21.8	12.0	7.3	24.8	38.9	17.9	22.5	23.0	39.7
Depreciation	4.5	9.7	6.2	2.0	0.7	1.8	1.1	3.7	6.1	5.8	2.6	2.5	1.5	2.7	7.0	4.1
Earnings Before Interest &Taxes	27.2	32.5	22.5	9.0	8.6	4.2	6.2	5.0	6.6	4.0	11.7	6.9	5.3	7.7	20.2	15.6
Nonoperating Income (Expense)	0.7	1.1	2.9	0.3	0.4	0.7	0.3	0.1	0.4	0.1	0.6	0.1	0.8	0.0	1.3	0.4
Interest Income (Expense)	(0.7)	0.7	2.9	0.0	0.0	0.0	1.5	0.3	3.3	1.0	1.1	1.0	0.5	1.0	1.9	1.6
Special Items-Income (Expense)	(0.0)	(6.3)	0.2	0.0	0.0	(0.3)	0.1	(0.3)	(0.8)	0.0	0.0	(1.0)	0.0	(0.2)	0.0	(0.1)
Pretax Income	27.1	26.7	22.8	9.2	9.0	4.6	5.1	4.5	2.9	3.1	11.2	5.1	5.6	6.5	19.7	14.4
Income Taxes-Total	9.1	5.1	7.8	3.5	2.8	1.3	(3.4)	1.9	0.8	1.2	3.0	1.6	2.0	2.4	7.1	5.6
Net Income (Loss)	18.0	21.6	15.0	5.8	6.2	3.3	8.5	2.9	(0.1)	2.0	8.4	3.4	3.6	6.8	12.6	8.9

EXHIBIT 1 | Common-Sized Financial Data and Ratios *(Continued)*

	Health Prod.		Beer		Computers		Books & Music		Paper		Tools		Retail		Newspapers	
	A	B	C	D	E	F	G	H	I	J	K	L	M	N	O	P
Market Data																
Beta	0.65	0.85	0.55	0.60	1.20	1.05	1.70	0.51	1.15	1.10	1.00	1.00	0.85	1.10	0.85	0.90
Price/Earnings	22.29	22.32	16.85	19.73	30.48	41.85	27.32	21.63	30.97	33.78	13.64	23.01	18.97	24.19	20.54	13.29
Price to Book	5.93	3.08	13.99	2.56	17.46	5.13	nmf	2.36	1.91	1.80	4.65	1.85	4.23	3.64	2.07	3.09
Dividend Payout	38.21	46.28	33.16	0.00	0.00	0.00	0.00	0.00	101.46	86.16	15.30	70.62	21.56	14.85	37.53	30.81
Liquidity																
Current Ratio	1.96	1.50	0.92	3.35	1.20	2.63	1.57	1.49	1.91	1.94	1.63	1.77	0.90	1.69	0.88	0.55
Quick Ratio	1.42	1.13	0.47	2.77	1.01	2.43	nmf	0.46	1.15	1.00	0.87	1.03	0.17	0.94	0.69	0.39
Asset Management																
Inventory Turnover	3.08	0.93	12.60	7.44	67.96	74.78	13.56	2.42	6.75	7.11	3.89	3.59	7.69	5.86	33.35	43.48
Receivables Turnover	7.06	5.47	21.87	18.68	12.23	8.28	nmf	72.11	8.68	11.64	5.82	4.42	192.73	8.31	10.98	8.50
Fixed Assets Turnover	4.67	2.86	1.72	12.67	30.68	12.03	29.42	6.54	1.43	1.86	7.63	7.50	4.50	2.77	3.43	2.59
Debt Management																
Total Debt/Total Assets	5.34	14.99	51.19	0.00	2.18	0.00	56.94	7.42	42.78	18.36	25.21	14.45	26.16	29.54	15.22	26.81
LT Debt/Shareholders' Equity	8.06	10.66	310.28	0.00	7.79	0.00	nmf	21.01	171.21	45.32	77.03	18.29	47.92	69.34	23.04	33.66
Interest Coverage After Tax	27.34	32.57	6.25	nmf	191.19	93.00	6.49	9.52	1.56	2.98	8.62	4.55	8.86	4.92	7.83	6.69
DuPont Analysis																
Net Profit Margin	17.97	21.58	15.00	5.76	6.18	3.33	8.50	2.53	1.87	1.96	8.17	3.39	3.59	4.02	12.65	8.86
Asset Turnover	0.93	0.44	0.97	2.23	2.31	1.11	2.56	1.43	0.73	1.20	1.11	1.09	2.54	1.47	0.48	0.85
Return on Equity	26.75	16.64	83.97	15.95	46.92	5.44	nmf	10.58	5.79	5.71	28.30	7.36	20.79	14.47	9.86	20.89

Sources of data: S&P's Research Insight; Value Line Investment Survey.

nmf = not a meaningful figure.

Krispy Kreme Doughnuts, Inc.

As the millennium began, the future for Krispy Kreme Doughnuts, Inc., smelled sweet. Not only could the company boast iconic status and a nearly cultlike following, it had quickly become a darling of Wall Street. Less than a year after its initial public offering, in April 2000, Krispy Kreme shares were selling for 62 times earnings and, by 2003, *Fortune* magazine had dubbed the company "the hottest brand in America." With ambitious plans to open 500 doughnut shops over the first half of the decade, the company's distinctive green-and-red vintage logo and unmistakable "Hot Doughnuts Now" neon sign had become ubiquitous.

At the end of 2004, however, the sweet story had begun to sour as the company made several accounting revelations, after which its stock price sank. From its peak in August 2003, Krispy Kreme's share price plummeted more than 80 percent in the next 16 months. Investors and analysts began asking probing questions about the company's fundamentals, but even by the beginning of 2005, many of those questions remained unanswered. **Exhibits 1** and **2** provide Krispy Kreme's financial statements for fiscal-years 2000 through 2004. Was this a healthy company? What had happened to the company that some had thought would become the next Starbucks? If almost everyone loved the doughnuts, why were so many investors fleeing the popular doughnut maker?

Company Background

Krispy Kreme began as a single doughnut shop in Winston-Salem, North Carolina, in 1937, when Vernon Rudolph, who had acquired the company's special doughnut recipe from a French chef in New Orleans, started making and selling doughnuts wholesale to supermarkets. Within a short time, Rudolph's products became so popular that he cut a hole in his factory's wall to sell directly to customers—thus was born the central Krispy Kreme retail concept: the factory store. By the late 1950s, Krispy Kreme had 29 shops in 12 states, many of which were operated by franchisees.

This case was prepared by Sean Carr under the direction of Robert F. Bruner of the Darden Graduate School of Business Administration. It was written as a basis for class discussion rather than to illustrate effective or ineffective handling of an administrative situation. Copyright © 2005 by the University of Virginia Darden School Foundation, Charlottesville, VA. All rights reserved. *To order copies, send an e-mail to* sales @dardenpublishing.com. *No part of this publication may be reproduced, stored in a retrieval system, used in a spreadsheet, or transmitted in any form or by any means—electronic, mechanical, photocopying, recording, or otherwise—without the permission of the Darden School Foundation.*

After Rudolph's death, in 1973, Beatrice Foods bought the company and quickly expanded it to more than 100 locations. Beatrice introduced other products, such as soups and sandwiches, and cut costs by changing the appearance of the stores and substituting cheaper ingredients in the doughnut mixture. The business languished, however, and by the early 1980s, Beatrice put the company up for sale.

A group of franchisees led by Joseph McAleer, who had been the first Krispy Kreme franchisee, completed a leveraged buyout of the company for $24 million in 1982. McAleer brought back the original doughnut formula and the company's traditional logo. It was also around this time that the company introduced the "Hot Doughnuts Now" neon sign, which told customers when fresh doughnuts were coming off the line. The company still struggled for a while, but by 1989, Krispy Kreme had become debt-free and had slowly begun to expand. The company focused on its signature doughnuts and added branded coffee in 1996. Scott Livengood, who became CEO in 1998 and chair the following year, took the company public in April 2000 in what was one of the largest initial public offerings (IPO) in recent years; one day after the offering, Krispy Kreme's share price was $40.63, giving the firm a market capitalization of nearly $500 million.

Krispy Kreme's Business

After the company's IPO, Krispy Kreme announced an aggressive strategy to expand the number of stores from 144 to 500 over the next five years. In addition, the company planned to grow internationally, with 32 locations proposed for Canada and more for the United Kingdom, Mexico, and Australia. **Exhibit 3** provides an overview of the company's store openings.

Krispy Kreme Doughnuts generated revenues through four primary sources: on-premises retail sales at company-owned stores (accounting for 27 percent of revenues); off-premises sales to grocery and convenience stores (40 percent); manufacturing and distribution of product mix and machinery (29 percent); and franchisee royalties and fees (4 percent). In addition to the traditional domestic retail locations, the company sought growth through smaller "satellite concepts," which relied on factory stores to provide doughnuts for reheating, as well as the development of the international market.

- *On-premises sales:* Each factory store allowed consumers to see the production of doughnuts; Krispy Kreme's custom machinery and doughnut-viewing areas created what the company called a "doughnut theater." In that way, Krispy Kreme attempted to differentiate itself from its competition by offering customers an experience rather than simply a product. Each factory store could produce between 4,000-dozen and 10,000-dozen doughnuts a day, which were sold both on- and off-premises.

- *Off-premises sales:* About 60 percent of off-premises sales were to grocery stores, both in stand-alone cases and on store shelves. The remainder were sold to convenience stores (a small percentage were also sold as private label). The company maintained a fleet of delivery trucks for off-premises sales.

- *Manufacturing and distribution:* Krispy Kreme's Manufacturing and Distribution (KKM&D) division provided the proprietary doughnut mixes and doughnut-making equipment to every company-owned and franchised factory store. This vertical integration allowed the company to maintain quality control and product consistency throughout the system. The company maintained its own manufacturing facilities for its mixes and machines, and it provided quarterly service for all system units. All franchisees were required to buy mix and equipment from Krispy Kreme. KKM&D also included the company's coffee-roasting operation, which supplied branded drip coffee to both company-owned and franchised stores.

- *Franchise royalties and fees:* In exchange for an initial franchise fee and annual royalties, franchisees received assistance from Krispy Kreme with operations, advertising and marketing, accounting, and other information-management systems. Franchisees that had relationships with the company before the IPO in 2000 were called Associates, and they typically had locations in heritage markets in the southeastern United States. Associates were not responsible for opening new stores. New franchisees were called Area Developers, and they were responsible for developing new sites and building in markets with high potential. Area Developers typically paid $20,000 to $50,000 in initial franchise fees and between 4.5 percent and 6 percent in royalties. Franchisees also contributed 1 percent of their annual total sales to the corporate advertising fund.

Roughly 60 percent of sales at a Krispy Kreme store were derived from the company's signature product, the glazed doughnut. This differed from Dunkin' Donuts, the company's largest competitor, for which the majority of sales came from coffee.

Holes in the Krispy Kreme Story

On May 7, 2004, for the first time in its history as a public company, Krispy Kreme announced adverse results. The company told investors to expect earnings to be 10 percent lower than anticipated, claiming that the recent low-carbohydrate diet trend in the United States had hurt wholesale and retail sales. The company also said it planned to divest Montana Mills, a chain of 28 bakery cafés acquired in January 2003 for $40 million in stock, and would take a charge of $35 million to $40 million in the first quarter. In addition, Krispy Kreme indicated that its new Hot Doughnut and Coffee Shops were falling short of expectations and that it had plans to close three of them (resulting in a charge of $7 million to $8 million). Krispy Kreme's shares closed down 30 percent, at $22.51 a share.

Then, on May 25, the *Wall Street Journal* published a story describing aggressive accounting treatment for franchise acquisitions made by Krispy Kreme.[1]

---

[1] Mark Maremont and Rick Brooks, "Krispy Kreme Franchise Buybacks May Spur New Concerns," *Wall Street Journal,* 25 May 2004.

According to the article, in 2003, Krispy Kreme had begun negotiating to purchase a struggling seven-store Michigan franchise. The franchisee owed the company several million dollars for equipment, ingredients, and franchise fees and, as part of the deal, Krispy Kreme asked the franchisee to close two underperforming stores and to pay Krispy Kreme the accrued interest on past-due loans. In return for those moves, Krispy Kreme promised to raise its purchase price on the franchise.

According to the *Journal,* Krispy Kreme recorded the interest paid by the franchisee as interest income and, thus, as immediate profit; however, the company booked the purchase cost of the franchise as an intangible asset, under reacquired franchise rights, which the company did not amortize. Krispy Kreme also allowed the Michigan franchise's top executive to remain employed at the company after the deal, but shortly after the deal was completed, that executive left. In accordance with a severance agreement, this forced Krispy Kreme to pay the executive an additional $5 million, an expense the company also rolled into the unamortized-asset category as reacquired franchise rights.

The company denied any wrongdoing with this practice, maintaining it had accounted for its franchise acquisitions in accordance with generally accepted accounting principles (GAAP). On July 29, however, the company disclosed that the U.S. Securities and Exchange Commission (SEC) had launched an informal investigation related to "franchise reacquisitions and the company's previously announced reduction in earnings guidance." Observers remained skeptical. "Krispy Kreme's accounting for franchise acquisitions is the most aggressive we have found," said one analyst at the time. "We surveyed 18 publicly traded companies with franchise operations, four of which had reacquired franchises, and they had amortized them. That clearly seems like the right thing to do."[2] Over the previous three years, Krispy Kreme had recorded $174.5 million as intangible assets (reacquired franchise rights), which the company was not required to amortize. On the date of the SEC announcement, Krispy Kreme's shares fell another 15 percent, closing at $15.71 a share.

Analysts' Reactions

Since the heady days of 2001, when 80 percent of the equity analysts following Krispy Kreme were making buy recommendations for the company's shares, the conventional wisdom about the company had changed. By the time the *Wall Street Journal* published the article about Krispy Kreme's franchise-reacquisition accounting practices in May 2004, only 25 percent of the analysts following Krispy Kreme were recommending the company as a buy; another 50 percent had downgraded the stock to a hold. **Exhibits 4** and **5** provide tables of aggregate analysts' recommendations and EPS (earnings per share) estimates. As Krispy Kreme's troubles mounted during the second half of 2004, analysts became increasingly pessimistic about the stock:

---

[2]"Did Someone Say Doughnuts? Yes, the SEC," *New York Times,* 30 July 2004.

Analyst	Comment	Date
John Ivankoe, J.P. Morgan Securities, Inc.	In addition to the possibility of an earnings restatement, we believe many fundamental problems persist, exclusive of any "low-carb" impact. Declining new-store volumes are indicative of a worsening investment model, and we believe restructured store-development contracts, a smaller store format, and reduced fees charged for equipment and ingredients sold to franchises are necessary.	July 29, 2004
Jonathan M. Waite, KeyBanc Capital Markets	We believe that the challenges KKD faces, including margin compression, lower returns, an SEC investigation, and product saturation, currently outweigh the company's positive drivers. In addition, shares of KKD are trading at 16.6× CY05 earnings versus its 15 percent growth rate. As such, we rate KKD shares HOLD.	Oct. 12, 2004
John S. Glass, CIBC World Markets	Krispy Kreme's balance sheet became bloated over the past two years by acquisition goodwill that will likely need to be written down. As a result, KKD's return on invested capital has plunged to about 10 percent versus 18 percent two years ago prior to these acquisitions. We'd view a balance sheet write-down, including eliminating a significant portion of the $170+ million in "reacquired franchise rights," as a first step in the right direction.	Nov. 8, 2004
Glenn M. Guard, Legg Mason	In our opinion, management was not focused on operations the way it should have been. As a result, too many units were opened in poor locations as the company tripled its unit base since 2000. Additionally, we believe that franchisees were not trained properly as to how best to run their off-premises business. As a result, we believe many units are losing money off-premises, and franchisees are not motivated to grow that business. It also appears to us that basic blocking and tackling, execution, and cost discipline were seriously lacking in both the company and franchise systems, resulting in inefficiencies.	Nov. 23, 2004

As the headlines about the SEC investigation and Krispy Kreme's other management issues continued (for example, Krispy Kreme's chief operating officer stepped down on August 16, 2004), observers looked more critically at the fundamentals of Krispy Kreme's business. In September, the *Wall Street Journal* published an article that focused attention on the company's growth:

> The biggest problem for Krispy Kreme may be that the company grew too quickly and diluted its cult status by selling its doughnuts in too many outlets, while trying to impress Wall Street. The number of Krispy Kreme shops has nearly tripled since early 2000, with 427 stores in 45 states and four foreign countries. Some 20,000 supermarkets, convenience stores, truck stops, and other outside locations also sell the company's doughnuts.
>
> Another issue is that Krispy Kreme has relied for a significant chunk of profits on high profit-margin equipment that it requires franchisees to buy for each new store. Its profits have also been tied to growth in the number of franchised stores, because of the upfront fee each must pay.[3]

---

[3]"Sticky Situation," *Wall Street Journal,* 3 September 2004.

In September 2004, Krispy Kreme announced that it would reduce its number of new stores for the year to about 60 from the previously announced 120.

Restatement Announced

On January 4, 2005, Krispy Kreme's board of directors announced that the company's previously issued financial statements for the fiscal year ended February 1, 2004 (FY2004) would be restated to "correct certain errors." The board determined that the adjustments, which principally related to the company's "accounting for the acquisitions of certain franchisees," would reduce pretax income for FY2004 by between $6.2 million and $8.1 million. The company also expected to restate its financial statements for the first and second quarters of FY2005.

Krispy Kreme also said it would delay the filing of its financial reports until the SEC's investigation had been resolved and the company's own internal inquiry was complete. However, the failure of the company to provide its lenders with financial statements by January 14, 2005, could constitute a default under the company's $150-million credit facility. In the event of such a default, Krispy Kreme's banks had the right to terminate the facility and to demand immediate payment for any outstanding amounts. Krispy Kreme's failure to file timely reports also placed the company at risk of having its stock delisted from the New York Stock Exchange (NYSE). By the end of the next day, Krispy Kreme's shares were trading at less than $10 a share.

Most analysts felt that Krispy Kreme's lenders would grant the company a waiver on its credit-facility default, and few felt the company was truly at risk of being delisted from the NYSE. The board's announcement, however, served only to raise more questions about the company. Since August 2003, the company had lost nearly $2.5 billion in its market value of equity. **Exhibit 6** illustrates the stock-price patterns for Krispy Kreme relative to the S&P 500 Composite Index. Were the revelations about the company's franchise accounting practices sufficient to drive that much value out of the stock? Were there deeper issues at Krispy Kreme that deserved scrutiny? **Exhibits 7, 8,** and **9** provide analytical financial ratios for Krispy Kreme and a group of comparable companies in the franchise food-service industry.

EXHIBIT 1 | Income Statements

Income Statement	($US thousands, except per-share amounts)					Three Months Ended		Three Months Ended	
	Jan. 30, 2000	Jan. 28, 2001	Feb. 3, 2002	Feb. 2, 2003	Feb. 1, 2004	May 5, 2003	May 2, 2004	Aug. 3, 2003	Aug. 1, 2004
Total revenues	220,243	300,715	394,354	491,549	665,592	148,660	184,356	159,176	177,448
Operating expenses	190,003	250,690	316,946	381,489	507,396	112,480	141,383	120,573	145,633
General and administrative expenses	14,856	20,061	27,562	28,897	36,912	8,902	10,664	9,060	11,845
Depreciation and amortization expenses	4,546	6,457	7,959	12,271	19,723	4,101	6,130	4,536	6,328
Arbitration award				9,075	(525)	(525)			
Provision for restructuring, Impairment charges and closing costs							7,543		1,802
Income from operations	10,838	23,507	41,887	59,817	102,086	23,702	18,636	25,007	11,840
Interest income	293	2,325	2,980	1,966	921	227	176	205	226
Interest expense	(1,525)	(607)	(337)	(1,781)	(4,409)	(866)	(1,433)	(997)	(1,366)
Equity loss in joint ventures		(706)	(602)	(2,008)	(1,836)	(694)	(575)	(802)	(399)
Minority interest		(716)	(1,147)	(2,287)	(2,072)	(616)	(126)	(616)	267
Other expense, net		(20)	(235)	(934)	(13)	(25)	(156)	(343)	114
Income before income taxes	9,606	23,783	42,546	54,773	94,677	21,728	16,522	22,454	10,682
Provision for income taxes	3,650	9,058	16,168	21,295	37,590	8,588	6,675	9,014	4,438
Discontinued operations[1]							34,285	439	480
Net income	5,956	14,725	26,378	33,478	57,087	13,140	(24,438)	13,001	5,764
Diluted earnings per share	0.15	0.27	0.45	0.56	0.92	0.22	(0.38)	0.21	0.09
Share price (fiscal year close)		16.22	39.85	30.41	35.64				
Number of shares outstanding (millions)	39.7	54.5	58.6	59.8	62.1	60.7	63.6	62.1	63.4

[1]Resulting from divestiture of Montana Mills.

Source of data: Company filings with the Securities and Exchange Commission (SEC).

EXHIBIT 2 I Balance Sheets

(in thousands)	Fiscal Year Ended					Three Months Ended	
	Jan. 30, 2000	Jan. 28, 2001	Feb. 3, 2002	Feb. 2, 2003	Feb. 1, 2004	May 2, 2004	Aug. 1, 2004
ASSETS							
Current Assets:							
Cash and cash equivalents	3,183	7,026	21,904	32,203	20,300	13,715	19,309
Short-term investments	0	18,103	15,292	22,976			
Accounts receivable	17,965	19,855	26,894	34,373	45,283	47,434	44,329
Accounts receivable, affiliates	1,608	2,599	9,017	11,062	20,482	20,740	19,933
Other receivables	794	2,279	2,771	884	2,363	3,169	4,868
Notes receivable, affiliates	0	0	0	0	458	4,404	5,440
Inventories	9,979	12,031	16,159	24,365	28,573	32,974	33,076
Prepaid expenses	3,148	1,909	2,591	3,478	5,399	4,675	6,749
Income taxes refundable	861		2,534	1,963	7,946	7,449	8,139
Deferred income taxes	3,500	3,809	4,607	9,824	6,453	13,280	20,005
Assets held for sale					36,856	3,374	3,325
Total current assets	**41,038**	**67,611**	**101,769**	**141,128**	**174,113**	**151,214**	**165,173**
Property and equipment, net	60,584	78,340	112,577	202,558	281,103	301,160	297,154
Deferred income taxes	1,398	0	0	0	0		
Long-term investments	0	17,877	12,700	4,344	0		
Long-term notes receivable, affiliates	0	0	0	1,000	7,609	2,988	2,925
Investments in unconsolidated joint ventures		2,827	3,400	6,871	12,426	10,728	9,921
Reacquired franchise rights, goodwill, other intangibles	0	0	16,621	49,354	175,957	176,078	176,045
Other assets	1,938	4,838	8,309	5,232	9,456	12,315	10,390
Total assets	**104,958**	**171,493**	**255,376**	**410,487**	**660,664**	**654,483**	**661,608**

EXHIBIT 2 | Balance Sheets   (*continued*)

(in thousands)	Fiscal Year Ended					Three Months Ended	
	Jan. 30, 2000	Jan. 28, 2001	Feb. 3, 2002	Feb. 2, 2003	Feb. 1, 2004	May 2, 2004	Aug. 1, 2004
LIABILITIES AND SHAREHOLDERS' EQUITY							
Current Liabilities:							
Accounts payable	13,106	8,211	12,095	14,055	18,784	18,866	18,817
Book overdraft	0	5,147	9,107	11,375	8,123	12,670	13,107
Accrued expenses	14,080	21,243	26,729	20,981	23,744	27,107	32,249
Arbitration award	0	0	0	9,075	0		
Revolving line of credit	0	3,526	3,871	0	0		
Current maturities of long-term debt	2,400	0	731	3,301	2,842	4,663	5,566
Short-term debt	0	0	0	900	0		
Income taxes payable	0	41	0	0	0		
Total current liabilities	**29,586**	**38,168**	**52,533**	**59,687**	**53,493**	**63,306**	**69,739**
Deferred income taxes	0	579	3,930	9,849	6,374	16,468	25,564
Compensation deferred (unpaid)	990	1,106	0	0	0		
Revolving lines of credit	0	0	0	7,288	87,000	72,000	62,000
Long-term debt, net of current portion	20,502	0	3,912	49,900	48,056	58,469	50,135
Accrued restructuring expenses	4,259	3,109	0	0	0		
Other long-term obligations	1,866	1,735	4,843	5,218	11,211	10,774	12,078
Total long-term liabilities	**27,617**	**6,529**	**12,685**	**72,255**	**152,641**	**157,711**	**149,777**
Minority interest		1,117	2,491	5,193	2,323	2,815	2,593
SHAREHOLDERS' EQUITY							
Common stock, no par value, 300,000 shares authorized; issued and outstanding		85,060	121,052	173,112	294,477	296,812	299,865
Common stock, 10 par value, 1,000 shares authorized: issued and outstanding	4,670						
Paid-in capital	10,805						
Unearned compensation		(188)	(186)	(119)	(62)	(47)	(31)
Notes receivable, employees	(2,547)	(2,349)	(2,580)	(558)	(383)	(383)	(383)
Nonqualified employee benefit plan assets		(126)	(138)	(339)	(369)	(264)	(264)
Nonqualified employee benefit plan liability		126	138	339	369	264	264
Accumulated other comprehensive income (loss)		609	456	(1,486)	(1,315)	(783)	(768)
Retained earnings	34,827	42,547	68,925	102,403	159,490	135,052	140,816
Total shareholders' equity	**47,755**	**125,679**	**187,667**	**273,352**	**452,207**	**430,651**	**439,499**
Total liabilities and shareholders' equity	**104,958**	**171,493**	**255,376**	**410,487**	**660,664**	**654,483**	**661,608**

Source of data: Company filings with the Securities and Exchange Commission (SEC).

EXHIBIT 3 | Store Growth

Store growth	Jan. 30, 2000	Jan. 28, 2001	Feb. 3, 2002	Feb. 2, 2003	Feb. 1, 2004
Total company factory stores					
Beginning of period	61	58	63	75	99
Stores openings	2	8	7	14	28
Store closings	(5)	(3)	(2)	(3)	(2)
Stores acquired from franchisees	0	0	7	13	16
End of period	58	63	75	99	141
Net change	*(3)*	*5*	*12*	*24*	*42*
% year-over-year growth		*9%*	*19%*	*32%*	*42%*
Total franchised factory stores					
Beginning of period	70	86	111	143	177
Unit openings	19	28	41	49	58
Unit closings	(3)	(3)	(2)	(2)	(3)
Stores transferred to company	0	0	(7)	(13)	(16)
End of period	86	111	143	177	216
Net change	*16*	*25*	*32*	*34*	*39*
% year-over-year growth		*29%*	*29%*	*24%*	*22%*
Total factory stores					
Beginning of period	131	144	174	218	276
Store openings	21	36	48	63	86
Store closings	(8)	(6)	(4)	(5)	(5)
End of period	144	174	218	276	357
Net change	*13*	*30*	*44*	*58*	*81*
% year-over-year growth		*21%*	*25%*	*27%*	*29%*
Percentage of total stores					
Company-owned	40.3%	36.2%	34.4%	35.9%	39.5%
Franchised	59.7%	63.8%	65.6%	64.1%	60.5%

Source of data: Company reports, case writer's analysis.

EXHIBIT 4 | Analysts' Recommendations

Period	Percentage Recommending:		
	Buy	Sell	Hold
14-Jun-01	80.0%	20.0%	0.0%
19-Jul-01	80.0%	20.0%	0.0%
16-Aug-01	80.0%	20.0%	0.0%
20-Sep-01	80.0%	20.0%	0.0%
18-Oct-01	80.0%	20.0%	0.0%
15-Nov-01	80.0%	20.0%	0.0%
20-Dec-01	80.0%	20.0%	0.0%
17-Jan-02	66.7%	33.3%	0.0%
14-Feb-02	57.1%	28.6%	14.3%
14-Mar-02	71.4%	28.6%	0.0%
18-Apr-02	66.7%	33.3%	0.0%
16-May-02	66.7%	33.3%	0.0%
20-Jun-02	71.4%	28.6%	0.0%
18-Jul-02	71.4%	28.6%	0.0%
15-Aug-02	71.4%	28.6%	0.0%
19-Sep-02	66.7%	33.3%	0.0%
17-Oct-02	57.1%	28.6%	14.3%
14-Nov-02	57.1%	28.6%	14.3%
19-Dec-02	50.0%	12.5%	37.5%
16-Jan-03	50.0%	12.5%	37.5%
20-Feb-03	62.5%	12.5%	25.0%
20-Mar-03	62.5%	12.5%	25.0%
17-Apr-03	62.5%	12.5%	25.0%
15-May-03	55.6%	11.1%	33.3%
19-Jun-03	66.7%	0.0%	33.3%
17-Jul-03	80.0%	0.0%	20.0%
14-Aug-03	83.3%	0.0%	16.7%
18-Sep-03	66.7%	16.7%	16.7%
16-Oct-03	66.7%	16.7%	16.7%
20-Nov-03	66.7%	16.7%	16.7%
18-Dec-03	42.9%	14.3%	42.9%
15-Jan-04	42.9%	14.3%	42.9%
19-Feb-04	28.6%	14.3%	57.1%
18-Mar-04	28.6%	14.3%	57.1%
15-Apr-04	37.5%	25.0%	37.5%
20-May-04	25.0%	25.0%	50.0%
17-Jun-04	25.0%	25.0%	50.0%
15-Jul-04	33.3%	11.1%	55.6%
19-Aug-04	28.6%	28.6%	42.9%
16-Sep-04	25.0%	37.5%	37.5%
14-Oct-04	14.3%	42.9%	42.9%
18-Nov-04	14.3%	42.9%	42.9%
16-Dec-04	14.3%	57.1%	28.6%
20-Jan-05	14.3%	57.1%	28.6%

Source of data: I/B/E/S (Thomson Financial/First Call).

EXHIBIT 5 | Consensus EPS Estimates

Estimate (Mean)	Estimate Date
$ 0.38	2-Jul-01
$ 0.43	24-Aug-01
$ 0.41	25-Oct-01
$ 0.44	16-Nov-01
$ 0.43	21-Dec-01
$ 0.62	8-Mar-02
$ 0.63	24-May-02
$ 0.63	3-Jun-02
$ 0.63	1-Jul-02
$ 0.64	29-Aug-02
$ 0.64	3-Sep-02
$ 0.63	8-Oct-02
$ 0.66	22-Nov-02
$ 0.65	10-Jan-03
$ 0.66	14-Feb-03
$ 0.87	20-Mar-03
$ 0.89	29-May-03
$ 0.90	30-Jul-03
$ 0.90	21-Aug-03
$ 0.91	15-Sep-03
$ 0.91	17-Dec-03
$ 0.92	27-Jan-04
$ 1.17	10-Mar-04
$ 1.00	7-May-04
$ 0.99	26-May-04
$ 0.98	24-Jun-04
$ 0.92	16-Aug-04
$ 0.59	27-Aug-04
$ 0.69	10-Sep-04
$ 0.65	13-Sep-04
$ 0.58	3-Nov-04
$ 0.45	23-Nov-04

Source of data: I/B/E/S (Thomson Financial/First Call).

EXHIBIT 6 | Stock-Price Patterns Relative to the S&P 500 Composite Index

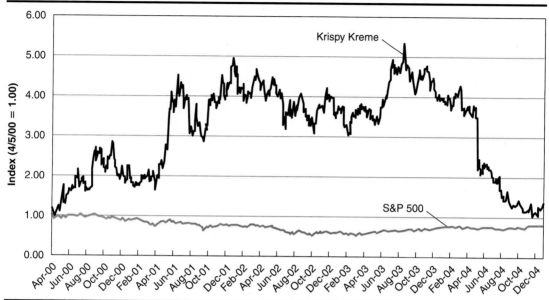

Source of data: Datastream.

EXHIBIT 7 | Analytical Financial Ratios for Krispy Kreme

	Fiscal Year Ended					
	Jan. 30, 2000	Jan. 28, 2001	Feb. 3, 2002	Feb. 2, 2003	Feb. 1, 2004	Ratio definitions
Liquidity ratios						
Quick (acid-test) ratio	1.05	1.46	1.63	1.96	2.72	(current assets-inventories)/curr.liab.
Current ratio	1.39	1.77	1.94	2.36	3.25	current assets/curr.liab.
Leverage ratios						
Debt-to equity (book)	47.96%	0.00%	2.47%	19.46%	11.26%	LT debt/shareholders' equity
Debt-to-capital	32.41%	0.00%	2.41%	16.29%	10.12%	LT debt/(shareholders' equity + debt)
Times interest earned	7.11	38.73	124.29	33.59	23.15	EBIT/interest expense
Assets to equity	2.20	1.36	1.36	1.50	1.46	total assets/shareholders' equity
Activity ratios						
Receivables turnover	10.81	12.16	10.19	10.61	9.70	sales/accounts receivables
Inventory turnover	19.04	20.84	19.61	15.66	17.76	cost of goods sold/inventory
Asset turnover	2.10	1.75	1.54	1.20	1.01	sales/total assets
Cash turnover	69.19	42.80	18.00	15.26	32.79	sales/cash and cash equivalents
Profitability ratios						
Return on assets	5.67%	8.59%	10.33%	8.16%	8.64%	net income/assets
Return on equity	12.47%	11.72%	14.06%	12.25%	12.62%	net income/shareholders' equity
Operating profit margin	4.92%	7.82%	10.62%	12.17%	15.34%	operating income/net sales
Net profit margin	2.70%	4.90%	6.69%	6.81%	8.58%	net income/sales

Source of data: Company filings with the Securities and Exchange Commission (SEC).

EXHIBIT 8 | Analytical Financial Ratios: Quick-Service Restaurants at End of FY2003

Company Name	Checkers	CKE	Domino's	Jack in the Box	Krispy Kreme	McDonald's	Panera Bread	Papa Johns	Sonic	Starbucks	Wendy's	Yum Brands
Sales-net (millions)	$190	$1,413	$1,333	$2,058	$666	$17,141	$356	$917	$447	$4,076	$3,149	$8,380
Liquidity ratios												
Quick ratio	0.96	0.47	0.60	0.23	2.72	0.49	1.34	0.33	0.77	0.76	0.61	0.26
Current ratio	1.42	0.76	0.99	0.63	3.25	0.76	1.58	0.77	0.92	1.52	0.88	0.55
Leverage ratios												
LT debt/equity (%)	33.97	262.97	(131.07)	61.82	11.26	77.97	0.00	38.30	62.53	0.21	39.39	183.57
Long-term debt/total capital(%)	25.36	72.45	421.90	38.20	10.12	43.81	0.00	26.98	38.11	0.21	28.26	64.74
Interest coverage before tax	6.99	(0.09)	2.05	5.44	23.15	6.93	1,014.10	8.93	14.09	nmf	9.25	5.79
Total assets/total equity	1.76	5.29	(0.62)	2.50	1.46	2.13	1.26	2.18	1.83	1.31	1.80	5.02
Activity ratios												
Receivables turnover	65.08	35.15	20.63	71.22	9.70	21.56	32.42	50.29	27.49	38.44	28.42	49.73
Inventory turnover	133.39	59.30	46.88	52.83	17.76	89.84	38.75	44.87	111.24	10.58	79.58	91.32
Total assets turnover	1.50	1.75	3.16	1.84	1.01	0.69	1.64	2.57	1.00	1.62	1.08	1.52
Cash turnover	12.00	38.83	40.90	147.12	32.79	41.64	8.74	110.73	40.31	10.84	17.12	46.04
Profitability ratios												
Return on assets (%)	12.23	(5.92)	8.66	6.26	8.64	5.91	12.46	9.79	10.75	9.83	7.46	11.00
Return on equity (%)	21.55	(31.30)	nmf	15.65	12.62	12.59	15.64	21.33	19.69	12.89	13.42	55.18
EBIT margin (%)	8.24	3.49	13.20	6.94	15.34	19.62	14.02	6.38	23.42	9.48	13.35	12.77
Net profit margin (%)	8.32	(3.24)	2.91	3.58	8.58	8.80	8.61	3.70	11.70	6.58	7.49	7.37

nmf = not a meaningful figure.

Source of data: Standard & Poor's *Research Insight*.

EXHIBIT 8 (continued) | Descriptions of Comparable Firms

Checkers Drive-in Restaurants, Inc.: Checkers is the #1 operator of drive-through fast-food restaurants, with more than 780 owned and franchised locations. Nearly 30% of its locations are company-owned.

CKE Restaurants, Inc.: CKE is a leading operator of quick-service food chains, with about 3,100 locations. CKE owns and operates more than a third of its restaurants; the rest are operated by franchisees.

Domino's Pizza, Inc.: Domino's is the world's #2 pizza chain, with more than 7,750 locations in more than 50 countries. Domino's stores are principally delivery locations and generally do not have any dine-in seating.

Jack in the Box Inc.: Jack in the Box operates and franchises over 2,000 of its flagship hamburger outlets in 17 states. More than 1,550 locations are company-owned, while the rest are franchised.

McDonald's Corp.: McDonald's is the world's #1 fast-food company by sales. With more than 31,000 flagship restaurants serving burgers and fries in more than 100 countries. Almost 30% of its locations are company-owned; the others are run by franchisees.

Panera Bread Company: Panera Bread is a leader in the quick-casual restaurant business, with more than 740 bakery cafés in about 35 states. Approximately 70% of its locations are operated by franchisees.

Papa John's International, Inc.: Papa John's is the #3 pizza chain, with 3,000 pizzerias across the United States and in 17 international markets. Papa John's owns and operates about 20% of its locations.

Sonic Corp.: The largest chain of quick-service drive-ins in the United States, Sonic operates about 535 restaurants and franchises more than 2,325 locations in 30 states.

Starbucks Corp.: The world's #1 specialty-coffee retailer, Starbucks operates and licenses more than 8,500 coffee shops in more than 30 countries. In addition, Starbucks markets its coffee through grocery stores, and licenses its brand for other food and beverage products.

Wendy's International, Inc.: Wendy's is the #3 hamburger chain by sales. There are almost 6,700 Wendy's restaurants worldwide; about 78% of them are franchised.

YUM! Brands, Inc.: YUM! Brands is one of the largest fast-food franchisers in the world, trailing only McDonald's in overall sales. It outnumbers the burger giant, however, in store locations, with more than 33,000 units in about 100 countries. (The company owns and operates almost a quarter of its stores and franchises most of the others.) The company's flagship brands include KFC, Pizza Hut, and Taco Bell. Yum! also owns A&W All-American Food Restaurants and Long John Silver's. Its long-term multibranding strategy (offering more than one of its brands at one site) has proven successful.

Source of data: Hoover's, Inc.

EXHIBIT 9 | Common-Sized Financial Statements: Limited-Service Restaurant
Averages and Krispy Kreme (KKD)

	2001	2002	2003	KKD 2003
Balance Sheet: Assets (%)				
Cash & equivalents	12.8	12.4	13.7	3.1
Trade receivables (net)	1.6	0.9	1.4	10.4
Inventory	4.0	3.3	3.8	4.3
All other current	2.6	2.6	3.5	8.6
Total current	21.0	19.2	22.4	26.4
Fixed assets (net)	54.7	57.0	55.0	42.5
Intangibles (net)	13.3	14.2	12.6	26.6
All other noncurrent	11.0	9.6	10.0	4.5
Total assets	100.0	100.0	100.0	100.0
Balance Sheet: Liabilities & Equity (%)				
Notes payable, short-term	4.7	5.6	5.8	0.0
Current maturity, long-term debt	6.1	6.0	6.8	0.4
Trade payables	9.2	7.4	9.3	2.8
Income taxes payable	0.2	0.2	0.3	0.0
All other current	13.9	16.9	14.0	4.8
Total current	34.1	36.1	36.4	8.1
Long-term debt	40.2	45.6	41.9	7.3
Deferred taxes	0.1	0.2	0.1	1.0
All other non-current	4.7	8.3	8.7	14.9
Shareholders' equity	20.9	9.9	12.9	68.4
Total liabilities & equity	100.0	100.0	100.0	100.0
Income Statement (%)				
Net sales	100.0	100.0	100.0	100.0
Operating expenses	56.3	55.6	58.1	76.2
Operating profit	4.0	4.7	4.0	15.3
All other expenses (net)	1.3	1.6	1.5	1.1
Profit before taxes	2.7	3.0	2.5	14.2

Source of data: *Annual Statement Studies:* 2004–2005, The Risk Management Association.

The Body Shop International PLC 2001: An Introduction to Financial Modeling

Finance bored the pants off me. I fell asleep more times than not.[1]
    —Anita Roddick, founder,
    The Body Shop International

Roddick, as self-righteous as she is ambitious, professes to be unconcerned [with financial results]…. "Our business is about two things: social change and action, and skin care," she snaps. "Social change and action come first. You money-conscious people… just don't understand." Well, maybe we don't, but we sure know this: Roddick is one hell of a promoter…. She and her husband, Gordon, own shares worth just under $300 million. Now that's social action.[2]

One of our greatest frustrations at The Body Shop is that we're still judged by the media and the City by our profits, by the amount of product we sell, whereas we want and have always wanted to be judged by our actions in the larger world, by the positive difference we make.[3]
    —Anita Roddick

In the late 1990s, The Body Shop International PLC, previously one of the fastest growing manufacturer-retailers in the world, ran aground. Although the firm had an annual revenue growth rate of 20 percent in the early to middle 1990s, by the late 1990s, revenue growth slowed to around 8 percent. New retailers of naturally based skin- and hair-care products entered the market, bringing intense competition for The Body Shop.

---

[1]Anita Roddick, *Body and Soul* (London: Ebury Press, 1991), 105.

[2]Jean Sherman Chatzky, "Changing the World," *Forbes* (March 2, 1992): 87.

[3]Anita Roddick, *Business as Unusual* (London: Thorsons, 2000), 56.

This case was prepared by Susan Shank and John Vaccaro under the direction of Robert Bruner and Robert Conroy. It was written as a basis for class discussion rather than to illustrate effective or ineffective handling of an administrative situation. The financial support of the Batten Institute for case development is gratefully acknowledged. Copyright © 2001 by the University of Virginia Darden School Foundation, Charlottesville, VA. All rights reserved. *To order copies, send an e-mail to* sales@dardenpublishing.com. *No part of this publication may be reproduced, stored in a retrieval system, used in a spreadsheet, or transmitted in any form or by any means—electronic, mechanical, photocopying, recording, or otherwise—without the permission of the Darden School Foundation.*

Amidst the competition, The Body Shop failed to maintain its brand image by becoming something of a mass-market line as it expanded into "almost every mall in America, as well as virtually every corner on Britain's shopping streets."[4]

Anita Roddick, founder of The Body Shop, stepped down as CEO in 1998,[5] after numerous unsuccessful attempts to reinvent the company. Patrick Gournay, an executive from the French food giant Danone SA came on board as CEO. However, problems persisted despite the management change. In fiscal year 2001, revenue grew 13 percent, but pretax profit declined 21 percent. Gournay said of the results, "This is below our expectations, and we are disappointed with the outcome."[6]

Nonetheless, Gournay was confident that a newly implemented strategy would produce improved results. The strategy consisted of three principal objectives: "To enhance The Body Shop brand through a focused product strategy and increased investment in stores; to achieve operational efficiencies in our supply chain by reducing product and inventory costs; and to reinforce our stakeholder culture."[7]

Suppose that Anita Roddick, the founder and co-chair of the board of directors, and Patrick Gournay, CEO, came to you in the spring of 2001, for assistance in short- and long-term planning for The Body Shop. As a foundation for this work, you will need to estimate The Body Shop's future earnings and financial needs. The challenge of this advisory work should not be underestimated. Anita Roddick is a strong-willed decision maker with little taste for finance or financial jargon. Your projections must not only be technically correct, but they must also yield practical insights and be straightforward. What you have to say and how you say it are equally important.

If you feel comfortable using **Exhibit 8** to prepare the next three years of financial statements and demonstrate The Body Shop's debt financing needs, you might be better served by scanning the next few sections on basic financial modeling and concentrate on the last section of the case ("Ms. Roddick Wants to Know"). From experience, however, a vast number of students have found the following exercises to be invaluable in their early understanding of financial modeling.

An Overview of Financial Forecasting

In seeking to respond to Roddick's request, you can draw on at least two classical forecasting methods and a variety of hybrids that use some of each method. The two classical forecasting methods are as follows:

> *T-account forecasting:* This method starts with a base year of financial statements (e.g., last year). Entries through double-entry bookkeeping determine how each account will change and what the resulting new balances will be.

---

[4]Sarah Ellisan, "Body Shop Seeks a Makeover—U.K. Cosmetics Retailer Confirms Sale Talks with Mexico's Grupo Omnilife—A Long and Difficult Fall from Grace," *Wall Street Journal Europe,* June 8, 2001.

[5]Anita Roddick remained on the company's board of directors and, together with her husband, Gordon Roddick, served as cochair.

[6]CEO report (The Body Shop International PLC preliminary results for the 53 weeks to March 3, 2001).

[7]CEO report (March 3, 2001).

While exactly true to the mechanics of how funds flow through the firm, this method is cumbersome and may require a degree of forecast information about transactions which are unavailable to many analysts outside (and even inside) a firm.

Percent-of-sales forecasting: This method starts with a forecast of sales and then estimates other financial statement accounts based on some presumed relationship between sales and that account. While simple to execute, this technique is easily misused. For instance, some naive analysts may assume that operational capacity can increase in fractional amounts parallel to increases in sales, but can an airline company really buy only half a jumbo jet? Operational capacity usually increases in "lumps," rather than by smooth amounts. The lesson here is that when you use this technique, you should scrutinize the percent-of-sales relationships to make sure they are reasonable.

The most widely used approach is a hybrid of these two. For instance, T-accounts are used to estimate shareholders' equity and fixed assets. Percent-of-sales is used to estimate income statements, current assets, and current liabilities, because these latter items may credibly vary with sales. Other items will vary as a percentage of accounts other than sales. Tax expense will usually be a percentage of pretax income, while dividends will vary with after-tax income, and depreciation will usually vary with gross fixed assets.

A Pencil-and-Paper Forecast

As an introduction to financial modeling, we will walk through the construction of a forecasted income statement and balance sheet, first with pencil and paper (just visualizing the steps may suffice) and later with a spreadsheet. In either case, you are preparing a pro forma (or projected) income statement and balance sheet for The Body Shop for 2002 (income statement for the entire year and balance sheet for year-end). All values should be in pounds sterling. Use the following assumptions as a guide:

Sales:	£422,733,000 (a 13% increase over 2001)
Cost of goods sold:	38% of sales
Operating expenses:	50% of sales
Interest expense:	6% of debt (about the current interest rate)
Profit before tax:	Sales minus COGS minus D&A minus interest
	30% of profit before tax (the going corporate tax rate in Britain)
Dividends:	£10.9 million (same as previous three years)
Earnings retained:	Profit after tax minus dividends
Current assets:	32% of sales
Fixed assets:	£110,600,000
Total assets:	Current assets plus fixed assets
Current liabilities:	28% of sales
Debt:	Total assets minus current liabilities minus shareholders' equity
Common equity:	£121,600,000 plus retentions to earnings

Income statement: Begin with sales, and use it to estimate COGS and operating expenses. For the time being, leave interest expense at zero since we do not yet know the amount of debt. Estimate profit before tax, tax expense, profit after tax, dividends, and earnings retained.

Balance sheet: Estimate current assets (32% of sales) and add that to £110,600,000 to get an estimate for total assets. Next, estimate current liabilities (28% of sales) and common equity. Debt becomes the "plug" figure that makes the two sides of the balance sheet balance. This amount is your estimate of the external financing needed by The Body Shop by year-end 2002. Estimate the plug by subtracting the amounts for current liabilities and common equity from total assets.

Iterate: Initially, you entered an interest expense of zero on the income statement, but this cannot be correct if debt is outstanding or if excess cash is invested in interest-earning instruments. This is a classic problem in finance arising from the dependence of the income statement and balance sheet on each other. Interest expense is necessary to estimate retained earnings, which is necessary to estimate debt. Let's call this the problem of "circularity." The way to deal with this problem is to insert your best estimate of interest expense in the income statement (using 6% × debt), then re-estimate the plug figure, then re-estimate interest expense, and so on. By iterating through the two statements five or six times, you will come to estimates of interest expense and debt that do not change very much further. Stop iterating when changes get to be small.

A Spreadsheet-Model Forecast

Fortunately, the tedium of iterating can be eliminated with the aid of a computer and spreadsheet software such as Excel. The specific commands reviewed here relate to Excel 2000. (These commands will appear in table form within the text.) The adaptation to other spreadsheet programs should be straightforward. Now, try the same forecast for The Body Shop using a computer spreadsheet.

Setup: Start with a clean spreadsheet. Set the recalculation mode to MANUAL so that the model will iterate only when you press CALC (F9). Also, set the number of iterations to one so that you will be able to see Excel re-estimate the plug figure and interest expense. You can set the number of iterations higher (Excel's default is 100), but Excel will converge on a solution after five or six iterations, so a setting of *1* is best to see the iterations in action. The commands are listed in **Table 1.**

TABLE 1 | Excel Spreadsheet Commands

Choose the <**Tools**> menu and then the <**Options**> menu item. Next, choose the <**Calculations**> tab; select the button next to <**Manual**>, and enter *1* in <**Maximum Iterations**>. Be sure the box next to <**Iterations**> is checked.

Saving: As you develop your model, be sure to save it every five minutes or so, just for insurance.

Format: Use the format in **Exhibit 1** as a guide to plan your worksheet. To facilitate sensitivity analysis, it is generally best to place the "Input Data" at the top of the worksheet. Next, develop the income statement just as you did on pencil and paper. Use **Exhibit 2** as a guide. Be sure to tie the cells to the proper percentage rate in the Input Data section. The first time through, enter *0* for interest. (This is very important for the iteration to work properly.) We will return to it later.

Now do the balance sheet. Again, be sure to tie the balance sheet together by formulas. With the basic format laid out, go back and enter the formula to calculate interest as "interest rate × debt." Press the (F9) key, and you should see the worksheet change. You should be able to press the (F9) key several more times until the numbers stop changing, which means the model has converged to a solution. You should have interest as exactly 6 percent of long-term liabilities and a balance sheet that balances.

Once you have seen how this works, you may want to have the model converge without having to press <CALC> several times. In order to do this, you must set the number of iterations you wish the spreadsheet to perform. Set the number of iterations back to *100* (Excel's default), and allow the computer to recalculate automatically. See Excel commands listed in **Table 2.**

TABLE 2

Choose the <**Tools**> menu, and then the <**Options**> menu item. Next, choose the <**Calculations**> tab; click on <**Automatic**>, and enter *100* in <**Maximum Iterations**>. Be sure the box next to <**Iterations**> is checked.

Note: Changing your iterations setting, combined with the circularity of the debt plug and interest expense (later we'll add the circularity of data tables) can lead to some confusing situations. It's easy to forget where you have your iterations set (more data tables lead to more circularity). When comparing your work to someone else's, be sure that both of you have the same iterations setting and have hit (F9) the same number of times (be sure you have either no data tables or the same data tables). Your worksheet should now look like **Exhibit 3.**

Projecting Farther

So far, you have managed to project The Body Shop's financial statements through 2002. Now, extend your projection to years 2003 and 2004. See **Table 3** for Excel commands. A simple way to do this is to copy your model for the two additional years. Before copying the formulas from column B to columns C and D, make sure that any references to your Input Data (cells B3 through B12) are absolute references as opposed to relative references. An absolute reference means that when you copy cells B16 through B35 to other parts of your spreadsheet, the cells are still linked back to the originals (i.e., B5). Otherwise, the program assumes that the cells should be linked to new cells, such as C5. To make a reference absolute, put in dollar signs—B3, instead of B3. Now you should be ready to copy.

TABLE 3

> Select the range of your data by highlighting it in the worksheet. Choose the <**Edit**> menu and then the <**Copy**> menu item. Highlight the cells where you want the copy to go. Choose the <**Edit**> menu and then the <**Paste**> menu item.

Note that you will have to change the equity formula for 2003 and 2004. For 2003, make the formula equal to 2002's equity plus 2003's additions to retained earnings. In addition, you should make sales grow by compounding. To do this, take 2002's sales × 2003's expected sales growth rate (say, 13%). As you enter these changes, you should see the effect ripple through your model.

When Debt Is Negative

Now modify the model to deal with the situation where the plug for debt is negative—this can happen routinely for firms with seasonal or cyclical sales patterns. Negative debt can be interpreted as excess cash. However, this is an odd way to show cash; a non-financial manager (like Roddick) might not appreciate this type of presentation. The solution is to add a line for excess cash on the assets side of the balance sheet and then set up three new lines below the last entry in the balance sheet:

Name	Formula
Trial Assets	Current Assets + Fixed Assets
Trial Liabilities and Equity	Current Liabilities + Equity
Plug	Trial Assets – Trial Liabilities

Now enter the following formula for "Excess Cash":

$$=IF(PLUG<0,-PLUG,0)$$

Instead of the word "PLUG," you should use the cell address for the actual plug number. The formula for DEBT is the following:

$$=IF(PLUG>0,+PLUG,0)$$

See **Exhibit 4** for an example of how your spreadsheet should look. To see how these modifications really work, change your COGS/SALES assumption to 0.45 and press (F9).

With excess cash, you should generate interest income instead of interest expense. In the event of an excess cash balance, to have your model treat interest as income rather than expense, you need to modify your interest expense formula as follows:

$$= +(B6*B34) - (B6*B28)$$

An example of the finished results appears in **Exhibit 5.**

Explore Sensitivities

After your model replicates the exhibit, you are ready to conduct a sensitivity analysis on the pro forma years by seeing how variations in the forecast assumptions will affect the financing requirements. A financial analyst might want to try the following variations (or more than one in combination):

- Suppose sales in 2002 will be £500 million.
- Suppose COGS runs at 45 percent of sales.
- Suppose dividends are increased to 60 percent of net income.
- Suppose The Body Shop must double its manufacturing capacity by adding a new £100 million facility in 2002.
- Assume inventories run higher than expected (model this by increasing current assets to 40 percent of sales).
- Assume that accounts-receivable collections improve so that current assets run at 28 percent of sales.
- Assume that operating expenses increase faster than sales.

What happens to the plug value (i.e., debt) under these different circumstances? In general, which assumptions in the "Input Data" section of your spreadsheet seem to have the biggest effect on future borrowing needs?

The "Data Table" is an invaluable tool for conducting a sensitivity analysis. It automatically calculates debt (or whatever else you want to focus on) as it varies across different values for a particular assumption—for instance, growth rates. In Excel, you can create a data table using a two-step process illustrated in the following examples. Suppose you want to estimate The Body Shop's debt required and excess cash generated at COGS/SALES ratios of .35, .38, .40, .42, .44, .45, and .48.

1. **Set up the table.** Move to a clean part of the spreadsheet and type the COGS/SALES ratios (.35, .38, .40, .42, .44, .45, and .48) in a column. At the top of the next column (one row above your first COGS/SALES ratio), enter the location of the value to be estimated, in this case, debt, or =B34. In the next column, type the cell location for excess cash, =B28. Your data table should be formatted as in **Exhibit 6.**

2. **Enter the data table commands. Table 4** gives the commands for setting up the data table.

TABLE 4

Highlight the cells that contain your COGS/SALES ratios and your cell references to Debt and Excess Cash. The cells to the right of your COGS/SALES ratios and below your cell references to Debt and Excess Cash are the cells to be filled in and should also be highlighted.

Choose the <**Data**> menu and then the <**Table**> menu item.

In the <**Column Input Cell**> box, enter the cell where your COGS/SALES assumption is B4.

The computer will fill in the table.

The additional circularity brought about by data tables can lead to some confusing results. To avoid this, be sure at this point to set the number of iterations to *at least 10.* The result should look like **Exhibit 7.**

The data table in **Exhibit 7** reveals that, at COGS/SALES ratios of 45 percent, the firm will need to borrow. This should trigger questions in your mind about what might cause that to happen, such as a price war or a surge in materials costs. Your spreadsheet can tell you about more sophisticated data-table formats. No financial analyst can afford to ignore this valuable tool. Armed with a data table, it's easy to go back and try variations in other input assumptions.

Note: Remember that data tables add more calculations that need to be iterated in your worksheet. When comparing your work to that of a fellow student, be sure your number of iterations are the same and you have roughly the same data tables in your files.

Ms. Roddick Wants to Know

Now that you have completed a simplified forecast, prepare a forecast based on the full range of accounts as actually reported by The Body Shop in 2001. **Exhibit 8** presents the results for the past three years. Please forecast all of the accounts individually for the next three years. You will see many familiar accounts, as well as some unusual accounts like minority interests.

For most accounts, you should extrapolate by using the same percentage of sales borne out by the preceding years' experience. You might use an average of the three historical years. You might want to use only the most recent year, or if you notice a significant upward or downward trend in an account, try growing or shrinking the percentage in the future years, according to your judgment. Whatever assumptions you decide upon, you should again isolate them at the top of your worksheet, so you can easily change an assumption and then have it flow through your worksheet. Additionally, this is very important for calculating sensitivities later, as you want to be able to point to one cell as the "Column Input Cell" in a data table.

Please make "overdrafts" the plug figure, and base interest expense (at 6%) on the overdrafts, current portion of long-term debt, and long-term liabilities. If you skipped to this section without doing the exercise above, you may differ from your fellow students in your treatment of the case where debt is negative.

Make your own assumptions regarding sales growth. Make other assumptions as needed. Be prepared to report to Roddick your answers to the following questions:

1. How did you derive your forecast? Why did you choose the "base-case" assumptions that you did?

2. Based on your pro forma projections, how much additional financing will The Body Shop need during this period?

3. What are the three or four most important assumptions or "key drivers" in this forecast? What is the effect on the financing need of varying each of these assumptions up or down from the base case? Intuitively, why are these assumptions so important?

4. Why are your findings relevant to a general manager like Roddick? What are the implications of these findings for her? What action should she take based on your analysis?

In discussing your analysis with Roddick, do not permit yourself to get mired in forecast technicalities or financial jargon. Focus your comments on your results. State them as simply and intuitively as you can. Do not be satisfied with simply presenting results. Link your findings to recommendations, such as key factors to manage, opportunities to enhance results, and issues warranting careful analysis. Remember that Roddick plainly admits she finds finance boring. Whenever possible, try to express your analysis in terms that she finds interesting, including people, customers, quality of natural products, and the health and dynamism of her business. Good luck!

EXHIBIT 1 | Format for Developing a Spreadsheet Model

	A	B
1	Input Data	
2		
3	SALES	422,733
4	COGS/SALES	0.38
5	OPERATING EXPENSES/SALES	0.50
6	INTEREST RATE	0.06
7	TAX RATE	0.30
8	DIVIDENDS	10,900
9	CURR. ASSETS/SALES	0.32
10	CURR. LIABS./SALES	0.28
11	FIXED ASSETS	110,600
12	STARTING EQUITY	121,600
13		
14	INCOME STATEMENT	2002
15		
16	SALES	
17	COGS	
18	OPERATING EXPENSES	
19	INTEREST EXPENSE (INCOME)	————
20	PROFIT BEFORE TAX	
21	TAX	————
22	PROFIT AFTER TAX	═══
23	DIVIDENDS	
24	EARNINGS RETAINED	
25		
26	BALANCE SHEET	2002
27		
28	CURRENT ASSETS	
29	FIXED ASSETS	————
30	TOTAL ASSETS	═══
31		
32	CURRENT LIABILITIES	
33	DEBT	
34	EQUITY	————
35	TOTAL LIAB. & NET WORTH	————

EXHIBIT 2 | Spreadsheet Formulas to Forecast 2002 Financials

	A	B
1	Input Data	
2		
3	SALES	422,733
4	COGS/SALES	0.38
5	OPERATING EXPENSES/SALES	0.50
6	INTEREST RATE	0.06
7	TAX RATE	0.30
8	DIVIDENDS	10,900
9	CURR. ASSETS/SALES	0.32
10	CURR. LIABS./SALES	0.28
11	FIXED ASSETS	110,600
12	STARTING EQUITY	121,600
13		
14	INCOME STATEMENT	2002
15		
16	SALES	+B3
17	COGS	+B4*B16
18	OPERATING EXPENSES	+B5*B16
19	INTEREST EXPENSE (INCOME)	+B6*B33
20	PROFIT BEFORE TAX	+B16-B17-B18-B19
21	TAX	+B7*B20
22	PROFIT AFTER TAX	+B20-B21
23	DIVIDENDS	+B8
24	EARNINGS RETAINED	+B22-B23
25		
26	BALANCE SHEET	2002
27		
28	CURRENT ASSETS	+B9*B16
29	FIXED ASSETS	+B11
30	TOTAL ASSETS	+B28+B29
31		
32	CURRENT LIABILITIES	+B10*B16
33	DEBT	+B30-B32-B34
34	EQUITY	+B12+B24
35	TOTAL LIAB. & NET WORTH	+B32+B33+B34

EXHIBIT 3 | Basic Forecasting Results for 2002

	A	B
1	Input Data	
2		
3	SALES	422,733
4	COGS/SALES	0.38
5	OPERATING EXPENSES/SALES	0.50
6	INTEREST RATE	0.06
7	TAX RATE	0.30
8	DIVIDENDS	10,900
9	CURR. ASSETS/SALES	0.32
10	CURR. LIABS./SALES	0.28
11	FIXED ASSETS	110,600
12	STARTING EQUITY	121,600
13		
14	INCOME STATEMENT	2002
15		
16	SALES	422,733
17	COGS	160,639
18	OPERATING EXPENSES	211,367
19	INTEREST EXPENSE (INCOME)	(1,171)
20	PROFIT BEFORE TAX	51,899
21	TAX	15,570
22	PROFIT AFTER TAX	36,329
23	DIVIDENDS	10,900
24	EARNINGS RETAINED	25,429
25		
26	BALANCE SHEET	2002
27		
28	CURRENT ASSETS	135,275
29	FIXED ASSETS	110,600
30	TOTAL ASSETS	245,875
31		
32	CURRENT LIABILITIES	118,365
33	DEBT	(19,520)
34	EQUITY	147,029
35	TOTAL LIAB. & NET WORTH	245,875

EXHIBIT 4 | Adjusting to Reflect Excess Cash

	A	B
1	Input Data	
2		
3	SALES	422,733
4	COGS/SALES	0.38
5	OPERATING EXPENSES/SALES	0.50
6	INTEREST RATE	0.06
7	TAX RATE	0.30
8	DIVIDENDS	10,900
9	CURR. ASSETS/SALES	0.32
10	CURR. LIABS./SALES	0.28
11	FIXED ASSETS	110,600
12	STARTING EQUITY	121,600
13		
14	INCOME STATEMENT	2002
15		
16	SALES	422,733
17	COGS	160,639
18	OPERATING EXPENSES	211,367
19	INTEREST EXPENSE (INCOME)	+(B6*B34)-(B6*B28)
20	PROFIT BEFORE TAX	40,706
21	TAX	14,247
22	PROFIT AFTER TAX	26,459
23	DIVIDENDS	10,900
24	EARNINGS RETAINED	15,559
25		
26	BALANCE SHEET	2002
27		
28	EXCESS CASH	=IF(B40<0,-B40,0)
29	CURRENT ASSETS	135,275
30	FIXED ASSETS	110,600
31	TOTAL ASSETS	+B29+B30+B28
32		
33	CURRENT LIABILITIES	118,365
34	DEBT	=IF(B40>0,+B40,0)
35	EQUITY	137,159
36	TOTAL LIAB. & NET WORTH	+B33+B34+B35
37		
38	TRIAL ASSETS	+B29+B30
39	TRIAL LIABILITIES AND EQUITY	+B33+B35
40	PLUG: DEBT (EXCESS CASH)	+B38-B39

EXHIBIT 5 | Finished Results for 2002, Reflecting Excess Cash

	A	B
1	Input Data	
2		
3	SALES	422,733
4	COGS/SALES	0.38
5	OPERATING EXPENSES/SALES	0.50
6	INTEREST RATE	0.06
7	TAX RATE	0.30
8	DIVIDENDS	10,900
9	CURR. ASSETS/SALES	0.32
10	CURR. LIABS./SALES	0.28
11	FIXED ASSETS	110,600
12	STARTING EQUITY	121,600
13		
14	INCOME STATEMENT	2002
15		
16	SALES	422,733
17	COGS	160,639
18	OPERATING EXPENSES	211,367
19	INTEREST EXPENSE (INCOME)	(1,171)
20	PROFIT BEFORE TAX	51,899
21	TAX	15,570
22	PROFIT AFTER TAX	36,329
23	DIVIDENDS	10,900
24	EARNINGS RETAINED	25,429
25		
26	BALANCE SHEET	2002
27		
28	EXCESS CASH	19,520
29	CURRENT ASSETS	135,275
30	FIXED ASSETS	110,600
31	TOTAL ASSETS	265,395
32		
33	CURRENT LIABILITIES	118,365
34	DEBT	0
35	EQUITY	147,029
36	TOTAL LIAB. & NET WORTH	265,395
37		
38	TRIAL ASSETS	245,875
39	TRIAL LIABILITIES AND EQUITY	265,395
40	PLUG: DEBT (EXCESS CASH)	(19,520)

EXHIBIT 6 | Setup for a Forecast with Data Table

	A	B	C	D	E	F
1	Input Data					
2						
3	SALES	422,733				
4	COGS/SALES	0.38				
5	OPERATING EXPENSES/SALES	0.50		Sensitivity Analysis		
6	INTEREST RATE	0.06		Of Debt and Excess Cash		
7	TAX RATE	0.30		To COGS/SALES Ratio		
8	DIVIDENDS	10,900				
9	CURR. ASSETS/SALES	0.32		COGS/SALES	DEBT	Ex. CASH
10	CURR. LIABS./SALES	0.28			=B34	=B28
11	FIXED ASSETS	110,600		0.35		
12	STARTING EQUITY	121,600		0.38		
13				0.40		
14	INCOME STATEMENT	2002		0.42		
15				0.44		
16	SALES	422,733		0.45		
17	COGS	160,639		0.48		
18	OPERATING EXPENSES	211,367				
19	INTEREST EXPENSE (INCOME)	(1,171)				
20	PROFIT BEFORE TAX	51,899				
21	TAX	15,570				
22	PROFIT AFTER TAX	36,329				
23	DIVIDENDS	10,900				
24	EARNINGS RETAINED	25,429				
25						
26	BALANCE SHEET	2002				
27						
28	EXCESS CASH	19,520				
29	CURRENT ASSETS	135,275				
30	FIXED ASSETS	110,600				
31	TOTAL ASSETS	265,395				
32						
33	CURRENT LIABILITIES	118,365				
34	DEBT	0				
35	EQUITY	147,029				
36	TOTAL LIAB. & NET WORTH	265,395				
37						
38	TRIAL ASSETS	245,875				
39	TRIAL LIABILITIES AND EQUITY	265,395				
40	PLUG: DEBT (EXCESS CASH)	(19,520)				

EXHIBIT 7 | Finished Forecast with Data Table

	A	B	C	D	E	F
1	Input Data					
2						
3	SALES	422,733				
4	COGS/SALES	0.38				
5	OPERATING EXPENSES/SALES	0.50		Sensitivity Analysis		
6	INTEREST RATE	0.06		Debt and Excess Cash		
7	TAX RATE	0.30		By COGS/SALES		
8	DIVIDENDS	10,900		COGS/SALES	DEBT	Ex. CASH
9	CURR. ASSETS/SALES	0.32			+B34	+B28
10	CURR. LIABS./SALES	0.28		0.35	0	28,787
11	FIXED ASSETS	110,600		0.38	0	19,520
12	STARTING EQUITY	121,600		0.40	0	13,342
13				0.42	0	7,165
14	INCOME STATEMENT	2002		0.44	0	987
15				0.45	2,102	0
16	SALES	422,733		0.48	11,369	0
17	COGS	160,639				
18	OPERATING EXPENSES	211,367				
19	INTEREST EXPENSE (INCOME)	(1,171)				
20	PROFIT BEFORE TAX	51,899				
21	TAX	15,570				
22	PROFIT AFTER TAX	36,329				
23	DIVIDENDS	10,900				
24	EARNINGS RETAINED	25,429				
25						
26	BALANCE SHEET	2002				
27						
28	EXCESS CASH	19,520				
29	CURRENT ASSETS	135,275				
30	FIXED ASSETS	110,600				
31	TOTAL ASSETS	265,395				
32						
33	CURRENT LIABILITIES	118,365				
34	DEBT	0				
35	EQUITY	147,029				
36	TOTAL LIAB. & NET WORTH	265,395				
37						
38	TRIAL ASSETS	245,875				
39	TRIAL LIABILITIES AND EQUITY	265,395				
40	PLUG: DEBT (EXCESS CASH)	(19,520)				

EXHIBIT 8 | Historical Financial Statements (£ in millions)

		Fiscal Year Ended Feb. 28			
	1999 (£)	1999 (% sales)	2000 (£)	2000 (% sales)	2001 (£)	2001 (% sales)

Income Statement						
Turnover	303.7	100.0	330.1	100.0	374.1	100.0
Cost of sales	127.7	42.0	130.9	39.7	149.0	39.8
Gross profit	176.0	58.0	199.2	60.3	225.1	60.2
Operating expenses						
– excluding exceptional costs	151.4	49.9	166.2	50.3	195.7	52.3
– exceptional costs[a]	4.5	1.5	0.0	0.0	11.2	3.0
Restructuring costs[b]	16.6	5.5	2.7	0.8	1.0	0.3
Net interest expense	0.1	0.0	1.5	0.5	4.4	1.2
Profit before tax	3.4	1.1	28.8	8.7	12.8	3.4
Tax expense	8.0	2.6	10.4	3.2	3.5	0.9
Profit/(loss) after tax	(4.6)	(1.5)	18.4	5.6	9.3	2.5
Ordinary dividends	10.9	3.6	10.9	3.3	10.9	2.9
Profit/(loss) retained	(15.5)	(5.1)	7.5	2.3	(1.6)	(0.4)

		Fiscal Year Ended Feb. 28			
	1999 (£)	1999 (% sales)	2000 (£)	2000 (% sales)	2001 (£)	2001 (% sales)

Balance Sheet						
Assets						
Cash	34.0	11.2	19.2	5.8	13.7	3.7
Accounts receivable	27.8	9.2	30.3	9.2	30.3	8.1
Inventories	38.6	12.7	44.7	13.5	51.3	13.7
Other current assets	12.5	4.1	15.6	4.7	17.5	4.7
Net fixed assets	87.8	28.9	104.7	31.7	110.6	29.6
Other assets[c]	0.0	0.0	6.0	1.8	6.7	1.8
Total assets	200.7	66.1	220.5	66.8	230.1	61.5
Liabilities and equity						
Accounts payable	13.0	4.3	20.5	6.2	10.7	2.9
Taxes payable	11.3	3.7	11.7	3.5	7.1	1.9
Accruals	10.8	3.6	15.6	4.7	11.5	3.1
Overdrafts	0.0	0.0	0.3	0.1	0.7	0.2
Other current liabilities	21.6	7.1	13.3	4.0	16.9	4.5
Long-term liabilities	28.0	9.2	36.7	11.1	61.2	16.4
Other liabilities[d]	1.7	0.6	1.0	0.3	0.4	0.1
Shareholders' equity	114.3	37.6	121.4	36.8	121.6	32.5
Total liabs. and equity	200.7	66.1	220.5	66.8	230.1	61.5

[a]Exceptional costs in 2001 included redundancy costs ($4.6 million), costs of supply chain development ($2.4 million) and impairment of fixed assets and goodwill ($4.2 million). The exceptional costs of $4.5 million in 1999 were associated with closing unprofitable shops and an impairment review of the remaining shops in the United States.

[b]Restructuring costs in 2001 and 2000 relate to the sale of manufacturing plants in Littlehampton, England, and to associated reorganization costs. Restructuring costs in 1999 arose from the realignment of the management structure of the business in the United States and the United Kingdom.

[c]Other assets in 2001 and 2000 represented receivables relating to the sale of the company's Littlehampton manufacturing plant.

[d]Other liabilities mostly included deferred taxes.

Padgett Paper Products Company

Negotiations with Padgett Paper Products Company had been going on for almost a year. Francis Libris hoped the time had come when they could be pushed to a mutually satisfactory conclusion. If not, Padgett might seek another bank as its source of funds. Alternatively, Libris would be subject to criticism by his superiors for failing to deliver on his commitment to manage and structure the relationship properly. Libris was vice president of the Caslon Trust Company of Richmond, Virginia, one of Virginia's largest banks. He was responsible for the Broad Street Commercial Lending Center of the bank, to which Padgett's account was assigned because its small executive offices were on an upper floor of the same building in which the center was located. It was a significant account for the center and important to its profitability.

Padgett had borrowed small amounts off and on from Caslon since it had first established an account with the bank in 1947. Even the acquisition of several small companies (for less than $1 million each) in the 1980s did not require high levels of debt. The acquisition of a long-coveted competitor at an attractive price on short notice in early 1996 brought Padgett suddenly to the bank, asking for an additional $3.6 million loan. Combined with the $3.6 million already outstanding at that time, Caslon's total exposure could rise to $7.2 million, well in excess of the $5 million advised credit line that had been approved for the company. The request was granted, nevertheless, under an internal guidance line of $8 million, and the rate was continued at prime. Libris had been working since then to structure the arrangements on a more orderly basis than 90-day notes with no protective covenants.

It was now January 1997. Libris hoped to have the new terms worked out so they could be reflected on the financial statements for the 1997 fiscal year that ended on April 30. There was a chance that a negotiation completed before the auditors finished their fieldwork, roughly two months after the April ending of Padgett's fiscal

This case was prepared by Paul H. Hunn, visiting lecturer, whose cooperation is acknowledged with appreciation. It was written as a basis for class discussion rather than to illustrate effective or ineffective handling of an administrative situation. Copyright © 1996 by the University of Virginia Darden School Foundation, Charlottesville, VA. All rights reserved. *To order copies, send an e-mail to* sales@dardenpublishing.com. *No part of this publication may be reproduced, stored in a retrieval system, used in a spreadsheet, or transmitted in any form or by any means—electronic, mechanical, photocopying, recording, or otherwise—without the permission of the Darden School Foundation.*

year, could be incorporated in the auditor's report. Libris preferred, however, to have the agreement signed before the end of the fiscal year to avoid this complication.

Libris wondered whether he should take a fresh look at the situation. He had originally tried to persuade Padgett's management to finance part of the company's requirements in the form of long-term debt from a life insurance company. When the financial vice president declined the private-placement proposal, Libris decided to see how the loan could be repaid to the bank within the period initially suggested by his superiors. As time had gone on, he began to think that those constraints might not be appropriate to the situation and that a more creative solution might prove acceptable both to departmental senior management and to Padgett's management. Because Libris knew he would have to get the approval of his superiors before he undertook a different initiative with Padgett's management, time was getting exceedingly short. He had to develop both the implications of the original decision and of any alternatives that appeared more attractive.

Padgett Paper Products Company

Padgett Paper Products Company, a closely held but publicly traded (over-the-counter) company, manufactured a variety of stationery products including notebooks, loose-leaf binders, forms, and filler paper for students and record-keeping purposes. The company was over 100 years old. Its ownership remained primarily with the descendants of the founders, now a large and widely spread group. Few family members were active in the company's management, and the major connection with most of the owners came in the form of a quarterly dividend check. A few members of the family depended on the dividends for most of their income. Most of the shareholders considered Padgett just another investment and an illiquid one at that, because the market for the company's stock was extremely thin. A significant payout was considered important by management.

Management, which was primarily professional, appeared competent, responsible, and reasonably effective. Its expertise was largely in operations, which were carried on at several plants in the Midsouth, and in marketing, which was controlled out of the executive office in Richmond. Management was not financially oriented, Libris had observed.

Padgett's customers were some 5,000 wholesalers and retailers in the United States and Canada. No single customer or small group of customers accounted for a substantial share of Padgett's sales. Terms were 2/10 net 30, but few customers took the discount. Many stretched payment for an additional 30 days. The business had a slight seasonal peak in the late summer when big back-to-school sales took place. Because the company tried to maintain level production to reduce unit cost in the highly competitive market, a seasonal variation of about $2 million occurred in its borrowing pattern. The peak occurred in the summer.

A consolidation had been taking place in the business since the late 1970s, initially caused by the high inflation rate of the period that made it difficult for small firms to finance their current assets. Financial difficulties and inventory problems resulting from the subsequent recession in the early 1980s further reduced the level of the competition. Changes in the tax rules periodically provided new impetus for the smaller companies to sell. The sharp drop in the stock market in October 1987 had frightened some owners into selling out. Most recently, a sudden increase in paper prices, which had risen over 50 percent from mid-1994 and exceeded the previous high prices of 1988/1989, had again created financial strains for firms such as Tri-State Tablet. Those pressures had become great enough, and the price-earnings multiples attractive enough because of the booming equity market, that many of the remaining owners (including Tri-State's) put their firms on the market. Tri-State had not been able to pass all the price increases through to its customers because of strong competition from large, integrated paper companies. In Padgett's case, a drop in its tax rate helped compensate for smaller margins.

Over the years, many of Padgett's competitors had been acquired by national corporations with strong marketing skills and good financial resources. The response of Padgett's management had been to acquire smaller companies that fit into its product or marketing needs. The acquisition of its competitor, Tri-State Tablet Company, in April 1996 was the culmination of those efforts.

Padgett's financial statements for fiscal year 1996 had been given an unqualified opinion by the national C.P.A. firm that audited them. Straight-line depreciation was used for reporting purposes with accelerated depreciation used for taxes. Inventory had been valued on a lower of cost (FIFO) or market basis despite the potential cash savings from the favorable tax effect if it changed to LIFO. Padgett's management had always concluded that it was not worth the complexity to change inventory accounting methods. Financial statements for the 1993–1996 fiscal years are presented in **Exhibits 1** and **2. Exhibit 3** is a standard computerized spread used by Caslon's credit department to organize a company's financial statements for analysis.

Padgett's Relationship with Caslon Trust

Caslon Trust had historically been Padgett's only lending bank and was the only lending bank in early 1997. Among the other benefits of that relationship, Padgett used Caslon Trust as the depository for its substantial Virginia and federal tax payments. So far, during the 1997 fiscal year, Padgett's average collected balance with Caslon had been $524,000. Affiliated companies and subsidiaries had balances that had averaged $231,000. The loan balances outstanding had ranged from $3.3 million to $7.2 million, with an average of $5.05 million. The loan had last been cleaned up for an extended period from March 31, 1993 to January 8, 1994.

Padgett maintained a small deposit relationship with the Phoenix Bank, a major North Carolina bank that had long been soliciting a more important role in the company's financial arrangements. In addition, several local banks were used to service the various plant locations.

The speed with which the Tri-State Tablet acquisition had been made had not allowed for careful planning of the financial arrangements. Libris's group management had been reluctant to double the loan to Padgett without a carefully structured financial program as well as appropriate protective covenants. With Libris's assurance that those questions could be quickly resolved, the group's senior vice president had authorized the loan and established a new temporary credit limit of $8 million. It had been expected, however, that the loan would be formally structured long before January 1997, which was a source of embarrassment to Libris. He knew he also would be embarrassed and his profit plan damaged, if he should lose the account to Phoenix.

Once the dust created by the acquisition had settled down, Libris met with John Ruhl, Padgett's financial vice president, to discuss the company's plans. Based on those conversations, Libris and Caslon's credit department prepared a preliminary financial forecast for Padgett's 1997–2000 fiscal years. Summary figures from that forecast are presented in **Exhibit 4.**

Libris was distressed to note that, even under what he thought were assumptions that minimized the need for funds, Padgett would still have $4.4 million in short-term debt on the books at the end of the fiscal year 2000. Assuming the company could generate about $1 million in "undedicated" cash each subsequent year, a total of eight years would be required to retire the debt. This was considerably longer than the typical bank five-year term loan that a company of Padgett's size might expect. Caslon was willing to stretch to six years for important relationships, but a seven-year term loan would be considered a bit long for a company such as Padgett, which did not enjoy the financial flexibility afforded firms having easy entry to the public capital markets.

Libris decided that a need of this duration appropriately called for insurance company financing. After he had met with officers of several companies, he wrote Ruhl to propose a 12- to 15-year loan and to quote terms an insurance company might offer. (Libris's letter is reproduced as **Exhibit 5.**) He also pointed out that Caslon might be able to structure an arrangement that would allow the bank to take the seasonal needs while the insurance company would take the long-term core requirements of $5 million.

Ruhl's response was emphatically negative. While he appreciated the information, he reported that management believed the current long-term fixed rates were too high. Although it was tempting to take advantage of the fact that long-term corporate rates had not yet returned to their early 1995 peak, his board was somewhat pessimistic about the future of the economy. "Politicians like low rates before elections," he said, "but they pay the piper afterward. I think they're pumping up the economy now. We'll probably have high rates soon after the election, and then we'll have a recession. Maybe that will be the time to lock in really low rates." He admitted, however, that a repeat of the interest-rate run-up of the 1970s would again have a serious effect on Padgett.

Furthermore, Padgett's management did not like the idea of an elaborate set of covenants. Ruhl said that he particularly disliked the type of covenant that could throw the company in default without management's explicit action. "Violation of a debt-capital ratio, for instance," explained Ruhl, "could occur as the result of an adverse year rather than anything we do. I don't mind agreeing not to borrow or pay dividends if certain conditions would result, but I just don't see agreeing to a lot of things that are out of my control. I can't see getting tied up in all these technicalities." Ruhl indicated that he did not see anything wrong with the present, friendly, informal loan. "After all," he said, "if you don't like what we're doing—anything at all—you can call your entire loan at the end of any 90-day period. Isn't this better protection for you than fancy agreements?"

In the months that followed this disappointing outcome, Libris met frequently with Ruhl to get a thorough understanding of the business. He planned to prepare a forecast of future needs that would accurately reflect Padgett management's thinking and his own insights into the company. By late in 1996, preliminary estimates for the 1997 fiscal year were becoming available so Libris could incorporate them into his forecasts. The forecasts, which were prepared showing the effects of 5 percent, 10 percent, and 15 percent growth in sales over the 1998–2000 fiscal years, are included as **Exhibit 6.**

Ruhl thought that this effort was most helpful, although he noted that two last-minute changes should be incorporated in the planning. First, he had finally persuaded Padgett's directors that a shift to LIFO inventory valuation would save more cash than the cost of implementing the system. LIFO would be adopted for the 1997 fiscal year, which would result in a tax benefit of $500,000. Second, management had decided to dispose of a redundant warehouse that had been part of the Tri-State acquisition. Management expected to receive $700,000 from the cash sale and tax refunds on the book loss.

Alternatives

Libris still thought that splitting the loan—maybe with the bank's own real estate department—had promise. For instance, Padgett owned outright a large, general-purpose warehouse. Its appraisal value of $3 million was more than the amount at which it was carried on the books. Although Libris was not an experienced real-estate lending officer, he believed the property would be attractive collateral for a mortgage loan. Another alternative might be to wait until the loan had been partly retired and then invite another bank to share the remainder for the duration of the repayment. Part of the loan could be rotated between banks to allow each a clean-up period of several months. Finally, he had discovered that Padgett's small Canadian operation was self-contained with a negligible amount of intercompany transfers and charges. With net current assets of $1.8 million to $2.0 million to offer as collateral and no direct debt, the Canadian subsidiary could probably raise $1.0 million from Canadian banks. The Canadian banks would require "charge," a form of security agreement, against all current assets of the subsidiary.

Although U.S. banking law and practice were not identical to Canadian and British practice with respect to "floating liens," asset-based finance might offer useful alternatives. It would be expensive to take effective security against Padgett's receivables because the company had so many customers and the average account was small. A factoring arrangement might be suitable, in which Padgett could sell its accounts on a non-recourse basis to a commercial finance company. Caslon Bank itself did not operate a factoring function, however. It would be necessary to find one that had experience in the paper distribution business or the costs of the factoring, which were usually about 2 percent of accounts purchased, would be too high. On the other hand, if Padgett factored its accounts, it could eliminate its credit department and would have no bad debts.

Caslon could always grant credit against the security of the accounts receivable even though the bank would not monitor the accounts as closely as a factor would. The loan would be limited to a percentage of receivables to provide some protection against losses. A security interest in the inventory also could be required, although the granting of this security could upset some major paper companies who were Padgett's sources of supply.

Money-Market Considerations and Pricing Aspects

Funds were readily available in the financial markets in January 1997. Although the prime rate had risen rapidly during 1994, rates had then declined modestly during 1995 and 1996 to 8.25 percent. The prime's low in recent years had been 6 percent from mid-1992 to early 1994. Thirty-day commercial paper was currently yielding 5.38 percent. The Treasury yield curve was relatively flat: 90-day bills yielded 5.04 percent; 1-year notes, 5.6 percent; 5-year notes, 6.10 percent; 10-year bonds, 6.59 percent; and 30-year bonds, 6.73 percent. During the recent election campaign, however, there had been much debate about whether the economy was growing too slowly or too rapidly. Rates had therefore been very volatile. Whenever the market began to suspect that the Federal Reserve would raise rates to curb inflation, rates spiked up.

The interest-rate volatility was an issue that Libris would have to address in preparing a proposal for Ruhl. Should the loan (or loans) be priced at a fixed rate or at a floating rate? Fixed-rate loans were generally offered at a premium of 2.5 percent to 1 percent above the floating rate.

In adjusting the prime rate to the conditions of the borrower, Caslon bank officers often used what they termed a "risk premium" system. This approach added or subtracted 25 basis points (2.5 percent) to the price for such factors as the size of the company's sales (add points for small size and lack of access to public markets), purpose, term, escalating versus level payments, debt profile, liquidity posture, and (subtract points for) relationship benefits (for example, balances, tax payments and corporate trust). Of course, the final rate had to be checked against the market, which in Padgett's case was highly competitive as the result of Phoenix's interest.

Because of the complications that had already been experienced and that were likely to arise while completing the negotiations, Libris knew that he had no more time to collect information. He had to work quickly toward a satisfactory resolution of the loan structure with Padgett's management.

EXHIBIT 1 | Income Statements for the Fiscal Years Ended April 30, 1993–96 (thousands of dollars except per-share figures)

	1993	1994	1995	1996
Net sales	$26,331	$27,219	$36,897	$41,308
Cost of goods sold	15,728	16,077	21,937	24,555
Depreciation and amortization	*	510	667	739
	$10,603	$10,632	$14,293	$16,014
General and admin. expense	5,814	5,087	7,139	7,821
Selling expense	—	1,878	2,603	3,147
Operating expenses	$ 5,814	$ 6,965	$ 9,742	$10,968
Operating profit	$ 4,789	$ 3,667	$ 4,551	$ 5,046
Interest expense	—	32	220	379
Other expenses (income)	83	(42)	(39)	(71)
Profit before taxes	$ 4,706	$ 3,677	$ 4,370	$ 4,738
Income taxes	2,702	1,893	2,216	2,132
Profit after taxes	$ 2,004	$ 1,784	$ 2,154	$ 2,606
Number of shares (000)	1,000	1,115	1,116	1,118
Earnings per share	$2.00	$1.60	$1.93	$2.33
Dividends per share	1.00	1.00	1.00	1.00

*Included in cost of goods sold in 1993.
—Included in general and administrative expenses in 1993.

EXHIBIT 2 | Balance Sheets as of April 30, 1993–96 (thousands of dollars)

	1993	1994	1995	1996
Assets				
Current Assets				
Cash and securities	$ 1,691	$ 266	$ 658	$ 834
Accounts receivable	4,734	5,542	6,350	7,754
Inventory	7,276	7,743	10,959	14,360
Prepayments and other	233	194	153	563
Total current assets	$13,934	$13,745	$18,120	$23,511
Property, plant, equip.	—	8,718	11,265	12,468
Less: accumulated deprec.	—	3,384	4,912	5,209
Net prop., plant, equip.	$ 4,797	$ 5,334	$ 6,353	$ 7,259
Other assets	59	257	386	224
Total assets	$18,790	$19,336	$24,859	$30,994
Liabilities and Owners' Equity				
Current Liabilities				
Short-term notes	$ —	$ —	$ 3,118	$ 7,221
Accounts payable	1,127	1,619	2,158	1,958
Accruals	395	397	703	1,014
Other current liabilities	271	251	418	824
Current portion, long-term debt	615	117	51	52
Total current liabilities	$ 2,408	$ 2,384	$ 6,448	$11,069
Long-term debt	338	221	507	455
Deferred taxes	538	568	714	756
Other liabilities	136	126	116	151
Total liabilities	$ 3,420	$ 3,299	$ 7,785	$12,431
Owners' Equity				
Common stock	5,587	5,587	5,587	5,587
Retained earnings	9,783	10,450	11,487	12,976
Total owners' equity	$15,370	$16,037	$17,074	$18,563
Total liabilities and net worth	$18,790	$19,336	$24,859	$30,994

EXHIBIT 3 | Cash Flow and Ratio Analysis, Fiscal Years Ended April 30, 1993–96 (dollar figures in thousands)

Cash Flow	1993	1994	1995	1996
Sources				
Profit after taxes plus deprec. and amort.*		$ 2,294	$ 2,821	$ 3,345
Deferred taxes		30	146	42
New long-term debt		—	337	—
New short-term debt		—	3,118	4,103
Accounts payable		492	539	(200)
Accruals		2	306	311
Other current liabilities		(20)	167	406
Other liabilities		(10)	(10)	35
Total sources		$ 2,788	$ 7,424	$ 8,042
Uses				
Dividends paid in cash		$ 1,117	$ 1,117	$ 1,117
Capital expenditure		979	1,575	1,530
Repayment of long-term debt		615	117	51
Accounts receivable		808	808	1,404
Inventory		467	3,216	3,401
Prepayments and other current assets		(39)	(41)	410
Other assets		198	129	(162)
Intangibles*		68	111	115
Total uses		$ 4,213	$ 7,032	$ 7,866
Change in cash and securities		$(1,425)	$ 392	$ 176
Working capital	$11,526	$11,361	$11,672	$12,442

Ratio Analysis	1993	1994	1995	1996
Profitability				
Sales growth	n.a.	3.4%	35.6%	12.0%
Gross profit margin	40.3%	39.1	38.7	38.8
Operating expenses/sales	22.1	25.6	26.4	26.5
Pretax margin	17.9	13.5	11.8	11.5
After-tax margin	7.6	6.6	5.8	6.3
Return on avg. owners' equity	n.a.	11.4	13.0	14.6
Return on total assets	10.7	9.2	8.7	8.4
EBIT/total assets	25.0	19.2	18.5	16.5
Dividend payout	50.2	62.6	51.9	42.9
Turnover on Sales				
Receivables	5.6×	4.9×	5.8×	5.3×
Inventory	3.6	3.5	3.4	2.9
Accounts payable	23.4	16.8	17.1	21.1
Working capital	2.3	2.4	3.2	3.3
Fixed asset	5.5	5.1	5.8	5.7
Net worth	1.7	1.7	2.2	2.2
Leverage				
Total debt/owners' equity	22.3%	20.6%	45.6%	67.0%
Long-term debt/owners' equity	2.2	1.4	2.9	2.4
Interest coverage	n.a.	115.9×	20.9×	13.5×
Liquidity				
Quick ratio	2.7×	2.4×	1.1×	0.8×
Current ratio	5.8	5.8	2.8	2.1

*Intangibles amortized as purchased.

n.a. = not applicable.

EXHIBIT 4 | Summary Figures from Preliminary Projection of Financial Position, Fiscal Years Ending April 30, 1997–2000 (millions of dollars)

	1997	1998	1999	2000
Sources of Funds				
Net sales	$55.2	$60.7	$66.8	$73.5
Profit after taxes	3.3	3.6	4.2	4.8
Noncash charges	.9	.9	1.0	1.1
Cash generated from operations	$ 4.2	$ 4.5	$ 5.2	$ 5.9
Disposition of assets	.2	—	—	—
Total sources	$ 4.4	$ 4.5	$ 5.2	$ 5.9
Uses of Funds				
Dividends	$ 1.1	$ 1.1	$ 1.1	$ 1.1
Increase in working capital*	2.4	2.4	3.1	3.6
Capital expenditures	1.0	1.0	1.0	1.0
	$ 4.5	$ 4.5	$ 5.2	$ 5.7
Effect on Short-Term Debt				
*Including retirement of short-term debt:	0.7	0.2	0.8	1.1
Leaving a balance in short-term debt of	$ 6.5	$ 6.3	$ 5.5	$ 4.4

Assumptions:

1. 10% sales growth
2. 6% to 6.5% after-tax margin
3. Accounts receivable turnover 5.7 (17.5% of sales)
4. Inventory turnover 3.6 (27.8% of sales)
5. Accounts payable turnover 21.3 (4.7% of sales)

Totals may not add because of rounding.

EXHIBIT 5 | Libris's Letter Outlining Proposed Term-Loan Arrangement

Caslon Trust Company
Broad Street Commercial Lending Center
1111 Broad Street
Richmond, Virginia

Francis X. Libris
Vice President and Manager

May 15, 1996

John Ruhl
Vice President–Finance
Padgett Paper Products Company
Richmond, Virginia

Dear John:

Thank you for the opportunity last week to review the financial plans you have for Padgett. This letter sets forth our thoughts relating to the need for properly incorporating your bank loan into those plans.

Currently, Padgett has $6,853,000 outstanding in short-term 90-day notes, and we understand that an additional $1.0 million to $1.5 million is likely to be borrowed to support new receivables of your new acquisition. This is in contrast with the circumstance of May 1994 when we financed your previous acquisition, and our loan outstanding increased from $500,000 to $1,850,000. At that time, an anticipated restructuring of the loan was postponed until a clearer definition of longer term corporate cash need could be ascertained.

In late 1995, we expressed an interest in discussing with you a restructuring of the current loan outstanding so that legitimately long-term funds could be sourced on a proper long-term basis. Our subsequent conversations and cash flow study were complicated by the anticipated major acquisition and its impact.

Enclosed is a copy of our most recent Padgett forecast, the results of which we have jointly reviewed. On balance, our feeling is that the forecast may tend to understate the cash requirement in that it assumes moderate sales growth, the upholding of traditional margins, and tight control over capital expenditures and dividends. The forecast does seem to indicate a long-term need of at least $5 million, which cannot be properly funded through the bank on anything resembling a full-payout term-loan basis.

Given what appears to be the clear nature of the need, it seems appropriate that financing discussions with an insurance company be initiated. This suggestion is rooted in our firm feeling that it is strategically unwise from the standpoint of the company, as well as that of the bank, to fulfill substantial long-term financial need through the continued use of 90-day notes.

On a confidential basis and without revealing your name, we have talked with three insurance companies within the last week. Discussions included the following generalized parameters for life-insurance company lending:

Amount:	no problem
Term:	12–15 years
Rate:	fixed, 9.5 percent minimum
Payback:	level payments desired but flexibility offered (e.g., three years of grace)
Prepayment:	all want protection designed to discourage it; however, there are provisions for prepayment without penalty if they were to turn you down for a requested increase in the amount and you were able to obtain a commitment from another source
Availability of money:	good

Caslon would continue to provide for Padgett's seasonal working-capital financing on a floating prime-rate basis. Our pricing, based on the structure of the long-term debt outlined, would probably be prime plus 0.5 percent.

We all recognize the fact that interest rates have started to rise again. Our Economics Department does not feel that long-term interest rates will see reduced levels in the foreseeable future. Financing demands on the capital markets are expected to continue strong, inflation psychology seems to be rising, the deficits are not yet under control, and any advantage to be gained in avoiding the long-term market is, at best, marginal. It might, in fact, be dangerous.

For any needs consistent with prudent bank lending, Caslon Trust stands ready to finance your business. Our desire to assist in every way we can is complete and sincere.

Sincerely,

Frank

Francis X. Libris
Vice President

EXHIBIT 6 | Projected Financial Statements for Fiscal Years Ending April 30, 1998–2000 Assuming 5 Percent, 10 Percent, and 15 Percent Sales Growth (dollar figures in millions except per-share amounts)

	1996 Actual	1997 Est.	5% Growth			10% Growth			15% Growth		
			1998	1999	2000	1998	1999	2000	1998	1999	2000
Income Statements											
Sales, net	$41.32	$57.80	$60.69	$63.72	$66.91	$63.58	$69.94	$76.93	$66.47	$76.44	$87.91
Cost of sales	24.56	36.08	37.27	38.86	40.81	39.05	42.65	46.93	40.82	46.61	53.61
Deprec. & amort.	0.74	0.94	0.91	1.00	1.10	0.91	1.00	1.10	0.91	1.00	1.10
General & admin.	7.82	10.23	10.75	11.29	11.87	11.27	12.42	13.69	11.81	13.64	15.72
Selling expense	3.15	4.61	4.84	5.09	5.35	5.08	5.60	6.15	5.30	6.11	7.03
Operating profit	$ 5.05	$ 5.94	$ 6.92	$ 7.48	$ 7.78	$ 7.27	$ 8.27	$ 9.06	$ 7.63	$ 9.08	$10.45
Interest expenses*	0.38	0.95	0.80	0.72	0.61	0.89	0.84	0.77	.97	1.01	1.05
Other exp. (income)	(.07)	(.71)	0.07	0.07	0.07	0.07	0.07	0.07	0.07	0.07	0.07
Pretax earnings	$ 4.74	$ 5.70	$ 6.05	$ 6.69	$ 7.10	$ 6.31	$ 7.36	$ 8.22	$ 6.59	$ 8.00	$ 9.33
After-tax earnings	2.61	3.42	3.63	4.01	4.26	3.79	4.42	4.93	3.95	4.80	5.60
Earnings per share on 1,118,000 shares	$ 2.33	$ 3.06	$ 3.25	$ 3.59	$ 3.81	$ 3.39	$ 3.95	$ 4.41	$ 3.54	$ 4.29	$ 5.01
Dividends per share	1.00	1.03	1.08	1.19	1.27	1.13	1.31	1.47	1.18	1.43	1.66

*Includes interest calculated on the cash deficit at 8.5%.

Note: Figures may not add because of rounding.

EXHIBIT 6 | (continued)

	1996 Actual	1997 Est.	5% Growth			10% Growth			15% Growth		
			1998	1999	2000	1998	1999	2000	1998	1999	2000
Balance Sheets											
Assets											
Cash (minimum)	$ .83	$ 1.17	$ 1.23	$ 1.29	$ 1.36	$ 1.29	$ 1.42	$ 1.56	$ 1.35	$ 1.55	$ 1.78
Excess cash	—	—	.01	.73	1.24	—	—	—	—	—	—
Acc. receivable	7.75	10.12	10.62	11.15	11.71	11.13	12.24	13.46	11.63	13.38	15.38
Inventory	14.36	16.18	16.99	17.84	18.74	17.80	19.58	21.54	18.61	21.40	24.61
Prepayments, etc.	.56	.23	.24	.26	.27	.26	.28	.31	.27	.31	.36
Total current assets	$23.51	$27.71	$29.10	$31.27	$33.32	$30.48	$33.52	$36.87	$31.86	$36.64	$42.14
Plant & equip.	12.47	13.27	14.27	15.27	16.27	14.27	15.27	16.27	14.27	15.27	16.27
Less: accum. deprec.	5.21	6.04	6.95	7.95	9.05	6.95	7.95	9.05	6.95	7.95	9.05
Net plant & equip.	$ 7.26	$ 7.23	$ 7.32	$ 7.32	$ 7.22	$ 7.32	$ 7.32	$ 7.22	$ 7.32	$ 7.32	$ 7.22
Other	.22	.11	.11	.11	.11	.11	.11	.11	.11	.11	.11
Total assets	$30.99	$35.05	$36.54	$38.71	$40.65	$37.91	$40.95	$44.20	$39.29	$44.07	$49.47
Liabilities and Owners' Equity											
Short-term notes	$ 7.22	$ 7.45	$ 6.29	$ 5.50	$ 4.35	$ 6.29	$ 5.50	$ 4.35	$ 6.29	$ 5.50	$ 4.35
Acc. payable	1.96	2.72	2.85	3.00	3.14	2.99	3.29	3.62	3.12	3.59	4.13
Accruals	1.01	1.44	1.52	1.59	1.67	1.59	1.75	1.92	1.66	1.91	2.20
Other	.82	1.15	1.21	1.33	1.40	1.27	1.39	1.53	1.33	1.61	1.85
Current portion, LTD	.05	.05	.05	.05	.05	.05	.05	.05	.05	.05	.05
Total current liab.	$11.06	$12.82	$11.93	$11.48	$10.61	$12.19	$11.98	$11.47	$12.45	$12.66	$12.58
Long-term debt	.46	.40	.35	.30	.25	.35	.30	.25	.35	.30	.25
Deferred taxes	.76	.80	.80	.80	.80	.80	.80	.80	.80	.80	.80
Other	.15	.20	.20	.20	.20	.20	.20	.20	.20	.20	.20
Cash deficit*	n.a.	n.a.	n.a.	n.a.	n.a.	1.02	1.37	1.89	2.02	3.44	5.23
Total liabilities	$12.43	$14.22	$13.28	$12.78	$11.86	$14.56	$14.65	$14.61	$15.82	$17.40	$19.06
Common stock	5.59	5.59	5.59	5.59	5.59	5.59	5.59	5.59	5.59	5.59	5.59
Retained earnings	12.98	15.24	17.67	20.34	23.18	17.76	20.71	24.00	17.88	21.09	24.82
Total owners' equity	$18.56	$20.83	$23.25	$25.93	$28.77	$23.35	$26.30	$29.59	$23.47	$26.68	$30.41
Total liability & owners' equity	$30.99	$35.05	$36.53	$38.71	$40.63	$37.91	$40.95	$44.20	$39.29	$44.07	$49.47

*Includes interest calculated on the cash deficit at 8.5%.

n.a. = not applicable.

EXHIBIT 6 | (continued)

	1996 Actual	1997 Est.	5% Growth			10% Growth			15% Growth		
			1998	1999	2000	1998	1999	2000	1998	1999	2000
Cash Flow											
Sources											
After-tax earnings		$ 3.42	$ 3.63	$ 4.01	$ 4.26	$ 3.79	$ 4.42	$ 4.93	$ 3.95	$ 4.80	$ 5.59
Noncash charges		.94	.91	1.00	1.10	.91	1.00	1.10	.91	1.00	1.10
Funds from operations		$ 4.36	$ 4.54	$ 5.01	$ 5.36	$ 4.70	$ 5.42	$ 6.03	$ 4.86	$ 5.80	$ 6.69
Deferred taxes		.04	—	—	—	—	—	—	—	—	—
Accounts payable		.76	.14	.14	.14	.27	.30	.33	.41	.47	.54
Accruals		.43	.07	.07	.08	.14	.16	.17	.22	.25	.29
Other and miscellaneous current liabilities		.33	.06	.12	.07	.12	.12	.14	.17	.27	.24
Other liabilities		.05	—	—	—	—	—	—	—	—	—
Other assets		.11	—	—	—	—	—	—	—	—	—
Total sources		$ 6.08	$ 4.81	$ 5.34	$ 5.65	$ 5.22	$ 6.00	$ 6.67	$ 5.66	$ 6.79	$ 7.76
Uses											
Dividends		$1.16	$1.21	$1.34	$1.42	$1.26	$1.47	$1.64	$1.31	$1.59	$1.86
Capital expenditures		.80	1.00	1.00	1.00	1.00	1.00	1.00	1.00	1.00	1.00
Short-term debt		(.23)	1.16	.79	1.15	1.16	.79	1.15	1.16	.79	1.15
Long-term debt		.05	.05	.05	.05	.05	.05	.05	.05	.05	.05
Minimum cash		.34	.06	.06	.06	.12	.13	.14	.18	.20	.23
Accounts receivable		2.36	.50	.53	.56	1.01	1.11	1.22	1.52	1.74	2.01
Inventory		1.82	.81	.85	.89	1.62	1.78	1.96	2.43	2.79	3.21
Prepay & def. charge		(.33)	.01	.01	.01	.02	.02	.03	.04	.04	.05
Intangibles		.11	—	—	—	—	—	—	—	—	—
Total uses		$6.08	$4.80	$4.63	$5.14	$6.24	$6.35	$7.19	$7.69	$8.20	$9.56
Net cash flow		—	0.02	0.71	0.51	(1.01)	(0.35)	(0.52)	(2.03)	(1.41)	(1.80)
Cumulative		—	0.02	0.73	1.24	(1.01)	(1.36)	(1.88)	(2.02)	(3.43)	(5.23)

EXHIBIT 6 | (continued)

	1996 Actual	1997 Est.	5% Growth			10% Growth			15% Growth		
			1998	1999	2000	1998	1999	2000	1998	1999	2000
Analytical Ratios											
Profitability											
Sales growth	12.0%	39.9%	5.0%	5.0%	5.0%	10.0%	10.0%	10.0%	15.0%	15.0%	15.0%
E.P.S. growth	20.7	31.4	6.2	10.3	6.3	10.8	16.5	11.2	15.5	21.4	16.5
Gross profit margin	38.8	35.9	38.6	39.0	39.0	38.6	39.0	39.0	38.6	39.0	39.0
Operating exp./sales	26.5	25.7	25.7	25.7	25.7	25.7	25.8	25.8	25.7	25.8	25.9
Pretax margin	11.5	10.3	10.0	10.5	10.6	9.9	10.5	10.7	9.9	10.5	10.6
After-tax margin	6.3	5.9	6.0	6.3	6.4	6.0	6.3	6.4	5.9	6.3	6.4
Return on average owners' equity	14.6	17.4	16.5	16.3	15.6	17.1	17.8	17.6	17.9	19.1	19.6
Return on total assets	8.4	9.8	9.9	10.4	10.5	10.0	10.8	11.2	10.1	10.9	11.3
EBIT/total assets	16.5	19.0	18.7	19.1	19.0	19.0	20.1	20.4	19.4	20.7	21.2
Dividend payout	42.9	33.8	33.3	33.3	33.3	33.3	33.3	33.3	33.2	33.2	33.2
Turnover											
Receivables	5.3×	5.7×	5.7×	5.7×	5.7×	5.7×	5.7×	5.7×	5.7×	5.7×	5.7×
Inventory	2.9	3.6	3.6	3.6	3.6	3.6	3.6	3.6	3.6	3.6	3.6
Accounts payable	21.1	21.3	21.3	21.3	21.3	21.3	21.3	21.3	21.3	21.3	21.3
Working capital	3.3	3.6	3.5	3.2	2.9	3.5	3.3	3.0	3.4	3.2	3.0
Fixed asset	5.7	8.0	8.3	8.7	9.3	8.7	9.6	10.6	9.1	10.4	12.2
Net worth	2.2	2.8	2.6	2.4	2.3	2.7	2.6	2.6	2.8	2.9	2.9
Leverage											
Total debt/owners' equity	67.0%	68.3%	57.1%	49.3%	41.3%	62.3%	55.7%	49.3%	67.4%	65.2%	62.7%
Long-term debt/ owners' equity	2.4	1.9	1.5	1.1	0.9	1.5	1.1	0.8	1.5	1.1	0.8
Interest coverage	13.5	7.0	8.7	10.3	12.6	8.0	9.6	11.1	7.5	8.3	8.9
Liquidity											
Quick ratio	0.8×	1.0×	1.0×	1.1×	1.3×	1.0×	1.1×	1.3×	1.1×	1.2×	1.4×
Current ratio	2.1	2.2	2.4	2.7	3.1	2.5	2.8	3.2	2.6	2.9	3.3
Working capital	$12.44	$14.89	$19.40	$29.98	$29.55	$18.29	$21.46	$25.23	$19.40	$23.98	$29.55

Kota Fibres, Ltd.

Ms. Pundir, the managing director and principal owner of Kota Fibres, Ltd., discovered the problem when she arrived at the parking lot of the company's plant one morning in early January 2001. Trucks filled with rolls of fiber yarns were being unloaded, but they had been loaded just the night before and had been ready to depart that morning. The fiber was intended for customers who had been badgering Pundir to fill their orders in a timely manner. The government tax inspector, who was stationed at the company's warehouse, would not clear the trucks for departure because the excise tax had not been paid. The tax inspector required a cash payment, but in seeking to draw funds for the excise tax that morning, Mr. Mehta, the bookkeeper, discovered that the company had overdrawn its bank account again—the third time in as many weeks. The truck drivers were independent contractors who refused to wait while the company and government settled their accounts. They cursed loudly as they unloaded the trucks.

This shipment would not leave for at least another two days, and angry customers would no doubt require an explanation. Before granting a loan with which to pay the excise tax, the branch manager of the All-India Bank & Trust Company had requested a meeting with Pundir for the next day to discuss Kota's financial condition and its plans for restoring the firm's liquidity.

Pundir told Mehta, "This cash problem is most vexing. I don't understand it. We're a very profitable enterprise, yet we seem to have to depend increasingly on the bank. Why do we need more loans just as our heavy selling season begins? We can't repeat this blunder."

Company Background

Kota Fibres, Ltd., was founded in 1962 to produce nylon fiber at its only plant in Kota, India, about 100 kilometers (km) south of New Delhi. By using new technology and domestic raw materials, the firm had developed a steady franchise among

This case was written by Thien T. Pham under the direction of Robert F. Bruner as a basis for class discussion rather than to illustrate effective or ineffective handling of an administrative situation. The financial support of the Batten Institute is gratefully acknowledged. Copyright © 2001 by the University of Virginia Darden School Foundation, Charlottesville, VA. All rights reserved. *To order copies, send an e-mail to* sales@dardenpublishing.com. *No part of this publication may be reproduced, stored in a retrieval system, used in a spreadsheet, or transmitted in any form or by any means—electronic, mechanical, photocopying, recording, or otherwise—without the permission of the Darden School Foundation.*

dozens of small, local textile weavers. It supplied synthetic fiber yarns used to weave colorful cloths for making saris, the traditional women's dress of India. On average, each sari required eight yards of cloth. An Indian woman typically would buy three saris a year. With India's female population at around 500 million, the demand for saris accounted for more than 12 billion yards of fabric. This demand was currently being supplied entirely from domestic textile mills that, in turn, filled their yarn requirements from suppliers such as Kota Fibres.

Synthetic-Textile Market

The demand for synthetic textiles was stable with year-to-year growth and predictable seasonal fluctuations. Unit demand increased with both population and national income. In addition, India's population celebrated hundreds of festivals each year, in deference to a host of deities, at which saris were traditionally worn. The most important festival, the Diwali celebration in mid-autumn, caused a seasonal peak in the demand for new saris, which in turn caused a seasonal peak in demand for nylon textiles in late summer and early fall. Thus, the seasonal demand for nylon yarn would peak in mid-summer. Unit growth in the industry was expected to be 15 percent per year.

Consumers purchased saris and textiles from cloth merchants located in the villages around the country. A cloth merchant was an important local figure usually well known to area residents; the merchant generally granted credit to support consumer purchases. Merchants maintained relatively low levels of inventory and built stocks of goods only shortly in advance of and during the peak selling season.

Competition among suppliers (the many small textile-weaving mills) to those merchants was keen and was affected by price, service, and the credit that the mills could grant to the merchants. The mills essentially produced to order, building their inventories of woven cloth shortly in advance of the peak selling season and keeping only maintenance stocks at other times of the year.

The yarn manufacturers competed for the business of the mills through responsive service and credit. The suppliers to the yarn manufacturers provided little or no trade credit. Being near the origin of the textile chain in India, the yarn manufacturers essentially banked the downstream activities of the industry.

Production and Distribution System

Thin profit margins had prompted Pundir to adopt policies against overproduction and overstocking, which would require Kota to carry inventories through the slack selling season. She had adopted a plan of seasonal production, which meant that the yarn plant would operate at peak capacity for two months of the year and at modest levels the rest of the year. That policy imposed an annual ritual of hirings and layoffs.

To help ensure prompt service, Kota Fibres maintained two distribution warehouses, but getting the finished yarn quickly from the factory in Kota to the customers was a challenge. The roads were narrow and mostly in poor repair. A truck could take

10 to 15 days to negotiate the trip between Calcutta and Kota, a distance of about 1,100 km, and except when they passed through cities, the highways had only one lane. When two cars or trucks met, they had to slow down and squeeze past each other or else stop and wait for the traffic to pass. Journeys were slow and dangerous, and accidents were frequent.

Company Performance

Kota Fibres had been consistently profitable. Moreover, sales had grown at an annual rate of 18 percent in the year 2000. Gross sales were projected to reach (Indian rupees) INR90.9 million in the fiscal year that ended December 31, 2001 (see **Exhibit 1**).[1] Net profits reached INR2.6 million in 2000. **Exhibits 2** and **3** present recent financial statements for the firm.

Reassessment

After the episode in the parking lot, Pundir and her bookkeeper went to her office to analyze the situation. She pushed aside the several items on her desk to which she had intended to devote her morning: a letter from a field sales manager requesting permission to grant favorable credit terms to a new customer (see **Exhibit 4**); a note from the transportation manager regarding a possible change in the inventory policy (**Exhibit 5**); a proposal from the purchasing agent regarding the delivery lead times of certain supplies (**Exhibit 6**); and a proposal from the operations manager for a scheme of level annual production (**Exhibit 7**).

To prepare a forecast on a business-as-usual basis, Pundir and Mehta agreed on various parameters. Cost of goods sold would run at 73.7 percent of gross sales—a figure that was up from recent years because of increasing price competition. Operating expenses would be about 6 percent of sales—also up from recent years to include the addition of a quality-control department, two new sales agents, and three young nephews with whom she hoped to build an allegiance to the Pundir family business. The company's income tax rate was 30 percent and, although accrued monthly, was actually paid quarterly in March, June, September, and December. The excise tax (at 15 percent of sales) was different from the income tax and was collected at the factory gate as trucks left to make deliveries to customers and the regional warehouses. Pundir proposed to pay dividends of INR500,000 per quarter to the 11 members of her extended family who held the entire equity of the firm. For years Kota had paid high dividends. The Pundir family believed that excess funds left in the firm were at greater risk than if the funds were returned to shareholders.

Mehta observed that sales collections in any given month had been running steadily at the rate of 40 percent of the last month's sales plus 60 percent of the sales from the month before last. The value of the raw materials purchased in any month represented on average 55 percent of the value of sales expected to be made two

---

[1]At the time, the rupee was pegged to the U.S. dollar at the rate of 46.5 rupees per dollar.

months later. Wages and other expenses in a given month were equivalent to about 34 percent of purchases in the previous month. As a matter of policy, Pundir wanted to see a cash balance of no less than INR750,000.

Kota Fibres had a line of credit at the All-India Bank & Trust Company, where it also maintained its cash balances. All-India's short-term interest rate was currently 14.5 percent, but Mehta was worried that inflation and interest rates might rise in the coming year. The seasonal line of credit had to be cleaned up for at least 30 days each year. The usual cleanup month had been October,[2] but Kota Fibres had failed to make a full repayment at that time. Only after strong assurances by Pundir that she would clean up the loan in November or December had the bank lending officer reluctantly agreed to waive the cleanup requirement in October. Unfortunately, the credit needs of Kota Fibres did not abate as rapidly as expected in November and December, and although his protests increased each month, the lending officer agreed to meet Kota's cash requirements with loans. Now he was refusing to extend any more seasonal credit until Pundir presented a reasonable financial plan for the company that demonstrated its ability to clean up the loan by the end of 2001.

Financial Forecast

Mehta hurriedly developed a monthly forecast of financial statements using the current operating assumptions (see **Exhibit 8**). As an alternative way of looking at the forecasted fund flows, Mehta also prepared a forecast of cash receipts and disbursements (**Exhibit 9**). The monthly T-accounts underlying the forecasts are given in **Exhibit 10,** and a summary of the forecast assumptions is in **Exhibit 11.**

Mehta handed over the forecast to Pundir with a graph showing projected sales and month-end debt outstanding (**Exhibit 12**). After studying the forecasts for a few moments, Pundir expostulated:

> This is worse than I expected. The numbers show that we can't repay All-India's loan by the end of December. The loan officer will not accept this forecast as a basis for more credit. We need a new plan, and fast. We need those loans in order to scale up for the most important part of our business season. Let's go over these assumptions in detail and look for any opportunities to improve our debt position.

Then, casting her gaze toward the stack of memos she had pushed aside earlier, she muttered, "Perhaps some of these proposals will help."

---

[2]The selection of October as the loan-cleanup month was imposed by the bank on the grounds of tradition. Seasonal loans of any type made by the bank were to be cleaned up in October. Pundir had seen no reason previously to challenge the bank's tradition.

EXHIBIT 1 | Summary of Monthly Sales, Actual for 2000 and Forecast for 2001 (in Rupees)

	2000 (Actual)	2001 (Forecast)
January	2,012,400	2,616,120
February	2,314,260	2,892,825
March	3,421,080	4,447,404
April	7,043,400	8,804,250
May	12,074,400	13,885,560
June	15,294,240	17,588,376
July	14,187,420	16,315,533
August	7,144,020	8,572,824
September	4,024,800	5,031,000
October	3,421,080	4,447,404
November	2,716,740	3,531,762
December	2,213,640	2,767,050
Year	**75,867,480**	**90,900,108**

EXHIBIT 2 | Annual Income Statements, Actual and Forecast (in Rupees)

	1999 (Actual)	2000 (Actual)	2001 (Forecast)
Gross sales	64,487,358	75,867,480	90,900,108
Excise tax	9,673,104	11,380,122	13,635,016
Net sales	54,814,254	64,487,358	77,265,092
Cost of goods	44,496,277	53,865,911	66,993,380
Gross profits	**10,317,978**	**10,621,447**	**10,271,712**
Operating expenses	3,497,305	4,828,721	5,454,006
Depreciation	769,103	908,608	1,073,731
Interest expense	910,048	1,240,066	1,835,620
Profit before tax	**5,141,521**	**3,644,052**	**1,908,355**
Income tax	1,542,456	1,093,216	572,506
Net profit	**3,599,065**	**2,550,837**	**1,335,848**

EXHIBIT 3 | Balance Sheets, Actual and Forecast (in Rupees)

	2000 (Actual)	2001 (Forecast)
Cash	762,323	750,000
Accounts receivable	2,672,729	3,715,152
Inventories	1,249,185	2,225,373
Total Current Assets	**4,684,237**	**6,690,525**
Gross PP&E	10,095,646	11,495,646
Accumulated depreciation	1,484,278	2,558,009
Net PP&E	8,611,368	8,937,637
Total Assets	**13,295,604**	**15,628,161**
Accounts payable	759,535	1,157,298
Notes to bank (deposits at bank)	684,102	3,463,701
Accrued taxes	0	(180,654)
Total Current Liabilities	**1,443,637**	**4,440,345**
Owners' equity	11,851,967	11,187,816
Total Liabilities and Equity	**13,295,604**	**15,628,161**

EXHIBIT 4 | Memo from Field Sales Manager

To: G. Pundir
From: A. Bajpai

January 7, 2001

As you know, Pondicherry Textiles is considering making us their prime yarn supplier for this year. Purchases would be in the neighborhood of INR6 million and are not reflected in our current sales forecast. Pondicherry would be one of our largest accounts. They have accepted our terms on price, but have asked for credit terms of 80 days, net. Unless we extend our credit terms, Pondicherry will not do business with us. We can expect that Pondicherry will purchase our yarn across the year in about the same pattern as our other customers.

If you approve this exception to our standard terms (45 days), the Pondicherry district sales office will meet its quarterly sales quota immediately. Please indicate your approval below.

Approved:

_____

EXHIBIT 5 | Memo from Transportation Manager

To: G. Pundir
From: R. Sikh

January 2, 2001

As you asked me to, I have been tracking our supply shipments in the last six months. The new road between Kota and New Delhi has improved reliability of the shipments significantly. Our supplier's new manufacturing equipment is now running consistently, and they have been meeting their shipment dates consistently. As a result, I would propose that we reduce our raw-material inventory requirement from 60 days to 30 days. This would reduce the amount of inventory we are carrying by one month, and should free up a lot of space in the warehouse. I am not sure if that will affect any other department since we will be buying the same amount of material, but it would make inventory tracking a lot easier for me. Please let me know so we can implement this in January.

EXHIBIT 6 | Memo from Purchasing Agent

To: G. Pundir
From: R. Mohan

January 5, 2001

Hibachi Chemicals of Yokohama has approached us with a proposal to supply us with poly-ester pellets on a "just-in-time" basis from their plant in Majala (20 km away). Those pellets account for 35 percent of our raw-material purchases. I am looking into the feasibility of this scheme—in particular, whether Hibachi can actually perform on that basis—and will report back in two weeks. If the proposal is feasible, it would reduce our inventory of pellets from 60 days outstanding to only 2 or 3 days.

EXHIBIT 7 | Memo from Operations Manager

To: G. Pundir
From: L. Gupta

January 7, 2001

You asked me to estimate the production efficiencies arising from a scheme of level annual production. In essence, there are significant advantages to be gained:

- Gross profit margin would rise by 2 percent or 3 percent, reflecting labor savings and production efficiencies gained from a stable work force and the absence of certain seasonal training and setup costs.
- Seasonal hirings and layoffs would no longer be necessary, permitting us to cultivate a stronger work force and, perhaps, to suppress labor unrest. You will recall that the unions have indicated that reducing seasonal layoffs will be one of their major negotiating objectives this year.
- Level production entails lower manufacturing risk. With the load spread throughout the year, we would suffer less from equipment breakdowns and could better match the routine maintenance with the demand on the plant and equipment.

EXHIBIT 8 | Monthly Forecast of Income Statements and Balance Sheets for 2001 (in Rupees)

	January	February	March	April	May	June	July	August	September	October	November	December
Gross sales	2,616,120	2,892,825	4,447,404	8,804,250	13,885,560	17,588,376	16,315,533	8,572,824	5,031,000	4,447,404	3,531,762	2,767,050
Excise taxes	392,418	433,924	667,111	1,320,638	2,082,834	2,638,256	2,447,330	1,285,924	754,650	667,111	529,764	415,058
Net sales	2,223,702	2,458,901	3,780,293	7,483,613	11,802,726	14,950,120	13,868,203	7,286,900	4,276,350	3,780,293	3,001,998	2,351,993
Cost of goods sold	1,928,080	2,132,012	3,277,737	6,488,732	10,233,658	12,962,633	12,024,548	6,318,171	3,707,847	3,277,737	2,606,909	2,039,316
Gross profit	295,622	326,889	502,557	994,880	1,569,068	1,987,486	1,843,655	968,729	568,503	502,557	399,089	312,677
Operating expenses	454,501	454,501	454,501	454,501	454,501	454,501	454,501	454,501	454,501	454,501	454,501	454,501
Depreciation	84,130	84,130	87,047	87,047	87,047	89,964	89,964	89,964	92,880	92,880	92,880	95,797
Interest expense (income)[1]	11,058	24,825	70,867	158,210	268,352	362,187	363,212	259,568	145,898	80,686	50,025	40,731
Profit before taxes	(254,068)	(236,566)	(109,858)	295,123	759,168	1,080,835	935,979	164,697	(124,776)	(125,510)	(198,317)	(278,352)
Income taxes	(76,220)	(70,970)	(32,957)	88,537	227,751	324,251	280,794	49,409	(37,433)	(37,653)	(59,495)	(83,506)
Net profit	(177,847)	(165,596)	(76,900)	206,586	531,418	756,585	655,185	115,288	(87,343)	(87,857)	(138,822)	(194,847)
Assets												
Cash[2]	750,000	750,000	750,000	750,000	750,000	750,000	750,000	750,000	750,000	750,000	750,000	750,000
Accounts receivable[3]	2,773,349	3,291,542	5,012,144	10,301,737	17,997,155	24,748,757	25,697,603	17,191,189	9,003,739	6,295,049	5,029,249	3,715,152
Inventories[4]	2,308,135	5,850,125	11,855,841	17,637,315	19,666,227	14,469,652	6,815,272	3,883,970	2,950,257	1,854,837	1,639,892	2,225,373
Total current assets	5,831,484	9,891,667	17,617,985	28,689,052	38,413,382	39,968,409	33,262,875	21,825,159	12,703,996	8,899,886	7,419,142	6,690,525
Net prop. plant & equip.[5]	8,527,237	8,443,107	8,706,060	8,619,013	8,531,966	8,792,002	8,702,038	8,612,075	8,869,194	8,776,314	8,683,434	8,937,637
Total assets	14,358,721	18,334,774	26,324,045	37,308,065	46,945,348	48,760,411	41,964,914	30,437,233	21,573,190	17,676,200	16,102,575	15,628,161
Liabilities and Owners' Equity												
Accounts payable[6]	1,614,553	4,010,818	6,805,539	8,842,088	8,142,024	3,883,534	1,935,531	1,614,553	1,110,950	690,358	1,039,007	1,157,298
Note payable—bank[7]	1,146,268	2,962,622	8,767,030	17,419,379	26,997,556	32,950,665	27,167,192	15,795,793	8,352,899	5,002,010	3,278,054	3,463,701
Accrued taxes[8]	(76,220)	(147,190)	(180,148)	(91,611)	136,140	0	280,794	330,203	0	(37,653)	(97,148)	(180,654)
Total current liabilities	2,684,601	6,826,250	15,392,421	26,169,856	35,275,720	36,834,199	29,383,517	17,740,548	9,463,849	5,654,715	4,219,913	4,440,345
Shareholders' equity[9]	11,674,120	11,508,524	10,931,623	11,138,209	11,669,627	11,926,212	12,581,397	12,696,685	12,109,341	12,021,484	11,882,662	11,187,816
Total liabilities & equity	14,358,721	18,334,774	26,324,045	37,308,065	46,945,348	48,760,411	41,964,914	30,437,233	21,573,190	17,676,200	16,102,575	15,628,161

[1]Interest expense = Notes Payable * 14.5%/12 months.
[2]See Exhibit 9.
[3]See panel 1, Exhibit 10.
[4]See panel 2, Exhibit 10.
[5]See panel 6, Exhibit 10.
[6]See panel 3, Exhibit 10.
[7]Plug figure.
[8]See panel 5, Exhibit 10.
[9]See panel 4, Exhibit 10.

EXHIBIT 9 | Schedule of Cash Receipts and Disbursements for 2001 (in Rupees)

	January	February	March	April	May	June	July	August	September	October	November	December
Assume:												
Sales	2,616,120	2,892,825	4,447,404	8,804,250	13,885,560	17,588,376	16,315,533	8,572,824	5,031,000	4,447,404	3,531,762	2,767,050
Purchases[1]	2,446,072	4,842,338	7,637,058	9,673,607	8,973,543	4,715,053	2,767,050	2,446,072	1,942,469	1,521,878	1,870,526	1,988,817
Debt outstanding	1,146,268	2,962,622	8,767,030	17,419,379	26,997,556	32,950,665	27,167,192	15,795,793	8,352,899	5,002,010	3,278,054	3,463,701
Receipts:												
Accts. rcvble. collected	2,515,500	2,374,632	2,726,802	3,514,657	6,190,142	10,836,774	15,366,686	17,079,239	13,218,449	7,156,094	4,797,562	4,081,147
New borrowings (repayments)	462,166	1,816,354	5,804,408	8,652,349	9,578,178	5,953,108	(5,783,473)	(11,371,400)	(7,442,894)	(3,350,889)	(1,723,956)	185,647
Disbursements:												
Accounts paid[2]	1,591,054	2,446,072	4,842,338	7,637,058	9,673,607	8,973,543	4,715,053	2,767,050	2,446,072	1,942,469	1,521,878	1,870,526
Capital expenditures	0	0	350,000	0	0	350,000	0	0	350,000	0	0	350,000
Interest payments	11,058	24,825	70,867	158,210	268,352	362,187	363,212	259,568	145,898	80,686	50,025	40,731
Excise tax paid	392,418	433,924	667,111	1,320,638	2,082,834	2,638,256	2,447,330	1,285,924	754,650	667,111	529,764	415,058
Operating expenses	454,501	454,501	454,501	454,501	454,501	454,501	454,501	454,501	454,501	454,501	454,501	454,501
Accrued income tax paid	0	0	0	0	0	460,390	0	0	292,770	0	0	0
Wages	540,958	831,665	1,646,395	2,596,600	3,289,026	3,051,005	1,603,118	940,797	831,665	660,439	517,438	635,979
Dividends	0	0	500,000	0	0	500,000	0	0	500,000	0	0	500,000
Subtotal: Disbursements	2,989,989	4,190,986	8,531,210	12,167,005	15,768,320	16,789,882	9,583,214	5,707,839	5,775,555	3,805,206	3,073,606	4,266,794
Receipts – Disbursements	(12,323)	0	0	0	0	0	0	0	0	0	0	0
Beginning of period cash balance	762,323	750,000	750,000	750,000	750,000	750,000	750,000	750,000	750,000	750,000	750,000	750,000
End of period cash balance	750,000	750,000	750,000	750,000	750,000	750,000	750,000	750,000	750,000	750,000	750,000	750,000

[1]Equal to 55 percent of sales in period (T+2).
[2]Equal to purchases in period (T-1).

143

EXHIBIT 10 | Forecast T-Accounts Supporting Financial Statements (in Rupees)

	January	February	March	April	May	June	July	August	September	October	November	December
1. Schedule of Accounts Receivable												
Beginning of period	2,672,729	2,773,349	3,291,542	5,012,144	10,301,737	17,997,155	24,748,757	25,697,603	17,191,189	9,003,739	6,295,049	5,029,249
Plus sales	2,616,120	2,892,825	4,447,404	8,804,250	13,885,560	17,588,376	16,315,533	8,572,824	5,031,000	4,447,404	3,531,762	2,767,050
Less collections, Last month[1]	885,456	1,046,448	1,157,130	1,778,962	3,521,700	5,554,224	7,035,350	6,526,213	3,429,130	2,012,400	1,778,962	1,412,705
Less collections, Month before last[2]	1,630,044	1,328,184	1,569,672	1,735,695	2,668,442	5,282,550	8,331,336	10,553,026	9,789,320	5,143,694	3,018,600	2,668,442
End of period	2,773,349	3,291,542	5,012,144	10,301,737	17,997,155	24,748,757	25,697,603	17,191,189	9,003,739	6,295,049	5,029,249	3,715,152

[1]40% of sales in period (T−1).
[2]60% of sales in period (T−2).

	January	February	March	April	May	June	July	August	September	October	November	December
2. Schedule of Inventories												
Beginning of period	1,249,185	2,308,135	5,850,125	11,855,841	17,637,315	19,666,227	14,469,652	6,815,272	3,883,970	2,950,257	1,854,837	1,639,892
Plus purchases[1]	2,446,072	4,842,338	7,637,058	9,673,607	8,973,543	4,715,053	2,767,050	2,446,072	1,942,469	1,521,878	1,870,526	1,988,817
Plus labor	540,958	831,665	1,646,395	2,596,600	3,289,026	3,051,005	1,603,118	940,797	831,665	660,439	517,438	635,979
Less shipments (COGS)	1,928,080	2,132,012	3,277,737	6,488,732	10,233,658	12,962,633	12,024,548	6,318,171	3,707,847	3,277,737	2,602,909	2,039,316
End of period	2,308,135	5,850,125	11,855,841	17,637,315	19,666,227	14,469,652	6,815,272	3,883,970	2,950,257	1,854,837	1,639,892	2,225,373

[1]Equal to 55 percent of sales in period (T+2).

	January	February	March	April	May	June	July	August	September	October	November	December
3. Schedule of Accounts Payable												
Beginning of period	759,535	1,614,553	4,010,818	6,805,539	8,842,088	8,142,024	3,883,534	1,935,531	1,614,553	1,110,950	690,358	1,039,007
+ Purchases[1]	2,446,072	4,842,338	7,637,058	9,673,607	8,973,543	4,715,053	2,767,050	2,446,072	1,942,469	1,521,878	1,870,526	1,988,817
− Payments[2]	1,591,054	2,446,072	4,842,338	7,637,058	9,673,607	8,973,543	4,715,053	2,767,050	2,446,072	1,942,469	1,521,878	1,870,526
End of period	1,614,553	4,010,818	6,805,539	8,842,088	8,142,024	3,883,534	1,935,531	1,614,553	1,110,950	690,358	1,039,007	1,157,298

[1]Equal to 55 percent of sales in period (T+2).
[2]Equal to purchases in period (T−1).

(continued)

EXHIBIT 10 I Forecast T-Accounts Supporting Financial Statements (in Rupees) *(continued)*

	January	February	March	April	May	June	July	August	September	October	November	December
4. Schedule of Shareholders' Equity												
Beginning of period	11,851,967	11,674,120	11,508,524	10,931,623	11,138,209	11,669,627	11,926,212	12,581,397	12,696,685	12,109,341	12,021,484	11,882,662
Plus net profit	(177,847)	(165,596)	(76,900)	206,586	531,418	756,585	655,185	115,288	(87,343)	(87,857)	(138,822)	(194,847)
Less dividends	0	0	500,000	0	0	500,000	0	0	500,000	0	0	500,000
End of period	11,674,120	11,508,524	10,931,623	11,138,209	11,669,627	11,926,212	12,581,397	12,696,685	12,109,341	12,021,484	11,882,662	11,187,816
5. Schedule of Accrued Taxes												
Beginning of period	0	(76,220)	(147,190)	(180,148)	(91,611)	136,140	0	280,794	330,203	0	(37,653)	(97,148)
Plus monthly tax expense (@ 30%)	(76,220)	(70,970)	(32,957)	88,537	227,751	324,251	280,794	49,409	(37,433)	(37,653)	(59,495)	(83,506)
Less quarterly tax payments	0	0	0	0	0	460,390	0	0	292,770	0	0	0
End of period	(76,220)	(147,190)	(180,148)	(91,611)	136,140	0	280,794	330,203	0	(37,653)	(97,148)	(180,654)
6. Schedule of Property, Plant, and Equipment												
Beginning gross PP&E	10,095,646	10,095,646	10,095,646	10,445,646	10,445,646	10,445,646	10,795,646	10,795,646	10,795,646	11,145,646	11,145,646	11,145,646
Plus capital expenditures	0	0	350,000	0	0	350,000	0	0	350,000	0	0	350,000
Ending gross PP&E	10,095,646	10,095,646	10,445,646	10,445,646	10,445,646	10,795,646	10,795,646	10,795,646	11,145,646	11,145,646	11,145,646	11,495,646
Monthly depreciation expense	84,130	84,130	87,047	87,047	87,047	89,964	89,964	89,964	92,880	92,880	92,880	95,797
Less cumulative depr'n.	1,568,408	1,652,539	1,739,586	1,826,633	1,913,680	2,003,643	2,093,607	2,183,571	2,276,451	2,369,332	2,462,212	2,558,009
Ending net PP&E	8,527,237	8,443,107	8,706,060	8,619,013	8,531,966	8,792,002	8,702,038	8,612,075	8,869,194	8,776,314	8,683,434	8,937,637

EXHIBIT 11 | Forecast Assumptions

Ratio of:	
Income tax/profit before tax	30%
Excise tax/Sales	15%
This month collections of last month's sales	40%
This month collections of month-before-last sales	60%
Purchases/Sales two months later	55%
Wages/Purchases	34%
Annual operating expenses/Annual sales	6%
Capital expenditures (every third month)	350,000
Interest rate on borrowings (and deposits)	14.5%
Minimum cash balance	750,000
Depreciation/Gross PP&E (per year)	10%
(per month)	0.83%
Dividends Paid (every third month)	500,000

EXHIBIT 12 | Trend of Certain Financial Accounts by Month (in Rupees)

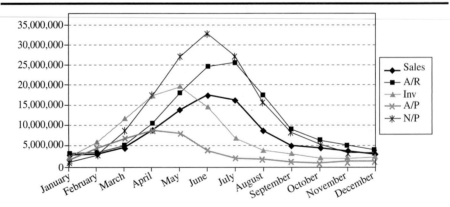

Deutsche Brauerei

In early January 2001, Greta Schweitzer arrived at Deutsche Brauerei[1] to participate in her first meeting of the board of directors. She had recently joined the board at the behest of her uncle, the managing director of the company. Lukas Schweitzer had told her that the board could use her financial expertise in addressing some questions that would come up in the near future, but he would not be specific as to the nature of those questions. The company was owned entirely by 16 uncles, aunts, and cousins from the Schweitzer family. Greta had received an MBA degree from a well-known business school and had worked for the past six years as a commercial-loan officer for a leading bank in Frankfurt, Germany. With the permission of the bank, she agreed to join the Deutsche Brauerei board.

The agenda for the January meeting of the directors consisted of three items of business: (1) approval of the 2001 financial budget, (2) declaration of the quarterly dividend, and (3) adoption of a compensation scheme for Oleg Pinchuk, the company's sales-and-marketing manager. Because she knew little about the company, Greta decided to visit it for a day before the first board meeting.

The Company

Deutsche Brauerei produced two varieties of beer, dark and light, for which it had won quality awards consistently over the years. Its sales and profits in 2000 were (euros) €92.1 million and €2.9 million, respectively.[2] (See **Exhibit 1** for historical and projected financial statements.) Founded in 1737, the Deutsche Brauerei had been in the Schweitzer family for 12 generations. An etching of Gustav Schweitzer, the founder, graced the label of each bottle of beer.

The company was located in a village just outside Munich, Germany. Its modern equipment was capable of producing 1.2 million hectoliters of beer a year. In 2000,

---

[1]In English, "Deutsche Brauerei" (DOI-cha BROI-reye) means "German brewery."

[2]In January 2001, the euro could be exchanged for about US$0.94.

the company sold 1.173 million hectoliters. This equipment was acquired in 1994, following a fire that destroyed the old equipment.

Because of its efficiency improvements and slightly larger size, the new equipment increased the potential output of the brewery. This additional capacity remained unused, however, until late 1998. In that year, Deutsche Brauerei expanded into Ukraine. Following the dissolution of the U.S.S.R., Lukas Schweitzer had envisioned a significant new market for high-quality beer in Eastern Europe, particularly in the former Soviet states, and resolved to penetrate that market. Ukraine was particularly attractive given its relatively larger population of 52 million and its strategic location within Central and Eastern Europe.

In 1995 and 1996, the Ukrainian government embarked on a wave of privatizations and market reforms. The Ukrainian government's posture convinced the Schweitzer family that it was a favorable time to enter the Ukrainian market. After analyzing various entry options, the Schweitzers decided to enter Ukraine through a network of independent distributors. Launched in 1998, Deutsche's beer was an overnight success. Accordingly, Lukas Schweitzer hired Oleg Pinchuk away from a major Ukrainian beer producer to market Deutsche's beer even more aggressively.

The beer won popularity for its full-bodied, malty taste. A factor extrinsic to the product—the fragmented nature of the Ukrainian beer industry—also provided easy entry opportunities for Deutsche Brauerei.

When the Russian debt crisis hit in 1998, the Ukrainian hryvna depreciated by 125 percent within three months (see **Exhibit 2**). The depreciation of the hryvna resulted in lower revenue, profit, and asset values when translated into deutsche marks (Germany's currency in 1998). Because of the popularity of Deutsche's beer, however, the increase in Deutsche Brauerei's volume sales more than offset the negative currency effects.[3] By early 2001, Ukrainian consumers accounted for 28 percent of Deutsche's sales. Further, Ukraine had accounted for most of the unit growth in Deutsche's sales over the past three years.

In Germany, Deutsche Brauerei served its markets through a network of independent distributors. Those distributors purchased Deutsche's beer, stored it temporarily in their own refrigerated warehouses, and ultimately sold it to *their* customers at the retail end of the distribution chain (e.g., stores, restaurants, and hotels). Oleg Pinchuk had adopted a different distribution strategy with regard to Ukraine.

Lunch with Uncle Lukas

After driving down from Frankfurt, Greta's visit began with a luncheon meeting with Lukas Schweitzer. Now 57, Lukas had worked at the brewery for his entire career. His experience had been largely on the production side of the brewery, where he had risen to the position of brewmaster before assuming general management of the company upon the retirement of his father. He said:

---

[3]For 2001 and 2002, the hryvna was not expected to depreciate materially against the euro. As **Exhibit 2** shows, the hryvna had held steady since the Russian default. In January 2001, (Ukrainian hryvna) UAG1 was equivalent to €0.20.

Over the long history of this company, the Schweitzers have had to be brewers, not marketers or finance people. As long as we made an excellent product, we always sold our output at the price we asked. Then, in the 1990s, I realized that we needed more than just production know-how. The collapse of the Berlin Wall, and then the dissolution of the Soviet Union, convinced me that tremendous opportunities existed in Eastern Europe. I hired Oleg Pinchuk to lead this initiative.

I'm quite pleased with what Oleg has been able to accomplish. He has organized five distributorships, taken us from 0 to 211 customer accounts, and set up warehousing arrangements—in 30 months, and on a small budget! He really produces results. I am afraid I will have to pay him a lot more money next year, if I am to keep him. As it is, I paid him €82,344 in 2000, consisting of a base salary of €40,000 and an incentive payment of €41,440, which is calculated as 0.5 percent of the annual sales increase in Ukraine. As you know from my letter to the board of directors, I am proposing increases in both his base salary (to €48,500) and incentive payment (to 0.6 percent of the annual sales increase).

Oleg was very helpful in pulling together the financial plan for 2001 (see **Exhibit 1**). It shows handsomely rising sales and profits! Also, he prepared various analytical presentations, including a sources-and-uses-of-funds statement (**Exhibit 3**) and a detailed ratio analysis (**Exhibit 4**). One very helpful analysis was the break-even chart[4] Oleg prepared (**Exhibit 5**). It shows that, as we increase our volume above the break-even volume, our profits rise disproportionately faster.

If we keep on this growth course, we'll exhaust our existing unused productive capacity by late 2001. The budget for 2001 calls for investment of €7 million in new plant and equipment. For 2002, Oleg has proposed that we invest €6.8 million in a state-of-the-art warehouse and distribution center in Ukraine. He argues that we won't be able to sustain our growth in Ukraine without those major investments. I haven't even begun thinking about how we will finance all this growth. In recent years, we have depended more on short-term bank loans than we used to. I don't know whether we should continue to rely on them to the extent that we have. Right now, we can borrow from our long-standing Hausbank at a 6.5 percent rate of interest.[5] Our banker asked me to meet with him next week to discuss our expansion plans; I'm guessing that he can't wait to get more of our business!

With the improved profits, I am proposing an increase in dividends for this quarter to a total of €698,000, one-fourth of the dividends projected to be paid in 2001. This should keep the Schweitzer family happy. As you know, half of our family stockholders are retirees and

---

[4]This chart shows the relationship between revenues, costs, and volume of output. For instance, revenues are calculated as the volume of hectoliters of beer sold times the unit price of €78.5 per hectoliter. Fixed costs (€24.6 million) remain constant as unit output varies, and are the sum of administration and selling expense plus depreciation. Variable costs are the sum of production costs, excise duties, and allowance for doubtful accounts, or €52.3 per hectoliter. At any given level of output, total costs are the sum of variable and fixed costs. Profits or losses are illustrated as the difference between the revenue and total-cost lines, but note carefully that "profit" here is implicitly defined as earnings before interest and taxes (EBIT). This analysis identifies the break-even volume, where revenues just equal total costs. Deutsche Brauerei's break-even volume was 938,799 hectoliters.

[5]In January 2001, the yield on short-term euro government debt was 4.58 percent.

rely on the dividend to help make ends meet. We have traditionally aimed for a 75 percent dividend payout from earnings each year, to serve our older relatives.

Lukas Schweitzer had been quite talkative during the meal, allowing Greta little opportunity to ask questions or offer her own opinions. She was disquieted by some of the statements she heard, however, and resolved to study the historical and forecast financials in detail. Then, quite abruptly, Uncle Lukas announced that lunch was done and he would take her to meet Oleg Pinchuk.

Meeting with Oleg Pinchuk

After the introductory pleasantries, Greta asked Pinchuk to describe his marketing strategy and achievements in Ukraine. He said:

Our beer almost sells itself; discount pricing and heavy advertising are unwarranted. The challenge is getting people to try it and getting it into a distribution pipeline, so that when the consumer wants to buy more, he or she can do so. But in 1998, the beer-distribution pipeline in Ukraine was nonexistent. I had to go there and set up distributorships from nothing; there were willing entrepreneurs, but they had no capital. I provided the best financing I knew how, in the form of trade-credit concessions. First, I extended credit to distributors in Ukraine who could not bear the terms we customarily gave our distributors in western Germany. I relaxed the terms for those new distributors from 2 percent 10, net 40, to 2 percent 10, net 80.[6] Even on these terms, our distributors are asking for more time to pay; I plan to relax the payment deadline to 90 days. I am confident that we will collect on all of those receivables; my forecast assumes that bad debts as a percentage of accounts receivable will amount to only 2 percent.

These distributors are real entrepreneurs. They started with nothing but their brains. They have great ambitions and learn quickly. Some of them have gotten past due on their payments to us, but I suspect that they will catch up in due course. Virtually all the retailers and restaurateurs we supply are expanding and enhancing their shops, buying modern equipment, and restocking their own inventories—all without the support of big banks like yours in Frankfurt! Most of those retailers can't get bank credit; their "bootstrap" financing is ingenious and admirable. A little delay in payment is understandable. Where we see great opportunity in these distributors, the banks see no collateral, low profits, negative cash flow, and high risk. I know these distributors better than the banks know them. I think we'll make a profit on our investment there. My analysis (see **Exhibit 6**) suggests that we are earning a very high return on our investment in receivables in Ukraine. We borrow at 6.5 percent from our bank in the West, and use those funds to finance receivables in Ukraine that give us a return of about 130 percent!

I should add that the other parts of my marketing strategy involve field warehousing, to permit rapid response to market demand, and quite a lot of missionary activity, to see that our beer receives the proper placement in stores and restaurants. My policy on field

---

[6]"2 percent 10, net 40" means that Deutsche's customer can take a 2 percent discount if payment is made within 10 days of the invoice and that, otherwise, the full payment is due within 40 days.

inventories has been to support the fragile distributor network by carrying a substantial part of the inventory on behalf of the distributor. This resulted in a sizable increase in inventory for the company in 1999 and 2000.

These new marketing policies have paid off handsomely in terms of our unit growth in the new federal states. Sales in Ukraine grew 47 percent in 2000—a rate of increase that I aim to sustain for the foreseeable future. Without my changes in credit and inventory policy, we would have realized only a small fraction of our current level of sales there. In 2001, I hope to establish five more distributors and place our beer in 100 more stores and restaurants.

Greta inquired about the signs of global economic recession. Pinchuk seemed relatively unconcerned. He said, "I don't think Ukraine will be affected. Last year the economy grew 7 percent, and this year it is predicted to grow 10 percent. I expect unit sales in Ukraine to rise significantly in 2001." At the close of their meeting, Greta asked for information on Deutsche's credit customers. Pinchuk supplied several files from which Greta extracted the summary information in **Exhibit 7.**

Conclusion

After a lengthy dinner that evening, at which she met the other directors, Greta returned to the information she had gathered that day. She would need to form an opinion on the three matters coming before the board the next day (the financial plan, the dividend declaration, and the compensation plan for Pinchuk). She also wanted to study the company's reliance on debt financing. The other directors would be interested to know why, if the company was operating so profitably above its break-even volume, it needed to borrow so aggressively. Greta also wondered about the wisdom of Deutsche's aggressive penetration of Ukraine: did rapid sales growth necessarily pay off in terms of more profits or dividends? All this would take more study. She yawned and then poured herself a cup of coffee before returning to scrutinize the numbers.

EXHIBIT 1 | Historical and Projected Income Statements and Balance Sheets (fiscal year ended December 31; all figures in € thousands)

	1997 (Actual)	1998 (Actual)	1999 (Actual)	2000 (Actual)	2001 (Proj'd)	2002 (Proj'd)
Income Statements						
1 Sales: Germany	62,032	62,653	64,219	66,216	68,203	70,249
2 Sales: Ukraine	—	4,262	17,559	25,847	37,479	48,722
3 Net sales	62,032	66,915	81,779	92,064	105,682	118,971
operating expenses:						
4 Production costs and expenses	32,258	35,366	44,271	49,827	61,393	71,609
5 Admin. and selling expenses	12,481	13,014	16,274	18,505	18,500	18,500
6 Depreciation	3,609	4,314	5,844	6,068	6,766	7,448
7 Excise duties	9,143	9,108	10,486	11,557	11,625	13,087
8 Total operating expenses	(57,491)	(61,802)	(76,874)	(85,957)	(98,284)	(110,644)
9 Operating profit	4,541	5,113	4,904	6,106	7,398	8,327
10 Allowance for doubtful accounts	(5)	(7)	(38)	(24)	(201)	(60)
11 Interest expense	(1,185)	(1,064)	(1,046)	(1,304)	(1,468)	(1,634)
12 Earnings before taxes	3,351	4,042	3,821	4,779	5,729	6,633
13 Income taxes	(1,132)	(1,396)	(1,510)	(1,864)	(2,005)	(2,322)
14 Net earnings	2,219	2,646	2,311	2,915	3,724	4,311
Dividends on:						
15 Dividends to all common shares	1,669	1,988	1,734	2,186	2,793	3,234
16 Retentions of earnings	550	658	577	729	931	1,078
Balance Sheets						
Assets						
1 Cash	5,366	8,183	9,813	11,048	12,682	14,277
2 Accounts receivable						
Germany	6,933	7,142	7,222	7,517	7,661	7,891
Ukraine	—	424	4,090	6,168	9,241	12,014
Allowance for doubtful accounts	(69)	(76)	(113)	(137)	(338)	(398)
3 Inventories	6,133	6,401	7,817	12,889	14,795	16,656
4 Total current assets	18,363	22,075	28,829	37,485	44,042	50,439
5 Investments & other assets	3,102	3,189	3,416	3,520	3,500	3,500
6 Gross property, plant, & equipt.	58,435	58,435	60,682	60,682	67,663	74,485
7 Accumulated depreciation	(23,404)	(27,719)	(33,562)	(39,631)	(46,397)	(53,845)
8 Net Property, plant, & equipt.	35,031	30,716	27,120	21,052	21,266	20,639
9 Total assets	56,496	55,981	59,365	62,057	68,808	74,579
Liabilities and Stockholders' Equity						
10 Bank borrowings (short term)	2,987	10,236	12,004	13,089	17,862	21,372
11 Accounts payable	3,578	3,755	4,103	4,792	5,284	5,949
12 Other current liabilities	7,397	7,361	8,996	10,127	11,625	13,087
13 Total current liabilities	13,962	21,352	25,103	28,009	34,771	40,407
14 Long term debt: Bank borrowings	16,107	7,544	6,601	5,658	4,715	3,772
15 Shareholders' equity	26,427	27,085	27,661	28,390	29,321	30,399
16 Total liabs. & stockholders' equity	56,496	55,981	59,365	62,057	68,808	74,579

Source: Casewriter analysis.

EXHIBIT 2 | Historical Exchange Rates: Ukrainian Hryvna to Deutsche Mark/Euro

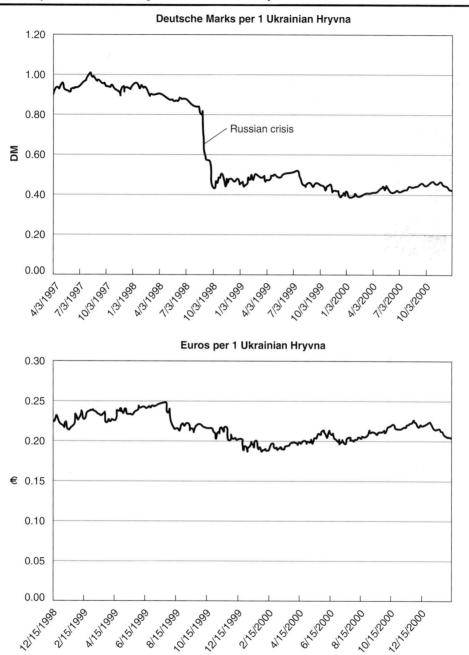

Source: http://www.oanda.com/convert/fxhistory.

EXHIBIT 3 | Sources-and-Uses-of-Funds Statements (fiscal year ending December 31; all figures in € thousands)

	1997 (Actual)	1998 (Actual)	1999 (Actual)	2000 (Actual)	2001 (Proj'd)	2002 (Proj'd)
Sources of Funds						
1 Net income		2,646	2,311	2,915	3,724	4,311
2 Increases in allowance for doubtful accts.		7	38	24	201	60
3 Depreciation		4,314	5,844	6,068	6,766	7,448
4 Increases in short-term debt		7,249	1,768	1,085	4,773	3510
5 Increases in accounts payable		177	348	690	492	664
6 Increases in other current liabilities		(36)	1,635	1,131	1,498	1,462
7 **Total Sources of Cash**		**14,357**	**11,943**	**11,913**	**17,454**	**17,456**
Uses of Funds						
8 Dividend payments		1,988	1,734	2,186	2,793	3,234
9 Increases in cash balance		2,817	1,630	1,234	1,634	1,595
10 Increases in accts. receivable (Germany)		209	79	296	144	230
11 Increases in accts. receivable (Ukraine)		424	3,665	2,078	3,074	2,772
12 Increases in inventories		267	1,417	5,072	1,906	1,861
13 Increases in other assets		87	227	104	(20)	0
14 Reductions in long-term debt		8,563	943	943	943	943
15 Capital expenditures		0	2,247	0	6,980	6,822
16 **Total Uses of Cash**		**14,357**	**11,943**	**11,913**	**17,454**	**17,456**

Source: Casewriter analysis.

EXHIBIT 4 | Ratio Analyses of Historical and Projected Financial Statements (fiscal year ended December 31)

	1997 (Actual)	1998 (Actual)	1999 (Actual)	2000 (Actual)	2001 (Proj'd)	2002 (Proj'd)
Profitability						
1 Operating profit margin (%)	7.3%	7.6%	6.0%	6.6%	7.0%	7.0%
2 Average tax rate (%)	33.8%	34.5%	39.5%	39.0%	35.0%	35.0%
3 Return on sales (%)	3.6%	4.0%	2.8%	3.2%	3.5%	3.6%
4 Return of equity (%)	8.4%	9.8%	8.4%	10.3%	12.7%	14.2%
5 Return on net assets (%)	6.5%	7.4%	6.9%	8.4%	9.3%	9.7%
6 Return on assets (%)	3.9%	4.7%	3.9%	4.7%	5.4%	5.8%
Leverage						
7 Debt/Equity ratio (%)	72.3%	65.6%	67.3%	66.0%	77.0%	82.7%
8 Debt/Total capital (%)	41.9%	39.6%	40.2%	39.8%	43.5%	45.3%
9 EBIT/Interest (x)	3.8	4.8	4.7	4.7	5.0	5.1
Asset Utilization						
10 Sales/Assets	1.10	1.20	1.38	1.48	1.54	1.60
11 Sales growth rate (%)	4.0%	7.9%	22.2%	12.6%	14.8%	12.6%
12 Assets growth rate (%)	6.0%	−0.9%	6.0%	4.5%	10.9%	8.4%
13 Receivables growth rate (%)	4.0%	9.1%	49.5%	21.0%	23.5%	17.8%
14 Receivables growth rate: Germany	4.0%	3.0%	1.1%	4.1%	1.9%	3.0%
15 Receivables growth rate: Ukraine	0.0%	nmf	863.5%	50.8%	49.8%	30.0%
16 Days in receivables	40.8	41.3	50.5	54.3	58.4	61.1
17 Days in receivables: Germany	40.8	41.6	41.0	41.4	41.0	41.0
18 Days in receivables: Ukraine	nmf	36.3	85.0	87.1	90.0	90.0
19 Payables to sales	5.8%	5.6%	5.0%	5.2%	5.0%	5.0%
20 Inventories to sales	9.9%	9.6%	9.6%	14.0%	14.0%	14.0%
Liquidity						
21 Current ratio	1.32	1.03	1.15	1.34	1.27	1.25
22 Quick ratio	0.88	0.73	0.84	0.88	0.84	0.84

Notes: These financial ratios show the performance of the firm in four important areas:

Profitability is measured both in terms of *profit or expense margins* (lines 1–3) and as *investment returns* (lines 4–6). Investors will focus on the latter measures of profitability.

Leverage ratios measure the use of short-term and long-term debt financing by the firm. In general, higher usage of debt increases the risk of the firm. Higher ratios of debt to equity and to capital (lines 7 and 8) suggest higher financial risk. The ratio of EBIT to interest expense measures the ability of the firm to "cover" its interest payments; lower levels of this ratio suggest higher risk (line 9).

Asset-utilization ratios measure the efficiency of asset use. For instance, the sales-to-assets ratio (line 10) shows how many euros of sales are generated per euro of assets; a higher figure suggests more efficiency, while a lower figure suggests less efficiency. Over the long term, differences in the growth rates of sales (line 11) and assets (line 12) can lead to production problems of over- or undercapacity. Days in receivables (lines 16–18) shows how many days it takes to collect the average credit sale; the longer it takes, the greater the investment in receivables.

Liquidity ratios measure the resources available to meet short-term financial commitments. The current ratio (line 21) is the ratio of all current assets to all current liabilities. The quick ratio (line 22) is the ratio of only cash and receivables (i.e., those assets that can be liquidated quickly) to all current liabilities.

nmf = not a meaningful figure.

EXHIBIT 5 | Break-Even Chart

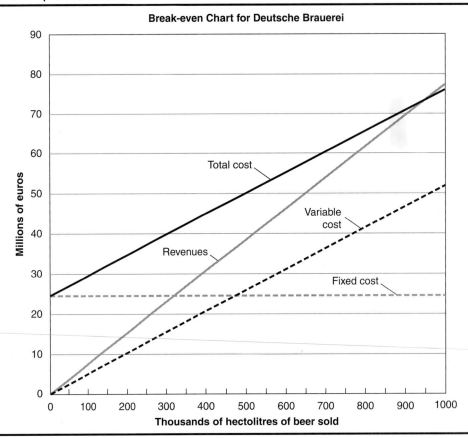

Break-even Chart for Deutsche Brauerei

Source: Casewriter analysis.

EXHIBIT 6 | Oleg Pinchuk's Analysis of the Return on Investment from Investment in Accounts
Receivable in Ukraine

To: Lukas Schweitzer

From: Oleg Pinchuk

The following table illustrates the high profitability we have achieved on our investment in receivables in Ukraine.
We can look forward to a return of about 120–130 percent on our receivables from the East.

The return on investment is calculated as follows:

$$Return\ on\ investment = \frac{Marginal\ after\text{-}tax\ profit\ contribution}{Required\ marginal\ investment}$$

The numerator is simply the profits we earn on new sales each year in Ukraine. It excludes the fixed costs
because we assume those costs have been covered: we want to focus only on the *marginal* events. Also, it
assumes that, without the extension of credit, no sales growth would occur in Ukraine. The denominator is Deutsche's
investment in the receivables. This is *not* the face amount of the receivables; it is only the cash outlay for the product
underlying the receivable. Accordingly, for 2001, the calculation is:

$$Investment\ in\ accounts\ receivable\ (AR) = (Variable\ costs \div Sales) \times Change\ in\ AR$$
$$= (€52.31 \div €78.49) \times €3{,}073{,}536 = €2{,}048{,}512$$

Assumptions

Revenue per HL (€)	78.49
Variable Costs per HL (€)	52.31
Contribution Percentage	33%
Tax Rate	35%

	1997 (Actual)	1998 (Actual)	1999 (Actual)	2000 (Actual)	2001 (Proj'd)	2002 (Proj'd)
Sales in Ukraine (€, thousands)	—	4,262	17,559	25,847	37,479	48,722
Change in sales (€, thousands)	—	4,262	13,297	8,288	11,631	11,244
Variable costs on the marginal sales	—	(2,841)	(8,863)	(5,524)	(7,752)	(7,494)
Contribution on the marginal sales	—	1,421	4,435	2,764	3,879	3,750
Taxes on the marginal contribution	—	(497)	(1,552)	(967)	(1,358)	(1,312)
Marginal After-tax Profits (€ thousands)	—	924	2,883	1,797	2,521	2,437
Variable costs/Sales	—	67%	67%	67%	67%	67%
Change in accounts receivable, Ukraine (€ thousands)	—	424	3,665	2,078	3,074	2,772
Investment in Accts. Receivable (€ thousands)	—	283	2,443	1,385	2,049	1,848
Return on Marginal Investment in Receivables	0%	327%	118%	130%	123%	132%

EXHIBIT 7 | Selected Information on Deutsche's Distributors in Ukraine

Deutsche Distributors by City:	Kharkiv	Dnipropetrovsk	Odessa	Donetsk	Kiev	Composite Ratios, German Beer-Distribution Industry
Income Data						
Net sales, 2000	€2,530,935	€2,024,748	€2,812,150	€843,645	€3,475,255	n.a.
Operating profit/sales	1.8%	2.2%	3.0%	1.1%	3.5%	3.7%
Pretax profit/sales	1.7%	1.9%	2.3%	0.7%	3.1%	3.5%
Assets (as % of total)						
Trade receivables	12.9%	13.5%	16.5%	19.5%	13.0%	12.0%
Inventory	15.1%	19.0%	30.0%	25.0%	22.0%	31.0%
Fixed assets	33.1%	29.1%	25.0%	21.0%	28.0%	24.0%
Total	100.0%	100.0%	100.0%	100.0%	100.0%	100.0%
Liabilities						
Short-term bank borrowings	0.1%	2.1%	1.5%	2.5%	4.0%	15.0%
Trade payables	29.2%	32.2%	28.7%	37.5%	19.0%	16.3%
Total current liabs.	35.0%	41.0%	33.2%	43.2%	27.0%	39.4%
Long-term debt	2.5%	0.0%	3.0%	0.0%	5.0%	16.0%
Net worth	32.5%	59.0%	63.8%	56.2%	68.0%	44.6%
Total	100.0%	100.0%	100.0%	100.0%	100.0%	100.0%
Ratios						
Current ratio	1.1	1.2	1.1	0.9	1.6	1.4
Days' sales outstanding	27.7	25.9	27.4	39.5	19.8	19.4
Sales/assets	2.0	1.9	2.2	1.8	2.4	2.3
Pretax profit/assets	2.9%	3.6%	5.1%	1.3%	7.4%	8.0%
Debt/equity	8.0%	3.6%	7.1%	4.4%	13.2%	69.5%

Source: Casewriter analysis.

n.a. = not applicable.

ServerVault: "Reliable, Secure, and Wicked Fast"

In early July 2000, Patrick Sweeney and Jim Zinn, respectively the president/CEO and CFO of ServerVault, prepared for a series of meetings with private investors and venture capital firms from which they hoped to raise the capital to grow their firm. ServerVault had been founded eight months before and had demonstrated the efficacy of its business model. Now Sweeney and Zinn sought to implement an ambitious plan of expansion. They knew that prospective investors would want an estimate of the firm's rate of cash consumption, known as the "burn rate." Therefore, they sought to have a forecast of the next two and a half years for the firm's statement of cash flows (SOCF) prepared on a monthly basis in order to reflect their plan of expansion. From this they hoped to identify the timing and amount of funds to be sought in the firm's capital-raising program.

Hosting Industry Overview

Companies in the hosting industry offered businesses and individuals the infrastructure to operate Internet-based applications, ranging from simple Web sites to sites featuring complex commercial transactions. Web sites were streamed into the Internet from powerful desktop-size computers, called "servers." Hosting companies offered physical space for the servers and supporting services. Web-hosting customers, like the customers of other outsourcing services, used the service to avoid the attention and expense of maintaining hardware or providing personnel to make Internet applications work. Hosting offered investors an "infrastructure play" in the Internet world. They offered an analogy to describe the role of hosting: "We are the arms merchant to the Internet. We don't care who's fighting, just as long as they continue to fight." Because infrastructure players supplied the capacity to compete on the fast-growing

This case was prepared by J. Chadwick Rynbrandt and Robert F. Bruner from field research. Some financial data have been disguised; some other information has been simplified to clarify the issues. It is intended to serve as the basis for classroom discussion rather than to illustrate effective or ineffective managerial action. Copyright © 2000 by the University of Virginia Darden School Foundation, Charlottesville, VA. All rights reserved. *To order copies, send an e-mail to* sales@dardenpublishing.com. *No part of this publication may be reproduced, stored in a retrieval system, used in a spreadsheet, or transmitted in any form or by any means—electronic, mechanical, photocopying, recording, or otherwise—without the permission of the Darden School Foundation.* Rev. 11/01.

Internet and generated cash flows from their inception, the capital market rewarded those firms with high valuation multiples. According to one analyst, Web-hosting companies faced a bright future as "they ride two transforming tailwinds . . . growth of the Internet and the trend toward business outsourcing."[1]

The industry featured three hosting business models: shared, co-location, and managed. **Exhibit 1** summarizes the characteristics of each. At the most basic level, all types of hosting offered the minimum "power, pipes, and paint." That is, they rented space in a building with constantly available power and Internet connections. From there, the three business models varied:

- **Shared** hosting put multiple customers on one server to share memory, processing power, and server space. Customers who had simple Internet needs usually preferred this option where they shared a host-owned server with other customers. Leading shared hosting providers (with 1999 revenues in millions of dollars) were PSINet ($555), Verio ($258), and Concentric ($147).[2]

- **Co-location** customers rented building space instead of hard-drive space. Hosts in this segment targeted customers who owned and managed their own servers but lacked a highly powered, cooled space and a reliable connection to the Internet. In some cases, co-location providers offered additional services (e.g., data backup). Leading co-location hosting providers (with 1999 revenues in millions of dollars) were BBN/GTE Internetworking ($1,036), Exodus Communications ($242), Qwest ($143), and Global Center ($79).

- **Managed** hosting introduced more value-added services to the hosting customer, mainly managing the equipment and applications of the customer. Companies with a significant Internet presence or high volume e-commerce would be more likely to choose this complete outsourcing solution. Leading managed hosting providers (with 1999 revenues in millions of dollars) were Digex ($59.8), IBM ($47), and Data Return ($7.1). ServerVault most likely would be classified in this segment, though Sweeney argued that ServerVault offered a much higher level of service than other firms in this group.

Hosting companies could differentiate themselves beyond type of service. Other important elements of hosting service were the level of physical and electronic security and the stability of power and Internet connections. Hosts offering the highest service provided completely reliable access to the server ("100 percent availability")—anything that might compromise access to the server, such as a damaged machine or a lost Internet connection, would be mitigated through the redundancy of capacity and system security.

Exhibit 2 shows the rapid growth expected in each of the three segments. By 2004, total revenues in the industry would approach $13 billion. The "managed" segment of service was expected to account for the majority of growth. The "shared" and "co-location" segments, in contrast, would not see much growth and would likely turn into commodity markets. Pricing pressure would be strong, so a hosting company that

---

[1]Jim Linnehan, Kevin Monroe, John Sharko, Peter DeCaprio, and Kent Siefers, "Hosting the New Economy: A White Paper on the Hosting Service Industry," Thomas Weisel Partners, 29 March 2000.

[2]The classification of firms into the three categories and their revenues are drawn from Linnehan, et al.

wanted to compete in that segment would need to find a differentiable service that made its customers less price-sensitive. An alternative strategy was to acquire the services necessary to make it a player in the "managed" segment—recent announcements[3] of acquisition talks had generated a flurry of speculation about the industry.

ServerVault's Business

ServerVault was founded in early 1999, when Patrick Sweeney, a second-generation IT professional and a high tech director at the real estate firm Trammell Crow, convinced Jim Zinn, former CFO of Capital One, to support Sweeney's attempt to carve out a niche in the hosting industry. Zinn joined first as an investor and then as CFO of the startup.

With ServerVault, Sweeney and Zinn created a company that served a segment of hosting customers who were Internet-reliant and security-savvy. ServerVault wanted customers whose Internet applications were so important that security and reliability drove the selection of a hosting provider. They were also targeting customers who wanted the end-to-end solution that "managed" hosting provided. At the core, ServerVault's promise was to provide "managed" hosting services that, according to the firm's motto, were "reliable, secure, and wicked fast."

ServerVault differentiated itself most clearly in the "secure" part of its promise. The firm offered seven layers of security protection **(Exhibit 3).** The result was a level of protection that met the U.S. Department of Defense security standards. For example, the physical layer (i.e., the facility) included a vault-like structure within an already-secure building. The vault, also known as the data center, contained row after row of server racks, each holding up to 25 machines. The vault was specially manufactured to be able to withstand the most destructive forces of nature. Reaching the vault required passing through a "man-trap" where visitors were screened for proper authorization to enter the facility. Once at the vault, only those ServerVault employees who had total security clearances could enter; for security reasons, customers were required to take a virtual tour.

ServerVault's promises of reliability and speed were met by redundant bandwidth and power supply. Each facility had four to five providers of Internet access. Should access to one of them become unavailable, traffic was instantly rerouted to another available bandwidth. Similarly, each facility had multiple electricity generators that were able to provide ample electricity should a power outage occur.

ServerVault derived revenue from three sources: one-time setup fees for new servers, monthly hosting fees, and fees for additional value-added services. Each facility was designed to generate four or five times more revenue per square foot than those of its competitors. The cash costs for the business occurred mainly upfront. Building each facility required a significant investment. The variable cost of adding

---

[3]Exodus Communications had announced preliminary talks to acquire Global Crossing, Ltd.'s Global-Center, Inc., unit for about $6.5 billion in stock. Nippon Telegraph & Telephone Corporation agreed to acquire Verio, Inc., and WorldCom Corporation acquired Digex's parent, Intermedia Communications, Inc., for $3 billion in stock plus $3 billion in assumed debt.

servers and maintaining them was comparatively small. Thus, when a ServerVault facility reached maximum capacity, it produced a significant and reliable stream of cash that amply covered the total costs. The challenge for Sweeney and Zinn was to fill each facility as quickly as possible because, once a facility had been built, the majority of expenses had been incurred. Every additional server hosted in a facility contributed a large profit over its variable costs. Sweeney mused that the hosting facilities were similar in their economics to a newly completed hotel waiting for guests.

Plans for Growth

As Sweeney and Zinn looked forward, they faced a major decision regarding the pace of expansion. Their first small-scale facility in the Washington, D.C., area was complete and was starting to fill up. Given the "land rush" that was taking place in the hosting market, Sweeney and Zinn felt pressure to gain a first-mover advantage by building additional facilities as quickly as possible. They planned to build a second, full-size facility in Dulles, Virginia, in September 2000. After that, they planned to establish a European presence in Dublin, Ireland, by opening a facility in January 2001. Other high-potential areas for future facilities included Silicon Valley, Boston, Austin (Texas), and Asia.

ServerVault faced two major constraints on its expansion. First, growth required employees. Each facility required 20 to 30 full-time employees, and ServerVault wanted to "hire only the best." But, as the best could be very hard to find, the job market affected the rate at which the firm could expand. In addition, ServerVault's corporate staff was still growing and refining their skills to optimally support the facilities.

The second constraint, cash, was even more pressing in the minds of Sweeney and Zinn. **Exhibit 4** shows the statement of cash flows for the first six months of 2000 for ServerVault. After raising enough money in 1999 to start the first facility and to build the corporate staff, ServerVault faced a cash crunch in May 2000. Accordingly, Sweeney and Zinn obtained a $2 million bridge loan from an Irish venture capitalist.[4] The $2 million would support operations for a few months, but in order to build any more facilities, a major capital infusion was needed. In the next few days, Sweeney and Zinn would need to decide how much capital they needed and when they needed it, given their growth plans.

Financial Forecast

Answering those important questions required a monthly forecast of ServerVault's cash flows for the next three years. Sweeney and Zinn discussed several assumptions that would be needed to build the forecast:

- **Capital expenditures.** Each new facility would cost $5 million to $6 million and could hold approximately 5,000 servers, depending on size. Assuming that

---

[4]The bridge loan would convert into equity at the next issuance of equity. Because the Irish investor had invested its capital months before new equity would be issued, the Irish loan would convert to shares at a discounted price per share. So, for example, if new equity were issued in September 2000 at $10 per share, the Irish investor would be allowed to convert its $2 million loan to equity at a price of $8 per share.

ServerVault could raise as much capital as it needed, Zinn estimated that it could add one more facility (Dulles) by the end of 2000, followed by one each quarter beginning in January 2001. Sweeney believed that the corporate staff could not support faster expansion. An alternative assumption for the forecast was for ServerVault to build a new facility only when it reached capacity in existing facilities.

- **Server costs.** Because ServerVault planned to own the servers in its facilities, it would need to purchase them as customer demand ramped up. ServerVault wanted to offer its customers a choice of server manufacturers. Zinn estimated that, on average, new servers (including the necessary software) would cost $3,000 each, representing an average mix of different configurations.

- **Server revenue.** Zinn compiled a forecast for growth in the number of servers hosted. He assumed a growth rate that started at 50 percent and gradually decreased to 10 percent by the end of the three-year period. His estimates are contained in **Exhibit 5.** For planning purposes, Zinn also estimated that the one-time setup fees for new servers would be $500 each (net of sales-force commissions).[5] Monthly recurring hosting fees were conservatively estimated to be $750 per server.

- **Services revenue.** Additional value-added services were offered on a server-by-server basis. Zinn believed that ServerVault would initially start at $50 of service revenue per server per month.

- **Operating expenses.** Each facility required people and bandwidth to operate. Zinn and ServerVault's manager of human resources estimated that each facility would require 20 to 30 people at an average cost of $7,000 per month per person, including benefits. ServerVault's redundant bandwidth design would translate into monthly expenses of $25,000 per month for each facility. Two other operating expenses were relevant to the forecast—marketing and administrative. ServerVault's growth plans would require aggressive marketing in the form of advertising and discounts. Zinn believed that marketing expenses would be run at $100,000 per month for the rest of 2000, $150,000 per month during 2001, and $200,000 per month for 2002. As for administrative expenses, Zinn estimated that $50,000 per month would cover the corporate staff, utilities, and miscellaneous items.

Financing Needs

Given their experience over the past months, Sweeney and Zinn knew that they would need funding soon. Friends, family, and "angel" investors[6] had provided the funds to get the business off the ground. Then, in May, the $2-million bridge loan came at a pivotal time, when their cash balance had declined to about $100,000. They expected that a similar "crunch point" would arise in the future.

---

[5]The setup fee for new servers was actually projected to grow each year.

[6]Startup companies typically went through different rounds of financing as they grew. In many cases, an entrepreneur's friends, family, or individual "angel" investors provided seed capital at the very beginning. Once those sources of funds ran dry, startups would then seek a significant investment from a venture capital or private equity fund to launch the high-growth phase of the business.

Accordingly, Sweeney and Zinn turned their eyes toward the two meetings that awaited them. Both were with venture capitalists who were interested in taking an equity stake in ServerVault in exchange for a cash investment. The amount to be raised would depend on capital market conditions and the appetite of investors. One might hypothesize an issue of equity capital in July 2000 that would raise as little as $5 million or as much as $15 million. This reflected recent conditions in the market for "new economy" sector equities and for venture capital: between March and June 2000, the NASDAQ index had plummeted 40 percent, reflecting investor disillusionment with prospects in that sector. One journalist wrote:

> America's Internet companies continue to burn prodigious amounts of cash, raising the prospect that dozens more will disappear from the landscape over the next 12 months. But the deteriorating cash position of the Internet universe as a whole masks the fact that an important change is taking place: The players are rapidly becoming separated into winners and losers.[7]

Against that backdrop, Sweeney and Zinn knew that, among other topics, the investors would cover three questions. First, how long could ServerVault go without any additional cash? Second, how much cash should they aim to raise in the next round of financing in order to keep the company going for the 12 months beyond that point? Third, when would ServerVault become a net producer of cash rather than a net user?

As he reviewed the existing and potential competition in the managed segment of the hosting industry, Patrick Sweeney observed: "One big problem is that people are promising what they can't deliver. We *can* deliver what we promise. But the general gap between talk and delivery means we have to sell harder to our investors and customers." Nevertheless, he was confident that the market would recognize and reward ServerVault's value proposition.

Now was the time to seize the opportunity through a program of rapid expansion of the number of facilities. Investors would want to know: How much cash should the firm seek to raise? When? What would be ServerVault's burn rate and the key drivers of that rate?

---

[7] Jack Willoughby, "Smoldering: 'Net Companies, still Burning Cash, try to Conserve Tinder," *Barron's,* 2 October 2000, 38.

EXHIBIT 1 | Comparison of Different Types of Hosting

	Shared	Co-location	Managed
Who is responsible for "power, pipes, and paint"?	Host	Host	Host
Who manages the equipment?	Host	Customer	Host
Is the server shared among customers or dedicated to one?	Shared	Dedicated	Dedicated
Are value-added services offered?	Rarely	Occasionally	Always
Who are the typical customers?	Small businesses and individuals that want a Web page	Businesses that own and manage their own servers	Businesses that want a complete, outsourced solution
What is the primary benefit?	Hard-drive space on an Internet server	Building space for servers, with power, cooling, and connectivity	Security, application maintenance, and outsourced technical staff

EXHIBIT 2 | Projected Size of Web-Hosting Segments

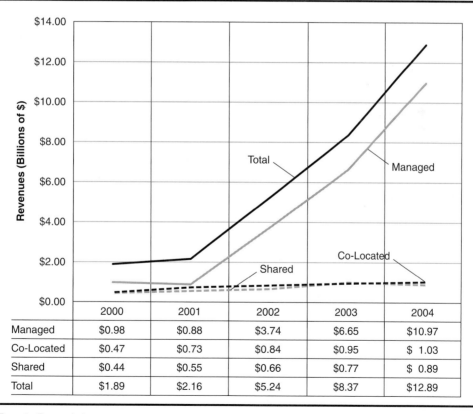

	2000	2001	2002	2003	2004
Managed	$0.98	$0.88	$3.74	$6.65	$10.97
Co-Located	$0.47	$0.73	$0.84	$0.95	$ 1.03
Shared	$0.44	$0.55	$0.66	$0.77	$ 0.89
Total	$1.89	$2.16	$5.24	$8.37	$12.89

Source: Forrester Research, Inc.

EXHIBIT 3 | Seven Layers of Security at ServerVault

Application

To support familiar Internet applications like HTTP, FTP, Telnet, and Mail, ServerVault provides robust messaging, security, and directory services, including redundant ACE servers for one-time password authentication and SSL certificate distribution for secure VPN-based systems management. Extensive use of parallel and load balancing systems ensures that your content is available.

Presentation

To provide data translation and reformatting between different applications, ServerVault has adopted the industry's best network management and monitoring solutions. The information from all of those systems flows through a single fault-tolerant real-time management application, and converts the network statistics into a real-time heads-up picture of current performance and emerging security threats.

Session

Providing logical connections between machines, the session layer supports information delivery for all Internet applications. This layer protects against DoS attacks, logs all session-level activity for trend analysis and demand planning, and flags any traffic sequences containing attack profiles or signatures.

Physical

ServerVault's connections to the outside world follow multiple physical paths and do not share dependencies on any external equipment. This makes it impossible for a single incident outside of our facilities to disrupt service. The data center is shielded and armored, and provides total protection from fire, shock, gasses, moisture, and all electromagnetic wave energy from the outside world. Access to the facility is limited to ServerVault employees, and armed guards make sure it stays that way.

Transport

To ensure reliable communications from client and server, ServerVault's multilayer network switches understand traffic classification at this layer in order to make sure time-sensitive or priority traffic is given preferential treatment.

Network

ServerVault's multiprovider attachments and private-peering provide fully fault-tolerant high-speed WAN connections that do not depend on any single carrier. In addition, multiple hoses can be viewed as one from the outside world, balancing the load for high-demand Web sites, and providing another level of backup if any of the servers should fail.

Data Link

ServerVault's core network is fully fault-tolerant along all of its link-paths using technologies such as gigabit-channel Ethernet and multihoming techniques. So, if a port or a piece of equipment should fail, your service stays up. Guaranteed.

Source: Company brochure.

EXHIBIT 4 | Statement of Cash Flows (direct method)

	Jan-00	Feb-00	Mar-00	Apr-00	May-00	Jun-00
Cash Flows from Operating Activities:						
Operating revenues						
Setup	1,000	2,500	3,000	5,000	6,000	7,500
Hosting	2,420	6,440	10,480	18,540	26,200	35,480
Services	445	350	600	1,150	1,900	2,325
Total sources	3,865	9,290	14,080	24,690	34,100	45,305
Operating Expenses						
Bandwidth	(3,790)	(3,790)	(6,115)	(5,591)	(5,591)	(11,678)
Marketing	(3,500)	(22,250)	(51,750)	(57,250)	(51,750)	(79,800)
Salaries	(28,250)	(45,100)	(54,570)	(56,600)	(61,520)	(62,200)
G&A (including corporate)	(9,584)	(15,484)	(16,884)	(22,530)	(30,160)	(39,910)
Total uses	(45,124)	(86,624)	(129,319)	(141,971)	(149,021)	(193,588)
Net cash produced (used) by operating activities	(41,259)	(77,334)	(115,239)	(117,281)	(114,921)	(148,283)
Cash Flows from Investing Activities:						
Capital expenditures						
Computer hardware	(9,800)	(14,265)	(17,770)	(31,220)	(36,150)	(44,890)
Facilities	(10,180)	(81,100)	(29,540)	(27,590)	—	—
Net cash produced (used) by investing activities	(19,980)	(95,365)	(47,310)	(58,810)	(36,150)	(44,890)
Cash Flows from Financing Activities:						
External funding	47,500	50,000	10,000	—	2,000,000	—
Net cash produced (used) by financing activities	47,500	50,000	10,000	—	2,000,000	—
NET MONTHLY CASH INFLOW (OUTFLOW)	(13,739)	(122,699)	(152,549)	(176,091)	1,848,929	(193,173)
CASH POSITION						
Beginning balance	575,000	561,261	438,562	286,013	109,922	1,958,851
Ending cash balance	561,261	438,562	286,013	109,922	1,958,851	1,765,678

EXHIBIT 5 | Three-Year Forecast of Server Growth

	Jan-00	Feb-00	Mar-00	Apr-00	May-00	Jun-00	Jul-00	Aug-00	Sep-00	Oct-00	Nov-00	Dec-00
New facilities	0	0	0	0	0	0	0	0	1	0	0	0
Total facilities	1	1	1	1	1	1	1	1	2	2	2	2
New servers	3	5	6	10	12	15	25	35	65	90	115	135
Total servers	3	8	14	24	36	51	76	111	176	266	381	516

	Jan-01	Feb-01	Mar-01	Apr-01	May-01	Jun-01	Jul-01	Aug-01	Sep-01	Oct-01	Nov-01	Dec-01
New facilities	1	0	0	1	0	0	1	0	0	1	0	0
Total facilities	3	3	3	4	4	4	5	5	5	6	6	6
New servers	206	221	236	271	291	311	351	376	401	447	477	502
Total servers	722	943	1179	1450	1741	2053	2404	2780	3182	3628	4105	4607

	Jan-02	Feb-02	Mar-02	Apr-02	May-02	Jun-02	Jul-02	Aug-02	Sep-02	Oct-02	Nov-02	Dec-02
New facilities	1	0	0	1	0	0	1	0	0	1	0	0
Total facilities	7	7	7	8	8	8	9	9	9	10	10	10
New servers	547	547	582	647	692	737	807	862	917	997	1062	1132
Total servers	5153	5700	6282	6929	7621	8358	9165	10027	10945	11942	13004	14137

Source: Case writer and company analysis.

PART 3

Estimating the Cost of Capital

"Best Practices" in Estimating the Cost of Capital: Survey and Synthesis

In recent decades, theoretical breakthroughs in such areas as portfolio diversification, market efficiency, and asset pricing have converged into compelling recommendations about the cost of capital to a corporation. By the early 1990s, a consensus had emerged prompting such descriptions as "traditional . . . textbook . . . appropriate," "theoretically correct" and "a useful rule of thumb and a good vehicle."[1] Beneath this general agreement about cost of capital theory lies considerable ambiguity and confusion over how the theory can best be applied. The issues at stake are sufficiently important that differing choices on a few key elements can lead to wide disparities in estimated capital cost. The cost of capital is central to modern finance touching on investment and divestment decisions, measures of economic profit, performance appraisal and incentive systems. Each year in the United States, corporations undertake more than $500 billion in capital spending. Since a difference of a few percent in capital costs can mean a swing in billions of expenditures, how firms estimate the cost is no trivial matter.

The purpose of this paper is to present evidence on how some of the most financially sophisticated companies and financial advisers estimate capital costs. This evidence is valuable in several respects. First, it identifies the most important ambiguities in the application of cost-of-capital theory, setting the stage for productive debate and research on their resolution. Second, it helps interested companies benchmark their cost-of-capital

---

[1]The three sets of quotes come, in order, from Ehrhardt (1994), Chapter 1; Copeland et al. (1990), p. 190; and Brealey and Myers (1993), p. 197.

This chapter was written by Robert F. Bruner, Kenneth M. Eades, Robert S. Harris, and Robert C. Higgins. Bruner, Eades, and Harris are professors at the Darden School, University of Virginia. Higgins is a professor at the University of Washington. The authors thank Todd Brotherson for excellent research assistance, and gratefully acknowledge the financial support of Coopers & Lybrand and the University of Virginia Darden School Foundation. The research would not have been possible without the cooperation of the 37 companies surveyed. These contributions notwithstanding, any errors remain the authors'. This chapter appeared in *Journal of Financial Practice and Education* (Spring 1998), and appears here with the permission of the Financial Management Association International, University of South Florida, College of Business Administration, Tampa, FL 33620-5500 (telephone: 813-974-2084).

estimation practices against best-practice peers. Third, the evidence sheds light on the accuracy with which capital costs can be reasonably estimated, enabling executives to use the estimates more wisely in their decision making. Fourth, it enables teachers to answer the inevitable question, "How do companies really estimate their cost of capital?"

The paper is part of a lengthy tradition of surveys of industry practice. Among the more relevant predecessors, Gitman and Forrester (1977) explored "the level of sophistication in capital budgeting techniques" among 103 large, rapidly growing businesses, finding that the internal rate of return and the payback period were in common use. Although the authors inquired about the level of the firm's discount rate, they did not ask how the rate was determined. Gitman and Mercurio (1982) surveyed 177 Fortune 1000 firms about "current practice in cost of capital measurement and utilization," concluding that "the respondents' actions do not reflect the application of current financial theory." Moore and Reichert (1983) surveyed 298 Fortune 500 firms on the use of a broad array of financial techniques, concluding among other things, that 86 percent of firms surveyed use time-adjusted capital budgeting techniques. Bierman (1993) surveyed 74 Fortune 100 companies reporting that all use some form of discounting in their capital budgeting and 93 percent use a weighted-average cost of capital. In a broad-ranging survey of 84 Fortune 500 large firms and Forbes 200 best small companies, Trahan and Gitman (1995) report that 30 percent of respondents use the capital asset pricing model.

This paper differs from its predecessors in several important respects. Existing published evidence is based on written, closed-end surveys sent to a large sample of firms, often covering a wide array of topics and commonly using multiple-choice or fill-in-the-blank questions. Such an approach often yields response rates as low as 20 percent and provides no opportunity to explore subtleties of the topic. Instead, we report the result of a telephone survey of a carefully chosen group of leading corporations and financial advisers. Another important difference is that the intent of existing papers is most often to learn how well accepted modern financial techniques are among practitioners, while we are interested in those areas of cost-of-capital estimation where finance theory is silent or ambiguous and practitioners are left to their own devices.

The following section gives a brief overview of the weighted-average cost of capital. The research approach and sample selection are discussed in Section II. Section III reports the general survey results. Key points of disparity are reviewed in Section IV. Section V discusses further survey results on risk adjustment to a baseline cost of capital, and Section VI offers conclusions and implications for the financial practitioner.

I. The Weighted-Average Cost of Capital

A key insight from finance theory is that any use of capital imposes an opportunity cost on investors; namely, funds are diverted from earning a return on the next best equal-risk investment. Since investors have access to a host of financial market opportunities, corporate uses of capital must be benchmarked against these capital market alternatives. The cost of capital provides this benchmark. Unless a firm can earn in excess of its cost of capital, it will not create economic profit or value for investors.

A standard means of expressing a company's cost of capital is the weighted average of the cost of individual sources of capital employed. In symbols, a company's weighted-average cost of capital (or WACC) is

$$\text{WACC} = (W_{\text{debt}}(1 - t)K_{\text{debt}}) + (W_{\text{preferred}}K_{\text{preferred}}) + (W_{\text{equity}}K_{\text{equity}}) \quad (1)$$

where:

K = Component cost of capital

W = Weight of each component as percent of total capital

t = Marginal corporate tax rate

For simplicity, this formula includes only three sources of capital; it can be easily expanded to include other sources as well.

Finance theory offers several important observations when estimating a company's WACC. First, the capital costs appearing in the equation should be current costs reflecting current financial market conditions, not historical, sunk costs. In essence, the costs should equal the investors' anticipated internal rate of return on future cash flows associated with each form of capital. Second, the weights appearing in the equation should be market weights, not historical weights based on often arbitrary, out-of-date book values. Third, the cost of debt should be after corporate tax, reflecting the benefits of the tax deductibility of interest.

Despite the guidance provided by finance theory, use of the weighted-average expression to estimate a company's cost of capital still confronts the practitioner with a number of difficult choices.[2] As our survey results demonstrate, the most nettlesome component of WACC estimation is the cost of equity capital; for unlike readily available yields in bond markets, no observable counterpart exists for equities. This forces practitioners to rely on more abstract and indirect methods to estimate the cost of equity capital.

II. Sample Selection

This paper describes the results of a telephone survey of leading practitioners. Believing that the complexity of the subject does not lend itself to a written questionnaire, we wanted to solicit an explanation of each firm's approach told in the practitioner's own words. Though our interviews were guided by a series of questions, these were sufficiently open-ended to reveal many subtle differences in practice.

Since our focus is on the gaps between theory and application rather than on average or typical practice, we aimed to sample practitioners who were leaders in the field. We began by searching for a sample of corporations (rather than investors or financial advisers) in the belief that they had ample motivation to compute WACC carefully and

---

[2]Even at the theoretical level, Dixit and Pindyck (1994) point out that the use of standard net present value (NPV) decision rules (with, for instance, WACC as a discount rate) does not capture the option value of being able to delay an irreversible investment expenditure. As a result, a firm may find it better to delay an investment even if the current NPV is positive. Our survey does not explore the ways firms deal with this issue; rather we focus on measuring capital costs.

to resolve many of the estimation issues themselves. Several publications offer lists of firms that are well regarded in finance;[3] of these, we chose a research report, *Creating World-Class Financial Management: Strategies of 50 Leading Companies* (1992), which identified firms,

> selected by their peers as being among those with the best financial management. Firms were chosen for excellence in strategic financial risk management, tax and accounting, performance evaluation and other areas of financial management . . . . The companies included were those that were mentioned the greatest number of times by their peers.[4]

From the 50 companies identified in this report, we eliminated 18 headquartered outside North America.[5] Of those remaining, five declined to be interviewed, leaving a sample of 27 firms. The companies included in the sample are given in **Exhibit 1.** We approached the most senior financial officer first with a letter explaining our research, and then with a telephone call. Our request was to interview the individual in charge of estimating the firm's WACC. We promised our interviewees that, in preparing a report on our findings, we would not identify the practices of any particular company by name— we have respected this promise in the presentation that follows.

In the interest of assessing the practices of the broader community of finance practitioners, we surveyed two other samples:

- *Financial advisers.* Using a "league table" of merger and acquisition advisers presented in Institutional Investor issues of April 1995, 1994, and 1993, we drew a sample of 10 of the most active[6] advisers. We applied approximately[7] the same set of questions to representatives of these firms' merger and acquisition departments. We wondered whether the financial advisers' interest in promoting deals might lead them to lower WACC estimates than those estimated by operating companies. This proved not to be the case. If anything, the estimating techniques most often used by financial advisers yield higher, not lower, capital cost estimates.

- *Textbooks and trade books.* From a leading textbook publisher we obtained a list of the graduate-level textbooks in corporate finance having the greatest unit sales

---

[3]For instance, *Institutional Investor* and *Euromoney* publish lists of firms with the best CFOs, or with special competencies in certain areas. We elected not to use these lists because special competencies or a stellar CFO might not indicate a generally excellent finance department.

[4]*Creating World-Class Financial Management: Strategies of 50 Leading Companies,* Research Report No. 1-110, Business International Corporation, New York, 1992 (238 pages), pages vii–viii. This survey was based upon a written questionnaire sent to CEOs, CFOs, controllers, and treasurers, followed up by a telephone survey.

[5]Our reasons for excluding these firms were the increased difficulty of obtaining interviews, and possible difficulties in obtaining capital market information (such as betas and equity market premiums) that might preclude using American practices. The enlargement of this survey to firms from other countries is a subject worthy of future study.

[6]*Activity* in this case was defined as four-year aggregate deal volume in mergers and acquisitions. The sample was drawn from the top 12 advisers, using their *average* deal volume over the 1993–95 period. Of these 12 firms, 2 chose not to participate in the survey.

[7]Specific questions differ, reflecting that financial advisers infrequently deal with capital budgeting matters and that corporate financial officers infrequently value companies.

in 1994. From these, we selected the top four. In addition, we drew on three trade books that discuss the estimation of WACC in detail.

Names of advisers and books included in these two samples are shown in **Exhibit 1.**

III. Survey Findings

The detailed survey results appear in **Exhibit 2.** The estimation approaches are broadly similar across the three samples in several dimensions:

- Discounted cash flow (DCF) is the dominant investment-evaluation technique.
- WACC is the dominant discount rate used in DCF analyses.
- Weights are based on *market,* not book, value mixes of debt and equity.[8]
- The after-tax cost of debt is predominantly based on *marginal* pretax costs, and *marginal* or *statutory* tax rates.
- The capital asset pricing model (CAPM) is the dominant model for estimating the cost of equity. Some firms mentioned other multifactor asset pricing models (e.g., arbitrage pricing theory), but these were in the small minority. No firms cited specific modifications of the CAPM to adjust for any empirical shortcomings of the model in explaining past returns.[9]

These practices differ sharply from those reported in earlier surveys.[10] First, the best-practice firms show much more alignment on most elements of practice. Second, they base their practice on financial economic models rather than on rules of thumb or arbitrary decision rules.

On the other hand, disagreements exist within and among groups on how to apply the CAPM to estimate cost of equity. The CAPM states that the required return (K) on any asset can be expressed as

$$K = R_f + \beta(R_m - R_f) \tag{2}$$

where:

R_f = Interest rate available on a risk-free bond

R_m = Return required to attract investors to hold the broad market portfolio of risky assests

β = the relative risk of the particular asset

---

[8]The choice between target and actual proportions is not a simple one. Because debt and equity costs clearly depend on the proportions of each employed, it might appear that the actual proportions must be used. However, if the firm's target weights are publicly known and if investors expect the firm soon to move to these weights, then observed costs of debt and equity may anticipate the target capital structure.

[9]For instance, even research supporting the CAPM has found that empirical data are better explained by an intercept higher than a risk-free rate and a price of beta risk less than the market risk premium. Ibbotson (1994) offers such a modified CAPM, in addition to the standard CAPM and other models, in its cost of capital service. Jagannathan and McGrattan (1995) provide a useful review of empirical evidence on the CAPM.

[10]Gitman and Forrester (1977), and Gitman and Mercurio (1982).

According to CAPM, then, the cost of equity, K_{equity}, for a company depends on three components: returns on risk-free bonds (R_f); the stock's equity beta, which measures risk of the company's stock relative to other risky assets ($\beta = 1.0$ is average risk); and the market risk premium ($R_m - R_f$) necessary to entice investors to hold risky assets generally versus risk-free bonds. In theory, each of these components must be a forward-looking estimate. Our survey results show substantial disagreements on all three components.

Comments on Risk-Free Rates

Some of our best-practice companies noted that their choice of a bond market proxy for a risk-free rate depended specifically on how they were proposing to spend funds. We asked, "What do you use for a risk-free rate?" and heard the following:

- "Ten-year Treasury bond or other duration Treasury bond if needed to better match project horizon."
- "We use a three- to five-year Treasury note yield, which is the typical length of our company's investment. We match our average investment horizon with maturity of debt."

The Risk-Free Rate of Return

As originally derived, the CAPM is a single-period model, so the question of which interest rate best represents the risk-free rate never arises. But in a many-period world typically characterized by upward-sloping yield curves, the practitioner must choose. Our results show the choice is typically between the 90-day T-bill yield and a long-term Treasury bond yield. (Because the yield curve is ordinarily relatively flat beyond 10 years, the choice of which particular long-term yield to use is not a critical one.)[11] The difference between realized returns on the 90-day T-bill and the 10-year T-bond has averaged 150 basis points over the long run; so choice of a risk-free rate can have a material effect on the cost of equity and WACC.[12]

The 90-day T-bill yields are more consistent with the CAPM as originally derived and reflect truly risk-free returns in the sense that T-bill investors avoid material loss in value from interest rate movements. However, long-term bond yields more closely

---

[11]In early January 1996, the differences between yields on the 10- and 30-year T-bonds was about 35 basis points. Some aficionados will argue that there is a difference between the 10- and 30-year yields. Ordinarily the yield curve declines just slightly as it reaches the 30-year maturity—this has been explained to us as the result of life insurance companies and other long-term buy-and-hold investors who are said to purchase the long bond in significant volume. It is said that these investors command a lower liquidity premium than the broader market, thus driving down yields. If this is true, then the yields at this point of the curve may be due not to some ordinary process of rational expectations, but rather to an anomalous supply–demand imbalance, which would render these yields less trustworthy. The counterargument is that life insurance companies could be presumed to be rational investors too. As buy-and-hold investors, they will surely suffer the consequences of any irrationality and therefore have good motive to invest for yields "at the market."

[12]This was estimated as the difference in arithmetic mean returns on long-term government bonds and U.S. Treasury bills over the years 1926 to 1994, given in Ibbotson Associates (1995).

reflect the default-free holding period returns available on long-lived investments and thus more closely mirror the types of investments made by companies.

Our survey results reveal a strong preference on the part of practitioners for long-term bond yields. Of both corporations and financial advisers, 70 percent use Treasury-bond yield maturities of 10 years or greater. None of the financial advisers and only 4 percent of the corporations used the Treasury-bill yield. Many corporations said they matched the term of the risk-free rate to the tenor of the investment. In contrast, 43 percent of the books advocated the T-bill yield, while only 29 percent used long-term Treasury yields.

Beta Estimates

Finance theory calls for a forward-looking beta, one reflecting investors' uncertainty about the future cash flows to equity. Because forward-looking betas are unobservable, practitioners are forced to rely on proxies of various kinds. Most often this involves using beta estimates derived from historical data and published by such sources as Bloomberg, Value Line, and Standard & Poor's.

The usual methodology is to estimate beta as the slope coefficient of the market model of returns:

$$R_{it} = \alpha_i + \beta_i(R_{mt}) \tag{3}$$

where:

R_{it} = Return on stock i in time period (e.g., day, week, month) t

R_{mt} = Return on the market portfolio in period t

α_i = Regression constant for stock i

β_i = Beta for stock i

In addition to relying on historical data, use of this equation to estimate beta requires a number of practical compromises, each of which can materially affect the results. For instance, increasing the number of time periods used in the estimation may improve the statistical reliability of the estimate, but risks the inclusion of stale, irrelevant information. Similarly, shortening the observation period from monthly to weekly, or even daily, increases the size of the sample but may yield observations that are not normally distributed and may introduce unwanted random noise. A third compromise involves choice of the market index. Theory dictates that R_m is the return on the market portfolio, an unobservable portfolio consisting of *all* risky assets, including human capital and other nontraded assets, in proportion to their importance in world wealth. Beta providers use a variety of stock market indices as proxies for the market portfolio on the argument that stock markets trade claims on a sufficiently wide array of assets to be adequate surrogates for the unobservable market portfolio.

The following table shows the compromises underlying the beta estimates of three prominent providers and their combined effect on the beta estimates of our sample companies. Note, for example, that the mean beta of our sample companies according to Bloomberg is 1.03, while the same number according to Value Line is 1.24. **Exhibit 3** provides a complete list of sample betas by publisher.

Compromises Underlying Beta Estimates and Their Effect on Estimated Betas of
Sample Companies

	Bloomberg*	Value Line	Standard & Poor's
Number of observations	102	260	60
Time interval	Weekly over 2 years	Weekly over 5 years	Monthly over 5 years
Market index proxy	S&P 500	NYSE composite	S&P 500
Sample mean beta	1.03	1.24	1.18
Sample median beta	1.00	1.20	1.21

*With the Bloomberg service it is possible to estimate a beta over many differing time periods, market indices, and smoothed or unadjusted. The figures presented here represent the base-line or default-estimation approach used if one does not specify other approaches.

Over half of the corporations in our sample (item 10, **Exhibit 2**) rely on published sources for their beta estimates, although 30 percent calculate their own. Among financial advisers, 40 percent rely on published sources, 20 percent calculate their own, and another 40 percent use what might be called "fundamental" beta estimates. These are estimates which use multifactor statistical models drawing on fundamental indices of firm and industry risk to estimate company betas. The best-known provider of fundamental beta estimates is the consulting firm BARRA.

Within these broad categories, the following comments indicate that a number of survey participants use more pragmatic approaches, which combine published beta estimates or adjust published estimates in various heuristic ways.

We asked our sample companies, "What do you use as your volatility or beta factor?" A sampling of responses shows that the choice is not always a simple one:

- "[We use] adjusted betas reported by Bloomberg. At times, our stock has been extremely volatile. If at a particular time the factor is considered unreasonably high, we are apt to use a lower (more consistent) one."

- "We begin with the observed 60-month covariance between our stock and the market. We also consider Value Line, BARRA, S&P betas for comparison and may adjust the observed beta to match assessment of future risk."

- "We average Merrill Lynch and Value Line figures and use Bloomberg as a check."

- "We do not use betas estimated on our stock directly. Our company beta is built up as a weighted average of our business segment betas—the segment betas are estimated using pure-play firm betas of comparable companies."

Equity Market Risk Premium

This topic prompted the greatest variety of responses among survey participants. Finance theory says the equity market risk premium should equal the excess return expected by investors on the market portfolio relative to riskless assets. How one measures expected future returns on the market portfolio and on riskless assets are problems left to practitioners. Because expected future returns are unobservable, all survey respondents extrapolated historical returns into the future on the presumption that past experience heavily conditions future expectations. Where respondents chiefly differed was in their use of *arithmetic* versus *geometric* average historical equity returns and in their choice of realized returns on T-bills versus T-bonds to proxy for the return on riskless assets.

The arithmetic mean return is the simple average of past returns. Assuming the distribution of returns is stable over time and that periodic returns are independent of one another, the arithmetic return is the best estimator of expected return.[13] The geometric mean return is the internal rate of return between a single outlay and one or more future receipts. It measures the compound rate of return investors earned over past periods. It accurately portrays historical investment experience. Unless returns are the same each time period, the geometric average will always be less than the arithmetic average and the gap widens as returns become more volatile.[14]

Based on Ibbotson Associates' (1995) data from 1926 to 1995, the matrix below illustrates the possible range of equity market risk premiums depending on use of the geometric as opposed to the arithmetic mean equity return and on use of realized returns on T-bills as opposed to T-bonds.[15] Even wider variations in market risk premiums can arise when one changes the historical period for averaging. Extending U.S. stock experience back to 1802, Siegel (1992) shows that historical market premiums have changed over time and were typically lower in the pre-1926 period. Carleton and Lakonishok (1985) illustrate considerable variation in historical premiums using different time periods and methods of calculation even with data since 1926.

The Equity Market Risk Premium ($R_m - R_f$)

	T-Bill Returns	T-Bond Returns
Arithmetic mean return	8.5%	7.0%
Geometric mean return	6.5%	5.4%

Of the texts and trade books in our survey, 71 percent support use of the arithmetic mean return over T-bills as the best surrogate for the equity market risk premium. For long-term projects, Ehrhardt advocates forecasting the T-bill rate and using a different cost of equity for each future time period. Kaplan and Ruback (1995) studied the equity risk premium implied by the valuations in highly leveraged transactions and estimated a mean premium of 7.97 percent, which is most consistent with the arithmetic mean and T-bills. A minority view is that of Copeland, Koller, and Murrin (1990,

---

[13]Several studies have documented significant negative autocorrelation in returns—this violates one of the essential tenets of the arithmetic calculation, since if returns are not serially independent, the simple arithmetic mean of a distribution will not be its expected value. The autocorrelation findings are reported by Fama and French (1986), Lo and MacKinlay (1988), and Poterba and Summers (1988).

[14]For large samples of returns the geometric average can be approximated as the arithmetic average minus one-half the variance of realized returns. Ignoring sample size adjustments, the variance of returns in the current example is .09 yielding an estimate of $.10 - 1/2(.09) = .055 = 5.5\%$ versus the actual 5.8% figure. Kritzman (1994) provides an interesting comparison of the two types of averages.

[15]These figures are drawn from Table 2–1, Ibbotson (1995), where the R_m was drawn from the "Large Company Stocks" series, and R_f drawn from the "Long-Term Government Bonds" and "U.S. Treasury Bills" series.

pp. 193–94) writing on behalf of the Corporate Financial Practice at McKinsey & Company: "We believe that the geometric average represents a better estimate of investors' expected returns over long periods of time." Ehrhardt (1994) recommends use of the geometric mean return if one believes stockholders are "buy-and-hold" investors.

Half of the financial advisers queried use a premium consistent with the arithmetic mean and T-bill returns, and many specifically mentioned use of the arithmetic mean. Corporate respondents, on the other hand, evidenced more diversity of opinion and tend to favor a lower market premium: 37 percent use a premium of 5 to 6 percent, and another 11 percent use an even lower figure.

Comments Regarding Market Risk Premium

"What do you use as your market risk premium?" A sampling of responses from our best-practice companies shows the choice can be a complicated one.

- "Our 400-basis-point market premium is based on the historical relationship of returns on an actualized basis and/or investment bankers' estimated cost of equity based on analysts' earnings projections."
- "We use an Ibbotson arithmetic average starting in 1960. We have talked to investment banks and consulting firms with advice from 3 to 7 percent."
- "A 60-year average of about 5.7 percent. This number has been used for a long time in the company and is currently the subject of some debate and is under review. We may consider using a time horizon of less than 60 years to estimate this premium."
- "We are currently using 6 percent. In 1993 we polled various investment banks and academic studies on the issue as to the appropriate rate and got anywhere between 2 and 8 percent, but most were between 6 and 7.4 percent."

Comments from financial advisers also were revealing. While some simply responded that they use a published historical average, others presented a more complex picture.

- "We employ a self-estimated 5 percent (arithmetic average). A variety of techniques are used in estimation. We look at Ibbotson data and focus on more recent periods, around 30 years (but it is not a straight 30-year average). We use smoothing techniques, Monte Carlo simulation, and a dividend discount model on the S&P 400 to estimate what the premium should be, given our risk-free rate of return."
- "We use a 7.4 percent arithmetic mean, after Ibbotson, Sinquefeld. We used to use the geometric mean following the then scholarly advice, but we changed to the arithmetic mean when we found later that our competitors were using the arithmetic mean and scholars' views were shifting."

Comments in our interviews (see box above) suggest the diversity among survey participants. While most of our 27 sample companies appear to use a 60-plus-year historical period to estimate returns, one cited a window of less than 10 years, two cited windows of about 10 years, one began averaging with 1960 and another with 1952 data.

This variety of practice should not come as a surprise, since theory calls for a forward-looking risk premium, one that reflects current market sentiment and may change with market conditions. What is clear is that there is substantial variation as practitioners try to operationalize the theoretical call for a market risk premium. A glaring result is that few respondents specifically cited use of any forward-looking method to supplement or replace reading the tea leaves of past returns.[16]

IV. The Impact of Various Assumptions for Using CAPM

To illustrate the effect of these various practices, we estimated the hypothetical cost of equity and WACC for Black & Decker, which we identified as having a wide range in estimated betas, and for McDonald's, which has a relatively narrow range. Our estimates are "hypothetical" in that we do not adopt any information supplied to us by the companies but rather apply a range of approaches based on publicly available information as of late 1995. **Exhibit 4** gives Black & Decker's estimated costs of equity and WACCs under various combinations of risk-free rate, beta, and market risk premiums. Three clusters of practice are illustrated, each in turn using three betas as provided by S&P, Value Line, and Bloomberg (unadjusted). The first approach, as suggested by some texts, marries a short-term risk-free rate (90-day T-bill yield) with Ibbotson's arithmetic mean (using T-bills) risk premium. The second, adopted by a number of financial advisers, uses a long-term risk-free rate (30-year T-bond yield) and a risk premium of 7.2 percent (the modal premium mentioned by financial advisers). The third approach also uses a long-term risk-free rate but adopts the modal premium mentioned by corporate respondents of 5.5 percent. We repeated these general procedures for McDonald's.

The resulting ranges of estimated WACCs for the two firms are as follows:

	Maximum WACC	Minimum WACC	Difference in Basis Points
Black & Decker	12.80%	8.50%	430
McDonald's	11.60%	9.30%	230

The range from minimum to maximum is large for both firms, and the economic impact is potentially stunning. To illustrate this, the present value of a level perpetual annual stream of $10 million would range between $78 million and $118 million for Black & Decker, and between $86 million and $108 million for McDonald's.

Given the positive but relatively flat slope of the yield curve in late 1995, most of the variation in our illustration is explained by beta and the equity market premium assumption. Variations can be even more dramatic, especially when the yield curve is inverted.

---

[16]Only two respondents (one advisor and one company) specifically cited forward-looking estimates, although others cited use of data from outside sources (e.g., a company using an estimate from an investment bank) where we cannot identify whether forward-looking estimates were used. Some studies using financial analyst forecasts in dividend growth models suggest market risk premiums average in the 6 to 6.5 percent range and change over time with higher premiums when interest rates decline. See for instance, Harris and Marston (1992). Ibbotson (1994) provides industry-specific cost-of-equity estimates using analysts' forecasts in a growth model.

V. Risk Adjustments to WACC

Finance theory is clear that a single WACC is appropriate only for investments of broadly comparable risk: A firm's overall WACC is a suitable benchmark for a firm's average risk investments. Finance theory goes on to say that such a company-specific figure should be adjusted for departures from such an average risk profile. Attracting capital requires payment of a premium that depends on risk.

We probed whether firms use a discount rate appropriate to the risks of the flows being valued in questions on types of investment (strategic vs. operational), terminal values, synergies, and multidivisional companies. Responses to these questions displayed in **Exhibit 3** do not display much apparent alignment of practice. When financial advisers were asked how they value parts of multidivision firms, all 10 firms surveyed reported that they use different discount rates for component parts (item 17). However, only 26 percent of companies always adjust the cost of capital to reflect the risk of individual investment opportunities (item 12). Earlier studies (summarized in Gitman and Mercurio (1982) reported that between a third and a half of firms surveyed did not adjust for risk differences among capital projects. These practices stand in stark contrast to the recommendations of textbooks and trade books: The books did not explicitly address all subjects, but when they did, they were uniform in their advocacy of risk-adjusted discount rates.

A closer look at specific responses reveals the tensions as theory based on traded financial assets is adapted to decisions on investments in real assets. Inevitably, a fine line is drawn between use of financial market data versus managerial judgments. Responses from financial advisers illustrate this. As shown in **Exhibit 2,** all advisers use different capital costs for valuing parts (e.g., divisions) of a firm (item 17); only half ever select different rates for synergies or strategic opportunities (item 18); only 1 in 10 state any inclination to use different discount rates for terminal values and interim cash flows (item 16). Two simplistic interpretations are that (1) advisers ignore important risk differences or (2) material risk differences are rare in assessing factors such as terminal values. Neither of these fits; our conversations with advisers reveal that they recognize important risk differences but deal with them in a multitude of ways. Consider comments from two prominent investment banks who use different capital costs for valuing parts of multidivision firms. When asked about risk adjustments for prospective merger synergies, these same firms responded as follows:

- "We make these adjustments in cash flows and multiples rather than in discount rates."
- "Risk factors may be different for realizations of synergies, but we make adjustments to cash flows rather than the discount rate."

While financial advisers typically value existing companies, corporations face further challenges. They routinely must evaluate investments in new products and technologies. Moreover, they deal in an administrative setting that melds centralized (e.g., calculating a WACC) and decentralized (e.g., specific project appraisal) processes. As the next box of comments illustrates, these complexities lead to a blend of approaches for dealing with risk. A number of respondents mentioned specific rate adjustments to distinguish between divisional capital costs, international versus domestic investments, and leasing versus nonleasing situations. In other instances, however, these same respondents favored cash-flow adjustments to deal with risks.

Why do practitioners risk-adjust discount rates in one case and work with cash-flow adjustments in another? Our interpretation is that risk-adjusted discount rates are more likely used when the analyst can establish relatively objective financial market benchmarks for what rate adjustments should be. At the business (division) level, data on comparable companies provide cost-of-capital estimates. Debt markets provide surrogates for the risks in leasing cash flows. International financial markets shed insights on cross-country differences. When no such market benchmarks are available, practitioners look to other methods for dealing with risks. Lacking a good market analog from which to glean investor opinion (in the form of differing capital costs), the analyst is forced to rely more on internal focus. Practical implementation of risk-adjusted discount rates thus appears to depend on the ability to find traded financial assets that are comparable in risk to the cash flows being valued and then to have financial data on these traded assets.

Comments Regarding Adjustments for Project Risk

When asked whether they adjusted discount rates for project risk, companies provided a wide range of responses:

- "No, it's difficult to draw lines between the various businesses we invest in, and we also try as best we can to make adjustments for risk in cash-flow projections rather than in cost of capital factors . . . . We advocate minimizing adjustments to cost of capital calculations and maximizing understanding of all relevant issues (e.g., commodity costs and international/political risks)." At another point the same firm noted that "for lease analysis only the cost of debt is used."
- "No [we don't risk adjust cost of capital]. We believe there are two basic components: (1) projected cash flows, which should incorporate investment risk, and (2) discount rate." The same firm noted, however, "For international investments, the discount rate is adjusted for country risk." and "For large acquisitions, the company takes significantly greater care to estimate an accurate cost of capital."
- "No, but use divisional costs of capital to calculate a weighted average company cost of capital . . . for comparison and possible adjustment."
- "Yes, we have calculated a cost of capital for divisions based on pure play betas and also suggest subjective adjustments based on each project. Our feeling is that use of divisional costs is the most frequent distinction in the company."
- "Rarely, but at least on one occasion we have, for a whole new line of business."
- "We do sensitivity analysis on every project."
- "For the most part we make risk adjustments qualitatively; i.e., we use the corporate WACC to evaluate a project, but then interpret the result according to the risk of the proposal being studied. This could mean that a risky project will be rejected even though it meets the corporate hurdle rate objectives."
- "No domestically; yes internationally—we assess a risk premium per country and adjust the cost of capital accordingly."

The pragmatic bent of application also comes to the fore when companies are asked how often they reestimate capital costs (item 13, **Exhibit 2**). Even for those firms that reestimate relatively frequently, the next box of comments shows that they draw an important distinction between estimating capital costs and policy changes about the capital cost figure used in the firm's decision making.

Firms consider administrative costs in structuring their policies on capital costs. For a very large venture (e.g., an acquisition), capital costs may be revisited each time. On the other hand, only large material changes in costs may be fed into more formal project evaluation systems. Firms also recognize a certain ambiguity in any cost number and are willing to live with approximations. While the bond market reacts to minute basis-point changes in investor return requirements, investments in real assets, where the decision process itself is time-consuming and often decentralized, involve much less precision. To paraphrase one of our sample companies, we use capital costs as a rough yardstick rather than the last word in project evaluation.

Our interpretation is that the mixed responses to questions about risk adjusting and reestimating discount rates reflect an often sophisticated set of practical trade-offs; these involve the size of risk differences, the quality of information from financial markets, and the realities of administrative costs and processes. In cases where there are material differences in perceived risk, a sufficient scale of investment to justify the effort, no large scale administrative complexities, and readily identifiable information from financial markets, practitioners employ risk adjustments to rates quite routinely. Acquisitions, valuing divisions of companies, analysis of foreign versus domestic investments, and leasing versus nonleasing decisions were frequently cited examples. In contrast, when one or more of these factors is not present, practitioners are more likely to employ other means to deal with risks.

Comments Regarding Reestimating WACC

How frequently do you reestimate your company's cost of capital? Here are responses from best-practice companies:

- "We usually review it quarterly but would review more frequently if market rates changed enough to warrant the review. We would only announce a change in the rate if the recomputed number was materially different than the one currently being used."
- "We reestimate it once or twice a year, but we rarely change the number that the business units use for decision and planning purposes. We expect the actual rate to vary over time, but we also expect that average to be fairly constant over the business cycle. Thus, we tend to maintain a steady discount rate within the company over time."
- "Usually every six months, except in case of very large investments, in which it is reestimated for each analysis."
- "Whenever we need to, such as for an acquisition or big investment proposal."
- "Reevaluate as needed (e.g., for major tax changes), but unless the cost of capital change is significant (a jump to 21 percent, for instance), our cutoff rate is not changed; it is used as a *yardstick* rather than the last word in project evaluation."
- "Probably need a 100-basis-point change to publish a change. We report only to the nearest percent."

VI. Conclusions

Our research sought to identify the "best practice" in cost-of-capital estimation through interviews of leading corporations and financial advisers. Given the huge annual expenditure on capital projects and corporate acquisitions each year, the wise selection of discount rates is of material importance to senior corporate managers.

The survey revealed broad acceptance of the WACC as the basis for setting discount rates. In addition, the survey revealed general alignment in many aspects of the estimation of WACC. The main area of notable disagreement was in the details of implementing the capital asset pricing model (CAPM) to estimate the cost of equity. This paper outlined the varieties of practice in CAPM use, the arguments in favor of different approaches, and the practical implications.

In summary, we believe that the following elements represent "best current practice" in the estimation of WACC:

- Weights should be based on *market-value* mixes of debt and equity.

- The after-tax cost of debt should be estimated from *marginal* pretax costs, combined with *marginal* or *statutory* tax rates.

- CAPM is currently the preferred model for estimating the cost of equity.

- Betas are drawn substantially from published sources, preferring those betas using a long interval of equity returns. Where a number of statistical publishers disagree, best practice often involves judgment to estimate a beta.

- Risk-free rate should match the tenor of the cash flows being valued. For most capital projects and corporate acquisitions, the yield on the U.S. government Treasury bond of 10 or more years in maturity would be appropriate.

- Choice of an equity market risk premium is the subject of considerable controversy both as to its value and method of estimation. Most of our best-practice companies use a premium of 6 percent or lower, while many texts and financial advisers use higher figures.

- Monitoring for changes in WACC should be keyed to major changes in financial market conditions, but should be done at least annually. Actually flowing a change through a corporate system of project valuation and compensation targets must be done gingerly and only when there are material changes.

- WACC should be risk adjusted to reflect substantive differences among different businesses in a corporation. For instance, financial advisers generally find the corporate WACC to be inappropriate for valuing different parts of a corporation. Given publicly traded companies in different businesses, such risk adjustment involves only modest revision in the WACC and CAPM approaches already used. Corporations also cite the need to adjust capital costs across national boundaries. In situations where market proxies for a particular type of risk class are not available, best practice involves finding other means to account for risk differences.

Best practice is largely consistent with finance theory. Despite broad agreement at the theoretical level, however, there remain several problems in application that can lead to wide divergence in estimated capital costs. Based on these remaining problems, we believe that further applied research on two principal topics is warranted. First, practitioners need additional tools for sharpening their assessment of relative risk. The variation in company-specific beta estimates from different published sources can create large differences in capital cost estimates. Moreover, use of risk-adjusted discount rates appears limited by lack of good market proxies for different risk profiles. We believe that appropriate use of averages across industry or other risk categories is an avenue worth exploration. Second, practitioners could benefit from further research on estimating equity market risk premiums. Current practice displays large variations and focuses primarily on averaging past data. Use of expectational data appears to be a fruitful approach. As the next generation of theories gradually sharpen our insights, we feel that research attention to implementation of existing theory can make for real improvements in practice.

Finally, our research is a reminder of the old saying that too often in business we measure with a micrometer, mark with a pencil, and cut with an ax. Despite the many advances in finance theory, the particular "ax" available for estimating company capital costs remains a blunt one. Best-practice companies can expect to estimate their weighted-average cost of capital with an accuracy of no more than plus or minus 100 to 150 basis points. This has important implications for how managers use the cost of capital in decision making. First, do not mistake capital budgeting for bond pricing. Despite the tools available, effective capital appraisal continues to require thorough knowledge of the business and wise business judgment. Second, be careful not to throw out the baby with the bath water. Do not reject the cost of capital and attendant advances in financial management because your finance people are not able to give you a precise number. When in need, even a blunt ax is better than nothing.

References

Aggarwal, Raj. "Corporate Use of Sophisticated Capital Budgeting Techniques: A Strategic Perspective and a Critique of Survey Results." *Interfaces* 10, no. 2 (April 1980), pp. 31–34.

Bierman, Harold J. "Capital Budgeting in 1992: A Survey." *Financial Management* 22, no. 3 (Autumn 1993), p. 24.

Brealey, Richard, and Stewart Myers. *Principles of Corporate Finance.* 4th ed. New York: McGraw-Hill, 1991.

Brigham, Eugene, and Louis Gapenski. *Financial Management, Theory and Practice.* 6th ed. Chicago: Dryden Press, 1991.

Carleton, Willard T., and Josef Lakonishok. "Risk and Return on Equity: The Use and Misuse of Historical Estimates." *Financial Analysts Journal* 4, no. 1 (January–February 1985), pp. 38–48.

Copeland, Tom; Tim Koller; and Jack Murrin. *Valuation: Measuring and Managing the Value of Companies.* 2nd ed. New York: John Wiley & Sons, 1994.

Dixit, Avinash K., and Robert S. Pindyck. *Investment under Uncertainty.* Princeton, NJ: Princeton University Press, 1993.

————. "The Options Approach to Capital Investment." *Harvard Business Review* 73, no. 3 (May–June 1995), pp. 105–15.

Ehrhardt, Michael. *The Search for Value: Measuring the Company's Cost of Capital.* Boston: HBS Press, 1994.

Fama, Eugene F., and Kenneth R. French. "Dividend Yields and Expected Stock Returns." *Journal of Financial Economics* 22, no. 1 (October 1986), pp. 3–25.

Gitman, Lawrence J. *Principles of Managerial Finance.* 6th ed. New York: HarperCollins, 1991.

Gitman, Lawrence J., and John R. Forrester, Jr. "A Survey of Capital Budgeting Techniques Used by Major U.S. Firms." *Financial Management* 6, no. 3 (Fall 1977), pp. 66–71.

Gitman, Lawrence J., and Vincent Mercurio. "Cost of Capital Techniques Used by Major U.S. Firms: Survey and Analysis of Fortune's 1000." *Financial Management* 11, no. 4 (Winter 1982), pp. 21–29.

Harris, Robert S., and Felicia C. Marston. "Estimating Shareholder Risk Premia Using Analysts' Growth Forecasts." *Financial Management* 21, no. 2 (Summer 1992), pp. 63–70.

Ibbotson Associates. *1995 Yearbook: Stocks, Bonds, Bills, and Inflation.* Chicago: Author, 1995.

————. *1994 Yearbook: Cost of Capital Quarterly.* Chicago: Author, October 1994.

Jagannathan, Ravi, and Ellen R. McGrattan. "The CAPM Debate." *The Federal Reserve Bank of Minneapolis Quarterly Review* 19, no. 4 (Fall 1995), pp. 2–17.

Kaplan, Steven N., and Richard S. Ruback. "The Valuation of Cash Flow Forecasts: An Empirical Analysis." *Journal of Finance* 50, no. 4 (September 1995), pp. 1059–93.

Kritzman, Mark. "What Practitioners Need to Know . . . About Future Value." *Financial Analysts Journal* 50, no. 3 (May–June 1994), pp. 12–15.

Lo, Andrew W., and A. Craig MacKinlay. "Stock Market Prices Do Not Follow Random Walks: Evidence from a Simple Specification Test." *Review of Financial Studies* 1, no. 1 (Spring 1988), pp. 41–46.

Moore, James S., and Alan K. Reichert. "An Analysis of the Financial Management Techniques Currently Employed by Large U.S. Companies." *Journal of Business Finance and Accounting* 10, no. 4 (Winter 1983), pp. 623–45.

Poterba, James M., and Lawrence H. Summers. "A CEO Survey of U.S. Companies' Time Horizons and Hurdle Rates." *Sloan Management Review* 37, no. 1 (Fall 1995), pp. 43–53.

————. "Mean Reversion in Stock Prices: Evidence and Implications." *Journal of Financial Economics* 22, no. 1 (October 1988), pp. 27–59.

Ross, Stephen; Randolph Westerfield; and Jeffrey Jaffe. *Corporate Finance* 4th ed. Chicago: Irwin, 1996.

Schall, Lawrence D.; Gary L. Sundem; and William R. Geijsbeek, Jr. "Survey and Analysis of Capital Budgeting Methods." *Journal of Finance* 33, no. 1 (March 1978), pp. 281–92.

Siegel, Jeremy J. "The Equity Premium: Stock and Bond Returns Since 1802." *Financial Analysts Journal* 48, no. 1 (January–February 1992), pp. 28–46.

Trahan, Emery A., and Lawrence J. Gitman. "Bridging the Theory-Practice Gap in Corporate Finance: A Survey of Chief Financial Officers." *Quarterly Review of Economics & Finance* 35, no. 1 (Spring 1995), pp. 73–87.

EXHIBIT 1 | Three Survey Samples

Company Sample	Adviser Sample	Textbook/Trade Book Sample
Advanced Micro Devices	CS First Boston	Textbooks
Allergan	Dillon, Read	Brealey and Myers
Black & Decker	Donaldson, Lufkin, Jenrette	Brigham and Gapenski
Cellular One	J. P. Morgan	Gitman
Chevron	Lehman Brothers	Ross, Westerfield & Jaffe
Colgate-Palmolive	Merrill Lynch	Trade Books
Comdisco	Morgan Stanley	Copeland, Koller & Murrin
Compaq	Salomon	Ehrhardt
Eastman Kodak	Smith Barney	Ibbotson Associates
Gillette	Wasserstein Perella	
Guardian Industries		
Henkel		
Hewlett-Packard		
Kanthal		
Lawson Mardon		
McDonald's		
Merck		
Monsanto		
PepsiCo		
Quaker Oats		
Schering-Plough		
Tandem		
Union Carbide		
U.S. West		
Walt Disney		
Weyerhauser		
Whirlpool		

Note: For the full titles of textbooks and trade books, please see the preceding list of references.

EXHIBIT 2 | General Survey Results

	Corporations	Financial Advisers	Textbooks/Trade Books
1. Do you use DCF techniques to evaluate investment opportunities?	89% Yes, as a primary tool 7% Yes, only as a secondary tool 4% No	100% rely on DCF, comparable companies multiples, comparable transactions multiples. Of these, 10% DCF is primary tool. 10% DCF is used mainly "as a check." 80% Weight the three approaches depending on purpose and type of analysis.	100% Yes
2. Do you use any form of a cost of capital as your discount rate in your DCF analysis?	89% Yes 7% Sometimes 4% N/A	100% Yes	100% Yes
3. For your cost of capital, do you form any combination of capital cost to determine a WACC?	85% Yes 4% Sometimes 4% No 7% N/A	100% Yes	100% Yes

4. What weighting factors do you use?
  a. target vs. current debt/equity?
  b. market vs. book weights?
	Target/Current *Market/Book*
	52% Target 59% Market
	15% Current 15% Book
	26% Uncertain 19% Uncertain
	7% N/A 7% N/A
		Target/Current *Market/Book*
		90% Target 90% Market
		10% Current 10% Book
			Target/Current *Market/Book*
			86% Target
			           100% Market
			14% Current

5. How do you estimate your before tax cost of debt?	52% Marginal cost 37% Current average 4% Uncertain 7% N/A	60% Marginal cost 40% Current average	71% Marginal cost 29% No explicit recommendation
6. What tax rate do you use?	52% Marginal or statutory 37% Average historical 4% Uncertain 7% N/A	60% Marginal or statutory 30% Average historical 10% Uncertain	71% Marginal or statutory 29% No explicit recommendation
7. How do you estimate your cost of equity? (If you do not use CAPM, skip to question 12).	81% CAPM 4% Modified CAPM 15% N/A	80% CAPM 20% Other (including modified CAPM)	100% Primarily CAPM Other methods mentioned: dividend-growth model arbitrage pricing model
8. As usually written, the CAPM version of the cost of equity has three terms: a risk-free rate, a volatility or beta factor, and a market risk premium. Is this consistent with your company's approach?	85% Yes 0% No 15% N/A	90% Yes 10% N/A	100% Yes

EXHIBIT 2 | *(continued)*

	Corporations	Financial Advisers	Textbooks/Trade Books
9. What do you use for the risk-free rate?	4% 90-day T-bill 7% 3–7 year Treasuries 33% 10-year Treasuries 4% 20-year Treasuries 33% 10–30 year Treasuries 4% 10 yrs. or 90-day; depends 15% N/A (Many said they match the term of the risk-free rate to the tenor of the investment)	10% 90-day T-bill 10% 5–10 year Treasuries 30% 10–30 year Treasuries 40% 30-year Treasuries 10% N/A	43% T-bills 29% LT Treasuries 14% Match tenor of investment 14% Don't say
10. What do you use as your volatility or beta factor?	52% Published source 3% Financial adviser's estimate 30% Self-calculated 15% N/A	30% Fundamental beta (e.g., BARRA) 40% Published source 20% Self-calculated 10% N/A	100% mention availability of published sources
11. What do you use as your market risk premium?	11% Use fixed rate of 4–4.5% 37% Use fixed rate of 5–6% 4% Use geometric mean 4% Use arithmetic mean 4% Use average of historical and implied 15% Use financial adviser's estimate 7% Use premium over Treasuries 3% Use Value Line estimate 15% N/A	10% Use fixed rate of 5% 50% Use 7–7.4% (Similar to arithmetic) 10% LT arithmetic mean 10% Both LT arithmetic and geometric mean 10% Spread above Treasuries 10% N/A	71% Arithmetic historical mean 15% Geometric historical mean 14% Don't say
12. Having estimated your company's cost of capital, do you make any further adjustments to reflect the risk of individual investment opportunities?	26% Yes 33% Sometimes 41% No	Not asked	86% Adjust beta for investment risk 14% Don't say
13. How frequently do you reestimate your company's cost of capital?	4% Monthly 19% Quarterly 11% Semiannually 37% Annually 7% Continually/every investment 19% Infrequently 4% N/A (Generally, many said that in addition to scheduled reviews, they reestimate as needed for significant events such as acquisitions and high-impact economic events)	Not asked	100% No explicit recommendation

EXHIBIT 2 | (*concluded*)

	Corporations	Financial Advisers	Textbooks/Trade Books
14. Is the cost of capital used for purposes other than project analysis in your company? (For example, to evaluate divisional performance?)	51% Yes 44% No 4% N/A	Not asked	100% No explicit discussion
15. Do you distinguish between strategic and operational investments? Is cost of capital used differently in these two categories?	48% Yes 48% No 4% N/A	Not asked	29% Yes 71% No explicit discussion
16. What methods do you use to estimate terminal value? Do you use the same discount rate for the terminal value as for the interim cash flows?	Not asked	30% Exit multiples only 70% Both multiples and perpetuity DCF model 70% Use same WACC for TV 20% No response 10% Rarely change	71% Perpetuity DCF model 29% No explicit discussion 100% No explicit discussion of separate WACC for terminal value
17. In valuing a multidivisional company, do you aggregate the values of the individual divisions, or just value the firm as a whole? If you value each division separately, do you use a different cost of capital for each one?	Not asked	100% Value the parts 100% Use different WACCs for separate valuations	100%: Use distinct WACC for each division
18. In your valuations do you use any different methods to value synergies or strategic opportunities (e.g., higher or lower discount rates, options valuation)?	Not asked	30% Yes 50% No 20% Rarely	29%: Use distinct WACC for synergies 71% No explicit discussion
19. Do you make any adjustments to the risk premium for changes in market conditions?	Not asked	20% Yes 70% No 10% N/A	14% Yes 86% No explicit discussion
20. How long have you been with the company? What is your job title?	Mean: 10 years All senior, except one	Mean: 7.3 years 4 MDs, 2 VPs, 4 associates	N/A

EXHIBIT 3 | Betas for Corporate Survey Respondents

	Bloomberg Betas		Value Line Betas	S&P Betas	Range Maximum–Minimum
	Raw	Adjusted[1]			
Advanced Micro	1.20	1.13	1.70	1.47	0.57
Allergan	0.94	0.96	1.30	1.36	0.42
Black & Decker	1.06	1.04	1.65	1.78	0.74
Cellular One			Not listed		
Chevron	0.70	0.80	0.70	0.68	0.12
Colgate-Palmolive	1.11	1.07	1.20	0.87	0.33
Comdisco	1.50	1.34	1.35	1.20	0.30
Compaq Computer	1.26	1.18	1.50	1.55	0.37
Eastman Kodak	0.54	0.69	nmf	0.37	0.32
Gillette	0.93	0.95	1.25	1.30	0.37
Guardian Industries			Not listed		
Henkel			Not listed		
Hewlett-Packard	1.34	1.22	1.40	1.96	0.74
Kanthal			Not listed		
Lawson Mardon			Not listed		
McDonald's	0.93	0.96	1.05	1.09	0.16
Merck	0.73	0.82	1.10	1.15	0.42
Monsanto	0.89	0.93	1.10	1.36	0.47
PepsiCo	1.12	1.08	1.10	1.19	0.11
Quaker Oats	1.38	1.26	0.90	0.67	0.71
Schering-Plough	0.51	0.67	1.00	0.82	0.49
Tandem Computers	1.35	1.23	1.75	1.59	0.52
Union Carbide	1.51	1.34	1.30	0.94	0.57
U.S. West	0.61	0.74	0.75	0.53	0.22
Walt Disney	1.42	1.28	1.15	1.22	0.27
Weyerhauser	0.78	0.85	1.20	1.21	0.43
Whirlpool	0.90	0.93	1.55	1.58	0.68
¯Mean	1.03	1.02	1.24	1.18	0.42
Median	1.00	1.00	1.20	1.21	0.42
Standard deviation	0.31	0.21	0.29	0.41	0.19

[1]Bloomberg's adjusted beta is $\beta_{adj} = (.66)\beta_{raw} + (.33)1.00$.

nmf = not a meaningful figure.

EXHIBIT 4 | Variations in Cost-of-Capital (WACC) Estimates for Black & Decker Using Different Methods of Implementing the Capital Asset Pricing Model*

1. Short-term rate plus arithmetic average historical risk premium (recommended by some texts)
   R_f = 5.36%, 90-day T-bills
   $R_m - R_f$ = 8.50%, Ibbotson arithmetic average since 1926

Beta Service	Cost of Equity (K_e)	Cost of Capital (WACC)
Bloomberg, β = 1.06	14.40%	9.70%
Value Line, β = 1.65	19.40%	12.20%
S&P, β = 1.78	20.50%	12.80%

2. Long-term rate plus risk premium of 7.20% ("modal" practice of financial advisers surveyed)
   R_f = 6.26%, 30-year T-bonds
   $R_m - R_f$ = 7.20%, modal response of financial advisers

Beta Service	Cost of Equity (K_e)	Cost of Capital (WACC)
Bloomberg, β = 1.06	13.90%	9.40%
Value Line, β = 1.65	18.10%	11.60%
S&P, β = 1.78	19.10%	12.10%

3. Long-term rate plus risk premium of 5.50% ("modal" practice of corporations surveyed)
   R_f = 6.26%, 30-year T-bonds
   $R_m - R_f$ = 5.50%, modal response of corporations

Beta Service	Cost of Equity (K_e)	Cost of Capital (WACC)
Bloomberg, β = 1.06	12.10%	8.50%
Value Line, β = 1.65	15.30%	10.20%
S&P, β = 1.78	16.10%	10.50%

*In all cases the CAPM is used to estimate the cost of equity, the cost of debt is assumed to be 7.81 percent based on a Baa rating, the tax rate is assumed to be 38 percent, and debt is assumed to represent 49 percent of capital.

Nike, Inc.: Cost of Capital

On July 5, 2001, Kimi Ford, a portfolio manager at NorthPoint Group, a mutual fund management firm, pored over analyst write-ups of Nike, Inc., the athletic shoe manufacturer. Nike's share price had declined significantly from the start of the year. Ford was considering buying some shares for the fund she managed, the NorthPoint Large-Cap Fund, which invested mostly in Fortune 500 companies with an emphasis on value investing. Its top holdings included ExxonMobil, General Motors, McDonald's, 3M and other large-cap, generally old-economy stocks. While the stock market declined over the last 18 months, NorthPoint Large-Cap had performed extremely well. In 2000, the fund earned a return of 20.7 percent even as the S&P 500 fell 10.1 percent. The fund's year-to-date returns at the end of June, 2001 stood at 6.4 percent versus the S&P 500's minus 7.3 percent.

Only a week ago, on June 28, 2001, Nike held an analysts' meeting to disclose its fiscal year 2001 results.[1] However, the meeting had another purpose: Nike management wanted to communicate a strategy for revitalizing the company. Since 1997, Nike's revenues had plateaued at around $9 billion, while net income had fallen from almost $800 million to $580 million (see **Exhibit 1**). Nike's market share in U.S. athletic shoes had fallen from 48 percent in 1997 to 42 percent in 2000.[2] In addition, recent supply-chain issues and the adverse effect of a strong dollar had negatively affected revenue.

At the meeting, management revealed plans to address both top-line growth and operating performance. To boost revenue, the company would develop more athletic shoe products in the mid-priced segment[3]—a segment that it had overlooked in recent years. Nike also planned to push its apparel line, which, under the recent leadership

---

[1]Nike's fiscal year ended in May.

[2]Robson, Douglas, "Just Do…Something: Nike's insularity and foot-dragging have it running in place," *BusinessWeek,* July 2, 2001.

[3]Sneakers in this segment sold for $70-$90 a pair.

This case was prepared from publicly available information by Jessica Chan under the supervision of Professor Robert F. Bruner. The financial support of the Batten Institute is gratefully acknowledged. This case was written as a basis for class discussion rather than to illustrate effective or ineffective handling of an administrative situation. Copyright © 2001 by the University of Virginia Darden School Foundation, Charlottesville, VA. All rights reserved. *To order copies, send an e-mail to* sales@dardenpublishing.com. *No part of this publication may be reproduced, stored in a retrieval system, used in a spreadsheet, or transmitted in any form or by any means—electronic, mechanical, photocopying, recording, or otherwise—without the permission of the Darden School Foundation.* Rev. 10/05.

of industry veteran Mindy Grossman,[4] had performed extremely well. On the cost side, Nike would exert more effort on expense control. Finally, company executives reiterated their long-term revenue growth targets of 8-10 percent, and earnings growth targets of above 15 percent.

Analyst reactions were mixed. Some thought the financial targets to be too aggressive; others saw significant growth opportunities in apparel and in Nike's international businesses.

Kimi Ford read all the analyst reports that she could find about the June 28 meeting, but the reports gave her no clear guidance: a Lehman Brothers report recommended a 'Strong Buy' while UBS Warburg and CSFB analysts expressed misgivings about the company and recommended a 'Hold'. Ford decided instead to develop her own discounted-cash-flow forecast to come to a clearer conclusion.

Her forecast showed that at a discount rate of 12 percent, Nike was overvalued at its current share price of $42.09 (see **Exhibit 2**). However, she had done a quick sensitivity analysis that revealed Nike was *under*valued at discount rates below 11.2 percent. Since she was about to go into a meeting, she requested her new assistant, Joanna Cohen, to estimate Nike's cost of capital.

Cohen immediately gathered all the data she thought she might need (**Exhibits 1 through 4**) and set out to work on her analysis. At the end of the day, she submitted her cost of capital estimate and a memo (**Exhibit 5**) explaining her assumptions to Ford.

---

[4]Mindy Grossman joined Nike in September 2000. She was the former president and chief executive of Jones Apparel Group's Polo Jeans division.

EXHIBIT 1 I Consolidated Income Statements

Year Ended May 31 (In millions except per-share data)	1995	1996	1997	1998	1999	2000	2001
Revenues	$4,760.8	$6,470.6	$9,186.5	$9,553.1	$8,776.9	$8,995.1	$9,488.8
Cost of goods sold	2,865.3	3,906.7	5,503.0	6,065.5	5,493.5	5,403.8	5,784.9
Gross profit	**1,895.6**	**2,563.9**	**3,683.5**	**3,487.6**	**3,283.4**	**3,591.3**	**3,703.9**
Selling and administrative	1,209.8	1,588.6	2,303.7	2,623.8	2,426.6	2,606.4	2,689.7
Operating income	**685.8**	**975.3**	**1,379.8**	**863.8**	**856.8**	**984.9**	**1,014.2**
Interest expense	24.2	39.5	52.3	60.0	44.1	45.0	58.7
Other expense, net	11.7	36.7	32.3	20.9	21.5	23.2	34.1
Restructuring charge, net	—	—	—	129.9	45.1	(2.5)	—
Income before income taxes	**649.9**	**899.1**	**1,295.2**	**653.0**	**746.1**	**919.2**	**921.4**
Income taxes	250.2	345.9	499.4	253.4	294.7	340.1	331.7
Net income	**$ 399.7**	**$ 553.2**	**$ 795.8**	**$ 399.6**	**$ 451.4**	**$ 579.1**	**$ 589.7**
Diluted earnings per common share	$1.36	$1.88	$2.68	$1.35	$1.57	$2.07	$2.16
Average shares outstanding (diluted)	294.0	293.6	297.0	296.0	287.5	279.8	273.3
Growth (%)							
Revenue		35.9	42.0	4.0	(8.1)	2.5	5.5
Operating income		42.2	41.5	(37.4)	(0.8)	15.0	3.0
Net income		38.4	43.9	(49.8)	13.0	28.3	1.8
Margins (%)							
Gross margin		39.6	40.1	36.5	37.4	39.9	39.0
Operating margin		15.1	15.0	9.0	9.8	10.9	10.7
Net margin		8.5	8.7	4.2	5.1	6.4	6.2
Effective tax rate (%)*		38.5	38.6	38.8	39.5	37.0	36.0

*The U.S. statutory tax rate was 35%. The state tax varied yearly from 2.5% to 3.5%.

Source: Company's 10-K SEC filing, UBS Warburg.

EXHIBIT 2 | Discounted Cash Flow Analysis

	2002	2003	2004	2005	2006	2007	2008	2009	2010	2011
Assumptions:										
Revenue growth (%)	7.0	6.5	6.5	6.5	6.0	6.0	6.0	6.0	6.0	6.0
COGS/sales (%)	60.0	60.0	59.5	59.5	59.0	59.0	58.5	58.5	58.0	58.0
S&A/sales (%)	28.0	27.5	27.0	26.5	26.0	25.5	25.0	25.0	25.0	25.0
Tax rate (%)	38.0	38.0	38.0	38.0	38.0	38.0	38.0	38.0	38.0	38.0
Current assets/sales (%)	38.0	38.0	38.0	38.0	38.0	38.0	38.0	38.0	38.0	38.0
Current liabilities/sales (%)	11.5	11.5	11.5	11.5	11.5	11.5	11.5	11.5	11.5	11.5
Yearly depreciation and capex equal each other.										
Cost of capital (%)	12.0									
Terminal value growth rate (%)	3.0									
Discounted Cash Flow										
Operating income	$ 1,218.4	$1,351.6	$1,554.6	$1,717.0	$1,950.0	$2,135.9	$2,410.2	$2,554.8	$2,790.1	$2,957.5
Taxes	463.0	513.6	590.8	652.5	741.0	811.7	915.9	970.8	1,060.2	1,123.9
NOPAT	755.4	838.0	963.9	1,064.5	1,209.0	1,324.3	1,494.3	1,584.0	1,729.9	1,833.7
Capex, net of depreciation	—	—	—	—	—	—	—	—	—	—
Change in NWC	8.8	(174.9)	(186.3)	(198.4)	(195.0)	(206.7)	(219.1)	(232.3)	(246.2)	(261.0)
Free cash flow	764.1	663.1	777.6	866.2	1,014.0	1,117.6	1,275.2	1,351.7	1,483.7	1,572.7
Terminal value										17,998.7
Total flows	764.1	663.1	777.6	866.2	1,014.0	1,117.6	1,275.2	1,351.7	1,483.7	19,571.5
Present value of flows	$ 682.3	$ 528.6	$ 553.5	$ 550.5	$ 575.4	$ 566.2	$ 576.8	$ 545.9	$ 535.0	$6,301.5
Enterprise value	$11,415.7									
Less: current outstanding debt	$ 1,296.6									
Equity value	$10,119.1									
Current shares outstanding	271.5									
Equity value per share at 12%	**$ 37.27**									

Current share price: **$ 42.09**

Sensitivity of equity value to discount rate:	
Discount rate	**Equity value**
8.00%	$ 75.80
8.50%	67.85
9.00%	61.25
9.50%	55.68
10.00%	50.92
10.50%	46.81
11.00%	43.22
11.17%	**42.09**
11.50%	40.07
12.00%	37.27

Note: Terminal value is estimated using the constant growth model:

$$TV = \frac{FCF_{10} * (1 + \text{Terminal value growth rate})}{\text{WACC} - g}$$

$$TV = \frac{\$1,572.7 * (1.03)}{12\% - 3\%}$$

EXHIBIT 3 | Consolidated Balance Sheets

	As of May 31,	
(In millions)	**2000**	**2001**
Assets		
Current assets:		
Cash and equivalents	$ 254.3	$ 304.0
Accounts receivable	1,569.4	1,621.4
Inventories	1,446.0	1,424.1
Deferred income taxes	111.5	113.3
Prepaid expenses	215.2	162.5
Total current assets	3,596.4	3,625.3
Property, plant and equipment, net	1,583.4	1,618.8
Identifiable intangible assets and goodwill, net	410.9	397.3
Deferred income taxes and other assets	266.2	178.2
Total assets	**$ 5,856.9**	**$ 5,819.6**
Liabilities and shareholders' equity		
Current liabilities:		
Current portion of long-term debt	$ 50.1	$ 5.4
Notes payable	924.2	855.3
Accounts payable	543.8	432.0
Accrued liabilities	621.9	472.1
Income taxes payable	—	21.9
Total current liabilities	2,140.0	1,786.7
Long-term debt	470.3	435.9
Deferred income taxes and other liabilities	110.3	102.2
Redeemable preferred stock	0.3	0.3
Shareholders' equity:		
Common stock, par	2.8	2.8
Capital in excess of stated value	369.0	459.4
Unearned stock compensation	(11.7)	(9.9)
Accumulated other comprehensive income	(111.1)	(152.1)
Retained earnings	2,887.0	3,194.3
Total shareholders' equity	3,136.0	3,494.5
Total liabilities and shareholders' equity	**$ 5,856.9**	**$ 5,819.6**

Source: Company 10-K SEC filing.

EXHIBIT 4 | Capital Market and Financial Information On or Around July 5, 2001

Current yields on U.S. Treasuries

3-month	3.59%
6-month	3.59%
1-year	3.59%
5-year	4.88%
10-year	5.39%
20-year	5.74%

Historical Equity Risk Premiums (1926–1999)

Geometric mean	5.90%
Arithmetic mean	7.50%

Current Yield on Publicly Traded Nike Debt*

Coupon	6.75% paid semi-annually
Issued	07/15/96
Maturity	07/15/21
Current Price	$95.60

Nike Historic Betas

1996	0.98
1997	0.84
1998	0.84
1999	0.63
2000	0.83
YTD 06/30/00	0.69
Average	0.80

Consensus EPS estimates:

FY 2002	FY 2003
$2.32	$2.67

Nike Share Price Performance Relative to S&P500:

January 2000 to July 5, 2001

Nike share price on July 5, 2001: $ 42.09

Dividend History and Forecasts

Payment Dates	31-Mar	30-Jun	30-Sep	31-Dec	Total
1997	0.10	0.10	0.10	0.10	0.40
1998	0.12	0.12	0.12	0.12	0.48
1999	0.12	0.12	0.12	0.12	0.48
2000	0.12	0.12	0.12	0.12	0.48
2001	0.12	0.12			

Value Line Forecast of Dividend Growth from '98-00 to '04-'06: 5.50%

*Data have been modified for teaching purposes.

Sources of data: Bloomberg Financial Services, Ibbotson Associates Yearbook 1999, Value Line Investment Survey, IBES.

EXHIBIT 5 | Joanna's Analysis

TO:	Kimi Ford
FROM:	Joanna Cohen
DATE:	July 6, 2001
SUBJECT:	Nike's Cost of Capital

Based on the following assumptions, my estimate of Nike's cost of capital is 8.4 percent:

Single or Multiple Costs of Capital?

The first question I considered was whether to use single or multiple costs of capital given that Nike has multiple business segments. Aside from footwear, which makes up 62 percent of revenue, Nike also sells apparel (30 percent of revenue) that complement its footwear products. In addition, Nike sells sport balls, timepieces, eyewear, skates, bats, and other equipment designed for sports activities. Equipment products account for 3.6 percent of revenue. Finally, Nike also sells some non-Nike branded products such as Cole-Haan dress and casual footwear, and ice skates, skate blades, hockey sticks, hockey jerseys and other products under the Bauer trademark. Non-Nike brands account for 4.5 percent of revenue.

I asked myself whether Nike's business segments had different enough risks from each other to warrant different costs of capital. Were their profiles really different? I concluded that it was only the Cole-Haan line that was somewhat different; the rest were all sports-related businesses. However, since Cole-Haan makes up only a tiny fraction of revenues, I did not think it necessary to compute a separate cost of capital. As for the apparel and footwear lines, they are sold through the same marketing and distribution channels and are often marketed in "collections" of similar design. I believe they face the same risk factors, as such, I decided to compute only one cost of capital for the whole company.

Methodology for Calculating the Cost of Capital: WACC

Since Nike is funded with both debt and equity, I used the Weighted Average Cost of Capital (WACC) method. Based on the latest available balance sheet, debt as a proportion of total capital makes up 27.0 percent and equity accounts for 73.0 percent:

Capital Sources	Book Values	
Debt		
Current portion of long-term debt	$ 5.4	
Notes payable	855.3	
Long-term debt	435.9	
	$1,296.6	→ 27.0% of total capital
Equity	$3,494.5	→ 73.0% of total capital

Cost of Debt

My estimate of Nike's cost of debt is 4.3 percent. I arrived at this estimate by taking total interest expense for the year 2001 and dividing it by the company's average debt balance.[1] The rate is lower than Treasury yields but that is because Nike raised a portion of its funding needs through Japanese yen notes, which carry rates between 2.0 percent to 4.3 percent.

After adjusting for tax, the cost of debt comes out to 2.7 percent. I used a tax rate of 38 percent, which I obtained by adding state taxes of 3 percent to the U.S. statutory tax rate. Historically, Nike's state taxes have ranged from 2.5 percent to 3.5 percent.

---

[1]Debt balances as of May 31, 2000 and 2001 were $1,444.6 and $1,296.6 respectively.

EXHIBIT 5 | *(continued)*

Cost of Equity

I estimated the cost of equity using the Capital Asset Pricing Model (CAPM). Other methods such as the Dividend Discount Model (DDM) and the Earnings Capitalization Ratio can be used to estimate the cost of equity. However, in my opinion, CAPM is the superior method.

My estimate of Nike's cost of equity is 10.5 percent. I used the current yield on 20-year Treasury bonds as my risk-free rate, and the compound average premium of the market over Treasury bonds (5.9 percent) as my risk premium. For beta I took the average of Nike's beta from 1996 to the present.

Putting it All Together

Inputting all my assumptions into the WACC formula, my estimate of Nike's cost of capital is 8.4 percent.

$$\text{WACC} = K_d (1 - t) * D/(D + E) + K_e \quad * E/(D + E)$$
$$= 2.7\% \quad * 27.0\% \quad + 10.5\% * 73.0\%$$
$$= 8.4\%$$

Coke versus Pepsi, 2001

On December 4, 2000, PepsiCo, Inc., and the Quaker Oats Company issued a joint press release announcing their merger. The terms of the merger stated that PepsiCo would acquire Quaker Oats in a stock-for-stock deal valuing Quaker at around $14 billion.

Judging by the share-price reactions to the announcement, observers viewed the deal as yet another setback for Coca-Cola. By acquiring Quaker Oats, PepsiCo would gain access to Gatorade and control 83.6 percent of the sports drink market. PepsiCo already possessed extremely strong brands in the noncarbonated-beverages segment, such as Aquafina, Tropicana, and Lipton. Now through Gatorade, PepsiCo would consolidate

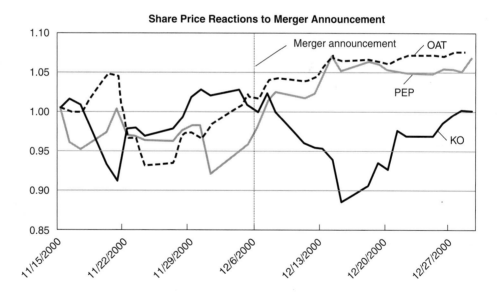

Share Price Reactions to Merger Announcement

This case was prepared by Jessica Chan under the supervision of Robert F. Bruner. It was written as a basis for class discussion rather than to illustrate effective or ineffective handling of an administrative situation. The financial support of the Batten Institute is gratefully acknowledged. Copyright © 2001 by the University of Virginia Darden School Foundation, Charlottesville, VA. All rights reserved. *To order copies, send an e-mail to* sales@dardenpublishing.com. *No part of this publication may be reproduced, stored in a retrieval system, used in a spreadsheet, or transmitted in any form or by any means—electronic, mechanical, photocopying, recording, or otherwise—without the permission of the Darden School Foundation.* Rev. 10/02.

its lead even further. Analysts estimated that PepsiCo would control around 33 percent of the U.S. noncarbonated-beverage market after the Gatorade acquisition, far ahead of Coca-Cola's 21 percent.[1] A report by UBS Warburg stated:

> Given PEP's [PepsiCo's] #1 rank in the faster-growth segment and its improving competitive position in CSDs [carbonated soft drinks], we believe PEP could, over the long term, threaten Coca-Cola's lead in the domestic beverage category in all channels except fountain.[2]

Carolyn Keene, consumer analyst at the mutual fund firm Siegel, Parker and Lauck (SPL), wondered how this latest announcement would affect the two companies' prospects for value creation. Historically, Coca-Cola had trounced PepsiCo in terms of value created as measured by "EVA,"[TM] or economic value-added **(Exhibit 1)**. She wondered if the trend would be reversed, given the recent developments. To develop a view, she decided to perform an EVA analysis for Coca-Cola and PepsiCo for 2001–2003. She hoped it would reveal which of the two companies would be the more attractive investment over the next few years.

Company Background: The Coca-Cola Company

In 2000, the Coca-Cola Company's (ticker symbol: KO) annual sales were $20.5 billion, and its market value reached $110.1 billion. The company was the largest manufacturer, distributor, and marketer of soft-drink concentrates and syrups[3] in the world. It also marketed and distributed a variety of noncarbonated-beverage products, which included Minute Maid orange juice, Fruitopia, Dasani bottled water, and Nestea, among others.

From 1993 to 1998, the Coca-Cola Company had consistently garnered the first or second spot in *Fortune*'s annual ranking of the top wealth creators. One of the main reasons for this was the company's strategy of spinning off its bottling operations to avoid consolidation on its balance sheet. This move, implemented in 1985, contributed to a dramatic rise in returns on equity from 23 percent to as much as 57 percent over the last two decades **(Exhibit 2)**.

Recently, however, the company had run into difficulties. The Asian financial crisis, South America's difficulties, and Russia's devaluation of the ruble all hurt KO. But business mistakes by Doug Ivester, CEO from 1997 to 1999, aggravated the situation.

---

[1]"Deal Ensures Pepsi Outdistancing Coke on the Flat," *South China Morning Post,* 6 December 2000.

[2]Caroline Levy, David Palmer, and Elyse Sakowitz, "PepsiCo, Inc.—Strong Buy," UBS Warburg, 5 December 2000.

[3]The Coca-Cola Company did not actually bottle and distribute its soft drink products. Rather, the company manufactured concentrate and syrups that were then sold to authorized bottlers that were either majority- or minority-owned by KO or completely independent. Those bottlers then combined the syrup or concentrate with carbonated water and sweetener, packaged the finished drinks in authorized containers bearing the Coca-Cola trademark, and then sold them to retailers and wholesalers. Thus, KO's main source of profit was from the syrup.

An example of one such mistake occurred in November 1999, when M. Douglas Ivester, CEO of Coca-Cola, instituted a 7.7 percent price hike on syrup, a rate that was double that of the usual increases. The Coca-Cola Company's bottlers were infuriated, and felt that Ivester was gouging them in order to increase KO's profits. In response, the bottlers raised prices for the first time in years to improve profitability, resulting in a decrease in volume **(Exhibit 3).** During Ivester's approximately two-year term, net income fell by 41 percent. The company's board of directors eased Ivester out in December 2000.

Douglas Daft, head of Coca-Cola's Middle and Far East and Africa groups, was chosen to succeed Ivester. Upon taking over, Daft immediately instituted major organizational changes such as cutting staff and reducing bureaucracy. But perhaps the most important change was his acknowledgment that KO needed to be a dominant player in the noncarbonated-beverages market. In contrast to Ivester, who had insisted on pushing the company's core soft-drink brands—Coca-Cola, Fanta, Sprite, and Diet Coke—Daft and his executives worked hard to come up with new, noncarbonated products.

Some analysts were optimistic that the change in management would return the Coca-Cola Company to its glory days. Perhaps through improved relations with bottlers and acquisitions of noncarbonated beverages, KO would return to the pre-1998 profit margins. Other analysts were less enthusiastic. One thing was certain, however; with PepsiCo's invigorated management, KO would need to get back on its feet as quickly as it could.

Company Background: PepsiCo, Inc.

In 2000, PepsiCo, Inc., was a $20 billion company involved in the snack food, soft drink, and noncarbonated beverage businesses. The company sold and distributed salty and sweet snacks under the Frito-Lay trademark and manufactured concentrates of Pepsi, Mountain Dew, and other brands to sell to franchised bottlers. The company also produced and distributed juices and other noncarbonated beverages.[4] Snack foods accounted for roughly two-thirds of PepsiCo's sales and operating income, while beverages accounted for the remainder.

Positioning PepsiCo as a focused snack-and-beverage company in 2000 was due mostly to the efforts of Roger Enrico, CEO from 1996 to 2000. During his tenure, Enrico instituted a massive overhaul at PepsiCo. In 1997, he sold off the fast-food chains KFC, Taco Bell, and Pizza Hut, ridding PepsiCo of a business that had long been a drag on returns. In 1999, he spun off Pepsi's capital-intensive bottling operations into an independent public company. By spinning off the bottling operations, PepsiCo would be left with just the higher-margin business of selling concentrate to bottlers.[5] At the same time, independent PepsiCo bottlers would be able to raise capital

---

[4]Yahoo Finance.

[5]In a price war, "it's the bottlers' margins that get flattened, while the 'parent' companies enjoy higher sales volume because of the low prices. The concentrate business . . . can have gross margins of 80%, compared with between 35% and 40% for bottling," according to Nikhil Deogun, "PepsiCo's Sale of Bottling-Business Stake isn't being Greeted with 'Dotcom' Hype," *Wall Street Journal,* 26 March 1999, C1.

on their own, freeing up cash flow within the parent company for other uses. Enrico also took aggressive steps to make PepsiCo a "total beverage company." He brokered the acquisitions of Tropicana, the market leader in orange juice, and Quaker Oats, whose Gatorade brand dominated the energy-drink market.

During Enrico's term, PepsiCo's return on equity almost doubled, from 17 percent in 1996 to 30 percent in 2000. (See **Exhibit 2** for historical returns and **Exhibit 1** for a historical EVA analysis.) On Wall Street, analysts were upbeat about PepsiCo's prospects.

Industry Overview and Competitive Events

In 2000, the beverage industry was undergoing a rapid transformation: the noncarbonated drinks segment, although still representing only a small fraction of the beverage market, had grown by 62 percent in volume over the last five years, while soft-drink-volume growth had been sluggish.[6] According to *Beverage Digest,* the share of the carbonated soft drink industry fell from 71.3 percent in 1990 to 60.5 percent in 2000.

In soft drink volume, PepsiCo still lagged behind Coke, although it seemed to have caught up somewhat in recent years **(Exhibit 3).** In the fall of 1999, for instance, PepsiCo, for the first time in its history, occupied two of the top three places for U.S. soft-drink brands on store shelves as its Mountain Dew dislodged Diet Coke from third place.[7]

Recent developments at both companies signaled an aggressive new round of competition. Below is a summary of recent competitive moves by both companies in several beverage categories.

Soft Drinks

Over the last five years, Pepsi had launched aggressive and exciting marketing campaigns (e.g., "Generation Next," "Joy of Pepsi") that helped boost volume and visibility. In addition, Pepsi launched the "Power of One" campaign—a strategy that entailed moving Pepsi drinks next to Frito-Lay chips on store shelves to entice shoppers to pick up a Pepsi when they bought chips. This strategy also helped boost both Frito-Lay and Pepsi's volumes. In response to the success of the Pepsi campaigns, in the summer of 2000, Coca-Cola resorted to a number of tactics, such as veering away from its traditional feel-good ads and launching trendier ones. Unfortunately, the new ads were highly unpopular and elicited negative reactions from customers and bottlers.[8] Coca-Cola pulled the ads and replaced them with the "Life Tastes Good" series, which marked a return to Coke's traditional "feel-good" themes, while being trendy at the same time.

---

[6]McCarthy, "Buffeted: Coke's Muddle over Quaker," *Economist* (25 November 2000).

[7]John A. Byrne, "PepsiCo's New Formula: How Roger Enrico is Remaking the Company," *BusinessWeek* (10 April 2000).

[8]The ads were produced by the Cliff Freeman Ad Agency, famous for its controversial dot-com ad in which gerbils were shown being shot out of a cannon. One Coke commercial featured a grandmother in a wheelchair who throws a tantrum when she discovers there is no Coke at a family reunion.

Noncarbonated Beverages

Coke and PepsiCo raced to position themselves in this important and fast-growing market segment:

> *Orange juice:* In 1998, PepsiCo acquired Tropicana, the clear market leader in orange juice. Tropicana held more than 40 percent of the total chilled orange juice market and 70 percent of the not-from-concentrate orange juice segment in the United States. Coke's Minute Maid had less than 20 percent of the chilled orange juice market.

> *Bottled water:* PepsiCo test-marketed Aquafina as early as 1994, while Coke, with its Dasani brand, did not enter the bottled-water market until 1999. Aquafina was the number one ranked bottled-water brand in the U.S. market in 2000.

> *Iced tea:* PepsiCo's Lipton boasted a 16-point-share lead over Coca-Cola's Nestea.

> *Sports drinks*: Pending the Federal Trade Commission's approval of the PepsiCo-Quaker Oats deal, PepsiCo would own Gatorade, which held 83 percent of the U.S. sports-drink market. Coca-Cola's Powerade was a distant second at 11 percent.

> *Specialty drinks:* PepsiCo, in alliance with Starbucks, introduced the highly popular Starbucks Frappuccino in 1996. It took Coca-Cola until 2000 to announce that it was going to test-market a frozen coffee beverage. In October 2000, PepsiCo beat Coca-Cola in acquiring South Beach Beverage Company, maker of the SoBe brand of teas and fruit juices.

Financial Comparison

Analysts expected that the coming months would be among the most exciting in the Coke-Pepsi saga. It would be interesting to see how the revived "cola wars" would play out. In the meantime, a look at some performance measures might provide clues as to what the future held.

- *Ratio analysis:* **Exhibits 4** and **5** present a variety of analytical ratios computed from the financial statements of each firm.

- *Economic profit analysis:* Also known as economic value-added, EVA can be used to estimate the value created or destroyed by comparing a firm's cash operating profits or net operating profits after tax (NOPAT) against a capital charge:

$$EVA = NOPAT - (\text{Weighted-average cost of capital}^9 \times \text{Invested capital})$$

Alternatively, the formula could be written as:

$$EVA = (\text{Return on invested capital} - WACC) \times \text{Invested capital}$$

Return on invested capital (ROIC), as the name suggests, could be calculated by dividing NOPAT by invested capital. The second formula highlights the idea that a "spread" earned beyond a company's cost of capital results in value creation.

---

[9]WACC.

Conclusion

Coke and Pepsi had created one of the strongest rivalries in business history. Carolyn Keene now wanted to develop a view about the two companies' future performances. She obtained pro forma projections for the two firms from reports prepared by analysts at Credit Suisse First Boston[10] **(Exhibits 6** and **7),** and gathered information about current capital-market conditions **(Exhibit 8).** She also took out her guidelines for estimating the components of EVA **(Exhibit 9).** It would be nice to finish her analysis before going off for Christmas break.

---

[10]KO forecasts were obtained from the report "Third Quarter Review of 10Q: Flat Revenue and Varied Operating Performance," by Andrew Conway, Chris O'Donnell, and Corey Horsch, Credit Suisse First Boston Equity Research, 19 November 2001. PepsiCo forecasts were obtained from the report "A Balanced Formula for Growth," by Conway, O'Donnell, and Horsch, Credit Suisse First Boston Equity Research, 8 November 2001.

EXHIBIT 1 | Historical EVA^{TM} Estimation and Return Comparisons for Coca-Cola Company and PepsiCo, Inc.

The Coca-Cola Company ($MM)

	1994	1995	1996	1997	1998	1999	2000
NOPAT	2,547	2,783	2,583	3,381	3,178	2,605	2,349
Invested capital	7,769	8,466	9,649	13,825	15,896	15,644	15,864
Return on invested capital	32.8%	32.9%	26.8%	24.5%	20.0%	16.6%	14.8%
WACC	12.2%	11.4%	13.4%	12.9%	11.1%	9.9%	8.4%
ROIC-WACC Spread	20.6%	21.4%	13.4%	11.6%	8.9%	6.8%	6.4%
EVA	1,602	1,814	1,292	1,601	1,422	1,063	1,016

PepsiCo, Inc. ($MM)

	1994	1995	1996	1997	1998	1999	2000
NOPAT	2,122	2,204	1,892	1,922	2,522	1,794	2,292
Invested capital	22,507	27,009	26,823	16,392	19,439	12,849	13,146
Return on invested capital	9.4%	8.2%	7.1%	11.7%	13.0%	14.0%	17.4%
WACC	11.5%	11.0%	10.5%	11.6%	10.8%	9.9%	8.3%
ROIC-WACC Spread	−2.1%	−2.8%	−3.4%	0.1%	2.2%	4.1%	9.1%
EVA	(464)	(760)	(916)	24	428	522	1,201

Source: Case writer estimates.

EXHIBIT 2 | Return on Equity and Return on Asset Comparisons, Coca-Cola and PepsiCo

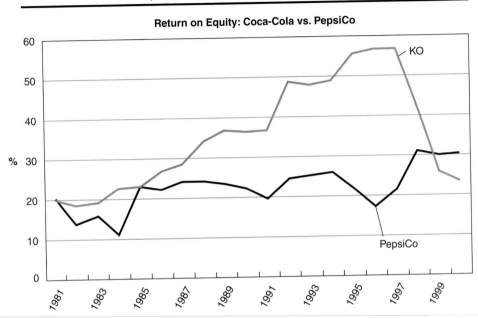

Return on Equity: Coca-Cola vs. PepsiCo

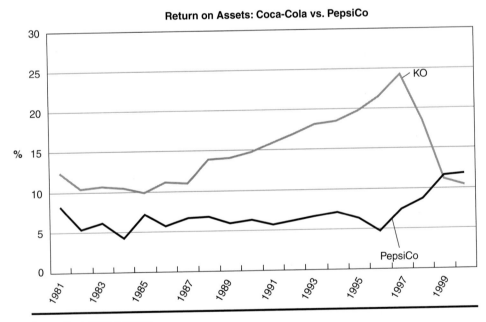

Return on Assets: Coca-Cola vs. PepsiCo

Source: Case writer estimates.

EXHIBIT 3 | U.S. Soft-Drink Market Shares and Volume, Coca-Cola and PepsiCo

	1990	1991	1992	1993	1994	1995	1996	1997	1998	1999	2000
Coca-Cola											
Gallonage (in millions)	4,915.5	5,038.4	5,108.9	5,310.0	5,580.8	5,915.4	6,223.9	6,473.0	6,764.4	6,730.5	6,737.2
Growth	4.0%	2.5%	1.4%	3.9%	5.1%	6.0%	5.2%	4.0%	4.5%	−0.5%	0.1%
Market share	41.0%	41.3%	41.3%	41.7%	42.0%	42.9%	43.8%	44.1%	44.6%	44.1%	44.0%
Market share gain/(loss)	0.6%	0.3%	0.0%	0.4%	0.3%	0.9%	0.9%	0.3%	0.5%	−0.5%	−0.1%
PepsiCo											
Gallonage (in millions)	3,970.5	4,010.2	3,827.6	3,899.0	4,070.6	4,201.8	4,370.2	4,500.2	4,704.1	4,732.3	4,736.1
Growth	3.0%	1.0%	−4.6%	1.9%	4.4%	3.2%	4.0%	3.0%	4.5%	0.6%	0.1%
Market share	33.1%	32.9%	30.9%	30.6%	30.7%	30.6%	30.8%	30.7%	31.0%	31.0%	30.9%
Market share gain/(loss)	0.1%	−0.2%	−2.0%	−0.3%	0.1%	−0.1%	0.2%	−0.1%	0.3%	0.0%	−0.1%
Soft Drink Industry											
Gallonage (in millions)	11,996.1	12,200.4	12,473.2	12,722.7	13,275.0	13,752.9	14,199.5	14,665.8	15,160.6	15,251.6	15,328.0
Growth	2.6%	1.7%	2.2%	2.0%	4.3%	3.6%	3.2%	3.3%	3.4%	0.6%	0.5%

Source: Compiled from *Beverage World*.

EXHIBIT 4 | Analytical Financial Ratios for the Coca-Cola Company

Coca-Cola Company	1994	1995	1996	1997	1998	1999	2000
Activity Analysis							
Average days outstanding	31.24	32.61	32.83	31.73	32.06	31.92	31.71
Working capital turnover	(16.33)	(11.27)	(10.62)	(8.90)	(6.14)	(5.49)	(6.52)
Fixed assets turnover	3.59	3.60	3.87	4.33	4.36	3.79	3.32
Total asset turnover	1.08	1.12	1.15	1.12	1.05	0.92	0.93
Liquidity Analysis							
Current ratio	0.64	0.59	0.80	0.75	0.87	0.90	0.87
Cash ratio	0.25	0.18	0.22	0.21	0.18	0.18	0.20
Cash from operations ratio	0.54	0.45	0.47	0.47	0.35	0.39	0.38
Long-Term Debt and Solvency Analysis							
Debt-equity ratio	0.67	0.75	0.73	0.61	0.65	0.65	0.61
Times interest earned	18.63	14.80	13.69	19.38	17.93	11.82	8.26
Fixed charge coverage ratio	10.02	9.87	7.18	8.99	8.70	6.03	5.77
Capital expenditure ratio	3.83	3.55	3.50	3.69	3.98	3.63	4.89
Cash from operations-debt ratio	0.96	0.82	0.77	0.78	0.55	0.62	0.63
Profitability Analysis							
Operating margin	22.9%	22.3%	21.1%	26.5%	26.4%	20.1%	18.0%
Net profit margin	15.8%	16.6%	18.8%	21.9%	18.8%	12.3%	10.6%
ROA	16.8%	17.7%	19.1%	21.1%	22.9%	17.3%	11.5%
ROE	44.3%	48.1%	51.7%	48.0%	46.1%	37.1%	25.8%
Financial leverage effect*	70.1%	68.9%	74.2%	89.2%	82.6%	71.1%	61.0%
Growth							
Sales	15.9%	11.4%	2.9%	1.7%	−0.3%	5.3%	3.3%
Book assets	15.4%	8.4%	7.4%	4.5%	13.4%	12.9%	−3.6%
Net income before unusual gain/loss	16.7%	16.9%	16.9%	18.2%	−14.4%	−31.2%	−10.4%
Adjusted NOPAT	19.5%	8.6%	−2.8%	27.7%	−0.7%	−19.8%	−7.3%
Net income	17.4%	16.9%	16.9%	18.2%	−14.4%	−31.2%	−10.4%
Operating income	19.5%	8.6%	−2.8%	27.7%	−0.7%	−19.8%	−7.3%

*Net income/operating income

Source: Company 10-K Filings with SEC.

EXHIBIT 5 | Analytical Financial Ratios for PepsiCo, Inc.

PepsiCo	1994	1995	1996	1997	1998	1999	2000
Activity Analysis							
Average days outstanding	25.33	26.89	28.39	40.71	37.59	37.25	31.28
Working capital turnover	(34.07)	513.67	200.28	20.98	(28.69)	(12.86)	38.78
Fixed assets turnover	1.64	1.72	1.82	1.42	1.57	1.55	2.05
Total asset turnover	1.17	1.20	1.27	0.94	1.05	1.01	1.14
Liquidity Analysis							
Current ratio	0.96	1.06	1.00	1.47	0.55	1.10	1.17
Cash ratio	0.28	0.29	0.15	0.68	0.05	0.28	0.34
Cash from operations ratio	0.71	0.72	0.82	0.80	0.41	0.80	0.99
Long-Term Debt and Solvency Analysis							
Debt-equity ratio	1.39	1.73	1.97	0.71	1.24	0.44	0.33
Times interest earned	4.96	4.38	4.24	5.57	6.54	7.76	14.59
Fixed charge coverage ratio	3.03	2.72	2.48	3.41	3.09	3.73	4.36
Capital expenditure ratio	1.65	1.78	1.83	2.27	2.29	2.71	3.67
Cash from operations-debt ratio	0.39	0.30	0.32	0.69	0.40	0.99	1.62
Profitability Analysis							
Operating margin	11.3%	9.9%	8.0%	12.7%	11.6%	13.8%	15.8%
Net profit margin	6.2%	5.3%	3.6%	10.2%	8.9%	10.1%	10.7%
ROA	7.2%	6.4%	4.6%	9.6%	9.3%	10.2%	12.2%
ROE	24.1%	24.7%	23.0%	16.9%	32.1%	30.0%	29.0%
Financial leverage effect*	54.6%	54.7%	53.8%	45.1%	80.5%	77.1%	72.7%
Growth							
Sales	13.3%	6.7%	4.6%	−33.9%	6.8%	−8.9%	0.3%
Book assets	4.6%	2.6%	−3.6%	−18.0%	12.7%	−22.5%	4.5%
Net income before unusual gain/loss	12.3%	−10.0%	−28.5%	29.8%	33.7%	2.9%	6.5%
Adjusted NOPAT	10.1%	−6.7%	−14.8%	4.6%	−2.9%	9.1%	14.4%
Net income	10.3%	−8.3%	−28.5%	86.4%	−7.0%	2.9%	6.5%
Operating income	10.1%	−6.7%	−14.8%	4.6%	−2.9%	9.1%	14.4%

*Net income/operating income

Source: Company 10-K Filings with SEC.

EXHIBIT 6 | Income-Statement and Balance-Sheet Forecasts for Coca-Cola

Coca-Cola Company
($ MM except per-share amounts)

Income Statement	2001E	2002E	2003E
Net operating revenue	$20,223	$21,234	$22,508
Cost of goods sold	6,092	6,285	6,617
Gross profit	14,131	14,949	15,891
Selling expense	7,508	7,569	7,985
General & admin.	1,224	1,248	1,273
	8,732	8,817	9,258
Operating income	5,399	6,132	6,633
Interest income	295	244	254
Interest expense	(310)	(280)	(264)
Equity income	197	227	261
Other income/(deductions), net	24	(10)	(10)
Pretax income	5,605	6,313	6,874
Income taxes	1,682	1,894	2,062
Net income	$ 3,923	$ 4,419	$ 4,812
Supplemental information:			
Depreciation	$ 489	$ 542	$ 597
Amortization	295	295	295
Cash taxes	1,738	1,957	2,131
Capital expenditures	$ 700	$ 750	$ 750

Accumulated goodwill amortization at the end of 2000 was expected to be $192 million.
The reader should assume net income reflects the deduction of depreciation and amortization.

Balance Sheet	2001E	2002E	2003E
Cash & equivalents	$ 2,238	$ 2,406	$ 2,432
A/R, net	1,838	1,930	2,046
Inventories	1,015	1,048	1,103
Prepaid expenses & other	1,834	1,868	1,964
Total current assets	6,925	7,252	7,545
Investments in bottlers	5,962	6,189	6,449
Marketable securities	2,364	2,364	2,364
PP&E	7,334	8,084	8,834
Less: acc. depreciation	(2,935)	(3,476)	(4,073)
Net PP&E	4,399	4,608	4,761
Goodwill & other	1,783	1,488	1,193
Total assets	$21,434	$21,901	$22,311
A/P & accrued liabilities	$ 3,796	$ 3,868	$ 4,066
Loans and notes payable	3,600	3,500	3,400
Current portion of long-term debt	154	153	2
Accrued income taxes	643	724	788
Total current liabilities	8,193	8,245	8,256
Long-term debt	681	528	526
Other	991	991	991
Deferred income taxes	302	239	170
Total liabilities	10,167	10,003	9,943
Common stock	870	870	870
Additional paid-in capital	3,196	3,196	3,196
Retained earnings	23,466	26,097	29,067
Accumulated other comprehensive losses	(2,722)	(2,722)	(2,722)
Treasury stock	(13,543)	(15,543)	(18,043)
Total equity	11,267	11,898	12,368
Total liabilities and equity	$21,434	$21,901	$22,311

Source (except for accumulated goodwill amortization): "Third Quarter Review of 10Q: Flat Revenue and Varied Operating Performance," by Andrew Conway, Chris O'Donnell, and Corey Horsch, Credit Suisse First Boston Equity Research, 19 November 2001.

EXHIBIT 7 | Income-Statement and Balance-Sheet Forecasts for PepsiCo

Pepsico
($ MM except per-share amounts)

Income Statement	2001E	2002E	2003E
Revenues			
Beverages	$10,553	$11,307	$12,116
Frito-Lay	14,498	15,373	16,273
Quaker Foods	2,042	2,109	2,179
	27,093	28,789	30,568
Operating Profit			
Beverages	1,667	1,818	1,976
Frito-Lay	2,675	2,955	3,239
Quaker Foods	408	426	446
Synergies	—	60	90
Corporate expense	(365)	(374)	(382)
	4,385	4,885	5,369
Net interest expense	148	92	37
Equity income	157	186	239
Pretax income	4,394	4,979	5,571
Provision for taxes	1,406	1,593	1,783
Net income	$ 2,988	$ 3,386	$ 3,788
Supplemental information:			
Depreciation	$ 900	$ 950	$ 1,000
Amortization	236	295	295
Cash taxes	1,142	1,245	1,504
Capital expenditures	$ 1,860	$ 1,583	$ 1,528

Accumulated goodwill amortization at the end of 2000 was expected to be $751 million.
The reader should assume net income reflects the deduction of depreciation and amortization.

Balance Sheet	2001E	2002E	2003E
Cash	$ 1,775	$ 3,677	$ 2,457
Investments	466	466	466
Cash and equivalents	2,241	4,143	2,923
A/R, net	2,292	2,435	2,585
Inventories	1,284	1,364	1,449
Prepaid exp. & other	886	942	1,000
Total noncash current assets	4,462	4,741	5,034
PP&E	7,449	8,021	8,493
Intangibles	4,556	4,556	4,556
Investments in unconsol. affiliated	3,095	3,235	3,414
Other	952	1,019	1,090
Total assets	$22,757	$25,716	$25,511
Short-term borrowings	$ 202	—	—
Current portion of long term debt	281	444	64
Accts payable & other current liabs	5,017	5,284	5,573
Total current liabilities	5,500	5,728	5,637
Long term debt	2,106	1,825	1,381
Other liabilities	4,244	4,541	4,859
Deferred income taxes	1,625	1,974	2,252
Total liabilities	13,475	14,068	14,129
Preferred stock			
Common stock & add'l paid-in capital	690	690	690
Retained earnings	18,420	20,786	23,520
Treasury stock	(8,434)	(8,434)	(11,434)
Accumulated comprehensive loss	(1,394)	(1,394)	(1,394)
Total equity	9,282	11,648	11,382
Total liabilities and equity	$22,757	$25,716	$25,511

Source (except for depreciation, amortization, and accum. goodwill amortization): "A Balanced Formula for Growth," by Andrew Conway, Chris O'Donnell, and Corey Horsch, Credit Suisse First Boston Equity Research, 8 November 2001.

EXHIBIT 8 | Capital-Market Information on December 4, 2000

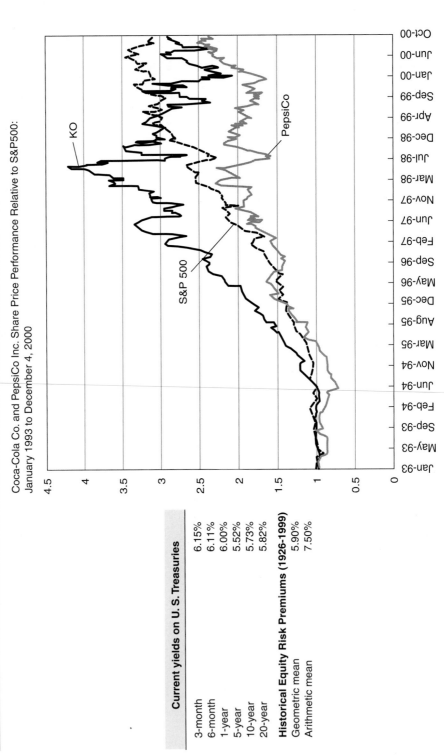

Coca-Cola Co. and PepsiCo Inc. Share Price Performance Relative to S&P500:
January 1993 to December 4, 2000

Current yields on U. S. Treasuries	
3-month	6.15%
6-month	6.11%
1-year	6.00%
5-year	5.52%
10-year	5.73%
20-year	5.82%
Historical Equity Risk Premiums (1926-1999)	
Geometric mean	5.90%
Arithmetic mean	7.50%

EXHIBIT 8 | Capital-Market Information on December 4, 2000   (*continued*)

The Coca-Cola Company		PepsiCo, Inc	
Publicly Traded Debt		*Publicly Traded Debt*	
Coupon	5.75% paid semi-annually	Coupon	5.75% paid semi-annually
Maturity	4/30/2009	Maturity	1/15/2008
Current price	91.54	Current price	93.26
Rating	A1	Rating	A2

Historic Betas		*Historic Betas*	
1994	0.88	1994	1.05
1995	0.83	1995	1.07
1996	1.19	1996	0.93
1997	1.11	1997	0.96
1998	0.97	1998	1.03
1999	0.71	1999	0.73
2000	0.44	2000	0.42
Average	0.88	Average	0.88

Dividend History and Forecasts

Paymt Dates	31-Mar	30-Jun	30-Sep	31-Dec	Total
1996	—	0.125	0.125	0.25	0.50
1997	—	0.14	0.14	0.28	0.56
1998	—	0.15	0.15	0.30	0.60
1999	—	0.16	0.16	0.32	0.64
2000	—	0.17	0.17	0.34 E	0.68

Dividend History and Forecasts

Paymt Dates	31-Mar	30-Jun	30-Sep	31-Dec	Total
1996	0.20	0.115	0.115	—	0.43
1997	0.23	0.125	0.125	—	0.48
1998	0.25	0.13	0.13	—	0.51
1999	0.26	0.135	0.135	—	0.53
2000	0.27	0.14	0.14	—	0.55

E = estimate

Value Line Forecast of Dividend Growth from '97-99 to '03-'05:	7.50%	Value Line Forecast of Dividend Growth from '97-99 to '03-'05:	7.50%
Value Line EPS Estimate for FY 2001:	$1.75	Value Line EPS Estimate for FY 2001:	$1.63
Coke share price on December 4, 2000:	$62.75	PepsiCo share price on December 4, 2000:	$43.81
Outstanding shares (in millions):		Outstanding shares (in millions):	
Basic	2,477	Basic	1,446
Diluted	2,487	Diluted	1,475

Sources of data: Bloomberg Financial Services, Ibbotson Associates Yearbook 1999, Value Line Investment Survey, IBES.

EXHIBIT 9 | Some Guidelines for Estimating Components of EVA

- **NOPAT.** Net operating profit after taxes (NOPAT) is calculated with the aim of arriving at the actual cash generated by the concern. Adjustments might include adding back goodwill amortization and other noncash expenses. Taxes must similarly be adjusted to reflect only actual cash taxes. Depreciation is not added back to NOPAT despite being a noncash expense, because of the assumption that depreciation represents a true economic cost (i.e., it is the amount that must be reinvested to maintain operations at the existing level). For consistency, invested capital is measured net of depreciation.

- **Invested capital.** Invested capital means, simply, the amount of capital invested in the business. It may be calculated either from the asset side or from the liabilities + equity side of the balance sheet. The latter is the simpler method.

  Invested capital includes debt, equity, and other near-capital items that represent economic value employed on behalf of the firm, such as the present value of operating leases, write-offs and cumulative losses, and accumulated goodwill amortization. The rationale for including losses and write-offs in continuing capital is that these represent unproductive assets, or failed investment. Were they excluded from the capital equation, the sum would only count successful efforts and not accurately reflect the performance of the firm. Accumulated goodwill amortization likewise needs to be included in invested capital because it represents a true investment. Excess cash not needed for operations, such as marketable securities, may be deducted from the invested capital base.

- **Cost of capital.** The capital charge applied against NOPAT should be based on a blend of the costs of all the types of capital the firm employs, or the weighted-average cost of capital.

$$\text{WACC} = K_d(1 - t) \times D/(D + E) + K_e \times E/(D + E)$$

where: K_d = Cost of debt

  t = Effective marginal tax rate

  K_e = Cost of equity

  D = Total debt

  E = Total equity

The cost of debt (used for both debt and leases) is the annual rate consistent with each firm's bond rating. The cost of equity may be estimated in a variety of ways[1]—a usual practice is to use the capital-asset pricing model:

$$K_e = R_f + \beta(R_m - R_f)$$

where:

  R_f = Risk-free rate, typically the yield on 10-year U.S. Treasury bonds

  β = Beta, a measure of the volatility of a company's stock price with respect to market movements

  $R_m - R_f$ = Market-risk premium, the additional return investors require over the risk-free rate to compensate them for investing in companies[2]

[1]Other ways of estimating the cost of equity include the dividend-growth and earnings-capitalization models.

[2]The two market premiums frequently used are 7.5%, which is an arithmetic average of annual market returns over the Treasury-bill rate from 1926 to 1998, and 5.9%, which is a compound or geometric average of market returns over Treasury bonds from 1926 to 1998. Source: Ibbotson Associates 1999 *Yearbook*.

Teletech Corporation, 2005

> ### Raider Dials Teletech
>
> #### "Wake-Up Call Needed," Says Investor
>
> New York—The reclusive billionaire Victor Yossarian has acquired a 10 percent stake in Teletech Corporation, a large regional telecommunications firm, and has demanded two seats on the firm's board of directors. The purchase was revealed yesterday in a filing with the Securities and Exchange Commission, and separately in a letter to Teletech's CEO, Maxwell Harper. "The firm is misusing its resources and not earning an adequate return," the letter said. "The company should abandon its misguided entry into computers, and sell its Products and Systems segment. Management must focus on creating value for shareholders." Teletech issued a brief statement emphasizing the virtues of a link between computer technology and telecommunications.
>
> *Wall Street Daily News,* 15 October 2005

Margaret Weston, Teletech Corporation's chief financial officer (CFO), learned of Victor Yossarian's letter late one evening in early October 2005. Quickly, she organized a team of lawyers and finance staff to assess the threat. Maxwell Harper, the firm's chief executive officer (CEO), scheduled a teleconference meeting of the firm's board of directors for the following afternoon. Harper and Weston agreed that before the meeting they needed to fashion a response to Yossarian's assertions about the firm's returns.

Ironically, returns had been the subject of debate within the firm's circle of senior managers in recent months. A number of issues had been raised about the hurdle rate used by the company when evaluating performance and setting the firm's annual capital budget. As the company was expected to invest nearly $2 billion in capital projects in the coming year, gaining closure and consensus on those issues had become an important priority for Weston. Now, Yossarian's letter lent urgency to the discussion.

This case was written by Robert F. Bruner, with the assistance of Sean D. Carr. It is dedicated to the memory of Professor Robert F. Vandell, a scholar in corporate finance and investment analysis and the author of an antecedent case upon which the present case draws. Teletech Corporation is a fictional company, reflecting the issues facing actual firms, and is used as a basis for class discussion rather than to illustrate effective or ineffective handling of an administrative situation. The financial support of the Batten Institute is gratefully acknowledged. Copyright © 2005 by the University of Virginia Darden School Foundation, Charlottesville, VA. All rights reserved. *To order copies, send an e-mail to* sales@dardenpublishing.com. *No part of this publication may be reproduced, stored in a retrieval system, used in a spreadsheet, or transmitted in any form or by any means—electronic, mechanical, photocopying, recording, or otherwise—without the permission of the Darden School Foundation.*

In the short run, Weston needed to respond to Yossarian. In the long run, she needed to assess the competing viewpoints on Teletech's returns, and she had to recommend new policies as necessary. What *should* the hurdle rates be for Teletech's two business segments, Telecommunications Services and its newer Products and Systems unit? Was the Products and Systems segment really paying its way?

The Company

The Teletech Corporation, headquartered in Dallas, Texas, defined itself as a "provider of integrated information movement and management." The firm had two main business segments: Telecommunications Services, which provided long-distance, local, and cellular telephone service to business and residential customers, and the Products and Systems segment, which engaged in the manufacture of computing and telecommunications equipment.

In 2004, Telecommunications Services had earned a return on capital (ROC)[1] of 9.10 percent; Products and Systems had earned 11 percent. The firm's current book value of net assets was $16 billion, consisting of $11.4 billion allocated to Telecommunications Services, and $4.6 billion allocated to Products and Systems. An internal analysis suggested that Telecommunications Services accounted for 75 percent of the market value (MV) of Teletech, while Products and Systems accounted for 25 percent. Overall, it appeared that the firm's prospective ROC would be 9.58 percent. Top management applied a hurdle rate of 9.30 percent to all capital projects and in the evaluation of the performance of business units.

Over the past 12 months, Teletech's shares had not kept pace with the overall stock market or with industry indexes for telephone, equipment, or computer stocks. Securities analysts had remarked on the firm's lackluster earnings growth, pointing especially to increasing competition in telecommunications, as well as disappointing performance in the Products and Systems segment. A prominent commentator on TV opined, "There's no precedent for a hostile takeover in this sector but, in the case of Teletech, there is every reason to try."

Telecommunications Services

The Telecommunications Services segment provided long-distance, local, and cellular telephone service to more than 7 million customer lines throughout the Southwest and Midwest. Revenues in this segment grew at an average rate of 3 percent over the 2000–2004 period. In 2004, segment revenues, net operating profit after tax (NOPAT), and net assets were $11 billion, $1.18 billion, and $11.4 billion, respectively.

Since the court-ordered breakup of the Bell System telephone monopoly in 1983, Teletech had coped with the gradual deregulation of its industry through aggressive expansion into new services and geographical regions. Most recently, the firm had been a leading bidder for cellular telephone operations and for licenses to offer personal communications services (PCS). In addition, the firm had purchased a number of telephone-operating companies through privatization auctions in Latin America.

---

[1]Return on capital was calculated as the ratio of net operating profits after tax (NOPAT) to capital.

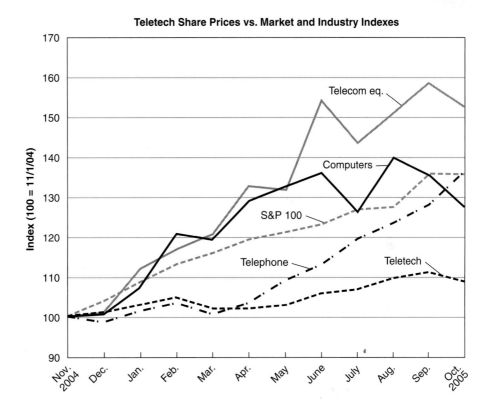

Teletech Share Prices vs. Market and Industry Indexes

Finally, the firm had invested aggressively in new technology—primarily, digital switches and optical-fiber cables—in an effort to enhance its service quality. All of those strategic moves had been costly: the capital budget in this segment had varied between $1.5 billion and $2 billion in each of the previous 10 years.

Unfortunately, profit margins in the telecommunications segment had been under pressure for several years. Government regulators had been slow to provide rate relief to Teletech for its capital investments. Other leading telecommunications providers had expanded into Teletech's geographical markets and invested in new technology and quality-enhancing assets. Teletech's management noted that large cable-TV companies had aggressively entered the telecommunications market and continued the pressure on profit margins.

Nevertheless, Teletech was the dominant service provider in its geographical markets and product segments. Customer surveys revealed that the company was the leader in product quality and customer satisfaction. Its management was confident that the company could command premium prices no matter how the industry might evolve.

Products and Systems

Before 2000, telecommunications had been the company's core business, supplemented by an equipment-manufacturing division that produced telecommunications components. In 2000, the company acquired a leading computer-workstation manufacturer with the goal of applying state-of-the-art computing technology to the design of telecommunications equipment. The explosive growth in the microcomputer market and the increased usage of telephone lines to connect home- and office-based computers with mainframes convinced Teletech's management of the potential value of marrying telecommunications equipment with computing technology. Using Teletech's capital base, borrowing ability, and distribution network to catapult growth, the Products and Systems segment increased its sales by nearly 40 percent in 2004. This segment's 2004 NOPAT and net assets were $480 million and $4.6 billion, respectively.

The Products and Systems segment was acknowledged as a technology leader in the industry. While this accounted for its rapid growth and pricing power, maintenance of that leadership position required sizable investments in research and development (R&D) and fixed assets. The rate of technological change was increasing, as witnessed by sudden major write-offs by Teletech on products that, until recently, management had thought were still competitive. Major computer manufacturers were entering the telecommunications-equipment industry. Foreign manufacturers were proving to be stiff competition for bidding on major supply contracts.

Focus on Value at Teletech

We will create value by pursuing business activities that earn premium rates of return.
—Teletech Corporation mission statement (excerpt)

Translating Teletech's mission statement into practice had been a challenge for Margaret Weston. First, it had been necessary to help managers of the segments and business units understand what *creating value* meant. Because the segments and smaller business units did not issue securities in the capital markets, the only objective measure of value was the securities prices of the whole corporation—but the activities of any particular manager might not be significant enough to drive Teletech's securities prices. Therefore, the company had adopted a measure of value creation for use at the segment and business-unit level that would provide a proxy for the way investors would view each unit's performance. This measure, called economic profit, multiplied the excess rate of return of the business unit by the capital it used:

$$Economic\ profit\ =\ (ROC - Hurdle\ rate) \times Capital\ employed$$

where:

$$ROC\ =\ Return\ on\ capital\ =\ \frac{NOPAT}{Capital}$$

$$NOPAT\ =\ Net\ operating\ profit\ after\ taxes$$

Each year, the segment and business-unit executives were evaluated on the basis of economic profit. This measure was an important consideration in strategic decisions about capital allocation, manager promotion, and incentive compensation.

The second way in which the value-creation perspective influenced managers was in the assessment of capital-investment proposals. For each investment, projected cash flows were discounted to the present using the firm's hurdle rate to give a measure of the net present value (NPV) of each project. A positive (or negative) NPV indicated the amount by which the value of the firm would increase (or decrease) if the project were undertaken. The following shows how the hurdle rate was used in the familiar NPV equation:

$$Net\ present\ value\ =\ \sum_{t=1}^{n}\left[\frac{Free\ cash\ flow_t}{(1\ +\ Hurdle\ rate)^t}\right]\ -\ Initial\ investment$$

Hurdle Rates

The hurdle rate used in the assessments of economic profit and NPV had been the focus of considerable debate in recent months. This rate was based on an estimate of Teletech's weighted average cost of capital (WACC). Management was completely satisfied with the intellectual relevance of a hurdle rate as an expression of the opportunity cost of money. The notion that the WACC represented this opportunity cost had been hotly debated within the company, and while its measurement had never been considered wholly scientific, it was generally accepted.

Teletech was "split-rated" between A− and BBB+. An investment banker recently suggested that, at those ratings, new debt funds might cost Teletech 5.88 percent (about 3.53 percent after a 40 percent tax rate). With a beta of 1.15, the cost of equity might be about 10.95 percent. At market-value weights of 22 percent for debt and 78 percent for equity, the resulting WACC would be 9.30 percent. **Exhibit 1** summarizes the calculation. The hurdle rate of 9.30 percent was applied to all investment and performance-measurement analyses at the firm.

Arguments for Risk-Adjusted Hurdle Rates

How the rate should be used within the company in evaluating projects was another point of debate. Given the differing natures of the two businesses and the risks each one faced, differences of opinion arose at the segment level over the appropriateness of measuring all projects against the corporate hurdle rate of 9.30 percent. The chief advocate for multiple rates was Rick Phillips, executive vice president of Telecommunications Services, who presented his views as follows:

> Each phase of our business is different. They must compete differently and must draw on capital differently. Given the historically stable nature of this industry, many telecommunications companies can raise large quantities of capital from the debt markets. In operations comparable to Telecommunications Services, 50 percent of the necessary capital is raised in the debt markets at interest rates reflecting solid A quality, on average. This is better than Teletech's corporate bond rating of A−/BBB+.
>
> I also have to believe that the cost of equity for Telecommunications Services is lower than it is for Products and Systems. Although the Products and Systems segment's sales growth and profitability have been strong, its risks are high. Independent equipment manufacturers are financed with higher-yielding BB-rated debt and a greater proportion of equity.

In my book, the hurdle rate for Products and Systems should reflect those higher costs of funds. Without the risk-adjusted system of hurdle rates, Telecommunications Services will gradually starve for capital, while Products and Systems will be force-fed—that's because our returns are less than the corporate hurdle rate, and theirs are greater. Telecommunications Services lowers the risk of the whole corporation, and should not be penalized.

Here's a rough graph of what I think is going on (**Figure 1**): Telecommunications Services, which can earn 9.10 percent on capital, is actually profitable on a risk-adjusted basis, even though it is not profitable compared to the corporate hurdle rate. The triangle shape on the drawing shows about where Telecommunications Services is located. My hunch is that the reverse is true for Products and Systems (P&S), which promises to earn 11.0 percent on capital. P&S is located on the graph near the little circle. In deciding how much to loan us, lenders will consider the composition of risks. If money flows into safer investments, over time the cost of their loans to us will decrease.

FIGURE 1

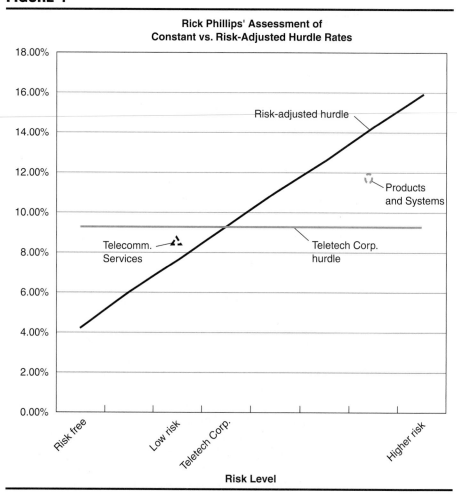

Our stockholders are equally as concerned with risk. If they perceive our business as being more risky than other companies are, they will not pay as high a price for our earnings. Perhaps this is why our price-to-earnings ratio is below the industry average most of the time. It is not a question of whether we adjust for risk—we already do, informally. The only question in my mind is whether we make those adjustments systematically or not.

While multiple hurdle rates may not reflect capital-structure changes on a day-to-day basis, over time they will reflect prospects more realistically. At the moment, as I understand it, our real problem is an inadequate and very costly supply of equity funds. If we are really rationing equity capital, then we should be striving for the best returns on equity for the risk. Multiple hurdle rates achieve that objective.

Implicit in Phillips's argument, as Weston understood it, was the notion that if each segment in the company had a different hurdle rate, the costs of the various forms of capital would remain the same. The mix of capital used, however, would change in the calculation. Low-risk operations would use leverage more extensively, while the high-risk divisions would have little to no debt funds. This lower-risk segment would have a lower hurdle rate.

Opposition to Risk-Adjusted Hurdle Rates

While several others within Teletech supported Phillips's views, opposition was strong within the Products and Systems segment. Helen Buono, executive vice president of Products and Systems, expressed her opinion as follows:

All money is green. Investors can't know as much about our operations as we do. To them the firm is a black box; they hire us to take care of what is inside the box, and judge us by the dividends coming out of the box. We can't say that one part of the box has a different hurdle rate than another part of the box if our investors don't think that way. Like I say, all money is green: all investments at Teletech should be judged against one hurdle rate.

Multiple hurdle rates are illogical. Suppose that the hurdle rate for Telecommunications Services was much lower than the corporate-wide hurdle rate. If we undertook investments that met the *segment* hurdle rate, we would be destroying shareholder value because we weren't meeting the *corporate* hurdle rate.

Our job as managers should be to put our money where the returns are best. A single hurdle rate may deprive an underprofitable division of investments in order to channel more funds into a more profitable division, but isn't that the aim of the process? Our challenge today is simple: we must earn the highest absolute rates of return that we can get.

In reality, we don't finance each division separately. The corporation raises capital based on its overall prospects and record. The diversification of the company probably helps keep our capital costs down and enables us to borrow more in total than the sum of the capabilities of the divisions separately. As a result, developing separate hurdle rates is both unrealistic and misleading. All our stockholders want is for us to invest our funds wisely in order to increase the value of their stock. This happens when we pick the most promising projects, irrespective of the source.

Margaret Weston's Concerns

As Weston listened to these arguments, presented over the course of several months, she became increasingly concerned about several related considerations. First, Teletech's corporate strategy had directed the company toward integrating the two segments. One effect of using multiple hurdle rates would be to make justifying high-technology research and application proposals more difficult, as the required rate of return would be increased. On the one hand, she thought, perhaps multiple hurdle rates were the right idea, but the notion that they should be based on capital costs rather than strategic considerations might be wrong. On the other hand, perhaps multiple rates based on capital costs should be used, but, in allocating funds, some qualitative adjustment should be made for unquantifiable strategic considerations. In Weston's mind, the theory was certainly not clear on how to achieve strategic objectives when allocating capital.

Second, using a single measure of the cost of money (the hurdle rate or discount factor) made the NPV results consistent, at least in economic terms. If Teletech adopted multiple rates for discounting cash flows, Weston was afraid that the NPV and economic-profit calculations would lose their meaning and comparability across business segments. To her, a performance criterion had to be consistent and understandable, or it would not be useful.

In addition, Weston was concerned about the problem of attributing capital structures to divisions. In the Telecommunications Services segment, a major new switching station might be financed by mortgage bonds. In Products and Systems, however, it was impossible for the division to borrow directly; indeed, any financing was only feasible because the corporation guaranteed the debt. Such projects were considered highly risky—at best, perhaps, warranting only a minimal debt structure. Also, Weston considered the debt-capacity decision difficult enough for the corporation as a whole, let alone for each division. Judgments could only be very crude.

In further discussions with others in the organization about the use of multiple hurdle rates, Weston discovered two predominant themes. One argument held that investment decisions should never be mixed with financing decisions. A firm should first decide what its investments should be and then determine how to finance them most efficiently. Adding leverage to a present-value calculation would distort the results. The use of multiple hurdle rates was simply a way of mixing financing with investment analysis. This argument also held that a single rate made the risk decision clear-cut. Management could simply adjust its standard (NPV or economic profit) as the risks increased.

The contrasting line of reasoning noted that the WACC tended to represent an average market reaction to a mixture of risks. Lower-than-average-risk projects should probably be accepted even when they did not meet the weighted-average criterion. Higher-than-normal-risk projects should provide a return premium. While the multiple-hurdle-rate system was a crude way to achieve this end, at least it was a step in the right direction. Moreover, some argued that Teletech's objective should be to maximize return on equity funds, and because equity funds were and would remain a comparatively scarce resource, a multiple-rate system would tend to maximize returns to stockholders better than a single-rate system would.

To help resolve these issues, Weston asked her assistant, Bernard Ingles, to summarize the scholarly thought regarding multiple hurdle rates. His memorandum is given in **Exhibit 2.** She also requested that Ingles obtain samples of firms comparable with the Telecommunications Services segment and the Products and Systems unit that might be used in deriving segment WACCs. A summary of the data is given in **Exhibit 3.** Information on capital-market conditions in October 2005 is given in **Exhibit 4.**

Conclusion

Weston could not realistically hope that all the issues before her would be resolved in time to influence Victor Yossarian's attack on management. But the attack did dictate the need for an objective assessment of the performance of Teletech's two segments—the choice of hurdle rates would be very important in the analysis. She did want to institute a pragmatic system of appropriate hurdle rates (or one rate), however, that would facilitate judgments in the changing circumstances faced by Teletech. What were the appropriate hurdle rates for the two segments? Was the Products and Systems segment underperforming, as suggested by Yossarian? How should Teletech respond to the raider?

EXHIBIT 1   I   Summary of the WACC Calculation for Teletech Corporation and Segment Worksheet

	Corporate	Telecommunications Services	Products and Systems
MV asset weights	100%	75%	25%
Bond rating	A−/BBB+	A	BB
Pretax cost of debt	5.88%	5.74%	7.47%
Tax rate	40%	40%	40%
After-tax cost of debt	3.53%	3.44%	4.48%
Equity beta	1.15	*1.04*	*1.40*
R_f	4.62%		
R_M	10.12%		
R_M-R_f	5.50%		
Cost of equity	10.95%	*10.34%*	*12.32%*
Weight of debt	22.2%	*27.1*	*9.2*
Weight of equity	77.8%	*72.9*	*90.8*
WACC	**9.30%**	*8.47%*	*11.67%*

Avg of peers (handwritten annotations)

Sources of data: *Bloomberg LP, S&P Research Insight, case writer's analysis.*

EXHIBIT 2 | Theoretical Overview of Multiple Hurdle Rates

To: Margaret Weston
From: Bernard Ingles
Subject: Segment cost-of-capital theory
Date: October 2005

You requested an overview of the theories on multiple hurdle rates. Without getting into the minutiae, the theories boil down to the following points:

1. The central idea is that required returns should be driven by risk. This is the dominant view in the field of investment management, and is based on a mountain of theory and empirical research stretching over several decades. The extension of this idea from investment management to corporate decision making is, at least in theory, straightforward.

2. An underlying assumption is that the firm is transparent (i.e., that investors can see through the corporate veil and evaluate the activities going on inside). No one believes firms are *completely* transparent, or that investors are perfectly informed. But financial accounting standards have evolved toward making the firm more transparent. And the investment community has grown tougher and sharper in its analysis. Teletech now has 36 analysts publishing both reports and forecasts on the firm. The reality is that for big publicly held firms, transparency is not a bad assumption.

3. Another underlying assumption is that the value of the whole enterprise is simply the sum of its parts—this is the concept of value additivity. We can define "parts" as either the business segments (on the left-hand side of the balance sheet) or the layers of the capital structure (on the right-hand side of the balance sheet). Market values have to balance.   *ASSETS*   *= CAPITAL*

$$MV_{Teletech} = (MV_{Telecommunication\ Services} + MV_{Products + Systems}) = (MV_{debt} + MV_{equity})$$

If those equalities did not hold, then a raider could come along and exploit the inequality by buying or selling the whole and the parts. This is arbitrage. By buying and selling, the actions of the raider would drive the MVs back into balance.

4. Investment theory tells us that the only risk that matters is nondiversifiable risk, which is measured by beta. Beta indicates the risk that an asset will add to a portfolio. Since we assume that an investor is diversified, we also assume she seeks a return for only the risk that she cannot shed, which is the nondiversifiable risk. The important point here is that the beta of a portfolio is equal to a weighted average of the betas of the portfolio components. Extending this to the corporate environment, the asset beta for the firm will equal a weighted average of the components of the firm—again, the components of the firm can be defined in terms of either the right-hand side or the left-hand side of the balance sheet.

$$\beta_{Teletech\ Assets} = (w_{Tel.Serv.}\ \beta_{Tel.Serv.} + w_{P+S}\ \beta_{P+S}) = (w_{debt}\beta_{debt} + w_{equity}\beta_{equity})$$

Where:

$$w = percentage\ weights\ based\ on\ market\ values.$$

$$\beta_{Tel.\ Serv.,}\beta_{P+S} = Asset\ betas\ for\ business\ segments.$$

$$\beta_{debt} = \beta\ for\ the\ firm's\ debt\ securities.$$

$$\beta_{equity} = \beta\ of\ firm's\ common\ stock\ (given\ by\ Bloomberg,\ etc.)$$

This is a very handy way to model the risk of the firm, for it means that we can use the capital asset pricing model to estimate the cost of capital for a segment (i.e., using segment asset betas).

5. Given the foregoing, it follows that the weighted average of the various costs of capital (*K*) for the firm (WACC), which is the theoretically correct hurdle rate, is simply a weighted average of segment WACCs:

$$WACC_{Teletech} = (w_{Tel.Serv.}\ WACC_{Tel.Serv.}) + (w_{P+S}WACC_{P+S})$$

EXHIBIT 2 | (continued)

Where:

$$w = \text{percentage weights based on market values.}$$

$$WACC_{Tel.\ Serv.} = (w_{debt,\ Tel.\ Serv.}\ K_{debt,\ Tel.\ Serv.}) + (w_{equity,\ Tel.\ Serv.}\ K_{equity,\ Tel.\ Serv.})$$

$$WACC_{P+S} = (w_{debt,\ P+S}\ K_{debt,\ P+S}) + (w_{equity,\ P+S}\ K_{equity,\ P+S})$$

6. The notion in point number 5 may not hold exactly in practice. First, most of the components in the WACC formula are estimated with some error. Second, because of taxes, information asymmetries, or other market imperfections, assets may not be priced strictly in line with the model—for a company like Teletech, it is reasonable to assume that any mispricings are just temporary. Third, the simple two-segment characterization ignores a hidden third segment: the corporate treasury department that hedges and aims to finance the whole corporation optimally—this acts as a shock absorber for the financial policies of the segments. Modeling the WACC of the corporate treasury department is quite difficult. Most companies assume that the impact of corporate treasury is not very large, and simply assume it away. As a first cut, we could do this too, although it is an issue we should revisit.

Conclusions

• In theory, the corporate WACC for Teletech is appropriate *only* for evaluating an asset having the same risk as the whole company. It is not appropriate for assets having different risks than the whole company.

• Segment WACCs are computed similarly to corporate WACCs.

• In concept, the corporate WACC is a weighted average of the segment WACCs. In practice, the weighted average concept may not hold, due to imperfections in the market and/or estimation errors.

• If we start computing segment WACCs, we must use the cost of debt, cost of equity, and the weights *appropriate to that segment.* We need a lot of information to do this correctly, or else we really need to stretch to make assumptions.

EXHIBIT 3 | Samples of Comparable Firms

Company Name	2004 Revenues ($ millions)	Equity Beta	Bond Rating	Book Val. Debt/Total Capital	Price to Book	Mkt. Val. Debt/Capital	Mkt. Val. Debt/Equity	Price/Earnings
Teletech Corporation	16,000	1.15	A−/BBB+	40%	3.0	22%	78%	12.9
Telecommunications Services Industry								
Alltel Corp.	8,246	1.00	A	44.7	2.4	23.2%	30.1%	15.4
AT&T Corp.	30,537	1.10	BB+	67.5	2.0	36.6%	57.7%	(2.4)
BellSouth Corp.	20,350	1.00	A	53.9	2.1	22.9%	29.7%	16.7
Centurytel Corp.	2,411	1.05	BBB+	48.7	1.3	37.0%	58.8%	13.3
Citizens Communications Co.	2,193	1.00	BB+	75.9	3.5	47.7%	91.1%	65.0
IDT Corp.	2,217	1.05	NA	4.6	1.2	2.1%	2.1%	(19.3)
SBC Communications Inc.	40,787	1.05	A	43.7	1.9	20.0%	25.0%	19.6
Sprint Corp.	27,428	1.15	A−	58.0	2.4	30.3%	43.4%	(43.1)
Verizon Communications Inc.	71,283	1.00	A+	40.0	2.6	24.1%	31.8%	12.5
Average		1.04		48.55	2.15	27.1%	41.1%	8.65
Telecommunications Equipment Industry								
Avaya Inc.	4,057	1.35	BB	54.5	3.5	4.4%	4.6%	18.3
Belden CDT Inc.	966	1.45	NA	23.6	1.2	17.5%	21.3%	38.7
Commscope Inc.	1,153	1.10	BB	41.6	2.0	22.4%	28.9%	10.3
Corning Inc.	3,854	1.45	BBB−	44.4	5.4	11.8%	13.4%	(11.1)
Harris Corp.	2,519	1.05	BBB−	24.5	2.7	10.7%	11.9%	21.9
Lucent Technologies Inc.	9,045	1.75	B	129.0	(26.0)	30.1%	43.0%	6.0
Nortel Networks Corp.	9,828	1.75	NA	45.7	3.0	20.7%	26.0%	(51.8)
Plantronics Inc.	560	1.20	NA	0.7	4.2	0.2%	0.2%	17.0
Scientific-Atlanta Inc.	1,708	1.45	NA	0.5	2.6	0.1%	0.1%	20.7
Average		1.39		40.50	(0.15)	13.1%	16.6%	7.77
Computer and Network Equipment Industry								
EMC Corp.	8,229	1.55	BBB	1.1	2.9	0.4%	0.4%	34.3
Gateway Inc.	3,650	1.35	NA	64.2	5.5	11.8%	13.4%	(4.2)
Hewlett-Packard Corp.	79,905	1.45	A−	16.9	1.7	7.8%	8.5%	18.5
Int'l. Business Machines Corp.	96,293	1.10	A+	51.4	4.1	8.4%	9.1%	15.2
Lexmark Int'l. Inc.	5,314	1.15	NA	6.8	4.2	1.4%	1.4%	15.5
NCR Corp.	5,984	1.20	NA	12.8	3.3	4.5%	4.8%	21.1
Seagate Technology	6,224	1.20	NA	28.6	4.4	10.0%	11.1%	25.0
Storage Technology Corp.	2,224	1.15	NA	0.9	2.4	0.3%	0.3%	18.2
Western Digital Corp.	3,047	1.80	NA	12.6	4.8	2.9%	3.0%	16.7
Average		1.33		21.70	3.70	5.3%	5.8%	17.81

Sources of data: *Value Line Investment Survey, S&P Research Insight.*

EXHIBIT 4 I   Debt-Capital-Market Conditions, October 2005

Corporate Bond Yields		U. S. Treasury Securities	
Industrials			
AAA	5.44%	3-month	3.56%
AA	5.51%	6-month	3.99%
A	5.74%	2-year	4.23%
		3-year	4.23%
BBB	6.23%	5-year	4.25%
BB	7.47%	10-year	4.39%
B	8.00%	30-year	4.62%
Phones			
A	6.17%		
BBB	6.28%		
Utilities			
A	5.69%		
BBB	6.09%		

Source of data: *Bloomberg LP.*

The Boeing 7E7

We still have a lot to get done as we move toward authority to offer the 7E7 to our customers. The team is making great progress—understanding what our customer wants, developing an airplane that meets their needs, and defining a case that will demonstrate the value of the program.
—**Michael Bair, Boeing Senior Vice President**[1]

In early 2003, Boeing announced plans to design and sell a new, "super-efficient" jet dubbed the 7E7, subsequently called the "Dreamliner." However, news over the next six months depressed the market for aircrafts, which were already in sharp contraction. The United States went to war against Iraq, spasms of global terrorism offered shocking headlines, and a deadly illness called SARS resulted in global travel warnings. For those and other reasons, airline profits were the worst seen in a generation. This seemed like an incredible environment in which to launch a major new airframe project. Nevertheless, on June 16, 2003, at the prestigious Paris Air Show, Michael Bair, the leader of the 7E7 project, announced that Boeing was making "excellent progress on the development of the 7E7 and continues to be on track to seek authority to offer the airplane."[2]

In order to proceed with the project, Bair sought a firm commitment from Boeing's board of directors in early 2004. If the board approved the plan, he could start collecting orders from airlines and expect passengers to start flying on the new jets in 2008. Between now and his recommendation to the board, he would need to complete a valuation of the 7E7 project and gain the support of Boeing's CEO, Philip Condit, and the other senior managers. Would the financial analysis show that this project would be profitable for Boeing's shareholders?

---

[1]"Bair Provides Update on Boeing 7E7 Dreamliner," *Le Bourget*, 16 June 2003.

[2]"Bair Provides Update."

This case was prepared by Professors James Tompkins and Robert F. Bruner using public information. It was written as a basis for class discussion rather than to illustrate effective or ineffective handling of an administrative situation. Copyright © 2004 by the University of Virginia Darden School Foundation, Charlottesville, VA. All rights reserved. *To order copies, send an e-mail to* sales@dardenpublishing.com. *No part of this publication may be reproduced, stored in a retrieval system, used in a spreadsheet, or transmitted in any form or by any means—electronic, mechanical, photocopying, recording, or otherwise—without the permission of the Darden School Foundation.*

Origins of the 7E7 Project

Boeing had not introduced a new commercial aircraft since it rolled out the highly successful 777 in 1994. Later in the 1990s, however, Boeing announced and then cancelled two new commercial-aircraft programs. The most prominent of those was the "Sonic Cruiser," which promised to fly 15 percent to 20 percent faster than any commercial aircraft and bragged of a sleek and futuristic design. Unfortunately, after two years of developing the Sonic Cruiser, Boeing's potential customers were sending the message that passengers were not willing to pay a premium price for a faster ride. Boeing was now long overdue to develop a product that would pull it out of its financial slump, as well as help it regain the commercial-aircraft sales that the company had lost over the years to Airbus, its chief rival.

With the 7E7, an Airbus executive argued that Boeing seemed to be promising a "salesperson's dream and engineer's nightmare."[3] The 7E7, while carrying between 200 and 250 passengers, would be capable of both short, domestic flights as well as long, international hauls. It would use 20 percent less fuel than existing planes of its projected size and be 10 percent cheaper to operate than Airbus's A330-200. At a time when major airlines were struggling to turn a profit, less fuel, cheaper operating costs, and long or short distance flexibility would be a very attractive package at the right price.

Skeptics of the 7E7 were not in short supply and suggested that the name "Dreamliner" was appropriate. To make the plane more fuel efficient, the 7E7 would be the first commercial aircraft built primarily with carbon-reinforced material, which was both stronger and lighter than the traditional aluminum. In addition, Boeing promised greater fuel efficiency by using a more efficient engine. Boeing claimed that the use of composites would also reduce its manufacturing costs. The goal would be to design a plane with fewer components that could be assembled in 3 days as opposed to the current 20 days that it took to rivet together the Boeing 767. The use of composite materials, however, had its risks. Composite materials were suspected as a contributory cause to a 2001 plane crash in New York and, therefore, would have to overcome regulatory scrutiny. Boeing would also have to change its production methods radically. The last time Boeing made a major production change was in 1997 in an effort to cut costs. However, because the process was not smooth, it resulted in two production lines being shut down for 30 days and hundreds of missed airline deliveries.

The ability to produce a short- and long-distance aircraft would also have to overcome engineering obstructions. Analysts argued that building a plane that would do short hops in Asia and long trans-Atlantic flights would require two versions of the plane with different wingspans.[4] Boeing engineers considered the possibility of snap-on wing extensions. The question was whether this would be too costly, as well as being technically feasible.

Finally, there was the matter of Boeing's board. Two of the most powerful members of the 11-person board, Harry Stonecipher and John McDonnell, were rumored

---

[3]"Will Boeing's New Idea Really Fly?" *BusinessWeek*, 23 June 2003.

[4]Noted by Richard Aboulafia, a senior analyst at Teal Group Corporation, in "Will Boeing's New Idea Really Fly?"

to have raised serious concerns regarding the cost of the 7E7. While the cost of developing the 7E7 project could be as high as $10 billion, there was an imminent veto threat if that number did not shrink by billions. More specifically the board wanted to keep 7E7 development costs down to only 40 percent of what it took to develop the 777. An additional pressure from the board was to keep the 7E7 per-copy costs to only 60 percent of the 777 costs. In response, Philip Condit, Boeing's CEO and chair, was quoted as saying that "Boeing has a responsibility to develop jetliners for less."[5] He knew, however, that if Boeing did not take bold risks in the commercial-aircraft industry that their days as a serious competitor to Airbus were numbered.

Commercial-Aircraft Industry

In 2002, two companies, Boeing and Airbus, dominated the large plane (100+ seats) commercial-aircraft industry. While Boeing historically held the lead in this market, through a number of measures Airbus became number one. In 2002, Airbus received 233 commercial orders compared to Boeing's 176 orders, representing a 57 percent unit market share and an estimated 53.5 percent dollar value market share.[6]

Airbus S.A.S.

Airbus was understandably proud of its growth. Established in 1970 by a consortium of European companies, it took Airbus 23 years to deliver its first 1000 aircraft, another six years to deliver the next 1000, and only another three years (by 2002) to pass the 3000 aircraft milestone.[7] In 1999, for the first time in its history, Airbus recorded more plane orders than its rival, Boeing.

Airbus's large plane commercial-aircraft products included the A300/310, A320, A330/340, and A380 families. Airbus touted the A300/310 family as having the flexibility to serve short-, medium-, and extended-range routes. The widebody, twin-engine aircraft was considered mid-size, with a typical passenger configuration of about 250 passengers. This family first flew passengers in 1983, and it was this aging fleet that provided a replacement opportunity for Boeing's 7E7. However, while Boeing was betting on the future demand for mid-size aircraft, Airbus announced its A380, superjumbo four-engine jet in 2000. The A380 was due to fly in 2006 with a 550-passenger configuration and long distance range of up to 8000 miles. It would be the largest passenger aircraft ever built.

The Boeing Company

Boeing was split into two primary segments: commercial airplanes and integrated defense systems. In 2002, it was awarded $16.6 billion in defense contracts, second

---

[5]"Losing Ground to Airbus, Boeing Faces a Key Choice," *Wall Street Journal,* 21 April 2003.

[6]"2002 Commercial Results," www.airbus.com.

[7]In 2001, Airbus formally became a single integrated entity through the transfer of Airbus related assets to the newly incorporated company. European Aeronautic Defense and Space Company (EADS) owned 80% of the new company, and BAE systems owned the remaining 20%.

only to Lockheed Martin with $17.0 billion. **Exhibit 1** shows that in 2002, each segment earned Boeing's revenues almost equally. In addition, while commercial-aircraft revenues had been falling, defense revenues had been rising. Analysts believed that Boeing was able to transfer significant amounts of technology from the defense R&D to the commercial-aircraft segment.

The commercial-aircraft segment produced and sold six main airframes designed to meet the needs of the short- to long-range markets: the 717, 737, and 757 standard-body models and the 747, 767, and 777 wide-body models. As of December 31, 2002, Boeing had undelivered units under firm order for 1,083 commercial aircraft and had a declining backlog of about $68 billion. For 2003, it projected 280 commercial-aircraft deliveries and expected between 275 and 300 in 2004. Boeing estimated that in 2003, the revenues for its commercial-airplane segment would be approximately $22 billion, down from $28 billion in 2002. Recognizing the negative impact of the September 11th attacks on commercial-aircraft demand, Boeing cut the production rates for 2002 in half in order to maintain profitability in that segment.

Exhibits 2 and **3** show Boeing's balance sheet and income statement respectively. While Boeing's earnings were down significantly from 2001 to 2002, most of this was the result of an accounting change (SFAS No. 142). However, a drop in commercial-airplane deliveries from 527 in 2001 to 381 in 2002 also contributed to the decline.

Demand for Commercial Aircraft

The long-term outlook for aircraft demand seemed positive.[8] Boeing's *Market Outlook* said the following:

> In the short term, air travel is influenced by business cycles, consumer confidence, and exogenous events. Over the long-term, cycles smooth out, and GDP, international trade, lower fares, and network service improvements become paramount. During the next 20 years, economies will grow annually by 3.2 percent, and air travel will continue its historic relationship with GDP by growing at an average annual rate of 5.1 percent.

As shown in **Exhibit 4,** Boeing's 20-year forecast from 2003 to 2022, was for 24,276 new commercial aircraft, in 2002 valued at $1.9 trillion. The company predicted a composition of 4,303 smaller regional jets (fewer than 90 seats); 13,647 single-aisle airplanes; 5,437 intermediate twin-aisle airplanes; and 889 747-size or larger airplanes. This prediction reflected a world fleet that would more than double, with one-fourth of the market coming from aircraft replacement and three-fourths from projected passenger and cargo growth.

Exhibit 5 illustrates Airbus's 20-year predictions for the years 2000–2020. Although the report was dated 2002, because of the September 11 attacks, numbers included the year 2000, to serve as a benchmark year. For that period, Airbus predicted the delivery

---

[8]The primary sources for commercial-aircraft demand estimates include Boeing's *2003 Current Market Outlook* and Airbus's *2002 Global Market Forecast 2001–2020*. While both reports recognized the negative effects of "exogenous events" such as September 11, 2001, they both agreed on a healthy long-term outlook.

of 15,887 new commercial aircraft in 2002, with a value of $1.5 trillion. This included 10,201 single-aisle aircraft; 3,842 twin-aisle aircraft; 1,138 very large aircraft, and 706 freighters. The 15,887-unit forecast did not include planes with less than 90 seats.

Although Boeing and Airbus's numbers are not directly comparable due to the slightly different time periods and aircraft classifications, it appeared that Airbus was more optimistic about the market for large aircraft than Boeing was. While Airbus predicted it to be a $270 billion market, including 1,138 passenger units, Boeing projected only $214 billion with 653 passenger units. Boeing, however, estimated that the share of intermediate-size planes would increase from 18 percent to 22 percent. In its forecast, Boeing acknowledged that intermediate-size airplanes would economically allow airlines to fly the increased frequencies, city pairs, and nonstop flights requested by passengers. According to a recent study by Frost & Sullivan, they believed that the Airbus market projection for the A380 was "over-optimistic."[9]

Aircraft Development and Lifecycle

The development of a new airframe was characterized by huge initial cash outflows that might require between one and two decades to recoup. For example, the development costs for the Boeing 777 were rumored to be $7 billion. Any pricing would not only have to recoup the upfront development costs but also the production costs. In addition, pricing would be subject to rigorous, competitive pressures. In short, because of the financial strains a new product line might create, each new aircraft was a "bet the ranch" proposition. Over time, survival in the industry depended on introducing successful products and having the deep financial pockets with which to survive the initially gushing cash flow.

While aircraft sales were subject to short-term, cyclical deviations, there was some degree of predictability in sales. Sales would typically peak shortly after the introduction of the new aircraft, and then fall. Thereafter, sales would rise and fall as derivatives of the aircraft were offered. **Exhibit 6** shows the cycles for the first 20 years of the 757 and 767 sales.

The 7E7

The concept of the Boeing 7E7 was driven by customer requirements. Boeing originally announced in March 2001 its plans to build the Sonic Cruiser, a plane that would fly just below the speed of sound. The success of the Cruiser depended on whether passengers would pay a premium for a faster flight. However, potential airplane customers who had been interested in the Cruiser during a robust, commercial-air travel market were now focusing on survival. The events of September 11 and the bursting of the technology bubble led to a significant decline in airplane orders. As a result, Boeing solicited updated feedback from a number of potential customers who

---

[9]"An Ongoing Rivalry," *Avionics Today*, August 2003.

would soon need to replace their aging fleet of mid-range planes, such as the 757s, 767s, A300s, A310s, A321s, and A330s. Overwhelmingly, the revised message from customers was for a plane with lower operating costs.

Based on discussions with over 40 airlines throughout the world, Bair identified a fresh market to replace mid-size planes, based not only on lower operating costs, but also on the creation of a mid-size plane that could travel long distances, a feat previously viable by only large planes, such as the 747. Such flexibility would allow airlines to offer nonstop service on routes that required long-range planes but did not justify the subsequent larger size. Bair estimated there to be more than 400 city pairs (e.g., Atlanta–Athens) that could be served efficiently on a nonstop basis by the 7E7.

Boeing was considering two new members for the 7E7 family, a basic and a stretch version. **Exhibit 7** gives Boeing's description of the two configurations. Other improvements for passengers included wider aisles, lower cabin altitude, and increased cabin humidity. In addition, the planes would include systems that provided in-flight entertainment, Internet access, real-time airplane systems and structure health monitoring, and crew connectivity. Furthermore, Boeing claimed the 7E7 would have the smallest sound "footprint" with the quietest takeoff and landing in its class.

Boeing projected a demand for between 2,000 and 3,000 planes of the 7E7 type within 20 years of each one entering service. A study by Frost & Sullivan predicted the sale of "at least 2,000 B7E7s."[10] However, the demand was highly dependent on whether Boeing could deliver the promised 20 percent cheaper fuel costs and the range flexibility in a mid-size aircraft. Furthermore, if the range flexibility did require snap-on wings, such a design may significantly increase the building costs of the aircraft. Not only did Boeing face the engineering uncertainty of being able to deliver such an aircraft, but also the risk of its duplication by Airbus. Airbus had already stated that if the fuel efficiency was primarily generated by new engine designs, then it would simply order the more efficient engines for its planes. Any uncertainty in the 7E7 plane specifications and risk of competition clearly put downward pressure on both the price Boeing could demand, as well as the number of units it would be able to sell.

Financial Forecast and Analysis

Exhibit 8 contains a 20-year forecast of free cash flows from the Boeing 7E7 project consistent with public information released by Boeing, Airbus, analysts, and other experts in the field. See the **Appendix** for detailed forecast assumptions. The primary implication of the forecast is that the 7E7 project would provide an internal rate of return (IRR) close to 16 percent. This assumes that Boeing would not only deliver the promised plane specifications, but that Airbus would be unable to replicate the 7E7's efficiencies.

Based on both analysts' and Boeing's expectations, the base case assumes that Boeing could sell 2,500 units in the first 20 years of delivery. Pricing was estimated using 2002 prices for Boeing's 777 and 767. The 7E7 would be a hybrid of the two

---

[10]"An Ongoing Rivalry"

planes in terms of the number of passengers and range. By interpolating between the 777 and 767 prices, it was possible to estimate the value placed on the range and number of passengers. Using this methodology, without any premium for the promised lower operating costs, the minimum price for the 7E7 and 7E7 Stretch was estimated to be $114.5 million and $144.5 million, respectively, in 2002. The forecast assumed that customers would be willing to pay a 5 percent price premium for the lower operating costs.

The IRR, which is consistent with "base case" assumptions, was 15.7 percent. But, the estimate of IRR was sensitive to variations in different assumptions. In particular, some obvious uncertainties would be the number of units that Boeing would be able to sell and at what price. For example, if Boeing only sold 1,500 units in the first 20 years, then, as shown in **Exhibit 9,** the IRR would drop to 11 percent. This might occur if air travel demand worsened, or if Airbus entered this segment with a new competing product.

Additional unknown variables were the development costs and the per-copy costs to build the 7E7. Boeing's board was anxious to minimize those costs. The forecast assumes $8 billion for development costs; however, analyst estimates were in the $6 billion to $10 billion range. The cost to manufacture the 7E7 was also subject to great uncertainty. On the one hand, engineers were challenged to build a mid-size aircraft with long-range capabilities. The engineering design to achieve this could push building costs up significantly. Conversely, if Boeing succeeded in using composite materials, which required a fraction of the normal assembly time, then construction costs would be lower. Consistent with Boeing's history, the base case assumes 80 percent as the percentage of cost of goods sold to sales. As shown in **Exhibit 9,** however, the IRR of the 7E7 was very sensitive to keeping production costs low.

Cost of Capital

Boeing's weighted-average cost of capital (WACC) could be estimated using the following well-known formula:

$$\text{WACC} = (\text{percent Debt})(r_d)(1 - t_c) + (\text{percent Equity})(r_e)$$

where:

$$r_d = \text{Pretax cost of debt capital}$$
$$t_c = \text{Marginal effective corporate tax rate}$$
$$\text{percent Debt} = \text{Proportion of debt in a market-value capital structure}$$
$$r_e = \text{Cost of equity capital}$$
$$\text{percent Equity} = \text{Proportion of equity in a market-value capital structure}$$

Exhibit 10 gives information about betas and debt/equity ratios for Boeing and comparable companies. **Exhibit 11** provides data about Boeing's outstanding debt issues. While Boeing's marginal effective tax rate had been smaller in the past, it currently was expected to be 35 percent. In June 2003, the yield on the three-month U.S. Treasury bill was 0.85 percent, and the yield on the 30-year Treasury bond was 4.56 percent. On June 16, 2003, Boeing's stock price closed at $36.41.

Analysts pointed out that Boeing actually consisted of two separate businesses: the relatively more stable defense business and the conversely more volatile commercial business. Defense corporations were the beneficiaries when the world became unstable due to the terrorist attacks on September 11, 2001. Furthermore, the United States, along with some of its allies, went to war against Iraq on March 20, 2003. While Bush declared an end to major Iraqi combat operations on May 1, 2003, as of June 16, the death toll in Iraq continued to rise on a daily basis. A different type of risk emanated with the outbreak of SARS. On February 1, 2003, China announced the discovery of the deadly and contagious illness that subsequently spread to Canada and Australia. As of June 16, travel warnings were still outstanding. Thus, the question arose of whether one should estimate Boeing's cost of capital to serve as a benchmark-required rate of return. Would a required return on a portfolio of those two businesses be appropriate for evaluating the 7E7 project? If necessary, how might it be possible to isolate a required return for commercial aircraft?

Conclusion

Within the aircraft-manufacturing industry, the magnitude of risk posed by the launching of a major new aircraft was accepted as a matter of course. With huge, upfront, capital costs in an environment of intense technology and price competition, there was no guarantee of success or major significant losses if the gamble did not pay off. At a time of great political and economic uncertainty, Michael Bair said:

> Clearly, we have to make a compelling business proposition. It could be [that] we'll still be in a terrible business climate in 2004. But you can't let what's happening today cause you to make bad decisions for this very long business cycle. This plane is very important to our future.[11]

Central to any recommendation that Bair would make to Boeing's board of directors was an assessment of the economic profitability of the 7E7 project. Would the project compensate the shareholders of Boeing for the risks and use of their capital? Were there other considerations that might mitigate the economic analysis? For instance, to what extent might organizational and strategic considerations influence the board? If Boeing did not undertake the 7E7, would it be conceding leadership of the commercial-aircraft business to Airbus?

---

[11]"New Team, Name for Boeing 'Super-Efficient' Jet," *Seattle Times,* 30 January 2003.

EXHIBIT 1 | Revenues, Operating Profits, and Identifiable Assets by Segment for the
Boeing Company

	2002	2001	2000
Revenues			
Commercial airplanes	$28,387	$35,056	$31,171
Integrated defense systems	24,957	22,815	19,963
Accounting eliminations and other	725	1,047	187
Total	$54,069	$58,918	$51,321
Operating Profit			
Commercial airplanes	$2,847	$2,632	$2,736
Integrated defense systems	2,009	2,965	$1,002
Accounting eliminations and other	(988)	(1,701)	(680)
Total	$3,868	$3,896	$3,058
Identifiable Assets			
Commercial airplanes	$9,726	$10,851	$10,367
Integrated defense systems	12,753	12,461	12,579
Unallocated and other	29,863	25,666	20,588
Total	$52,342	$48,978	$43,534

Source: Boeing Company, 2002 Annual Report.

EXHIBIT 2 | Boeing Balance Sheets ($ in millions)

	2002	2001
Assets		
Cash and cash equivalents	$2,333	$633
Accounts receivable	5,007	5,156
Inventories, net of advances, progress billings, and reserves	6,184	7,559
Other current assets	3,331	3,497
Total current assets	16,855	16,845
Customer and commercial financing–net	10,922	9,345
Property, plant, and equipment–net	8,765	8,459
Goodwill and other acquired intangibles–net	3,888	6,447
Prepaid pension expense	6,671	5,838
Deferred income taxes and other assets	5,241	2,044
Total assets	$52,342	$48,978
Liabilities and Shareholders' Equity		
Accounts payable and other liabilities	$13,739	$14,237
Short-term debt and current portion of long-term debt	1,814	1,399
Other current liabilities	4,257	4,930
Total current liabilities	19,810	20,566
Accrued retiree health-care and pension-plan liability	11,705	5,922
Long-term debt	12,589	10,866
Other liabilities	542	799
Shareholders' equity:		
Common shares	1,831	4,994
Retained earnings	14,262	14,340
Treasury shares	(8,397)	(8,509)
Total shareholders' equity	7,696	10,825
Total liabilities and shareholders' equity	$52,342	$48,978

Source: Boeing Company, 2002 Annual Report.

EXHIBIT 3 | Boeing Income Statements ($ in millions; except per-share data)

	2002	2001
Sales and other operating revenues	$54,069	$58,198
Cost of products and services	45,499	48,778
General and administrative expense	2,534	2,389
Research and development expense	1,639	1,936
Impact of September 11, 2001 charges/(recoveries)	(2)	935
Other operating expenses	531	264
Earnings from operations	3,868	3,896
Other income/(expense)	42	318
Interest and debt expense	(730)	(650)
Earnings before income taxes	3,180	3,564
Income taxes[1]	861	738
Net earnings before cumulative effect of accounting change	2,319	2,826
Cumulative effect of accounting change, net of tax	(1,827)	1
Net earnings	$492	$2,827
Earnings per share	$0.62	$3.46

Source: Boeing Company, 2002 Annual Report.

[1]Boeing's average tax rate consistent with reported financial performance for 2002 was 27 percent. Yet Boeing's marginal effective tax rate was 35 percent.

EXHIBIT 4 | Boeing Delivery Distribution Forecast 2003–2022

Seat Category	Models	2002 Dollars (billions)	Passenger Units Freighter Units Total Units
Single-aisle			
Small and intermediate regional jets	Fewer than 90 seats Regional jets	96.5	4,303 0
			4,303
90–170	717-200 737-600/-700/-800	575.5	11,249 58
	A318/A319/A320 Larger regional jets		11,307
171–240	737-900 757	170.0	2,307 33
	A321		2,340
Twin-aisle			
230–310 (181–249)	767 A300	370.7	2,521 272
	A310 A330-200		2,793
311–399 (250–368)	777 A330-300	488.3	2,482 162
	A340		2,644
Large			
747 and larger (>400)	747-400 A380	214.0	653 236
			889
Total		**1,915.0**	**23,515** 761
			24,276

Source: Boeing Company.

EXHIBIT 5 | Airbus Delivery Distribution Forecast, 2000–2020

Seat Category (number of seats)	Examples of Models	2002 Dollars (billions)	Units
Single-aisle (passenger) (100–210)	A318, A319, A320, A321	609	10,201
Twin-aisle (passenger) (250–400)	A330, A340	524	3,842
Very large (passenger) (>400)	A380	270	1,138
Freighters		106	706
Total		**1,509**	**15,887**

Source: Boeing Company.

EXHIBIT 6 | Lifecycle of Unit Sales (Averaged across the Boeing 757 and 767)

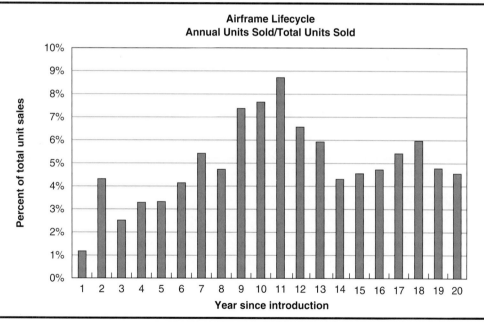

Source: Boeing Company Web site, www.boeing.com.

EXHIBIT 7 | Description of Product Configurations for the Baseline and Stretch Models of the 7E7

Boeing 7E7 Baseline Model	**Boeing 7E7 Stretch**
Brief Description:	**Brief Description:**
The Boeing 7E7 Baseline is a super-efficient airplane with new passenger-pleasing features. It will bring the economics of large jet transports to the middle of the market, using 20% less fuel than any other airplane its size.	The Boeing 7E7 Stretch is a slightly bigger version of the 7E7 Baseline. Both are super-efficient airplanes with new passenger-pleasing features. The Stretch will bring the economics of large jet transports to the middle of the market, using 20% less fuel than any other airplane its size.
Seating:	**Seating:**
200 passengers in three-class configuration 300 + in single-class configuration	250 passengers in three-class configuration 350 + in single-class configuration
Range:	**Range:**
6,600 nautical miles	8,000 nautical miles
Configuration:	**Configuration:**
Twin-aisle	Twin-aisle
Cross Section:	**Cross Section:**
226 inches	226 inches
Wing Span:	**Wing Span:**
186 feet	186 feet
Length:	**Length:**
182 feet	202 feet
Cruise Speed:	**Cruise Speed:**
Mach 0.85	Mach 0.85
Cargo Capacity after Passenger Bags:	**Cargo Capacity after Passenger Bags:**
5 pallets + 5 LD3 containers	6 pallets + 8 LD3 containers
Program Milestones:	**Program Milestones:**
Authority to offer: Late 2003/Early 2004 Assembly start: 2005 First flight: 2007 Certification/entry into service: 2008	Entry into service 2010 likely, but depends on marketplace

Source: Boeing Company.

EXHIBIT 8 | Forecast of Boeing 7E7 Free Cash Flows ($ in millions)

Assumptions	
Initial price of 7E7	$136.95
Initial price of 7E7 Stretch	$170.87
Cost of goods sold (% of sales)	80%
Working capital requirement (WCR) as a % of sales	6.7%
General, selling, and administrative (GS&A) as a % of sales	8%
R&D expense (% of sales)	2.3% (excluding 2004–2007)
Capital expenditure (% of sales)	0.16% (excluding 2004–2007)
Development costs (2004–2009)	$8,000
Total number of planes: yrs 1–20	2,500
Total number of planes: yrs 20–30	Same as year 20
Inflation	2%
Marginal effective tax rate	35%

	2004	2005	2006	2007	2008
Revenues					
Planes delivered					
7E7 planes					30
7E7 Stretch planes					30
7E7 price					0
7E7 Stretch price					$136.95
Total product revenues					
Cost of goods sold					4,108.64
Gross profit					3,286.91
Depreciation	7.50	29.44	102.23	117.06	821.73
GS&A expense					123.78
Operating profit (before R&D)	(7.50)	(29.44)	(102.23)	(117.06)	308.15
R&D expense	300.00	900.00	3,000.00	900.00	389.80
Pretax profit	(307.50)	(929.44)	(3,102.23)	(1,017.06)	694.50
Taxes (or tax credit)	(107.63)	(325.30)	(1,085.78)	(355.97)	(304.69)
After-tax profit	(199.88)	(604.13)	(2,016.45)	(661.09)	(106.64)
Capital expenditure	100.00	300.00	1,000.00	300.00	(198.05)
Depreciation add-back	7.50	29.44	102.23	117.06	206.57
Change in WCR					123.78
					275.28
Annual free cash flow	$(292.38)	$(874.70)	$(2,914.22)	$(844.03)	$(556.13)

EXHIBIT 8 | (continued)

	2009	2010	2011	2012	2013
Revenues					
Planes delivered	108	64	82	84	104
7E7 planes	108	51	41	42	52
7E7 Stretch planes	0	13	41	42	52
7E7 price	$139.69	$142.49	$145.34	$148.24	$151.21
7E7 Stretch price		170.87	174.28	177.77	181.33
Total product revenues	15,086.93	9,488.14	13,104.49	13,692.60	17,291.79
Cost of goods sold	12,069.55	7,590.51	10,483.59	10,954.08	13,833.44
Gross profit	3,017.39	1,897.63	2,620.90	2,738.52	3,458.36
Depreciation	123.80	115.66	108.67	102.83	99.64
GS&A expense	1,131.52	711.61	982.84	1,026.94	1,296.88
Operating profit (before R&D)	1,762.06	1,070.36	1,529.40	1,608.75	2,061.83
R&D expense	647.00	218.23	301.40	314.93	397.71
Pretax profit	1,115.06	852.13	1,227.99	1,293.82	1,664.12
Taxes (or tax credit)	390.27	298.25	429.80	452.84	582.44
After-tax profit	724.79	553.89	798.19	840.98	1,081.68
Capital expenditure	124.14	15.18	20.97	21.91	27.67
Depreciation add-back	123.80	115.66	108.67	102.83	99.64
Change in WCR	735.55	(375.12)	242.30	39.40	241.15
Annual free cash flow	$(11.09)	$1,029.48	$643.60	$882.50	$912.51

	2014	2015	2016	2017	2018
Revenues					
Planes delivered	136	119	185	192	219
7E7 planes	68	60	93	96	110
7E7 Stretch planes	68	59	92	96	109
7E7 price	$154.23	$157.32	$160.46	$163.67	$166.95
7E7 Stretch price	184.95	188.65	192.42	196.27	200.20
Total product revenues	23,064.59	20,569.48	32,626.19	34,554.82	40,185.75
Cost of goods sold	18,451.67	16,455.59	26,100.95	27,643.86	32,148.60
Gross profit	4,612.92	4,113.90	6,525.24	6,910.96	8,037.15
Depreciation	99.95	100.84	103.70	106.87	110.54
GS&A expense	1,729.84	1,542.71	2,446.96	2,591.61	3,013.93
Operating profit (before R&D)	2,783.12	2,470.35	3,974.57	4,212.48	4,912.68
R&D expense	530.49	473.10	750.40	794.76	924.27
Pretax profit	2,252.64	1,997.25	3,224.17	3,417.72	3,988.40
Taxes (or tax credit)	788.42	699.04	1,128.46	1,196.20	1,395.94
After-tax profit	1,464.21	1,298.21	2,095.71	2,221.52	2,592.46
Capital expenditure	36.90	32.91	52.20	55.29	64.30
Depreciation add-back	99.95	100.84	103.70	106.87	110.54
Change in WCR	386.78	(167.17)	807.80	129.22	377.27
Annual free cash flow	$1,140.48	$1,533.31	$1,339.41	$2,143.88	$2,261.44

EXHIBIT 8 | (*continued*)

	2019	2020	2021	2022	2023
Revenues					
Planes delivered	165	149	108	115	119
7E7 planes	83	75	54	58	60
7E7 Stretch planes	82	74	54	57	59
7E7 price	$170.29	$173.69	$177.17	$180.71	$184.32
7E7 Stretch price	204.20	208.29	212.45	216.70	221.03
Total product revenues	30,878.29	28,440.04	21,039.33	22,833.05	24,100.43
Cost of goods sold	24,702.63	22,752.03	16,831.46	18,266.44	19,280.34
Gross profit	6,175.66	5,688.01	4,207.87	4,566.61	4,820.09
Depreciation	112.89	114.85	115.88	117.16	118.63
GS&A expense	2,315.87	2,133.00	1,577.95	1,712.48	1,807.53
Operating profit (before R&D)	3,746.89	3,440.15	2,514.04	2,736.97	2,893.92
R&D expense	710.20	654.12	483.90	525.16	554.31
Pretax profit	3,036.69	2,786.03	2,030.13	2,211.81	2,339.61
Taxes (or tax credit)	1,062.84	975.11	710.55	774.13	818.86
After-tax profit	1,973.85	1,810.92	1,319.59	1,437.68	1,520.75
Capital expenditure	49.41	45.50	33.66	36.53	38.56
Depreciation add-back	112.89	114.85	115.88	117.16	118.63
Change in WCR	(623.60)	(163.36)	(495.85)	120.18	84.91
Annual free cash flow	$2,660.94	$2,043.63	$1,897.65	$1,398.13	$1,515.90

	2024	2025	2026	2027	2028
Revenues					
Planes delivered	136	150	120	115	115
7E7 planes	68	75	60	58	58
7E7 Stretch planes	68	75	60	57	57
7E7 price	$188.01	$191.77	$195.61	$199.52	$203.51
7E7 Stretch price	225.46	229.96	234.56	239.26	244.04
Total product revenues	28,115.61	31,630.06	25,810.13	25,209.53	25,713.72
Cost of goods sold	22,492.49	25,304.05	20,648.10	20,167.63	20,570.98
Gross profit	5,623.12	6,326.01	5,162.03	5,041.91	5,142.74
Depreciation	116.20	105.31	62.54	50.92	43.54
GS&A expense	2,108.67	2,372.25	1,935.76	1,890.72	1,928.53
Operating profit (before R&D)	3,398.25	3,848.45	3,163.73	3,100.27	3,170.68
R&D expense	646.66	727.49	593.63	579.82	591.42
Pretax profit	2,751.60	3,120.96	2,570.09	2,520.45	2,579.26
Taxes (or tax credit)	963.06	1,092.33	899.53	882.16	902.74
After-tax profit	1,788.54	2,028.62	1,670.56	1,638.29	1,676.52
Capital expenditure	44.98	50.61	41.30	40.34	41.14
Depreciation add-back	116.20	105.31	62.54	50.92	43.54
Change in WCR	269.02	235.47	(389.94)	(40.24)	33.78
Annual free cash flow	$1,590.73	$1,847.86	$2,081.74	$1,689.12	$1,645.13

continued

EXHIBIT 8 | (*continued*)

	2029	2030	2031	2032	2033
Revenues					
Planes delivered	115	115	115	115	115
7E7 planes	58	58	58	58	58
7E7 Stretch planes	57	57	57	57	57
7E7 price	$207.58	$211.73	$215.96	$220.28	$224.69
7E7 Stretch price	248.92	253.90	258.98	264.16	269.44
Total product revenues	26,228.00	26,752.56	27,287.61	27,833.36	28,390.03
Cost of goods sold	20,982.40	21,402.05	21,830.09	22,266.69	22,712.02
Gross profit	5,245.60	5,350.51	5,457.52	5,566.67	5,678.01
Depreciation	39.86	41.10	42.13	43.19	44.07
GS&A expense	1,967.10	2,006.44	2,046.57	2,087.50	2,129.25
Operating profit (before R&D)	3,238.64	3,302.97	3,368.82	3,435.98	3,504.68
R&D expense	603.24	615.31	627.62	640.17	652.97
Pretax profit	2,635.39	2,687.66	2,741.21	2,795.81	2,851.71
Taxes (or tax credit)	922.39	940.68	959.42	978.53	998.10
After-tax profit	1,713.00	1,746.98	1,781.78	1,817.28	1,853.61
Capital expenditure	41.96	42.80	43.66	44.53	45.42
Depreciation add-back	39.86	41.10	42.13	43.19	44.07
Change in WCR	34.46	35.15	35.85	36.57	37.30
Annual free cash flow	$1,676.45	$1,710.13	$1,744.41	$1,779.37	$1,814.96

	2034	2035	2036	2037
Revenues				
Planes delivered	115	115	115	115
7E7 planes	58	58	58	58
7E7 Stretch planes	57	57	57	57
7E7 price	$229.18	$233.77	$238.44	$243.21
7E7 Stretch price	274.83	280.33	285.93	291.65
Total product revenues	28,957.83	29,536.99	30,127.73	30,730.28
Cost of goods sold	23,166.26	23,629.59	24,102.18	24,584.22
Gross profit	5,791.57	5,907.40	6,025.55	6,146.06
Depreciation	44.59	45.33	45.25	45.08
GS&A expense	2,171.84	2,215.27	2,259.58	2,304.77
Operating profit (before R&D)	3,575.14	3,646.80	3,720.72	3,796.21
R&D expense	666.03	679.35	692.94	706.80
Pretax profit	2,909.11	2,967.45	3,027.78	3,089.41
Taxes (or tax credit)	1,018.19	1,038.61	1,059.72	1,081.29
After-tax profit	1,890.92	1,928.84	1,968.06	2,008.12
Capital expenditure	46.33	47.26	48.20	49.17
Depreciation add-back	44.59	45.33	45.25	45.08
Change in WCR	38.04	38.80	39.58	40.37
Annual free cash flow	$1,851.14	$1,888.10	$1,925.52	$1,963.65

EXHIBIT 9 | Sensitivity Analysis of Project IRRs by Price, Volume, Development, and Production Costs

Unit Volume (First 20 Years)	Price Premium Above Expected Minimum Price			
	0%	5%	10%	15%
1,500	10.5%	10.9%	11.3%	11.7%
1,750	11.9%	12.3%	12.7%	13.1%
2,000	13.0%	13.5%	13.9%	14.4%
2,250	14.1%	14.6%	15.1%	15.5%
2,500	15.2%	*15.7%*	16.1%	16.6%
2,750	16.1%	16.6%	17.1%	17.6%
3,000	17.1%	17.6%	18.1%	18.6%

Development Costs	Cost of Goods Sold as a Percentage of Sales			
	78%	80%	82%	84%
$6,000,000,000	21.3%	18.7%	15.9%	12.6%
$7,000,000,000	19.4%	17.0%	14.4%	11.3%
$8,000,000,000	17.9%	*15.7%*	13.2%	10.3%
$9,000,000,000	16.6%	14.5%	12.1%	9.4%
$10,000,000,000	15.5%	13.5%	11.2%	8.6%

Note: The IRR consistent with "base case" assumptions is 15.7% and is indicated in italics in the table.

Source: Case writer's analysis.

EXHIBIT 10 | Information on Comparable Companies (Specially calculated betas estimated from daily stock and market returns over the periods indicated)

	Boeing	Lockheed Martin	Northrop Grumman	Raytheon
Percentage of revenues derived from government (defense and space)	46%	93%	91%	73%
Estimated betas				
1. Value Line[1]	1.05	0.60	0.70	0.80
2. Calculated against the S&P 500 index:[2]				
60 months	0.80	0.36	0.34	0.43
21 months	1.03	0.38	0.31	0.46
60 trading days	1.45	0.34	0.27	0.66
3. Calculated against the NYSE composite index:[2]				
60 months	1.00	0.49	0.44	0.59
21 months	1.17	0.44	0.36	0.53
60 trading days	1.62	0.37	0.30	0.73
Effective marginal tax rate	0.35	0.35	0.35	0.35
Market-value debt/equity ratios	0.525	0.410	0.640	0.624

Sources: Case writer's analysis and *Value Line Investment Survey.*

[1]Value Line betas are calculated from a regression analysis between the weekly percentage change in price of a stock and the weekly percentage changes of the New York Stock Exchange Composite Index. The beta is calculated using the last five years of data.

[2]Regression periods for the 60-day, 21-month, and 60-month begin on March 20, 2003, September 17, 2001, and June 16, 1998, respectively. Regression periods end on June 16, 2003.

EXHIBIT 11 | Outstanding Bonds of the Boeing Company as of June 2003 ($ values in millions)

Debt Amount	Debt Rating	Coupon	Maturity	Price	Yield To Maturity
$202	A-	7.625%	2/15/2005	106.175	3.911%
$298	A-	6.625%	6/1/2005	105.593	3.393%
$249	A-	6.875%	11/1/2006	110.614	3.475%
$175	A-	8.100%	11/15/2006	112.650	4.049%
$349	A-	9.750%	4/1/2012	129.424	5.470%
$597	A-	6.125%	2/15/2013	103.590	4.657%
$398	A-	8.750%	8/15/2021	127.000	6.239%
$300	A-	7.950%	8/15/2024	126.951	5.732%
$247	A-	7.250%	6/15/2025	114.506	6.047%
$249	A-	8.750%	9/15/2031	131.000	6.337%
$173	A-	8.625%	11/15/2031	138.974	5.805%
$393	A-	6.125%	2/15/2033	103.826	5.850%
$300	A-	6.625%	2/15/2038	106.715	6.153%
$100	A-	7.500%	8/15/2042	119.486	6.173%
$173	A-	7.825%	4/15/2043	132.520	5.777%
$125	A-	6.875%	10/15/2043	110.084	6.191%

Note: This table does not include the outstanding debt of Boeing's financing subsidiary, Boeing Capital Corporation.

Sources: Boeing Company 10-Q, Bloomberg Financial Services, and Mergent Online.

APPENDIX | Assumptions Underlying the Forecast of Cash Flows

Revenue Estimation

In order to project revenues for the project, several assumptions were made about the expected demand and timing for the units, their price, and price increases.

Demand: Boeing estimated that in the first 20 years they would sell 2,000–3,000 units.[1] Frost & Sullivan, aviation industry analysts, predicted at least 2,000 units.[2] Analysis assumes 2,500 units in years 1 through 20. Years 20–30 assume unit sales equal to year 20. First delivery of 7E7 expected in 2008 and 7E7 Stretch in 2010.

Timing of demand: Units sold per year is the percentage of the total units in the first 20 years as shown in **Exhibit 6. Exhibit 6** uses an historical average of the 757 and 767 unit sales during their first 20 years. The Boeing 7E7 is expected to be a replacement aircraft for the 757 and 767. Analysis assumes the 7E7 Stretch accounts for only 20 percent of unit sales in its first year of delivery and 50 percent thereafter. If the total number of unit sales per year is an odd number, the 7E7 units are rounded up and the 7E7 Stretch are rounded down.

Price: The expected price of the 7E7 and Stretch version is a function of the 767 and 777 prices in 2002. Using range and capacity as the primary variables, the 7E7 and 7E7 Stretch would be expected to have a minimum price of $114.5 million and $144.5 million respectively in 2002 dollars. This does not include a premium for the expected lower operating costs and flexibility of the 7E7. The analysis assumes a 5 percent price premium as a benchmark, resulting in expected prices of $120.2 million and $151.7 million in 2002.

Rate of price increases: Aircraft prices are assumed to increase at the rate of inflation. Inflation is assumed to be 2 percent per year until 2037.

Expense Estimation

Cost of goods sold: The average cost of goods sold for Boeing's commercial-aircraft division was 80 percent over the three-year period 2000–2002. The range was 77.9 percent to 81.1 percent. The analysis assumes 80 percent as the COGS.

General, selling, and administrative expense: The average general, selling, and administrative expense for Boeing was 7.5 percent over the three-year period 2000–2002. The range was 7.4 percent to 7.7 percent. The analysis assumes 7.5 percent as the general, selling, and administrative expense.

Depreciation: Boeing depreciated its assets on an accelerated basis. The forecast uses 150 percent declining balance depreciation with a 20-year asset life and zero salvage value as the base.

Research and development as a percentage of sales: The average research and development expense for Boeing's commercial-aircraft division as a percentage of commercial-aircraft sales was 2.3 percent over the three-year period 2000–2002. The range was 1.8 percent to 2.7 percent. During that period, Boeing did not have any extraordinary new commercial-aircraft development expenses. The analysis, therefore, assumes 2.3 percent as the estimated research and development expense. That does not include the initial research and development costs required to design and develop the 7E7.

Tax expense: Boeing's expected marginal effective tax rate was 35 percent.

Other Adjustments to Cash Flow

Capital expenditures: The 1998–2002 average for capital expenditures as a percentage of sales was 0.93 percent. During this period, Boeing did not have any extraordinary new commercial-aircraft development expenses. At the time, Boeing had six families of aircraft: the 717, 737, 747, 757, 767, and 777. The average capital expenditures per family line, as a percentage of sales, was therefore 0.16 percent. This does not include the initial capital expenditure costs required to develop and build the 7E7.

Change in working capital requirements (WCR): For the years 2000–2002, Boeing had negative working capital due to factors such as advance customer payments. The analysis assumes that the commercial segment of Boeing would require positive working capital. The years prior to 2000, Boeing had positive working capital. The 1997–1999, three-year average of working capital as a percentage of sales is 6.7 percent with a range from 3.5 percent to 11.2 percent. The analysis assumes this percentage.

---

[1] "New Team, Name for Boeing 'Super-Efficient' Jet," *Seattle Times,* 30 January 2003, 1.

[2] "An Ongoing Rivalry," *Aviation Today,* August 2003.

APPENDIX | (continued)

Initial development costs: Development costs include the research and capital requirements needed to design and build the 7E7. Analysts estimated between $6 billion and $10 billion.[3] The analysis assumes $8 billion. Assuming a launch in 2004, analysts expected spending to peak in 2006. Timing of the development costs are assumed to be 2004: 5 percent, 2005: 15 percent, 2006: 50 percent, 2007: 15 percent, 2008: 10 percent, and 2009: 5 percent. It is estimated that 75 percent of the initial development costs are research and development expenses, while the remaining 25 percent are capital expenditures.

[3]"Boeing Plays Defense," *Business Week,* 3 June 2003.

Source: Case writer's analysis.

PART 4

Capital Budgeting and Resource Allocation

The Investment Detective

The essence of capital budgeting and resource allocation is a search for good investments in which to place the firm's capital. The process can be simple when viewed in purely mechanical terms, but a number of subtle issues can obscure the best investment choices. The capital-budgeting analyst, therefore, is necessarily a detective who must winnow bad evidence from good. Much of the challenge is in knowing what quantitative analysis to generate in the first place.

Suppose you are a new capital-budgeting analyst for a company considering investments in the eight projects listed in **Exhibit 1.** The chief financial officer of your company has asked you to rank the projects and recommend the "four best" that the company should accept.

In this assignment, only the quantitative considerations are relevant. No other project characteristics are deciding factors in the selection, except that management has determined that projects 7 and 8 are mutually exclusive.

All the projects require the same initial investment, $2 million. Moreover, all are believed to be of the same risk class. The firm's weighted average cost of capital has never been estimated. In the past, analysts have simply assumed that 10 percent was an appropriate discount rate (although certain officers of the company have recently asserted that the discount rate should be much higher).

To stimulate your analysis, consider the following questions:

1. Can you rank the projects simply by inspecting the cash flows?

2. What criteria might you use to rank the projects? Which quantitative ranking methods are better? Why?

3. What is the ranking you found by using quantitative methods? Does this ranking differ from the ranking obtained by simple inspection of the cash flows?

4. What kinds of real investment projects have cash flows similar to those in **Exhibit 1?**

EXHIBIT 1 I Projects' Free Cash Flows (dollars in thousands)

Project number: Initial investment		1 ($2,000)	2 ($2,000)	3 ($2,000)	4 ($2,000)	5 ($2,000)	6 ($2,000)	7 ($2,000)	8 ($2,000)
Year	1	$330	$1,666		$ 160	$280	$2,200*	$1,200	($350)
	2	330	334*		200	280		900*	(60)
	3	330	165		350	280		300	60
	4	330			395	280		90	350
	5	330			432	280		70	700
	6	330			440*	280			1,200
	7	330*			442	280			$2,250*
	8	$1,000			444	280*			
	9				446	280			
	10				448	280			
	11				450	280			
	12				451	280			
	13				451	280			
	14				452	280			
	15			$10,000*	($2,000)	$280			
Sum of cash flow benefits		$3,310	$2,165	$10,000	$3,561	$4,200	$2,200	$2,560	$4,150
Excess of cash flow over initial investment		$1,310	$165	$8,000	$1,561	$2,200	$200	$560	$2,150

*Indicates year in which payback was accomplished.

Fonderia di Torino S.p.A.

In November 2000, Francesca Cerini, managing director of Fonderia di Torino S.p.A.,[1] was considering the purchase of a Vulcan Mold-Maker automated molding machine. This machine would prepare the sand molds into which molten iron was poured to obtain iron castings. The Vulcan Mold-Maker would replace an older machine and would offer improvements in quality and some additional capacity for expansion. Similar molding-machine proposals had been rejected by the board of directors for economic reasons on three previous occasions, most recently in 1999. This time, given the size of the proposed expenditure of about (euros) €1 million,[2] Cerini was seeking a careful estimate of the project's costs and benefits and, ultimately, a recommendation of whether to proceed with the investment.

The Company

Fonderia di Torino specialized in the production of precision metal castings for use in automotive, aerospace, and construction equipment. The company had acquired a reputation for quality products, particularly for safety parts (i.e., parts whose failure would result in loss of control for the operator). Its products included crankshafts, transmissions, brake calipers, axles, wheels, and various steering-assembly parts. Customers were original-equipment manufacturers (OEM), mainly in Europe. OEMs were becoming increasingly insistent about product quality, and Fonderia di Torino's response had reduced the rejection rate of its castings by the OEMs to 70 parts per million.

This record had won the company coveted quality awards from BMW, Ferrari, and Peugeot, and had resulted in strategic alliances with those firms: Fonderia di

---

[1]S.p.A. stands for *Societa per Azioni,* literally, a business under share ownership, like a public corporation in the United States.

[2]In November 2000, the exchange rate between the euro and the U.S. dollar was about €1.17: $1.00.

This case was prepared by Robert F. Bruner from field research and public information and draws its structure and some data from an antecedent case written by Brandt Allen. Fonderia di Torino is a fictional company representing the issues that faced actual firms. The author gratefully acknowledges the financial support of the Batten Institute. It was written as a basis for class discussion rather than to illustrate effective or ineffective handling of an administrative situation. Copyright © 2001 by the University of Virginia Darden School Foundation, Charlottesville, VA. All rights reserved. *To order copies, send an e-mail to* sales@ dardenpublishing.com. *No part of this publication may be reproduced, stored in a retrieval system, used in a spreadsheet, or transmitted in any form or by any means—electronic, mechanical, photocopying, recording, or otherwise—without the permission of the Darden School Foundation.* Rev. 12/01.

Torino and the OEMs exchanged technical personnel and design tasks; in addition, the OEMs shared confidential market-demand information with Fonderia di Torino, which increased the precision of the latter's production scheduling. In certain instances, the OEMs had provided cheap loans to Fonderia di Torino to support capital expansion. Finally, the company received relatively long-term supply contracts from the OEMs and had a preferential position for bidding on new contracts.

Fonderia di Torino, located in Milan, Italy, had been founded in 1912 by Francesca Cerini's great-grandfather, Benito Cerini, a naval engineer, to produce castings for the armaments industry. In the 1920s and 1930s, the company expanded its customer base into the automotive industry. Although the company barely avoided financial collapse in the late 1940s, Benito Cerini predicted a postwar demand for precision metal casting and positioned the company to meet it. From that time, Fonderia di Torino grew slowly but steadily; its sales for calendar-year 2000 were expected to be €280 million. It was listed for trading on the Milan stock exchange in 1991, but the Cerini family owned 55 percent of the common shares of stock outstanding. (The company's beta was 1.25.)[3]

The company's traditional hurdle rate of return on capital deployed was 14 percent. (This rate had not been reviewed since 1984.) In addition, company policy sought payback of an entire investment within five years. At the time of the case, the market value of the company's capital was 33 percent debt and 67 percent equity. The debt consisted entirely of loans from Banco Nazionale di Milano bearing an interest rate of 6.8 percent. The company's effective tax rate was about 43 percent, which reflected the combination of national and local corporate income-tax rates.

Francesca Cerini, age 57, had assumed executive responsibility for the company 20 years earlier, upon the death of her father. She held a doctorate in metallurgy and was the matriarch of an extended family. Only a son and a niece worked at Fonderia di Torino, however. Over the years, the Cerini family had sought to earn a rate of return on its equity investment of about 18 percent—this goal had been established by Benito Cerini and had never once been questioned by management.

The Vulcan Mold-Maker Machine

Sand molds used to make castings were prepared in a semi-automated process at Fonderia di Torino in 2000. Workers stamped impressions in a mixture of sand and adhesive under heat and high pressure. The process was relatively labor intensive, required training and retraining to obtain consistency in mold quality, and demanded some heavy lifting from workers. Indeed, medical claims for back injuries in the molding shop had doubled since 1998 as the mix of Fonderia di Torino's casting products shifted toward heavy items. (Items averaged 25 kilograms in 2000.)

The new molding machine would replace six semi-automated stamping machines that, together, had originally cost €415,807. Cumulative depreciation of €130,682 had

---

[3]The rate of return on euro-denominated bonds issued by E.U. governments was 5.3 percent. Francesca Cerini assumed that the equity risk premium would be 6 percent. Also, she believed that current bond yields impounded an expected inflation rate of 3 percent for the near future.

already been charged against the original cost; annual depreciation on those machines had been averaging €47,520 a year. Fonderia di Torino's management believed that those semi-automated machines would need to be replaced after six years. Cerini had received an offer of €130,000 for the six machines.

The current six machines required 12 workers per shift[4] (24 in total) at €7.33 per worker per hour, plus the equivalent of 3 maintenance workers, each of whom was paid €7.85 an hour, plus maintenance supplies of €4,000 a year. Cerini assumed that the semi-automated machines, if kept, would continue to consume electrical power at the rate of €12,300 a year.

The Vulcan Mold-Maker molding machine was produced by a company in Allentown, Pennsylvania. Fonderia di Torino had received a firm offering price of €850,000 from the Allentown firm. The estimate for modifications to the plant, including wiring for the machine's power supply, was €155,000. Allowing for shipping, installation, and testing, the total cost of the Vulcan Mold-Maker machine was expected to be €1.01 million, all of which would be capitalized and depreciated for tax purposes over eight years. (Cerini assumed that, at a high and steady rate of machine utilization, the Vulcan Mold-Maker would need to be replaced after the eighth year.)

The new machine would require two skilled operators (one per shift), each receiving €11.36 an hour (including benefits), and contract maintenance of €59,500 a year, and would incur power costs of €26,850 yearly. In addition, the automatic machine was expected to save at least €5,200 yearly through improved labor efficiency in other areas of the foundry.

With the current machines, more than 30 percent of the foundry's floor space was needed for the wide galleries the machines required; raw materials and in-process inventories had to be staged near each machine in order to smooth the workflow. With the automated machine, almost half of that space would be freed for other purposes (although at present there was no need for new space).

Certain aspects of the Vulcan Mold-Maker purchase decision were difficult to quantify. First, Cerini was unsure whether the tough collective-bargaining agreement her company had with the employees' union would allow her to lay off the 24 operators of the semi-automated machines. Reassigning the workers to other jobs might be easier, but the only positions needing to be filled were those of janitors, who were paid €4.13 an hour. The extent of any labor savings would depend on negotiations with the union. Second, Cerini believed that the Vulcan Mold-Maker would result in even higher levels of product quality and lower scrap rates than the company was now boasting. In light of the ever-increasing competition, this outcome might prove to be of enormous, but currently unquantifiable, competitive importance. Finally, the Vulcan Mold-Maker had a theoretical maximum capacity that was 30 percent higher than that of the six semi-automated machines; but those machines were operating at only 90 percent of capacity, and Cerini was unsure when added capacity would be needed. The latest economic news suggested that the economies of Europe were headed for a slowdown.

---

[4]The foundry operated two shifts a day. It did not operate on weekends or holidays. At maximum, the foundry would produce for 210 days a year.

Compass Records

Still bleary-eyed after an all-night drive from North Carolina, Alison Brown sat in the office below her recording studio near Nashville's famed "Music Row." It was late June 2005, and she had a moment to reflect on Compass Records, the artist-run record company that she and her husband, Garry West, had founded ten years ago. The past few years had brought them great success, but managing the daily myriad decisions for the business remained a challenge. Foremost in her mind was whether to offer a recording contract to a talented new folk musician, Adair Roscommon, whose demo CD she was now listening to in her office.

Compass Records' tenth anniversary was a major milestone for a company in the intense and unforgiving music business. With a roster of well-known and successful artists under contract, Compass had carved out a niche as an established player in the folk and roots musical genres. But unlike executives at the major record companies who typically had large budgets, every decision made by Brown and West regarding new musicians could have a major impact on their business. Compass could scarcely afford to squander resources on an artist in whom Brown and her husband did not believe strongly.

Brown was an acclaimed folk musician about whom the entertainment industry magazine *Billboard* once wrote: "In Brown's hands, the banjo is capable of fluid musical phrases of boundless beauty." Brown's assessment of another folk musician's artistic merit, therefore, had tremendous value, and she liked Adair Roscommon's work. Brown was also a former investment banker with an MBA who clearly understood Roscommon's potential as an investment for Compass. Intuitively, Brown grasped the implications of adding a risky asset, such as a new musician, to Compass Records' growing portfolio.

The central question for Brown, when contemplating any new musician, was whether to license that artist's music for a limited period of time or to produce and own the artist's master recording outright. In the short term, it was cheaper for Compass to license a recording, but it also limited the company's potential profit.

This case was prepared by Sean D. Carr, under the supervision of Robert F. Bruner and Professor Kenneth M. Eades of the Darden Graduate School of Business Administration. Certain persons and events in the case have been disguised, and some details have been simplified for expositional clarity. The case is intended to serve as a basis for class discussion rather than to illustrate effective or ineffective handling of an administrative situation. Copyright © 2005 by the University of Virginia Darden School Foundation, Charlottesville, VA. All rights reserved. *To order copies, send an e-mail to* sales@dardenpublishing.com. *No part of this publication may be reproduced, stored in a retrieval system, used in a spreadsheet, or transmitted in any form or by any means—electronic, mechanical, photocopying, recording, or otherwise—without the permission of the Darden School Foundation.*

If Compass Records purchased a musician's master recording and the album failed to take off, however, the company risked owning a significantly impaired asset. This issue and a host of others gathered momentum in Brown's mind while the gentle melodies of Roscommon's demo filled the thick southern air in her office.

Alison Brown and Compass Records

Alison Brown grew up in a family of lawyers, and had she not been influenced by music at an early age, she might have ended up becoming a lawyer, too. After moving with her family to La Jolla, California, when she was 11, she immersed herself in banjo playing and developed a burgeoning talent. By the time she was 14, Brown was playing publicly, and by 15, she had won the Canadian National Five-String Banjo Championship. In 1980, Brown carried her passion for playing the banjo with her to Cambridge, Massachusetts, where she earned degrees in history and literature from Harvard University. She spent her extracurricular time traveling the bluegrass circuit in New England, and continued to develop herself as an artist.

Still thinking that music was an avocation and not a career, Brown enrolled at the University of California–Los Angeles, where she earned an MBA in 1986. Afterward, she accepted a position as an associate in the public-finance department at Smith Barney in San Francisco. During the next two years, Brown continued to kindle her passion for the banjo, even though playing publicly was incompatible with her new life as a banker. Brown eventually realized that she had a calling. "I knew people who would wake up in the morning and get in the shower and think about how they were going to refund a particular bond issue," Brown once said. "I would wake up in the morning and think about music." During a six-month hiatus from her office job, Brown was invited to play for the award-winning band Alison Krauss and Union Station. That job lasted three years and launched Brown into a new career.

By 1992, not only had Brown been named Banjo Player of the Year by the International Bluegrass Association, but she had also released her first album, which was nominated for a Grammy.[1] After leaving Alison Krauss, she accepted an invitation to join the world tour of folk-pop artist Michelle Shocked, where she met her future husband, Garry West. "About two months into [the tour] we realized there were a lot of things we wanted to do," West later said. "We were in Sweden, sitting around over strong coffee and pastries, wondering how we could encompass our vision of the good life: an outlet for our work, other recordings, publishing, and management." As Brown described it, they laid out their vision on the "proverbial napkin," and mapped out a plan for a business that would satisfy their needs.

In 1993, Brown and West started Small World Music and Video in Nashville, Tennessee, selling folk, world, and environmental records produced by a company they had discovered while on tour in Australia with Michelle Shocked. That same year,

---

[1]The Grammy Awards were presented by the Recording Academy, an association of recording-industry professionals, for outstanding achievement. The Grammies were awarded based on the votes of peers rather than on popular or commercial success. The awards were named for the trophy, a small, gilded statuette of a gramophone.

they were approached by a potential investor who had heard an interview that Brown had done on National Public Radio and who believed in what Brown and West wanted to do. With support from that investor, the two started producing their own projects and, in 1995, they launched the Compass Records label.[2]

By 2005, Brown and West's intuitive strategy was serving them well. Compass Records had grown to include nearly 50 artists under contract, and the company averaged about 20 releases a year. Their label was largely centered on roots music, and included marquee names like Victor Wooten, who was considered one of the best bass players in the world; Kate Rusby, a sensation among fans of traditional Anglo-Irish music; Colin Hay, the former front man and songwriter for the group Men At Work; Glenn Tilbrook, the former lead songwriter for the 1980s pop group Squeeze; Fairport Convention, one of the inventors of the folk-rock sound; and, of course, the dynamic bluegrass-jazz fusion of Alison Brown, who won a Grammy for her 2000 release, *Fair Weather*.

Compass Records in Context

Within the context of the global music business, Compass Records was tiny. The $32-billion music recording industry was dominated by a handful of large, multinational corporations, which accounted for 86 percent of the market for global recorded music. Those companies included Universal Music Group, with 29 percent; Sony/BMG, with 30 percent; Warner Music Group, with 16 percent; and EMI, with 11 percent. See **Figure 1** for a pie chart showing the percentages.

The major labels' dominance, deep pockets, and global distribution systems helped them to survive a turbulent and uncertain decade in the music industry. While the global market for recorded music had grown from $2 billion, in 1969, to $40 billion, in 1995, it had stagnated ever since. According to the Recording Industry Association of America (RIAA), the industry had registered no growth in any single year since 1995. By 2003, the recorded-music sector had shrunk to 1993 levels ($32 billion), and annual dollar sales were estimated to have declined at a compound annual growth rate of 5 percent.

As the major labels battled to preserve their slices of the shrinking pie, a number of new independent labels,[3] such as Compass Records, had begun to emerge. Smaller and more nimble, these companies saw opportunities in markets where the major record companies could ill-afford to go given the scale of their economies. "The trouble with those huge corporations is that they have to have enough sales volume on a

---

[2]A record label was a brand created by a company that specialized in manufacturing, distributing, and promoting audio and video recordings in various formats, including CDs, LPs, DVD-Audio, Super Audio CDs, and cassettes. The name was derived from the paper label at the center of the original gramophone record.

[3]Technically, an independent record label, or indie, operated without the funding or distribution network of one of the major record labels. In practice, the boundaries between majors and independents were ambiguous. Some independents, especially those with a successful roster of performing artists, received funding from major labels, and many independent labels relied on a major label for international licensing deals and distribution arrangements.

FIGURE 1 |

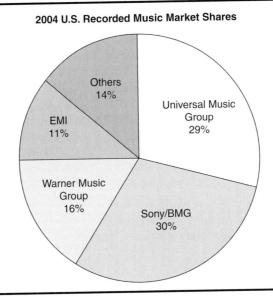

2004 U.S. Recorded Music Market Shares

Source: Nielsen *Soundscan*, Morgan Stanley Research.

release to feed this huge infrastructure," said Brown. "And yet something like 98 percent of all records sell fewer than 5,000 copies, so if your benchmark is a million, or even 100,000, you're obviously overlooking a lot of good music that sells well enough to deserve being out there."

Brown estimated that 40 percent of Compass Records' albums sold 5,000 units or more; only a few of her artists were popular enough to sell more than 20,000 units. "For a major label, 5,000 units is a failure," Brown said. "Only an indie can make this a success." Compass Records turned a profit on 80 percent of its titles in 2005 (versus a 10 percent success rate for the major labels). **Exhibits 1** and **2** provide Compass Records' balance sheet and income statement for the fiscal year ended December 31, 2004. **Exhibit 3** offers the company's historical income and expenses.

Music-Business Fundamentals

Recording Contracts

Recording contracts were agreements between a record label and an artist whereby the label had the right to promote and market recordings of the artist's music. Under such contracts, the record company could either license an artist's finished recordings for a limited period of time or produce the recordings and own them indefinitely. If the label negotiated to "produce and own," it was entitled to exploit the music through the sales of CDs and electronic downloads, as well as through licensing the music to other record companies or to firms that wished to use the music in other media, such as commercials, television, or film. When Compass Records opted to produce and own a master recording,[4] the artist received no payment up front.

Under a licensing contract, the record label licensed a work that had already been recorded and packaged. It had the right to exploit that recording only for a predetermined period of time, typically five to seven years. Unlike a contract to produce and own a master, a licensing contract obligated the label to pay the artist an up-front fee (advance), which was intended to defray some of the costs the artist had incurred in developing the album. Compass generally negotiated advances of $3,000 to $5,000. If the artist sought a very large advance (i.e., $20,000 or more), Brown believed that it made more sense to own the master recording instead. Under a licensing arrangement, additional costs included updates to the album's packaging (around $500) and touch-ups to the master itself, although generally not required. Marketing and promotional costs associated with the licensed recording were usually the same as those for the purchased master.

Certain recording contracts also gave the record company options on additional albums by the artist (with a purchased master, the label usually had three options, although it was not uncommon to have seven or eight options). Those options were particularly important with new artists because the label made significant up-front investments to launch a new act for which the company might not realize a return until three or four records down the road. Recording contracts customarily gave record companies the exclusive right to record an artist during the term of the agreement. If an artist failed to fulfill her obligations, most contracts permitted the company to suspend the contract. An artist could also request to be released from the contract, which the company might be willing to grant if it were repaid its recording costs and/or granted a percentage on the sales of the artist's records released by another company.

Royalties and Recoupment

Regardless of the type of recording contract, record labels paid royalties[5] to artists for the use and sale of their music. The two most common types of royalties were *mechanical royalties,* which were paid to songwriters and music publishers[6] for the use of their musical compositions, and *recording artist royalties,* which were paid to an artist for the recorded performance of those compositions. Each type of royalty worked somewhat differently.

In 2005 in the United States, mechanical royalties were fixed at a statutory rate of $0.085 per song. If the song were included on a CD, then the record company would pay the artist and/or the publisher that amount for each CD unit sold. Many

---

[4]A master recording, or master, was an original recording from which copies were made.

[5]A royalty was a payment to the owner for the use of the owner's property, especially patents, copyrighted works, and franchises.

[6]A music publisher was a company that worked with a songwriter to promote her musical compositions. Publishers negotiated partial or total ownership of an artist's copyright for her work, and she received a share of the mechanical royalties from the use of that work, typically about 50 percent.

record contracts, especially those with artists who were both the songwriter and the recording artist, included a *controlled composition*[7] *clause.* Because those artists received both mechanical and recording royalties, the clause allowed the label to limit its mechanical expense. Compass Records, for instance, often negotiated a 10-song per CD maximum for mechanicals, which capped the mechanical expense at $0.85 per CD sold.

Recording artist royalties were not determined statutorily, but were negotiated between the artist and the record label. The recording royalty varied widely, and often depended on the stature of the artist. It ranged between 8 percent and 25 percent of the suggested retail price of the album. Recording artist royalties also differed with the type of contract. At Compass Records, the average recording artist royalty for an owned master recording was $1.45 per unit sold, whereas the royalty for a licensed recording was around $1.75 per unit sold. Recording royalties were generally lower for produce-and-own contracts because the record label was underwriting the expense of album production.

The record label, however, did not pay any recording artist royalties until certain costs incurred in making and promoting the album had been recouped. All the costs of recording and preparing the music for manufacture were recoupable. About 50 percent of the marketing and promotional costs were recoupable. For licensing contracts, the advance was completely recoupable. An artist reimbursed the record label for those recoupable costs at her contracted royalty rate. For example, if the artist's royalty rate was $1.45, the record label reduced the amount of the total recoupable expense by $1.45 for every unit sold. When the label had recovered all recoupable expenses, the artist would begin to collect the recording artist royalties. (Mechanical royalties were not subject to the requirement that recoupable expenses be recovered first.)

Record companies' justification for the practice of recouping certain costs from an artist was that the label had invested its resources and had borne the financial risk of making and promoting the album. Some labels argued that this was similar to a joint venture in which production costs and overhead were repaid before the partners divided any profits. As an accounting matter, Compass Records recorded its recoupable costs as an asset on its balance sheet. On average, the company expensed those costs after two years.

Production and Manufacturing

If a record label negotiated a contract to produce and own an artist's master recording, the cost of producing that recording would depend on the size of the project, the complexity of the recording, and the level of perfection desired. The costs for producing an album would typically include fees for producers, arrangers, copyists, engineers, and background musicians, as well as the charges for studio and equipment rental, mixing, and editing. For relatively new artists signed by a major label, those costs could range between $80,000 and $150,000 for a single album, while established artists were known to run up production costs in excess of $500,000.

---

[7]A controlled composition was a piece of music that was written or owned by the recording artist.

As a small independent label, Compass Records incurred production costs that were significantly lower than the major labels'. Compass even had an advantage over some other indie labels because Brown and West had acquired a recording studio in May 2004. The wood-paneled, digital studio, which had cost Compass about $100,000 to equip, gave the label and its artists more flexibility in the creative process and saved the company about $500 a day, which it would otherwise have spent on studio rental. Compass Records might spend between $15,000 and $25,000 to produce an album.

Regardless of whether a record company opted to license or to produce and own an artist's album, the next major expense for the label was the manufacturing of the CDs. The manufacturing cost—which included pressing the CD, purchasing the standard jewel case, shrink-wrapping, and attaching a label to the top spine—was about $0.70 per unit. There was an additional unit cost of about $0.20 for printing the booklet and other materials contained inside the CD case. Compass had an arrangement with a CD manufacturer in Minneapolis, Minnesota, whereby the minimum initial order required was 1,000 units; thereafter, Compass could order in increments of 500. Because the manufacturer could turn around an order in three to five days, Brown and West tried to keep very tight control over their inventory.

Marketing and Distribution

For the major record labels, promoting an album depended on obtaining regular airplay on radio stations around the country. This process began with an album mail-out, which provided free copies of the recording to radio stations and music journalists. For a small independent label like Compass, promotional efforts were highly specialized and targeted. Compass focused on local radio programs and record stores in coordination with the performer's tour schedule. A typical album mail-out for Compass Records included 2,000 CD units. Compass usually negotiated a reduced rate of $0.50 per unit with its manufacturer for making the promotional CDs; the postage and collateral materials cost an additional $2 per unit. None of those costs were recoupable.

For Compass's artists, a major component of the marketing effort was venue sales at live concerts. Fans of folk, Celtic, and roots music were often known to postpone purchases of an album by a favorite artist until they could buy it at the concert, even if the album was locally available in stores. To encourage local fans to attend concerts by new artists, therefore, Compass usually paid for local print-advertising campaigns ($3,000), posters and press photos ($500), e-card mailings ($1,000), and the services of an independent radio promoter ($2,500).

With respect to CD distribution, major labels had divisions that handled the placement of millions of units worldwide. Independent labels such as Compass, however, secured deals with independent distributors to place their albums in regional retail outlets. Domestic distributors charged the label a fee; for Compass, this fee was 21 percent of the standard wholesale price of $11.45 per unit. The distribution of recorded music was also subject to a return privilege. All unsold CDs or cassettes were completely returnable by retailers. "This business is 100 percent consignment," Brown said. Compass was paid only for the CD units that sold, not for the number shipped. Retailers returned unsold units to the distributor, which then returned them to the record company.

FIGURE 2 |

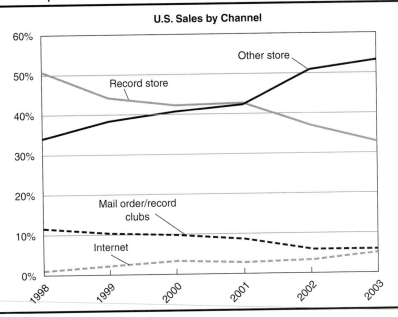

Source: Recording Industry Association of America.

Because of the return privilege, Compass typically manufactured about 30 percent more units than it estimated would actually sell at retail outlets; the company would usually write those units off after two years.

At the retail level, there had been a major shift from specialty record shops to mass-market and on-line retailers (see **Figure 2**). Record stores' share of U.S. music sales declined from 51 percent, in 1998, to 33 percent, in 2003, while the mass-market stores' share grew from 34 percent to 53 percent over the same period. Getting a record well placed with the large retailers was expensive. Brown estimated that Compass might spend around $5,000 for a new artist on in-store listening stations and other retail programs. The average retail list price for a Compass CD was $17.98 per unit.

Retailers gave an album only about 90 days from its release date to generate meaningful consumer demand; if that failed to occur, they exercised their return privilege. Therefore, in order to ensure high demand by an album's release date, sufficient publicity and promotion had to occur months in advance. "From a financial point of view," Brown said, "that means incurring all your recording, preproduction, and manufacturing costs six months or more before you will ever see any return." To keep an album available in the stores, a record label had to sell at least 50 percent of the total forecast sales in the first three months after the release date, and perhaps reach 75 percent in the first year. After that, sales might fall off quickly, with most of the remaining inventory sold the following year.

The Roscommon Decision

Adair Roscommon, an Irish singer who played fiddle, mandolin, and guitar, had been called "the Dublin folk scene's hottest up-and-comer" by one reviewer. She had begun her musical career as a teenager with the Irish traditional band Fairlea Brigham, and after reading history at Trinity University in Ireland, Roscommon started writing her own songs and touring with other artists in the United Kingdom and the United States. Her self-released 2003 album, *Swallows Fly,* did well—she sold 2,500 copies of the album from her van—and led to her being voted "Best New Artist of 2004" by the listeners of the influential Boston folk radio station WUMB. That local success caught the attention of Alison Brown. She liked how Roscommon combined the sophisticated, modern folk music of her native Ireland with the soulful strains of bluegrass; she had a sharp, accessible sound that was both classic and modern.

Brown and her husband believed strongly in Roscommon as an artist, but they were still undecided about whether Compass's contract with her should be to produce and own her next master or simply to license the finished recording. Purchasing her music would mean producing a master recording, which Compass Records would then own and from which it could potentially generate revenues indefinitely. Licensing the recording might be less expensive on the front end, but there was a finite life to the future cash flows associated with the recording. "If you fund a master, then it costs more than if you license [a finished recording]," Brown said, "but licensing means renting the material."

On the one hand, Brown believed she could negotiate a deal to produce Roscommon's next recording for $20,000, which included the standard options to produce and own three additional albums. As part of the deal, Compass would also negotiate a copublishing arrangement with Roscommon. Typically, an artist such as Roscommon, who wrote all her own songs, would split 50 percent of the mechanical royalties earned on an album with a music publisher, with which she would contract to promote her written compositions. Under this deal, however, Compass would be the publisher of the songs on the album. If Brown and her husband chose this alternative, therefore, Compass would effectively reduce their mechanical royalty expenses by half.

On the other hand, if Compass licensed Roscommon's finished recording, Brown thought the advance would be about $3,000, and Roscommon might be willing to include a performance-based option in the contract. With this option, if Compass achieved a sales target of 10,000 units, then it would earn the right to license her next album. "If we succeed with Roscommon under the license deal and make her a more well-known and viable act," Brown thought, "it's very possible that another label could swoop in with cash and promises of bigger things and reap the benefit of Compass's investment in her." Thus, having this additional clause in the licensing deal offered Brown some security. "We have a good feeling about her long-term potential," she said, "but we realize it may not show itself for a few albums."

Brown and West thought hard about their projections for Roscommon's album. "Only 1 in 20 albums will be the grand slam," Brown thought. For Compass, a grand slam might be 50,000 units, but success would depend on the up-front recording and marketing costs. They estimated that Compass could safely sell 5,000 units of Roscommon's album in the United States through its domestic distributor. Because Roscommon already had a fan base overseas, they also believed they could generate international sales through distributors in other regions. Brown forecast sales of another 2,000 units in the United Kingdom, Ireland, and Europe; 1,000 units in Japan, New Zealand, and Australia; and 500 in Canada.[8] Roscommon herself could also probably sell at least 1,500 CDs from her van; she would pay Compass $6 per unit, and she would receive no artist or mechanical royalties on sales from her van. Brown used the industry's standard 12 percent discount rate for her analysis. Compass Records' marginal corporate tax rate was 40 percent.

At Compass, Brown had historically preferred to license rather than to own records. "It gives me the chance to wait and see," she said. But it wasn't always so simple. Compass's new distribution agreements in Europe and Asia created opportunities to sell an artist's CDs in new markets around the world, and Compass's recently built studio made producing an album easier and cheaper.

"We used to own only about 30 percent of the whole catalog for an artist, but with the studio we now own about half of them. The only rule of thumb is our experience," Brown said. She knew that an artist's success depended heavily on how active they were. A new artist that toured heavily and consistently could achieve 50 percent of their total sales at venues alone. "The rest just seems to come down to karma," Brown thought. "One thing we've learned is that you can't sell a record before its time; the hard part is guessing whether or not it's an artist's time."

---

[8] For sales in the United Kingdom, Ireland, and Europe, Compass typically received (euros) EUR7 per unit. For sales in Japan, Australia, and New Zealand, Compass received (U.S. dollars) USD6.50 per unit; for Canadian sales, Compass received USD7.00 per unit. Compass's international distributors did not charge an additional distribution fee. In mid June 2005, the USD/euro exchange rate was 1.224.

EXHIBIT 1 | Compass Records' Balance Sheet

		Dec. 31, 2004
Assets		
Current assets:		
Cash		$ 68,074
Accounts receivable		1,038,026
Other current assets		801,850
Total current assets		1,907,949
Fixed assets		433,608
Other assets:		
Accumulated amortization		(53,393)
Organizational costs		22,293
Start-up costs		3,510
Recoupable artist costs		908,226
Total other assets:		880,636
Total Assets		**$3,222,193**
LIABILITIES & EQUITY		
Liabilities		
Accounts payable		$ 280,907
Short-term debt		48,282
Other current liabilities:		
Accrued royalties payable	304,736	
Royalty reserve account	322,737	
Payroll tax payable	35,102	
Sales tax payable	8,108	
Credit card rec. issues	(567)	
Franchise tax payable	(5,670)	
Foreign taxes payable	6,105	
Line of credit	1,024,216	
Total other current liabilities		1,694,767
Total Liabilities		**$2,023,956**
Equity		
Paid-in capital		$270,000
Additional paid-in capital		530,053
Retained earnings		398,184
Total Equity		**$1,198,236**
Total Liabilities & Equity		**$3,222,193**

EXHIBIT 2 | Compass Records' Income Statement

	Jan–Dec 2004
Ordinary Income/Expense	
Income	
CDs	$4,634,967
Downloaded music	141
Consignment merchandise	1,625
Videos	2,225
DVDs	52,280
Studio rental income	14,128
Total Income	**$4,705,366**
Cost of Goods Sold	
Cassettes	$ 724
CDs	767,858
DVDs	7,006
Videos	805
Merchandise	210
Consignment	145
Total Cost of Goods Sold	**$ 776,748**
Gross Profit	**$3,928,618**
Expense	
Distribution expenses	$ 781,771
Royalty expense	570,565
Payroll expenses	466,542
General and administrative	576,583
Payroll tax expense	38,754
Other tax expense	15,786
Miscellaneous	36,167
Advertising	334,225
Promotion expense	71,116
Mailing expense	154,761
Travel & entertainment	48,558
Tour support	25,477
Graphic artist fees	33,064
Project expenses	24,244
Project costs not recouped	(3,375)
Total Expense	**$3,950,985**
Net Ordinary Income	**$ 754,381**
Other income	34,511
Net Income	**$ 788,892**

EXHIBIT 3 | Compass Records' Historical Income and Expenses

Year	Total Revenues	Expenses
2003	$2,702,840	$2,720,477
2002	2,734,773	2,755,426
2001	3,097,362	2,877,749
2000	2,898,315	3,075,899
1999	3,039,806	2,900,359
1998	1,343,050	1,389,010
1997	911,588	962,912
1996	770,094	906,439
1995	837,748	866,908

Diamond Chemicals plc (A): The Merseyside Project

Late one afternoon in January 2001, Frank Greystock told Lucy Morris, "No one seems satisfied with the analysis so far, but the suggested changes could kill the project. If solid projects like this can't swim past the corporate piranhas, the company will never modernize."

Morris was plant manager of Diamond Chemicals' Merseyside Works in Liverpool, England. Her controller, Frank Greystock, was discussing a capital project that Morris wanted to propose to senior management. The project consisted of a (British pounds) £9-million expenditure to renovate and rationalize the polypropylene production line at the Merseyside plant in order to make up for deferred maintenance and to exploit opportunities to achieve increased production efficiency.

Diamond Chemicals was under pressure from investors to improve its financial performance because of both the worldwide economic slowdown and the accumulation of the firm's common shares by a well-known corporate raider, Sir David Benjamin. Earnings per share had fallen to £30.00 at the end of 2000 from around £60.00 at the end of 1999. Morris thus believed that the time was ripe to obtain funding from corporate headquarters for a modernization program for the Merseyside Works—at least she had believed so until Greystock presented her with several questions that had only recently surfaced.

Diamond Chemicals and Polypropylene

Diamond Chemicals, a major competitor in the worldwide chemicals industry, was a leading producer of polypropylene, a polymer used in an extremely wide variety of products (ranging from medical products to packaging film, carpet fibers, and

This case was prepared by Robert F. Bruner as a basis for class discussion rather than to illustrate effective or ineffective handling of an administrative situation. Diamond Chemicals is a fictional company reflecting the issues facing actual firms. The author wishes to acknowledge the helpful comments of Dr. Frank H. McTigue, the literary color of Anthony Trollope, and the financial support of the Citicorp Global Scholars Program. Copyright © 2001 by the University of Virginia Darden School Foundation, Charlottesville, VA. All rights reserved. *To order copies, send an e-mail to* sales@dardenpublishing.com. *No part of this publication may be reproduced, stored in a retrieval system, used in a spreadsheet, or transmitted in any form or by any means—electronic, mechanical, photocopying, recording, or otherwise—without the permission of the Darden School Foundation.*

automobile components) and known for its strength and malleability. Polypropylene was essentially priced as a commodity.

The production of polypropylene pellets at Merseyside began with propylene, a refined gas received in tank cars. Propylene was purchased from four refineries in England that produced it in the course of refining crude oil into gasoline. In the first stage of the production process, polymerization, the propylene gas was combined with a diluent (or solvent) in a large pressure vessel. In a catalytic reaction, the polypropylene precipitated to the bottom of the tank and was then concentrated in a centrifuge.

The second stage of the production process compounded the basic polypropylene with stabilizers, modifiers, fillers, and pigments to achieve the desired attributes for a particular customer. The finished plastic was extruded into pellets for shipment to the customer.

The Merseyside production process was old, semicontinuous at best, and, therefore, higher in labor content than its competitors' newer plants. The Merseyside plant was constructed in 1967.

Diamond Chemicals produced polypropylene at Merseyside and in Rotterdam, Holland. The two plants were of identical scale, age, and design. The managers of both plants reported to James Fawn, executive vice president and manager of the Intermediate Chemicals Group (ICG) of Diamond Chemicals. The company positioned itself as a supplier to customers in Europe and the Middle East. The strategic-analysis staff estimated that, in addition to numerous small producers, seven major competitors manufactured polypropylene in Diamond Chemicals' market region. Their plants operated at various cost levels. **Exhibit 1** presents a comparison of plant sizes and indexed costs.

The Proposed Capital Program

Morris had assumed responsibility for the Merseyside Works only 12 months previously, following a rapid rise from the entry position of shift engineer nine years before. When she assumed responsibility, she undertook a detailed review of the operations and discovered significant opportunities for improvement in polypropylene production. Some of those opportunities stemmed from the deferral of maintenance over the preceding five years. In an effort to enhance the operating results of the Works, the previous manager had limited capital expenditures to only the most essential. Now, what previously had been routine and deferrable was becoming essential. Other opportunities stemmed from correcting the antiquated plant design in ways that would save energy and improve the process flow: (1) relocating and modernizing tank-car unloading areas, which would enable the process flow to be streamlined; (2) refurbishing the polymerization tank to achieve higher pressures and thus greater throughput; and (3) renovating the compounding plant to increase extrusion throughput and obtain energy savings.

Morris proposed an expenditure of £9 million on this program. The entire polymerization line would need to be shut down for 45 days, however, and because the Rotterdam plant was operating near capacity, Merseyside's customers would buy from competitors. Greystock believed the loss of customers would not be permanent. The benefits would be a lower energy requirement[1] as well as a 7 percent greater manufacturing throughput. In addition, the project was expected to improve gross margin (before depreciation and energy savings) from 11.5 percent to 12.5 percent. The engineering group at Merseyside was highly confident that the efficiencies would be realized.

Merseyside currently produced 250,000 metric tons of polypropylene pellets a year. Currently, the price of polypropylene averaged £541 per ton for Diamond Chemicals' product mix. The tax rate required in capital-expenditure analyses was 30 percent. Greystock discovered that any plant facilities to be replaced had been completely depreciated. New assets could be depreciated on an accelerated basis[2] over 15 years, the expected life of the assets. The increased throughput would necessitate a one-time increase of work-in-process inventory equal in value to 3.0 percent of cost of goods. Greystock included in the first year of his forecast preliminary engineering costs of £500,000, which had been spent over the preceding nine months on efficiency and design studies of the renovation. Finally, the corporate manual stipulated that overhead costs be reflected in project analyses at the rate of 3.5 percent times the book value of assets acquired in the project per year.[3]

Greystock had produced the discounted-cash-flow (DCF) summary given in **Exhibit 2.** It suggested that the capital program would easily hurdle Diamond Chemicals' required return of 10 percent for engineering projects.

Concerns of the Transport Division

Diamond Chemicals owned the tank cars with which Merseyside received propylene gas from four petroleum refineries in England. The Transport Division, a cost center, oversaw the movement of all raw, intermediate, and finished materials throughout the company and was responsible for managing the tank cars. Because

---

[1]Greystock characterized the energy savings as a percentage of sales and assumed that the savings would be equal to 1.25 percent of sales in the first 5 years and 0.75 percent in years 6–10. Thereafter, without added aggressive "green" spending, the energy efficiency of the plant would revert to its old level, and the savings would be zero. He believed that the decision to make further environmentally oriented investments was a separate choice (and one that should be made much later) and, therefore, that to include such benefits (of a presumably later investment decision) in the project being considered today would be inappropriate.

[2]The company's capital-expenditure manual suggested the use of double-declining-balance (DDB) depreciation, even though other more aggressive procedures might be permitted by the tax code. The reason for this policy was to discourage jockeying for corporate approvals based on tax provisions that could apply differently for different projects and divisions. Prior to senior-management's approval, the controller's staff would present an independent analysis of special tax effects that might apply. Division managers, however, were discouraged from relying heavily on those effects. In applying the DDB approach to a 15-year project, the formula for accelerated depreciation was used for the first 10 years, after which depreciation was calculated on a straight-line basis. This conversion to straight line was commonly done so that the asset would depreciate fully within its economic life.

[3]The corporate-policy manual stated that new projects should be able to sustain a reasonable proportion of corporate overhead expense. Projects that were so marginal as to be unable to sustain those expenses and also meet the other criteria of investment attractiveness should not be undertaken. Thus, all new capital projects should reflect an annual pretax charge amounting to 3.5 percent of the value of the initial asset investment for the project.

of the project's increased throughput, Transport would have to increase its allocation of tank cars to Merseyside. Currently, the Transport Division could make this allocation out of excess capacity, although doing so would accelerate from 2005 to 2003 the need to purchase new rolling stock to support the anticipated growth of the firm in other areas. The purchase would cost £2 million. The rolling stock would have a depreciable life of 10 years,[4] but with proper maintenance, the cars could operate much longer. The rolling stock could not be used outside Britain because of differences in track gauge.

A memorandum from the controller of the Transport Division suggested that the cost of the tank cars should be included in the initial outlay of Merseyside's capital program. But Greystock disagreed. He told Morris:

> The Transport Division isn't paying one pence of actual cash because of what we're doing at Merseyside. In fact, we're doing the company a favor in using its excess capacity. Even *if* an allocation has to be made somewhere, it should go on the Transport Division's books. The way we've always evaluated projects in this company has been with the philosophy of "every tub on its own bottom"—every division has to fend for itself. The Transport Division isn't part of our own Intermediate Chemicals Group, so they should carry the allocation of rolling stock.

Accordingly, Greystock had not reflected any charge for the use of excess rolling stock in his preliminary DCF analysis, given in **Exhibit 2.**

The Transport Division and Intermediate Chemicals Group reported to separate executive vice presidents, who reported to the chairman and chief executive officer of the company. The executive VPs received an annual incentive bonus pegged to the performance of their divisions.

Concerns of the ICG Sales and Marketing Department

Greystock's analysis had led to questions from the director of Sales. In a recent meeting, the director had told Greystock:

> Your analysis assumes that we can sell the added output and thus obtain the full efficiencies from the project, but as you know, the market for polypropylene is extremely competitive. Right now, the industry is in a downturn and it looks like an oversupply is in the works. This means that we will probably have to shift capacity away from Rotterdam toward Merseyside in order to move the added volume. Is this really a gain for Diamond Chemicals? Why spend money just so one plant can cannibalize another?

The vice president of Marketing was less skeptical. He said that with lower costs at Merseyside, Diamond Chemicals might be able to take business from the plants of competitors such as Saône-Poulet or Vaysol. In the current severe recession, competitors would fight hard to keep customers, but sooner or later the market would

---

[4]The Transport Division depreciated rolling stock using DDB depreciation for the first eight years and straight-line depreciation for the last two years.

revive, and it would be reasonable to assume that any lost business volume would return at that time.

Greystock had listened to both the director and the vice president, and chose to reflect no charge for a loss of business at Rotterdam in his preliminary analysis of the Merseyside project. He told Morris:

> Cannibalization really isn't a cash flow; there is no check written in this instance. Anyway, if the company starts burdening its cost-reduction projects with fictitious charges like this, we'll never maintain our cost competitiveness. A cannibalization charge is rubbish!

Concerns of the Assistant Plant Manager

Griffin Tewitt, the assistant plant manager and Morris's direct subordinate, proposed an unusual modification to Greystock's analysis during a late-afternoon meeting with Greystock and Morris. Over the past few months, Tewitt had been absorbed with the development of a proposal to modernize a separate and independent part of the Merseyside Works, the production line for ethylene-propylene-copolymer rubber (EPC). This product, a variety of synthetic rubber, had been pioneered by Diamond Chemicals in the early 1960s and was sold in bulk to European tire manufacturers. Despite hopes that this oxidation-resistant rubber would dominate the market in synthetics, in fact, EPC remained a relatively small product in the European chemical industry. Diamond, the largest supplier of EPC, produced the entire volume at Merseyside. EPC had been only marginally profitable to Diamond because of the entry by competitors and the development of competing synthetic-rubber compounds over the past five years.

Tewitt had proposed a renovation of the EPC production line at a cost of £1 million. The renovation would give Diamond the lowest EPC cost base in the world and would improve cash flows by £25,000 ad infinitum. Even so, at current prices and volumes, the net present value (NPV) of this project was -£750,000. Tewitt and the EPC product manager had argued strenuously to the company's executive committee that the negative NPV ignored strategic advantages from the project and increases in volume and prices when the recession ended. Nevertheless, the executive committee had rejected the project, basing its rejection mainly on economic grounds.

In a hushed voice, Tewitt said to Morris and Greystock:

> Why don't you include the EPC project as part of the polypropylene line renovations? The positive NPV of the poly renovations can easily sustain the negative NPV of the EPC project. This is an extremely important project to the company, a point that senior management doesn't seem to get. If we invest now, we'll be ready to exploit the market when the recession ends. If we don't invest now, you can expect that we will have to exit the business altogether in three years. Do you look forward to more layoffs? Do you want to manage a shrinking plant? Recall that our annual bonuses are pegged to the size of this operation. Also remember that, in the last 20 years, no one from corporate has monitored renovation projects once the investment decision was made.

Concerns of the Treasury Staff

After a meeting on a different matter, Frank Greystock described his dilemmas to Andrew Gowan, who worked as an analyst on Diamond Chemicals' Treasury staff. Gowan scanned Greystock's analysis, and pointed out:

> . . . cash flows and discount rate need to be consistent in their assumptions about inflation. The 10 percent hurdle rate you're using is a nominal target rate of return. The Treasury staff thinks this impounds a long-term inflation expectation of 3 percent per year. Thus, Diamond Chemicals' real (that is, zero inflation) target rate of return is 7 percent.

The conversation was interrupted before Greystock could gain a full understanding of Gowan's comment. For the time being, Greystock decided to continue to use a discount rate of 10 percent because it was the figure promoted in the latest edition of Diamond Chemicals' capital-budgeting manual.

Evaluating Capital-Expenditure Proposals at Diamond Chemicals

In submitting a project for senior management's approval, the project's initiators had to identify it as belonging to one of four possible categories: (1) new product or market, (2) product or market extension, (3) engineering efficiency, or (4) safety or environment. The first three categories of proposals were subject to a system of four performance "hurdles," of which at least three had to be met for the proposal to be considered. The Merseyside project would be in the engineering-efficiency category.

1. *Impact on earnings per share:* For engineering-efficiency projects, the contribution to net income from contemplated projects had to be positive. This criterion was calculated as the average annual earnings per share (EPS) contribution of the project over its entire economic life, using the number of outstanding shares at the most recent fiscal year-end (FYE) as the basis for the calculation. (At FYE2000, Diamond Chemicals had 92,891,240 shares outstanding.)

2. *Payback:* This criterion was defined as the number of years necessary for free cash flow of the project to amortize the initial project outlay completely. For engineering-efficiency projects, the maximum payback period was six years.

3. *Discounted cash flow:* DCF was defined as the present value of future cash flows of the project (at the hurdle rate of 10 percent for engineering-efficiency proposals) less the initial investment outlay. This net present value of free cash flows had to be positive.

4. *Internal rate of return:* IRR was defined as being the discount rate at which the present value of future free cash flows just equaled the initial outlay—in other words, the rate at which the NPV was zero. The IRR of engineering-efficiency projects had to be greater than 10 percent.

Conclusion

Morris wanted to review Greystock's analysis in detail and settle the questions surrounding the tank cars and the potential loss of business volume at Rotterdam. As

Greystock's analysis now stood, the Merseyside project met all four investment criteria:

1. Average annual addition to EPS = £0.018
2. Payback period = 3.6 years
3. Net present value = £9.0 million
4. Internal rate of return = 25.9 percent

Morris was concerned that further tinkering might seriously weaken the attractiveness of the project.

EXHIBIT 1 | Comparative Information on the Seven Largest Polypropylene Plants in Europe

	Plant Location	Built in	Plant Annual Output (metric tons)	Production Cost per Ton (indexed to low-cost producer)
CBTG A.G.	Saarbrün	1981	350,000	1.00
Diamond Chem.	Liverpool	1967	250,000	1.09
Diamond Chem.	Rotterdam	1967	250,000	1.09
Hosche A.G.	Hamburg	1977	300,000	1.02
Montecassino SpA	Genoa	1961	120,000	1.11
Saône-Poulet S.A.	Marseille	1972	175,000	1.07
Vaysol S.A.	Antwerp	1976	220,000	1.06
Next 10 largest plants			450,000	1.19

Source: Case writer's analysis.

EXHIBIT 2 | Greystock's DCF Analysis of the Merseyside Project (financial values in millions of British pounds)

Assumptions

Annual output (metric tons)	250,000	Discount rate	10.0%
Output gain/Original output	7.0%	Depreciable life (years)	15
Price/ton (pounds sterling)	541	Overhead/Investment	3.5%
Inflation rate (prices and costs)	0.0%	Salvage value	0
Gross margin (ex. Deprec.)	12.50%	WIP inventory/Cost of goods	3.0%
Old gross margin	11.5%	Months downtime, construction	1.5
Tax rate	30.0%	After-tax scrap proceeds	0
Investment outlay (mill.)	9.00	Preliminary engineering costs	0.5
Energy savings/Sales Yr. 1-5	1.25%		
Yr. 6-10	0.8%		
Yr. 11-15	0.0%		

Year	0 Now	1 2001	2 2002	3 2003	4 2004	5 2005	6 2006	7 2007	8 2008	9 2009	10 2010	11 2011	12 2012	13 2013	14 2014	15 2015
1. Estimate of incremental gross profit																
New output (tons)		267,500	267,500	267,500	267,500	267,500	267,500	267,500	267,500	267,500	267,500	267,500	267,500	267,500	267,500	267,500
Lost output—construction		(33,438)														
New sales (millions)		126.63	144.72	144.72	144.72	144.72	144.72	144.72	144.72	144.72	144.72	144.72	144.72	144.72	144.72	144.72
New gross margin		13.8%	13.8%	13.8%	13.8%	13.8%	13.3%	13.3%	13.3%	13.3%	13.3%	12.5%	12.5%	12.5%	12.5%	12.5%
New gross profit		17.41	19.90	19.90	19.90	19.90	19.18	19.18	19.18	19.18	19.18	18.09	18.09	18.09	18.09	18.09
Old output		250,000	250,000	250,000	250,000	250,000	250,000	250,000	250,000	250,000	250,000	250,000	250,000	250,000	250,000	250,000
Old sales		135.25	135.25	135.25	135.25	135.25	135.25	135.25	135.25	135.25	135.25	135.25	135.25	135.25	135.25	135.25
Old gross profit		15.55	15.55	15.55	15.55	15.55	15.55	15.55	15.55	15.55	15.55	15.55	15.55	15.55	15.55	15.55
Incremental gross profit		1.86	4.34	4.34	4.34	4.34	3.62	3.62	3.62	3.62	3.62	2.54	2.54	2.54	2.54	2.54
2. Estimate of incremental depreciation																
New depreciation		1.20	1.04	0.90	0.78	0.68	0.59	0.51	0.44	0.38	0.33	0.43	0.43	0.43	0.43	0.43
3. Overhead		0.32	0.32	0.32	0.32	0.32	0.32	0.32	0.32	0.32	0.32	0.32	0.32	0.32	0.32	0.32
4. Prelim. engineering costs		0.50														
5. Pretax incremental profit		(0.16)	2.99	3.13	3.25	3.35	2.72	2.80	2.87	2.92	2.98	1.79	1.79	1.79	1.79	1.79
6. Tax expense		(0.05)	0.90	0.94	0.97	1.01	0.82	0.81	0.86	0.88	0.89	0.54	0.54	0.54	0.54	0.54
7. After-tax profit		(0.11)	2.09	2.19	2.27	2.35	1.90	1.95	2.01	2.05	2.08	1.25	1.25	1.25	1.25	1.25
8. Cash flow adjustments	(9.00)															
Less capital expenditures	(9.00)															
Add back depreciation		1.20	1.04	0.90	0.78	0.68	0.59	0.51	0.44	0.38	0.33	0.43	0.43	0.43	0.43	0.43
Less added WIP inventory		0.31	-0.47	0.00	0.00	0.00	0.00	0.00	0.00	0.00	0.00	0.00	0.00	0.00	0.00	0.00
After-tax scrap proceeds		0.00														
9. Free cash flow	(9.00)	1.40	2.66	3.09	3.06	3.02	2.49	2.47	2.45	2.43	2.41	1.68	1.68	1.68	1.68	1.68

NPV = **9.00**

IRR = **25.9%**

Diamond Chemicals plc (B): Merseyside and Rotterdam Projects

James Fawn, executive vice president of the Intermediate Chemicals Group (ICG) of Diamond Chemicals, met with his financial analyst, John Camperdown, to review two mutually exclusive capital-expenditure proposals. The firm's capital budget would be submitted for approval to the board of directors in early February 2001, and any projects proposed by Fawn for the ICG had to be forwarded to the chief executive officer of Diamond Chemicals soon for his review. Plant managers in Liverpool and Rotterdam had independently submitted expenditure proposals, each of which would expand the polypropylene output of their respective plants by 7 percent.[1] Diamond Chemicals' strategic-analysis staff argued strenuously that a company-wide increase in polypropylene output of 14 percent made no sense, but half that amount did. Thus, Fawn could not accept *both* projects; he could sponsor only one for approval by the board.

Corporate policy was to evaluate projects based on four criteria: (1) net present value (NPV) computed at the appropriate cost of capital, (2) internal rate of return (IRR), (3) payback, and (4) growth in earnings per share. In addition, the board of directors was receptive to "strategic factors"—considerations that might be difficult to quantify. The manager of the Rotterdam plant, Elizabeth Eustace, argued vociferously that her project easily hurdled all the relevant quantitative standards and that it had important strategic benefits. Indeed, Eustace had interjected those points in two recent meetings

---

[1]Background information on Diamond Chemicals and the polypropylene business is given in "Diamond Chemicals plc (A): The Merseyside Project," (Case 20).

This case was prepared by Robert F. Bruner as a basis for class discussion rather than to illustrate effective or ineffective handling of an administrative situation. Diamond Chemicals is a fictional company, reflecting the issues facing actual firms. The author wishes to acknowledge the helpful comments of Dr. Frank H. McTigue, the literary color of Anthony Trollope, and the financial support of the Citicorp Global Scholars Program. Copyright © 2001 by the University of Virginia Darden School Foundation, Charlottesville, VA. All rights reserved. *To order copies, send an e-mail to* sales@dardenpublishing.com. *No part of this publication may be reproduced, stored in a retrieval system, used in a spreadsheet, or transmitted in any form or by any means—electronic, mechanical, photocopying, recording, or otherwise—without the permission of the Darden School Foundation.*

with senior management and at a cocktail reception for the board of directors. Fawn expected to review the proposal from Lucy Morris, manager of the Liverpool plant, at the meeting with Camperdown, but Fawn suspected that neither proposal dominated the other on all four criteria. Fawn's choice would apparently not be straightforward.

The Proposal from Merseyside, Liverpool

The project for the Merseyside plant entailed the enhancement of existing facilities and the production process. Based on the type of project and the engineering studies, the potential benefits of the project were fairly certain (see "Diamond Chemicals plc (A): The Merseyside Project," [Case 20] for a detailed discussion of this project). To date, Morris, manager of Merseyside Works, had limited her discussions about the project to conversations with Fawn and Camperdown. Camperdown had raised various exploratory questions about the project and had presented preliminary analyses of it to managers in marketing and transportation for their comments. The revised analysis emerging from those discussions would be the focus of the discussion with Camperdown in the forthcoming meeting.

Camperdown had indicated that Morris's final memo on the project was short, only three pages. Fawn wondered whether this memo would satisfy his remaining questions.

The Rotterdam Project

Elizabeth Eustace's proposal consisted of a 90-page document replete with detailed schematics, engineering comments, strategic analyses, and financial projections. The basic discounted cash flow (DCF) analysis is presented in **Exhibit 1** and shows that the project had an NPV of (British pounds) £14 million and an IRR of 17.9 percent. Accounting for a worst-case scenario, which assumed erosion of Merseyside's volume equal to the gain in Rotterdam's volume, the NPV was £11.6 million.

In essence, Eustace's proposal called for the expenditure of £8 million, spread over three years, to convert the plant's polymerization line from batch to continuous-flow technology and to install sophisticated state-of-the-art process controls throughout the polymerization and compounding operations. The heart of the new system would be an analog computer driven by advanced software written by a team of engineering professors at an institute in Japan. The three-year-old process-control technology had been used on a smaller polypropylene production facility in Japan and had produced significant improvements in cost and output. Other major producers were known to be evaluating this system for use in their plants.

Eustace explained that installing the sophisticated new system would not be feasible without also obtaining a continuous supply of propylene gas. She proposed to obtain this gas by pipeline from a refinery five kilometers away (rather than by railroad tank cars sourced from three refineries). Diamond Chemicals had an option to purchase a pipeline and its right-of-way for £3.5 million, which Eustace had included in her £8-million estimate for the project; then, for relatively little cost, the pipeline could be extended to the Rotterdam plant and refinery at the other end. The option had been purchased several years earlier. A consultant had informed Eustace that to purchase a right-of-way at today's prices and to lay a comparable pipeline would cost approximately £6 million, a value at which the consultant believed the right-of-way could be sold today at auction. The consultant also forecast that the value of the right-of-way would be £35 million in 15 years.[2] This option was set to expire in six months.

Some senior Diamond Chemicals executives firmly believed that if the Rotterdam project were not undertaken, the option on the right-of-way should be allowed to expire unexercised. The reasoning was summarized by Jeffrey Palliser, chairman of the executive committee:

> Our business is chemicals, not land speculation. Simply buying the right-of-way with the intention of reselling it for a profit takes us beyond our expertise. Who knows when we could sell it, and for how much? How distracting would this little side venture be for Elizabeth Eustace?

Younger members of senior management were more willing to consider a potential investment arbitrage on the right-of-way.

Eustace expected to realize the benefit of this investment (i.e., a 7 percent increase in output) gradually over time, as the new technology was installed and shaken down and as the learning-curve effects were realized. She advocated a phased-investment program (as opposed to all at once) in order to minimize disruption to plant operations and to allow the new technology to be calibrated and fine-tuned.

Given the complexity of the technology and the extent to which it would permeate the plant, the system would be very expensive to dismantle. Practically, there would be no going back once the decision had been made to install the new controls. Eustace's project would represent an irrevocable commitment to the analog technology at the Rotterdam plant.

Fawn recalled that the strategic factors to which Eustace referred had to do with the obvious cost and output improvements expected from the new system, as well as from an advantage from being the first major European producer to implement the new technology. Being the first to implement the technology probably meant a head start in moving down the learning curve toward reducing costs as the organization became familiar with the technology. Eustace argued:

> The Japanese, and now the Americans, exploit the learning-curve phenomenon aggressively. Fortunately, they aren't major players in European polypropylene, at least for now. This is a once-in-a-generation opportunity for Diamond Chemicals to leapfrog its competition through the exploitation of new technology.

---

[2]The right-of-way had several commercial uses. Most prominently, the Dutch government had expressed an interest in using the right-of-way for a new high-speed railroad line. The planning for this line had barely begun, however, which suggested that land-acquisition efforts were years away. Moreover, government budget deficits threatened the timely implementation of the rail project. Another potential user was Medusa Communications, an international telecommunications company that was looking for pathways along which to bury its new optical-fiber cables. Power companies and other chemical companies or refineries might also be interested in acquiring the right-of-way.

In an oblique reference to the Merseyside proposal, Eustace went on to say:

> There are two alternatives to implementation of the analog process-control technology. One is a series of myopic enhancements to existing facilities, but this is nothing more than sticking one's head in the sand, for it leaves us at the mercy of our competitors who *are* making choices for the long term. The other alternative is to exit the polypropylene business, but this amounts to walking away from the considerable know-how we've accumulated in this business and from what is basically a valuable activity. Our commitment to analog controls makes the right choice at the right time.

The analog process-control system seemed to be the most advanced on the market. There were rumors, however, that an engineering design team at Glüsingen University in Germany was testing a radically different process-control technology—based on lasers, spectral chromatography, and digital computing—and that it was outperforming the Japanese system on cost reduction and output improvement by a factor of 1.1:1. If those rumors were true, such a system might become commercially available within five years. While it would be possible to switch to the German technology in five years, doing so would mean entirely writing off the investment in the Japanese system.

Fawn wondered how to take the potential new technology into account in making his decision. Even if he recommended the Merseyside project today, the new controls (either Japanese or German, if the latter were successfully commercialized) could also later be installed at Merseyside; any such new controls would supplant, rather than duplicate, the improvements achieved from the currently proposed enhancements at Merseyside. Lucy Morris, the plant manager at Merseyside, told James Fawn that she preferred to "wait and see" before entertaining a technology upgrade at her plant. Fawn believed that the flexibility to change technologies differed between the Rotterdam and Merseyside proposals, and this difference might affect the value of the respective projects.[3]

Conclusion

James Fawn wanted to give this choice careful thought because the plant managers at Merseyside and Rotterdam seemed to have so much invested in their own proposals. He wished that the capital-budgeting criteria would give a straightforward indication of the relative attractiveness of the two mutually exclusive projects. He wondered by what rational analytical process he could extricate himself from the ambiguities of the present measures of investment attractiveness. Moreover, he wished he had a way to evaluate the primary technological difference between the two proposals: (1) the Rotterdam project, which firmly committed Diamond Chemicals to the new-process technology, or (2) the Merseyside project, which did not, but which did retain the flexibility to allow the technology in the future.

---

[3]Using Monte Carlo simulation, Morris had estimated that the cash returns from both the German and Japanese technologies had standard deviations of 8 percent and that the correlation of the two returns was predictably high: 80 percent. The nominal risk-free rate of return was about 5.5 percent. The view of Diamond's engineers was that the German digital-based process-control system would emerge in the next five years or not emerge at all and that the probability of successful commercialization of the German technology was 50 percent.

EXHIBIT 1 | Analysis of Rotterdam Project (financial values in millions of British pounds)

Assumptions

Annual output (metric tons)	250,000		
Output gain per year/Prior Year	2.0%	Discount rate	10.0%
Maximum possible output	267,500	Depreciable life (years)	15
Price/ton (pounds sterling)	541	Overhead/Investment	3.5%
Inflation (prices and costs)	0.0%	Salvage value	0
Gross margin growth rate/Year	0.80%	WIP inventory/Cost of goods sold	3.0%
Maximum possible gross margin	16.0%	Terminal value of right-of-way	35
Old gross margin	11.5%	Months downtime, construction	
Tax rate	30.0%		

Investment outlay (millions): Now 3.5 | 2001 2.5 | 2002 1 | 2003 1

Months downtime, construction: 2001 5 | 2002 4 | 2003 3 | 2004 0

Year	0 Now	1 2001	2 2002	3 2003	4 2004	5 2005	6 2006	7 2007	8 2008	9 2009	10 2010	11 2011	12 2012	13 2013	14 2014	15 2015
1. Estimate of incremental gross profit																
New output		255,000	260,100	265,302	267,500	267,500	267,500	267,500	267,500	267,500	267,500	267,500	267,500	267,500	267,500	267,500
Lost output—construction		(106,250)	(86,700)	(66,326)												
New sales (millions)		80.47	93.81	107.65	144.72	144.72	144.72	144.72	144.72	144.72	144.72	144.72	144.72	144.72	144.72	144.72
New gross margin		11.6%	11.8%	12.1%	12.5%	13.0%	13.6%	14.4%	15.3%	16.0%	16.0%	16.0%	16.0%	16.0%	16.0%	16.0%
New gross profit		9.33	11.05	12.99	18.02	18.76	19.67	20.80	22.17	23.15	23.15	23.15	23.15	23.15	23.15	23.15
Old output		250,000	250,000	250,000	250,000	250,000	250,000	250,000	250,000	250,000	250,000	250,000	250,000	250,000	250,000	250,000
Old sales		135.25	135.25	135.25	135.25	135.25	135.25	135.25	135.25	135.25	135.25	135.25	135.25	135.25	135.25	135.25
Old gross profit		15.55	15.55	15.55	15.55	15.55	15.55	15.55	15.55	15.55	15.55	15.55	15.55	15.55	15.55	15.55
Incremental gross profit		(6.23)	(4.50)	(2.57)	2.47	3.20	4.12	5.25	6.62	7.60	7.60	7.60	7.60	7.60	7.60	7.60
2. Estimate of incremental depreciation																
Yr. 1 outlays		0.33	0.29	0.25	0.22	0.19	0.16	0.14	0.12	0.11	0.09	0.12	0.12	0.12	0.12	0.12
Yr. 2 outlays			0.14	0.12	0.10	0.09	0.08	0.07	0.06	0.05	0.04	0.05	0.05	0.05	0.05	0.05
Yr. 3 outlays				0.15	0.13	0.11	0.09	0.08	0.07	0.06	0.05	0.05	0.05	0.05	0.05	0.05
Total, new depreciation		0.33	0.43	0.53	0.45	0.39	0.33	0.29	0.25	0.21	0.18	0.22	0.22	0.22	0.22	0.22
3. Overhead		0	0	0	0	0	0	0	0	0	0	0	0	0	0	0
4. Pretax incremental profit		(6.56)	(4.94)	(3.09)	2.02	2.81	3.79	4.96	6.37	7.39	7.42	7.38	7.38	7.38	7.38	7.38
5. Tax expense		(1.97)	(1.48)	(0.93)	0.61	0.84	1.14	1.49	1.91	2.22	2.23	2.21	2.21	2.21	2.21	2.21
6. After-tax profit		(4.59)	(3.46)	(2.17)	1.41	1.97	2.65	3.47	4.46	5.17	5.19	5.17	5.17	5.17	5.17	5.17
7. Cash flow adjustments																
Add back depreciation		0.33	0.43	0.53	0.45	0.39	0.33	0.29	0.25	0.21	0.18	0.22	0.22	0.22	0.22	0.22
Less added WIP inventory		1.46	(0.35)	(0.36)	(0.96)	0.02	0.03	0.03	0.04	0.03						
Capital spending	3.50	2.50	1.00	1.00												
Terminal value, land																35.00
8. Free cash flow	(3.50)	(8.21)	(3.68)	(2.28)	2.83	2.34	2.96	3.73	4.67	5.35	5.38	5.39	5.39	5.39	5.39	40.39

DCF, Rotterdam = 14.01
IRR, Rotterdam = 17.9%

continued

EXHIBIT 1 | Analysis of Rotterdam Project (financial values in millions of British pounds) *(continued)*

Year	0 Now	1 2001	2 2002	3 2003	4 2004	5 2005	6 2006	7 2007	8 2008	9 2009	10 2010	11 2011	12 2012	13 2013	14 2014	15 2015
9. Adjustment for erosion in Merseyside volume:																
Lost Merseyside output		—	—	—	17,500	17,500	17,500	17,500	17,500	17,500	17,500	17,500	17,500	17,500	17,500	17,500
Lost Merseyside revenue		—	—	—	9.47	9.47	9.47	9.47	9.47	9.47	9.47	9.47	9.47	9.47	9.47	9.47
Lost Merseyside gross profits		—	—	—	1.09	1.09	1.09	1.09	1.09	1.09	1.09	1.09	1.09	1.09	1.09	1.09
Lost gross profits after taxes		—	—	—	0.76	0.76	0.76	0.76	0.76	0.76	0.76	0.76	0.76	0.76	0.76	0.76
Change in Merseyside inventory		—	—	—	0.28	0.28	0.28	0.28	0.28	0.28	0.28	0.28	0.28	0.28	0.28	0.28
Total effect on free cash flow		—	—	—	(0.48)	(0.48)	(0.48)	(0.48)	(0.48)	(0.48)	(0.48)	(0.48)	(0.48)	(0.48)	(0.48)	(0.48)
DCF, erosion Merseyside **(2.45)**																
DCF, Rotterdam adjusted for full erosion at Merseyside = 11.57																
Cash flows after erosion	(3.50)	(8.21)	(3.68)	(2.28)	2.35	1.86	2.48	3.25	4.19	4.88	4.90	4.91	4.91	4.91	4.91	39.91
IRR 16.56%																

Genzyme/GelTex Pharmaceuticals Joint Venture

In early 1997, Greg Phelps, EVP of Genzyme Corporation, met with members of a joint-venture negotiating team to develop proposed terms of a joint-venture agreement. The venture would combine capabilities of Genzyme and GelTex Pharmaceuticals to market GelTex's first product, RenaGel. GelTex was an early-stage biotech research company with two products in its pipeline. GelTex had neither the capital nor the marketing organization to launch RenaGel. Therefore, the company had been looking for a partner that would contribute cash and marketing expertise in exchange for a share of profits in a joint venture.

Genzyme had revenues of $518 million in 1996, and had grown rapidly through the innovative use of joint ventures and alliances. The joint venture with GelTex was attractive to Genzyme for several reasons. In addition to the benefit of increasing earnings through the sale of RenaGel, the joint venture would represent an excellent fit for Genzyme's specialty therapeutics and allow the firm to tap new markets. Also, building a strong partnership with GelTex might enable Genzyme to strike the same kind of deal for GelTex's second product, CholestaGel, which was targeting a much larger segment, the multibillion-dollar market of anticholesterol drugs.

Greg Phelps was eager to conclude a deal and launch the venture with GelTex. Important questions, however, had to be addressed before consummating an agreement.

- *What was the likely enterprise value of the joint venture?* This estimate would need to reflect the risks inherent in investing in a drug not yet approved by the U.S. Food and Drug Administration (FDA). Also, the joint-venture team would need to determine the best way to value a business with no operating history and an uncertain future.

This case was prepared by Pierre Jacquet, MD, PhD, MBA '98, and Robert Bruner and Samuel E. Bodily. The cooperation of Genzyme is gratefully acknowledged. Certain financial data regarding the venture have been disguised. It was written as a basis for class discussion rather than to illustrate effective or ineffective handling of an administrative situation. Copyright © 1999 by the University of Virginia Darden School Foundation, Charlottesville, VA. All rights reserved. *To order copies, send an e-mail to* sales@dardenpublishing.com. *No part of this publication may be reproduced, stored in a retrieval system, used in a spreadsheet, or transmitted in any form or by any means—electronic, mechanical, photocopying, recording, or otherwise—without the permission of the Darden School Foundation.*

- *How much of the venture should Genzyme acquire?* Typically, joint ventures between pharmaceutical firms and biotech companies featured an unequal division of interests (e.g., 80 percent pharma and 20 percent biotech). Phelps, however, wanted to consider the possible benefits of a 50:50 balance of interests.

- *How much should Genzyme pay for its interest?* Initial discussions had focused on a lump-sum payment of $27.5 million for a 50 percent interest. But the amount of any payment would depend on answers to the previous questions, on the assessment of risks, and on the impact on Genzyme's earnings. Accounting rules required that Genzyme expense investments that occurred before the venture received FDA approval. After approval, Genzyme could capitalize the investment and amortize it over the life of the venture.

Phelps turned to his team for analysis of those issues and proposals for GelTex.

Genzyme Corporation

Genzyme Corporation, headquartered in Cambridge, Massachusetts, was the fourth-largest biotech company in the United States. Unlike pharmaceutical companies that manufactured drugs through chemical processes, biotech companies used living organisms or their products to generate drugs. The company's sales reached $518 million in 1996 through researching, developing, manufacturing, and marketing products for human health care. Genzyme was founded as an enzyme-manufacturing company in 1981 by Henry Blair, a Tufts University scientist whose vision was to develop enzymes for use in diagnosis.[1] The first opportunity to turn Genzyme's expertise into a new therapeutic came with Ceredase, a treatment for Gaucher's disease. The drug was approved for sale in the United States in March 1991 to treat patients suffering moderate to severe symptoms of Gaucher's disease, a market of some 3,000 people.

Two years later, the company launched a recombinant form of Ceredase and started to enter new markets—surgical, pharmaceutical, diagnostic, and genomic products—through strategic alliances, joint ventures, and acquisitions. Such diversity allowed Genzyme to play a leadership role in a broad range of cutting-edge technologies and therapies, according to Genzyme's chair, president, and CEO, Henri A. Termeer.[2] The company's diversity came from its three[a] divisions—Genzyme General; Genzyme Tissue Repair; and a subsidiary, Genzyme Transgenics—each with its own common stock traded on the NASDAQ **(Exhibit 1).**

The wide array of technologies provided Genzyme with an excellent platform for achieving breakthroughs in major unmet medical needs. Rather than concentrate efforts on the next big hit, however, the company had decided to manage its R&D like a portfolio by outsourcing innovations through partnerships. Genzyme's strategy was to supplement its internal R&D with strategic alliances with external companies in order to access high-quality products in late-stage development.

---

[a] A fourth division, Genzyme Molecular Oncology, would be founded by the end of 1997.

The GelTex Opportunity

In early 1997, Genzyme was approached by GelTex's management team to form an alliance for launching RenaGel. Genzyme and GelTex had had a long-term relationship. Besides the fact that the boards of directors of both companies had common members, Henry Blair, the founder of Genzyme, had helped found GelTex in 1991.

History

GelTex was founded to develop ideas generated by George Whitesides, a professor of polymer chemistry at Harvard. Cofounder Dr. James Tananbaum, who worked with Whitesides, developed the initial patents that composed GelTex's technology base. Tananbaum brought along two more founders with business expertise, Bob Carpenter and Henry Blair.

As Carpenter commented in an interview for the *Boston Business Journal:*[3]

> The company was set up very quickly. We invited 10 of our friends to dinner, all of whom were either scientists or biotech-company executives. And then Professor Whitesides and I pitched our idea to the invited guests. By the time dessert was served, $875,000 had been put on the table and GelTex was born.

The money lasted a year. In July 1993, another $6.8 million was raised from venture capitalists, and the company moved its makeshift lab from the North Shore of Boston to a 4,000-square-foot facility in Lexington. At the time, there were only four employees. In August 1994, another $10 million was raised in a third round of financing, and the company moved to its present location in Waltham, Massachusetts.

In November 1995, the company completed an initial public offering of its common stock, selling 2,875,000 common shares, with net proceeds to the company of $26.2 million after deducting offering costs. GelTex had 45 employees at the time of the joint-venture deal with Genzyme and had committed to a strategic alliance for RenaGel with two partners: Chugai Pharmaceuticals for marketing and distribution in Asia, and Dow Chemical for drug manufacturing. The possible joint venture between Genzyme and GelTex would concern only the U.S. and European markets.

Technology

Many drug-delivery companies had looked at polymers, which had the attractive features of being nonreactive in the body and able to store relatively large quantities of drug for slow release. GelTex had the innovative, reverse idea to find polymers that could soak up substances in the body. With that approach, GelTex set out to develop orally available polymers, or "hydrogels," that could absorb and eliminate, through their efficient binding surface areas, toxic substances from the human gastrointestinal tract.[4] During the digestive process, the intestinal tract delivered nutrients and water to the bloodstream and eliminated waste products and indigestible materials though the bowel. Absorption of nutrients, electrolytes, water, and certain digestive substances such as bile acid was controlled by the intestinal wall, which acted as a gateway from the intestines to the bloodstream. Once they entered the digestive tract, GelTex polymers absorbed water and expanded like a sponge, thereby increasing the surface area of available binding sites. The spongelike material helped trap the target substance and eliminated it from the intestinal tract, even at low dosage levels.

The target markets for GelTex's technology were patients with conditions treatable in the gastrointestinal tract, including the large markets of patients with elevated cholesterol, elevated phosphorus levels, certain infectious diseases, and inflammatory conditions of the intestine. The company's lead products were RenaGel (which bound dietary phosphates in patients with chronic kidney dysfunction) and CholestaGel (which bound bile acid to lower cholesterol absorption from the gastrointestinal tract).

Strategy

GelTex's overall strategy was to become a "virtual" company that took its products far enough into development to create value without building huge operating infrastructures. As stated by Mark Skaletsky, GelTex's CEO, the company's strategy was simple.[4] Instead of creating a big corporate infrastructure, the company minimized costs by hiring a handful of experts to oversee work in key areas and then outsourcing most of the actual work. By curtailing its expenses, GelTex had generally minimized its need for capital. When it did need money, the company, from the beginning, had been successful tapping private investors and venture-capital firms.

While GelTex farmed out a lot of work, it was still maintaining its own staff of 30 researchers and some support personnel, in addition to the core managers. The five areas that were being outsourced included preclinical testing, manufacturing, medical services, regulatory affairs, and business development. Depending on their area of supervision, all five individuals who oversaw the outsourcing and who also served as the company's management team were working with outside contractors, consultants, clinical-research organizations, and the FDA to get the work accomplished in their respective areas of responsibility.

RenaGel

Healthy individuals' kidneys maintained a delicate balance between phosphorus and calcium levels in the blood by excreting excess phosphorus in the urine. In patients with chronic kidney failure, the kidneys were unable to remove enough phosphorus to maintain this critical balance. The resulting increased level of phosphorus, called hyperphosphatemia, resulted in the production of parathyroid hormone, which broke down bone to release calcium into the blood in an effort to re-establish the calcium-phosphorus balance. This process was responsible for bone demineralization, calcification of the circulatory system, and other serious complications.

When administered through the gastrointestinal tract, RenaGel was able to bind with phosphorus and decrease its absorption into the bloodstream. The drug was expected to be effective in restoring the calcium-phosphorus balance in patients with chronic renal failure. Moreover, compared with other drugs available for this condition, RenaGel simplified administration of therapy for physicians and was associated with less-toxic effects.

Kidney-Failure Market

In 1997, there were nearly 1 million patients in the United States with chronic renal failure; of those, an estimated 210,000 required dialysis to survive. All of those patients had lost the ability to excrete phosphorus and were prescribed phosphate binders; hence, they were all candidates for RenaGel. The U.S. dialysis-patient population had grown at a compounded annual rate of 8 percent over the last 10 years, driven by multiple factors including the aging of the population, increases in the incidence of diabetes, and increased utilization of dialysis. Europe had roughly 165,000 dialysis patients, with the population growing at approximately 6 percent annually; the Japanese market had roughly a population of 130,000 dialysis patients, growing at the same rate as the European population.[4, 5]

Current Treatment and Competition

The initial treatment in patients with chronic renal failure sought to maintain the level of phosphorus in the blood within normal limits by reducing the amount of phosphate in the diet. Sources of phosphates included eggs, dairy products, and meat products. This prevention therapy only worked in 10 percent of dialysis patients, leaving 90 percent to proceed to drug therapy.

There was only one drug approved by the FDA for lowering phosphate levels: Braintree Pharmaceuticals' PhosLo (calcium acetate), which required a prescription. Analysts estimated that PhosLo had about 50 percent of the market.[3] The rest of the market was filled by generic over-the-counter drugs: calcium carbonate and aluminum hydroxide. Both drugs created severe side effects and were not used chronically because of their high level of toxicity.[5]

There were also several drugs under development for the treatment of hyperphosphatemia. Most of those products were in an early stage of clinical development and were vitamin-D analogues that would act synergistically rather than competing with RenaGel.[5]

Patents and Stage of Clinical Development

GelTex had received a U.S. patent for RenaGel, as well as for a broader class of phosphate-binding agents. After having successfully completed phase I and phase II studies, GelTex announced, in early January 1997, positive preliminary results from a phase III study that encompassed 172 patients at 17 different medical centers. Two months later, GelTex reported positive results from a second phase III clinical trial on 82 patients and was planning to file for a new drug approval (NDA) with the Food and Drug Administration by the end of 1997.

Development Risks for Drugs

Products in the biotech industry were characterized by many unique features, which made them difficult to value. Once a product was marketed, the revenues, costs, and product potential could be estimated with comparative ease. Given the long time frame between idea inception, regulatory approval, and product marketing as well as the small number of ideas that ultimately resulted in a marketable product, however, biotech drugs were subject to numerous uncertainties.

There were three major risk factors in each pharmaceutical/biotech development project: the probability of clinical success or failure at progressive stages of development, delays in the development and approval process, and uncertainty of the future revenue stream (if any) of the resultant product.[6]

Clinical Risk

One feature of the biotechnology industry that made valuation so complex was the product lifecycle. A biotech drug had two distinct lifecycles, the development lifecycle and the product lifecycle. The development lifecycle was critical to the value of a product because large capital resources were needed to sustain the significant levels of R&D. It was estimated that more than 80 percent of biotech projects failed during that cycle for economic and regulatory reasons.[7]

The development lifecycle of a drug could be divided into six distinct stages through which any drug would have to progress in order to reach the marketplace:[1]

- *Preclinical research:* A drug that showed potential was tested in the laboratory and in animals to assess its safety and to analyze its biological effects. If the drug proved safe and demonstrated the desired biological effects, the firm filed a notice for an investigational new drug (IND) with the FDA. If the FDA did not object within 30 days, the company could proceed to conduct clinical testing with humans using the new compound. It was estimated that only 1 in 5,000 compounds that were considered under development entered the preclinical-testing phase.[8]

- *Phase I trial:* The phase I trial in clinical testing was designed to determine the safety and pharmacological properties of the drug. Each drug was typically tested in 20 or more healthy volunteers.

- *Phase II trial:* The phase II trials were designed to evaluate the effectiveness of the drug and to identify side effects. Tests were typically conducted with several hundred volunteers, some of whom received the drug and some of whom received a placebo.

- *Phase III trial:* The phase III trials measured the effect of the drug on a large sample of hundreds of patients over several years. Those trials helped ascertain long-term side effects and provided information on the effectiveness of a range of doses administered to a mix of patients.

- *Registration:* Upon completion of the phase III trials, firms were required to file an NDA or a product-license application (PLA) with the FDA and submit documentation of all relevant data for review.

- *Regulatory review:* The FDA created a special advisory committee for each NDA and PLA that made the final recommendation as to whether the drug should be released for commercial sale. Safety monitoring continued even after approval.

To value the clinical risk of a biotech drug, one could consider its stage of clinical development and its probability to make it to market. As shown in **Exhibit 2**, a drug in phase III trial, such as RenaGel was in early 1997, had a 65 percent probability to move on through FDA filing to FDA approval and thus make it to market launch.

Development Time before Market Launch

As a drug progressed through the different clinical stages, the revenue stream generated through market launch drew closer. It took several years for a drug in phase III to reach the market. The uncertainty surrounding FDA approval was compounded by the impact of changing regulations and governmental policies as well as by the arrival of competing compounds. With regard to RenaGel, an expeditious response from the FDA would occur one year after filing, that is, in 1998. Because of the encouraging results of RenaGel's phase III studies, management believed that RenaGel would be launched in the United States at the beginning of 1999 and in Europe at the beginning of 2000. The team assumed a 20 percent probability of a one-year launch delay in the United States (and therefore in Europe) beyond those dates and a 10 percent probability of a two-year delay.

Market Success

Once a drug received FDA approval, uncertainties remained concerning its market success. Depending on market conditions (e.g., competition, health-care policies, and market need), the average lifecycle of a biotech drug was estimated to be around 13 to 14 years, with the peak penetration rate reached within the first five years.[9] Drug sales generally peaked between years five and seven after market launch and started to decline by year nine because of the entrance of new or improved products. Currently, there was no serious competition for RenaGel in the hyperphosphatemia market, but many drugs were under development. For RenaGel, the team projected (conservatively) that the lifecycle of the drug would be as low as 10 years and as high as 20 years, with the most likely outcome 13 years.

Financial Projections for RenaGel

Analysts on Genzyme's joint-venture team decided to use a discounted cash flow analysis to value the venture as an enterprise. As the analysts were building financial projections, however, they realized that there were many uncertainties associated with RenaGel. A typical discounted cash flow analysis would not unveil the different outcomes of the venture and their relative values. The team wondered whether running a Monte Carlo simulation for the different assumptions would be helpful to price the venture and to design its term structure.

Forecast of Income Statement

Because many factors varied predictably with the volume of sales, the primary variable forecasted was RenaGel revenues. Once approved for the U.S. market, the drug was expected to enter the European market the following year. The Genzyme RenaGel joint venture would not supply the Asian market because GelTex had already licensed drug development and commercialization rights in those countries to Chugai Pharmaceuticals.

It was estimated that 90 percent of the U.S. market would be eligible for the drug, while the ratio might be lower (70 percent) for the European market. Many factors were expected to influence revenues.

- *Peak penetration rate in the market:* Based on different marketing analyses and analysts' reports, the best guess was a 50 percent peak penetration rate at year five, with a range from 20 percent to 59 percent (giving an average of 43 percent). Whatever the value of that peak rate, the analysts assumed that the pattern of penetration over time would be similar and thus the market penetration at any time would be proportional to the peak. The pattern of penetration over time assumed by the team is contained in the first complete line of **Exhibit 3.**

- *Compliance:* Not all patients who used the drug would do so faithfully, even with a doctor strongly recommending its use. The team believed that the most likely compliance rate would be 92 percent, and was prepared for a number as low as 75 percent or as high as 94 percent. Based on those numbers, the average compliance rate would be 87 percent.

- *Price per patient:* The annual price of the drug per patient would depend on many things, including how many pills the patient used and competitive pressures on the price that could be charged for the pill. The joint-venture team had worked up a figure of $1,000 as the average annual price per patient. This figure was based on an estimate of $1,100 as the most likely outcome, with a range from $600 to $1,300.

Although the variable costs of the drug were hard to pinpoint, they were not the most critical variable in the success of the drug. The team members decided to use the average industry gross profit margin of 70 percent for their analysis. They also believed that a gross profit margin for RenaGel could not be pinpointed and that the standard deviation around that number would be about 5 percent.

The target market for RenaGel could reach 200,000 patients. Instead of targeting patients with chronic renal failure, however, the joint venture would market the drug to doctors with the largest patient populations. The analysts believed that a sales force of 45 people would be enough to serve the market. They prepared a schedule of the sales force and marketing costs as a percentage of sales revenue over time **(Exhibit 3)**. Each member of the sales force would cost $200,000, rising at 5 percent a year.

The team realized that the marketing costs could turn out to be higher or lower than this schedule. The team assumed that the costs could be as low as 87 percent of the schedule or as much as 20 percent higher, and the most likely outcome was that they would be 93 percent of the schedule (which produced an average of exactly 100 percent). General and administrative costs were assumed to be 40 percent of the cost of the sales force.

Forecast of Free Cash Flows

Net working capital for the joint venture would comprise a 45-day collecting period for receivables, a 90-day period for RenaGel inventory, and a 45-day period for payables. The team forecasted capital expenditures of $14 million, split over the first three years of the venture **(Exhibit 4).**

The last decision that had to be made by Genzyme's joint-venture team was choosing a cost of capital for discounting the cash flows of the joint venture. A common practice in the biotech industry was to use a 20 percent–25 percent discount rate for products in advanced clinical trials. The weighted-average costs of capital for Genzyme and GelTex were, respectively, 14.75 percent and 23 percent on March 15, 1997.

Conclusion

Exhibit 4 shows the estimated value to Genzyme of a hypothetical 50 percent interest in the joint venture to be $44,896 million; subtracting a payment of $27.5 million gives a net present value (NPV) to Genzyme of $17,396 million. Phelps observed that this estimate hinged on many assumptions that were uncertain. He wondered about the effect of this uncertainty on the expected value of the joint venture, and on the likelihood that the NPV would turn out to be negative. He wanted to revisit the impact of uncertainty, and then to develop its implications for the amount and timing of investment.

Endnotes

[1] Elizabeth O. Teisberg. "Genzyme Corporation: Strategic Challenges with Ceredase." Harvard Business School, 1994. Case 9-793-120.

[2] Annual Report: Top Biotechnology Companies. *MedAdNews* 1997; 16: 8–60.

[3] Ellie McCormack. "GelTex Pharmaceuticals Stays Ahead of the Game." *Boston Business Journal*, 9 June 1995.

[4] Alex Zisson, Robert J. Olan. GelTex Pharmaceuticals, Inc.: Company Report. Hambrecht & Quist Institutional Research, 15 May 1996.

[5] Barbara Dau Hoffman. GelTex Pharmaceuticals. Vector Securities International. 10 March 1997.

[6] V. Walter Bratic, Patricia Tilton, and Mira Balakrishnan. "Navigating through a Biotechnology Valuation." *Journal of Biotechnology in Healthcare* 4 (1997): 207–216.

[7] Mark Edwards. "A New Approach to the Evaluation of Biopharmaceutical R&D Projects and Value Creation by Strategic Alliances." Recombinant Capital. 1994.

[8] J.F. Beary. "The Drug Development and Approval Process in the 90s." Office of Research and Development, Pharmaceutical Research and Manufacturers of America, Washington, D.C.

[9] D. Larry Smith. "Valuation of Life Sciences Companies: An Empirical and Theoretical Approach." Hambrecht & Quist. 4 January 1994.

EXHIBIT 1 | Ownership Structure of Genzyme Corporation and Affiliates

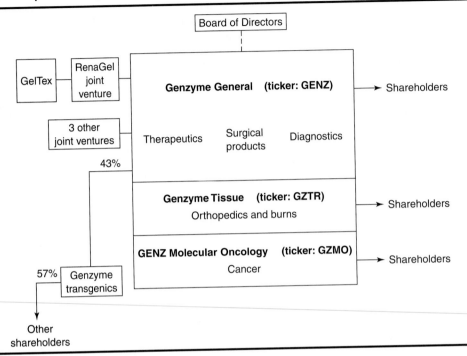

EXHIBIT 2 | Transition Probability, Probability of Market Entrance, and Development Periods for Biotech Drugs

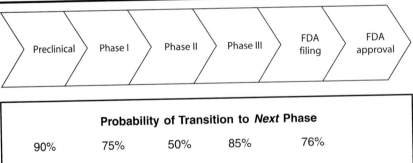

EXHIBIT 3 | Forecast of Income Statement

Genzyme Price for JV	$27,500	Genzyme Share of JV	50%

Uncertainties

FDA approval, launch	1	Compliance (%)	87%
Launch delay (years)	0	Gross profit (%)	70%
Peak penetration rate	43%	Marketing cost multiplier	1
Price per patient ($)	1000	Life of drug	14

Assumptions

	1	0
Market launch probability	65%	35%
U.S. growth rate	8%	
Europe growth rate	6%	
Discount rate	20%	

Results

JV Enterprise Value	$89,793
Genzyme NPV	$17,396
GelTex NPV	$44,896

RenaGel market performance	1997	1998	1999	2000	2001	2002	2003	2004	2005	2006	2007	2008	2009	2010	2011	2012
Market penetration, no launch																
delay	0%	0%	4%	9%	22%	34%	43%	43%	43%	43%	42%	41%	40%	39%	37%	34%
Actual penetration	0%	0%	4%	9%	22%	34%	43%	43%	43%	43%	42%	41%	40%	39%	37%	34%
U.S. patients	210,000	226,800	244,944	264,540	285,703	308,559	333,244	359,903	388,695	419,791	453,374	489,644	528,816	571,121	616,811	666,156
Eligibility	90%	90%	90%	90%	90%	90%	90%	90%	90%	90%	90%	90%	90%	90%	90%	90%
Total U.S. customers	—	—	9,479	20,475	55,283	95,530	128,965	139,282	150,425	162,459	171,947	180,018	190,326	198,921	205,287	206,242
Europe patients	165,000	174,900	185,394	196,518	208,309	220,807	234,056	248,099	262,985	278,764	295,490	313,219	332,012	351,933	373,049	395,432
Europe eligibility	70%	70%	70%	70%	70%	70%	70%	70%	70%	70%	70%	70%	70%	70%	70%	70%
Total European customers	—	—	—	5,915	12,540	33,231	56,361	74,678	79,158	83,908	88,942	92,393	94,939	98,517	101,059	102,362
Total customer base	—	—	9,479	26,391	67,824	128,761	185,326	213,960	229,584	246,367	260,889	272,411	285,265	297,438	306,346	308,603
Total revenues ($000s)	—	—	8,247	22,960	59,007	112,022	161,234	186,145	199,738	214,339	226,974	236,998	248,181	258,771	266,521	268,485
Gross profit ($000) 70%	—	—	5,773	16,072	41,305	78,416	112,863	130,302	139,816	150,038	158,882	165,898	173,726	181,140	186,565	187,939
Expenses																
Sales force (number)	—	15	30	45	45	45	45	45	45	45	45	45	45	45	45	45
Sales force ($000s)	—	3,150	6,615	10,419	10,940	11,487	12,061	12,664	13,297	13,962	14,660	15,393	16,163	16,971	17,819	18,710
Marketing costs (% of sales)	—	—	65%	30%	15%	8%	5%	5%	5%	5%	5%	5%	5%	5%	5%	5%
Marketing costs ($000s)	—	—	5,361	6,888	8,851	8,962	8,062	9,307	9,987	10,717	11,349	11,850	12,409	12,939	13,326	13,424
G&A (% of sales force)	—	—	40%	40%	40%	40%	40%	40%	40%	40%	40%	40%	40%	40%	40%	40%
G&A ($000)	800	800	2,646	4,167	4,376	4,595	4,824	5,066	5,319	5,585	5,864	6,157	6,465	6,788	7,128	7,484
R&D ($000)	4,000	3,000	3,000	3,000	3,000	3,000	3,000	3,000	3,000	3,000	3,000	3,000	3,000	3,000	3,000	3,000
Depreciation ($000)	400	400	950	950	950	950	950	950	950	950	950	950	950	950	950	950
Total expense ($000)	5,200	7,350	18,572	25,424	28,116	28,993	28,897	30,987	32,553	34,214	35,823	37,350	38,987	40,648	42,223	43,569
EBIT ($000)	(5,200)	(7,350)	(12,799)	(9,352)	13,188	49,423	83,967	99,315	107,264	115,824	123,059	128,548	134,740	140,492	144,341	144,371
Tax ($000) @: 38%	—	—	—	—	5,012	18,781	31,907	37,740	40,760	44,013	46,762	48,848	51,201	53,387	54,850	54,861
Net income ($000)	(5,200)	(7,350)	(12,799)	(9,352)	8,177	30,642	52,059	61,575	66,503	71,811	76,296	79,700	83,539	87,105	89,492	89,510

EXHIBIT 4 | Forecast of Free Cash Flows ($000)

	1997	1998	1999	2000	2001	2002	2003	2004	2005	2006	2007	2008	2009	2010	2011	2012
Net Income	(5,200)	(7,350)	(12,799)	(9,352)	8,177	30,642	52,059	61,575	66,503	71,811	76,296	79,700	85,539	87,105	89,492	89,510
Change in Net Working Capital																
Receivables (days) 45	—	—	1,017	2,831	7,275	13,811	19,878	22,949	24,625	26,425	27,983	29,219	30,598	31,903	32,859	33,101
Inventories (days) 90	—	—	610	1,698	4,365	8,287	11,927	13,770	14,775	15,855	16,790	17,531	18,359	19,142	19,715	19,861
Payables (days) 45	—	—	(305)	(849)	(2,182)	(4,143)	(5,963)	(6,885)	(7,388)	(7,928)	(8,395)	(8,766)	(9,179)	(9,571)	(9,858)	(9,930)
Investment in working capital	—	—	1,322	3,680	9,457	17,954	25,842	29,834	32,013	34,353	36,378	37,985	39,777	41,474	42,716	43,031
Net change in working capital	—	—	(1,322)	(2,358)	(5,777)	(8,497)	(7,887)	(3,993)	(2,178)	(2,340)	(2,025)	(1,607)	(1,792)	(1,697)	(1,242)	(315)
Capital expenditure	(3,500)	(2,500)	(8,000)	—	—	—	—	—	—	—	—	—	—	—	—	—
Add back depreciation	400	400	950	950	950	950	950	950	950	950	950	950	950	950	950	950
Free Cash Flows	(8,300)	(9,450)	(21,170)	(10,760)	3,349	23,095	45,122	58,533	65,275	70,421	75,221	79,043	82,696	86,358	89,200	90,145
Terminal value																43,031
Adjusted Free Cash Flows	(8,300)	(9,450)	(21,170)	(10,760)	3,349	23,095	45,122	58,533	65,275	70,421	75,221	79,043	82,696	86,358	89,200	133,176
Genzyme Investment	$27,500															

	JV	Genzyme	Geltex
Enterprise value (000)	89,793	44,896	44,896
Genzyme Investment NPV	$27,500		
Genzyme NPV	17,396		

Euroland Foods S.A.

In early January 2001, the senior management committee of Euroland Foods was to meet to draw up the firm's capital budget for the new year. Up for consideration were 11 major projects that totaled more than (euro) EUR316 million. Unfortunately, the board of directors had imposed a spending limit on capital projects of only EUR120 million; even so, investment at that rate would represent a major increase in the firm's current asset base of EUR965 million. Thus, the challenge for the senior managers of Euroland Foods was to allocate funds among a range of compelling projects: new-product introduction, acquisition, market expansion, efficiency improvements, preventive maintenance, safety, and pollution control.

The Company

Euroland Foods, headquartered in Brussels, Belgium, was a multinational producer of high-quality ice cream, yogurt, bottled water, and fruit juices. Its products were sold throughout Scandinavia, Britain, Belgium, the Netherlands, Luxembourg, western Germany, and northern France. (See **Exhibit 1** for a map of the company's marketing region.)

The company was founded in 1924 by Theo Verdin, a Belgian farmer, as an off-shoot of his dairy business. Through his keen attention to product development and shrewd marketing, the business grew steadily over the years. The company went public in 1979, and, by 1993, was listed for trading on the London, Frankfurt, and Brussels exchanges. In 2000, Euroland Foods had sales of almost EUR1.6 billion.

Ice cream accounted for 60 percent of the company's revenue; yogurt, which was introduced in 1982, contributed about 20 percent. The remaining 20 percent of sales was divided equally between bottled water and fruit juices. Euroland Foods's flagship brand name was "Rolly," which was represented by a fat dancing bear in farmer's clothing. Ice cream, the company's leading product, had a loyal base of customers who sought out its high-butter-fat content, large chunks of chocolate, fruit, nuts, and wide range of original flavors.

This case was prepared by Casey Opitz and Robert F. Bruner and draws certain elements from an antecedent case by them. All names are fictitious. The financial support of the Batten Institute is gratefully acknowledged. It was written as a basis for class discussion rather than to illustrate effective or ineffective handling of an administrative situation. Copyright © 2001 by the University of Virginia Darden School Foundation, Charlottesville, VA. All rights reserved. *To order copies, send an e-mail to* sales@dardenpublishing.com. *No part of this publication may be reproduced, stored in a retrieval system, used in a spreadsheet, or transmitted in any form or by any means—electronic, mechanical, photocopying, recording, or otherwise—without the permission of the Darden School Foundation.*

Euroland Foods sales had been static since 1998 (see **Exhibit 2**), which management attributed to low population growth in northern Europe and market saturation in some areas. Outside observers, however, faulted recent failures in new-product introductions. Most members of management wanted to expand the company's market presence and introduce more new products to boost sales. Those managers hoped that increased market presence and sales would improve the company's market value. The company's stock was currently at 14 times earnings, just below book value. This price/earnings ratio was below the trading multiples of comparable companies, and it gave little value to the company's brands.

Resource Allocation

The capital budget at Euroland Foods was prepared annually by a committee of senior managers, who then presented it for approval to the board of directors. The committee consisted of five managing directors, the président directeur-général (PDG), and the finance director. Typically, the PDG solicited investment proposals from the managing directors. The proposals included a brief project description, a financial analysis, and a discussion of strategic or other qualitative considerations.

As a matter of policy, investment proposals at Euroland Foods were subject to two financial tests: payback and internal rate of return (IRR). The tests, or hurdles, had been established in 1999 by the management committee and varied according to the type of project as shown in **Table 1.**

TABLE 1 | Project Hurdles

Type of Project	Minimum Acceptable IRR	Maximum Acceptable Payback Years
1. New product or new markets	12%	6 years
2. Product or market extension	10%	5 years
3. Efficiency improvements	8%	4 years
4. Safety or environmental	No test	No test

In January 2001, the estimated weighted-average cost of capital (WACC) for Euroland Foods was 10.6 percent.

In describing the capital-budgeting process, the finance director, Trudi Lauf, said:

> We use the sliding scale of IRR tests as a way of recognizing differences in risk among the various types of projects. Where the company takes more risk, we should earn more return. The payback test signals that we are not prepared to wait for long to achieve that return.

Ownership and the Sentiment of Creditors and Investors

Euroland Foods's 12-member board of directors included three members of the Verdin family, four members of management, and five outside directors who were prominent managers or public figures in northern Europe. Members of the Verdin family combined owned 20 percent of Euroland Foods's shares outstanding, and company executives combined owned 10 percent of the shares. Venus Asset Management, a mutual-fund management company in London, held 12 percent. Banque du Bruges et des Pays Bas held 9 percent and had one representative on the board of directors. The remaining 49 percent of the firm's shares were widely held. The firm's shares traded in Brussels and Frankfurt, Germany.

At a debt-to-equity ratio of 125 percent, Euroland Foods was leveraged much more highly than its peers in the European consumer-foods industry. Management had relied on debt financing significantly in the past few years to sustain the firm's capital spending and dividends during a period of price wars initiated by Euroland. Now, with the price wars finished, Euroland's bankers (led by Banque du Bruges) strongly urged an aggressive program of debt reduction. In any event, they were not prepared to finance increases in leverage beyond the current level. The president of Banque du Bruges had remarked at a recent board meeting:

> Restoring some strength to the right-hand side of the balance sheet should now be a first priority. Any expansion of assets should be financed from the cash flow after debt amortization until the debt ratio returns to a more prudent level. If there are crucial investments that cannot be funded this way, then we should cut the dividend!

At a price-to-earnings ratio of 14 times, shares of Euroland Foods common stock were priced below the average multiples of peer companies and the average multiples of all companies on the exchanges where Euroland Foods was traded. This was attributable to the recent price wars, which had suppressed the company's profitability, and to the well-known recent failure of the company to seize significant market share with a new product line of flavored mineral water. Since January 2000, all the major securities houses had been issuing "sell" recommendations to investors in Euroland Foods shares. Venus Asset Management had quietly accumulated shares during this period, however, in the expectation of a turnaround in the firm's performance. At the most recent board meeting, the senior managing director of Venus gave a presentation, in which he said:

> Cutting the dividend is unthinkable, as it would signal a lack of faith in your own future. Selling new shares of stock at this depressed price level is also unthinkable, as it would impose unacceptable dilution on your current shareholders. Your equity investors expect an improvement in performance. If that improvement is not forthcoming, or worse, if investors' hopes are dashed, your shares might fall into the hands of raiders like Carlo de Benedetti or the Flick brothers.[1]

At the conclusion of the most recent meeting of the directors, the board voted unanimously to limit capital spending to EUR120 million in 2001.

Members of the Senior Management Committee

Seven senior managers of Euroland Foods would prepare the capital budget. For consideration, each project had to be sponsored by one of the managers present. Usually

---

[1]De Benedetti of Milan and the Flick brothers of Munich were leaders of prominent hostile-takeover attempts in recent years.

the decision process included a period of discussion followed by a vote on two to four alternative capital budgets. The various executives were well known to each other:

Wilhelmina Verdin (Belgian), PDG, age 57. Granddaughter of the founder and spokesperson on the board of directors for the Verdin family's interests. Worked for the company her entire career, with significant experience in brand management. Elected "European Marketer of the Year" in 1982 for successfully introducing low-fat yogurt and ice cream, the first major roll-out of this type of product. Eager to position the company for long-term growth but cautious in the wake of recent difficulties.

Trudi Lauf (Swiss), finance director, age 51. Hired from Nestlé in 1995 to modernize financial controls and systems. Had been a vocal proponent of reducing leverage on the balance sheet. Also, voiced the concerns and frustrations of stockholders.

Heinz Klink (German), managing director for Distribution, age 49. Oversaw the transportation, warehousing, and order-fulfillment activities in the company. Spoilage, transport costs, stock-outs, and control systems were perennial challenges.

Maarten Leyden (Dutch), managing director for Production and Purchasing, age 59. Managed production operations at the company's 14 plants. Engineer by training. Tough negotiator, especially with unions and suppliers. A fanatic about production-cost control. Had voiced doubts about the sincerity of creditors' and investors' commitment to the firm.

Marco Ponti (Italian), managing director of Sales, age 45. Oversaw the field sales force of 250 representatives and planned changes in geographical sales coverage. The most vocal proponent of rapid expansion on the senior-management committee. Saw several opportunities for ways to improve geographical positioning. Hired from Unilever in 1993 to revitalize the sales organization, which he successfully accomplished.

Fabienne Morin (French), managing director for Marketing, age 41. Responsible for marketing research, new-product development, advertising, and in general, brand management. The primary advocate of the recent price war, which, although financially difficult, realized solid gains in market share. Perceived a "window of opportunity" for product and market expansion and tended to support growth-oriented projects.

Nigel Humbolt (British), managing director for Strategic Planning, age 47. Hired two years previously from a well-known consulting firm to set up a strategic planning staff for Euroland Foods. Known for asking difficult and challenging questions about Euroland's core business, its maturity, and profitability. Supported initiatives aimed at growth and market share. Had presented the most aggressive proposals in 2000, none of which were accepted. Becoming frustrated with what he perceived to be his lack of influence in the organization.

The Expenditure Proposals

The forthcoming meeting would entertain the following proposals in **Table 2**:

TABLE 2 | Project Proposals

Project	Expenditure (euro millions)	Sponsoring Manager
1. Replacement and expansion of the truck fleet	33	Klink, distribution
2. A new plant	45	Leyden, production
3. Expansion of a plant	15	Leyden, production
4. Development and roll-out of snack foods	27	Morin, marketing
5. Plant automation and conveyer systems	21	Leyden, production
6. Effluent-water treatment at four plants	6	Leyden, production
7. Market expansion southward	30	Ponti, sales
8. Market expansion eastward	30	Ponti, sales
9. Development and introduction of new artificially sweetened yogurt and ice cream	27	Morin, marketing
10. Networked, computer-based inventory-control system for warehouses and field representatives	22.5	Klink, distribution
11. Acquisition of a leading schnapps brand and associated facilities	60	Humbolt, strategic planning

1. Replacement and expansion of the truck fleet: Heinz Klink proposed to purchase 100 new refrigerated tractor-trailer trucks, 50 each in 2001 and 2002. By doing so, the company could sell 60 old, fully depreciated trucks over the two years for a total of EUR4.05 million. The purchase would expand the fleet by 40 trucks within two years. Each of the new trailers would be larger than the old trailers and afforded a 15 percent increase in cubic meters of goods hauled on each trip. The new tractors would also be more fuel- and maintenance-efficient. The increase in the number of trucks would permit more flexible scheduling and more efficient routing and servicing of the fleet than at present and would cut delivery times and, therefore, possibly inventories. It would also allow more frequent deliveries to the company's major markets, which would reduce the loss of sales caused by stock-outs. Finally, expanding the fleet would support geographical expansion over the long term.

As shown in **Exhibit 3,** the total net investment in trucks of EUR30 million and the increase in working capital to support added maintenance, fuel, payroll, and inventories of EUR3 million was expected to yield total cost savings and added sales potential of EUR11.6 million over the next seven years. The resulting IRR was estimated to be 7.8 percent, marginally below the minimum 8 percent required return on efficiency projects. Some of the managers wondered if this project would be more properly classified as "efficiency" than "expansion."

2. A new plant: Maarten Leyden noted that Euroland Foods yogurt and ice-cream sales in the southeastern region of the company's market were about to exceed the capacity of its Melun, France, manufacturing and packaging plant. At present, some of the demand was being met by shipments from the company's newest, most efficient facility, located in Strasbourg, France. Shipping costs over that distance were high, however, and some sales were undoubtedly being lost when the marketing effort could not be supported by delivery. Leyden proposed that a new manufacturing and packaging plant be built in Dijon, France, just at the current southern edge of the Euroland Foods marketing region, to take the burden off the Melun and Strasbourg plants.

The cost of that plant would be EUR37.5 million and would entail EUR7.5 million for working capital. The EUR21 million worth of equipment would be amortized over seven years, and the plant over ten years. Through an increase in sales and depreciation and the decrease in delivery costs, the plant was expected to yield after-tax cash flows totaling EUR35.6 million and an IRR of 11.3 percent over the next 10 years. This project would be classified as a market extension.

3. Expansion of a plant: In addition to the need for greater production capacity in Euroland Foods's southeastern region, its Nuremberg, Germany, plant had reached full capacity. This situation made the scheduling of routine equipment maintenance difficult, which, in turn, created production scheduling and deadline problems. This plant was one of two highly automated facilities that produced the Euroland Foods's entire line of bottled water, mineral water, and fruit juices. The Nuremberg plant supplied central and western Europe. (The other plant, near Copenhagen, Denmark, supplied the Euroland Foods northern European markets.)

The Nuremberg plant capacity could be expanded by 20 percent for EUR15 million. The equipment (EUR10.5 million) would be depreciated over seven years, and the plant over ten years. The increased capacity was expected to result in additional production of up to EUR2.25 million a year, yielding an IRR of 11.2 percent. This project would be classified as a market extension.

4. Development and roll-out of snack foods: Fabienne Morin suggested that the company use the excess capacity at its Antwerp spice- and nut-processing facility to produce a line of dried fruits to be test-marketed in Belgium, Britain, and the Netherlands. She noted the strength of the Rolly brand in those countries and the success of other food and beverage companies that had expanded into snack food production. She argued that the Euroland Foods's reputation for wholesome, quality products would be enhanced by a line of dried fruits and, further, that name association with the new product would probably even lead to increased sales of the company's other products among health-conscious consumers.

Equipment and working-capital investments were expected to total EUR22.5 million and EUR4.5 million, respectively, for this project. The equipment would be depreciated over seven years. Assuming the test market was successful, cash flows from the project would be able to support further plant expansions in other strategic locations. The IRR was expected to be 13.4 percent, slightly above the required return of 12 percent for new-product projects.

5. Plant automation and conveyer systems: Maarten Leyden also requested EUR21 million to increase automation of the production lines at six of the company's older plants. The result would be improved throughput speed and reduced accidents, spillage, and production tie-ups. The last two plants the company had built included conveyer systems that eliminated the need for any heavy lifting by employees. The systems reduced the chance of injury by employees; at the six older plants, the company had sustained an average of 223 missed-worker days per year per plant in the last two years because of muscle injuries sustained in heavy lifting. At an average hourly total compensation rate of EUR14.00 an hour, more than EUR150,000 a year were thus lost, and the possibility always existed of more serious injuries and lawsuits. Overall, cost savings and depreciation totaling EUR4.13 million a year for the project were expected to yield an IRR of 8.7 percent. This project would be classed in the efficiency category.

6. Effluent-water treatment at four plants: Euroland Foods preprocessed a variety of fresh fruits at its Melun and Strasbourg plants. One of the first stages of processing involved cleaning the fruit to remove dirt and pesticides. The dirty water was simply sent down the drain and into the Seine or Rhine Rivers. Recent European Community directives called for any wastewater containing even slight traces of poisonous chemicals to be treated at the sources, and gave companies four years to comply. As an environmentally oriented project, this proposal fell outside the normal financial tests of project attractiveness. Leyden noted, however, that the water-treatment equipment could be purchased today for EUR6 million; he speculated that the same equipment would cost EUR15 million in four years when immediate conversion became mandatory. In the intervening time, the company would run the risks that European Community regulators would shorten the compliance time or that the company's pollution record would become public and impair the image of the company in the eyes of the consumer. This project would be classed in the environmental category.

7 and 8. Market expansions southward and eastward: Marco Ponti recommended that the company expand its market southward to include southern France, Switzerland, Italy, and Spain, and/or eastward to include eastern Germany, Poland, the Czech Republic, Slovakia, and Austria. Ponti believed the time was right to expand sales of ice cream, and perhaps yogurt, geographically. In theory, the company could sustain expansions in both directions simultaneously, but practically, Ponti doubted that the sales and distribution organizations could sustain both expansions at once.

Each alternative geographical expansion had its benefits and risks. If the company expanded eastward, it could reach a large population with a great appetite for frozen dairy products, but it would also face more competition from local and regional ice cream manufacturers. Moreover, consumers in eastern Germany, Poland, and Slovakia did not have the purchasing power that consumers to the south did. The eastward expansion would have to be supplied from plants in Nuremberg, Strasbourg, and Hamburg.

Looking southward, the tables were turned: more purchasing power and less competition but also a smaller consumer appetite for ice cream and yogurt. A southward expansion would require building consumer demand for premium-quality yogurt and ice cream. If neither of the plant proposals (proposals 2 and 3) was accepted, then the southward expansion would need to be supplied from plants in Melun, Strasbourg, and Rouen.

The initial cost of either proposal was EUR30 million of working capital. The bulk of this project's costs was expected to involve the financing of distributorships, but over the 10-year forecast period, the distributors would gradually take over the burden of carrying receivables and inventory. Both expansion proposals assumed the rental of suitable warehouse and distribution facilities. The after-tax cash flows were expected to total EUR56.3 million for southward expansion and EUR48.8 million for eastward expansion.

Marco Ponti pointed out that southward expansion meant a higher possible IRR but that moving eastward was a less risky proposition. The projected IRRs were 21.4 percent and 18.8 percent for southern and eastern expansion, respectively. These projects would be classed in the market-extension category.

9. *Development and introduction of new artificially sweetened yogurt and ice cream:* Fabienne Morin noted that recent developments in the synthesis of artificial sweeteners were showing promise of significant cost savings to food and beverage producers as well as stimulating growing demand for low-calorie products. The challenge was to create the right flavor to complement or enhance the other ingredients. For ice cream manufacturers, the difficulty lay in creating a balance that would result in the same flavor as was obtained when using natural sweeteners; artificial sweeteners might, of course, create a superior taste.

In addition, EUR27 million would be needed to commercialize a yogurt line that had received promising results in laboratory tests. This cost included acquiring specialized production facilities, working capital, and the cost of the initial product introduction. The overall IRR was estimated to be 20.5 percent.

Morin stressed that the proposal, although highly uncertain in terms of actual results, could be viewed as a means of protecting present market share, because other high-quality ice-cream producers carrying out the same research might introduce these products; if the Rolly brand did not carry an artificially sweetened line and its competitors did, the brand might suffer. Morin also noted the parallels between innovating with artificial sweeteners and the company's past success in introducing low-fat products. This project would be classed in the new-product category of investments.

10. *Networked, computer-based inventory-control system for warehouses and field representatives.* Heinz Klink had pressed unsuccessfully for three years for a state-of-the-art computer-based inventory-control system that would link field sales representatives, distributors, drivers, warehouses, and possibly even retailers. The benefits of such a system would be shorter delays in ordering and order processing, better control of inventory, reduction of spoilage, and faster recognition of changes in demand at the customer level. Klink was reluctant to quantify these benefits, because they could range between modest and quite large amounts. This year, for the first time, he presented a cash-flow forecast, however, that reflected an initial outlay of EUR18 million for the system, followed by EUR4.5 million in the next year for ancillary equipment. The inflows reflected depreciation tax shields, tax credits, cost reductions in warehousing, and reduced inventory. He forecast these benefits to last for only three years. Even so, the project's IRR was estimated to be 16.2 percent. This project would be classed in the efficiency category of proposals.

11. *Acquisition of a leading schnapps[2] brand and associated facilities.* Nigel Humbolt had advocated making diversifying acquisitions in an effort to move beyond

---

[2]Any of various strong dry liquors, such as a strong Dutch gin. Definition borrowed from *American Heritage*® *Dictionary of the English Language,* 4th ed.

the company's mature core business but doing so in a way that exploited the company's skills in brand management. He had explored six possible related industries in the general field of consumer packaged goods and determined that cordials and liqueurs offered unusual opportunities for real growth and, at the same time, market protection through branding. He had identified four small producers of well-established brands of liqueurs as acquisition candidates. Following exploratory talks with each, he had determined that only one company could be purchased in the near future, namely, the leading private European manufacturer of schnapps, located in Munich.

The proposal was expensive: EUR25 million to buy the company and EUR30 million to renovate the company's facilities completely while simultaneously expanding distribution to new geographical markets. The expected returns were high: after-tax cash flows were projected to be EUR198.5 million, yielding an IRR of 27.5 percent. This project would be classed in the new-product category of proposals.

Conclusion

Each member of the management committee was expected to come to the meeting prepared to present and defend a proposal for the allocation of Euroland Foods's capital budget of EUR120 million. **Exhibit 3** summarizes the various projects in terms of their free cash flows and the investment-performance criteria.

EXHIBIT 1 | Nations Where Euroland Foods Competed

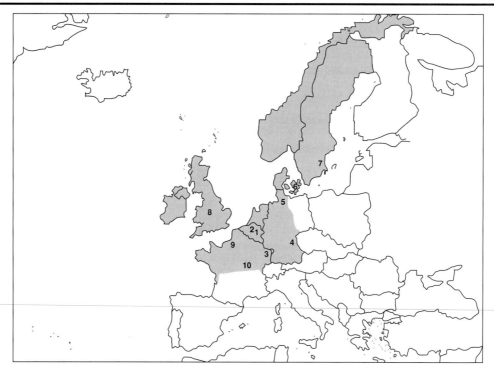

Note: The shaded area on this map reveals the principal distribution region of Euroland's products. Important facilities are indicated by the following figures:

1	Headquarters, Brussels, Belgium
2	Plant, Antwerp, Belgium
3	Plant, Strasbourg, France
4	Plant, Nuremberg, Germany
5	Plant, Hamburg, Germany
6	Plant, Copenhagen, Denmark
7	Plant, Svald, Sweden
8	Plant, Nelly-on-Mersey, England
9	Plant, Caen, France
10	Plant, Melun, France

EXHIBIT 2 | Summary of Financial Results (all values in euro millions, except per-share amounts)

	Fiscal Year Ending December		
	1998	**1999**	**2000**
Gross sales	1,614	1,608	1,611
Net income	77	74	56
Earnings per share	1.13	1.08	0.81
Dividends	30	30	30
Total assets	716	870	984
Shareholders' equity (book value)	559	640	697
Shareholders' equity (market value)	1,271	1,258	784

EXHIBIT 3 | Free Cash Flows and Analysis of Proposed Projects[1] (all values in euro millions)

Project	1	2	3	4	5	6	7	8	9	10
	Expand Truck Fleet[3]	New Plant (Dijon, France)	Expanded Plant (Nuremberg, Germany)	Snack Foods	Automation and Conveyer Systems	Southward Expansion[5]	Eastward Expansion[5]	Artificial Sweetener	Inventory-Control System	Strategic Acquisition[6]
Investment										
Property	30.00	37.50	15.00	22.50	21.00	0.00	0.00	22.50	22.50	45.00
Working capital	3.00	7.50	0.00	4.50	0.00	30.00	30.00	4.50	0.00	15.00
Year	EXPECTED FREE CASH FLOWS[4]									
0	−17.10	−45.00	−15.00	−9.00	−21.00	−30.00	−30.00	−27.00	−18.00	−25.00
1	−11.85	3.00	1.88	−9.00	4.13	5.25	4.50	4.50	8.25	−30.00
2	4.50	7.50	2.25	−9.00	4.13	6.00	5.25	6.00	8.25	7.50
3	5.25	8.25	2.63	4.50	4.13	6.75	6.00	6.75	7.50	13.50
4	6.00	9.00	3.00	4.50	4.13	7.50	6.75	7.50		16.50
5	6.75	9.38	3.38	6.00	4.13	8.25	7.50	7.50		19.50
6	7.50	9.75	3.75	6.75	4.13	9.00	8.25	7.50		22.50
7	10.50	10.13	2.25	7.50	4.13	9.75	9.00	7.50		25.50
8		7.50	2.25	8.25		10.50	9.75	7.50		28.50
9		7.88	2.25	9.00		11.25	10.50	7.50		31.50
10		8.25	2.25	9.75		12.00	11.25	7.50		88.50
Undiscounted Sum	11.55	35.63	10.88	29.25	7.88	56.25	48.75	42.75	6.00	198.50
Payback (years)	6	6	6	7	6	5	5	5	3	5
Maximum payback accepted	4	5	5	6	4	6	6	6	4	6
IRR	7.8%	11.3%	11.2%	13.4%	8.7%	21.4%	18.8%	20.5%	16.2%	27.5%
Minimum accepted ROR	8.0%	10.0%	10.0%	12.0%	8.0%	12.0%	12.0%	12.0%	8.0%	12.0%
Spread	−0.2%	1.3%	1.2%	1.4%	0.7%	9.4%	6.8%	8.5%	8.2%	15.5%
NPV at Corp. WACC (10.6%)	−2.88	1.49	0.41	3.74	−1.31	17.99	13.49	13.43	1.75	69.45
NPV at Minimum ROR	−0.19	2.81	0.82	1.79	0.48	14.85	10.62	10.97	2.67	59.65
Equivalent Annuity[2]	−0.04	0.46	0.13	0.32	0.09	2.63	1.88	1.94	1.03	10.56

[1]The effluent treatment program is not included in this exhibit.

[2]The equivalent annuity of a project is that level annual payment that yields a net present value equal to the NPV at the minimum required rate of return for that project. Annuity corrects for differences in duration among various projects. In ranking projects on the basis of equivalent annuity, bigger annuities create more investor wealth than smaller annuities.

[3]This reflects EUR16.5 million spent both initially and at the end of year one.

[4]Free cash flow = Incremental profit or cost savings after taxes + Depreciation − Investment in fixed assets and working capital.

[5]Franchisees would gradually take over the burden of carrying receivables and inventory.

[6]EUR25 million would be spent in the first year, EUR30 million in the second, and EUR5 million in the third.

Star River 星河 Electronics Ltd.

On July 5, 2001, her first day as chief executive officer (CEO) of Star River Electronics Ltd., Adeline Koh confronted a host of management problems. One week earlier, Star River's president and CEO had suddenly resigned to accept a CEO position with another firm. Koh had been appointed to fill the position—starting immediately. Several items in her in-box that first day were financial in nature, either requiring a financial decision or with outcomes that would have major financial implications for the firm. That evening, Koh asked to meet with her assistant, Andy Chin, to begin addressing the most prominent issues.

Star River Electronics and the Optical-Disc-Manufacturing Industry

Star River Electronics had been founded as a joint venture between Starlight Electronics Ltd., U.K., and an Asian venture-capital firm, New Era Partners. Based in Singapore, Star River's sole business mission was to manufacture CD-ROMs as a supplier to major software companies. In no time, Star River had gained fame in the industry for producing high-quality discs.

The popularity of optical and multimedia products created rapid growth for the CD-ROM manufacturing industry in the mid-1990s. Accordingly, small manufacturers proliferated, creating an oversupply that pushed prices down by as much as 40 percent. Consolidation followed as less efficient producers began to feel the pinch.

Star River Electronics survived the shakeout thanks to its sterling reputation. While other CD-ROM manufacturers floundered, volume sales at the company grew at a robust rate in the past two years. Unit prices, however, had declined because of price competition and the growing popularity of substitute storage devices, particularly digital video discs (DVDs). The latter had 14 times more storage capacity and threatened to displace CD-ROMs. Although CD-ROM *disc drives* comprised 93 percent of all optical-disc-drive shipments in 1999, a study predicted that this number would fall to 41 percent by 2005,

This case is derived from materials originally prepared by Robert Bruner, Robert Conroy, and Kenneth Eades. The firms and individuals in the case are fictitious. The financial support of the Batten Institute is gratefully acknowledged. It was written as a basis for class discussion rather than to illustrate effective or ineffective handling of an administrative situation. Copyright © 2001 by the University of Virginia Darden School Foundation, Charlottesville, VA. All rights reserved. *To order copies, send an e-mail to sales@dardenpublishing.com. No part of this publication may be reproduced, stored in a retrieval system, used in a spreadsheet, or transmitted in any form or by any means—electronic, mechanical, photocopying, recording, or otherwise—without the permission of the Darden School Foundation.*

while the share of DVD drives would rise to 59 percent.[1] Star River had begun to experiment with DVD manufacturing, but DVDs still accounted for less than 5 percent of its sales at fiscal year-end 2001. With new installed capacity, however, the company hoped to increase the proportion of revenue from DVDs.

Financial Questions Facing Adeline Koh

That evening, Koh met with Andy Chin, a promising new associate whom she had brought along from New Era Partners. Koh's brief discussion with Chin went as follows:

KOH: Back at New Era we looked at Star River as one of our most promising venture-capital investments. Now it seems that such optimism may not be warranted—at least until we get a solid understanding of the firm's past performance and its forecast performance. Did you have any success on this?

CHIN: Yes, the bookkeeper gave me these: the historical-income statements [Exhibit 1] and balance sheets [Exhibit 2] for the last four years. The accounting system here is still pretty primitive. However, I checked a number of the accounts, and they look orderly. So I suspect that we can work with these figures. From these statements, I calculated a set of diagnostic ratios [Exhibit 3].

KOH: I see you have been busy. Unfortunately, I can't study these right now. I need you to review the historical performance of Star River for me, and to give me any positive or negative insights that you think are significant.

CHIN: When do you need this?

KOH: At 7:00 a.m. tomorrow. I want to call on our banker tomorrow morning and get an extension on Star River's loan.

CHIN: The banker, Mr. Tan, said that Star River was "growing beyond its financial capabilities." What does that mean?

KOH: It probably means that he doesn't think we can repay the loan within a reasonable period. I would like you to build a simple financial forecast of our performance for the next two years (ignore seasonal effects), and show me what our debt requirements will be at the fiscal years ending 2002 and 2003. I think it is reasonable to expect that Star River's sales will grow at 15 percent each year. Also, you should assume capital expenditures of SGD54.6 million[2] for DVD manufacturing equipment, spread out over the next two years and depreciated over seven years. Use whatever other assumptions seem appropriate to you based on your historical analysis of results. For this forecast, you should assume that any external funding is in the form of debt.

CHIN: But what if the forecasts show that Star River cannot repay the loan?

KOH: Then we'll have to go back to Star River's owners, New Era Partners and Star River Electronics U.K., for an injection of equity. Of course, New Era Partners

---

[1]Global Industry Analysts, Inc., "TEAC—Facts, Figures and Forecasts," 5.

[2]SGD = Singaporean dollars.

would rather not invest more funds unless we can show that the returns on such an investment would be very attractive, and/or that the survival of the company depends on it. Thus, my third request is for you to examine what returns on book assets and book equity Star River will offer in the next two years and to identify the "key-driver" assumptions of those returns. Finally, let me have your recommendations about operating and financial changes I should make based on the historical analysis and the forecasts.

CHIN: The plant manager revised his request for a new packaging machine and thinks these are the right numbers [see the plant manager's memorandum in **Exhibit 4**]. Essentially, the issue is whether to invest now or wait three years to buy the new packaging equipment. The new equipment can save significantly on labor costs but carries a price tag of SGD1.82 million. My hunch is that our preference between investing now versus waiting three years will hinge on the discount rate.

KOH: [laughing] The joke in business school was that the discount rate was always 10 percent.

CHIN: That's not what my business school taught me! New Era always uses a 40 percent discount rate to value equity investments in risky start-up companies. But Star River is reasonably well established now and shouldn't require such a high-risk premium. I managed to pull together some data [see **Exhibit 5**] on other Singaporean electronics companies with which to estimate the required rate of return on equity.

KOH: Fine. Please estimate Star River's weighted-average cost of capital and assess the packaging-machine investment. I would like the results of your analysis tomorrow morning at 7:00.

EXHIBIT 1 | Historical Income Statements for Fiscal Year Ended June 30 (SGD 000)

	1998	1999	2000	2001
Sales	71,924	80,115	92,613	106,042
Operating expenses:				
Production costs and expenses	33,703	38,393	46,492	53,445
Admin. and selling expenses	16,733	17,787	21,301	24,177
Depreciation	8,076	9,028	10,392	11,360
Total operating expenses	58,512	65,208	78,185	88,983
Operating profit	13,412	14,908	14,429	17,059
Interest expense	5,464	6,010	7,938	7,818
Earnings before taxes	7,949	8,897	6,491	9,241
Income taxes*	2,221	2,322	1,601	2,093
Net earnings	5,728	6,576	4,889	7,148
Dividends to all common shares	2,000	2,000	2,000	2,000
Retentions of earnings	3,728	4,576	2,889	5,148

*The expected corporate tax rate was 24.5%.

EXHIBIT 2 | Historical Balance Sheets for Fiscal Year Ended June 30 (SGD 000)

	1998	1999	2000	2001
Assets:				
Cash	4,816	5,670	6,090	5,795
Accounts receivable	22,148	25,364	28,078	35,486
Inventories	23,301	27,662	53,828	63,778
Total current assets	50,265	58,697	87,996	105,059
Gross property, plant & equipment	64,611	80,153	97,899	115,153
Accumulated depreciation	(4,559)	(13,587)	(23,979)	(35,339)
Net property, plant & equipment	60,052	66,566	73,920	79,814
Total assets	110,317	125,262	161,916	184,873
Liabilities and Stockholders' Equity:				
Short-term borrowings (bank)[1]	29,002	37,160	73,089	84,981
Accounts payable	12,315	12,806	11,890	13,370
Other accrued liabilities	24,608	26,330	25,081	21,318
Total current liabilities	65,926	76,296	110,060	119,669
Long-term debt[2]	10,000	10,000	10,000	18,200
Shareholders' equity	34,391	38,967	41,856	47,004
Total liabilities and stockholders' equity	110,317	125,263	161,916	184,873

[1]Short-term debt was borrowed from City Bank at an interest rate equal to Singaporean prime lending rates + 1.5 percent. Current prime lending rates were 5.2 percent. The benchmark 10-year Singapore treasury bond currently yielded 3.6 percent.

[2]Two components made up the company's long term debt. One was a SGD10 million loan that had been issued privately in 1996 to New Era Partners and to Star River Electronics Ltd., U.K. This debt was subordinate to any bank debt outstanding. The second component was a SGD8.2 million from a 5-year bond issued on a private placement basis last July 1, 2000 at a price of SGD97 and a coupon of 5.75% paid semi-annually.

EXHIBIT 3 | Ratio Analyses of Historical Financial Statements

	1998	1999	2000	2001
Profitability				
Operating margin (%)	18.6%	18.6%	15.6%	16.1%
Tax rate (%)	27.9%	26.1%	24.7%	22.6%
Return on sales (%)	8.0%	8.2%	5.3%	6.7%
Return on equity (%)	16.7%	16.9%	11.7%	15.2%
Return on assets (%)	5.2%	5.2%	3.0%	3.9%
Leverage				
Debt/equity ratio	1.13	1.21	1.99	2.20
Debt/total capital (%)	0.53	0.55	0.67	0.69
EBIT/interest (x)	2.45	2.48	1.82	2.18
Asset Utilization				
Sales/assets	65.2%	64.0%	57.2%	57.4%
Sales growth rate (%)	15.0%	11.4%	15.6%	14.5%
Assets growth rate (%)	8.0%	13.5%	29.3%	14.2%
Days in receivables	112.4	115.6	110.7	122.1
Payables to COGS	36.5%	33.4%	25.6%	25.0%
Inventories to COGS	69.1%	72.1%	115.8%	119.3%
Liquidity				
Current ratio	0.76	0.77	0.80	0.88
Quick ratio	0.41	0.41	0.31	0.34

EXHIBIT 4 | Plant Manager's Memo Regarding New Packaging Equipment

---

MEMORANDUM

TO: Adeline Koh, President and CEO, Star River Electronics
FROM: Esmond Lim, Plant Manager
DATE: June 30, 2001
SUBJECT: New Packaging Equipment

Although our CD packaging equipment is adequate at current production levels, it is terribly inefficient. The new machinery on the market can give us significant labor savings as well as increased flexibility with respect to the type of packaging used. I recommend that we go with the new technology. Should we decide to do so, the new machine can be acquired immediately. The considerations relevant to the decision are included in this memo.

Our current packaging equipment was purchased five years ago as used equipment in a liquidation sale of a small company. Although the equipment was inexpensive, it is slow, requires constant monitoring and is frequently shut down for repairs. Since the packaging equipment is significantly slower than the production equipment, we routinely have to use overtime labor to allow packaging to catch up with production. When the packager is down for repairs, the problem is exacerbated and we may spend several two-shift days catching up with production. I cannot say that we have missed any deadlines because of packaging problems, but it is a constant concern around here and things would run a lot smoother with more reliable equipment. In 2002 we will pay about SGD15,470 per year for maintenance costs. The operator is paid SGD63,700 per year for his regular time, but he has been averaging SGD81,900 per year because of the overtime he has been working. The equipment is on the tax and reporting books at SGD218,400 and will be fully depreciated in three years time (we are currently using the straight-line depreciation method for both tax and reporting purposes and will continue to do so). Because of changes in packaging technology, the equipment has no market value other than its worth as scrap metal. But its scrap value is about equal to the cost of having it removed. In short, we believe the equipment has no salvage value at all.

The new packager offers many advantages over the current equipment. It is faster, more reliable, more flexible with respect to the types of packaging it can perform, and will provide enough capacity to cover all our packaging needs in the foreseeable future. With suitable maintenance, we believe the packager will operate indefinitely. Thus, for the purposes of our analysis, we can assume that this will be the last packaging equipment we will ever have to purchase. Because of the anticipated growth at Star River, the current equipment will not be able to handle our packaging needs by the end of 2004. Thus, if we do not buy new packaging equipment by this year's end, we will have to buy it after three years time anyway. Since the speed, capacity, and reliability of the new equipment will eliminate the need for overtime labor, we feel strongly that we should buy now rather than wait another three years.

The new equipment currently costs SGD1.82 million which we would depreciate over 10 years at SGD182,000 per year. It comes with a life-time factory maintenance contract that covers all routine maintenance and repairs at a price of SGD3,640 for the initial year. The contract stipulates that the price after the first year will be increased by the same percentage as the rate of increase of the price of new equipment. Thus if the manufacturer continues to increase the price of new packaging equipment at 5 percent per annum as it has in the past, our maintenance costs will rise by 5 percent also. We believe that this sort of regular maintenance should insure that the new equipment will keep operating in the foreseeable future without the need for a major overhaul.

Star River's labor and maintenance costs will continue to rise due to inflation at approximately 1.5 percent per year over the long term. Because the manufacturer of the packaging equipment has been increasing its prices at about 5 percent per year, we can expect to save SGD286,878 in the purchase price by buying now rather than waiting three years. The marginal tax rate for this investment would be 24.5 percent.

EXHIBIT 5 | Data on Comparable Companies and Capital-Market Conditions

Name	% of Sales from CD-ROM and/or DVD Production	Price/ Earnings Ratio	Beta	Book D/E	Book Value per Share	Market Price per Share	Number of Shares Outstanding (millions)	Last Annual Dividend	5-Year Earnings Growth Forecast
Sing Studios, Inc.	20%	9.0	1.07	0.23	1.24	1.37	9.3	1.82	4.0%
Wintronics, Inc.	95%	NMF	1.56	1.70	1.46	6.39	177.2	0.15	15.7%
STOR-Max Corp.	90%	18.2	1.67	1.30	7.06	27.48	89.3	none	21.3%
Digital Media Corp.	30%	34.6	1.18	0.00	17.75	75.22	48.3	none	38.2%
Wymax, Inc.	60%	NMF	1.52	0.40	6.95	22.19	371.2	1.57	11.3%

Note: NMF means not a meaningful figure. This arises when a company's earnings or projected earnings are negative.

Singapore's equity market risk premium could be assumed to be close to the global equity market premium of 6 percent, given Singapore's high rate of integration into global markets.

Descriptions of Companies

Sing Studios, Inc.

This company was founded 50 years ago. Its major business activities historically had been production of original-artist recordings, management and production of rock-and-roll road tours, and personal management of artists. It entered the CD-production market in the 1980s, and only recently branched out into the manufacture of CD-ROMs. Most of its business, however, related to the manufacture and sale of MIDI (Music Instrument Digital Interface) CDs.

Wintronics, Inc.

This company was a spin-off from a large technology-holding corporation in 1981. Although the company was a leader in the production of CD-ROMs and DVDs, it has recently suffered a decline in sales. Infighting among the principal owners has fed concerns about the firm's prospects.

STOR-Max Corp.

This company, founded only two years ago, had emerged as a very aggressive competitor in the area of CD-ROM and DVD production. It was Star River's major competitor and its sales level was about the same.

Digital Media Corp.

This company had recently been an innovator in the production of DVDs. Although DVD manufacturing was not a majority of its business (film production and digital animation were its main focus), the company was projected to be a major competitor within the next three years.

Wymax, Inc.

This company was an early pioneer in the CD-ROM and DVD industries. Recently, however, it had begun to invest in software programming and had been moving away from disc production as its main focus of business.

PART 5

Management of the Firm's Equity: Dividends, Repurchases, Initial Offerings

Gainesboro Machine Tools Corporation

In mid-September 2005, Ashley Swenson, chief financial officer (CFO) of Gainesboro Machine Tools Corporation, paced the floor of her Minnesota office. She needed to submit a recommendation to Gainesboro's board of directors regarding the company's dividend policy, which had been the subject of an ongoing debate among the firm's senior managers. Compounding her problem was the uncertainty surrounding the recent impact of Hurricane Katrina, which had caused untold destruction across the southeastern United States. In the weeks after the storm, the stock market had spiraled downward and, along with it, Gainesboro's stock, which had fallen 18 percent, to $22.15. In response to the market shock, a spate of companies had announced plans to buy back stock. While some were motivated by a desire to signal confidence in their companies as well as in the U.S. financial markets, still others had opportunistic reasons. Now, Ashley Swenson's dividend-decision problem was compounded by the dilemma of whether to use company funds to pay shareholder dividends or to buy back stock.

Background on the Dividend Question

After years of traditionally strong earnings and predictable dividend growth, Gainesboro had faltered in the past five years. In response, management implemented two extensive restructuring programs, both of which were accompanied by net losses. For three years in a row since 2000, dividends had exceeded earnings. Then, in 2003, dividends were decreased to a level below earnings. Despite extraordinary losses in 2004, the board of directors declared a small dividend. For the first two quarters of 2005, the board declared no dividend. But in a special letter to shareholders, the board committed itself to resuming payment of the dividend as soon as possible—ideally, sometime in 2005.

This case was written by Robert F. Bruner and Sean Carr, research assistant, and is dedicated to Professors Robert F. Vandell and Pearson Hunt, the authors of an antecedent case, long out of print, that provided the model for the economic problem in this case. "Gainesboro" is a fictional firm, though it draws on dilemmas of contemporary companies. The financial support of the Batten Institute is gratefully acknowledged. Copyright © 2005 by the University of Virginia Darden School Foundation, Charlottesville, VA. All rights reserved. *To order copies, send an e-mail to* sales@dardenpublishing.com. *No part of this publication may be reproduced, stored in a retrieval system, used in a spreadsheet, or transmitted in any form or by any means—electronic, mechanical, photocopying, recording, or otherwise—without the permission of the Darden School Foundation.*

In a related matter, senior management considered embarking on a campaign of corporate-image advertising, together with changing the name of the corporation to "Gainesboro Advanced Systems International, Inc." Management believed that the name change would help improve the investment community's perception of the company.

Overall, management's view was that Gainesboro was a resurgent company that demonstrated great potential for growth and profitability. The restructurings had revitalized the company's operating divisions. In addition, the newly developed machine tools designed on state-of-the-art computers showed signs of being well received in the market, and promised to render the competitors' products obsolete. Many within the company viewed 2005 as the dawning of a new era, which, in spite of the company's recent performance, would turn Gainesboro into a growth stock. The company had no Moody's or Standard & Poor's rating because it had no bonds outstanding, but Value Line rated it an "A" company.[1]

Out of this combination of a troubled past and a bright future arose Swenson's dilemma. Did the market view Gainesboro as a company on the wane, a blue-chip stock, or a potential growth stock? How, if at all, could Gainesboro affect that perception? Would a change of name help to positively frame investors' views of the firm? Did the company's investors expect capital growth or steady dividends? Would a stock buyback instead of a dividend affect investors' perceptions of Gainesboro in any way? And, if those questions could be answered, what were the implications for Gainesboro's future dividend policy?

The Company

Gainesboro Corporation was founded in 1923 in Concord, New Hampshire, by two mechanical engineers, James Gaines and David Scarboro. The two men had gone to school together and were disenchanted with their prospects as mechanics at a farm-equipment manufacturer.

In its early years, Gainesboro had designed and manufactured a number of machinery parts, including metal presses, dies, and molds. In the 1940s, the company's large manufacturing plant produced armored-vehicle and tank parts and miscellaneous equipment for the war effort, including riveters and welders. After the war, the company concentrated on the production of industrial presses and molds, for plastics as well as metals. By 1975, the company had developed a reputation as an innovative producer of industrial machinery and machine tools.

In the early 1980s, Gainesboro entered the new field of computer-aided design and computer-aided manufacturing (CAD/CAM). Working with a small software company, it developed a line of presses that could manufacture metal parts by responding to computer commands. Gainesboro merged the software company into its operations and, over the next several years, perfected the CAM equipment. At the same time, it developed a superior line of CAD software and equipment that would allow an engineer

---

[1] Value Line's financial-strength ratings, from A++ to C, were a measure of a company's ability to withstand adverse business conditions and were based on leverage, liquidity, business risk, company size, and stock-price variability, as well as analysts' judgments.

to design a part to exacting specifications on a computer. The design could then be entered into the company's CAM equipment, and the parts could be manufactured without the use of blueprints or human interference. By the end of 2004, CAD/CAM equipment and software were responsible for about 45 percent of sales; presses, dies, and molds made up 40 percent of sales; and miscellaneous machine tools were 15 percent of sales.

Most press and mold companies were small local or regional firms with limited clientele. For that reason, Gainesboro stood out as a true industry leader. Within the CAD/CAM industry, however, a number of larger firms, including Autodesk, Inc., Cadence Design, and Synopsys, Inc., competed for dominance of the growing market.

Throughout the 1990s, Gainesboro helped set the standard for CAD/CAM, but the aggressive entry of large foreign firms into CAD/CAM and the rise of the U.S. dollar dampened sales. In the late 1990s and early 2000s, technological advances and aggressive venture capitalism fueled the entry of highly specialized, state-of-the-art CAD/CAM firms. Gainesboro fell behind some of its competition in the development of user-friendly software and the integration of design and manufacturing. As a result, revenues slipped from a high of $911 million, in 1998, to $757 million, in 2004.

To combat the decline in revenues and to improve weak profit margins, Gainesboro took a two-pronged approach. First, it devoted a greater share of its research-and-development budget to CAD/CAM in an effort to reestablish its leadership in the field. Second, the company underwent two massive restructurings. In 2002, it sold two unprofitable lines of business with revenues of $51 million, sold two plants, eliminated five leased facilities, and reduced personnel. Restructuring costs totaled $65 million. Then, in 2004, the company began a second round of restructuring by altering its manufacturing strategy, refocusing its sales and marketing approach, and adopting administrative procedures that allowed for a further reduction in staff and facilities. The total cost of the operational restructuring in 2004 was $89 million.

The company's recent consolidated income statements and balance sheets are provided in **Exhibits 1** and **2.** Although the two restructurings produced losses totaling $202 million in 2002 and 2004, by 2005 the restructurings and the increased emphasis on CAD/CAM research appeared to have launched a turnaround. Not only was the company leaner, but also the research led to the development of a system that Gainesboro's management believed would redefine the industry. Known as the Artificial Workforce, the system was an array of advanced control hardware, software, and applications that could distribute information throughout a plant.

Essentially, the Artificial Workforce allowed an engineer to design a part on CAD software and input the data into CAM equipment that could control the mixing of chemicals or the molding of parts from any number of different materials on different machines. The system could also assemble and can, box, or shrink-wrap the finished product. The Artificial Workforce ran on complex circuitry and highly advanced software that allowed the machines to communicate with each other electronically. Thus, a product could be designed, manufactured, and packaged solely by computer no matter how intricate it was.

Gainesboro had developed applications of the product for the chemicals industry and for the oil- and gas-refining industries in 2004 and, by the next year, it had created applications for the trucking, automobile-parts, and airline industries.

By October 2004, when the first Artificial Workforce was shipped, Gainesboro had orders totaling $75 million. By year end, the backlog was $100 million. The future for the product looked bright. Several securities analysts were optimistic about the product's impact on the company. The following comments paraphrase their thoughts:

> The Artificial Workforce products have compelling advantages over competing entries, which will enable Gainesboro to increase its share of a market that, ignoring periodic growth spurts, will expand at a real annual rate of about 5 percent over the next several years.

> The company is producing the Artificial Workforce in a new automated facility, which, when in full swing, will help restore margins to levels not seen in years.

> The important question now is how quickly Gainesboro will be able to ship in volume. Manufacturing mishaps and missing components delayed production growth through May 2005, putting it about six months beyond the original target date. And start-up costs, which were a significant factor in last year's deficits, have continued to penalize earnings. Our estimates assume that production will proceed smoothly from now on and that it will approach the optimum level by year's end.

Gainesboro's management expected domestic revenues from the Artificial Workforce series to total $90 million in 2005 and $150 million in 2006. Thereafter, growth in sales would depend on the development of more system applications and the creation of system improvements and add-on features. International sales through Gainesboro's existing offices in Frankfurt, Germany; London, England; Milan, Italy; and Paris, France; and new offices in Hong Kong, China; Seoul, Korea; Manila, Philippines; and Tokyo, Japan, were expected to provide additional revenues of $150 million by as early as 2007. Currently, international sales accounted for approximately 15 percent of total corporate revenues.

Two factors that could affect sales were of some concern to Gainesboro. First, although the company had successfully patented several of the processes used by the Artificial Workforce system, management had received hints through industry observers that two strong competitors were developing comparable products and would probably introduce them within the next 12 months. Second, sales of molds, presses, machine tools, and CAD/CAM equipment and software were highly cyclical, and current predictions about the strength of the U.S. economy were not encouraging. As shown in **Exhibit 3,** real GDP (gross domestic product) growth was expected to hover at a steady but unimpressive 3.0 percent over the next few years. Industrial production, which had improved significantly since 2001, would likely indicate a trend slightly downward next year and the year after that. Despite the macroeconomic environment, Gainesboro's management remained optimistic about the company's prospects because of the successful introduction of the Artificial Workforce series.

Corporate Goals

A number of corporate objectives had grown out of the restructurings and recent technological advances. First and foremost, management wanted and expected the firm to grow at an average annual compound rate of 15 percent. A great deal of corporate planning had been devoted to that goal over the past three years and, indeed, second-quarter financial data suggested that Gainesboro would achieve revenues of about $870 million in 2005, as shown in **Exhibit 1.** If Gainesboro achieved a 15 percent compound rate of growth through 2011, the company could reach $2.0 billion in sales and $160 million in net income.

In order to achieve that growth goal, Gainesboro management proposed a strategy relying on three key points. First, the mix of production would shift substantially. CAD/CAM and peripheral products on the cutting edge of industrial technology would account for three-quarters of sales, while the company's traditional presses and molds would account for the remainder. Second, the company would expand aggressively in the international arena, whence it hoped to obtain half of its sales and profits by 2011. This expansion would be achieved through opening new field sales offices around the world. Third, the company would expand through joint ventures and acquisitions of small software companies, which would provide half of the new products through 2011; in-house research would provide the other half.

The company had had an aversion to debt since its inception. Management believed that small amounts of debt, primarily to meet working-capital needs, had their place, but that anything beyond a 40 percent debt-to-equity ratio was, in the oft-quoted words of Gainesboro cofounder David Scarboro, "unthinkable, indicative of sloppy management, and flirting with trouble." Senior management was aware that equity was typically more costly than debt, but took great satisfaction in the company's "doing it on its own." Gainesboro's highest debt-to-capital ratio in the past 25 years (22 percent) had occurred in 2004, and was still the subject of conversations among senior managers.

Although eleven members of the Gaines and the Scarboro families owned 13 percent of the company's stock and three were on the board of directors, management placed the interests of the outside shareholders first. (Shareholder data are provided in **Exhibit 4.**) Stephen Gaines, board chair and grandson of the cofounder, sought to maximize growth in the market value of the company's stock over time.

At 61, Gaines was actively involved in all aspects of the company's growth. He dealt fluently with a range of technical details of Gainesboro's products, and was especially interested in finding ways to improve the company's domestic market share. His retirement was no more than four years away, and he wanted to leave a legacy of corporate financial strength and technological achievement. The Artificial Workforce, a project that he had taken under his wing four years earlier, was finally beginning to bear fruit. Gaines now wanted to ensure that the firm would also soon be able to pay a dividend to its shareholders.

Gaines took particular pride in selecting and developing promising young managers. Ashley Swenson had a bachelor's degree in electrical engineering and had been a systems analyst for Motorola before attending graduate school. She had been hired in 1995, fresh out of a well-known MBA program. By 2004, she had risen to the position of CFO.

Dividend Policy

Gainesboro's dividend and stock-price histories are presented in **Exhibit 5.** Before 1999, both earnings and dividends per share had grown at a relatively steady pace, but Gainesboro's troubles in the early 2000s had taken their toll on earnings. Consequently, dividends were pared back in 2003 to $0.25 a share—the lowest dividend since 1990. In 2004, the board of directors declared a payout of $0.25 a share, despite reporting the largest per-share earnings loss in the firm's history and despite, in effect, having to borrow to pay that dividend. In the first two quarters of 2005, the directors did not declare a dividend. In a special letter to shareholders, however, the directors declared their intention to continue the annual payout later in 2005.

In August 2005, Swenson contemplated her choices from among the three possible dividend policies to decide which one she should recommend:

- *Zero-dividend payout:* This option could be justified in light of the firm's strategic emphasis on advanced technologies and CAD/CAM, and reflected the huge cash requirements of such a move. The proponents of this policy argued that it would signal that the firm now belonged in a class of high-growth and high-technology firms. Some securities analysts wondered whether the market still considered Gainesboro a traditional electrical-equipment manufacturer or a more technologically advanced CAD/CAM company. The latter category would imply that the market expected strong capital appreciation, but perhaps little in the way of dividends. Others cited Gainesboro's recent performance problems. One questioned the "wisdom of ignoring the financial statements in favor of acting like a blue chip." Was a high dividend in the long-term interests of the company and its stockholders, or would the strategy backfire and make investors skittish?

  Swenson recalled a recently published study that found that firms were displaying a lower propensity to pay dividends. The study found that the percentage of firms paying cash dividends had dropped from 66.5 percent, in 1978, to 20.8 percent, in 1999.[2] In that light, perhaps the market would react favorably, if Gainesboro adopted a zero dividend-payout policy.

- *40 percent dividend payout or a dividend of around $0.20 a share:* This option would restore the firm to an implied annual dividend payment of $0.80 a share, the highest since 2001. Proponents of this policy argued that such an announcement was justified by expected increases in orders and sales. Gainesboro's investment banker suggested that the market might reward a strong dividend that would bring the firm's payout back in line with the 36 percent average within the electrical-industrial-equipment industry and with the 26 percent average in the machine-tool industry. Still others believed that it was important to send a strong signal to shareholders, and that a large dividend (on the order of a 40 percent payout) would suggest that the company had conquered its problems and that its directors were confident of its future earnings. Supporters of this view argued that borrowing to pay dividends was consistent with the behavior of most firms. Finally, some older managers opined that a growth rate in the range of 10 percent to 20 percent should accompany a dividend payout of between 30 percent and 50 percent.

- *Residual-dividend payout:* A few members of the finance department argued that Gainesboro should pay dividends only after it had funded all the projects that offered

---

[2]Eugene Fama and Kenneth French, "Changing Firm Characteristics or Lower Propensity to Pay," *Journal of Financial Economics* 60 (April 2001): 3–43.

positive net present values (NPV). Their view was that investors paid managers to deploy their funds at returns better than they could otherwise achieve, and that, by definition, such investments would yield positive NPVs. By deploying funds into those projects and returning otherwise unused funds to investors in the form of dividends, the firm would build trust with investors and be rewarded through higher valuation multiples.

Another argument in support of that view was that the particular dividend policy was "irrelevant" in a growing firm: any dividend paid today would be offset by dilution at some future date by the issuance of shares needed to make up for the dividend. This argument reflected the theory of dividends in a perfect market advanced by two finance professors, Merton Miller and Franco Modigliani.[3] To Ashley Swenson, the main disadvantage of this policy was that dividend payments would be unpredictable. In some years, dividends could even be cut to zero, possibly imposing negative pressure on the firm's share price. Swenson was all too aware of Gainesboro's own share-price collapse following its dividend cut. She recalled a study by another finance professor, John Lintner,[4] which found that firms' dividend payments tended to be "sticky" upward—that is, dividends would rise over time and rarely fall, and that mature, slower-growth firms paid higher dividends, while high-growth firms paid lower dividends.

In response to the internal debate, Swenson's staff pulled together **Exhibits 6** and **7,** which present comparative information on companies in three industries—CAD/CAM, machine tools, and electrical-industrial equipment—and a sample of high- and low-payout companies. To test the feasibility of a 40 percent dividend-payout rate, Swenson developed the projected sources-and-uses of cash statement provided in **Exhibit 8.** She took the boldest approach by assuming that the company would grow at a 15 percent compound rate, that margins would improve over the next few years to historical levels, and that the firm would pay a dividend of 40 percent of earnings every year. In particular, the forecast assumed that the firm's net margin would hover between 4 percent and 6 percent over the next six years, and then increase to 8 percent in 2011. The firm's operating executives believed that this increase in profitability was consistent with economies of scale to be achieved upon the attainment of higher operating output through the Artificial Workforce series.

Image Advertising and Name Change

As part of a general review of the firm's standing in the financial markets, Gainesboro's director of Investor Relations, Cathy Williams, had concluded that investors misperceived the firm's prospects and that the firm's current name was more consistent with its historical product mix and markets than with those projected for the future.

---

[3]M. H. Miller and F. Modigliani, "Dividend Policy, Growth, and the Valuation of Shares," *Journal of Business* 34 (October 1961): 411–433.

[4]J. Lintner, "Distribution of Incomes of Corporations among Dividends, Retained Earnings, and Taxes," *American Economic Review* 46 (May 1956): 97–113.

Williams commissioned surveys of readers of financial magazines, which revealed a relatively low awareness of Gainesboro and its business. Surveys of stockbrokers revealed a higher awareness of the firm, but a low or mediocre outlook on Gainesboro's likely returns to shareholders and its growth prospects. Williams retained a consulting firm that recommended a program of corporate-image advertising targeted toward guiding the opinions of institutional and individual investors. The objective was to enhance the firm's visibility and image. Through focus groups, the image consultants identified a new name that appeared to suggest the firm's promising new strategy: Gainesboro Advanced Systems International, Inc. Williams estimated that the image-advertising campaign and name change would cost approximately $10 million.

Stephen Gaines was mildly skeptical. He said, "Do you mean to raise our stock price by 'marketing' our shares? This is a novel approach. Can you sell claims on a company the way Procter & Gamble markets soap?" The consultants could give no empirical evidence that stock prices responded positively to corporate-image campaigns or name changes, though they did offer some favorable anecdotes.

Conclusion

Swenson was in a difficult position. Board members and management disagreed on the very nature of Gainesboro's future. Some managers saw the company as entering a new stage of rapid growth and thought that a large (or, in the minds of some, any) dividend would be inappropriate. Others thought that it was important to make a strong public gesture showing that management believed that Gainesboro had turned the corner and was about to return to the levels of growth and profitability seen in the 1980s and '90s. This action could only be accomplished through a dividend. Then there was the confounding question about the stock buyback. Should Gainesboro use its funds to repurchase stocks instead of paying out a dividend? As Swenson wrestled with the different points of view, she wondered whether Gainesboro's management might be representative of the company's shareholders. Did the majority of public shareholders own stock for the same reason, or were their reasons just as diverse as those of management?

EXHIBIT 1 | Consolidated Income Statements (dollars in thousands, except per-share data)

| | For the Years Ended December 31 | | | Projected |
	2002	2003	2004	2005
Net sales	$858,263	$815,979	$756,638	$870,000
Cost of sales	540,747	501,458	498,879	549,750
Gross profit	317,516	314,522	257,759	320,250
Research & development	77,678	70,545	75,417	77,250
Selling, general, & administrative	229,971	223,634	231,008	211,500
Restructuring costs	65,448	0	89,411	0
Operating profit (loss)	(55,581)	20,343	(138,077)	31,500
Other income (expense)	(4,500)	1,065	(3,458)	(4,200)
Income (loss) before taxes	(60,081)	21,408	(141,534)	27,300
Income taxes (benefit)	1,241	8,415	(750)	9,282
Net income (loss)	($61,322)	$ 12,993	($140,784)	$ 18,018
Earnings (loss) per share	($3.25)	$ 0.69	($7.57)	$ 0.98
Dividends per share	$ 0.77	$ 0.25	$ 0.25	$ 0.39

Note: The dividends in 2005 assume a payout ratio of 40%.

EXHIBIT 2 | Consolidated Balance Sheets (dollars in thousands)

	For the Years Ended December 31		Projected 2005
	2003	2004	
Cash & equivalents	$ 13,917	$ 22,230	$ 25,665
Accounts receivable	208,541	187,235	217,510
Inventories	230,342	203,888	217,221
Prepaid expenses	14,259	13,016	15,011
Other	22,184	20,714	21,000
Total current assets	489,242	447,082	496,407
Property, plant, & equipment	327,603	358,841	410,988
Less depreciation	167,414	183,486	205,530
Net property, plant, & equipment	160,190	175,355	205,458
Intangible assets	9,429	2,099	1,515
Other assets	15,723	17,688	17,969
Total assets	**$674,583**	**$642,223**	**$721,350**
Bank loans	$ 34,196	$ 71,345	$ 74,981
Accounts payable	36,449	34,239	37,527
Current portion of long-term debt	300	150	1,515
Accruals and other	129,374	161,633	183,014
Total current liabilities	200,318	267,367	297,037
Deferred taxes	16,986	13,769	16,526
Long-term debt	9,000	8,775	30,021
Deferred pension costs	44,790	64,329	70,134
Other liabilities	2,318	5,444	7,505
Total liabilities	273,411	359,683	421,224
Common stock, $1 par value	18,855	18,855	18,835
Capital in excess of par	107,874	107,907	107,889
Cumulative translation adjustment	(6,566)	20,208	26,990
Retained earnings	291,498	146,065	156,875
Less treasury stock at cost:			
1990–256,151; 1991–255,506	(10,490)	(10,494)	(10,464)
Total shareholders' equity	401,172	282,541	300,126
Total liabilities & equity	**$674,583**	**$642,223**	**$721,350**

Note: Projections assume a dividend-payout ratio of 40%.

EXHIBIT 3 | Economic Indicators and Projections (all numbers are percentages)

					Projected		
	2001	2002	2003	2004	2005	2006	2007
Three-month Treasury bill rate (at auction)	3.4	1.6	1.0	1.4	3.2	4.2	4.7
Ten-year Treasury note yield	5.0	4.6	4.0	4.3	4.3	4.8	5.7
AAA corporate bond rate	7.1	6.5	5.7	5.6	5.3	5.9	6.8
Percentage change in:							
Real gross domestic product	0.8	1.9	3.0	4.3	3.3	2.9	3.2
Producer prices, finished goods	2.0	(1.3)	3.2	3.5	1.2	(0.2)	0.1
Industrial production	(3.4)	(0.6)	0.3	4.5	3.7	3.4	4.8
Consumption of durable goods	4.3	6.5	7.4	6.0	2.4	4.2	4.5
Consumer spending	2.5	3.1	3.3	3.5	2.9	2.9	2.8
GDP deflator	2.4	1.7	1.8	2.1	1.9	1.7	1.9

Sources of data: *Value Line Investment Survey,* 26 August 2005; *U.S. Economic Outlook,* Global Insight, September 2004.

EXHIBIT 4 | Comparative Stockholder Data, 1994 and 2004 (in thousands of shares)

	1994		2004	
	Shares	Percentage	Shares	Percentage
Founders' families	2,390	13%	2,421	13%
Employees and families	3,677	20%	3,155	17%
Institutional investors				
Growth-oriented	2,390	13%	1,138	6%
Value-oriented	1,471	8%	2,421	13%
Individual investors				
Long-term retirement	6,803	37%	4,806	26%
Short-term; trading-oriented	919	5%	2,421	13%
Other; unknown	735	4%	2,239	12%
Total	18,385	100%	18,600	100%

Note: The investor-relations department identified these categories from company records. The type of institutional investor was identified from promotional materials stating the investment goals of the institutions. The type of individual investor was identified from a survey of subsamples of investors.

EXHIBIT 5 | Per-Share Financial and Stock Data[1]

| Year | Sales/ Share | EPS[2] | DPS[2] | CPS[2] | Stock Price | | | Avg. P/E | Payout Ratio | Avg. Yield | Shares Outstanding (millions) |
					High	Low	Avg.				
1989	$14.52	$0.45	$0.18	$0.97	$20.37	$9.69	$14.48	32.4	40%	1.2%	15.49
1990	16.00	0.74	0.22	1.29	21.11	10.18	14.85	20.2	30%	1.5%	15.58
1991	22.25	0.89	0.27	1.43	21.23	8.20	13.50	15.1	30%	2.0%	16.04
1992	25.64	1.59	0.31	2.05	18.50	10.18	13.35	8.4	19%	2.3%	17.87
1993	27.19	2.29	0.40	2.83	22.48	12.17	18.36	8.0	17%	2.2%	18.08
1994	30.06	2.59	0.57	3.25	23.84	18.01	21.00	8.1	22%	2.7%	18.39
1995	31.66	2.61	0.72	3.34	26.70	18.25	22.73	8.7	27%	3.1%	18.76
1996	37.71	2.69	0.81	3.60	29.43	19.50	24.23	9.0	30%	3.4%	18.76
1997	40.69	2.56	0.86	3.62	39.74	20.12	29.48	11.5	34%	2.9%	18.78
1998	48.23	3.58	0.92	4.81	40.98	27.32	33.98	9.5	26%	2.7%	18.88
1999	43.59	2.79	1.03	4.25	38.74	21.36	31.82	11.4	37%	3.2%	18.66
2000	42.87	0.65	1.03	2.23	47.19	29.55	36.81	57.0	160%	2.8%	18.66
2001	41.48	0.35	1.03	2.00	40.23	26.82	31.26	89.9	297%	3.3%	18.66
2002	45.52	(3.25)	0.77	2.86	30.75	22.13	26.45	nmf	nmf	2.9%	18.85
2003	43.28	0.69	0.25	1.99	71.88	50.74	61.33	88.2	35%	0.4%	18.85
2004	$40.68	($7.57)	$0.25	($0.97)	$39.88	$18.38	$29.15	nmf	nmf	0.9%	18.60

nmf = not a meaningful figure.

[1] Adjusted for a 3-for-2 stock split in January 1995 and a 50% stock dividend in June 1997.

[2] EPS: earnings per share; CPS: cash earnings per share; DPS: dividend per share.

EXHIBIT 6 | Comparative Industry Data, August 2005

		Annual Growth Rate of Cash Flow (%)						
	Sales ($mm)	Last 5 Years	Next 3-5 Years	Current Payout Ratio (%)	Current Dividend Yield (%)	Debt/ Equity (%)[1]	Insider Ownership (%)	P/E Ratio (x)
Gainesboro Machine Tools Corp.	504	(1.5)	15.0	0.0	0.0	28.0	30.0	nmf
CAD/CAM companies (software and hardware)								
Autodesk, Inc.	1,234	4.5	10.5	6.0	0.3	0.0	3.2	25.3
Ansys, Inc.	135	16.5	13.0	0.0	0.0	0.0	4.4	23.3
Cadence Design	1,198	(1.5)	6.0	0.0	0.0	24.7	3.5	21.4
Intergraph Corp.	551	(8.0)	12.0	0.0	0.0	0.2	3.1	25.7
Mentor Graphics	711	4.5	2.0	0.0	0.0	65.5	5.9	21.9
Moldflow Corp.	49	nmf	11.5	0.0	0.0	0.0	15.4	36.2
Parametric Technology Corp.	660	(6.5)	6.0	0.0	0.0	0.0	5.4	33.4
Synopsys, Inc.	1,092	6.5	6.0	0.0	0.0	0.0	5.6	26.5
Electrical-industrial equipment manufacturers								
Cooper Industries, Inc.	4,463	1.5	3.0	39.0	2.4	30.6	1.0	16.4
Emerson Electric Company	15,615	2.5	3.5	54.0	2.6	43.3	0.8	20.5
Hubbell Inc.	1,993	5.0	6.0	52.0	3.0	21.1	2.9	17.6
Thomas & Betts Corp.	1,516	(10.0)	5.0	0.0	0.0	60.2	2.4	17.7
Machine tool manufacturers								
Actuant Corp.	976	(21.5)	12.5	0.0	0.0	180.8	5.9	19.1
Lincoln Electric Holdings, Inc.	1,334	2.5	10.0	32.0	2.2	28.4	5.2	15.0
Milacron, Inc.	774	(15.5)	(2.5)	0.0	0.0	468.1	4.6	nmf
Snap-on Inc.	2,407	5.0	3.5	71.0	3.1	18.3	3.0	22.9

nmf = not a meaningful figure.

[1] Based on book values.

Source of data: *Value Line Investment Survey,* August 2005.

EXHIBIT 7 | Selected Healthy Companies with High and Zero Dividend-Payouts, August 2005

	Industry	Expected Return on Total Capital (next 3–5 years)	Expected Growth Rate of Dividends (next 3–5 years)	Current Dividend Payout	Current Dividend Yield	Expected Growth Rate of Sales (next 3–5 years)	Current P/E Ratio
High-Payout Companies							
Crescent Real Estate Equities Co.	Real estate investment trust	5.0	nmf	123.0	8.9	nmf	12.4
Equity Office Properties Trust	Real estate investment trust	5.5	nmf	96.6	7.2	nmf	nmf
Frontline, Ltd.	Oil transport	20.0	9.0	115.0	35.3	(5.0)	3.2
Scudder High Income Trust	Investment management	nmf	nmf	96.4	9.2	nmf	nmf
TEPPCO Partners, LP	Pipeline operations	12.0	3.5	104.0	6.7	5.0	24.3
UIL Holdings	Electric utility	4.5	0.0	112.0	6.0	5.5	18.7
Zero-Payout Companies							
Amgen Inc.	Biotechnology	17.5	0.0	0.0	0.0	18.5	26.5
Cisco Systems, Inc.	Network systems	49.0	0.0	0.0	0.0	16.0	21.6
Coach, Inc.	Luxury retail	22.5	0.0	0.0	0.0	20.5	25.8
eBay Inc.	Internet auction	26.0	0.0	0.0	0.0	32.0	74.7
Oracle Corporation	Software	31.0	0.0	0.0	0.0	14.5	17.9
Research in Motion Limited	Telecommunications	13.5	0.0	0.0	0.0	30.0	nmf
Yahoo! Inc.	Internet/media	14.5	0.0	0.0	0.0	31.0	nmf

nmf = not a meaningful figure.

Source of data: *Value Line Investment Survey*, August 2005.

EXHIBIT 8 | Projected Sources-and-Uses Statement Assuming a 40% Payout Ratio[1] (dollars in millions)

Assumptions:	2005	2006	2007	2008	2009	2010	2011	
1. Sales Growth Rate	15%	15%	15%	15%	15%	15%	15%	
2. Net Income as % of Sales	2.1%	4.0%	5.0%	5.5%	6.0%	5.6%	8.0%	
3. Dividend-Payout Ratio	40.0%	40.0%	40.0%	40.0%	40.0%	40.0%	40.0%	

Projections:	2005	2006	2007	2008	2009	2010	2011	Total 2005-11
Sales	$870.1	$1,000.7	$1,150.8	$1,323.4	$1,521.9	$1,750.1	$2,012.7	$9,629.6
Sources:								
Net income	$ 18.1	$ 40.0	$ 57.5	$ 72.8	$ 91.3	$ 98.0	$ 160.0	$ 537.8
Depreciation	$ 22.5	$ 25.5	$ 30.0	$ 34.5	$ 40.5	$ 46.5	$ 52.5	$ 252.0
Total	$ 40.6	$ 65.5	$ 87.5	$ 107.3	$ 131.8	$ 144.5	$ 212.5	$ 789.8
Uses:								
Capital expenditures	$ 43.8	$ 50.4	$ 57.5	$ 66.2	$ 68.5	$ 78.8	$ 90.6	$ 455.7
Change in working capital	$ 19.5	$ 22.4	$ 25.8	$ 29.6	$ 34.0	$ 38.5	$ 44.3	$ 214.1
Total	$ 63.3	$ 72.8	$ 83.3	$ 95.8	$ 102.4	$ 117.3	$ 134.9	$ 669.8
Excess cash/(borrowing needs)	$ (22.7)	$ (7.3)	$ 4.2	$ 11.5	$ 29.4	$ 27.2	$ 77.6	$ 120.0
Dividend	$ 7.2	$ 16.0	$ 23.0	$ 29.1	$ 36.5	$ 39.2	$ 64.0	$ 215.1
After dividend Excess cash/(borrowing needs)	$ (29.9)	$ (23.3)	$ (18.8)	$ (17.6)	$ (7.2)	$ (12.0)	$ 13.6	$ (95.1)

Note: Dividend calculated as 40% of net income.

[1]This analysis ignores the effects of borrowing on interest and amortization. It includes all increases in long-term liabilities and equity items other than retained earnings.

341

JetBlue Airways IPO Valuation

My neighbor called me the other day and she said, "You have an interesting little boy." Turns out, the other day she asked my son Daniel what he wanted for Christmas. And he said, "I want some stock." "Stock?" she said. "Don't you want video games or anything?" "Nope," he said, "I just want stock. JetBlue stock."

—David Neeleman,
CEO and Founder, JetBlue Airways

It was April 11, 2002, barely two years since the first freshly painted JetBlue plane rolled out at the company's home base at New York City's John F. Kennedy (JFK) Airport. JetBlue's first years had been good ones. Despite the challenges facing the U.S. airline industry following the aircraft terrorist attacks of September 2001, the company remained profitable and was growing aggressively. To support their growth trajectory and offset portfolio losses by their venture capital investors, management was ready to raise additional capital through a public equity offering. A video summary of the IPO pricing decision by JetBlue CFO John Owen can be found at http://it.darden.virginia.edu/JetBlue/streaming_links.htm. **Exhibits 1** through **4** provide selections from JetBlue's initial public offering (IPO) prospectus—the name for the document required by the SEC to inform investors about the details of the equity offering.

After nearly two weeks of road-show meetings with the investment community, the JetBlue management team had just finished their final investor presentation and was heading for Chicago's Midway Airport. With representatives of co-lead manager Morgan Stanley and the JetBlue board patched in on a conference call, it was time for the group to come to an agreement on the offering price of the new shares. The initial price range for JetBlue shares communicated to potential investors was from $22 to $24. Facing sizeable excess demand for the 5.5 million shares planned in the IPO, management had recently filed an increase in the offering price range to $25 to $26. Yet, even at that price range, most of the group thought the stock faced "blow-out"

This case was prepared by Professor Michael J. Schill with the assistance and cooperation of John Owen (JetBlue), Garth Monroe (MBA '05), and Cheng Cui (MBA '04). It was written as a basis for class discussion rather than to illustrate effective or ineffective handling of an administrative situation. Copyright © 2003 by the University of Virginia Darden School Foundation, Charlottesville, VA. All rights reserved. *To order copies, send an e-mail to sales@dardenpublishing.com. No part of this publication may be reproduced, stored in a retrieval system, used in a spreadsheet, or transmitted in any form or by any means—electronic, mechanical, photocopying, recording, or otherwise—without the permission of the Darden School Foundation. Rev. 8/04.*

demand. After months of preparation, it was time to set the price. The underwriters were anxious to distribute the shares that evening and NASDAQ was prepared for JBLU (the company's ticker symbol) to begin trading on the exchange in the morning.

JetBlue Airways

In July 1999, David Neeleman, 39, announced his plan to launch a new airline that would bring "humanity back to air travel." Despite the fact that the U.S. airline industry had witnessed 87 new airline failures over the previous twenty years, Neeleman was convinced that his commitment to innovation in people, policies, and technology could keep his planes full and moving.[1] His vision was shared by an impressive new management team and a growing group of investors. Ex-Continental Airlines vice-president, David Barger, had agreed to become the new JetBlue president and COO. John Owen had left his position as executive vice president and former treasurer for Southwest Airlines to fill the CFO role at JetBlue. Neeleman had received strong support for his business plan from the venture capital community. He had quickly raised $130 million in funding from such high profile firms as Weston Presidio Capital, Chase Capital Partners, and George Soros's private equity firm, Quantum Industrial Partners.

Within seven months, JetBlue had secured a small fleet of Airbus A320 aircraft and initiated service from JFK to Fort Lauderdale, Florida, and Buffalo, New York. By late summer 2000, routes had been added to two other Florida cities (Orlando and Tampa), two other northern cities (Rochester and Burlington, Vermont), and two California cities (Oakland and Ontario). The company continued to grow rapidly through early 2002 and now operated 24 aircraft flying 108 flights per day to 17 destinations.

JetBlue's early success was often attributed to Neeleman's extensive experience with airline startups. As a University of Utah student in his early 20s, Neeleman began managing low-fare flights between Salt Lake City and Hawaii. His company, Morris Air, became a pioneer in ticketless travel and was later acquired by low-fare leader Southwest Airlines. Neeleman stayed only briefly with Southwest, leaving to assist in the launching of Canadian low-fare carrier WestJet while waiting out the term of his non-compete agreement with Southwest. Simultaneously, Neeleman also developed the e-ticketing system, Open Skies, which was acquired by Hewlett-Packard in 1999.

Neeleman acknowledged that JetBlue's strategy was built on the goal of fixing everything that "sucks" about airline travel. He offered passengers a unique flying experience by providing new aircraft, simple and low fares, leather seats, free LiveTV at every seat, pre-assigned seating, reliable performance, and high-quality customer service. JetBlue focused on point-to-point service to large metropolitan areas with high average fares or highly traveled markets that were underserved. JetBlue's operating strategy had produced the lowest cost per available seat mile of any of the major U.S. airlines in 2001—6.98 cents versus an industry average of 10.08 cents.

With its strong capital base, JetBlue had acquired a fleet of new Airbus A320 aircraft. The JetBlue fleet was not only more reliable and fuel-efficient than other airline fleets but also afforded greater economies of scale, because the airline only had one

---

[1] Jeff Sweat, "Generation Dot-Com Gets Its Wings," *Information Week*, January 1, 2001.

model of aircraft. JetBlue management believed in leveraging advanced technology. For instance, all their pilots used laptop computers in the cockpit to calculate the weight and balance of the aircraft and to access their manuals in electronic format during the flight. JetBlue was the first U.S. airline to secure cockpits with bulletproof Kevlar doors and security cameras in response to the September 11 hijackings.

JetBlue had made significant progress in establishing a strong brand by seeking to be identified as a safe, reliable, low-fare airline that was highly focused on customer service and by providing an enjoyable flying experience. JetBlue was well positioned in New York, the nation's largest travel market, with approximately 21 million potential customers in the metropolitan area. Much of JetBlue's customer service strategy relied on building strong employee morale through generous compensation and passionately communicating the company vision to employees.

The Low-Fare Airlines

In 2002, the low-fare business model was gaining momentum in the U.S. airline industry. Southwest Airlines, the pioneer in low-fare air travel, was the dominant player among low-fare airlines. Southwest had been successful following a strategy of high-frequency, short-haul, point-to-point, low-cost air travel service. Southwest flew more than 64 million passengers a year to 58 cities, making it the fourth largest carrier in America and in the world. Financially, Southwest had also been extremely successful—in April 2002 Southwest's market capitalization was larger than all other U.S. airlines combined. (**Exhibits 5** and **6** provide financial data on Southwest Airlines from Value Line and Mergent).

Following the success of Southwest, a flurry of new low-fare airlines emerged. These airlines adopted much of the Southwest low-cost model, including flying to secondary airports adjacent to major metropolitan areas and focusing on few aircraft types to minimize maintenance complexity. In addition to JetBlue, current low-fare U.S. airlines included AirTran, America West, ATA, and Frontier. An established regional airline, Alaska Air, was adopting a low-fare strategy. A number of the low-fare airlines had been more resilient in the aftermath of the aircraft disasters of September 11. (**Exhibit 7** shows current market multiple calculations for U.S. airlines.) Low-fare airlines had also appeared in markets outside the United States with Ryanair and easyJet in Europe and WestJet in Canada. (**Exhibit 8** provides historical growth rates of revenue and equipment for low fare airlines.)

The most recent IPOs among low-fare airlines were of non-U.S. airlines. Ryanair, WestJet, and easyJet had gone public with trailing EBIT multiples of 8.5 times, 11.6 times and 13.4 times, respectively, and first day returns of 62 percent, 25 percent and 11 percent, respectively.[2]

---

[2]The "first-day return" was the realized return based on the difference between the IPO share price and the market share price at the close of the first day of exchange-based trading. The term "trailing EBIT (earnings before interest and taxes) multiple" was defined as [Book debt+IPO price*Post IPO shares outstanding]/[Most recent year's EBIT]. The term "leading EBIT multiple" referred to an EBIT multiple based on a future year's forecasted EBIT estimate.

The IPO Process

The process of "going public" (selling publicly traded equity for the first time) was an arduous process that typically required about three months. **Exhibit 9** provides a timeline for the typical IPO.[3] A comment on the IPO process by JetBlue CFO John Owen can be found at http://it.darden.virginia.edu/JetBlue/streaming_links.htm.

Private firms needed to fulfill a number of prerequisites prior to initiating the equity issuance process. Firms had to generate a credible business plan, gather a qualified management team, create an outside board of directors, prepare audited financial statements, performance measures and projections, and develop relationships with investment bankers, lawyers, and accountants. Frequently firms held "bake-off" meetings with potential investment banks to discuss the equity issuance process with a number of candidates before selecting a lead underwriter. Important characteristics of an underwriter included the proposed compensation package, previous track record, analyst research support, distribution capabilities, and after-market market-making support.

After establishing the prerequisites, the equity issuance process began with an organization or "all hands" meeting. This meeting was attended by all key participants of the process, including management, underwriters, accountants, and legal counsel for both the underwriters and issuing firm. The meeting was designed to plan the process and agree on the specific terms. Throughout the process, additional meetings could be called to discuss problems and review progress. Following the initiation of the equity issuance process, the SEC prohibited the company from publishing information outside the prospectus. The company could continue established, normal advertising activities, but any increased publicity designed to raise the awareness of the company's name, products, or geographic presence that created a favorable attitude towards the company's securities could be considered illegal. This requirement was known as the "quiet period."

The underwriter's counsel generally prepared a "letter of intent" that provided most of the terms of the underwriting agreement but was not legally binding. The underwriting agreement described the securities to be sold, set forth the rights and obligations of the various parties, and established the underwriter compensation. Since the underwriting agreement was not signed until the offering price was determined (just before distribution began), both the firm and the underwriter were free to pull out of the agreement anytime before the offering date. If the firm did withdraw the offer, the letter of intent generally required the firm to reimburse the underwriter for direct expenses.

The Securities and Exchange Commission required that firms selling equity in public markets solicit the commission's approval. The filing process required preparation of the prospectus (Part I of the registration statement), answers to specific questions,

---

[3]This section draws from Michael C. Bernstein and Lester Wolosoff, *Raising Capital: Grant Thornton LLP Guide for Entrepreneurs*; Frederick Lipman, *Going Public*; Coopers and Lybrand, *A Guide to Going Public*; and Craig G. Dunbar, *The Effect of Information Asymmetries on the Choice of Underwriter Compensation Contracts in IPOs*, Ph.D. Dissertation, University of Rochester.

copies of the underwriting contract, company charter and by-laws, and a specimen of the security (all included in Part II of the registration statement), all of which required extensive attention by all parties on the offering team. One of the important features of the registration process was the performance of "due-diligence" procedures. Due-diligence referred to the process of providing reasonable grounds that there was nothing in the registration statement that was significantly untrue or misleading and was motivated by the liability to all parties participating in the registration statement for any material misstatements or omissions. The due-diligence procedure involved such things as reviewing company documents, contracts, and tax returns, visiting company offices and facilities, soliciting "comfort letters" from company auditors, and interviewing company and industry personnel.

During this period, the lead underwriter began to form the underwriting "syndicate." The syndicate was composed of a number of investment banks who agreed to buy portions of the offering at the offer price less the underwriting discount. In addition to the syndicate members, dealers were enlisted to sell a certain number of shares on a "best-efforts" basis. The dealers received a fixed reallowance or concession for each share sold. The selling agreement provided the contract among members of the syndicate. The agreement provided power of attorney to the lead underwriter, stipulated the management fee that each syndicate member was required to pay the lead underwriter, the share allocations, and the dealer reallowance or concessions. Since the exact terms of the agreement were not specified until approximately 48 hours before selling began, the agreement did not become binding until just before the offering. The original contract specified a range of expected compensation levels. The selling agreement was structured so that the contract became binding with oral approval of the contract via telephone by the syndicate members after the effective date.

The SEC review process started when the registration statement was filed and the statement was assigned to a branch chief of the Division of Corporate Finance. As part of the SEC review, the statement was given to accountants, attorneys, analysts, and industry specialists. The SEC review process was legislated in the Securities Act of 1933, which aspired to "provide full and fair disclosure of the character of securities sold in interstate commerce."[4] Under the Securities Act, the registration statement became effective 20 days after the filing date. However, if the commission found anything in the registration statement that was regarded as materially untrue, incomplete, or misleading, the branch chief sent the registrant a letter of comment detailing the deficiencies. Following a letter of comment, the issuing firm was required to correct and return the amended statement to the SEC. Unless an acceleration was granted by the SEC, the amended statement restarted the 20-day waiting period.

While the SEC was reviewing the registration statement, the underwriter was engaged in book-building activities. Building the book involved surveying potential investors to construct a schedule of investor demand for the new issue. To generate investor interest, the preliminary offering prospectus or "red herring" (since the preliminary prospectus was required to have "Preliminary Prospectus" printed on the

---

[4] Securities Act of 1933, Preamble.

cover in red ink) was printed and offered to potential investors. Underwriters generally organized a one- to two-week "road show" tour during this period. The road shows allowed managers to discuss their investment plans, display their management potential, and answer questions from financial analysts, brokers, and institutional investors in a variety of locations throughout the country or sometimes abroad. Finally, companies could place "tombstone ads" in various financial periodicals announcing the offering and listing the members of the underwriting syndicate.

By the time the registration statement was ready to become effective, the underwriter and offering firm management negotiated the final offering price and underwriters' discount. The negotiated price depended on perceived investor demand and current market conditions (e.g., price multiples of comparable companies, previous offering experience of industry peers). Once the underwriters and management agreed on the offering price and discount, the underwriting agreement was signed, and the final registration amendment was filed with the SEC. The company and underwriter generally requested acceleration by the SEC of the final pricing amendment, which was generally granted immediately over the telephone. The offering was now ready for public sale. The final pricing and acceleration of the registration statement generally happened within a few hours.

During the morning of the effective day, the lead underwriter confirmed the selling agreement with the members of the syndicate. Following the selling agreement confirmation, selling began. Members of the syndicate sold shares of the offering through oral solicitations to potential investors. Since investors were required to receive a final copy of the prospectus with the confirmation of sale and the law allowed investors to back out of purchase orders upon receipt of the final prospectus, the offering sale was not realized until underwriters actually received payment. Underwriters would generally cancel orders if payment was not received within five days of the confirmation.

SEC Rule 10b-7 permitted underwriters to engage in price stabilization activities for a limited period during security distribution. Under this rule, underwriters often posted stabilizing bids at or below the offer price, which provided some price stability during the initial trading of an IPO.

The offering settlement or closing occurred seven to ten days after the effective date, as specified in the underwriting agreement. At this meeting, the firm delivered the security certificates to the underwriters and dealers, and the lead underwriters delivered the prescribed proceeds to the firm. In addition, the firm traditionally delivered an updated comfort letter from the company's independent accountants. Following the offering, the underwriter generally continued to provide valuable investment banking services by providing research literature and market-making services for the company.

The IPO Decision

There was some debate among the JetBlue management team regarding the appropriate pricing policy for the IPO shares. Morgan Stanley reported that the deal was highly oversubscribed by investors (i.e., demand exceeded supply). Analysts and reporters were overwhelmingly enthusiastic about the offering. (**Exhibit 10** contains a selection of recent analyst and reporter comments.) With such strong demand, some members of the group worried that the current pricing range still left too much money on the table. Moreover, they felt that raising the price sent a strong signal of confidence to the market.

The contrasting view held that increasing the price might compromise the success of the deal. In management's view, a successful offering entailed not only raising the short-term capital requirements, but also maintaining access to future capital raisings and providing positive returns to the crewmembers (employees) and others involved in directed IPO share purchases. Since maintaining access to capital markets was considered vital to JetBlue's aggressive growth plans, discounting the company's IPO price seemed like a reasonable concession to ensure a successful deal and generate a certain level of investor buzz. Being conservative on the offer price seemed particularly salient considering the risks of taking an infant New York airline public just six months after the 9/11 disaster. (**Exhibit 11** provides expected aggregate industry growth and profitability forecasts from the Value Line Investment Survey. **Exhibit 12** shows the share price performance of airlines over the past eight months.)

By April 2002, the U.S. economy had been stalling for nearly two years. The Federal Reserve had attempted to stimulate economic activity by reducing interest rates to their lowest level in a generation. Current long-term U.S. Treasuries traded at a yield of 5 percent, short-term rates were at 2 percent, and the market risk premium was estimated to be 5 percent.

Exhibit 13 provides a financial forecast for the company based on the JetBlue management team's forecast of aircraft acquisitions.

EXHIBIT 1 | Selections from JetBlue Prospectus

The Offering

Common stock offered	5,500,000 shares
Common stock estimated to be outstanding immediately after this offering	40,578,829 shares
Over-allotment option	825,000 shares
Use of proceeds	We intend to use the net proceeds, together with existing cash, for working capital and capital expenditures, including capital expenditures related to the purchase of aircraft.
Dividends	We have not declared or paid any dividends on our common stock. We currently intend to retain our future earnings, if any, to finance the further expansion and continued growth of our business.
Proposed NASDAQ National Market symbol	JBLU

Results of Operations

	Three Months Ended				
	Dec 31, 2000	Mar 31, 2001	Jun 30, 2001	Sep 30, 2001	Dec 31, 2001
			(unaudited)		
Operating Statistics:					
Revenue passengers	523,246	644,419	753,937	791,551	926,910
Revenue passenger miles (000)	469,293	600,343	766,350	863,855	1,051,287
Available seat miles (000)	623,297	745,852	960,744	1,131,013	1,370,658
Load factor	75.3%	80.5%	79.8%	76.4%	76.7%
Breakeven load factor	79.4%	73.2%	70.6%	74.6%	76.2%
Aircraft utilization (hours per day)	11.8	13.1	13.1	12.8	11.8
Average fare	$ 90.65	$ 96.15	$ 101.01	$ 101.66	$ 99.37
Yield per passenger mile (cents)	10.11	10.32	9.94	9.29	8.76
Passenger revenue per available seat mile (cents)	7.61	8.31	7.93	7.10	6.72
Operating revenue per available seat mile (cents)	7.85	8.56	8.16	7.30	6.97
Operating expense per available seat mile (cents)	8.03	7.55	7.01	6.93	6.68
Departures	4,620	5,283	6,332	6,936	7,783
Average stage length (miles)	833	871	937	1,007	1,087
Average number of operating aircraft during period	9.2	10.5	13.2	15.9	19.4
Full-time equivalent employees at period end	1,028	1,350	1,587	1,876	2,116
Average fuel cost per gallon (cents)	103.38	86.03	83.24	79.53	60.94
Fuel gallons consumed (000)	8,348	9,917	12,649	14,958	17,571
Percent of sales through jetblue.com during period	32.6%	37.6%	39.4%	45.1%	51.3%

EXHIBIT 2 | JetBlue Airways Corporation Balance Sheets (in thousands)

| | December 31, | | | December 31, | |
	2001	2000		2001	2000
ASSETS			**LIABILITIES**		
Cash and cash equivalents	$117,522	$34,403	Accounts payable	$24,549	$12,867
Receivables, less allowance	20,791	21,633	Air traffic liability	51,566	27,365
Inventories, less allowance	2,210	1,133	Accrued salaries, wages and benefits	18,265	5,599
Prepaid expenses and other	3,742	2,744	Other accrued liabilities	15,980	5,255
			Short-term borrowings	28,781	15,138
Total current assets	144,265	59,913	Current maturities of long-term debt	54,985	24,800
Flight equipment	364,681	163,060			
Predelivery deposits for flight			Total current liabilities	194,126	91,024
equipment	125,010	91,620	Long-term debt	290,665	137,110
	489,691	254,680	Deferred credits & other liabilities	10,708	6,595
Less accumulated depreciation	9,523	2,334	Convertible redeemable preferred stock	210,441	163,552
	480,168	252,346	**COMMON STOCKHOLDERS' EQUITY**		
Other property and equipment	29,023	18,290	Additional paid-in capital	44	44
Less accumulated depreciation	4,313	1,632	Accumulated deficit	3,889	487
			Unearned compensation	(33,117)	(54,684)
Total property and equipment	24,710	16,658		(2,983)	—
Other assets	504,878	269,004	Total common stockholders' equity (deficit)	(32,167)	(54,153)
Total Assets	24,630	15,211	Total Liabilities & Common Stockholders' Equity	$673,773	$344,128
	$673,773	$344,128			

EXHIBIT 3 | JetBlue Airways Corporation Statements of Operations (in thousands, except per share amounts)

	Year Ended December 31,		
	2001	2000	1999
Operating revenues:			
Passenger	$310,498	$101,665	$ —
Other	9,916	2,953	—
Total operating revenues	320,414	104,618	—
Operating expenses:			
Salaries, wages, and benefits	84,762	32,912	6,000
Aircraft fuel	41,666	17,634	4
Aircraft rent	32,927	13,027	324
Sales and marketing	28,305	16,978	887
Landing fees and other rents	27,342	11,112	447
Depreciation and amortization	10,417	3,995	111
Maintenance, materials, and repairs	4,705	1,052	38
Other operating expenses	63,483	29,096	6,405
Total operating expenses	293,607	125,806	14,216
Operating income (loss)	26,807	(21,188)	(14,216)
Other income (expense)			
Airline stabilization act compensation	18,706	—	—
Interest expense	(14,132)	(7,395)	(705)
Capitalized interest	8,043	4,487	705
Interest income and other	2,491	2,527	685
Total other income (expense)	15,108	(381)	685
Income (loss) before income taxes	41,915	(21,569)	(13,531)
Income tax expense (benefit)	3,378	(239)	233
Net income (loss)	38,537	(21,330)	(13,764)
Preferred stock dividends	(16,970)	(14,092)	(4,656)
Net income (loss) applicable to common stockholders	$ 21,567	($35,422)	($18,420)
Earnings (loss) per common share:			
Basic	$ 9.88	($27)	($37)
Diluted	$ 1.14	($27)	($37)
Pro forma basic (unaudited)	$ 1.30		

EXHIBIT 4 | JetBlue Airways Corporation Statements of Cash Flows (in thousands)

	Year Ended December 31,		
	2001	**2000**	**1999**
Cash Flows from Operating Activities			
Net income (loss)	$38,537	($21,330)	($13,764)
Adjustments to reconcile net income (loss) to net cash provided by (used in) operating activities:			
Depreciation	9,972	3,889	111
Amortization	445	106	—
Deferred income taxes	3,373	—	—
Other, net	5,960	3,892	619
Changes in certain operating assets and liabilities:			
Decrease (increase) in receivables	430	(21,622)	—
Increase in inventories, prepaid expenses and other	(2,120)	(3,354)	(340)
Increase in air traffic liability	23,788	26,173	—
Increase in accounts payable and other accrued liabilities	30,894	15,070	6,818
Net cash provided by (used in) operating activities	111,279	2,824	(6,556)
Cash Flows from Investing Activities			
Capital expenditures	(233,775)	(205,759)	(12,463)
Predelivery deposits for flight equipment, net	(54,128)	(27,881)	(50,713)
Increase in security deposits	(1,952)	(7,939)	(5,302)
Purchases of short-term investments	—	(20,923)	—
Proceeds from maturities of short-term investments	—	21,392	—
Other, net	—	(20)	1,026
Net cash used in investing activities	(289,855)	(241,130)	(67,452)
Cash Flows from Financing Activities			
Proceeds from issuance of convertible redeemable preferred stock	29,731	51,322	80,671
Proceeds from issuance of common stock	25	130	69
Proceeds from issuance of long-term debt	185,000	137,750	—
Proceeds from short-term borrowings	28,781	15,138	—
Proceeds from aircraft sale and leaseback transactions	72,000	70,000	—
Repayment of long-term debt	(35,254)	(18,577)	—
Repayment of short-term borrowings	(15,138)	—	—
Other, net	(3,450)	(1,300)	—
Net cash provided by financing activities	261,695	254,463	80,740
Increase In Cash and Cash Equivalents	83,119	16,157	6,732
Cash and cash equivalents at beginning of year	34,403	18,246	11,514
Cash and cash equivalents at end of year	$17,522	$34,403	$18,246

EXHIBIT 5 | Selections from Value Line Tear Sheet for Southwest Airlines

Recent stock price	$20.69			
P/E ratio	49.3			
Dividend yield	0.1%			
Beta	1.10			
Financial statement forecast	2001	2002E	2003E	2005E/2007E
Total debt ($ mill)	$1,842			
Revenue ($ mill)	$5,555	$6,000	$7,100	$10,300
Operating margin	17.1%	18.0%	24.5%	27.0%
Tax rate	31.0%	38.5%	38.5%	38.5%
Common shares outstanding (mill)	776.8	785.0	795.0	815.0

Soft demand and pricing pressures will probably put a damper on Southwest Airlines top-line growth. Although the carrier is faring better than most, it is still clearly a challenge to fill seats, which have been 61.2% occupied so far in 2002. That's almost 10% below last year's level. We attribute the decline to a 9.1% drop in traffic, owing to reduced demand, combined with 4.5% growth in capacity. Clearly, travelers have responded positively to reduced ticket prices. But we believe that additional fare cuts will be necessary to generate the traffic growth needed to support top-line growth. We do not expect year-over-year revenue comparisons to be positive until the second half of the year. The top line should advance by a total of 7%-8% in 2002. A significantly stronger economy ought to lead to an advance of 15%-20% next year.

Although still under pressure, margins should show overall improvement in 2002. Declining expenditures for fuel, commissions, and aircraft rentals should help to offset increasing wage and maintenance costs. We look for the operating margin to widen throughout the year, and for share net to rebound 18% in 2002. Business should show much improvement in 2003, allowing for a full earnings recovery.

Profitability enhancements are likely over the long haul, too. An ongoing efficiency program aims to improve maintenance and inspection procedures and automate some airport operations. The increasing move to ticketless travel should yield additional savings. And commission expenses are likely to decline further, as online ticket sales grow.

Modest system expansion is likely for 2002. Although no plans have been announced, we think it is likely that the airline will add one or two cities to its East Coast network later this year.

Southwest stock has worthwhile capital-appreciation potential to 2005-2007. As a long-term investment, we believe LUV shares are attractively priced, based on our 3-5 year earnings-growth projections. Due to the stock's recent poor price momentum, however, it carries an untimely rank for relative price performance over the next six to 12 months.

— Warren Thorpe, Value Line Investment Survey, March 15, 2002

EXHIBIT 6 | Southwest Airlines: Current Debt Outstanding

Issue	Moody's rating	Amount outstanding	Maturity date	Yield to maturity
Short-term bank debt	NA	$475 million	NA	NA
Floating rate secured notes	NA	$200 million	2004	NA
Private notes 5.10–6.10	NA	$614 million	2006	NA
Floating rate French bank debt	NA	$ 52 million	2012	NA
8.75 note	Baa1	$100 million	Oct-2003	5.65%
8.00 note	Baa1	$100 million	Feb-2005	5.91%
7.875 debenture	Baa1	$100 million	Sep-2007	7.41%
7.375 debenture	Baa1	$100 million	Feb-2027	8.68%
Capital leases	NA	$109 million	NA	NA

NA = not applicable.

Source: Mergent's Bond Record; Southwest Annual Report.

EXHIBIT 7 | Recent Valuation Multiples

	Actual for 2001						Estimates for 2002	
	Price/ Share	Book Equity/ Share	Book Debt/ Share	EBITDA/ Share	EBIT/ Share	Earnings/ Share	EBIT/ Share	Earnings/ Share
	(1)	(2)	(3)	(4)	(5)	(6)	(7)	(8)
AirTran	6.6	0.5	4.0	1.2	0.8	0.3	0.8	0.3
Alaska Air	29.1	32.1	33.8	3.3	−1.7	−1.5	2.7	−0.8
America West	3.5	12.5	10.2	−4.3	−6.2	−4.4	−4.5	−4.1
AMR	22.3	35.1	69.3	−7.0	−16.2	−11.5	12.4	−3.9
ATA	15.0	10.8	32.9	8.5	−2.0	−2.6	−6.4	−7.2
Continental	26.2	20.9	82.0	9.8	1.4	−1.6	11.1	−1.2
Delta	29.3	32.7	70.3	−1.4	−11.8	−9.9	8.4	−3.1
Frontier	17.0	5.4	0.0	3.2	3.0	2.0	0.6	0.4
Midwest	14.6	8.3	2.7	−0.1	−1.6	−1.1	1.6	0.8
Northwest	15.7	−5.1	66.9	1.6	−4.4	−5.0	7.2	−2.5
Ryanair	32.1	5.5	3.3	1.3	0.9	0.7	1.2	0.9
Southwest	18.5	5.3	1.8	1.5	1.1	0.7	1.4	0.7
United	13.5	59.6	186.2	−37.0	−56.1	−39.6	NA	−15.4
WestJet	15.9	2.8	1.0	2.1	1.3	0.8	1.6	0.6

	Trailing					Leading	
	Market to Book Multiple	Total Capital Multiple	EBITDA Multiple	EBIT Multiple	PE Multiple	EBIT Multiple	PE Multiple
	[1/2]	[(1+3)/(2+3)]	[(1+3)/4]	[(1+3)/5]	[1/6]	[(1+3)/7]	[1/8]
AirTran	13.5	2.4	8.6	13.0	25.3	13.9	20.0
Alaska Air	0.9	1.0	19.2	−37.1	−19.3	23.3	−38.8
America West	0.3	0.6	−3.2	−2.2	−0.8	−3.0	−0.8
AMR	0.6	0.9	−13.1	−5.7	−1.9	7.4	−5.7
ATA	1.4	1.1	5.6	−23.8	−5.7	−7.5	−2.1
Continental	1.3	1.1	11.0	77.0	−16.7	9.8	−22.4
Delta	0.9	1.0	−71.6	−8.4	−3.0	11.8	−9.4
Frontier	3.2	3.2	5.3	5.7	8.4	26.6	45.9
Midwest	1.8	1.6	−298.3	−11.0	−13.5	11.2	17.4
Northwest	−3.1	1.3	51.6	−18.8	−3.1	11.5	−6.3
Ryanair	5.8	4.0	26.4	38.5	44.0	30.3	34.1
Southwest	3.5	2.9	13.4	18.6	27.6	14.3	28.4
United	0.2	0.8	−5.4	−3.6	−0.3	NA	−0.9
WestJet	5.6	4.4	8.1	12.7	19.6	10.6	26.9

NA = not applicable.

Data source: Actual numbers for 2001 are from company annual reports. Estimates for 2002 are from Value Line when available, otherwise consensus analyst estimates are used. All stock prices are quoted as of December 31, 2001. Ryanair figures are based on the respective American Deposit Receipt prices. Westjet figures are in Canadian dollars. One U.S. dollar = 1.5870 Canadian dollars as of March 31, 2002. The calculation procedure for the valuation multiples in the lower panel is based on the numbered variables defined in the upper panel.

EXHIBIT 8 | Historical Annual Growth Rates for Low-Fare Airlines

Year	$ Revenue Growth					$ Gross Equipment Growth				
	AirTran	ATA	Frontier	Ryanair	Southwest	AirTran	ATA	Frontier	Ryanair	Southwest
1972					−20%					177%
1973					5%					55%
1974					28%					61%
1975					32%					54%
1976					51%					35%
1977					101%					59%
1978					42%					66%
1979					46%					68%
1980					32%					57%
1981					35%					27%
1982					45%					23%
1983					18%					35%
1990					10%		11%			17%
1991					14%		24%			11%
1992					20%		23%			28%
1993		1%			21%		5%			36%
1994	456%	21%			18%	2204%	4%			13%
1995	186%	18%	49%		13%	175%	17%	186%		11%
1996	−4%	2%	125%	20%	10%	−40%	22%	66%	25%	19%
1997	49%	20%	39%	NA	16%	−4%	15%	26%	15%	12%
1998	18%	21%	56%	NA	19%	108%	−1%	50%	29%	9%
1999	−20%	39%	105%	39%	19%	15%		50%	11%	14%
2000	35%	23%	79%	68%	16%	24%		43%	21%	19%
2001	−22%	−58%	237%	NA	12%	7%		−6%	NA	−2%

NA = not applicable.

EXHIBIT 9 | Life Cycle of a Typical U.S. IPO Transaction

Event time (in days)	Event
<0	Underwriter selection meeting.
0	Organization "all hands" meeting. "Quiet period" begins.
15–44	Due diligence. Underwriter interviews management, suppliers, and customers; reviews financial statements; drafts preliminary registration statement. Senior management of underwriter gives ok on issue.
45	Registration (announcement) date. Firm files registration statement with SEC; registration statement is immediately available to the public.
45–75	SEC review period. SEC auditor reviews for compliance with SEC regulations. Underwriter assembles syndicate and prepares road show.
50	Distribute preliminary prospectus ("red herring").
60–75	Road show. Underwriters and issuing firm management present offering to interested institutional investors and build book of purchase orders.
75–99	Letters of comment received from SEC; amendments filed with SEC.
99	Effective date. Underwriter and firm price offering. SEC gives final approval of registration statement.
100	Public offering date. Stock issued and begins trading.
108	Settlement date. Underwriter distributes proceeds to issuing firm.
After market	Underwriter may support new equity by acting as market maker and distributing research literature on issuing firm.

EXHIBIT 10 | Analyst and Reporter Quotes

"The bottom line is really very simple. Neeleman saw a gaping hole and flew a plane through it. Get on this baby, because this is as close to a sure thing as it gets." —Lisa DiCarlo, Forbes

"People are going to have a high appetite for [JetBlue stock]." —Ray Neidl, ABN Amro.

"JetBlue took to the skies in 2000 and surprised the airline sector when it reported its first profit only a year later. Passengers are drawn to the low fares, leather seats and free live TV on board. And Wall Street admires JetBlue for its experienced management team and winning formula, one made popular by the success of Southwest Airlines." —Suzanne Pratt, Nightly Business Report

"JetBlue is off to a good start. But to say it deserves the valuation of Southwest, which has not had a year without profits for 27 years, might be a stretch." —Jim Corridore, Standard & Poor's

"[JetBlue] has a management team with real expertise, and they're executing very well." —Marc Baum, IPO Group

"It's a very young company that's still going to need to make a lot of investment over the next 5 to 10 years. There's not going to be a lot of free cash flow." —Jonathan Schrader, Morningstar

"What's important here is that the business model is solid and they aren't deviating from it." —Helane Becker, Buckingham Research

"Everyone I've talked to that's flown with them has been delighted." —Jim Broadfoot, Ivy Emerg. Growth Fund

"This is an industry where the failure rate is very high for new entrants." —Patrick Murphy, Former Assistant Secretary of Department of Transportation

"It's a fantastic airline. It's also something that you need to personally experience... There's live TV, all-leather seats that are comfortable, and the crew has an attitude that is one of service. It's ingrained and installed in them and as a result, they treat passengers differently. I think they have cornered the market on perhaps the way flying ought to be." —Clark Snyder, LiveTV

Sources: *BusinessWeek, BBC News, Nightly Business Report, New York Metro.*

EXHIBIT 11 | Historical Financial Performance and Analysts' Financial Forecasts
for Air Transport Industry

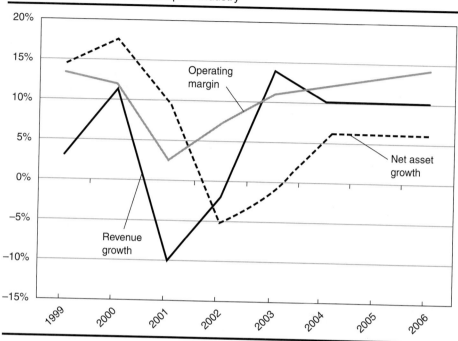

Source: Value Line Investment Survey, March 2002.

EXHIBIT 12 | Recent Share-Price Performance for Airlines

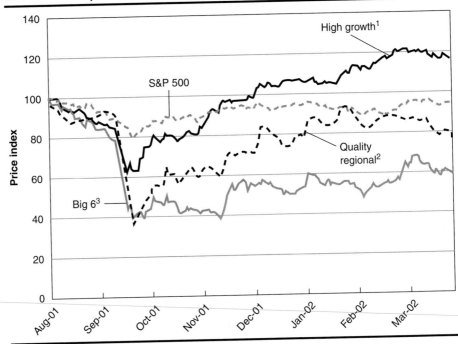

[1]High-growth airlines include Southwest Airlines, Ryanair, easyJet, and WestJet.
[2]Quality regional airlines include Atlantic Coast and Skywest.
[3]Big 6 airlines include American, Continental, Delta, Northwest, United, and US Airways.

EXHIBIT 13 | JetBlue Financial Forecast

$ figures in millions	2001	2002E	2003E	2004E	2005E	2006E	2007E	2008E	2009E	2010E
Number of aircraft	21	34	48	62	74	86	98	108	113	117
Revenue/plane	$15.3	$17.6	$18.4	$19.2	$20.1	$21.0	$21.9	$22.8	$23.8	$24.9
Expected inflation rate		16%	4%	4%	4%	4%	4%	4%	4%	4%
Operating margin	8.4%	10.0%	11.5%	12.1%	12.7%	13.4%	13.4%	13.4%	13.4%	13.4%
Depreciation per aircraft	$ 0.5	$ 0.5	$ 0.5	$ 0.6	$ 0.6	$ 0.6	$ 0.7	$ 0.7	$ 0.7	$ 0.8
Net capex per incremental aircraft	$21.3	$22.3	$23.5	$24.6	$25.9	$27.1	$28.5	$29.9	$31.4	$33.0
Expected inflation rate		5%	5%	5%	5%	5%	5%	5%	5%	5%
Net working capital (NWC) turnover (revenue/NWC)	9.4	9.4	9.4	9.4	9.4	9.4	9.4	9.4	9.4	9.4
Financial forecast										
Revenue	$ 320	$ 600	$ 884	$1,192	$1,485	$1,802	$2,114	$2,466	$2,694	$2,912
Cash expenses	283	502	723	975	1,215	1,474	1,753	2,016	2,202	2,380
Depreciation	10	18	26	36	45	54	65	75	83	90
Earnings before interest and taxes (EBIT)	27	80	134	181	226	274	326	375	410	443
Taxes (tax rate=34%)	9	27	46	62	77	93	111	127	139	151
Net operating profit after tax (NOPAT)	18	53	89	120	149	181	215	247	270	292
Capital expenditure	234	290	328	345	310	326	342	299	270	292
Net working capital	$ 34	$ 63	$ 94	$ 126	$ 157	$ 191	$ 227	$ 261	$ 285	$ 308

Source: JetBlue management forecast and case writer analysis.

Purinex, Inc.

To lead the world in discovering, developing & commercializing novel therapeutic compounds acting on the purine receptors in order to save and improve patients' lives.

   Company mission statement

In June 2004, Purinex, Inc., a pharmaceutical company with several clinically and commercially promising drugs in development, had reached a turning point. Sometime in the next four to twelve months, the company stood an excellent chance of establishing a partnership with a major pharmaceutical company. That partnership would enable Purinex to develop one of its leading compounds into a drug for the treatment of one of the world's deadliest and most widespread diseases. The company had no sales or earnings, however, and there was only enough cash on hand to last 11 months.

Gilad Harpaz, Purinex's chief financial officer, believed that if a partnership deal came through, the company would be in an excellent position to carry out its mission. Moreover, securing a deal was practically a prerequisite for any eventual initial public offering,[1] which was an attractive exit strategy for many of the company's investors. But, as things stood, it was unclear whether the firm could stay afloat until such a partnership could be consummated.

Harpaz believed that the company could either attempt to secure financing now or wait until it struck a partnership deal. "But if we wait," Harpaz thought, "the terms of a deal would get a lot worse." Harpaz, a former officer in the Israeli special forces who had earned a graduate degree in business, considered how to structure this decision. What were the probabilities that a collaboration with a pharmaceutical company would actually happen? How would the company stay above water until that occurred? Besides insolvency, what were the other risks to the company under these circumstances?

---

[1] An initial public offering (IPO) was the first sale of stock to the public by a private company. IPOs were often issued by smaller, younger companies seeking capital to expand, but could also be done by large privately owned companies looking to become publicly traded.

Purinex, Inc.

Purinex was a drug-discovery and -development company based in Syracuse, New York, that sought to commercialize therapeutic compounds based on its purine drug-development platform. Purine was a naturally occurring molecule that played an important role in numerous biochemical processes. Purinex had developed a process for creating small molecules that acted as selective agonists (activators) or antagonists (blockers) for specific purine receptors in the cell membrane.[2] These molecules could initiate physiological responses or block the activation of receptors by endogenously produced signaling molecules. Purinex's goal was to develop products that evoked a receptor-specific pharmacodynamic effect without producing undesirable outcomes that could result from interactions with other receptors.

The company had 14 employees and maintained a chemistry laboratory a few miles from its main office. Purinex's intellectual-property portfolio consisted of more than 35 patents pending or issued in the purine field. The company planned to take its new receptor-selective drugs into clinical trials to address a broad range of potential indications. In June 2004, the most promising indications for its compounds were for the treatment of diabetes and sepsis.

Diabetes

Diabetes was a long-term condition that affected the body's ability to process glucose and hampered its use of other nutrients, such as protein and fat. Glucose, a common product of digestion, circulated in the blood to the body's cells, where it served as one of the chief sources of energy. Diabetes disrupted the body's mechanisms for moving glucose out of the bloodstream and using it in cells. As a result, levels of blood glucose (blood sugar) stayed excessively high, leading to serious health complications over time.

High levels of blood glucose affected the eyes, kidneys, and the nervous system. In addition, diabetes increased the risk of atherosclerosis, which narrowed arteries, especially those carrying blood to the heart, brain, and legs. Diabetes affected more than 100-million people worldwide, and was among the most common causes of death and disability in North America and Europe. Purinex had a patent on the use of any purine antagonist for the treatment of diabetes and its related conditions within the United States. The company had also developed a series of proprietary antagonist molecules that showed great promise in preclinical studies of diabetes. Potential annual sales for this drug were believed to be $4 billion.

Sepsis

Sepsis was a serious medical condition caused by a severe infection leading to a systemic inflammatory response. The more critical subsets of sepsis included severe sepsis (sepsis with acute organ dysfunction) and septic shock (sepsis with refractory arterial hypotension). Septicemia was sepsis of the bloodstream (blood poisoning) and

---

[2] An *agonist* promoted certain kinds of cellular activity by binding to a cell's receptor. An *antagonist* prevented certain types of cellular reactions by blocking other substances from binding to a cell's receptor.

was caused by bacteremia, which was the presence of bacteria in the bloodstream. The systemic inflammatory response syndrome led to widespread activation of inflammation and coagulation pathways. This could progress to dysfunction of the circulatory system and, even under optimal treatment, into multiple-organ dysfunction syndrome and, eventually, death.

Sepsis was more common and more dangerous in the elderly, immunocompromised, and critically ill patients. It occurred in 2 percent of all hospitalizations, and accounted for as much as 25 percent of intensive care unit (ICU) bed utilization. It was a major cause of death in ICUs worldwide, with mortality rates that ranged from 20 percent for sepsis to 40 percent for severe sepsis to more than 60 percent for septic shock. In the United States, sepsis was the leading cause of death in noncoronary ICU patients, and the tenth leading cause of death overall. One problem in the management of septic patients was the delay in administering the right treatment after the sepsis had been diagnosed.

One of Purinex's agonists for the treatment of sepsis had been shown (in animals) to have limited side effects and to be fast acting and effective at treating sepsis, even if treatment were significantly delayed after onset of the disease. Further, it had been proved safe in humans in a phase I clinical trial. Harpaz estimated that annual sales for this product could be around $500 million.

Development of Pharmaceutical Drugs

In 2005, the pharmaceutical industry remained one of the world's most dynamic economic sectors, with more than $530 billion in global sales. Although pharmaceuticals continued to grow faster than most other segments of the economy, some analysts predicted a softening in its growth over the next five years. As part of an effort to remain competitive, many large pharmaceutical firms had moved aggressively to partner with smaller firms in the biotechnology sector[3] in order to identify the next generation of drug candidates. In recent years, the U.S. biotechnology industry had mushroomed, as sector revenues grew from $8 billion, in 1992, to nearly $40 billion, at the end of 2003.

Collectively, the biotechnology industry devoted a higher percentage of its sales to research and development (R&D) than did any other major U.S. industry. According to Standard & Poor's, R&D spending by biotechnology firms was close to 40 percent of the industry's revenues. This high percentage was largely because many biotechnology companies did not generate revenues. R&D spending by public biotechnology companies was $17 billion in 2003 and $12.5 billion in 2002. Among the reasons for the high R&D costs was that the drug development and approval process was lengthy and risky. According to a June 2001 study by the Boston Consulting Group (BCG), the total cost to develop a new human-therapeutic compound was $880 million; a 2003 report by Tufts University placed that cost at $897 million (in 2000 dollars). The BCG report estimated that drug-development failures accounted for 75 percent of the total R&D cost.

---

[3] In its broadest sense, *biotechnology* referred to the use of biological processes to solve problems or to make useful products in agribusiness, biology-based environmental remediation, biodefense, and drug research and development by small pharmaceutical firms.

While the total development time for a drug was highly variable, it took 10 to 15 years, on average, to move a drug from preclinical development to marketing approval. The process for discovering, developing, and gaining approval for new therapeutics consisted of several distinct steps: early discovery, preclinical development, clinical trials, and regulatory filing and review. **Exhibit 1** illustrates schematically the phases of development for a new compound.

According to a number of studies, the preclinical phase accounted for about 40 percent of the time and resources required to bring a new compound to market. The preclinical stage included target identification, target validation, assay development,[4] primary and secondary screening, lead optimization, and preclinical studies. The significant challenges of the preclinical phase were exemplified by a rule of thumb adopted by Pfizer, Inc. On average, it took about 7 million primary screen candidates to produce one new chemical entity.

In the United States, the drug-approval process was overseen by the Food and Drug Administration (FDA), which required extensive testing to ensure drug safety and efficacy. The drug manufacturer had to undertake three sequential sets of clinical tests before applying for regulatory approval. The FDA estimated that, out of every 20 drugs that entered clinical testing, on average, 13 or 14 would successfully complete phase I. Of those, about 9 would complete phase II; only 2 would likely survive phase III. On average, only 5 percent to 10 percent of drugs entering clinical trials were ultimately approved for marketing, often after several attempts.

Access to Capital

Given the magnitude of R&D requirements, early-stage biotechnology firms needed sufficient access to capital. Typically, biotechnology entities were funded through seed money from individual angel investors[5] or venture-capital[6] (VC) firms. According to Burrill & Company, a private merchant bank specializing in life sciences, funding from such sources for North American biotechnology firms was $2.6 billion in 2002 and more than $2.8 billion in 2003. A recent report by Standard & Poor's indicated that funding for most biotechnology firms would remain attractive, but "…we see deal terms remaining clearly less attractive than the valuation premiums that were commanded in 2000, when the market was in a euphoric state."

If a firm had a promising investigational drug candidate, it could also seek an alliance with a larger pharmaceutical or biotechnology company. The larger company

---

[4]An assay was a test that measured a biological response or assessed physical attributes, or, as here, referred to a screening process for new drug candidates.

[5]Angel investors were individuals who provided financing to small start-ups or entrepreneurs. Angel investors were often friends or relatives of the firm's principals, but they could also be sophisticated and experienced investors. Angel investors were rarely involved in the firm's management, but they could add value through their contacts and expertise.

[6]Venture capital was a broad term that referred to the financing provided by professional/institutional investors to start-up firms and small businesses with perceived growth potential. Venture capital was often a very important source of funding for new firms that might not have access to capital markets and that usually entailed high risk for investors, but that had the potential for above-average returns.

could provide up-front fees, R&D funding, milestone payments,[7] royalties,[8] and, possibly, copromotion rights. In addition, the company could supply production facilities or sales organizations, often in return for marketing rights under licensing arrangements. **Exhibit 2** describes the terms of recent partnership deals between biotechnology and pharmaceutical firms. **Exhibit 3** provides the median and mean values of a broad sample of those deals at each stage of the drug development process.

The number of collaborative agreements between "Big Pharma" (large-capitalization pharmaceutical firms) and biotechnology entities had increased steadily in recent years. According to Burrill & Company, such partnering arrangements had reached $8.9 billion in 2003, up from $7.5 billion in 2002. These partnering deals were expected to surpass $10 billion in 2004. **Exhibit 4** depicts the relative proportion of funding sources for North American biotechnology firms in 2003.

Investment and Financing Decisions

In June 2004, Purinex had a broad range of technologies under development, two of which had applications appropriate for partnership deals with a larger pharmaceutical company: a preclinical stage antagonist program for the treatment of diabetes and an agonist program for the treatment of sepsis that had completed a phase I clinical trial.

Over the past several months, Purinex had initiated discussions with several, large, well-capitalized pharmaceutical companies regarding a possible collaboration for both compounds. Two companies had come forward with preliminary term sheets: one sought a deal for the treatment of sepsis, and the other wanted a deal for diabetes. Each proposed deal would entitle Purinex to receive a combination of up-front fees, milestone payments, and royalties, as described in **Table 1**:

TABLE 1 I Combinations of Monies to be Received for Each Deal

	Sepsis	Diabetes
Up-front	$5 million	$8 million
Milestones (total, undiscounted[9])	$108 million	$80 million
Royalty	10.0%	12.0%

Harpaz believed there was about a 75 percent chance that Purinex would secure a partnership with a pharmaceutical company for either sepsis or diabetes sometime during the next four to twelve months. If that partnership occurred, he estimated a 60 percent

---

[7] Milestone payments were a series of payments made upon the successful completion of certain triggering events in the drug development process.

[8] A royalty was a payment to an owner for the use of property, especially patents, copyrighted works, or franchises. Royalties were usually calculated as a percentage of the revenues obtained through the use of the property.

[9] Harpaz's initial practice was to assess partnership deal terms on an undiscounted basis; but where time allowed and forecast assumptions were available, he would do further analysis.

probability that it would be a deal for sepsis. If a partnership did not occur during the next four to twelve months, Harpaz believed there was a very strong chance—perhaps a 95 percent probability—that a different partnership with a third company for the diabetes application would occur about a year later. This later deal would likely have half the value of the one he was currently considering.

Harpaz thought it unlikely that Purinex would form partnership deals for both sepsis and diabetes. The company's management believed it was important for Purinex to retain at least one of those programs in order to maintain the firm's viability as a strategic acquisition target or as a possible IPO candidate ("so as not to sell off all of the crown jewels," he thought). Therefore, he believed the two deals were mutually exclusive.

Harpaz remained very concerned that Purinex had only $700,000 in cash on hand. The firm's burn rate[10] was about $60,000 a month (Purinex had no sales or earnings other than income from federal research grants, which offset about $100,000 of the company's $160,000 in monthly expenses). Because the sepsis and diabetes partnerships were so uncertain in the short term, Harpaz was considering three options for his firm. Each option came with its own risks:

- **Venture-capital round:** Purinex could seek to raise a one-time round of financing from a VC firm. VC firms had expressed serious interest in biotechnology investments lately, and Purinex showed great promise. Harpaz believed it would take about three months to secure $10 million from a VC firm, and that VC firms would likely give the company a premoney valuation[11] of $15 million. The VC financing would come with a significant number of restrictions, including preferences for board appointments, antidilution rights, liquidity, participation, and positive and negative covenants.

- **Wait six months:** Purinex could simply wait in the expectation that either the sepsis deal or the diabetes deal would come through. Purinex's current owners would then retain complete control of the company, which Harpaz believed could be valued at $25 million. While Purinex had about twelve months of cash available, the company could only wait about six months before securing additional financing. If either the sepsis or the diabetes deal failed to happen during the next six months, Purinex would be forced into a down-round[12] scenario with potential investors. Under those dire circumstances, Harpaz believed that the premoney valuation for Purinex would drop to $8 million or possibly as low as $5 million.

---

[10]The burn rate was the rate at which a new company depleted its capital to finance operations before it began to generate a positive cash flow. The burn rate was usually quoted in terms of cash spent per month.

[11]Premoney valuation was the value of a company before external financing alternatives were added to its balance sheet.

[12]A down round was a round of financing in which investors purchased stock from a company at a lower valuation than the one placed on the company by earlier investors. Down rounds caused the dilution of economic value for existing investors, which often meant that the company founders' stock or options were worth much less or possibly nothing at all. For start-up firms in a down round, VC firms would typically impose more onerous covenants, dictate a lower premoney valuation, and even remove current management.

- **Angel round:** A third option for the company would be to undertake another one-time round of financing from a number of angel investors. Harpaz did not think Purinex could raise as much from angel investors as it could from VC firms—probably only $2 million. But with angel investors, Harpaz could probably ensure a higher firm valuation—about $17.5 million—and a diverse group of angels would not demand many preferences. It would take about six months to complete an angel round of financing.

In the back of his mind, Harpaz knew that if the firm were well capitalized, it would have a better chance of securing a collaboration with a major pharmaceutical firm and getting a better deal;[13] there was a "credibility value" in being adequately funded. How could the firm survive until that happened? What was the best way to finance the firm, yet also maximize the value of the firm today? Certainly, there was value in having the founders and current principals maintain control of the company, but what was that worth? "There are certain risks we're willing to take, and certain ones we're not," Harpaz thought to himself. "We are in the technology risk business, not the finance risk business." How could he evaluate all those risk-and-return scenarios?

---

[13] Harpaz believed that a round of VC funding could possibly increase the value of a pharma deal by 10 percent.

EXHIBIT 1 | The Drug-Development Process

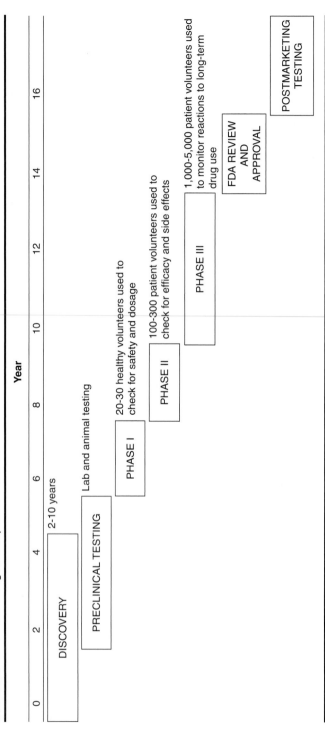

Source of data: Ernst & Young, LLP, *Biotechnology Industry Report: Convergence 2000* (cited in the *Guide to Biotechnology*, The Biotechnology Industry Organization BIO).

EXHIBIT 2 | Recent Biotechnology/Pharmaceutical Partnering Deals

Companies	Date	Details of the Deals
Curagen/TopoTarget	Jun–04	Histone deacetylase inhibitor: $5 million (m) in equity, $5m in license fees, plus $41m in milestones and royalties; deal includes rights to follow-up compounds at $1m license fee and $30m in milestones per product
Serono/4SC	May–04	Licenses worldwide rights to small-molecule dihydroorotate dehydrogenase inhibitors for autoimmune disorders—up-front, R&D funding and milestones, plus undisclosed royalties
Arqule/Roche	Apr–04	E2F pathway: $15m up-front, $276m in milestones, plus undisclosed royalties
Lundbeck/Merck	Feb–04	Gaboxadol, sleep deprivation: $70m up-front plus $200m in milestones plus royalties plus copromotion rights to undisclosed Merck product
Biostratum/NovoNordisk	Jan–04	Cancer project focused on Anti-laminin 5 antibodies: $80m milestones per antibody plus royalties and undisclosed royalties
Array Biopharma/AZ	Dec–03	Oncology: $10m up-front, $85m milestones, R&D funding plus milestones
Neurogean/Merck	Dec–03	Neurology/pain: $42m up-front, $118m in milestones, plus R&D funding plus milestones
MorphoSys/Pfizer	Dec–03	Five-year license, $50m in potential milestones plus royalties
Actelion/Merck	Dec–03	Renin inhibitor: $10m up-front, $262m in milestones
Neurosearch/GSK	Dec–03	Central nervous system area: $82m in guaranteed payments plus $200m in "bioworld payments"

Source of data: Credit Suisse First Boston.

EXHIBIT 3 I Mean and Median Terms of Partnership-Deal Licensing (in millions of dollars)

	Preclinical Stage	Phase I	Phase II	Phase III
Total Value				
Mean	$82.7	$268.0	$212.3	$227.0
Median	$57.0	$200.4	$179.5	$247.5
Up-front				
Mean	$30.2	$32.6	$44.6	$42.7
Median	$19.0	$11.7	$25.0	$32.0
Milestones				
Mean	$72.9	$213.0	$196.6	$241.7
Median	$62.0	$184.6	$120.0	$200.0

Source of data: Credit Suisse First Boston, citing *Biocentury* (2003–February 2004).

EXHIBIT 4 I Financings in the North American Biotechnology Industry, 2003

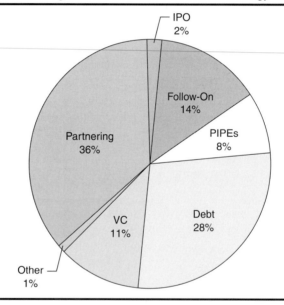

Note: PIPEs were private investments in public entities.

Source of data: Burrill & Company.

PART 6

Management of the Corporate Capital Structure

An Introduction to Debt Policy and Value

Many factors determine how much debt a firm takes on. Chief among them ought to be the effect of the debt on the value of the firm. Does borrowing create value? If so, for whom? If not, then why do so many executives concern themselves with leverage?

If leverage affects value, then it should cause changes in either the discount rate of the firm (that is, its weighted-average cost of capital) or the cash flows of the firm.

1. Please fill in the following:

	0% Debt/ 100% Equity	25% Debt/ 75% Equity	50% Debt/ 50% Equity
Book value of debt	0	$2,500	$5,000
Book value of equity	$10,000	$7,500	$5,000
Market value of debt	0	$2,500	$5,000
Market value of equity	$10,000	$8,350	$6,700
Pretax cost of debt	.05	.05	.05
After-tax cost of debt	.033	.033	.033
Market value weights of:			
Debt	0	—	—
Equity	1.0	—	—
Levered beta	.8	—	—
Risk-free rate	.05	.05	.05
Market premium	.06	.06	.06
Cost of equity	—	—	—
Weighted-average cost of capital (WACC)	—	—	—
EBIT	$ 1,485	$1,485	$1,485
− Taxes (@ 34%)	—	—	—
EBIAT	—		
+ Depreciation	$500	$ 500	$ 500
− Capital expense	$ (500)	$ (500)	$ (500)
Change in net working capital	0	0	0
Free cash flow	—	—	—

Why does the value of assets change? Where, specifically, do those changes occur?

2. In finance, as in accounting, the two sides of the balance sheet must be equal. In the previous problem, we valued the asset side of the balance sheet. To value the other side, we must value the debt and the equity, and then add them together.

	0% Debt/ 100% Equity	25% Debt/ 75% Equity	50% Debt/ 50% Equity
Cash flow to creditors:			
Interest	0	$ 125	$ 250
Pretax cost of debt	.05	.05	.05
Value of debt:			
(Interest/k_d)	—	—	—
Cash flow to shareholders:			
EBIT	$1,485	$1,485	$1,485
− Interest	0	$ (125)	$ (250)
Pretax profit	—	—	—
Taxes (@ 34%)	—	—	—
Net income	—	—	—
+ Depreciation	$ 500	$ 500	$ 500
− Capital expense	$ (500)	$ (500)	$ (500)
+ Change in net working capital	0	0	0
− Debt amortization	0	0	0
Residual cash flow (RCF)	—	—	—
Cost of equity	—	—	—
Value of equity (RCF/k_e)	—	—	—
Value of equity plus value of debt	—	—	—

As the firm levers up, how does the increase in value get apportioned between the creditors and the shareholders?

3. In the preceding problem, we divided the value of all the assets between two classes of investors: creditors and shareholders. This process tells us where the change in value is *going,* but it sheds little light on where the change is *coming from.* Let's divide the free cash flows of the firm into *pure business flows* and cash flows resulting from *financing effects.* Now, an axiom in finance is that you should discount cash flows at a rate consistent with the risk of those cash flows. Pure business flows should be discounted at the unlevered cost of equity (i.e., the cost of capital for the unlevered firm). Financing flows should be discounted at the rate of return required by the providers of debt.

	0% Debt/ 100% Equity	25% Debt/ 75% Equity	50% Debt/ 50% Equity
Pure business cash flows:			
EBIT	$1,485	$1,485	$1,485
Taxes (@ 34%)	$ (505)	$ (505)	$ (505)
EBIAT	$ 980	$ 980	$ 980
+ Depreciation	$ 500	$ 500	$ 500
− Capital expense	$ (500)	$ (500)	$ (500)
+ Change in net working capital	0	0	0
Free cash flow (FCF)	$ 980	$ 980	$ 980
Unlevered beta	.8	.8	.8
Risk-free rate	.05	.05	.05
Market premium	.06	.06	.06
Unlevered WACC	—	—	—
Value of pure business flows: (FCF/unlevered WACC)	—	—	—
Financing cash flows			
Interest	—	—	—
Tax reduction	—	—	—
Pretax cost of debt	.05	.05	.05
Value of financing effect: (Tax reduction/pretax cost of debt)	—	—	—
Total value (sum of values of pure business flows and financing effects)	—	—	—

The first three problems illustrate one of the most important theories in finance. This theory, developed by two professors, Franco Modigliani and Merton Miller, revolutionized the way we think about capital-structure policies. The M&M theory says:

$$\text{Value of assets} = \text{Value of debt} + \text{Value of equity} = \text{Value of unlevered firm} + \text{Value of debt tax shields}^1$$

$$\wedge \qquad\qquad \wedge \qquad\qquad\qquad \wedge$$

Problem 1   Problem 2   Problem 3

4. What remains to be seen, however, is whether shareholders are better or worse off with more leverage. Problem 2 does not tell us because there we computed total value of equity, and shareholders care about value *per* share. Ordinarily, total value will be a good proxy for what is happening to the price per share, but in the case of a relevering firm, that may not be true. Implicitly, we assumed that, as our firm in problems 1–3 levered up, it was repurchasing stock on the open market

---

[1]Debt tax shields can be valued by discounting the future annual tax savings at the pretax cost of debt. For debt, that is assumed to be outstanding in perpetuity, the tax savings is the tax rate, t, times the interest payment, k × D. The present value of this perpetual savings is tkD/k = tD.

(you will note that EBIT did not change, so management was clearly not investing the proceeds from the loans into cash-generating assets). We held EBIT constant so that we could see clearly the effect of financial changes without getting them mixed up in the effects of investments. The point is that, as the firm borrows and repurchases shares, the total value of equity may decline, but the price per share may *rise*.

Now, solving for the price per share may seem impossible because we are dealing with two unknowns—share price and the change in the number of shares:

$$\text{Share price} = \frac{\text{Market value of equity}}{\text{Original shares} - \text{Repurchased shares}}$$

But by rewriting the equation, we can put it in a form that can be solved:

$$\text{Share price} = \frac{\text{Original market value of equity} + \text{Value of financing effect}}{\text{Number of original shares}}$$

Referring to the results of problem 2, let's assume that all the new debt is equal to the cash paid to repurchase shares. Please complete the following table:

	0% Debt/ 100% Equity	25% Debt/ 75% Equity	50% Debt/ 50% Equity
Total market value of equity	—	—	—
Cash paid out	—	—	—
Number of original shares	1,000	1,000	1,000
Total value per share	—	—	—

5. In this set of problems, is leverage good for shareholders? Why? Is levering/unlevering the firm something that shareholders can do for themselves? In what sense should shareholders pay a premium for shares of levered companies?

6. From a macroeconomic point of view, is society better off if firms use more than zero debt (up to some prudent limit)?

7. As a way of illustrating the usefulness of the M&M theory and consolidating your grasp of the mechanics, consider the following case and complete the worksheet. On March 3, 1988, Beazer PLC (a British construction company) and Shearson Lehman Hutton, Inc. (an investment-banking firm) commenced a hostile tender offer to purchase all the outstanding stock of Koppers Company, Inc., a producer of construction materials, chemicals, and building products. Originally, the raiders offered $45 a share; subsequently, the offer was raised to $56 and then finally to $61 a share. The Koppers board asserted that the offers were inadequate and its management was reviewing the possibility of a major recapitalization.

To test the valuation effects of the recapitalization alternative, assume that Koppers could borrow a maximum of $1,738,095,000 at a pretax cost of debt of 10.5 percent and that the aggregate amount of debt will remain constant in perpetuity. Thus, Koppers will take on additional debt of $1,565,686,000 (that is, $1,738,095,000 minus $172,409,000). Also assume that the proceeds of the loan would be paid as an extraordinary dividend to shareholders. **Exhibit 1** presents Koppers' book- and market-value balance sheets, assuming the capital structure before recapitalization. Please complete the worksheet for the recapitalization alternative.

EXHIBIT 1 | Koppers Company, Inc. (values in thousands)

	Before Recapitalization	After Recapitalization
Book-Value Balance Sheets		
Net working capital	$ 212,453	
Fixed assets	601,446	
Total assets	$ 813,899	
Long-term debt	$ 172,409	
Deferred taxes, etc.	195,616	
Preferred stock	15,000	
Common equity	430,874	
Total capital	$ 813,899	
Market-Value Balance Sheets		
Net working capital	$ 212,453	
Fixed assets	1,618,081	
Present value (PV) debt tax shield	58,619	
Total assets	$1,889,153	
Long-term debt	$ 172,409	
Deferred taxes, etc.	0	
Preferred stock	15,000	
Common equity	1,701,744	
Total capital	$1,889,153	
Number of shares	28,128	
Price per share	$ 60.50	
Value to Public Shareholders		
Cash received	0	
Value of shares	$1,701,744	
Total	1,701,744	
Total per share	$ 60.50	

Structuring Corporate Financial Policy: Diagnosis of Problems and Evaluation of Strategies

This note outlines a diagnostic and prescriptive way of thinking about corporate financial policy. Successful diagnosis and prescription depend heavily on thoughtful creativity and careful judgment, so the note presents no cookie-cutter solutions. Rather, it discusses the elements of good *process* and offers three basic stages in that process:

Description: The ability to describe a firm's financial policies (which have been chosen either explicitly or by default) is an essential foundation of diagnosis and prescription. Part I of this note defines "financial structure" and discusses the design elements by which a senior financial officer must make choices. This section illustrates the complexity of a firm's financial policies.

Diagnosis: One derives a "good" financial structure by triangulating from benchmark perspectives. Then one compares the idealized and actual financial structures, looking for opportunities for improvement. Part II of this note is an overview of three benchmarks by which the analyst can diagnose problems and opportunities: (1) the expectations of investors, (2) the policies and behavior of competitors, and (3) the internal goals and motivations of corporate management itself. Other perspectives may also exist. Parts III, IV, and V discuss in detail the estimation and application of the three benchmarks. These sections emphasize artful homework and economy of effort by focusing on key considerations, questions, and information. The goal is to derive insights unique to each benchmark, rather than to churn data endlessly.

Prescription: Action recommendations should spring from the insights gained in description and diagnosis. Rarely, however, do unique solutions or ideas exist; rather, the typical chief financial officer (CFO) must have a *view* about competing suggestions. Part VI addresses the task of comparing competing proposals. Part VII presents the conclusion.

Part I: Identifying Corporate Financial Policy: The Elements of Its Design

You can observe a lot just by watching.
  —Yogi Berra

The first task for financial advisers and decision makers is to understand the firm's *current* financial policy. Doing so is a necessary foundation for diagnosing problems and prescribing remedies. This section presents an approach for identifying the firm's financial policy, based on a careful analysis of the *tactics* by which that policy is implemented.

The Concept of Corporate Financial Policy

The notion that firms *have* a distinct financial policy is startling to some analysts and executives. Occasionally, a chief financial officer will say, "All I do is get the best deal I can whenever we need funds." Almost no CFO would admit otherwise. In all probability, however, the firm has a more substantive policy than the CFO admits to. Even a management style of myopia or opportunism is, after all, a policy.

Some executives will argue that calling financing a "policy" is too fancy. They say that financing is reactive: it happens after all investment and operational decisions have been made. How can reaction be a policy? At other times, one hears an executive say, "Our financial policy is simple." Attempts to characterize a financial structure as reactive or simplistic overlook the considerable richness of choice that confronts the financial manager.

Finally, some analysts make the mistake of "one-size-fits-all" thinking; that is, they assume that financial policy is mainly driven by the economics of a certain industry and they overlook the firm-specific nature of financial policy. Firms in the same, well-defined industry can have very different financial policies. The reason is that financial policy is a matter of *managerial choice.*

"Corporate financial policy" is a set of broad *guidelines* or a preferred *style* to guide the raising of capital and the distribution of value. Policies should be set to support the mission and strategy of the firm. As the environment changes, policies should adapt.

The analyst of financial policy must come to terms with its ambiguity. Policies are guidelines; they are imprecise. Policies are products of managerial choice rather than the dictates of an economic model. Policies change over time. Nevertheless, the framework in this note can help the analyst define a firm's corporate financial policy with enough focus to identify potential problems, prescribe remedies, and make decisions.

The Elements of Financial Policy

Every financial structure reveals underlying financial policies through the following seven elements of financial-structure design:[1]

---

[1]For economy, this note will restrict its scope to these seven items. One can, however, imagine dimensions other than the ones listed here.

1. *Mix* of classes of capital (such as debt versus equity, or common stock versus re-tained earnings): *How heavily does the firm rely on different classes of capital? Is the reliance on debt reasonable in light of the risks the firm faces and the nature of its industry and technology?* Mix may be analyzed through capitalization ratios, debt-service coverage ratios, and the firm's sources-and-uses-of-funds statement (where the analyst should look for the origins of the new additions to capital in the recent past). Many firms exhibit a pecking order of financing: they seek to fulfill their funding needs through the retention of profits, then through debt, and, finally, through the issuance of new shares. *Does the firm observe a particular pecking order in its acquisition of new capital?*

2. *Maturity structure of the firm's capital:* To describe the choices made about the maturity of outstanding securities is to be able to infer the judgments the firm made about its priorities—for example, future financing requirements and oppor-tunities or relative preference for refinancing risk[2] versus reinvestment risk.[3] A risk-neutral position with respect to maturity would be where the life of the firm's assets equals the life of the firm's liabilities. Most firms accept an inequality in one direction or the other. This might be due to ignorance or to sophistication: managers might have a strong internal "view" about their ability to reinvest or re-finance. Ultimately, we want managers to maximize value, not minimize risk. The absence of a perfect maturity hedge might reflect managers' better-informed bets about the future of the firm and markets. Measuring the maturity structure of the firm's capital can yield insights into the bets that the firm's managers are appar-ently making. The standard measures of maturity are term to maturity, average life, and duration. *Are the lives of the firm's assets and liabilities roughly matched? If not, what gamble is the firm taking (i.e., is it showing an appetite for refunding risk or interest-rate risk)?*

3. *Basis of the firm's coupon and dividend payments:* In simplest terms, basis ad-dresses the firm's preference for fixed or floating rates of payment and is a useful tool in fathoming management's judgment regarding the future course of interest rates. Interest-rate derivatives provide the financial officer with choices condi-tioned by caps, floors, and other structured options. Understanding management's basis choices can reveal some of the fundamental bets management is placing, even when it has decided to "do nothing." *What is the firm's relative preference for fixed or floating interest rates? Are the firm's operating returns fixed or floating?*

---

[2]Refinancing risk exists where the life of the firm's assets is *more* than the life of the firm's liabilities. In other words, the firm will need to replace (or "roll over") the capital originally obtained to buy the asset. The refinancing risk is the chance that the firm will be unable to obtain funds on advantageous terms (or at all) at the rollover date.

[3]Reinvestment risk exists where the life of the firm's assets is *less* than the life of the firm's liabilities. In other words, the firm will need to replace, or roll over, the investment that the capital originally financed. Reinvestment risk is the chance that the firm will be unable to reinvest the capital on advantageous terms at the rollover date.

4. *Currency* addresses the global aspect of a firm's financial opportunities: These opportunities are expressed in two ways: (a) management of the firm's exposure to foreign exchange-rate fluctuations, and (b) the exploitation of unusual financing possibilities in global capital markets. Exchange-rate exposure arises when a firm earns income (or pays expenses) in a variety of currencies. Whether and how a firm hedges this exposure can reveal the "bets" that management is making regarding the future movement of exchange rates and the future currency mix of the firm's cash flows. The financial-policy analyst should look for foreign-denominated securities in the firm's capital and for swap, option, futures, and forward contracts—all of which can be used to manage the firm's foreign-exchange exposure. The other way that currency matters to the financial-policy analyst is as an indication of the management's willingness to source its capital "offshore." This is an indication of sophistication and of having a view about the parity of exchange rates with security returns around the world. In a perfectly integrated global capital market, the theory of interest rate parity would posit the futility of finding bargain financing offshore. But global capital markets are not perfectly integrated, and interest rate parity rarely holds true everywhere. Experience suggests that financing bargains may exist temporarily. Offshore financing may suggest an interest in finding and exploiting such bargains. *Is the currency denomination of the firm's capital consistent with the currency denomination of the firm's operating cash flows? Do the balance sheet footnotes show evidence of foreign-exchange hedging? Also, is the company, in effect, sourcing capital on a global basis or is it focusing narrowly on the domestic capital markets?*

5. *Exotica:* Every firm faces a spectrum of financing alternatives, ranging from plain-vanilla bonds and stocks to hybrids and one-of-a-kind, highly tailored securities.[4] This element considers management's relative preference for financial innovation. Where a firm positions itself on this spectrum can shed light on management's openness to new ideas, intellectual originality and, possibly, opportunistic tendencies. As a general matter, option-linked securities often appear in corporate finance where there is some disagreement between issuers and investors about a firm's prospects. For instance, managers of high-growth firms will foresee rapid expansion and vaulting stock prices. Bond investors, not having the benefit of inside information, might see only high risk—issuing a convertible bond might be a way to allow the bond investors to capitalize the risk[5] and to enjoy the creation of value through growth in return for accepting a lower current yield. Also, the circumstances under which exotic securities were issued are often fascinating episodes in a company's history. *Based on past financings, what is the firm's appetite for issuing exotic securities? Why have the firm's exotic securities been tailored as they are?*

---

[4]Examples of highly tailored securities include exchangeable and convertible bonds, hybrid classes of common stock, and contingent securities, such as a dividend-paying equity issued in connection with an acquisition.

[5]In general, the call options embedded in a convertible bond will be more valuable depending on the greater the volatility of the underlying asset.

6.   *External control*: Any management team probably prefers little outside control. One must recognize that, in any financial structure, management has made choices about subtle control trade-offs, including *who* might exercise control (for example, creditors, existing shareholders, new shareholders, or a raider) and the control *trigger* (for example, default on a loan covenant, passing a preferred stock dividend, or a shareholder vote). How management structures control triggers (for example, the tightness of loan covenants) or forestalls discipline (perhaps through the adoption of poison pills and other takeover defenses) can reveal insights into management's fears and expectations. Clues about external control choices may be found in credit covenants, collateral pledges, the terms of preferred shares, the profile of the firm's equity holders, the voting rights of common stock, corporate bylaws, and antitakeover defenses. *In what ways has management defended against or yielded to external control?*

7.   *Distribution* seeks to determine any patterns in (a) the way the firm markets its securities (i.e., acquires capital), and (b) the way the firm delivers value to its investors (i.e., returns capital). Regarding marketing, insights emerge from knowing where a firm's securities are listed for trading, how often the shares are sold, and who advises the sale of securities (the adviser that a firm attracts is one indication of its sophistication). Regarding the delivery of value, the two generic strategies involve dividends or capital gains. Some companies will pay low or no dividends and force their shareholders to take returns in the form of capital gains. Other companies will pay material dividends, even borrowing to do so. Still others will repurchase shares, split shares, and declare extraordinary dividends. Managers' choices about delivering value yield clues about management's beliefs regarding investors and the company's ability to satisfy investors' needs. *How have managers chosen to deliver value to shareholders, and with whose assistance have they issued securities?*

A Comparative Illustration

The value of looking at a firm's financial structure through these seven design elements is that the insights they provide can become a basis for developing a broad, detailed picture of the firm's financial policies. Also, the seven elements become an organizational framework for the wealth of financial information on publicly owned companies.

Consider the examples of Eli Lilly and Company, a leading manufacturer and marketer of pharmaceuticals and animal-health products, and Genentech, Inc., a biotechnology company focused on developing products in oncology, immunology, and pulmonary medicine. Sources such as the *Mergent Industrial Manual* and the *Value Line Investment Survey* distill information from annual reports and regulatory filings and permit the analyst to draw conclusions about the seven elements of each firm's financial policy. Drawing on the financial results for 2004, analysts may glean the following insights about the policies of Eli Lilly and Genentech from **Table 1.**

As **Table 1** shows, standard information available on public companies yields important contrasts in their financial policies. Note that the insights are *informed*

TABLE 1 | Financial Policies for Eli Lilly and Genentech

Elements of Financial Policy	Eli Lilly and Company	Genentech, Inc.
MIX	**Moderate debt** • Debt/assets = 19% • Debt/capital = 30% • Sold equity in 1972, 1973, 1978 • S&P credit rating: AA • Acquisitions financed with combinations of cash and stock	**Equity orientation** • Debt/assets = 4% • Debt/capital = 6% • Sold equity in 1980, 1985, 1999, 2000 • S&P credit rating: A+ • Acquisitions financed with cash
MATURITY	**Medium- to long-term** • Average life = 16.3 years • 64% @ 5 to 15 years • 36% @ 30 years	**Short-term** • Maintains a single 2-year issue
BASIS	**Fixed rates** • 91% of debt is at a fixed rate	**Floating rates** • Variable interest, with minimum 1.2% rate
CURRENCY	**Exclusively U.S. dollars**	**Exclusively U.S. dollars**
EXOTICA	**No exotics** • Modest use of leases	**No exotics**
CONTROL	**Favors large stockholders** • Debt unsecured and callable • Lilly Foundation owned 13.4% of the stock	**Significant investor** • Roche Holdings Inc. owned 56.1% of outstanding common stock • Increased authorized shares from 300 million in 2000 to 3 billion in 2004
DISTRIBUTION	**Steady dividends** • Average payout: 47% • Numerous stock splits • Participating preferred available **Various advisers** • Morgan Stanley & Co.; Goldman, Sachs & Co.; J.P Morgan; Deutsche Banc; Merrill Lynch & Co., among others **Broadly international** • Subsidiaries and affiliates in over 40 major countries	**Capital gains** • Rapid growth and high returns • No dividends • Stock splits in 1999, 2000, 2004 **Single adviser** • Hambrecht & Quist **Some international** • Subsidiaries in Canada, Switzerland, Japan, Germany, United Kingdom, and the Netherlands

guesses: neither of those firms explicitly describes its financial policies. Nonetheless, with practice and good information, the validity of the guesses can be high.

Eli Lilly and Genentech present distinctly different policy profiles. While Genentech's policy is conservative in almost every dimension, Lilly's is somewhat more aggressive. Two such firms would warrant very different sets of questions by a director or an outside financial adviser. The key idea is that financial policies can be characterized by the tracks they leave. Good strategic assessment begins with good tracking of current or past policy.

Part II: General Framework for Diagnosing Financial-Policy Opportunities and Problems

Having parsed the choices embedded in the firm's financial structure, one must ask, "Were these the *right* choices?" What is "right" is a matter of the context and the clientele to which management must respond. A firm has many potential claimants.[6] The discussion that follows will focus on the perspectives of competitors, investors, and senior corporate managers.

1. *Does the financial policy create value?*

   From the standpoint of investors, the best financial structure will (a) maximize shareholder wealth, (b) maximize the value of the entire firm (i.e., the market value of assets), and (c) minimize the firm's weighted-average cost of capital (WACC). When those conditions occur, the firm makes the best trade-offs among the choices on each of the seven dimensions of financial policy. This analysis is all within the context of the *market* conditions.

2. *Does the financial policy create a competitive advantage?*

   Competitors should matter in the design of corporate financial policy. Financial structure can enhance or constrain competitive advantage mainly by opening or foreclosing avenues of competitive response over time. Thus, a manager should critically assess the strategic options created or destroyed by a particular financial structure. Also, assuming that they are reasonably well managed, competitors' financial structures are probably an indicator of good financial policy in a particular industry. Thus, a manager should want to know how his or her firm's financial structure compares with the peer group. In short, this line of thinking seeks to evaluate the relative position of the firm in its competitive environment on the basis of financial structure.

3. *Does the financial policy sustain senior management's vision?*

   The internal perspective tests the appropriateness of a capital structure from the standpoint of the expectations and capacities of the corporate organization itself. The analyst begins with an assessment of corporate strategy and the resulting

---

[6]With a moment's reflection, the analyst will call up a number of claimants (stakeholders or clientele), whose interests the company might serve. Managers, customers, and investors are often the first to come to mind. Creditors (for example, bankers) often have interests that differ from those of the equity investors. Workers (and unions) often make tangible claims on the firm. Governments, through their taxing and regulatory powers, do so as well. One might extend the list to environmentalists and other social activists. The possibilities are almost limitless. For economy, this discussion treats only the three perspectives that yield the most insight about financial policy.

stream of cash requirements and resources anticipated in the future. The realism of the plan should be tested against expected macroeconomic variations, as well as against possible but unexpected financial strains. A good financial structure meets the classic maxim of corporate finance, "Don't run out of cash": in other words, the ideal financial structure adequately funds the growth goals and dividend payouts of the firm without severely diluting the firm's current equity owners. The concept of self-sustainable growth provides a straightforward test of this ideal.

The next three sections will discuss these perspectives in more detail. All three perspectives are unlikely to offer a completely congruent assessment of financial structure. The investor's view looks at the *economic* consequences of a financial structure; the competitor's view considers *strategic* consequences; the internal view addresses the firm's *survival and ambitions*. The three views ask entirely different questions. An analyst should not be surprised when the answers diverge.

Rather like estimating the height of a distant mountain through the haze, the analyst develops a concept of the best financial structure by a process of *triangulation*. Triangulation involves weighing the importance of each of the perspectives as each one *complements* the other rather than as it substitutes for the other, identifying points of consistency, and making artful judgments where the perspectives diverge.

The goal of this analysis should be to articulate concretely the design of the firm's financial structure, preferably in terms of the seven elements discussed in Part I. This exercise entails developing notes, comments, and calculations for every one of the cells of this analytical grid:

Elements of Financial Structure	Current Structure	Investor View	Competitor View	Internal View	Evaluation/ Comments
1. Mix					
2. Maturity					
3. Basis					
4. Currency					
5. Exotica					
6. External Control					
7. Distribution					

No chart can completely anticipate the difficulties, quirks, and exceptions that the analyst will undoubtedly encounter. What matters most, however, is the way of thinking about the financial-structure design problem that encourages both critical thinking and organized, efficient digestion of information.

Figure 1 summarizes the approach presented in this section. Good financial-structure analysis develops three complementary perspectives on financial structure, and then blends those perspectives into a prescription.

FIGURE 1 | Overview of Financial-Structure Analysis

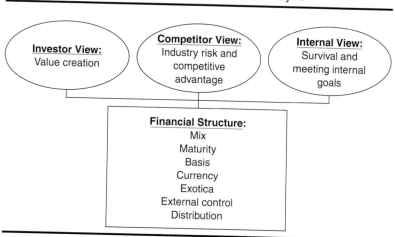

Part III: Analyzing Financial Policy from the Investors' Viewpoint[7]

In finance theory, the investors' expectations should influence all managerial decisions. This theory follows the legal doctrine that firms should be managed in the interests of their owners. It also recognizes the economic idea that if investors' needs are satisfied after all other claims on the firm are settled, then the firm must be healthy. The investors' view also confronts the reality of capital market discipline. The best defense against a hostile takeover (or another type of intrusion) is a high stock price. In recent years, the threat of capital market discipline has done more than any academic theory to rivet the management's attention to *value creation*.

Academic theory, however, is extremely useful in identifying value-creating strategies. Economic value is held to be the present value of expected future cash flows discounted at a rate consistent with the risk of those cash flows. Considerable care must be given to the estimation of cash flows and discount rates (a review of discounted cash flow [DCF] valuation is beyond the scope of this note). Theory suggests that leverage can create value through the *benefits of debt tax shields* and can destroy value through the *costs of financial distress*. The balance of those costs and benefits depends upon specific capital market conditions, which are conveyed by the debt and equity costs that capital providers impose on the firm. Academic theory's bottom line is as follows:

> An efficient (i.e., value-optimizing) financial structure is one that simultaneously minimizes the weighted-average cost of capital and maximizes the share price and value of the enterprise.

[7]Excellent summaries of the investors' orientation are found in Tom Copeland, Tim Koller, and Jack Murrin, *Valuation: Measuring and Managing the Value of Companies,* 2nd ed. (New York: Wiley, 1994); and Alfred Rappaport, *Creating Shareholder Value,* 2nd ed. (New York: Free Press, 1997).

The investors' perspective is a rigorous approach to evaluating financial structures: valuation analysis of the firm and its common stock under existing and alternative financial structures. The best structure will be one that creates the most value.

The phrase *alternative financial structures* is necessarily ambiguous, but should be interpreted to include a wide range of alternatives, including leveraged buyouts, leveraged recapitalizations, spin-offs, carve-outs, and even liquidations. However radical the latter alternatives may seem, the analyst must understand that investment bankers and corporate raiders routinely consider those alternatives. To anticipate the thinking of those agents of change, the analyst must replicate their homework.

Careful analysis does not rest with a final number, but rather considers a range of elements:

Cost of Debt   The analysis focuses on yields to maturity and the spreads of those yields over the Treasury yield curve. Floating rates are always effective rates of interest.

Cost of Equity   The assessment uses as many approaches as possible, including the capital asset pricing model, the dividend discount model, the financial leverage equation, the earnings/price model, and any other avenues that seem appropriate. Although it is fallible, the capital asset pricing model has the most rigor.

Debt/Equity Mix   The relative proportions of types of capital in the capital structure are important factors in computing the weighted-average cost of capital. All capital should be estimated on a *market value* basis.

Price/Earnings Ratio, Market/Book Ratio, Earnings before Interest and Taxes (EBIT) Multiple   Comparing those values to the average levels of the entire capital market or to an industry group can provide an alternative check on the valuation of the firm.

Bond Rating   The creditors' view of the firm is important. Standard & Poor's and Moody's publish average financial ratios for bond-rating groups. Even for a firm with no publicly rated debt outstanding, a simple ratio analysis can reveal a firm's likely rating category and its current cost of debt.

Ownership   The relative mix of individual and institutional owners and the presence of block holders with potentially hostile intentions can help shed light on the current pricing of a firm's securities.

Short Position   A large, short-sale position on the firm's stock can indicate that some traders believe a decline in share price is imminent.

To conclude, the first rule of financial-policy analysis is: *Think like an investor.* The investor's view assesses the value of a firm's shares under alternative financial structures and the existence of any strongly positive or negative perceptions in the capital markets about the firm's securities.

Part IV: Analyzing Financial Policy from a Competitive Perspective

The competitive perspective matters to senior executives for two important reasons. First, it gives an indication about (1) standard practice in the industry, and (2) the strategic position of the firm relative to the competition. Second, it implies rightly that finance can be a strategic competitive instrument.[8]

The competitive perspective may be the hardest of the three benchmarks to assess. There are few clear signposts in industry dynamics, and, as most industries become increasingly global, the comparisons become even more difficult to make. Despite the difficulty of this analysis, however, senior executives typically give an inordinate amount of attention to it. The well-versed analyst must be able to assess the ability of the current policy (and its alternatives) to maintain or improve its competitive position.

This analysis does not proceed scientifically, but rather evolves iteratively toward an accurate assessment of the situation.[9] The steps might be defined as follows:

1. Define the universe of competitors.

2. Spread the data and financial ratios on the firm and its competitors in comparative fashion.

3. Identify similarities and, more importantly, differences. Probe into anomalies. Question the data and the peer sample.

4. Add needed information, such as a foreign competitor, another ratio, historical normalization, etc.

5. Discuss or clarify the information with the CFO or industry expert.

As the information grows, the questions will become more probing. What is the historical growth pattern? Why did the XYZ company suddenly increase its leverage or keep a large cash balance? Did the acquisition of a new line actually provide access to new markets? Are the changes in debt mix and maturity or in the dividend policy related to the new products and markets?

Economy of effort demands that the analyst begin with a few ratios and data that can be easily obtained (from Value Line, 10-Ks, etc.). If a company is in several industries and does not have pure competitors, choose group-divisional competitors and, to the extent possible, use segment information to devise ratios that will be valid, e.g., operating income to sales, rather than an after-tax equivalent). Do not forget information that may be outside the financial statements and may be critical to competitive survival, such as geographic diversification, research and development

---

[8] For a discussion of finance as a competitive instrument, see the classic work by William E. Fruhan Jr., *Financial Strategy: Studies in the Creation, Transfer, and Destruction of Shareholder Value* (Homewood, IL: Irwin, 1979).

[9] A good overview of industry and competitor analysis may be found in Michael Porter, *Competitive Analysis* (New York: Free Press, 1979). An excellent survey of possible information sources on firms is in Leonard M. Fuld, *Competitor Intelligence* (New York: Wiley, 1985).

expenditures, and union activity. For some industries, other key ratios are available through trade groups, such as same-store sales and capacity analyses. Whatever the inadequacy of the data, the comparisons will provide direction for subsequent analysis.

The ratios and data to be used will depend on the course of analysis. An analyst could start with the following general types of measures with which to compare a competitor group:

1. *Size:* sales, market value, number of employees or countries, market share.

2. *Asset productivity:* return on assets (ROA), return on invested capital, market to book value.

3. *Shareholder wealth:* price/earnings (P/E), return on market value.

4. *Predictability:* Beta, historical trends.

5. *Growth:* 1- to 10-year compound growth of sales, profits, assets, and market value of equity.

6. *Financial flexibility:* debt-to-capital, debt ratings, cash flow coverage, estimates of the cost of capital.

7. *Other significant industry issues:* unfunded pension liabilities, postretirement medical benefit obligations, environmental liabilities, capacity, research and development expense to sales, percentage of insider control, etc.

One of the key issues to resolve in analyzing the comparative data is whether all the peer-group members display the same results and trends. Inevitably, they will not—which begs the question, why not? Trends in asset productivity and globalization have affected the competitors differently and elicited an assortment of strategic responses. These phenomena should stimulate further research.

The analyst should augment personal research efforts with the work of industry analysts. Securities analysts, consultants, academicians, and journalists—both through their written work and via telephone conversations—can provide valuable insights based on their extensive, personal contacts in the industry.[10]

Analyzing competitors develops insights into the range of financial structures in the industry and the appropriateness of your firm's structure in comparison. Developing those insights is more a matter of qualitative judgment than of letting the numbers speak for themselves. For instance:

1. Suppose your firm is a highly leveraged computer manufacturer with an uneven record of financial performance. Should it unlever? You discover that the peer group of computer manufacturers is substantially equity financed, owing largely to the rapid rate of technological innovation and the predation of a few large players in the industry. The *strategic rationale* for low leverage is to survive the business and short product lifecycles. Yes, it might be good to unlever.

---

[10]See, for example, *Nelson's Guide to Securities Research* for a directory of securities analysts. The Frost & Sullivan *Predicast* and the indexes to the *Wall Street Journal* can give quick overviews of industry trends.

2. Suppose your firm is an airline that finances its equipment purchases with flotations of commercial paper. The average life of the firm's liabilities is 4 years, while the average life of the firm's assets is 15 years. Should the airline refinance its debt using securities with longer maturity? You discover that the peer group of airlines finances its assets with leases, equipment-trust certificates, and project-finance deals that almost exactly match the economic lives of assets and liabilities. The *strategic rationale* for lengthening the maturity structure of liabilities is to hedge against yield-curve changes that might adversely affect your firm's ability to refinance, yet still leave its peer competitors relatively unaffected.

3. Here is a trickier example. Your firm is the last nationwide supermarket chain that is publicly held. All other major supermarket chains have gone private in leveraged buyouts (LBO). Should your firm lever up through a leveraged share repurchase? Competitor analysis reveals that other firms are struggling to meet debt service payments on already thin margins and that a major shift in customer patronage may be under way. You conclude that price competition in selected markets would trigger realignment in market shares in your firm's favor, because the competitors have little pricing flexibility. In that case, adjusting to the industry-average leverage would not be appropriate.

Part V: Diagnosing Financial Policy from an Internal Perspective[11]

Internal analysis is the third major screen of a firm's financial structure. It accounts for the expected cash requirements and resources of a firm, and tests the consistency of a firm's financial structure with the profitability, growth, and dividend goals of the firm. The classic tools of internal analysis are the forecast cash flow, financial statements, and sources-and-uses of funds statements. The standard banker's credit analysis is consistent with this approach.

The essence of this approach is a concern for (1) the preservation of the firm's *financial flexibility,* (2) the *sustainability* of the firm's financial policies, and (3) the *feasibility* of the firm's strategic goals. For example, the firm's long-term goals may call for a doubling of sales in five years. The business plan for achieving that goal may call for the construction of a greenfield plant in year one, and then regional distribution systems in years two and three. Substantial working capital investments will be necessary in years two through five. How this growth is to be financed has huge implications for your firm's financial structure *today.* Typically, an analyst addresses this problem by forecasting the financial performance of the firm, experimenting with different financing sequences and choosing the best one, then determining the structure that makes the best foundation for that financing sequence. This analysis implies the need to maintain future financial flexibility.

---

[11] An excellent overview of the "in-house" view of a firm's financial policies may be found in Gordon Donaldson, *Managing Corporate Wealth: The Operation of a Comprehensive Financial Goals System* (New York: Praeger, 1984).

Financial Flexibility

Financial flexibility is easily measured as the excess cash and unused debt capacity on which the firm might call. In addition, there may be other reserves, such as unused land or excess stocks of raw materials, that could be liquidated. All reserves that could be mobilized should be reflected in an analysis of financial flexibility. Illustrating with the narrower definition (cash and unused debt capacity), one can measure financial flexibility as follows:

1. Select a target minimum debt rating that is acceptable to the firm. Many CFOs will have a target minimum in mind, such as the BBB/Baa rating.

2. Determine the book value[12] debt/equity mix consistent with the minimum rating. Standard & Poor's, for instance, publishes average financial ratios, including debt/equity, that are associated with each debt-rating category.[13]

3. Determine the book value of debt consistent with the debt/equity ratio from step 2. This gives the amount of debt that would be outstanding, if the firm moved to the minimum acceptable bond rating.

4. Estimate financial flexibility using the following formula:

$$\text{Financial flexibility} = \text{Excess cash} + (\text{Debt at minimum rating} - \text{Current debt outstanding})$$

The amount estimated by this formula indicates the financial reserves on which the firm can call to exploit unusual or surprising opportunities (for example, the chance to acquire a competitor) or to defend against unusual threats (for example, a price war, sudden product obsolescence, or a labor strike).

Self-Sustainable Growth

A shorthand test for sustainability and internal consistency is the self-sustainable growth model. This model is based on one key assumption: over the forecast period, the firm sells no new shares of stock (this assumption is entirely consistent with the actual behavior of firms over the long run).[14] As long as the firm does not change its mix of debt and equity, the self-sustainable model implies that assets can grow only as fast as equity grows. Thus, the issue of sustainability is significantly determined by the firm's return on equity (ROE) and dividend payout ratio (DPO):

$$\text{Self-sustainable growth rate of assets} = \text{ROE} \times (1 - \text{DPO})$$

---

[12]Ideally, one would work with market values rather than book values, but the rating agencies compute their financial ratios only on a book value basis. Because this analysis, in effect, mimics the perspective of the rating agencies, the analyst must work with book values.

[13]See *CreditWeek,* published by Standard & Poor's.

[14]From 1950 to 1989, only 5 percent of the growth of the U.S. economy's business sector was financed by the sale of new common stock. The most significant sources were short-term liabilities, long-term liabilities, and retained earnings, in that order.

The test of feasibility of any long-term plan involves comparing the growth rate implied by this formula and the *targeted* growth rate dictated by management's plan. If the targeted growth rate equals the implied rate, then the firm's financial policies are in balance. If the implied rate exceeds the targeted rate, the firm will gradually become more liquid, creating an asset deployment opportunity. If the targeted rate exceeds the implied rate, the firm must raise more capital by selling stock, levering up, or reducing the dividend payout.

Management policies can be modeled finely by recognizing that ROE can be decomposed into various factors using two classic formulas:

DuPont system of ratios: $ROE = P/S \times S/A \times A/E$

P/S = profit divided by sales or net margin; a measure of profitability
S/A = sales divided by assets; a measure of asset productivity
A/E = assets divided by equity; a measure of financial leverage

Financial-leverage equation:[15] $ROE = ROTC + [(ROTC - K_d) \times (D/E)]$

$ROTC$ = return on total capital
K_d = cost of debt
D/E = debt divided by equity; a measure of leverage

Inserting either of those formulas into the equation for the self-sustainable growth rate gives a richer model of the drivers of self-sustainability. One sees, in particular, the importance of internal operations. The self-sustainable growth model can be expanded to reflect explicitly measures of a firm's operating and financial policies.

The self-sustainable growth model tests the internal consistency of a firm's operating and financial policies. *This model, however, provides no guarantee that a strategy will maximize value.* Value creation does not begin with growth targets; growth per se does not necessarily lead to value creation, as the growth-by-acquisition strategies of the 1960s and '70s abundantly illustrated. Also, the adoption of growth targets may foreclose other, more profitable strategies. Those targets may invite managers to undertake investments yielding less than the cost of capital. Meeting sales or asset growth targets can destroy value. Thus, any sustainable growth analysis must be augmented by questions about the value-creation potential of a given set of corporate policies. These questions include (1) What are the magnitude and duration of investment returns as compared with the firm's cost of capital? and (2) With what alternative set of policies is the firm's share price maximized? With questions such as those, the investor orientation discussed in Part III is turned inward to double-check the appropriateness of any inferences drawn from financial forecasts of the sources-and-uses of funds statements and from the analysis of the self-sustainable growth model.

---

[15]This is the classic expression for the cost of equity, as originally presented in the work of the Nobel Prize winners, Franco Modigliani and Merton Miller.

Part VI: What Is Best?

Any financial structure evaluated against the perspectives of investors, competitors, and internal goals will probably show opportunities for improvement. Most often, CFOs choose to make changes at the margin rather than tinkering radically with a financial structure. For changes large and small, however, the analyst must develop a framework for judgment and prescription.

The following framework is a way of identifying the trade-offs among "good" and "bad," rather than finding the right answer. Having identified the trade-offs implicit in any alternative structure, it remains for the CFO and the adviser to choose the structure with the most attractive trade-offs.

The key elements of evaluation are as follows:

Flexibility: the ability to meet unforeseen financing requirements as they arise— those requirements may be favorable (for example, a sudden acquisition opportunity) or unfavorable (such as a product-tampering scare). Flexibility may involve liquidating assets or tapping the capital markets in adverse market environments or both. Flexibility can be measured by bond ratings, coverage ratios, capitalization ratios, liquidity ratios, and the identification of salable assets.

Risk: the predictable variability in the firm's business. Such variability may be due to both macroeconomic factors (such as consumer demand) and industry- or firm-specific factors (such as product lifecycles, or strikes before wage negotiations). To some extent, past experience may indicate the future range of variability in EBIT and cash flow. High leverage tends to amplify those predictable business swings. The risk associated with any given financial structure can be assessed by EBIT–EPS (earnings per share) analysis, break-even analysis, the standard deviation of EBIT, and beta. In theory, beta should vary directly with leverage.[16]

Income: this compares financial structures on the basis of value creation. Measures such as DCF value, projected ROE, EPS, and the cost of capital indicate the comparative value effects of alternative financial structures.

Control: alternative financial structures may imply changes in control or different control constraints on the firm as indicated by the percentage distribution of share ownership and by the structure of debt covenants.

Timing: asks the question whether the current capital-market environment is the right moment to implement any alternative financial structure, and what the implications for future financing will be if the proposed structure is adopted. The current market environment can be assessed by examining the Treasury yield curve, the trend in the movement of interest rates, the existence of any windows in the market for new issues of securities, P/E multiple trends, etc. Sequencing considerations are implicitly captured in the assumptions underlying the alternative DCF value estimates, and can

---

[16]This relationship is illustrated by the formula for estimating a firm's levered beta:

$$B_l = B_u \times [1 + (1 - t) \times D/E]$$

where: B_l = levered beta; B_u = unlevered beta; t = firm's marginal tax rate; and D/E = the firm's market-value debt-to-equity ratio.

be explicitly examined by looking at annual EPS and ROE streams under alternative financing sequences.

This framework of flexibility, risk, income, control, and timing (FRICT) can be used to assess the relative strengths and weaknesses of alternative financing plans. To use a simple example, suppose that your firm is considering two financial structures: (1) 60 percent debt and 40 percent equity (i.e., debt will be issued), and (2) 40 percent debt and 60 percent equity (i.e., equity will be issued). Also, suppose that your analysis of the two structures under the investor, competitor, and internal-analysis screens leads you to make this basic comparison:

	60% Debt	40% Debt
Flexibility	A little low, not bad BBB debt rating $50 million in reserves	High AA debt rating $300 million in reserves
Risk	High EBIT coverage = 1.5	Medium EBIT coverage = 3.0
Income	Good-to-high DCF value = $20/share	Mediocre DCF value = $12/share (dilutive)
Control	Covenants tight No voting dilution	Covenants not restrictive 10% voting dilution
Timing	Interest rates low today Risky sequence	Equity multiples low today Low-risk sequence for future

The 60 percent debt structure is favored on the grounds of income, control, and today's market conditions. The 40 percent debt structure is favored on the grounds of flexibility, risk, and the long-term financial sequencing. This example boils down to a decision between "eating well" and "sleeping well." It remains up to senior management to make the difficult choice between the two alternatives, while giving careful attention to the views of the investors, competitors, and managers.

Part VII: Conclusion

Description, diagnosis, and prescription in financial structuring form an iterative process. It is quite likely that the CFO in the eat-well/sleep-well example would send the analyst back for more research and testing of alternative structures. **Figure 2** presents an expanded view of the basic cycle of analysis and suggests more about the complexity of the financial-structuring problem. With time and experience, the analyst develops an intuition for efficient information sources and modes of analysis. In the long run, this intuition makes the cycle of analysis manageable.

FIGURE 2 | An Expanded Illustration of the Process of Developing a Financial Policy

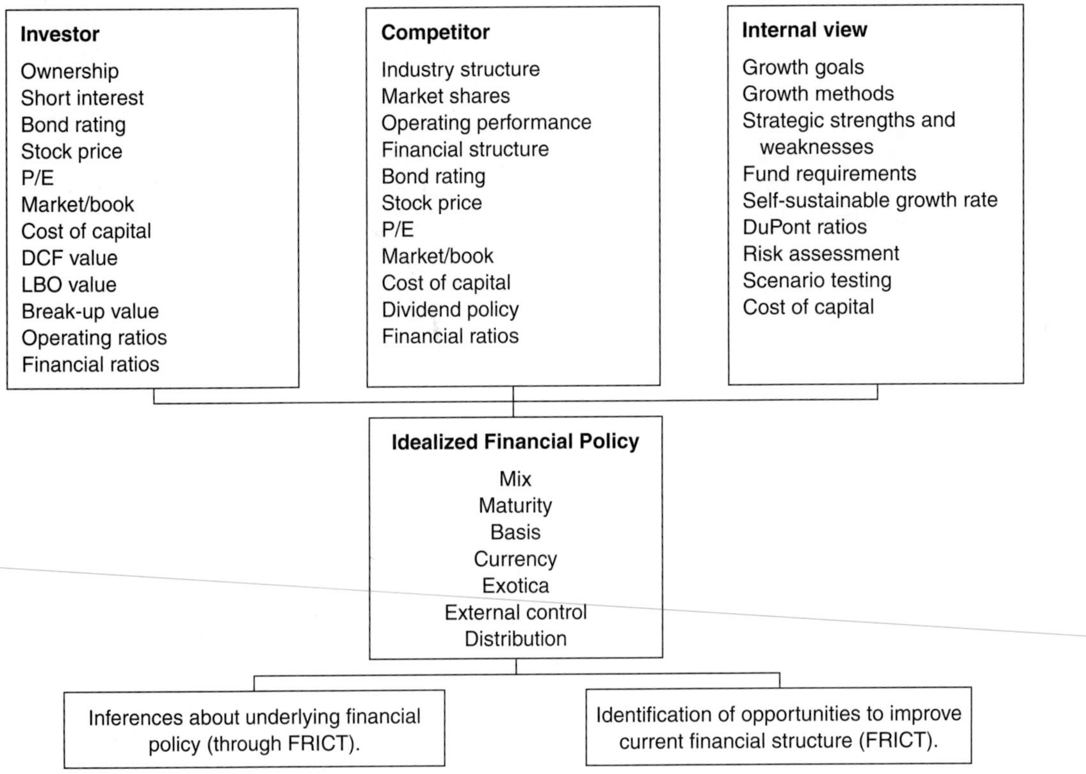

Investor

Ownership
Short interest
Bond rating
Stock price
P/E
Market/book
Cost of capital
DCF value
LBO value
Break-up value
Operating ratios
Financial ratios

Competitor

Industry structure
Market shares
Operating performance
Financial structure
Bond rating
Stock price
P/E
Market/book
Cost of capital
Dividend policy
Financial ratios

Internal view

Growth goals
Growth methods
Strategic strengths and
   weaknesses
Fund requirements
Self-sustainable growth rate
DuPont ratios
Risk assessment
Scenario testing
Cost of capital

Idealized Financial Policy

Mix
Maturity
Basis
Currency
Exotica
External control
Distribution

Inferences about underlying financial policy (through FRICT).

Identification of opportunities to improve current financial structure (FRICT).

The Wm. Wrigley Jr. Company: Capital Structure, Valuation, and Cost of Capital

Interest rates are at their lowest point in 50 years. Yet the use of debt financing by corporations is declining—this happens anyway in a recession. And some deleveraging is due to strategic changes in an industry, such as technological innovation or other developments that increase business risk. But corporate deleveraging seems to have gone too far. CEOs are missing valuable opportunities to create value for their shareholders. In the extreme case, you have mature firms who use no debt at all! Take the Wm. Wrigley Jr. Company, for instance. It has a leading market share in a stable low-technology business—it makes chewing gum—and yet has no debt. I bet that if we could persuade Wrigley's board to do a leveraged recapitalization through a dividend or major share repurchase, we could create significant new value. Susan, please run some numbers on the potential change in value. And get me the names and phone numbers of all of Wrigley's directors.

With those words, Blanka Dobrynin, managing partner of Aurora Borealis LLC, asked Susan Chandler, an associate, to initiate the research for a potential investment in Wrigley. Aurora Borealis was a hedge fund with about $3 billion under management and an investment strategy that focused on distressed companies, merger arbitrage, change-of-control transactions, and recapitalizations. Dobrynin had immigrated to the United States from Russia in 1991, and had risen quickly to become partner at a major Wall Street firm. In 2000, she founded Aurora Borealis to pursue an "active-investor" strategy. Her typical mode of operation was to identify opportunities for a corporation to restructure, invest significantly in the stock of the target firm, and then undertake a process of persuading management and directors to restructure. Now, in June 2002, Dobrynin could look back on the large returns from the use of that strategy.

Chandler noted that Wrigley's market value of common equity was about $13.1 billion. Dobrynin and Chandler discussed the current capital-market conditions and decided to focus on the assumption that Wrigley could borrow $3 billion at a credit rating between BB and B, to yield 13 percent. Chandler agreed to return soon to discuss the results of her research.

The Wm. Wrigley Jr. Company

Wrigley was the world's largest manufacturer and distributor of chewing gum. The firm's industry, branded consumer foods and candy, was intensely competitive and was dominated by a few large players. **Exhibit 1** gives product profiles of Wrigley and its peers. Over the preceding two years, revenues had grown at an annual compound rate of 10 percent (earnings at 9 percent), reflecting the introduction of new products and foreign expansion (**Exhibit 2**). Historically, the firm had been conservatively financed. At the end of 2001, it had total assets of $1.76 billion and no debt (**Exhibit 3**). As **Exhibit 4** shows, Wrigley's stock price had significantly outperformed the S&P 500 Composite Index, and was running slightly ahead of its industry index.

Estimating the Effect of a Leveraged Recapitalization

Under the proposed leveraged recapitalization, Wrigley would borrow $3 billion and use it either to pay an equivalent dividend or to repurchase an equivalent value of shares. Chandler knew that this combination of actions could affect the firm's share value, cost of capital, debt coverage, earnings per share, and voting control. Accordingly, she sought to evaluate the effect of the recapitalization on those areas. She gathered financial data on Wrigley and its peer companies (**Exhibit 5**).

Impact on Share Value

Chandler recalled that the effect of leverage on a firm could be modeled by using the adjusted present-value formula, which hypothesized that debt increased the value of a firm by means of shielding cash flows from taxes. Thus, the present value of debt tax shields could be added to the value of the unlevered firm to yield the value of the levered enterprise. The marginal tax rate Chandler proposed to use was 40 percent, reflecting the sum of federal, state, and local taxes.

Impact on Debt Rating

A key assumption in the analysis would be the debt rating for Wrigley, after assuming $3 billion in debt, and whether the firm could cover the resulting interest payments. Dobrynin had suggested that Chandler should assume Wrigley would borrow $3 billion at a rating between BB and B. Was a rating of BB/B likely? In that regard, Chandler gathered information on the average financial ratios associated with different debt-rating categories (**Exhibit 6**). Dobrynin thought that Wrigley's pretax cost of debt would be around 13 percent. Chandler sought to check that assumption against the capital-market information given in **Exhibit 7**.

Impact on Cost of Capital

Chandler knew that the maximum value of the firm was achieved when the weighted average cost of capital (WACC) was minimized. Thus, she intended to estimate what the cost of equity and the WACC might be if Wrigley pursued this capital-structure change. The projected cost of debt would depend on her assessment of Wrigley's debt rating after recapitalization and on current capital-market rates (summarized in **Exhibit 7**).

The cost of equity (K_E) could be estimated by using the capital asset pricing model. **Exhibit 7** gives yields on U.S. Treasury instruments, which afforded possible estimates of the risk-free rate of return. The practice at Aurora Borealis was to use an equity-market risk premium of 7.0 percent. Wrigley's beta would also need to be relevered to reflect the projected recapitalization.

Chandler wondered whether her analysis covered everything. Where, for instance, should she take into account potential costs of bankruptcy and distress or the effects of leverage as a signal about future operations? More leverage would also create certain constraints and incentives for management. Where should those be reflected in her analysis?

Impact on Reported Earnings Per Share

Chandler intended to estimate the expected effect on earnings per share (EPS) that would occur at different levels of operating income (EBIT) with a change in leverage. The beginnings of an EBIT/EPS analysis are presented in **Exhibit 8**.

Impact on Voting Control

The Wm. Wrigley Jr. Company had 232.441 million shares outstanding. A repurchase of shares would alter that amount. The Wrigley family controlled 21 percent of the common shares outstanding and 58 percent of Class B common stock, which had superior voting rights to the common stock.[1] Assuming the Wrigley family did not sell any shares, how would the share-repurchase alternative affect the family's voting-control position in the company?

Conclusion

Although Susan Chandler's analysis followed a familiar path, each company that she had analyzed differed in important respects from previous firms. Blanka Dobrynin paid her to run numbers and, more importantly, to find the differences wherein hidden threats and opportunities lay. Running the numbers was easy for Chandler; drawing profitable insights from them was not.

---

[1] Shares of Class B common stock had 10 votes each; ordinary common shares had one vote each. Class B shares were restricted in their sale or transfer and could be converted into ordinary common shares on a 1:1 basis. Thus, for purposes of computing per-share values, the total number of shares outstanding for Wrigley consisted of the sum of common shares (189.8 million) and Class B shares (42.641 million), a total of 232.441 million shares.

EXHIBIT 1 | Description of Industry Peer Firms

Company	Description
Cadbury Schweppes plc	Cadbury Schweppes plc made and distributed confectionary and beverage products worldwide. Sold 51% stake in Coca-Cola and Schweppes Beverages Ltd. in 1997; beverage brands in 160 international markets in 1999. In 1998, owned 40% of American Bottling. Licensed Cadbury to Hershey in U.S. Acquired Dr. Pepper/7Up in '95; Hawaiian Punch in '99; and Snapple in '00. Segment sales/operating profits in '01: beverages, 43%/61%; confectionary, 57%/39%. Sales by region: U.K., 21%; U.S., 42%; Australia, 10%; other (including Europe), 27%. Had 36,460 employees. Bond rating: BBB/Baa2.
Hershey Foods Corp.	Hershey Foods Corp. was the largest U.S. producer of chocolate and nonchocolate confectionary products (major brands: Hershey's, Reese's, Cadbury, Kit Kat, Sweet Escapes, TasteTations, Jolly Rancher, Good & Plenty, and Milk Duds). Sold majority of pasta operations in 1/99. Acquired Cadbury U.S. in 9/88; Henry Heide in 12/95; and Leaf North America in 12/96. Advertising costs: 4.2% of '01 sales. '01 depreciation rate: 6.6%. Had 14,400 employees; 40,300 shareholders. Hershey Trust Co. owns 11.5% of common stock and 99.6% of Class B. Bond rating: A+/A1.
Kraft Foods Inc.	Kraft Foods Inc. was the largest branded food and beverage company headquartered in the U.S. and second largest worldwide. The company marketed many of the world's leading food brands, including Kraft cheese, Maxwell House coffee, Nabisco cookies and crackers, Philadelphia cream cheese, Oscar Mayer meats, and Post cereals. Its products were sold in more than 145 countries. North American sales accounted for 74% of '01 sales; international, 26%. Acquired Nabisco in 12/00. Had about 14,000 employees. Philip Morris owns 84% of its common stock(3/02 proxy). Bond rating: BBB+/A3.
Tootsie Roll Industries, Inc.	Tootsie Roll Industries, Inc., produced candy. Products included Tootsie Roll, Tootsie Pop, Tootsie Bubble Pop, and Mason Dots. Acquired Brach's Confections' Andes Candies in 5/00; Warner-Lambert's former chocolate/caramel brands (Junior Mints, Sugar Daddy, Charleston Chew, and Pom Poms) in 9/88; Cella Confections in 7/85. Five plants in U.S., one in Mexico. Int'l ops. (Mexico and Canada): 7% of '01 sales. Had about 1,950 employees. M. J. & E. R. Gordon control 74% of voting power. Bond rating: N/A.
The Wm. Wrigley Jr. Company	The Wm. Wrigley Jr. Company was the world's largest manufacturer and seller of chewing gums, specialty gums, and gum base. Principal brands: Doublemint, Spearmint, Juicy Fruit, Big Red, WinterFresh, Extra, Orbit, Freedent. Amurol Products subsidiary made novelty gums, including Bubble Tape, Big League Chew; markets Hubba Bubba bubble gum. Foreign sales: 58% of 2001 total, 58% of pretax profit. Had 10,800 employees; 38,701 common shareholders. William Wrigley Jr. owned 21% of common stock and 58% of Class B. Bond rating: N/A.

Sources of information: *Value Line Investment Survey;* Bloomberg LP.

402

EXHIBIT 2 | Income Statements for the Wm. Wrigley Jr. Company

(in thousands, except per-share amounts)	Year Ended December 31		
	2001	**2000**	**1999**
Earnings			
Net sales	**$ 2,429,646**	$ 2,145,706	$ 2,061,602
Cost of sales	**997,054**	904,266	904,183
Gross profit	**1,432,592**	1,241,440	1,157,419
Selling, general and administrative expenses	**919,236**	778,197	721,813
Operating income	**513,356**	463,243	435,606
Investment income	**18,553**	19,185	17,636
Other expense	**(4,543)**	(3,116)	(8,812)
Earnings before income taxes	**527,366**	479,312	444,430
Income taxes	**164,380**	150,370	136,247
Net earnings	**$ 362,986**	$ 328,942	$ 308,183
Per-Share Amounts			
Net earnings per share of common stock	**$ 1.61**	$ 1.45	$ 1.33
Dividends paid per share of common stock	**$ 0.745**	$ 0.70	$ 0.66

Source of data: Company regulatory filings.

EXHIBIT 3 | Consolidated Balance Sheets for the Wm. Wrigley Jr. Company

(in thousands of dollars)	2001	2000
ASSETS		
Current assets:		
Cash and equivalents	$ 307,785	$ 300,599
Short-term investments, at amortized cost	25,450	29,301
Accounts receivable	239,885	191,570
Inventories		
Finished goods	75,693	64,676
Raw materials and supplies	203,288	188,615
	278,981	253,291
Other current assets	46,896	39,728
Deferred income taxes - current	14,846	14,226
Total current assets	913,843	828,715
Marketable equity securities, at fair value	25,300	28,535
Deferred charges and other assets	115,745	83,713
Deferred income taxes - noncurrent	26,381	26,743
Property, plant, and equipment (at cost)		
Land	39,933	39,125
Buildings and building equipment	359,109	344,457
Machinery and equipment	857,044	756,050
	1,256,086	1,139,632
Less accumulated depreciation	571,717	532,598
Net property, plant and equipment	684,379	607,034
TOTAL ASSETS	$1,765,648	$1,574,740
LIABILITIES AND STOCKHOLDERS' EQUITY		
Current liabilities:		
Accounts payable	$ 91,225	$ 73,129
Accrued expenses	128,406	113,779
Dividends payable	42,711	39,467
Income and other taxes payable	68,437	60,976
Deferred income taxes - current	1,455	859
Total current liabilities	332,234	288,210
Deferred income taxes - noncurrent	43,206	40,144
Other non-current liabilities	113,921	113,489
Common stock	12,646	12,558
Class B convertible stock	2,850	2,938
Additional paid-in capital	1,153	346
Retained earnings	1,684,337	1,492,547
Treasury stock	(289,799)	(256,478)
Accumulated other comprehensive income	(134,900)	(119,014)
Total stockholders' equity	1,276,287	1,132,897
TOTAL LIABILITIES AND STOCKHOLDERS' EQUITY	$1,765,648	$1,574,740

Source of data: Company regulatory filings.

EXHIBIT 4 | Stock-Price Performance of the Wm. Wrigley Jr. Company (value of $1,000 investment: June 1, 2000, to June 7, 2002)

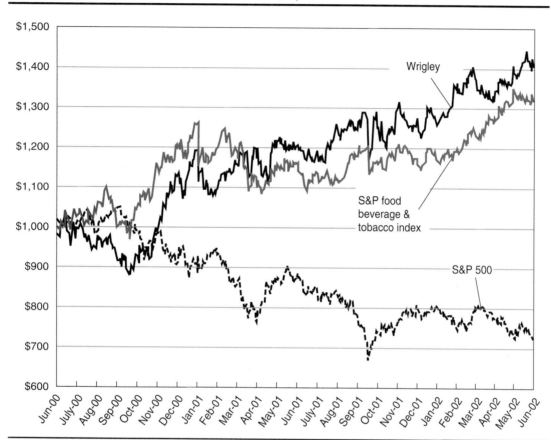

Source of data: Datastream, with casewriter's analysis.

EXHIBIT 5 | Financial Characteristics of Major Confectionary Firms

Company Name	Recent Price	Common Shares Outstanding (millions)	Market Value of Equity (millions)	Book Value of Equity (millions)	Total LT Debt (millions)	LT Debt/ (LT Debt + Book Value of Equity)	LT Debt/ (LT Debt + Mkt Value of Equity)	LT Debt/Book Value of Equity	LT Debt/ Mkt Value of Equity
Cadbury Schweppes plc	$ 26.66	502.50	$ 13,397	$ 5,264	$ 2,264	30.07%	14.46%	43.01%	16.90%
Hershey Foods Corp.	$ 65.45	136.63	$ 8,942	$ 2,785	$ 869	23.77%	8.85%	31.18%	9.71%
Kraft Foods	$ 38.82	1,735.00	$ 67,353	$ 39,920	$ 8,548	17.64%	11.26%	21.41%	12.69%
Tootise Roll Industries Inc.	$ 31.17	51.66	$ 1,610	$ 509	$ 8	1.45%	0.46%	1.47%	0.47%
Wm. Wrigley Jr. Co.	$ 56.37	232.44	$ 13,103	$ 1,276	—	0.00%	0.00%	0.00%	0.00%
S&P 500 Composite	$ 1,148.08					18.23%	8.76%	24.27%	9.94%

Company Name	Beta	EPS	Price/ Earnings	Cash Dividend	Dividend Payout	Dividend Yield	Interest Coverage Before Tax	Compound Growth of EPS Past 5 Yrs	Firm Value/ EBITDA
Cadbury Schweppes plc	0.60	1.39	15.20	$ 0.67	44.0%	2.50%	4.6x	6.50%	10.3
Hershey Foods Corp.	0.60	2.74	20.40	$ 1.16	41.0%	2.00%	11.1x	6.50%	11.4
Kraft Foods	nmf	1.17	18.70	$ 0.26	12.0%	1.50%	3.4x	nmf	10.1
Tootise Roll Industries Inc.	0.65	1.30	24.00	$ 0.28	22.0%	0.90%	nmf	12.50%	14.6
Wm. Wrigley Jr. Co.	0.75	1.61	29.30	$ 0.75	46.0%	1.50%	nmf	9.00%	22.6
S&P 500 Composite	1.00	18.78	40.55					-49.57%	

nmf = not a meaningful figure.

Source of data: *Value Line Investment Survey.*

EXHIBIT 6 | Key Industrial Financial Ratios by Credit Rating

	Investment Grade				Non-Investment Grade	
	AAA	AA	A	BBB	BB	B
EBIT interest coverage (x)	23.4	13.3	6.3	3.9	2.2	1.0
Funds from operations/total debt (%)	214.2	65.7	42.2	30.6	19.7	10.4
Free operating cash flow/total debt (%)	156.6	33.6	22.3	12.8	7.3	1.5
Return on capital (%)	35.0	26.6	18.1	13.1	11.5	8.0
Operating income/sales (%)	23.4	24.0	18.1	15.5	15.4	14.7
Long-term debt/capital (%)	(1.1)	21.1	33.8	40.3	53.6	72.6
Total debt/capital, incl. short-term debt (%)	5.0	35.9	42.6	47.0	57.7	75.1

Source of data: Standard & Poor's *CreditStats*, September 8, 2003.

Definitions:

EBIT interest coverage divides earnings before interest and taxes (EBIT) by gross interest expense (before subtracting capitalized interest and interest income).

FFO/total debt divides funds from operations (FFO) by total debt. FFO is defined as net income from continuing operations, depreciation and amortization, deferred income taxes, and other noncash items/Long-term debt + current maturities + commercial paper, and other short-term borrowings.

Free operating cash flow/total debt. Free operating cash flow is defined as FFO − capital expenditures − (+) increase (decrease) in working capital (excluding changes in cash, marketable securities, and short-term debt)/Long-term debt+ current maturities, commercial paper, and other short-term borrowings.

Total debt/EBITDA. Long-term debt + current maturities, commercial paper, and other short-term borrowing/Adjusted earnings from continuing operations before interest, taxes, and depreciation and amortization.

Return on capital. EBIT/Average of beginning of year and end of year capital, including short-term debt, current maturities, long-term debt, noncurrent deferred taxes, minority interest, and equity (common and preferred stock).

Total debt/capital. Long-term debt + current maturities, commercial paper, and other short-term borrowings/Long-term debt + current maturities, commercial paper, and other short-term borrowings + shareholders' equity (including preferred stock) + minority interest.

Source of data: Standard & Poor's *Corporate Ratings Criteria* (New York: Standard & Poor's, 2005), 42.

EXHIBIT 7 | Capital-Market Conditions as of June 7, 2002

U.S. Treasury Obligations	Yield
3 mos.	1.670%
6 mos.	1.710%
1 yr.	2.310%
2 yr.	3.160%
3 yr.	3.660%
5 yr.	4.090%
7 yr.	4.520%
10 yr.	4.860%
20 yr.	5.650%

Other Instruments	Yield
U.S. Federal Reserve Bank discount rate	1.730%
LIBOR (1 month)	1.840%
Certificates of deposit (6 month)	1.980%
Prime interest rates	4.750%

Corporate Debt Obligations (10 year)	Yield
AAA	9.307%
AA	9.786%
A	10.083%
BBB	10.894%
BB	12.753%
B	14.663%

U.S. Treasury Yield Curve

June 7, 2002

Source of data: Bloomberg LP; Federal Reserve Bank Reports.

EXHIBIT 8 | EPS versus EBIT Analysis

Assumptions

Before recapitalization

Interest rate on debt _____

Pre-recap debt _____

Tax rate _____

Before recapitalization

	Worst case	Most likely	Best case
Operating income (EBIT)			
Interest expense			
Taxable income			
Taxes			
Net income			
Shares outstanding			
Earnings per share			

Assumptions

After recapitalization

Interest rate on debt _____

Pre-recap debt _____

Tax rate _____

After recapitalization

	Worst case	Most likely	Best case
Operating income (EBIT)			
Interest expense			
Taxable income			
Taxes			
Net income			
Shares outstanding			
Earnings per share			

Deluxe Corporation

In the late summer of 2002, Rajat Singh, a managing director at Hudson Bancorp, was reflecting on the financial policies of Deluxe Corporation, the largest printer of paper checks in the United States. Earlier in the year, Deluxe had retired all of its long-term debt, and the company had not had a major bond issue in more than 10 years. Simultaneously, the company had been pursuing an aggressive program of share repurchases, the latest of which was nearly complete. So far, those actions had proven successful; investors had responded well to the share repurchases, and the company's stock was at its highest level in nearly 10 years. But Singh, who had been retained by Deluxe's board of directors to provide guidance on the company's financial strategy, saw dangers looming for Deluxe that would require the company's managers to do more.

Deluxe Corporation was the dominant player in the highly concentrated and competitive check-printing industry. Deluxe's sales and earnings growth, however, had been in a slow decline as the company struggled to fight a relentless wave of technological change. Since the advent of on-line payment methods and the rising popularity of credit and debit cards, consumers' usage of paper checks had fallen steadily. In response, Deluxe's chair and chief executive officer (CEO), Lawrence J. Mosner, had led a major restructuring of the firm whereby he rationalized its operations, reduced its labor force, and divested several noncore businesses. Singh sensed that those measures would only carry the company so far and that the board was looking for other alternatives.

Singh surmised that there would eventually be a tipping point at which the demand for paper checks would fall precipitously. In this challenging operating environment, Singh was convinced that Deluxe would need continued financial flexibility to fend off the eventual disintegration of its core business. Singh had already told the board that the company had probably gone as far as it could with share repurchases, and the time for a new round of debt financing was at hand. The board had asked Singh for a detailed plan in five days, and had insisted that, as part of the plan, he undertake a complete assessment of the firm's overall debt policy, focusing primarily on the appropriate mix of debt and equity. In the not-too-distant future, Deluxe's financial and strategic choices would be severely constrained, and Singh believed it was essential that the company's financial policies afford it the necessary funding and flexibility to steer a path to survivability.

Modest Beginnings

Deluxe Corporation was founded in 1915 by a chicken-farmer-turned-printer in a one-room print shop in St. Paul, Minnesota. Then known as Deluxe Check Printers, the company was a pioneer in the emerging check-printing business, and specialized in imprinting personalized information on checks and checkbooks. Deluxe became a publicly traded company in 1965, and traded on the New York Stock Exchange in 1980 under the name Deluxe Corporation. The company was the largest provider of checks in the United States, serving customers through more than 10,000 financial institutions. Deluxe processed more than 100 million check orders each year—nearly half of the U.S. market. American consumers wrote more than 42 billion checks annually, although check usage had declined in recent years.

Between 1975 and 1995, the peak years of check usage in the United States, Deluxe Corporation's revenues grew at a compound annual rate of 12 percent. This rate, however, had declined over the past decade as checks lost share to the electronic forms of payment, such as ATMs, credit cards, debit cards, and Internet bill-paying systems. As those new forms of payment created a highly fragmented payment industry, check printing itself remained highly concentrated, with only a few firms controlling 90 percent of the market. Deluxe competed primarily with two other companies, John Harland and Clarke American, a subsidiary of U.K.-based Novar **(Figure 1).** With a proliferation of alternative payment systems, the check-printing business faced an annual decline of 1 percent–3 percent in check demand, a trend that most industry analysts expected to continue.

FIGURE 1 | U.S. Check-Printing Market Share

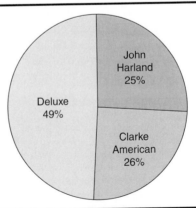

Source of data: D.A. Davidson & Co.

Recent Financial Performance

With the prospect of a precipitous decline in demand for paper checks emerging in the late 1990s, Deluxe undertook a major reorganization during which it divested non-strategic businesses and dramatically reduced the number of its employees and facilities. The company went from 62 printing plants to 13, reduced its labor force from 15,000 to 7,000, outsourced information technology functions, improved manufacturing efficiencies, and divested nearly 20 separate businesses. The resulting reductions in operating expenses helped reverse Deluxe's earnings slump in 1998, despite the continued softening in revenue growth.

In 2000, Deluxe announced a major strategic shift with the spinoff of its technology-related subsidiaries, eFunds and iDLX Technology Partners, in an initial public offering. The subsidiary eFunds provided electronic-payment products and services (e.g., electronic transaction processing, electronic funds transfer, and payment protection services) to the financial and retail industries; iDLX offered technology-related consulting services to financial services companies. Deluxe's CEO, Mosner, believed that Deluxe offered more value to shareholders as a pure-play company. While he admitted that the eventual demise of the paper-check business was a certainty, he insisted that there were still growth opportunities for the company:

> We don't want to abandon the core business too soon. Instead, you mine all you can out of the core business before [moving on]. We have a very good business, a very solid business with high levels of profitability. We feel we can generate revenues and profits on our core business not only today but over the next five years.[1]

With the spinoff of eFunds and iDLX, management abandoned its plan for Deluxe to offer products and services targeting the electronic-transfer market and refocused on its core business. Repositioning the firm as a pure-play check-printing company made sense to investors, and the company's stock price rose on the news.

Following the spinoff, Mosner reorganized Deluxe's remaining paper-payments segment around three primary business units. Financial Services sold checks to consumers through financial institutions, with institutional clients typically entering into three-to-five-year supplier contracts. Direct Checks sold to consumers through direct mail and the Internet. The Business Services segment sold checks, forms, and related products through financial institutions and directly to small businesses, targeting firms with no more than 20 employees. See **Figure 2** for data on Deluxe's 2001 sales by segment.

According to some analysts, the Business Services segment ultimately held the most promise for Deluxe because it could allow the company to bundle or cross-sell a variety of products and services to the growing small-business sector. Rather than simply grow its number of individual customers, as it had done in the past with its check business, Business Services could generate growth in the number of products

---

[1]Dee DePass, "Cashing Out: Even Deluxe Corp. Admits That Paper Checks Are Headed for the Dust Heap of History," *Star-Tribune Newspapers of the Twin Cities*, 17 January 2002.

FIGURE 2 | Deluxe Corp. Sales by Segment, 2001

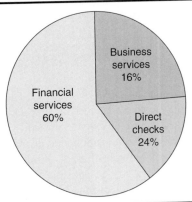

Source of data: Company reports.

or services it sold *per* customer. Furthermore, there were several regional companies active in this sector that had the potential to be strategic partners for Deluxe.

By year-end 2001, the market had responded favorably to the spinoff and restructuring efforts—the firm's share price had grown by more than 65 percent over the year, outperforming the S&P 500 Index, which had fallen nearly 20 percent. Over the preceding decade, however, the firm's share price growth had lagged the broad market indexes. **Exhibit 1** gives a 10-year summary of the financial characteristics of the firm, including share prices and data on comparable market performance. From 1998 to 2001, Deluxe Corporation's compound annual rate of sales growth was −4.0 percent, which reflected the growing maturity of the market for paper checks in the United States. Consistent with the perceived maturity of the market segment, Deluxe's 2001 price earnings ratio (P/E) of 11.0× hovered well below the broader market's P/E of 29.5×.

Concerns about revenue growth and declining demand for printed checks were echoed in the comments of analysts who followed the firm. Despite a positive assessment of the firm's recent ability to improve margins, one analyst covering Deluxe was guarded:

> [W]e remain cautious concerning Deluxe's long-term prospects for earnings growth, until the company can improve profitability in its core [Financial Services] check printing segment. At present, this seems like a tough proposition, given a relatively mature market, intense price competition, the growth in electronic payments, and consolidation in the banking sector.[2]

Rajat Singh knew that Deluxe's board members had many of the same concerns, but also knew that they believed the analyst community had taken a shortsighted view of the company's potential. In fact, Deluxe's most recent annual report stated, "While

---

[2]David Gallen, *Value Line Investment Survey*, 24 May 2002.

the check printing industry is mature, our existing leadership position in the market place contributes to our financial strength."[3] The U.S. Federal Reserve Board's 2001 *Bank Payment Study* indicated that checks still remained consumers' most preferred method of noncash payment, representing 60 percent of all retail noncash payments. The company's management believed that it was well positioned to extract value from this business and to explore noncheck offerings that would closely leverage Deluxe's core competencies. **Exhibits 2** and **3** give the latest years' income statements and balance sheets for Deluxe Corporation.

Current and Future Financing

Against this backdrop, Singh assessed the current and future financing requirements of the firm. From time to time, Deluxe required additional financing for such general corporate purposes as working capital, capital asset purchases, possible acquisitions, repayment of outstanding debts, dividend payments, and repurchasing the firm's securities. To meet those short-term financing needs, Deluxe could draw upon the following debt instruments:

- **Commercial paper:**[4] Deluxe maintained a $300-million commercial-paper program, which carried a credit rating of A1/P1. "The risk of a downgrade of Deluxe's short-term credit rating is low," Singh thought. "If for any reason, they were unable to access the commercial paper markets, they would rely on their line of credit for liquidity." Deluxe had $150 million in commercial paper outstanding, at a weighted-average interest rate of 1.85 percent.

- **Line of credit:** Deluxe also had $350 million available under a committed line of credit, which would expire in August 2002, and $50 million under an uncommitted line of credit. During 2001, the company drew no amounts on its committed line of credit. The average amount drawn on the uncommitted line during 2001 was $1.3 million, at a weighted-average interest rate of 4.26 percent. At year-end, no amount was outstanding on this line of credit.

- **Medium-term notes**: Deluxe had a shelf registration[5] for the issuance of up to $300 million in medium-term notes. No such notes had been issued or were outstanding.

In February 2001, Deluxe paid off $100 million of its 8.55 percent long-term unsecured and unsubordinated notes, which it had issued in 1991.

---

[3]Deluxe Corporation Annual Report (2001), 25–26.

[4]Commercial paper was an unsecured, short-term obligation issued by a corporation, typically for financing accounts receivable and inventories. It was usually issued at a discount reflecting prevailing market interest rates, and its maturity ranged from 2 to 270 days.

[5]Shelf registration was a term used to describe the U.S. Securities and Exchange Commission's rule that gave a corporation the ability to comply with registration requirements up to two years before a public offering for a security. With a registration on the shelf, the company could quickly go to market with its offering when conditions became more favorable.

In January 2001, the company's board of directors approved a stock-repurchase program, which authorized the repurchase of up to 14 million shares of Deluxe common stock, or about 19 percent of total shares outstanding. By year-end, the company had spent about $350 million to repurchase 11.3 million shares. This program followed a share-repurchase program initiated in 1999, which called for the repurchase of 10 million shares, or about 12.5 percent of the firm's shares outstanding at the time. Deluxe funded these repurchases with cash from operations and from issuances of commercial paper. **Exhibit 1** summarizes the firm's share repurchase activity in recent years. Singh believed the board would continue to pursue an aggressive program of share repurchases.

In addition to possible buybacks and strategic acquisitions, Singh reviewed other possible demands on the firm's resources. He believed that cash dividends would be held constant for the foreseeable future. He also believed that capital expenditures would be about equal to depreciation for the next few years. Although sales might grow, working capital turns should decline, resulting in a reduction in net working capital in the first year, followed by increases later on. Both of those effects reflected the tight asset management under the new CEO. **Exhibit 4** gives a five-year forecast of Deluxe's income statement and balance sheet. This forecast was consistent with the lower end of analysts' projections for revenue growth and realization of the benefits of Deluxe's recent restructuring. The forecast assumed that the existing debt would be refinanced with similar debt, but did not assume major share repurchases. The forecast would need to be revised to reflect the impact of any recommended changes in financial policy.

Considerations in Assessing Financial Policy

In addition to assessing Deluxe's internal financing requirements, Singh recognized that his policy recommendations would play an important role in shaping the perceptions of the firm by bond-rating agencies and investors.

Bond rating[6]

Deluxe's senior debt, which had matured in February 2001, had been rated A+ by Standard & Poor's and A1 by Moody's. (**Exhibit 5** presents the bond-rating definitions for this and other rating categories.) A+/A1 were investment-grade ratings, as were the next lower rating grades, BBB/Baa. Below that, however, were noninvestment-grade ratings (BB/Ba), which were often referred to as high yield or junk debt. Some large institutional investors (for example, pension funds and charitable trusts) were barred from investing in noninvestment-grade debt, and many individual investors shunned it as well. For that reason, the yields on noninvestment-grade debt over U.S. Treasury securities (i.e., spreads) were typically considerably higher than the spreads for investment-grade issues. For pertinent data on the rating categories, see **Figures 3** and **4.**

---

[6]A firm's bond rating, which was based on an analysis of the issuer's financial condition and profitability, reflected the probability of defaulting on the issue. The convention in finance was that the firm's bond rating referred to the rating on the firm's *senior* debt, with the understanding that any subordinated debt issued by the firm would ordinarily have a lower bond rating. For instance, Deluxe's senior debt had the split BBB/Baa3 rating, while its subordinated convertible bonds were rated BB/Ba. Standard & Poor's, Moody's Investors Service, and Fitch Investors Service were bond-rating services.

FIGURE 3 | Default Rates by Rating Category, 2001

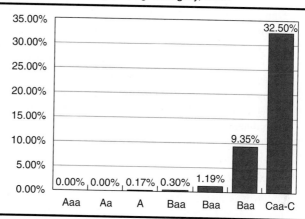

Source of data: Moody's Investors Service, February 2002.

The ability to issue noninvestment-grade debt depended, to a much greater degree than did investment-grade debt, on the strength of the economy and on favorable credit market conditions. On that issue, Rajat Singh said:

> You don't pay much of a penalty in yield as you go from A to BBB. There's a range over which the risk you take for more leverage is de minimus. But you pay a big penalty as you go from BBB to BB. The penalty is not only in the form of higher costs, but also in the form of possible damage to the Deluxe brand. We don't want the brand to be sullied by an association with junk debt.

FIGURE 4 | Number of New Issues by Rating Category, 2005

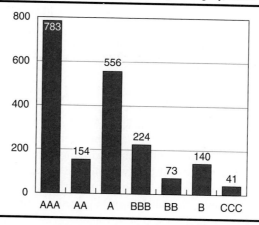

Source of data: Standard & Poor's *RatingsDirect*.

For those reasons, Singh sought to preserve an investment-grade rating for Deluxe. But where in the investment-grade range should Deluxe be positioned? **Exhibit 6** gives the financial ratios associated with the various rating categories.

While the rating agencies looked closely at a number of indicators of credit quality, Deluxe's managers paid particular attention to the ratio of earnings before interest and taxes (EBIT) to interest expense. **Exhibit 7** illustrates Deluxe's EBIT-coverage ratios for the past 10 years. Singh's recommendations for the company would require the selection of an appropriate target bond rating. Thereafter, Singh would have to recommend to the board the minimum and maximum amounts of debt that Deluxe could carry to achieve the desired rating.

Flexibility

Singh was aware that choosing a target debt level based on an analysis of industry peers might not fully capture the flexibility that Deluxe would need to meet its own possible future adversities. Singh said:

> Flexibility is how much debt you can issue before you lose the investment-grade bond rating. I want flexibility, and yet I want to take advantage of the fact that, with more debt, you have lower cost of capital. I am very comfortable with Deluxe's strategy and internal financial forecasts for its business; if anything, I believe the forecasts probably underestimate, rather than overestimate, its cash flows. But let's suppose that a two-sigma adverse outcome would be an EBIT close to $200 million—I can't imagine in the worst of times an EBIT less than that.

Accordingly, Singh's final decision on the target bond rating would have to be one that maintained reasonable reserves against Deluxe's worst-case scenario.

Cost of Capital

Consistent with management's emphasis on value creation, Singh believed that choosing a financial policy that minimized the cost of capital was important. He understood that exploitation of debt tax shields could create value for shareholders—up to a reasonable limit, but beyond that limit, the costs of financial distress would become material and would cause the cost of capital to rise. Singh relied on Hudson Bancorp's estimates of the pretax cost of debt and cost of equity by rating category (see **Exhibit 8**).

The cost of debt was estimated by averaging the current yield-to-maturity of bonds within each rating category. The cost of equity (K_e) was estimated by using the capital asset pricing model (CAPM). The cost of equity was computed for each firm by using its beta and other capital market data. The individual estimates of K_e were then averaged within each bond-rating category. Singh reflected on the relatively flat trend in the cost of equity within the investment-grade range, and he understood that changes in leverage within the investment-grade range were not regarded as material to investors. Nonetheless, it remained for Singh to determine which rating category provided the lowest cost of capital.

Current Capital-Market Conditions

Any policy recommendations would need to acknowledge the feasibility of implementing those policies today as well as in the future. **Exhibit 9** presents information about current yields in the U.S. debt markets. The current situation in the debt markets was favorable as the U.S. economy continued its expansion. The equity markets seemed to be pausing after a phenomenal advance in prices. The outlook for interest rates was stable, although any sign of inflation might cause the Federal Reserve to lift interest rates. Major changes in taxes and regulations were in abeyance, at least until the outcome of the next round of presidential elections.

Conclusion

Rajat Singh leafed through the analyses and financial data he had gathered for his presentation to Deluxe Corporation's board of directors. Foremost in his mind were the words of the company's chief financial officer, Douglas Treff, who had said to a group of securities analysts barely a week earlier:

> Let me anticipate a question which many of you are pondering. What now? Our board of directors and the management team are committed to maximizing shareholder value. Our past actions have demonstrated that commitment. We have spun off a business, eFunds, at the end of 2000, to unleash the value of two different types of companies. Over the past 18 months, we have returned more than $600 million to shareholders through cash dividends and share repurchases. Therefore, be assured that we are evaluating options that will continue to create value for our fellow shareholders.[7]

Clearly, Singh's plan would have to afford Deluxe low costs and continued access to capital under a variety of operating scenarios in order for the firm to pursue whatever options it was considering. This would require him to test the possible effects of downside scenarios on the company's coverage and capitalization ratios under alternative debt policies. He reflected on the competing goals of value creation, flexibility, and bond rating. He aimed to recommend a financial policy that would balance those goals and provide guidance to the board of directors and the financial staff regarding the firm's target mix of capital. With so many competing factors to weigh, Singh believed that it was unlikely that his plan would be perfect. But then he remembered one of his mentor's favorite sayings: "If you wait until you have a 99 percent solution, you'll never act; go with an 80 percent solution."

---

[7]Fair Disclosure Financial Network, transcript of Earnings Release Conference Call, 18 July 2002.

EXHIBIT 1 | Deluxe Corporation's 10-Year Financial Summary (in millions of U.S. dollars except per-share values)

		At Fiscal Years Ended December 31								
	1992	1993	1994	1995	1996	1997	1998	1999	2000	2001
Selected Income Statement Information										
Net sales	$1,534.4	$1,581.8	$1,747.9	$1,858.0	$1,895.7	$1,919.4	$1,931.8	$1,650.5	$1,262.7	$1,278.4
Operating expenses	$ 722.2	$ 739.5	$ 797.3	$ 819.4	$ 862.4	$ 806.7	$ 805.9	$ 688.9	$ 417.9	$ 421.1
Profit from operations	$ 812.2	$ 842.3	$ 950.6	$1,038.6	$1,033.3	$1,112.7	$1,125.9	$ 961.6	$ 844.8	$ 857.2
Interest expense	$ 15.4	$ 10.3	$ 11.3	$ 14.7	$ 12.0	$ 9.7	$ 9.7	$ 9.5	$ 10.8	$ 5.6
Net earnings	$ 202.8	$ 141.9	$ 140.9	$ 87.0	$ 65.5	$ 44.7	$ 143.1	$ 203.0	$ 161.9	$ 185.9
Common shares, end of year (000s)	83,797	82,549	82,375	82,364	82,056	81,326	80,481	72,020	72,555	64,102
Common shares repurchased (000s)	(2,197)	(1,341)	(1,191)	(1,414)	(1,715)	(1,833)	(9,573)	(48)	(11,332)	(3,898)
Common shares issued (000s)	949	1,167	1,181	1,106	985	988	1,112	583	2,890	1,255
Earnings per share[1]	$ 2.42	$ 2.09	$ 1.71	$ 1.15	$ 1.65	$ 2.15	$ 2.34	$ 2.64	$ 2.34	$ 2.70
Dividend per share	$ 1.34	$ 1.42	$ 1.46	$ 1.48	$ 1.48	$ 1.48	$ 1.48	$ 1.48	$ 1.48	$ 1.48
Selected Balance Sheet Information										
Working capital	$ 330.9	$ 386.9	$ 224.5	$ 130.4	$ 12.3	$ 108.1	$ 131.0	$ 167.8	$ 14.0	$ 116.6
Net property, plant, & equipment	$ 389.0	$ 401.6	$ 461.8	$ 494.2	$ 446.9	$ 415.0	$ 340.1	$ 294.8	$ 174.0	$ 149.6
Total assets	$1,199.6	$1,252.0	$1,256.3	$1,295.1	$1,176.4	$1,148.4	$1,171.5	$ 992.6	$ 649.5	$ 537.7
Long-term debt	$ 115.5	$ 110.8	$ 110.9	$ 111.0	$ 108.9	$ 110.0	$ 106.3	$ 115.5	$ 10.2	$ 10.1
Common stockholders' equity	$ 829.8	$ 801.2	$ 814.4	$ 780.4	$ 712.9	$ 610.2	$ 606.6	$ 417.3	$ 262.8	$ 78.6
Book value: LT debt/capital	12.2%	12.1%	12.0%	12.5%	13.3%	15.3%	14.9%	21.7%	3.7%	11.4%
Market value: LT debt/capital	2.9%	3.6%	4.9%	4.4%	3.9%	3.8%	3.5%	5.5%	0.6%	0.4%
Selected Valuation Information (year-end)										
Deluxe Corp. stock price	$ 46.75	$ 36.25	$ 26.38	$ 29.00	$ 32.75	$ 34.50	$ 36.56	$ 27.44	$ 25.27	$ 41.58
S&P 500 Composite Index	418.17	464.30	462.62	576.70	700.92	941.64	1,072.32	1,281.91	1,364.44	1,104.61
Deluxe Corp. average P/E[2]	17.60x	19.00x	17.40x	25.90x	20.60x	15.40x	14.30x	12.70x	10.20x	11.01x
S&P 500 Composite average P/E[2]	24.38x	24.11x	18.36x	16.92x	20.26x	23.88x	27.45x	31.43x	26.29x	29.50x
Deluxe Corp. market/book ratio	4.72x	3.73x	2.67x	3.06x	3.77x	4.60x	4.85x	4.74x	6.98x	33.91x
Deluxe Corp. beta	1.00	1.00	1.00	0.95	0.90	0.95	0.85	0.90	0.90	0.85
Yield on 20-year T-bonds	7.67%	6.48%	8.02%	6.01%	6.73%	6.02%	5.39%	6.83%	5.59%	5.74%
Yield on 90-day T-bills	3.08%	3.01%	5.53%	4.96%	5.07%	5.22%	4.37%	5.17%	5.73%	1.71%
Total annual ret. on large co. stocks	7.67%	9.99%	1.31%	37.43%	23.07%	33.36%	28.58%	21.04%	−9.11%	−11.88%

[1] Primary earnings though 1997, then diluted.

[2] P/E ratios are computed on earnings before restructuring charges, litigation award, and other extraordinary items.

Sources of data: Standard & Poor's *Research Insight; Value Line Investment Survey;* Datastream Advance; Ibbotson Associates, Stocks, *Bonds Bills & Inflation Yearbook 2002.*

EXHIBIT 2 | Deluxe Corporation's Consolidated Statements of Income
(in millions of U.S. dollars)

	Years Ended December 31	
	2001	**2000**
Revenue	$1,278.4	$1,262.7
Cost of goods sold	453.8	453.0
Selling, general, and admin. expense	514.4	518.2
Goodwill amortization expense	6.2	5.2
Asset impairment and disposition losses	2.1	7.3
Total costs	976.4	983.8
Profit/(loss) from operations	302.0	278.9
Interest income	2.4	4.8
Other income	(1.2)	1.2
Interest expense	(5.6)	(11.4)
Earnings/(loss) before taxes	297.6	273.4
Tax expense	111.6	104.0
Discontinued operations income/(loss)		(7.5)
Net earnings/(loss)	$ 185.9	$ 161.9

Source of data: Company regulatory filings.

EXHIBIT 3 | Deluxe Corporation's Consolidated Balance Sheets (in millions of U.S. dollars)

	2001	2000
Assets		
Current assets		
Cash and cash equivalents	$ 9.6	$ 80.7
Marketable securities	—	18.5
Trade accounts receivable – net	37.7	46.0
Inventories	11.2	11.3
Supplies	11.1	11.8
Deferred income taxes	4.6	7.4
Prepaid expenses and other	9.9	12.0
Total current assets	84.0	187.8
Long-term investments	37.7	35.6
Property, plant, and equipment – net	151.1	174.0
Intangibles – net	115.0	134.5
Goodwill–net	82.2	88.4
Other noncurrent assets	67.9	36.2
Total assets	$537.8	$656.4
Liabilities and Stockholders' Equity		
Current liabilities		
Accounts payable	$ 52.8	$ 44.7
Accrued liabilities	162.9	148.5
Short-term debt	150.0	—
Long-term debt due within one year	1.4	100.7
Total current liabilities	367.1	293.9
Long-term debt	10.1	10.2
Deferred income taxes	44.9	51.1
Other long-term liabilities	37.0	38.3
Total liabilities	459.1	393.5
Common stockholders' equity		
Common shares	64.1	72.6
Additional paid-in capital	—	44.2
Retained earnings	14.6	146.2
Unearned compensation	0.1	0.1
Accum. other comprehensive income	—	(0.2)
Total common stockholders' equity	78.7	262.9
Total liabilities and stockholders' equity	$537.8	$656.4

Source of data: Company regulatory filings.

EXHIBIT 4 | Deluxe Corporation's Financial Forecast, 2002–06 (in millions of U.S. dollars)

	Actual	Projected				
	2001	2002	2003	2004	2005	2006
Annual increase in sales	1.2%	1.4%	1.6%	2.0%	2.2%	2.4%
Operating profit/sales	23.6%	26.6%	26.7%	26.7%	26.7%	26.7%
Tax rate	37.0%	38.0%				
Working capital/sales	9.1%	9.1%				
Dividend payout ratio		52.0%				
Income Statement						
Net sales	$1,278.4	$1,296.3	$1,317.0	$1,343.4	$1,372.9	$1,405.9
Operating profit	302.0	344.8	351.6	358.7	366.6	375.4
Interest expense, net	3.2	4.0	4.0	4.0	4.0	4.0
Pretax income	298.8	340.8	347.6	354.7	362.6	371.4
Tax expense	111.6	129.5	132.1	134.8	137.8	141.1
Net income	187.1	211.3	215.5	219.9	224.8	230.3
Dividends	94.9	94.9	94.9	94.9	94.9	94.9
Retentions to earnings	$ 92.2	$ 116.4	$ 120.7	$ 125.0	$ 129.9	$ 135.4
Balance Sheet						
Cash	$ 9.6	$ 124.3	$ 243.1	$ 365.8	$ 493.0	$ 625.4
Working capital (without debt)	116.6	118.2	120.1	122.5	125.2	128.2
Net fixed assets	151.1	151.1	151.1	151.1	151.1	151.1
Total assets	277.2	393.6	514.3	639.3	769.3	904.6
Debt (long- and short-term)	161.5	161.5	161.5	161.5	161.5	161.5
Other long-term liabilities	37.0	37.0	37.0	37.0	37.0	37.0
Equity	78.7	195.2	315.8	440.9	570.8	706.2
Total capital	$ 277.2	$ 393.6	$ 514.3	$ 639.3	$ 769.3	$ 904.6
Free Cash Flows						
EBIT		$ 344.8	$ 351.6	$ 358.7	$ 366.6	$ 375.4
Less taxes on EBIT		(131.0)	(133.6)	(136.3)	(139.3)	(142.6)
Plus depreciation		50.0	50.0	50.0	50.0	50.0
Less capital expenditures		(50.0)	(50.0)	(50.0)	(50.0)	(50.0)
Less additions to/plus reductions in working capital		(1.6)	(1.9)	(2.4)	(2.7)	(3.0)
Free cash flow		$ 212.2	$ 216.1	$ 220.0	$ 224.6	$ 229.7

Source: Case writer's analysis, consistent with forecast expectations of securities analysts.

EXHIBIT 5 | Standard & Poor's Bond-Rating Definitions

Long-Term Issue Credit Ratings: Issue credit ratings are based, in varying degrees, on the following considerations:

- Likelihood of payment? Capacity and willingness of the obligor to meet its financial commitment on an obligation in accordance with the terms of the obligation.
- Nature and provisions of the obligation.
- Protection afforded by and relative position of the obligation in the event of bankruptcy, reorganization, or other arrangements under the laws of bankruptcy and other laws affecting creditors' rights.

The issue-rating definitions are expressed in terms of default risk. As such, they pertain to senior obligations of an entity. Junior obligations are typically rated lower than senior obligations, to reflect the lower priority in bankruptcy, as noted above. (Such differentiation applies when an entity has both senior and subordinated obligations, secured and unsecured obligations, or operating company and holding company obligations.) Accordingly, in the case of junior debt, the rating may not conform exactly to the category definition.

AAA
An obligation rated AAA has the highest rating assigned by Standard & Poor's. The obligor's capacity to meet its financial commitment on the obligation is extremely strong.

AA
An obligation rated AA differs from the highest-rated obligations only to a small degree. The obligor's capacity to meet its financial commitment on the obligation is very strong.

A
An obligation rated A is somewhat more susceptible to the adverse effects of changes in circumstances and economic conditions than are obligations in the higher-rated categories. The obligor's capacity to meet its financial commitment on the obligation, however, is still strong.

BBB
An obligation rated BBB exhibits adequate protection parameters. However, adverse economic conditions or changing circumstances are more likely to lead to a weakened capacity of the obligor to meet its financial commitment on the obligation.

BB, B, CCC, CC, and C
Obligations rated BB, B, CCC, CC, and C are regarded as having significant speculative characteristics. BB indicates the least degree of speculation and C indicates the highest. While such obligations will likely have some quality and protective characteristics, those characteristics may be outweighed by large uncertainties or major exposures to adverse conditions.

Plus (+) or minus (−)
The ratings from AA to CCC may be modified by the addition of a plus (+) or a minus (−) sign to show the obligation's relative standing within the major rating categories.

Source: Standard & Poor's *Bond Guide*, 2001.

EXHIBIT 5 | Moody's Bond-Rating Definitions   (*continued*)

Aaa Bonds that are rated Aaa are judged to be of the best quality. They carry the smallest degree of investment risk and are generally referred to as gilt edge. Interest payments are protected by a large or by an exceptionally stable margin and principal is secure. While the various protective elements are likely to change, such changes as can be visualized are most unlikely to impair the fundamentally strong position of such issues.

Aa Bonds that are rated Aa are judged to be of high quality by all standards. Together with the Aaa group, they compose what are generally known as high-grade bonds. They are rated lower than the best bonds because margins of protection may not be as large as in Aaa securities or fluctuations of protective elements may be of greater amplitude or there may be other elements present that make the long-term risks appear somewhat larger than in Aaa securities.

A Bonds that are rated A possess many favorable investment attributes and are to be considered upper-medium-grade obligations. Factors giving security to principal and interest are considered adequate, but elements may be present that suggest a susceptibility to impairment sometime in the future.

Baa Bonds that are rated Baa are considered medium-grade obligations (i.e., they are neither highly protected nor poorly secured). Interest payment and principal security appear adequate for the present, but certain protective elements may be lacking or may be characteristically unreliable over any great length of time. Such bonds lack outstanding investment characteristics and, in fact, have speculative characteristics as well.

Ba Bonds that are rated Ba are judged to have speculative elements; their future cannot be considered as well assured as the higher-rated categories. Often, the protection of interest and principal payments may be very moderate and thereby not well safeguarded during both good and bad times over the future. Uncertainty of position characterizes bonds in this class.

B Bonds that are rated B generally lack the characteristics of the desirable investment. Assurance of interest and principal payments or of maintenance of other terms of the contract over any long period may be small.

Caa Bonds that are rated Caa are of poor standing. Such issues may be in default or there may be present elements of danger with respect to principal or interest.

Ca Bonds that are rated Ca represent obligations that are speculative in a high degree. Such issues are often in default or have other marked shortcomings.

C Bonds that are rated C are the lowest-rated class of bonds, and issues so rated can be regarded as having extremely poor prospects for ever attaining any real investment standing.

Source: *Mergent Annual Bond Record*, 2002.

EXHIBIT 6 | Key Industrial Financial Ratios by Rating Categories

Key Industrial Financial Ratios (Three-year medians 2000–02)	Investment Grade				Noninvestment Grade	
	AAA	AA	A	BBB	BB	B
EBIT interest coverage (x)	23.4	13.3	6.3	3.9	2.2	1.0
EBITDA interest coverage (x)	25.3	16.9	8.5	5.4	3.2	1.7
Funds from operations/total debt (%)	214.2	65.7	42.2	30.6	19.7	10.4
Free operating cash flow/total debt (%)	156.6	33.6	22.3	12.8	7.3	1.5
Return on capital (%)	35.0	26.6	18.1	13.1	11.5	8.0
Operating income/sales (%)	23.4	24.0	18.1	15.5	15.4	14.7
Long-term debt/capital (%)	(1.1)	21.1	33.8	40.3	53.6	72.6
Total debt/capital, incl. short-term debt (%)	5.0	35.9	42.6	47.0	57.7	75.1

Standard & Poor's defined these ratios based on the book value of these items as follows:

EBIT interest coverage = EBIT/interest expense.

EBITDA interest coverage = (EBIT plus depreciation and amortization)/interest expense

Long-term debt/capital = long-term debt/(long-term debt + stockholders' equity)

Total debt/capital, incl. short-term debt = (short-term debt + long-term debt)/(short-term debt + long-term debt + stockholders' equity)

Source of data: Standard & Poor's *CreditStats.*

EXHIBIT 7 | Deluxe Corporation's Annual EBIT-Coverage Ratios

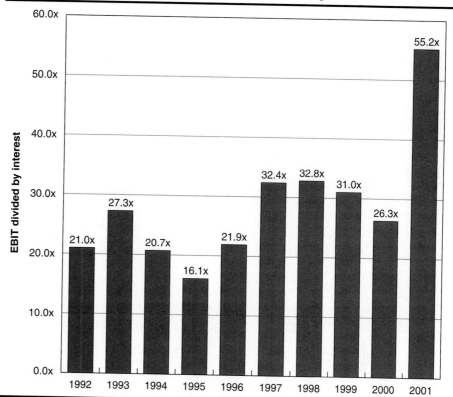

Source of data: Company regulatory filings; case writer's analysis.

EXHIBIT 8 | Capital Costs by Rating Category

	AAA	AA	A	BBB	BB	B
Cost of debt (pretax)	5.47%	5.50%	5.70%	6.30%	9.00%	12.00%
Cost of equity	10.25%	10.35%	10.50%	10.60%	12.00%	14.25%

Source of data: Hudson Bancorp.

EXHIBIT 9 | Capital-Market Conditions (as of July 31, 2002)

U.S. Treasury Obligations	Yield	Other Instruments	Yield
90-day bills	1.69%	Discount Notes	1.70%
180-day bills	1.68%	Certificates of Deposit (3-month)	1.72%
2-year notes	2.23%	Commercial Paper (6-month)	1.75%
3-year notes	2.79%	Term Fed Funds	1.78%
5-year notes	3.45%		
10-year notes	4.46%		
30-year notes	5.30%		

Corporate Debt Obligations (10-year)	Yield
AAA	5.51%
AA	5.52%
A	5.70%
BBB	6.33%
BB	9.01%
B	11.97%

Source of data: *Bloomberg LP, S&P's Research Insight, Value Line Investment Survey, Datastream Advance*

Rosario Acero S.A.[1]

In March 1997, Pablo Este sat in a comfortable chair in the living room of his home in Buenos Aires, reflecting on the future of the small steel mill he owned. The initial years of Rosario Acero S.A., the former Rosario Works of Giganto Acero S.A., had been one challenge after another—the divestiture of Rosario from Giganto, downsizing the operations and workforce, searching for new customers during the six-month Giganto Acero strike at a time when sales to Giganto Acero accounted for nearly half the company's total sales, and arguing with local bankers over the value of receivables due from customers facing possible bankruptcy.

Now, after six profitable quarters, the company prepared to issue its first long-term securities since its incorporation in 1993. The concern that Este faced in March 1997 was the type of capital to acquire. The company's size—revenues were below $35 million pesos[2]—definitely limited options, but Este, as majority shareholder and board chair of Rosario Acero S.A.'s board of directors, wanted to consider all the options available at the time.

Este had engaged Raul Martinez, an independent financial consultant, to investigate a private placement of eight-year senior notes with warrants. Martinez's initial report stated that Rosario Acero S.A. could raise its required $7.5 million at a coupon rate of 13 percent. Another option Este was interested in evaluating was an initial public offering of Rosario Acero S.A.'s stock through a local investment bank. And perhaps now was the time to sell the entire company to another firm.

---

[1] *Acero* is Spanish for steel. S.A. stands for *sociedad anonimo,* the equivalent of a corporation.

[2] The Argentine peso was fixed at a 1:1 exchange rate with the U.S. dollar. Local convention was to indicate the currency with the dollar sign.

The Company

History

Just two days after Christmas 1992, Giganto Acero announced the closing of 15 unprofitable business units, among which was the Rosario, Argentina, plant, operated by Giganto Acero since 1932. In April 1993, Pablo Este, a Rosario native, Harvard Business School graduate, and successful small business entrepreneur, was introduced by Rosario civic leaders to members of the plant's top management. After reviewing the situation, Este agreed to commit the necessary capital, time, and managerial expertise to save the operation and make the mill a viable company in Rosario. Giganto Acero would remain an important customer. After brief negotiations, Este and a group investment partners purchased the assets of the plant for $14 million, the bulk of which was financed by seller notes from Giganto Acero—Este and his partners invested only $250,000 in the equity of the firm. The plant began operating as Rosario Acero S.A. in July 1993.

Product Lines and Sales

Taking advantage of existing facilities and numerous opportunities to cut costs, Rosario's management positioned the company as a niche player in the industry. Rosario Acero S.A. sold a variety of cast- and fabricated-steel products to over 35 steel and other heavy-industry customers. The percentage of sales in each major product category for the years 1994–1996 is shown in **Exhibit 1.** Six product managers located in Rosario oversaw each of six product categories: rolling mill rolls, steel castings, staves, mill liners, continuous caster rolls, and miscellaneous products. The company employed five outside salespersons on straight salary, who were located in Buenos Aires and Rosario, Argentina; Montevideo, Uruguay; Sao Paulo, Brazil; and Santiago, Chile.

The vast majority of the company's sales were to integrated steel producers (Giganto Acero and Brasilia Metal together accounted for 65 percent of sales in 1994; 49 percent in 1995; and 42 percent in 1996) and to mini-mills. Those buyers were very different types of customers. The integrated producers tended to multisource orders, which made them less price-sensitive consumers than mini-mills; they also tended to place more value on their long-standing supplier relationships. Mini-mills tended to be price sensitive, and though they relied on a single supplier, they were more likely to consider purchasing from suppliers outside of Mercosur.[3]

The company's chief product was rolling mill rolls, which were like rolling pins found in a kitchen. Those rolls were sold in pairs, and were used to squeeze moving slabs of hot or cold steel into a certain shape and a specific thickness. Rolling mill rolls accounted for nearly half of the firm's net sales in 1996. The company estimated its gross margins on this product at 32 percent. The company ranked itself second in the Mercosur market for rolling mill rolls, with a 17 percent share.

---

[3]Mercosur was the South American free trade association formed by a treaty among Argentina, Brazil, and Uruguay.

Continuous caster rolls were used to channel molten steel as it was cooled during the casting process.[4] Repair and remachining of caster rolls was required on a regular basis. Rosario Acero S.A. provided the refurbishment, in addition to preparation of new rolls, to its customers who did not have the in-house capability to refurbish rolls. Company officials estimated gross margins on continuous caster rolls at 12 percent. The market for new rolls in Mercosur was approximately $25 million in 1996, so Rosario's sales gave it about a 13 percent share.

Rosario Acero S.A. produced both machined[5] (finished) and nonmachined (rough) steel castings in a variety of sizes from 1,500 to 45,000 kilograms for a diverse group of customers, including steel makers, cement producers, shipbuilders, automotive manufacturers, extrusion-press operators, and rock and coal crushers. One example of steel castings was the slag pot, a steel vessel used to receive the impurities thrown off from blast furnaces and reheating furnaces. The company estimated the total potential slag-pot market in Mercosur at $5 million, of which its share in the manufacture of small pots (those under 30,000 kilograms) was 80 percent. Overall, gross margins on rough castings were approximately 18 percent; gross margins on finished castings were just 2 percent.

Mill liner was a rolled-steel liner plate and lift-bar used in industrial grinding machines for grinding cement, pulverizing coal, and grinding high-silica sand for glass production. Rosario Acero S.A. produced mill liners from purchased parts at gross margins of 40 percent.

Facilities and Operations

All of Rosario Acero S.A.'s production took place at the company's sole facility in Rosario, Argentina. The plant housed two electric furnaces used to melt scrap metal for production (for a total melting capacity of 61,000 kilograms). All melting and pouring was done from 17:00 to 9:00 on weekdays, or on weekends, to minimize energy costs. This practice saved an estimated $50,000 in monthly electricity costs. Factory overhead accounted for 63 percent of Rosario Acero S.A.'s cost of goods sold.

Plant equipment and facilities had been well maintained under Giganto Acero's ownership, with capital spending totaling over $25 million from 1976–1989. Capital spending by Rosario Acero S.A. totaled $3 million from 1993 to March 1997, with additional spending planned from a portion of the long-term capital to be raised.

Rosario Acero S.A. relied on one primary source, located in Buenos Aires, for the scrap metal used in its production of rolls and castings. **Exhibit 2** lists scrap prices during the recent year. Within the structure of Rosario Acero S.A.'s costs, direct materials including scrap accounted for 26 percent of the cost of goods sold in 1996.

---

[4]Molten steel would be poured into rectangular boxes where it would harden into steel ingots. This process was known as casting the steel. More generally, there were two ways to shape steel: (1) bend, stretch, cut, drill, or squeeze it under pressure, or (2) pour it into a preformed mold where it would harden into the desired shape—the latter was casting.

[5]Machining was the process of shaping the steel through cutting or drilling.

As of the end of 1996, the company's plant operated seven days a week on three shifts, with an hourly work force of 816. The unionized work force, (40 percent semi-skilled, 60 percent skilled), earned an average hourly wage of $3.75 during 1996. Direct labor accounted for 11 percent of Rosario Acero S.A.'s cost of goods sold in 1996. All hourly employees were represented by the Union de Obreros Metalurgicos (Metalworkers' Union) under a contract that expired in June 1998. The hourly wage rate for comparable work was $4.25. Union leaders had told Pablo Este that the hourly employees would demand a better-than-competitive contract at the expiration of the current contract—this was to compensate the employees for staying with the firm through its difficulties.[6]

The company also operated with 118 administrative employees, and a new CEO, Enrique Salazar, was appointed in May 1996 to assume operational responsibility under Pablo Este. Other members of senior management under Giganto Acero's ownership held the same positions now, with the exception of the former company president, who had resigned in February 1997.

Six top managers other than Este held 25 percent of the stock outstanding at the end of 1996. Este held 58 percent. Este's investment partners held the balance of the shares outstanding.

The Steel Industry in 1997

In 1996, the Argentine steel industry enjoyed a moderately profitable year. Several factors accounted for this turnaround in the industry. First, capacity cutbacks and modernization programs of the past half decade paid off; the industry reached 80 percent capacity in 1996, with utilization for high-demand items near 100 percent. In addition, the birth of the Mercosur trade group promoted more trade by Argentine firms with customers in Brazil and Uruguay.

Forecasts for 1997 and the next three to five years were favorable, but were contingent on producers continuing their recent efforts to remain competitive in the industry. Domestic steel shipments were estimated to be 70 million metric tons, slightly below 1996 because of cutbacks in inventories rather than lower consumption. Imports were expected to continue their decline from the 1996 level of 20 million metric tons to less than 19 million tons in 1997.

Rosario Acero S.A.'s Outlook

Rosario Acero S.A.'s revenues and earnings had grown since the company began operations in July 1993. The company's balance sheets and income statements for this period are provided in **Exhibits 3** and **4**. Management predicted continued growth into the new century, with different product lines growing at different rates. Annualized rates of growth from 1996 to 2002 were projected by product line as follows:

---

[6]The financial forecasts by Pablo Este assumed modest increases in wage rates, consistent with expectations for competitive market conditions.

Product Line	1996 Sales (in millions)	1996–2002 Projected Growth Rate
Rolling mill rolls	$16.0	13.9%
Castings	9.0	1.4
Slag pots	1.4	19.6
Mill liners	1.6	14.5
Continuous caster rolls	3.3	5.7
Fabricated and other	3.5	6.8
Total	$34.8 Average	10.32%

In addition to continuing to serve present customers, Este wanted the company to pursue customers outside Mercosur. As yet, management had taken no action to investigate external markets, largely because of capital constraints on the firm.

Rosario Acero S.A.'s Financing Alternatives

Management sought $7.5 million in long-term capital for three purposes in early 1997: (1) $4.8 million to pay down the company's present working-capital line of credit, (2) $975,000 to repay long-term debt that would mature in mid-1997, and (3) the remaining $1,725,000 for capital improvements and general purposes. The company would retain its recently negotiated $5 million working-capital line of credit with Banco de Sol of Buenos Aires. This line, at 2 percent above the local lending base rate, was not secured by any collateral,[7] although Este had given a personal guarantee backed by specific commercial real estate he owned. The banker had emphatically stated that an increase in the line of credit and the release of Este from his guarantee would be out of the question without more long-term capital to support the loan, as well as a longer record of successful financial performance.

The private placement of eight-year notes recommended by Raul Martinez would have the terms set forth in **Exhibit 5.** The potential purchasers were two Spanish investment funds. The fee associated with issuing the placement through Martinez would be $52,000. The prospective investors demanded warrants with the debt, because of the firm's small size, relatively high leverage, and the absence of a long history of operating profitability. Martinez explained that the warrants were a kicker that increased the effective return to the investors. The covenants associated with this placement had yet to be negotiated. The Spanish investors told Martinez that the minimum acceptable EBIT coverage ratio (i.e., EBIT divided by interest expense) would be 2.0. As a foundation for valuing the warrants, Martinez estimated the average volatility of peer steel companies' shares at 0.35. Martinez had also determined that in several recent comparable private placements of debt, the effective annual cost of

---

[7]The custom of extending working-capital loans clean (i.e., unsecured by the firm's receivables and inventory) was due to the difficulties in Argentina in getting a perfected lien, and filing new paperwork to keep up the lien as the inventory and receivables rolled over.

the financing to the issuer had been between 14 percent and 16 percent, which represented a huge premium over the Argentine base lending rate of 8.5 percent.

A second financing alternative that Este considered was an initial public offering (IPO) of the company's stock. While the 233,000 shares of stock currently outstanding were not presently traded, six senior managers had been offered (and had accepted) a chance to invest three times since the company's inception at prices as follows:[8]

December 1994:	15,480 shares at $3.00/share
January 1995:	14,220 shares at $4.00/share
December 1996:	28,550 shares at $9.00/share

Those purchases accounted for management's 25 percent equity interest in the firm.

Fees associated with the IPO were expected to be about 8 percent, but they could be as low as 2 percent if a "best efforts" placement was selected rather than a guaranteed underwriting. Public trading of the stock would have implications for the shares held by top management and Este. For instance, Este wanted to see the issue open at a price higher than the $9 that managers had most recently paid for their shares of Rosario Acero S.A. For this reason, he had concluded that the size of the issue would have to be determined after a market value had been placed on the company.

The IPO market had recovered modestly since the Mexican peso crash of November 1994. By March 1997, the stock market had rebounded from the tequila effect of the peso crash. The Merval Index had risen over the previous three years, suggesting a growing optimism among equity investors in Argentina. The market for IPOs was following the same recovery route, although the volume of IPOs was still relatively light.

The success of IPOs in recent months had depended a great deal on the quality of the offering; issues in more stable and mature industries that appealed to the knowledgeable investors fared better than media and communications issues. A number of the recent IPOs involved privatizations of state-owned enterprises. Other IPOs were spinoffs from larger industrial groups who sought to rationalize their operations. One recent example was a spinoff of a subsidiary involved in a commodity fertilizer business that brought $22 per share on 11 million shares, surpassing expectations of $17 to $20 a share set for the issue prior to the November crash. In contrast was a retailer's first issue that had been planned for the end of November 1996. The company had expected to issue $9 million in equity, but it was forced to look elsewhere for funds when it could not locate another underwriter after its first banker withdrew.

Pablo Este had recently entertained the idea of selling Rosario Acero to another concern, although no specific price had been estimated for the company at that time. This option could be considered in more detail this time, as a means of obtaining funds or issuing stock to the public.

To value Rosario Acero S.A., Este had forecast the financial performance of the firm under either financing option, the debt and warrants issue (**Exhibits 6, 7,** and **8**)

---

[8]The number of shares currently outstanding (233,000), included those recent share sales.

or the equity issue (**Exhibits 9, 10,** and **11**). Also, he obtained average valuation multiples for mini-mills from a recent investment report. Those multiples indicated an average equity value of 1.5 times book value, 21 times 1996 earnings, and 18 times estimated 1997 earnings. Este also gathered information on several publicly held steel producers in Mercosur that were somewhat similar to Rosario Acero S.A. This information is contained in **Exhibit 12.** He wondered whether to simply average the results of all the peers given in that exhibit, or to exclude any. Picasso Acero, for instance, had experienced a turbulent year due to a strike and vandalism at its plant. Based on his own experience with leveraged buyouts (LBO), Este believed that a potential LBO purchaser might place a value on the company's equity by using a multiple of four times EBIT and then subtracting the total debt.

Interest rates over the past few years are provided in **Exhibits 13** and **14.** Research by Raul Martinez revealed that economists and financial institutions were forecasting annual rates of inflation between 2.5 percent and 4 percent, and real gross national product (GNP) growth at 1.5 percent to 6 percent.

Pablo Este was 66 years old and the patriarch of a large extended family. While he had no intention of retiring from Rosario's board of directors in the near future, he was concerned about the liquidity of his valuable investment in the firm. It was important to him and the other equity investors to increase the marketability of Rosario's common stock. Tempering any momentum to choose the IPO, however, was the cautious sentiment among senior management regarding the impact of any securities issuance on their administrative control of the firm.

Este realized that, as the board's chair, he could easily rely on someone else to explore the various options that might be available to Rosario Acero S.A. As the key framer of the company's success so far, however, he had an interest in seeing the board select the alternative that would best assure a continuation of that financial and employment success. With much information in front of him and all of his knowledge of Rosario Acero S.A. in his head, Pablo Este sat down to determine which long-term financing option he would support.

EXHIBIT 1 | Percentage of Company Sales by Product Line[1]

	1994	1995	1996	Feb. 1997[2]	Recent Gross Profit Margins
Rolls	40%	46%	46%	68%	32%
Castings	29	27	29	20	18 (rough)
					2 (finished)
Continuous caster rolls	4	6	9	6	12
Mill liners	8	5	5	2	40
Staves	0	3	1	1	
Other products	17	8	5	4	80 (small pots)
Services	2	4	4	0	
Total	100%	100%	100%	100%	

[1]Columns may not add to 100 because of rounding.

[2]1997 percentages based on bookings as of February 1997.

Source: Company records.

EXHIBIT 2 | Scrap Prices of Dealer Bundles (price per metric ton delivered from Buenos Aires)

Date of Estimate	Price Range
12/95	$96–$97
1/96	$99–$100
2/96	$104–$105
3/96	$98–$99
4/96	$93–$94
5/96	$103–$104
6/96	$114–$115
7/96	$115–$116
8/96	$119–$120
9/96	$131–$132
10/96	$159–$160
11/96	$159–$160
12/96	$144–$145
1/97	$139–$140

Source: Company records.

EXHIBIT 3 | Balance Sheets (pesos in thousands)

	As of December 31		
	1994	1995	1996
Cash	$ 119	$ 0	$ 245
Accounts receivable	3,077	3,845	6,846
Inventories	5,186	4,786	4,682
Other current assets	865	168	381
Total current assets	9,247	8,799	12,154
Property, plant, & equipment	13,938	14,054	14,210
Other	193	187	116
Total assets	$23,378	$23,040	$26,480
Working capital notes payable	$ 4,650	$ 4,998	$ 4,821
Current portion long-term debt	1,706	1,171	1,335
Accounts payable	3,313	3,048	4,663
Other current liabilities	804	1,993	2,315
Total current liabilities	10,473	11,210	13,134
Long-term debt	11,804	8,847	8,467
Deferred taxes & leases	312	1,258	1,282
Total liabilities	22,589	21,315	22,883
Common stock (par = $1/sh)	210	202	233
Additional paid-in capital	71	114	191
Retained earnings	508	1,409	3,173
Total owners' equity	789	1,725	3,597
Total liabilities & equity	$23,378	$23,040	$26,480

Source: Company financial statements.

EXHIBIT 4 | Income Statements (in thousands of pesos, except per-share data)

	As of December 31		
	1994	1995[1]	1996
Revenues	$25,084	$26,605	$34,836
Cost of goods sold (including depreciation)[2]	18,138	21,784	27,654
Selling, general, & administrative	3,598	3,767	3,959
Interest	1,586	1,461	1,098
Restructuring expenses	445	142	537
Profit before tax	1,317	(549)	1,588
Tax provision (benefit)	577	(285)	4
Income (loss) before extraordinary item	740	(264)	1,584
Extraordinary item[3]	265	1,165	179
Net income	$ 1,005	$ 901	$ 1,763
Earnings per share	$ 4.79	$ 4.46	$ 7.57

[1] Company loss in 1995 was attributed to sales lost as a result of a six-month strike against Giganto Acero, which was a major account for Rosario.

[2] COGS includes depreciation of $736,000 in 1994, $876,000 in 1995, and $935,000 in 1996.

[3] Extraordinary income resulted from the refunding of debt, net of applicable income taxes in 1995 and 1996. Credits on income taxes due to net operating loss carryovers resulted in extraordinary income in 1994.

Source: Company financial statements.

EXHIBIT 5 | Summary of Terms of Proposed Private Placement

Amount	$7,500,000
Issue	Senior notes with warrants
Maturity	Eight years due 2004
Takedown	Second quarter 1997
Interest Rate	13% per annum, payable semi-annually
Amortization	Interest only for the first six years. Mandatory principal payments of $1,875,000 in the seventh year, and $5,625,000 in the eighth year.

Optional Redemption

None for the first six years. Callable thereafter at the following redemption prices as a whole or in part:

Year 7	105%
Year 8	100% (no premium)

Warrants

The notes will be accompanied by an eight-year nondetachable warrant entitling the holder to purchase 40,000 shares of common stock at an exercise price of $1 per share. The warrant shares will be subject to anti-dilution provisions and will be adjusted for stock splits, stock dividends, recapitalizations, mergers, and the sale of stock, issuance of options, or securities or warrants convertible or issuable into common stock, all at a price in excess of $1 per share.

The number of warrant shares will be adjusted on a one-time basis depending on the average of net operating income for the years 1997 and 1998. Such adjustment will occur in the first quarter of 1999.

Net Operating Income	# of Shares	Percentage of Ownership
$6,000,000 or greater	40,000	15.0%
$5,999,999–$5,000,000	47,725	17.5%
$4,999,999–$4,000,000	56,250	20.0%
$3,999,999–$3,000,000	65,325	22.5%
less than $3,000,000	75,000	25.0%

Net operating income will be defined as stated in the company's audited financials, before interest and provision for income taxes, and will conform to generally accepted definitions of operating income.

Optional Put

The warrant shares can be put to the company, starting at the end of the fifth year by the holder of the warrant at a price per share equivalent to the then "appraised market value per share." Such value shall be calculated by taking operating income before taxes and interest for the latest four quarters and multiplying the sum by six, adding cash and marketable securities, and deducting short-term and long-term debt. This sum will be divided by fully diluted shares outstanding to arrive at an appraised market value per share. The warrant holder may not put in excess of 25% of his warrant shares to the company in any one year.

Provision for Early Redemption

Redemption of the senior notes before maturity would not be permitted.

Registration Rights

The warrant shares will be subject to one free right of registration after the company's initial public offering and unlimited rights to piggyback other public offerings of the stock, subject to consent of underwriters.

Restrictive Covenants on the Notes

To be negotiated.

Source: Raul Martinez, Second Draft of Private Placement Memorandum.

EXHIBIT 6 | Forecast of Income Statement: Growth Financed with the Privately Placed Debt and Warrants Issue (in millions of pesos, except per-share data)

Common Assumptions

Revenue growth rate	10.30%	Inventory/revenues	13.00%
COGS/revenues	78.00%	Other curr. assets/revenues	1.00%
SG&A/revenues	13.00%	Gross fixed assets/revenues	48.00%
Tax rate	34.00%	Accts. payable/revenues	14.00%
Depreciation/gross fixed assets	5.60%	Other curr. assets/revenues	7.00%
Cash/revenues	1.00%	Interest rate	10.00%
Accts. receivable/revenues	20.00%	Change in deferred tax/taxes	25.00%
Base lending rate	8.50%	Primary shares	233,000
		Fully diluted shares	273,000

	Actual	Projected					
	1996	1997	1998	1999	2000	2001	2002
Income Statement							
Revenues	$34.80	$38.38	$42.34	$46.70	$51.51	$56.81	$62.67
Cost of goods sold	(27.65)	(29.94)	(33.02)	(36.43)	(40.18)	(44.32)	(48.88)
Selling, general, & administrative	(3.96)	(4.99)	(5.50)	(6.07)	(6.70)	(7.39)	(8.15)
Earnings before interest and taxes	3.19	3.45	3.81	4.20	4.64	5.11	5.64
Interest (notes and old loans)[1]	(1.10)	(0.73)	(0.70)	(0.65)	(0.59)	(0.51)	(0.41)
Interest (new loan @ 13%)		(0.98)	(0.98)	(0.98)	(0.98)	(0.98)	(0.98)
Profit before taxes	2.09	1.75	2.13	2.57	3.07	3.63	4.26
Taxes	0.00	(0.59)	(0.72)	(0.88)	(1.04)	(1.23)	(1.45)
Profit after taxes	$ 2.09	$ 1.15	$ 1.41	$ 1.70	$ 2.03	$ 2.40	$ 2.81
Profit with extraordinary item	$ 1.76						
Earnings per share	$ 7.57	$ 4.96	$ 6.04	$ 7.29	$ 8.70	$10.28	$12.06

[1]The firm is assumed to borrow at the base rate plus 2%, and lend at the base rate less 2%.

EXHIBIT 7 | Forecast of Balance Sheets: Growth Financed with the Private Placement of Debt and Warrants (pesos in millions, except per-share data)

	Actual	Projected					
	1996	1997	1998	1999	2000	2001	2002
Balance Sheet							
Cash	$ 0.20	$ 0.38	$ 0.42	$ 0.47	$ 0.52	$ 0.57	$ 0.63
Accounts receivable	6.80	7.68	8.47	9.34	10.30	11.36	12.53
Inventory	4.70	4.99	5.50	6.07	6.70	7.39	8.15
Other current assets	0.40	0.38	0.42	0.47	0.52	0.57	0.63
Total current assets	12.10	13.43	14.82	16.34	18.03	19.88	21.93
Gross fixed assets	16.70	18.42	20.32	22.42	24.72	27.27	30.08
Accumulated depreciation	(2.50)	(3.53)	(4.67)	(5.93)	(7.31)	(8.84)	(10.52)
Net fixed assets	14.20	14.89	15.65	16.49	17.41	18.43	19.56
Other assets	0.10	0.10	0.10	0.10	0.10	0.10	0.10
Total assets	$26.40	$28.43	$30.57	$32.93	$35.54	$38.42	$41.59
Notes payable (excess cash)	$ 4.80	($0.76)	($0.84)	($0.81)	($1.00)	($1.44)	($2.17)
Accounts payable	4.60	5.37	5.93	6.54	7.21	7.95	8.77
Other current liabilities	2.30	2.69	2.96	3.27	3.61	3.98	4.39
Total current liabilities	11.70	7.30	8.05	9.00	9.82	10.49	10.99
Old long-term debt	9.80	7.43	7.23	6.73	6.23	5.73	5.23
New long-term debt		7.50	7.50	7.50	7.50	7.50	7.50
Deferred taxes	1.30	1.45	1.63	1.85	2.11	2.42	2.78
Total liabilities	22.80	23.67	24.41	25.07	25.66	26.14	26.50
Common stock	0.20	0.20	0.20	0.20	0.20	0.20	0.20
Paid-in surplus	0.20	0.20	0.20	0.20	0.20	0.20	0.20
Retained earnings	3.20	4.35	5.76	7.46	9.49	11.88	14.69
Total liabilities and equity	$26.40	$28.43	$30.57	$32.93	$35.54	$38.42	$41.59
Comparative Ratios							
EBIT/interest	2.90	2.03	2.27	2.58	2.96	3.45	4.08
EBIT/(interest + amort.)	1.93	0.36	1.95	2.00	2.06	2.11	2.16
Liabilities/equity	6.33	4.98	3.96	3.19	2.59	2.13	1.76
(Debt + notes)/equity	4.06	2.98	2.25	1.71	1.29	0.96	0.70
Profit/revenues	5.1%	3.0%	3.3%	3.6%	3.9%	4.2%	4.5%
Profit/equity	49.0%	24.3%	22.8%	21.6%	20.5%	19.5%	18.6%

EXHIBIT 8 | Forecast of Free Cash Flow: Growth Financed with Debt and Warrants (pesos in millions)

	Projected					
	1997	1998	1999	2000	2001	2002
Earnings before interest and taxes	3.45	3.81	4.20	4.64	5.11	5.64
Taxes	(1.17)	(1.30)	(1.43)	(1.58)	(1.74)	(1.92)
Earnings before interest and after taxes	2.28	2.51	2.77	3.06	3.37	3.72
Plus depreciation	1.03	1.14	1.26	1.38	1.53	1.68
Less capital expenditures	(1.72)	(1.90)	(2.09)	(2.31)	(2.55)	(2.81)
Less additions to net working capital	(0.17)	(0.55)	(0.61)	(0.67)	(0.74)	(0.82)
Free cash flow	1.41	1.20	1.33	1.46	1.61	1.78

EXHIBIT 9 | Forecast of Income Statements: Growth Financed with Equity, Shares Sold at $9 Each (pesos in millions, except per-share data)

Common Assumptions			
Revenue growth rate	10.30%	Inventory/revenues	13.00%
COGS/revenues	78.00%	Other curr. assets/revenues	1.00%
SG&A/revenues	13.00%	Gross fixed assets/revenues	48.00%
Tax rate	34.00%	Accts. payable/revenues	14.00%
Depreciation/gross fixed assets	5.60%	Other curr. liabs./revenues	7.00%
Cash/revenues	1.00%	Interest rate	10.00%
Accts. receivable/revenues	20.00%	Change in deferred tax/taxes	25.00%
Base lending rate	8.50%	1996 primary shares	233,000
		1997 + primary shares	1,066,333

	Actual	Projected					
	1996	1997	1998	1999	2000	2001	2002
Income Statement							
Revenues	$34.80	$38.38	$42.34	$46.70	$51.51	$56.81	$62.67
Cost of goods sold	(27.65)	(29.94)	(33.02)	(36.43)	(40.18)	(44.32)	(48.88)
Selling, general, & administrative	(3.96)	(4.99)	(5.50)	(6.07)	(6.70)	(7.39)	(8.15)
Earnings before interest and taxes	3.19	3.45	3.81	4.20	4.64	5.11	5.64
Interest (on notes and old loans)[1]	(1.10)	(0.68)	(0.60)	(0.50)	(0.37)	(0.23)	(0.07)
Interest (new loan @ 13%)		0.00	0.00	0.00	0.00	0.00	0.00
Profit before taxes	2.09	2.77	3.21	3.71	4.26	4.88	5.57
Taxes	0.00	(0.94)	(1.09)	(1.26)	(1.45)	(1.66)	(1.89)
Profit after taxes	$ 2.09	$ 1.83	$ 2.12	$ 2.45	$ 2.81	$ 3.22	$ 3.68
Profit with extraord. item	$ 1.76						
Earnings per share	$ 7.57	$ 1.72	$ 1.99	$ 2.29	$ 2.64	$ 3.02	$ 3.45

[1]The firm is assumed to borrow at the base rate plus 2%, and lend at the base rate less 2%.

EXHIBIT 10 | Forecast of Balance Sheets: Growth Financed with Equity, Shares Sold at $9 Each (in millions of pesos, except per-share data)

	Actual	Projected					
	1996	1997	1998	1999	2000	2001	2002
Balance Sheet							
Cash	$ 0.20	$ 0.38	$ 0.42	$ 0.47	$ 0.52	$ 0.57	$ 0.63
Accounts receivable	6.80	7.68	8.47	9.34	10.30	11.36	12.53
Inventory	4.70	4.99	5.50	6.07	6.70	7.39	8.15
Other current assets	0.40	0.38	0.42	0.47	0.52	0.57	0.63
Total current assets	12.10	13.43	14.82	16.34	18.03	19.88	21.93
Gross fixed assets	16.70	18.42	20.32	22.42	24.72	27.27	30.08
Accumulated depreciation	(2.50)	(3.53)	(4.67)	(5.93)	(7.31)	(8.84)	(10.52)
Net fixed assets	14.20	14.89	15.65	16.49	17.41	18.43	19.56
Other assets	0.10	0.10	0.10	0.10	0.10	0.10	0.10
Total assets	26.40	$28.43	$30.57	$32.93	$35.54	$38.42	$41.59
Notes payable (or excess cash)	4.80	($1.53)	($2.40)	($3.21)	($4.29)	($5.66)	($7.37)
Accounts payable	4.60	5.37	5.93	6.54	7.21	7.95	8.77
Other current liabilities	2.30	2.69	2.96	3.27	3.61	3.98	4.39
Total current liabilities	11.70	6.54	6.49	6.59	6.53	6.27	5.79
Old long-term debt	9.80	7.43	7.23	6.73	6.23	5.73	5.23
New long-term debt		0.00	0.00	0.00	0.00	0.00	0.00
Deferred taxes	1.30	1.54	1.81	2.12	2.49	2.90	3.37
Total liabilities	22.80	15.50	15.52	15.44	15.24	14.89	14.39
Common stock	0.20	1.20	1.20	1.20	1.20	1.20	1.20
Paid-in surplus	0.20	6.70	6.70	6.70	6.70	6.70	6.70
Retained earnings	3.20	5.03	7.15	9.59	12.41	15.63	19.30
Total liabilities and equity	$26.40	$28.43	$30.57	$32.93	$35.54	$38.42	$41.59
Comparative Ratios							
EBIT/interest	2.90	5.08	6.32	8.45	12.37	21.95	81.14
EBIT/(interest + amort.)	1.93	0.37	2.27	2.32	2.38	2.43	2.48
Liabilities/equity	6.33	1.20	1.03	0.88	0.75	0.63	0.53
(Debt + notes)/equity	4.06	0.46	0.32	0.20	0.10	0.00	−0.08
Profit/revenues	5.1%	4.8%	5.0%	5.2%	5.5%	5.7%	5.9%
Profit/equity	49.0%	14.2%	14.1%	14.0%	13.8%	13.7%	13.5%

EXHIBIT 11 | Forecast of Free Cash Flow: Growth Financed with Equity, Shares Sold at $9 Each (in millions of pesos)

	Projected					
	1997	**1998**	**1999**	**2000**	**2001**	**2002**
Earnings before interest and taxes	3.45	3.81	4.20	4.64	5.11	5.64
Taxes	(1.17)	(1.30)	(1.43)	(1.58)	(1.74)	(1.92)
Earnings before interest and after taxes	2.28	2.51	2.77	3.06	3.37	3.72
Plus depreciation	1.03	1.14	1.26	1.38	1.53	1.68
Less capital expenditures	(1.72)	(1.90)	(2.09)	(2.31)	(2.55)	(2.81)
Less additions to net working capital	(0.17)	(0.55)	(0.61)	(0.67)	(0.74)	(0.82)
Free cash flow	1.41	1.20	1.33	1.46	1.61	1.78

EXHIBIT 12 | Selected 1996 Data on Publicly Listed Peer Firms

Description of Business	
Acero Dali S.A. (AD)	Production and fabrication of steel reinforcing and merchant bars. Principal customers: building, road, and bridge contractors; municipal, county, and state agencies; concrete manufacturers; railroad, utility, and industrial companies. Marketing areas: Argentina, Uruguay, Brazil, and the Caribbean. Directors own 3% of stock.
Colon S.A. (CSA)	Makes and distributes furnace lining materials (69% of sales), mainly to the steel industry. Produces filter media, filters, and oil-control products. Mines a variety of ores and clays (14%). Insiders control about 55% of stock.
Greco Acero (GA)	Produces carbon steel products exclusively by the electric furnace method. Steel scrap is a major raw material. Makes 75% of sales in Argentina to steel service centers, fabricators, and hardware jobbers. Main markets: agriculture and construction. Escobar family owns about 45% of stock.
Velasguez S.A. (VAZ)	Manufactures steel and steel joists (holds 30% of regional market for joists). Major markets: construction, energy, rail, agriculture.
Picasso Acero S.A. (PI)	Leading processor of ferrous scrap (75% of sales) and nonferrous scrap (10%). Picasso family holds about 25% of stock; Tiger group about 15%. Sustained losses in the most recent year due to a strike, and strike-related vandalism at its plant.

(all values in pesos, except percentages)

Operating Information[1]	AD	CSA	GA	VAZ	PI
Sales	$381.0	$362.8	$397.4	$755.2	$117.1
Operating margin	55.6	11.7	26.0	144.9	(1.1)
Net income	16.9	7.5	10.3	46.4	(5.1)
Operating margin/sales	14.6%	3.2%	6.5%	19.2%	(0.9%)
Net Income/sales	4.4	2.1	2.6	6.1	(4.4%)
LT debt/capital (book)	40%	56%	22%	33%	42%
Total debt/capital (book)	57%	66%	40%	37%	65%
Total debt/equity (book)	1.33	1.94	0.67	0.59	1.86
Market equity/book equity	1.85	1.25	1.50	2.10	0.90
Total debt/equity (market)	0.72	1.55	0.44	0.28	2.06
Dividend payout ratio (3-year average)	27%	0%	15%[2]	12%	0%
Dividend yield	3.0%	0%	3.3%	1.0%	0%
P/E ratio	9.5	15.9	11.3	15.0	7.3
Beta	1.35	1.05	1.00	1.15	2.50
Stock price range	$44 1/2 – 18 1/4	$20 1/4 – 13 1/2	$24 1/4 – 11 1/8	$49 1/2 – 29 1/2	$54 – 18 3/4
Close March 1, 1997	$32 3/4	$18 5/8	$19 1/2	$42 1/2	$33
5-year annualized per-share growth projections					
Sales	10%		9%	10%	5%
Earnings	17%			12%	
Dividends	14%			12%	8%

[1]All operating information for most recent fiscal year as of March 1997 and in millions of pesos. Other information current as of March 1997 unless noted.

[2]Payout based on 1996 only. No dividends paid previously.

(All data are disguised.)

EXHIBIT 13 | Debt-Market Conditions

	March 1997
Average corporate bond yield	9.86%
Base lending rate	8.50
10-year Argentine T-bond	8.50
3-month Argentine T-bill	5.70%

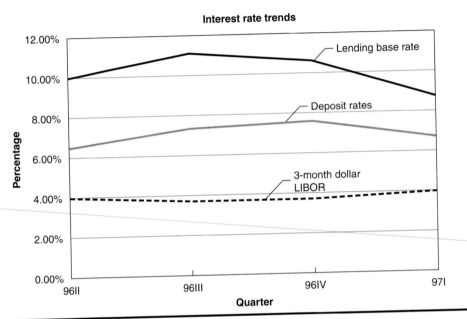

EXHIBIT 14 | Current Yields on Selected Debt Issues in South America

Company	Rating[1]	Form of Debt	Coupon	Mat. Date	Current Yield	Yield to Maturity
Sola S.A.	BBB	Notes	8.625%	2005	9.02%	9.41%
HABASA	BBB−	Subordinated notes	9.300	2003	10.35	10.49
Mercado S.A.	CCC+	Subordinated debent.	11.990	2005	16.89	13.05
Orientar S.A.	BBB−	Notes	10.500	2004	10.47	10.45
Serenidad S.A.	CCC−	Sen. sf. debent.	7.750	2004	12.86	17.42
Turismo S.A.	CCC+	Senior subord. notes	13.250	2003	13.25	13.25
Util S.A.	CCC	Sub. sf. debent.	5.000	2003	15.25	16.10
Tulipan S.A.	CCC−	Sinking fund debent.	8.100%	2005	15.88%	19.08%

[1] According to a well-known international debt-rating agency, "Debt rated BBB is believed to have a satisfactory capacity to pay interest and repay principal, although that capacity would decline readily if adverse economic conditions or changing circumstances should arise. . . . Debt rated . . . CCC . . . is predominantly speculative."

Recent Private Placement Yields, BBB- Issues			
	Company	**Form of Debt**	**Maturity Date**	**Coupon**
January	Grua S.A.	Fixed rate notes	2005	11.25%
	Globo S.A.	Sr. notes	2001	11.35
	Disquete S.A.	Sr. notes	2001	11.40
February	Energa S.A.	Sr. notes	2006	11.20
	Energa S.A.	Sr. notes	2002	11.60
	Vemco S.A.	Sub. secured notes	2001	11.50
March	Luza Solaro S.A.	Sec. non-recourse notes	2001	10.90
	Dorar S.A.	Sec. notes	1999	10.80
	Contrahacer S.A.	Sr. sec. notes	2002	10.85
	Coronar S.A.	Sr. notes	2001	10.20%

(Data have been disguised.)

Deutsche Bank Securities: Financing the Acquisition of Consolidated Supply S.A.

On November 20, 2003, Maria Ober, vice president of Deutsche Bank Securities, received a telephone call confirming that an important client intended to bid in an auction for a large hospital supply distributor and was seeking Deutsche Bank's assistance in arranging the financing. The call was no surprise: the client had briefed Deutsche Bank on the possibility of a bid regularly over the past six months. The seller had finally announced a firm deadline for receiving sealed bids for the target. An offering price and indication of financial commitment were due in two weeks.

The client was Intercontinental Capital, Ltd. (ICL), a major European leveraged buyout (LBO) sponsor. The target of the acquisition was a leading global supplier of medical products to hospitals and a subsidiary of AtlantisMed Systems, a major manufacturer of medical products and supplies. AtlantisMed was headquartered in the United States. The subsidiary, Consolidated Supply S.A. (CSSA), had global sales of $2.5 billion and was headquartered in Luxembourg.

Calling from Luxembourg, Louis Danton, a managing director with ICL, explained to Maria Ober that ICL contemplated a bid of $1.513 billion for CSSA, paid in cash—which represented a multiple of 9.2 times 2003 estimated (2003e) EBITDA. Danton also sketched a preliminary financial structure for the bid: ICL would invest $534 million in the equity of CSSA. Deutsche Bank would arrange total funded debt of $979 million, which would represent 6.0 times CSSA's 2003e EBITDA. ICL also sought a bridge loan facility from Deutsche Bank that would temporarily fund the deal until underwritten notes could be placed with investors after the closing of the acquisition. Ober responded that the leveraged finance team would begin work on the deal immediately and respond in a few days.

This case was prepared by Robert F. Bruner with the assistance of Sean Carr and the cooperation of Deutsche Bank Securities. Certain case facts and the identities of persons and companies in this case have been disguised. Copyright © 2005 by the University of Virginia Darden School Foundation, Charlottesville, VA. All rights reserved. *To order copies, send an e-mail to* sales@dardenpublishing.com. *No part of this publication may be reproduced, stored in a retrieval system, used in a spreadsheet, or transmitted in any form or by any means—electronic, mechanical, photocopying, recording, or otherwise—without the permission of the Darden School Foundation.* Rev. 12/05.

Ober knew that that if Deutsche Bank Securities arranged the financing on competitive terms, ICL would bring more business in the future. At the same time, the excesses of the last leveraged finance wave reminded all bankers of the need to structure sensible deals. She sought to evaluate Danton's contemplated bid price and financing proposal and to search for the structure that would be most attractive. The ideal solution would meet Deutsche Bank's credit, underwriting, and profitability standards, offer an attractive return to ICL, and win the auction.

Industry Overview and CSSA's Market Position

The hospital supply market was diversified across regions, products, and end-markets. North America, Europe, and the rest of the world accounted for 41 percent, 32 percent, and 27 percent of global industry revenue, respectively. Catheters, surgical equipment and instruments, and linens and gowns accounted for 36 percent, 36 percent, and 28 percent of revenues, respectively. Because of increases in surgical procedures and medical advances, ICL projected industry growth at 4 to 5 percent per annum—that compared with compound average growth from 1960 to 2000 in hospital-service research and development (R&D) spending of 7.6 percent.

Both demand and supply in the industry were highly fragmented. CSSA afforded distribution for more than 5,000 manufacturers (including itself) and offered a range of products exceeding 750,000 stocking units. More than 250,000 customers worldwide purchased products from CSSA. The customer base was diversified across a range of fields: hospitals, surgery centers, outpatient medical facilities, and medical offices.

CSSA competed with both third-party hospital and medical products distributors and product manufacturers' direct sales forces. Three firms led competition among the distributors: Medical and Scientific Supply (MASS), Spa and Hospital Distribution Corp., and CSSA. Together those three held a 28 percent share of the worldwide sales in the hospital supply market—CSSA alone accounted for 15 percent of the U.S. market and 13 percent of the European market. Among them, CSSA was the only firm focused solely on distribution; the other two also had large manufacturing operations. More than 70 percent of worldwide sales were handled through distributors such as CSSA. In Europe, CSSA was one of only two companies with sufficient brand franchise, infrastructure, systems support, and financial strength to service the entire market efficiently. The growing importance of offering a "one-stop shop" for all of the customers' hospital and medical equipment needs gave CSSA a competitive advantage against smaller firms.

The Company: Consolidated Supply S.A.

With sales of about \$2.5 billion,[1] CSSA distributed a range of products including catheters, surgical supplies, linens, instruments, protective clothing, and other hospital and medical products and offered a range of managed services including software consulting

---

[1] CSSA's financial reports were given in U.S. dollars. Many of CSSA's long-term supply contracts with global research firms were denominated in dollars. And it had been a matter of convenience to account for results in dollars, when CSSA was a subsidiary of AtlantisMed, a U.S.-headquartered firm.

and systems for supply-chain management, hazardous materials tracking systems, storeroom management, and purchases from third parties. Most of CSSA's products were consumable in nature, and thus ensured a steady recurring revenue stream. In 2003, approximately 57 percent of revenue was derived from customers with less than $750,000 of annual purchases, and no one customer represented more than 3 percent of total revenue. CSSA sought to be the principal provider of hospital supplies to its customer base. Already, the firm was the principal provider of hospital supplies to the majority of the largest global hospital systems, as well as the largest North American hospital buying consortia.

The firm operated 17 distribution centers in Europe and North America, 30 smaller regional centers, and numerous "just-in-time" delivery facilities near customer sites. The company processed about 50,000 orders per day. CSSA had specialized manufacturing facilities in Lille, France; Shanghai, China; Dortmund, Germany; Allentown, Pennsylvania; and San Diego, California. Products manufactured by CSSA accounted for approximately 2 percent of the firm's sales in 2003. As of December 2003, CSSA had approximately 6,100 employees worldwide, including 2,500 employees in North America and approximately 3,200 employees in Europe.

Management of CSSA focused on fiscal discipline, profitable revenue growth opportunities, and free cash flow generation. For the next five to 10 years, its executives intended to pursue a strategy focused on improved efficiency, an expanded line of private label products, and growing CSSA's "share of wallet" with key accounts. Management believed that it would be possible to lift the CCSA's EBITDA margin of 6.6 percent to a level more consistent with the margin of Medical and Scientific Supply (MASS), its primary competitor—that would improve the EBITDA margin by 350 basis points. The two firms' difference in margins was attributed to higher selling, general and administrative expenses at CSSA and MASS's greater reliance on self-manufactured and private label product sales, and its higher productivity and resultant lower sales, general, and administrative expenses (SG&A). CSSA's greater international presence accounted for some of the difference, given that a larger infrastructure was required to address a more fragmented, multilingual and multicultural marketplace. The firm's sales force of 1,200 served the market in 11 different languages, and 400 employees worked full-time at customer locations.

Historically, CSSA enjoyed stable sales growth and profitability, which resulted in substantial free cash flow generation.[2] About 75 percent of CSSA's revenues derived from repeat sales. The high service orientation of the firm and its ability to integrate into customers' purchasing and supply chain systems created "sticky" customer relationships with high switching costs. The capital intensity of the business was comparatively low (capital expenditures were projected at 1.1 percent of revenue).

---

[2]In 2003, CSSA was the target of litigation related to the distribution of products containing asbestos. To date, 19 asbestos-related claims had been filed against CSSA, of which 13 were settled out of court for an aggregate indemnity value of $3.1 million, including $150,000 of legal costs; six were still pending as the auction deadline approached.

CSSA's management team was experienced in the administration of a global distribution company. The top five executives had an average of 20 years' experience in the distribution field, with a minimum of 10 years' experience working at CSSA.

Exhibits 1 and **2** give CSSA's historical and projected income statements and balance sheets. **Exhibit 3** summarizes the forecast assumptions underlying this model. **Exhibit 4** summarizes information on recent acquisitions in CSSA's market space. Peer firms in the general field of distribution and logistics are summarized in **Exhibit 5.** The EBITDA/sales margins of the peer firms were generally higher than CSSA's because they derived a higher portion of their business from private label manufacturing.

Equity Investor

Intercontinental Capital, Ltd. (ICL) was one of the oldest and most respected private equity investment firms in the world. Since its founding in 1978, ICL had invested more than $4.5 billion in 36 businesses across a broad range of industries. ICL was currently managing a pool of equity capital of $3.5 billion on behalf of major pension funds, university endowments, and other leading financial institutions. CSSA represented a "classic" investment opportunity for ICL: a complicated extraction of a noncore, captive asset from a large multinational corporation. ICL had built its reputation through its successful execution of similar transactions.

Maria Ober knew that relationships with LBO sponsors were important sources of transactions in the current market environment. Each deal generated interest income and a host of fees from bond underwriting, loan syndication, agency, and mergers and acquisitions (M&A) advisory assignments. The volume of transactions in global investment banking was rising in 2003, but remained well below the peak of the last capital market cycle of deals. Financing highly leveraged transactions was a bright spot in the industry because of the high volume of deals (LBO sponsors were buying actively). Indeed, the outlook of some observers was that leveraged finance would account for half the profits of the investment banking industry in 2004. Those deals were also profitable. Including interest income and fees, the return on assets from one of these transactions could easily exceed 15 percent (on a pretax basis). For all those reasons, Ober wanted to serve ICL well in financing the CSSA acquisition.

Deutsche Bank

With total assets of EUR803 billion, Ober's institution was the largest bank in Germany. Based on all financings arranged in 2003, Deutsche Bank was the seventh-largest in the European Union and the fifth-largest in the United States.[3] Following its acquisition of Bankers Trust in 1999, Deutsche Bank extended its financial services into investment banking and capital markets trading. It was the fourth-ranked arranger of leveraged loans and acquisition financing and was involved in the financings for each of the 15 largest deals to date in 2003. It was the second-ranked global underwriter of high-yield bonds. Deutsche Bank employed 21 professionals in acquisition finance, divided between New York and London.

---

[3]Source of rankings data: Loan Pricing Corporation.

History of the Deal

Four years earlier, Deutsche Bank Securities had advised the owners of CSSA on the sale of that company to AtlantisMed. Then, as AtlantisMed's new product development program ran into stiff competition and that company needed to raise cash, Deutsche Bank proposed an initial public offering (IPO) for CSSA. Simultaneously, a number of strategic buyers approached AtlantisMed about acquiring CSSA; those included competitors of CSSA and firms that were close to CSSA in the value chain. Five LBO sponsors also expressed an interest in acquiring CSSA.

AtlantisMed evaluated the range of potential buyers and decided against continuing discussions with any buyer who might face the risk of an antitrust challenge. Since CSSA operated in numerous countries, the regulatory review process would be lengthy and risky. AtlantisMed wanted to sell quickly and to avoid creating a more powerful supplier to its own laboratories. Those criteria excluded the strategic buyers.

The remaining bidders were the five LBO sponsors. Three of the firms were based in the United States but had significant operations in Europe. The European firms were ICL and a large LBO firm in London. Maria Ober and Louis Danton discussed the implications of the competitive field. First, the bid prices would reflect the need for strategic buyers to earn internal rates of return (IRR) on the equity invested in excess of 30 percent. Second, in the absence of synergies, those buyers would look to operating improvements and the aggressive use of leverage to achieve the returns. Third, all five LBO sponsors were sophisticated clients of the global capital markets: they would seek the best terms available and would rely on their advisors to place the securities quickly and at low cost.

The Proposed Financing

Exhibit 6 gives the contemplated sources and uses of funds for the acquisition. **Exhibit 7** presents the pro forma capitalization of CSSA from 2004 to 2013 reflecting the amortization of permanent financing at conventional repayment terms. At closing, CSSA would have approximately $50.7 million in cash on its balance sheet, which would be used to repay the revolving loan and returned as a dividend to the seller immediately following the closing of the acquisition. Danton also stated that $10.9 million of CSSA's current bank debt could be "rolled over" or refinanced.

The senior secured credit facilities would be secured by 100 percent of the equity of CSSA and 65 percent of the equity of its foreign subsidiaries, along with all the other tangible and intangible assets, including all accounts receivables, contract rights, securities, U.S. patents, U.S. trademarks, other U.S. intellectual property, inventory, equipment, and real estate interests. CSSA would guarantee obligations by the parent and each of its subsidiaries. The senior secured credit facilities would be led by Deutsche Bank Securities, as follows:

- $111.25 million multicurrency revolving credit facility with a five-year maturity. The revolver would be available for general corporate purposes;
- $369.4 million U.S. dollar-denominated term loan facility with a seven-year maturity;
- $133.5 million euro-denominated term loan facility with a five-year maturity.

In addition, $462.9 million in unsecured notes would be placed by Deutsche Bank, as follows:

- $155.8 million, U.S. dollar-denominated senior unsecured notes with 10-year maturity.
- $307.1 million U.S. dollar-denominated senior subordinated notes with 10-year maturity.

A separate $462.9 million senior subordinated facility would serve as temporary financing until the placement of the unsecured notes in the high-yield capital markets would be completed. In the absence of a capital markets takeout, the temporary financing would be converted into $155.8 million of senior unsecured permanent financing with a maturity of eight years and $307.1 million of senior subordinated permanent financing with a maturity of 10 years. The temporary financing (the senior subordinated facility) would be subordinated to the revolver, and CSSA's subsidiaries would guarantee both the U.S. dollar term loan and the euro term loan.

The common equity base of this transaction would consist of an investment of $534 million by ICL. Louis Danton told Maria Ober that ICL's bid had the support of CSSA's senior management; as a group, they would invest $15 million of personal funds as part of ICL's equity investment.

Ober knew that Deutsche Bank would collect a range of fees for its financial advisory work for ICL, most of which were subject to negotiation with the client. But in relationships such as this one, the following fees might prevail:

- Commitment fee: Compensation for providing the letter of financial commitment. The fee was typically equal to 0.75 percent of the principal amount of the temporary financing outstanding and would be payable only upon successful completion of the transaction.
- Funding fee: Compensation for funding the temporary financing. The fee was typically equal to 1.5 percent of the amount of the financing and would be payable only upon successful completion of the transaction.
- Syndication fee: The fee for forming a syndicate of banks to take up the bank debt would be about 0.5 percent.
- Conversion fee: In the event that the temporary financing was not taken out by permanent financing, the amount outstanding would be converted to loans, for which Deutsche Bank would be paid a conversion fee equal to 2.5 percent of the senior permanent financing and 2.75 percent of the senior subordinated permanent financing.
- Underwriting fee: In the industry, underwriting fees for senior debt were between 1 percent and 2.25 percent of the outstanding; for subordinated debt, they were 2 to 3 percent of the outstanding. For placing the notes with investors, Deutsche Bank would receive a fee of 2.5 percent of the amount of senior subordinated notes placed, and 2.75 percent of the amount of senior subordinated notes placed. Should it be necessary to underwrite the placement of equity, the fee would be 5 to 7 percent of the gross proceeds at closing.

• Administrative agency fee: This fee was determined by a pricing grid and would typically equal $200,000 per year for loans of this type.

Conclusion

Ober assembled her acquisition finance team to complete the analysis of Danton's proposed bid price and financing. Various credit statistics associated with the financing proposal and projected financial performance are given in **Exhibit 8. Exhibit 9** presents a forecast of interest coverage and total capitalization ratios as a foundation for examining potential covenant compliance.

Exhibit 10 gives a simple DCF valuation of CSSA under the assumption of an exit from the investment in 2008 at a multiple of 9.2 times EBITDA, the same multiple as implied in the contemplated entry to the investment. The resulting internal rate of return (IRR) to Intercontinental Capital, Ltd. was estimated to be 21.3 percent. As the exhibit suggests, however, the IRR was sensitive to variations in the year of exit and the exit multiple. Ober wondered whether the return to ICL could be enhanced through alterations in the deal design.

Exhibits 11, 12, and **13** present information on loan ratings and current capital market conditions. The fees associated with this deal were subject to negotiation. As a point of departure for analysis, total fees and expenses for the deal might amount to $66.8 million. Ober wondered what the total return on assets to Deutsche Bank might be from this relationship. **Exhibit 14** suggested that the return on assets to Deutsche Bank would be 23.2 percent before taxes, including all fees, interest income, and principal flows.

She reminded her team that it would be desirable to reply with not only an evaluation of ICL's proposal, but also improvements that might enhance the transaction for all. Her reply would be expected in a few days. That would merely be the start of a detailed review of the transaction: a credit officer would review the credit risk of the financing, and the underwriting committee would examine the suitability of the loans for syndication and consider whether holding the loans in Deutsche Bank's own portfolio might be preferable.

EXHIBIT 1 | Historical and Projected Income Statements for CSSA

(fiscal year ended December 31)	Historical 2001	Historical 2002	Pro forma 2003	1 2004	2 2005	3 2006	4 2007	5 2008	6 2009	7 2010	8 2011	9 2012	10 2013
Consolidated revenues	$2,244.9	$2,335.4	$2,487.5	$2,549.8	$2,647.2	$2,750.3	$2,854.4	$2,967.1	$3,076.9	$3,190.8	$3,308.9	$3,431.4	$3,558.4
% growth	NA	4.0%	6.5%	2.5%	3.8%	3.9%	3.8%	3.9%	3.7%	3.7%	3.7%	3.7%	3.7%
Consolidated COGS (before D&A)	$1,674.6	$1,731.4	$1,843.4	$1,889.4	$1,958.9	$2,023.5	$2,106.6	$2,186.8	$2,264.6	$2,345.3	$2,428.7	$2,511.8	$2,601.2
% of sales	74.6%	74.1%	74.1%	74.1%	74.0%	73.9%	73.8%	73.7%	73.6%	73.5%	73.4%	73.2%	73.1%
Consolidated gross profit	$570.3	$604.0	$644.1	$660.4	$688.3	$717.8	$747.9	$780.4	$812.3	$845.6	$880.2	$919.6	$957.2
% margin	25.4%	25.9%	25.9%	25.9%	26.0%	26.1%	26.2%	26.3%	26.4%	26.5%	26.6%	26.8%	26.9%
Consolidated SG&A	$426.2	$459.7	$480.3	$484.5	$500.3	$517.1	$533.8	$551.9	$569.2	$587.1	$605.5	$624.5	$644.1
% margin	19.0%	19.7%	19.3%	19.0%	18.9%	18.8%	18.7%	18.6%	18.5%	18.4%	18.3%	18.2%	18.1%
Non-recurring items	0.0	0.0		0.0	0.0	0.0	0.0	0.0	0.0	0.0	0.0	0.0	0.0
Consolidated EBITDA	$144.1	$144.4	$163.8	$175.9	$187.9	$200.8	$214.1	$228.5	$243.1	$258.5	$274.6	$295.1	$313.1
% margin	6.4%	6.2%	6.6%	6.9%	7.1%	7.3%	7.5%	7.7%	7.9%	8.1%	8.3%	8.6%	8.9%
100% EBITDA				$175.9	$187.9	$200.8	$214.1	$228.5	$243.1	$258.5	$274.6	$295.1	$313.1
Restructuring charges				25.0	25.0	0.0	0.0	0.0	0.0	0.0	0.0	0.0	0.0
Other charges/(income)				6.0	6.0	6.0	6.0	6.0	6.0	6.0	6.0	6.0	6.0
Pension expense				9.0	9.6	1.9	2.0	2.3	2.3	2.3	2.3	2.3	2.3
Depreciation				31.3	31.5	31.6	31.7	31.9	32.0	32.0	32.0	32.0	32.0
Amortization of goodwill (nondeductible)				9.3	9.3	9.3	9.3	9.3	9.3	9.3	9.3	9.3	9.3
Amortization of new financing fees				4.2	4.2	4.2	4.2	4.2	4.2	4.2	4.2	4.2	4.2
EBIT				91.2	102.4	147.8	161.0	174.9	189.3	204.7	220.9	241.3	259.4
% margin				3.6%	3.9%	5.4%	5.6%	5.9%	6.2%	6.4%	6.7%	7.0%	7.3%

Pro Forma	Pro Forma	2004	2005	2006	2007	2008	2009	2010	2011	2012	2013
Interest expense											
Revolving credit facility	$0.1	$0.0	$0.0	$0.0	$0.0	$0.0	$0.0	$0.0	$0.0	$0.0	$0.0
Euro tranche	5.2	5.6	6.6	6.5	4.8	3.1	1.3	0.1	0.0	0.0	0.0
Term loan B	14.4	15.4	19.1	20.7	18.2	15.7	13.0	8.6	2.9	0.0	0.0
Term loan C	0.0	0.0	0.0	0.0	0.0	0.0	0.0	0.0	0.0	0.0	0.0
Existing third-party debt	0.4	0.5	0.6	0.7	0.7	0.7	0.7	0.7	0.7	0.7	0.7
Senior notes	12.1	12.1	12.1	12.1	12.1	12.1	12.1	12.1	12.1	12.1	12.1
Senior subordinated notes	27.6	27.6	27.6	27.6	27.6	27.6	27.6	27.6	27.6	27.6	27.6
Seller contingent notes–cash pay	0.0	0.0	0.0	0.0	0.0	0.0	0.0	0.0	0.0	0.0	0.0
Unused commitment fee	0.5	0.6	0.6	0.6	0.6	0.6	0.6	0.6	0.6	0.6	0.6
Total cash interest expense	60.4	61.7	66.6	68.2	63.9	59.7	55.2	49.7	43.9	41.0	41.0
HoldCo PIK notes		0.0	0.0	0.0	0.0	0.0	0.0	0.0	0.0	0.0	0.0
Total interest expense		61.7	66.6	68.2	63.9	59.7	55.2	49.7	43.9	41.0	41.0
Interest income on cash balance		0.1	0.2	0.2	0.2	0.2	0.2	0.0	0.3	0.9	2.1
Net interest expense		61.6	66.4	68.0	63.7	59.5	55.0	49.5	43.7	40.1	38.9
Pretax income		29.6	36.0	79.9	97.2	115.3	134.3	155.1	177.2	201.2	220.5
Income taxes		18.9	23.1	30.8	42.4	55.3	59.1	67.4	76.3	85.9	93.6
Deferred tax		(7.3)	(7.5)	1.1	(1.2)	(3.6)	0.0	2.3	(2.0)	(2.0)	(2.0)
Net income		18.0	20.4	48.0	56.0	63.6	75.2	85.4	103.0	117.4	128.9
Preferred stock dividend		0.0	0.0	0.0	0.0	0.0	0.0	0.0	0.0	0.0	0.0
Net income to common		$18.0	$20.4	$48.0	$56.0	$63.6	$75.2	$85.4	$103.0	$117.4	$128.9

Use ICL tax rate? Yes (No = 1)   1   1

Income tax calculation	2004	2005	2006	2007	2008	2009	2010	2011	2012	2013
Pretax income	$29.6	$36.0	$79.9	$97.2	$115.3	$134.3	$155.1	$177.2	$201.2	$220.5
– Nondeductible goodwill	9.3	9.3	9.3	9.3	9.3	9.3	9.3	9.3	9.3	9.3
– Nondeductible transaction fees	4.2	4.2	4.2	4.2	4.2	4.2	4.2	4.2	4.2	4.2
Taxable income	43.0	49.4	93.3	110.7	128.8	147.7	168.6	190.6	214.7	233.9
Cash income tax @ 40.0%	$17.2	$19.8	$37.3	$44.3	$51.5	$59.1	$67.4	$76.3	$85.9	$93.6

456

EXHIBIT 2 | Historical and Projected Balance Sheets for CSSA

(fiscal year ended December 31)	Opening 12/31/03	Adjustments +	Adjustments −	Closing 12/31/03	1 2004	2 2005	3 2006	4 2007	5 2008	6 2009	7 2010	8 2011	9 2012	10 2013
Cash	$50.7	$0.0	($50.7)	$0.0	$20.0	$20.0	$20.0	$20.0	$20.0	$20.0	$20.0	$30.9	$144.2	$267.4
Accounts receivables	355.0			355.0	384.6	393.2	405.3	414.1	430.4	446.3	462.8	480.0	497.7	516.2
Inventories	242.3			242.3	269.9	273.5	282.6	292.4	303.6	314.4	325.6	337.2	348.7	361.1
Prepaid & other	22.3			22.3	24.6	25.2	26.6	27.6	28.6	29.7	30.8	31.9	33.1	34.3
Note from AtlantisMed	0.0	7.3		7.3	0.0	0.0	0.0	0.0	0.0	0.0	0.0	0.0	0.0	0.0
Total current assets	**670.3**			**626.9**	**699.2**	**711.9**	**734.5**	**754.1**	**782.6**	**810.4**	**839.2**	**879.9**	**1,023.7**	**1,179.0**
PP&E	140.9			140.9	136.9	133.8	131.6	130.6	130.5	129.8	130.4	132.2	135.3	139.7
Deferred tax	20.1	29.9		50.0	55.4	58.5	53.0	49.8	49.0	49.0	49.0	49.0	49.0	49.0
Financing fees	0.0	66.8		66.8	62.6	58.4	54.2	50.1	45.9	41.7	37.5	33.4	29.2	25.0
Other long-term assets	36.8			36.8	39.9	42.7	40.3	39.9	41.5	40.0	40.0	40.0	40.0	40.0
Intangible assets and goodwill	739.1	264.7		1,003.7	994.5	985.2	976.0	966.7	957.5	948.2	939.0	929.7	920.4	911.2
Total assets	**$1,607.3**			**$1,925.2**	**$1,988.4**	**$1,990.5**	**$1,989.6**	**$1,991.1**	**$2,006.9**	**$2,019.2**	**$2,035.1**	**$2,064.3**	**$2,197.7**	**$2,343.8**
Accounts payable	$234.4			$234.4	$277.8	$309.4	$329.9	$346.5	$359.3	$372.1	$385.3	$399.1	$412.7	$427.4
Other current liabilities	84.1			84.1	91.9	95.4	99.1	102.9	106.9	110.9	115.0	119.2	123.6	128.2
Taxes payable	0.0			0.0	0.0	0.0	0.0	0.0	0.0	0.0	0.0	0.0	0.0	0.0
Total current liabilities	**318.5**			**318.5**	**369.7**	**404.8**	**429.0**	**449.4**	**466.2**	**482.9**	**500.3**	**518.3**	**536.3**	**555.6**
Revolver	0.0	2.4		2.4	0.0	0.0	0.0	0.0	0.0	0.0	0.0	0.0	0.0	0.0
Euro tranche	0.0	133.5		133.5	133.4	111.3	86.4	59.4	35.1	3.9	0.0	0.0	0.0	0.0
Term loan B	0.0	369.4		369.4	369.2	336.0	298.7	258.3	221.7	175.0	89.8	0.0	0.0	0.0
Term loan C	0.0			0.0	0.0	0.0	0.0	0.0	0.0	0.0	0.0	0.0	0.0	0.0
Senior notes	0.0	155.8		155.8	155.8	155.8	155.8	155.8	155.8	155.8	155.8	155.8	155.8	155.8
Senior subordinated notes	0.0	307.1		307.1	307.1	307.1	307.1	307.1	307.1	307.1	307.1	307.1	307.1	307.1
HoldCo PIK	0.0			0.0	0.0	0.0	0.0	0.0	0.0	0.0	0.0	0.0	0.0	0.0
Existing debt	228.8	10.9	(228.8)	10.9	10.9	10.9	10.9	10.9	10.9	10.9	10.9	10.9	10.9	10.9
Deferred tax liability	36.2			36.2	28.9	21.4	22.5	21.3	17.7	17.7	20.0	18.0	16.0	14.0
Pension liability/other	70.9	7.3		78.2	95.9	105.3	93.3	87.0	86.8	85.0	85.0	85.0	85.0	85.0
Total liabilities	**654.5**			**1,412.0**	**1,470.8**	**1,452.6**	**1,403.7**	**1,349.2**	**1,301.3**	**1,238.3**	**1,168.9**	**1,095.0**	**1,111.1**	**1,128.3**
PIK preferred	0.0	0.0		0.0	0.0	0.0	0.0	0.0	0.0	0.0	0.0	0.0	0.0	0.0
Other comprehensive income	0.0	0.0		0.0	(13.6)	(13.6)	(13.6)	(13.6)	(13.6)	(13.6)	(13.6)	(13.6)	(13.6)	(13.6)
Common equity	952.7	534.0	(973.6)	513.2	531.2	551.5	599.5	655.6	719.2	794.4	879.9	982.8	1,100.2	1,229.1
Total shareholders' equity	**952.7**			**513.2**	**517.6**	**537.9**	**585.9**	**642.0**	**705.6**	**780.8**	**866.3**	**969.2**	**1,086.6**	**1,215.5**
Total liabilities & shareholders' equity	**$1,607.3**			**$1,925.2**	**$1,988.4**	**$1,990.5**	**$1,989.6**	**$1,991.1**	**$2,006.9**	**$2,019.2**	**$2,035.1**	**$2,064.3**	**$2,197.7**	**$2,343.8**
Balance check	0.000			0.000	0.000	0.000	0.000	0.000	0.000	0.000	0.000	0.000	0.000	0.000
Net working capital	$301.1			$308.4	$309.5	$287.1	$285.5	$284.7	$296.4	$307.4	$318.9	$330.8	$343.2	$356.0

Source: Deutsche Bank Securities, Inc.

457

EXHIBIT 3 | Summary of Forecast Assumptions

Foreign Exchange Rates: The average EUR/USD exchange rate of 1.13 for the full year 2003 was assumed to remain constant throughout the projection period, 2004–08.

Sales: Consolidated revenue was projected to grow at a compounded annual rate of 4% over the projection period. This compared to forecast growth in the hospital supply products market of 4% to 5% per year, with third-party distributors likely to take incremental share from direct distribution and regional and/or niche distributors. CSSA's growth would be achieved primarily through expanding business with existing customers, aggressively pursuing selected growth markets in North America, and targeted cross-selling of products throughout Europe. Revenues in North America were forecast to grow at 4% per year; in Europe, revenue growth was projected at 3.5% per year.

Gross Profit: CSSA's gross margins were projected to improve from 25.9% in 2003 to 26.2% in 2008. That improvement would be obtained by improvements in product mix. The projections assumed a gross margin increase from 22.4% in 2003 to 23.6% in 2008, driven primarily by increased private label penetration, more aggressive sourcing from suppliers, and selected SKU rationalization.

Selling, General, and Administrative Expenses: SG&A expenses as a percentage of sales were projected to decline from 19.3% in 2003 to 18.6% in 2008, largely as a result of productivity improvements foreseen in Europe.

EBITDA: Through the combination of gross margin improvements and reductions in SG&A expenses mentioned above in both North America and Europe, consolidated EBITDA was projected to grow at a five-year CAGR of 6.6%, with EBITDA margins improving from 6.6% in 2003 to 7.6% in 2008.

Working Capital: The projections assume total working capital as a percentage of sales would decline from 11.6% (adjusted for currency) in 2003 to 8.9% in 2008. The improvement would be driven by a combination of payable, receivable and inventory management initiatives.

EXHIBIT 4 | Financial Data on Recent Acquisitions in Medical Products Logistics Management and Distribution

Announcement Date	Target Name	Acquirer Name	Transaction Value ($mil)	Per-Share Offer ($)	Enterprise Value ($mil)	Acquisition Technique	Enterprise Value as Multiple of:			Stock Premium (%)		
							Net Sales	EBITDA	EBIT	1 day prior	1 wk prior	4 wks prior
12/27/03	Skelton Catheters Supply	Costello Laboratories	408.1	15.4	415.1	Tender offer	6.57x	na	na	19.3%	25.6%	19.6%
12/1/03	Bene/Bio Corp.	Orchid Health	504.3	48.0	402.7	Tender offer	4.68x	17.93x	22.82x	0.0%	15.4%	3.7%
5/25/03	Institution Group	MASS Corp.	769.7	18.7	762.2	Tender offer	2.83x	13.15x	16.72x	1.1%	−1.3%	4.0%
3/10/03	Robin Holding AG	Wilhelm Distributors AG	1,175.0	489.7	1,183.2	Tender offer	4.88x	30.86x	48.90x	56.7%	55.0%	46.7%
9/31/2002	Distribuo Italia SpA	Leno Inc.	276.6	21.4	152.6	Stock swap	33.36x	na	na	36.2%	64.3%	74.4%
11/23/02	Loire Medecin S.A.	Wilma Rock A.G.	256.6	63.4	224.2	Tender offer	3.08x	16.63x	33.85x	30.5%	50.6%	63.1%
						Mean	**9.23x**	**19.64x**	**30.57x**	**24.0%**	**34.9%**	**35.3%**
						Median	**4.78x**	**17.28x**	**28.34x**	**24.9%**	**38.1%**	**33.2%**

na = not available.

Source: Thomson Financial SDC Platinum Database. Names, dates, and certain figures are disguised.

EXHIBIT 5 | Summary of Financial Information on Peer Firms in Logistics Management and Distribution

(Global medical supply firms listed for trading in the United States for 12 months ended September 30, 2003.)

Name	Medecin Toujours S.A.	Mendenhall Hospital Supply Ltd.	Osaka Medico	Deutsche Gesundheit Gmbh	Medical & Scientific Supply Corp.	Clinique Voltaire S.A.	Spa and Hospital Distr. Corp.	Caja de Techno S.A.	MEDIAN	MEAN
Headquarters Location	France	U.K.	Japan	Germany	U.S.	Swiss	U.S.	Spain		
Net revenues ($mil)	$750.33	$512.30	$94.40	$997.10	$2,400.50	$531.80	$1,388.70	$162.10	$641.07	$854.65
Gross margin	60.5%	42.1%	52.4%	64.0%	59.1%	73.5%	57.0%	78.6%	59.8%	60.9%
EBITDA margin	18.6%	27.7%	14.5%	25.7%	10.1%	28.8%	27.1%	51.1%	26.4%	25.5%
Net income ($mil)	$ 56.96	$ 66.91	$ 4.61	$ 77.09	$ 124.83	$ 64.85	$ 206.57	$ 50.75	$ 65.88	$ 81.57
Return on sales	7.59%	13.06%	4.89%	7.73%	5.20%	12.19%	14.88%	31.31%	10.0%	12.1%
Debt/equity (book)	47.7%	40.0%	13.3%	57.5%	63.1%	36.9%	24.3%	7.2%	0.38	0.36
Debt/equity (market)	16.1%	11.8%	4.9%	29.2%	13.9%	7.1%	6.1%	1.4%	0.09	0.11
Debt/capital (book)	32.7%	28.2%	11.8%	36.5%	43.0%	27.5%	20.7%	6.8%	0.28	0.26
Debt/capital (market)	13.9%	10.6%	4.7%	22.6%	12.2%	6.6%	5.7%	1.4%	0.09	0.10
Dividend yield	0.0%	0.0%	0.0%	0.0%	0.0%	0.0%	0.9%	0.0%	0.0%	0.1%
Beta	0.55	0.16	1.50	0.60	0.96	1.81	0.19	0.82	0.71	0.82
Enterprise value/sales	1.56	2.59	3.06	4.78	2.85	5.04	3.13	7.94	3.10	3.87
Enterprise value/EBIT	10.76	11.32	34.80	40.36	17.16	23.44	14.36	16.99	17.08	21.15
Enterprise value/EBITDA	8.38	9.35	21.10	18.61	13.22	17.47	11.54	15.54	14.38	14.40
Enterprise value/opng. CF	13.35	14.46	28.87	22.16	16.22	25.80	15.65	22.24	19.19	19.84
Enterprise value/FCF	26.74	17.42	392.81	27.37	37.82	39.79	18.81	29.59	28.48	73.79
Enterprise value/equity (book)	3.16	3.41	2.70	2.06	4.94	5.29	4.07	4.86	3.74	3.81
Total debt/enterprise value	0.15	0.12	0.05	0.28	0.13	0.07	0.06	0.01	0.09	0.11
P/E ratio	19.55	20.19	178.00	60.79	23.65	49.83	19.85	38.91	31.28	51.35
Market value of equity/sales	1.46	2.56	3.07	4.57	2.63	4.97	3.09	8.55	3.08	3.86
Market value of equity/EBIT	10.06	11.21	34.94	38.61	15.82	23.13	14.18	18.31	17.07	20.78
Market value of equity/EBITDA	7.84	9.25	21.18	17.81	12.18	17.24	11.39	16.74	14.46	14.21
Market value of equity/opng. CF	12.49	14.32	28.99	21.21	14.95	25.46	15.45	23.96	18.33	19.60
Market value of equity/FCF	25.02	17.25	394.46	26.19	34.86	39.27	18.56	31.88	29.03	73.43
Market value of equity/equity (book)	2.96	3.38	2.71	1.97	4.55	5.22	4.01	5.24	3.70	3.76

Source: Standard and Poor's *Research Insight.* Names and some figures have been disguised.

EXHIBIT 6 | Contemplated Sources and Uses of Funds for the Transaction

Sources of Funds	($mm)	% of Total Cap.	Mult. of 2003E EBITDA	Cumulative Multiple	Uses of Funds	($mm)
Revolver	2.4	0.2%	0.0	0.0	Purchase target company	1,435.3
Term loan euro denominated	133.5	8.8%	0.8	0.8	Cash on balance sheet	0.0
Term loan dollar denominated	369.4	24.4%	2.3	3.1	Fees & expenses	66.8
Existing third-party debt	10.9	0.7%	0.1	3.2	Rollover existing debt	10.9
Senior notes	155.8	10.3%	1.0	4.1		
Senior subordinated notes	307.1	20.3%	1.9	6.0		
PIK preferred	0.0	0.0%	0.0	6.0		
HoldCo PIK	0.0	0.0%	0.0	6.0		
Sponsor equity	534.0	35.3%	3.3	9.2		
Seller equity	0.0	0.0%	0.0	9.2		
Total sources of funds	**1,513.0**	**100.0%**	**9.2**	**9.2**	**Total uses of funds**	**1,513.0**

Source: Deutsche Bank Securities, Inc.

EXHIBIT 7 | Projection of Capitalization of CSSA

CAPITALIZATION	Pro Forma 2003	1 2004	2 2005	3 2006	4 2007	5 2008	6 2009	7 2010	8 2011	9 2012	10 2013
Cash	$ 0.0	$ 20.0	$ 20.0	$ 20.0	$ 20.0	$ 20.0	$ 20.0	$ 20.0	$ 30.9	$ 144.2	$ 267.4
Revolver	$ 2.4	$ 0.0	$ 0.0	$ 0.0	$ 0.0	$ 0.0	$ 0.0	$ 0.0	$ 0.0	$ 0.0	$ 0.0
Term loan A	133.5	133.4	111.3	86.4	59.4	35.1	3.9	0.0	0.0	0.0	0.0
Term loan B	369.4	369.2	336.0	298.7	258.3	221.7	175.0	89.8	0.0	0.0	0.0
Existing third-party debt	10.9	10.9	10.9	10.9	10.9	10.9	10.9	10.9	10.9	10.9	10.9
Total bank debt	**516.2**	**513.5**	**458.2**	**396.1**	**328.6**	**267.8**	**189.8**	**100.8**	**10.9**	**10.9**	**10.9**
Senior notes	155.8	155.8	155.8	155.8	155.8	155.8	155.8	155.8	155.8	155.8	155.8
Total senior debt	**672.0**	**669.3**	**614.0**	**551.8**	**484.4**	**423.5**	**345.6**	**256.5**	**166.7**	**166.7**	**166.7**
Senior subordinated notes	307.1	307.1	307.1	307.1	307.1	307.1	307.1	307.1	307.1	307.1	307.1
Total debt	**979.0**	**976.3**	**921.0**	**858.9**	**791.4**	**730.6**	**652.6**	**563.6**	**473.7**	**473.7**	**473.7**
HoldCo PIK	0.0	0.0	0.0	0.0	0.0	0.0	0.0	0.0	0.0	0.0	0.0
Total debt + PIK	**979.0**	**976.3**	**921.0**	**858.9**	**791.4**	**730.6**	**652.6**	**563.6**	**473.7**	**473.7**	**473.7**
Shareholders' equity	513.2	517.6	537.9	585.9	642.0	705.6	780.8	866.3	969.2	1,086.6	1,215.5
Total capitalization	**$1,492.2**	**$1,493.9**	**$1,459.0**	**$1,444.8**	**$1,433.4**	**$1,436.2**	**$1,433.5**	**$1,429.8**	**$1,443.0**	**$1,560.4**	**$1,689.3**
Cash available for debt service	na	$ 22.7	$ 55.3	$ 62.4	$ 67.2	$ 60.9	$ 77.9	$ 89.1	$ 100.7	$ 113.3	$ 123.2
Cumulative cash available for debt service	na	22.7	78.0	140.1	204.6	268.4	346.4	435.4	536.1	649.5	772.6
% of bank debt outstanding	102.2%	101.6%	90.7%	78.4%	65.0%	53.0%	37.6%	19.9%	2.2%	2.2%	2.2%

na = not available.

Source: Deutsche Bank Securities, Inc.

EXHIBIT 8 | Summary of Credit Statistics for the Financing as Contemplated and for Performance as Projected

CREDIT STATISTICS	2003	2004	2005	2006	2007	2008	2009	2010	2011	2012	2013
EBITDA/cash interest expense	2.7x	2.8x	2.8x	2.9x	3.3x	3.8x	4.4x	5.2x	6.2x	7.2x	7.6x
(EBITDA-capex)/cash interest expense	2.5x	2.4x	2.4x	2.5x	2.9x	3.3x	3.8x	4.5x	5.5x	6.3x	6.7x
EBITDA/total interest expense	2.7x	2.8x	2.8x	2.9x	3.3x	3.8x	4.4x	5.2x	6.2x	7.2x	7.6x
(EBITDA-capex)/total interest expense	2.5x	2.4x	2.4x	2.5x	2.9x	3.3x	3.8x	4.5x	5.5x	6.3x	6.7x
Bank debt/EBITDA	3.2x	2.9x	2.4x	2.0x	1.5x	1.2x	0.8x	0.4x	0.0x	0.0x	0.0x
Senior debt/EBITDA	4.1x	3.8x	3.3x	2.8x	2.3x	1.9x	1.4x	1.0x	0.6x	0.6x	0.5x
Total debt/EBITDA	6.0x	5.6x	4.9x	4.3x	3.7x	3.2x	2.7x	2.2x	1.7x	1.6x	1.5x
Total debt+PIK/EBITDA	6.0x	5.6x	4.9x	4.3x	3.7x	3.2x	2.7x	2.2x	1.7x	1.6x	1.5x

Source: Deutsche Bank Securities, Inc.

EXHIBIT 9 | Information on Covenant Compliance: Forecast Interest Coverage and Total Leverage

INTEREST COVERAGE RATIO

Fiscal year	2004					2005					2006				
Period (quarters)	1	2	3	4	Total	1	2	3	4	Total	1	2	3	4	Total
Quarter ended	31-Mar	30-Jun	30-Sep	31-Dec	31-Dec	31-Mar	30-Jun	30-Sep	31-Dec	31-Dec	31-Mar	30-Jun	30-Sep	31-Dec	31-Dec
Seasonal EBITDA contribution	25.0%	25.0%	25.0%	25.0%	100.0%	25.0%	25.0%	25.0%	25.0%	100.0%	25.0%	25.0%	25.0%	25.0%	100.0%
EBITDA	$44.0	$44.0	$44.0	$44.0	$175.9	$47.0	$47.0	$47.0	$47.0	$187.9	$50.2	$50.2	$50.2	$50.2	$200.8
Total numerator	$44.0	$44.0	$44.0	$44.0		$47.0	$47.0	$47.0	$47.0		$50.2	$50.2	$50.2	$50.2	
Consolidated cash interest expense:															
Revolver	$0.0	$0.0	$0.0	$0.0	$0.0	$0.0	$0.0	$0.0	$0.0	$0.0	$0.0	$0.0	$0.0	$0.0	$0.0
Term loan A	1.4	1.4	1.4	1.4	5.6	1.7	1.7	1.7	1.7	6.6	1.6	1.6	1.6	1.6	6.5
Term loan B	3.8	3.8	3.8	3.8	15.8	4.8	4.8	4.8	4.8	19.1	5.2	5.2	5.2	5.2	20.7
Existing third-party debt	0.1	0.1	0.1	0.1	0.5	0.1	0.1	0.1	0.1	0.6	0.2	0.2	0.2	0.2	0.7
Senior notes	6.0	6.0	6.0	6.0	12.1	6.0	6.0	6.0	6.0	12.1	6.0	0.0	6.0	0.0	12.1
Senior sub. notes	13.8	13.8	13.8	0.0	27.6	13.8	13.8	13.8	0.0	27.6	13.8	0.0	13.8	0.0	27.6
Unused commitment fee	0.1	0.1	0.1	0.1	0.6	0.1	0.1	0.1	0.1	0.6	0.1	0.1	0.1	0.1	0.6
Total cash interest expense	$25.3	$5.5	$25.3	$5.5	$61.7	$26.6	$6.7	$26.6	$6.7	$66.6	$27.0	$7.1	$27.0	$7.1	$68.2
Test period numerator	$44.0	$44.0	$44.0	$44.0		$47.0	$47.0	$47.0	$47.0		$50.2	$50.2	$50.2	$50.2	
Rolling 12-month numerator	NA	NA	NA	175.9		178.9	181.9	184.9	187.9		191.2	194.4	197.6	200.8	
Test period denominator	25.3	5.5	25.3	5.5		26.6	6.7	26.6	6.7		27.0	7.1	27.0	7.1	
Rolling 12-month denominator	NA	NA	NA	61.7		62.9	64.2	65.4	66.6		67.0	67.4	67.8	68.2	
Calculated 12-month rolling ratio				2.85x		2.84x	2.84x	2.83x	2.82x		2.85x	2.88x	2.91x	2.95x	
85% calculated 12-month rolling ratio				2.42x		2.42x	2.41x	2.40x	2.40x		2.42x	2.45x	2.48x	2.50x	
Proposed covenant minimum				2.00x		2.25x	2.25x	2.25x	2.25x		2.25x	2.25x	2.25x	2.25x	

TOTAL LEVERAGE RATIO

Fiscal year	2004					2005					2006				
Period (quarters)	1	2	3	4	Total	1	2	3	4	Total	1	2	3	4	Total
Quarter ended	31-Mar	30-Jun	30-Sep	31-Dec	31-Dec	31-Mar	30-Jun	30-Sep	31-Dec	31-Dec	31-Mar	30-Jun	30-Sep	31-Dec	31-Dec
Consolidated total debt:															
Revolver	$1.8	$1.2	$0.6	$0.0		$0.0	$0.0	$0.0	$0.0	$0.0	$0.0	$0.0	$0.0	$0.0	$0.0
Term loan A	133.5	133.4	133.4	133.4		127.9	122.3	116.8	111.3		105.1	98.8	92.6	86.4	
Term loan B	369.3	369.3	369.2	369.2		360.9	352.6	344.3	336.0		326.7	317.4	308.0	298.7	
Term loan C	0.0	0.0	0.0	0.0		0.0	0.0	0.0	0.0		0.0	0.0	0.0	0.0	
Assumed LC usage	0.0	0.0	0.0	0.0		0.0	0.0	0.0	0.0		0.0	0.0	0.0	0.0	
Senior notes	155.8	155.8	155.8	155.8		155.8	155.8	155.8	155.8		155.8	155.8	155.8	155.8	
Senior sub. notes	307.1	307.1	307.1	307.1		307.1	307.1	307.1	307.1		307.1	307.1	307.1	307.1	
Total debt	$967.4	$966.7	$966.0	$965.4		$951.6	$937.7	$923.9	$910.1		$894.5	$879.0	$863.5	$847.9	
Test period seasonalized EBITDA	$44.0	$44.0	$44.0	$44.0		$47.0	$47.0	$47.0	$47.0		$50.2	$50.2	$50.2	$50.2	$200.8
Rolling 12-month seasonalized EBITDA	NA	NA	NA	175.9		178.9	181.9	184.9	187.9		191.2	194.4	197.6	200.8	
Calculated ratio				5.49x		5.32x	5.15x	5.00x	4.84x		4.68x	4.52x	4.37x	4.22x	
120% case calculated ratio				6.58x		6.38x	6.18x	5.99x	5.81x		5.62x	5.43x	5.24x	5.07x	
Proposed covenant maximum				6.75x		6.50x	6.50x	6.25x	6.25x		5.75x	5.75x	5.75x	5.25x	

NA = not available.

Source: Deutsche Bank Securities, Inc.

EXHIBIT 10 | Estimation of Internal Rate of Return to Intercontinental Capital, Ltd.

Equity Allocation	Investment	Equity Ownership
PIK preferred stock	$0.0	0.0%
Seller equity	0.0	0.0%
Sponsor equity	534.0	100.0%
Total	**$534.0**	**100.0%**

Sponsor Equity	2003	2004	2005	2006	2007	2008
Initial investment	($534.0)					
Equity participation		0.0	0.0	0.0	0.0	1,400.3
	($534.0)	$0.0	$0.0	$0.0	$0.0	$1,400.3

IRR	21.3%

Exit Valuation	
Exit year	2008
Exit multiple	9.2x
Exit year EBITDA	$228.5
Exit valuation (total firm value)	**$2,110.9**
Revolver	$0.0
Euro tranche	35.1
Term loan B	221.7
Term loan C	0.0
Existing Debt	10.9
Senior notes	155.8
Senior subordinated notes	307.1
Seller contingent PIK notes	0.0
PIK preferred	0.0
Total debt & preferred stock	730.6
Less: accumulated cash	(20.0)
Net debt	$710.6
Allocation proceeds (equity value)	**$1,400.3**

	Diluted Equity Ownership				
	60.0%	70.0%	80.0%	90.0%	100.0%
8.0x	4.7%	7.9%	10.8%	13.5%	15.9%
8.5x	6.7%	10.1%	13.0%	15.7%	18.2%
Exit multiple 9.0x	8.6%	12.0%	15.1%	17.8%	20.3%
9.5x	10.4%	13.9%	16.9%	19.7%	22.3%
10.0x	12.1%	15.6%	18.7%	21.5%	24.1%

Source: Deutsche Bank Securities, Inc.

EXHIBIT 11 Information on Credit Rating Standards and Interest Rates

	Investment Grade				Non-investment Grade	
	AAA	**AA**	**A**	**BBB**	**BB**	**B**

Key Industrial Financial Ratios (Three-year medians 2000-2002)
Source of data: Standard & Poor's CreditStats, September 8, 2003.

	AAA	AA	A	BBB	BB	B
EBIT interest coverage (x)	23.4	13.3	6.3	3.9	2.2	1.0
EBITDA interest coverage (x)	25.3	16.9	8.5	5.4	3.2	1.7
Funds from operations/total debt (%)	214.2	65.7	42.2	30.6	19.7	10.4
Free operating cash flow/total debt (%)	156.6	33.6	22.3	12.8	7.3	1.5
Return on capital (%)	35.0	26.6	18.1	13.1	11.5	8.0
Operating income/sales (%)	23.4	24.0	18.1	15.5	15.4	14.7
Long-term debt/capital (%)	(1.1)	21.1	33.8	40.3	53.6	72.6
Total debt/capital, incl. short-term debt (%)	5.0	35.9	42.6	47.0	57.7	75.1

Spread over LIBOR for Syndicate-Funded Fully-Secured Senior Revolving and Term Debt (quoted in basis points)
Source: Case writer's estimates.

	AAA	AA	A	BBB	BB	B
Term of 1 year or less	10	20	50	100	200	300
Term of 2 years	11	22	55	110	220	330
Term of 3 years	12	24	60	120	240	360
Term of 4 years	14	28	70	140	280	420
Term of 5 years	16	32	80	160	320	480
Term of 6 years	17	34	85	170	340	510
Term of 7 years	18	36	90	180	360	540

Average Yields to Maturity of Fixed-Rate Long-Term Senior Bonds (%)
Source of data: Bloomberg, LP.

	AA+/AA	AA−	A	BBB	BBB−	BB
Term of 5 years	3.902	3.985	4.104	4.334	5.545	6.058
Term of 10 years	4.629	4.698	4.881	5.127	6.378	6.892
Term of 15 years	5.028	na	5.332	5.648	na	na
Term of 20 years	na	na	5.949	na	na	na

Definitions:

EBIT interest coverage divides earnings before interest and taxes (EBIT) by gross interest expense (before subtracting capitalized interest and interest income).

EBITDA interest coverage divides earnings before interest, taxes, depreciation, and amortization (EBITDA) by gross interest expense.

FFO/total debt divides funds from operations (FFO) by total debt. FFO is defined as net income from continuing operations, depreciation and amortization, deferred income taxes, and other non-cash items/Long-term debt + current maturities + commercial paper, and other short-term borrowings.

Free operating cash flow/total debt. Free operating cash flow is defined as FFO − capital expenditures − (+) increase (decrease) in working capital (excluding changes in cash, marketable securities, and short-term debt)/Long-term debt + current maturities, commercial paper, and other short-term borrowings.

Total debt/EBITDA. Long-term debt + current maturities, commercial paper, and other short-term borrowings/Adjusted earnings from continuing operations before interest, taxes, and depreciation and amortization.

Return on capital. EBIT/Average of beginning of year and end of year capital, including short-term debt, current maturities, long-term debt, noncurrent deferred taxes, minority interest, and equity (common and preferred stock).

Total debt/capital. Long-term debt + current maturities, commercial paper, and other short-term borrowings/Long-term debt + current maturities, commercial paper, and other short-term borrowings + shareholders' equity (including preferred stock) + minority interest.

na = not available.

Source: Standard & Poor's *Corporate Ratings Criteria 2005* (New York: Standard & Poor's Corporation, 42).

EXHIBIT 12 | Information on Capital Market Conditions at November 20, 2003

U.S. Treasury Obligations	Yield	Other Instruments	Yield
3 month bills	0.937%	U.S. Federal Reserve discount rate	0.750%
6 month bills	1.001%	U.S. certificate of deposit (30 day)	1.027%
2 year bonds	1.781%	U.S. commerical paper (30 day)	1.030%
3 year bonds	2.320%	LIBOR (30 day)	2.068%
5 year bonds	3.119%	UK Interbank (30 day)	3.813%
10 year bonds	4.152%	U.S. prime rate	4.000%
30 year bonds	5.009%		

Long-Term Corporate Debt Obligations	Yield	Price/earnings Ratios	
(European industrial)		S&P 500 Composite Index	30.2x
AA+/AA	5.028%	S&P Industrial	37.1x
AA−	4.698%	FTSE 350 Index	17.8x
A	5.949%	FTSE Chemicals	20.3x
BBB+	5.059%	FTSE Food Producers	10.6x
BBB	5.648%	DAX 30	11.7x
BBB−	6.378%		
BB	6.892%		

Source of data: Thomson Financial's *Datastream Advance*; Bloomberg LP.

EXHIBIT 13 | Trends in Equity Values for Selected Markets and Sectors

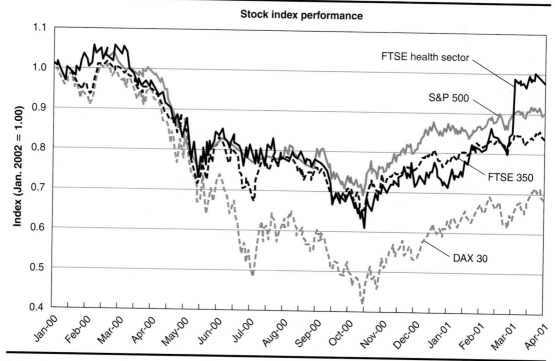

Source: Thomson Financial's *Datastream Advance*.

EXHIBIT 14 | Estimate of Return on Assets to Deutsche Bank and Cost of Funds to Intercontinental Capital, Ltd.

(Results are merely illustrative and not meant to suggest a recommendation.)

Key assumptions for senior bank credits

LIBOR =				1.160%						
Revolving loan spread over LIBOR (in basis points) =				250						
Term loan spread over LIBOR (in basis points) =				275						
Amount of revolving loan (US$ millions)				$2.4						
Amount of senior term loan (US$ millions)				$513.8						
Percentage of loans sold through syndication				80.0%						
Tax rate				40.0%						
Commitment fees on revolving loan (as percent of commitment, per year)				0.75%						
Agency fees on revolver and senior term loan (as a percent of outstandings)				0.5%						
Syndication fees on revolver and senior term loan (as a percent of initial balance)				0.5%						
Advisory and other fees (absolute amount in US$ millions)				$17.0						
Bond underwriting fee				2.5%						

Loan amortization: please indicate the outstandings in the table below.

	At closing	2005	2006	2007	2008	2009	2010	2011	2012
Revolver balance (max life: 5 years)	2.4	0.0	0.0	0.0	0.0	0.0	0.0	0.0	0.0
Sr. term balance (max life: 7 years)	513.8	513.5	458.2	396.1	328.6	267.8	189.8	100.8	10.9

Key assumptions for underwriting services: long-term debt, and preferred and common stock

		Cost before Fees
Long-term senior bonds to be underwritten or placed (US$ millions)	$155.8	7.8%
Subordinated bonds to be underwritten or placed (US$ millions)	$307.1	9.0%
Convertible bonds to be underwritten or placed (US$ millions)	$0.00	8.0%
Preferred stock to be underwritten or placed (US$ millions)	$0.00	9.5%
Common stock to be underwritten or placed (US$ millions)	$0.00	10.0%
Advisory and other fees (absolute amount in US$ millions)	$0.00	
Underwriting or placement fees (as % of amount issued)		
Long-term senior bonds	2.5%	
Subordinated bonds	3.0%	
Convertible bonds	3.0%	
Preferred stock	4.0%	
Common stock	5.0%	

Bank's View: Analysis of Return on the Client Relationship

	Pretax	After-tax
Total return on assets	23.17%	12.28%
ROA from senior bank credits only	9.66%	5.66%
Implied ROA from fees	13.51%	6.63%

Client's View: Analysis of Cost of Financing, after Fees

		Cost of new financing	
	Amount	Pretax	After-tax
Blended cost of all funds raised, after fees	$979.0	6.35%	3.81%
Cost of revolving loan	$2.4	3.85%	2.31%
Cost of senior term loan	$513.8	4.12%	2.47%
Cost of long-term senior bonds	$155.8	7.95%	4.77%
Cost of subordinated bonds	$307.1	9.28%	5.57%
Cost of convertible bonds	$0.0	8.25%	4.95%
Cost of preferred stock	$0.0	9.90%	9.90%
Cost of common stock	$0.0	10.53%	10.53%

EXHIBIT 14 | *(continued)*

	At closing	2005	2006	2007	2008	2009	2010	2011	2012
IRR of After-Tax Cash Flows Net of Funding Costs									
Net interest income									
Revolver		0.01	0.00	0.00	0.00	0.00	0.00	0.00	0.00
Senior term debt		2.83	13.36	11.75	9.96	8.20	6.29	4.00	1.54
Fees associated with senior debt									
Commitment fee	0.02								
Agency fee		2.58	2.57	2.29	1.98	1.64	1.34	0.95	0.50
Syndication fee	2.58								
Advisory and other fees	17.00								
Fees associated with placement or underwriting commitments									
Advisory and other fees	0.00								
Long-term bonds	3.89								
Subordinated bonds	9.21								
Convertible bonds	0.00								
Preferred stock	0.00								
Common stock	0.00								
Pretax income	32.70	5.41	15.93	14.04	11.95	9.84	7.63	4.94	2.04
Income tax	(13.08)	(2.16)	(6.37)	(5.62)	(4.78)	(3.94)	(3.05)	(1.98)	(0.82)
Debt amortization									
Revolver	(0.48)	(0.48)	0.00	0.00	0.00	0.00	0.00	0.00	0.00
Senior term	(102.76)	0.05	11.06	12.43	13.49	12.17	15.59	17.82	17.96
Total cash flow	($83.62)	$2.82	$20.62	$20.85	$20.66	$18.08	$20.17	$20.78	$19.19
IRR (ROA after taxes)=	**12.28%**								
IRR of Cash Flows before Funding Costs and Bank Taxes									
Gross Pretax									
Cash flow=	($70.54)	$4.99	$26.99	$26.47	$25.43	$22.02	$23.22	$22.76	$20.00
IRR (ROA after taxes)=	**23.17%**								

	At closing	2005	2006	2007	2008	2009	2010	2011	2012
Analysis of ROA on Senior Bank Credits Only									
Pretax net interest income									
Revolver		0.01	0.00	0.00	0.00	0.00	0.00	0.00	0.00
Senior term debt		2.83	13.36	11.75	9.96	8.20	6.29	4.00	1.54
Less: taxes		(1.13)	(5.34)	(4.70)	(3.99)	(3.28)	(2.52)	(1.60)	(0.61)
After-tax net interest income		1.70	8.02	7.05	5.98	4.92	3.78	2.40	0.92
Debt amortization									
Revolver	(0.48)	(0.48)	0.00	0.00	0.00	0.00	0.00	0.00	0.00
Senior term	(102.76)	0.05	11.06	12.43	13.49	12.17	15.59	17.82	17.96
Total cash flow	($103.24)	$1.27	$19.08	$19.48	$19.47	$17.09	$19.36	$20.21	$18.88
IRR (ROA after taxes)=	**5.66%**								
Pretax cash flow	($103.24)	$2.40	$24.42	$24.18	$23.45	$20.37	$21.88	$21.81	$19.50
IRR (ROA) before taxes=	**9.66%**								

Source: Case writer's analysis.

Threshold Sports, LLC

Carl Frischkorn closed the door and walked to his desk. As he sat down, he began to reflect on the meeting he had just attended in the conference room of Threshold Sports, LLC. There, Frischkorn had listened as company founders David Chauner and Gerard "Jerry" Casale Jr. discussed the company's growth plans. Among the most critical challenges before Threshold was financing. The firm's founders were certain they would need outside financing of $500,000 to grow according to their plans, but they were unsure what type of financing would best fit their needs, how to value the firm, and how to communicate that value to outsiders. Their task over the next few days would be to find answers. For help in the matter, they had sought the input of Frischkorn, a management consultant, angel investor, and chairman of Threshold Sports.

Founded three months earlier, in March 2000, Threshold Sports was a sports-marketing and event-production company focusing on the U.S. cycling market. Partners Jerry Casale and David Chauner had formed the limited-liability corporation to buy the cycling assets of Octagon Worldwide, the sports division of the advertising and marketing firm Interpublic Group (IPG). Through the newly formed Threshold, Casale and Chauner sought to market and produce, in the United States, competitive cycling events like those found throughout Europe.

The Cycling Market

Part of the Olympic Games since 1896, bicycle racing was popular as both an amateur and professional sport throughout the world. In Europe, both indoor and outdoor racing were extremely popular among amateurs and professionals. The professional circuit in Europe ran from February through October, and included the world's largest and most famous annual competitive cycling event, the prestigious Tour de France. The Tour, which covered about 2,256 miles over a four-week period, commanded a worldwide television audience of 1 billion viewers.

In the United States, the popularity of cycling was undeniable. In 1999, U.S. retailers sold a record 7.4 million bicycles. As of 2000, approximately 73 million Americans rode bicycles—outnumbering the ranks of skiers, golfers, and tennis players combined.

This case was prepared by Dorothy C. Kelly, CFA, under the supervision of Robert F. Bruner and Professor Kenneth M. Eades. It is intended for illustrative purposes only. Copyright © 2001 by the University of Virginia Darden School Foundation, Charlottesville, VA. All rights reserved. *To order copies, send an e-mail to sales@dardenpublishing.com. No part of this publication may be reproduced, stored in a retrieval system, used in a spreadsheet, or transmitted in any form or by any means—electronic, mechanical, photocopying, recording, or otherwise—without the permission of the Darden School Foundation.* Rev. 12/05.

Despite the popularity of cycling in the United States and the existence of a national cycling association (USA Cycling, known as USAC), both amateur and professional cycling in the United States lagged in development when compared with other sports. Often regarded simply as a pastime or method of transportation, amateur cycling lacked the community support and organization associated with other amateur sports, such as Little League baseball, YMCA soccer, or youth tennis. Likewise, professional cycling in the United States had yet to offer the level of competition and organization available in other sports such as football, baseball, basketball, or hockey, each of which had grown into a multibillion-dollar business **(Exhibit 1).** Although interest in cycling as a competitive sport had grown with the notable successes of American cyclists Greg LeMond and Lance Armstrong, professional U.S. cycling had yet to develop a signature competitive series such as the PGA Tour or offer an equivalent to the Tour de France.[1]

Threshold Sports

Threshold sought to fill the void in U.S. cycling by managing and producing European-style competitive cycling events. Threshold felt confident it could fill this small but attractive niche because of management's experience with event planning and relationships within the cycling world. For 15 years, COO Jerry Casale, 52, had staged cycling events, including national championship races as well as the cycling events of the 1996 Olympic Games. President and CEO David Chauner, 62, was a former Olympic cyclist and a member of the U.S. Bicycling Hall of Fame. In their collective careers as sports promoters, Chauner and Casale had been responsible for producing more than 100 professional cycling events.

On April 1, 2000, Threshold Sports obtained multiyear contracts from Octagon Marketing to host three major cycling events for the USAC: the First Union Cycling Series, the BMC Software Cycling Grand Prix, and the Saturn USPRO Cycling Tour. According to the terms of the deal, Threshold would pay Octagon an annual lease for the life of the First Union Series Title Sponsorship Agreement, while the Saturn and BMC contracts were assigned to Threshold at no cost.

The First Union Cycling Series consisted of four road races in the Philadelphia area. The crown jewel of the series was the popular First Union USPRO Cycling Championship, founded in 1985 by Chauner and Casale. The race attracted 700,000 spectators annually. First Union Bank had already committed to sponsoring the event for $1,150,000 a year for the duration of the five-year contract. Threshold management expected the series to generate annual revenues of approximately $2 million based on sponsorships and merchandising. Threshold would earn a management fee that started at $420,000 and increased to $510,000, and would pay annual lease payments of $200,000 in 2001, increasing to $260,000 in 2005. Profits generated after

---

[1]LeMond was the first American to win the Tour de France and went on to win the competition three times (1986, 1989, and 1990). Armstrong made headlines by winning the 1999 Tour less than three years after recovering from cancer. Armstrong was chosen to lead the 2002 Olympic Torch Relay in preparation for the 2002 Winter Olympics in Salt Lake City.

operating costs, lease payments, and management fees would be split 75 percent/ 25 percent between Threshold and Octagon Marketing, respectively.

The BMC Software Cycling Grand Prix was a series of four road races held in Austin, Houston, San Jose, and Boston. The Lance Armstrong Foundation managed the Austin event, while Threshold managed the other three events. According to the contract, which ran through 2003, Threshold's annual revenue for the series would be a minimum of $1,150,000 plus a 50 percent profit share with USAC.

Threshold also obtained an exclusive five-year license to develop and manage the USPRO Cycling Tour (PCT), a 17-event series that included both the First Union and BMC races. The Saturn automobile company had contracted to be title sponsor for both 1999 and 2000, with commitments of $700,000 for each year. For the 2000 PCT, Threshold had already attracted an additional $300,000 in sponsorships.

In addition to the contracts, Threshold purchased event-staging equipment from Octagon for $65,000—less than one-third its replacement value. Prior to its purchase by Octagon, the equipment had been the principal asset of Special Events Suppliers (SES), an equipment-leasing business operated by Jerry Casale. SES leased the equipment for concerts, city festivals, and parades (including the 1992 presidential inauguration parade). One of its highest-profile and most lucrative leases was a seven-figure contract for staging the 1996 Olympic cycling events in Atlanta.

Growth Prospects and Plans

In considering Threshold's long-term prospects, the founders reflected on the success of established sports such as the National Football League (NFL), Major League Baseball (MLB), and the National Basketball Association (NBA), which had television and merchandising contracts in the billions of dollars. The key, it seemed, was branding. According to Mark Holtzman, senior vice president for Consumer Products at NFL Properties, the league's marketing arm, "We see ourselves, like Disney or Tommy Hilfiger, as a brand that has extensions 365 days a year."[2]

Threshold's founders knew that problems in established sports—including strikes and lockouts—had created an opening for relative upstart sports such as the National Association for Stock Car Racing (NASCAR) and so-called extreme sports. Monday Night Football audiences were down 10 percent in 1998, in part, perhaps, because people were watching alternative sports on Disney's sports network ESPN. ESPN's household audiences for extreme sports such as skateboarding, snowboarding, sky surfing, and street luge had increased 119 percent from 1994 through 1998.[3] During the same period, sponsorship revenue for extreme sports had increased from $24 million to $135 million. NASCAR's growth was also impressive. Its television audience had increased each year since 1990, and by 1999, when it reached 250 million fans, was second only to the NFL. Sales, meanwhile, had grown from $80 million, in 1990,

---

[2]Richard Alm, "National Football League Revamps Marketing Strategy," *Dallas Morning News,* 9 September 2001.

[3]Karl Taro Greenfeld, "A Wider World of Sports," *Time* (9 November 1998).

to $1.13 billion, in 1999.[4] Threshold's owners hoped that they could grow their niche in a similar fashion.

In the near term, Threshold's founders believed that they could double revenues within three years by developing additional USAC racing events and leasing the company's staging equipment for noncompany events. The profit/loss projections for events and projects for the next five years are shown in **Exhibit 2.** The projected profit/loss statement for the firm is shown in **Exhibit 3.**

To reach its near-term goal, Threshold sought to stage at least one new major racing event and one lesser race in 2001. The following two years, they planned to do the same, for a total of six new races in three years. As of June 2000, the firm was in the process of developing races in San Francisco, New York, Atlanta, and Valley Forge:

San Francisco, CA	Threshold was negotiating with Tailwind Sports, manager of the U.S. Postal Service Cycling Team, to produce an event in San Francisco. Threshold expected to receive approximately $1.1 million in corporate sponsorships from the event, scheduled for September 9, 2001.
New York, NY	The New York City Sports Commission had endorsed Threshold to develop the New York City Cycling Championship.
Atlanta, GA	Threshold had formed a joint venture with Ivory Communications to develop a cycling event with organizations involved in the 1996 Olympic Games.
Valley Forge, PA	The Valley Forge Convention and Visitor's Bureau retained Threshold to plan and organize a weekend festival in October 2001. Called the American Cycling Jamboree, the festival would feature competitions, exhibitions, concerts, and demonstrations.

Financing Needs and Alternatives

Given Threshold's growth plans and current balance sheet **(Exhibit 4),** the founders agreed that the company needed additional financing to support the first growth phase. According to management's estimates, financing the development of the additional races would require approximately $500,000 in working capital. Because of their limited experience in finance, the principals approached Frischkorn for help in arranging the deal.

Frischkorn faced three significant challenges with regard to Threshold's financing needs. First, he needed to determine the type of securities to offer that would best suit the company's needs. Most importantly, he needed to determine the value of the company and thus the appropriate pricing of the offering. Finally, he needed to identify potential investors he might approach with the offering.

Frischkorn believed that the size, history, and character of the company favored a private placement rather than a public issue. Among the financing alternatives Threshold was considering were a common-stock offering, a convertible-preferred-stock offering, and debt financing.

---

[4]Data from National Association for Stock Car Racing and industry estimates.

Common Stock

To raise the needed capital, Threshold could issue additional common stock to new investors. Issuing common stock to other investors would dilute the voting interests of the current equity holders, and possibly dilute the stream of reported earnings per share.[5] The extent of any EPS dilution would depend on the profitability of projects funded by the new capital. Ultimately, the owners wondered whether any new equity financing would dilute the *market value* of their interest in Threshold.

Convertible Preferred Stock

Another option for Threshold was to issue convertible preferred stock, which, under pre-established terms, could be converted into the common stock of the company. Preferred stock carried no voting rights. Dividends could be suspended, but all preferred dividends would have to be paid in full before dividends could be paid to holders of common shares. (See **Appendix** for a structure under which Frischkorn believed convertible preferred stock might be issued.)

Debt Financing

Threshold would not qualify for investment-grade debt, and would therefore have to entice investors by offering high-yield debt if it were to issue a bond offering. Paying the interest associated with high-yield debt would seriously constrain Threshold's cash flow and thus its growth. A more likely, albeit short-term, source of debt financing would be a traditional revolving credit loan from Threshold's bank. According to Threshold's management, the firm's banker was willing to loan the company the necessary funds as long as principals Chauner and Casale personally guaranteed the loans. (See **Exhibit 5** for the terms under which Frischkorn believed a loan might be obtained.) Both founders had bristled at the idea of personal guarantees and had argued that the revolving credit could provide Threshold with the cash it needed in the short term, but was not a long-term solution for Threshold's capital needs.

As an angel investor, Frischkorn had garnered experience with each type of financing that Threshold was considering, but in those circumstances he had to weigh the advantages and disadvantages only from the investor's perspective. In the case of Threshold, he had to weigh the advantages and disadvantages of each type of financing from the *company's* perspective. He also had to consider the dilutive effects any deal might have on the voting control of the current owners (**Exhibit 6**).

Frischkorn thought about some of the other private placements in which he had been involved. He recalled that the more mature companies in which he had invested had frequently chosen debt offerings because of the tax advantages of paying interest

---

[5]In corporate-finance terms, "dilution" meant reduction. Its opposite was "accretion." Dilution could refer to any of three effects: (1) reduction in voting power, (2) reduction in such financial results as EPS, and (3) reduction in market value of the firm; these three effects were known respectively as control, accounting, and economic dilution.

over paying dividends. Many of the younger companies, meanwhile, had elected to issue common stock because it provided flexibility in terms of paying (or not paying) a dividend. Still, he recalled a number of deals in which the issuing company had chosen to offer preferred stock because it conveyed no voting rights and allowed some flexibility regarding the timing of dividends.

Placement

Placing the offering presented a challenge for Frischkorn. In Frischkorn's experience, risk-tolerant individual investors had usually provided the necessary capital for such deals even though they offered a relatively low yield compared with other investments. Risk-tolerant individual investors, interested in early-stage financing, found preferred stock attractive because of its liquidation preference. Most corporate investors Frischkorn had contacted were uninterested in providing such early-stage seed capital regardless of the tax advantage offered by preferred shares.[6]

Generally, Frischkorn had been successful in attracting investors for a number of the companies in which he was involved. But Threshold was different from Frischkorn's other investments, which included both old-economy start-ups and new-economy Internet plays. He believed that Threshold would appeal primarily to investors who were cycling enthusiasts or who had personal knowledge of the firm's key managers. He knew that he would have to screen potential investors carefully.[7]

Regardless of their individual circumstances or identities, all new and current Threshold investors would be interested in potential exit strategies. Frischkorn himself was keenly aware of at least two potential means of exit: the possible sale of the business to a large advertising agency or an initial public offering. In the near term, the former seemed more likely than the latter. IPG, Omnicom Group, and WPP Group were all public companies that acted as holding companies of individual marketing firms and were actively acquiring small, branded firms. A future sale to one of these umbrella organizations could offer an exit strategy to investors, provide Threshold with certain economies of scale, and still allow Threshold to maintain its own brand identity as well as some level of independence. Given Threshold's

---

[6]Individual investors reported all dividends from preferred issues as ordinary income, while corporate investors could, for tax-reporting purposes, exclude from income 70 percent of the dividends received from preferred issues.

[7]For a private placement, all investors in the offering had to qualify as "accredited investors," as defined under Regulation D of the Securities Act of 1933. Under Regulation D, an accredited investor was generally defined as:

(i) an individual who is a director or officer of the Company; or

(ii) an individual who has individual income in excess of $200,000 in each of the two most recent years, or joint income with that of his or her spouse in excess of $300,000 in each of such years, and who reasonably expects income in excess of such amounts in the current year; or

(iii) an individual who has an individual net worth, or a joint net worth with that of his or her spouse, in excess of $1,000,000.

relationship with Octagon, such a sale seemed the most likely outcome for now. A future public offering, while still a possibility, seemed a less likely exit strategy at the present time.

Valuation

A significant problem for Frischkorn was estimating Threshold's value. Based on his experience, Frischkorn knew that some investors would argue that the company was worth only what was visible on its balance sheet and would therefore suggest a traditional asset-valuation approach. In conversations, Chauner and Casale had argued vehemently that the firm was worth much more than what appeared on the balance sheet and should be valued based on its growth prospects. They favored valuing Threshold by using a discounted-cash-flow approach. Uncertain as to which valuation method would prevail, Frischkorn pointed out that any preferred-stock investor in Threshold would require at least a 20 percent rate of return, and a common-stock investor would probably seek returns in excess of 30 percent.

Complicating Frischkorn's appraisal was the changing investment environment and its impact on valuations. As seen in **Exhibit 7,** the NASDAQ had endured a dramatic correction in the three months since March 2000. Internet stocks had been hit particularly hard, but the decline had affected even nontech stocks. The abrupt change in public valuations had closed the IPO window for many companies and that, in turn, had impacted private valuations. According to venture capitalists, valuations had dropped significantly from March through May. Noting the change in climate, Rick Kroon, head of Donaldson Lufkin & Jenrette Securities' venture-capital arm, Sprout, observed, "The market will start to be more selective, and [venture capitalists will] wait until their companies are more mature before taking them public . . . . That's healthier for everyone in the long run."[8] Other venture capitalists concurred: "We're walking away from a lot of deals today that we wouldn't have only a few weeks ago . . . . These companies just aren't going to get funded, particularly by anyone involved in late-stage or expansion capital at all," said Matthew Cowan, a general partner at Bowman Capital.[9] Given the changing environment, Frischkorn concluded that angel investors buying common stock in such an immature company would require a return in excess of 30 percent.

While Frischkorn had been in his meeting, his associate Phil Peterson had performed some preliminary research for the Threshold deal. The report included information about current yields (**Exhibits 8** and **9**). It also included some analytical information about outstanding debt as well as preferred and convertible preferred securities (**Exhibits 10, 11,** and **12**).

An interesting aspect of the report concerned Peterson's search for "comparables." Initially, Peterson had encountered great difficulty finding firms, particularly U.S. firms, that matched Threshold's niche. Undeterred, he had collected information on a

---

[8]Suzanne McGee, "Deals & Deal Makers: Sky Is No Longer the Limit for Venture-Capital Firms," *Wall Street Journal,* 9 May 2000, C1.

[9]McGee, "Deals & Deal Makers."

number of publicly traded companies, including sports-marketing companies such as Magnum Sports and Entertainment, entertainment companies such as Disney, and advertising agencies such as Cordiant Communications Group (CRI) in London; Omnicom Group Inc. (OMC); WPP Group Plc (WPP), also in London; and Interpublic Group of Companies (IPG), the parent company of Octagon.

With the help of an investment-banking friend, Peterson had broadened his search and had discovered two other companies that could be described as sports-marketing event managers: Sports and Outdoor Media International PLC, in London (SOR); and Tow Co. Ltd., in Tokyo. According to the information available through Bloomberg Financial, SOR traded on the London Exchange. Tow was a privately held Japanese company that was currently preparing for a public offering. Fortunately, Peterson's friend had provided him with a copy of Tow's red-herring prospectus, which included basic financial information about the company as well as information about its market and growth prospects.

In an effort to estimate Threshold's growth prospects, Peterson gathered information from Multex Data Group. According to Multex, as a group, advertising agencies such as Cordiant, IPG, Omnicom, and WPP were expected to show profit growth of 31.17 percent in 2001 and 15.47 percent in 2002, while earnings of the S&P 500 were expected to climb 1.41 percent in 2001 and decline 9.95 percent in 2002. These estimates were significantly higher than the 11 percent growth estimated for both Tow and its market in the company's red herring.

Peterson included summary information about all the companies, their businesses, and their financials in his report (**Exhibits 13** and **14**), to which he attached a note dated June 15, 2000:

> Carl—Here's the information you requested on current market conditions and comparables. In our discussion this week, you asked about EBIT multiples for private companies. Although I am unable to provide the exact reference, I recently read in one of the financial journals that the EBIT multiple for private companies is 6. Let me know if you need anything else.—Phil

Conclusion

Frischkorn sat back and wondered, How does one value an entity whose primary asset is goodwill and the leases (or rights) to produce events? How does one create and then attribute value to a "brand" such as the Pro Cycling Tour? More specifically, how much was Threshold worth based on either an asset valuation or a DCF valuation? Was one type of financing more suitable than another for Threshold? Which was most appropriate? And what type of investors would be interested in this deal?

EXHIBIT 1 | Major U.S. Sports Organizations

Sports Organization	2000 Sales (in millions)	1-Yr. Sales Growth	Employees	Revenue/ Employee
Major League Baseball (MLB)	$3,177.0	12.00%	200	$15,888,000.00
National Basketball Association (NBA)	$2,164.0	126.50%	800	$ 2,705,000.00
National Football Association (NFL)	$3,602.2	10.10%	450	$ 8,004,888.89
National Hockey League (NHL)	$1,697.2	15.00%	289	$ 5,872,664.36

Source: "The NBA Shoots for the Net," *Industry Standard,* 24 April 2000
(http://www.thestandard.com/article/0,1902,14064,00.html?body_page+2).

EXHIBIT 2 | Estimated Event Income and Loss, 2001–05 (in thousands)

Projected Event Income	2001	2002	2003	2004	2005
First Union Series	$1,700	$1,800	$1,910	$2,125	$ 2,525
US PRO Tour	1,200	1,350	1,525	1,700	2,300
BMC Grand Prix	1,300	1,425	1,540	1,725	2,350
Pre-event consulting[1]	15	25	35	50	70
New event 1	500	575	660	750	900
New event 2	300	350	410	490	625
New event 3		500	580	675	850
New event 4		250	325	475	550
New event 5			500	565	725
New event 6			250	325	475
Total Event Income	**$5,015**	**$6,275**	**$7,735**	**$8,880**	**$10,170**
Operations Cost[2]					
First Union Series	$1,650	$1,700	$1,785	$1,925	$ 1,985
US PRO Tour	1,100	1,200	1,260	1,325	1,350
BMC Grand Prix	1,200	1,250	1,315	1,385	1,400
Octagon lease	200	225	236	248	260
New event 1	450	475	500	550	555
New event 2	275	300	330	365	380
New event 3		475	500	525	555
New event 4		225	245	255	265
New event 5			475	510	535
New event 6			225	250	260
Profit share	50	$ 88	$ 113	$ 220	$ 610
Total Operations Cost	**$4,925**	**$5,938**	**$6,984**	**$7,558**	**$ 8,155**
Net Event Income (Loss)	**$ 90**	**$ 338**	**$ 752**	**$1,322**	**$ 2,015**

[1]Pre-event consulting income refers to fees generated from consulting work performed to research a new event for a municipality.

[2]Operations cost for each contracted project includes a management fee to Threshold Sports.

EXHIBIT 3 | Estimated Fee Income and Loss, 2001–05 (in thousands)

	2001	2002	2003	2004	2005
Income					
Management-fee income	$1,150	$1,525	1,750	2,100	2,240
Special-projects income	80	80	90	105	110
Profit (loss) from racing events	90	337	752	1,322	2,015
Miscellaneous income	2	3	3	4	3
Total income	$1,322	$1,945	$2,595	$3,531	$4,368
Expenses					
Salaries and overhead	$1,104	$1,296	$1,495	$1,719	$1,977
Special projects	35	55	60	72	85
Depreciation	11	16	22	28	34
Capital expenditures	50	50	60	60	60
Expansion expense	40	55	100	200	225
New business	24	30	60	100	200
Total expenses	$1,264	$1,502	$1,797	$2,179	$2,581
Net profit (loss)	$ 58	$ 443	$ 798	$1,351	$1,787

EXHIBIT 4 | Balance Sheet for Fiscal Year Ended May 31, 2000

Assets	
Current assets	
Cash	$379,349
Accounts receivable	363,084
Other current assets	2,900
Total current assets	**$745,333**
Staging equipment	65,000
Total assets	**$810,333**
Liabilities and equity	
Liabilities	
Accounts payable	$133,590
Other current liabilities	9,937
Accrued expenses	322,000
Total liabilities	**$465,527**
Equity	
Net income	344,806
Total equity	**$344,806**
Total liabilities and equity	**$810,333**

EXHIBIT 5 | Terms of Revolving Credit Loan

Type of loan	Revolving credit line
Principal amount	Up to $500,000
Term	36 months
Annual interest rate	Prime + 4%
Current prime rate	9.10%
Security	Business equipment plus personal guarantee
Purpose of loan	Working capital
Payment due date	The fourth day of each month
Prepayment penalty	None

EXHIBIT 6 | Current Ownership Structure

	Holdings	Current Ownership
Class A Units		
David Chauner	12.0 units	40%
Jerry Casale	9.0 units	30
Robin Morton	3.0 units	10
Carl Frischkorn	3.0 units	10
Loren Smith	1.5 units	5
Frank Chauner	1.5 units	5
	30.0 units	100%

EXHIBIT 7 | Equity-Market Conditions: Closing Values and Trendlines

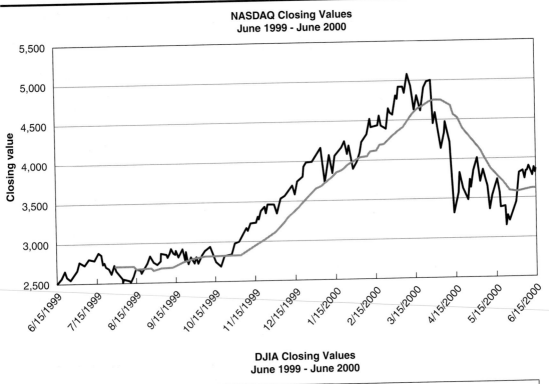

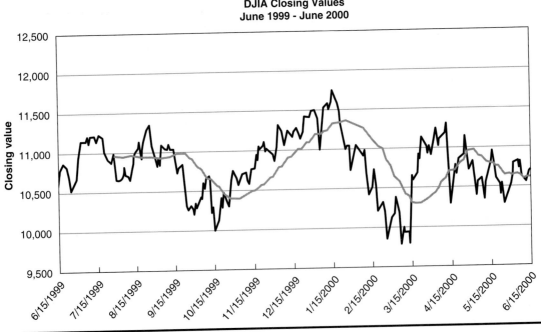

Source: Financial Forecast Center (www.forecasts.org).

EXHIBIT 8 | Capital-Market Conditions: Selected Interest Rates for Week Ended June 2, 2000

	Yield
Federal funds	6.53%
U.S. Treasury securities	
3 Month	5.78
1 Year	6.30
3 Year	6.60
5 Year	6.49
30 Year	6.00
Corporate bonds	
Aaa	7.83%
Baa	8.76

Source: Federal Reserve Statistical Release H.15, 5 June 2000.

Corporate Bond Yields According to Bond Rating and Maturity

Maturity	AAA	AA	A	BBB	BB+	BB/BB−	B
1	6.77	6.85	7.19	7.79	11.26	10.29	11.04
5	7.67	7.98	8.25	8.93	10.50	11.05	12.20
10	7.62	7.98	8.27	8.99	9.74	10.94	12.26
15	7.92	8.32	8.61	9.35	9.62	NA	NA
20	7.94	8.36	8.65	9.47	NA	NA	NA
25	7.92	8.36	8.66	NA	NA	NA	NA

Note: Data as of 5/30/2000. U.S. Industrials include Yankee bond issues. Minimum $100 million outstanding.
NA = not available.

Source: Standard & Poor's *CreditWeek* (7 June 2000): 46 (from Standard & Poor's Fixed Income Research-Bond Corp.).

EXHIBIT 9 | Market Conditions

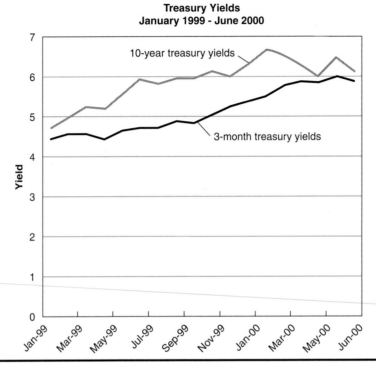

Source: The Federal Reserve Board of Governors Release H.15.

EXHIBIT 10 | Key Industrial Financial Ratios by Rating Category: Median Three-Year Ratios for 1996–98

Industrial Long-Term Debt	AAA	AA	A	BBB	BB	B	CCC
Pretax interest coverage (×)	12.9	9.2	7.2	4.1	2.5	1.2	(0.9)
EBITDA interest coverage (×)	18.7	14.0	10.0	6.3	3.9	2.3	0.2
Funds from operations/total debt (%)	89.7	67.0	49.5	32.2	20.1	10.5	7.4
Free operating cash flow/total debt (%)	40.5	21.6	17.4	6.3	1.0	(4.0)	(25.4)
Return on capital (%)	30.6	25.1	19.6	15.4	12.6	9.2	(8.8)
Operating income/sales (%)	30.9	25.2	17.9	15.8	14.4	11.2	5.0
Long-term debt/capital (%)	21.4	29.3	33.3	40.8	55.3	68.8	71.5
Total debt/capital (incl. short-term debt) (%)	31.8	37.0	39.2	46.4	58.5	71.4	79.4

Source: Wesley E. Chinn, *Adjusted Key U.S. Financial Ratios,* Standard & Poor's Research, 7 July 1999.

EXHIBIT 11 | Sample of Dividend Yields for Preferred Stocks, June 2000

Security	S&P Rating	Maturity Date	Dividend Yield
ABN AMRO Cap. Fd. II 7.125%	A+	3/31/04	9.0%
HSBC USA $2.8575	A+	9/30/07	7.2
Australia & New Zealand Bank 9.125%	A	2/24/03	9.3
NB Capital 8.35% Sr. A Dep.	A−	9/2/07	9.6
LaSalle RE Holding 8.75%	BB+	3/26/07	12.5
SEMCO Cap Tr I 10.25%	BB+	4/18/05	10.3
AICI Cap Trust 9%	B+	9/29/02	19.0
Host Marriott 10% B	B	4/28/05	12.1
United Dominion Realty 8.60% B	BBB	5/28/07	10.8
FelCor Lodging Trust 9% Dep	BB−	5/6/03	12.9
ONB Cap. Tr. I 9.50% Tru PS	BBB−	3/14/05	9.2

Source: Standard & Poor's *Stock Guide*, June 2000.

EXHIBIT 12 | Analytical Ratios on a Sample of Convertible Preferred Securities[1]

Security	Apache $2.015 C Cv Pfd	Chiquita Brands $3.75 cm CV B Pfd	Sealed Air $2.00 CV Pfd A	Standard Automotive 8.50% Sr CV Pfd	Superior Telecom 8.50% TR 1 cm CV Pfd	USX-US Steel Group 6.50% cm CV Pfd
S&P rating	BBB−	B−	BB	NR	CCC+	BB
Dividend yield	4.03%	18.11%	3.88%	11.64%	17.36%	8.80%
Conversion ratio[2]	0.8197	3.3333	0.8846	1.0000	1.1496	1.0840
Price of convertible pfd.	$50.06	$21.00	$51.50	$9.00	$27.00	$37.06
Price of underlying stock	$57.25	$ 4.00	$54.00	$6.69	$11.13	$21.06
Parity[3] (CV ratio × stock price)	$46.93	$13.33	$47.77	$6.69	$12.79	$22.83
Premium[4] ([CV price/parity] − 1)	6.67%	57.54%	7.81%	34.53%	111.10%	62.33%

[1] Financial data and calculations as of 6/15/00.

[2] Conversion ratio reflects the number of common shares to be received in exchange for one share of convertible preferred.

[3] Parity (also known as conversion parity price) is the common stock price at which immediate conversion would make sense.

[4] The premium reflects the mark-up of the convertible over parity. It is the percentage difference between the two.

Source: Bloomberg Financial and Standard & Poor's.

EXHIBIT 13 | Selected Marketing and Entertainment Companies

Name	Symbol[1]	Business	Description
Cordiant Communications Group	CRI (LN) *ADR:CDA*	Advertising services	A holding company whose subsidiaries operate in more than 70 countries. Businesses encompass advertising, merchandising, market research, direct marketing, public relations, and media services. Also provides services in television and multimedia production, as well as live conferences and exhibitions.
The Walt Disney Co.	DIS	Multimedia	Conducts operations in media networks, studio entertainment, theme parks and resorts, consumer products, and Internet and direct marketing. Produces motion pictures, television programs, and musical recordings as well as publishes books and magazines. Also operates ABC radio and television and theme parks.
Interpublic Group of Companies	IPG	Advertising services	An organization of advertising agencies and marketing service companies. Operates globally in sectors of advertising, independent media buying, direct marketing, healthcare communications, interactive consulting services, marketing research, promotions, experiential marketing, public relations, and sports marketing.
Magnum Sports & Entertainment Inc.[2]	MAGZ	Advertising services	Provides management, marketing, and commercial endorsement agency services to various sports entities.
Omnicom Group Inc.	OMC	Advertising services	Provides marketing communications and advertising services through global, national, and regional independent agency brands. Operates branded independent agencies in public relations, specialty advertising, and direct response and promotional marketing. Holds minority interests in other businesses.
Sports & Outdoor Media International Plc	SOR (LN)	Advertising services	Acts as a sports stadia advertising agent to major sports rights holders in U.K. and Australia, selling ground signage and other forms of advertising at cricket and rugby grounds. Also has a sports marketing and sponsorship consultancy business.
Tow Co., Ltd.[3]	NA	Advertising services	Plans, advertises, produces, and manages various types of events. Primarily manages exhibitions, ceremonies, festivals, product promotion campaigns, public service announcements, sporting events, and expositions. The company was privately held but was preparing to make its initial public offering in 7/00.
WPP Group Plc	WPP (LN) *ADR:WPPGY*	Advertising services	Operates a communications services group with 1,300 offices in 102 countries. Operations encompass advertising, media investment management, information and consultancy, public relations and public affairs, healthcare and specialist communications, and branding and identity services.

NA = not available.

[1] LN indicates the stock trades on the London Exchange. ADRs are available where noted.

[2] Formerly Worldwide Entertainment & Sports.

[3] Initial public offering of 1 million shares expected in July 2000, to be traded on the Tokyo Exchange (JP).

EXHIBIT 14 | Selected Financial Information on Comparable Companies for Fiscal Year 1999

Symbol	FY 1999 Sales (millions)	Shares Outstanding (millions)	FYE Share Price	Equity Market Value (millions)	Book Value (millions)	Total Debt (millions)	Total Debt to Equity	Total Debt-to-Equity Market Value	Price to Book	Price to Earnings	EBITDA Multiplier	100-Day Volatility (%)	Beta	Unlevered Beta
CRI (LN)	GBP335.80	228.80	GBP2.93	GBP670.38	(GBP40.20)	GBP84.00	NM	0.13	NM	35.73	15.09	47.9	1.10	NM
DIS	$23,435.00	2,069.00	$26.00	$53,794.00	$21,323.00	$11,693.00	0.55	0.22	2.63	44.32	10	41.6	0.86	0.65
IPG	$4,977.82	307.01	$57.69	$17,710.64	$1,846.08	$1,311.09	0.71	0.07	10.19	44.04	17.89	43.7	1.07	0.77
MAGZ	$1.12	3.49	$2.00	$6.98	$6.08	$0.12	0.02	0.02	5.73	NA	NA	NA	0.37	0.37
OMC	$5,130.55	177.49	$100.00	$17,749.00	$1,676.02	$842.00	0.50	0.05	11.43	49.75	19.65	41.3	1.02	0.78
SOR (LN)	GBP14.56	33.77	GBP0.83	GBP28.03	GBP12.48	GBP15.18	1.22	0.54	0.37	92.17	NA	53.1	0.33	0.19
TOW (JP)	JPY5,396.00	NA	NA	NA	JPY1,002.00	JPY1.95	0.95	NA	NA	NA	NA	NA	NA	NM
WPP (LN)	GBP9,345.90	774.54	GBP9.50	GBP7,358.13	GBP195.80	GBP515.10	1.58	0.07	23.88	42.84	24.1	50.8	0.86	0.44

Notes: NM = not meaningful; NA = not available. Volatility reflects most recent 100 days prior to 6/1/00. Volatility and beta values for foreign securities reflect those of ADRs.

GBP = British pounds; JPY = Japanese yen.

Source: Bloomberg Financial.

Appendix | Summary of Terms of Hypothetical Convertible-Preferred-Stock Offering

Amount:	$500,000 (maximum)
Securities:	A maximum of 10 convertible preferred Units
Price per unit:	$50,000 (original purchase price)
Cumulative preferred return:	To be determined. Initial proposal: 10 percent dividend on par value which shall accrue and be payable on a cumulative and noncompounding basis. If there are insufficient funds to pay the Cumulative Preferred Return in full, payment shall be made on a pro-rata basis. The Cumulative Preferred Return shall accrue annually commencing on the closing date of this offering and shall terminate on December 31, 2005.
Liquidation preference:	In the event of any liquidation, dissolution, or winding up of the Company, the holders of these Units will be entitled to receive (in preference to the holders of other interests) the initial investment less any capital distributions that may have previously been made plus all unpaid portions, if any, of the Cumulative Preferred Return.
Conversion privilege:	To be determined. Initial proposal for Units to be convertible at any time into shares of common stock at a strike price of 1.5 times most recent book value per share of common.
Holder redemption right:	Beginning March 31, 2005, and each anniversary thereof, Holders of these convertible preferred Units shall have the right to require the Company to redeem the convertible preferred Units.
Company redemption right:	The Company may redeem any convertible preferred Units, annually, by notice within 90 days following the end of each calendar year. The redemption price will be at par value.
Mandatory tax distribution:	For each calendar year Unit holders will receive a special cash distribution in an amount equal to 35 percent of the income allocated to such holders.
Voting rights:	Holders of convertible preferred Units shall not have voting rights.
Right of first refusal:	In the event that a holder wishes to sell or otherwise transfer its investment interest pursuant to a bona-fide offer from a third party, the holder shall first offer the investment interest to (i) the Company, and (ii) then to the nonselling holders, upon the same terms and conditions of the bona-fide offer.
Co-sale rights:	If any holder owning more than 25 percent of the Company intends to sell its interest pursuant to a third party offer, the nonselling holders may include their membership interests in the sale on a pro-rata basis.
Drag along rights:	If holders of membership interests that in the aggregate represent 50 percent or more of the Company elect to sell the Company pursuant to a sale of assets, sale of membership interests, merger or otherwise, such members may compel the remaining members to consent to, and participate in, such sale.
Preemptive right:	All Unit holders shall have a pro-rata right to participate in subsequent equity financings of the Company subject to customary exclusions.

Analysis of Financing Tactics: Leases, Options, and Foreign Currency

Merton Electronics Corporation

Patricia Merton, president and majority shareholder of Merton Electronics, was dissatisfied with her company's results over the past year (see **Exhibits 1** and **2**). Sales had risen by over 12 percent compared to the previous year, very close to budget, but at a considerably slower pace than what had been enjoyed during the previous three years. At the same time, 1997 earnings fell by more than 40 percent reflecting increasingly difficult market conditions. Margins had been flat or falling for the past three years, but 1997 was the worst. Operational improvements had been maintained, keeping working capital and cash needs under control. Also, she had secured additional long-term financing and an increase in the company's credit line. Although continued growth would require additional investment in new computer and office equipment, and other fixed assets, she expected this could be largely financed out of cash flow—if margins did not deteriorate further and working capital could be kept in line with sales.

Since its founding in 1950 by Thomas Merton, Merton Electronics had been a distributor for GEC, a large manufacturer of electrical and electronics products for consumer and institutional markets. Over the years, in addition to the GEC products, the company had added noncompeting lines of electrical appliances, records, compact discs, and cassettes. In 1980, it began to broaden its product lines by importing Japanese consumer electronics. Four years later, it entered into an exclusive import agreement with the Goldstone Corporation of Taiwan, a major producer of television and other electronic equipment. These products were distributed to retail firms and dealers throughout a broad geographical area.

By the beginning of the 1990s, the company had entered into the personal computer (PC) market distributing both hardware and software products. It became the national distributor for Fuji Electronics, a major Japanese manufacturer of PCs and related products, in September 1993. This had proven to be a fast growing market, accounting for more than half of total sales although only about a third of profits in 1997; this part of the business was becoming more and more competitive as price-cutting had become rampant from mail order and computer discount houses.

Patricia Merton had been working in the company for two years when her father, Thomas Merton, died in the spring of 1991. As the only family member with experience

---

This case was prepared by Professor Lee Remmers, INSEAD. Copyright © 1998, Lee Remmers, INSEAD. Rev. 2/98.

in the company, she succeeded him as president. Together with her mother, she controlled 65 percent of the share capital of the firm. The remaining shares were held by her father's brother and sister, their families, and a few long-service employees.

During the first weeks of 1998, she had been taking advantage of the relative calm that usually marked that time of the year. This was when they took the semi-annual inventory, tended to various small problems that had been pushed aside during the past few months, and thought about the future.

One of the things that continued to disturb her was the volatility of the yen, and more recently, the Taiwanese dollar (see **Exhibit 3**). Over half of the equipment sold in the PC, TV and VCR, and Hi-fi product lines were imported from Japanese suppliers. From a volume of about $20 million two years earlier, yen-denominated purchases had approached $27 million during the past 12 months. Annual purchases totaling another $4 million were from Taiwanese suppliers. With the volume expected in the consumer electronics and PC product lines, she foresaw purchases from Fuji Electronics, the company's principal supplier, and other Asian manufacturers to increase in the future.

Typical of Merton's Japanese suppliers, Fuji Electronics had always insisted on invoicing in yen. In contrast, at the beginning of their agreement, Goldstone Corporation had invoiced in U.S. dollars. This changed in 1989, when the company was informed that from then on, the Taiwan dollar would be used for billing.

Once an order was placed, the Asian suppliers shipped by airfreight normally within 60 days. Payment terms were 30 days from the end of the delivery month; hence the ¥284 million value of goods delivered in January 1998 would be paid at the end of February (see **Exhibit 4**). With few exceptions, the spot price on the last day of the month in which the order was placed was used for the invoice. This meant that Merton had on average a 90-day currency exposure for each order.

Two years earlier, towards the end of January 1996, concerned that the falling margins were at least partially due to the impact of a rising exchange rate, Patricia Merton had asked her general manager, Charles Brown, to gather some data on the monthly volume of purchases from Japanese suppliers as well as the yen–dollar exchange rates. The data gathered by Brown at the time astonished her. The effect of the yen's more or less continual appreciation against the dollar until the summer of 1995 meant that purchases during that period appeared to have cost the company significantly more—in dollar terms—than if the exchange rate had been stable. Fortunately, thanks to the popularity of the Fuji products, they had been able until 1995 to increase prices to partially offset their higher dollar costs. Also, the Japanese suppliers had absorbed some of the yen's rise by cutting prices significantly. But as the dollar fell through the ¥100 "barrier," it became more and more difficult to maintain margins. During the first four months of 1995, the rising yen translated into almost $1.1 million higher dollar cost of purchases. Although Brown did not prepare a detailed analysis of purchases before 1995, he estimated that "losses" were if anything considerably larger. On the other hand, his data had shown that between July and December 1995, a strengthening dollar produced "gains" of over $1.4 million. As a result of this analysis, they had sought the advice of their banker in January 1996.

Listening to his clients' story, the banker agreed that Merton did face significant currency risk. Further, he reminded them that since Merton Electronics imported a higher portion of its products from Japan than some of its principal competitors, its profit margins were much more sensitive to the value of the yen than theirs were. In view of this, he advised them to hedge their yen purchases. The bank would arrange hedges to cover the orders placed during the month. They agreed that this would be on a monthly basis to obtain the better rates relatively large transactions would provide. The hedges would, he explained, fix in advance the dollar cost of each month's orders. This would effectively remove the currency problem from their everyday concerns and allow them to concentrate on running the business. As for purchases from the Taiwanese suppliers, the banker told them the Taiwanese authorities managed their currency so that it stayed more or less fixed to the U.S. dollar, that even if it were to move it was likely to depreciate, and for these reasons, hedging would not be worthwhile. This advice was taken and since 1996, Merton had systematically hedged each yen purchase order; purchases from Taiwanese suppliers were not hedged.

Now, after two years, Patricia Merton thought it was time to review this policy. Once again she asked Brown to look at their experience over the past year, going back to January 1997. What this showed was completely different from the previous analysis. Although the yen was still volatile, it had mainly weakened against the dollar during this period. By hedging, the dollar cost of yen purchases had been about $25.5 million during 1997. If the purchases had not been hedged, but the yen bought on the spot market when the invoices came due, the dollar cost would have been about $24.6 million—almost $900,000 difference! This was almost exactly the pre-tax earnings for 1997. Extremely disturbed by what Brown told her, Patricia Merton immediately contacted the firm's banker and arranged to see him later in the day.

Merton's meeting with her banker was strained at the beginning. Somewhat defensive, he maintained that since neither he, nor anyone else for that matter, could have accurately predicted how the yen–dollar exchange rate would have moved during the past two years, hedging the exposures was the most prudent policy for Merton. Furthermore, with so much economic and political uncertainty in Japan and the rest of Asia at the present time, he could not recommend in good conscience a better solution to managing the yen risk. When Patricia Merton asked him why he had not encouraged them earlier to hedge the Taiwanese dollar payments, he recalled his advice at the time was that it had been basically pegged to the U.S. dollar for several years and anyway was difficult to hedge satisfactorily because of exchange controls imposed by the Taiwanese authorities. He reckoned that by following his recommendation not to hedge the Taiwanese dollar purchases, the U.S. dollar costs had been lower in 1997 by some $125,000 compared to what they would have been if hedged. Not entirely satisfied by his explanation, she asked him what he thought they should do now.

The issue boiled down to whether the company should take on currency risk or not, and if so, how much. With over 60 percent of its purchases subject to currency fluctuations, the banker stuck to his earlier view that the firm could not afford to ignore this risk. He admitted that, with hindsight, not hedging would have been the best policy over the past one to two years. This meant that Merton would have bought the foreign currency on the spot market each time payments to the Asian suppliers were made. This, he said, was essentially a bet on a stronger dollar—which turned out to be the case. Quickly checking the numbers, he noted that if the ¥880 million worth of goods on order or already invoiced at the end of January were to be settled at the current spot rate of ¥127, this would cost Merton about $6.93 million. As it stood, the company was already committed to pay $7.04 million since these purchases had been hedged when the goods were ordered. In other words, hedging appeared to have cost them some $110,000 at the present time. This lost opportunity would be larger or smaller depending on what the yen would do between now and when the invoices were settled. Nevertheless, he still would not advise the company to "do nothing" and expose itself to large possible currency losses in the future. Patricia Merton, as president and major shareholder of the company, would have to decide.

Accepting his arguments that it would be unwise to "do nothing," she thought it would be useful to review the various other alternative courses that the company might follow. Although the company had been using forward contracts for some 18 months to hedge the yen purchases, Merton felt she needed to have her memory refreshed, and asked the banker to outline once again how the different hedges worked.

According to the banker, there were two basic choices when hedging. It could "lock in" today an exchange rate that would be close to the current spot rate; the forward contracts they had been using provided this type of hedge. Or they could enter into an option contract that would set an upper bound on the cost of yen, but allow them to take advantage of cheaper yen if that should happen by the time the invoices had to be paid. The option would provide some of the advantages of not hedging, but limit the disadvantages—but at a cost.

To lock in an exchange rate, the banker went on, meant that the future price of a foreign currency—the future spot rate—would in effect be set today—in other words, the hedge was a bet on a stronger yen. This type of hedge insured that whatever the future spot rate might turn out to be, the effective price paid for yen would still be that which was agreed today. There were three ways to lock in an exchange rate: a forward contract, a money market transaction, and a currency futures contract. Each of these carried precisely defined terms with regard to price, maturity, and certain other performance measures. Any modifications in the terms of the contract, such as changing its maturity, would have to be negotiated and agreed with the party providing the hedge, possibly resulting in additional cost.

The forward contract hedge, which the company had used for the past 18 months, was an arrangement by which it bought from the bank a specified quantity of yen to be delivered at a specified date in the future—normally when the invoice had to be settled. The exchange rate was fixed at the outset. At ¥125.50, the 90-day forward rate was at present nearly 1.5 percent more "expensive" than the spot rate. With this hedge, Merton would receive yen from the bank on the agreed maturity date, pay the bank the amount of dollars at the forward exchange rate set earlier (¥125.50), and then use the yen to pay the Japanese suppliers.

The money market hedge was also an arrangement with the bank. Merton would buy yen today on the spot market and place it in a yen time deposit or some other yen asset until needed to pay the suppliers. The purchase of yen would be financed in dollars by a short-term loan or by using cash reserves if they were available.

The cost of this hedge would be the difference between the interest paid on the dollar loan and that received from the yen deposit. The banker reminded them that Merton could borrow dollars at 25 basis points[1] over the current prime rate (8.50 percent); but they would only earn at present ⅜ percent on a 3-month Euroyen time deposit, Japanese rates being at an all-time low (see **Exhibit 5** for rates).

The yen futures hedge was provided by an instrument traded on the Chicago Mercantile Exchange (CME).[2] Quotations for yen futures on January 22 appear in **Exhibit 6**. As protection against loss from currency fluctuations, this hedge was very similar to the forward contract provided by the bank. Merton would buy a sufficient number of futures to create the hedge. It could then wait until the futures contracts came to maturity and take delivery of the yen. Alternatively, if Merton decided the hedge was no longer needed before the futures contracts reached maturity, they could be sold. If a rise in the value of the yen meant it cost more dollars to settle the purchase account with the Japanese suppliers, it also meant that the futures would be sold at a profit, thereby providing an offset. However, the mechanics of futures contracts differ considerably from forwards. The contracts are made through a member of the futures exchange, usually a broker. Currency futures come in standard contract sizes (for the yen ¥12.5 million), and standard maturity dates (the third Wednesday of March, June, September, December). They are revalued daily (marked-to-market) with any profit or loss immediately settled between broker and client. To trade on the futures market, the client must open and maintain collateral (a margin account) with the broker. This changes from time to time, but at present, is a minimum of $1,500 per contract. In addition, the broker will charge a small commission.

The currency option contract was available from either banks or exchanges. Option contracts give the right but not the obligation to buy (a call) or to sell (a put) currency or some other asset within a specified period and at a predetermined price known as the strike or exercise price.

Bank or OTC[3] options can be tailored to meet the client's precise needs for maturity, amount, or currency. They are usually European-type options, that is, they may only be exercised at expiration. Most bank options are on spot currency. Merton's banker pointed out that besides dealing in "plain vanilla" (standard) call and put options, he could also offer them synthetic or exotic instruments. Synthetics were combinations of calls, puts, and sometimes forward contracts which were designed to meet particular risk/return objectives of a client. A so-called zero-cost option is one of the more widely used of these. Exotics were options that had some particular feature that gave the buyer a lower premium at the price of a more risky payoff.[4]

---

[1]A basis point is 1/100 of a percent, i.e., 0.0001. Basis points are generally used in pricing loans and certain other financial instruments. Rates are usually quoted on an annual basis.

[2]Currency futures are also traded on exchanges in London (LIFFE), Singapore (SIMEX), Sidney, and elsewhere in the world.

[3]OTC: over-the-counter.

[4]Among the most popular were average-rate and barrier or knockout options.

Like futures, exchange-traded options have standardized maturities and amounts. The expiration dates are similar to those for futures: March, June, September, and December. In addition, the American exchanges offer some "nearby" expiration dates (see **Exhibit 7**). For example, at the end of January, contracts were offered for February and April expiration as well as for the March and June standard months. Only a few major currencies are available. Most are priced in U.S. dollars, even those traded on European or Asian exchanges. They are usually so-called American-type options, in other words, they may be exercised at any time before expiration. Recently European-style options have been introduced on some exchanges—they can only be exercised at maturity. Those traded on the Philadelphia exchange are on spot currency. Chicago's CME and London's LIFFE contracts are on currency futures. To buy an option on an exchange, the full premium[5] must be paid in advance. To sell (or write) an option requires a specified margin to be maintained with the broker.

Besides going over the hedging instruments, the banker raised a number of other issues for Merton to consider. The company imported goods from its Japanese suppliers on a continuous basis throughout the year. If they did decide to continue hedging these purchases, should it be when the orders were placed as they have been doing up to now? Or should they wait until the time when the purchase invoice was actually received? What about hedging periodically for a longer period of 6 to 12 months once operating plans and budgets were agreed? Finally if they do continue to hedge, should it be for the entire amount at risk, however it was measured, or only some portion of it?

Merton's banker concluded by stressing there was no "correct" hedging approach. It depended on the particular needs and financial position of the company, and the attitudes of its management and shareholders towards risk. Whether or not the hedge was profitable would only be known ex post—when the supplier was paid. In the case of Merton Electronics, hedging yen during the past months turned out to be the wrong decision; in contrast, it was the correct decision for the Taiwanese dollar. If instead yen had strengthened against the dollar, locking in the rate would have been the correct decision. Further, he cautioned that hedging, under some competitive situations, could actually increase risk rather than decrease it.

The discussion left Merton nearly as baffled as when she arrived at the bank. On leaving, she told the banker that she needed a few days to decide what to do. Back at the office, Merton told Brown that she was pretty much convinced that they should begin to devote a bit more time and thought to managing their currency position. Although they had "lost" some $900,000 on yen purchases during the past few months from a rather simplistic "hedge everything" policy, there was clearly too much uncertainty for a "do-nothing" policy to be justified. The problem was to decide quickly what to do.

Anxious to resolve this matter quickly, Patricia Merton asked Brown to prepare a brief report on how their company's currency risk should be managed. In particular,

---

[5]The LIFFE exchange uses a margin system similar to that for futures trading. Hence, a specified minimum margin is maintained with the broker rather than paying a cash premium up-front.

she asked him to set out the relative advantages in terms of cost and risk for each of the alternatives that had been described to them by the banker. To provide a practical example, he could use the ¥300 million exposure arising from the goods that were ordered in January and which would be due for payment in April, 90 days from then. She suggested he use the January 22 market rates which they had picked up at the bank (see **Exhibit 5**) and, for the purpose of the analysis, assume that the suppliers would be paid and the hedges lifted on April 22. She also asked him to check out whether they would have been better off hedging with options over the past months than with forwards. She herself intended to give some thought to broader policy issues including whether they should hedge at all and, if so, how much, when, and under what circumstances?

EXHIBIT 1 | Comparative Income Statements (dollars in thousands)

	Year Ending 31 December 1996	Year Ending 31 December 1997
Sales revenue	$53,682	$60,392
Cost of goods sold	44,336	51,228
Gross margin	9,346	9,164
Variable expenses	3,277	3,687
Fixed expenses	3,652	4,009
Depreciation	171	207
Operating earnings (EBIT)	2,246	1,261
Interest expense	565	348
Earnings before taxes	1,681	913
Corporate taxes	581	301
Earnings after taxes	$ 1,100	$ 612

EXHIBIT 2 | Comparative Balance Sheets (dollars in thousands)

	31 December 1996	31 December 1997
Assets		
Current assets:		
Cash & deposits	$ 95	$ 115
Prepaid expenses	96	70
Accounts receivable	7,816	8,794
Inventories	8,880	9,350
	16,887	18,329
Fixed assets (net)	1,290	1,585
Goodwill	150	150
Total assets	$18,327	$20,064
Capital & Liabilities		
Current liabilities:		
Bank credit	$ 4,257	$ 2,237
Mortgage—current	150	150
Accrued expenses	392	359
Accounts payable:		
Domestic	2,215	2,497
Foreign (yen)	3,312	3,670[1]
	10,826	8,913
Mortgage loan	750	600
Subordinated loan	—	500
Capital stock	1,500	1,500
Retained earnings	5,751	6,313
Owners' equity	7,251	7,813
Total capital & liabilities	$18,327	$20,064

[1] Dollar value of foreign currency accounts payable (¥375.2 million at spot rate of ¥130.5/US$; Taiwan $ 25.9 million at spot rate of TWD 32.6/USD$).

EXHIBIT 3 | Foreign Exchange Data

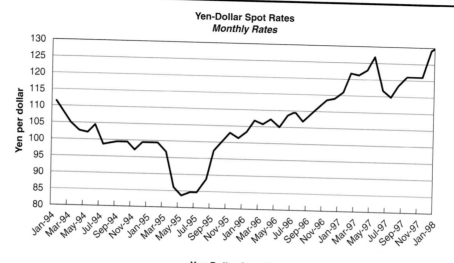

Yen-Dollar Spot Rates
Monthly Rates

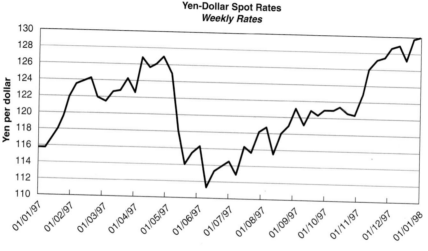

Yen-Dollar Spot Rates
Weekly Rates

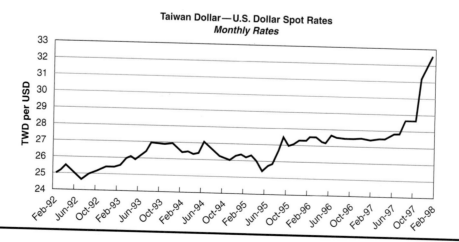

Taiwan Dollar—U.S. Dollar Spot Rates
Monthly Rates

EXHIBIT 4 | Actual and Forecasted Purchases from Japanese Suppliers, January 1997–April 1998

Purchase Amount ¥ Million	Order Date	Average ¥/$ Spot	Delivery & Invoice Date	Payment Date	Average ¥/$ Spot	Change in Order Value in $ 000
224.7	Jan 97	116	Mar 97	Apr 97	123	+110.2
261.1	Feb 97	122	Apr 97	May 97	127	+84.3
276.6	Mar 97	121	May 97	Jun 97	117	−78.2
271.1	Apr 97	123	Jun 97	Jul 97	115	−153.3
237.6	May 97	127	Jul 97	Aug 97	118	−142.7
192.2	Jun 97	117	Aug 97	Sept 97	121	+54.3
253.5	Jul 97	115	Sept 97	Oct 97	121	+109.3
294.5	Aug 97	118	Oct 97	Nov 97	121	+61.9
395.3	Sept 97	121	Nov 97	Dec 97	129	+202.6
330.8	Oct 97	121	Dec 97	Jan 98	130	+189.3
284.6	Nov 97	121	Jan 98	Feb 98	?	?
295.5	Dec 97	129	Feb 98	Mar 98	?	?
300.0	Jan 98	130	Mar 98	Apr 98	?	?
325.0	Feb 98	?	Apr 98	May 98	?	?
375.0	Mar 98	?	May 98	Jun 98	?	?
340.0	Apr 98	?	Jun 98	Jul 98	?	?

EXHIBIT 5 | Currency and Other Financial Market Data, January 22, 1998

Spot yen:	127.35–127.40 per $; $0.7849–$0.7852 per ¥100
90-day forward yen:	125.50–125.75 per $; $0.7952–$0.7968 per ¥100

90-day Euroyen interest rates:	3/8%–1/2% per annum
Japanese 10-year government bond yield:	1 3/4%
90-day Eurodollar interest rates:	5 1/2 %–5 5/8 % per annum
Merton short-term borrowing rate:	Prime (8 1/2%) + 25 basis points

March 98 yen futures (CME): $0.7928; June 1998 yen futures (CME): $0.8031

90-day yen call options (OTC): *127.35* $0.7852 strike–$0.0249 per 100 yen

125.50 $0.7968 strike–$0.0188 per 100 yen

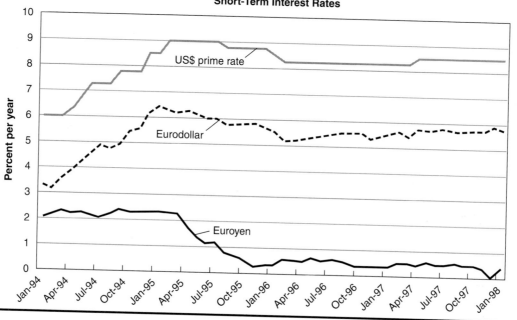

EXHIBIT 6 | Futures Prices

Japan Yen (CME)–12.5 million yen; $ per yen (.00)

	Open	High	Low	Settle	Change	Lifetime High	Lifetime Low	Open Interest
Mar	.7928	.7970	.7890	.7917	−.0024	.9375	.7512	88,937
Jun	.8046	.8046	.7950	.8017	−.0024	.9090	.7637	2,293
Sept	—	—	—	.8117	−.0024	.8695	.7735	413

Est. vol. 20,416; Vol. Th. 36,578; open int. 91,647, +608.

Source: *Wall Street Journal,* January 23–24, 1998.

EXHIBIT 7 | Futures Option Prices

Japanese Yen (CME) 12.5 million yen; cents per 100 yen

Strike Price	Calls—Settle Feb	Calls—Settle Mar	Calls—Settle Apr	Puts—Settle Feb	Puts—Settle Mar	Puts—Settle Apr
7,800	1.66	2.21		0.49	1.05	1.12
7,850	1.32	1.92		0.65	1.25	1.30
7,900	1.03	1.65		0.86	1.48	
7,950	0.80	1.42		1.12	—	—
8,000	0.62	1.21	2.08	1.45	2.02	
8,050	0.48	1.03	1.84	1.81	—	—

Est. vol. 4,445; Wed. 6,552 calls, 4,970 puts; Op. int. Wed. 49,854 calls, 65,330 puts.

Source: *Wall Street Journal,* January 23–24, 1998.

Carrefour S.A.

In the summer of 2002, with total sales of (euro) EUR53.9 billion from more than 5,200 stores, Carrefour S.A. was Europe's largest retailer. Over the past four years, Carrefour's growth had occurred almost entirely outside France and included several large acquisitions. In the past, Carrefour management had generally financed company growth through securities denominated in the currency of business operations. Its investment banks, Morgan Stanley and UBS Warburg, however, had recently suggested that Carrefour consider borrowing in British pounds sterling in order to take advantage of a borrowing opportunity in that currency. With a debt-financing requirement of EUR750 million, the bond issue would be one of Carrefour's largest. Now, in August 2002, the investment bankers expected that the 10-year Carrefour bonds would be priced at a coupon rate of 5¼ in euros, 5⅜ in British pounds, 3⅝ in Swiss francs, or 5½ in U.S. dollars.

Carrefour S.A.

In 1963, Carrefour altered the world of retailing with the introduction of the "hyper-market" concept in the small French town of Sainte-Geneviève-des-Bois, southeast of Paris. This format combined a supermarket, drugstore, discount store, and gas station into one massive, one-stop-shopping megastore. The original store had 2,500 square meters of retail space, 12 checkouts, and 400 parking spaces. The company expanded rapidly in France and beyond, opening its first store outside France (Belgium) in 1969, and outside Europe (Brazil) in 1975. In addition to strong organic growth, Carrefour pursued selective acquisitions, including notable mergers with Euromarche and Montlaur in 1991, and Promodes in 1999. **Exhibit 1** provides a history of Carrefour's store portfolio from 1992 to 2001.

Carrefour was profitable in all major operating regions. In 2001, the company generated operating profits of EUR2.8 billion on total net sales of EUR69.5 billion. Of that profit, 5 percent originated in Asia, 2 percent originated in Latin America, and

This case was prepared by Professor Michael J. Schill. It is based exclusively on public sources and contains some fictionalized content. It was written as a basis for class discussion rather than to illustrate effective or ineffective handling of an administrative situation. Copyright © 2005 by the University of Virginia Darden School Foundation, Charlottesville, VA. All rights reserved. *To order copies, send an e-mail to* sales@dardenpublishing.com. *No part of this publication may be reproduced, stored in a retrieval system, used in a spreadsheet, or transmitted in any form or by any means—electronic, mechanical, photocopying, recording, or otherwise—without the permission of the Darden School Foundation.*

26 percent originated in Europe outside France, with the remainder of profits coming from French operations. The regional-sales breakdown was 7 percent from Asia, 12 percent from Latin America, and 32 percent from Europe outside France. For Carrefour, 2001 was the first year that total sales outside France exceeded total domestic sales. Carrefour was the largest retailer in France, Belgium, Greece, and Spain. **Exhibit 2** details Carrefour's consolidated financial statements.

The company expected to maintain its expansion trajectory. Carrefour's CEO, Daniel Bernard, stated his expectation that, in 2002, the company would increase sales by 5 percent on constant exchange rates and increase recurring net income by 10–15 percent. He asserted that the company continued to gain market share in most of the countries where it operated, notably in Italy, Belgium, Brazil, and Argentina. Carrefour relaunched its expansion in China, with the opening of a store in Chengdu in June.[1]

Carrefour's Financing Policy

In each country, Carrefour operated primarily within the local economy when buying and selling products. Foreign-currency exposure on imported goods was generally hedged through currency-forward contracts.

In 2001, total Carrefour borrowings were EUR13.5 billion, of which EUR6.4 billion were in publicly traded bonds. Carrefour's debt was denominated in many currencies. **Exhibit 3** details the recent composition of Carrefour's borrowings by currency. Foreign-currency borrowing was generally hedged so that total debt requirements were currently 97 percent in euros.

Current Market Opportunities

As Carrefour management considered the bond-denomination decision, it also considered the current inflation, interest-rate, and exchange-rate environment.[2] Over the past three years, long-term bond yields had declined in all four currencies. The Swiss franc's interest rate, however, had consistently been the lowest rate. The decision also hinged on future movements in exchange rates. Over the past five years, the euro had depreciated against most major currencies. Should this trend continue, paying down foreign-currency debt with euro-denominated cash flow would become increasingly expensive. **Exhibits 4, 5,** and **6** provide information on trends in inflation, government-benchmark bond yields, and exchange rates in the various currencies. **Exhibits 7** and **8** provide information on prevailing current spot exchange rates and the yield curve.

---

[1]Carrefour S.A., news release, 13 June 2002.

[2]Because the bonds would be offered in the eurobond market, they would be subject to similar issuance costs, liquidity, and specifications regardless of the currency denomination. Eurobonds uniformly followed an annual coupon convention.

EXHIBIT 1 | Total Number of Consolidated Stores

	1992	1993	1994	1995	1996	1997	1998	1999	2000	2001
France	485	546	828	840	761	805	1,256	1,703	1,726	1,295
Spain	40	43	46	50	53	56	58	1,858	1,939	1,952
Portugal	2	2	2	2	2	3	4	278	277	281
Italy	0	1	6	5	6	6	6	52	413	305
Turkey	0	1	1	1	1	2	2	14	46	99
Poland						1	3	13	23	60
Czech Republic								3	6	9
Slovakia									2	2
Belgium										129
Switzerland										8
Greece								146	323	338
Argentina	6	7	9	12	15	18	21	128	361	400
Brazil	28	29	33	38	44	49	59	152	189	222
Mexico			2	7	13	17	19	17	18	19
Chile							1	2	3	4
Colombia							1	2	3	5
United States	2							2	3	5
Taiwan	5	7	8	10	13	17	21	23	24	26
Malaysia			1	1	2	3	5	6	6	6
China				2	3	7	14	20	24	24
Korea					3	3	6	12	20	22
Indonesia							1	5	7	8
Singapore						1	1	1	1	1
Hong Kong					1	2	4	4		
Thailand					2	6	7	9	11	15
Japan									1	3
Total	568	636	936	968	919	996	1,489	4,448	5,423	5,233

Source: Carrefour S.A., Annual Report, 2001.

EXHIBIT 2 | Financial Statements (in millions of euros)

	2001	2000
Sales, net of taxes	69,486	64,802
Cost of sales	53,875	49,920
Sales, general, & admin. exp.	11,729	11,236
Other income	645	763
Depreciation	1,702	1,685
EBIT	2,826	2,725
Interest expense	646	707
Income tax	586	650
Net income from recurring operations	1,594	1,369
Fixed assets	26,561	27,840
Inventories	5,909	5,716
Trade and supplier receivables	2,946	3,146
Other receivables	3,258	4,387
Cash and marketable securities	4,797	2,941
Total assets	43,470	44,031
Shareholders' equity	8,192	8,932
Provision for long-term liabilities	2,027	1,772
Borrowings	13,471	13,949
Trade payables and other debt	19,781	19,377
Total liabilities and shareholders' equity	43,470	44,031

EXHIBIT 3 | Breakdown of Borrowings by Currency (in millions of euros)

	2001	2000
Euro	12,267	12,201
Japanese yen	342	90
U.S. dollar	110	115
Argentine peso	238	903
Swiss franc	191	161
Norwegian krone	61	61
Turkish lire	49	65
Chinese yuan	39	28
Brazilian real	35	143
Malaysian ringgit	29	70
Colombian peso	26	7
Taiwanese dollar	25	71
Korean won	15	30
Others	15	3
Total	13,471	13,949

Source: Company documents.

EXHIBIT 4 | Trends in Inflation Rates (GDP deflator)

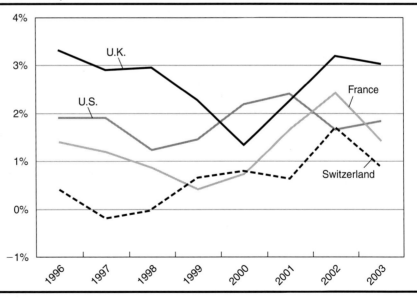

Source: Datastream.

EXHIBIT 5 | Trends in 10-Year Government-Benchmark Bond Yields

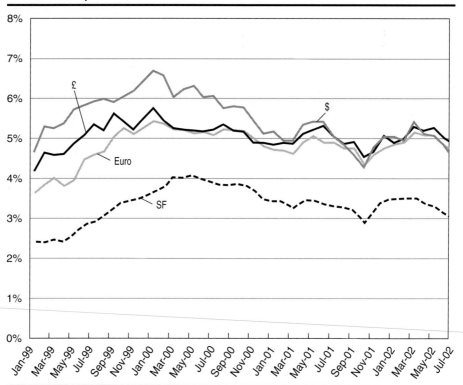

Source: Datastream.

EXHIBIT 6 | Trends in Foreign-Currency Spot Rates

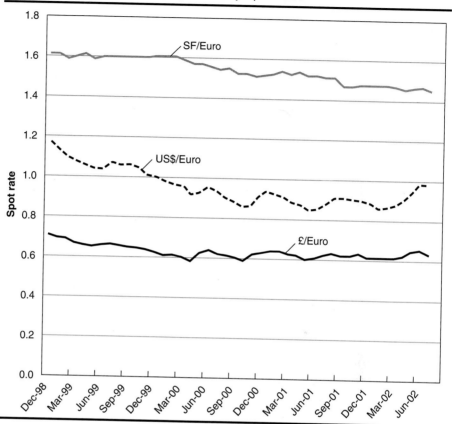

Source: Datastream.

EXHIBIT 7 | Cross-Exchange Rates (spot prices, 7/31/2002)

Row Currency/ Column Currency	Euro	British Pound	Swiss Franc	U.S. Dollar
Euro	1.000	1.593	0.688	1.020
British pound	0.628	1.000	0.432	0.640
Swiss franc	1.453	2.315	1.000	1.482
U.S. dollar	0.980	1.562	0.675	1.000

Source: Datastream.

EXHIBIT 8 | Risk-Free Rates by Currency Denomination[1]

Maturity	Euro	British Pound	Swiss Franc	U.S. Dollar
1-year	3.514%	4.258%	1.125%	2.099%
2-year	3.816	4.622	1.713	2.767
3-year	4.110	4.910	2.172	3.432
4-year	4.342	5.088	2.498	3.922
5-year	4.530	5.190	2.743	4.308
6-year	4.688	5.249	2.948	4.619
7-year	4.819	5.292	3.120	4.873
8-year	4.928	5.331	3.267	5.081
9-year	5.017	5.358	3.394	5.264
10-year	5.087	5.374	3.499	5.413

[1]Rates equal to zero-curve fixed-to-floating swap rates.

Source: Datastream.

National Railroad Passenger Corporation ("Amtrak"): Acela Financing

On April 30, 1999, Arlene Friner, CFO of Amtrak, instructed her treasury staff to review a leveraged-lease proposal from BNY Capital Funding LLC (BNYCF). Several weeks earlier, Amtrak and its adviser, Babcock & Brown Financial Corporation, had invited financial institutions to submit lease-financing proposals for Amtrak's planned purchase of locomotives and high-speed train sets.[1] The equipment would be utilized on the "Acela" line, Amtrak's new brand that was designed to differentiate Amtrak passenger trains and service in the Northeast Corridor from the existing service.[2] Acela, scheduled to begin service in late 1999, promised to offer faster trip times and premium service (**Exhibit 1**).

Friner and her staff had gone over the proposals and agreed that BNYCF was among those that offered the best terms. Now, she had to decide whether Amtrak should finance the equipment purchases using BNYCF's leveraged-lease proposal or borrow money and purchase the equipment on its own.

Company Background

In 1970, the U.S. Congress created the National Railroad Passenger Corporation (Amtrak) to ensure that "modern, efficient intercity passenger-rail service would

---

[1] A train set consisted of one first-class coach car, one bistro car, three coach cars, one end-coach car, and two power cars.

[2] Babcock and Brown memorandum, 1.

This case was prepared by Jessica Chan, under the supervision of Robert F. Bruner. The author wishes to thank Lisa Levine of the Equipment Leasing and Finance Foundation, Dennis Neumann and Barbara Dering of BNY Capital Funding LLC, and Raj Srinath of Amtrak. The financial support of the Batten Institute is gratefully acknowledged. It was written as a basis for class discussion rather than to illustrate effective or ineffective handling of an administrative situation. Copyright © 2001 by the University of Virginia Darden School Foundation, Charlottesville, VA. All rights reserved. *To order copies, send an e-mail to* sales@dardenpublishing.com. *No part of this publication may be reproduced, stored in a retrieval system, used in a spreadsheet, or transmitted in any form or by any means—electronic, mechanical, photocopying, recording, or otherwise—without the permission of the Darden School Foundation.* Rev. 12/05.

remain an integral part of the national transportation system."[3] The government mandated Amtrak to take over the rail-passenger operations of private railroads. Since then, Amtrak had become the primary provider of passenger-rail service in the United States. Amtrak's national network provided service to more than 20 million intercity passengers and operated 516 stations in 44 states.

Historically, Amtrak had received annual subsidies from the federal government. In 1997, however, Congress passed the Amtrak Reform and Accountability Act (ARAA), which stipulated that Amtrak eliminate its reliance on federal subsidies by 2002. After 2002, no federal funds could be used for Amtrak's operating expenses. This represented a formidable challenge, as Amtrak had never been profitable in its 30-year history. (See **Exhibits 2** and **3** for Amtrak's historical income statements and latest balance sheet.) Thus, to meet Congress's goal of operating self-sufficiency by 2002, Amtrak developed a radical new business plan, the centerpiece of which was a high-speed rail service that was projected to bring in net annual revenues of $180 million by fiscal-year 2002.[4]

Acela

In its Northeast Corridor, which served routes from Virginia to Maine,[5] Amtrak branded this new high-speed rail service "Acela":

> Acela is designed to be more than high-speed trains—it is a brand representing a new way of doing business. Acela was designed to bring high speed and high quality to Northeast Corridor passengers. The Acela service will offer faster trip times, comfortable amenities, and highly personalized service. Acela is the latest and boldest step by Amtrak to change its rail service into a more customer-focused, commercially driven, premium transportation service.[6]

The Acela trains, designed to operate as fast as 150 miles an hour (241.35 kilometers an hour), promised to reduce travel time significantly. For instance, the trip from Washington, D.C., to Boston, which currently took 7 hours and 30 minutes, would take 5 hours and 50 minutes on the high-speed trains.[7] The first high-speed trains, the Acela Express, were scheduled to begin service between New York City and Boston in late 1999, while the New York–Washington leg would be added within a year. The full high-speed service was expected to be in place by the fall of 2000.

---

[3]Executive Summary: 1999 Assessment of Amtrak's Financial Needs through 2002.

[4]Amtrak's fiscal year ended September 30.

[5]Amtrak was organized along three strategic business units (SBUs): Amtrak Northeast Corridor, Amtrak Intercity, and Amtrak West. The Northeast Corridor included all the routes in the Northeast from Virginia to Maine; Amtrak West included the West Coast routes in California and the Pacific Northwest, and extended to Vancouver, British Columbia. Amtrak Intercity was the remainder of the system, across the middle of the country.

[6]Babcock and Brown memorandum, 3.

[7]Information provided by Raj Srinath, senior director of Corporate Finance, Amtrak.

The Equipment

To operate the Acela Regional Service as planned, Amtrak needed to purchase 15 dual-cab, high-horsepower electric locomotives and 20 high-speed train sets. Each train set consisted of one first-class coach car, one bistro car, three coach cars, one end coach car, and two power cars. The estimated total cost for all the equipment was around $750 million:

	No.	Cost	Aggregate Cost
High-speed locomotives	15	$ 7,161,300	$ 107,419,500
Train sets	20	$ 32,129,050	$ 642,581,000
Total			$ 750,000,500

The train sets and locomotives had estimated useful lives of 25 years and residual values equivalent to approximately 15 percent of the original equipment cost. Amtrak used straight-line depreciation for accounting purposes and seven-year MACRS[8] for tax purposes. Amtrak was subject to the corporate income tax rate of 38 percent.

Friner had already been able to arrange financing for all the equipment save for six locomotives and seven train sets, which totaled $267.9 million in value. This was the amount (not $750 million) for which she was considering the BNYCF leveraged-lease proposal.

Financing Options

Three options were available for Amtrak to gain use of the equipment: (1) borrow money to fund the purchase, (2) lease the equipment from a financial institution such as BNYCF, or (3) rely on federal sources for funding.

Borrow and Buy

A major bank had offered to underwrite a bond issuance for Amtrak with a 20-year term at 6.75 percent per annum. This arrangement would call for Amtrak to make semiannual payments of $12.303 million, beginning in December 1999. The locomotives and train sets would serve as collateral for the loan. A member of the treasury staff suggested that one drawback to this alternative was that Amtrak had recently issued debt—as such, the public market might already be saturated with Amtrak paper.

---

[8]Modified Accelerated Cost Recovery System. See **Exhibit 6** for a seven-year MACRS schedule.

Lease

BNYCF had proposed a leveraged-lease[9] structure for the transaction (**Exhibit 4**). BNY Capital Funding LLC, a wholly owned subsidiary of the Bank of New York, would act as lessor. It would provide the equity funds needed to finance the purchase. The Export Development Corporation (EDC) of Canada would be the sole lender and debt provider, agreeing to provide 80 percent of the required funds. The equity investor, BNYCF, would provide the remaining 20 percent and would receive lease payments only after the debtor had been paid.

The equity and debt funds on closing would flow through Wilmington Trust, an independent third party to the transaction that acted as owner-trustee. The rental payments would also flow through Wilmington Trust, which would distribute the payments to either EDC or BNYCF.

Under the lease proposal, Amtrak would have to make semiannual payments according to the schedule provided in **Exhibit 5**. At the end of the lease term, Amtrak could buy the equipment from BNYCF at the higher of terminal or fair market value.[10] Amtrak also had an early-buyout option, whereby it could acquire the equipment from BNYCF in 2017 for $126.6 million.

Rely on Federal Sources

Theoretically, Amtrak could use federal monies to fund the Acela equipment purchases. Although Congress had mandated that Amtrak could not use federal subsidies for operating expenses, it had agreed to continue funding Amtrak for capital appropriations. Purchase of the Acela equipment would be considered a capital-asset acquisition and, as such, federal grant monies could be used. But Friner and her staff considered federal grants to be a "premium and precious" commodity; thus, Amtrak preferred to use the grant money to fund capital projects that could not be easily and cost-effectively financed, such as safety, right-of-way and infrastructure-related projects, and major overhauls. Acela train sets and other rolling stock, however, could be very efficiently financed through the capital markets.

Conclusion

Arlene Friner needed to make a decision soon. The timely commencement of the Acela service was crucial to Amtrak's prospects for self-sufficiency. She needed to arrange financing immediately if the equipment were to be delivered on time.

---

[9]There were three common types of financial leases. Direct leases were those in which the lessor purchased the equipment or asset and rented it out to the lessee. In sale-and-leaseback arrangements, the lessee already owned the asset but sold it to a lessor and leased it back. Leveraged leases were those in which the lessor borrowed money to fund part of the purchase of assets, pledging the lease contract as security for the loan.

[10]Using historical data, the treasury staff estimated that the standard deviation of the market-value fluctuations of train sets and locomotives was 25 percent. The 17-year risk-free rate currently stood at 5.78 percent. The treasury staff also calculated Amtrak's WACC to be 11.8 percent.

EXHIBIT 1 | About Acela

Northeast Travel

Ride the
Acela

New World-Class Service From Amtrak®.

Acela,^{SM} A blend of "acceleration" and "excellence."
Acela^{SM} (pronounced ah-CELL-ah) represents the
Amtrak® commitment to excel. To make your journey the best it
can be at every stage — from faster, more efficient reservation
systems to striking new and renovated stations to premium on-
board services. Acela Express^{SM} is the name of the sleek new
high-speed trains you'll see in the Northeast this year.

amtrak.com
30% off
Book online today!

1+1=3
On Acela
Express

But Acela means more than fast trains. It stands for leading
technology, superior comfort and modern amenities. With three
levels of service — Express, Regional and Commuter — Acela
offers an unparalleled standard of travel for every guest on every
train. A standard that includes consistently professional, highly
personalized service; new and refurbished trains with a
contemporary interior design; convenient connections to a wide
variety of destinations across the U.S. and thoughtful touches for
your pleasure and comfort. Simply stated, Acela puts top priority
on your time and provides a pleasant travel experience. It's
Amtrak's commitment to the way you choose to travel.

At 150 MPH, This is Not Your Ordinary Train Trip.

If your life is on the fast track, **Acela Express**^{SM} is
Amtrak's top-of-the-line ride to business or pleasure in
the Northeast. The new 150-mph Acela Express trains will replace
Metroliner®this year. These trains are designed to offer state-of-the-
art equipment and premium service to travelers who expect nothing
but the best. We're even improving our station locations — we've
added a new Route 128 station near Boston and updated Penn
Station in New York.

Reserved First class and Business class seating accommodate your
busy agenda with comfort, upscale business amenities and polished
professional service.

Plush seats with foot-rests and adjustable head cushions invite you
to relax and recharge. Listen to music, enjoy a gourmet-to-go snack
or sandwich. When there's work to do, you have an electrical outlet
at your seat, adjustable lighting and a large tray table for your laptop.
You can hold a meeting at one of our 32 conference tables located
throughout the train. Or take a break in the bistro-like atmosphere of
the Cafe car, where there's beer on tap and news on the TV screen.
Aboard Acela Express, it's all about how you use your time.

Source: http://amtrak.com/savings/acela.html. Note: Image has been modified to fit page.

EXHIBIT 2 | Income Statement (values in millions of U.S. dollars)

	Fiscal Year Ending September 30				
	1994	1995	1996	1997	1998
Revenues					
Passenger-related and other	$1,152	$1,177	$1,213	$1,341	$1,392
Commuter	184	213	234	242	260
Reimbursable	77	107	108	91	91
Federal payments	—	—	—	—	542
Total revenues	**$1,413**	**$1,497**	**$1,555**	**$1,674**	**$2,285**
Expenses					
Salaries, wages, and benefits	$1,330	$1,241	$1,236	$1,299	$1,448
Train operations	358	321	321	365	356
Facility and office related	153	172	181	187	190
Maintenance-of-way goods and services	45	73	59	46	52
Advertising and sales	91	90	109	98	102
Interest	185	144	149	160	181
Depreciation and amortization	245	230	238	242	294
Other	83	34	25	39	15
One-time charges/(gains)	(244)	—	—	—	—
Total expenses	**2,246**	**2,305**	**2,318**	**2,436**	**2,638**
Operating income/(loss)	**($833)**	**($808)**	**($763)**	**($762)**	**($353)**
Exclude federal payments and related interest					577
Operating loss restated	**($833)**	**($808)**	**($763)**	**($762)**	**($930)**
Federal grants					
Federal operating grant	$352	$392	$285	$223	$202
Excess railroad retirement taxes	150	150	120	142	142
Federal capital—interest	—	—	—	42	—
Federal capital—progressive overhaul and other	—	—	36	37	82
Total federal grants	**$502**	**$542**	**$441**	**$444**	**$426**
Net loss	**($331)**	**($266)**	**($322)**	**($318)**	**($504)**

Source of data: Amtrak annual report.

EXHIBIT 3 | Balance Sheet (values in millions of U.S. dollars)

	FY Ending Sept. 30, 1998
ASSETS	
Current assets	
Cash and equivalents	$ 274.7
Temporary cash investments	409.7
Accounts receivable, net	88.7
Materials and supplies	91.6
Other current assets	3.4
Total current assets	868.1
Property, plant, and equipment	9,456.4
Less accumulated depreciation	(3,106.9)
Net property, plant, and equipment	6,349.5
Other assets and deferred charges	87.6
Total assets	$ 7,305.3
LIABILITIES AND CAPITALIZATION	
Current liabilities	
Accounts payable	$ 270.8
Accrued expenses and other current liabilities	186.7
Deferred ticket revenue	61.4
Current maturities of long-term debt and capital-lease obligations	102.2
Total current liabilities	621.1
Long-term debt and capital lease obligations	
Capital-lease obligations	1,213.1
Equipment and other debt	322.5
	1,535.6
Other liabilities and deferred credit	
Deferred federal payments	457.0
Casualty reserves	136.2
Postretirement employee-benefits obligation	118.4
Environmental reserve	35.4
Advances from railroads and commuter agencies	20.6
Other	1.5
	769.1
Total liabilities	2,925.8
Capitalization	
Preferred stock	10,939.7
Common stock	93.9
Other paid-in capital	6,471.3
Accumulated comprehensive loss	(13,125.4)
	4,379.5
Total liabilities and capitalization	$ 7,305.3

Source of data: Amtrak annual report.

EXHIBIT 4 | BNY Capital Funding LLC's Proposed Leveraged-Lease Structure

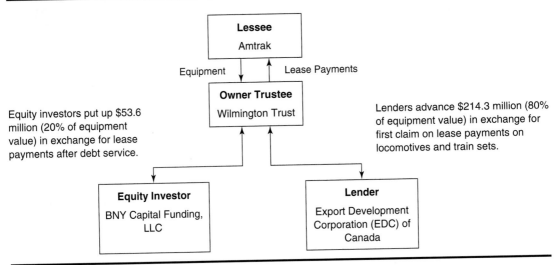

Equity investors put up $53.6 million (20% of equipment value) in exchange for lease payments after debt service.

Lenders advance $214.3 million (80% of equipment value) in exchange for first claim on lease payments on locomotives and train sets.

Note: Diagram based on illustration in *Principles of Corporate Finance* by Richard Brealey and Stewart Myers, 5th ed., p. 755.

EXHIBIT 5 | BNY Capital Funding LLC's Proposed Lease-Payment Schedule (in dollars)

Date Due		Amount
1999	June	$ —
	Dec.	200,102
2000	June	3,761,228
	Dec.	7,965,652
2001	June	10,022,594
	Dec.	10,316,948
2002	June	8,617,634
	Dec.	10,360,645
2003	June	9,828,570
	Dec.	10,367,985
2004	June	8,607,823
	Dec.	10,418,573
2005	June	9,683,063
	Dec.	10,435,186
2006	June	8,580,151
	Dec.	11,599,993
2007	June	7,338,339
	Dec.	11,468,211
2008	June	9,475,208
	Dec.	15,792,709
2009	June	7,765,741
	Dec.	20,224,322
2010	June	5,067,035
	Dec.	15,872,556
2011	June	4,121,823
	Dec.	22,807,129
2012	June	3,336,587
	Dec.	23,645,133
2013	June	2,662,913
	Dec.	24,055,367
2014	June	1,957,919
	Dec.	20,017,608
2015	June	6,067,613
	Dec.	6,287,652
2016	June	12,292,315
	Dec.	21,394,788
2017	June	6,551,924
	Dec.	18,107,167
2018	June	8,612,133
	Dec.	13,469,295
2019	June	8,864,543
	Dec.	6,654,238
2020	June	2,035,748
	Dec.	1

EXHIBIT 6 | Seven-Year MACRS Depreciation Schedule[1] (in percentages of depreciable investment)

Year	% Depreciated
1	14.29
2	24.49
3	17.49
4	12.49
5	8.93
6	8.93
7	8.93
8	4.45

[1] Because of the half-year convention, seven-year MACRS involved eight years of depreciation expenses.

Primus Automation Division, 2002

In early 2002, Tom Baumann, an analyst in the Marketing and Sales Group of the Factory Automation Division of Primus Corporation, had to recommend to the division sales manager, Jim Feldman, the terms under which Primus would lease one of its advanced systems to Avantjet Corporation, a manufacturer of corporate-jet aircraft. Specifically, Baumann was weighing a choice among four alternative sets of lease terms.

The problem of analyzing and setting lease terms was relatively new to Baumann and had arisen only a month earlier, when Avantjet informed Baumann and Feldman that its pending purchase of the factory-automation system had been put on indefinite hold. Avantjet's CEO had just ordered a moratorium on any capital expenditures that might negatively affect Avantjet's income statement and balance sheet. Baumann was not completely surprised by Avantjet's decision. Just recently, the *Wall Street Journal* had singled out Avantjet's declining stock price and worsening balance sheet as an example of manufacturers' deteriorating condition during the economic recession.

Only three months earlier, Baumann and Feldman had won an apparent competition for Avantjet's business over Primus's leading competitors, Faulhaber Gmbh of Germany and Honshu Heavy Industries of Japan. Baumann feared that Avantjet's temporizing would give those two competitors an opportunity to renew their selling efforts to Avantjet.

Feldman challenged Baumann to find a way to make the sale: "Help me salvage this deal or we won't make our sales budget for the year. Also, given the steep competition, we might lose the customer altogether on future sales." Baumann explored a range of creative financing terms, such as leasing, that might remove Avantjet's reluctance to proceed. He concluded that structuring the transaction as a lease might save the deal. Now, choosing the annual lease payment remained the only detail to be settled before returning to Avantjet with a proposal.

This case was prepared by Robert Hengelbrok, under the supervision of Robert F. Bruner and with the assistance of Sean D. Carr. It was written as a basis for class discussion rather than to illustrate effective or ineffective handling of an administrative situation. Copyright © 2005 by the University of Virginia Darden School Foundation, Charlottesville, VA. All rights reserved. *To order copies, send an e-mail to* sales@ dardenpublishing.com. *No part of this publication may be reproduced, stored in a retrieval system, used in a spreadsheet, or transmitted in any form or by any means—electronic, mechanical, photocopying, recording, or otherwise—without the permission of the Darden School Foundation.*

Primus Automation Division

Primus Automation, a division of a large, worldwide manufacturing and services firm, was an innovative producer of world-class factory-automation products and services, with operations in the United States, Europe, and Asia. Primus's products included programmable controllers, numerical controls, industrial computers, manufacturing software, factory-automation systems, and data communication networks.

The business environment had changed dramatically over the past year. Slower economic growth, coupled with increased competition for market share, had been forecast for the next few years. Still, a recent resurgence in the U.S. manufacturing base—due to the weakened dollar driving up U.S. exports—was spurring factory automation. Cross-continental industry alliances and an accelerated rate of new product introductions had heightened industry rivalries.

Primus Automation's objectives were to maintain leadership in market share, increase sales by 15 percent a year, and achieve its targets for net income and working capital turnover. Those objectives were to be realized by providing the most responsive customer service, attaining a strong share position in the high volume-growing segments, and offering leading-technology products based on industry standards.

Meeting the objectives required stimulating the demand by creating new incentives for purchasing automation equipment. Many of the unsophisticated users of automation equipment in the United States needed to be educated in analyzing capital expenditures, tax incentives, and alternative methods for acquiring the needed equipment. Division executives had discussed various asset-financing approaches as a means of assisting with the placement of their systems.

Asset-Financing Approaches

Baumann discussed with Primus's division executives the variety of ways a firm might acquire the use of a Primus Automated Factory System. First, the customer could purchase a system with cash or with borrowed funds, either unsecured or collateralized by the equipment. Second, the firm could acquire the equipment through a conditional sale in which the title would pass to the firm upon the receipt of the final payment. Finally, the customer could lease the equipment in one of two ways: (1) via a cancelable *operating lease,* which would carry a term that was less than the economic life of the property; or (2) via a noncancelable financial *capital lease* that would span the entire economic life of the property.

Capital versus Operating Leases

Baumann reviewed his notes on the rules defining the two types of leases. To be classified as a capital lease under the guidelines of Financial Accounting Standards Board (FASB) Statement No. 13,[1] the lease had to meet one or more of the following four criteria:

---

[1]*Statement of Financial Accounting Standards No. 13: Accounting for Leases,* Financial Accounting Standards Board (November 1976), 7–9.

a.   Ownership of the asset transferred by the end of the lease term.

b.   The lease contained a bargain-purchase option, whereby the lessee had to pay the fair market value for the property at the end of the lease.

c.   The lease term was equal to 75 percent or more of the economic life of the property.

d.   The present value of the lease payments over the lease term was equal to or greater than 90 percent of the fair market value of the leased property at the beginning of the lease.

If the lease qualified as a capital lease, then the lessee would be required to depreciate the equipment by showing it as an asset and a liability on its balance sheet. The lessee could not deduct the lease payment from its income taxes. At the end of the lease, the lessee retained ownership and bore the risk of early changes in the asset's value.

If the lease met none of the foregoing criteria, it would be classified as an operating lease. As an operating lease, the lease payments would be treated as an ordinary expense, deductible from taxable income. The leased property would not appear on the lessee's balance sheet and, after the lease term, would revert to the lessor.

Primus Automation had never before offered leasing and was unfamiliar with the actual workings of leasing arrangements. Fortunately, the Equipment Finance Division of Primus's parent company had extensive leasing expertise and assisted Baumann in his research. As he dug out some of the information that the division had sent him, Baumann realized that this was the first application of his efforts and he wanted to make sure he understood all the nuances involved with leasing.

Avantjet

Baumann had heard that Avantjet's vice president of operations was determined to get an automation system to cut costs and accelerate his company's production line. A large backlog of orders for both new jets and the retrofitted older models had put new demands on production. Without such a system, it would be very difficult to meet promised deliveries. In addition, Baumann knew that Avantjet's capital-budgeting process included all major expenditures—new construction and capital leases—but excluded operating leases.

The risk of obsolescence and the ability to upgrade equipment weighed heavily in Avantjet's decision. Overall, the most important factor was cash flow, because Avantjet wanted to avoid any additional unplanned expenditures in 2002. Avantjet was very capital intensive and was only marginally profitable because it was so highly leveraged. (**Exhibits 1** and **2** show Avantjet's income statement and balance sheet.)

With that in mind, Baumann wondered how he was going to find a way to resolve all the issues. He knew that many companies had turned to leasing to address some of those concerns. Although many of the large firms in the airframe industry were not as cash strapped as the small- and medium-sized shops, it was worthwhile to find out what classes of customers would benefit financially from leasing. Baumann surmised that tax rates and cost-of-capital disparities between the lessor and lessee might be critical drivers in any lease arrangement.

Primus's Competitors

Several months earlier, when Avantjet was reviewing system proposals from Primus, Honshu, and Faulhaber, Baumann and Feldman learned from Avantjet that all three systems were roughly equivalent but differed in pricing. **Table 1** summarizes the pricing options then available:

TABLE 1 I Summary of the available pricing options (in US$)

System Manufacturer	Purchase Price of System If Avantjet Were to Buy	Quoted Annual Lease Expense and Guaranteed Residual Value[2] for 5-Year Operating Lease
Faulhaber Gmbh	$759,000	$170,000; 15% residual value
Honshu Heavy Industries	$737,000	$163,000; 24% residual value
Primus Automation Division	$715,000	Not previously quoted

Baumann had learned from industry newsletters that foreign manufacturers sometimes exploited their allegedly lower costs of capital as a competitive weapon in designing financing terms for their customers. Baumann wondered whether this was apparent in the lease terms proposed by Faulhaber and Honshu, and planned to estimate the effective lease costs under their respective proposals.

Primus's Lease Proposal

The particular deal that Feldman had called Baumann about was a proposal for a $715,000 factory-automation system. This equipment would enable Avantjet to operate a group of workstations from a central control site while gaining valuable feedback and planning capabilities. Realizing that he had to find out more about Avantjet's motives for delaying the project, Baumann quizzed Feldman about Avantjet's performance and requirements. Feldman told Baumann that Avantjet's last CEO had been replaced by a senior executive from outside the firm who was more concerned about the bottom line and the balance sheet than he was about making capital expenditures that had long paybacks.

With that in mind, Baumann began to assess this particular deal. The price of the total package was $715,000. Baumann assumed that Avantjet's primary alternative to leasing was to borrow the purchase price of the equipment on a five-year, interest-bearing term loan payable in equal annual amounts due at the end of each year. The Equipment Finance Division also quoted Baumann four alternatives for a five-year operating lease with equal annual payments (due at the beginning of each year) that varied depending on Avantjet's actual tax rate and cost of debt. At the end of the lease

---

[2]Residual value was the estimated fair value of a leased asset at the end of the lease term. Because future values were difficult to predict, residual values were often highly subjective. Equipment leases typically stipulated a guaranteed residual value.

term, renewal was subject to negotiation between the two parties. Factory-automation equipment was classified as technological equipment with a five-year life. Five-year MACRS[3] depreciation rates, based on the full value of the property, were as follows in **Table 2:**

TABLE 2 I Five-Year MACRS

Income Tax Depreciation Rate Schedule	
Year	Percentage
1	20.00
2	32.00
3	19.20
4	11.52
5	11.52

In order to structure it as an operating lease, the Equipment Finance Division required an 11.2729 percent residual guarantee from Baumann's division. Baumann did not know how sensitive to the residual assumption the results would be. Because his division was trying to move into leasing to bolster sales, he figured that it might be willing to assume some of the risk of the equipment's value declining substantially in five years. Primus Automation might also have to assist the Equipment Finance Division in remarketing the equipment to another user, if a new lease were not signed when the original lease expired. (**Exhibit 3** lists the various pricing and leasing terms.)

To analyze leasing scenarios, Baumann created a leasing model (**Exhibits 4** and **5**) for computing the net present value (NPV) and the internal rate of return (IRR) of cash flows to get a better understanding of which alternative would be the least costly to Avantjet. The scenario with the lowest present value would be the cheapest financing alternative. The IRR represented the effective cost of the lease financing. If that rate were below the after-tax cost of debt, leasing would be the more attractive method of financing.

Although Baumann guessed that Avantjet had about the same borrowing cost as Primus (about 9.5 percent), he suspected that Avantjet was in a lower tax bracket. Baumann decided to run some sensitivity analyses with a zero marginal tax rate. With such a low tax rate, Avantjet could not fully exploit the tax savings on interest and depreciation.

Small- and medium-sized firms probably paid higher interest rates than Primus and could save money if Primus financed the equipment and passed on some of the financing savings to them. Leasing terms might be adjusted to exchange tax benefits for lower lease rates. Baumann's analysis used the after-tax cost of debt as the discount rate, but Baumann thought he might want to use a higher discount rate, perhaps

---

[3]MACRS stood for modified accelerated cost recovery system. It was a method of accelerated depreciation allowed under the U.S. Tax Code. Under MACRS, depreciation deductions were determined without regard to the asset's residual value.

the weighted-average cost of capital, based on the greater risk involved with leasing high-technology equipment.

A thorough sensitivity analysis based on various discount and tax rates might help to determine under what circumstances a customer might want to lease. Sample calculations for four lease rates that Primus might offer different customers are presented in **Exhibit 6.** With a variety of options and scenarios to propose to Avantjet, depending on actual tax and hurdle rates, Baumann believed that Primus had a good chance of resurrecting the deal and meeting its sales goals for 2002. Moreover, this experience would assist Primus in offering lease proposals to its future customers.

EXHIBIT 1 | Avantjet's Statement of Income ($000)

	2001	2000	1999
Sales	$576,327	$575,477	$432,522
Other income	9,985	6,976	9,677
Gross income	586,312	582,453	442,199
Cost of goods sold	425,076	423,443	325,016
Selling, general, & admin.	43,624	36,215	35,632
Research & development	13,773	12,873	9,064
Interest	84,062	87,259	27,002
Total expenses	566,535	559,790	396,714
Income before taxes	19,777	22,662	45,485
Taxes	9,690	11,105	22,288
Net income	$ 10,087	$ 11,557	$ 23,197

Source: Company records.

EXHIBIT 2 | Avantjet's Balance Sheet ($000)

	2001	2000
Assets		
Current assets:		
Cash and temporary investments	$ 19,918	$ 27,263
Accounts receivable	37,791	37,307
Inventories	310,180	323,101
Prepaid expenses	13,928	13,362
Total current assets	381,817	401,033
Property, plant, and equipment:		
Land	2,245	2,245
Buildings	30,654	30,229
Machinery and equipment	26,932	21,244
Furniture and fixtures	1,683	1,520
Construction in progress	1,668	885
	63,182	56,123
Less accumulated depreciation	12,634	8,267
Net property, plant, and equipment	50,548	47,856
Other assets	640,369	648,339
Total assets	$1,072,734	$1,097,228
Liabilities and stockholders' equity		
Current liabilities:		
Long-term debt	$ 592	$ 563
Accounts payable	42,355	38,760
Notes payable	4,750	5,764
Accrued compensation, interest, and other liabilities	39,627	43,855
Deposits and progress payments	146,964	160,946
Total current liabilities	234,288	249,888
Long-term notes payable to banks	646,633	671,225
Deferred income taxes	42,661	41,498
	689,294	712,723
Common stockholders' equity:		
Common stock	3,385	3,027
Capital in excess of par value	74,081	69,770
Retained earnings	72,017	62,156
Less common stock in treasury	(331)	(336)
Total stockholders' equity	149,152	134,617
Total liabilities and stockholders' equity	$1,072,734	$1,097,228

Source: Company records.

EXHIBIT 3 | Terms under Hypothetical Leasing and Borrow-and-Buy Strategies

Loan ("Borrow-and-Buy")	
5-year term loan	
Payment in arrears	$715,000
Equipment cost	$0
Cash down payment	$715,000
Loan amount	
Lease	Annual payments (in advance)
5-year net lease	$155,040
Leasing option #1	$160,003
Leasing option #2	$162,350
Leasing option #3	$164,760
Leasing option #4	
Both Methods	11.2729%
Guaranteed residual value:	
(required by Primus Equipment Finance Division)	0%
Investment tax credit	Five-year MACRS
Depreciation	

EXHIBIT 4 | Sample Calculation of the Present Value of Cash Outflows: Scenario A, Lease Payment 2 ($160,003)[1]

| Tax rate: | 34.00% | Equipment cost: $715,000 |
| Pretax interest rate | 9.50% | Lease payment: $160,003 |

Year	Interest Payment after Tax[2]	Principal Payment[2]	Five-Year MACRS[3] Depr. Rate	Depr. before Tax	Depr. Tax Savings	Residual Cash Flow after Tax[4]	Loan Cash Outflow[5]	Lease Cash Outflow[6]
0							$ 0	$105,602
1	$ 44,831	$118,287	20.00%	$143,000	($48,620)		$114,498	$105,602
2	$ 37,414	$129,524	32.00%	$228,800	($77,792)		$ 89,146	$105,602
3	$ 29,293	$141,829	19.20%	$137,280	($46,675)		$124,447	$105,602
4	$ 20,400	$155,303	11.52%	$ 82,368	($28,005)		$147,698	$105,602
5	$ 10,663	$170,057	11.52%	$ 82,368	($28,005)	($67,199)	$ 85,515	$ 0
Sum	$142,600	$715,000	94.24%	$673,816	($229,097)	($67,199)	$561,303	$528,010
NPV							$469,273	$469,273

[1]This table illustrates the calculation of net present value (NPV) for the two methods of equipment financing: the loan financing alternative (also called borrow-and-buy) and the lease financing. Because these cash flows are net outflows or expenses, the alternative with the lower net present value will be more attractive to the customer.

[2]See "Loan Amortization Table."

[3]Modified Accelerated Cost Recovery System (MACRS).

[4]The residual cash flow equals the sale proceeds less the tax expense on the gain or loss from the sale. The tax expense equals the tax rate times the differences between sale proceeds and net book value of the asset (see separate calculation below).

[5]Loan cash flows are the sum of after-tax interest payments, principal payments, depreciation tax shield (shown as a negative value because it reduces expenses), and value captured from the sale of the residual asset (also negative). Loan-financing cash flows occur *in arrears*.

[6]Lease cash flows equal the assumed lease payment less the tax shield. Lease payments are made *in advance*.

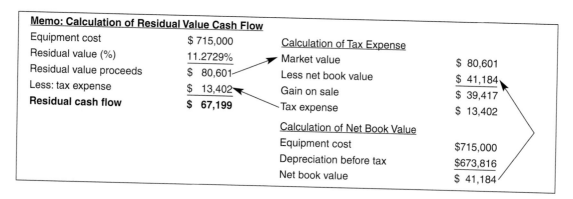

Memo: Calculation of Residual Value Cash Flow

Equipment cost	$ 715,000	Calculation of Tax Expense	
Residual value (%)	11.2729%	Market value	$ 80,601
Residual value proceeds	$ 80,601	Less net book value	$ 41,184
Less: tax expense	$ 13,402	Gain on sale	$ 39,417
Residual cash flow	**$ 67,199**	Tax expense	$ 13,402
		Calculation of Net Book Value	
		Equipment cost	$715,000
		Depreciation before tax	$673,816
		Net book value	$ 41,184

EXHIBIT 5 | Sample Calculation of the Internal Rate of Return: Scenario A, Lease Payment 2 ($160,003)[1]

Year	Lease Payment after Tax[2]	Forgone Tax Savings Associated with Depreciation[2]	Forgone Residual Value after Tax[2]	Initial Purchase Price Saved	Lease Payment Less Incremental Cash Flow
0	($105,602)			$715,000	$609,398
1	($105,602)	($48,620)			($154,222)
2	($105,602)	($77,792)			($183,394)
3	($105,602)	($46,675)			($152,277)
4	($105,602)	($28,005)			($133,607)
5	$0	($28,005)	($67,199)		($95,204)
Sum	($528,010)	($229,097)	($67,199)	$715,000	($109,307)
IRR					**6.27%**

[1]This table illustrates the calculation of the internal rate of return (IRR) associated with lease financing. The IRR is the effective after-tax cost of the lease financing and is useful for comparison with the cost of alternative forms of financing. Because this is a calculation based on *costs* to the customer, a lower IRR will be more attractive to the customer.

[2]See "Sample Calculation of the Present Value of Cash Outflows."

EXHIBIT 6 | Summary Table of the NPV and IRR for the Four Tax and Cost-of-Capital Scenarios

Scenario	A	B	C	D
Effective tax rate	34.0%	34.0%	0.0%	0.0%
Pretax cost of debt	9.5%	13.0%	9.5%	13.0%
After-tax cost of debt	6.27%	8.58%	9.50%	13.00%
NPV of loan ("borrow-and-buy")	$469,273	$484,546	$663,800	$671,253
IRR of loan ("borrow-and-buy")	6.27%	8.58%	9.50%	13.00%
Leasing option #1	$155,040	$155,040	$155,040	$155,040
NPV of leasing option #1	$454,717			
IRR of lease	5.32%			
Lease advantage over borrowing	$ 14,556			
Leasing option #2	$160,003	$160,003	$160,003	$160,003
NPV of leasing option #2	$469,273			
IRR of lease	6.27%			
Lease advantage over borrowing	$0			
Leasing option #3	$162,350	$162,350	$162,350	$162,350
NPV of leasing option #3	$476,156			
IRR of lease	6.72%			
Lease advantage over borrowing	($6,883)			
Leasing option #4	$164,760	$164,760	$164,760	$164,760
NPV of leasing option #4	$483,225			
IRR of lease	7.19%			
Lease advantage over borrowing	($13,952)			
Faulhaber Gmbh				
NPV of loan				
NPV of lease				
IRR of lease				
Lease advantage over borrowing				
Honshu Heavy Industries				
NPV of loan				
NPV of lease				
IRR of lease				
Lease advantage over borrowing				

Note: Calculations for shaded cells are presented in Exhibits 4 and 5.

Corning, Inc.: Zero Coupon Convertible Debentures Due November 8, 2015 (A)

On November 8, 2000, Corning announced that it would issue $2.7 billion in zero-coupon convertible debentures priced at $741.923 per $1,000 principal amount. The initial public offering (IPO) price yielded 2 percent per annum to maturity, compounded semiannually. A summary of terms is given in **Exhibit 1.** Concurrent with the offering, Corning also conducted a separate public offering of 30 million shares of its common stock at $71.25 per share.[1] Neither offering was contingent upon completion of the other. The entire financing would raise around $4.8 billion.

Corning planned to use the proceeds of both offerings to fund its acquisition of Pirelli S.p.A.'s 90 percent interest in Optical Technologies USA, Pirelli's optical-components and -devices business. The total acquisition consideration was approximately $3.6 billion in cash. The acquisition agreement had been announced on September 27, 2000, and pended regulatory approval. Observers agreed, however, that the acquisition was likely to be completed.

The issue of the Corning zero-coupon convertibles came to the attention of Julianna Coopers, an investment analyst at the Paradigm Group of mutual funds. The Paradigm Group offered 36 different funds and managed more than $50 billion in assets. Coopers and her group handled Paradigm's Convertible Securities Fund, which sought "high returns through a combination of current income and capital appreciation."

Coopers had been tasked with assessing the new issue of Corning convertibles. That day, she needed to decide whether to recommend purchasing some of the

---

[1] www.ipo.com.

This case was prepared by Jessica Chan, under the supervision of Robert F. Bruner. It was written as a basis for class discussion rather than to illustrate effective or ineffective handling of an administrative situation.

bonds for the Convertible Securities Fund. Her task was to assess the risk of the bond issue, and judge the adequacy of the yield, offering price, and the conversion terms.

The Company

Corning, Inc., competed in three broadly defined operating segments: Telecommunications, Advanced Materials, and Information Display. The Telecommunications division accounted for roughly 70 percent of company's revenue. **Exhibit 2** contains a breakdown of sales and net income by operating segment. **Exhibit 3** provides a detailed breakdown of the products within each operating segment.

Corning was the world's largest manufacturer of optical fiber and amplifiers, with a 50 percent share of the optical fiber market, twice that of its nearest competitor, Lucent. At the time of the offering, the fiber market was in a sold-out state, and Corning had presold the next 18 months of its entire fiber manufacturing capacity.[2] Worldwide demand for fiber grew by 40 percent in 1999, and management expected the same robust growth rate for 2000. Going forward, industry analysts expected the annual growth rate for fiber to be between 20 and 25 percent through 2002, although there was some debate about a potential fiber glut.

Within the company's Telecommunications division, its photonics business increased at a triple-digit annual rate. The photonics business manufactured products that enhanced the flexibility and performance of communications networks. Those products boosted, combined, separated, and connected optical signals transmitted over fiber optic networks. Because of strong demand, Corning expanded capacity for photonics six-fold over the next 18 months.[3]

The nontelecommunications businesses of Corning also performed impressively. The company was the number-one supplier of flat-panel glass for LCDs (liquid crystal displays) used in PC screens, televisions, digital cameras, and other devices, and commanded roughly a 60 percent world market share. Demand for the flat-panel displays grew at around 40 percent per annum, amid stable pricing. The flat-panel business was expected to reach roughly $500 million in 2000, and to hit $1 billion in a few years.[4] In addition, Corning's biotechnology-related products were experiencing a healthy demand. This segment was expected to grow by 30 to 35 percent annually, led by DNA-analysis products.[5]

A rich valuation for Corning shares testified to the rosy outlook for the company. Corning's average P/E ratio for the past month had been roughly 94× the estimated 2000 earnings and 75× the estimated 2001 earnings, compared with an average of around 30× for the S&P 500. (**Exhibit 4** contains a history of Corning's share-price

---

[2] Gavin Duffy and T. Peter Andrew, *Corning: Charging Ahead at the Speed of Light* (A.G. Edwards report), 6 November 2000.

[3] Timothy Anderson and B. Alexander Henderson, *Corning, Inc.: Initiating Coverage with a Buy* (Salomon Smith Barney report), 20 September 2000.

[4] Anderson and Henderson, *Corning, Inc.*

[5] Anderson and Henderson, *Corning, Inc.*

performance and its P/E ratios.) However, Corning's future was also fraught with risks. The most pressing concerns related to the following:[6]

Dependence on service providers: Service providers required huge investments for network expansion and capacity building. There was a risk that, as investors became more aware of the capital-intensive nature of the business, funding for service providers would dry up, in turn affecting demand for Corning's products.

Potential supply glut in the fiber market: Some industry analysts suggested that excess fiber capacity was beginning to emerge. They argued that if all the fiber in the ground were lit, it would be more than enough to support all bandwidth needs for some time. In contrast, other analysts expressed the view that there was currently not enough equipment to light and connect all the fiber in the ground. Corning did not think that an oversupply was approaching.

The end of major long-haul carriers' fiber build-outs: In the past few years, Corning had benefited as major U.S. long-haul carriers such as MCI, Sprint, and AT&T deployed fiber rapidly. Now, after the ramp-ups, build-outs by major U.S. carriers were likely to slow down, just as Corning increased its fiber manufacturing capacity. This meant that Corning would have to shift its reliance to overseas and metro carrier markets. While overseas growth was expected to be strong, foreign-service providers were also smaller and seen as more risky.

Technological change: The market for Corning's products was characterized by rapidly changing technologies, evolving industry standards, and frequent new product introductions. Corning's success would depend heavily on the timely and successful introduction of new products and on its ability to address competing technologies.[7]

Analyzing the Convertible-Bond Offering

After reading the prospectus for the convertible bond offering, Coopers began her analysis by putting together a table of metrics that convertible bond traders traditionally used for evaluating converts. **Exhibit 5** shows the results of her work.

After studying **Exhibit 5,** Coopers decided to value the converts directly. She believed that doing so would be better than relying on the traditional ratios to arrive at an independent judgment. In valuing the converts directly, she relied on the idea that converts were actually hybrid securities composed of a straight bond and one or more embedded options, such as the right to convert the bond to common stock. The value, V, of a convertible bond was therefore just the sum of the straight bond's value and the values of the embedded options:

$$V_{CV \ Bond} = V_{Straight \ Bond} + V_{Option \ 1} + V_{Option \ 2} + \ldots + V_{Option \ n}$$

By valuing each component directly, she could arrive at an appropriate price for the convert. She began with the straight bond portion, which was easier to value. Straight bonds were usually evaluated on the adequacy of their yield to maturity relative to the risk and maturity of the bond. If Coopers used the offering price of

---

[6] Anderson and Henderson, *Corning, Inc.*

[7] Corning prospectus for zero-coupon convertible debentures due November 8, 2015.

$741.923 and the principal repayment of $1,000, the yield to maturity would come out to 2 percent.[8] She knew, however, that this did not properly reflect all the elements of the convert, as the price of $741.923 should contain both the value of the bond and the embedded options. Instead, the true value of the straight bond portion could be estimated by using yields on similarly rated corporate bonds. She reviewed Corning's recent ratings **(Exhibit 6),** computed its debt and coverage ratios pro forma for the convertible bond and equity issuances, and compared her results with statistics for different bond-rating categories **(Exhibit 7).** She then put together a sample of straight debt issuances of similarly rated companies **(Exhibit 8)** and proceeded to value the bond portion of the converts.

Valuing the Conversion Option

Next, Coopers attempted to value the conversion option. "The right to convert is effectively an American call option that allows me to buy Corning shares at $89.062 per share anytime between now and the next 15 years. Right now, the stock is trading at $71.25 per share, so I wouldn't convert at this time. But there is a value to my owning an option to convert when conversion becomes favorable. I can use the Black-Scholes option pricing model to value that option."[9]

"The most important assumption I need to feed into the model is the volatility of Corning stock, since the value of my call option depends to a large extent on the stock price. The more volatile the stock, the more valuable my call option is because the distribution of potential stock prices is wider." She gathered data on Corning's dividend history **(Exhibit 9),** as well as data on the historical volatilities of Corning, its peer firms, and the main stock indexes **(Exhibit 10).** She also gathered data to compute Corning's implied volatilities by using recently traded Corning options **(Exhibit 11).**

"Another important assumption is the risk-free rate. The Black-Scholes model uses this rate to obtain the present value of the expected payoff[10] from the option." Coopers checked the current yields on U.S. Treasuries **(Exhibit 12).**

As she entered her assumptions into the model, Coopers reminded herself that after obtaining the value of the conversion option, she would need to adjust for dilution in order to account for the conversion of the bond into shares and for the issuance of new common stock in connection with the company's concurrent stock offering.

---

[8] $741.923 today would grow to $1,000 in 15 years, if it earned 2 percent compounded semiannually.

[9] Strictly speaking, the Black-Scholes model should be used to value only European options. But because American options were usually held to maturity in order to preserve the time value of the option, they could essentially be thought of as European options. The exception was when a stock underlying an American call option paid a large enough dividend. In that case, an investor might exercise the call option well before maturity in order to obtain the dividend. In such instances, it was not appropriate to use the Black-Scholes model.

[10] The payoff was the difference between the stock price and the exercise price, if the difference was positive. If it was negative, the payoff was zero.

Valuing the Redemption Option

After valuing the conversion option, Coopers observed that the terms of the bond offering allowed Corning to call (redeem) the bond issue anytime after November 8, 2005. Thus, the redemption provision gave Corning flexibility to repay the bond early. Effectively, the company was "long" a call on the convert and the bondholder was "short" a call.

Coopers thought more carefully about the redemption option, and tried to visualize the circumstances in which Corning might redeem the convertible bond. If interest rates declined, bond prices should theoretically go up. But Corning could, by virtue of its redemption option, call in the bonds at prices well below their market value. Coopers thought "With a noncallable bond, as yields decline, the bond value rises. But with callable bonds, the increase in price tops out, because of the expectation that the issuer will exercise the option to refund the bond with cheaper debt." See **Figure 1.**

FIGURE 1 |

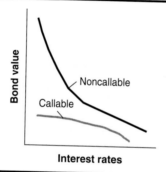

Interest rates

Coopers noted, however, that in the case of most convertible bonds, refunding the bond with cheaper debt almost never made sense because the convertibles usually carried very low coupons. With a low coupon rate, interest rates would have to fall dramatically before it became economically attractive to refund the bond with another, even lower coupon issue or to use interest-generating cash to repay the bond. Instead, redemption provisions had a different purpose: to permit the issuer to force conversion of the bonds into common stock.[11] Of course, this only occurred when the conversion option was in the money.

---

[11] Rapidly growing companies often forced conversion in order to expand their base of equity capital as a foundation for greater debt financing. Creditors usually made lending decisions on the basis of conventional definitions of debt and equity. The conventional definitions might ignore economic reality. An in-the-money convertible bond traded like, and was economically similar to, common equity. From that standpoint, forced conversion to expand the borrowing capacity of the firm was unnecessary window dressing. Nevertheless, very few issuers of convertible bonds permitted them to run their full term as debt.

"Without being forced to convert to stock by some threat of redemption, I might continue to hold the convertible bond even if the option is in the money.[12] But with this redemption option, Corning could force me to make the conversion. From my standpoint, being forced to do anything is a negative. Therefore, this redemption provision has to reduce the value of the bond." Valuing redemption provisions was complicated, however, because the likelihood that the firm would call the bond early depended on two key drivers: interest rates and stock prices.[13] Coopers could not simulate those variables by using her Black-Scholes model. Rather, she would have to build a spreadsheet that accurately modeled this complexity. Because Coopers was in a hurry, she asked one of her firm's derivatives experts to help her. He came back an hour later with the following values for the redemption option based on the different volatility assumptions shown in **Table 1**.

TABLE 1 |

Volatility	0.25	0.75	1.25
Redemption-option value (per bond)[14]	$103.18	$284.98	$336.66

Other Embedded Options

Coopers reviewed the term sheet to see if there were any other embedded options for which she had not accounted. She noticed another option that allowed investors to sell back the debentures to Corning on two specified dates: November 8, 2005, and November 8, 2010. She thought, "Effectively, this is a put option. In fact, these are actually two put options. But the interrelatedness of the two puts makes this option difficult to value. The existence of the 2010 option depends on whether or not I exercise the 2005 option, and that, in turn, depends on whether redemption is favorable at that point."

Given the complexity of valuing the put options, Coopers again asked the derivatives expert for help. He came back with the estimates shown in **Table 2**.

TABLE 2 |

Volatility	0.25	0.75	1.25
Put-option value (per bond)[15]	$96.9	$166.25	$273.1

Finally, Coopers noticed the change-in-control provision that gave bondholders the right to require Corning to repurchase the converts if the company became the subject of a merger or acquisition. She noted, "This option is favorable for me because it protects me against the possibility of someone buying the company and loading it

---

[12] Investors tended to hold convertible bonds until just before maturity in order to preserve the time value of the option.

[13] It was rational for the issuer to call the bond if the redemption price of the bond was less than either its bond-equivalent value (present value of principal and interest) or its equity-equivalent value (current stock price times the conversion ratio of the bond).

[14] Estimated by using a binomial option-pricing model.

[15] Estimated by using a binomial option-pricing model.

up with debt. But Corning is a large firm with a large equity base and a good operating history; I think it is very unlikely that the company would be bought. Therefore, I will assign no value to this option."

A Further Test of Reality

Before she could make her final decision on whether to invest in the Corning bonds, Coopers needed to think carefully about several things. First was Corning's stock-price performance. Its stock currently traded at $71.25, but only a year earlier it traded at less than half that amount. Much of the run-up had to do with what investors saw as a white-hot market for optical-fiber technology. At its current price, Corning's P/E ratio was very high. But then again, Corning's stock had hit $113 earlier in the year. "Perhaps the conversion option, which effectively allows me to buy stock at $89, is not so bad considering the high that the stock has reached. I have to consider this very carefully. If the share price falls, I will be left holding a bond that has a yield to maturity of only 2 percent."

She decided to analyze how valuable the firm would need to be in order to put the conversion option in the money. She reviewed the prospectus, which illustrated both the company's actual capitalization at September 30, 2000, and its capitalization as adjusted to give effect to the convertible bond offering and the concurrent offering of common stock (**Exhibit 13**).

FIGURE 2 |

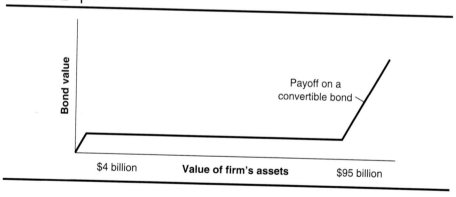

"The company's total debt is around $4 billion. As long as the total value of its assets does not fall below $4 billion, the convertible bonds are worth at least their aggregate principal amount of $2.71 billion (see **Figure 2**). Now what will the value of the assets need to be in order for the bond to be worth more as equity? Well, my break-even price for equity is the exercise price of $89.0625 per share. There are going to be 988.7 million shares outstanding after the concurrent equity offering. In addition, the company has issued stock options in connection with the recent acquisitions totaling 30 million shares. If all options are exercised, including those embedded in the convertible-bond offering, there will be another 53 million shares all in all.[16] Thus, the total number of shares will be 1.0413 billion. If I multiply this by my break-even price, I get a total equity value of $92.7 billion. Adding the company's existing long-term debt of around $2 billion, my calculations tell me that the market value of Corning's assets must be around $95 billion for my bond to be worth more as equity. As it stands right now, the market value of Corning's assets stands at around $65 billion."

Coopers wondered whether the market value of Corning's assets would reach $95 billion before 2015. She also thought about potential further dilution. Corning had been on an acquisition roll in recent months and might continue to acquire more companies given its current capacity constraints. If so, how would that affect the convertible bonds' holders?

Coopers pondered those questions as she prepared her final report to give to her fund's portfolio manager.

---

[16] If call options were exercised, shares from the convertible bond offering were calculated as follows: total principal amount of $2,712,546,000 divided by $1,000 principal per debenture = 2,712,546 debentures. Each debenture was convertible into 8.3304 shares, for a total of 22,596,593 shares.

EXHIBIT 1 | Summary of Terms of the Offering

Securities offered	$2,712,546,000 aggregate principal amount at maturity of our zero-coupon convertible debentures due November 8, 2015. The debentures are senior unsecured obligations of Corning.
Offering price	$741.923 per $1,000 principal amount at maturity.
Interest	We will not pay interest on the debentures prior to maturity.
Maturity date	November 8, 2015.
Conversion right	You may convert the debentures into shares of our common stock initially at a conversion rate of 8.3304 shares for each debenture at any time before the close of business on November 8, 2015, unless we have previously redeemed or repurchased the debentures. The initial conversion rate is equivalent to an initial conversion price of approximately $89.0625 per share, which is based on the IPO price of the debentures. The conversion rate may be adjusted in certain circumstances.
Original issue discount	For U.S. federal income tax purposes, we are offering each debenture at an original issue discount equal to the principal amount at maturity of each debenture less the IPO price. You should be aware that, although we will not pay interest on the debentures until maturity, U.S. investors must include original issue discount as the discount accrues in their gross income for U.S. federal income tax purposes prior to the conversion, redemption, sale, or maturity of the debentures (even if such debentures are ultimately not converted, redeemed, sold, or paid at maturity).
Use of proceeds	We plan to use a portion of the net proceeds from this offering and our concurrent common stock offering to fund the Pirelli acquisition. If the Pirelli acquisition is not completed, or if we receive proceeds from those offerings in excess of what we require to fund the Pirelli acquisition, we will use those proceeds for general corporate purposes.
Optional redemption by Corning	We may redeem some or all the debentures at our option at any time on or after November 8, 2005, at a redemption price equal to the IPO price plus the accrued original issue discount through the redemption date.
Repurchase at option of holders	You may require us to repurchase some or all of your debentures on November 8, 2005, and November 8, 2010, at repurchase prices specified in this prospectus supplement.
Repurchase at option of holders upon a change in control	If we are the subject of a change in control, you may require us to repurchase some or all of your debentures at a price equal to the IPO price plus accrued original issue discount through the repurchase date.

Source: Corning prospectus.

Note: This exhibit has been modified from its original form for instructional purposes.

EXHIBIT 2 | Sales and Net Income Breakdown by Operating Segment

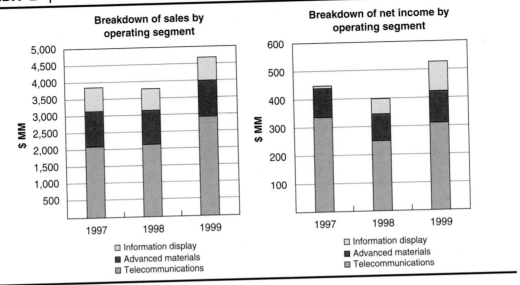

Source: Company Offering memorandum.

EXHIBIT 3 | Products within the Three Major Business Segments

Telecommunications

- Optical fiber (single mode and multimode)
  Long haul, submarine, metro area and premise networks.

- Corning Cable Systems (formerly Siecor, Siemens Communications Cables)
  Fiber optic and copper cabling.
  Related hardware including: assemblies, interconnects, splicers, and test equipment.
  Submarine, cable TV and private networks.

- Photonics
  Products for the routing, switching, and amplification of optical signals.
  Dense wave division multiplexing (DWDM) modules.
  Optical amplifier modules.
  Components such as thin-film filters, multiclad couplers, and fiber bragg gratings.
  Optical cross connects.
  Pump and transmission lasers.

Information Display

- Glass for flat-panel and active matrix liquid crystal displays (AMLCD)
  Flat-panel glass for notebook computer screens, desktop monitors, digital cameras, PDAs, and automotive navigational displays.

- Glass panels and funnels for televisions and CRTs (conventional video components) and projection video lens assemblies.

Advanced Materials

- Environmental products
  Component parts for catalytic converters.

- Semiconductor materials
  Fused silica lens assemblies used by semiconductor manufacturers in microlithography techniques for etching transistor lines onto silicon wafers.

- Science products
  Various materials used to enhance drug discovery process by enabling high-speed drug testing.

Source: Gavin Duffy and T. Peter Andrew, *Corning: Charging Ahead at the Speed of Light* (A.G. Edwards report), 6 November 2000.

EXHIBIT 4 | Historical Stock Price Information

	1995	1996	1997	1998	1999	2000[1]	52-week hi-lo from November 8, 2000
Stock Price							
High	10.4	13.0	21.7	15.0	43.0	113.3	High 113.33
Low	7.1	8.1	11.3	7.8	15.2	74.0	Low 27.35
Average	8.8	10.3	15.6	12.1	22.6	34.6	Average 68.16
Beta (average)	0.87	0.81	0.95	0.83	1.06	1.53	
Corning P/E[2]							
High	27.69	30.83	31.97	31.69	64.47	169.92	
Low	23.67	25.61	20.74	17.84	34.33	77.13	
Average	25.22	27.55	27.68	24.09	41.21	114.17	
S&P 500 P/E							
High	17.60	21.15	24.82	32.27	35.82	32.37	
Low	15.96	16.89	19.32	22.77	28.91	26.20	
Average	16.61	19.21	22.34	26.75	32.46	29.52	
P/E premium/(discount)							
High	57.3%	45.8%	28.8%	−1.8%	80.0%	424.9%	
Low	48.3%	51.6%	7.3%	−21.6%	18.8%	194.4%	
Average	51.9%	43.4%	23.9%	−9.9%	27.0%	286.8%	

[1]Through November 8, 2000.

[2]Based on monthly data.

Source of data: Bloomberg Financial Services, S&P's Research Insight Database.

EXHIBIT 5 | Convertible Debt Comparables

	(a) Bond Rating	(a) Yield to Maturity	(b) Bond Price (for $1,000 par value)	(c) Conversion Ratio	(d) Conversion Price per Share	Current Stock Price	(e) Conversion Premium per Share	(f) Interest Income per Bond	(g) Dividend Income per Bond	(h) Income Spread per Bond	(i) Premium Payback Period
Corning 2015	A2	2.00%	741.9	8.33	89.06	71.25	25.0%	—	2.00	(2.00)	(74.2)
Baker Hughes (Sr.) (Zero) 2008	A2	Flat	792.5	18.60	42.61	34.38	23.9%	—	8.56	(8.56)	(17.9)
Deere & Co. 5 1/2s 2001	A		3,372.5	91.58	36.83	36.81	0.0%	55.0	80.59	(25.59)	(0.1)
E'town Corp. 6 3/4s 2012	A–	0.49%	1,685.0	25.00	67.40	67.38	0.0%	63.4	51.00	12.40	0.0
Hewlett Packard (Zero) 2017	A+	Flat	693.7	15.09	45.97	46.50	–1.1%	—	4.83	(4.83)	1.7
Loews Corp. 3 1/2s 2010	A+	6.35%	822.5	15.38	53.48	34.56	54.7%	35.0	7.69	27.31	10.7
Magna Int'l. 5s 2002	A–	6.66%	970.0	13.38	72.49	44.88	61.5%	50.0	15.39	34.61	10.7
Motorola Inc. (Zero) 2013	A	Flat	800.0	21.36	37.45	24.94	50.2%	—	3.42	(3.42)	(78.2)
Oak Industries 4 7/8s 2008	A–		4,930.0	64.43	76.52	76.50	0.0%	47.8	15.46	32.34	0.0
Omnicom Group 2 1/4s 2013	A		1,852.5	20.07	92.30	92.25	0.1%	22.5	14.05	8.45	0.1
Potomac Elec. Pwr. (Sr) 5s 2002	A–		960.0	29.50	32.54	22.88	42.2%	50.0	48.97	1.03	276.7
Times Mirror (Zero) 2017	A–		587.5	14.57	40.32	37.06	8.8%	—	5.83	(5.83)	(8.2)
USF&G Corp. (Zero) 2009	A	Flat	865.0	16.64	51.98	51.25	1.4%	—	17.97	(17.97)	(0.7)
Young & Rubicam 3s 2005	A–	2.94%	1,000.3	11.38	87.90	66.88	31.4%	30.0	2.73	27.27	8.8

Definitions of terms:

a) Return from principal and interest only.

b) Current quote

c) Number of shares to be received in exchange for $1,000 par value of bond.

d) Obtained by dividing the *bond price* by the *conversion ratio*. This is effectively the price that an investor pays for the common stock and is also known as the exercise price.

e) The premium of the exercise price over the current stock price.

f) Annual interest income per $1,000 bond.

g) The annual dividend income that would be received by converting into the underlying common stock. Calculated by multiplying the annual dividend per common share by the conversion ratio.

h) The difference between interest income and dividend income per bond. In effect this represents the income differential between converting and not converting.

i) Obtained by dividing the dollar conversion premium per share by the income spread per share. The higher the ratio, the less favorable it is to convert.

Source of data: *Standard and Poor's Bond Guide*, November 2000.

All issues cited are convertible bond debentures outstanding in November 2000.

EXHIBIT 6 | Credit-Rating History for Selected Corning Offerings

Rating History for Senior Unsecured Debt—Moody's		Rating History for LT Local Issuer Credit—S&P	
Rating	Effective	Rating	Effective
A2	2/2/2000	A*−	9/27/2000
A3	12/24/1996	A	5/14/1996
A2	1/21/1992	A+	3/21/1991
A1	11/29/1982	AA−	3/10/1982
Aa3	4/26/1982	AA−	11/9/1973

*−denotes a negative outlook.

Rating Scale Comparison

Moody's	S&P
Aaa	AAA
Aa1	AA+
Aa2	AA
Aa3	AA−
A1	A+
A2	A
A3	A−
Baa1	BBB+
Baa2	BBB
Baa3	BBB−
Ba1	BB+
Ba2	BB
Ba3	BB−
B1	B+
B2	B
B3	B−
Caa1	CCC+
Caa2	CCC+
Caa3	CCC−

Ratings Definitions:

Moody's Investors Service: Long-Term Debt Ratings

A   Bonds which are rated A possess many favorable investment attributes and are to be considered as upper medium-grade obligations. Factors giving security to principal and interest are considered adequate, but elements may be present which suggest a susceptibility to impairment sometime in the future.

Standard & Poor's Long-Term Issuer Credit Ratings

A   An obligor rated 'A' has STRONG capacity to meet its financial commitments but is somewhat more susceptible to the adverse effects of changes in circumstances and economic conditions than obligors in higher-rated categories.

Source: Bloomberg Financial Services.

EXHIBIT 7 | Key Industrial Financial Ratios by Rating Category: Median Three-Year Ratios for 1996–1998

Industrial Long-Term Debt	AAA	AA	A	BBB	BB	B	CCC	Corning Pro-Forma for Convertible Bond and Equity Offerings
Pretax interest coverage ($\times$)	12.9	9.2	7.2	4.1	2.5	1.2	–0.9	5.02
EBITDA interest coverage ($\times$)	18.7	14	10	6.3	3.9	2.3	0.2	8.05
Funds from operations/total debt (%)	89.7	67	49.5	32.2	20.1	10.5	7.4	20.9
Free operating cash flow/total debt (%)	40.5	21.6	17.4	6.3	1	–4	–25.4	–2.1
Return on capital (%)	30.6	25.1	19.6	15.4	12.6	9.2	–8.8	3.67
Operating income/sales (%)	30.9	25.2	17.9	15.8	14.4	11.2	5	14
Long-term debt/capital (%)	21.4	29.3	33.3	40.8	55.3	68.8	71.5	28.2
Total debt/capital (incl. short-term debt) (%)	31.8	37	39.2	46.4	58.5	71.4	79.4	29

Sources: Chinn, Wesley E., *Standard & Poor's Research*, "Adjusted Key U.S. Financial Ratios", July 7, 1999; casewriter estimates.

EXHIBIT 8 | Sample of Comparable Straight Current Coupon Bonds

Issuer	S&P Rating	Maturity	Yield to Maturity
AirTouch Communications	A	2008	7.56%
American Stores	A−	2017	7.99
Bell Atlantic	A+	2012	7.73
Coca-Cola Enterprises	A	2017	7.81
Corning Inc.	A	2013	7.50
Walt Disney Co.	A	2015	7.90
Enron Oil and Gas	A−	2008	7.70
IBM	A+	2019	7.65
Lucent Technologies	A	2028	7.87
New York Tel. Co.	A+	2013	7.47
Nordstrom, Inc.	A	2009	8.11
Southwest Airlines	A−	2027	7.95
WorldCom Inc.	A−	2010	7.45
	Mean		7.75%
	Median		7.73%
	Standard Deviation		0.21%

Source: *Standard and Poor's Bond Guide,* October 2000.

EXHIBIT 9 | Corning's Dividend History

Payment Dates	31-Mar	30-Jun	30-Sep	31-Dec	Full Year
1997	0.06	0.06	0.06	0.06	0.24
1998	0.06	0.06	0.06	0.06	0.24
1999	0.06	0.06	0.06	0.06	0.24
2000	0.06	0.06	0.06		

Source: Bloomberg; *Value Line Investment Survey.*

EXHIBIT 10 | Estimates of Historical Volatilities as of November 8, 2000

	1 Mo.	3 Mos.	6 Mos.	1 Yr.
Corning	123.56	85.74	77.63	79.67
JDS Uniphase	140.07	90.14	91.56	95.42
Lucent	159.76	100.95	83.01	77.88
Ciena	144.15	102.11	98.64	110.26
Average	**141.89**	**94.74**	**87.71**	**90.81**
Dow Jones Industrial Average	22.36	16.24	16.57	19.93
S&P 500 Index	25.81	17.98	18.63	20.92
Nasdaq 100 Index	66.45	47.72	51.31	51.51

Source: Bloomberg Financial Services.

EXHIBIT 11 | Premiums for Corning Options on the Chicago Board Options Exchange: Closing Prices as of November 7, 2000

		Calls: Last		Puts: Last	
Option & NY Close	**Strike Price**	**Nov**	**May**	**Nov**	**May**
$68.50	$70.00	$3.25	no option	$4.75	no option
68.50	70.00	no option	15.50	no option	14.50
68.50	80.00	0.75	no option	12.63	no option
68.50	83.38	0.44	no option	16.13	no option
Days to maturity		17	193	17	193

Source: *The Wall Street Journal,* November 8, 2000.

EXHIBIT 12 | Capital Market Conditions around November 8, 2000

Yields on U.S. Treasuries

3-month	6.34%
1-year	6.14
3-year	5.79
5-year	5.68
7-year	5.78
10-year	5.70
30-year	5.76

Yields on Corporates, by Rating

Aaa	7.53%
Baa	8.35

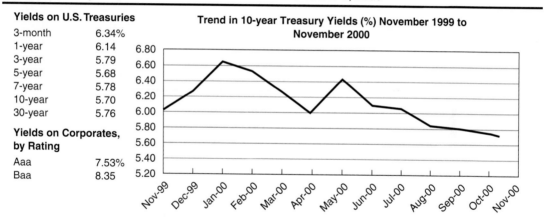

Trend in 10-year Treasury Yields (%) November 1999 to November 2000

Trend in S&P 500 Index: November 1999 to November 2000

Source: Bloomberg Financial Services; Federal Reserve Board Releases.

EXHIBIT 13 | Actual and Pro Forma Balance Sheet

	September 30, 2000	
	Actual	As Adjusted
	(in millions)	
Cash and short-term investments	1,237.5	5,286.9
Current maturities of long-term debt and short-term notes payable	111.4	111.4
Loans payable beyond one year	1,946.3	1,946.3
Zero coupon convertible debentures	—	2,012.5
Minority interest in subsidiary companies	138.7	138.7
Convertible preferred stock	8.9	8.9
Common shareholders' equity		
Common stock, issued:	6,600.0	8,678.0
958.7 million actual and 988.7 million as adjusted	2,113.7	2,113.7
Retained earnings	(746.9)	(746.9)
Treasury stock	(114.6)	(114.6)
Accumulated other comprehensive loss		
Total common shareholders' equity	7,852.2	9,930.2
Total capitalization	9,946.1	14,036.6
Debt to equity ratio	26.2%	41.0%
Debt to capitalization	20.8%	29.1%

Source: Corning prospectus.

Enron Corporation's Weather Derivatives (A)

Everybody talks about the weather, but nobody does anything about it.[1]

In October 2000, Mary Watts, the chief financial officer of Pacific Northwest Electric (PNW), a utility servicing the Pacific Northwest region of the United States, reviewed the financial plan for PNW's 2000–01 forthcoming winter season. Winter temperatures affected the firm's revenues: the colder the season, the greater the electricity usage. She recalled that the last few years had offered a warmer-than-average winter climate, resulting in adverse financial results for PNW. The weather, combined with rapid deregulation in PNW's market area, meant that the firm reported substantially no EPS growth from 1995 to 1999, in an otherwise buoyant economic setting. PNW's stock price had suffered accordingly. On her desk was a report from a weather-advisory service predicting another unseasonably warm winter.

Watts remembered a recent conversation with Mike James, a representative of Enron Corporation. James had presented a new "weather-derivative" product from Enron that he claimed could minimize PNW's weather-related volume risk. Watts wondered how these derivatives worked, and how they might be used to help restore PNW's credibility in the capital markets. Should she consider purchasing Enron's weather-protection products for the upcoming winter season? She would need to decide soon about the use of these derivatives if she wanted to put in place a hedge for the winter months ahead.

---

[1]Charles Dudley Warner, in an editorial in the *Hartford Courant,* 1897.

This case was prepared from field research by Mari Capestany and Professors Robert Bruner and Samuel Bodily. It is intended to serve as a basis for class discussion rather than to illustrate effective or ineffective managerial decision making. Certain names, facts, and financial data have been disguised to preserve confidential information and/or sharpen the managerial issues in the case. The resulting presentation, however, reasonably reflects the actual managerial setting. The assistance and cooperation of Enron Corporation is gratefully acknowledged. Copyright © 2000 by the University of Virginia Darden School Foundation, Charlottesville, VA. All rights reserved. *To order copies, send an e-mail to sales@dardenpublishing.com. No part of this publication may be reproduced, stored in a retrieval system, used in a spreadsheet, or transmitted in any form or by any means—electronic, mechanical, photocopying, recording, or otherwise—without the permission of the Darden School Foundation. Rev. 12/01.*

Pacific Northwest Electric

PNW was a significant producer of electric power, with primary coverage in parts of Oregon, Washington, Northern California, Idaho, and Montana. Its revenues in 1999 were $11 billion; net income was $800 million. Earnings per share were $1.04 in 1999, up from $1.03 in 1995. Noting the basically flat EPS trend for PNW and expressing concern for the firm's dividend coverage, securities analysts were reluctant to advocate holding PNW's shares. Thus, the utility's share price underperformed broad market indexes and indexes of the utility industry. Watts estimated that the warmer-than-usual weather of the past four years had accounted for about two-thirds of the firm's underperformance in earnings.

PNW was a capital-intensive firm, spending about $1 billion a year in capital projects. The firm's recent record of financial performance held important implications for PNW's ability to finance its capital spending. First, it contributed to a higher cost of capital for PNW. The firm's share prices had been more volatile than usual for a public utility, yielding a higher beta and cost of equity. Similarly, the firm's debt rating had slipped from A− to BBB+, producing a cost of debt higher by 75 basis points at the margin. In the former environment of return regulation, it might have been possible for PNW to recover the higher capital costs from consumers. But in the current deregulating environment, where consumers could purchase power from a variety of producers on the power grid, cost disadvantages would lead to a loss of market share. Second, slippage in financial performance might restrict the firm's access to capital in a restrictive financial climate.

Weather Risk

The U.S. Department of Commerce estimated that at least $1 trillion of the total U.S. gross national product (about $7 trillion) was sensitive to variations in weather. This reflected economic sectors as disparate as agriculture, apparel retailing, and ski resorts that depended on *appropriate* variations in weather. "Weather" subsumed a variety of specific conditions such as temperature, wind, precipitation, type of precipitation, storms and hurricanes, haze, and "misery" (i.e., the combination of heat and humidity)—adverse changes in any of these could correlate with lost demand, lost workdays, or generally lost ability to fill demand. Theoretically, any of these forms of weather risk could be the focus of risk hedging by firms. Indeed, it was possible to purchase insurance from catastrophic loss due to extreme events such as tornadoes, tsunamis, and floods. But only since 1997 could companies purchase protection from the more normal variations in weather.

Of paramount concern to the U.S. public utility industry was variation in temperatures. "Weather risk is the biggest independent variable in the power business," noted an industry publication.[2] Customer demand for power was highly correlated with seasonal temperatures. Unexpected decreases in demand (e.g., from a warm winter or cool summer) could have a detrimental impact on a company's earnings. One analyst noted that over a "recent 15-year period . . . temperature variations in 10 major

[2]*Energy & Power Risk Management* 2, no. 8 (December 1997–January 1998).

population centers in the U.S. caused the cost of energy consumed for space heating and cooling to vary by an average of $3.6 billion per year."[3] Utilities typically determined their seasonal budgets from historical averages of temperature and demand. However, if winter temperatures, for example, were warmer than average, customers used less heat—therefore, utilities' revenues fell below budget. Historically, utilities and Wall Street had discounted weather-related earnings' volatility because weather was seen as an uncertainty that could not be hedged. Weather risk was therefore a company's exposure to volume changes as a result of variability in temperature.

The utility industry measured weather conditions in terms of heating or cooling degree-days (HDD, CDD). Degree-days were determined by the deviation of the average daily temperature from an established benchmark of 65 degrees Fahrenheit. It was assumed that, at 65 degrees, customers used neither heat nor air conditioning. Therefore, a mean temperature of 55° on February 1, 2000, would equal 10 heating degree-days (65° − 55°) for that day. Weather conditions for a particular season were stated in terms of degree-days accumulated across the entire period.

The *risk* associated with temperature lay in the uncertainty surrounding the mean temperature for a season. Effects such as El Niño[4] and La Niña[5] created cyclical variations in temperature. And over the past 100 years, there had been an unmistakable increase in temperature—this was attributed, variously, to global warming and "heat-island" effects.[6] Compounding matters were possible asymmetries in risk exposure across competitors in an industry. Competitors might be fully exposed, partially hedged, or fully hedged regarding weather risk—these differences in exposure might elicit different competitive reactions to variations in weather. For instance, the fully hedged firm might seek to exploit adversity imposed on the unhedged firm.

Motives and Instruments for Hedging Weather Risk

Firms might seek to manage their exposure to weather risk for a variety of reasons:[7]

- *Smooth revenues* or compensate for the loss of demand. An ice-cream manufacturer might seek insurance against an unseasonably cool summer.

---

[3]*Energy & Power Risk Management* 2, no. 8

[4]The El Niño effect was a cyclical warming of the tropical region of the Pacific Ocean associated with increased rainfall in the southern United States, drought in the western Pacific region, warmer winters in the north-central United States, and cooler winters in the Southeast and Southwest of the United States. The name meant "little boy" in Spanish, and derived from the arrival of this effect around Christmas. El Niño occurred on an approximate seven-year cycle.

[5]La Niña was a countervailing cooling of the tropical Pacific Ocean that tended to occur after El Niños, and was associated with warmer-than-normal winter temperatures in the southeastern United States and cooler temperatures in the Northwest.

[6]A "heat island" reflected the increased retention of radiant energy from the sun, associated with the increased mass of cities, paved roads, use of concrete construction, etc. Cities such as Orlando, Florida, and Phoenix, Arizona, which had grown rapidly in the preceding 30 years, reported significant increases in mean temperature, associated with the heat-island effect.

[7]The following points draw upon *Managing Weather* (Enron Corporation, 1999).

- *Cover excess costs.* An unexpected frost could destroy crops and raise the costs for a consumer-foods manufacturer. Industrial consumers of energy might seek to hedge against "spikes" in the cost of purchased electricity associated with peak-load demand in the summer.

- *Reimburse lost-opportunity costs.* Ideally, manufacturers would produce, and retailers would stock, the exact quantity of product that customers would buy. Weather introduced uncertainty into estimates of customer demand. In the event of stock-outs, businesses lost the opportunity to sell their products. Firms might seek to hedge this risk (e.g., the ice-cream manufacturer might seek weather insurance against stock-outs in an unseasonably hot summer).

- *Stimulate sales.* Customers might delay their purchase decision until a seasonal trend in weather became apparent. Cruise lines, resorts, and ski-lift operators witnessed this behavior annually. Firms might use weather derivatives to back up their "money-back guarantee" of consumer satisfaction.

- *Diversify investment portfolios.* Financial investors might seek to exploit the low correlation between returns associated with weather and returns from other financial instruments. Weather derivatives could potentially reduce risk and/or increase returns in a portfolio.

The first weather-protection contract was arranged in August 1997 between Enron Capital and Trade Resources (ECT) and an eastern U.S. electric utility. Enron Corporation was the world's leading integrated natural gas and electricity company. The company delivered physical commodities, risk management, and financial services to provide energy solutions to customers around the world. By 2000, Enron had been named "most innovative company" by *Fortune* magazine for five years in a row.

Upon discovering a methodology for hedging its own weather risk, Enron believed that this innovation could be useful for its customers as well, and set out to create customized products to help customers manage their own weather risk. Enron's weather-protection products were targeted at power producers and utilities or any company that was exposed to volume risk as a result of changes in weather. A big challenge facing Enron and other marketers of weather-protection products was that utilities were very slow, conservative, and resistant to the use of derivative financial instruments.

Although historically utilities hedged only price risk (through the use of futures), the introduction of weather-protection products allowed "companies to protect against weather conditions adversely affecting volume-related revenues."[8] Specifically, weather derivatives provided protection against the deviation of actual cumulative degree-days from an established threshold. Degree-days were calculated using the average temperature readings for a predetermined geographic location (usually the closest airport) as measured by the National Weather Service. Depending on the sensitivity of demand to cumulative degree-days, the utility was able to determine how much margin it would lose if seasonal temperatures deviated from the average. The degree-day threshold was

---

[8]*Hedging Weather Risk* (Enron Corporation, 1998).

determined by the utility's level of risk tolerance: how much income it was willing to lose as a result of weather variability. (Most weather-derivative contracts were short term, with an average transaction period of five months.) If, at the end of the transaction period, the actual cumulative degree-days were below the established threshold, the utility would receive a payment to offset the loss in income associated with lost demand (volume).

Weather-protection products could take on several structures:[9]

- A *floor* provided the customer with downside protection when the underlying variable, such as degree-days, *fell below* the established threshold. The upside opportunity remained unconstrained. The payout for the floor was equal to the degree-day differential times a price per degree-day ($/dd). Most sellers of weather derivatives, however, were unwilling to accept all the downside risk associated with a floor and therefore set a payout limit.

- A *ceiling cap* provided the customer with compensation if the underlying weather variable went *above* a predetermined level. The seller of the ceiling cap paid this compensation to the buyer. A midwestern state might buy a snowfall ceiling cap that would compensate it if snowfall exceeded a certain level—this payment would help to reimburse the state for excessive snow-removal expenses. Temperature ceiling caps could be stated in degree-days or payout limits.

- A *collar* was a two-part transaction in which a customer bought a cap or a floor to provide financial protection against adverse weather conditions and simultaneously sold a floor or a cap at a different strike price that limited its financial upside if weather were favorable. The second part (the sale) helped to finance the first part (the purchase of the insurance).

- A *swap* allowed the customer to generate a fixed revenue stream. If actual degree-days were less (greater) than the threshold, the utility received a payment equal to the degree-day differential times an agreed-upon price per degree-day ($/dd). If actual degree-days were greater (less) than the threshold, the utility paid the seller. A swap was generally similar to the collar in its economic effect, except that it offered a single trigger level, whereas the collar offered two. For instance, a utility might enter into a 30-day HDD swap with a reference temperature of 65° Fahrenheit. If the actual average temperature turned out to be 55°, the utility was due 300 degree-days (30 × [65 − 55]) multiplied by the amount of money agreed upon for each degree-day.

- *Futures contracts* could be purchased on the Chicago Mercantile Exchange (CME), and were introduced for trading in 1999. Generally, a futures contract was a legal agreement to deliver or accept a commodity at a specified time and at an agreed-upon price. The CME contracts were specifically designed around temperature variations (i.e., HDD or CDD). The buyer and seller agreed upon a price for a contract tailored to a specific month, one of 12 city locations, and an

---

[9]The description of instruments paraphrases a discussion in *Managing Weather.*

HDD/CDD index level. Variations in temperature above or below the value led to a daily cash settlement between the buyer and seller.

- *Option on a futures contract.* The CME also permitted trading in options on futures.

An important difference between the exchange-traded contracts, on the one hand, and the insurance and tailored weather-protection contracts, on the other hand, lay in their accounting treatment. Under the new FAS Rule 133, risk hedges of all sorts would need to be marked-to-market frequently *so long as the hedge was pegged to a market index.* One prominent auditor remarked that most weather derivatives would not require this accounting treatment because inches of rainfall or heating degree-days would be outside the scope of the rule.[10]

The Market for Weather Protection

Several markets converged in weather-protection instruments:

- *Insurance.* The insurance industry provided weather-related protection, typically for catastrophic events such as hurricanes, floods, and tornadoes. Players in this market sought to pool risks across a large number of insured parties. So long as the insured events were independent, cross-sectionally and over time, pooling would pay. Typically, coverage arranged through insurance companies was tailored and dealt with catastrophic events.

- *Capital and commodities markets.* In 1997, Enron had originated standardized contracts in weather protection that were relatively liquid securities and dealt with standard variations in weather. In 1999, the CME began trading in weather futures and options, which also were standardized contracts. The rise of this market as a second source for weather protection reflected the growing trend of *securitization* of assets through capital markets. Market makers in weather derivatives included Enron, Koch Energy Trading, Aquila Energy, Southern Company Energy Marketing, and Duke Power—firms with a historical basis in the energy industry.

One participant observed that "the truth is that the convergence of these two industries is well under way . . . the question isn't which industry wins the battle for business, but what these institutions, whatever their background, will look like, and who will best be able to meet customer demands."[11]

Potential users of weather protection were widely distributed throughout the U.S. economy. Some of the most active players were heating-oil distributors and local gas distributors, firms that, because of their deregulated markets, could not pass along the costs of weather variation to customers. Public utilities were significantly exposed

---

[10]Based on a remark by Deirdre Schiela, partner at PricewaterhouseCoopers, quoted in "No Hedging for Weather Derivatives?" *American Banker and Bond Buyer CFO Alert* (October 12, 1998).

[11]William Jewett, senior vice president and chief underwriting officer of Centre Re, a division of Zurich Reinsurance, quoted in "New Kids on the Capital Markets Block; Reinsurers Want Not Only to Securitize Every Insurance Risk Imaginable, but to Go Head-to-Head with Wall Street in Other Key Areas Too," *Investment Dealer's Digest* (August 3, 1998).

to weather risk but were slow to come into the weather-protection market because of regulations that permitted them to pass along costs to consumers. Enron's objective was to balance the market for weather protection through aggregation of contracts.

Determining PNW's Need for Weather Protection

PNW's winter season lasted from November through March. Mary Watts would need to make a decision soon about hedging PNW's weather risk. The first step in her analysis was to determine how sensitive PNW's earnings were to changes in weather. She gathered historical weather information and calculated the correlation of PNW's winter demand to historical seasonal heating degree-days. Watts remembered hearing that the average temperature of metropolitan areas was increasing because of increased population, automobiles, and other demographic trends. Watts's weather data would have to be adjusted for this historical trend or else she might run the risk of under-valuing the cost of protection. The load data would also need to be trend adjusted to eliminate the impact of increased overall demand due to new customers. Watts's analysis revealed that seasonal demand had a 91.7 percent correlation with a 1 percent change in cumulative seasonal heating degree-days.

Using PNW's residential tariffs and its cost to generate the power to supply demand, Watts could calculate the gross margin per heating degree-day and the loss in income for a corresponding loss in volume. She could then translate that loss in income to a \$/HDD. On average, PNW received \$60.30/MWh for power sold to residential customers and paid \$20/MWh to generate or purchase power to supply its demand.

Because PNW was exposed to volume risk if weather were warmer than average, PNW would want protection from winter heating degree-days falling significantly below the average. Watts believed that PNW would accept no more than a 5 percent variability in HDD.

Hypothetical Weather-Derivative Contract for PNW

Exhibit 1 presents a hypothetical contract of the sort that Enron would negotiate with PNW to cover its weather exposure for the forthcoming winter. The contract specified that, in return for the initial purchase of the contract, PNW would receive a one-time payment at the expiration of the contract as determined by the extent of the adverse deviation from the HDD target. (See **Exhibit 2** for a glossary of terms.)

The Decision

Mary Watts knew that PNW was a very conservative company that would not be persuaded easily to use derivative hedging products. Although PNW's revenues were extremely sensitive to weather conditions, weather protection required a rather sizable up-front premium. But because 2000–01 was expected to be an unseasonably warm winter, the impact on earnings could be devastating. Given the unpredictability of weather, however, PNW might not want to hedge all its weather exposure; this would also minimize the cost of protection by effectively reducing the $/HDD. Moreover, the cost of protection could be reduced if Watts chose a lower HDD threshold.

EXHIBIT 1 | Sample Contract

[Date]

[Counterparty Name – ABC Co]
[Address]
[Address]
Attention: [Name]

Fax No.:
Telephone No.:

Re: FLOOR TRANSACTION Contract No. WR[ ]

Reference is made to the Master Agreement dated as of [ ] (the "Agreement") between ABC Co and XYZ Co pursuant to which this Confirmation is delivered and to which the Transaction contemplated herein is subject.

This is confirmation of the following Transaction:

Option Type:	HDD Weather Floor
Notional Amount:	$20,000 Per Heating Degree Day
Trade Date:	October 23, 2000
Effective Date:	November 1, 2000
Termination Date:	March 31, 2001
Premium Payment Details:	ABC Co shall pay XYZ $[premium] two Business Days after the Trade Date.
Determination Period:	The period from and including the Effective Date to and including the Termination Date.
Payment Date(s):	The fifth Business Day after the Floating Amount for the Determination Period is determinable, **provided, however,** that a one time adjustment in the amount paid will be made by the appropriate party, if applicable, if the National Climatic Data Center ("NCDC") makes any correction or adjustment to the reported daily high and low temperatures within 95 days of the end of the Determination Period for any day within the Determination Period.
Fixed Amount Payer: (Buyer of the Floor)	ABC Co
Floating Amount Payer: (Seller of the Floor)	XYZ Co
Strike Amount:	400 HDD
Floating Amount:	The sum of the Heating Degree Days ("HDD") for each day during the applicable Determination Period.
	HDD for each day is equal to the greater of (i) 65 minus the non-rounded average of the daily high and daily low temperatures in degrees Fahrenheit from and including 12:01 AM on that day to and including 12:00 AM on the next day local time as measured by the National Weather Service ("NWS"), and reported by the NCDC, for the Reference Weather Station or (ii) zero. The daily high and low temperatures measured by the NWS and reported by the NCDC

shall be rounded to whole numbers prior to the calculation of HDDs as follows: if the first number after the decimal point is five (5) or greater then the whole number shall be increased by one (1), and if the first number after the decimal point is less than five (5) then the whole number shall remain unchanged (the "Rounding Convention").

Reference Weather Station: Seattle-Tacoma International Airport, Washington.

Fallback Reference Weather Station: If for any day during the Determination Period a daily high or daily low temperature is unavailable for the Reference Weather Station then the missing temperature(s) for that day at such Reference Weather Station shall be calculated in accordance with the following procedure: (i) the daily high (if the missing temperature is a daily high) or daily low (if the missing temperature is a daily low) temperature for the corresponding day of each of the previous 30 years at such Reference Weather Station shall be identified as reported in Fahrenheit by the NCDC (which numbers as reported by the NCDC shall not be rounded by the parties) and an average temperature shall be determined, which average temperature shall be determined to and including four decimal points; (ii) in accordance with the above procedures, the daily high or daily low temperature as appropriate shall be determined for the corresponding day of each of the previous 30 years at the Weather Station at Portland, Oregon Airport (the "Fallback Reference Weather Station") as reported in Fahrenheit by the NCDC (which numbers as reported by the NCDC shall not be rounded by the parties), and an average temperature shall be determined, which average temperature shall be determined to and including four decimal points; (iii) the average temperature generated in (ii) above shall be subtracted from the average temperature generated in (i) above (with the resulting number (whether positive or negative) referred to as the "Average Temperature Difference Number"); (iv) the daily high or daily low temperature as appropriate for the corresponding Fallback Reference Station for the day for which the daily high or daily low temperature is missing for the Reference Weather Station shall be identified as reported in Fahrenheit by the NCDC (which number as reported by the NCDC shall not be rounded); and (v) the temperature determined in (iv) shall be adjusted by adding the Average Temperature Difference Number if it is a positive number and subtracting the absolute value of the Average Temperature Difference Number if it is a negative number, with the resulting number being rounded in accordance with the Rounding Convention. The final rounded whole number determined in (v) shall be deemed the daily high or daily low temperature as appropriate for the Reference Weather Station for the relevant day and shall be the number used to make the calculations as required pursuant to the procedures set forth in the "Floating Amount" above.

Data Sources: The data used to determine the Floating Amount (and to the extent required, data for any Fallback Reference Weather Station) shall be obtained from the NCDC's official website located at http://www.nndc.noaa.gov/cgi-bin/nndc/ph2_lcd_v2.cgi, or any successor thereto; provided, however, if data is not reported for any particular day at such website, then the data for such day shall be obtained from the website for the appropriate Regional Climate Data Center located at http://www.nws.noaa.gov/regions.shtml, or any successor thereto; and provided further to the extent that (i) the NCDC data is corrected or adjusted within 95 days of the end of the Determination Period or (ii) the data is temporarily sourced from the Regional Climate Data Center, then the data for such new, adjusted or corrected number(s) shall be obtained from the NCDC's official website located at http://www4.ncdc.noaa.gov/cgi-win/wwcgi.dll?WWNolos~Product~ PB-078. Notwithstanding the foregoing, if neither the Regional Climate Data Center nor the NCDC issues data for the Reference Weather Station, then the procedures set forth under "Fallback Reference Weather Station(s)" shall be utilized to determine the missing data.

Strike Amount Differential:	The amount equal to the excess (if a positive number) of (i) the Strike Amount over (ii) the Floating Amount.
Payment Amount:	Notwithstanding any provision of the Agreement to the contrary, if the Strike Amount is greater than the Floating Amount, the Floating Amount Payer shall pay the Fixed Amount Payer an amount in US Dollars equal to the product of (i) the Notional Amount and (ii) the Strike Amount Differential, which amount shall be due and payable on the applicable Payment Date, **provided, however,** that the maximum amount payable by the Floating Amount Payer shall not exceed $800,000.

EXHIBIT 2 | Glossary of Terms

Demand: The rate at which power is being used by consumers.

Energy: Actual electrical flow, sold on an hourly, monthly, or similar basis.

IPP: The passing of PURPA (1978) gave rise to Qualified Facilities, which were cogeneration facilities selling surplus power to the utilities. Since EPA Act of 1992, IPPs are now also often referred to as EWGs.

Kilowatt (KW): One thousand watts.

Kilowatt-hour (KWh): One kilowatt of power supplied for a continuous period of one hour. This is the principal unit used for pricing retail electrical energy.

Load: The electric current being transmitted or demanded.

Megawatt (MW): One million watts or one thousand kilowatts.

Megawatt-hour (MWh): One thousand kilowatt-hours.

Power Marketer: A company that buys and resells electricity, and therefore assumes economic risk in the transactions. Power Marketers are usually independent entities, although some electric utilities have set up their own marketing operations. Power Marketers are responsible for arranging the transmission of power to the purchaser.

Public Utility Regulatory Policies Act, 1978 (PURPA): PURPA was passed as part of the National Energy Act. It set out to create incentives for the development of cogeneration facilities. Qualifying Facilities (QFs) had to produce electric and thermal power and could sell all or only their excess electric power to utilities. Utilities were required to purchase this power at their Full Avoided Cost.

Tick Size: Notional amount of a contract—the dollars per HDD to be paid out.

Watt: The standard measure of electricity's capacity to do work. It is the voltage (pressure) multiplied by the amperage (or speed).

PART 8

Valuing the Enterprise: Acquisitions and Buyouts

Arcadian Microarray Technologies, Inc.

In August 2005, negotiations neared conclusion for a private equity investment by Sierra Capital Partners in Arcadian Microarray Technologies, Inc. The owners of Arcadian, who were also its senior managers, proposed to sell a 60 percent equity interest to Sierra Capital for $40 million. The proceeds of the equity sale would be used to finance the firm's growth. Sierra Capital's due diligence study of Arcadian had revealed a highly promising high-risk investment opportunity. It remained for Rodney Chu, a managing director with Sierra Capital, to negotiate the specific price and terms of investment. Chu aimed to base his negotiating strategy on an assessment of Arcadian's economic value and to structure the interests of Sierra Capital and the managers of Arcadian to create the best incentives for value creation.

Chu's analysis so far had focused on financial forecasting of equity cash flows. The final steps would be to estimate a terminal value for the company (also called "continuing value") and to discount the cash flows and terminal value to the present. He also sought an assessment of forecast assumptions. In that regard, he requested help from Paige Simon, a new associate with Sierra Capital.

Sierra Capital Partners

Sierra Capital, located in Albuquerque, New Mexico, had been organized in 1974 as a hedge fund, though over the years it had a successful record of private equity investments and had gradually shifted its activities to this area. The firm had $2 billion under management, and its portfolio consisted of 64 investments, about evenly split between venture capital investments and participations in leveraged buyouts. Sierra Capital focused almost entirely on the life sciences sector. Like other investors, however, the firm had been burned by several flameouts following the boom in biotechnology stocks in 2000, when many rising young firms' blockbuster discoveries failed to materialize. Sierra Capital's mantra now when evaluating investments was, "NRDO: no research, development only."

Arcadian Microarray Technologies, Inc.

Following the completion of the Human Genome Project[1] in 2003, which sought to map the entire human DNA sequence,[2] several companies had developed technologies for researchers to exploit the mountain of new data. Specifically, those products helped scientists find the links between the variations in a person's genetic code and their predisposition to disease. It was hoped that ultimately this would usher in an era when disease diagnosis, treatment, and prevention could be tailored to an individual's unique genetic identity.

Arcadian Microarray Technologies, Inc., headquartered in Arcadia, California, was founded in 2003 by seven research scientists, two of whom had been major contributors to the Human Genome Project itself and were leaders in the field of genomics.[3] The team had developed a unique DNA scanning device in the form of a waferlike glass chip that could allow scientists to analyze thousands of human genes or gene fragments at one time, rather than individually. The gene chips, also called DNA microarrays, made it possible to identify specific sequence variations in an individual's genes, some of which could be associated with disease. Arcadian's business consisted of two segments:

- *DNA microarrays.* Arcadian's DNA microarrays were created using semiconductor-manufacturing technology. The chips were only a few centimeters in size, and had short, single-stranded DNA segments spread across their surface. Arcadian's chips were unique because they could hold up to one billion DNA types—more than any other microarray currently available. That was ground-breaking technology that would afford low-cost and virtually error-free detection of a wide range of medical conditions. Development of the chip technologies was finished, and the products were moving rapidly through the Food and Drug Administration (FDA) approval process; because of their noninvasive and diagnostic nature, they might be available for sale within 12 months.

- *Human therapeutics.* The search for vaccines and antibiotics with which to fight incurable diseases was potentially the most economically attractive segment, and Arcadian leveraged its leading-edge DNA-testing platform to conduct proprietary research in this area. Management's long-term strategy was to use external funding (through joint venture arrangements with well-capitalized pharmaceutical

---

[1] The Human Genome Project (HGP), completed in April 2003, was an international research program to map and understand all human genes. The HGP revealed that there are probably between 30,000 and 40,000 human genes, and the research provided detailed information about their structure, organization, and function.

[2] Sequencing is a means of determining the exact order of the chemical units within a segment of DNA.

[3] Genomics is the study of an organism's genome and its use of genes. A genome is an organism's complete set of deoxyribonucleic acid (DNA), a chemical compound that contains the genetic instructions needed to develop and direct the activities of every organism. Each of the estimated 30,000 genes in the human genome carries information for making all the proteins required by an organism, a process called *gene expression*.

firms) to the fullest extent possible to carry the firm until its first major proprietary breakthrough. But despite external funding, Arcadian still faced significant capital requirements stemming from investment in infrastructure, staffing, and its own proprietary research program.

Arcadian's management believed that applications for its DNA microarray technology would pay off dramatically and quickly: by the year 2013 they believed the firm's revenues (namely, sales of proprietary products, underwritten research, and royalties) would top $1 billion. Rodney Chu was less optimistic, believing that the FDA approval process would slow down the commercialization of Arcadian's new products. The cash flow forecasts of management and of Chu are given in **Exhibits 1** and **2.** Chu assumed the firm would not finance itself with debt; thus, the forecasted free cash flows were identical with equity cash flows.

In assessing Arcadian, Chu looked toward two publicly held companies in the general field of molecular diagnostics.

- *Affymetrix, Inc.* based in Santa Clara, California, was the pioneer in the development of DNA microarrays and was at that time the world's leading provider of gene expression technology. Its patented GeneChip® product was widely used for molecular biology research and had been cited in more than 3,000 peer-reviewed publications. On December 27, 2004, Affymetrix's GeneChip was the first microarray approved by the FDA for in-vitro use, which represented a major step toward the use of DNA microarrays in a clinical setting. The firm's beta was 1.30; its price/expected earnings ratio was 50.09; its price/book ratio was 8.56; price/sales was 7.49; and price/free cash flow was 97.50. The firm had $120 million in debt outstanding. The firm's sales had grown from $290 million in 2002, to $301 million in 2003, to $346 million in 2004, and to an expected $380 million in 2005. The company paid no dividend.

- *Illumina, Inc.* of San Diego, California, developed a microarray design that attached hundreds of thousands of biological sensors to submicroscopic glass beads that could seek out and latch onto specific sequences of DNA. The company's proprietary BeadArray technology used fiber optics to achieve this miniaturization of arrays that enabled a new scale of experimentation. With negative historical and expected earnings, the firm's price/earnings ratio was meaningless; however, the firm traded at 8.46 times book value, and 8.82 times sales. Illumina's revenues were $10 million in 2002, $28 million in 2003, and $51 million in 2004, and were expected to be about $73 million in 2005.

Having been burned by the biotech bust, securities analysts were now cautious about the fledgling gene diagnostics industry. "The human genome period ushered in a new wealth of information about our genes and at the time there was a lot of hoopla about the ability to cure disease," said one analyst. "In reality, human biology and genetics are complicated."[4] DNA-based medical testing, made possible by gene

---

[4]Aaron Geist, analyst with Robert W. Baird & Co., quoted in "Success Is All in the Genes," *Investor's Business Daily,* 18 July 2005, A12.

expression diagnostic technology, was at the edge of the legal envelope, and the field was quickly being flooded with entrepreneurial research scientists. The FDA approval process was at best uncertain in this area, and established firms experienced internal clashes over direction.

The Idea of Terminal Value

To assist him in the final stages of preparing for the negotiations, Rodney Chu called in Paige Simon, who had just joined the firm after completing an undergraduate degree. To lay the groundwork for the assignment, Chu began by describing the concept of terminal value:

CHU: Terminal value is the lump-sum of cash flow at the *end* of a stream of cash flows—that's why we call it "terminal." The lump sum represents either (a) the proceeds to us from exiting the investment, or (b) the present value (at that future date) of all cash flows beyond the forecast horizon.

SIMON: Because they are way off in the future, terminal values really can't be worth worrying about, can they? I don't believe most investors even think about them.

CHU: Terminal values are worth worrying about for two reasons. First, they are present in the valuation of just about every asset. For instance, in valuing a U.S. Treasury bond, the terminal value is the return of your principal at the maturity of the bond.

SIMON: Some investors might hold to maturity, but the traders who really set the prices in the bond markets almost never hold to maturity.

CHU: For traders, terminal value equals the proceeds from selling the bonds when you exit from each position. You can say the same thing about stocks, currencies, and all sorts of hard assets. Now, the second main reason we worry about terminal value is that in the valuation of stocks and whole companies, terminal value is *usually a very big value driver.*

SIMON: I don't believe it. Terminal value is a distant future value. The only thing traders care about is dividends.

CHU: I'll bet you that if you took a random sample of stocks—I'll let you throw darts at the financial pages to choose them—and looked at the percentage of today's share price *not* explained by the present value of dividends for the next five years, you would find

> Simon's first task: Present and explain the data in **Exhibit 3.**

that the unexplained part would dominate today's value. I believe that the unexplained part is largely due to terminal value.[5]

SIMON: I'll throw the darts, but I still don't believe it—I'll show you what I find.

---

[5] The unexplained part could also be due to option values that are not readily captured in a discounted cash flow valuation.

Varieties of Terminal Values

CHU: We can't really foresee terminal value, we can only *estimate* it. For that reason, I like to draw on a wide range of estimators as a way of trying to home in on a best guess of terminal value. The estimators include (a) accounting book value, (b) liquidation value, (c) multiples of income, and (d) constant growth perpetuity value. Each of those has advantages and disadvantages, as my chart here shows (**Exhibit 4**). I like the constant growth model best and the book value least, but they all give information, so I look at them all.

SIMON: Do they all agree?

CHU: They rarely agree. Remember that they are imperfect estimates. It's like picking the point of central tendency out of a scatter diagram or triangulating the height of a tree, using many different points of observation from the ground. It takes a lot of careful judgment because some of the varieties of terminal value are inherently more trustworthy than others. From one situation to the next the different estimators have varying degrees of appropriateness. In fact, even though I usually disregard book value, there are a few situations in which it might be a fair estimate of terminal value.

SIMON: Like what?

CHU: Give it some thought; you can probably figure it out. Give me some examples of where the various estimators would be appropriate or inappropriate. But remember that no single estimator will give us a "true" value. Wherever possible, we want to use a variety of approaches.

> Simon's second task: Consider the approaches described in **Exhibit 4.**

Taxes

SIMON: What about taxes in terminal values? Shouldn't I impose a tax on the gain inherent in any terminal value?

CHU: Sure, if you are a taxpaying investor and if it is actually your intent to exit the investment at the forecast horizon. But lots of big investors in the capital markets (such as pension funds and university endowments) do not pay taxes. And other investors really do not have much tax exposure because of careful tax planning. Finally, in mergers and acquisitions analysis and most kinds of capital budgeting analysis, the most reasonable assumption is to *buy and hold,* in perpetuity. Overall, the usual assumption is *not* to tax terminal values. But we all need to ask the basic question at the start of our analysis, is the investor likely to pay taxes?

Liquidation vs. Going Concern Values

SIMON: Now I'm starting to get confused. I thought "terminal" meant the end—and now you're talking about value in perpetuity. If terminal value is really the ending value, shouldn't we be talking about a *liquidation value*? Liquidation values are easy to estimate: we simply take the face value of net working capital, add the proceeds of selling any fixed assets, and subtract the long-term debt of the company.

CHU: *Easy* isn't the point. We have to do what's economically sensible. For instance, you wouldn't want to assume that you would liquidate Microsoft in three years just because that's as far into the future as you can forecast. Microsoft's key assets are software, people, and ideas. The value of those will never get captured in a liquidator's auction. The real value of Microsoft is in a stream of future cash flows. When we come to a case such as Microsoft, we see the subtlety of "terminal value"—in the case of *most* companies, it means "continuing value" derived from the going concern of the business. Indeed, many assets live well beyond the forecast horizon. Terminal value is just a summary (or present value) of the cash flows beyond the horizon.

SIMON: So when would you use liquidation value?

CHU: I've seen it a lot in corporate capital budgeting, cases like machines, plants, natural resources projects, etc. The assets in those cases have definite lives. But companies and *businesses* are potentially very long-lived and should be valued on a going concern basis. But I still look at liquidation value because I might find some interesting situations where liquidation value is higher than going concern value. Examples would be companies subject to oppressive regulation or taxation and firms experiencing weird market conditions—in the late 1970s and early 1980s, most oil companies had a market value *less* than the value of their oil reserves. You don't see those situations very often, but still it's worth a look.

Market Multiples and Constant Growth Valuation

SIMON: Aren't multiples the best terminal value estimators? They are certainly the easiest approach.

CHU: I use them, but they've got disadvantages, as my chart (**Exhibit 4**) shows. They're easy to use, but too abstract for my analytical work. I want to get really close to the assumptions about value, and for that reason, I use this version of the constant growth valuation model to value a firm's assets:

$$TV_{Firm} = \frac{FCF \times (1 + g_{FCF}^{\infty})}{WACC - g_{FCF}^{\infty}}$$

"FCF" is free cash flow. "WACC" is weighted average cost of capital. And "g^{∞}" is the constant growth rate of free cash flows to infinity. This model was derived from an infinitely long DCF valuation formula.

$$PV_{Firm} = \frac{FCF_0 \times (1 + g_{FCF}^{\infty})}{(1 + WACC)} + \frac{FCF_0 \times (1 + g_{FCF}^{\infty})^2}{(1 + WACC)^2}$$
$$+ \frac{FCF_0 \times (1 + g_{FCF}^{\infty})^3}{(1 + WACC)^3} + \cdots + \frac{FCF_0 \times (1 + g_{FCF}^{\infty})^{\infty}}{(1 + WACC)^{\infty}}$$

If the growth rate is constant over time, this infinitely long model can be condensed into the easy-to-use constant growth model.

When I'm valuing equity instead of assets, I use the constant-growth valuation formula, but with equity-oriented inputs:

$$TV_{Equity} = \frac{Residual\ cash\ flow \times (1 + g_{RCF}^{\infty})}{Cost\ of\ equity - g_{RCF}^{\infty}}$$

Residual Cash Flow (RCF) is the cash flow which equity-holders can look forward to receiving—a common name for RCF is dividends. A key point here is that the growth rate used in this model should be the growth rate appropriate for the type of cash flow being valued; and the capital cost should be appropriate for that cash flow as well.

You may have seen the simplest version of the constant growth model—the one that assumes zero growth—which reduces to dividing the annual cash flow by a discount rate.

SIMON: Sure, I have used a model like that to price perpetual preferred stocks. In the numerator, I inserted the annual dividend; in the denominator I inserted whatever we thought the going required rate of return will be for that stream.

CHU: If you insert some positive growth rate into the model, the resulting value gets bigger. In a growing economy, the assumption of growing free cash flows is quite reasonable. Sellers of companies always want to persuade you of their great growth prospects. If you buy the optimistic growth assumptions, you'll have to pay a higher price for the company. But the assumption of growth can get unreasonable if pushed too far. Many of the abuses of this model have to do with the little infinity symbol, ∞: the model assumes *constant growth at the rate, g, to infinity.*

"Peter Pan" Growth: WACC < g

SIMON: Right! If you assume a growth rate greater than WACC, you'll get a *negative* terminal value.

CHU: That's one instance in which you cannot use the constant growth model. But think about it: WACC less than g *can't* happen; a company cannot grow to infinity at a rate greater than its cost of capital. To illustrate why, let's rearrange the constant growth formula to solve for WACC:

$$WACC = \frac{FCF_{Next\ period}}{Value\ of\ firm_{Current\ period}} + g_{FCF}^{\infty}$$

If WACC is less than g, then the ratio of FCF divided by the value of the firm would have to be *negative.* Since the value of the healthy firm to the investors cannot be less than zero,[6] the source of negativity must be FCF—that means the firm is absorbing rather than throwing off cash. Recall that in the familiar constant growth terminal value formula, FCF is the flow that compounds to infinity at the rate g. Thus, if FCF is negative, then the entire stream of FCFs must be negative— the company is like Peter Pan: *it never grows up;* it never matures to the point where it throws off positive cash flow. That is a crazy implication because investors would not buy securities in a firm that never paid a cash return. In short, you cannot use the constant growth model where WACC is less than g, nor would you want to because of the unbelievable implications of that assumption.

Using Historical Growth Rates; Setting Forecast Horizons

CHU: A more common form of abuse of this model is to assume a very high growth rate, simply by extrapolating the past rate of growth of the company.

SIMON: Why isn't the past growth rate a good one?

CHU: Companies typically go through life cycles. A period of explosive growth is usually followed by a period of maturity and/or decline. Take a look at the three deals in this chart (**Exhibit 5**): a startup of an animation movie studio in Burbank, California; a bottling plant in Mexico City; and a high-speed private toll road in Los Angeles.

- **Movie studio.** The studio has a television production unit with small but steadily growing revenues and a full feature-length film production unit with big but uncertain cash flows. The studio does not reach stability until the 27th year. The stability is largely due to the firm's film library, which should be sizable by then. After year 27, exploiting the library through videos and re-releases will act as a shock absorber, dampening swings in cash flow due to the production side of the business. Also, at about that time, we can assume that the studio reaches production capacity.

- **Bottling plant.** The bottler must establish a plant and an American soda brand in Mexico, which accounts for the initial negative cash flows and slow growth. Then, as the brand takes hold, the cash flows increase steeply. Finally, in year 12, the plant reaches capacity. After that, cash flows grow mainly at the rate of inflation.

- **Toll road.** The road will take 18 months to build, and will operate at capacity almost immediately. The toll rates are government-regulated, but the company will be allowed to raise prices at the rate of inflation. The cash flows reach stability in year 3.

A key point of judgment in valuation analysis is to *set the forecast horizon at that point in the future where stability or stable growth begins.* You can't use past rates

---

[6] This is a sensible assumption for healthy firms, under the axiom of the limited liability of investors: investors cannot be held liable for claims against the firm, beyond the amount of their investment in the firm. However, in the cases of punitive government regulations or an active torts system, investors may be compelled to "invest" further in a losing business. Examples would include liabilities for cleanup of toxic waste, remediation of defective breast implants, and assumption of medical costs of nicotine addiction. In those instances, the value of the firm to investors could be negative.

of growth of cash flows in each of these three projects because the explosive growth of the past will not be repeated. Frankly, over long periods of time, it is difficult to sustain cash flow growth much in excess of the economy. If you did, you would wind up owning everything!

SIMON: So at what year in the future would you set the horizon and estimate a terminal value for those three projects? And what growth rate would you use in your constant growth formula for them? Uh-oh. I know: "Figure it out for yourself."

> Simon's third task: Assess the forecast horizons for the three projects. See **Exhibit 5.**

Growth Rate Assumption

CHU: There are two classic approaches for estimating the growth rate to use in the constant-growth formula. The first is to use the self-sustainable growth rate formula,

$$g^\infty = ROE \times (1 - DPO)$$

That equation assumes that the firm can only grow as fast as it adds to its equity capital base (through the return on equity, or "ROE," less any dividends paid out, indicated through the dividend payout ratio, or "DPO"). I'm not a big fan of that approach because most naive analysts simply extrapolate *past* ROE and DPO without really thinking about the future. Also it relies on accounting ROE and can give some pretty crazy results.[7]

The second approach assumes that nominal growth of a business is the sum of *real growth* and *inflation.* In more proper mathematical notation the formula is:

$$g^\infty_{Nominal} = \left[(1 + g^\infty_{Units}) \times (1 + g^\infty_{Inflation}) \right] - 1$$

That formula uses the Fisher Formula, which holds that the nominal rate of growth is the product of the rate of inflation and the "real" rate of growth.[8] We commonly think of real growth as a percentage increase in units shipped. But in rare instances, real growth could come from price increases due, for instance, to a monopolist's power over the market. For simplicity, I just use a short version of the model (less precise, though the difference in precision is not material):

$$g^\infty_{Nominal} = g^\infty_{Units} + g^\infty_{Inflation}$$

Now, this formula focuses you on two really interesting issues: the real growth rate in the business, and the ability of the business to pass along the effects of inflation. The consensus inflation outlook in the United States today calls for about a 2 percent inflation rate indefinitely. We probably have not got the political consensus in the United States to drive inflation to zero, and the Federal Reserve has shown strong resistance to letting inflation rise much higher. Well, if inflation

---

[7] For a full discussion of the self-sustainable growth rate model, see "A Critical Look at the Self-Sustainable Growth Rate Concept" (UVA-F-0951).

[8] Economist Irving Fisher derived this model of economic growth.

is given, then the analyst can really focus her thinking on the more interesting issue of the real growth rate of the business.

The real growth rate is bound to vary by industry. Growth in unit demand of consumer staple products (such as adhesive bandages) is probably determined by the growth rate of the population—less than 1 percent in the United States. Growth in demand for luxury goods is probably driven by growth of real disposable income—maybe 3 percent today. Growth in demand for industrial commodities like steel is probably about equal to the real rate of growth of GNP—about 3 percent on average through time. In any event, all of those are small numbers.

When you add those real growth rates to the expected inflation rate today, you get a small number—that is intuitively appealing since over the very long run, the increasing maturity of a company will tend to drive its growth rate downward.

Terminal Value for Arcadian Microarray Technologies

CHU: We're negotiating to structure an equity investment in Arcadian. We and management disagree on the size of the cash flows to be realized over the next 10 years (see **Exhibits 1** and **2**). I'm willing to invest cash on the basis of *my* expectations, but I'm also willing to agree to give Arcadian's management a contingent payment if they achieve *their* forecast. To begin the structuring process, I needed valuations of Arcadian under their and our forecasts. We have the cash flow forecasts, and we both agree that the weighted average cost of capital (WACC) should be 20 percent—that's low for a typical venture capital investment, but given that Arcadian's research and development (R&D) partners are bearing so much of the technical risk in this venture, I think it's justified. All I needed to finish the valuation was a sensible terminal value assumption—I've already run a sensitivity analysis using growth rates to infinity ranging from 2 to 7 percent (see **Exhibit 6**). The rate at which the firm grows will place different demands on the need for physical capital and net working capital—the higher the growth rate, the greater the capital requirements. So, in computing the terminal value using the constant growth model, I adjusted the free cash flow for these different capital requirements. Here are the scenarios I ran (in millions of U.S. dollars):

> Simon's fourth task: Interpret **Exhibit 6.**

Nominal Growth Rate to Infinity	Capital Expenditures in Terminal Year, Net of Depreciation	Net Working Capital Investment in Terminal Year
2%	$0 million	$0 million
3%	−$ 5	−$3
4%	−$12	−$5
5%	−$15	−$7
6%	−$20	−$8
7%	−$28	−$9

Arcadian's management believes that they can grow at 7 percent to infinity, assuming a strong patent position on breakthrough therapeutics. I believe that a lower growth rate is justified, though I would like to have your recommendation on what that rate should be. Should we be looking at the population growth rate in the United States (about 1 percent per year), or the real growth rate in the economy (about 3 percent per year), or the historical real growth rate in pharmaceutical industry revenues (5 percent per year)? Are there other growth rates we should be considering?

> Simon's fifth task: What drives g^{∞}?

We ought to test the reasonableness of the DCF valuations against estimates afforded by other approaches. Estimates of book and liquidation values of the company are not very helpful in this case, but multiples estimates would help. Price/earnings (P/E) multiples for Arcadian are expected to be 15 to 20 times at the forecast horizon—that is considerably below the P/Es for comparable companies today, but around the P/Es for established pharmaceutical companies. Price/book ratios for comparable companies today are around 8.5 times; Arcadian's book value of equity is $3.5 million. Please draw on any other multiples you might know about. We do not foresee Arcadian paying a dividend for a long time.

> Simon's sixth task: Estimate terminal values using multiples and prepare present-value estimates using them.

SIMON: That makes me skeptical about the whole concept. Terminal value for a high-tech company will be an awfully mushy estimate. How do you estimate growth? How sensitive is terminal value to variations in assumed growth rates? And with several terminal value estimates, how do you pick a "best guess" figure necessary to complete the DCF analysis? And once you've done all that, how far apart are the two valuations?

CHU: You need to help me find intelligent answers to those questions. Please let me have your recommendations about terminal values, their assumptions, and ultimately, about what you believe is a sensible value range today for Arcadian, from our standpoint and management's. By "value range," I mean high and low estimates of value for the equity of Arcadian that represent the bounds within which we will start negotiating (the low value), and above which we will abandon the negotiations.

> Simon's seventh task: Triangulate value ranges and recommend a deal structure.

Conclusion

Later, Rodney Chu reflected on the investment opportunity in Arcadian. It looked as if management's asking price was highly optimistic; $40 million would barely cover the cash deficit Sierra had projected for 2005. That implied that further rounds of financing would be needed for 2006 and beyond. But buying into

> Chu's task: Assess early exit values and their impact on the decision.

Arcadian now was like buying an option on future opportunities to invest—the price of that option was high, but the potential payoff could be immense if the examples of Affymetrix and Illumina were accurate reflections of the potential value creation in this field. Indeed, it was reasonable to assume that Arcadian could go public in an initial public offering (IPO) shortly after a major breakthrough pharmaceutical was announced. An IPO would accelerate the exit from this investment. If an IPO occurred, Sierra Capital would not sell its shares in Arcadian, but instead would distribute the Arcadian shares tax-free to clients for whom Sierra Capital was managing investments. Chu wondered how large the exit value might be, and what impact an early exit would have on the investment decision.

EXHIBIT 1 | Arcadian Microarray Technologies Cash Flow Forecast, by Arcadian Management (values in millions of U.S. dollars)

	Actual 2004	2005	2006	2007	2008	2009	2010	2011	2012	2013	2014
INCOME STATEMENT											
Sales											
Clinical microarrays	$0	$1	$15	$56	$107	$181	$249	$274	$282	$285	$289
Research microarrays	2	12	28	45	75	110	135	165	190	210	225
Royalties and other revenue	0	0	2	13	52	106	146	166	174	186	189
Human therapeutics	0	0	0	0	8	57	171	250	330	352	362
Total sales	**2**	**13**	**45**	**114**	**242**	**454**	**701**	**855**	**976**	**1,033**	**1,065**
Cost of sales	7	10	21	41	84	159	246	322	335	350	361
Gross profits	**(5)**	**3**	**24**	**73**	**158**	**295**	**455**	**533**	**641**	**683**	**704**
Contract revenue	16	21	23	15	12	4	3	3	3	3	3
Operating expenses											
Research & development	14	20	24	18	21	21	32	43	51	52	50
Selling, general, & admin.	12	15	24	45	93	176	259	323	369	372	349
Total expenses	**26**	**35**	**48**	**63**	**114**	**197**	**291**	**366**	**420**	**424**	**399**
Other income	3	2	2	0	(3)	(10)	(25)	(38)	(43)	(37)	(20)
Income before taxes	**(12)**	**(9)**	**1**	**25**	**53**	**92**	**142**	**132**	**181**	**225**	**288**
Taxes	0	0	5	9	19	32	57	76	89	90	85
Net income	**($12)**	**($9)**	**($4)**	**$16**	**$35**	**$60**	**$85**	**$56**	**$92**	**$135**	**$203**
FREE CASH FLOW											
Net income	($12)	($9)	($4)	$16	$35	$60	$85	$56	$92	$135	$203
Noncash items	0	1	2	2	6	10	18	19	15	8	(1)
Working capital	(4)	(8)	(12)	(22)	(63)	(101)	(118)	(100)	(61)	1	39
Capital expenditures	(15)	(6)	(5)	(23)	(53)	(93)	(111)	(98)	(66)	(10)	(10)
Free cash flow	**($31)**	**($22)**	**($19)**	**($27)**	**($76)**	**($124)**	**($126)**	**($123)**	**($20)**	**$134**	**$231**

Source: Case writer's analysis.

EXHIBIT 2 | Arcadian Microarray Technologies Cash Flow Forecast, by Sierra Capital Analysts (values in millions of U.S. dollars)

	Actual 2004	2005	2006	2007	2008	2009	2010	2011	2012	2013	2014	2015
INCOME STATEMENT												
Sales												
Clinical microarrays	$0	$0	$2	$11	$22	$36	$56	$71	$85	$95	$106	$114
Research microarrays	2	4	11	22	40	59	89	135	145	160	185	199
Royalties and other revenue	0	1	4	7	12	15	25	50	60	75	91	105
Human therapeutics	0	0	0	0	0	0	0	14	56	80	110	140
Total sales	**2**	**5**	**17**	**40**	**74**	**110**	**170**	**270**	**346**	**410**	**492**	**558**
Cost of sales	7	17	20	25	39	54	72	96	124	142	154	160
Gross profits	**(5)**	**(12)**	**(3)**	**15**	**35**	**56**	**98**	**174**	**222**	**268**	**338**	**398**
Contract revenue	16	22	22	15	12	4	4	4	4	4	4	4
Operating expenses												
Research & development	14	23	25	27	29	33	37	44	52	53	54	58
Selling, general, & admin.	12	21	25	32	44	64	87	104	127	138	136	136
Total expenses	**26**	**44**	**50**	**59**	**73**	**96**	**124**	**147**	**179**	**191**	**191**	**194**
Other income	3	0	0	1	(1)	(2)	(2)	(3)	(2)	0	0	3
Income before taxes	**(12)**	**(34)**	**(31)**	**(29)**	**(27)**	**(38)**	**(24)**	**28**	**45**	**80**	**152**	**210**
Taxes	0	0	(0)	1	4	(13)	4	11	15	27	39	48
Net income	**($12)**	**($34)**	**($31)**	**($30)**	**($31)**	**($25)**	**($28)**	**$17**	**$30**	**$53**	**$112**	**$162**
FREE CASH FLOW												
Net income	($12)	($34)	($31)	($30)	($31)	($25)	($28)	$17	$30	$53	$112	$162
Noncash items	2	3	3	3	4	6	8	10	14	18	20	23
Working capital	(6)	(6)	(6)	(7)	(14)	(17)	(19)	(20)	(28)	(16)	(6)	(6)
Capital expenditures	(15)	(9)	(9)	(9)	(10)	(11)	(15)	(18)	(24)	(27)	(28)	(30)
Free cash flow	**($31)**	**($46)**	**($43)**	**($43)**	**($51)**	**($47)**	**($54)**	**($11)**	**($8)**	**$28**	**$98**	**$149**

Source: Case writer's analysis.

EXHIBIT 3 | Paige Simon's Dart-Selected Sample of Firms with Analysis of Five-Year Dividends as a Percentage of Stock Price

	Recent Price	Annual Dividend	Projected Five-Year Dividend Growth (%)	Beta	Equity Cost	Present Value of Five Years' Dividends	Percent of Market Price Not Attributable to Dividends
BNSF	$53	$0.64	13.0%	0.95	11.2%	$3.36	94%
Caterpillar	49	0.80	10.0	1.20	12.6	3.74	92
Cooper Industries	67	1.40	0.0	1.20	12.6	4.98	93
Cummins, Inc.	82	1.20	1.0	1.35	13.4	4.30	95
Deluxe Corporation	33	1.48	1.5	0.80	10.4	5.79	82
RR Donnelley	34	1.04	3.5	0.95	11.2	4.21	88
Dun & Bradstreet	64	0.00	0.0	0.80	10.4	0.00	100
Eaton Corp.	63	1.08	13.5	1.10	12.0	5.62	91
Emerson Electric Co.	70	1.60	7.5	1.10	12.0	7.08	90
Equifax	33	0.11	3.5	1.10	12.0	0.44	99
FedEx Corporation	81	0.29	13.0	1.10	12.0	0.00	100
Fluor Corporation	63	0.64	4.0	1.20	12.6	2.54	96
Honeywell Int'l. Inc.	34	0.75	3.0	1.35	13.4	2.84	92
Illinois Tool Works, Inc.	82	1.00	8.5	1.05	11.7	4.58	94
Kelly Services	29	0.40	11.0	0.95	11.2	1.99	93
ServiceMaster	14	0.43	2.5	0.80	10.4	1.73	87
Sherwin-Williams Co.	46	0.68	11.0	1.00	11.5	3.36	93
Smurfit-Stone Cont. Co.	10	0.00	0.0	1.30	13.1	0.00	100
Tenneco	17	0.00	0.0	1.75	15.5	0.00	100
Weyerhauser Co.	68	1.60	7.5	1.15	12.3	7.03	90
						Average	93%

Note: To illustrate the estimate of 94% for Burlington Northern, the annual dividend of $0.64 was projected to grow at 13.0% per year to $0.72 in 2006, $0.82 in 2007, $0.92 in 2008, $1.04 in 2009, and $1.18 in 2010. The present value of those dividends discounted at 11.2% was $3.36. That equaled about 6% of Burlington Northern's stock price, $53.00. The complement, 94%, is the portion of market price not attributable to dividends.

Source of data: *Value Line Investment Survey* for prices, dividends, growth rates, and betas. Other items calculated by case writer.

EXHIBIT 4 | Key Terminal Value Estimators

Approach	Advantages	Disadvantages
Book Value	—Simple —"Authoritative"	—Ignores some assets and liabilities —Historical costs: backward-looking —Subject to accounting manipulation
Liquidation Value	—Conservative	—Ignores "going concern" value —(Dis)orderly sale?
Replacement Value	—"Current"	—Replace *what?* —Subjective estimates
Multiples, Earnings Capitalization —Price/Earnings —Value/EBIT —Price/Book	—Simple —Widely used	—"Earnings" subject to accounting manipulation —"Snapshot" estimate: may ignore cyclical, secular changes —Depends on comparable firms: ultimately just a measure of relative, not absolute value
Discounted Cash Flow	—Theoretically based —Rigorous —Affords many analytical insights —Cash focus —Multiperiod —Reflects time value of money	—Time-consuming —Risks "analysis paralysis" —Easy to abuse, misuse —Tough to explain to novices

EXHIBIT 5 | Cash Flows of Three Deals with Differing Rates of Development (values in millions of U.S. dollars)

Year	Movie Studio	Bottling Plant	Toll Road
1	($20)	($20)	($20)
2	(40)	(60)	90
3	(60)	(100)	169
4	(20)	5	172
5	0	10	176
6	20	20	179
7	30	40	183
8	50	65	187
9	75	115	190
10	100	150	194
11	90	180	198
12	80	190	202
13	60	200	206
14	55	204	210
15	70	208	214
16	85	212	219
17	95	216	223
18	105	221	227
19	130	225	232
20	150	230	237
21	140	234	241
22	160	239	246
23	190	244	251
24	225	249	256
25	240	254	261
26	230	259	266
27	255	264	272
28	260	269	277
29	265	275	283
30	270	280	288
31+	Steady growth to infinity.		

Projected cash flows by investment

Source : Case writer's analysis.

EXHIBIT 6 | Sensitivity Analysis of Arcadian Terminal Value and Present Value By Variations in Terminal Value Scenarios (values in millions of U.S. dollars)

Arcadian's View

	2%	3%	4%	5%	6%	7%
Annual growth rate to infinity						
Weighted average cost of capital	20%	20%	20%	20%	20%	20%
Annual capex (net of depr'n.) 2015	$0	($5)	($12)	($15)	($20)	($28)
Annual addition to NWC 2015	—	(3)	(5)	(7)	(8)	(9)
Adjusted free cash flow 2015	202	194	185	180	174	165
Terminal value 2014	1,142	1,173	1,200	1,257	1,314	1,355
PV of terminal value 2014	185	189	194	203	212	219
PV free cash flows 2005–2014	($151)	($151)	($151)	($151)	($151)	($151)
Total Present Value	**$33**	**$38**	**$43**	**$52**	**$61**	**$68**

Sierra Capital's View

	2%	3%	4%	5%	6%	7%
Annual growth rate to infinity						
Weighted average cost of capital	20%	20%	20%	20%	20%	20%
Annual capex (net of depr'n.) 2016	$0	($5)	($12)	($15)	($20)	($28)
Annual addition to NWC 2016	—	(3)	(5)	(7)	(8)	(9)
Adjusted free cash flow 2016	185	177	168	163	157	148
Terminal value 2015	1,049	1,073	1,093	1,142	1,189	1,219
PV of terminal value 2015	141	144	147	154	160	164
PV free cash flows 2005–2015	($118)	($118)	($118)	($118)	($118)	($118)
Total Present Value	**$23**	**$26**	**$29**	**$35**	**$42**	**$46**

Source: Case writer's analysis.

Yeats Valves and Controls Inc.

On May 2, 2000, W. B. "Bill" Yeats, chairman, CEO, and founder of Yeats Valves and Controls Inc. (YVC), met with Kate Porter, his long-time adviser, investment banker, and a member of the Yeats Valves board of directors. The pair met to prepare for the final negotiations about the proposed acquisition of Yeats Valves by TSE International Corporation. Serious negotiations for combining the two companies had started in March, following casual conversations, which dated back to late 1999. Those initial talks focused on broad motives for each side to reach an agreement, and on the social issues, such as management and compensation in the new firm. The final term sheet on which the definitive agreement would be drafted and signed was still open for negotiation.

Porter and Yeats had worked together to craft the outline of the agreement. So far, the social terms of the merger had been broached, although the specific details remained to be settled. YVC would become a subsidiary of TSE. Bill Yeats would remain as YVC's CEO.

Yeats had never thought seriously about a possible sellout before last November, when he had his 62nd birthday. "I began to wonder what would happen to the company after I retired or died," he reminded Kate Porter. "I've got a good top-management team here, but they are all specialists. I don't think any one of them could step in and run the show alone. It's a tough business to learn, and I don't think I could find a successor very easily—nor train him quickly. There's stability in the TSE International combination that's worth something personally to me."

"In your eagerness to sell, just don't leave too much value on the table," Kate Porter said. "YVC's prospects are brighter than ever. You have technology to die for. With our intellectual property and new products coming along, there is a lot of hidden value in this company that's not reflected on the balance sheet. Be a realist about the value."

Bill Yeats agreed. "There are lots of reasons for me to want to see the acquisition take place. However, I want to make sure it's also going to be good for our shareholders. They've put a lot of faith in me at very critical times in the company's history, and I wouldn't want to let them down."

Yeats Valves and Controls Inc.

Yeats Valves and Controls Inc., headquartered in Innisfree, California, was principally engaged in the manufacture of specialty valves and heat exchangers. The firm had many standard items, but nearly 40 percent of its volume and more than 50 percent of its profits derived from special applications for the defense and aerospace industries. Such products required extensive engineering work of the kind only a few firms were capable of matching. Yeats had a reputation for engineering excellence in the most complex phases of the business and, as a result, often did prime contract work on highly technical devices for the government.

Yeats was an outgrowth of a small company organized in 1980 for engineering and developmental work on an experimental heat exchanger product. In 1987, as soon as the product was brought to the commercial stage, the company was organized to acquire the patents and properties, both owned and leased, of the engineering corporation. Bill Yeats, who founded the engineering firm, founded Yeats Valves and continued as its CEO.

The raw materials used by the company were obtainable in ample supply from a number of competitive suppliers. Marketing arrangements presented no problems; sales to machinery manufacturers were made directly by a staff of skilled sales engineers. Auden Company, a large concern in a related field, was an important foreign channel of distribution under a nonexclusive distributor arrangement. About 15 percent of Yeats Valves' sales came from Auden. Foreign sales through Auden and direct through Yeats Valves' own staff accounted for 30 percent of sales. Half of the foreign sales originated in emerging economies, mainly Brazil, Korea, and Mexico. The other half originated in the United Kingdom, Italy, and Germany.

Although the foreign-currency crises in the mid-1990s had temporarily interrupted sales growth for the company, better economic conditions in the markets of developed countries, together with its recent introduction of new products for the aerospace and defense industries offered the company excellent prospects for improved performance. As such, sales in the first quarter of 2000 grew 20–25 percent over the corresponding period in 1999, whereas many of Yeats Valves' competitors were experiencing limited growth. **Exhibits 1** and **2** show the most recent balance sheet for Yeats Valves and Controls Inc. and income statements from 1995 forward. **Exhibit 3** presents five years of projected sales, earnings, and other data for Yeats Valves.

The Yeats Valves plants, all of modern construction, were organized for efficient handling of small production orders. The main plant was served by switch tracks in a 15-car dock area of a leading railroad, and additionally served by a truck area for the company's own fleet of trucks. From 1997 to 1999, net additions to property totaled $7.6 million. Bill Yeats, outstanding in research in his own right, had always stressed the research and development of improved products, with patent protection, although the company's leadership was believed to be based on its head start in the field and its practical experience.

The success of Yeats Valves and Controls Inc. had brought numerous overtures from companies looking for diversification, plant capacity, management efficiency, financial resources, or an offset to cyclical business. For instance, when Yeats Valves went public in 1986, Auden Company, which later held 20 percent of Yeats Valves' common stock, advanced a merger proposal. Word of the proposal reached the financial commentators, who reported possible action by the U.S. Department of Justice in antitrust proceedings. Although lawyers for Yeats Valves were confident that they had a ready defense in an antitrust suit, the practical question was one of whether such a legal victory on principle would offset perhaps two or more years of litigation, possibly to the U.S. Supreme Court. Lawsuits did not build a business, as Yeats noted at the time, and they used up time and energy that management should devote to the company's operating problems. Hence, the idea was not further developed.

As Bill Yeats neared retirement, however, the idea of selling the company to a bigger firm seemed almost necessary. Compelling reasons existed in addition to his impending retirement[1] and the problem of management succession. First, the company needed a deep-pocketed partner to expand, and to bankroll more research and development (R&D) projects. Conducting research to continue developing leading-edge products for aerospace and defense required sizeable investments. Second, Yeats believed that the company would benefit from gaining access to a large marketing and distribution network. Yeats Valves was highly successful in its own niche, but Yeats concluded that more segments could be tapped if Yeats Valves' products were more aggressively marketed and more widely available. Third, as the company continued to grow, it would need to gain production know-how for high-volume manufacturing. Yeats Valves did not have this kind of expertise. Finally, there had been an increasing trend of consolidation in Yeats Valves' industry over the last year. Yeats feared that without a well-financed partner, the company would be swamped by competition. Thus, when the merger opportunity with TSE International Corporation came along in 1999, Yeats determined to make it work as best as he could.

Bill Yeats believed that YVC had alternatives to this deal. Rockheed-Marlin Corporation, a large defense contractor (or any of a number of others), might be induced to make an offer for Yeats Valves, though Yeats preferred TSE International Corporation as a merger partner. YVC and TSE might establish a joint venture of some sort, though Bill Yeats suspected that joint ventures faced the same kinds of integration problems as did acquisitions; as a result, he thought joint ventures were an inferior alternative. YVC could move forward alone, but that would require raising large sums of new debt and equity to finance the rapid expansion of the firm's "widening gyre" program. Yeats was concerned that he might lose voting control of the firm regardless. It seemed to him that doing a deal with a known and friendly partner today would prepare the way for an orderly transition for himself and the firm.

Bill Yeats and Tom Eliot had known each other for four years, having been introduced at an industry conference where they were both speakers. As founders and significant stockholders of their firms, they liked and respected each other. Talks of a possible combination seemed to gain momentum following the announcement by Yeats Valves of a U.S. government contract to develop an advanced hydraulic-controls system code-named Widening Gyre for use in a wide array of commercial and military

---

[1] For Yeats' estate-planning purposes, selling his shares in Yeats Valves would also work to his advantage.

applications in aerospace, automotive, and transportation industries. The Widening Gyre program had already generated valuable patents, numerous options for ongoing R&D. Bill Yeats and his team were most interested in the R&D aspects of the program, and hoped that TSE or some other partner would assume the work on commercialization, and numerous possible product extensions. Yeats insisted that the financial forecasts for his firm were conservative, and included only the most predictable benefits of the Widening Gyre. He told Kate Porter, "I hope TSE will recognize the intellectual capital we have built up for the Widening Gyre program. We're all very excited about it; it could be really big. We have one high-profile government contract. But right now the forecasts don't show its promise. And the stock price doesn't reflect our growth prospects. How should we build it into our negotiations?"

TSE International Corporation

TSE International Corporation was incorporated in 1970. By 2000, the company manufactured products ranging from advanced industrial components to chains, cables, nuts and bolts, castings and forgings, and other similar products, and they sold them, for the most part indirectly, to various industrial users. One division produced parts for aerospace propulsion and control systems with a broad line of intermediate products. A second division produced a wide range of nautical navigation assemblies and allied products. The third division manufactured a line of components for missile and fire-control systems. Those products were all well regarded by TSE's customers, and each was a significant factor in its natural market. Financial statements for TSE International are provided in **Exhibits 4** and **5**—the firm's debt was currently rated Baa. Porter had obtained an analysts' consensus forecast of TSE's earnings, dividends, and cash flow items as shown in **Exhibit 6.**

The company's raw material supply, in the form of sheets, plates, and coils—of various metals—came from various producers. The TSE International plants were modern, ample, equipped with substantially new machinery, and adequately served by railroad sidings. The firm was considered a low-cost producer, made possible by unusual production knowledge. TSE International was also known as a tough competitor.

The Current Situation

During the early part of 2000, a series of group meetings had taken place between Yeats and Eliot and their respective company's counsel. From the very start of the negotiations for combining the two companies, the merits of alternative methods had been considered by counsel for both parties. A straight common-for-common exchange was expected to be the most likely outcome, although Yeats was willing to consider an assets-for-stock exchange. Both methods would be structured to provide a deferment of the tax liability. Whatever terms were finally worked out, the agreement would be subject to the approval of the stockholders of both companies.

YVC had 560 stockholders. Roughly 70 percent of the stock was held within the board of directors and their families, including 20 percent owned by Auden Company and 40 percent owned by Bill Yeats. Yeats had kept the board of directors fully informed throughout the discussions with TSE International. The proposed merger was discussed with the president of Auden Company, whose approval was necessary because of his company's 20 percent interest. Although the Auden executives were not convinced that the proposal had strict business merit, they decided not to object but, instead, gave notice that they would sell their company's holdings of Yeats Valves stock. Auden Company was about to undertake a new expansion of its own, and its executives were not disposed to keep minority interests in a company like TSE International Corporation. However, they saw no reason for not maintaining their satisfactory relationships with the Yeats Valves enterprise when it should become a TSE International division.

Social terms of the merger needed to be confirmed. YVC's management team and employees would remain intact; no layoffs were contemplated. Bill Yeats sought a grant of five-year options to purchase 80,000 shares of TSE International stock at 90 percent of its market price at the close of the acquisition, and an incentive bonus between $50,000 and $200,000 per year. Yeats' current salary at YVC was $300,000 per year.

Kate Porter, as a director of Yeats Valves, had been kept fully informed regarding the merger discussions. She was intrigued with the possibility that Yeats Valves might be more fully valued if it were part of a larger, more diversified enterprise. Yeats Valves had recently traded at a price-earnings ratio of 10.3 times, perhaps reflecting the risks associated with a small, concentrated enterprise, possibly vulnerable to competition from larger firms. The American Stock Exchange listing of TSE International would be attractive to some shareholders, although Porter's firm had earned significant commissions specializing in handling Yeats Valves' NASDAQ trading. **Exhibit 7** shows recent market prices of Yeats Valves and TSE International shares.[2] **Exhibit 8** provides valuation information on exchange-listed possible peer firms of Yeats Valves and TSE International. **Exhibit 9** presents information on recent acquisitions within Yeats Valves' industry. **Exhibit 10** presents money market and stock return data for recent years. Porter believed that a 40 percent marginal tax rate was warranted for both TSE and Yeats.

"Kate, what do you think of the merger?" Yeats asked his friend as they sat down to analyze the deal. "It looks good to me, yet maybe I've gotten too close to the situation to uncover all the things I should be seeing. I also worry that our people, who have gotten used to an independent, entrepreneurial culture here at Yeats Valves, would have trouble adjusting at a big firm like TSE International. Do you think that the merger will benefit Yeats Valves? And, if so, what is the minimum price we should ask to ensure that our stockholders profit from this merger?"

"April, 2000 was pretty cruel to those dot-com companies," Bill Yeats said. "Our firm is different. We've got a great growth outlook, but our valuation is still low. Is this merger a move that will help fetch a better multiple? Or, should we wait to see if our efforts are better rewarded?" With that comment, Yeats passed the following clipping to Kate Porter:

---

[2] TSE International's stock had a beta of 0.85; the beta for Yeats Valves and Controls was 1.50, based on the most recent year's trading prices.

Modest Valuations—In light of currently modest share prices, we believe that the number of acquisitions will increase in the future. Some valuations are so low, in fact, managers are considering leveraged buyouts of their individual companies . . . . We advise most investors to delay additional commitments until the stock market settles.[3]

---

[3] *Value Line Investment Survey,* 5 May 2000, 1301.

EXHIBIT 1 | Yeats Valves and Controls Inc. Consolidated Balance Sheet as of December 31, 1999 (dollar figures in thousands)

Assets

Cash		
U.S. Treasury tax notes and other Treasury obligations		$ 1,884
Due from U.S. Government		9,328
Accounts receivable net[1]		868
Inventories, at lower of cost or market[2]		2,316
Other current assets		6,888
		116
Total current assets		$21,400
Investments		1,768
Plant, property, and equipment, at cost		
Land[3]	$ 92	
Buildings	6,240	
Equipment[3]	18,904	
Less: allowance for depreciation	7,056	
	$18,180	
Construction in process	88	
Total plant, property, and equipment, net		$18,268
Patents		156
Cash value of life insurance		376
Deferred assets		156
Total assets		$42,124

Liabilities and Stockholders' Equity

Accounts payable	
Wages and salaries accrued	$ 2,016
Employees' pension cost accrued	504
Tax accrued	208
Dividends payable	72
Provision for federal income tax	560
	1,200
Total current liabilities	$ 4,560
Deferred federal income tax	800
Common stock, par $0.50, authorized and outstanding 1,440,000 shares	720
Capital surplus	7,680
Earned surplus	28,364
Total equity	$36,764
Total liabilities and stockholders' equity	$42,124
Current ratio	4.69
Quick ratio	3.16

[1]Allowance for doubtful accounts: $190,392 (probably conservative).

[2]Obsolete inventories were written off semi-annually.

[3]Equivalent land in the area had a market value of $320,000, and the building had an estimated market worth of $16.8 million. Equipment had a replacement cost of approximately $24 million, but a market value of about $16 million in an orderly liquidation.

EXHIBIT 2 | Yeats Valves and Controls Inc. Summary of Earnings and Dividends, Years Ended December 31, 1995–1999 (dollar figures in thousands, except per-share figures)

	1995	1996	1997	1998	1999	(Unaudited) Three Months Ended 3/30 1999	(Unaudited) Three Months Ended 3/30 2000
Sales	$36,312	$34,984	$35,252	$45,116	$49,364	$11,728	$14,162
Cost of goods sold	25,924	24,200	24,300	31,580	37,044	8,730	10,190
Gross profit	10,388	10,784	10,952	13,536	12,320	2,998	3,972
Administrative	2,020	2,100	2,252	2,628	2,936	668	896
Other income, net	92	572	108	72	228	14	198
Income before taxes	8,460	9,256	8,808	10,980	9,612	2,344	3,274
Taxes	3,276	3,981	3,620	4,721	4,037	1,009	1,391
Net income	$ 5,184	$ 5,275	$ 5,188	$ 6,259	$ 5,575	$ 1,335	$ 1,883
Depreciation	$ 784	$ 924	$ 1,088	$ 1,280	$ 1,508	$ 364	$ 394
Cash dividends	$ 1,680	$ 2,008	$ 2,016	$ 2,304	$ 2,304	$ 576	$ 753
Earnings per common share	$ 3.74	$ 3.61	$ 3.60	$ 4.35	$ 3.87	$ 0.93	$ 1.31
Cash dividends declared:							
Per preferred share	$ 5.00	$ 1.25					
Per common share	$ 1.00	$ 1.40	$ 1.40	$ 1.60	$ 1.60	$ 0.40	$ 0.52
Capital expenditures	—	$ 1,826	$ 2,011	$ 2,213	$ 2,433	$ 2,675	$ 2,675
Working capital needs	—	$ 3,492	$ 3,867	$ 4,289	$ 4,757	$ 5,273	$ 5,273
Percent payout to common stock	27.8%	38.2%	38.9%	36.8%	41.3%	43.1%	40.0%
Ratio analysis							
Sales	100.0	100.0	100.0	100.0	100.0	100.0	100.0
Cost of goods sold	71.4	69.2	68.9	70.0	75.0	74.4	72.0
Gross profit	28.6	30.8	31.1	30.0	25.0	25.6	28.0
Administrative	5.6	6.0	6.4	5.8	5.9	5.7	6.3
Other income, net	0.3	1.6	0.3	0.2	0.5	0.1	1.4
Income before fed. taxes	23.3	26.5	25.0	24.3	19.5	20.0	23.1
Net income	14.3	15.1	14.7	13.9	11.3	11.4	13.3

EXHIBIT 3 | Yeats Valves and Controls Inc. Forecast of Sales, Earnings, and Other Items for Years Ending December 31, 2000–2004 (dollar figures in thousands except per-share amounts)

	Actual	Projected				
	1999	2000	2001	2002	2003	2004
Sales	$49,364	$59,600	$66,000	$73,200	$81,200	$90,000
Cost of goods sold	37,044	42,316	47,850	52,704	58,058	63,900
Gross profit	12,320	17,284	18,150	20,496	23,142	26,100
Administrative	2,936	3,612	4,024	4,464	4,952	5,492
Other income, net	228	240	264	288	320	352
Income before taxes	9,612	13,912	14,390	16,320	18,510	20,960
Taxes	4,037	5,565	5,756	6,528	7,404	8,384
Net income	$ 5,575	$ 8,347	$ 8,634	$ 9,792	$11,106	$12,576
Depreciation	$ 1,508	$ 1,660	$ 1,828	$ 2,012	$ 2,212	$ 2,432
Cash dividends	$ 2,304	$ 2,304	$ 2,880	$ 3,456	$ 4,320	$ 5,184
Earnings per share	$ 3.87	$ 5.80	$ 6.00	$ 6.80	$ 7.71	$ 8.73
Dividends per share	$ 1.60	$ 1.60	$ 2.00	$ 2.40	$ 3.00	$ 3.60
Capital expenditures	—	$ 1,826	$ 2,011	$ 2,213	$ 2,433	$ 2,675
Working capital needs	—	$ 3,492	$ 3,867	$ 4,289	$ 4,757	$ 5,273
Ratio analysis						
Sales	100.0	100.0	100.0	100.0	100.0	100.0
Cost of goods sold	75.0	71.0	72.5	72.0	71.5	71.0
Gross profit	25.0	29.0	27.5	28.0	28.5	29.0
Administrative	5.9	6.1	6.1	6.1	6.1	6.1
Other income, net	0.5	0.4	0.4	0.4	0.4	0.4
Income before fed. taxes	19.5	23.3	21.8	22.3	22.8	23.3
Net income	11.3	14.0	13.1	13.4	13.7	14.0

EXHIBIT 4 | TSE International Corporation Consolidated Balance Sheet as of December 31, 1999 (dollar figures in thousands)

Assets

Cash		$ 46,480
U.S. government securities, at cost		117,260
Trade accounts receivable		241,761
Inventories, at lower of cost or market		179,601
Prepaid taxes and insurance		2,120
Total current assets		$ 587,222
Investment in wholly-owned Canadian subsidiary		158,081
Investment in supplier corporation		104,000
Cash value of life insurance		3,920
Miscellaneous assets		2,160
Property, plant, and equipment, at cost:		
Buildings, machinery, equipment	$671,402	
Less: allowances for depreciation and amortization	260,001	
Property, plant and equipment, net	$411,402	
Land	22,080	
Property, plant, equipment, and land, net		$ 389,321
Patents, at cost, less amortization		1,120
Total assets		$1,245,825

Liabilities and Stockholders' Equity

Notes payable to bank	$ 5,795
Accounts payable and accrued expenses	90,512
Payrolls and other compensation	38,399
Taxes other than taxes on income	3,052
Provision for federal taxes on income refund, estimated	32,662
Current maturities of long-term debt	30,900
Total current liabilities	$ 201,320
Note payable to bank[1]	119,100
Deferred federal income taxes	29,668
2% cumulative convertible preferred stock, $20 par,	27,783
1,389,160 shares outstanding[2]	
Common stock, $2 par; 96,000,000 shares authorized;	125,389
62,694,361 shares issued	
Capital surplus[3]	21,904
Retained earnings	720,661
Total equity	$ 895,737
Total liabilities and stockholders' equity	$1,245,825

[1]$150,000,000 note, payable semi-annually beginning June 30, 2000; $30,900,000 due within one year, shown in current liabilities. One covenant required company not to pay cash dividends, except on preferred stock, or to make other distribution on its shares or acquire any stock, after December 31, 1999, in excess of net earnings after that date.

[2]Issued in January 1999; convertible at rate of 1.24 common share to one preferred share; redeemable beginning in 2004; sinking fund beginning in 2004.

[3]Resulting principally from the excess of par value of 827,800 shares of preferred stock over the pay value of common-share issues in conversion in 1999.

EXHIBIT 5 | TSE International Corporation Summary of Consolidated Earnings and Dividends for Years Ended December 31, 1995–1999 (dollars in thousands except per-share amounts)

	1995	1996	1997	1998	1999
Net sales	$1,623,963	$1,477,402	$1,498,645	$1,980,801	$2,187,208
Cost of products sold	1,271,563	1,180,444	1,140,469	1,642,084	1,793,511
Gross profit	352,400	296,958	358,176	338,717	393,697
Selling, general, and administrative	58,463	69,438	74,932	87,155	120,296
Earnings before federal income taxes	293,937	227,520	283,244	251,562	273,401
Tax expense	126,393	95,558	116,130	101,882	109,360
Net earnings	$ 167,544	$ 131,962	$ 167,114	$ 149,679	$ 164,041
Depreciation	$ 19,160	$ 20,000	$ 21,480	$ 24,200	$ 26,800
Cash dividends declared	$ 85,754	$ 77,052	$ 53,116	$ 77,340	$ 92,238
Net earnings per common share	$ 2.55	$ 1.86	$ 2.01	$ 1.92	$ 2.23
Cash dividends declared					
Per common share	$ 1.39	$ 1.25	$ 0.86	$ 1.25	$ 1.49
Per preferred share	$ 0.00	$ 0.00	$ 0.00	$ 0.00	$ 0.40
Cash payout	51.2%	58.4%	31.8%	51.7%	56.2%
Ratio analysis					
Sales	100.0	100.0	100.0	100.0	100.0
Cost of goods sold	78.3	79.9	76.1	82.9	82.0
Gross profit	21.7	20.1	23.9	17.1	18.0
Selling, general, and administrative	3.6	4.7	5.0	4.4	5.5
Income before federal taxes	18.1	15.4	18.9	12.7	12.5
Net income	10.3	8.9	11.2	7.6	7.5

EXHIBIT 6 | TSE International Corporation Forecast of Sales, Earnings, and Other Items for Years Ending December 31, 2000–2004 (dollar figures in thousands, except per-share amounts)

	Actual			Projected		
	1999	2000	2001	2002	2003	2004
Sales	$2,187,208	$2,329,373	$2,480,785	$2,642,037	$2,813,769	$2,996,658
Cost of goods sold	1,793,511	1,910,086	2,034,244	2,166,470	2,307,291	2,457,260
Gross profit	393,697	419,287	446,541	475,567	506,478	539,398
Selling, general, and admin.	120,296	125,786	131,482	140,028	146,316	155,826
Income before tax	273,401	293,501	315,060	335,539	360,162	383,572
Tax expense	109,360	117,400	126,024	134,215	144,065	153,429
Net income	$ 164,041	$ 176,101	$ 189,036	$ 201,323	$ 216,097	$ 230,143
Depreciation	$ 26,800	$ 27,950	$ 29,770	$ 31,700	$ 33,170	$ 35,960
Cash dividends	$ 92,238	$ 102,083	$ 108,715	$ 115,780	$ 125,185	$ 133,314
Earnings per share[1]	$ 2.23	$ 2.39	$ 2.54	$ 2.71	$ 2.93	$ 3.12
Divs. per shr. common stock[1]	$ 1.49	$ 1.58	$ 1.69	$ 1.80	$ 1.94	$ 2.07
Div. per shr. preferred stock[2]	$ 0.40					
Ratio analysis						
Sales	100.0	100.0	100.0	100.0	100.0	100.0
Cost of goods sold	82.0	82.0	82.0	82.0	82.0	82.0
Gross profit	18.0	18.0	18.0	18.0	18.0	18.0
Selling, general, and admin.	5.5	5.4	5.3	5.3	5.2	5.2
Income before tax	12.5	12.6	12.7	12.7	12.8	12.8
Net income	5.0	5.0	5.1	5.1	5.1	5.1

[1]62,694,361 common shares in 1999. Thereafter, 64,416,919 shares reflecting conversion of the preferred stock.

[2]1,389,160 preferred shares in 1999. Conversion into 1,722,558 shares of common stock assumed in 2000.

EXHIBIT 7 | Market Prices of Yeats Valves and Controls Inc. and TSE International Corporation Common Stock, 1995–YTD (year to date) 2000 (in dollars per share)

| | Yeats Valves and Controls | | | TSE International | | | | |
| | Common Stock | | | Common Stock | | | Preferred Stock | |
	High	Low	Close	High	Low	Close	High	Low
1995	$16.25	$ 8.75	$15.00	$12.31	$10.06	$11.88		
1996	24.75	14.00	22.63	14.37	11.77	13.16		
1997	25.00	20.00	22.25	12.82	9.28	11.13		
1998 Quarter Ended:								
March 31	24.38	20.75	21.50	14.13	12.83	13.96		
June 30	22.75	20.38	21.00	13.70	12.05	11.79		
September 30	22.75	20.38	21.50	12.83	10.49	11.27		
December 31	24.38	20.13	21.00	12.40	11.27	11.88		
1999 Quarter Ended:								
March 31	23.50	20.00	21.75	11.60	10.21	10.67	13.61	12.22
June 30	23.63	19.88	22.00	11.60	10.90	10.90	13.15	12.05
September 30	22.75	20.00	22.50	13.61	11.14	13.61	14.23	12.37
December 31	30.00	22.25	28.50	17.01	13.30	16.78	17.32	13.77
2000 Quarter Ended:								
March 31	32.13	26.00	31.50	20.73	15.08	20.69	17.32	13.99
May 1, 2000	$39.75	$38.90	$39.75	$22.58	$18.31	$21.98	$17.63	$15.36

EXHIBIT 8 | Information on Peer Firms in the Industrial Machinery Sector

	Price/ Earnings Ratio	Beta	Dividend Yield	Expected Rate of Growth to 2005	Debt/ Capital
CASCADE CORP. Designs, manufactures, and markets hydraulically actuated products.	8.2×	0.85	4.0%	12.5%	49%
CURTISS-WRIGHT CORPORATION Manufactures precision components in motion (42%), flow control (36%), and metal treatment (36% of sales).	10.3×	0.65	1.4%	10.0%	8%
FLOWSERVE CORP. Makes, designs, and markets fluid handling equipment (pumps, valves, and mechanical seals).	11.0×	0.80	Nil	6.5%	39%
IDEX CORP. Designs, manufactures, and markets industrial pumps, compressors, and a wide range of industrial products.	14.6×	1.10	1.9%	9.0%	42%
ROPER INDUSTRIES Operates in three segments: industrial controls, fluid handling, and analytical instrumentation.	16.3×	0.75	0.9%	15.5%	39%
TECUMSEH PRODUCTS Manufactures compressors, condensers, and pumps for commercial, industrial, and agricultural applications. Foreign sales and exports totaled 43% of 1999 sales.	7.0×	0.65	3.0%	8.5%	1%
THOMAS INDUSTRIES Leading manufacturer of compressors and vacuum pumps.	10.7×	0.85	1.6%	9.5%	16%
WATTS INDUSTRIES Designs, manufactures, and sells an extensive line of valves for the plumbing & heating and water-quality markets.	10.4×	nmf	2.9	14.0	36

nmf = not meaningful figure.
Source of data: *Value Line Investment Survey,* 5 May 2000.

EXHIBIT 9 | Information on Selected Recent Merger & Acquisition Transactions in the Industrial Machinery and Aerospace Sectors

Effective Date	Acquirer	Business	Target	Business	Transaction Size ($mm)	Target Net Sales Last 12 Months ($mm)	Equity Value/Target Net Income	Equity Value/Target Book Value	Enterprise Value/Target Net Sales	Enterprise Value/Target Operating Income	Enterprise Value/Target Cash Flow	Enterprise Value/Net Income	Premium (Discount) 4 Weeks Prior to Announcement Date
10/20/2000	General Electric Co.	Electrical, construction	Honeywell Int'l. Inc.	Aerospace, automotive	45,204.7	31,052.0	24.70	4.8	1.61	16.85	11.98	27.36	54.63
6/11/1999	United Technologies Corp.	Aircraft engines, defense	Sundstrand Corp.	Aerospace, industrial equip.	4,408.3	2,024.0	16.70	6.8	2.13	11.40	9.37	18.66	54.08
12/15/1999	AlliedSignal Inc.	Aircraft engines, radar	Tristar Aerospace Co.	Aerospace hardware	269.8	205.1	10.00	2.7	1.37	7.92	7.49	15.52	65.22
7/10/2000	Meritor Automotive Inc.	Car, truck equipment	Arvin Industries Inc.	Auto parts, accessories	1,138.4	3,010.3	7.50	1.1	0.38	8.99	4.84	14.37	22.20
10/12/2000	DaimlerChrysler AG	Automobiles and trucks	Detroit Diesel	Diesel, alternative engines	581.2	2,256.2	12.20	1.3	0.29	8.48	5.22	14.78	77.78
8/19/1999	Goldman Industrial Group	Metal-working machinery	Bridgeport Machines	Metal-cutting tools	57.0	197.0	29.00	0.8	0.37	11.40	9.37	18.66	53.85
2/24/2000	Siemens Energy & Automation	Electronic parts	Moore Products Corp.	Control instruments	168.6	168.9	63.00	2.5	0.96	26.76	15.53	62.08	79.38
6/17/1999	TI Group PLC	Metal products	Walbro Corp.	Fuel system components	630.3	697.4	19.80	4.0	0.79	13.44	7.14	44.87	na
6/19/2000	Ingersoll-Rand Co.	Industrial machinery	Hussmann Int'l. Inc.	Refrigeration systems	1,837.2	1,306.8	27.30	7.2	1.45	15.24	12.48	33.01	109.95

na = not available.
Source of data: Thomson Financial's *SDC Platinum*.

EXHIBIT 10 | Capital Market Interest Rates and Stock Price Indexes (average percentage per annum except for May 1, 2000, which offers closing prices)

	1997	1998	1999	May 1, 2000
U.S. Treasury Yields				
3-month bills	5.06%	4.78%	4.64%	6.60%
30-year bonds	6.61%	5.58%	5.87%	5.98%
Corporate Bond Yields by Rating				
Aaa	7.27%	6.53%	7.05%	8.67%
Aa	7.48%	6.80%	7.36%	9.15%
A	7.54%	6.93%	7.53%	9.35%
Baa	7.87%	7.22%	7.88%	9.60%
Stock Market				
S&P 500 Index	873	1,085	1,327	1,481
Price/earnings ratio	15.9×	17.4×	19.4×	18.8×
Industrial Machinery Stocks				
Price/earnings ratio	12.9×	13.9×	14.9×	15.0×
Dividend yield	1.8%	1.5%	1.6%	1.6%

N.B.: The geometric average equity market-risk premium for the period 1926–1999 was about 5.5%. The arithmetic average equity market-risk premium for that period was about 7.2%.

Sources of data: *Value Line Investment Survey,* 5 May 2000; *Federal Reserve Bulletin,* April 2000; *Wall Street Journal,* 2 May 2000.

Chrysler Corporation: Negotiations between Daimler and Chrysler

In January 1998, Jürgen Schrempp, chief executive officer (CEO) of Daimler-Benz A.G., approached Chrysler Corporation's chairman and CEO, Robert Eaton, about a possible merger, acquisition, or deep strategic alliance between their two firms. As Schrempp argued:

> The two companies are a perfect fit of two leaders in their respective markets. Both companies have dedicated and skilled work forces and successful products, but in different markets and different parts of the world. By combining and utilizing each other's strengths, we will have a preeminent strategic position in the global marketplace for the benefit of our customers. We will be able to exploit new markets, and we will improve return and value for our shareholders.[1]

Schrempp recounted later:

> I just presented the case, and I was out again. The meeting lasted about 17 minutes. I don't want to create the impression that he was surprised. When the meeting was over, I said, "If you think I'm naïve, this is nonsense I'm talking, just tell me." He smiled and said, "Just give me a chance. We have done some evaluation as well, and I will phone you in the next two weeks." I think he phoned me in a week or so.[2]

Independently Eaton had concluded that some type of combination of Chrysler with another major automobile firm was needed. The firm was currently financially

[1] Press release, Daimler-Benz A.G., 6 May 1998.

[2] "Gentlemen, Start Your Engines," *Fortune* (8 June 1998): 140.

This case was prepared from public information by Robert F. Bruner, Petra Christmann, and Robert Spekman and with the assistance of Brian Kannry and Melinda Davis. It is intended to be used in a negotiation exercise with "Daimler-Benz A.G.: Negotiations between Daimler and Chrysler" (Case 54 in Instructor's Manual). The financial support of the Darden Partnership Program and the Darden School Foundation is gratefully acknowledged. Copyright © 1998 by the University of Virginia Darden School Foundation, Charlottesville, VA. All rights reserved. *To order copies, send an e-mail to* sales@dardenpublishing.com. *No part of this publication may be reproduced, stored in a retrieval system, used in a spreadsheet, or transmitted in any form or by any means—electronic, mechanical, photocopying, recording, or otherwise—without the permission of the Darden School Foundation.* Rev. 12/01.

healthy, but industry overcapacity and huge prospective investment outlays called for an even larger type of global competitor. Before seeing Schrempp, Eaton had polled investment bankers for their ideas about a major automotive merger, and had spoken with executives from BMW on this topic.

Eaton replied positively to Schrempp's idea of an industrial combination. Now the task of forging the details of the agreement to combine lay ahead. Robert Eaton appointed a small task force of business executives and lawyers to represent Chrysler in the detailed negotiations. Eaton challenged this team on several counts: exploit the benefits of combination; preserve and strengthen the Chrysler brands; minimize the adverse effects of combination on employees and executives; and maximize shareholder value. Eaton reflected on the variety of terms the Chrysler team might seek and immediately convened a meeting to begin planning the team's negotiation strategy. Eaton said,

> My number one criterion is that [any deal] has got to be a long-term upside with no negative short-term impact. It's got to be good for the shareholders. That's my—and my board's—fiduciary responsibility.[3]

Chrysler Corporation

In 1920, Walter P. Chrysler, a multimillionaire and the president of Buick at age 45, stormed out of the head office of General Motors with the idea of starting his own car company. The Chrysler Corporation was officially launched in 1924 with the introduction of the Chrysler Six and rapidly grew to become the third largest automaker in America. While Chrysler managed to survive the Great Depression intact, labor problems and rampant mismanagement brought the company to the brink of financial ruin multiple times (e.g., 1956, 1965, and 1993), but most notably in 1980. Under the leadership of Lee Iacocca and with the support of federal loan guarantees, Chrysler managed to turn itself around one more time, returning to profitability in 1982. While the late 1980s proved tough for the industry as a whole, the introduction and meteoric rise of the family minivan (a market controlled 47 percent by Chrysler as of 1996), coupled with the 1987 acquisition and subsequent exploitation of the Jeep brand name, left Chrysler the envy of the U.S. auto market by the mid-1990s. As *Fortune* magazine stated in late 1996, "If a vehicle is in demand and generates high profit margins, you can bet Chrysler's making it."[4] While Chrysler's success and relatively conservative management style attracted praise from industry observers, it also attracted the attention of Las Vegas billionaire Kirk Kerkorian, who with the help of retired Lee Iacocca, mounted a hostile bid for Chrysler in 1995. The (U.S. dollar) $55 per share ($27.50 today following a 2-for-1 stock split in 1996) not only failed to win the approval of Chrysler's board, but also turned out to be largely unfinanced, leaving Chrysler to continue under its current management.

---

[3]John Pepper, "Why Eaton Cut the Deal," *Detroit News,* 7 May 1998, http://www.detnews.com.

[4]Susan E. Kuhn, "Auto Stocks: Today's Big Steal," *Fortune* (25 November 1996): 204–205.

Chrysler Products

Chrysler focused heavily on trucks in its product offering. In 1997, trucks, including minivans, accounted for about two-thirds of Chrysler's vehicle sales in the United States and cars accounted for about one-third. Chrysler's trucks included sport-utility vehicles, such as the Jeep Wrangler, Jeep Cherokee, and the Dodge Durango; pick-up trucks such as the Dodge Ram; and minivans such as the Plymouth Voyager.

One of Chrysler's most successful products was the minivan, which Chrysler invented in 1983. Dodge Caravan/Plymouth Voyager, the world's most successful minivan, was first introduced in 1984. Chrysler had dominated the segment ever since. In 1997, minivans accounted for about one-third of Chrysler's truck sales. Chrysler's profitability was high in the sport-utility market despite increased competition from new products, especially at the top and bottom ends of the market.

Chrysler's cars were sold under the Chrysler, Dodge, and Plymouth brand names. Chrysler's larger cars (such as the Stratus) were priced similarly to those of Mercedes-Benz's lower-middle class cars (in size), namely the C-Class. While Chrysler's cars were much larger and more powerful than the Mercedes of comparable price, they lacked Mercedes's attention to detail in manufacturing and brand image. At the bottom end of the range, Chrysler offered the Dodge/Plymouth Neon.

Chrysler's Product Development and Manufacturing Strategy

Chrysler was best known for its short cycle of concept-to-market for new products, low development costs, efficient plants, good supplier relations, and creative styling. Vehicle development time for Chrysler declined to 24 months in 1996 from 60 months in 1988. The efficiency in the product development process could be mainly attributed to platform teams—autonomous groups that consisted of all the professionals required to design and produce a new car—which were introduced by Chrysler in 1989. Chrysler's innovation was to put all the engineers and designers assigned to a specific project together on a single floor, along with representatives of marketing, finance, purchasing, and even outside suppliers, and to grant them considerable autonomy. Close contact kept the teams fast and efficient. The teams used target pricing, in which the cost of the car was determined at the beginning of the process, not the end. Chrysler had consistently performed better than its target time and budget goals. The system worked so well that in 1991 Chrysler dissolved most of its functional groups and reassigned its members to four platform teams—small car, large car, minivan, and Jeep/truck. Harbour & Associates, a consulting firm in Troy, Michigan, estimated that Chrysler's research and development (R&D) costs per vehicle were $550, compared to over $2,000 per vehicle for Mercedes.

Since 1989, Chrysler had narrowed its supplier base from 2,500 companies to 1,140 and had fundamentally changed the way it worked with those that remained. Suppliers were offered long-term contracts, were involved in the design process for new cars, and were encouraged to make cost-saving suggestions through an initiative called SCORE (supplier cost reduction effort) introduced in 1989. This initiative yielded $2.5 billion in savings from its inception until mid-1998.[5] As a result, Chrysler was the least vertically integrated of the big three U.S. automakers. It purchased 75 percent of its components, versus 50 percent at Ford and 30 percent at GM in early 1998.[6]

Unlike other U.S. auto manufacturers, which had improved the bottom line almost entirely by cutting costs, Chrysler's profits surged by introducing new models. Its vehicle lineup was known as one of the most innovative in the industry. The LH series (Chrysler Concorde, Dodge Intrepid, and Eagle Vision), introduced in the 1993 model year, was Chrysler's first new car platform in a decade. These cars were very well received in the marketplace and were largely credited as being a major factor contributing to Chrysler's latest turnaround.

Chrysler's International Strategy

In the 1990s, Chrysler substantially internationalized its sales. International vehicle sales (i.e., outside North America) rose from less than 50,000 units in 1990 to 237,060 units in 1997, but were still accounting for less than 10 percent of Chrysler's total unit sales. The Jeep name was invaluable to Chrysler's gradual international spread, due to the appeal and name recognition the Jeep enjoyed in large parts of the world. Chrysler's American Motors acquisition in 1987 included Jeep.

Latin America was a focus of Chrysler's geographic expansion. Sales of its products increased by more than 100 percent in this region from 1996 to 1997. Venezuela, with retail sales of 20,716 units, was the number one Latin American market for Chrysler, making Chrysler fourth in market share in that country behind Toyota, GM, and Ford. The automaker produced the Jeep Grand Cherokee and Cherokee sport-utility vehicles, and the Neon passenger car at its Carabobo Assembly Plant in Valencia, Venezuela, for local distribution and export to Colombia and Ecuador. In 1998, Chrysler planned to open a new 950,000-square-meter manufacturing facility in Curitiba, Brazil, to assemble the Dodge Dakota pickup truck, adding Jeep Cherokee production to the Cordoba plant in Argentina, opening a parts warehouse/technical training center in Buenos Aires, Argentina, and breaking ground on a $500 million joint venture engine plant with BMW in Brazil. (The 40,000-square-meter engine plant was to be an adjacent facility to the Dodge Dakota assembly plant.) Because the range of import duties for Venezuela, Argentina, and Brazil was 60 to 70 percent, Chrysler opted to produce vehicles in those countries, contrasting with a general preference to establish an international presence via importing its domestically produced vehicles.

Chrysler had been completely absent from Europe for many years. Since it came back in 1990, it was very successful with the Voyager, which was built in Graz, Austria, for the European market. However, Chrysler was far from the leadership position it had in the U.S. minivan market. Leading minivan manufacturers in Europe were Ford and

---

[5]Debra Walker, "Supply Chain Collaboration Saved Chrysler $2.5 Billion and Counting," *Supply Chain Management* (August 1998): 60.

[6]These data are drawn from a table titled "Estimated Levels of Integration and Production Parts Purchasing," *Automotive News Europe*, 19 January 1998.

Volkswagen (VW), which accounted for about one-third of European minivan sales in 1997, and Renault, which surpassed Ford and Volkswagen in 1998 by adding the stretched Grand Espace to its product line. Ford and Volkswagen sold three basically identical models—Ford Galaxy, VW Sharan, and Seat Alhambra—produced in a joint venture factory in Portugal. Chrysler's overall market share in Europe was still only 0.7 percent in 1997, partly due to the lack of car models for the European market. The Vision/Concorde/Intrepid was too large for Europe, the Stratus had attracted mainly buyers for the four- to-five-passenger convertible, and the Neon had too many popular European competitors. Another primary reason for Chrysler's comparatively modest impact on the European market was its still rather thin sales network.

Daimler-Benz A.G.

Gottlieb Daimler and Karl Benz were two German rival carmakers at the turn of the previous century. While both Daimler and Benz achieved individual success in the early 1900s, the challenge of rebuilding Germany after World War I, as well as competing with the burgeoning Ford Motor Company, led the two companies to merge in 1926 to form Daimler-Benz. While the company shifted to military production during World War II, Daimler began manufacturing cars again in 1947. By the 1980s, Daimler and its Mercedes brand had become synonymous with premier quality and craftsmanship. Flush with success, Daimler began a program of diversification in the mid-1980s, intending to transform the company into a self-described "integrated technology group," with product lines ranging from transportation to aerospace to microelectronics to white goods. Unfortunately, a string of largely unprofitable acquisitions in the late 1980s left Daimler unfocused and inefficient, culminating in a staggering (German deutsche marks) DEM5.7 billion loss for 1995 (the largest peacetime loss ever by a German company). Under the direction of new chief executive, Jürgen Schrempp, Daimler began to shed unprofitable business units, to return the company to its core business of making high quality automobiles, and to move towards a more "American-style" management designed to enhance shareholder value. By 1997, the company had returned to profitability on record sales.

Daimler-Benz Diversification under Reuter

Under chairman Edzard Reuter, who took office in 1987, Daimler undertook a series of acquisitions, amounting to an estimated $6.2 billion, that turned Daimler-Benz into one of the world's biggest industrial conglomerates. Reuter reorganized the company into a holding structure with four separate companies in 1989: Mercedes for cars and trucks, Dasa for aerospace, Daimler-Benz InterServices (Debis) for financial and computer services, and AEG for engineering. To refocus the company from defense to civilian aircraft, Dasa, under the leadership of Jürgen Schrempp, acquired 51 percent of the money-losing Dutch Fokker Company, a maker of short- and intermediate-range propeller and jet passenger planes, in 1993.

During Reuter's chairmanship, Gerhard Liener, Daimler's chief financial officer (CFO), pushed for a listing of the company on the New York Stock Exchange (NYSE), which necessitated publishing the company's returns under American accounting rules.

These accounting rules required Daimler to report on current operations, which revealed a huge operating loss of $3.3 billion in 1993. Of the four holding companies, only Debis reported a profit. Reuter faced a barrage of criticism, especially as the new companies remained the loss-makers while Mercedes-Benz swung back to big profits in 1994. Jürgen Schrempp replaced Reuter as chairman in 1995.

Jürgen Schrempp

Jürgen Schrempp was born in the western German city of Freiburg in 1944. Following his school education, he joined Daimler as a motor mechanic apprentice at the Mercedes-Benz Freiburg branch in 1967. He later went to the university to train as an engineer and returned to Daimler-Benz. From 1967, Schrempp worked in a number of different areas at Daimler-Benz. In 1974, he was appointed to the management team of the South African subsidiary, Mercedes-Benz of South Africa, initially in the service division and after 1980 as the board member responsible for engineering. In 1982, Schrempp took over as president of Euclid, Inc., of Cleveland, Ohio, at the time a 100 percent subsidiary of Daimler-Benz and manufacturer of extremely heavy-duty trucks. Schrempp told headquarters that it would cost too much to fix the unit and recommended its sale. The board took his advice, and after Schrempp successfully divested the unit, he returned as vice president, in 1984, to Mercedes-Benz of South Africa. In 1985, he was appointed president of the South African subsidiary. Two years later, he was called back to Stuttgart to join the Daimler-Benz management board and head the Daimler-Benz aerospace subsidiary. He orchestrated the purchase of the Dutch aircraft maker Fokker, which was part of Reuter's diversification program, a move that later on turned out to be a mistake.

Daimler-Benz Restructuring under Schrempp

When Schrempp took charge, cuts in defense spending were hurting the aerospace unit's military operations. Meanwhile, airlines were canceling commercial aircraft orders to be competitive in the deregulated airline market, thus effectively pinching the Airbus operation. More than 300 supposedly firm orders were cancelled in late 1994 and early 1995. This represented more than half of the company's backlog and the equivalent of about 30 months' production. The worldwide truck business was slumping and the Mercedes auto operations had not yet recovered from the early 1990s onslaughts of Lexus and Infiniti.

During his tenure as chairman, Schrempp proved to be a master of boardroom politics; he could make decisions quickly and was willing to take risks. Schrempp focused on shareholder value, something that was not typically done by European companies. Daimler's top executives were not in the habit of putting stockholders first. To sell the idea of shareholder value, Schrempp started calling colleagues at random and asking them for Daimler's current stock price. At first, he said, "Seven did not know and three were wrong. Nowadays they can tell me." Schrempp instituted the rule that every single business at Daimler had to achieve a 12 percent return on capital (ROC) or be capable of achieving a 12 percent return on capital in the foreseeable future. If it could not, it would be sold. Such a rule was very uncommon for German companies. This rule resulted in a reduction of the total number of businesses from 35 to 23. Major

TABLE 1 | Daimler-Benz Operating Profits and Revenues by Division (in millions of DEM)

	1997		1996	
	Operating Profit	Revenues	Operating Profit	Revenues
Passenger cars	3,132	53,892	3,090	46,652
Commercial vehicles	481	39,140	(354)	32,152
Aerospace	432	15,286	(196)	13,053
Services	457	15,498	288	13,143
Directly managed businesses	(129)	7,555	(585)	8,014

divestitures were the sale of the company's unprofitable electrical engineering business (AEG), and the closure of the aircraft maker, Fokker. In addition, Schrempp demanded superior performance from the rest of the company's units. Despite the resistance of the strong German unions, he reduced the workforce by 10 percent.

In the beginning of 1997, Schrempp reorganized Daimler-Benz into five divisions that contained 23 business units. The divisions were passenger cars, commercial vehicles, aerospace, services, and directly managed businesses (rail systems, automotive electronics, MTU/diesel engines).

Critics in Germany said that Schrempp was a renegade supporter of "Anglo-Saxon" corporate ethics, who put Daimler-Benz's share price before the welfare of workers and disrupted the long-standing social contract between employers and labor by destroying thousands of jobs and squeezing pay and benefits. Schrempp's relations with labor were difficult. His most famous clash with employees came over their sick benefits, which he attempted to cut back in 1996. The decision, not followed by other companies, triggered such an uproar he was forced to back down. On the other hand, Schrempp won praise from investors. So far the results of the restructuring had been impressive. After a record net loss in 1995 of $3.17 billion, one of the biggest annual losses in European corporate history, Daimler posted profits of about $1.6 billion for 1996 and $1.8 billion before a tax credit in 1997.

Daimler-Benz Aerospace Segment

In the aerospace business, Daimler became more productive and efficient. Three of ten plants were closed, and new production methods helped to reduce cycle time between plane order and delivery by 50 percent. Schrempp also decided to stop financing the company's struggling Dutch airline maker, NV Fokker, and write off the entire investment. In the process, Schrempp proved to be a master of boardroom politics. He acknowledged his role in buying the company a few years earlier and asked for a vote of confidence from the board. The board backed him in full. "I am the first top man who has blown out DEM2.3 billion [by investing in 51 percent of Fokker] and who say without a doubt, this was my fault. While other managers have been fired for DEM50 million, I'm still here. And I think I'm not even arrogant—just very self assured."[7]

---

[7]Andrea Rothman and Rupert Spiegelberg, "Flamboyant Daimler Executive Is Famous for His Risk-Taking," *Seattle Times,* 7 May 1998, D1.

In addition, Airbus started a new effort to capture market share from the world leader Boeing. Key to this plan was enlarging the Airbus family of planes, bringing out new models that ate into categories where Boeing now had an effective monopoly. This new strategy, combined with strong airline orders and the weak German mark, resulted in Airbus's recovery. In 1997, orders rose nearly 50 percent to an all-time high of 460 planes, valued at nearly $30 billion, giving Airbus 45 percent of the world market. As a result, Daimler-Benz's aerospace division (Dasa) reported 1997 operating profits of DEM432 million on revenues of DEM15,286 million after posting losses in 1995 and 1996.

Daimler-Benz Commercial-Vehicle Segment

When Schrempp took control, the truck business had been hurt by a combination of weak European markets, fierce price competition from Volvo and Scania, Daimler's outmoded truck and bus designs, and the company's high-cost production methods. In Europe, Daimler addressed these problems through the production of a series of new heavy-duty trucks, lighter trucks, and vans. In addition, the company went head-to-head with its unions, stretching the boundaries of Germany's collective bargaining agreements to the limit to negotiate productivity agreements plant-by-plant.

Many truck operations were relocated to places like Turkey and Brazil, so that roughly half of all Daimler truck production moved outside Germany. Daimler's U.S. truck operation, Freightliner, was in a different position; the company had been boosting market share since the early 1990s. Freightliner's share in the North American market in heavy-duty Class 8 tractor-trailer cabs rose from 23 percent, in 1995, to 29 percent, in 1996, and 30 percent in 1997. The aim was to increase the share to more than 40 percent by 2000. That effort was helped by the 1997 purchase of Ford Heavy Trucks. The decision to buy Ford's heavy-duty truck operations took only two weeks. "Under the previous system it would have taken six to eight months," said Schrempp.[8]

Daimler-Benz Passenger-Car Segment

The automotive division was hurt in the early 1990s by the new luxury cars introduced by Toyota's Lexus, Honda's Acura, and Nissan's Infiniti. These cars compared in quality, comfort, and styling to Mercedes cars, but they cost much less. Part of the price difference was due to exchange rates, which gave the Japanese a temporary advantage. Germany's high labor costs hurt Daimler too. At more than $30 an hour plus benefits, the labor cost was the world's highest. Daimler also suffered from antiquated and inefficient production methods. By one account, while it took 20 hours to build a Lexus, it took between 60 and 80 hours to make a Mercedes. The wakeup call from Japan was not ignored by Mercedes, but there was considerable resistance to change at the top, and progress was slow. One of Schrempp's first moves after being appointed chairman was, like the truck operations, to face down the powerful unions and hammer out new plant contracts that would boost productivity and cut costs.

---

[8]Greg Steinmetz and Brandon Mitchener, "Under Schrempp, Daimler Switches Focus to Cars, Profit," *Wall Street Journal,* 7 May 1998, B1.

Car-Segment Growth Strategy and Models

Mercedes-Benz specialized in top-quality luxury vehicles, and even the company's middle-class cars were choice models, costing more than comparably sized competitors. Schrempp was convinced that, to survive, Mercedes had to grow. Growth, he figured, meant expanding downmarket. The basic aim was to lessen the company's dependence on pricey models like the S-class. Mercedes's strategy was not to enter the mass market, but rather to establish premium niches within every part of it—a niche for people who would pay premium for prestige and perceived quality. In essence, Mercedes was trying to enter the mass market without becoming part of it, a feat Mercedes managed to pull off with its C-class, unveiled in 1982. With that example in mind, Schrempp put his authority behind the M-class sport utility-vehicle, the A-class town car, and the Smart car joint venture with Swatch. In addition to that, he extended the existing product lines in the E-class, the C-class, and the S-class by introducing new models. As Schrempp saw things, the common factor of all the cars was that they served not a mass market but a niche of people who were prepared to pay extra for perceived quality and the Mercedes name. That, he figured, offered some protection from down auto cycles.

The M-class sport-utility vehicle, built in Mercedes's facility in Tuscaloosa, Alabama that had opened in 1997, had a list price starting at about $35,000 and competed with the likes of the Ford Explorer and the Jeep Grand Cherokee. The facility was Mercedes's first major foray into car making outside Germany. The M-class was very successful since its launch in late 1997. In early 1998, a potential buyer had to wait up to eight months for delivery. There were plans to increase the production capacity of the Alabama plant by 20 percent in 1999, from 65,000 to 80,000 units a year, with some designated for export to Europe.

The A-class, a small commuter car that thus far had only been marketed in Europe, was surrounded by controversy from the beginning. It was the least expensive Mercedes to date (at about $14,000), it was small, and had only an 82-horsepower engine. Most of the controversy stemmed from the fact that the car failed to pass the so-called Elk test performed by Swedish auto journalists, a no-brakes, high-speed violent swerve to simulate avoiding a large animal that had wandered out on the highway. The front-wheel-drive car flipped over, threatening Daimler with a huge marketing disaster. Daimler's stock dropped on the news by 25 percent to a low of $63, and the company was forced to back down from blaming the journalists. Schrempp put together a task force of what he called "our most brilliant people" to come up with a solution. Nineteen days later, they released a plan that included a halt on all A-class sales and a change in the car design to lower the chassis, put on wider tires and install "electronic stabilizing runners" on the inside of the wheel, at a cost of $200 million. By January 1998, after the changes had been made, the car passed the test and sales resumed. Daimler estimated that it could sell the 150,000 A-class cars that it could make in a year. After Daimler fixed the problems with the A-class and posted healthy 1997 results, the shares recovered and resumed their ascent. Schrempp knew he was walking a tightrope: "If we make a mistake, it would not only affect the profitability of the A-class, it would have a negative impact on Mercedes generally."[9] By 1999,

---

[9]Paul Klebnikov, "Mercedes-Benz' Bold Niche Strategy," *Forbes* (8 September 1997): 68.

TABLE 2 | Daimler-Benz Passenger-Car Sales, 1997

			Units (000)	% Change from 1996	Price Category
World			715	11	
	A-class		7		$14,000
	C-class		349	24	$35,000
		CLK	22		$40,000
		SLK	47		
	E-class		277	−5	
	S-/SL-class		63	−8	$65,000
	M-class		16		$34,000
	G-class		3	−23	
Europe			477	8	
Western Europe (excluding Germany)			194	11	
Germany			277	5	
North America			130	40	
USA (retail sales)			122	35	
Latin America			7	11	
Far East (excluding Japan)			28	−7	
Japan (new registrations)			42	2	
Middle East			9	1	
Republic of South Africa			12	−18	

Mercedes hoped to be producing 200,000 A-class vehicles in Germany and another 70,000 in a new $400 million plant in Brazil.

The Smart car, being built by Daimler, was the product of an 81/19 percent joint venture of Daimler-Benz and SMH A.G., the Swiss maker of Swatch watches. The car was a tiny two-seater designed for city use. It was never expected to sell in the United States. This car would be built in a new factory in France, with an annual capacity of 200,000 units.

Daimler had also introduced a stream of new models, including the new E-class, wagons for the C-class, and the new SLK, a small roadster, which had a steel roof that retracted into the trunk. This car, which was selling at $40,000, followed BMW's Z3 and Porsche's Boxster to open up a completely new sports-car niche in the United States—somewhere between the $20,000 Mazda Miata and a $70,000 Porsche 911. The SLK pursued a more youthful image for Mercedes. Waiting lists for this car were as long as two years in the middle of 1997. In 1997, Daimler introduced its CLK coupe, followed by a CLK convertible. In 1998, Daimler was expected to introduce an all-new luxury S-class model, followed perhaps in 2001 or 2002 by the Maybach, an even more luxurious car that (the prototype suggested) could come with such features as a hot-and-cold drink bar, an in-car personal computer, and a large-screen TV.

Passenger-car sales by model and by geographic area are shown in **Table 2.**

In 1997, global automotive sales increased by only 3 percent; however, Daimler sales increased by 11 percent, one of the biggest increases of any major automaker. This success was primarily due to the market success of the new vehicles and favorable exchange rates.

TABLE 3 | Daimler-Benz Vehicle Operations by Geographic Area

	Production Locations	Sales Organization Locations	Revenues (in millions DEM)	Personnel
Europe	21	3,435	55,966	171,778
North America	10	655	19,190	15,321
South America	4	468	4,683	13,128
Africa	3	272	3,077	3,815
Australia/Oceania	1	186	1,044	682
Asia	7	931	7,672	2,618

Daimler-Benz Car-Segment Design and Production

To achieve its goal of producing cheaper cars without penalizing profitability, Daimler was breaking the rules on how to succeed in the auto business. Conventional wisdom suggested that automakers should reduce the number of different platforms on which they built its different chassis. That was what Toyota, Chrysler, and VW had done. But Mercedes was producing a new platform for each of its new car lines and expected money on each at a production level that was below the breakeven point for the bigger full-line manufacturers. By sharing platforms "it is certainly cost-effective, but I don't think it's the way to do it. If you just put a different body on the same base, all you are doing is fooling customers. That's not the way to win sales," said Schrempp.[10] Daimler-Benz reduced its level of vertical integration, but at 40 percent, Daimler was still more vertically integrated than Chrysler at 25 percent.

Daimler-Benz Car Segment's International Strategy

Daimler sold its cars worldwide and had a global distribution network. As depicted in **Table 3,** Daimler was also increasingly locating automotive production outside Germany. More than two-thirds of Daimler's total revenues originated outside Germany, and more than one-third of its stock was held internationally.

Ownership of Daimler-Benz Equity

Deutsche Bank had cut its interest in Daimler from 28 to 21.7 percent. Deutsche Bank had at times taken the lead in strategic decisions at Daimler. It engineered the appointment of Edzard Reuter as chairman of Daimler's management board in 1987, and supported Daimler's diversification strategy in the 1980s. German institutional investors held about 48 percent of Daimler's shares. The Emirate of Kuwait owned about 13 percent.

Unlike the single boards found in the United States, German companies had a management board (*Vorstand*), composed solely of executives charged with a company's day-to-day operations, and a supervisory board (*Aufsichtsrat*), which represented a company's largest shareholders and its workers and oversaw the management board. The system gave each board certain checks and balances so that neither dominated the firm.

---

[10] Jay Palmer, "Shake-Up Artist: Daimler-Benz Chairman Jürgen Schrempp Has Knocked the Dust off Mercedes, Restoring Hope for European Manufacturers," *Barrons* (23 March 1998): 35.

Daimler-Benz Labor Unions

Germany had a dual system of worker representation. At the company level, workers had the right to participate in management decisions. Under the German system of codetermination, almost half of the seats of the Aufsichtsrat had to be filled with labor representatives in large enterprises. While they could be outvoted in the Aufsichtsrat, their access to information and decision making gave them a stronger hand in labor negotiations. Worker councils (*Betriebsräte*) also represented the interests of the workers at the company level. They had a voice in social and personnel matters.

At the national level, 17 large labor unions, which were organized on an industry basis, were primarily responsible for industry-wide collective bargaining of wages and salaries and other matters, such as shortening the workweek and vacation time. IG Metall, the powerful metalworkers union, which had 2.7 million members, represented automobile industry workers.

Compared with other countries, the collective bargaining process for wages was accompanied by relatively few strikes in Germany. Reasons contributing to this low strike rate were the existing conflict-resolution mechanisms; German labor law, which obliged management and labor groups to seek peaceful solutions to conflicts; and generally cooperative relationships between capital and labor.

Executive Compensation

Compensation for German executives was significantly lower than for their American counterparts. Executive pay in German firms had to be reviewed by the supervisory board of a company. In addition, German companies were not required to disclose executive pay to the same extent as U.S. companies (by the U.S. Securities and Exchange Commission). Daimler disclosed pay only on an aggregate basis, and reported that, in 1997, the 10 executives on the management board received total remuneration of DEM20 million,[11] or $11.3 million at a recent exchange rate of DEM1.77 to the dollar. Schrempp currently made about $2.5 million a year. In comparison, Chrysler chairman and CEO Robert Eaton made $16 million in 1997.

Under Schrempp, Daimler was the first German company to offer stock options to its executives. The union members on the supervisory board opposed Schrempp's decision to offer stock options to management, but he prevailed on an 11-to-9 vote within the board. Another proposal, to create an incentive pay plan that rewarded employees based on their contribution to overall profits, passed more easily. All 150,000 Mercedes workers would qualify for a bonus.

Trends In the Global Automobile Industry

As of early 1998, recent events suggested that the competitive landscape of the automobile industry had changed permanently. While the announcement of alliances and mergers was a steady occurrence over the years, the nature and frequency of these

---

[11]Daimler-Benz 1997 Annual Report, 80.

deals had become more intense. Price Waterhouse estimated that, worldwide in 1997, auto firms struck 750 mergers or alliances, with a total value of $28 billion. Consistent with both the airlines and the telecommunications industries, there was a more assertive attempt to consolidate players in the industry, thereby creating a new form of competition—the truly global car company. Only a small number of automakers (e.g., Toyota, VW, Ford, and GM) had the capability to go global without major acquisitions. These first-tier firms could pursue a worldwide strategy by buying smaller producers with recognized name brands. The mantra became, "If you wish to succeed, you have to be worldwide." Standard & Poor's DRI predicted that, over the next 10 years, there would be a reduction in the number of international producers, with the current 39 being reduced to about 20 major companies.

Car manufacturers had been operating internationally for many years. They had exported models to other countries, assembled and engineered cars and trucks for foreign markets, and sourced from non-U.S. suppliers for years. In addition, these firms had taken equity stakes in numerous foreign partners. The list included, for example, Ford and Jaguar, Ford and Mazda, GM and Saab, GM and Suzuki, and BMW and Rover. Yet efforts to form truly global companies were different. Simply put, there were few successes at building and distributing a *global car*. The motivations driving Chrysler and Daimler-Benz extended beyond the development of a global car. Typically, consolidation was driven by a series of factors.

These factors were responses to the pressures of a dynamic, changing industry. It was too simple to say that the world was changing. There were relentless cost and time pressures, where the design and introduction of new and innovative models had to be completed in shorter time periods and less expensively. Adding to the complexity was the fact that consumer tastes were changing, the Internet lowered barriers to information transfer, product introduction, and commonality among processes, and products became the path to the bottom line.[12] At the extreme, there was talk about the era of the virtual customer who was integrated into a manufacturing process that was fed by global suppliers and that fed into worldwide distribution. However, there were a number of recent trends that appeared to lie at the heart of the recent consolidation wave.

Overcapacity

The industry was plagued by excess capacity. Through consolidation, assembly plants could be rationalized; carmakers in Western Europe already had the capacity to produce 30 percent more cars than they could sell.[13] The result was idle equipment, wasted investments, underutilized workers, and subnormal returns. The tension around these conditions created the political pressure against shutting domestic plants, laying off workers, and searching for lower-cost labor and manufacturing sites in developing countries. Ironically, this movement of manufacturing to developing countries partly exacerbated the problem of excess capacity. Many of the plants (for example, those in Asia)

---

[12]David Smith, "US Automakers Take a New Spin; the World Has Changed and So Have They," *Ward's Auto World* 34, no. 3: 38.

[13] Anne Swardson, "European Carmakers' Traffic Jam," *Washington Post*, 10 September 1998, C1.

had been built with the government's blessing as an attempt to promote manufacturing and create fairly high-paying jobs, not to mention that a home-grown auto industry was a matter of national pride. Emerging economies, such as Brazil, saw an automotive industry as a means to increase its ability to export products and stimulate internal growth. Yet a number of the smaller companies in Asia particularly were at risk, like Kia and Hyundai. While not acquisition targets per se, both were likely to be sought as joint venture partners. Many believed that the consolidation would take out capacity, which in turn would reduce the pricing pressures caused by the worldwide excess production capacity.

Development Costs

The costs associated with all aspects of new model development made it very difficult for a small manufacturer to survive, since these costs were allocated over a smaller volume of cars. Development costs included design and tooling, emissions engineering, electronics, and manufacturing process design. Other nonproduction costs associated with manufacturing included the expense of linking suppliers and dealers electronically and on a global basis. Attempts to shorten the production and the design cycles would pay off over time but also require a substantial initial investment. A dramatic redesign of a car could include the use of lighter weight materials, the use of alternative fuel sources, and changes to both the engine and the braking system. The price tag for these changes would worry even the largest companies.

Sourcing and Supply-Chain Costs

In part, the consolidation in the industry was driven by a desire to lower the costs of purchased materials by combining purchasing functions and exercising greater power as a result. Typically, firms attempted to reap price concessions from suppliers based on sheer volume. Beyond the savings that accrued through volume, there were gains to be made in the use of common parts. When Chrysler began purchasing the same air-bag part from Robert Bosch (who previously supplied Mercedes), the cost to both fell 40 percent, since Bosch could now justify dedicated production in Mexico. Smart sourcing also had a component that affected the revenue side of the equation: By working more closely with key suppliers, carmakers could leverage their suppliers' expertise and other sources of competitive advantage. Honda, for example, attributed significant gains in its ability to design and produce new models at lower costs to the input and expertise of its key suppliers.

Market Access and Product Diversity

The ability of niche manufacturers to survive over the long term was limited by both geography and the narrow focus of their product lines. At the core of merger discussions in the automotive industry of the 1990s was the notion of complementarity and the potential partners' ability to fill gaps in both markets and products. One assumption was that only full product line, global producers would survive. Market access was affected by both existing distribution networks and the national policy dictating the manner in which a foreign automaker might enter the host country. In some instances, local production might be required, or there might be rules regarding a certain percentage of local content in the cars sold. Although the merger failed, part of the rationale for the Volvo-Renault marriage was a complementarity in market presence. In addition, the products lines did not overlap much and on the surface seemed to fill gaps in the other's offerings. BMW was attracted to Rover because its products broadened its product offering without diluting the upmarket BMW image with smaller cars and sports-utility vehicles. BMW's strategy was to encourage Rover's *Britishness* with big investments in the United Kingdom, while sharing parts and improving quality and distribution.[14]

Legal and Financial Considerations

It was likely that the consolidation among companies would provide access to capital and capital markets that might have been limited because of either regional biases or size considerations. To be global in scope and size not only bestowed more favorable rates on the issuance of stock or debt, but also broadened the range of available financial markets. For instance, as a benefit of consolidation, a foreign-based company might trade in the United States as a global stock rather than through the use of American depositary receipts (ADRs) that carry both complex regulatory issues and often added expense. The point was that such global firms set the pace for the globalization of the equity markets. In addition, a second-order effect was the governance structure of the newly consolidated company and the question of which country's laws would take precedence. There might be less governmental control and say in how the newly formed global firm behaved as compared to when the individual companies were separate entities. To some extent, competing on the world scene might reduce the regulatory power/influence of local national governments.

For Chrysler and Daimler-Benz, there were a number of gains to be achieved through their merger. **Table 4** summarizes the advantages to both. The question remained whether each gained equally. Although Schrempp and Eaton contemplated a merger of equals, creating the third largest automaker in the world, Daimler-Benz might appear to be the more senior partner because of its size.

Strategic Alternatives

As companies examined the options available to them to join forces and attempted to accomplish goals that would be difficult to achieve alone, there were a number of alternatives to consider. The automotive industry in recent years had witnessed a number of alliances (some in which equity stakes were taken and others where there was no exchange of ownership), joint ventures, mergers, and acquisitions.

Mergers

In a merger, companies (such as Chrysler and Daimler-Benz) agreed to an exchange of stock that resulted in the joint ownership of a new company. Typically, the two

---

[14] Brandon Mitchener, "BMW-Rover Deal Offers Clues to Future Daimler-Benz," *Wall Street Journal Interactive,* 29 May 1998.

TABLE 4 | Potential Benefits to Both Chrysler and Daimler-Benz

Benefits to Chrysler	Shared Benefits	Benefits to Daimler-Benz
• Boosts nonexistent position in Europe • Improved quality from Daimler-Benz engineering • Gives a European manufacturing base • Might gain from luster of Mercedes name plate • Broadens line to luxury end • Uses some production capacity around the world • Improves technical capability, lowers warranty costs • Improved safety features available	• $1.4 billion in pretax cost savings, expected in 1999; expected to grow to $3.0 billion in 2001 and to grow at rate of inflation thereafter • Purchasing power • Better capacity utilization • Technology transfer	• Expands manufacturing and dealership operations in U.S. • Creates opportunity for joint development, at lower costs • Expands production ability in the U.S. • Combines with trucks, the lighter lines from Chrysler • Helps align cost structure • Borrows creative styling • Jeep adds to the image for sports-utility vehicle (urban and rugged)

companies, in a friendly exchange of stock, combined to achieve cost savings through the elimination of redundant facilities and other mechanisms through which cost savings were gained. In addition, they often pursued opportunities that would be hard to achieve alone. Schrempp and Eaton expected, for example, to realize pretax cost savings of $1.4 billion in 1999 through the exchange of components and technology, combined purchasing, and shared distribution networks. Eaton's staff believed that these synergies would grow to $3.0 billion by 2001 and grow at the rate of inflation in the U.S. dollar thereafter. (These synergies are *not* reflected in the exhibits that accompany this case.) There were also a number of other benefits that resulted from learning by both partners from each other and incorporating the best practices of both in the merged company.

Alliances

Unlike a merger, an alliance combined separate companies for the purposes of the collaborative efforts delineated by the partners. However, the separate organizations remained autonomous businesses, each retaining its own governance structure and operating processes and principles. Joint activities, shared decision making, coordination of activities, open lines of communications, etc. were all part of the glue that held the alliance together.

An alliance was a quasi-organizational form in which separate and distinct firms joined to accomplish goals that would be difficult to achieve alone. The challenge was to develop a management process to encourage the joint cooperative efforts of the partners. To the extent that one entered an alliance with a traditional "command and control" mentality, one would find that it could be difficult to accomplish one's ends. One cannot control what one does not own.

Alliances, if properly formed and nurtured, could accomplish the same goals as one might in a vertically integrated firm, without the added cost burden. Alliances were collaborative ventures in which companies acknowledged their interdependence and acted in the interest of the alliance. Unlike a merged or acquired entity, there remained the possibility of opportunistic behavior whereby one partner acted in its own self-interest to the detriment of the other. That is, alliance partners had multiple tasks: they worked together to accomplish joint goals but also maintained individual agendas and objectives. When these different goals conflicted, the alliance suffered and the proposed advantages were lost. In this regard alliances were quite fragile and subject to pressures and tensions not found in ventures where two or more firms relinquished their sovereignty to become one centrally managed and controlled organization with one set of goals. Although alliance contracts were likely to be used to formalize the terms and conditions of the relationship, alliances were held together by trust and commitment to the shared vision of the alliance partners.

Joint Ventures

Joint ventures (JVs) were another form of alliance in which partners joined selected assets and formed a separate entity, which became jointly owned by the partners. One primary difference between JV alliances and the alliance forms discussed above were the degree of embeddedness between the partners. JV partners committed resources (e.g., people, factories, dollars, technology) and these assets became commingled in the joint venture; thus, their ability to exit the relationship was often more tedious. Also, joint ventures tended to have more formal agreements between partners, based mainly on the fact that partners had formally commingled assets in this newly formed separate entity.

There was a joint governance structure for the JV that was jointly administered by the partners, depending on their equity-sharing agreement. While most managers believed they would prefer to be the dominant shareholder (e.g., equity interest in excess of 50 percent), there was a compelling argument for equal equity-sharing joint ventures. This argument was based on the belief that equal shares in the JV would lead to greater commitment and a willingness on the part of the partners to work hard to overcome problems in the JV. Again, the elements of trust and commitment were important and served to complement the joint-venture agreement that nominally set the structure of the relationship.

Joint-venture partners sometimes struggled in their ability to determine equitably the value of each partner's contribution to the alliance. For example, one partner might bring hard assets to the JV and the other would bring intellectual capabilities (e.g., innovations, technology, knowledge of markets). The problem became how to determine a fair exchange rate. Simply, the question might arise: How many new ideas equal a factory worth $5 million converted to the needs of the joint venture?

Preferred Relationships

Of the four relationship types discussed here, preferred relationships was the least formal and therefore the most volatile in the sense that it was viewed as more transactional in nature and more subject to the whims of the partners. Ties and linkages tended to be loose and viewed as less long term in nature. For instance, parties might decide to trade with each other, and might do so for many years. However, the level of communication and the content of information shared never went beyond the transaction at hand. In an

TABLE 5 | An Array of Relationships

	← Low	Ownership	High →		
Commitment HIGH Long-term focus	Strategic Sourcing		Joint Ventures	Joint Venture	Acquisition Merger
↑	Evergreen contracts	Just-in-time and standard outsourcing	R&D partnerships to co-develop	Co-manufacturing/ production	
↓	Preferred suppliers	Reseller relationships	Shared info about markets R&D		
Commitment LOW Short-term focus	Commodity purchasing order	Collaborative advertising			
Degree of commitment	Loose linkages	Standard resources	Shared funds	Shared equity	Wholly owned

alliance, as opposed to these more arms-length dealings, partners tended to exchange information germane to longer-term plans and strategic requirements over time.

Preferred relationships suggested that, all things being equal, partners would continue to interact but there was a much less episodic nature to the relationship. Commitment to the relationship tended to be lower than in any of the other relationships mentioned above. These kinds of relationships were often found between buyers and suppliers where one was given the status of a preferred supplier by virtue of certain standards being met (e.g., certification and ISO9002). In addition, there might exist a long-term relationship through which both parties shared a degree of comfort and trust. At the same time, the ability to disengage was relatively easy to do both because of the nature of the linkages and the fact that the psychological bonds between partners was relatively low.

Table 5 compares the various relationship types discussed here. Chrysler's negotiation team would need to assess these alternative forms of combination, giving particular attention to the relative attractiveness of the outright acquisition of Chrysler by Daimler versus the other types of deals. Schrempp had specifically mentioned an acquisition; it was Robert Eaton's expectation that the negotiating team would seriously explore this path as a first course of action. But ultimately, Chrysler's board of directors would want some justification for why outright acquisition dominated other types of deals as a way to exploit the benefits of combination.

History of the Merger Discussions[15]

At the Detroit International Auto Show in mid-January 1998, Jürgen Schrempp, CEO of Daimler-Benz, visited with Robert Eaton, chairman and CEO of Chrysler. Schrempp discussed with Eaton some of his thoughts about the likelihood of consolidation in the

---

[15] This section draws details from the F-4 Registration statement by Chrysler Corporation, submitted to the U.S. Securities and Exchange Commission (SEC).

worldwide automotive industry and suggested it might be mutually beneficial if Daimler-Benz and Chrysler were to consider a merger. Eaton indicated that Chrysler had been conducting its own studies of the industry and had similar views. Eaton said that he would telephone Schrempp within the next couple of weeks. Toward the end of January, Eaton telephoned Schrempp to suggest a meeting early in February. On February 5, 1998, the Chrysler board was briefed on the discussion between Schrempp and Eaton.

On February 12, 1998, Eaton and Gary Valade, executive vice president and chief operating officer (COO) of Chrysler, met with Schrempp and Eckhard Cordes, the Daimler-Benz board member responsible for corporate development and directly managed businesses, to discuss the possibility of combining the two companies. Following this discussion, they decided to consult with their respective financial advisers and to meet again on February 18, 1998.

On February 17 and 18, 1998, Cordes and representatives of Goldman Sachs (the merger adviser to Daimler) met with Valade and representatives of Credit Suisse First Boston (the merger adviser to Chrysler) to discuss various transaction structures. During the course of these discussions, Valade stated that it was important to Chrysler that any potential transaction maximize value for its stockholders, that it be tax-free to Chrysler's U.S. stockholders, and tax-efficient for DaimlerChrysler AG, that it have the postmerger governance structure of a merger-of-equals, that it have the optimal ability to be accounted for as a pooling of interests, that it result in the combination of the respective businesses of Daimler-Benz and Chrysler into one public company. Cordes indicated that it was important to Daimler-Benz that any potential transaction maximize value for its stockholders, that it be tax-free to Daimler-Benz's German stockholders and tax-efficient for DaimlerChrysler AG, and that the surviving entity of any combination be a German stock corporation, thereby enhancing the likelihood of acceptance of the transactions by all important constituencies of Daimler-Benz. During these meetings, various tax, corporate, and management issues were discussed with a view to developing a transaction structure that would accommodate the parties' objectives.

Valade and Cordes were scheduled to meet again in the first week of March, to discuss the progress of their working teams. At this time, Valade requested that Daimler-Benz provide Chrysler with its preliminary thoughts on valuation.

Valuation and Earnings per Share (EPS) Analysis

Exhibits 2 through **9** present forecasts of financial statements for both companies, as well as discounted cash flow (DCF) valuations using the free-cash-flow/weighted-average cost of capital (WACC) approach. The analysts' financial model actually estimated value using three DCF approaches (WACC, adjusted present value, and equity residual), and used two ways to estimate terminal values (constantly growing perpetuities and multiples of earnings). Analysts could also consider the firms' current stock price, latest book value, and valuations based on various industry average multiples. **Table 6** summarizes the estimates of value of Chrysler and Daimler shares in U.S. dollars.

The Chrysler deal team would also need to consider the financial reporting impact of any deal structure. Merely for illustration, **Exhibit 10** summarizes the calculations of earnings per share dilution that might result from a share-for-share exchange. This

TABLE 6 | Key Valuation Results

	US$/Share	
Valuation of Chrysler's Equity		
Recent share price	$ 40.75	
Book value per share	$ 16.82	
DCF estimates with terminal values using:	Multiples[1]	Constant Growth[2]
WACC approach	$ 64.53	$64.34
Equity residual approach	$ 60.71	$60.67
Adjusted present value (APV)	$ 70.34	$70.34
Multiples estimates using industry averages (see exh. 13)		
Price/earnings (P/E) times forward EPS	$ 76.76	
Price/cash flow times forward cash flow from operations	$101.58	
Market/book value times book value	$ 38.00	
Valuation of Daimler's Equity		
Recent share price	$ 99.63	
Book value per share	$ 68.03	
DCF estimates with terminal values using:	Multiples[1]	Constant Growth[2]
WACC approach	$ 86.95	$86.12
Equity residual approach	$ 55.79	$57.20
Adjusted present value (APV)	$ 82.84	$82.84
Multiples estimates using industry averages (see exh. 13)		
Price/earnings times forward EPS	$ 60.06	
Price/cash flow times forward cash flow from operations	$ 85.21	
Market/book value times book value	$153.71	

[1]Terminal value multiples for Chrysler are 4 times EBITDA for the WACC and APV approaches, and 8.5 times earnings for the P/E approach. For Daimler, the multiples are 6.5 and 16.

[2]Constant growth rates used in estimating terminal values are 3% for Chrysler, and 4% for Daimler.

illustration assumes an exchange ratio of one share of Daimler stock per one share of Chrysler stock, and reveals earnings dilution of 25.6 percent in 1997 for Daimler, followed by earnings accretion in subsequent years. In contrast, if the merger were accounted for as a purchase, Daimler's earnings dilution for 1997 would be 34.2 percent. **Exhibit 10** also shows that Chrysler would contribute 46.9 percent of Newco's revenues, and 60.8 percent of its EBITDA.

Exhibits 11 and **12** present the longer-term financial and stock-price histories of both companies in the form of reports from *Value Line Investment Survey*. **Exhibit 13** gives information on peer firms in the automobile manufacturing industry. **Exhibit 14** gives the recent stock-price history of both firms, as well as estimates of their betas and sigmas, or percentage volatility of their stock prices, based on trading on the New York Stock Exchange. **Exhibit 15** presents details on the debt capitalization of both firms. **Exhibit 16** gives information on recent mergers-and-acquisitions activity; **Exhibit 17** offers details on a selection of acquisitions in the automobile industry. **Exhibit 18** presents data on recent macroeconomic trends in the United States and Germany. **Exhibit 19** gives information on capital-market conditions prevailing in the United States and Germany at the end of February 1998.

Negotiation of Detailed Acquisition Terms

Gary Valade and the Chrysler negotiating team could contemplate a variety of dimensions for the deal:

- *Price or value.* How much value should Chrysler shareholders receive in consideration for the sale of their firm?

- *Form of payment.* Initially, Eaton and Schrempp had contemplated a stock-for-stock transaction. However, once the negotiators got into the detailed deal design, there was a possibility that the deal could be structured in terms of cash for stock or fixed-income securities for stock. Indeed, some sort of contingent payment could be included in the consideration given for Chrysler's shares. If a stock-for-stock deal were proposed, the two sides would need to state an explicit *exchange ratio* indicating how many shares of Daimler were to be received for one share of Chrysler. A separate ratio might indicate the exchange of employee stock options for the buyer's shares, though ordinarily this was based on the assumption of the option into stock, and therefore was not necessarily required. A related issue was whether the exchange ratio was to be fixed, or could vary within limits as the stock prices of Daimler and Chrysler varied up to the date of closing. It might take six months to consummate an acquisition of this size, once the merger announcement was made. These limits, popularly called a *collar*, defined the range within which the stock prices of the two firms would be allowed to vary before any adjustment in the deal terms might be made. If the negotiators agreed to a collar, it would be necessary to specify the limits within which the stock prices could vary without triggering an adjustment in the exchange ratio, and the adjustments to be made if the stock prices exceeded those limits.

- *Merger or acquisition.* The transaction could be structured as a merger of equals or as an acquisition of one firm by another. The Chrysler side was mainly interested in a merger of equals. Shareholders might be influenced in their voting by the appearance of one firm dominating the other, regardless of the economic reality of the deal.

- *Need for shareholder vote.* Shareholder voting provisions influenced deal design in that they affected the speed with which the deal could be closed and the possibility for interference by large shareholder groups. In the United States, a vote of the shareholders required the distribution of a prospectus and proxy statement and the scheduling of a special shareholders meeting. The concern about interference was typically important for acquirers, who feared second-guessing by investors or outsiders. Two types of deals would require votes by Daimler shareholders. The first was where a large number of new shares would be created, as in a large stock-for-stock acquisition. The second was a statutory merger in which both firms would be extinguished and an entirely new firm ("Newco") would emerge— this would require a vote of both firms' shareholders.

- *Accounting treatment.* In the United States at the time, merging firms could account for the merger on a *purchase* basis, or a *pooling-of-interests* basis. Generally, pooling accounting resulted in higher earnings per share for the new firm, because it did not entail the creation of goodwill that had to be amortized under U.S. generally accepted accounting principles (GAAP). In order for the transaction to be accounted for on a pooling basis, it had to meet several tests, of which the primary ones were (1) continuity of ownership interests (at least 80 percent of the previous shareholders of the acquired firm had to remain as shareholders of the new firm); (2) equal size of the two firms; (3) each entity must have been independent of the other for two years prior to the deal; (4) the combination must be effected in a single transaction—contingent payouts were not permitted in pooling transactions; (5) the acquiring firm must issue only common stock in exchange for substantially all the voting common stock of the other company (e.g., 90 percent); and (6) the new firm must not dispose of a significant portion of assets within two years after the merger.

- *Treatment for major shareholders.* Deutsche Bank, the largest German financial institution, held a 21.7 percent interest in Daimler-Benz. Deutsche Bank held several seats on (and the chairmanship of) Daimler's board, and was instrumental in appointing Jürgen Schrempp as CEO in 1994 in a push for shareholder value maximization. Also, the Emirate of Kuwait held 13 percent of Daimler's stock. Kirk Kerkorian held approximately 14 percent of Chrysler's stock through his holding company, Tracinda Corporation. In 1994 and 1995, Kerkorian had threatened Chrysler with a hostile takeover attempt, claiming the firm was underperforming and that it was sitting on too much cash ($8 billion). Chrysler fended off Kerkorian's advances with promises to increase the dividend, accelerate share repurchases, and relax the poison-pill trigger from 10 to 15 percent of shares outstanding. While Kerkorian had agreed to a standstill on his attempts to take over the firm, his interest was large enough to influence other investors in any Chrysler shareholder vote on a deal. Kerkorian was known to be a sophisticated investor who would probably favor a tax-deferred deal. Deutsche Bank, the Emirate of Kuwait, and Kerkorian would emerge from a stock-for-stock acquisition as significant shareholders in the new firm. Therefore, it would be advisable to obtain advance support from these interested parties.

- *Tax treatment.* Some deal structures could trigger an immediate tax liability for the selling (Chrysler) shareholders, on the difference between the cost basis of their shares and the consideration received. Other structures would defer this liability. Generally, the tax-deferred deals (or "tax-free" deals, as popularly called) entailed the acquisition of the target firm's stock with the stock of the buyer, or the buyer's subsidiary. Deals that entailed payment with cash or notes or that entailed the purchase of assets would trigger an immediate tax liability. An opinion of a tax adviser and, ultimately, a ruling (or "letter") from the U.S. Internal Revenue Service would confirm whether any contemplated structure was to be taxable or tax-free.

- *Applicable law.* The new corporation could be incorporated in Germany or the United States. If incorporated in Germany, it would be subject to German law. If incorporated in the United States, U.S. law would apply.

- *Governance.* The merger agreement would need to specify the location of headquarters, treatment of workers (especially, the distribution of board seats to

Daimler's principal labor union, IG Metall, or to the United Auto Workers), the election of directors generally, and the individual to be named CEO of the firm. Under the German Co-Determination Law of 1976, a firm of Daimler's size would have a supervisory board (much like an American board of directors) and a management board. German law required a supervisory board of 20 members, 10 of whom were appointed by shareholders and the others by employees—German law specifically required that corporations must have 49 percent labor representation on their supervisory boards. The terms of the deal could specify in advance whether and how the Daimler and Chrysler sides were to divide up the 10 supervisory directors, as well as the size and composition (Daimler versus Chrysler) of the management board.

- *Union recognition.* Daimler operated a nonunionized factory in Alabama. In a combination between Daimler and Chrysler, it was likely that Chrysler's union, the United Auto Workers, would require that the UAW be recognized as the bargaining agent for that plant.

- *Official language.* It was customary in cross-border mergers and acquisitions for the deal terms to specify the official language for the firm, postconsummation.

- *Executive compensation.* The contract might also specify any senior executive compensation for the foreseeable future. This would be important if the analysts sought to equalize the compensation across the newly merged firm.

- *Listing on stock exchanges.* Considering the combined shareholders of both companies, a stock-for-stock deal would leave American and German shareholders with a major interest in a multinational firm. If shares were listed outside the home country of the shareholders, it would make those shares somewhat less liquid and less attractive. Agreeing in advance on where the shares were to be listed would influence the shareholders in their vote on any merger or acquisition.

EXHIBIT 1 | Chrysler Corporation Unit-Sales Trends

	1997	1996	Change
U.S. Retail Market:			
Car sales	736,530	832,633	(96,103)
Car market share	8.9%	9.7%	−0.8%
Truck sales (including minivans)	1,567,258	1,618,193	(50,935)
Truck market share	21.7%	23.4%	−1.7%
Combined car and truck sales	2,303,788	2,450,826	(147,038)
Combined car and truck market share	14.9%	15.9%	−1.0%
Minivans only	518,445	—	na
Minivan market share	44.4%	—	na
U.S. and Canadian Retail Market:			0.0%
Combined car and truck sales	2,559,950	2,690,340	(130,390)
Combined car and truck market share	15.1%	16.1%	−1.0%
North America:			
Combined car and truck sales	2,649,542	—	na
Combined car and truck market share			
Worldwide:			
Combined car and truck sales	2,886,981	2,958,800	(71,819)
International shipments (outside North America)	237,000	224,000	13,000

na = not available.

Source: *Chrysler Corporation Annual Report.*

EXHIBIT 2 | Chrysler Corporation Income Statements (values in millions of U.S. dollars, except per-share amounts)

	1995	1996	1997	1998	1999	Projected 2000	2001	2002
Revenues	$53,195.0	$61,397.0	$61,147.0	$64,815.8	$68,704.8	$72,827.1	$77,196.7	$81,828.5
Cost of good sold (excluding depreciation)	41,304.0	45,842.0	46,743.0	49,547.6	52,520.4	55,671.7	59,012.0	62,552.7
Selling, general, & administrative	5,227.0	6,144.0	6,145.0	6,513.7	6,904.5	7,318.8	7,757.9	8,223.4
EBITDA	6,664.0	9,411.0	8,259.0	8,754.5	9,279.8	9,836.6	10,426.8	11,052.4
Depreciation	2,220.0	2,312.0	2,696.0	3,194.7	3,406.7	3,631.4	3,869.7	4,122.2
Amortization of goodwill & intangibles	0.0	0.0	0.0	39.3	38.3	37.4	36.4	35.5
Other expense (income)	0.0	0.0	0.0	0.0	0.0	0.0	0.0	0.0
Earnings before interest and taxes	4,444.0	7,099.0	5,563.0	5,520.5	5,834.8	6,167.8	6,520.7	6,894.7
Interest (income)	0.0	0.0	0.0	(412.3)	(437.0)	(463.2)	(491.0)	(520.5)
Interest expense—straight debt	995.0	1,007.0	1,006.0	1,014.4	995.3	963.8	932.4	900.9
Interest expense—convertible debt	0.0	0.0	0.0	0.0	0.0	0.0	0.0	0.0
Interest expense—revolver	0.0	0.0	0.0	(11.7)	(66.2)	(147.9)	(225.6)	(305.6)
Pretax income	3,449.0	6,092.0	4,557.0	4,930.1	5,342.7	5,815.1	6,304.9	6,819.9
Income taxes	1,328.0	2,372.0	1,752.0	1,893.2	2,051.6	2,233.0	2,421.1	2,618.9
Minority interest	0.0	0.0	0.0	0.0	0.0	0.0	0.0	0.0
Extraordinary item (income)	96.0	191.0	0.0	0.0	0.0	0.0	0.0	0.0
Net income	2,025.0	3,529.0	2,805.0	3,037.0	3,291.1	3,582.1	3,883.8	4,201.1
Straight preferred dividends	0.0	0.0	0.0	0.0	0.0	0.0	0.0	0.0
Convertible preferred dividends	21.0	3.0	1.0	0.0	0.0	0.0	0.0	0.0
Net income to common	$ 2,004.0	$ 3,526.0	$ 2,804.0	$ 3,037.0	$ 3,291.1	$ 3,582.1	$ 3,883.8	$ 4,201.1
Earnings per share:								
Basic	$2.68	$4.83	$4.15	$5.02	$5.44	$5.92	$6.42	$6.95
Fully diluted	$2.56	$4.74	$4.09	$4.77	$5.17	$5.63	$6.10	$6.60

EXHIBIT 3 | Chrysler Corporation Balance Sheets (values in millions of U.S. dollars)

	1995	1996	1997	1998	1999	Projected 2000	2001	2002
Cash and equivalents	$ 8,125.0	$ 7,752.0	$ 7,848.0	$ 8,318.9	$ 8,818.0	$ 9,347.1	$ 9,907.9	$10,502.4
Accounts receivable	2,003.0	2,126.0	1,646.0	1,744.8	1,849.4	1,960.4	2,078.0	2,202.7
Inventory	4,448.0	5,195.0	4,738.0	5,022.3	5,323.6	5,643.0	5,981.6	6,340.5
Other current assets	14,608.0	14,268.0	15,711.0	16,653.7	17,652.9	18,712.1	19,834.8	21,024.9
Total current assets	29,184.0	29,341.0	29,943.0	31,739.6	33,644.0	35,662.6	37,802.3	40,070.5
Property, plant, & equipment	20,468.0	23,052.0	27,082.0	31,082.3	35,322.6	39,817.3	44,581.7	49,632.0
Accumulated depreciation	7,873.0	8,147.0	9,114.0	12,308.7	15,715.4	19,346.8	23,216.5	27,338.6
Net property, plant, & equipment	12,595.0	14,905.0	17,968.0	18,773.6	19,607.2	20,470.5	21,365.2	22,293.3
Goodwill & other intangibles	2,082.0	1,995.0	1,573.0	1,533.7	1,495.3	1,457.9	1,421.5	1,386.0
Equity in income of affiliates	0.0	0.0	0.0	0.0	0.0	0.0	0.0	0.0
Other long-term assets	9,895.0	9,943.0	10,934.0	10,934.0	10,934.0	10,934.0	10,934.0	10,934.0
Total assets	$53,756.0	$56,184.0	$60,418.0	$62,980.9	$65,680.5	$68,525.0	$71,523.1	$74,683.8
Accounts payable	$ 8,290.0	$ 8,981.0	$ 9,512.0	$10,082.7	$10,687.7	$11,328.9	$12,008.7	$12,729.2
Other current liabilities (excl. short-term debt)	7,032.0	8,864.0	9,717.0	10,300.0	10,918.0	11,573.1	12,267.5	13,003.5
Total current liabilities	15,322.0	17,845.0	19,229.0	20,382.7	21,605.7	22,902.0	24,276.2	25,732.7
Straight debt	14,193.0	13,396.0	15,485.0	15,485.0	15,029.8	14,574.7	14,119.5	13,664.4
Convertible debt	0.0	0.0	0.0	0.0	0.0	0.0	0.0	0.0
Revolver				(377.9)	(1,759.2)	(3,013.1)	(4,263.2)	(5,595.9)
Total debt	14,193.0	13,396.0	15,485.0	15,107.1	13,270.6	11,561.5	9,856.3	8,068.5
Deferred taxes	0.0	0.0	0.0	1,537.2	2,566.2	3,268.4	3,761.4	4,120.8
Minority interest	0.0	0.0	0.0	0.0	0.0	0.0	0.0	0.0
Other long-term liabilities	13,282.0	13,372.0	14,342.0	14,342.0	14,342.0	14,342.0	14,342.0	14,342.0
Total liabilities	42,797.0	44,613.0	49,056.0	51,369.1	51,784.5	52,074.0	52,235.8	52,264.0
Straight preferred stock	0.0	0.0	0.0	0.0	0.0	0.0	0.0	0.0
Convertible preferred stock	0.0	0.0	0.0	0.0	0.0	0.0	0.0	0.0
Common stock (Par + APIC)	4,679.0	2,742.0	757.0	(1,043.0)	(1,043.0)	(1,043.0)	(1,043.0)	(1,043.0)
Retained earnings	6,280.0	8,829.0	10,605.0	12,654.8	14,939.0	17,494.0	20,330.3	23,462.8
Total liabilities & stockholders' equity	$53,756.0	$56,184.0	$60,418.0	$62,980.9	$65,680.5	$68,525.0	$71,523.1	$74,683.8

EXHIBIT 4 | Chrysler Corporation Discounted Cash Flow Valuation (values in millions of U.S. dollars, except as noted)

Discounted Cash Flow Analysis: WACC Method	Projected				
	1998	1999	2000	2001	2002
Net income	$ 3,037.0	$ 3,291.1	$ 3,582.1	$ 3,883.8	$ 4,201.1
Interest expense	1,002.7	929.1	815.9	706.8	595.2
Tax effect of interest expense	(385.0)	(356.8)	(313.3)	(271.4)	(228.6)
After-tax interest expense	617.6	572.3	502.6	435.4	366.7
Net operating profit after tax (NOPAT)	3,654.6	3,863.4	4,084.7	4,319.2	4,567.7
Depreciation	3,194.7	3,406.7	3,631.4	3,869.7	4,122.2
Amortization	39.3	38.3	37.4	36.4	35.5
Deferred taxes	1,537.2	1,029.0	702.2	492.9	359.4
Minority interest	0.0	0.0	0.0	0.0	0.0
Income from affiliates	0.0	0.0	0.0	0.0	0.0
Other noncash items	0.0	0.0	0.0	0.0	0.0
Changes in net working capital (NWC)	2,676.0	(182.3)	(193.2)	(204.8)	(217.1)
Cash flow from operations	11,101.8	8,155.1	8,262.5	8,513.4	8,867.8
Capital expenditures	(4,000.3)	(4,240.3)	(4,494.7)	(4,764.4)	(5,050.3)
Other	0.0	0.0	0.0	0.0	0.0
Free Cash Flow	7,101.6	3,914.8	3,767.8	3,749.0	3,817.5
Terminal value (perpetuity)	0.0	0.0	0.0	0.0	59,696.5
Total Free Cash Flows to Capital Providers	$ 7,101.6	$ 3,914.8	$ 3,767.8	$ 3,749.0	$63,514.0
Valuation					
Firm value	$56,227.4	$54,297.2	$55,178.6	$56,432.3	$57,957.7
Plus: excess cash	2,848.0	3,318.9	3,818.0	4,347.1	4,907.9
Less: debt outstanding	15,485.0	15,107.1	13,270.6	11,561.5	9,856.3
Less: minority interest	0.0	0.0	0.0	0.0	0.0
Less: preferred stock	0.0	0.0	0.0	0.0	0.0
Equity value	43,590.4	42,508.9	45,726.0	49,217.9	53,009.4
Value per Share	**$64.53**	**$70.28**	**$75.60**	**$81.37**	**$87.64**
WACC Calculation					
Debt/market equity	35.5%	35.5%	29.0%	23.5%	18.6%
Relevered beta	0.91	0.91	0.88	0.86	0.84
Cost of Equity (K_e)	11.1%	11.1%	10.9%	10.8%	10.6%
WACC	9.2%	9.2%	9.3%	9.5%	9.6%

EXHIBIT 5 | Daimler-Benz A.G. Income Statements (values in DEM millions, except per-share amounts)

	1995	1996	1997	Projected 1998	1999	2000	2001	2002
Revenues	DEM102,985.0	DEM106,339.0	DEM124,050.0	DEM133,974.0	DEM144,691.9	DEM156,267.3	DEM168,768.7	DEM182,270.1
Cost of goods sold (excluding depreciation)	75,581.0	77,816.0	91,422.0	98,735.8	106,634.6	115,165.4	124,378.6	134,328.9
Selling, general, & administrative	26,203.0	21,534.0	23,096.0	24,943.7	26,939.2	29,094.3	31,421.9	33,935.6
EBITDA	1,201.0	6,989.0	9,532.0	10,294.6	11,118.1	12,007.6	12,968.2	14,005.6
Depreciation	8,661.0	4,908.0	5,198.0	3,826.8	4,241.6	4,689.6	5,173.4	5,696.0
Amortization of equip. on operating leases	2,444.0	2,018.0	2,323.0	2,807.7	2,339.7	1,949.8	1,624.8	1,354.0
Other expense (income)	(1,742.0)	(1,402.0)	(1,620.0)	(2,679.5)	(2,893.8)	(3,125.3)	(3,375.4)	(3,645.4)
EBIT	(8,162.0)	1,465.0	3,631.0	6,339.6	7,430.7	8,493.6	9,545.3	10,601.1
Interest (income)	(2,113.0)	(1,368.0)	(1,589.0)	(1,830.2)	(2,175.0)	(2,469.1)	(2,737.7)	(2,997.2)
Interest expense—straight debt	1,184.0	865.0	933.0	2,215.2	2,207.4	2,207.4	2,207.4	2,207.4
Interest expense—convertible debt	0.0	0.0	0.0	0.0	0.0	0.0	0.0	0.0
Interest expense—revolver	0.0	0.0	0.0	0.0	0.0	0.0	0.0	0.0
Pretax income	(7,233.0)	1,968.0	4,287.0	5,954.6	7,398.2	8,755.3	10,075.6	11,390.8
Income taxes	(1,620.0)	(712.0)	(1,074.0)	2,381.8	2,959.3	3,502.1	4,030.2	4,556.3
Minority interest	116.0	(89.0)	189.0	0.0	0.0	0.0	0.0	0.0
Extraordinary item (income)	0.0	0.0	(2,908.0)	0.0	0.0	0.0	0.0	0.0
Net income	(5,729.0)	2,769.0	8,080.0	3,572.8	4,438.9	5,253.2	6,045.4	6,834.5
Straight preferred dividends	0.0	0.0	0.0	0.0	0.0	0.0	0.0	0.0
Convertible preferred dividends	0.0	7.0	38.0	0.0	0.0	0.0	0.0	0.0
Net income to common	DEM (5,729.0)	DEM 2,762.0	DEM 8,042.0	DEM 3,572.8	DEM 4,438.9	DEM 5,253.2	DEM 6,045.4	DEM 6,834.5
Earnings per share:								
Basic	nmf	5.37	15.59	6.91	8.59	10.17	11.70	13.23
Fully diluted	nmf	5.35	15.30	6.80	8.45	10.00	11.51	13.01

nmf = not a meaningful figure.

EXHIBIT 6 | Daimler-Benz A.G. Balance Sheets (values in DEM millions)

	1995	1996	1997	1998	Projected 1999	2000	2001	2002
Cash and equivalents	DEM 12,176.0	DEM 14,340.0	DEM 20,520.0	DEM 25,235.1	DEM 29,139.4	DEM 32,588.8	DEM 35,853.3	DEM 39,075.8
Accounts receivable	10,581.0	10,864.0	12,006.0	12,966.5	14,003.8	15,124.1	16,334.0	17,640.8
Inventory	14,329.0	13,602.0	14,390.0	15,541.2	16,784.5	18,127.3	19,577.4	21,143.6
Other current assets	14,188.0	15,009.0	20,838.0	22,505.0	24,305.4	26,249.9	28,349.9	30,617.9
Total current assets	51,274.0	53,815.0	67,754.0	76,247.8	84,233.1	92,090.0	100,114.6	108,478.0
Property, plant, & equipment	63,983.0	65,231.0	69,376.0	77,057.7	85,354.0	94,314.0	103,990.8	114,441.7
Accumulated depreciation	47,407.0	47,006.0	48,720.0	52,546.8	56,788.3	61,477.9	66,651.3	72,347.2
Net Property, plant, & equipment	16,576.0	18,225.0	20,656.0	24,511.0	28,565.7	32,836.1	37,339.5	42,094.5
Goodwill & other intangibles	10,330.0	13,892.0	16,846.0	14,038.3	11,698.6	9,748.8	8,124.0	6,770.0
Equity in income of affiliates	4,813.0	3,536.0	3,453.0	3,453.0	3,453.0	3,453.0	3,453.0	3,453.0
Deferred taxes and other	19,105.0	22,993.0	28,390.0	28,390.0	28,390.0	28,390.0	28,390.0	28,390.0
Total assets	DEM102,098.0	DEM112,461.0	DEM137,099.0	DEM146,640.1	DEM156,340.4	DEM166,518.0	DEM177,421.1	DEM189,185.5
Accounts payable	7,378.0	9,027.0	11,079.0	11,965.3	12,922.5	13,956.3	15,072.9	16,278.7
Other current liabilities (excl. short-term debt)	16,703.0	17,160.0	20,230.0	21,848.4	23,596.3	25,484.0	27,522.7	29,724.5
Total current liabilities	24,081.0	26,187.0	31,309.0	33,813.7	36,518.8	39,440.3	42,595.5	46,003.2
Straight debt	22,285.0	28,850.0	39,302.0	39,302.0	39,302.0	39,302.0	39,302.0	39,302.0
Convertible debt	0.0	0.0	0.0	0.0	0.0	0.0	0.0	0.0
Revolver	0.0	0.0	0.0	0.0	0.0	0.0	0.0	0.0
Total debt	22,285.0	28,850.0	39,302.0	39,302.0	39,302.0	39,302.0	39,302.0	39,302.0
Deferred taxes	3,460.0	2,253.0	2,003.0	6,293.4	9,841.9	12,936.1	15,762.8	18,442.9
Minority interest	1,324.0	936.0	1,170.0	1,170.0	1,170.0	1,170.0	1,170.0	1,170.0
Other long-term liabilities	28,088.0	27,842.0	28,230.0	28,230.0	28,230.0	28,230.0	28,230.0	28,230.0
Total liabilities	79,238.0	86,068.0	102,014.0	108,809.2	115,062.7	121,078.5	127,060.3	133,148.1
Straight preferred stock	0.0	0.0	0.0	0.0	0.0	0.0	0.0	0.0
Convertible preferred stock	0.0	0.0	0.0	0.0	0.0	0.0	0.0	0.0
Common stock (par + APIC)	6,589.0	7,360.0	8,577.0	8,577.0	8,577.0	8,577.0	8,577.0	8,577.0
Retained earnings	16,271.0	19,033.0	26,508.0	29,254.0	32,700.7	36,862.5	41,783.8	47,460.4
Total liabilities & stockholders' equity	DEM102,098.0	DEM112,461.0	DEM137,099.0	DEM146,640.1	DEM156,340.4	DEM166,518.0	DEM177,421.1	DEM189,185.5

EXHIBIT 7 | Daimler-Benz A.G. Discounted Cash Flow Valuation (values in millions of U.S. dollars, except as noted)

			Projected		
Discounted Cash Flow Analysis: WACC Method	**1998**	**1999**	**2000**	**2001**	**2002**
Net income	$ 2,030.0	$ 2,565.9	$ 3,090.1	$ 3,598.4	$ 4,117.2
Interest expense	1,258.6	1,276.0	1,298.5	1,313.9	1,329.8
Tax effect of interest expense	(503.5)	(510.4)	(519.4)	(525.6)	(531.9)
After-tax interest expense	755.2	765.6	779.1	788.4	797.9
Net operating profit after tax (NOPAT)	2,785.2	3,331.4	3,869.2	4,386.8	4,915.0
Depreciation	2,174.3	2,451.8	2,758.6	3,079.4	3,431.3
Amortization	1,595.3	1,352.4	1,146.9	967.1	815.7
Deferred taxes	2,437.8	2,051.1	1,820.1	1,682.5	1,614.5
Minority interest	0.0	0.0	0.0	0.0	0.0
Income from affiliates	0.0	0.0	0.0	0.0	0.0
Other noncash items	0.0	0.0	0.0	0.0	0.0
Changes in net working capital	(723.9)	(795.3)	(874.1)	(955.3)	(1,044.1)
Cash flow from operations	8,268.6	8,391.4	8,720.7	9,160.6	9,732.4
Capital expenditures	(4,364.6)	(4,795.5)	(5,270.6)	(5,760.0)	(6,295.7)
Other	0.0	0.0	0.0	0.0	0.0
Unlevered free cash flow	3,904.0	3,595.9	3,450.1	3,400.6	3,436.7
Terminal value (EBITDA multiple)	0.0	0.0	0.0	0.0	54,841.3
Cash flows to capital providers	$ 3,904.0	$ 3,595.9	$ 3,450.1	$ 3,400.6	$58,278.0
Valuation					
Firm value	$50,083.3	$50,460.4	$51,235.2	$52,267.4	$53,492.3
Plus: excess cash	8,818.2	11,696.6	14,199.6	16,421.9	18,586.3
Less: debt outstanding	22,330.7	22,717.9	23,118.8	23,394.0	23,675.9
Less: minority interest	664.8	676.3	688.2	696.4	704.8
Less: preferred stock	0.0	0.0	0.0	0.0	0.0
Equity Value	35,906.0	38,762.8	41,627.8	44,598.9	47,697.9
Price per share	$ 69.48	$ 75.01	$ 80.56	$ 86.31	$ 92.30
Price per share	*DEM122.29*	*DEM129.77*	*DEM136.95*	*DEM145.00*	*DEM153.22*
WACC Calculation					
Debt/market equity	62.2%	58.6%	55.5%	52.5%	49.6%
Relevered beta	1.06	1.04	1.03	1.01	1.00
Cost of Equity (K_e)	11.9%	11.8%	11.7%	11.6%	11.6%
WACC	8.7%	8.8%	8.8%	8.9%	8.9%

EXHIBIT 8 | Daimler-Benz A.G. Income Statements (values in millions of U.S. dollars)

	1995	1996	1997	1998	1999	Projected 2000	2001	2002
Revenues	$71,517	$68,606	$69,302	$76,122	$83,637	$91,922	$100,458	$109,801
Cost of goods sold (excluding depreciation)	52,487	50,204	51,074	56,100	61,639	67,744	74,035	80,921
Selling, general, & administrative	18,197	13,893	12,903	14,173	15,572	17,114	18,703	20,443
EBITDA	834	4,509	5,325	5,849	6,427	7,063	7,719	8,437
Depreciation	6,015	3,166	2,904	2,174	2,452	2,759	3,079	3,431
Amortization of equip. on operating leases	1,697	1,302	1,298	1,595	1,352	1,147	967	816
Other expense (income)	(1,210)	(905)	(905)	(1,522)	(1,673)	(1,838)	(2,009)	(2,196)
EBIT	(5,668)	945	2,028	3,602	4,295	4,996	5,682	6,386
Interest (income)	(1,467)	(883)	(888)	(1,040)	(1,257)	(1,452)	(1,630)	(1,806)
Interest expense	822	558	521	1,259	1,276	1,298	1,314	1,330
Pretax income	(5,023)	1,270	2,395	3,383	4,276	5,150	5,997	6,862
Income taxes	(1,125)	(459)	(600)	1,353	1,711	2,060	2,399	2,745
Minority interest	81	(57)	106	0	0	0	0	0
Extraordinary item (income)	0	0	(1,625)	0	0	0	0	0
Net income	(3,978)	1,786	4,514	2,030	2,566	3,090	3,598	4,117
Preferred dividends	0	5	21	0	0	0	0	0
Net income to common	($3,978)	$1,782	$4,493	$2,030	$2,566	$3,090	$3,598	$4,117
Shares outstanding (average- basic)	513,000	513,900	515,700	516,748	516,748	516,748	516,748	516,748
Earnings per share (basic)	nmf	$3.47	$8.71	$3.93	$4.97	$5.98	$6.96	$7.97

nmf = not a meaningful figure.

EXHIBIT 9 | Daimler-Benz A.G. Balance Sheets (values in millions of U.S. dollars)

	1995	1996	1997	1998	1999	2000	2001	2002
						Projected		
Cash and equivalents	$ 8,456	$ 9,252	$11,464	$14,338	$16,844	$19,170	$ 21,341	$ 23,540
Accounts receivable	7,348	7,009	6,707	7,367	8,095	8,897	9,723	10,627
Inventory	9,951	8,775	8,039	8,830	9,702	10,663	11,653	12,737
Other current assets	9,853	9,683	11,641	12,787	14,049	15,441	16,875	18,444
Total current assets	35,607	34,719	37,851	43,323	48,690	54,171	59,592	65,348
Property, plant, & equipment	44,433	42,085	38,758	43,783	49,338	55,479	61,899	68,941
Accumulated depreciation	32,922	30,326	27,218	29,856	32,826	36,163	39,673	43,583
Net property, plant, & equipment	11,511	11,758	11,540	13,927	16,512	19,315	22,226	25,358
Goodwill & other intangibles	7,174	8,963	9,411	7,976	6,762	5,735	4,836	4,078
Equity in income of affiliates	3,342	2,281	1,929	1,962	1,996	2,031	2,055	2,080
Deferred taxes and other	13,267	14,834	15,860	16,131	16,410	16,700	16,899	17,102
Total assets	$70,901	$72,555	$76,592	$83,318	$90,370	$97,952	$105,608	$113,967
Accounts payable	$ 5,124	$ 5,824	$ 6,189	$ 6,798	$ 7,470	$ 8,210	$ 8,972	$ 9,806
Other current liabilities (excl. short-term debt)	11,599	11,071	11,302	12,414	13,639	14,991	16,383	17,906
Total current liabilities	16,723	16,895	17,491	19,212	21,109	23,200	25,354	27,713
Straight debt	15,476	18,613	21,956	22,331	22,718	23,119	23,394	23,676
Total debt	15,476	18,613	21,956	22,331	22,718	23,119	23,394	23,676
Deferred taxes	2,403	1,454	1,119	3,576	5,689	7,609	9,383	11,110
Minority interest	919	604	654	665	676	688	696	705
Other long-term liabilities	19,506	17,963	15,771	16,040	16,318	16,606	16,804	17,006
Total liabilities	55,026	55,528	56,991	61,823	66,510	71,223	75,631	80,210
Common stock (par + APIC)	4,576	4,748	4,792	4,873	4,958	5,045	5,105	5,167
Retained earnings	11,299	12,279	14,809	16,622	18,902	21,684	24,871	28,591
Total liabilities & stockholders' equity	$70,901	$72,555	$76,592	$83,318	$90,370	$97,952	$105,608	$113,967

EXHIBIT 10 | EPS and Dilution Analysis, Pooling-of-Interests Transaction (100% Stock)

Transaction Assumptions

Target name	Chrysler Corp.
Acquiror name	Daimler-Benz
Transaction type	
(1 = pooling; 2 = purchase)	1
% cash (input % for all transaction types)	0.0%
Refinance target debt	
(1 = yes; 2 = no)	2
Refinancing rate:	
Yield-to-maturity on 10-year Treasuries	5.4%
Spread	0.7%
Refinancing rate	6.1%
Current weighted: average cost of debt	
(Interest expense / debt balance)	6.5%
Effective tax rate	38.4%
Base year for combination	1997

Note: Combination model excludes effect of transaction expenses (i.e., legal, banking, accounting fees).

Transaction Adjustments (in millions of U.S. dollars, except per-share amounts)

Pro Forma Net Income (diluted)	1997	1998E	1999E
Daimler-Benz's net income	$4,492.7	$2,030.0	$2,565.9
Chrysler Corp.'s net income	2,804.0	3,037.0	3,291.1
Unadjusted combined	$7,296.7	$5,066.9	$5,856.9

Adjustments to net income: expenses (−) or credits (+)

	1997	1998E	1999E
Goodwill amortization	$0.0	$0.0	$0.0
New interest income (expense)	748.3	748.3	748.3
Refinancing adjustments	0.0	0.0	0.0
Assumed combination synergies	0.0	0.0	1,400.0
Pretax adjustments	748.3	748.3	2,148.3
Income taxes on adjustments	(287.7)	(287.7)	(825.9)
After-tax adjustments	460.6	460.6	1,322.4
Adjusted net income	$7,757.3	$5,527.5	$7,179.3
Pro forma EPS	$6.48	$4.62	$6.00

Current Valuation	Chrysler Corp.	Daimler-Benz
Price per share	$40.75	$99.63
Merger price	$99.63	
Implied premium	144.5%	
Exchange ratio	1.0000	
Shares outstanding (in millions)	648.4	516.7
Options / SARs / converts	31.7	7.51
Total postdeal shares	680.1	524.3

Earnings per share (basic)	1997	1998E	1999E
Chrysler Corp.	$4.15	$5.02	$5.44
Daimler-Benz	$8.71	$3.93	$4.97
Source of projections	Model		

1997 financial data (in millions of U.S. dollars)	Chrysler Corp.	Daimler-Benz
Revenues	$61,147.0	$69,301.7
EBITDA	8,259.0	5,325.1
EBIT	5,563.0	2,028.5
Net income to common	2,804.0	4,492.7
Existing goodwill amortization	0.0	1,297.8
Total cash & equivalents	7,848.0	11,463.7
Excess cash	2,848.0	8,670.4
Goodwill	1,573.0	9,411.2
Total assets	60,418.0	76,591.6
Total debt	15,485.0	21,956.4
Preferred equity	0.0	0.0
Common equity	$11,362.0	$19,600.6

Goodwill Created	
Cost of equity acquired	na
Plus: liabilities assumed	na
Less: excess cash	na
Total consideration	na
Less: adjusted value of assets	na
Goodwill created in transaction	na
Goodwill amortization period	na

Adjusted Asset Value	
Total assets	na
Less: goodwill	na
Less: excess cash	na
Plus: assumed asset write-up	na
Adjusted value of assets	na

Summary Outputs—Pooling of Interests (100% Stock)

Pro Forma Earnings Impact	1997	1998E	1999E
Daimler-Benz's standalone EPS	$8.71	$3.93	$4.97
Newco's combined EPS	$6.48	$4.62	$6.00
Accretion / (dilution)	−25.6%	17.6%	20.8%
Additional pretax synergies required for no dilution (in millions of U.S. dollars)	$4,336.9	$0.0	$0.0

1997 Contribution Analysis	Chrysler Corp.	Daimler-Benz
Revenues	46.9%	53.1%
EBITDA	60.8%	39.2%
Newco shares	680.1	516.7
% ownership	56.8%	43.2%

na = not available.

EXHIBIT 11 | *Value Line* Report on Chrysler Corporation

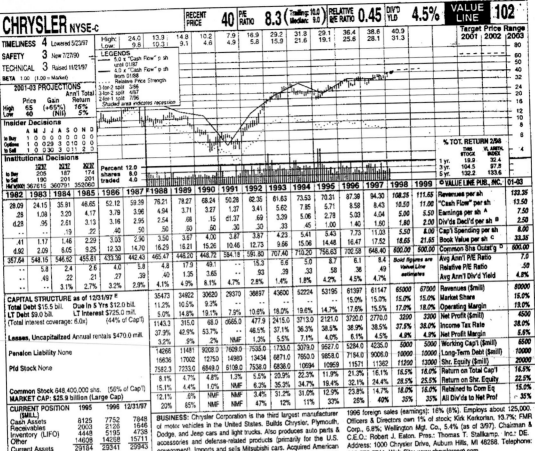

CHRYSLER NYSE-C

| RECENT PRICE | **40** | P/E RATIO | **8.3** | (Trailing: 10.0 / Median: 9.0) | RELATIVE P/E RATIO | **0.45** | DIV'D YLD | **4.5%** | VALUE LINE | **102** |

TIMELINESS 4 Lowered 5/23/97
SAFETY 3 New 7/27/90
TECHNICAL 3 Raised 11/21/97
BETA 1.00 (1.00 = Market)

2001-03 PROJECTIONS
	Price	Gain	Ann'l Total Return
High	65	(+65%)	16%
Low	40	(Nil)	5%

Target Price Range 2001 | 2002 | 2003

LEGENDS
5.0 x "Cash Flow" p sh until 01/87
4.0 x "Cash Flow" p sh from 01/88
· · · · Relative Price Strength
3-for-2 split 3/86
3-for-2 split 4/87
2-for-1 split 7/96
Shaded area indicates recession

Insider Decisions
	A	M	J	J	A	S	O	N	D
to Buy	1	0	0	0	0	0	0	0	0
Options	1	0	0	29	3	0	10	0	0
to Sell	1	0	0	30	3	0	11	2	0

Institutional Decisions
	1Q97	2Q97	3Q97
to Buy	205	187	174
to Sell	190	201	201
Hld's(000)	367615	360791	352060

% TOT. RETURN 2/98
	THIS STOCK	VL ARITH. INDEX
1 yr.	19.9	32.4
3 yr.	104.5	97.8
5 yr.	132.2	133.6

1982	1983	1984	1985	1986	1987	1988	1989	1990	1991	1992	1993	1994	1995	1996	1997	1998	1999	© VALUE LINE PUB., INC.	01-03
28.09	24.15	35.81	46.65	52.12	59.39	76.21	78.27	68.24	50.28	62.35	61.63	73.53	70.31	87.39	94.30	108.35	111.65	Revenues per sh	133.35
.28	1.08	3.20	4.17	3.79	3.96	4.94	3.71	3.27	1.37	3.41	5.62	7.85	5.71	8.58	8.43	10.50	11.00	"Cash Flow" per sh	13.50
d.28	.95	2.61	3.13	3.16	2.95	2.54	.68	.15	d1.37	.69	3.39	5.06	2.78	5.03	4.04	5.00	5.50	Earnings per sh A	7.50
· ·	· ·	.19	.22	.40	.50	.50	.60	.60	.30	.30	.33	.45	1.00	1.40	1.60	1.80	2.00	Div'd Decl'd per sh B	2.50
· ·	· ·	· ·	· ·	· ·	· ·	· ·	· ·	· ·	· ·	· ·	4.23	5.41	5.43	7.73	11.03	5.50	8.00	Cap'l Spending per sh	8.00
.41	1.17	1.46	2.29	3.03	2.90	3.50	3.67	4.00	3.87	3.87	9.66	15.06	14.48	16.47	17.52	18.65	21.65	Book Value per sh C	33.35
d.92	2.09	6.05	9.25	12.33	14.70	16.29	16.21	15.26	10.46	12.73	707.40	710.20	756.63	702.58	648.40	600.00	600.00	Common Shs Outst'g D	600.00
357.64	548.15	546.62	455.61	433.39	442.43	465.47	446.20	448.72	584.18	591.80						Bold figures are		Avg Ann'l P/E Ratio	7.0
· ·	5.8	2.4	2.6	4.0	5.8	4.8	17.9	49.1	· ·	15.3	6.6	5.0	8.7	6.1	8.4	Value Line estimates		Relative P/E Ratio	.50
· ·	.49	.22	.21	.27	.39	.40	1.35	3.65	· ·	.93	.39	.33	.58	.38	.49			Avg Ann'l Div'd Yield	4.8%
· ·	· ·	3.1%	2.7%	3.2%	2.9%	4.1%	4.9%	8.1%	4.7%	2.8%	1.4%	1.8%	4.2%	4.5%	4.7%				

CAPITAL STRUCTURE as of 12/31/97 E
Total Debt $15.5 bill. Due In 5 Yrs $12.0 bill.
LT Debt $9.0 bill. LT Interest $725.0 mill.
(Total interest coverage: 6.0x) (44% of Cap'l)

Leases, Uncapitalized Annual rentals $470.0 mill.

Pension Liability None

Pfd Stock None

Common Stock 648,400,000 shs. (56% of Cap'l)
MARKET CAP: $25.9 billion (Large Cap)

	35473	34922	30620	29370	36897	43600	52224	53195	61397	61147	65000	67000	Revenues ($mill)	80000
	11.2%	10.5%	9.3%	· ·	· ·	· ·	· ·	· ·	· ·	· ·	15.0%	15.0%	Market Share	15.0%
	5.0%	14.8%	19.1%	7.9%	10.6%	18.0%	19.6%	14.7%	17.6%	15.5%	17.0%	18.0%	Operating Margin	19.0%
	1143.3	315.0	68.0	d665.0	477.9	2415.0	3713.0	2121.0	3720.0	2770.0	3200	3300	Net Profit ($mill)	4500
	37.9%	42.9%	53.7%	· ·	46.5%	37.1%	36.3%	38.5%	38.9%	38.5%	37.5%	38.0%	Income Tax Rate	38.0%
	3.2%	.9%	.2%	NMF	1.3%	5.5%	7.1%	4.0%	6.1%	4.5%	4.9%	4.9%	Net Profit Margin	5.6%
	14266	11481	9208.0	7609.0	7535.0	1733.0	3079.0	9527.0	5284.0	4235.0	5000	5000	Working Cap'l ($mill)	6500
	16636	17002	12750	14980	13434	6871.0	7650.0	9858.0	7184.0	9006.0	10000	10000	Long-Term Debt ($mill)	10000
	7582.3	7233.0	6849.0	6109.0	7538.0	6838.0	10694	10959	11571	11362	11200	13000	Shr. Equity ($mill)	20000
	8.1%	4.7%	4.8%	1.3%	5.5%	20.9%	22.3%	11.9%	21.3%	16.1%	16.5%	18.0%	Return on Total Cap'l	16.5%
	15.1%	4.4%	1.0%	NMF	6.3%	35.3%	34.7%	19.4%	32.1%	24.4%	28.5%	25.5%	Return on Shr. Equity	22.5%
	12.1%	.6%	NMF	NMF	3.4%	31.2%	31.0%	12.9%	23.8%	14.7%	18.0%	16.0%	Retained to Com Eq	15.0%
	20%	85%	NMF	NMF	47%	12%	11%	33%	26%	40%	35%	35%	All Div'ds to Net Prof	35%

CURRENT POSITION
($MILL.)	1995	1996	12/31/97
Cash Assets	8125	7752	7848
Receivables	2003	2126	1646
Inventory (LIFO)	4448	5195	4738
Other	14608	14268	15711
Current Assets	**29184**	**29341**	**29943**
Accts Payable	8290	8981	9512
Debt Due	4335	6212	6479
Other	7032	8864	9717
Current Liab.	**19657**	**24057**	**25708**

ANNUAL RATES
of change (per sh)	Past 10 Yrs.	Past 5 Yrs.	Est'd '95-'97 to '01-'03
Sales	5.5%	3.5%	8.0%
"Cash Flow"	7.0%	21.5%	10.0%
Earnings	4.0%	· ·	12.0%
Dividends	13.5%	13.5%	11.0%
Book Value	5.0%	2.0%	13.0%

QUARTERLY REVENUES ($ mill.)
Cal-endar	Mar.31	Jun.30	Sep.30	Dec.31	Full Year
1995	13613	12516	12009	15057	53195
1996	14956	15839	14356	16246	61397
1997	16116	14388	13176	17500	61147
1998	16000	16000	16000	17000	65000
1999	16000	17000	17000	17000	67000

EARNINGS PER SHARE A
Cal-endar	Mar.31	Jun.30	Sep.30	Dec.31	Full Year
1995	.80	.18	.46	1.34	2.78
1996	1.32	1.39	.93	1.39	5.03
1997	1.46	.70	.65	1.23	4.04
1998	1.50	1.40	.70	1.40	5.00
1999	1.50	1.50	1.00	1.50	5.50

QUARTERLY DIVIDENDS PAID B
Cal-endar	Mar.31	Jun.30	Sep.30	Dec.31	Full Year
1994	.10	.10	.125	.125	.45
1995	.20	.20	.25	.25	.90
1996	.30	.30	.35	.35	1.30
1997	.40	.40	.40	.40	1.60
1998	.40				

BUSINESS: Chrysler Corporation is the third largest manufacturer of motor vehicles in the United States. Builds Chrysler, Plymouth, Dodge, and Jeep cars and light trucks. Also produces auto parts & accessories and defense-related products (primarily for the U.S. government). Imports and sells Mitsubishi cars. Acquired American Motors Corp. in 1987. Sold Gulfstream Aerospace Corp. in 1990. 1996 foreign sales (earnings): 16% (8%). Employs about 125,000. Officers & Directors own 1% of stock; Kirk Kerkorian, 13.7%; FMR Corp., 6.8%; Wellington Mgt. Co., 5.4% (as of 3/97). Chairman & C.E.O.: Robert J. Eaton. Pres.: Thomas T. Stallkamp. Inc.: DE. Address: 1000 Chrysler Drive, Auburn Hills, MI 48288. Telephone: 810-576-5741. Web Site: www.chryslercorp.com.

Although the coming year will likely be a tough one for auto makers, Chrysler's earnings should rebound, to $5.00 a share, in 1998. Marketing costs will probably increase to about 10% of revenues, versus 9% in 1997. Incentives levels, which we had expected to trend downward this year, are slated to remain around $1,100–$1,200 a unit, owing to protracted price competition. However, there are a number of positives here. Chrysler's margins should benefit from a richer product mix, including the new Dodge *Durango* and *LH* sedans, and about $1.5 billion in cost reductions stemming from higher manufacturing efficiencies, lower warranty expenses, and the Score Program, which aims to share cost savings with the company's suppliers. In addition, a lower tax rate and 7%–8% fewer shares outstanding ($2 billion of stock buybacks are planned for this year) should give Chrysler's 1998 share net a significant boost.

Over $10 billion is at management's disposal. The balance sheet boasts nearly $8 billion in cash, the pension fund is overfunded by $2 billion, and a separate trust holds $1 billion. The money has generally been intended to protect against an economic downturn. But management recently intimated that the funds would possibly be used to make an acquisition in the wake of the Asian financial crisis. Such a move would potentially improve Chrysler's long-term growth prospects, but doing so would come with sizable risks. Alternatively, the cash could be returned to shareholders through faster dividend increases and share repurchases.

High-yielding Chrysler stock is up by nearly 15% since our December report. Still, our momentum-based Timeliness system ranks these shares to lag the year-ahead market. Over the coming 3 to 5 years, though, this equity seems to offer worthwhile total-return prospects, based on our projections through 2001–2003. As the most profitable company of the Big Three domestic auto manufacturers, Chrysler is well positioned to capitalize on the expanding U.S. economy. Investors should keep in mind, however, that Chrysler's business is highly cyclical, which could make for some volatility.
Nick Primavera   *March 13, 1998*

(A) Primary earnings through 1996, diluted thereafter. Excludes nonrecurring gain (losses): '97, 5¢; '96, (26¢); '95, (13¢); '93, ($6.40); '91, (27¢). Next earnings report due late May. (B) Next dividend declared mid-May. Next ex date early June. Dividend payment dates: 15th of January, April, July, October. (C) Includes intangibles. In '97: $1.6 billion, $2.47/sh. (D) In millions, adjusted for stock splits.

Company's Financial Strength	B++
Stock's Price Stability	50
Price Growth Persistence	60

EXHIBIT 12 | *Value Line* Report on Daimler-Benz A. G.

DAIMLER-BENZ (ADR) NYSE-DAI

RECENT PRICE	85	
P/E RATIO	22.8	(Trailing: 23.7 / Median: NMF)
RELATIVE P/E RATIO	1.23	
DIV'D YLD	0.8%	
VALUE LINE	103	

TIMELINESS 4 Lowered 12/19/97

SAFETY 3 New 12/17/93

TECHNICAL 4 Raised 3/13/98

BETA .90 (1.00 = Market)

2001-03 PROJECTIONS
	Price	Gain	Ann'l Total Return
High	125	(+45%)	11%
Low	80	(-5%)	Nil

Insider Decisions

NOT REPORTED

U.S. Institutional Decisions
	1Q'97	2Q'97	3Q'97
to buy	21	23	28
to sell	16	13	13
shares (000)	8791	9655	9866

Percent shares traded	0.6 0.4 0.2

High/Low prices: 54.2/36.4, 46.7/33.8, 50.9/31.8, 48.8/32.3, 55.3/43.3, 51.8/43.1, 68.8/50.8, 87.1/63.1, 84.9/56.3

Target Price Range 2001 2002 2003

LEGENDS
- 6.0 x "Cash Flow" p sh
- Relative Price Strength
- Shaded area indicates recession

% TOT. RETURN 2/98
	THIS STOCK	VL ARITH. INDEX
1 yr.	15.3	32.4
3 yr.	74.5	97.8
5 yr.	141.8	133.6

On Oct. 3, 1993, Daimler-Benz AG became the first German company listed on the New York Stock Exchange, after it agreed to report its results under U.S. generally accepted accounting principles (GAAP). Deutsche Bank, the biggest shareholder, sold 15 mill. American Depositary Receipts at $46.75 in Daimler's first secondary offering on Jan. 27, 1994. Daimler issued rights permitting holders of common shares & ADRs to subscribe for stock equal to 10% of holdings, at a 20% discount to market price, DM 640/share ($38.35/ADR).

CAPITAL STRUCTURE as of 6/30/97
Total Debt $17896 mill. Due in 5 Yrs $14000 mill.
LT Debt $6896 mill. LT Interest $650.0 mill.
(Total interest coverage: 6.5x)
(30% of Cap'l)
Leases, Uncapitalized $591.6 mill.
Pension Liability None in '96 vs. $8949 mill. in '95
Pfd Stock None
Common Stock 515,396,362 mill. shares
(70% of Cap'l)
MARKET CAP: $43.8 billion (Large Cap)

CURRENT POSITION
	1995	1996	6/30/97
Cash Assets	7340	9312	9473
Receivables	12733	19428	10593
Inventory (Avg Cst)	10947	8833	8474
Other	4685	5818	5493
Current Assets	35705	43391	34033
Accts Payable	5015	5400	11864
Debt Due	8398	9934	11000
Other	9389	12302	2139
Current Liab.	22802	27636	25003

ANNUAL RATES
of change (per ADR)	Past 10 Yrs.	Past 5 Yrs.	Est'd '94-'96 to '01-'03
Sales	--	2.5%	4.5%
"Cash Flow"	--	.5%	4.0%
Earnings	--	-20.5%	NMF
Dividends	--	-9.5%	NMF
Book Value	--	-2.5%	5.0%

SEMIANNUAL REVENUES ($ mill.)
Calendar	Jun.30	Dec.31	Full Year
1995	33359	38550	71909
1996	28864	40193	69057
1997	31051	36949	68000
1998	34500	40000	74500
1999	36500	42000	78500

EARNINGS PER ADR B
Calendar	Jun.30	Dec.31	Full Year
1995	d2.13	d.17	d2.30
1996	.99	2.48	3.47
1997	1.07	2.63	3.70
1998	1.10	2.65	3.75
1999	1.15	2.80	3.95

GROSS QUARTERLY DIV'DS PAID C
Calendar	Mar.31	Jun.30	Sep.30	Dec.31	Full Year
1994	--	.482	--	--	.48
1995	--	.788	--	--	.79
1996	--	--	--	--	--
1997	--	.647	--	--	.65
1998					

Statistical Array

	1988	1989	1990	1991	1992	1993	1994	1995	1996	1997	1998	1999	© VALUE LINE PUB., INC. 01-03	
Trans. Rate(DM/$) A	1.77	1.69	1.50	1.52	1.62	1.94	1.55	1.44	1.54	1.80	1.80	1.80		1.80
Revenues per ADR	96.61	103.79	122.74	134.41	131.03	108.13	130.89	139.99	133.99	131.80	144.40	151.55		181.75
"Cash Flow" per ADR	--	--	9.79	12.27	10.83	6.21	11.19	10.78	12.21	11.25	11.80	12.35		15.10
Earnings per ADR B	--	--	1.27	3.44	1.31	d3.03	1.10	d2.30	3.47	3.70	3.75	3.95		4.90
Gross Div'ds Decl'd ADR C	.68	.71	.80	.86	.80	.41	.71	--	.71	.70	.85	.85		1.20
Cap'l Spending per ADR	--	--	7.82	8.12	8.92	5.87	8.69	7.49	8.36	7.55	7.55	7.70		8.55
Book Value per ADR D	--	--	37.83	36.70	29.08	37.02	30.90	33.26	31.00	34.90	37.65		48.10
Equiv ADRs Outst'g E	429.80	435.50	464.38	465.06	464.27	465.93	512.99	513.69	515.40	516.00	516.00	518.00		520.00
Avg Ann'l P/E Ratio	--	--	36.8	12.0	33.2	--	44.9	--	16.2	20.5	Bold figures are Value Line estimates			21.0
Relative P/E Ratio	--	--	2.73	.77	2.01	--	2.94	--	1.01	1.18				1.50
Avg Ann'l Div'd Yield	--	--	1.7%	2.1%	1.8%	1.0%	1.4%	--	1.3%	.9%				1.2%
Revenues ($mill)	41523	45202	57000	82507	60833	50380	67145	71909	69057	68000	74500	78500		94500
Operating Margin	--	--	2.2%	2.6%	2.4%	NMF	6.0%	4.2%	6.6%	8.0%	8.5%	8.5%		8.0%
Depreciation ($mill)	--	--	3813.3	4109.9	4420.4	4302.1	5178.1	6716.7	4497.7	3900	4150	4350		5300
Net Profit ($mill)	--	--	930.7	1598.7	609.3	d1409	563.9	d1179	1793.6	1900	1950	2050		2550
Income Tax Rate	--	--	63.1%	31.8%	61.8%	--	70.1%	--	--	22.0%	40.0%	40.0%		40.0%
Net Profit Margin	--	--	1.6%	2.6%	1.0%	NMF	.8%	NMF	2.6%	2.8%	2.6%	2.6%		2.7%
Working Cap'l ($mill)	--	--	16211	17834	12352	15030	12903	15755	17000	19000	21000			28000
Long-Term Debt ($mill)	--	--	4396.1	4285.2	3864.4	8787.1	5087.5	7718.1	5700	6700	6700			7500
Shr. Equity ($mill)	--	--	17595	17040	13547	18990	15875	17140	16000	18000	19500			25000
Return on Total Cap'l	--	--	8.6%	4.4%	NMF	2.9%	NMF	8.1%	9.0%	8.5%	8.5%			8.5%
Return on Shr. Equity	--	--	9.1%	3.6%	NMF	3.0%	NMF	10.5%	12.0%	11.0%	10.5%			10.0%
Retained to Com Eq	--	--	6.8%	1.3%	NMF	1.3%	NMF	10.4%	9.5%	8.5%				7.5%
All Div'ds to Net Prof	--	--	43%	25%	65%	NMF	56%	NMF	0%	17%	19%	21%		25%

BUSINESS: Daimler-Benz AG is Germany's largest ind'l co. Major businesses: Mercedes-Benz, the world's leading maker of luxury cars ('96 unit sales: 645,000) and commercial vehicles (340,700 units); Daimler-Benz Aerospace, aircraft, space systems, defense prods., 38% stake in Airbus consortium; Daimler-Benz InterServices (Debis), info. technology, fin'l services. Other businesses: rail systems, microelectronics, diesel engines. Labor costs: 26% of '96 revs.; R&D, 5.2%. '96 deprec. rate: 10.6%. Has 290,000 emple., 450,000 shrhldrs. Major shrhldrs: Deutsche Bank, 23%; gov't of Kuwait, 13% ('96 annual report). Chrmn.: Jurgen Schrempp. Inc.: Germany. Addr: 70546 Stuttgart, Germany. U.S. office: 375 Park Ave., New York, NY 10152. Tel.: 212-909-9727.

Daimler-Benz is likely to show only a slight increase in share earnings this year. Although we expect continued strength in the company's businesses (see below), fewer tax loss carryforwards are likely to result in a much higher tax rate in 1998. Share earnings should reach $3.75, just $0.05 higher than our $3.70 estimate for 1997.

Sales at Mercedes-Benz are likely to grow by about 10%. Demand for the new M-Class sport-utility vehicle is far outpacing supply. Production will increase 20% this year. To meet demand, Mercedes will also boost production of the new CLK and SLK roadsters and most of the models in the core C-, E-, and S-Class lines. Meanwhile, the company's venture into smaller cars has hit another snag. The introduction of the Smart car, a micro-compact that Daimler is producing in a joint venture with Switzerland's SMH Swiss Corp., will be delayed until October. The delay follows the stability problems in Mercedes' new subcompact car, the A-Class, which the company has agreed to rectify at a cost of over $100 million this year. **Commercial vehicle sales are likely to** continue to improve as well. New products and aggressive pricing helped Mercedes increase its market share in Europe last year. In North America, the acquisition of Ford's heavy-truck business should boost sales and income in what is likely to be the world's strongest market for commercial vehicles.

The aerospace division is benefiting from rising demand for civil aircraft. New orders were up nearly 15% at the end of December, pointing to another year of double-digit sales growth. Plus, profitability has improved as the mark has slipped against the dollar.

This ADR is ranked to trail the year-ahead market. Out to 2001-2003, its appreciation potential falls short of the *Value Line* median.

Christopher M. Joseph   March 13, 1998

Sales (and Operating Margins) by Business Line
	1994	1997	1998	1999
Autos & Trucks	49670(3.6%)	46500(4.0%)	51000(5.0%)	54000(5.0%)
Aerospace	8429(d1.5%)	8000(1.0%)	9000(2.0%)	9600(2.0%)
Info & Fin'l Svcs	7013(2.7%)	8000(3.0%)	8700(3.0%)	9000(3.0%)
Other	4938(d7.7%)	5500(4.0%)	5800(4.0%)	6000(4.0%)
Company Total*	69057(2.1%)	68000(3.5%)	74500(4.0%)	78500(4.0%)

*After depreciation

(A) At yearend. (B) Diluted earnings, based on U.S. acctg. Excl. nonrecurring gains/(losses): '91, (77¢); '92, 48¢; '93, 99¢; '94, 24¢; '95, ($5.37). Next eqg. report early April.

(C) Before 10% German withholding tax. Next div'd mtg. early April. Goes ex-div'd May. Div'd pmt. date: May 23. Excl. proceeds from sale of rights: '89, $9.65; '94, $9.60.

(D) Incl. intangibles: In '96, $1267.0 mill. $2.46/ADR. (E) In millions. Each ADR represents one common share.

Company's Financial Strength	B+
Stock's Price Stability	75
Price Growth Persistence	25
Earnings Predictability	NMF

EXHIBIT 13 | Comparable Automobile Manufacturers (values in millions of U.S. dollars, except as noted)

		Price Feb-98	1997 Revenues	1997 Profits	1997 EPS	1998E EPS[1]	1997 Cash Flow/ Share	Trailing P/E	Forward P/E	Price/ Cash Flow	Shares Outstanding	Long-term Debt	Debt/ Total Cap	Market Book Value	Beta[2]
United States															
Ford Motor		37 9/16	$153,627	$6,920	$5.75	$5.38	$11.97	6.5	7.0	3.1	1,194	$80,245	64%	1.51	0.86
General Motors		68 15/16	166,445	6,276	8.70	7.97	22.82	7.9	8.6	3.0	721	41,972	46%	2.67	0.96
Chrysler		40 3/4	61,147	2,804	4.15	5.01	8.43	9.8	8.1	4.8	648	9,006	25%	2.33	0.85
Navistar		30 3/8	$ 6,321	$ 150	$1.65	$2.60	$ 3.33	18.4	11.7	9.1	72	$ 1,316	37%	2.83	1.03
Average: U.S.							$11.64	10.67	8.86	5.03			43%	2.33	0.93
Japan															
Honda Motor		70 3/8	$45,111	$1,960	$4.02	$4.40	$6.39	17.5	16.0	11.0	487	$ 5,096	13%	4.55	0.80
Nissan Motor		8 7/8	49,358	382	0.30	0.55	3.34	29.6	16.1	2.7	1,257	12,554	53%	0.92	0.66
Toyota Motor		54 7/8	$87,807	$3,416	$1.79	$2.35	$3.81	30.7	23.4	14.4	1,902	$16,006	13%	2.70	0.63
Average: Japan							$4.51	25.92	18.49	9.36			26%	2.72	0.70
Europe															
Daimler-Benz		99 5/8	$68,951	$1,764	$3.38	$3.75	$11.50	29.5	26.6	8.7	517	$9,564	16%	2.69	0.86
Volvo		27 1/8	$23,118	$ 400	$0.88	$2.20	$ 2.99	30.8	12.3	9.1	442	$2,913	20%	1.59	0.71
BMW	DEM	1,475	60,137	1,246	50.63	59.50	412.99	29.1	24.8	3.6	25	10,516	22%	3.59	0.88
Peuqeot Citröen	FRF	867	186,785	(2,768)	(55.24)	48.20	336.97	nmf	18.0	2.6	50	17,004	28%	0.82	0.88
Fiat	ITL	6,292	89,658	2,417	459.90	379.60	2,141.76	13.7	16.6	2.9	5	10,938	25%	1.35	0.73
Audi	DEM	1,450	22,410	367	85.35	125.00	536.28	17.0	11.6	2.7	4	-	0%	2.93	0.68
Renault	FRF	212	207,912	5,427	22.79	16.00	48.88	9.3	13.3	4.3	238	30,760	38%	1.16	0.78
Average: Europe							nmf	21.57	17.59	4.84			21%	2.02	0.79
Average: All Firms								19.22	15.29	5.86			29%	2.26	0.81

nmf = not a meaningful figure.

Note: Data is taken from Value Line Investment Survey and Bloomberg, and may not match exactly with other data given in the case.
[1] Domestic EPS estimates are taken from Nelson's; international EPS estimates are taken from Value Line and IBES.
[2] Beta is calculated against the S&P in all cases and is based on weekly observations between March 1996 and February 1998.

EXHIBIT 14 | Recent Stock-Price Information for Chrysler Corporation and Daimler-Benz A.G.

Chrysler Corporation		Daimler-Benz (ADR[1] in millions of U.S. dollars)		Ratio of Chrysler to Daimler
Month	Stock Price	Month	Stock Price	
May-96	$ 33.31	May-96	$ 53.50	0.6227
Jun-96	$ 31.25	Jun-96	$ 53.00	0.5896
Jul-96	$ 28.38	Jul-96	$ 53.13	0.5341
Aug-96	$ 29.25	Aug-96	$ 54.25	0.5392
Sep-96	$ 28.63	Sep-96	$ 58.25	0.4914
Oct-96	$ 33.63	Oct-96	$ 64.50	0.5213
Nov-96	$ 35.50	Nov-96	$ 67.31	0.5274
Dec-96	$ 33.00	Dec-96	$ 71.00	0.4648
Jan-97	$ 34.88	Jan-97	$ 71.13	0.4903
Feb-97	$ 34.00	Feb-97	$ 76.00	0.4474
Mar-97	$ 30.00	Mar-97	$ 73.13	0.4103
Apr-97	$ 30.00	Apr-97	$ 78.00	0.3846
May-97	$ 31.88	May-97	$ 80.13	0.3978
Jun-97	$ 32.88	Jun-97	$ 82.13	0.4003
Jul-97	$ 37.19	Jul-97	$ 73.50	0.5060
Aug-97	$ 35.13	Aug-97	$ 80.75	0.4350
Sep-97	$ 36.81	Sep-97	$ 67.31	0.5469
Oct-97	$ 35.25	Oct-97	$ 69.44	0.5077
Nov-97	$ 34.31	Nov-97	$ 71.00	0.4833
Dec-97	$ 35.19	Dec-97	$ 68.75	0.5118
Jan-98	$ 34.81	Jan-98	$ 79.75	0.4365
Feb-98	$ 38.75	Feb-98	$ 99.63	0.3890
High: $ 38.75		High: $ 99.63		0.6227
Low: $ 28.38		Low: $ 53.00		0.3846
Average: $ 33.36		Average: $ 70.25		0.4835
Adjusted beta[2]: 0.85		Adjusted beta[2]: 0.97		
Volatility[3]: 25.83%		Volatility[3]: 29.39%		

[1]ADR = American depository receipt.

[2]Beta was calculated with respect to the S&P 500 Index from weekly data over the period 5/03/96 to 3/01/98 and adjusted for beta's tendency to converge to 1 according to the formula: Adjusted beta = (0.67)* Raw beta + (0.33)* 1.00.

[3]Volatility was calculated from daily data for the 260 most recent trading days.

Source of data: Bloomberg Financial Service.

EXHIBIT 15 | Long-Term Debt Structure as of December 31, 1997 (values in millions of U.S. dollars)

Chrysler Corporation				
	1997	**1996**	**LTD Repayment Schedule**	
Chrysler Corp. debentures due 2027–2097	$ 1,588.0	$ 265.0	1998	$ 2,638.0
Chrysler Corp. notes due 1999–2020	689.0	1,467.0	1999	3,423.0
Chrysler Finance Corp. senior notes due 1999–2018	9,335.0	8,437.0	2000	2,363.0
Chrysler Finance Corp. mortgage notes and capital leases	32.0	13.0	2001	431.0
			2002	470.0
Total	$11,644.0	10,182.0	Thereafter	2,319.0
Less current portion	2,638.0	2,998.0		$11,644.0
Total long-term debt (LTD)	$ 9,006.0	$7,184.0		

Daimler-Benz				
	1997	**1996**	**LTD Repayment Schedule**	
Bonds and notes due 1999–2007	$ 5,619.0	$4,720.0	1998	$ 669.8
Long-term bank loans due 1999–2019	3,769.3	3,261.3	1999	1,315.1
Liabilities to affiliated companies due 1999–2004	309.5	245.2	2000	1,750.8
Capital leases and residual-value guarantees	589.9	370.3	2001	1,553.6
			2002	1,426.3
Total	$10,287.7	$8,596.8	Thereafter	3,572.1
Less current portion	669.8	313.5		$10,287.7
Total long-term debt (LTD)	$ 9,617.9	$8,283.2		

Source: Chrysler and Daimler-Benz 1997 Annual Reports.

EXHIBIT 16 | Recent Acquisition Activity in the United States (values in billions of U.S. dollars, except as noted)

	2nd Quarter 1997		3rd Quarter 1997		4th Quarter 1997		Ist Quarter 1998	
	# Deals	Value	# Deals	Value	# Deals	Value	# Deals	Value
All Activity:								
U.S. acquisitions	1,365	$167.60	1,581	$178.10	1,719	$172.60	1,420	$162.70
Non-U.S. acquisitions	141	19.10	174	18.00	205	25.10	138	18.50
U.S. acquisitions, Non-U.S.	287	22.10	279	17.80	256	23.40	256	25.10
Total	1,793	208.80	2,034	213.90	2,180	221.10	1,814	206.30
# reporting price	739		877		1,051		809	
Divestitures only[1]	613	51.90	666	43.00	686	72.40	505	76.30
# reporting price	271		336		402		286	
Leveraged buyouts (LBOs) only[1]	23	2.10	25	0.60	22	1.80	16	0.50
# reporting price	9		10		9		8	

[1]Included in all activity.

Twelve-Month Moving-Average Stock Premiums

1 Month before Announcement		1 Week before Announcement	
2Q97	35.31%	2Q97	29.53%
3Q97	47.97%	3Q97	39.61%
4Q97	36.51%	4Q97	28.34%
1Q98	37.11%	1Q98	31.61%

Mode of Payment

	Combined[1]	Cash	Stock
2Q97	18%	54%	29%
3Q97	17%	57%	26%
4Q97	15%	59%	26%
1Q98	17%	58%	24%

[1]"Combined" includes mixture of cash and stock.

Source of data: Mergers & Acquisitions, July/August 1998.

Sales Volumes of Target Companies 4/1/97 to 3/31/98

Sales[1]	# Firms
$1–$5	154
$5.1–$10	144
$10.1–$15	103
$15.1–$25	184
$25.1–$35	103
$35.1–$50	107
$50.1–$75	104
$75.1–$100	65
$100.1–$500	301
$500–	179

[1]Sales are in millions.

EXHIBIT 17 | Recent Jumbo M&A Activity Greater than $10 Billion (in millions of U.S. dollars, except as noted)

Nonfinancial Companies						
Acquiror	Target	Date	Value	P/E	Premium to Stock Price One Week Prior	Outcome
Tracinda Corp.	Chrysler	Apr-95	$21,618	5.40	37.50%	Withdrawn
Walt Disney	Capital Cities/ABC	Jul-95	$18,837	25.40	25.20%	Completed
SBC Communications	Pacific-Telesis	Apr-96	$16,490	15.50	36.20%	Completed
WorldCom	MFS Communications	Jan-97	$13,596	nmf	60.00%	Completed
CSX Corp.	Conrail	Jun-97	$10,436	58.40	60.30%	Withdrawn
Bell Atlantic	NYNEX Corp.	Aug-97	$21,346	19.50	−0.40%	Completed
Boeing Corp.	McDonnell Douglas	Aug-97	$13,359	nmf	22.70%	Completed
CUC International	HFS Incorporated	Dec-97	$11,343	40.30	3.00%	Completed
Lockheed Martin	Northrup Grumman	Feb-98	$11,831	28.00	41.20%	Withdrawn
Starwood Lodging	ITT Corp.	Feb-98	$13,748	24.70	98.30%	Completed

Financial Companies						
Acquiror	Target	Date	Value	P/E	Premium to Stock Price One Week Prior	Outcome
Chemical Banking Corp.	Chase Manhattan Corp.	Mar-96	$10,446	10.70	7.50%	Completed
Wells Fargo	First Interstate Corp.	Apr-96	$10,930	13.10	36.30%	Completed
Dean Witter Discover	Morgan Stanley	Feb-97	$10,573	10.70	12.80%	Completed
Nationsbank	Barnett	Jan-98	$14,822	25.00	43.90%	Completed

nmf = not a meaningful figure.

Source of data: Securities Data Company, Bloomberg.

EXHIBIT 18 | Recent Economic Data for Germany and the United States

	Unemployment			Inflation (CPI[1])			Annual GDP[2] Growth			Industrial Production		
	U.S.	Germany (Total)	Germany (West)	U.S.	Germany (Total)	Germany (West)	U.S.	Germany (Total)	Germany (West)	U.S.	Germany (Total)	Germany (West)
1991	7.30%		5.70%	3.10%		4.20%	0.39%		3.30%	0.30%	−0.10%	
1992	7.40%		6.50%	2.90%	3.30%	3.40%	3.70%	0.90%	0.30%	4.40%	−5.00%	−5.50%
1993	6.50%	9.60%	8.10%	2.70%	4.20%	3.30%	2.40%	−0.20%	−0.90%	3.80%	−1.50%	−2.60%
1994	5.40%	9.30%	8.20%	2.70%	2.50%	2.50%	3.30%	3.40%	2.70%	6.80%	6.80%	5.90%
1995	5.60%	9.90%	8.60%	2.50%	1.80%	1.50%	2.10%	0.00%	−0.20%	2.30%	−4.90%	−5.10%
1996	5.30%	10.80%	9.50%	3.30%	1.40%	1.40%	3.90%	2.10%	1.90%	4.70%	3.10%	2.50%
1997	4.70%	11.80%	9.90%	1.70%	1.80%	1.70%	3.80%	2.30%	2.50%	5.70%	3.20%	3.70%
1998	4.50%	11.00%	9.30%	1.70%	1.20%	1.10%	3.60%	2.50%	2.60%	3.20%	1.60%	1.70%

[1]CPI = consumer price index.

[2]GDP = gross domestic product.

Source: Bloomberg Financial Service.

EXHIBIT 19 | Current Capital-Market Conditions

Prime Rates on Senior Bank Loans

	Germany	U.S.
1988		10.50%
1989		10.50%
1990		10.00%
1991		7.50%
1992		6.00%
1993		6.00%
1994		8.50%
1995		8.75%
1996	6.75%	8.25%
1997	6.62%	8.50%
Jan-98		8.50%
Feb-98	6.55%	8.50%

Recent Money Rates (February 27th, 1998)

	Germany	U.S.
LIBOR	3.76%	5.78%
3-mo. T-bill	3.43%	5.30%
6-mo. T-bill	3.48%	5.31%
1-yr. T-bill	3.66%	5.39%
3-yr. T-note	4.15%	5.53%
5-yr. T-note	4.49%	5.57%
10-yr. T-bond	4.93%	5.61%
30-yr. T-bond	5.49%	5.91%

Stock Market Indexes

	Germany (DAX)	U.S. (S&P 500)
1988	1,328	278
1989	1,790	353
1990	1,398	330
1991	1,578	417
1992	1,545	436
1993	2,267	467
1994	2,107	459
1995	2,254	616
1996	2,889	741
1997	4,250	970
Jan-98	4,440	980
Feb-98	4,710	1,049

U.S. Corporate Bond Ratings & Yields[1]

	AAA	A	BBB	BB
Dec-97	6.17%	6.44%	6.62%	7.85%
Jan-98	5.90%	6.21%	6.49%	7.64%
Feb-98	6.06%	6.37%	6.58%	7.76%

[1]Based on 10-year yields from the Bloomberg Index for selected Industrials.

Sources: Bloomberg, Federal Reserve Bulletin.

S&P Bond Ratings

Chrysler Corp.	A2/A
Daimler-Benz	A1/A+

Yield to Maturities of Selected Issues as of 2/27/98

Chrysler		Daimler-Benz	
7.95%/00	6.12%	10%/99	6.02%
6.95%/02	6.19%	6.625%/00	6.00%
7.45%/27	6.84%	6%/02	6.10%
7.45%/97	7.02%	7.375%/06	6.36%

Sources: Bloomberg.

Palamon Capital Partners/ TeamSystem S.p.A.

We want to make money by investing in change.
  —Louis Elson, Managing Partner, Palamon Capital Partners

In February 2000, Louis Elson looked over the London skyline and reflected on the international private equity industry and the investment processes that would be necessary for success in this increasingly competitive field. Elson, a managing partner of the U.K.-based private equity firm Palamon Capital Partners, was specifically considering an investment in TeamSystem S.p.A., an Italian software company. Palamon was interested in TeamSystem for the growth opportunity that it represented in a fast-changing market. Palamon had an opportunity to purchase a 51 percent stake in TeamSystem for (euro) EUR25.9 million. In preparing a recommendation to his colleagues at Palamon, Elson planned to assess TeamSystem's strategy, value the firm, identify important risks, evaluate proposed terms of the investment, and consider alternative exit strategies.

International Private Equity Industry

The international private equity industry was segmented into three sectors. Venture capital funds made high-risk early-stage investments in startup companies. Generalist private equity funds provided expansionary funding or transitional funding that allowed small companies to grow and eventually go public. Leveraged buyout funds financed the acquisitions (often by management) of preexisting companies that had the capacity to take on debt and make radical improvements in operations.

Private equity funds raised capital primarily from individual investors, pension funds, and endowments that were interested in more attractive risk/return investment propositions than the public capital markets offered. Funds existed all over the world,

This case was prepared by Chad Rynbrandt from interviews, under the direction of Robert F. Bruner, with the assistance of Sean D. Carr. Some details have been simplified for expositional clarity. The cooperation of Palamon Capital Partners is gratefully acknowledged, as is the financial support of the Batten Institute. Copyright © 2001 by the University of Virginia Darden School Foundation, Charlottesville, VA. All rights reserved. *To order copies, send an e-mail to* sales@dardenpublishing.com. *No part of this publication may be reproduced, stored in a retrieval system, used in a spreadsheet, or transmitted in any form or by any means—electronic, mechanical, photocopying, recording, or otherwise—without the permission of the Darden School Foundation.* Rev. 12/05.

but, not surprisingly, North America had the largest number of funds and largest dollar value of capital invested as of 1999. Europe and Asia had the next largest private equity industries. **Exhibit 1** presents the number and dollar values of private equity funds by global geographic region.

Most private equity markets saw rapid growth in the 1990s. In Europe, the amount of new capital raised grew from EUR4.4 billion in 1994 to EUR25.4 billion in 1999. Correspondingly, the amount of capital invested by the funds more than quadrupled from EUR5.5 billion to EUR25.1 billion over the same period. **Exhibit 2** summarizes the amount of new capital raised and the amount invested through the 1990s. Some key players in the mid-market sector in Europe included Duke Street Capital (EUR650 million fund based in the United Kingdom), Mercapital (EUR600 million fund based in Spain), and Nordic Capital (EUR760 million fund based in Sweden). Large investment banks such as Dresdner, Deutsche Bank, and Banca de Roma also had notable private equity presences.

Louis Elson and Palamon Capital Partners

Louis Elson began working in private equity in 1990, when he joined E.M. Warburg, Pincus & Co. Soon after joining the firm, he began focusing on European transactions and, in 1992, decided to relocate permanently to Europe. Elson became a partner of Warburg, Pincus in 1995 and was an integral part of a team that built a US$1.3 billion portfolio of equity investments for the firm. The portfolio contained more than 40 investments in seven different European countries. In late 1998, Elson and another of his partners, Michael Hoffman, saw a unique window of opportunity in the European private equity industry. They believed that the European economic landscape was changing in a way that benefited smaller, middle-market companies. Therefore, Elson and Hoffman recruited two additional partners and began laying the foundation for what would eventually become Palamon Capital Partners.

By August 1999, Elson and Hoffman had raised a fund of EUR440 million. They accomplished that despite macroeconomic obstacles like the Russian debt default by marketing their unique pan-European private equity experience. With the fund closed, Elson and Hoffman grew the Palamon team to nine professionals. They hired people with experience in private equity, investment banking, corporate finance, and management consulting. Consistent with Elson and Hoffman's original vision, the Palamon team used their breadth of experience to build a portfolio of investments that would provide investors with a unique risk profile and substantial long-term returns. Essentially, Palamon was a generalist private equity fund that served the segment of investor that was interested in less risk than venture capital, but more risk than the leveraged buyout funds. Accordingly, Palamon targeted a 35 percent return on a single portfolio investment, and 20 to 25 percent blended net return on a portfolio, with an investment horizon of approximately six years. Louis Elson said:

> Our investors include large American public sector pension funds, corporate pension funds, major financial institutions, and large endowment funds. They look for us to beat the return on the S&P Index by 500 basis points per year on average. We have the best

chance of getting funded again if we can beat this target, adjusting of course for risk. We look to pick up good businesses at attractive prices, and then add value through active involvement with them.

Like other generalist funds, Palamon's investment strategy was to make "bridge" investments in companies that wanted to move from small, private ownership to the public capital markets. Unlike many private equity funds, however, Palamon did not restrict itself to one specific European country, nor did it limit its scope to one industry. Instead, Palamon focused more broadly on small to midsized European companies in which it could acquire a controlling stake for between EUR10 million and EUR50 million.

For companies that fit Palamon's profile, the transition from private to public ownership required both funding and management ability. Palamon, therefore, complemented its financial investments with advisory services to increase the probability that the portfolio companies would successfully make it to the public markets. Elson was optimistic about Palamon's investment strategy. As Elson sat in his office, Palamon was finalizing its first investment, a Spanish Internet content company, Lanetro, S.A., and had three other investments (including TeamSystem) in the pipeline.

Investment Process

Palamon's investment process began with the development of an investment thesis that would typically involve a market undergoing significant change, which might be driven by deregulation, trade liberalization, new technology, demographic shifts, and so on. Within the chosen market, Palamon looked for attractive investment opportunities, using investment banks, industry resources, and personal contacts. The search process was time-consuming, with only 1 percent of the opportunities making it through to the next phase, due diligence, which involved thorough research into the history, performance, and competitive advantages of the investment candidate. Typically, only one company made it through that final screen to provide Palamon with a viable investment alternative.

Palamon brought its deal-making experience to bear in shaping the specific terms of investment. Carefully tailored agreements could increase the likelihood of a successful outcome, both by creating the right incentives for operating managers to achieve targets, and by timing the delivery of cash returns to investors in ways consistent with the operating strategy of the target. Deal negotiations covered many issues including price, executive leadership, and board composition. Once a deal had been completed, Palamon then offered value-added support to management.

To close the process, Palamon searched for the best exit alternative, one that would help them fully realize a return on the fund's investment. Classic exit alternatives included sale of the firm through an initial public offering in a stock market, and sale of the firm to a strategic buyer. **Exhibit 3** provides more detail about Palamon's process and the firm's investment screening criteria.

TeamSystem S.p.A.

Palamon's theme-based search generated the opportunity to invest in TeamSystem S.p.A. In early 1999, even before Palamon's fund had been closed, Elson had concluded that the payroll servicing industry in Italy could provide a good investment opportunity because of the industry's extreme fragmentation and constantly changing regulations. History had shown that governments in Italy adjusted their policies as often as four times a year. For Palamon, the space represented a ripe opportunity to invest in a company that would capitalize on the need of small companies to respond to this legislative volatility. With the help of a boutique investment bank and industry contacts, Palamon approached two leading players in the market. Neither company was suitable to Palamon, but both identified their most respected competitor as TeamSystem. Palamon approached TeamSystem directly and found a good fit. Due diligence was done and, by the end of the year, a specific investment proposal had taken shape. It was the one Elson now considered.

TeamSystem was founded in 1979 in Pesaro, Italy. Since its founding, the company had grown to become one of Italy's leading providers of accounting, tax, and payroll management software for small-to-medium-size enterprises (SMEs). Led by cofounder and chief executive officer (CEO) Giovanni Ranocchi, TeamSystem had built up a customer base of 28,000 firms, representing a 14 percent share of the Italian market.

TeamSystem offered its customers a compelling value proposition. The company's software integrated a business's financial information and automated tedious and complex administrative functions. The software also enabled SMEs and their financial advisors to stay on top of the frequently changing regulatory environment. To that end, TeamSystem continually invested in development to keep its software current. Customers were given access to product upgrades in exchange for a yearly maintenance fee that the company collected (in addition to the initial purchase price of the software). TeamSystem had excelled in customer service and developed loyal customers. Nearly 95 percent of its customers renewed their maintenance contracts every year.

In 1999, TeamSystem generated sales of (lira) ITL60.5 billion (EUR31.3 million) and EBIT (earnings before interest and taxes) of ITL18.5 billion (EUR9.5 million). Those results continued a strong pattern of growth for TeamSystem. Since 1996, sales had grown at an annualized rate of 15 percent and operating margins improved. As a result, EBIT had grown at an annualized rate of 31.6 percent over the same period. **Exhibit 4** provides additional detail on TeamSystem's historical sales and profitability from 1996 through 1999. **Exhibit 5** contains balance sheet information for the same period.

As Elson looked through the numbers, he noted the current lack of debt on TeamSystem's balance sheet. In his opinion, that represented an opportunity to bring TeamSystem to a more effective capital structure that might lower the company's cost of capital. Elson also noted the "pro forma" label on both financial statements. TeamSystem, given its private ownership and multicompany structure, did not have audited consolidated financial information for the previous five years.

Industry Profile

The Italian accounting, tax, and payroll management software industry in which TeamSystem operated was highly fragmented. More than 30 software providers vied for the business of 200,000 SMEs with the largest having a 15 percent share of the market;

TeamSystem ranked number two with its 14 percent share. All of the significant players in the industry were family-owned companies that did not have access to international capital markets. **Exhibit 6** shows 1998 revenues for the nine largest players.

Analysts predicted that two things would characterize the future of the industry—consolidation and growth. Consolidation would occur because few of the smaller companies would be able to keep up with the research and development demands of a changing industry. Analysts pointed to three acquisitions in 1998–99 as the start of that trend. As for growth, experts predicted 9 percent annual growth over the period 1999–2002. That growth would come primarily from increased personal computer (PC) penetration among SMEs, greater end-user sophistication, and continued computerization of administrative functions.

The Transaction

After reviewing TeamSystem's past performance and the state of the industry, Elson returned his attention to the specifics of the TeamSystem investment. The most recent proposal had offered EUR25.9 million for 51 percent of the common (or ordinary) shares in a multipart structure that also included a recapitalization to put debt on the balance sheet:

- Palamon would invest ITL50.235 billion (EUR25.9 million) in the ordinary shares (i.e., common equity) of TeamSystem S.p.A. Those shares would be purchased from existing shareholders of TeamSystem. Giovanni Rannochi would maintain a 20 percent shareholding, while noncore employees would be diluted from holdings ranging from 3 percent to 8 percent to just 1 percent each after completion.

- More than half of TeamSystem's ITL28.5 billion of cash was to be distributed to existing shareholders via two dividend payments before Palamon's investment: an ITL8.5 billion dividend to existing TeamSystem shareholders in April 2000, and a ITL6.5 billion dividend to be paid at time of closing. A cash balance of ITL13.5 billion would remain.

- With Palamon's assistance, TeamSystem would borrow ITL46 billion from Deutsche Bank, in a seven-year loan, offering a three-year principal repayment holiday and an initial cost of 1.0 percent over base rates (Italian government bonds). Shareholders would receive the proceeds of the debt at time of closing in another special dividend.

- Excess real estate would be sold by TeamSystem, thus removing the distraction of unrelated property investments. A group of existing shareholders had made an offer to purchase ITL2.1 billion of real estate at book value if the transaction closed.

The sources and uses of funds in the transaction are summarized in **Exhibit 7**. An income statement and balance sheet for TeamSystem, pro forma the transaction, are given in **Exhibits 8** and **9**. Palamon, as a majority shareholder, would have full effective control of TeamSystem, although the existing shareholders would have a number of minority protection rights. For example, Palamon would be unable to dismiss Ranocchi for a two-year period. But Palamon would have the ability to deliver

100 percent of the shares of the company to a trade buyer should that be the appropriate exit. Furthermore, more than 40 percent of the cash to be paid to the departing shareholders would be held in escrow for a period of at least two years, under Palamon's control.

Valuation

To properly evaluate the deal, Elson had to develop a view about the value of TeamSystem. He faced some challenges in that task, however. First, TeamSystem had no strategic plan or future forecast of profitability. Elson only had four years of historical information. If Elson were to do a proper valuation, he would need to estimate the future cash flows that TeamSystem would generate given market trends and the value that Palamon could add. His best guess was that TeamSystem could grow revenues at 15 percent per year for the next few years, a pace above the expected market growth rate of 9 percent, followed by a 6 percent growth rate in perpetuity.[1] He also thought that Palamon's professionals could help Ranocchi improve operating margins slightly. Lastly, Elson believed that a 14 percent discount rate would appropriately capture the risk of the cash flows. That rate reflected three software companies' trading on the Milan stock exchange, whose betas averaged 1.44 and unlevered betas averaged 1.00.

The second challenge Elson faced was the lack of comparable valuations in the Italian market. Because most competitors were family-owned, there was very little market transparency. The nearest matches he could find were other European and U.S. enterprise resource planning (ERP)[2] companies and accounting software companies. The financial profiles of those comparable firms are contained in **Exhibits 10** and **11**. See also exchange rates and capital market conditions in **Exhibits 12** and **13**. Looking through the data, Elson noticed the high growth expectations (greater than 20 percent) for the software firms and correspondingly high valuation multiples.

Risks

Elson was concerned about more than just the valuation, however. He wanted to evaluate carefully the risks associated with the deal, specifically:

- *TeamSystem's management team might not be able to make the change to a more professionally run company.* The investment in TeamSystem was a bet on a small private company that Elson hoped would become a dominant, larger player. The CEO, Ranocchi, had successfully navigated the last five years of growth, but had, by his own admission, created a management group that relied on him for almost

---

[1]This was roughly the sum of an expected long-term inflation rate in the euro of 3 percent, and long-term real economic growth in Europe of 3 percent.

[2]Enterprise resource planning (ERP) systems were commercial software packages that promised the seamless integration of all the information flowing through a company: financial, accounting, supply chain, customer, and human resources information.

every decision. From conversations and interviews, Elson concluded that Ranocchi could take the company forward, but he had concerns about the ability of the supporting cast to deliver in a period of continued growth.

- *TeamSystem was facing an inspection by the Italian tax authorities.* The inspection posed a financial risk and therefore could serve as a significant distraction for management. Further, because it was open-ended, the inspection might delay the company's ability to go public. Elson had quantified the risk, however, through sensitivity and scenario analysis, and believed that the expected monetary impact of the inspection was low.

- *The company might not be able to keep up with technological change.* While the company had begun to adapt to technological changes such as new programming languages, it still had some products on older platforms that would require significant reprogramming. In addition, the Internet posed an immediate threat if TeamSystem's competitors adapted to it more quickly than TeamSystem did.

Finally, Elson wanted to make sure that he could capture the value that TeamSystem might be able to create in the next few years. Exit options were, therefore, also an important consideration.

Conclusion

Elson looked at all the information that covered his desk and pondered the recommendation he should make to his partners. How much was a 51 percent stake really worth? What might explain the valuation results? What nonprice considerations should he make part of the deal? How might Palamon feasibly capture the value from the investment? Were the risks serious enough to compromise the value of the investment?

EXHIBIT 1 | Size of Regional Private Equity Markets, 1999

Region	Number of Funds	Total Value of Funds (in U.S.$ millions)
North America	8,376	892,598
Europe	2,556	160,749
Asia	1,360	60,582
Middle East	130	6,469
Australia/Oceania	155	5,741
Central/South America	42	5,044
Africa	13	1,711

Source of data: Thomson Securities Data/Venture Xpert.

EXHIBIT 2 | Historical Data on European Private Equity Market

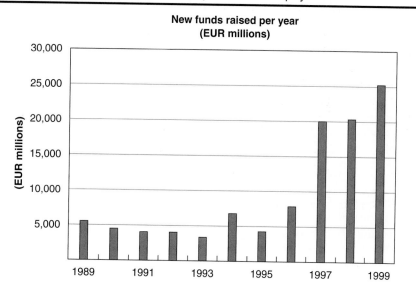

New funds raised per year
(EUR millions)

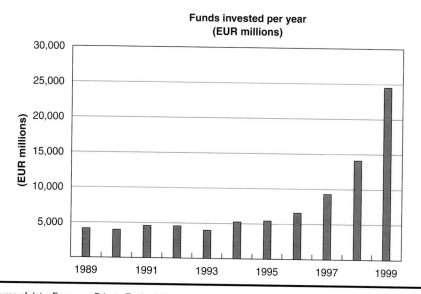

Funds invested per year
(EUR millions)

Source of data: European Private Equity & Venture Capital Association.

EXHIBIT 3 | Screening Criteria and Investment Process

Investment Process

Palamon utilizes an investment process that has been proven over the past decade through economic cycles and across geographic regions. The process is underpinned by a core set of investment principles, which can be summarized by stage of the investment process.

- Determination of Investment Focus—Identify sectors undergoing significant changes, develop industry knowledge, and take a contrarian stance when appropriate.
- Pro-Active Deal Sourcing—Proactively pursue investment opportunities within identified sectors.
- Rigorous Due Diligence—Execute comprehensive yet focused company due diligence; concentrate on "deal breakers" early on.
- Sophisticated Deal Structuring—Base structuring on a sound knowledge of local practices without relying necessarily on ineffective customs; align objectives with the entrepreneur; avoid excess leverage.
- Value-Added Support—Provide strategic direction to portfolio companies; make international network of advisors and expertise available to management teams; commit to longer time horizons sufficient to ensure scope for company growth.
- Proven Realization Strategies—Prepare for liquidity events; utilize in-house expertise to access public market capital or organize trade sales, creating exit options for all shareholders.

Investment Screening Criteria

The partners of Palamon are especially rigorous in their investment selection criteria, identifying those characteristics that will foster high growth combined with manageable risk. The following key elements are sought in each investment made:

- Superior management with unique capabilities and experience
- Leadership in core markets which are either expanding robustly or are experiencing dislocation due to technological, regulatory, or competitive changes
- High potential for operating leverage
- Opportunity to access alternative markets
- Access to undervalued assets

Source: http://www.palamon.com/ (accessed 19 December 2005).

EXHIBIT 4 | TeamSystem S.p.A. Pro Forma Historical Income Statement (values in ITL millions)

	1996	1997	1998	1999
Total sales	39,665	42,922	50,694	60,499
Cost of materials	(9,979)	(11,430)	(12,258)	(15,179)
Cost of service	(9,380)	(8,692)	(10,889)	(12,389)
Rents and leasing	(328)	(394)	(1,493)	(1,553)
Total operating cost	**(19,687)**	**(20,516)**	**(24,640)**	**(29,121)**
Salaries	(4,875)	(5,382)	(6,282)	(7,151)
Social contributions	(1,855)	(2,047)	(1,917)	(2,011)
Other personnel costs	(456)	(481)	(572)	(753)
Total personnel costs	**(7,186)**	**(7,910)**	**(8,771)**	**(9,915)**
Other operating costs	(2,793)	(3,052)	(3,133)	(1,339)
EBITDA	**9,999**	**11,444**	**14,150**	**20,124**
Depreciation & amortization	(1,052)	(1,427)	(1,355)	(1,636)
EBIT	**8,947**	**10,017**	**12,795**	**18,488**
Interest expense	(185)	(144)	(154)	(210)
Non-operating income	1,800	1,305	1,132	1,283
Pretax profit	**10,563**	**11,178**	**13,773**	**19,562**
Taxes	(5,870)	(6,699)	(6,437)	(9,525)
Earnings before minorities	4,693	4,479	7,336	10,036
Elimination of intercompany investment	(30)	(13)	(139)	(287)
Net income	**4,663**	**4,466**	**7,197**	**9,749**

Source: Palamon memorandum.

EXHIBIT 5 | TeamSystem S.p.A. Pro Forma Historical Balance Sheet (values in ITL millions)

	1996	1997	1998	1999
ASSETS				
Cash	13,092	19,134	21,144	28,513
Marketable securities				
Receivables	13,257	14,957	16,328	19,443
Inventory	1,333	1,087	1,195	1,235
Total current assets	27,682	35,178	38,667	49,191
Intangible assets	14	22	18	21
Land, PP&E	4,962	2,080	2,489	3,681
Other tangible assets	729	668	1,140	2,055
Deferred costs	327	1,947	1,738	1,865
Securities and other	1,434	1,173	1,229	1,226
Total assets	35,148	41,068	45,281	58,039
LIABILITIES				
Accounts payable	7,661	8,932	8,969	9,669
Tax and other payables	6,796	9,827	8,660	9,956
Deferred income and accruals	1,200	1,127	1,257	4,156
Long-term liabilities	2,688	2,094	2,235	3,055
Total liabilities	18,345	21,980	21,121	26,836
SHAREHOLDERS' EQUITY AND MINORITY INTEREST				
Capital	4,580	4,580	4,580	4,580
Reserves	6,636	9,442	11,662	15,884
Operating income	4,584	4,405	7,132	9,660
(Less special dividend)				
Total shareholders' equity	15,800	18,427	23,374	30,124
Minority interest	1,003	661	786	1,079
Total shareholders' equity and minority interest	16,803	19,088	24,160	31,203
Total shareholders' equity and liabilities	35,148	41,068	45,281	58,039

Source: Palamon memorandum.

EXHIBIT 6 | Revenues for Top Companies in Italian Payroll Software Industry, 1998

Company	Revenues (ITL billions)
TeamSystem	50.7
Inaz Paghe	47.0
Osra	38.0
Sistemi	37.0
Zuchetti	36.0
Esa Software	35.0
Omega Data	34.4
Axioma	26.0
Dylog Italia	25.0

Source: Palamon memorandum.

EXHIBIT 7 | Sources/Uses of Cash in Proposed Leveraged Restructuring (values in ITL millions)

Sources:	
Debt	46,000
Excess cash	15,000
	61,000
Uses:	
Special dividend—April 2000	8,500
Special dividend—closing	52,500
	61,000

Note: This table refers strictly to the leveraged recapitalization of TeamSystem. Ignored in this table are (1) the ITL50.235 billion purchase of shares by Palamon from investors in TeamSystem and (2) a purchase of TeamSystem real estate for ITL2.1 billion by investors. Palamon would not receive any of the special dividends.

EXHIBIT 8 | TeamSystem S.p.A. Pro Forma Income Statement (values in ITL millions)

	1996	1997	1998	1999	2000	2001	2002	2003	2004	2005	2006	2007	Assumptions
Total sales	39,665	42,922	50,694	60,499	15% 69,573	15% 80,009	15% 92,011	6% 97,532	6% 103,383	6% 109,586	6% 116,162	6% 123,131	growth
Cost of materials	(9,979)	(11,430)	(12,258)	(15,179)									45% of sales
Cost of service	(9,380)	(8,692)	(10,889)	(12,389)									
Rents and leasing	(328)	(394)	(1,493)	(1,553)									
Total operating cost	(19,687)	(20,516)	(24,640)	(29,121)	(31,308)	(36,004)	(41,405)	(43,889)	(46,523)	(49,314)	(52,273)	(55,409)	
Salaries	(4,875)	(5,382)	(6,282)	(7,151)									15.5% of sales
Social contributions	(1,855)	(2,047)	(1,917)	(2,011)									
Other personnel costs	(456)	(481)	(572)	(753)									
Total personnel costs	(7,186)	(7,910)	(8,771)	(9,915)	(10,784)	(12,401)	(14,262)	(15,117)	(16,024)	(16,986)	(18,005)	(19,085)	
Other operating costs	(2,793)	(3,052)	(3,133)	(1,339)	(2,783)	(3,200)	(3,680)	(3,901)	(4,135)	(4,383)	(4,646)	(4,925)	4% of sales
EBITDA	9,999	11,444	14,150	20,124	24,699	28,403	32,664	34,624	36,701	38,903	41,237	43,712	
Depreciation & amortization	(1,052)	(1,427)	(1,355)	(1,636)	(835)	(900)	(975)	(1,010)	(1,046)	(1,085)	(1,126)	(1,170)	25% of PP&E and intangibles
EBIT	8,947	10,017	12,795	18,488	23,863	27,503	31,689	33,614	35,655	37,818	40,111	42,542	
Interest expense	(185)	(144)	(154)	(210)	(3,160)	(3,160)	(3,160)	(2,765)	(1,975)	(1,185)	(395)	—	6.87% interest
Non-operating income	1,800	1,305	1,132	1,283	561	1,157	1,855	2,091	2,408	2,813	3,310	4,507	5% return on market-able securities
Pretax profit	10,563	11,178	13,773	19,562	21,265	25,500	30,383	32,939	36,088	39,446	43,026	47,049	
Taxes	(5,870)	(6,699)	(6,437)	(9,525)	(10,207)	(12,240)	(14,584)	(15,811)	(17,322)	(18,934)	(20,652)	(22,584)	48% of pretax profit
Earnings before minorities	4,693	4,479	7,336	10,036	11,058	13,260	15,799	17,129	18,766	20,512	22,373	24,465	
Elimination of intercompany investment	(30)	(13)	(139)	(287)									
Net income	4,663	4,466	7,197	9,749	11,058	13,260	15,799	17,129	18,766	20,512	22,373	24,465	

Source: Case writer's analysis.

EXHIBIT 9 | TeamSystem S.p.A. Pro Forma Balance Sheet (values in ITL millions)

	1996	1997	1998	1999	2000	2001	2002	2003	2004	2005	2006	2007	Assumptions
ASSETS													
Cash	13,092	19,134	21,144	28,513	13,500	15,202	17,482	18,531	19,643	20,821	22,071	23,395	19.0% of sales
Marketable securities	13,257	14,957	16,328	19,443	11,224	23,143	37,096	41,816	48,165	56,253	66,196	90,144	plug figure
Receivables					20,872	24,003	27,603	29,259	31,015	32,876	34,848	36,939	30.0% of sales
Inventory	1,333	1,087	1,195	1,235	1,391	1,600	1,840	1,951	2,068	2,192	2,323	2,463	2.0% of sales
Total current assets	27,682	35,178	38,667	49,191	46,988	63,948	84,021	91,557	100,891	112,142	125,438	152,941	
Intangible assets	14	22	18	21	20	20	20	20	20	20	20	20	
Land, PP&E	4,962	2,080	2,489	3,681	1,581	1,581	1,581	1,581	1,581	1,581	1,581	1,581	
Other tangible assets	729	668	1,140	2,055	1,739	2,000	2,300	2,438	2,585	2,740	2,904	3,078	2.5% of sales
Deferred costs	327	1,947	1,738	1,865	2,087	2,400	2,760	2,926	3,102	3,288	3,485	3,694	3.0% of sales
Securities and other	1,434	1,173	1,229	1,226	1,391	1,600	1,840	1,951	2,068	2,192	2,323	2,463	2.0% of sales
Total assets	35,148	41,068	45,281	58,039	53,807	71,549	92,523	100,473	110,245	121,962	135,751	163,776	
LIABILITIES													
Accounts payable	7,661	8,932	8,969	9,669	11,132	12,802	14,722	15,605	16,541	17,534	18,586	19,701	16.0% of sales
Tax and other payables	6,796	9,827	8,660	9,956	11,132	12,802	14,722	15,605	16,541	17,534	18,586	19,701	16.0% of sales
Deferred income and accruals	1,200	1,127	1,257	4,156	3,479	4,000	4,601	4,877	5,169	5,479	5,808	6,157	5.0% of sales
Long term liabilities	2,688	2,094	2,235	3,055	46,000	46,000	46,000	34,500	23,000	11,500	—	—	
Total liabilities	18,345	21,980	21,121	26,836	71,742	75,604	80,044	70,587	61,252	52,047	42,980	45,559	
SHAREHOLDERS' EQUITY AND MINORITY INTEREST													
Capital	4,580	4,580	4,580	4,580	4,580	4,580	4,580	4,580	4,580	4,580	4,580	4,580	
Reserves	6,636	9,442	11,662	15,884	24,544	(24,398)	(11,138)	4,661	21,789	40,555	61,067	83,440	
Operating income	4,584	4,405	7,132	9,660	11,058	13,260	15,799	17,129	18,766	20,512	22,373	24,465	
(Less special dividend)					(61,000)								
Total shareholders' equity	15,800	18,427	23,374	30,124	(19,818)	(6,558)	9,241	26,369	45,135	65,647	88,020	112,486	
Minority interest	1,003	661	786	1,079	1,883	2,504	3,238	3,517	3,859	4,269	4,751	5,732	3.5% of equity
Total shareholders' equity and minority interest	16,803	19,088	24,160	31,203	(17,935)	(4,054)	12,479	29,886	48,994	69,915	92,771	118,218	
Total shareholders' equity and liabilities	35,148	41,068	45,281	58,039	53,807	71,549	92,523	100,473	110,245	121,962	135,751	163,776	

DEBT REPAYMENT

	2000	2001	2002	2003	2004	2005	2006
Starting balance	46,000						
Principal due	0%	0%	0%	25%	25%	25%	25%
Payment	—	—	—	(11,500)	(11,500)	(11,500)	(11,500)

Source: Case writer's analysis.

657

EXHIBIT 10 | Valuation Measures for Publicly Traded Enterprise Resource Planning (ERP) Software Companies

	Adjusted Market Value[1] as a Multiple of:			Equity Market Value as a Multiple of:			Long-Term Projected EPS Growth[2]	CY 1999 P/E to Long-Term Growth Rate	Growth Rates 1 Year		Long-Term Margins	
	Long-Term Revenues	Long-Term Operating Income	EPS	CY 1999 EPS Est.[2]	CY 2000 EPS Est.[2]	CY 2001 EPS Est.[2]			Rev.	EBIT	EBIT	Net
Tier 1—Large ERP Players												
Baan	4.0 ×	nmf	nmf	nmf	nmf	nmf	26%	nmf	8.2%	nmf	-38.0%	-40.2%
JD Edwards	1.6 ×	26.2 ×	37.9 ×	nmf ×	95.0 ×	74.9 ×	27%	nmf	44.2%	77.0%	6.2%	5.0%
Oracle	6.8 ×	32.0 ×	47.8 ×	42.1 ×	34.4 ×	27.8 ×	24%	143%	23.6%	32.7%	21.2%	14.6%
Peoplesoft	2.3 ×	23.6 ×	nmf	nmf ×	54.8 ×	44.3 ×	24%	231%	61.1%	41.7%	9.9%	2.1%
SAP	8.3 ×	42.1 ×	75.2 ×	61.9 ×	45.8 ×	36.6 ×	25%	182%	41.9%	17.4%	19.7%	11.1%
Low	1.6 ×	23.6 ×	37.9 ×	42.1 ×	34.4 ×	27.8 ×	24%	143%	8.2%	17.4%	-38.0%	-40.2%
Mean	4.6 ×	31.0 ×	53.6 ×	52.0 ×	57.5 ×	45.9 ×	25%	185%	35.8%	42.2%	3.8%	-1.5%
High	8.3 ×	42.1 ×	75.2 ×	61.9 ×	95.0 ×	74.9 ×	27%	231%	61.1%	77.0%	21.2%	14.6%
Tier 2—Middle Market Accounting Software Companies												
Great Plains Software Inc.	4.8 ×	8.1 ×	56.1 ×	48.2 ×	37.8 ×	28.0 ×	35%	108%	57.5%	590.5%	58.9%	9.5%
Intuit Inc.	5.8 ×	42.8 ×	43.6 ×	62.4 ×	52.4 ×	43.2 ×	21%	247%	12.8%	40.1%	13.6%	16.3%
Epicor Software	1.5 ×	nmf	na	54.2 ×	18.1 ×	14.2 ×	28%	66%	na	na	-10.0%	-10.2%
Sage Group PLC	16.0 ×	58.5 ×	84.3 ×	71.1 ×	58.2 ×	43.0 ×	35%	165%	25.9%	26.6%	27.4%	17.7%
Symix	0.7 ×	8.2 ×	12.6 ×	13.5 ×	12.1 ×	9.4 ×	28%	43%	48.4%	68.0%	8.4%	5.1%
Low	0.7 ×	8.1 ×	12.6 ×	13.5 ×	12.1 ×	9.4 ×	21%	43%	12.8%	26.6%	-10.0%	-10.2%
Mean	5.8 ×	29.4 ×	49.2 ×	49.9 ×	35.7 ×	27.6 ×	29%	126%	36.2%	181.3%	19.7%	7.7%
High	16.0 ×	58.5 ×	84.3 ×	71.1 ×	58.2 ×	43.2 ×	35%	247%	57.5%	590.5%	58.9%	17.7%
Tier 3—Others												
Agresso	0.8 ×	40.2 ×	42.0 ×	15.6 ×	7.7 ×	3.5 ×	121%	6%	266.4%	3209.1%	2.1%	1.8%
Intentia	1.6 ×	-69.2 ×	nmf	62.1 ×	29.5 ×	na	na	na	51.7%	115.6%	-2.4%	-5.5%
Navision	17.6 ×	79.6 ×	126.9 ×	41.6 ×	32.0 ×	na	na	na	91.5%	137.9%	22.1%	14.0%
Brain International	3.1 ×	nmf	nmf	72.7 ×	31.8 ×	na	na	na	23.1%	-66.0%	-0.2%	1.1%
Low	0.8 ×	-69.2 ×	42.0 ×	15.6 ×	7.7 ×	3.5 ×	121%	6%	23.1%	-66.0%	-2.4%	-5.5%
Mean	5.8 ×	16.9 ×	84.5 ×	48.0 ×	25.3 ×	3.5 ×	121%	6%	108.2%	849.2%	5.4%	2.9%
High	17.6 ×	79.6 ×	126.9 ×	72.7 ×	32.0 ×	3.5 ×	121%	6%	266.4%	3209.1%	22.1%	14.0%

nmf = not a meaningful figure.

na = not available.

CY = Calendar year.

[1] Based on adjusted market capitalization, which is defined as equity market value + long-term debt – cash & equivalents.

[2] Based on I/B/E/S estimates.

Source of data: Thomson Financial's *Datastream Advance*.

EXHIBIT 11 | Financial Data for Selected Enterprise Resource Planning (ERP) Software Companies (values in thousands of U.S. dollars, except per-share data)

	Equity Market Value	Long-Term Debt	Cash & Equiv.	Adjusted Market Value[1]	Revenues	Operating Income	EPS	CY 2000 EPS Est.[2]	CY 2001 EPS Est.[2]	Book Value	Total Assets
Tier 1 - Large ERP Players											
Baan	2,637,618	200,546	121,697	2,716,467	674,664	(256,446)	$ (1.35)	$ 0.08	$ 0.10	112,821	696,510
JD Edwards	1,829,385	—	211,782	1,617,603	1,001,263	61,842	$ 0.45	$ 0.18	$ 0.23	583,996	950,473
Oracle	62,282,746	301,140	2,562,764	60,021,122	8,827,252	1,872,881	$ 0.87	$ 1.21	$ 1.50	3,695,267	7,259,654
Peoplesoft	3,611,452	—	498,155	3,113,297	1,333,095	131,978	$ 0.05	$ 0.26	$ 0.32	664,292	1,440,605
SAP	41,907,460	718,858	693,411	41,932,907	5,052,321	995,535	$ 5.33	$ 8.76	$ 10.96	2,096,138	4,083,069
Tier 2 - Middle Market Accounting Software Companies											
Great Plains Software	767,893	—	123,683	644,210	134,907	79,489	$ 0.86	$ 1.28	$ 1.72	133,193	180,252
Intuit Inc.	6,476,010	36,043	1,761,200	4,750,853	814,889	111,009	$ 2.15	$ 1.79	$ 2.17	1,673,405	2,469,865
Epicor Software	154,977	—	47,304	107,673	73,688	(7,333)	na	$ 0.21	$ 0.27	122,196	199,735
Sage Group	5,997,648	136,046	78,171	6,055,523	377,477	103,595	$ 0.58	$ 0.83	$ 1.13	11,187	650,375
Symix	84,421	4,109	3,261	85,269	123,010	10,374	$ 0.91	$ 0.95	$ 1.22	36,749	73,346
Tier 3 - Others											
Agresso	88,554	1,398	18,680	71,272	85,973	1,771	$ 0.04	$ 0.24	$ 0.53	40,804	89,789
Intentia	557,217	36,833	12,655	581,395	352,988	(8,400)	$ (0.72)	$ 0.74	na	104,085	275,714
Navision	655,707	—	6,285	649,422	36,875	8,155	$ 0.20	$ 0.80	na	9,540	25,127
Brain International	256,499	19,991	39,283	237,207	76,686	(164)	$ 0.13	$ 1.26	na	65,365	107,844

na = not available.

CY = Calendar year.

[1] Based on adjusted market capitalization, which is defined as equity market value + long-term debt – cash & equivalents.

[2] Based on I/B/E/S estimates.

Source of data: Thomson Financial's Datastream Advance.

EXHIBIT 12 | Recent ITL/EUR Exchange Rates

On January 1, 1999, the European Community fixed the ITL/EUR conversion rate at 1,936.27. The exchange rates that follow were estimated through euro vs. dollar exchange rates,[1] and are proxies for open market rates of exchange.

Date	ITL/EUR
September 1999	1696.3
October 1999	1740.1
November 1999	1901.8
December 1999	1912.6
January 2000	2055.0

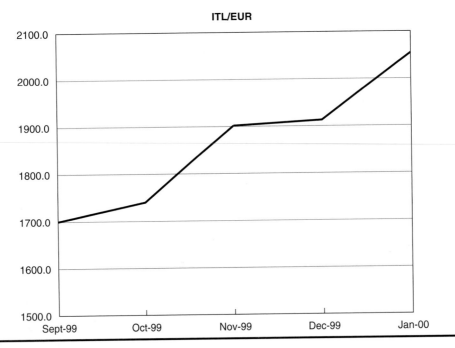

ITL/EUR

Source of data: Bloomberg LP.

[1]For instance, in September 1999, the EUR/USD exchange rate was 1.0684, and the ITL/USD exchange rate was 1812.32. Dividing the ITL/USD rate by the EUR/USD rate yields an implied ITL/EUR rate of 1696.3.

EXHIBIT 13 | Capital-Market Conditions, February 2000

Instrument	Yield
EURIBOR[1]	
90-day	3.41%
6-month	3.78%
1-year	4.11%
Government Bonds	
(euro-denominated)	
Italy, April 2004	6.00%
Italy, July 2007	5.87%
Italy, March 2011	9.25%
Euro area,[2] **5 years**	5.16%
Euro area, 7 years	5.45%
Euro area, 10 years	5.61%

Equity Market Index	Price/Earnings Multiple
Milan MIB30 Index	37.87
FTSE 100 Index (London)	28.75
DAX Index (Frankfurt)	57.47

Sources of data: *ECB Monthly Bulletin,* European Central Bank (March 2000); Bloomberg LP.

[1]EURIBOR stands for euro interbank offered rates.

[2] Euro area bond yields are harmonized national government bond yields weighted by the nominal outstanding amounts of government bonds in each maturity band.

General Mills' Acquisition of Pillsbury from Diageo PLC

On December 8, 2000, management of General Mills, Inc., recommended that its shareholders authorize the creation of more shares of common stock and approve a proposal for the company to acquire the worldwide businesses of Pillsbury from Diageo PLC. This transaction called for an exchange of shares of General Mills for the Pillsbury subsidiary that would leave Diageo as the largest shareholder in General Mills. Furthermore, it was agreed that, just before the transaction, Pillsbury would borrow about $5 billion and pay a special dividend to Diageo. Finally, General Mills would obtain a contingent commitment from Diageo that would pay General Mills up to $642 million on the first anniversary of the transaction, depending on General Mills' stock price. The proxy statement carried the opinions of General Mills' financial advisers that the transaction was fairly priced. Yet shareholders and securities analysts were puzzled by the contingent payment. What was it? Why was it warranted in this transaction? Would this deal create value for General Mills' shareholders? In light of answers to these questions, should General Mills' shareholders approve this transaction?

General Mills, Inc.

Headquartered in Minneapolis, Minnesota, General Mills was a major manufacturer and marketer of consumer foods, with revenues of about $7.5 billion in fiscal-year 2000. The firm's market capitalization was about $11 billion. It was the largest producer of yogurt and the second-largest producer of ready-to-eat breakfast cereals in the United States. The firm's segments included Big G cereals, Betty Crocker desserts, baking and dinner-mix products, snack products, and yogurt marketed under the Yoplait and Colombo brands. Each of these businesses in the United States was mature

This case was prepared by Robert F. Bruner from public information, with research assistance by Dennis Hall. It was written as a basis for class discussion rather than to illustrate effective or ineffective handling of an administrative situation. Copyright © 2001 by the University of Virginia Darden School Foundation, Charlottesville, VA. All rights reserved. *To order copies, send an e-mail to sales@dardenpublishing.com. No part of this publication may be reproduced, stored in a retrieval system, used in a spreadsheet, or transmitted in any form or by any means—electronic, mechanical, photocopying, recording, or otherwise— without the permission of the Darden School Foundation.* Rev. 12/01.

and offered relatively low organic growth. The firm pursued expansion opportunities overseas through company-owned businesses and through a cereal joint venture with Nestlé and a snack joint venture with PepsiCo. Through a program of aggressive share repurchases in the 1990s, the firm had increased its book value debt-to-equity ratio dramatically compared with its peers.

Diageo PLC

Diageo, headquartered in the United Kingdom, had been formed in 1997 through the merger of GrandMet and Guinness, making it one of the world's leading consumer-goods companies. Its product portfolio consisted of prominent alcoholic-beverage brands such as Smirnoff, Johnnie Walker, Guinness, J&B, Gordon's, and Tanqueray, as well as the Burger King fast-food chain and Pillsbury. Pillsbury had been acquired by GrandMet, acting as a "white-knight" acquirer to save Pillsbury from acquisition by Sir James Goldsmith, a well-known raider.

The Pillsbury Company

Pillsbury produced and marketed refrigerated dough and baked goods under the familiar Dough Boy character, canned and frozen vegetables under the familiar Green Giant brand, Old El Paso Mexican foods, Progresso soups, Totino's frozen pizzas, and other food products. Pillsbury had been headquartered in Minneapolis, Minnesota, as an independent company, and still had significant administrative operations there. Revenues for the company in fiscal-year 2000 were about $6.1 billion.

Origin of the Transaction

Seeking to build growth momentum, General Mills studied areas of potential growth and value creation in the spring of 1998. This had generated some smaller acquisitions and a general receptivity to acquisition proposals by the firm. In early 2000, the firm's financial advisers suggested that Diageo might be interested in selling Pillsbury, in an effort to focus Diageo on its beverage business, and that Pillsbury would complement General Mills' existing businesses.

In March 2000, Diageo's chief operating officer contacted General Mills' chairman and chief executive officer (CEO) to explore a possible sale of Pillsbury. General Mills submitted its proposed deal terms to Diageo in June 2000—the total proposed payment was $10.0 billion. Diageo submitted an asking price of $10.5 billion. The two sides would budge no further, and it looked as if the negotiations would founder. General Mills did not want to issue more than one-third of its post-transaction shares to Diageo, and believed that its shares were undervalued in the stock market. Diageo believed it was necessary to value General Mills' shares at the current trading prices.

In an effort to bridge the difference in positions, the two firms agreed upon including in the terms of the deal a contingent payment on the first anniversary of the transaction that would depend on General Mills' share price. James Lawrence, chief financial officer of General Mills, said, "We genuinely believe this is a way in which they could have their cake and we could eat it, too. There's no question in my mind that, absent this instrument, we wouldn't have been able to reach this deal." David Van Benschoten, General Mills' treasurer, added that the contingent payment was another example of the "development of the use of [options] in the past 20 years as finance has come to first understand, and work with, the constructs of optionality."[1]

On July 16, 2000, the boards of General Mills and Diageo approved the final terms. On July 17, the two firms issued press releases announcing the deal. In the week following the announcement, the shares of General Mills lost 8 percent of their value, net-of-market. But in late August, investors began to bid upward the General Mills share price, perhaps in response to the publication of the merger proxy statement and prospectus, and on news that the operating losses at Pillsbury had narrowed further than analysts had expected in fiscal-year 2000. That fall, General Mills was the subject of several "buy" recommendations. **Exhibit 1** gives the recent trading history of shares in General Mills.

Motives for the Transaction

In its proxy statement, General Mills declared that acquiring Pillsbury would create value for shareholders by providing opportunities for accelerated sales and earnings growth. These opportunities would be exploited through product innovation, channel expansion, international expansion, and productivity gains. The resulting product portfolio would be more balanced. The combined firm would rank fifth in size among competitors, based on global food sales.

In addition to growth, the deal would create opportunities to save costs. Management expected pretax savings of $25 million in fiscal 2001, $220 million in 2002, and $400 million by 2003. Supply-chain improvements (i.e., consolidation of activities and application of best practices in purchasing and logistics); efficiencies in selling, merchandising, and marketing; and, finally, the streamlining of administrative activities would generate these savings.

Terms of the Transaction

The transaction proposed that an acquisition subsidiary of General Mills would merge with the Pillsbury Company, with Pillsbury surviving as a wholly owned subsidiary of General Mills. The agreement outlined several features:

- *Payment of shares.* General Mills would issue 141 million shares of its common stock to Diageo shareholders. After the transaction, Diageo would own about 33 percent of General Mills' outstanding shares. When the board of directors approved the merger in July, the company's shares traded at around $34.00–$37.00. In the first week of December, the company's shares traded at around $40.00–$42.00.

---

[1]Steven Lipin, "First Roll out a Tool to Save Doughboy Deal," *Wall Street Journal,* July 21, 2000, C1.

- *Assumption of Pillsbury debt.* General Mills agreed to assume the liabilities of Pillsbury at the closing, an amount expected to be $5.142 billion of debt. The Pillsbury debt would consist of about $142 million in existing debt and $5.0 billion in new borrowings, which Pillsbury would distribute to Diageo before closing. Terms of the new debt were conditional upon the consent of General Mills, for which a primary concern was that it should not lose its investment-grade bond rating.

- *Contingent payment by Diageo to General Mills.* At the closing, Diageo would establish an escrow fund of $642 million. Upon the first anniversary of the closing, Diageo was required to pay from this fund an amount to General Mills depending on General Mills' share price:

  - *$642 million,* if the average daily share price for 20 days was $42.55 or more.

  - *$0.45 million,* if the average daily share price was $38.00 or less. This price reflected the price at which General Mills was trading at the time the deal was negotiated.

  - *Variable amount,* if the average daily share price was between $38.00 and $42.55. Diageo would retain the amount by which $42.55 would exceed the average daily share price for 20 days, times the number of General Mills shares held by Diageo.

Some financial professionals called this a "claw-back" provision because it would reclaim some value for General Mills if its share price rose. Still other professionals referred to this as a "contingent value right" (CVR), a kind of collar that lived beyond the closing of the deal. CVRs were unusual corporate-finance devices that were used to give the seller confidence in the value of the buyer's shares.

Merrill Lynch estimated that the transaction costs for this deal would amount to $55 million.

Conclusion

In evaluating this proposal, analysts considered current capital-market conditions (see **Exhibit 2**). **Exhibit 3** presents a calculation of the historical share-price volatility of General Mills from the past year's weekly stock prices, ending December 8, 2000—this volatility was 0.248. Using the same method to estimate the *historical volatility* for the year ending July 17, 2000 (the date of announcement of the deal) yielded an estimate of 0.249. Analysts knew that it would be possible to estimate the *implied volatility* from traded options on General Mills' shares (prices on these options are given in **Exhibit 4**). **Exhibit 5** presents the volatilities and financial characteristics of General Mills' peer firms. Contingent payments of the sort used in this transaction were rare; **Exhibit 6** outlines some prominent transactions where they had been used previously, mainly in combinations of pharmaceutical firms.

Analysts wondered why the contingent payment was used in this deal, and why it would be attractive to either side. Most importantly, they puzzled over the implications of the contingent payment for the cost of the deal to General Mills' shareholders. Finally, they sought to determine whether the total deal was fairly priced from the standpoint of shareholders of General Mills. The financial advisers of General Mills presented valuation analyses of Pillsbury and General Mills as a foundation for an assessment of the deal terms (see **Exhibit 7** for a summary of the valuation analyses). Nevertheless, some securities analysts remained uncertain about the deal:

> The deal is dilutive . . . we are concerned with the company's expectations that the acquisition will be dilutive to earnings until fiscal 2004. [General Mills] notes the deal will be accretive to EBITDA by fiscal 2002, suggesting the investment community focus on this metric. However, we prefer to monitor traditional earnings growth in order to track a company's progress.[2]

> The sizable jump in debt concerns us. After the merger is complete, [General Mills] will have borrowings totaling more than $8.5 billion. To help manage the high leverage, the company will likely suspend any share repurchases, using the funds expected to be received [from asset sales] . . . to work down the large debt load.[3]

Ultimately, these analysts sought to make a recommendation about how General Mills' shareholders should vote on the proposed merger: for or against?

---

[2]*Value Line Investment Survey* (August 11, 2000): 1477.

[3]*Value Line Investment Survey* (November 10, 2000): 1476.

EXHIBIT 1 | Weekly Stock Price of General Mills (GIS) Compared to the
S&P 500 Index (Prices indexed to 1.00 at January 3, 2000)

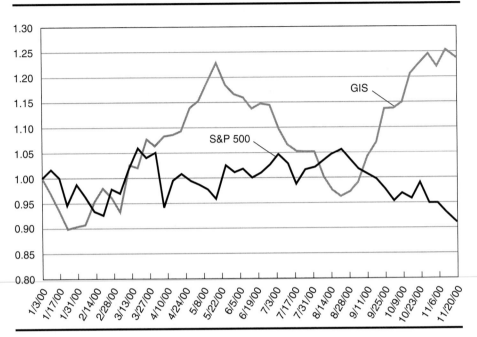

Source of price data: Bloomberg Financial Services.

EXHIBIT 2 | Current Capital-Market Conditions at December 8, 2000

	December 8, 2000
Equity Market Indexes	
Dow Jones Industrial Average	10,373
S&P 500 Index	1,315
NASDAQ OTC Composite Index	2,645
Change in Equity Market Indexes over Last 12 Months	
Dow Jones Industrial Average	−5.6%
S&P 500 Index	−5.8%
NASDAQ OTC Composite Index	−21.1%
U.S. Treasury Yields	
Bills (90 days)	6.09%
Bonds	
1 year	5.22%
2 years	5.43%
5 years	5.32%
10 years	5.43%
20 years	5.74%
30 years	5.64%
Corporate Benchmark Rates	
Prime rate of lending	9.50%
LIBOR	6.45%

Sources of data: *Wall Street Journal* (December 8, 2000); *Value Line Investment Survey.*

EXHIBIT 3 | Estimation of General Mills Stock-Price Volatility across 53 Weeks, November 29, 1999 to November 27, 2000

Date	Weekly Closing Prices	Price Relative	Log of Price Relative	Squared Error of Price Relative
29-Nov-99	$36.56			
6-Dec-99	$33.55	0.918	-0.086	0.007731
13-Dec-99	$32.47	0.968	-0.033	0.001212
20-Dec-99	$32.65	1.006	0.006	0.000013
27-Dec-99	$34.45	1.055	0.054	0.002695
3-Jan-00	$32.67	0.948	-0.053	0.003028
10-Jan-00	$31.76	0.972	-0.028	0.000914
17-Jan-00	$30.61	0.964	-0.037	0.001518
24-Jan-00	$29.39	0.960	-0.040	0.001802
31-Jan-00	$29.51	1.004	0.004	0.000005
7-Feb-00	$29.58	1.002	0.002	0.000000
14-Feb-00	$31.15	1.053	0.052	0.002505
21-Feb-00	$32.07	1.029	0.029	0.000721
28-Feb-00	$31.46	0.981	-0.019	0.000444
6-Mar-00	$30.49	0.969	-0.031	0.001111
13-Mar-00	$33.52	1.100	0.095	0.008646
20-Mar-00	$33.28	0.993	-0.007	0.000085
27-Mar-00	$35.16	1.057	0.055	0.002816
3-Apr-00	$34.63	0.985	-0.015	0.000293
10-Apr-00	$35.43	1.023	0.023	0.000430
17-Apr-00	$35.43	1.000	0.000	0.000004
24-Apr-00	$35.61	1.005	0.005	0.000010
1-May-00	$37.27	1.046	0.045	0.001882
8-May-00	$37.63	1.010	0.010	0.000062
15-May-00	$38.98	1.036	0.035	0.001101
22-May-00	$40.14	1.030	0.029	0.000752
29-May-00	$38.73	0.965	-0.036	0.001418
5-Jun-00	$38.12	0.984	-0.016	0.000320
12-Jun-00	$37.88	0.994	-0.006	0.000071
19-Jun-00	$37.08	0.979	-0.021	0.000538
26-Jun-00	$37.45	1.010	0.010	0.000062
3-Jul-00	$37.41	0.999	-0.001	0.000009
10-Jul-00	$35.81	0.957	-0.044	0.002092
17-Jul-00	$34.82	0.972	-0.028	0.000893
24-Jul-00	$34.33	0.986	-0.014	0.000263
31-Jul-00	$34.27	0.998	-0.002	0.000014
7-Aug-00	$34.33	1.002	0.002	0.000000
14-Aug-00	$32.73	0.953	-0.048	0.002477
21-Aug-00	$31.86	0.974	-0.027	0.000823
28-Aug-00	$31.43	0.986	-0.014	0.000243
4-Sep-00	$31.74	1.010	0.010	0.000061
11-Sep-00	$32.36	1.019	0.019	0.000298
18-Sep-00	$33.96	1.050	0.048	0.002150
25-Sep-00	$35.01	1.031	0.030	0.000808
2-Oct-00	$37.20	1.063	0.061	0.003454
9-Oct-00	$37.07	0.997	-0.003	0.000028
16-Oct-00	$37.45	1.010	0.010	0.000065
23-Oct-00	$39.37	1.051	0.050	0.002320
30-Oct-00	$40.05	1.017	0.017	0.000232
6-Nov-00	$40.74	1.017	0.017	0.000223
13-Nov-00	$39.81	0.977	-0.023	0.000630
20-Nov-00	$40.99	1.030	0.029	0.000742
27-Nov-00	$40.49	0.988	-0.012	0.000200
Sum:		52.132	0.102	0.060218
Average:	35.0548	1.003	0.002	0.001158

Number of price relatives:	52
Number of stock prices:	53
Adjusted weekly variance:	0.001181
Annual variance:	0.061
Annual Standard Deviation (sigma):	**0.248**

Comment: In this table, stock prices are converted into price relatives (which are simply the ratio of today's price to yesterday's price). Then the price relatives are transformed into logarithmic values (in order to normalize the distribution). In the right-hand column, the squared deviations of the logarithmic values are computed from their mean value (0.002). The weekly variance is computed by dividing the sum of the right-hand column (.060218) by the number of price relatives (52) and then multiplying by a correction factor (52/51) to adjust for sampling bias. The annual variance is obtained by multiplying the weekly variance by 52. The standard deviation is the square root of annual variance. For a more detailed discussion of this estimation procedure, see J. Cox and M. Rubinstein, *Options Markets* (Englewood Cliffs, N.J.: Prentice-Hall, 1985), pp. 255–58.

Source of data: Bloomberg Financial Services.

EXHIBIT 4 | Prices of Call and Put Options on General Mills Shares

Option	Call	Put
July 19, 2000		
Stock Price = $35.00		
Expires July 22, 2000, Strike = $35	$0.25	$0.375
Expires October 21, 2000, Strike = $40	$0.50	$5.375
December 14, 2000		
Stock Price = $39.9375		
Expires January 20, 2001, Strike = $45	$0.50	None traded

Note: The 90-day T-bill yield at December 14 was 5.92 percent. In mid-July, the 90-day T-bill yield was 6.14 percent.

Source of data: *Wall Street Journal* (July 20, 2000, and December 15, 2000).

EXHIBIT 5 | Financial Data on Firms Comparable to General Mills

Company and Business	P/E	Previous Year's Food Sales ($bn)[1]	Previous Year's Sales ($bn)[1]	Beta	Expected Sales Growth[2]	Expected Earnings Growth[2]	Expected Dividend Yield[2]	Long-Term Debt-to-Equity Ratio	Total Debt-to-Equity Ratio	Sigma[3]
General Mills, Inc. Cereals, desserts, flour, baking mixes, dinner and side dishes, snacks, beverages, and yogurt products.	19.8	$10.9	$16.7	0.65	8.5%	11.5%	1.10%	6.719	12.048	0.248
ConAgra Foods, Inc. Packaged foods (shelf-stable foods, frozen foods), refrigerated foods, agricultural products.	20.7	$17.1	$25.4	0.80	4.5%	12.5%	0.90%	1.287	2.391	0.398
PepsiCo, Inc. Snack foods, beverages, and juice.	30.6	$ 7.9	$20.4	0.85	5.5%	11.0%	0.56%	0.383	0.399	0.287
Unilever Plc Foods, detergents, personal & home care products.	na	$ 7.2	$43.6	0.75	1.5%	8.5%	0.76%	0.160	0.326	0.425
Sara Lee Corporation Packaged meats, frozen-baked goods, coffee and tea, shoe care, body care, insecticides, air fresheners, intimates.	11.2	$ 6.9	$17.5	0.75	3.0%	8.5%	0.58%	2.951	5.266	0.388
H. J. Heinz Company Ketchup, condiments and sauces, frozen food, soups, beans and pasta meals, tuna and seafood products, infant food.	22.9	$ 5.1	$ 9.4	0.70	4.5%	9.0%	1.57%	2.163	2.365	0.311
Campbell Soup Company Soup and sauces, biscuits and confectionery, and foodservice.	19.7	$ 4.8	$ 6.3	0.80	3.0%	1.0%	0.90%	9.050	23.850	0.375
Kellogg Company Cereals, cereal bars, toaster pastries, frozen waffles, bagels, and other products.	18.8	$ 4.4	$ 7.0	0.70	5.5%	7.0%	1.10%	0.699	2.164	0.365
Hershey Foods Corporation Chocolate and non-chocolate confectionery, pasta and grocery items.	25.2	$ 4.0	$ 4.0	0.65	6.0%	9.0%	1.12%	0.600	0.790	0.361
Quaker Oats Company Hot and cold cereals, pancake mixes and syrups, grain-based snacks, cornmeal, hominy grits, rice products, and pasta.	37.0	$ 2.4	$ 4.7	0.65	5.0%	11.5%	1.14%	1.539	1.730	0.337

na = not available.

[1] Sales for fiscal year ending before July 17, 2000. PepsiCo's next earliest fiscal year ended in December 1999.

[2] Expected sales, earnings, and dividend yield for the five years from 2000 to 2005.

[3] Sigma (volatility) was estimated for the 54 weeks before and including July 17, 2000.

Source of data: *Value Line Investors Services* and casewriter analysis.

EXHIBIT 6 | Terms of Other Contingent-Payment Schemes in Mergers and Acquisitions (M&A)

Deal	Eli Lilly and Company Buys 100% of Equity in Hybritech, Inc.	Rhône-Poulenc Acquires 68% of Equity in Rorer Group, Inc.	Dow Chemical Acquires 67% of Equity in Marion Laboratories	Roche Holding Ltd. Acquires 60% of Equity in Genentech
Closing date	February 1986	July 1990	July 1989	February 1990
Total est. payment (US$)	$412.8 million	$1,600 million	$5,700 million	$1,295 million
General structure	One-stage exchange per each Hybritech share: (1) $22.00 cash or par value of 10-yr. convertible notes paying 6.75%. Conversion price = $66.31 per share. (2) 1.4 warrants to buy Lilly common stock at $75.98 per share. (3) One contingent-payment unit (CPU) paying up to $22.00 in dividends over 10 years.	Three-stage transaction: (1) Cash tender offer for 50.1% of stock in Rorer. At $36.50 for 43.2 million shares, the initial cash outlay is $1,577 million. (2) Rhône-Poulenc (RP) transfers its worldwide human pharmaceuticals business to Rorer. Rorer pays RP $20 million and assumes $265 million of RP debt. Rorer issues million new common shares to RP. (3) RP issues 41.8 million contingent value rights (CVRs).	Two-step transaction: (1) Dow acquires 38.9% of Marion through a cash tender offer at $38 per share. 2) Dow contributes its pharmaceutical subsidiary, Merrill-Dow, and 92 million CVRs in exchange for new Marion shares.	Two-step transaction: (1) Roche purchases a 20% interest in Genentech through the purchase of newly issued shares at $22 per share. (2) All non-Roche common shares are exchanged for $18 cash and ½ share of redeemable common stock. Following the transaction, public shareholders will own 40% of voting stock; Roche will own 60%.
Contingent terms	Annual dividend of CPU equal to: [6% of sales + 20% of gross profits - ($11 million × (1.35^t)] divided by number of Hybritech shares. t = years since 1986. Sales and gross profits are for Hybritech.	CVR entitles holders to receive from RP the amount by which $98.26 a share exceeds either a $52.00 floor price or the average market value of Rorer's share price 60 days before the rights' maturity date of July 31, 1993. Maximum payout $46.26 per share. RP has the right to extend maturity of CVRs for an additional year to July 31, 1994. In that event, the ceiling rises from $98.26 to $106.12. Maximum payout increased to $54.12.	Similar to RP's CVR: a put spread guarantees shareholder returns within a predetermined range of stock prices through 1992.	Redeemable common stock entitles Roche to redeem the shares at predetermined prices until June 1995. Thereafter, these shares will automatically convert into an equal number of regular common shares. Redemption price starts at $38.00 at closing and rises $1.25 per quarter to the maximum of $60 per share in April-June 1995.

673

EXHIBIT 7 | Valuation Estimates by General Mills' Financial Advisers

	Valuation Based on Comparable Firms	Valuation Based on Comparable Transactions	Valuation Based on Discounted Cash Flow Analysis
Analysis of Pillsbury			
Analysis by Evercore Partners:	LTM EBITDA: $8.6–$12.11 billion LTM EBIT: $8.97–$12.87 billion	LTM EBITDA: $10.59 billion LTM EBIT: $13.21 billion	Without synergies: $8.4–$10.5 billion With synergies: $11.3–$14.2 billion
Analysis by Merrill Lynch:	$8.598–$10.78 billion based on LTM EBITDA and LTM EBIT	$9.553–$12.44 billion based on LTM EBITDA and LTM EBIT	Without synergies: $9.184–$11.204 billion With synergies: $11.836–$13.489 billion
Analysis of General Mills			
Stock price at July 14, 2000:	$36.31/share		
Analysis by Evercore Partners:	LTM EBITDA: $34.60/share LTM EBIT: $37.17/share LTM price/earnings: $41.17/share	Comparable transactions are not an applicable basis for valuation of General Mills because the firm is not a target in this transaction.	$34.69–$42.15/share
Analysis by Merrill Lynch:	$31.75–$42.25/share		$38.50–$46.75/share

LTM = latest twelve months.

Note: Evercore's analyses were expressed in terms of valuation multiples rather than dollar figures. To permit easier comparison with the Merrill Lynch figures and to simplify student analysis, the Evercore multiples were converted into dollar figures using several simplifying assumptions.

Source of information: General Mills Definitive Merger Proxy Statement and Prospectus, filed with the U.S. Securities and Exchange Commission (August 22, 2000).

Printicomm's Proposed Acquisition of Digitech: Negotiating Price and Form of Payment

In December 1998, Jay Risher sat in his office at Printicomm seeking to structure the price and form of payment for the acquisition of Digitech. Risher was the vice president and controller of Printicomm, a communications company that offered "end-to-end" printing services by combining production capabilities with the ability to create finished copy and distribute the printed materials. He had identified Digitech as an attractive acquisition candidate and negotiated a letter of intent granting Printicomm the exclusive right to negotiate the purchase of Digitech. That exclusivity period would expire in two weeks.

Due-diligence research revealed that the value of Digitech depended crucially on the managerial know-how of the two leaders of the firm. Risher had gained the agreement of these two individuals to remain with Printicomm for five years to manage the Digitech operations. With the benefit of their leadership, Risher concluded that the value of Digitech would be no greater than $30 million. These individuals believed, however, that Digitech was worth $40 million. With the closing of the transaction approaching, Risher needed to decide on the appropriate deal structure to use given the existing disparity in the valuation of Digitech and the importance of retaining key Digitech employees after the acquisition.

Risher was impressed with the recent growth of Digitech and the likely prospects for future growth. Digitech's revenues had grown from $7 million, in

This case was prepared from field research by Scott Stiegler, under the supervision of Robert F. Bruner. All names and financial data have been disguised. It was written as a basis for class discussion rather than to illustrate effective or ineffective handling of an administrative situation. Copyright © 1999 by the University of Virginia Darden School Foundation, Charlottesville, VA. All rights reserved. *To order copies, send an e-mail to* sales@dardenpublishing.com. *No part of this publication may be reproduced, stored in a retrieval system, used in a spreadsheet, or transmitted in any form or by any means—electronic, mechanical, photocopying, recording, or otherwise—without the permission of the Darden School Foundation.* Rev. 12/01.

1995, to $24 million, in 1998 (see **Exhibit 1** for historical income statements). This rapid growth was attributable to the addition of several key large corporate accounts, which represented almost 40 percent of total revenue in 1997. Printicomm's acquisition of Digitech made strategic sense because of the complementarity of the company's products and markets, and offered the prospect of significant growth potential. In addition, Risher thought that significant cost and revenue synergies might be realized after the acquisition.

Frank Greene, the founder and owner of Digitech, was 60 years old and wanted to sell the firm to achieve some investment liquidity before retirement. He was quite proud of the fact that the success of Digitech was totally a function of the hard work, knowledge, and expertise displayed by himself and his chief operating officer, Jepson "Jep" Buckingham. Greene wanted to retire within the next few years to spend more time with his grandchildren. But walking away from Digitech would be difficult for Greene because he had a rather strong emotional bond with his enterprise and the welfare of its loyal employees. He had chosen to sell the business at this time because he had felt that the current marketplace was offering attractive valuations for companies like Digitech. Greene mentioned to Risher that he had recently seen several other firms like his sell for 10 to 12 times EBITDA. Although Greene was ready to recognize a return on his investment in Digitech by selling, he told Risher that he was willing to continue to run the day-to-day operations of Digitech until he retired.

Negotiations for the acquisition began in August 1998, when Printicomm made a tentative offer of $11 million for Digitech.[1] Because Digitech's value was so strongly a function of the owner's continued involvement, Risher did not initially feel comfortable employing a financial forecast in excess of five years. Given Greene's and Buckingham's continued involvement for a period of five years and effective conveyance of their know-how to Printicomm, Risher was prepared to pay a maximum going-concern enterprise value of approximately $30 million. This valuation was based on both a discounted-cash-flow analysis **(Exhibit 1)** and a review of comparable public companies **(Exhibit 2)** that were prepared by Risher in his valuation analysis (see also **Exhibit 3** for yields on U.S. Treasury securities). Greene was firmly convinced that his business was worth at least 10 times EBITDA, for an enterprise value of $40 million. Digitech financed itself with no debt.

The last negotiation between the two parties ended with Printicomm bidding $28 million and Digitech holding firmly at a price of $40 million. Given the strategic importance of this acquisition, Risher did not want the deal to fall apart over valuation, yet he was not willing to bid in excess of his estimate of $30 million as the maximum estimate of the enterprise value of Digitech. Risher also knew that other competitors would move quickly to acquire Digitech if Printicomm failed in its attempt. Printicomm's exclusive right to negotiate the acquisition of Digitech would end in two weeks. Greene appeared unwilling to budge from his latest asking price.

---

[1]This value was based on the present value of cash flows over the next five years, excluding a terminal value. Printicomm typically opened with a bid based on this type of valuation for companies like Digitech, where intellectual property was a major component of the value.

In an effort to continue negotiating, Risher considered the possibility of proposing an earnout for the transaction. For simplicity, Risher had decided to propose two different earnout structures to Greene at the next meeting. The first earnout structure would extend payments to Greene and Buckingham over the next five years based on Digitech's achieving certain operating-income targets. Because the five-year plan left Printicomm exposed for a long time, Risher planned to incorporate high earnout targets into this structure. The second earnout structure would provide for contingent payments only over the next three years. Risher believed that the earnout targets should be lower for this structure as there was less uncertainty about the future in the shorter time frame. The key would be setting the earnout targets in each structure so that Risher and Greene could each arrive at an acceptable enterprise valuation based on their views of the future.

Printicomm

Printicomm was headquartered in Palo Alto, California, with key production facilities in Georgia, Massachusetts, North Carolina, Colorado, Maryland, New York, and Texas. The company was capable of handling electronic submissions of print copy throughout the United States and from 70 major cities abroad. Printicomm provided customers with integrated, "end-to-end" information and communication solutions, which involved a full range of creative, production, and distribution services.

The company was organized around two business units: Professional Communications, serving customers that published information, and Marketing Communications, serving customers that created and conveyed marketing messages. To those two markets, Printicomm offered services ranging across message creation, production, distribution, and fulfillment for well-defined market niches. Printicomm's services included corporate-identity marketing, advertising, custom publishing, direct marketing, financial communication, interactive media, point-of-purchase marketing, promotional marketing, specialty packaging, software duplication, catalog production, magazine and journal production, and general commercial printing.

Professional Communications

Printicomm Journal Services

PrinticommJS was one of the world's largest producers of scientific, technical, and medical journals. This business unit provided traditional composition, printing, and distribution services, as well as a full complement of digital services, reprint, archiving, and content management for commercial and not-for-profit associations and special-interest publishers. PrinticommJS offered a full range of solutions for publishers of journals, magazines, and other time-sensitive information. In order for PrinticommJS to remain an industry leader in journal services, it was critical for the unit to stay focused on the rapid technological advances within the industry. The vision for PrinticommJS was to create a "total digital pathway" that would enable complete digital workflows and the creation of a flexible digital content data base.

Marketing Communications

PrinticommCom

PrinticommCom was a major integrated marketing firm that, in addition to its creative capabilities, offered in-house printing, production, and distribution. PrinticommCom's tactical capabilities included print and broadcast advertising, direct marketing, catalog and collateral design, publication development, and new media. The integrative approach of PrinticommCom had proved to be attractive to customers interested in dealing with a one-stop shop that could be held accountable for all aspects of a communications program.

Printicomm Financial Communications

Among the top-five financial printers in the nation, PrinticommFC specialized in the creation, production, and distribution of documents (electronic and traditional) to regulatory agencies and the investing community in more than 70 cities worldwide. In addition to the private- and public-business sectors, PrinticommFC's primary markets included commercial- and investment-banking institutions, mutual-fund companies, legal firms, and insurance companies.

Printicomm Graphic Solutions

PrinticommGS was in the business of integrating printing solutions with a wide variety of high-quality graphic-communications services and consultation. Through its Corporate Partnership initiative, PrinticommGS offered analysis that reduced overhead, streamlined procurement systems, and provided innovative solutions to graphic-communications challenges. It provided state-of-the-art commercial prepress and printing, data archiving and management for repurposing content for electronic applications, finishing and binding, and a full array of mailing services. PrinticommGS also was the home of Printicomm Catalog Services, which specialized in providing end-to-end solutions in the catalog industry.

Printicomm Point of Purchase

PrinticommPOP focused on merchandising strategies and creative development, primarily for the quick-service-restaurant, beverage, retail, motor-sports, hospitality, and travel industries. PrinticommPOP handled in-house design, print production and assembly, on-demand production services, kit packing, fulfillment, and data-base management.

Printicomm Specialty Packaging and Promotional Printing

Printicomm Specialty Packaging and Promotional Printing produced CDs and floppy disks that served as distinguishable advertising vehicles, as well as collateral materials that communicated marketing messages. Its services included structural design, production, and distribution of high-quality, full-color external and internal packaging, dimensional mailers, corporate-identity materials, product literature, computer documentation, and catalogs.

Printicomm Technology Solutions

A turnkey operation for software solutions, PrinticommTS handled CD and floppy-disk duplication, label printing, fulfillment and distribution, and inventory and logistics management. PrinticommTS paired its comprehensive in-house services with strategic outsourcing relationships for auxiliary services needed by clients in the high-tech industry and by those who wanted to incorporate technology into their customer offerings.

Over the past five years, Printicomm had completed 22 acquisitions in an effort to expand and enhance its capabilities. Those acquisitions primarily involved premier marketing-, communications-, and publication-services companies that complemented Printicomm's strong core printing competence. Three of the acquisitions involved various earnout structures, most of which were economically successful. Because of the strong element of "intellectual capital" that typified the acquired companies in these transactions, reinvestment needs and asset values were not typically material elements of valuation. Printicomm found earnout structures to be a useful vehicle for substituting the risk of future cash flows from buyer to seller rather than seeking to mitigate risk by increasing its hurdle rate for the transaction.

Digitech

Frank Greene had started Digitech 10 years earlier, after becoming frustrated working as a senior software engineer for a large technology firm. Soon after starting his firm, Greene recruited a former colleague, Jepson "Jep" Buckingham, from their previous employer. Buckingham displayed a brilliance for creative programming and energized the development of important new products. One year after start-up, Digitech had a market hit with Print-now software. Sales of this product spurred revenues to more than $15 million by 1992. However, because of marketing-channel constraints and the fact that a large well-financed competitor quickly entered this market niche, the new product's life cycle was short-lived.

Digitech's sales sputtered until the development of its Marketelegence software in 1995, which was the trademarked name for solutions for advertisers and publishers. Marketelegence used interactive technology to manage marketing messages from creation to ultimate placement to consumers. All photography and graphics were digitized and stored, and the message-and-data repository was linked to a page-layout program. In 1997, sales of this software skyrocketed with the addition of several major new large corporate customers. These customers represented more than 40 percent of 1999's expected sales. Digitech had a great product but was severely constrained by its lack of marketing-channel development and understanding. In Risher's view, management was focused on the development of new products, but lacked the managerial depth to operate a rapidly growing firm the size of Digitech.

Industry Highlights

Commercial printing was one of the nation's oldest and largest manufacturing activities. The industry was highly fragmented, with approximately 52,000 printing establishments and one million employees that were dispersed geographically throughout the United States. In 1998, the top 500 printers represented less than 1 percent of the total population of printers, while their revenues accounted for 34 percent of the total $73 billion in sales. Most printers competed on the regional, state, and local level rather than the national level.

Most products of the U.S. commercial printing industry targeted the diverse needs of domestic consumers and businesses. The industry's economic fortunes tracked fluctuations in the nation's GDP, and were closely tied to the level of U.S. advertising expenditures. Changes in U.S. demographics typically had a swift impact on the markets for printed products. Expansion of the school-age population generated more comics, textbooks, juvenile books, and youth-oriented periodicals. Growth in the number of households promoted the interests of producers of direct mailers, newspaper inserts, and catalogs. New-business formation created markets for trade advertising, forms, directories, and financial and legal printing. An increase in the number of senior citizens increased the demand for newspapers and books.

Commercial printing was a mature industry that was undergoing a significant transition. Forces affecting U.S. commercial printing included changes in technology, shifts in the industry's structural dynamics, changes in the demand for print advertising, and imposition of new electronic media on traditional print markets.

Traditional printing operations had long been centered on analog technology, a process dependent on photographic film, light-sensitive printing plates, solvent-based inks, and an array of chemicals and developers. This traditional technology was rapidly being replaced by digital technology. As a result, thousands of typesetting firms had been rendered obsolete by digital type produced on desktop computers. Also gone were the many platemaking and color-separation shops whose film-based skills had become worthless as digital processors produced color-corrected films or the digital text and images were applied directly to printing plates. Digital technology was also being applied to printing presses themselves, which yielded cost-effective, full-color, short production runs of text- and image-variable printed products that had been cost-prohibitive before the advent of digital imaging.

The rapid technological changes in the industry had led to increasing consolidation as players sought economies of scale while attempting to retain a marketing focus that was sensitive to local and regional printing opportunities. A wave of merger-and-acquisition activities, supported by a growing U.S. economy and rising stock market, was consolidating ownership among a few dominant players. The most successful consolidators in the industry displayed many of the same qualities. First, they were geographically dispersed and had a specific business strategy. Second, they defined themselves as either a high-value-added printer providing extra services in a specialized market niche or a specialized low-cost producer in a narrow market niche. The goal of these firms was to become a one-stop shop that met all their clients' communications needs.

While commercial printing's value of shipments closely paralleled GDP fluctuations, the industry was largely dependent on U.S. expenditures on print advertising. Since 1980, U.S. advertising through various print media had held steady at approximately 60 percent of total advertising expenditures. Although print advertising's trends in the 1990s showed overall growth in nominal dollars, gains in advertising expenditures among print media varied significantly. Marginal growth was expected in the advertising revenues of newspapers and periodicals, while higher advertising growth was expected in the direct-mail, catalog, and insert segments. The increased use of digital printing equipment was expected to enable U.S. printers to respond more rapidly to any changes in print demand that might arise from fluctuations in advertising expenditures.

Although total demand in the United States for printed products continued to expand, the electronic media provided strong competition. Examples included CD-ROMs, which reduced the need for technical manuals, encyclopedias, and directories; Web sites on the Internet, which provided electronic access to digital catalogs, annual reports, and other company information; and e-mail, including electronic commerce, which lessened the demand for newsletters and printed business information and forms. The Internet was used on a regular basis at work or at home by more than 29 million U.S. residents 18 or older. This sector represented 15 percent of the U.S. adult population. A doubling of this Internet-accessed sector over the next decade was virtually assured, guaranteeing further inroads in the demand for selected printed products.

A series of favorable factors was expected to support the growth of U.S. printed-product output over the next five years. The U.S. population was projected to reach 280.4 million by 2003, an increase of 8.1 million. Higher levels of educational attainment and increasing personal income were expected to accompany this population growth. A rising U.S. economy, coupled with growth in aggregate demand for print advertising, was expected to support an inflation-adjusted annual growth rate of 2 percent in the value of industry shipments over the next five years. Competition from the electronic media was expected to reduce U.S. markets for some printed products, but commercial printing's aggregate demand was projected to stay relatively aligned with growth in the nation's economy. The costs of the printing industry's principal material input, paper, were expected to increase over the next five years, adversely affecting printers' profit margins.

Support for the Acquisition of Digitech

Printicomm was at a unique historical inflection point, where the skills and competencies with which its businesses had originally achieved success were less able to sustain profit growth and margins necessary for quality investment. This slow erosion of print margins and the increasing difficulty of maintaining or growing revenues had severely strained future internal growth. Continuing innovation in graphic reproduction threatened to render current equipment obsolete and further increase industry overcapacity, forcing the demise or further consolidation of remaining companies.

Printicomm's strategy in this rapidly changing industry was to grow its business through strategic acquisitions that would provide the company with additional competitive advantages in its selected niches of the commercial-printing industry. Risher believed that the acquisition of Digitech would have a significant positive impact on the performance of both the Printicomm Journal Services and Printicomm Point of

Purchase divisions. Digitech's Marketelegence software would enhance the capabilities of these divisions by providing customers with the latest electronic marketing solutions.

Alternatives

Given the difficulty of the negotiations to date, Risher reflected on the strategic alternatives before him.

Develop Capability Internally

One alternative for Printicomm was to develop Digitech's technology in-house. The time and expense of creating a viable software program with the capabilities of Marketelegence were likely to be high, but failure to reach a reasonable purchase price for Digitech might make this a good option. According to some of Risher's rough calculations, it would cost Printicomm $50 million to develop the technology. Moreover, it would take approximately two years for Printicomm to have a working prototype that could compete in the marketplace.

Find Another Company to Purchase

Risher knew that it was not too late to try to acquire an alternative company. There were a number of other small software companies that had developed their own forms of digital technology for the commercial printing industry, but Risher believed that Digitech's technology was superior to that of the current competition and was worth a premium price, if necessary. Risher also knew that Greene possessed strong managerial skills and that his level of qualifications would be difficult to find in another target company. In addition, it would be frustrating to start negotiations with a new company given the time and energy already spent on the Digitech transaction.

Fixed-Price Deal

Negotiations up to this point had focused on determining a fixed price for the acquisition of Digitech. A fixed-price deal would certainly be the easiest to consummate, requiring only a standard purchase-and-sale agreement that highlighted the total consideration in amount and form. Unfortunately, the two parties remained relatively far apart on their respective notions of a fair valuation for Digitech's business. Risher was also concerned that if Printicomm paid a premium price for Digitech, Digitech's management would have little incentive to stay on at Digitech and continue to grow the business. Risher thought that the retention of Greene and Buckingham was critical to integrating the companies and transferring business knowledge between the two companies.

Earnout

Given his concerns about valuation and management retention, Risher had begun to consider the idea of using an earnout to move this potential transaction forward. Risher recalled that an earnout was an acquisition payment mechanism whereby some portion of the purchase price of the acquired company (Digitech) would be paid by the acquiring company (Printicomm) only if Digitech attained certain agreed-upon performance goals after the closing. Risher knew that there were three key elements in creating a successful earnout. First, the earnout should be based on achievable performance goals that increased the value of Digitech in the hands of Printicomm after the closing. Second, Digitech's management should receive adequate compensation for creating that value. Third, the earnout should provide Digitech's management with the resources and operating freedom necessary to achieve its performance goals.

Risher knew that an earnout made a lot of sense from an economic perspective and, if designed appropriately, could be viewed as a win-win situation for both parties. He also knew that the two key drivers that could be negotiated in designing an earnout were the time period and the earnout targets. As a result, Risher decided to develop two different earnout structures to present to Greene at their next meeting. The two proposals would offer alternatives that were on either side of the spectrum with regard to time period and earnout targets.

The first earnout structure would extend payments to Greene and Buckingham over the next five years, based on Digitech's achieving certain operating income targets. Because this five-year plan left Printicomm exposed for a long time, Risher wanted to incorporate high earnout targets into the structure. Risher decided to set the targets as follows: 1999—$2.5 million; 2000—$3.0 million; 2001—$3.0 million; 2002—$3.5 million; 2003—$3.5 million. These targets were purposely set close to Printicomm's projected operating income numbers for Digitech so that Printicomm would pay additional monies only for performance above the expected level. Risher also believed that the dollars paid out at closing could be set at the relatively low value of $20 million because of the potential future value offered to Digitech with a five-year earnout period.

The second earnout structure would provide for contingent payments only over the next three years. Risher believed that the earnout targets should be lower for this structure as there was less uncertainty about the future in this shorter time frame. Risher decided to set the targets as follows: 1999—$2.0 million; 2000—$2.5 million; 2001—$2.5 million. These relatively low targets provided Digitech with a good opportunity to earn additional monies in the earnout, but were still not expected to cost Printicomm much over the shorter time frame. Because the shorter time frame provided Digitech with less time to capture value from the earnout, Risher believed that the dollars at closing would need to approximate the $28 million fixed-price offer that was already on the table.

The tax treatment of the earnout payments was under consideration by Printicomm's counsel. If Printicomm could deduct the payments as expenses, the cost of an earnout would be materially lower. But it was possible that the earnout payments might be viewed as a dividend (i.e., paid from after-tax earnings). As a starting point, Risher decided to make the more conservative assumption, namely, that the earnout payments were not a deductible expense.

Each earnout would be valued differently by Printicomm and Digitech, based on their respective views of the future. Risher decided that he would use a simulation-based valuation model that would use expected distributions for key value drivers.

Risher believed that the key drivers of future value for Digitech were sales growth and profit margin. As a result, he set out to determine the appropriate distributions for those variables from Printicomm's perspective. He projected that sales would grow by at least 5 percent a year, with a maximum growth rate of 15 percent. He further estimated that the most likely growth rate for future sales was 10 percent. Risher also decided that the same distribution of expected values could be used for expected future profit margins.

In order to anticipate how Digitech might view an earnout proposal, Risher decided to repeat the analysis, using the distributions that Digitech would likely use for the key drivers in its analysis. Risher reviewed the projections prepared by Digitech, and concluded that Digitech's minimum expected future sales growth was 10 percent. He also determined that Digitech's maximum expected sales growth was 30 percent, with the most likely growth rate equaling 20 percent. Risher believed that the distribution for expected profit margins was slightly tighter, with a range of 15 to 25 percent, with 20 percent being the most likely.

After designing the two earnout options and determining the distributions for the key value drivers from the perspectives of both parties, Risher thought it was time to simulate the values of the earnout proposals in order to determine the attractiveness of each earnout. Based on this analysis of the two proposed earnouts, he wondered which structure he would recommend to Greene and why.

EXHIBIT 1 | Historical and Projected Income Statements and Cash Flows

Years Ended	Actuals Reported by Digitech							Projection by Printicomm			
	1992	1993	1994	1995	1996	1997	1998	Est 1999	Est 2000	Est 2001	Est 2002
Sales	$15,350	$10,633	$11,313	$6,747	$7,400	$18,651	$23,450	$28,140	$32,361	$36,244	$39,506
Nominal sales growth		−31%	6%	−40%	10%	152%	26%	20%	15%	12%	9%
Cost of goods sold	9,655	8,700	8,890	5,096	3,850	14,800	16,850	21,867	24,868	27,539	30,018
Selling, general, & administrative	2,500	1,900	1,950	2,200	2,400	2,600	2,600	3,374	3,837	4,249	4,632
Depreciation and amortization	55	55	55	55	65	65	65	84	96	106	116
Total expenses	12,210	10,655	10,895	7,351	6,315	17,465	19,515	25,326	28,801	31,895	34,766
Operating income	$3,140	$(22)	$418	$(604)	$1,085	$1,186	$3,935	$2,814	$3,560	$4,349	$4,741
Operating ratio	80%	100%	96%	109%	85%	94%	83%	90%	89%	88%	88%
Operating income after taxes								$1,688	$2,136	$2,610	$2,844
Plus depreciation and amortization								$84	$96	$106	$116
Less capital expenditures								$(281)	$(324)	$(362)	$(395)
Less additions to working capital								$(563)	$(647)	$(725)	$(790)
								929	1,261	1,628	1,775
								$929	$1,261	$1,628	$1,775

1% This year's sales.
2% This year's sales.

DCF Valuation: Printicomm's View
Discount Rate   10%
Terminal Growth Rate   5%
PV of total free cash flows $30,267

	Projection by Digitech			
	Est 1999	Est 2000	Est 2001	Est 2002
Sales	$28,609	$34,331	$40,167	$45,389
Nominal sales growth	22%	20%	17%	13%
Cost of goods sold	21,985	25,789	30,173	34,096
Selling, general, & administrative	3,392	3,979	4,656	5,261
Depreciation	85	99	116	132
Total expenses	25,462	29,868	34,945	39,488
Operating income	$3,147	$4,463	$5,222	$5,901
Operating ratio	89%	87%	87%	87%
Operating income after taxes	$1,888	$2,678	$3,133	$3,540
Plus depreciation and amortization	$85	$99	$116	$132
Less capital expenditures	$(286)	$(343)	$(402)	$(454)
Less additions to working capital	$(572)	$(687)	$(803)	$(908)
	1,115	1,747	2,044	2,310
	$1,115	$1,747	$2,044	$2,310

1% This year's sales.
2% This year's sales.

DCF Valuation: Digitech's View
Discount Rate   10%
Terminal Growth Rate   5%
PV of total free cash flows $40,285

EXHIBIT 2 | Selected Industry Comparables (dollars in millions, except for per-share data)

Company	Shares Outstanding (mill)	Share Price 31 Dec, 96 ($)	Beta (Lev.)	Beta (Unlev.)	Market Value Equity ($ mill)	Net Debt ($ mill)	Firm Value ($ mill)	Book Value ($ mill)	Revenues ($ mill)	EBIT ($ mill)	Net Income ($ mill)	1999E EPS	EBITDA
Champion Industries	9.714	$ 10.25	0.54	0.49	$100	$17.86	$117	$ 90.62	$123.06	$ 7.87	$4.15	$1.14	$11.49
Cunningham Graphics Intl.	5.305	$ 15.25	na	na	$ 81	$ 2.4	$ 83	6.3	$ 53.15	$ 3.51	$4.01	$1.05	$ 4.20
Baldwin Technology A	14.920	$ 5.625	0.53	0.43	$ 84	$33.11	$117	$126.91	$231.41	$14.39	$9.02	$0.57	$18.37
Polyvision Corp.	14.093	$2.0625	0.25	0.23	$ 29	$ 3.36	$ 32	na	$ 34.17	$ 1	$ 1	$0.09	$ 2
PrimeSource Corp.	6.529	$ 6.625	0.62	0.42	$ 43	$34.15	$ 77	$ 105.1	$453.05	$ 9	$ 4	$0.89	$ 12
Tufco Technologies	4.426	$ 5.00	0.10	0.07	$ 22	$ 17.7	$ 40	$ 65	$ 76.97	$ 2	$ 0	$0.13	$ 5
IPI Inc.	4.734	$3.4375	na	na	$ 16	$ 0.05	$ 16	$ 32.48	$ 8.53	$ 1.95	$2.03	$0.43	$ 2.37

Enterprise Value as a Multiple of:

	Revenues	EBIT	Net Income	EBITDA
Champion Industries	$1.0	$14.9	$ 28.3	$10.2
Cunningham Graphics Intl.	$1.6	$23.7	$ 20.8	$19.8
Baldwin Technology A	$0.5	$ 8.1	$ 13.0	$ 6.4
Polyvision Corp.	$0.9	$23.3	$ 32.1	$18.3
PrimeSource Corp.	$0.2	$ 8.3	$ 18.9	$ 6.6
Tufco Technologies	$0.5	$17.8	$120.7	$ 8.2
IPI Inc.	$1.9	$ 8.4	$ 8.0	$ 6.9
Low	$0.2	$ 8.1	$ 8.0	$ 6.4
High	$1.9	$23.7	$120.7	$19.8
Median	$0.9	$14.9	$ 20.8	$ 8.2

Equity Value as a Multiple of:

	1999E EPS	Book Value
Champion Industries	$ 9.0	$ 1.1
Cunningham Graphics Intl.	$14.5	$12.8
Baldwin Technology A	$ 9.8	$ 0.7
Polyvision Corp.	$22.9	na
PrimeSource Corp.	$ 7.4	$ 0.4
Tufco Technologies	$38.5	$ 0.3
IPI Inc.	$ 8.0	$ 0.5
Low	$ 7.4	$ 0.3
High	$38.5	$12.8
Median	$ 9.8	$ 0.6

na = not available.

Source: Bloomberg Financial Services and case writer's analysis.

EXHIBIT 3 | Yields on U.S. Treasury Securities

Maturity	Current	1 Year Ago
1 Year	4.69%	5.55%
2 Year	5.00	5.69
3 Year	5.04	5.70
4 Year	5.08	5.73
5 Year	5.11	5.75
10 Year	5.22	5.74
30 Year	5.57	5.90

Source: *The Wall Street Journal.*

Structuring Repsol's Acquisition of YPF S.A. (A)

Repsol will seek to negotiate with YPF to achieve a successful integration of the two companies.
—Repsol S.A.[1]

It was a shock to Alfonso Cortina, Repsol's chief executive, when he was cold-shouldered at his first YPF board meeting.... The Argentine company, under the leadership of Roberto Monti, appeared determined to resist Mr. Cortina's efforts to start integrating the companies' activities.[2]

In early April 1999, Repsol chair and chief executive officer (CEO) Alfonso Cortina reflected on the resistance of YPF to his firm's overtures. Repsol was the dominant oil company in Spain and the thirteenth largest in the world in reserves. Seeking oil reserves and the advantages of larger scale, Cortina had embarked on a strategy of acquiring oil assets throughout Latin America. He began to acquire Yacimientos Petroliferos Fiscales S.A. (YPF) when the Argentine government announced that it would sell its block of shares in the firm. YPF was the largest oil company in Argentina, and the twelfth largest in reserves. YPF management had resisted negotiating a friendly acquisition. To complete a takeover of the firm, Cortina would need to appeal directly to the shareholders in the form of a tender offer to purchase their shares. Unsolicited tender offers were extremely rare events in cross-border merger and acquisitions (M&A) and especially between developed and developing economies. It was very important to Repsol's management that any offer would receive the support of YPF's shareholders and repel potential competitors. A tender offer of that magnitude would be the biggest ever by a Spanish company, and the biggest ever in the energy sector.

---

[1]"Presentation to Security Analysts on 22 January 1999," Repsol's Web site, www.repsol.com, accessed January 27, 2000.

[2]"Repsol: The Winner Must Oil the Wheels," *Financial Times,* accessed at ft.com-Mergers and Acquisitions/Case studies, 27 January 2000.

This case was prepared from public information by Fernanda Pasquarelli and Pablo I. Ciano under the supervision of Professor Robert F. Bruner. The financial support of the Batten Institute is gratefully acknowledged. Copyright © 2000 by the University of Virginia Darden School Foundation, Charlottesville, VA. All rights reserved. *To order copies, send an e-mail to* sales@dardenpublishing.com. *No part of this publication may be reproduced, stored in a retrieval system, used in a spreadsheet, or transmitted in any form or by any means—electronic, mechanical, photocopying, recording, or otherwise—without the permission of the Darden School Foundation.* Rev. 12/01.

The first step in planning the tender offer was to settle on the amount of consideration Repsol would pay for the 85 percent of YPF it did not already own. Cortina had decided to offer $44.78[3] per YPF share. The next step would be to determine the form of payment and financing for the offer. Repsol could offer cash, shares of Repsol stock, or conceivably, a mix of the two. Any cash offer would need to be financed by an issue of debt or equity securities, since the cash reserves of the firm would not meet the total payment of $13.438 billion. Cortina contemplated the three possible financing alternatives. He wondered what the comparative advantages and disadvantages of the alternatives were and how they should be analyzed.

History of the Transaction

In January 1998, the Argentine government announced its intention to sell its 20.56 percent holding in YPF that remained after the firm's privatization several years earlier. But unexpected volatility in the equity markets caused the auction to be delayed. In September, the government invited 16 companies to bid for a block of 14.99 percent, with a minimum price of $38 per share. Of the 16 invitees, only six signed the confidentiality agreement to gain access to private information about YPF and to gain the right to bid in an auction for the block of YPF shares. These included Repsol, ENI S.p.A. of Italy, Consolidated Natural Gas of Pittsburgh, Argentina's Perez Companc S.A., and Britain's BP Amoco PLC.

On January 20, 1999, Repsol won the bidding at the minimum price of $38 per share, reflecting the absence of any other bidders. That bid was at a 30 percent premium to the market price of a few days earlier, $29.25. "It's a steal,"[4] analyst Vinod Sehgal remarked, noting that Repsol would be acquiring YPF's energy reserves at a comparatively cheap price of $3.65 per barrel. Another analyst team[5] opined that the bid was in line with the prevailing EBITDA multiples.

A news report noted:

> Repsol is now likely to start a long and arduous courtship with YPF's loyal shareholders in an attempt to convince them that further integration with Repsol, and its Argentine oil and gas subsidiary Astra . . . makes sense . . . YPF's bylaws say that any buyer who pays a premium for 15 percent of the company's shares or more must pay all other shareholders the similar premium in cash. That rule makes an all-cash tender offer for YPF difficult. . . . Repsol is likely to solicit a vote for an extraordinary shareholders meeting and then ask for a change in bylaws allowing for a tender offer via a stock swap. That move is bound to meet with some opposition, if only because there is a wise perception that Repsol has badly

---

[3]Figures in this case are quoted in U.S. dollars, consistent with general practice in international oil transactions, and cross-border M&A. Also note that the Argentine peso was convertible into the dollar at parity (i.e., one for one).

[4]Quotation of Vinod Sehgal in "Repsol Wins Stake in YPF with $2 Billion Bid," *Wall Street Journal*, 21 January 1999.

[5]Irene Himona, Rachel Beaver, and Andrew Whittock, "Repsol-YPF: A Quantum Leap," ABN AMRO, September 6, 1999.

managed Astra, which it purchased a few years ago. "It has not struck my attention that Repsol is noted for its ability to cut costs and merge companies," said [one money manager].[6]

The Argentine government would maintain a "golden share."[7] The government would support a Repsol tender offer for the balance of YPF for a period of three years, including supporting changes to YPF's bylaws to facilitate an acquisition. Any third party interested in launching a tender offer for 100 percent of YPF would have to pay a premium of 25 percent over the price paid by Repsol for its block of YPF.

The securities markets expected Repsol's management to announce plans to increase control in YPF. Therefore, Alfonso Cortina wanted to make a public announcement before the end of April. It was time to choose a form of payment (stock for stock or all cash) and financing (debt, equity, or a combination) for the transaction. Cortina understood that to meet investors' expectations and to minimize the cost of the acquisition he needed to assess conditions in the current debt and equity global capital markets especially the increasing risk in emerging economies and volatile oil prices.

Industry Outlook

After a long period of weak oil prices, 1999 was likely to be a year of recovery. Prices had been depressed in 1998, due to the Asian financial crisis, the expansion of Iraqi oil exports, and warm winters in Europe and North America. But oil prices had increased unexpectedly in recent months, increasing the attractiveness of firms with proven reserves. Inventories of oil in the United States and Asia were contracting as a consequence of strong demand. That, combined with OPEC's compliance with a landmark agreement reached in March to boost sagging oil prices by slashing daily output by 7 percent, was driving prices up. The rebound began in late March, and industry analysts predicted that it would likely continue in the future, taking crude prices toward $18 to $20 per barrel. **Exhibit 1** shows oil price fluctuations during the last nine years.

Spot oil prices were trading at around $25 per barrel for January 2000 deliveries. Traders seemed anxious about what would happen in March 2000, when the actual OPEC agreement would expire. At one meeting, the oil cartel representatives expressed their interest in stable prices. With strong demand, observers speculated that they might increase production. Industry players still remembered OPEC's inaction for production restraint during 1998 that drove prices to a 30-year low, below $10 per barrel, seriously damaging the sector's profitability.

---

[6]Irene Himona, Rachel Beaver, and Andrew Whittock,

[7]Golden shares were a common feature of most privatizations of state-owned enterprises. They were first introduced by the British government in its privatization program that began in the 1980s under the leadership of Prime Minister Margaret Thatcher. In YPF's case, the golden share would permit the government to exercise veto power in (1) a merger of YPF with any other company, (2) acquisition by any other company of more than 50 percent of the capital, (3) sales of significant assets involved in exploration and production activities, or (4) dissolution of the company. Unclear was the possible influence of this golden share on the management of YPF.

The natural gas sector also looked promising, especially in Latin America which was enjoying strong demand coupled with the final stages of industry deregulation. The construction of various cross-border pipelines would reduce supply/demand imbalances and would make the product available to countries with perennial need for gas. Experts forecasted expected growth rates of natural gas volumes at 25 percent for Brazil, 12 percent for Chile, and 5 percent for Argentina.

A recent wave of very large mergers had suddenly changed the paradigm of competition in the oil industry. **Exhibit 2** compares recently announced "jumbo" deals with Repsol's contemplated takeover of YPF. Second-tier firms in America and Europe realized that they were too small to compete with the giants for the biggest of the multibillion-dollar projects in risky but important places such as China and Africa. Yet they were not sufficiently focused to compete effectively against niche firms with geographic or technical specialties.

An industry analyst likened the current merger madness to "the rush to find a partner, any partner, at a school dance after the big boys have picked the best ones." He suggested that remaining firms could try to succeed alone, but to do so they would have to rethink their strategies.

Repsol S.A.

Repsol was an international integrated oil and gas company. In 1998, it had the largest revenue of any industrial company in Spain. Compared with other large competitors, it was the "oil company without any oil,"[8] with 1.1 billion barrels in proven reserves, ranking it thirteenth after YPF, which had 3.1 billion barrels.

Repsol was founded in 1987, when the Spanish government consolidated various state-owned oil and gas assets. Spain sold 24 percent of the firm to public investors in 1987, another 66 percent in 1996, and the remaining holdings in April 1997. Its shares were quoted on the Madrid Stock Exchange and in the form of ADRs[9] on the New York Stock Exchange.

Repsol had operations in 26 countries. Since 1996, the firm had been pursuing a strategy to create a new geographical dimension to its operations in markets with high growth potential. Latin America was the center of Repsol's strategy and accounted for $3 billion invested in the region since 1995. In Latin America, Repsol saw excellent opportunities to reinforce important pillars of its corporate strategy, in particular, the desire to strengthen its upstream business and to strengthen its gas business, exploiting the links to electricity generation. Prior to the YPF bid, Repsol had acquired refining assets in Peru, and 67 percent of Astra, the fifth-largest energy company in Argentina. Astra derived the bulk of its earnings from exploration and production, and became a platform for the acquisition of other oil assets in Argentina. Cortina intended

---

[8]*Wall Street Journal*, 21 January 1999.

[9]ADRs (American Depositary Receipts) were receipts issued by U.S. banks to American buyers as a convenient substitute for direct ownership of stock in foreign companies. ADRs were traded on stock exchanges and in the over-the-counter market. Foreign companies issued ADRs as a way of reaching the American stock market.

to merge YPF with Astra,[10] which, if it pushed through, would require Repsol to dispose of assets in order to satisfy Argentine antitrust authorities.

Exhibit 3 gives Repsol's financial statements for 1996, 1997, and 1998. Repsol's share price had risen 27 percent to $16.74 at the end of March 1999, from $13.62 at the end of September 1998, reflecting the rise in oil prices in early 1999, and the market's reaction to the YPF deal. Historically, Repsol's price/earnings (P/E) ratio had been similar to those of its European rivals but below the P/E ratios of major U.S. competitors. With a market capitalization of $15 billion, Repsol was perceived as a neutral or "hold" stock by securities analysts. Analysts agreed that if Repsol succeeded in a full acquisition of YPF, then the increase in size of the company, its more balanced revenue mix, and its geographical diversity, would help the shares trade at higher earnings and cash flow multiples than in the past.

YPF S.A.

YPF was Argentina's largest company, with a market capitalization of $15 billion. It was engaged in the exploration, development, and production of oil and natural gas, in electricity-generation activities, and in the refining, marketing, transportation and distribution of oil, as well as in a wide range of petroleum products, petroleum derivatives, petrochemicals and liquid petroleum gas. **Exhibit 4** gives YPF's recent financial statements.

YPF played a key role in Argentina's energy industry, accounting for 51 percent of the total estimated crude oil production, 58 percent of the total domestic and export sales of Argentine natural gas, 51 percent of the total refining capacity, and 37 percent of all service stations. The company had been pursuing an aggressive expansion strategy, mainly through joint ventures in areas in which it held concessions.

As part of the government privatization program, YPF completed an initial public offering in 1993. As a result, the Argentine government's ownership of YPF's equity was reduced from 100 percent to approximately 20 percent. **Exhibit 5** contains the current YPF structure of equity ownership. In addition, YPF restructured its internal organization and significantly reduced the number of its employees, from more than 51,000 in December 1990, to 7,500 by December 1993. In December 1998, YPF had approximately 9,500 employees. Thanks to this restructuring, the firm outperformed its peer group of Latin-American oil companies and generally was regarded as an efficiently run firm.

Despite its low cost structure, strong management, commanding position in Argentina's downstream industries, and the strong export potential of natural gas to Brazil, YPF's future performance could be affected by certain risk factors, such as economic and political risks in Argentina and other countries where YPF had operations and volatility in oil prices. Argentina's economy experienced periods of slow or negative growth, high inflation, currency devaluation, and the imposition of exchange

---

[10]"CMS Keeps Eye on YPF-Repsol Merger," *Alexander's Gas & Oil Connections, Company News, Latin America,* June 11, 1999, www.gasandoil.com (accessed 27 January 2000).

rate control measures. In 1991, the currency board system[11] that Argentina adopted brought more uncertainty about the peso because it differed from an orthodox currency board system. "An orthodox currency board system had no central bank and no room for discretionary monetary policy. Argentina's monetary system, in contrast, had a central bank with room for discretionary monetary policy."[12] Moreover, YPF's revenues in dollars and costs in pesos increased the risks of any change in the exchange rate policy in Argentina.

The tight link between Argentina and other emerging countries amplified uncertainty about the timing of this transaction. Emerging economies seemed to be recovering from the financial collapse that began with the Russian debt moratorium in August 1998, and was followed by the Brazilian currency devaluation on January 13, 1999 (five days before the Argentine auction of YPF shares). Investors remained reluctant to invest in emerging economies.

Foreign petroleum exploration, development, and production activities were subject to a variety of regulatory and political risks, including: foreign exchange controls from other countries, expropriation of property, and risks of loss in countries due to civil strife and guerilla activities. Such risks might interrupt YPF's operations. **Exhibit 6** presents the actual sovereign ratings for all the countries where YPF had operations, as well as capital market conditions.

Fluctuations in oil prices would affect the timing and reduce the amount of projected capital expenditures related to explorations and development activities which, in turn, could have a negative effect on YPF's ability to replace reserves. The ability to replace reserves was a crucial factor for companies in the commodity sector, because it suggested the company's ability to continue in the business. Credit ratings and cost of financing depended not only on the level of reserves but also on their estimated average life. For this reason, YPF's exposure to oil prices could ultimately increase investors' concerns about the future outlook for YPF.

M&A Environment[13]

M&A activity worldwide exploded from 1994 to 1998: the value of announced European transactions had grown at a compound average rate of 42 percent. In the first quarter of 1999, announced deals in Europe amounted to $449 billion, compared with $128 billion a year earlier. This reflected increases in both the number of deals and in the average transaction size. European M&A activity was driven by both global influences, such as deregulation, globalization, buoyant equity markets, etc., and European-specific influences, such as the creation of the European Monetary Union,

---

[11]Steve H. Hanke and Kurt Schuler, "A Dollarization Blueprint for Argentina," *Foreign Policy Briefing,* Cato Institute, March 11, 1999, 1. Note: Under Argentina's currency board system, the peso traded at a fixed rate one to one with the dollar and was convertible on demand.

[12]Hanke and Schuler, 8.

[13]This section draws certain facts from presentations at the Mergers and Acquisitions Conference, Credit Suisse First Boston, May 14, 1999.

pressure by governments to create "national champions," and consolidation of previously fragmented markets.

In Latin America, many of the same forces exerted influence on M&A activity, though with an emerging markets twist. Generally, the liberalization of markets through trade, deregulation, and privatization pushed firms to use their resources more efficiently. The rise of regional trading blocs, such as Mercosur, and globalization made it attractive for foreign buyers to establish regional platforms for business activities and further acquisitions in key markets. As business and capital markets matured, equity market volatility in those markets gradually declined. Strengthening business fundamentals and relatively low valuations meant that business assets might be acquired at reasonable prices. Those factors combined to create a compelling argument for foreign and domestic firms to seek acquisitions in emerging markets.

M&A activity in Latin America had increased at a compound rate of 58 percent from 1995 to 1998. Latin American deal volumes in 1997 and 1998 were greater than the previous 10 years combined. European-based acquirers had increased their activity four-fold between 1996 and 1998. Acquisition activity was not slowed by the Brazilian crisis in early 1999. Seventy-five percent of recent transactions were in Brazil, Argentina, and Mexico. Seventy-three percent of M&A volume occurred in capital-intensive industries.

Motives for the Acquisition

Repsol management noted several advantages from this transaction:

*   *Geographical diversification.* YPF would deepen Repsol's business base in Argentina and give it a material presence in other Latin American countries.

*   *Business diversification.* Repsol's activities were concentrated in the "downstream" segment of the oil industry: refining and marketing. YPF had a substantial presence in exploration and production. Also, YPF would add a significant activity in natural gas.

*   *Acquisition of reserves.* The transaction would convey YPF's substantial reserves at relatively low average price.

*   *Competitive preemption.* Acquiring this dominant competitor in Latin America would deny other oil companies access to this market. YPF had a strong brand in Latin America.

*   *Critical mass.* The transaction would elevate Repsol in the league tables of integrated oil companies (see **Table 1**). This would permit the exploitation of some economies of scale. More importantly, it would create the financial strength to permit exploration for new reserves and more aggressive marketing.

The precipitous decline in oil prices during 1998 (West Texas Intermediate grade was down by 34 percent over that year), had encouraged several high profile consolidations in the oil and gas sector. Cost savings, economies of scale, concentration and consolidation of capital spending motivated those mergers. Repsol's full takeover of YPF, however, was driven by a strategic step to take advantage of a unique opportunity.

For Repsol, the acquisition of YPF represented an opportunity to meet a number of its ambitions quickly. It would create an entity with a much better balance in a business sense, given that YPF's upstream business counterbalanced Repsol's orientation to the downstream. **Exhibit 7** shows the impact of the acquisition on Repsol's revenue sources. For both companies, the combined entity represented a geographical diversification from focused country-based current operations.

The acquisition reflected Repsol's four strategic objectives:[14]

Table 1	Rank of Repsol-YPF among European and American Integrated Oil Companies:
Total assets	8th
Operating revenues	9th
Operating income	7th
Net income	6th
Oil & gas production	9th
Oil & gas reserves	7th
Service stations	8th

1. Grow upstream: YPF would strengthen Repsol's upstream business; oil and gas reserves would grow by more than four times; oil and gas production would rise by 4.3 times.

2. Expand internationally: YPF would triple Repsol's presence in Latin America with 50 percent of the new group's total assets.

3. Diversify into gas/power generation: YPF would raise gas production eightfold.

4. Retain domestic market share: YPF's acquisition would complement Repsol's dominance in the Spanish market.

Synergies

Repsol's operating management believed that a combination of Repsol and YPF would yield synergies in three areas:

- Cost savings after tax of $80 million in 1999, rising to $300 million to $350 million by the end of 2000, achieved primarily through merging YPF and Astra. That savings amounted to 1.6 percent of the combined cost base of the two firms in 1998, and compared with 7.1 percent savings in the BP-Amoco deal. Some analysts believed that this estimate was too conservative and that the cost savings might amount to $500 million by 2002.

- More focused capital expenditure. By combining the two entities, the sum of the two companies' capital expenditure in the period 1999-2002 could be reduced from $15.6 billion to $13.6 billion, which would conserve cash as well as reduce net interest expense.

- Better balance between upstream and downstream operations. A better balance would generate increases in revenue from the enhanced integration and capital efficiency of the new group. Those pretax synergies would start at $50 million in 1999 and 2000, and were expected to reach $200 million in 2003.

---

[14]Himona, Beaver, and Whittock.

Repsol's managers also expected to divest noncore assets by 2002, yielding $2.5 billion after taxes.

Financial Effects of the Combination

Analysts believed that the new company, compared to the old Repsol, would have lower earnings volatility due to its more balanced source of profits (upstream versus downstream). At the same time it would have increased sensitivity to oil prices as a consequence of higher exposure to exploration and production activities. In sum, Repsol-YPF would enjoy lower earnings volatility at the expense of higher oil price sensitivity.

The acquisition of YPF by Repsol might increase Repsol's financial risk. The cost of capital might increase due to the political and economic risks that operations in an emerging region would bring. If the cost of capital were higher in developing countries than in developed countries, then it would seem that YPF's cost of capital would be higher than Repsol's. Combining the two firms could, therefore, result in a higher weighted-average cost of capital (WACC) after acquisition than for Repsol on a stand-alone basis, since 40 percent of the assets were going to be located in Argentina.

Repsol's capital structure and cost of capital would both be affected by the transaction. First, the diversification of business activities would affect the perceived *operating risk* of the new firm. Second, any choice of form of payment and transaction financing would affect the perceived *financial risk* of the firm. The cost of capital would be affected by leverage choices and investors' beliefs about default risk. **Exhibit 8** describes the calculation of the WACC for YPF (12.55 percent), Repsol (8.14 percent) and the new firm, Repsol-YPF (10.6 percent, if the all-debt financing alternative were chosen, or 11.07 percent with all-equity financing).

Form of Payment

Repsol's management intended to make a tender offer to buy the 85.01 percent of YPF's shares that it did not own, at a price of $44.78 a share. A tender offer was simply a bid to acquire shares of another firm, made directly to the shareholders of the target. Cortina needed to make a final recommendation on the form of payment (i.e., cash, Repsol shares, or a combination).

A reporter wrote:

> Repsol had always planned to mount a stock rather than a cash offer to secure control of its prey. But with the YPF board opposed, a messy struggle to change YPF's statutes . . . appeared inevitable.[15]

Endesa, a Spanish electric power company, had acquired the Chilean power company Enersis, and had attempted to assume control through a change in the latter's bylaws, but encountered resistance from Enersis. The cash deal seemed to be the easiest option to implement, because the acquisition could have been made based on the current YPF bylaws. The difficulty Endesa experienced in Chile did not set a promising precedent.

---

[15]"Repsol: The Winner Must Oil the Wheels," *Financial Times,* ft.com-Mergers and Acquisitions/Case studies (accessed 27 January 2000).

In a cash transaction, YPF's shareholders would receive a fixed price and would not participate in any additional gains or losses after the acquisition. Depending upon their expectations and uncertainties in the market, this option could be very attractive. This alternative would also signal the serious intention of Repsol's management to achieve the strategic synergies and to implement the growth strategy in Latin America.

In view of YPF's and Repsol's similar size, however, some analysts believed a cash offer would be outside Repsol's financing capabilities. In addition, the short-term balance sheet risk that would be created by the abrupt increase in debt concerned Cortina. Financing would have to be arranged almost simultaneously with the cash offer to minimize the balance sheet risk and persuade YPF shareholders that Repsol could consummate the transaction.

On the other hand, a stock-for-stock deal offered important advantages. It would not be immediately taxable to YPF shareholders. Depending on the final price and capital gains obtained, YPF's shareholders might prefer a stock deal over cash in order to defer taxes. But a stock-for-stock deal might not be the best alternative given that Repsol's shares had recently underperformed the European market index by 19 percent.

Financing a Possible Cash Bid

To support a cash bid, Repsol would have to put together a financing consortium to provide $13.4 billion of cash. But Alfonso Cortina needed to decide on the most effective way to finance this cash outlay in the long run. The financial staff had analyzed three alternatives for financing a cash bid based on certain assumptions.

Alternative 1: Financing with Debt

Cortina explored financing a $13.4 billion cash offer by issuing a global bond. The possible terms of such an offer were not completely certain. Cortina asked his finance staff to recommend the possible structure of a globally issued bond including, currency, maturity structure, coupon rate, fixed/floating rate, required yield, covenants, placement, etc. There were many variables to be defined in a short period of time.

The success of the bond issue would depend on the current situation in the debt capital markets. Two important crises recently affected the debt market. The first, triggered by the Russian debt moratorium in August 1998, caused a huge outflow of foreign investment from emerging economies, mainly in Asia and Latin America. The second crisis occurred in early January 1999, when Brazil sustained one of the most dramatic currency devaluations in its history. Once more, investors moved their portfolios to less risky instruments, such as U.S. Treasury bonds.

Even though there were many uncertainties in the debt capital markets, Repsol's management was aware that debt financing tended to be cheaper than equity. If Repsol were successful in issuing the global bond, its net debt could move up sharply. Repsol's board was eager to capture the value represented by the tax benefits originating from tax shields. Moreover, the decrease in the combined enterprise's cost of capital was a factor that would create value for shareholders, especially in a scenario with the future acquisitions and capital expenditures that YPF was already projecting.

Possibly enhancing the chance of debt financing was the fact that Repsol had already proven it could do a global bond offering. In early February 1999, Repsol issued a global bond for 1.1 billion euros at an interest rate of 3.81 percent, or only 45 basis points above the benchmark German government five-year bond rate. This was the largest fixed income offer carried out by a Spanish company in international financial markets and the second-largest ever denominated in euros. The purpose of the issue was to refinance the payment by Repsol for the Argentine government's shares in YPF.

Still, Cortina was reluctant to accept the debt offering as the best way to finance the tender offer for YPF's shares. A sudden increase in Repsol's leverage would almost certainly trigger a downgrade in Repsol's debt ratings and an increase in the cost of debt. **Exhibit 9** gives the S&P rating categories associated with different financial ratios. Cortina was determined to maintain a solid investment-grade rating—indeed, he aimed for a rating of no less than a single-A during 2000. In addition to the predictable effect on debt rating, increased leverage would undermine Repsol's ability to meet unforeseen financing requirements as they arose. **Exhibit 10** presents an assessment of the probability of default for Repsol under the three financing alternatives.

YPF's strength in upstream activities meant that the oil price level and trend would be crucial in determining the profitability of the new company. The all-debt option was highly sensitive to price changes since the company's repayment capacity was strongly linked to the macro conditions in the sector.

Among the many other concerns he had, Alfonso Cortina was not sure about investors' reactions to this huge debt issuance. There was also uncertainty about the final price or yield of the bond given the recent global financial crises in Russia and Brazil. Was the market ready for financing new investments in emerging markets? Was there liquidity for a $13.4 billion bond offer? How would the market react to the offer? What would a bond issue signal to the investor community?

According to the industry practice and to Repsol practice, long-term bonds were the most typical source of debt finance. In the 1990s, investment-grade corporations issued bonds with maturities ranging from eight to 17 years and coupon rates from 6 to 8 percent. Cortina, however, was aware that market conditions might have changed.

To keep the investment-grade rating, the maturity would have to be shorter, around five years. And the coupon rate would have to include a spread of 300 basis points over U.S. Treasury yields, reflecting the uncertainties relating to the size of the deal and the timing of the debt issuance in the capital markets.

Alternative 2: Financing a Cash Transaction with an Issue of Common Equity

The second option consisted of a bridge loan followed by a global stock issuance after the acquisition had been consummated.[16] Although the Latin American debt capital market was showing some signs of recovery after the Brazilian devaluation, with bond yields falling at a fast pace and the equity capital market rebounding to record highs, analysts were not convinced that the financial crisis was completely under control.

---

[16]A global offering would include listings in the following stock exchanges: Madrid, New York, London, Frankfurt, and Buenos Aires.

Even though the outlook for the equity capital markets was cloudy, Cortina wanted to examine the implications of an equity transaction as an alternative to financing the $13.4 billion cash payment.

An issue of common equity offered some significant advantages. With an all-equity financing, the combined enterprise would maintain or expand its unused debt capacity, and as a consequence, would be prepared to take advantage of sudden acquisition opportunities, especially considering YPF's strategy of aggressive growth in Latin America. Under that option, Repsol could maintain its coverage ratios and its credit ratings.

On the other hand, Repsol's board was concerned about the impact of an all-equity transaction on the cost of capital of the enterprise. How would the benefit of less gearing impact the cost of capital? Would the less-leveraged firm bring more focus on business risk?

Repsol's shareholders were also concerned not only about the impact on earnings due to dilution, but also about the stock price reaction after the announcement of the financing. Demand for Repsol and YPF shares could be seriously affected by investors' perceptions about the future value of the enterprise. An all-equity transaction would be highly dependent on Repsol's share price. Was Repsol's stock being traded at a fair value? Overvaluation or undervaluation of the stock could bring key information about investors' perceptions regarding the value of the new enterprise. **Exhibit 11** shows YPF's and Repsol's historic stock prices.

Another issue that concerned management about the all-equity option was which type of investor would be the target clientele for Repsol's new shares. At the time of deciding between an all-cash or all-stock offer, it was clear that exchanging the YPF shares for paper in Repsol—a Spain-based company—would have led to a large proportion of those holders selling their Repsol shares after the deal since most of YPF shares were held in emerging markets funds where the shares in new Repsol-YPF would not fit the pure emerging markets profile. It was not clear how the market would view a combined company that had 50 percent of its assets in developing countries. Assessing that perception was important to determine the potential demand for and success of the new shares offering.

Alternative 3: Finance a Cash Offer with a Mix of Debt and Equity

A third option consisted of a mix of equity, equity-linked instruments, and debt. The finance staff modeled the following structure:

1. A global syndicated bank loan would finance the cash offer. This loan would be repaid by a series of issuances of long-term securities.

2. Issuance of $7.5 billion of common equity within six months of the transaction.

3. Refinance the remainder of the debt with $6 billion of long-term public debt issues. This would occur in a 12-to-18-month time frame. That debt would carry a 9 percent coupon rate at an A-rating, assuming Repsol could meet the requirements for that rating.

This alternative was by far the most complex and would need to be completed in more than one phase. Less reliance on equity financing would reduce the dilution in earnings per share for the current Repsol shareholder, but it would also result in higher leverage.

This alternative, while bringing the advantages and disadvantages of the two pure ones, also added a timing concern. Given the complexity of the transaction, it required a medium-term schedule of debt and equity issuances that would keep management busy in order to correctly launch each transaction. That fact could bring anxiety to the market that would prefer management to focus more on the implementation of the merger and less on the financial side of the deal.

Exhibit 12 provides a valuation analysis for the combined enterprise. **Exhibit 13** presents the balance sheet for Repsol-YPF under the three financing alternatives. **Exhibit 14** presents an analysis of potential EPS dilution under the all-debt alternative. **Exhibit 15** gives comparative financial information on peer firms in the oil sector.

Conclusion

Alfonso Cortina reviewed the analysis and assembled data. It remained for him to examine the tradeoffs among the alternatives and make a recommendation. He would want to give special attention to how he should frame his recommendation to Repsol's board of directors. Strategic goals would be a significant influence on the board's willingness to endorse a recommendation. All of this would need to occur quickly to preempt any actions by competitors and any turbulence in capital markets and oil markets.

EXHIBIT 1 | Oil Prices, 1991–99

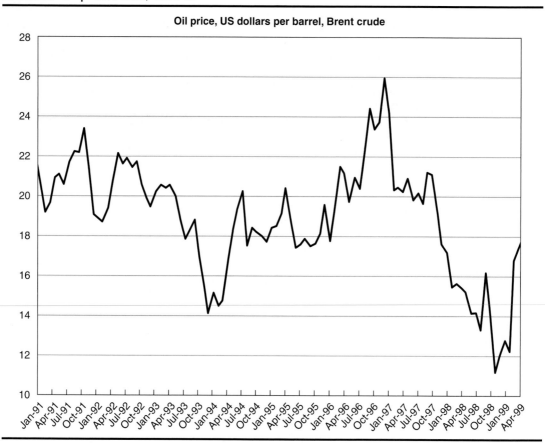

Source of data: Bloomberg Financial Services.

EXHIBIT 2 | Information on Selected Recent Jumbo M&A Transactions

Buyer Target	Exxon Mobil	British Petroleum Amoco	BP Amoco Atlantic Richfield	Repsol YPF
Announcement date	1-Dec-98	11-Nov-98	1-Apr-99	tba
Value of equity bid only ($ bn)	$78,945	$48,174	$27,233	$13,438
Value of equity bid and debt assumed ($ bn)	$86,399	$55,040	$33,702	$17,437
Form of payment	Stock	Stock	Stock	tba
Accounting	Pooling	Pooling	Purchase	tba
Lockup option	Exxon received right to acquire 14.9% of Mobil at 3.1% discount from offer price.	Amoco granted BP an option to acquire up to 19.9% of shares at 72% discount from offer price.	None	14.99% pre-existing stake from Argentine government auction
Attitude	Friendly	Friendly	Friendly	Unsolicited
Valuation multiples for target				
Price/book	4.19	3.07	3.53	2.19
Price/earnings	27.89	23.18	nmf	27.31
Enterprise value/sales	1.37	1.60	3.12	3.65
Enterprise value/EBITDA	na	9.33	133.20	9.41
Enterprise value/operating income	5.28	16.66	na	na
Premium of bid over stock price 4 weeks prior	32%	22%	54%	42%

tba = to be announced.

na = not available.

Source of data: Securities Data Company, Merger and Acquisitions Transactions Database.

EXHIBIT 3 | Repsol Financial Statements (values in millions of U.S. dollars, except per-share amounts)

Balance Sheet	1997	1998
Cash	$ 1,088	$ 1,144
Accounts receivable	2,907	3,185
Inventory	1,365	1,142
Total current assets	5,360	5,472
Total non current assets	12,884	13,033
Total Assets	**$18,244**	**$18,505**
Accounts payable	$ 3,520	$ 3,674
Short-term debt	1,716	2,574
Total current liabilities	5,236	6,248
Total non current liabilities	4,382	3,617
Total Liabilities	**9,617**	**9,866**
Minority interest	1,873	1,629
Shareholders' equity	6,754	7,010
Total Liabilities & Shareholders' Equity	**$18,244**	**$18,505**

Income Statement	1996	1997	1998
Net Sales	**$21,891**	**$21,920**	**$22,227**
Cost of sales	(20,325)	(20,324)	(20,285)
Operating income	1,566	1,596	1,942
Amortization of goodwill	(7)	(26)	(28)
Other income (expenses), net	(11)	39	(62)
Net financial items	(64)	(171)	(200)
Net income before tax	1,484	1,438	1,652
Income tax	(436)	(416)	(465)
Minority interest	(109)	(161)	(162)
Net income before preferred stock dividends	939	861	1,025
Net Income	**$939**	**$861**	**$1,025**
Shares outstanding (millions)	900	900	900
Earnings per Share	**$1.04**	**$0.96**	**$1.14**

N.B.: Shares outstanding and earnings per share are restated to reflect a stock split and recapitalization of Repsol that occurred in April 1999.

EXHIBIT 4 | YPF Financial Statements (values in millions of U.S. dollars, except per-share amounts)

Balance Sheet	1996	1997	1998	1999E	2000E	2001E
Cash	$ 90	$ 142	$ 70	$ 88	$ 279	$ 409
Accounts receivable	1193	1132	1177	1070	1193	1316
Inventory	282	324	308	329	362	400
Total current assets	1,565	1,598	1,555	1,487	1,834	2,125
Total non current assets	10,519	11,163	11,591	11926	12369	12824
Total Assets	**$12,084**	**$12,761**	**$13,146**	**$13,413**	**$14,203**	**$14,949**
Accounts payable	$ 886	$ 882	$ 788	$ 839	$ 935	$ 1031
Debt (short- and long-term)	1,485	2,088	1,634	1652	1668	1684
Total current liabilities	2,371	2,970	2,422	2,491	2,603	2,715
Total non current liabilities	3,189	2,698	3,364	3230	3425	3419
Total Liabilities	**5,560**	**5,668**	**5,786**	**5,721**	**6,028**	**6,134**
Minority interest	150	153	151	160	171	185
Shareholders' equity	6,374	6,940	7,209	7532	8004	8630
Total Liabilities & Shareholders' Equity	**$12,084**	**$12,761**	**$13,146**	**$13,413**	**$14,203**	**$14,949**

Income Statement	1996	1997	1998	1999E	2000E	2001E
Net Sales	**$5,937**	**$6,144**	**$5,500**	**$5,649**	**$5,846**	**$6,128**
Cost of sales	(3,616)	(3,730)	(3,594)	(3,594)	(3,594)	(3,594)
Gross Profit	**2,321**	**2,414**	**1,906**	**2,055**	**2,252**	**2,534**
Selling, general, & administrative expenses	(782)	(782)	(760)	(760)	(760)	(760)
Operating income (EBIT)	1,539	1,632	1,146	1,295	1,492	1,774
Income on long-term investments	25	37	26	25	45	50
Other income (expenses), net	(93)	(50)	(44)	(15)	(18)	(35)
Net financial items	(246)	(239)	(264)	(316)	(280)	(285)
Net income before tax	1,225	1,380	864	989	1,239	1,504
Income tax	(369)	(479)	(264)	(306)	(382)	(466)
Minority interest	(12)	(15)	(11)	(10)	(12)	(13)
Net income before preferred stock dividends	844	886	589	673	845	1,025
Dividend requir.on pref.stock of controlled companies	(27)	(9)	(9)	(2)	0	0
Net Income	**$ 817**	**$ 877**	**$ 580**	**$ 671**	**$ 845**	**$1,025**
Shares outstanding (millions)	353	353	353	353	353	353
Earnings per Share	**$ 2.31**	**$ 2.48**	**$ 1.64**	**$ 1.90**	**$ 2.39**	**$ 2.90**

Cash Flow	1996	1997	1998	1999E	2000E	2001E
Cash Flow from Operating Activities						
Net income	$ 817	$ 877	$ 580	$ 671	$ 846	$ 1,025
Adjustments						
Depreciation and amortization	1,065	1,093	1,061	1,131	1,230	1,323
Change in assets and liabilities	810	75	(1)	247	67	76
Net Cash Flow from Operating Activities	**$ 2,692**	**$ 2,045**	**$ 1,640**	**$ 2,049**	**$ 2,143**	**$2,424**
Cash Flow from Investing Activities						
Acquisition of fixed assets	(1,817)	(1,593)	(1,351)	(1,400)	(1,600)	(1,700)
Acquisitions of long-term investments and intangible assets	(76)	(151)	(122)	(129)	(137)	(145)
Net proceeds on sale of investments	43	50	(67)	(71)	(75)	(80)
Other	28	39	31	33	34	36
Net Cash Flow from Investing Activities	**$(1,822)**	**$(1,655)**	**$(1,509)**	**$(1,567)**	**$(1,778)**	**$(1,889)**
Cash Flow from Financing Activities						
Proceeds from loans	$ 1,964	$52	$ 115	$ 0	$ 0	$ 0
Preferred shares redemption	(281)	(63)	0	0	0	0
Payments of loans	(2,261)	0	0	(100)	200	0
Dividends paid	(293)	(319)	(326)	(349)	(373)	(399)
Net Cash Flow from Financing Activities	**$ (871)**	**$ (330)**	**$ (211)**	**$ (449)**	**$ (173)**	**$ (399)**

EXHIBIT 5 | YPF Shareholding Structure Before and After Argentine Government Sale

Shareholding Structure as of December 1998

YPF shares outstanding included 353,000,000 shares of common stock, with a par value of 10 Argentine pesos and one vote per share, which were fully subscribed, paid-in and authorized for stock exchange listing. There had been no change in the number of shares since YPF's privatization in 1993. At the end of December 1998, YPF's shares were divided into four classes, as detailed below:

Owner	Number of Shares	Type of Share	Percentage of Capital Stock
Government[1]	72,602,289	Class A	20.56%
Provinces	16,552,797	Class B	4.68
Employees	1,505,475	Class C	4.26
Public[2]	263,339,439	Class D	70.50

[1]The Argentine government owned one "golden share" and could retain it indefinitely.
[2]50% of the public shares were held by U.S. investors, mainly emerging market mutual funds.

YPF Shareholding Structure as of February 1, 1999

In January 1999, the Argentine government sold to Repsol 52,914,700 Class A shares in block (14.99% of YPF's shares) at $38 per share, which were converted to Class D shares.

Owner	Number of Shares	Type of Share	Percentage of Capital Stock
Government[1]	19,687,589	Class A	5.57%
Provinces	16,552,797	Class B	4.68
Repsol	52,914,700	Class D	14.99
Employees	1,505,475	Class C	4.26
Public	263,339,439	Class D	70.50

[1]The Argentine government kept the "golden share."

EXHIBIT 6 | Capital Market Conditions, April 5, 1999

Treasury Obligations	U.S. Yields	Spanish Yields
90-day bills	4.38%	2.77%
1-year notes	4.66	2.84
5-year notes	5.05	3.47
10-year bonds	5.18	4.24
30-year bonds	5.62	5.14

Other Instruments	Yield	
Federal discount rate	4.75%	
Commercial paper		
60 days	5.03	
90 days	5.04	
Certificates of deposit		
3 months	4.87	
1 year	5.05	
LIBOR		
3 months	5.00	
6 months	5.05	
12 months	5.24	
Bank prime rates		
Argentina	8.73	
United States	7.75	

Source of data: Bloomberg Financial Services.

Sovereign	Date	Long-Term Rating
Argentina	Apr-97	BB
Brazil	Jan-99	B+
Chile	Jul-95	A−
Colombia	May-98	BBB−
Costa Rica	Jul-97	BB
El Salvador	Apr-99	BB+
Indonesia	Mar-99	CCC+
Mexico	Oct-98	BB
Peru	Dec-97	BB
Russia	Jan-99	Default
South Africa	Mar-98	BB+
Spain	Mar-99	AA+
United States	Jun-89	AAA
Venezuela	Aug-98	B+

Source of data: Standard&Poor's - Sovereign Ratings History, April 1999.

EXHIBIT 7 | Distribution of Repsol Revenues Before and After the Transaction

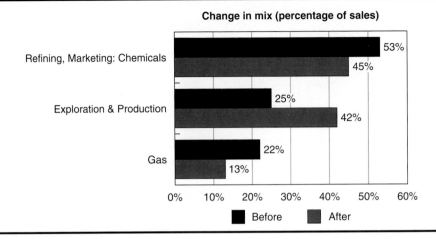

Change in mix (percentage of sales)

Source of data: "Quantum Leap," ABN AMRO Bank, September 1, 1999.

EXHIBIT 8 | Estimation of WACC for Repsol's Acquisition of YPF (suitable for valuing U.S. dollar cash flows)

	Repsol in Spain (stand-alone)	YPF in Argentina (stand-alone)	Combined Repsol-YPF Debt Financing	Combined Repsol-YPF Mixed Financing	Combined Repsol-YPF Equity Financing
Pretax cost of debt (%)	3.9%	6.0%	9.0%	8.2%	7.0%
Tax rate (%)	34%	34%	34%	34%	34%
Post-tax cost of debt (%)	**2.6%**	**4.0%**	**5.9%**	**5.4%**	**4.6%**
Asset beta	0.57	0.56	0.56	0.56	0.56
Beta in local market/relevered beta	0.80	0.75	0.96	0.78	0.68
Risk-free rate (%) for U.S. $ investment	5.0%	5.0%	5.0%	5.0%	5.0%
Country beta versus U.S. market	1.15	2.00	1.59	1.59	1.59
Adjustment to U.S. risk-free rate for country risk	1.0%	3.0%	2.0%	2.0%	2.0%
Global equity market risk premium	6.0%	6.0%	6.0%	6.0%	6.0%
Cost of equity without country risk premium	**9.80%**	**9.50%**	**10.77%**	**9.70%**	**9.08%**
Cost of equity with country risk premium	**11.52%**	**17.00%**	**16.18%**	**14.47%**	**13.50%**
BV debt/(BV debt+MV equity)	38%	34%	51.6%	36.9%	23.7%
MV equity/(BV debt+MV equity)	62%	66%	48.4%	63.1%	76.3%
WACC with Country Risk Premium	**8.14%**	**12.55%**	**10.90%**	**11.13%**	**11.40%**
WACC without Country Risk Premium	**7.07%**	**7.61%**	**8.28%**	**8.12%**	**8.03%**
Market value of equity (U.S. $ millions)	$15,066	$15,807			
Weight of Repsol and YPF market values	49%	51%			

Repsol's recently issued five-year euro-denominated bonds yielded 3.81%.[1] The outlook was that Repsol bonds would be priced to yield 3.9% for 1999–2003 if Repsol remained on a stand-alone basis. Spanish government bonds were returning 5.2%; Repsol's beta was 0.8 and the Spanish market risk premium over the United States was 1%.

Weighted-Average Cost of Capital (WACC) Calculation Methodology
The financial forecasts are given in U.S. dollars. Therefore, the appropriate WACC is a dollar-based estimate, but reflecting the risks associated with doing business in Spain and Argentina. Estimating a WACC across borders must account for differences in political risk (through the political risk premium (pi) added to the U.S. risk-free rate), and equity market risk (through the use of a country beta that is multiplied by the beta in the local market). Accordingly, the general cross-border cost of equity model is an expanded version of the capital-asset pricing model (CAPM):

$$K_e = Rf_{US} + \pi + [\beta_{Country} \times \beta_{Firm} \times (\text{Equity Market Risk Premium})]$$

Source: Case writers' analysis.

[1] At the time, yields on U.S. dollar- and euro-denominated instruments were similar.

EXHIBIT 9 | Median Financial Ratios Associated with Long-Term Debt Rating Categories (estimated for 1996–1998)

	AAA	AA	A	BBB	BB	B
EBIT interest coverage (x)	12.9	9.2	7.2	4.1	2.5	1.2
EBITDA interest coverage (x)	18.7	14.0	10.0	6.3	3.9	2.3
Funds flow/total debt (%)	89.7	67.0	49.5	32.2	20.1	10.5
Free operating cash flow/total debt (%)	40.5	21.6	17.4	6.3	1.0	-4.0
Return on capital (%)	30.6	25.1	19.6	15.4	12.6	9.2
Operating income/sales (%)	30.9	25.2	17.9	15.8	14.4	11.2
Long-term debt/capital (%)	21.4	29.3	33.3	40.8	55.3	68.6
Total debt/capital (including short-term debt) (%)	31.8	37.0	39.2	46.4	58.5	71.4

Source of data: Standard & Poor's Corporation, *Corporate Ratings Criteria*, 1999, 112.

EXHIBIT 10 | Analysis of Default Risk for the Year 2000 Associated with the Three Financing
Alternatives[1]

To: Alfonso Cortina, Chief Executive Officer
From: Carmelo Lopez, Chief Financial Officer

In an effort to estimate the default risk of Repsol-YPF under the three financing alternatives, the finance staff has
prepared an estimate of the probability of not being able to meet interest payments. Specifically, default was defined as EBIT falling below interest expense. The probability was estimated across the three financing alternatives, and a range of possible cost-saving synergies. We know that there are other benefits from the merger and
restructuring, but decided to ignore them for the sake of conservatism. The assessed probabilities of default are
given in the following table:

	Sensitivity Analysis for Synergies:						
	Interest Coverage				**Probability of Interest Coverage < 1**		
	Debt	**Mix**	**Equity**		**Debt**	**Mix**	**Equity**
Cost Savings in Millions							
$ 50	1.2608	1.6656	2.9564	$ 50	24.05%	8.68%	1.21%
$150	1.2968	1.7131	3.0409	$150	21.13%	7.24%	0.94%
$250	1.3328	1.7607	3.1253	$250	18.43%	5.99%	0.72%
$350	**1.3688**	**1.8083**	**3.2098**	**$350**	**15.95%**	**4.92%**	**0.55%** Base Case
$450	1.4048	1.8559	3.2943	$450	13.70%	4.01%	0.41%
$550	1.4409	1.9035	3.3787	$550	11.68%	3.23%	0.31%

Methodology

The simulations essentially run a sensitivity analysis of the EBIT coverage ratios under different oil price assumptions. We began by defining which business activities are exposed to oil price volatility. Two main sources appear:
Upstream and downstream operating income. For both, we considered a triangle distribution of the oil prices
based on the market's expectations and historical experience:

• Upstream operating income: this segment was calculated by taking the company's output prediction in barrels of
  oil, and subtracting the direct costs of this operation.
• Downstream operating income: this segment has different subproducts that are exposed to changes in oil prices
  in different ways. For the sake of simplicity, we took Repsol's stand-alone sensitivity to oil prices (since its income was mainly from downstream activities) and applied the same figure to the combined enterprise downstream business
• Sensitivity summary: we added or subtracted all non-oil-price-sensitive charges to the operating income, and arrived at a Group EBIT.s

[1]Case writers' analysis.   (*continued*)

EXHIBIT 10 | Analysis of Default Risk for the Year 2000 (*Continued*)

Analysis of Default Risk under Three Financing Alternatives

Detailed Results for "Base Case" of Cost Saving Synergies of $350 Million

Running the simulation through 1,000 trials on a base case scenario of $350 million in cost-saving synergies yields the graphs below, and these results for the coverage ratio:

	All Debt	Mix of Debt and Equity	All Equity
Minimum	0.550	0.727	1.291
Mean	1.368	1.808	3.210
Maximum	2.307	3.049	5.412
Probability of Default	15.95%	4.92%	0.55%

Graphs of "Base Case" Probability Distributions of Coverage Ratio

Probability distribution of Repsol's EBIT coverage ratio if bid for YPF is financed by a blend of debt and equity.

Probability distribution of Repsol's EBIT coverage ratio if bid for YPF is financed entirely by an issue of debt.

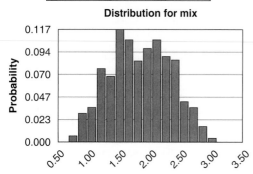

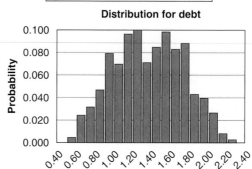

Probability distribution of Repsol's EBIT coverage ratio if an issue of equity finances bid for YPF.

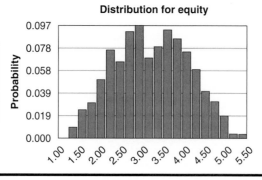

EXHIBIT 11 | Recent Stock Prices of Repsol and YPF (values in U.S. dollars)

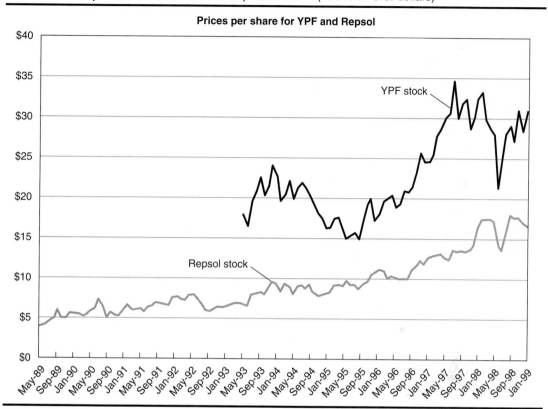

Source of data: Bloomburg Financial Services.

EXHIBIT 12 | Forecast of Free Cash Flows for Repsol, YPF, and the Combined Firm, Repsol-YPF
(values in millions of U.S. dollars, except as noted)

Assumptions:	YPF	Repsol	Combined		
Terminal value growth rate (%)	4.0%	2.0%	3.0%		
WACC (%)	12.5%	8.1%	10.6%		
Tax rate (%)	34.0%	34.0%	34.0%		
Goodwill			$6,229		
Return on assets			8%		

YPF Free Cash Flow	1999E	2000E	2001E	2002E	2003E
Earnings before interest and taxes (EBIT)	$1,295	$1,492	$1,774	$2,046	$ 2,291
Taxes	440	507	603	696	779
Earnings after tax	855	985	1,171	1,350	1,512
+ Depreciation	1,160	1,185	1,230	1,250	1,310
− Capital expenditures	(1,460)	(1,680)	(1,810)	(1,940)	(1,960)
− Increase in working capital	(65)	(75)	(89)	(102)	(115)
Free Cash Flow	490	415	502	558	748
Terminal value					9,093
Total Free Cash Flow	$ 490	$ 415	$ 502	$ 558	$ 9,840

Repsol Free Cash Flow	1999E	2000E	2001E	2002E	2003E
Earnings before interest and taxes (EBIT)	$1,948	$2,285	$2,554	$2,754	$ 2,889
Taxes	662	777	868	936	982
Earnings after tax	1,286	1,508	1,686	1,818	1,907
+ Depreciation	1,121	1,205	1,269	1,310	1,337
− Capital expenditures	(2,140)	(2,098)	(1,653)	(1,417)	(1,539)
− Increase in working capital	(97)	(114)	(128)	(138)	(144)
Free Cash Flow	169	501	1,174	1,573	1,560
Terminal value					25,917
Total Free Cash Flow	$ 169	$ 501	$1,174	$1,573	$27,478

Repsol-YPF Synergy Cash Flow Effects	1999E	2000E	2001E	2002E	2003E
Sales of assets	$ —	$1,000	$1,000	$ 500	$ —
Adjustment to EBIT after sale of assets	—	(53)	(106)	(132)	(132)
Cost savings after tax	80	250	350	400	450
Revenue enhancement after costs and taxes	7	14	14	21	28
Reductions in capex less lost depreciation tax shields	393	386	380	373	366
Goodwill tax shield	$ 106	$ 106	$ 106	$ 106	$ 106

Source: Case writers' analysis.

EXHIBIT 13 | Balance Sheet of the Combined Firm, Pro Forma the Acquisition under the Three Financing Alternatives Assuming Purchase Accounting (values in millions of U.S. dollars, except per-share amounts)

Amount to be financed	$ 13,438

Financing Alternatives

		Percentage
Debt	$ 6,000	45%
Equity	$ 7,438	55%
Assumed price per share	$20.41	
Option chosen	Mixed financing	

Gearings (Book values)

	Pro-Forma 100% Debt	Pro-Forma 100% Equity	Pro-Forma Mixed financing
Total debt	$22,838	$ 9,400	$15,400
Total equity	$ 7,073	$20,511	$14,511
Total capital	$29,911	$29,911	$29,911
Debt/equity	323%	46%	106%
Debt/capital	76.4%	31.4%	51.5%
Equity/capital	23.6%	68.6%	48.5%

Balance Sheet Repsol-YPF	Repsol	YPF	Adjustments	Pro-Forma 100% Debt	Pro-Forma 100% Equity	Pro-Forma Mixed Financing
Assets						
Cash	$ 148	$ 70		$ 218	$ 218	$ 218
Accounts receivable	3,462	1,177		4,639	4,639	4,639
Inventory	2,337	308		2,645	2,645	2,645
Total current assets	5,947	1,555		7,502	7,502	7,502
Goodwill/asset revaluation*			$6,229	6,229	6,229	6,229
Total non current assets	14,940	11,591		26,531	26,531	26,531
Total Assets	**$20,887**	**$13,146**		**$40,262**	**$40,262**	**$40,262**
Liabilities						
Accounts payable	$ 1,146	$788		$ 1,934	$ 1,934	$ 1,934
Loans	2,798	1,252		4,050	4,050	4,050
Other	1,046	241		1,287	1,287	1,287
Taxes payable	1,801	141		1,942	1,942	1,942
Total Current Liabilities	**$ 6,791**	**$ 2,422**		**$ 9,213**	**$ 9,213**	**$ 9,213**
Long-term notes and accounts payable	$ 56	$ 53		$ 109	$ 109	$ 109
Loans	2,663	2,578		5,241	5,241	5,241
Other	2,533	733		3,266	3,266	3,266
New debt from acquisition			$6,000	13,438	—	6,000
Total non current liabilities	5,252	3,364		22,054	8,616	14,616
Total Liabilities	**$12,043**	**$ 5,786**		**$31,267**	**$17,829**	**$23,829**
Minority interest	$ 996	$ 151		$ 1,147	$ 1,147	$ 1,147
Preferred shares	775			775	775	775
New shares issued			$ 364			364
New shares premium account			$7,074		13,438	7,074
Shareholders' equity	7,073	7,209		7,073	20,511	14,511
Total Liabilities & Shareholders' Equity	**$20,887**	**$13,146**		**$40,262**	**$40,262**	**$40,262**

Source: Case writers' analysis.

EXHIBIT 14 | Analysis of Earnings per Share Dilution/Accretion (values in millions of U.S. dollars, except per-share amounts)

Pro-Forma Earnings Repsol-YPF		1999E	2000E	2001E	2002E	2003E
Repsol operating income (EBIT)		$1,948	$2,285	$2,554	$ 2,754	$ 2,989
YPF operating income (EBIT)		1,295	1,492	1,774	2,046	2,391
Operating income before goodwill and amortization		3,243	3,777	4,328	4,800	5,380
Existing goodwill & amortization		(40)	(40)	(40)	(40)	(40)
New depreciation of assets written-up		(69)	(69)	(69)	(69)	(69)
New goodwill & amortization over 20 years		(311)	(311)	(311)	(311)	(311)
Existing net financial expense		(684)	(713)	(652)	(623)	(590)
New financial expense	9.00%	(257)	(385)	(228)	(81)	56
Total interest expense		(941)	(1,098)	(880)	(704)	(534)
Other expense (income)		(15)	(18)	(35)	(40)	(50)
Associates income		25	45	50	55	60
Pre tax income		1,892	2,286	3,043	3,691	4,435
Taxes	34%	(643)	(777)	(1,034)	(1,255)	(1,508)
Minorities		(178)	(193)	(212)	(233)	(256)
Reported Net Income		**1,071**	**1,315**	**1,796**	**2,203**	**2,671**
Cost savings after tax		80	250	350	400	450
Revenue enhancement		50	100	100	150	200
Reported Net Income with Synergies		**$1,201**	**$1,565**	**$2,146**	**$ 2,603**	**$ 3,121**
Number of original shares (millions)		900	900	900	900	900
New shares (millions)		364	364	364	364	364
Total shares (millions)		1,264	1,264	1,264	1,264	1,264
Repsol original earnings per share (EPS)		$ 1.23	$ 1.45	$ 1.71	$ 1.88	$ 2.1
New Repsol-YPF EPS excluding synergies		$ 0.85	$ 1.04	$ 1.42	$ 1.74	$ 2.11
New Repsol-YPF EPS including synergies		$ 0.95	$ 1.24	$ 1.70	$ 2.06	$ 2.47
Dilution (including synergies)		**−29.5%**	**−17.1%**	**−0.8%**	**8.7%**	**14.9%**
Debt Repayment						
Net income with synergies		$1,201	$1,565	$2,146	$ 2,603	$ 3,121
Depreciation		2,371	2,525	2,684	2,843	2,979
Goodwill & amortization		351	351	351	351	351
Equity income		(25)	(45)	(50)	(55)	(60)
Minorities		178	193	212	233	256
Operating cash flow		**$4,076**	**$4,590**	**$5,344**	**$ 5,975**	**$ 6,648**
Dividends	45%	$ (540)	$ (704)	$ (966)	$(1,171)	$(1,405)
Preferred dividends	7.5%	(90)	(117)	(161)	(195)	(234)
Capital expenditures (Capex)		(3,549)	(3,743)	(3,872)	(3,872)	(3,892)
Capex savings		400	400	400	400	400
Capex after savings		(3,149)	(3,343)	(3,472)	(3,472)	(3,492)
Cash from disposals		—	1,000	1,000	500	—
Financing cash flows		(3,779)	(3,165)	(3,599)	(4,339)	(5,131)
Cash Available for Debt Repayment		**$ 297**	**$1,425**	**$1,745**	**$ 1,637**	**$ 1,517**
Debt outstanding		$6,000	$5,703	$4,278	$ 2,533	$ 897
Debt repayment		$ 297	$ 1,425	$1,745	$ 1,637	$ 1,517
Balance	$6,000	$5,703	$4,278	$2,533	$ 897	$ (621)

Source: Case writers' analysis.

EXHIBIT 15 | Financial Comparison of Repsol (Stand-Alone) with Other Major Integrated Oil Companies

	Sector Average	Total	Shell	Chevron	ENI S.p.A.	Texaco	BP Amoco	Exxon Mobil	ELF	Repsol
Valuation Ratios										
Beta	0.80	0.85	0.81	0.57	0.94	0.32	na	na	0.84	1.00
Price to book	3.65	3.34	3.52	3.32	2.61	2.61	4.78	4.59	3.51	1.95
Price to cash flow	29.9	14.3	19.16	15.72	6.75	13.38	23.17	18.9	9.13	6.1
Price to earnings (1999)	na	21.8	26.2	31.3	15.2	30.6	30.9	27.9	24.0	18.6
Market capitalization (billion)	na	30.48	67.09	62.44	48.98	29.52	166.3	270.1	34.96	16.27
Growth Rates (%)										
Sales—5 yr. growth	8.49%	3.33%	−0.3%	−3.8%	0.8%	−1.4%	nmf	nmf	0.2%	na
Earnings per share—5 yr. growth	10%	9.13%	−40.0%	1.0%	42.9%	−14.2%	nmf	nmf	37.0%	na
Capital expenditures—5 yr. growth	20.68%	10.19%	9.0%	3.2%	0.3%	5.9%	nmf	nmf	−5.7%	na
Financial Strength										
Current ratio	1.11	1.37	0.88	0.75	1.02	1.15	0.95	0.77	1.11	0.87
Total debt to equity	0.59	0.44	0.29	0.48	0.59	0.61	0.33	0.29	0.53	0.61
Interest coverage	10.05	nmf	4.6	4.63	nmf	2.98	6.92	17.39	4.32	na
Profitability Ratios (%)										
Earnings before interest, taxes, and depreciation margin	15.6%	11.1%	14.6%	16.3%	27.9%	9.3%	18.4%	11.0%	16.1%	7.4%
Operating margin	4.3%	6.1%	6.0%	8.5%	13.1%	3.0%	10.7%	5.7%	4.5%	8.7%
Net profit margin	2.9%	3.8%	2.5%	3.2%	8.5%	2.0%	4.9%	4.1%	1.9%	4.6%
Management Effectiveness										
Return on net assets - 5 yr. average	4.8	4.03	5.4	5.62	5.74	5.18	na	na	1.85	5.15
Return on equity - 5 yr. average	10.49	7.95	10.29	12.62	20.49	13.57	na	na	4.11	14.50

nmf = not a meaningful figure.

na = not available.

Source of data: "Market Guide," BT Alex Brown Forecasts, May 1999.

Hostile Takeovers: A Primer for the Decision Maker

The game of professional investment is intolerably boring and overexacting to anyone who is entirely exempt from the gambling instinct; whilst he who has it must pay to this propensity the appropriate toll.

—John Maynard Keynes[1]

1. Introduction: Takeovers Are Games

A hostile tender offer ("takeover") begins with an unsolicited offer by a bidder to purchase a majority or all of the target firm's shares. The bidder will set the offer for a particular period of time, at a price, and a form of payment, and may attach conditions to the offer. The target will ordinarily undertake evasive maneuvers. Research shows that the hostile bidder consummates a deal in about 20 percent of the cases. In roughly 30 percent of the cases, the target is acquired by another, usually "friendly," firm. And in the remainder of the cases, the target remains independent. The complexity, uncertainty, and drama of these events seem to defy an easy grasp.

Keynes's famous words afford a basis for understanding, analyzing, and designing or repelling hostile tender offers: takeovers are *games*. In the arena of mergers and acquisitions (M&A), the professional investor that Keynes cites is the arbitrageur. One can understand these events and the arbitrageur better by studying them the way one studies a game:

- Gain the perspective of the various players in the takeover scenario, their motives, and behaviors.

- Master important rules and defenses that constrain the players.

- Anticipate the paths that outcomes may take.

---

[1]Quoted in Adam Smith [George J. W. Goodman], *The Money Game* (New York: Dell, 1969), 16.

The analytics of hostile tender offers significantly entail the assessment of probabilities. Takeover attempts are bets on uncertain outcomes. The players' strategies are aimed at tilting the odds in one's favor. The homework necessary to assess these odds and play them well surely constitutes Keynes's "appropriate toll." Of course, understanding the game is no assurance of likely success—it also takes skill. As John McDonald said about poker,

> A knowledge of mathematical probabilities will not make a good poker player, but a total disregard for them will make a bad one.[2]

2. Be Aware of the Players, both on the Field and off

One begins an introduction to a game by surveying the people gathered around the table.

> *Attacker* (or, in street parlance, *bidder*). The popular press and halls of government view bidders rather harshly, for it is the bidders who propose to wrest control, close plants, lay off workers, and take other actions to enrich themselves. A more benign view is that bidders are *entrepreneurs* who, through research and initiative, discover profitable opportunities. The hostile tender offer is the action taken to begin to harvest the profit.

> *Defender* or *target is* the profitable opportunity. Usually, targets have underperformed against one or more benchmarks, about which the target managers are doing little, or are floundering in attempts to improve performance. The bidder may see hidden or underutilized assets that could be sold or businesses that are draining cash and could be restructured or closed.

It is naïve to see the hostile tender offer as a contest simply between bidder and target. The field is considerably more complicated. Viewed through a lens of economics, the contest embraces the following kinds of players:

> *Free riders versus the bidder.* Free riders are shareholders who may not be well informed but who suspect that the bidder knows something they don't and who are tempted to participate in some of the profits flowing to the bidder. These shareholders seek to ride free in harvesting the profitable opportunity. The bidder would like to quell the free riders, because they reduce the bidder's profit.

> *Groups within the target.* One of the worst mistakes is to view the target as a solid bloc of decision makers. In reality, the target harbors important divisions that the bidder can exploit:

>> *Managers versus directors.* Usually, senior target company managers lose their jobs following a successful hostile takeover. Even if they do not lose them, salaries and perquisites tend to be distributed less freely. In short, target managers have a strong incentive to oppose a hostile bid. A firm's directors, however, are bound by legal doctrines of the duties of care and loyalty to maximize the welfare of shareholders.

---

[2]John McDonald, *Strategy in Poker, Business & War* (New York: W.W. Norton, 1989), 22.

Failing to do so exposes directors to micromanagement by courts of law and possible personal liability for past errors. Obviously, the interests of managers and directors can diverge. The *target's board of directors* is at the fulcrum of pressure and can reverse management's strategy in the game through such means as rescinding the firm's antitakeover defenses and declaring an auction for the firm.

Insiders versus outside directors. The board itself may consist of subgroups that harbor divergent interests. Inside directors are usually also managers. Other directors who side with the manager-directors may have links by marriage or work experience that tie them by loyalty more closely to managers than to shareholders.

Large shareholders versus small shareholders. Not all target shareholders are equal; their relative voting power can have an influence on the board of directors.

Other potential buyers who would have an interest in acquiring the target but have yet to enter a bid. These might include friendly buyers (also called "white knights") and friendly investors in special controlling securities (also called "white squires").[3]

Arbitrageurs who make a living betting on price movements in takeovers. Once a takeover is announced, the "arbs" (as they are more popularly known) practically absorb all loose shares sloshing around in the stock market, and almost certainly become the crucial deciders of any contest—for this reason, they deserve careful examination.

3. The Arb Is the Consummate Economic Actor

The arbs' outlook is rationalistic, impatient, and always oriented toward value maximization. Appeals to loyalty, tradition, or some vague plan will have little influence over them. They like immediate cash profits. Arbitrageurs are short-term investors driven only by economic motives. They invest funds in takeover situations and recapitalizations and try to limit the exposure to the likelihood of a deal not being consummated. They often provide liquidity to investors who do not wish to wait out a battle for corporate control.

Consider the example[4] of a target company that receives an offer of $60 a share for all the shares of the company. If the shares are trading at $40 a share when the offer is announced, one could make a profit of $20 by buying instantaneously and holding until the transaction is completed. Unfortunately, the stock exchange would probably suspend trading in the stock as investors flood the market with orders to buy or sell. When order has been regained, the stock will resume trading at a point where there are both buyers and sellers at the same price. At that point, the shares may be trading at $57 or $58 a share. Institutions and private investors would be able to sell shares immediately to the arbs at $57, reaping a $17 gain. The $3

---

[3]Warren Buffett has played the "white squire" to several firms, most notably Gillette. He has purchased convertible preferred stock, which, if converted, would represent a material minority of shares outstanding. The shares represented in these white-squire positions require added investment on the part of a hostile bidder and thus have a deterrent effect.

[4]This example was drawn from "Takeover! 1997 (A): The Target Company: Global Foods Corporation," a Darden case study (UVA-F-1170), coauthored by Robert Bruner, John P. McNicholas, and Edward Rimland.

difference, or spread, can be viewed as compensation to investors for any remaining uncertainty about whether the transactions will be consummated and for the time remaining to closing the deal. The bidder's share price declines $3 upon the announcement, to close at $50, and remains there until the end of the arb's holding period.

The task for the arb is to evaluate the likelihood of the deal's being consummated and structure an investment position based on that view. The arb will seek to create a hedged position whose risk is determined by the deal rather than by general market conditions. A typical arbitrage position following a hostile-takeover announcement would be to take a "long" position in the shares of the target company and a "short" position in the shares of the bidder—this reflects the typical movement of share prices at the announcement of hostile bids, but the structure also cushions the arb against general movements in the stock market.

3. a. Return to the Arbitrageur

The following example calculates the return to the arb in the transaction described above:

(1) Position Taken: 100 Target Company shares bought at $57; 100 Bidder Company shares sold short at $50.

(2) Date Position Taken: June 1, 1996

(3) Date Shares Tendered: June 28, 1996

(4) Date Proceeds Received: July 10, 1996

(5) Total Time Involvement: 40 days

(6) Capital Employed:

Assets

Long 100 shares of Target × $57/share =	$5,700

Liabilities and Capital

Short 100 shares of Bidder × $50/share =	$5,000
Borrowed 100 shares of Bidder =	($5,000)
Bank Borrowings (70% of Assets) =	$3,990
Capital (30% of Assets) =	1,710
Total	$5,700

(7) Net Spread Calculation:

$300	Gross Spread (Target: [$60 − $57] × 100 shares) plus (Buyer: [$50 − $50] × 100 shares)
(43)	Interest Cost (10% for 40 days on credit of $3,990)
(20)	Short Dividends Forgone
30	Long Dividends Received
$267	Net Spread or Return on Investment

(8) Annualized Return on Capital

$$\text{Average Capital Employed} = \frac{40 \text{ days}}{365 \text{ days}} \times \$1,710 = \$187$$

$$\text{Annualized Return on Capital Employed} = \frac{\$267}{\$187} = 142\%$$

While this is a high apparent return on capital, the arb could sustain a sizable loss if the hostile bid does not succeed. Note also that this return on investment (ROI) is very sensitive to small variations in waiting period and dollar return.

3. b. The Arb's Choice Between Tendering into a Hostile Bid and Waiting for the Target's Recapitalization

In deciding where to tender their shares in a contest for corporate control, the arbs will determine which offer gives them the highest annualized return on their invested capital. To continue our example, an arb would prefer $60 on July 10 as opposed to payment of $61 received in September. With capital costs of 30 to 40 percent per year, the timing of cash flows received is crucial to their decision. Lastly, the decision of arbs to tender their shares to a raider will, in almost all cases, mean that a company will not have ample time to complete its own recapitalization if it is calculated to have a lower blended value.

Assume the target company decides to mount its own recapitalization plan by buying back 35 percent of its shares at $85 a share. Furthermore, assume that the stub share (i.e., a share of the common stock remaining after the recapitalization) will be estimated to trade at approximately $55 a share afterward.

$$\text{Blended value} = (35\% \times \$85) + (65\% \times \$55) = \$65.50$$

Note that an arb would prefer a blended value of $65.50 if that value could be delivered on a timely basis.

More usually, risk arbitrageurs will play both sides of a hostile tender offer, taking a long position in the shares of the target and a short position in the shares of the bidder. One of the leading arbs, Guy Wyser-Pratte, has written,

> An arbitrageur is not an investor in the formal sense of the word: i.e., he is not normally buying or selling securities because of their investment value. He is, however, committing capital to the "deal"—the merger, tender offer, recapitalization, etc.—rather than to the particular security. He must thus take a position in the deal in such a way that he is at the risk of the deal, and not at the risk of the market.[5]

As Wyser-Pratte suggests, the arb will be extremely sensitive to the values underlying the deal, and to its outcome. To illustrate why, consider **Table 1,** which expands the results of the example given above and gives the annualized rates of return associated with different holding periods and payoffs.

---

[5]Guy P. Wyser-Pratte, *Risk Arbitrage II* (New York: New York University, Salomon Brothers Center for the Study of Financial Institutions, Monograph 1982–3–4), 7.

TABLE 1 | Sensitivity Analysis of Annualized Rate of Return to Variation in Length of Holding Period and Expected Payoff from Investment

		Expected Value Per Share								
		$ 55	$ 57	$ 59	$ 60	$ 61	$ 63	$ 65	$ 67	$ 69
	20	−226%	−13%	201%	308%	414%	628%	841%	1055%	1268%
	25	−186%	−15%	156%	241%	327%	497%	668%	839%	1010%
	30	−159%	−16%	126%	197%	268%	411%	553%	695%	838%
	35	−139%	−17%	105%	166%	227%	349%	471%	593%	715%
Days in	40	−125%	−18%	89%	142%	195%	302%	409%	516%	622%
Holding	45	−113%	−19%	76%	124%	171%	266%	361%	456%	551%
Period	50	−104%	−19%	66%	109%	152%	237%	322%	408%	493%
	55	−97%	−19%	58%	97%	136%	213%	291%	369%	446%
	60	−91%	−20%	51%	87%	123%	194%	265%	336%	407%
	65	−86%	−20%	46%	78%	111%	177%	243%	308%	374%
	70	−81%	−20%	41%	71%	102%	163%	224%	285%	346%
	75	−77%	−20%	36%	65%	93%	150%	207%	264%	321%
	80	−74%	−21%	33%	59%	86%	139%	193%	246%	300%

Note: Shaded cell indicates example case in text.

The table reveals that seemingly small variations (e.g., $2.00) in expected payoffs produce sizable swings in returns—returns vary directly with payoffs. The table also shows that returns vary inversely with holding period—the longer the period, the smaller the returns.[6] Plainly, a takeover consummated in 20 days results in dramatically higher returns than those taking 40 and 80 days.

The implication of **Table 1** is that the arb will be extremely sensitive to variations in time and payoff. This sensitivity means that bidders and targets that seek the support of arbs must tailor their tactics to exploit this sensitivity.

4. The Arb Assesses a Recapitalization Proposal in Terms of Blended Value

One common response by takeover targets is to initiate a leveraged recapitalization of the firm. This entails borrowing substantially and paying a large one-time dividend to all shareholders and/or a large one-time share repurchase. Asset sales or other restructuring tactics may also be involved. The result is a highly levered acquisition target that is probably less attractive to a hostile bidder. The arb assesses the share-repurchase recapitalization as a blend of values.

---

[6]The inverse relationship between holding period and return is true for all but the left-most column, in which the return is less negative the longer the period. This is because, at short holding periods, the annualization multiple (365 divided by days in holding period) has a huge effect in amplifying a negative return to be even more negative. For longer periods, the annualization impact is less pronounced.

Assume the target company decides to mount its own recapitalization plan by buying back 35 percent of its shares at $85 a share pro rata among all shares. Furthermore, assume that the stub share[7] will be estimated to trade at approximately $55 a share after the recapitalization is completed. The share value to the arb of this recapitalization is a blend of the two:

$$\text{Blended value} = (35\% \times \$85) + (65\% \times \$55) = \$65.50$$

In this example, note that an arb would prefer a blended value of $65.50 realized from the recapitalization (as opposed to the raider's $60 offer), if that value could be delivered on a timely basis. To continue the previous example, if the arb realizes a value of $65.50 per share, the return on investment for 40 days will be 48 percent,[8] and the annualized return will be 436 percent. As this second example illustrates, the high leverage of the arb's position causes the returns to swing dramatically with small changes in the gross spread per share.

In deciding where to tender their shares in a contest for corporate control, the arbs will determine which offer (i.e., the hostile bid or the recapitalization) gives them the highest annualized return on their invested capital. To continue our example, an arb would probably prefer $60 cash on July 10 as opposed to cash and securities of $65.50 received on October 10.[9] With capital costs of 30 to 40 percent per year, the timing of cash flows received is crucial to the arbs' decision. Lastly, the arbs' decision to tender their shares to a raider will, in almost all cases, mean that a company will not have ample time to complete its own recapitalization if it is calculated to have a lower blended value.

5. Takeover Defenses Alter the Probabilities of Outcomes

Target management can undertake a series of maneuvers to delay or completely stop the consummation of a hostile acquisition. These are commonly known as "antitakeover defenses." Courts have shown strong reluctance to invalidate these defenses without some proof of conflict of interest, negligence, or fraud on the part of target management.

Classified boards dictate the election of a fraction of the total directors each year, thus delaying the attainment of control by the bidder through domination of the board.

The supermajority amendment to the bylaws specifies that a large percentage of the currently outstanding common shares must approve a merger between the company and an acquirer. Generally, acquirers would be hesitant to make an offer for a company if they believed they would not be able to complete the merger.

---

[7]"Stub shares" are the shares of a company that remain after a major recapitalization. For instance, if a parent company decided, in the face of a hostile tender offer, to sell off two of its major business lines and borrow a significant amount of money to buy back two-thirds of its shares, the shares left over would be called stub shares.

[8]The gross spread is $65.50 − $57 × 100 shares, or $850 on the position in the target, and $50 − $50 × 100 shares, or zero on the position in the buyer. Deducting interest of $43.73 and dividends forgone from the short sale of $20 and adding dividends received of $30 give a net spread of $816.27. Dividing the net spread by capital committed of $1,710 gives a return on capital of 48%, which is annualized to 436%.

[9]Assuming a 40% annual discount rate, the present value of $65.50 received in four months is $58.55.

The *fair-price amendment to the bylaws* requires that all selling shareholders receive the same price from a buyer. This prevents the implementation of a two-tier, or "freeze-out," tender offer, in which a controlling block of shares is purchased at a premium and the remaining minority is purchased at a discount.

Golden parachutes grant target management generous severance payments if they are fired following an acquisition. This has the effect of raising the cost of acquisition to a bidder.

A *leveraged recapitalization* by the target entails borrowing heavily and paying a large one-time dividend to target shareholders. Thus, a hostile acquirer will need to assume a large debt burden from the target. Moreover, many debt provisions in highly leveraged recapitalizations include *poison puts*, which make the debt immediately payable upon a change of control of the target firm. Thus, the bidder must be prepared to refinance the target's debt upon acquisition.

The *shareholder right* (or "poison pill," as it is commonly called) is a nondetachable right to obtain common shares at nominal cost. All shareholders participate in the right except for an "interested person" who acquires more shares than allowed under the rights plan. Thus, the plan discriminates against an unwanted acquirer in favor of all other shareholders, making the acquisition more expensive (e.g., 25 to 50 percent more) than otherwise. Typically, the right is effective for 10 years unless extended by the board of directors. Nondetachable rights are distributed pro rata to all common stockholders as a stock dividend. The rights are automatically transferred with the shares of common stock to which they relate but do not become exercisable (and indeed are not even represented by separate instruments) until the occurrence of a "triggering event." At that point, separate instruments representing the rights are distributed to shareholders. The rights detach from the common shares and become separately tradable.

- *Triggering event, "interested person."* The triggering event is defined as the acquisition by any person (or group of persons acting in concert) of a certain percentage (today, typically 10 percent) of outstanding common stock without the prior consent of the firm's board of directors. Such an acquirer is known as an "interested person." An "interested person" may not exercise the rights.

- *"Flip in" and "flip over" provisions.* The rights plan may contain either "flip in" or "flip over" provisions or both. "Flip over" provisions apply only when the "interested person," having acquired voting control of the firm, attempts to merge the firm into itself. At that point, holders of the rights become entitled to purchase common shares of the surviving firm at nominal value. "Flip in" provisions entitle the holders to purchase common shares of the target firm at nominal value. Both the "flip in" and "flip over" provisions impose significant economic dilution on the "interested person."

- *Redemption.* The board of directors may redeem the rights at any time prior to the triggering event and for 10 days thereafter at the redemption price of $0.01 per right. The rights become irredeemable after a 10-day "window."

- *Qualified offer, "dead hand" provision.* The board may also choose to exempt a qualified offer from the operations of the rights plan. A "qualified offer" is defined as an all-cash, any-and-all-shares tender offer or merger proposal that has been approved by the board. After a "change of control," defined as the replacement of 50 percent of the board in a proxy contest, the rights may be redeemed only by a majority of (but at least two) "continuing directors." A "continuing director" is defined as a person who was a member of the target board at the time the rights plan was adopted or was nominated by a majority of the directors then in office or their nominees.

Poison pills are by far the most effective defense in the corporate arsenal. Pills have never been deliberately triggered, and, unless rescinded by target directors, are virtually guaranteed to halt a hostile takeover. But the poison-pill defense is not without weaknesses. On occasion, courts have required boards to rescind poison pills. Some targets have successfully appealed to directors and shareholders to rescind pills (usually, this is accompanied by a large acquisition premium).

6. Court Decisions, Laws, and Regulations Affect the Game Considerably

Government intervention in hostile takeovers influences the takeover process considerably. At the federal government level in the United States, securities law has been oriented toward creating a "level playing field" in the spirit of enhancing competition among bidders. Antitrust law has been oriented toward protecting consumers and generally enhancing competition in product markets. At the state government level, antitakeover laws have been oriented toward simply preventing unwanted takeovers. These and other laws and regulations constrain the behavior of bidders and targets and affect the odds of successful acquisition. The following government-imposed requirements give a sense of the constraints on bidder and target managements.

A. The acquisition of shareholdings in excess of 5 percent of a target's shares must be disclosed within 10 days to the Securities and Exchange Commission (Rule 13-D). Arbitrageurs, major trading houses, and financial institutions employ runners to transmit copies of these 13-D filings with the SEC immediately to their employers. Disclosures of major changes in shareholding become rapidly impounded in share prices. The effect of this requirement is to telegraph the intentions of a bidder to the target and the rest of the market, well in advance of acquiring control through open market purchases.

B. A tender offer must remain open 20 business days (Rule 14e-1(a)). Before the Williams Act, raiders could set a relatively short time to expiration of the offer, compelling hasty decision making on the part of the target shareholders and preventing action by target management. The effect of this rule is to give the target a window in which to organize a defense or a counterproposal to the arbs.

C. The bidder must honor all shares tendered into the offering pro rata, rather than on a first-come, first-served basis (Rule 14d-8). This relieves some of the target shareholders' compulsion to decide quickly in order to get in line early—offers for a controlling interest (e.g., 51 percent) rather than 100 percent of shares might be intended to induce a shareholder stampede. Similarly, this rule defuses somewhat the impact of the two-tier tender offer.

D. Target shareholders may withdraw their tenders for any reason in the first 15 days of a tender offer (Rule 14d-7(a)(1)). This permits shareholders greater flexibility in responding to competing offers, should they appear.

E. Tender offer time periods are extended by 10 days if a competing offer appears (Rule 14d-7(a)(1)).

F. Directors must exercise duties of care and loyalty to the shareholders (case law). This extremely important doctrine prevents directors from giving much weight to the considerations of other stakeholders in the firm. Directors must do what is best for the shareholders first and must do so in an informed and diligent manner.

G. Directors and managers must disclose *material* information about the company to the public (case law). For instance, receipt of a bona fide certain offer to buy a company that is communicated to management under some circumstances must be communicated to shareholders. However, what is "material" is a key matter of judgment. If management receives an offer, then they must determine, with or without the assistance of an investment banker, if the offer is bona fide. For instance, an offer made by someone without financial support may not be deemed bona fide. If the offer is deemed bona fide, then, at the very least, the board of directors should be notified. At that point, legal counsel should be sought to determine whether to disclose the offer. The company should never lie to the press because to do so would make it liable to charges of fraud. The company may elect, as a matter of corporate policy, not to comment on market rumors.

H. If it is determined that the company is to be sold, the directors must sell it to the highest bidder (case law, the "Revlon Decision").

I. The courts are disinclined to intervene in, or second-guess, management decision making unless gross negligence or fraud can be proved. This is the "Business Judgment Rule" doctrine in U.S. federal courts. This puts the burden of proof on the bidder if the bidder seeks to have a court invalidate a target's antitakeover defenses.

J. In the event that a management group conducts an auction for the company, managers must be careful to maintain a level playing field during the auction process. They can give no bidder a preferred advantage in the bidding process.

7. Selling Shareholders Face a Prisoner's Dilemma

The decision whether to sell into a tender offer creates an unusual conflict of interests for the selling shareholders of target companies. On the one hand, by waiting and not tendering, they may get a higher offer down the road—or management might reveal some hidden value justifying a higher share price and bid offer. On the other hand, by selling now they lock in a certain value. The only way to find out whether there is more value in the target firm is for target shareholders to band together, delay in tendering into the bidder's offer, and wait to see if a higher value (or bid) emerges. The problem is that unified action among a highly atomistic shareholder group is difficult, if not impossible, to engineer.

TABLE 2 |

		Prisoner B	
		Doesn't Confess	Confesses
Prisoner A	Doesn't Confess	I. A gets 5 years B gets 5 years	II. A gets 8 years B gets 3 years
	Confesses	III. A gets 3 years B gets 8 years	IV. A, B get 10 years each

This is the classic problem of the "prisoner's dilemma."[10] In this hypothetical case, two robbers are arrested by the police in the belief that they acted together in committing a crime. The prisoners are separated in different cells and interrogated independently. The prosecutor encourages each prisoner to confess and implicate the other. If neither prisoner confesses, the prosecutor believes the court can be convinced to send the suspects to jail for five years. If both prisoners confess *and* implicate each other, the court will send the suspects to jail for 10 years. If one prisoner confesses and implicates the other, and the other neither confesses nor implicates, the one who confesses will get three years (time off for assisting the prosecution), and the other will get eight years. The "prisoner's dilemma" is whether to confess or not, and offers four possible outcomes, represented in **Table 2.**

Plainly, quadrants II and III are the best outcomes for the two prisoners individually because they result in lower jail terms for each. But if *both* prisoners take the incentive offered, they will wind up with the longest sentence, 10 years each. The safest course of action is for neither to confess, as it results in a jail term materially shorter than 8 or 10 years and not much longer than 3 years. Unfortunately, with the prisoners separated and unable to communicate, the collaboration and mutual assurances necessary to achieve quadrant I are unlikely.

The "prisoner's dilemma" illustrates how opportunism and the absence of joint action result in the least desirable outcomes. The model has been used to explain a wide range of phenomena in business and finance. The key here is in anticipating the probabilities and actions of other players in the game.

The decision facing target shareholders (especially arbs) is similar. **Table 3** recasts the prisoner's dilemma into a takeover setting. Here, two shareholders contemplate a two-tier tender offer of $80 cash paid per share for the first 51 percent of shares and $60 in securities for the rest. Target shareholders face the payoffs shown in the cells of **Table 3,** associated with either tendering immediately or waiting. With an immediate tender, the investor accepts the raider's offer. If both wait, the offer is defeated and the raider must raise its offer. If only one waits, the waiting shareholder becomes a minority investor in the firm and eventually sells to the raider at a much-reduced price.

---

[10]The prisoner's dilemma was first discussed in Anatol Rapoport and A.M. Chammah, *Prisoner's Dilemma* (Ann Arbor: University of Michigan Press, 1965).

TABLE 3 I

		Investor B	
		Wait	**Sell into Offer**
Investor A	**Wait**	I. A gets $100/share B gets $100/share	II. A gets $60/share B gets $80/share
	Sell into Offer	III. A gets $80/share B gets $60/share	IV. A, B get $70 each*

*The $70 payoff in quadrant IV assumes proration of the front-end and back-end payments, 50% times $80 plus 50% time $60.

If the target shareholders act in concert and wait, they may obtain better information and a better price for their firm (quadrant I). If some sell into the tender offer while others wait, those who sell may obtain a better deal than those who wait and wind up being minority shareholders in a firm that is dominated by the bidder. Absent joint action and communication, if all shareholders sell into the tender offer, the bidder takes the firm at the price he offered (quadrant IV).

To the extent that takeovers conform to this model, the "prisoner's dilemma" has important implications for bidders and target shareholders:

- Bidders benefit and target shareholders lose by the asymmetrical structure of pay-offs and the difficulty of taking joint action among target shareholders.

- To heighten the bidder's benefit (and achieve quadrant IV), the bidder should structure the asymmetry of incentives to the target shareholders to motivate all to "defect" to accept the bid. This might be achieved by offering one high and relatively certain price to those who tender early, and another, lower, and less certain payment to those who tender late. Also, the bidder might send signals consistent with a likely future "minority shareholder freeze-out." The classic achievement here is the "two-tier" tender offer: cash is offered to shareholders who participate in the bidder's offer for 51 percent of the firm, to be followed by shares or high-yield bonds for the shareholders who delay and tender late, participating in the last 49 percent of the purchase. A minority that holds out entirely might see the assets of the firm stripped and sold piecemeal to the bidder—in essence, liquidating the target. In 1997, Hilton Hotels Corporation bid $55 a share for ITT Corporation: for the first 50.1 percent of shares, Hilton would pay cash; for the rest of the shares outstanding, Hilton would pay $55 in shares of stock. The consideration was structured to be equivalent in value, though the cash payment appealed much more to arbitrageurs.

- A key problem for arbs and other target firms' shareholders is to assess the probability of other shareholders' actions. Nowhere does the gamelike nature appear in takeovers more than in this fact: like the cardplayer who must assess the hands and probabilities of other players, the arb in this situation must assess the likely actions of other investors.

- Collaboration among selling shareholders may pay. This may explain the appearance of ad hoc committees of target shareholder groups and the appeals to take action together.

- Securities-regulation regimes that favor equitable treatment of all shareholders and "level playing field" conditions will discourage asymmetrical incentives leading to quadrant IV outcomes.

- Time is very valuable to the target shareholders and is the enemy of the bidder. Searching for a white-knight buyer, developing a recapitalization plan, or mounting defenses takes time. To the extent that the bidder can hasten the target shareholders' decision process, the less effective the target management's evasive action is bound to be.

8. To Set a Bid Price, Think Like an Investor

Given the panoply of laws and takeover defenses, the bidder faces the reality that the main instrument of success is *deal design*. The range of possible elements of acquisition terms includes price, form of payment (fixed, semifixed, contingent, side), timing, commitments, and incentives. The bidder's task in a hostile takeover is to fashion terms so that the acquisition succeeds, while preserving as much value as possible for the bidder. In the discussion that follows, the focus will be on price, though, in reality, form of payment and the other dimensions will be very important considerations as well.

Given that arbitrageurs are the significant decision makers in a hostile tender offer, it is reasonable to assume that the highest price offered takes the company. The bidder presumably will offer to purchase shares at a premium to the preexisting share price. The key issue is how large the premium should be. The range of choice for the bid premium will be bounded on the high side by the bidder's most optimistic estimate of the target's intrinsic value (using discounted cash flow, multiples, and other valuation approaches to achieve this "high" value). At first glance, it would seem that the low end of the premium range would be determined by the preexisting share price. But the bidder needs to assume the possibility that the target might undertake a self-initiated restructuring to release value to its shareholders in excess of the current share price—a leveraged restructuring, for example. Because it is reasonable to assume that target management want to keep their jobs and that restructuring is the only alternative available if a white knight cannot be induced to enter the bidding, then, in effect, this restructuring value becomes the other bound in the range of bid premia. Exactly where within this range the bidder will choose to make an offer is a matter of how likely the bidder believes a competing bidder will enter the action.

The advice to a bidder in a situation like this is to *think like the target shareholder*. The shareholder's choice is simple: accept the tender offer if:

$$\text{Value of tendering} \geq \text{Expected value of not tendering}$$

Because the value of the bidder's offer can be reasonably estimated, the core of the analysis lies in estimating the value of not tendering (EVNT). EVNT is a simple average of share prices under two uncertain outcomes: (1) no shares are tendered to the raider, the takeover fails, and share prices subside to the ex ante price;[11] and (2) no shares are tendered to the raider, but they are tendered to a higher competing bidder who buys the firm. These prices are multiplied by their probability of occurrence and then summed:

$$\text{EVNT} = (\text{Share Price}_{\text{No Competing Bid}} \times \text{Probability}_{\text{No Competing Bid}}) + \\ (\text{Share Price}_{\text{Competing Bid}} \times \text{Probability}_{\text{Competing Bid}})$$

Thus, to succeed in the bidding, the raider must set the bid price somewhat higher than EVNT. Of course, this requires estimates of probabilities and the dollar offer of a competing bidder. If a decision maker is uncomfortable with this judgment, the EVNT formula could be solved in reverse for those probabilities and competing bid prices that yield outcomes just better or worse than the bidder's possible offers. Then, the bidder can make some judgment about the reasonableness of the range of competing offers and probabilities as a final step to preparing a bid price.

To illustrate how the EVNT equation can be used to help frame a bidder's analysis, consider the following example. A hostile bidder wants to prepare an initial bid for ABC Corp. ABC's current share price is $45. Under an aggressive restructuring plan (calling for asset sales and a leveraged recapitalization), ABC would be worth $65 a share. The hostile bidder envisions some synergies with ABC, which, if applied entirely to the value of ABC, would justify a maximum bid of $77 a share. Plainly, the hostile bidder would like to appropriate as much of the middle range for itself as possible. At what price should the bidder commence the hostile offer?

As discussed earlier, the raider's strategy will be heavily influenced by the target's ability to counter with a value-creating restructuring plan. Thus, the raider could consider two scenarios:

- *Possibility A: Target does not restructure.* In this instance, if the raider's bid fails to attract the requisite number of shares, the target's share price could be presumed to fall back to the ex ante level, $45.

- *Possibility B: Target announces a restructuring.* Here the shareholders would be unlikely to part with their shares for less than $65 if they were highly confident of the target's ability to deliver this value. For simplicity, let's assume that the restructuring value is highly likely.

Table 4 gives EVNT for various combinations of competing bid prices and probabilities in the first scenario. The shaded area indicates the break even values for each probability and bid that the raider must top in order to motivate the arbs to favor the raider's bid. For instance, a competing bid of $70 and a 50 percent probability suggest that the raider must bid *more* than $57.50 to motivate the arbs to tender their shares to the bidder. The task of the bidder must be to assess whether any other firm

---

[11]When a hostile tender offer is successfully deflected, we observe that the target share price tends to subside back toward the level prevailing ex ante. Whether it returns to the ex ante price exactly will depend on expectations of further takeover bids or possible changes in management policies.

TABLE 4 I EVNT If the "Default Value" Is the Target's Ex Ante Share Price (Possibility A)

		Value of Competing Bid									
		$45.00	$50.00	$55.00	$60.00	$65.00	$70.00	$75.00	$80.00	$85.00	$90.00
Probability	10%	$45.00	$45.50	$46.00	$46.50	$47.00	$47.50	$48.00	$48.50	$49.00	$49.50
of a	25%	$45.00	$46.25	$47.50	$48.75	$50.00	$51.25	$52.50	$53.75	$55.00	$56.25
Competing	50%	$45.00	$47.50	$50.00	$52.50	$55.00	$57.50	$60.00	$62.50	$66.00	$67.50
Bid	75%	$45.00	$48.75	$52.50	$56.25	$60.00	$63.75	$67.50	$71.25	$75.00	$78.75
	90%	$45.00	$49.50	$54.00	$58.50	$63.00	$67.50	$72.00	$76.50	$81.00	$85.50

could possibly afford $70 a share, which is the same as asking whether the probability of a bid at $70 is really 50 percent.

Table 5 summarizes the results for the second scenario. Comparing the shaded areas of both tables shows that the target's restructuring considerably reduces the buyer's room to maneuver.

This analysis shows the enormous advantage that accrues to the first mover in hostile tender offers. Arbs must weigh the concrete offer by the first bidder against uncertain offers by potential competing bidders. Uncertainty discounts the value of these potential competitors so that a relatively high probability of a high bid is required to dissuade arbs from tendering into a certain offer.

The practitioner (bidder or target) can use this analysis as follows:

1. Bound the bidding range on the low side by either the ex ante share price or the value per share produced by any restructuring plan.

2. Set an upper limit on the bidding range, determined by the value of the target firm and reflecting all synergies and optimistic assumptions about operations and the ability to use financial leverage aggressively.

3. Estimate the EVNTs for various combinations of competing bids and probabilities—this is equivalent to the shaded areas in **Tables 4** and **5.**

4. After reflecting on competing bidders, their bid prices, and the likelihood of their entry into the contest, set an offering price that slightly exceeds the EVNT for that cell in your table.

TABLE 5 I EVNT If the "Default Value" Is Driven by the Target's Restructuring (Possibility B)

		Value of Competing Bid									
		$45.00	$50.00	$55.00	$60.00	$65.00	$70.00	$75.00	$80.00	$85.00	$90.00
Probability	10%	$63.00	$63.50	$64.00	$64.50	$65.00	$65.50	$66.00	$66.50	$67.00	$67.50
of a	25%	$60.00	$61.25	$62.50	$63.75	$65.00	$66.25	$67.50	$68.75	$70.00	$71.25
Competing	50%	$55.00	$57.50	$60.00	$62.50	$65.00	$67.50	$70.00	$72.50	$75.00	$77.50
Bid	75%	$50.00	$53.75	$57.50	$61.25	$65.00	$68.75	$72.50	$76.25	$80.00	$83.75
	90%	$47.00	$51.50	$56.00	$60.50	$65.00	$69.50	$74.00	$78.50	$83.00	$87.50

Finally, EVNT offers general insights into two classic competing strategies: (1) start with a high bid and (2) start with a low bid. Each has advantages and disadvantages:

- *Bid high.* A high initial bid is known in M&A parlance as a "bear hug"—presumably referring to the apparent expression of affection that kills all resistance. This strategy deters competitors and pressures the target's directors to accept the offer. Knowing this and seeing the high offer, arbs will tend to support the bid. Accordingly, the high-bid strategy probably wins the contest. The chief disadvantage of this strategy is that it gives value to target shareholders that might have been retained by the bidder with a lower-priced opening bid. Generally, this strategy is appropriate where the bidder fears other competitors or is impatient.

- *Bid low.* This has the advantage of saving the gains from takeover for the bidder. But it may attract competing bidders and almost certainly invites the target to announce an internal restructuring. This approach probably leads to a longer contest. The risk to the bidder is higher. Generally, this strategy is appropriate where the bidder is patient and/or confident of there being no or few other competing bidders.

9. Conclusion: The Game Has Implications for Design and Defense of Takeovers

The discussion in this note suggests that practitioners need to assess and exploit uncertainty in the design and execution of hostile offers. Specific implications include the following:

- Clarity about the value of the target is an absolutely essential foundation for takeover attack and defense. Value should be estimated from a variety of perspectives: current stand-alone status, status if restructured or recapitalized, value to the primary hostile bidder with synergies, and value to potential competing bidders with their synergies. At the very least, this valuation effort anticipates the likely analysis of arbitrageurs who will figure importantly in deciding the contest.

- The hostile bidder should take actions that shorten the time to outcome, that forestall collaboration among target shareholders, that preempt potential competitors, that reduce investor uncertainty about the value of the bid, and that generally pressure the target board to cooperate. The target firm should do the opposite: delay, explore restructuring and white-knight bidders, cast uncertainty on the hostile bidder and its bid, and generally pressure the target board not to cooperate.

- The focus of both attacker and defender should be the investor, particularly the arbitrageur. The arb is unimpressed with appeals to loyalty, tradition, or vague strategies. Cash value delivered in timely fashion will be decisive. Winning the game, then, is largely a matter of maximizing value.

- Government influence in the takeover game is immense. Courts and government agencies can intervene in the game, often in unpredictable ways. An important second "front" for both attacker and defender to manage is the observance and exploitation of case law.

Selected Readings

Auerbach, Alan J. *Mergers and Acquisitions*. Chicago: University of Chicago Press, 1988.

Brams, Steven J. *Rational Politics, Decisions, Games, and Strategy*. Boston: Academic Press, 1985.

Bruner, Robert F. *Applied Mergers and Acquisitions.* Hoboken, New Jersey: John Wiley & Sons, Inc., 2004.

Fleischer, Arthur, Jr., and Alexander R. Sussman. *Takeover Defense*. 5th ed. New York: Aspen Publishers, 1997.

Gilson, Ronald J., and Bernard S. Black. *The Law and Finance of Corporate Acquisitions*. 2nd ed. Westbury, NY: The Foundation Press, 1995.

McDonald, John. *Strategy in Poker, Business & War*. New York: W.W. Norton, 1989.

Rapoport, Anatol, and A. M. Chammah. *Prisoner's Dilemma*. Ann Arbor: University of Michigan Press, 1965.

Smith, Adam [George J. W. Goodman]. *The Money Game*. New York: Dell, 1969.

Thaler, Richard H. *The Winner's Curse: Paradoxes and Anomalies of Economic Life*. Princeton, NJ: Princeton University Press, 1992.

Wyser-Pratte, Guy P. *Risk Arbitrage II*. New York: New York University, Salomon Brothers Center for the Study of Financial Institutions, Monograph 1982–3–4.

General Electric's Proposed Acquisition of Honeywell

You got a commitment from our management team that's delivered to make this the most successful acquisition in industrial history. And I tell you we're going to do that, and that's what's going to happen here . . . Look at product line by product line, component by component by component and there is no index by any calculation one can make anywhere that says there is one issue. From an emotional standpoint one might make a comment about it, but from any factual base, this is the cleanest deal you'll ever see.

—John F. Welch Jr., October 23, 2000[1]

On March 1, 2001, Jessica Gallinelli, managing director of Bancroft Capital Management, heard surprising and somewhat disturbing news about the proposed bid by General Electric Company (GE) for Honeywell International Inc. Despite recent public assurances about the deal from GE's chair and chief executive officer (CEO), John F. "Jack" Welch Jr., the antitrust regulatory authority of the European Commission (EC) announced that it had initiated a review of the proposed merger. Gallinelli, whose fund owned a large stake in Honeywell, considered that major development and wondered whether Bancroft should alter its investment.

Immediately, Gallinelli instructed her associate to provide background material on the merger, an assessment of the probability that the merger would be approved by antitrust regulators in the United States and Europe, and valuation analyses to assist Gallinelli in assessing Bancroft's investment in Honeywell. She needed to decide quickly whether to hold or sell her fund's 10 million shares in Honeywell and its short position of 10 million shares in GE. As a risk arbitrageur, she thought prices would respond rapidly to the EC's announcement. She remembered Jack Welch's confidence

---

[1]Honeywell International Inc., U.S. Securities and Exchange Commission File No.: 1–8974.

from five months earlier that this was "the cleanest deal you'll ever see," and she wondered whether that was still the case.

Background on GE's Bid for Honeywell

On Thursday, October 19, 2000, GE's Jack Welch was visiting the New York Stock Exchange (NYSE), when he noticed something unusual in Honeywell's stock price. "I was looking at the ticker and Honeywell's stock was up, like 10 bucks," he said. "I couldn't understand it."[2] A reporter explained to him at the time that Honeywell and United Technologies Corporation (UTC) had just initiated merger discussions. Reportedly, UTC would pay 0.74 shares of its own stock for each share of Honeywell. Such a merger would create a company that could become a dominant supplier in the aerospace market and an effective competitor with GE.

Welch had been prepared for that news. Late the next morning, Welch called Honeywell's chair and CEO, Michael Bonsignore, to present GE's own bid for Honeywell at a 1:1 share-for-share exchange ratio. After Honeywell's attorneys delivered the news to UTC that GE had entered with a superior offer, UTC's chief executive, George David, told Bonsignore that UTC would walk away from their deal if Honeywell's board did not approve the UTC merger proposal by 2:30 p.m. Honeywell could not meet that deadline, however, and UTC dropped its offer, deciding not to enter into a bidding war with GE. **Exhibit 1** provides a timeline of the events surrounding the competing bids for Honeywell. **Exhibits 2** and **3** offer a history of Honeywell, GE, and UTC stock prices during this period.

On Saturday, October 21, after hearing that Jack Welch, who had been planning to retire, pledged to remain as head of GE through the acquisition period, Honeywell's board agreed to the GE offer at a slightly increased price of 1.055 GE shares for each share of Honeywell, plus assumed debt. GE formally announced the deal on Sunday, October 22, 2000. The company submitted the required regulatory filings to the U.S. Department of Justice (DOJ) on November 15, 2000, and notified the EC of the proposed merger on February 4, 2001.

General Electric Company[3]

In March 2001, General Electric was one of the largest and most diversified corporations in the world. It generated $130 billion in revenues in segments as diverse as aircraft engines, plastics, financial services, and television production. Jack Welch had served as the company's iconic chair and CEO for the previous 20 years, during which time he made GE the most valuable company in the world and led it to break one revenue and earnings record after another. Welch led more than 1,700 acquisitions and pushed GE into many new markets.

---

[2]Matt Murray et al., "Extended Tour: On Eve of Retirement, Jack Welch Decides to Stick around a Bit—Blockbuster Move to Acquire Honeywell Puts Wrench in GE Succession Race—A Deal He Couldn't Pass Up," *Wall Street Journal*, 23 October 2000, A1.

[3]http://www.ge.com/en/company/companyinfo/at_a_glance/hist_leader.htm (accessed 19 December 2005).

The company traced its roots to 1876, when famed inventor Thomas Alva Edison opened a laboratory in Menlo Park, New Jersey, where he developed a wide range of commercially successful electrical devices. By 1890, Edison had organized many of his businesses into the Edison General Electric Company, which merged with the Thomson-Houston Company in 1892 to form the General Electric Company. GE was listed in the original Dow Jones Industrial Index in 1896, and was the only company to have remained part of the index to date.

Honeywell International Inc.

Honeywell International Inc. was a diversified technology and manufacturing corporation with $25 billion in revenues in segments that included aerospace products and services, power generation systems, and specialty chemicals. It was formed upon the merger of AlliedSignal Inc. and Honeywell Inc. in December 1999, and employed approximately 120,000 people in 95 countries.

Honeywell's history began in 1885, when Albert Butz patented the furnace regulator and alarm, invented a thermostat called the "damper flapper," and formed the Butz Thermo-Electric Regulator Company. The company was eventually acquired by the Minneapolis Heat Regulator Company, which merged with Honeywell Heating Specialty Company in 1927. That company became Honeywell Inc. in 1963. Among numerous innovations, the company invented the electric autopilot and the round thermostat, and it had operations related to gyroscopes, security systems, and computers. It acquired Sperry Aerospace in 1986 and had become a leader in certain aerospace markets by 2000.

In December 1999, Honeywell Inc. completed a $16 billion merger with AlliedSignal, in a deal widely praised by Wall Street analysts. The merger of Honeywell and AlliedSignal was expected to enhance the competitive strengths of each company, and the CEOs predicted that these synergies, combined with cost reductions, would increase earnings per share by at least 20 percent per year. Six months after completion of the deal, however, Honeywell's CEO, Michael Bonsignore, explained to investors that expected growth would not meet that prediction, and would instead be in the 12 percent to 14 percent range. Indeed, Honeywell board members did not think the company could make significant improvement for another 18 months to two years, and there was some speculation that a potential deal with a company such as UTC or GE could provide Bonsignore with an opportunity for "a graceful exit."[4]

Merger Considerations

Upon hearing the news of UTC's offer for Honeywell, Jack Welch realized that such a combination could threaten GE's competitive position in several aerospace markets. By making its own bid for Honeywell, GE would not only keep Honeywell out of UTC's grasp, thereby prohibiting UTC from becoming the leading avionics and engines provider, but would also materially increase its own market power. A top

---

[4]Murray et al.

industry analyst observed at the time, "GE essentially will become a gate in the [aerospace] business as no other company has before, and given their likely profitability, it's hard to imagine how you would set up a competing entity of comparable scale."[5]

GE also expected to remain dominant in the market for commercial jet engines. From 1990 to 1999, it controlled 59 percent of the market with its closest competitors Pratt & Whitney (a division of UTC) and Rolls-Royce plc far behind, at 16 percent and 13 percent, respectively. Honeywell would add to GE's business portfolio another line of turbofan power plants concentrated in the lower-thrust class, in addition to a wide array of aircraft subsystems, such as avionics, environmental controls and aircraft landing systems, inventory logistics services, repair and overhaul, and spare parts for the commercial aircraft market. Comparable firms and their relevant ratios are given in **Exhibit 4,** and comparable transactions appear in **Exhibits 5** and **6.**

Welch was particularly enthusiastic about the potential synergies for the merged companies. "Honeywell's core group of businesses—avionics, automated controls, performance materials, and its new microturbine technology—are a perfect complement to four of GE's major businesses [Aircraft Engines, Industrial Systems, Plastics, and Power Systems]," Welch said. "Not only are the businesses a perfect fit, but so are the people and processes. GE's operating system and social architecture, coupled with both companies' common culture based on the initiatives of Six Sigma, services, globalization, and e-business are also a perfect fit."[6] Furthermore, cost and revenue synergies of $3 billion were projected to arise from GE's merger with Honeywell, most likely through employee layoffs and more efficient processes.

Despite the potential merger benefits, there were also risks to consider. This would be the largest acquisition GE had ever contemplated. Although GE had established a reputation for its mergers and acquisitions expertise, its typical strategy was to purchase small companies that could be easily integrated, both structurally and culturally. Within Honeywell there were financial problems and cultural integration issues related to its recent merger with AlliedSignal. Honeywell also had certain low-margin, slow-growth businesses that could drag down GE's historically high returns. Welch had to consider potential legal and political roadblocks as well, mainly antitrust concerns in both the United States and European Union (EU), and potential protectionist policies in the EU that would oppose the increasing power of major American firms.

Antitrust Concerns

As of March 2001, American and European regulators had divergent views regarding corporate mergers. The DOJ assessed whether the merger would substantially lessen

---

[5]"GE Outmaneuvers UTC and Snares Honeywell; Large-Scale Mergers May Be Back in Vogue in the Aerospace Industry, and at this Stage, It's Anybody's Guess Where this Next Round of Consolidation Might Lead," *Aviation Week* (October 30, 2000): 28.

[6]Robert P. Mader, "General Electric to Buy Honeywell," *Contractor* (November 2000): 5.

competition, and subsequently, how prices and product innovation would be affected. The legal standard for evaluating mergers in the EU, on the other hand, measured the companies' degree of industry dominance, and whether or not the merged entity would have increased dominance in its associated industries.

Procedural differences between the DOJ and the EC also affected their respective decision analysis. In the United States, even after the DOJ or the U.S. Federal Trade Commission approved a merger, other parties could still file a lawsuit to prevent the deal. That was not the case in Europe, where the European Commission's decision to approve or block a merger was final. Further, whereas American authorities generally disregarded competitor complaints about a potential deal and may have even considered them a reason to allow a deal, European authorities respected the views of competitors and were willing to bar a deal due to their pleas.

The majority of media reports following the announcement of the proposed GE-Honeywell combination suggested that it presented no problems to antitrust officials. There was minimal overlap in the companies' aerospace products, and all other products were largely complementary. Certain observers, however, believed the deal would raise antitrust scrutiny, especially in Europe. Antitrust officials did not typically endorse mergers between an industry's biggest players. In addition, various experts foresaw both vertical (a company's ability to tie or bundle its products) and horizontal (overlapping product lines, such as jet-engine controls) antitrust concerns.

On March 1, 2001, the European Commission made its surprising decision to open a full investigation into the proposed GE-Honeywell transaction. The EC's move was a personal blow for Welch, who spoke twice the previous day with Mario Monti, the EC's antitrust chief, arguing that GE and Honeywell's products were complementary and that "the trend toward open systems would allow customers to 'mix and match' different suppliers."[7] The EC's decision to challenge the merger destroyed GE's plans to complete the deal by March or April, and signaled that the companies might have to make significant concessions before obtaining approval.

Specifically, the EC expressed concerns over the increased market power of the combined firm, and the additional leverage that GE would have over competitors and customers. It worried that the merged company could dominate the market for avionics, on-board systems, and engines, with deep discounts pushing out competitors and the bundling of products forcing engine customers to purchase avionics through deals with GE's leasing arm, GE Capital Aviation Services (GECAS). The EC acknowledged that this increased competition would lower prices for customers in the short run, but expressed fear that GE's rivals would face eroding margins and not be able to keep up in the long run, thereby decreasing competition, reducing product development in the industry, and enabling GE to increase prices.

The EC also announced plans to investigate the financial clout that GE could wield through GECAS, which purchased aircraft that it later leased or sold to airlines and cargo carriers. It was already one of the largest aircraft buyers in the world, and many industry officials feared that the addition of Honeywell's products to GE's

---

[7]Michael A. Taverna, "Europe May Oppose GE-Honeywell Merger," *Aviation Week* (March 5, 2001): 44.

current product mix would give GECAS too much power over its customers, which it could leverage to sell more of the combined company's products. A spokesman for GE said that GECAS bought a range of engines aside from GE models, that aircraft purchasers could typically choose the engine brand they wanted installed on their aircraft, and that GE had been "very careful for years" to avoid a conflict on the issue and had never faced antitrust problems.[8]

Gallinelli's Considerations

Jessica Gallinelli wondered how the news from Europe would affect the value of her fund's arbitrage position, which had remained long by 10 million shares of Honeywell[9] and short by 10 million shares of GE, with 70 percent of invested capital borrowed at 15 percent interest.[10] Just one point of opposition would be fatal to the deal. She wondered what the probability was that both the DOJ and the EC would approve the merger. Gallinelli planned to consider the regulators' different methods and criteria when evaluating mergers. In addition, she intended to look at historical precedents to help predict the outcome of the current case. Gallinelli noted that since the EC began reviewing mergers in 1990, it only blocked one of more than 400 of those proposed by American companies, namely the merger between WorldCom and Sprint. This deal was also blocked by American authorities.

Gallinelli also planned to consider relevant personality and political issues. Mario Monti was known for opposing large mergers. Both Monti and the U.S. assistant attorney general, Charles James, had personal interests in the outcome of the case, as both their respective careers depended on their results as regulators. Jack Welch was respected by all but seen by many as extremely arrogant, and his attitude and approach to the merger could affect its outcome. The EC might not want two large American companies to gain more power relative to European competitors. On the other hand, the EC might not want to be responsible for harming the already tense U.S.–EU trade relationship.

How would the unexpected news that the EC was initiating an investigation of the deal affect the stock prices of GE and Honeywell? (**Exhibits 7, 8, 9,** and **10** provide a forecast of the financial performance for Honeywell and a completed valuation analysis. Capital market information appears in **Exhibits 11** and **12**.) Should Bancroft Capital Management sell its position in Honeywell, or should it maintain it? Should it alter its short position in GE?

---

[8]Philip Shishkin, "GE Purchase of Honeywell Faces Scrutiny in Europe—Competitors Are Concerned that Combined Firm Will be too Powerful," *Wall Street Journal*, 7 February 2001, A22.

[9]Options on Honeywell's shares were currently trading at prices that implied volatilities ranging from 33.04 percent to 51.77 percent, with a mean of 41.20 percent.

[10]Gallinelli had entered into the long and short positions simultaneously on October 20, 2000.

EXHIBIT 1 | GE–Honeywell Key Events Timeline

Date	Event
October 19, 2000	• Media reports potential merger between United Technologies Company (UTC) and Honeywell
October 20, 2000	• Honeywell board meets to discuss merger with UTC • Jack Welch (GE's CEO) contacts Michael Bonsignore (Honeywell's CEO) to indicate merger interest at an exchange ratio of 1:1 • Bonsignore tells UTC that Honeywell has received another proposal • UTC terminates discussions with Honeywell
October 21, 2000	• Welch meets with Bonsignore and increases the exchange ratio to 1.055 GE shares for each Honeywell share • Honeywell board approves merger
October 22, 2000	• GE board approves merger and announces Honeywell acquisition
November 15, 2000	• Regulatory filing made with U.S. Department of Justice (DOJ)
February 4, 2001	• European Commission (EC) notified of proposed merger
March 1, 2001	• EC initiates review of proposed GE–Honeywell combination

EXHIBIT 2 | Trading History of Honeywell, GE, and UTC Stock

Date	HON $US	GE $US	UTX $US	S&P 500 Index
1-Sep-00	35.55	52.71	58.03	1,520.77
5-Sep-00	35.83	52.09	57.33	1,507.08
6-Sep-00	36.85	53.16	59.72	1,492.25
7-Sep-00	34.48	53.16	59.43	1,502.51
8-Sep-00	31.55	53.96	57.91	1,494.50
11-Sep-00	32.95	53.79	58.85	1,489.26
12-Sep-00	33.35	53.22	58.85	1,481.99
13-Sep-00	33.80	53.22	58.90	1,484.91
14-Sep-00	33.85	53.16	59.90	1,480.87
15-Sep-00	32.90	51.14	59.84	1,465.81
18-Sep-00	32.22	51.81	60.25	1,444.51
19-Sep-00	32.45	51.36	58.61	1,459.90
20-Sep-00	31.55	51.03	59.43	1,451.34
21-Sep-00	32.00	50.69	58.26	1,449.05
22-Sep-00	32.73	51.64	61.30	1,448.72
25-Sep-00	32.05	52.32	62.47	1,439.03
26-Sep-00	32.39	52.26	62.82	1,427.21
27-Sep-00	31.44	53.56	64.40	1,426.57
28-Sep-00	32.84	53.16	66.92	1,458.29
29-Sep-00	32.11	52.21	64.93	1,436.51
2-Oct-00	32.45	52.84	63.88	1,436.23
3-Oct-00	33.52	53.34	66.10	1,426.46
4-Oct-00	34.14	53.18	66.04	1,434.32
5-Oct-00	33.02	53.96	68.09	1,436.28
6-Oct-00	32.90	53.68	67.39	1,408.99
9-Oct-00	33.29	52.84	65.57	1,402.03
10-Oct-00	32.84	52.44	67.21	1,387.02
11-Oct-00	32.50	51.15	66.92	1,364.59
12-Oct-00	31.55	49.22	63.64	1,329.78
13-Oct-00	31.21	51.48	65.22	1,374.17

Source: http://finance.yahoo.com (accessed on September 26, 2005).

Note: UTC's stock ticker is "UTX."

EXHIBIT 2 | Trading History of Honeywell, GE, and UTC Stock *(continued)*

Date	HON $US	GE $US	UTX $US	S&P 500 Index
16-Oct-00	32.28	52.16	67.44	1,374.62
17-Oct-00	31.77	50.24	65.22	1,349.97
18-Oct-00	30.37	50.13	63.99	1,342.13
19-Oct-00	32.34	50.24	59.90	1,388.76
20-Oct-00	41.46	47.08	60.84	1,396.93
23-Oct-00	45.01	44.93	59.43	1,395.78
24-Oct-00	48.05	48.21	60.54	1,398.13
25-Oct-00	47.09	47.81	59.90	1,364.90
26-Oct-00	47.04	47.08	62.24	1,364.44
27-Oct-00	46.42	47.19	62.94	1,379.58
30-Oct-00	48.45	48.77	64.46	1,398.66
31-Oct-00	48.50	49.50	65.34	1,429.40
1-Nov-00	48.22	49.17	64.23	1,421.22
2-Nov-00	46.99	48.49	64.34	1,428.32
3-Nov-00	46.54	48.15	62.82	1,426.69
6-Nov-00	47.66	49.22	65.34	1,432.19
7-Nov-00	48.90	49.62	63.70	1,431.87
8-Nov-00	48.22	49.28	63.35	1,409.28
9-Nov-00	48.39	49.28	63.58	1,400.14
10-Nov-00	48.11	48.66	61.95	1,365.98
13-Nov-00	45.63	46.46	61.83	1,351.26
14-Nov-00	46.76	47.64	63.00	1,382.95
15-Nov-00	46.54	47.42	62.98	1,389.81
16-Nov-00	46.59	47.53	64.38	1,372.32
17-Nov-00	46.14	46.86	65.15	1,367.72
20-Nov-00	44.55	45.21	64.80	1,342.62
21-Nov-00	45.12	45.84	65.73	1,347.35
22-Nov-00	43.65	43.86	65.91	1,322.36
24-Nov-00	43.99	44.60	67.55	1,341.77
27-Nov-00	43.99	44.37	65.68	1,348.97
28-Nov-00	44.44	44.99	64.21	1,336.09
29-Nov-00	43.70	44.88	65.15	1,341.91
30-Nov-00	44.10	44.76	66.50	1,314.95
1-Dec-00	45.18	46.06	66.20	1,315.23

Source: http://finance.yahoo.com (accessed on September 26, 2005).

Note: UTC's stock ticker is "UTX."

EXHIBIT 2 | Trading History of Honeywell, GE, and UTC Stock *(continued)*

Date	HON $US	GE $US	UTX $US	S&P 500 Index
4-Dec-00	45.80	46.63	68.14	1,324.97
5-Dec-00	47.89	48.89	71.25	1,376.54
6-Dec-00	47.89	48.72	70.78	1,351.46
7-Dec-00	47.61	48.32	70.72	1,343.55
8-Dec-00	49.30	49.85	70.25	1,369.89
11-Dec-00	49.93	49.95	67.85	1,380.20
12-Dec-00	47.16	47.70	69.02	1,371.18
13-Dec-00	47.16	47.87	67.26	1,359.99
14-Dec-00	45.74	46.46	66.85	1,340.93
15-Dec-00	43.31	44.99	66.85	1,312.15
18-Dec-00	45.00	46.06	69.31	1,322.74
19-Dec-00	44.22	45.28	70.19	1,305.60
20-Dec-00	41.61	42.85	68.85	1,264.74
21-Dec-00	41.89	43.24	70.43	1,274.86
22-Dec-00	43.20	44.15	71.37	1,305.97
26-Dec-00	43.42	44.54	72.95	1,315.19
27-Dec-00	43.02	43.67	74.89	1,328.92
28-Dec-00	43.37	43.89	73.89	1,334.22
29-Dec-00	42.80	43.44	73.83	1,320.28
2-Jan-01	40.03	39.64	70.66	1,283.27
3-Jan-01	43.54	43.32	70.55	1,347.56
4-Jan-01	43.48	43.55	69.08	1,333.34
5-Jan-01	42.46	42.87	66.79	1,298.35
8-Jan-01	41.33	41.28	67.96	1,295.86
9-Jan-01	40.43	40.44	66.32	1,300.80
10-Jan-01	40.88	40.49	67.85	1,313.27
11-Jan-01	42.86	42.19	69.37	1,326.82
12-Jan-01	42.06	41.40	66.38	1,318.32
16-Jan-01	43.31	42.93	66.61	1,326.65
17-Jan-01	43.42	42.31	67.73	1,329.47
18-Jan-01	44.22	43.16	68.61	1,347.97
19-Jan-01	43.77	42.59	66.73	1,342.54

Source of data: http://finance.yahoo.com (accessed on September 26, 2005).

Note: UTC's stock ticker is "UTX."

EXHIBIT 2 | Trading History of Honeywell, GE, and UTC Stock *(continued)*

Date	HON $US	GE $US	UTX $US	S&P 500 Index
22-Jan-01	42.57	41.45	67.50	1,342.90
23-Jan-01	43.31	42.31	68.32	1,360.40
24-Jan-01	42.86	41.96	68.55	1,364.30
25-Jan-01	42.80	41.63	70.96	1,357.51
26-Jan-01	42.01	40.44	68.67	1,354.95
29-Jan-01	41.43	40.21	69.12	1,364.17
30-Jan-01	42.85	41.91	69.89	1,373.73
31-Jan-01	42.74	41.66	70.41	1,366.01
1-Feb-01	43.19	41.89	69.63	1,373.47
2-Feb-01	43.15	41.93	69.45	1,349.47
5-Feb-01	44.71	43.36	69.68	1,354.31
6-Feb-01	44.55	43.13	69.83	1,352.26
7-Feb-01	43.92	42.54	69.73	1,340.89
8-Feb-01	44.13	42.71	70.44	1,332.53
9-Feb-01	42.70	41.37	70.32	1,314.76
12-Feb-01	44.38	43.05	70.43	1,330.17
13-Feb-01	44.05	42.73	72.68	1,318.80
14-Feb-01	43.12	41.92	72.52	1,315.92
15-Feb-01	44.05	43.48	74.40	1,326.61
16-Feb-01	43.78	42.59	73.70	1,301.53
20-Feb-01	44.68	43.21	74.17	1,278.94
21-Feb-01	44.20	42.86	74.52	1,255.27
22-Feb-01	43.77	42.68	73.88	1,252.82
23-Feb-01	42.69	41.84	72.75	1,245.86
26-Feb-01	44.21	43.48	73.88	1,267.65
27-Feb-01	43.73	43.49	75.01	1,257.94
28-Feb-01	42.44	42.13	73.38	1,239.94
1-Mar-01	41.82	41.60	73.47	1,241.23

Source of data: //finance.yahoo.com (accessed on September 26, 2005).

Note: UTC's stock ticker is "UTX."

EXHIBIT 3 | Historical Stock Performance for Honeywell, GE, and the S&P 500 Index

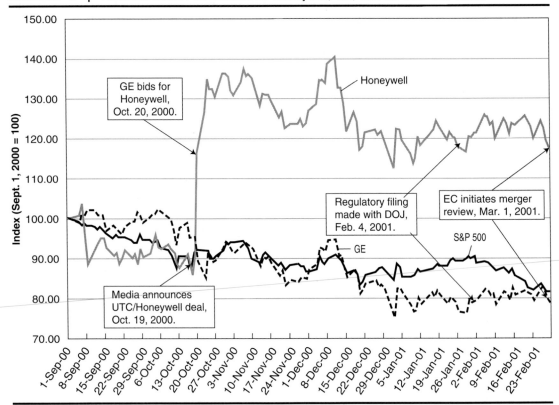

EXHIBIT 4 | Financial Data for Comparable Firms (values in millions of U.S. dollars, except per-share amounts)

Company	Market Capitalization	Six-Month Avg. Price	Beta	Book Value per Share	Total Assets	Cash	Net Debt	Total Liabilities
Emerson Electric Co.	$ 28,691	$62.76	0.659	$14.98	$ 15,164	$ 281	$ 4,319	$ 8,762
Textron Inc.	$ 7,599	$43.89	0.893	$28.28	$ 16,370	$ 289	$ 6,974	$ 12,376
Tyco International Ltd.	$ 95,528	$54.98	0.953	$10.11	$ 40,404	$ 1,265	$ 9,734	$ 23,371
United Technologies	$ 36,671	$66.58	1.304	$16.29	$ 25,364	$748	$ 4,063	$ 17,270
General Electric Co.	$460,759	$46.74	1.242	$ 5.08	$437,006	$13,223	$188,089	$386,514
Honeywell Int'l. Inc.	$ 37,615	$41.36	0.988	$12.02	$ 25,175	$ 1,196	$ 4,427	$ 15,468

Company	Shares Outstanding	Sales	EBIT	EBITDA	Net Income	Market Value Equity	Enterprise Value	Book Value
Emerson Electric Co.	427.48	$ 15,545	$ 2,541	$ 3,219	$ 1,422	$ 26,828	$ 31,148	$ 6,403
Textron Inc.	140.93	$ 13,090	$ 1,580	$ 2,074	$ 218	$ 6,186	$ 13,160	$ 3,994
Tyco International Ltd.	1684.51	$ 28,932	$ 5,750	$ 7,189	$ 4,520	$ 92,614	$102,348	$17,033
United Technologies	470.31	$ 26,583	$ 3,140	$ 3,748	$ 1,808	$ 31,313	$ 35,376	$ 8,094
General Electric Co.	9932.01	$128,051	$29,606	$37,342	$12,735	$464,222	$652,311	$50,492
Honeywell Int'l. Inc.	807.29	$ 25,023	$ 3,629	$ 4,624	$ 1,659	$ 33,390	$ 37,817	$ 9,707

Company	EPS	Enterprise Value as a Multiple of:				Market Value of Equity as a Multiple of:	
		Sales	EBIT	EBITDA	Net Income	EPS Book	Value
Emerson Electric Co.	$3.33	2.00	10.56	8.33	21.90	18.86	4.19
Textron Inc.	$1.55	1.01	3.91	2.98	60.36	28.37	1.55
Tyco International Ltd.	$2.68	3.54	16.11	12.88	22.64	20.49	5.44
United Technologies	$3.84	1.33	9.97	8.35	19.57	17.32	3.87
General Electric Co.	$1.28	5.09	15.68	12.43	51.22	36.45	9.19
Honeywell Int'l. Inc.	$2.06	1.51	9.20	7.22	22.79	20.13	3.44
Median		1.76	10.27	8.34	22.72	20.31	4.03

Source of data: Standard and Poor's *Research Insight.*

EXHIBIT 5 | Financial Data for Comparable Transactions: Aerospace Industry

Target Name Acquirer Name	McDonnell Douglas Boeing	Sundstrand United Technologies	Gulfstream Aerospace General Dynamics	Median
Announcement date	12/17/1996	2/22/1999	5/17/1999	
Transaction value ($mil)	$15,282	$4,355	$5,687	$5,687
Equity value ($mil)	$13,359	$4,408	$5,420	$5,420
Long-term debt / equity	0.81	0.54	1.24	0.81
Total debt/equity	0.89	0.85	1.59	0.89
Target price/equity	na	17.50	22.00	19.75
Target price/book	4.60	7.00	24.10	7.00
Enterprise value/net sales	1.12	2.16	2.23	2.16
Enterprise value/cash flow	10.09	9.58	12.69	10.09
Enterprise value/EBIT	12.19	11.64	13.92	12.19
Equity value/net income	na	17.19	22.22	19.71
Offer price/book value	4.62	6.99	24.09	6.99
Offer price/EPS	na	17.54	21.98	19.76
Stock price/book value (4 weeks prior)	3.85	4.54	16.72	4.54
Premium overstock price:				
1 day prior (%)	0.62	20.69	28.44	20.69
1 week prior (%)	22.71	31.93	34.48	31.93
1 month prior (%)	20.08	54.08	44.14	44.14
Consideration offered	stock	cash, stock, and collar	stock	

na = not available.

Source of data: Thomson SDC Platinum.

EXHIBIT 6 | Financial Data for Comparable Transactions: Jumbo Deals[a]

Target Name Acquirer Name	GTE Bell Atlantic	Amoco BP	US WEST Quest	Texaco Chevron	Median
Announcement date	7/28/1998	6/30/1998	6/14/1999	10/16/2000	
Transaction value ($mil)	$71,324	$55,040	$56,306	$43,318	$55,673
Equity value ($mil)	$53,415	$48,174	$56,307	$42,872	$50,794
Long-term debt/equity	1.91	0.35	9.39	0.50	1.21
Total debt/equity	2.41	0.45	10.91	0.56	1.49
Target price/equity	23.20	23.20	28.00	15.30	23.20
Target price/book	6.80	3.10	45.10	2.80	4.95
Enterprise value/net sales	2.92	1.60	4.49	0.94	2.26
Enterprise value/cash flow	8.16	9.33	10.63	8.35	8.84
Enterprise value/EBIT	14.61	16.66	18.60	12.37	15.64
Equity value/net income	23.52	22.84	31.47	15.55	23.18
Offer price/book value	6.76	3.07	45.14	2.79	4.92
Offer price/EPS	23.17	23.18	28.01	15.34	23.18
Stock price/book value (4 weeks prior)	7.12	na	30.14	2.38	7.12
Premium over stock price:					
1 day prior (%)	−2.72	na	32.48	17.68	17.68
1 week prior (%)	−2.72	na	50.11	22.55	22.55
1 month prior (%)	−4.94	na	49.77	17.51	17.51
Consideration offered	stock	stock	stock, liab.	stock, liab.	

[a]Jumbo deals are those whose transaction value is $40 billion or more.

na = not available.

Source of data: Thomson SDC Platinum.

EXHIBIT 7 | Honeywell International Pro Forma Modeling Assumptions

	Actual			2000	Forecast				
	1997	1998	1999	2000	2001E	2002E	2003E	2004E	2005E
Annual growth rate in sales[1]		4.7%	0.8%	5.4%	5.5%	5.5%	5.5%	5.5%	5.5%
Costs and expenses									
Cost of goods sold[2]	77.5%	75.1%	77.9%	76.3%	75.0%	75.0%	75.0%	75.0%	75.0%
Selling, general, and admistative expenses[2]	13.1%	12.8%	13.5%	12.5%	12.0%	12.0%	12.0%	12.0%	12.0%
Annual depreciation as % of prior yr. PPE[2]			0.1%	1.2%	1.8%	1.8%	1.8%	1.8%	1.8%
Interest rate on borrowings[3]					7.6%	7.6%	7.6%	7.6%	7.6%
Taxes[1]	32.2%	31.3%	31.5%	30.8%	31.0%	31.0%	31.0%	31.0%	31.0%
Balance sheet items									
Cash and cash equivalents[2]		4.3%	8.4%	4.8%	4.8%	4.8%	4.8%	4.8%	4.8%
Accounts and notes receivable[2]		16.6%	16.4%	18.5%	18.5%	18.5%	18.5%	18.5%	18.5%
Inventories[2]		14.7%	14.5%	14.9%	14.7%	14.7%	14.7%	14.7%	14.7%
Other current assets[2]		4.2%	4.6%	4.4%	4.4%	4.4%	4.4%	4.4%	4.4%
Property, plant, and equipment—gross[2]		53.7%	53.5%	49.8%	49.0%	49.0%	49.0%	49.0%	49.0%
Accounts payable[2]		8.6%	9.0%	9.4%	9.0%	9.0%	9.0%	9.0%	9.0%
Short-term borrowings[2]		0.6%	1.3%	0.4%	0.8%	0.8%	0.8%	0.8%	0.8%
Commercial paper[2]		7.5%	8.5%	4.8%	6.9%	6.9%	6.9%	6.9%	6.9%
Current maturities of long-term debt[2]		1.2%	1.2%	1.5%	1.3%	1.3%	1.3%	1.3%	1.3%
Accrued liabilities[2]		14.6%	14.9%	12.7%	14.0%	14.0%	14.0%	14.0%	14.0%
Common shares (millions)	804.4	799.6	790.3	801.4	801.4	801.4	801.4	801.4	801.4
Dividend as a percentage of earnings[2]	26.4%	25.3%	34.2%	36.1%	30.5%	31.5%	33.1%	32.8%	32.0%

[1] Figure taken from the *Value Line Investment Survey*.

[2] Percentage of sales estimate.

[3] Yield on 10-year A-rated corporate bond.

Note: These base case assumptions are drawn from analysts' forecasts and case writer's assumptions, and they reflect Honeywell's outlook at March 1, 2001.

EXHIBIT 8 | Honeywell International Pro Forma Financial Statements (values in millions of U.S. dollars, except per-share amounts)

INCOME STATEMENT	Actual				2001E	2002E	Forecast			
	1997	1998	1999	2000	2001E	2002E	2003E	2004E	2005E
Net sales	$22,499	$23,555	$23,735	$25,023	$26,399	$27,851	$29,383	$30,999	$32,704
Costs, expenses, and other									
Cost of goods sold	17,444	17,689	18,495	19,090	19,799	20,888	22,037	23,249	24,528
Selling, general, and administrative expenses	2,940	3,008	3,216	3,134	3,168	3,342	3,526	3,720	3,924
(Gain) on sale of nonstrategic businesses	(303)		(106)	(112)					
Equity in (income) of affiliated companies	(191)	(162)	(76)	89					
Other (income) expense	(87)	(27)	(307)	(57)					
EBIT	**2,696**	**3,047**	**2,513**	**2,879**	**3,432**	**3,621**	**3,820**	**4,030**	**4,252**
Interest and other financial charges	277	275	265	481	671	621	567	507	439
Income before taxes	**2,419**	**2,772**	**2,248**	**2,398**	**2,761**	**3,000**	**3,253**	**3,523**	**3,813**
Taxes	778	869	707	739	856	930	1,008	1,092	1,182
Net income	**$ 1,641**	**$1,903**	**$1,541**	**$ 1,659**	**$ 1,905**	**$ 2,070**	**$ 2,244**	**$ 2,431**	**$ 2,631**
EBITDA	2,696	3,047	2,529	3,036	3,656	3,854	4,065	4,289	4,525
Dividends	434	481	527	599	581	652	742	797	841
Retained earnings	1,207	1,422	1,014	1,060	1,324	1,417	1,502	1,633	1,789
EPS (basic)	$ 2.04	$ 2.38	$ 1.95	$ 2.07	$ 2.38	$ 2.58	$ 2.80	$ 3.03	$ 3.28

continued

EXHIBIT 8 | Honeywell International Pro Forma Financial Statements (values in millions of U.S. dollars, except per-share amounts) *(continued)*

BALANCE SHEET	1997	Actual			2001E	Forecast			
	1997	1998	1999	2000	2001E	2002E	2003E	2004E	2005E
Current assets									
Cash and cash equivalents		$ 1,018	$ 1,991	$ 1,196	$ 1,267	$ 1,337	$ 1,410	$ 1,488	$ 1,570
Accounts receivable		3,899	3,896	4,623	4,877	5,146	5,429	5,727	6,042
Inventories		3,456	3,436	3,734	3,878	4,091	4,316	4,554	4,804
Other current assets		981	1,099	1,108	1,164	1,228	1,295	1,366	1,441
Total current assets		**9,354**	**10,422**	**10,661**	**11,186**	**11,801**	**12,450**	**13,135**	**13,858**
Investments and long-term receivables		1,792	782	748	748	748	748	748	748
Property, plant, and equipment—gross		12,657	12,703	12,460	12,936	13,647	14,398	15,190	16,025
Accumulated depreciation		7,057	7,073	7,230	7,454	7,687	7,933	8,192	8,465
Property, plant, and equipment—net		5,600	5,630	5,230	5,481	5,960	6,465	6,998	7,560
Goodwill and other intangible assets—net		4,365	4,660	5,898	5,898	5,898	5,898	5,898	5,898
Other assets		1,627	2,033	2,638	2,638	2,638	2,638	2,638	2,638
Total assets		**$22,738**	**$23,527**	**$25,175**	**$25,952**	**$27,045**	**$28,199**	**$29,417**	**$30,701**
Current liabilities									
Accounts payable		$ 2,018	$ 2,129	$ 2,364	$ 2,375	$ 2,505	$ 2,643	$ 2,788	$ 2,942
Short-term borrowings		133	302	110	200	211	223	235	248
Commercial paper		1,773	2,023	1,192	1,832	1,932	2,039	2,151	2,269
Current maturities of long-term debt		284	284	380	345	364	384	405	427
Accrued liabilities		3,437	3,534	3,168	3,708	3,912	4,127	4,354	4,594
Total current liabilities		**7,645**	**8,272**	**7,214**	**8,460**	**8,925**	**9,416**	**9,934**	**10,480**
Other liabilities (plug)		7,010	6,656	8,254	6,427	5,638	4,799	3,866	2,814
Shareowners' equity		8,083	8,599	9,707	11,031	12,448	13,950	15,583	17,373
Minority interests		37	46	34	34	34	34	34	34
Total liabilities and shareowners' equity		**$22,738**	**$23,527**	**$25,175**	**$25,952**	**$27,045**	**$28,199**	**$29,417**	**$30,701**

Source: Case writer's analysis.

EXHIBIT 9 | Honeywell International Discounted Cash Flow (DCF) Valuation and Valuation Summary (values in million of U.S. dollars, except per-share amounts)

Period	1997	1998	1999	2000	2001E	2002E	2003E	2004E	2005E
	-4	-3	-2	-1	1	2	3	4	5
EBIT	$2,696	$3,047	$2,513	$2,879	$3,432	$3,621	$3,820	$4,030	$4,252
− Taxes	778	869	707	739	856	930	1,008	1,092	1,182
Net operating profit after tax	1,918	2,178	1,806	2,140	2,576	2,691	2,812	2,938	3,070
+ Depreciation			16	157	224	233	246	259	273
Subtotal	1,918	2,178	1,822	2,297	2,800	2,924	3,057	3,197	3,343
− Change in net working capital			441	605	(15)	411	434	458	483
− Capital investment			30	(243)	476	711	751	792	835
Free cash flow from operations	$1,918	$2,178	$1,351	$1,935	$2,340	$1,801	$1,873	$1,947	$2,025
Terminal value									$59,639
Total free cash flow					$2,340	$1,801	$1,873	$1,947	$61,664

DCF of Honeywell	$43,379
Less debt	(6,427)
Equity value	36,953
Per share	**$46.11**

Weighted average cost of capital (WACC)	10.69%
W_e	75.05%
W_d	24.95%
K_e	12.49%
K_d	7.62%
Tax rate	31.00%
Risk-free rate (U.S. Treasury, 30-year)	5.29%
Risk premium	6.00%
Beta (est. from *Value Line Investment Survey*)	1.20

Present value (PV) of terminal value	$35,899
Constant growth model:	
$(CF_n(1 + g)/(K - g))/(1 + K)^5$	
Perpetual growth rate	5.27%
Inflation	2.70%
Real	2.50%
Resulting terminal value estimate	
NOPAT $(1 + g)/(K - g)$	$59,639

Sensitivity Analysis	
Rev. growth	DCF/share
Base Case	$46.11
2.0%	$45.53
4.0%	$45.86
6.0%	$46.19
8.0%	$46.52
10.0%	$46.85

continued

EXHIBIT 9 | Honeywell International Discounted Cash Flow (DCF) Valuation and Valuation Summary (values in million of U.S. dollars, except per-share amounts) *(continued)*

Valuation Summary Honeywell International		Multiples		Enterprise Value		Equity Value	
		Low	High	Low	High	Low	High
Free cash flow (FCF)				**$35,177**	**$54,696**	**$28,750**	**$48,270**
valuation	Per share					$ 35.87	$ 60.23
Comparable firms:							
Enterprise value as a							
multiple of:	**2000 revenue**	1.01	2.00	25,156	50,139	18,729	43,713
	Per share					23.37	54.54
	2000 EBIT	9.20	16.11	26,489	55,280	20,062	48,853
	Per share					25.03	60.96
	2000 EBITDA	7.22	12.88	21,923	39,112	15,496	32,685
	Per share					19.33	40.78
	2000 net income	19.57	22.79	32,461	37,817	26,034	31,390
	Per share					32.48	39.17
Equity value as a							
multiple of:	**2000 EPS**	17.32	20.49			28,732	33,994
	Per share					35.85	42.42
	2000 book value	3.44	5.44			33,390	52,780
	Per share					41.66	65.86
Comparable transactions:							
(Aerospace and Jumbo)							
Enterprise value as a							
multiple of:	**2000 revenue**	0.94	2.92	23,522	73,067	17,095	66,640
	Per share					21.33	83.15
	2000 EBIT	11.64	18.60	33,512	53,549	27,085	47,123
	Per share					33.79	58.80
Equity value as a							
multiple of:	**2000 net income**	15.55	31.47			25,797	52,209
	Per share					32.19	65.14
Offer price as a							
multiple of:	**2000 book value**	2.79	6.99			27,083	67,852
	Per share					33.79	84.66
	2000 EPS	15.34	28.01			25,442	46,472
	Per share					31.75	57.98
Premium over							
stock price:	**One day prior**	(2.72)	32.48			32,324	44,021
	Per share					40.33	54.93
	One week prior	(2.72)	50.11			25,245	38,955
	Per share					31.50	48.61
	One month prior	(4.94)	54.08			24,037	38,960
	Per share					29.99	48.61
Recent trading prices						30.37	49.93
Median equity value						**$25,797**	**$46,472**
	Per share					$ 32	$ 56

Source : Case writer's analysis.

EXHIBIT 10 | Honeywell Valuation Triangulation (per-share amounts in U.S. dollars)

Valuation Method	High Value	Low Value	Difference
DCF	$60.23	$35.87	$24.36
Peer firms	$50.62	$29.62	$21.00
Recent market prices	$49.93	$30.37	$19.56
Peer transactions	$62.74	$31.83	$30.90

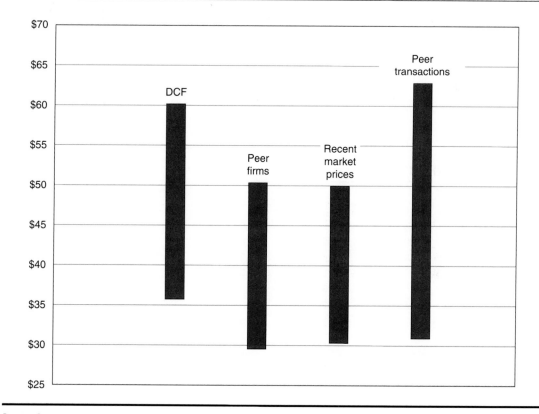

Source: Case writer's analysis.

EXHIBIT 11 | Yields on U.S. Government Bonds

as of Mar. 1, 2001	
3-month	4.843%
6-month	4.679%
2-year	4.402%
3-year	4.607%
5-year	4.646%
10-year	4.872%
30-year	5.292%

Source of data: Bloomberg LP.

EXHIBIT 12 | Yields on U.S. Corporate Bonds

	as of Mar. 1, 2001			
	AAA	A	BBB+	BB
3-month	5.370%	5.731%	5.936%	7.550%
6-month	5.145%	5.516%	5.682%	7.502%
1-year	4.998%	5.379%	5.555%	7.473%
2-year	5.037%	5.506%	5.712%	7.579%
3-year	5.233%	5.682%	6.034%	7.773%
4-year	5.321%	5.790%	6.121%	7.880%
5-year	5.497%	5.917%	6.297%	8.034%
7-year	5.692%	6.112%	6.589%	8.266%
8-year	5.799%	6.229%	6.735%	8.421%
9-year	5.887%	6.326%	6.745%	8.479%
10-year	5.868%	6.326%	6.735%	8.517%
15-year	6.170%	6.735%	7.172%	8.932%
20-year	6.307%	6.988%	7.347%	9.086%

Source of data: Bloomberg LP.

The Hilton–ITT Wars

Professor William Z. Ripley of Harvard, the leading authority on corporations in the 1920s, warned President Calvin Coolidge that "prestidigitation, double-shuffling, honey-fugling, hornswoggling, and skulduggery" were threatening the entire economic system. Plus ça change, plus c'est la même chose.[1]
  —Rand V. Araskog, CEO of ITT

Surprised by the announcement of ITT Corporation's (ITT) restructuring proposal, on July 17, 1997, Matthew J. Hart, the chief financial officer of Hilton Hotels Corporation (Hilton), reviewed the valuation analysis of ITT (see the **Appendix**) and pondered the next step in his firm's hostile tender-offer contest for ITT. Hilton had commenced the tender offer on January 27, 1997. The financial community had responded favorably, but ITT's management had resisted firmly, selling assets and even refusing to call an annual meeting. Because ITT had a strong "poison-pill" antitakeover defense in place, it would be necessary to replace ITT's board and for that board to rescind the poison-pill defense before Hilton could consummate its purchase of ITT. But ITT had delayed calling an annual meeting at which a new board could be elected. In the six months since the initial Hilton offer, ITT had developed its "trivestiture" proposal, which it hoped would successfully fend off Hilton.

ITT Corporation's tax-free "trivestiture" proposal would split the company into three independent companies:

1. ITT Destinations, Inc., which would consist of the gaming and lodging businesses and own the Caesars and Sheraton brands;

2. ITT Information Services, Inc., which would publish international telephone directories;

3. ITT Educational Services, Inc., which would own and operate a chain of technical schools.

---

[1] Rand V. Araskog, *The ITT Wars* (New York: Henry Holt and Company, 1989), 228.

Under the proposal, ITT shareholders would get a share each of ITT Destinations and ITT Information Services and 0.25 share of ITT Educational Services. ITT also announced a self-tender offer for 30 million shares (25 percent of the outstanding shares) at $70 a share and a tender for $2 billion of outstanding public debt. This proposal was to be put to a vote at the upcoming annual meeting of ITT shareholders.[2] Any attempt to acquire ITT Destinations after the restructuring would endanger the tax-free status of the trivestiture and the acquirer would be saddled with a $1.4 billion tax liability. Also, ITT Destinations had only one-third of its directors up for retirement every year, slowing the pace of any possible takeover of that business unit. The trivestiture appeared to be an attempt to lift ITT's share price by creating highly focused companies in three distinct industries through a tax-efficient separation and then delivering cash to shareholders through the self-tender.[3]

Hilton Hotel Corporation

Hilton Hotel Corporation was the seventh-largest hotel company, with 1996 sales of approximately $3.9 billion and assets of approximately $7.6 billion. The company developed, owned, managed, and franchised hotel-casinos, resorts, hotel properties, and vacation-ownership resorts. The firm operated 241 Hilton hotels, casino-resorts, and riverboat casinos in 40 states and 11 Conrad International hotel-casinos in 10 countries around the world.[4]

ITT Corporation

ITT was formerly a wholly owned subsidiary of a Delaware corporation known as ITT Corporation (Old ITT). On December 19, 1995, Old ITT (renamed ITT Industries) distributed to its shareholders all the outstanding shares of common stock of ITT and ITT Hartford Group, Inc. In 1998, ITT Corporation was no longer affiliated with ITT Industries or ITT Hartford Group, Inc.

In 1996, ITT Corporation was one of the world's largest hotel and gaming companies. It had sales of approximately $6.6 billion and assets of approximately $9.3 billion. Its core assets included ITT Sheraton, one of the world's largest hotel companies, with approximately 410 hotels and resorts in 60 countries, and Caesars World, the leading brand name in the gaming industry, with major casinos in Atlantic City, Las Vegas, and Lake Tahoe. Other assets included ITT Educational Services, ITT World Directories, and ownership interest in Madison Square Garden (in partnership with Cablevision) and in New York television station WBIS+ (in partnership with Dow Jones).[5]

---

[2]Tom Lowry, "ITT Splits Three Ways to Fend Off Hilton," *USA Today,* July 17, 1997, B3.

[3]ITT Corporation Investor Presentation, July 16, 1997.

[4]Hilton Hotel Corporation Annual Report and 10-K Statement, 1996.

[5]ITT Corporation Annual Report and 10-K Statement, 1996.

Hilton's Hostile Offer and ITT's Initial Responses

On January 27, 1997, Hilton offered to pay $55 a share in cash for 50.1 percent of ITT shares and $55 a share in stock for the rest. The acquisition would be accounted for as a purchase transaction. (See **Exhibit 1** for a complete summary of the offer.) If successful, this transaction would be the biggest takeover ever in the lodging and gaming industry. Many analysts believed that the ITT acquisition would make Hilton the world's biggest hotel and casino company. With ITT Sheraton's larger international presence, Hilton would be in a much stronger position to compete in the worldwide hotel industry. Moreover, ITT's "Caesars" brand name would solidify Hilton's presence in Atlantic City and Las Vegas. W. Bruce Turner, gaming and lodging analyst at Salomon Brothers, said, "The combination of Hilton and ITT represents a once-in-a-lifetime opportunity to create an unduplicatable global franchise twice as large as any hotel rival and four times as large as any gaming company."[6]

Wall Street was very excited about this tender offer; Hilton's shares increased 10 percent following the announcement, an unusual move for the stock of an acquiring company (**Exhibit 2** gives the share price of both firms during the period of the tender offer). Turner observed, "It's an indication of the market's enthusiasm for the proposal and the value Hilton could bring."[7]

Both ITT Corporation and Hilton Corporation were in a race to dominate the lodging and gaming industry. They competed for the same customers, more or less, in their main business segments, lodging and gaming. Both were acquiring hotel properties in the luxury and midscale markets. In the 1990s, it was cheaper to acquire than build. In the gaming business, ITT acquired Caesars World, Inc., in 1995; Hilton outbid ITT to acquire Bally Entertainment Corporation in 1996. This was not the only time that ITT and Hilton had crossed paths directly. ITT had approached Hilton to acquire its hotel business in 1960 and its hotel and gaming business in 1994. On both occasions, ITT's offer was rebuffed.

The hostile tender offer was no surprise because ITT management had declined to negotiate a friendly acquisition by Hilton. Even after the tender offer, ITT management refused to meet with Hilton management. While there was no negotiation, there was verbal jousting. Rand Araskog, ITT's chairman, said,

> We've never bothered to talk with Hilton, and our board has turned down their bid because we are a much better company with a brighter future, given the superior quality and location of our hotels and gaming facilities. Our Sheraton brand name is in the Four Seasons class, and no gaming operation has quite the same image that our Caesars operation has.[8]

---

[6]Jonathan Laing, "Nasty Bout," *Barron's*, September 29, 1997, 34.

[7]Laing.

[8]Laing, 33.

Stephen Bollenbach, CEO of Hilton, said,

> What Araskog has shown ever since we made our first offer in late January is that he will do anything just to try to fend us off and preserve his own job. That includes dumping so-called core assets, sacrificing 65 percent of his headquarters staff, riding roughshod over the interest of shareholders, and turning his company into a junk credit. He has spent his entire career acting like a beneficiary rather than as a steward of ITT assets, living like a sultan of Brunei in the process. And even more pathetic, he has been acting like a super-weenie, hiding behind his board and advisers and refusing to talk with us.[9]

The Hilton offer of $55 a share amounted to a 29 percent premium over ITT's share price of $43, and was timed to exploit the imminent ITT general meeting at which all of ITT's directors would be up for reelection. At the annual meeting, Bollenbach planned to ask ITT shareholders to elect up to 25 Hilton nominees to the ITT board. These nominees were expected to facilitate the proposed merger. Hilton also planned to ask the ITT shareholders to repeal any bylaw amendments that ITT might adopt before the annual meeting that could interfere with the offer, the merger, or the election of Hilton's nominees—chief among these would be to waive the activation of ITT's poison-pill antitakeover defense.

On February 12, 1997, ITT management rejected Hilton's offer, arguing, "The interests of ITT shareholders as well as ITT employees, suppliers, creditors, and customers would be best served by ITT's continued independence." ITT management cited the following reasons to support its decision:[10]

1. The Hilton offer did not reflect the inherent value of ITT. ITT's response stated, "In the opinion of our financial advisers, Goldman Sachs and Lazard Freres, the Hilton proposal is inadequate."

2. The merger would lead to cannibalization and conflicts among properties managed by Sheraton and Hilton.

3. Hilton's proposal to license the Sheraton and Four Points names for franchising could lead to termination of numerous contracts.

4. The offer raised several potential antitrust and gaming-law issues.

In an effort to defend itself, ITT management deferred the general meeting by six months and initiated litigation to claim relief from the misappropriation and misuse of confidential ITT information acquired by Hilton after its recent acquisition of Bally Entertainment.

Hilton reacted immediately to ITT's rejection. It filed an injunction to force ITT to hold its annual meeting in May. It also communicated the following to the capital market:

- A potential annual synergy cash flow of more than $100 million in this transaction, pointing to Bollenbach's ability to squeeze out a $60 million annual synergy cash flow from the Bally acquisition as an illustration of his ability to realize the stated synergies;

---

[9]Laing, 33.

[10]ITT Corporation press release, July 17, 1997.

- A strategy to create value for ITT's shareholders by monetizing and selling non-core assets of ITT;
- A history of poor shareholder-value creation by current ITT managers, who were more interested in cashing in than performance.[11]

Following the unsolicited $6.5 billion hostile-takeover bid by Hilton, ITT started an aggressive effort to sell assets—the objective was to raise its stock price and keep Hilton from winning the takeover battle. In effect, ITT management sought to take the kinds of actions that Hilton management had proposed to do after the merger.

- February: Reduction in headquarters staff from 200 to 75
- February–March: Sale of investments in Alcatel Alsthom for $830 million
- April: Sale of interest in Madison Square Garden for $650 million
- May: Sale of interest in WBIS+ for $128.75 million

  Sale of five Sheraton hotels for $200 million

These actions by ITT resulted in an increase in share price to $63.50. Also, management refused to hold an annual meeting at which Hilton's proposal might be heard and voted upon. On April 4, 1997, the U.S. District Court for the District of Nevada denied Hilton's motion for a preliminary injunction requiring ITT to hold its annual meeting in May.

Countering the Trivestiture

Now, on July 17, 1997, Matthew Hart knew that Hilton would have to fight this battle on two fronts: in the courtrooms and in the capital markets. Analysts' and arbitrageurs' expectations, as well as fear of a white knight and the repurchase of shares by ITT at $70 a share, convinced Hart that Hilton would have to raise its bid for ITT. He was unsure, however, what the next bid should be, what legal action he should initiate, and what message he should send to investors and the financial community.

As a foundation for considering the next steps, it would be necessary to take the view of investors and arbitrageurs who held ITT's shares. First, one needed to evaluate the bidding for a target's shares in light of the target's estimated intrinsic value. (The **Appendix** presents an estimate of value consistent with analysts' expectations before the bidding began.) Hart would want to update this analysis to reflect recent events and ITT's press releases. Second, it would be necessary to model the investor's decision and work backward from that to the bid by Hilton that reflected Hart's assessment of an even higher bid by ITT or a third party—this was the analysis based on the Expected Value of Not Tendering (EVNT). In short, intrinsic value and EVNT would provide benchmarks against which Hart could evaluate Hilton's past bidding for ITT and the range of possible future bids. Hart wanted to make sure that his next bid would compel the ITT board of directors to accept the Hilton offer.

---

[11]Over the 16 years of Araskog's chairmanship, ITT was able to deliver an average annual gain of only around 10 percent. The S&P over the same period gained nearly 16 percent per annum. Despite ITT's lackluster performance, Araskog earned a compensation of $11.4 million in 1990, a period when ITT's return to shareholders was in the bottom 30 percent of America's 406 largest corporations. In 1995, he negotiated a $13.5 million compensation package for himself.

EXHIBIT 1 | Comparison of the Terms of the Actual Tender Offer and Proposed Tender Offer

	Actual Tender Offer as of January 28, 1997	Suggested Terms of Tender Offer Originally Proposed in Appendix
Offer	$55 a share cash and stock bid	$65–$70 a share cash and stock bid
Terms	$55 a share in cash for 50.1% of outstanding ITT shares and Hilton shares worth $55 in exchange for the remaining 49.9% of ITT shares	$65–$70 a share in cash for 50.1% of outstanding ITT shares and Hilton shares worth $65–$70 in exchange for the remaining 49.9% of ITT shares
Assumed debt	$4 billion	$4 billion
Total value	$10.5 billion	$11.7 billion to $12.3 billion
Offer expiry date	February 28, 1997	One month from date of offer
Approvals	Hilton and ITT shareholders Gaming regulators Antitrust regulators National Basketball Association National Hockey League Federal Communications Commission	Hilton and ITT shareholders Gaming regulators Antitrust regulators National Basketball Association National Hockey League Federal Communications Commission
Collar	Unspecified	Specified, based on Hilton's expected share price immediately after announcement of offer

Source: Casewriter's analysis.

EXHIBIT 2 | ITT Corporation's Share Price versus S&P 500 from January 1, 1996, to July 17, 1997

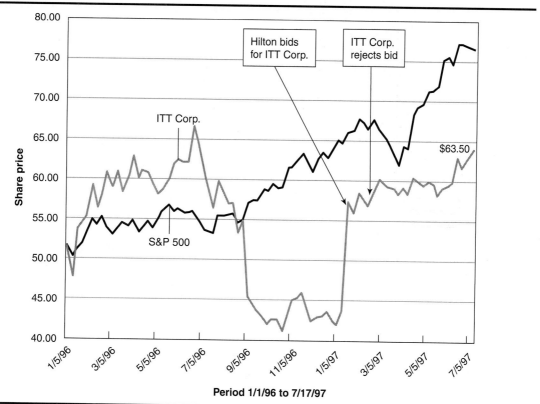

continued

EXHIBIT 2 | Hilton Hotel Corporation's Share Price versus S&P 500 from January 1, 1996, to July 17, 1997   (*continued*)

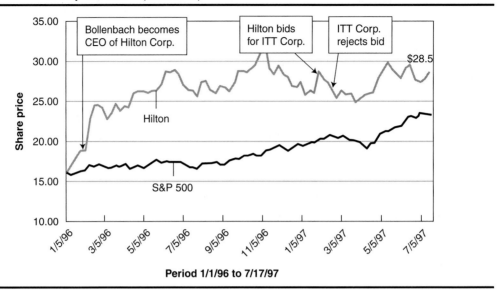

Period 1/1/96 to 7/17/97

To: Matthew J. Hart,
           Chief Financial Officer
           Hilton Hotels Corporation

From: Jane Smith, Director
           Corporate Planning

Subject: Tender Offer for ITT Corporation

Date: December 31, 1996

This memo summarizes our valuation of ITT, and the proposed strategy for acquiring the firm. Sections and Exhibits are as follows.

1. Strategic Motives for the Transaction
2. The Tender Offer
3. Pricing and Timing of the Tender Offer
4. Suggested Terms of Proposed Tender Offer
5. Implementation of the Tender Strategy
6. Comparison of ITT Corporation and Hilton Hotel Corporation
7. Industry and Competitive Outlook
8. Valuation of Proposed Acquisition of ITT Corporation

        Valuation Methodology

        Exhibit A1 - Summary Valuation of ITT Corporation

        Exhibit A2 - Valuation of ITT's Lodging Business

        Exhibit A3 - Valuation of ITT's Gaming Business

        Exhibit A4 - Valuation of ITT's Information Services Business – ITT Education

        Exhibit A5 - Valuation of ITT's Information Services Business – ITT Directories

        Exhibit A6 - Valuation of ITT's Entertainment Business

        Exhibit A7 - Valuation of ITT's Investments

        Exhibit A8 - Valuation of Unallocated Corporate Overhead

        Exhibit A9 - Valuation of Merger Synergies

        Additional Financial Data

        Exhibit A10 - Comparable Transactions

        Exhibit A11 - Comparable Companies

This appendix is a fictitious memorandum prepared from public information. The views and analysis herein are consistent with observations of knowledgeable observers outside of ITT and Hilton. This is intended to represent the range of concerns attendant to making a hostile tender offer and to stimulate student analysis rather than to illustrate effective or ineffective managerial decision making.

1. Strategic Motives for the Transaction

This acquisition is consistent with Hilton's corporate strategy of global expansion of its lodging business and market leadership of its gaming business. With the acquisition of the Sheraton Hotels, The Luxury Collection, Ciga and Four Points Hotels, Hilton will bolster its international presence in the lodging industry. The increase in capacity to 230,973 rooms will make Hilton the sixth largest lodging corporation in the world. Also, the proposed franchising arrangement with HFS will ensure the domestic and international expansion of the Sheraton and Hilton brands. The acquisition of the Caesars gaming business will add considerable muscle to Hilton's existing gaming operations. The critical size achieved will enable Hilton to emerge as a giant of the gaming industry with brands such as Caesars, Bally, Sheraton, and Hilton Casinos in its portfolio of gaming assets. Additionally, the critical size and international presence achieved by this merger will enable the realization of synergies in the following areas.

1. International expansion through Sheraton's global presence will bring benefits of global diversification.

2. The consolidation of reservation services, catering, marketing, and bakeries will result in pre tax annual cost savings of more than $100–115 million. Also, the company will have increased bargaining power in negotiation with food and beverage suppliers, insurance brokers, telephone and telecommunication companies, and computer hardware and software vendors.

3. Reduced capital expenditure will result in increased cash flow. This will enable Hilton to pay larger dividends to shareholders.

2. The Tender Offer

It is proposed that Hilton Hotel Corporation make an unsolicited tender offer for any and all common shares of ITT Corporation. As you know, we have approached ITT management and attempted to negotiate a friendly merger. Despite the unwillingness of ITT management to negotiate, we continue to believe that this combination offers substantial economic benefits that could enhance the wealth of both Hilton and ITT shareholders. Thus, we propose proceeding with a hostile tender offer and recommend the strategy set forth below:

- Integration of ITT hotels and casinos into the Hilton system.
- Eliminate duplicative selling, general and administrative expense, to be derived in part from the disposal of ITT senior management.
- Franchising of the Sheraton name to HFS Inc.
- Sale and/or monetization (through spin-offs or carve-outs) of noncore assets.

To be successful, this tender must be made at an opportune time and at a significant premium to the market price of ITT shares. It will also be necessary to comply with SEC disclosures, Section 13 and Section 14 of the Williams Act of 1968, Insider Trading sanctions, Racketeer Influenced and Corrupt Organizations Act of 1970,

Nevada State Business Laws, Securities & Exchange Act of 1934, ITT's internal bylaws and antitrust regulations.

3. Pricing and Timing of the Tender Offer

In light of the current gaming and lodging industry dynamics, we believe there is a low probability of a competitive bidder with the financial resources and management capacity to run ITT. However, based on comparable transactions we believe that a premium of about 50 percent over the current $43–$46.50 share price range would be appropriate, implying a bid price range of $65–$70 per share. A tender offer in this range is higher than ITT's breakup value and will appeal to ITT's shareholders and will discourage other acquirers from entering into a bidding war. Moreover, with a high price, the probability of a successful tender offer is higher. The high probability will attract the support of risk arbitrageurs ("arbs") who, shortly after the tender offer, will likely become the critical swing "voters" in the control contest. If we can gain the support of the arbs, it is likely that our offer will succeed.

Late January is an ideal time to voice this tender offer to ITT management because:

1. ITT shares are expected to remain undervalued.

2. ITT's entire board of directors is up for reelection. This is a golden opportunity to oust all of the ITT directors at the next annual meeting.

3. A merger between ITT and Hilton may result in the cancellation of ITT's Tampa Hotel Project. The ambiguity around the merger will have a negative impact on ITT's projected earnings and ITT's share price.

4. Suggested Terms of the Proposed Tender Offer

Offer:	$65–$70 a share cash and stock bid.
Terms:	$65–$70 a share in cash for 50.1% of outstanding ITT shares and Hilton shares worth $65–$70 in exchange for the remaining 49.9% of ITT shares.
Assumed debt:	$4 billion
Total value:	$11.7 to $12.3 billion
Nature:	Hostile tender offer
Offer expiry date:	One month from offer date and prior to June 1997
Consummation subject to these approvals:	Hilton and ITT shareholders Gaming regulators Antitrust regulators National Basketball Association National Hockey League Federal Communications Commission
Collar:	Specified, based on Hilton's expected share price immediately after announcement of offer.

5. Implementation of the Tender Offer Strategy

a. Purchase 4.9 percent of ITT's shares before the announcement. At 5 percent, Hilton must file a Form 13-D with the Securities and Exchange Commission, thus announcing to the public its interest in Hilton. By purchasing just less than 5 percent, Hilton acquires a "toe-hold" number of votes, and a bloc of shares on which to profit if Hilton's bid is topped by another firm.

b. Commence the tender offer with a public announcement of the tender price, and with direct solicitation of major institutional stockholders in ITT. The key points of persuasion are the attractive offer (at $65–$70 per share) and the abysmal record of current ITT management. The offer must be outstanding for 20 business days before Hilton can purchase shares.

c. Restructure the ITT board of directors, and rescind the poison pill anti takeover defense. At the Shareholder meeting Hilton management must ask ITT shareholders:

- To elect up to 25 Hilton nominees to the ITT board. These nominees will help facilitate the proposed merger.

- To sanction this merger and repeal any bylaw amendments that ITT management might adopt before the annual meeting that could interfere with the offer, the merger, or the election of Hilton's nominees.

It is essential that ITT's poison pill be rescinded—without this, the acquisition of ITT will become prohibitively expensive. ITT's bylaws give ITT's board the right to rescind the poison pill. Hence, restructuring ITT's board is essential.

The restructured board should give attention to other considerations as well:

- Possibly limiting "golden parachute" payments, compensation to ITT management because of change in ownership.

- Possibly limiting stock option exercise because of change in ITT ownership and management.

- Managing the redemption of debt securities as a result of change in ITT ownership and management.

- Limiting the negotiation of contracts that are not in the interest of the merged company.

- Terminating defensive litigation.

d. Licensing the Sheraton name to HFS Inc. After the ITT acquisition, Hilton should consider licensing the Sheraton Brand to Hospitality Franchising Services Inc. (HFS), which franchises Ramada, Days Inn, and Howard Johnson hotels. HFS would license Sheraton's franchise and management systems. The agreement with HFS should ensure that HFS pays a fee for the Sheraton trademark and shares earnings with Hilton from the franchise and management fees. This arrangement will give Hilton a secure cash flow stream from HFS and promote healthy competition between the Hilton and Sheraton brands.

e. **Sale or Monetization of Noncore Assets.** ITT Corporation consists of four distinct businesses: gaming, lodging, entertainment (Madison Square Garden) and information systems (ITT Education and ITT Directories). They also have a 5 percent stake in Alcatel Alsthom, a French chemical company. As Hilton is interested in the gaming and lodging assets of ITT, it will be financially prudent to monetize the information systems assets and sell off noncore assets, the entertainment business, and Alcatel Alsthom investments. The monies realized from the sale and monetization of noncore assets should be used to pay down the debt incurred during the acquisition.

f. **Financing the Acquisition.** The acquisition should be financed from a combination of internal and external sources. We recommend that Hilton use available cash, working capital, and existing borrowing facilities and also issue public debt. It should be possible to finance the acquisition in this manner, and maintain Hilton Hotel Corporation's debt rating at "Baa1."

6. Comparison of ITT Corporation and Hilton Hotel Corporation

a. Corporate Strategy[1]

ITT Corporation	Hilton Hotel Corporation
To deliver near term value to shareholders while maintaining and building a platform for superior long-term growth and profitability.	1. Access favorable capital markets and utilize strong balance sheet. 2. Take advantage of current economic conditions to acquire full-service hotels. 3. Be a winner in the consolidation of the gaming industry. 4. Invest in our brand through domestic franchising and expanding our international presence.

b. Investor Base[2]

Equity Ownership	ITT Corporation	Hilton Hotel Corporation
Management	4%	27%
Banks	12%	11%
Insurance companies	13%	3%
Asset managers	40%	30%
Mutual funds	22%	23%
Others	9%	6%

---

[1]Hilton Hotel Corporation and ITT Corporation Annual Reports and 10-K Statements, 1996.

[2]O'Neil Database, December 1996.

c. Properties by Ownership Type[3]

	ITT Corporation		Hilton Hotel Corporation	
	Properties	Rooms	Properties	Rooms
Owned or partially-owned hotels	68	22,856	31	23,092
Managed hotels	135	50,415	28	16,776
Franchised hotels	208	51,691	177	45,050
Owned, partially-owned, managed, or franchised casinos	11	3,179	13	17,914
Riverboat casinos	1	0	5	0
TOTAL	**423**	**128,141**	**254**	**102,832**

d. Financial Performance[4]

	ITT Corporation		Hilton Hotel Corporation	
	1996	1995	1996	1995
Revenues	$ 6,597	$ 6,252	$ 3,940	$ 3,555
Operating income	$ 728	$ 568	$ 329	$ 355
Net income	$ 249	$ 147	$ 82*	$ 173
Total assets	$ 9,275	$ 8,692	$ 7,577	$ 3,443
Long-term debt	$ 3,894	$ 3,575	$ 2,606	$ 1,070
Shareholders' equity	$ 3,074	$ 2,936	$ 3,211	$ 1,254
Shares outstanding	117	117	194	194
Earnings per share (EPS)	$ 2.11	$ 1.26	$ 0.42	$ 0.89

Note: All financials, other than per-share data, are in millions. ITT's financials adjusted for 1995 reorganization.

*Includes extraordinary loss of $74 million.

e. Recent Corporate Events[5]

ITT Corporation	Hilton Hotel Corporation
In January 1995, ITT completed a cash tender offer for the outstanding shares of Caesars World Inc., a gaming corporation, for approximately $1.76 billion.	In February 1996, Steven F. Bollenbach was named president and chief executive officer of Hilton Hotel Corporation.
In March 1995, MSG, a partnership between subsidiaries of ITT and Cablevision Systems Corporation acquired the business of Madison Square Garden Corporation for approximately $1 billion.	In June 1996, Hilton acquired Bally Entertainment Corporation and became the world's largest casino gaming company.
In July 1996, ITT in partnership with Dow Jones and Co. purchased a television station WNYC-TV (now renamed as WBIS+) from the City of New York for $207 million.	In August 1996, Hilton formed a strategic alliance with Ladbrook Group PLC (current owners of the Hilton name outside the United States) to reunite the Hilton brand on a worldwide basis.

[3] ITT Corporation and Hilton Hotel Corporation Annual Reports and 10-K Statements, 1996.

[4] ITT and Hilton Annual Reports and 10-K Statements, 1996.

[5] ITT and Hilton Annual Reports and 10-K Statements, 1996.

f. Share Price Analysis

ITT Corporation	Hilton Hotel Corporation
Based on **Figure A1** we conclude that in 1996, ITT shares under performed the S&P Index by 32 percent. Total return to shareholders during this period was −16 percent. This poor performance is mainly due to shareholder expectations of poor returns from the gaming business segment.	Based on **Figure A1** we conclude that in 1996 Hilton's share price outperformed the S&P Index by 50 percent. Total return to shareholders during this period was 68 percent. This has been mainly due to its aggressive growth strategy and market expectation of continued economic prosperity for this industry as a whole.

FIGURE A1 | Hilton Hotel Corporation, ITT Corporation, and S&P 500 Index Performance from January 1, 1996, to December 31, 1996

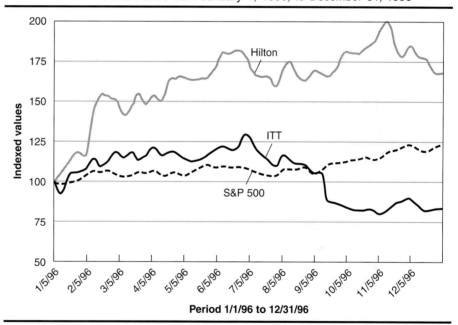

7. Industry and Competitive Outlook

a. Lodging Operations[6]

We expect Average Daily Rates (ADR) to increase at rates higher than the overall inflation rate of the U.S. economy. Demand for hotel rooms will be fueled by moderate economic growth; however, there are indications that the robust growth experienced by the industry during 1995 and 1996 will soon ease. U.S. unemployment at 5.5 percent will lead to a hike in the federal minimum wage and this will affect labor costs and margins adversely. Also, the $5.2 billion investment in hotel construction in 1996 is expected to create increased capacity and competition, which will reduce the growth rate of ADR.

---

[6]S&P 500 Industry Report, October 1996.

Internationally, the emerging economies of Latin America, Eastern Europe, Southeast Asia, and China will fuel international growth of this industry. As foreign direct investment to various regions increases, there will be a demand for luxury, mid-scale, and budget hotels. New construction, strategic joint ventures or cross-border acquisition and expansion of local hotel chains will fulfill this demand.

Many analysts believe that due to the absence of capacity in full-service hotels in the luxury and midscale segments, it is more attractive (less costly) for companies to acquire existing properties. This market opportunity has resulted in a spate of equity issuance and mergers-and-acquisitions activity. Recently, Double Tree Corporation bought Red Lion Hotels for $1.2 billion and Marriott International bought Renaissance Hotel Group for $1 billion. For now, hotel companies and REITs are focused on acquisitions in their peer groups. Down the road, they are going to look further afield towards acquisition of other real-estate-related businesses including ski resorts and casino operations.

b. Gaming Operations[7]

Revenues continue to rise in the gaming industry, but the conditions for long-term sustainable double-digit growth in the United States have weakened. No new states have approved non-Native American casinos since mid-1993. Although the development of glamorous and distinctive new facilities in Las Vegas and Atlantic City should boost the number of gambling visitors, for many Americans, a visit to a casino still requires a long-distance trip by plane, car, or bus. Riverboat gambling has mushroomed in popularity in the past decade as additional states—Illinois, Indiana, Iowa, Louisiana, Mississippi and Missouri—have approved the practice. This is an area of differentiation and one that will be very profitable in the long run.

Though geographic expansion prospects for the gaming industry look weak and analysts believe that the industry is plagued with overcapacity, gaming companies have taken a long-term perspective and have started attracting family customers by establishing themselves as destination resorts. Food prices, room rates and entertainment income have skyrocketed and serious revenue streams have begun to flow as gaming companies have reinvented themselves to be in the "business of selling excitement." So, if casino operations do not make money, the gaming businesses are insulated with higher room rates, lower food costs, and revenues from nongaming entertainment.

c. Assessment of ITT World Directories[8]

One of the most important factors currently affecting the business of ITT World Directories is the changing competitive environment in the member states of the European Union in which it publishes telephone directories. Historically, the national telephone service provider in countries in the European Union awarded an exclusive

---

[7]S&P 500 Industry Report, October 1996.

[8]ITT Corporation 10-K Statement, 1996.

contract for the provision of directories. ITT World Directories lost its exclusive contract with the national provider of telecommunications services in Belgium (Belgacom) and the Netherlands (PTT Telekom) in 1994 and 1993, respectively. In Belgium, ITT World Directories now actively competes with BDS, a joint venture between the local telecommunications provider, Belgacom, and a subsidiary of GTE Corporation. In the Netherlands, ITT World Directories now actively competes with directories published by a joint venture between the local telecommunications provider, PTT Telekom, and Telemedia Group. Although currently there is no meaningful competition for directory services in the other principal countries in which ITT World Directories operates, there can be no assurance that such conditions will continue.

d. Assessment of ITT Educational[9]

The postsecondary education market in the United States is highly fragmented and competitive, with no private or public institution enjoying a significant market share. ITT Technical Institutes compete for students with four-year and two-year degree-granting institutions, which include not-for-profit public and private colleges and proprietary institutions, as well as with alternatives to higher education, such as military service or immediate employment. Competition among educational institutes is believed to be based on the quality of the educational program, perceived reputation of the institution, cost of the program and employability of graduates. Certain public and private colleges may offer programs similar to those of ITT Technical Institutes at a lower tuition cost due in part to government subsidies, foundation grants, tax-deductible contributions, or other financial resources not available to proprietary institutions. Other proprietary institutions offer programs that compete with those of the ITT Technical Institutes. Certain of ITT Educational's competitors in both the public and private sectors have greater financial and other resources than ITT Educational.

8. Valuation of Proposed Acquisition of ITT Corporation

As ITT consists of four strategic business units (SBUs), break-up valuation methodology has been used to value the corporation. We derived the estimate of each SBU by triangulating[10] from the results of several valuation techniques:

1. Comparable Companies
2. Comparable Transactions
3. Discounted Cash Flow

---

[9]ITT Corporation 10-K Statement, 1996.

[10]"Triangulate" is a term used by valuation practitioners to suggest the process of finding the likely intrinsic value of an asset from several estimates of value. This process entails judgment about the efficacy of the different value estimates (e.g., DCF, multiples) as well as valuation practice within the industry.

The comparable companies and comparable transaction valuations involved the use of enterprise value multiples (Revenue, EBIT, EBITDA, Adj. EBITDA, and Net Income), and equity value multiples (PE's and Book to Market). To ensure the accuracy of the valuation these multiples were derived from financials of pure plays from each business segment.

The discounted cash flow valuation makes use of the capital asset pricing model to determine the discount rate. All discount rates were calculated based on pure-play betas and target-capital structures. For the purpose of valuation, terminal values were based on constant growth model. As a sanity check, other methods to calculate terminal values were also used.

EXHIBIT A1 I Summary Valuation of ITT Corporation (in millions of U.S. dollars, except per-share amounts)

Business Units	Valuation		
	Pessimistic	Best Guess	Optimistic
1. Lodging	$ 4,200	$ 6,000	$ 7,000
2. Gaming	2,300	2,800	3,300
3. Information services			
Education	330	425	498
Directories	880	1,050	1,280
4. Entertainment			
MSG	500	500	500
WBIS+	104	104	104
5. Investments	877	877	877
6. Corporate-level expenses	(999)	(999)	(999)
Value of enterprise	**$ 8,193**	**$ 10,757**	**$ 12,559**
Less value of debt	(4,000)	(4,000)	(4,000)
Value of equity without synergy	**$ 4,193**	**$ 6,757**	**$ 8,559**
Shares outstanding	116.37	116.37	116.37
Per-share value of equity without synergy	**$ 36.04**	**$ 58.07**	**$73.55**
Value of synergy	900	1,149	1,300
Value of equity with synergy	**$ 5,093**	**$ 7,906**	**$ 9,859**
Shares outstanding (millions)	116.37	116.37	116.37
Per-share value of equity with synergy	**$ 43.77**	**$ 67.94**	**$ 84.73**

EXHIBIT A2 | Valuation of ITT's Lodging Business (in millions of U.S. dollars, except as noted)

	1997	1998	1999	2000	2001
EBIT	$ 465	$ 577	$ 645	$ 707	$ 763
(Less) taxes	(186)	(231)	(258)	(283)	(305)
(Add) depreciation	173	189	209	229	249
Subtotal	**452**	**535**	**595**	**653**	**707**
Change in noncurrent assets and liabilities	(21)	7	12	11	10
Change in working capital	390	16	30	28	26
Net capital investment	(465)	(431)	(534)	(532)	(530)
Free Cash Flow	$ 355	$ 127	$ 102	$ 159	$ 213
Terminal Value					$ 5,882

Discounted Cash Flow of ITT Lodging $ 4,009

WACC	10.90%	**Present Value of Terminal Value** (Constant Growth Model)	$ 3,507
W_e	84.46%	$(CF_n (1 + g) / (K - g)) / (1+K)^5$	
W_d	15.54%		
K_e	12.07%	Growth rate	7.01%
K_d	7.55%	Inflation	2.70%
R_f	6.44%	Real	4.20%
R_p	5.40%		
Beta	1.04	**Other Terminal Value Estimates**	
		NOPAT/K	$ 3,853
		NOPAT $(1 - i)/(K - g)$	$10,815

Valuation Summary—Lodging	Multiples		Value	
	Low	High	Low	High
Free Cash Flow Valuation			$ 3,100	$ 4,500
Enterprise Value as a Multiple of 1996:				
1 Revenue	1.03	12.45	4,566	55,191
2 EBIT	16.71	31.49	6,199	11,683
3 Net income	34.35	58.87	6,321	10,833
4 EBITDA	13.39	25.71	6,641	12,752
5 Adj. EBITDA	23.14	30.80	3,271	4,354
6 Net assets	2.19	3.67	—	—
Equity Value as a Multiple of:				
1 1996 EPS (actual)	29.24	32.00	5,380	5,888
2 1997 EPS (estimated)	21.43	27.21	5,161	6,553
3 1998 EPS (estimated)	16.57	22.35	5,102	6,882
Triangulated Enterprise Value			$ 4,200	$7,000

Source: Case writer's analysis.

EXHIBIT A3 | Valuation of ITT's Gaming Business (in millions of U.S. dollars, except as noted)

	1997	1998	1999	2000	2001
EBIT	$ 233	$ 254	$ 271	$ 306	$ 327
(Less) taxes	(93)	(101)	(108)	(122)	(131)
(Add) depreciation & amortization	120	131	135	139	143
Subtotal	260	283	298	323	339
Change in noncurrent assets and liabilities	26	5	7	5	8
Change in working capital	31	(4)	(3)	(6)	(3)
Net capital investment	(914)	(297)	(108)	(108)	(109)
Free Cash Flow	$ (598)	$ (11)	$ 195	$ 213	$ 235
Terminal Value					$3,929

Discounted Cash Flow of ITT Gaming $ 2,361

WACC	9.11%	**Present Value of Terminal Value** (Constant Growth Model)	$ 2,540
W_e	77.54%	$(CF_n (1 + g) / (K - g))/(1+K)^5$	
W_d	22.46%		
K_e	10.44%	Growth rate	2.96%
K_d	7.55%	Inflation	2.70%
R_F	6.44%	Real	0.25%
R_p	5.40%		
Beta	0.74	**Other Terminal Value Estimates**	
		NOPAT/K	$ 1,286
		NOPAT $(1 - i)/(K - g)$	$ 1,904

Valuation Summary—Gaming	Multiples		Value	
	Low	High	Low	High
Free Cash Flow Valuation			$ 2,300	$ 3,000
Enterprise Value as a Multiple of 1996:				
1 Revenue	1.72	3.64	2,210	4,677
2 EBIT	8.97	16.30	1,893	3,439
3 Net income	21.73	35.21	797	1,292
4 EBITDA	6.72	12.47	1,902	3,529
5 Adj. EBITDA	9.78	13.26	1,762	2,389
6 Net assets	1.34	2.40	—	—
Equity Value as a Multiple of:				
1 1996 EPS (actual)	16.51	23.58	606	865
2 1997 EPS (estimated)	13.31	22.73	365	624
3 1998 EPS (estimated)	11.60	19.23	852	1,413
Triangulated Enterprise Value			$ 2,300	$ 3,300

Source: Case writer's analysis.

EXHIBIT A4 I   Valuation of ITT's Education Business (in millions of U.S. dollars, except as noted)

	1997	1998	1999	2000	2001
EBIT	$ 24	$ 27	$ 31	$ 35	$ 40
(Add) depreciation	7	8	9	10	11
(Less) taxes	(9)	(11)	(12)	(14)	(16)
Subtotal	21	24	27	30	34
Change in noncurrent assets and liabilities	0	0	0	0	0
Change in working capital	6	8	9	10	11
Net capital investment	(8)	(8)	(9)	(10)	(10)
Free Cash Flow	$ 19	$ 24	$ 27	$ 31	$ 35
Terminal Value					$637

Discounted Cash Flow of ITT Education $485

WACC	9.77%	**Present Value of Terminal Value** (Constant Growth Model)	$ 400
W_e	100.00%	$(CF_n (1 + g)/(K - g))/(1 + K)^5$	
W_d	0.00%		
K_e	9.77%	Growth rate	
K_d	0.00%	Inflation	3.98%
R_F	6.50%	Real	2.70%
R_p	5.40%		1.25%
Beta	0.61	**Other Terminal Value Estimates**	
		NOPAT /K	$ 244
		NOPAT $(1 - i)/(K - g)$	$ 412
		NOPAT $[1/K + i(R - K)/K(K - g)]$	$ 465

Valuation Summary—Education	Multiples	Values	
		Low	**High**
Free Cash Flow Valuation		$400	$550
Market Capitalization as on 12/31/96			642
Enterprise Value as a Multiple of 1996:			
1 Revenue	2.92		678
2 EBIT	25.08		441
3 Net income	38.47		456
4 EBITDA	20.25		468
5 Net assets	4.13		536
Equity Value as a Multiple of:			
1 1996 EPS (actual)	36.21		429
2 1997 EPS (estimated)	30.00		424
3 1998 EPS (estimated)	23.33		376
4 1996 Book Value	16.91		1,162
Triangulated Enterprise Value		**$400**	**$600**

Source: Case writer's analysis.

EXHIBIT A5 | Valuation of ITT's Directories Business (in millions of U.S. dollars, except as noted)

	1997	1998	1999	2000	2001
EBIT	$ 218	$ 215	$ 209	$ 203	$ 203
Net of depreciation + capital investment	1	57	1	1	0
Taxes	(87)	(86)	(84)	(81)	(81)
Change in working capital	1	57	1	1	0
Free Cash Flow	$ 133	$ 243	$ 127	$ 124	$ 122
Terminal Value					$1,268
Discounted Cash Flow of ITT Directories	$1,378				

WACC	9.76%	**Present Value of Terminal Value** (Constant Growth Model)	$ 796
W_e	78.03%	$(CF_n (1 + g)/(K - g))/(1 + K)^5$	
W_d	21.97%		
K_e	11.03%	Growth rate	0.00%
K_d	8.69%	Inflation	0.00%
R_F	6.50%	Real	0.00%
R_p	5.40%		
Beta	0.84	**Other Terminal Value Estimates**	
		Book value	$ 317
		NOPAT / K	$1,251

Valuation Summary—Directories	Multiples		Value	
	Low	High	Low	High
Free Cash Flow Valuation			$ 1,000	$ 1,400
Enterprise Value as a Multiple of 1996:				
1 Revenue	0.76	2.24	491	1,449
2 EBIT	11.73	16.29	2,503	3,477
3 Net income	13.92	21.68	1,755	2,733
5 Net assets	1.04	1.89	421	766
Equity Value as a Multiple of:				
1 1996 EPS (actual)	12.80	13.00	1,613	1,639
2 1997 EPS (estimated)	11.82	12.66	1,544	1,653
3 1998 EPS (estimated)	10.82	10.33	1,399	1,336
Triangulated Enterprise Value			**$1,100**	**$1,600**

Source: Case writer's analysis.

EXHIBIT A6 | Valuation of ITT's Entertainment Business (in millions of U.S. dollars)

MSG Sport Properties	
Book value	$500.00
WBIS+ TV Station	
Book value	$103.50

As both acquisitions were made in 1995–96, their book values are assumed to provide a reasonable estimate of their fair market values.

Sources: Financial statements and 10-K statement.

EXHIBIT A7 | Valuation of ITT's Investments (in millions of U.S. dollars)

Fair market value of 7.5 million shares of Alcatel Alsthom	$599
Equity in 20%–50% owned companies	$261
Other investments	$ 17
Value of total investments	**$877**

Sources: Financial statements and 10-K Report.

EXHIBIT A8 | Valuation of Unallocated Corporate Overhead (in millions of U.S. dollars)

	1997	1998	1999	2000	2001
Pre tax impact of corporate-level expenses	$100	$104	$108	$112	$ 117
After-tax Impact of corporate-level expenses	$ 60	$ 62	$ 65	$ 67	$ 70
Terminal value of corporate-level expenses					$1,216
Present Value of Corporate-level Expenses	**$999**				

Assumptions:	
WACC	10.00%
Growth rate	4.00%
Tax rate	40%

Source: Case writer's analysis.

EXHIBIT A9 I   Valuation of Merger Synergies (in millions of U.S. dollars)

	1997	1998	1999	2000	2001
Pre tax impact of synergies	$ 115	$120	$124	$129	$ 135
After-tax impact of synergies	$ 69	$ 72	$ 75	$ 78	$ 81
Terminal value of synergies					$1,398
Present Value of Synergies	$1,149				

	Low	High
Value Range of Synergies	$900	$1,300

Assumptions:	
WACC	10.00%
Growth rate	4.00%
Tax rate	40%

Source: Case writer's analysis.

EXHIBIT A10 | Comparable Transactions

Selected Gaming and Lodging M&A Transactions (in millions of U.S. dollars, except per-share amounts)

Date Announced	Acquirer & Target	Implied Equity Purchase Price/Share	Implied Aggregate Equity Purchase Price	Total Announced Transaction Value	Enterprise Value as a Multiple of:			
					LTM EBITDA	CFY EBITDA	CFY + 1 EBITDA	LTM Net Income
Lodging Comparables								
Jan-97	Extended Stay America/ Studio Plus Hotel	$22.86	$ 287.00	$ 253.60	26.4	22.6	11.1	55.2
Dec-96	Marriot International/ Renaissance Hotel Group	$32.70	$1,000.00	$1,061.90	16.4	16.5	13.9	30.0
Aug-96	Double Tree Corporation/ Red Lion Hotels	$30.49	$ 977.60	$1,154.40	15.8	10.0	9.3	30.3
				Low	15.8	10.0	9.3	30.0
				High	26.4	22.6	13.9	55.2
				Mean	19.5	16.4	11.4	38.5
Gaming Comparables								
Aug-96	Sun International Hotels/ Griffin Gaming & Entertainment	$22.00	$ 198.10	$ 271.80	5.6	6.5	6.5	20
May-96	Hilton Hotels/ Bally Entertainment	$26.59	$2,050.30	$3,097.00	11.1	10	9.1	58.8
Apr-96	Boyd Gaming Corporation/ Par A Dice Gaming Corp	$18.25	$ 174.60	$ 186.00	5.3	na	na	na
Mar-96	Hollywood Park/ Boomtown	$6.33	$ 56.80	$ 147.80	6.3	na	na	na
Mar-95	Circus Circus/ Gold Strike Resorts	na	$ 443.50	$ 590.40	8.3	na	na	na
Dec-94	ITT Corporation/ Caesars World	$67.50	$1,754.00	$1,824.50	9.6	7.7	7	23.8
				Low	5.3	6.5	6.5	20.0
				High	11.1	10.0	9.1	58.8
				Mean	7.7	8.1	7.5	34.2

LTM = last twelve months.
CFY = calender fiscal year.
na = not available.

EXHIBIT A11 | Comparable Companies

Selected Gaming, Lodging, Education and Publishing Comparables (in millions of U.S. dollars, except per-share amounts)

	Enterprise Value as Multiple of:						Market Value of Equity as a Multiple of:			
	Revenues	EBIT	Net Income	EBITDA	Adj. EBITDA	Net Assets	1996 EPS	1997 E EPS	1998 E EPS	Book Value
Lodging										
Marriot International 1996	0.91	14.64	30.09	11.73	24.35	1.92	24.67	22.10	18.73	5.58
HFS Inc. 1996	13.00	32.87	61.46	26.84	32.15	2.45	46.32	22.46	17.37	3.83
Promus Hotel Corp. 1996	7.49	18.94	27.34	14.94	17.77	2.82	23.70	20.15	16.55	6.15
DoubleTree Hotels 1996	7.73	60.82	90.17	46.34	79.82	1.37	44.55	28.48	22.17	2.23
Gaming										
Circus Circus 1996	3.50	17.24	46.27	12.46	17.42	1.76	34.72	20.22	17.63	3.30
Mirage Resorts 1996	3.19	14.31	21.04	10.95	15.08	2.10	20.40	19.66	16.63	3.00
MGM Grand 1996	3.09	13.31	22.35	10.00	13.49	2.03	17.10	15.85	14.53	2.08
Harrah Entertainment 1996	1.82	9.53	29.26	7.14	10.39	1.56	20.92	17.28	13.25	2.73
Publishing										
McGraw-Hill 1996	1.67	12.16	10.39	9.65	na	1.41	9.30	8.54	7.82	3.35
Donnelley 1996	1.03	15.99	29.55	17.47	na	1.41	21.03	20.48	16.71	2.91
Dun & Bradstreet 1996	2.39	14.40	38.60	10.02	na	2.39	30.45	13.57	12.50	−9.39
Education										
National Education Corp. 1996	2.21	18.99	29.13	15.33	na	3.13	26.29	21.79	16.94	12.28
Entertainment										
Florida Panthers 1995–96	19.75	na	na	na	na	14.20	na	na	na	1.61
Boston Celtics 1995–96	2.62	10.67	10.74	10.47	na	1.22	8.64	372.92	na	7.25
Media—TV Stations										
King World Productions 1995–96	2.05	7.08	9.05	7.05	na	2.66	9.27	9.65	9.83	1.84
Paxon Communications Corporation 1995–96	4.32	na	na	22.84	na	1.29	na	na	na	0.53

na = not available.

Source: Bloomberg, Value Line, and Case writer's analysis.